The Oxford

Color

Portuguese Dictionary

The Oxford Color Portuguese Dictionary

PORTUGUESE–ENGLISH
Còmpiled by John Whitlam

ENGLISH–PORTUGUESE
Compiled by Lia Correia Raitt

OXFORD
UNIVERSITY PRESS

OXFORD
UNIVERSITY PRESS

Great Clarendon Street, Oxford OX2 6DP

Oxford University Press is a department of the University of Oxford.
It furthers the University's objective of excellence in research, scholarship,
and education by publishing worldwide in

Oxford New York

Auckland Bangkok Buenos Aires Cape Town Chennai
Dar es Salaam Delhi Hong Kong Istanbul Karachi Kolkata
Kuala Lumpur Madrid Melbourne Mexico City Mumbai
Nairobi São Paulo Shanghai Taipei Tokyo Toronto

Oxford is a registered trade mark of Oxford University Press
in the UK and in certain other countries

Published in the United States
by Oxford University Press Inc., New York

© Oxford University Press 1999

British Library Cataloguing in Publication Data
Data available

Library of Congress Cataloging in Publication Data
Data available

ISBN-13: 978-0-19-860273-6
ISBN-10: 0-19-860273-1

10 9 8 7 6 5

Typeset in Nimrod and Arial
by PureTech India Ltd
Printed in China

Contents/Índice

Preface/Prefácio   vi–vii

Introduction/Introdução   viii–ix

Proprietary terms/Nomes comerciais   x

Pronunciation/Pronúncia

    Portuguese/Português   xi–xv

    English/Inglês   xvi–xvii

European Portuguese   xviii–xix

Abbreviations/Abreviaturas   xx–xxii

Portuguese-English   **1–180**
Português-Inglês

English-Portuguese   **181–430**
Inglês-Português

Portuguese verbs/Verbos portugueses   431–436

Skill-related fitness

hea...

flexibility

cardi...

muscular fit...

muscular strength

muscular endurance

body composition

agility

balance

power

reaction time

coordination

speed

norm-referenced tests

criterion- "

health-related fitness ...

... standards .

reface

The Oxford Color Portuguese Dictionary has been written for speakers of both Portuguese and English and contains the most useful words and expressions in use today.

The dictionary provides a handy and comprehensive reference work for tourists, students, and business people who require quick and reliable answers to their translation needs.

Thanks are due to: Dr John Sykes, Prof. A. W. Raitt, Commander Virgílio Correia, Marcelo Affonso, Eng. Pedro Carvalho, Eng. Vasco Carvalho, Dr Iva Correia, Dr Ida Reis de Carvalho, Eng. J. Reis de Carvalho, Prof. A. Falcão, Bishop Manuel Falcão, Dr M. Luísa Falcão, Prof. J. Ferraz, Prof. M. de Lourdes Ferraz, Drs Ana and Jorge Fonseca, Mr Robert Howes, Irene Lakhani, Eng. Hugo Pires, Prof. M. Kaura Pires, Dr M. Alexandre Pires, Ambassador L. Pazos Alonso, Dr Teresa Pinto Pereira, Dr Isabel Tully, Carlos Wallenstein, Ligia Xavier, and Dr H. Martins and the members of his Mesa Lusófona at St Antony's College, Oxford.

Prefácio

O *Oxford Color Portuguese Dictionary* foi escrito por pessoas de língua portuguesa e inglesa, e contém as palavras e expressões mais úteis em uso atualmente.

O dicionário constitui uma obra de referência prática e abrangente para turistas, estudantes e pessoas de negócios que necessitam de respostas rápidas e confiáveis para as suas traduções.

Agradecimentos a: Dr John Sykes, Prof. A. W. Raitt, Comandante Virgílio Correia, Marcelo Affonso, Eng. Pedro Carvalho, Eng. Vasco Carvalho, Dr Iva Correia, Dr Ida Reis de Carvalho, Eng. J. Reis de Carvalho, Prof. A. Falcão, Bispo Manuel Falcão, Dr M. Luísa Falcão, Prof. J. Ferraz, Prof. M. de Lourdes Ferraz, Drs Ana e Jorge Fonseca, Mr Robert Howes, Eng. Hugo Pires, Prof. M. Laura Pires, Dr M. Alexandre Pires, Embaixador L. Pazos Alonso, Dr Teresa Pinto Pereira, Dr Isabel Tully, Carlos Wallenstein, e Dr H. Martins e os membros de sua Mesa Lusófona do St Antony's College, em Oxford.

Introduction

The swung dash (∼) is used to replace a headword, or that part of a headword preceding the vertical bar (|).

In both English and Portuguese, only irregular plural forms are given. Plural forms of Portuguese nouns and adjectives ending in a single vowel are formed by adding an s (e.g. *livro, livros*). Those ending in *n, r, s* where the stress falls on the final syllable, and *z*, add *es* (e.g. *mulher, mulheres, falaz, falazes*). Nouns and adjectives ending in *m* change the final *m* to *ns* (e.g. *homem, homens, bom, bons*). Most of those ending in *ão* change their ending to *ões* (e.g. *estação, estações*).

Portuguese nouns and adjectives ending in an unstressed *o* form the feminine by changing the *o* to *a* (e.g. *belo, bela*). Those ending in *or* become *ora* (e.g. *trabalhador, trabalhadora*). All other masculine–feminine changes are shown at the main headword.

English and Portuguese pronunciation is given by means of the International Phonetic Alphabet. It is shown for all headwords, and for those derived words whose pronunciation is not easily deduced from that of a headword.

Portuguese verb tables will be found in the appendix.

Introdução

O sinal (~) é usado para substituir o verbete, ou parte deste precedendo a barra vertical (|).

Tanto em inglês como em português, somente as formas irregulares do plural são dadas. As formas regulares do plural dos substantivos ingleses recebem um *s* (ex. *teacher, teachers*), ou *es* quando terminarem em *ch, sh, s, ss, us, x* ou *z* (ex. *sash, sashes*). Os substantivos terminados em *y* e precedidos por uma consoante, mudam no plural para *ies* (ex. *baby, babies*).

O passado e o particípio passado dos verbos regulares ingleses são formados pelo acréscimo de *ed* á forma infinitiva (ex. *last, lasted*). Os verbos terminados em *e* recebem *d* (ex. *move, moved*). Aqueles terminados em *y* têm o *y* substituído por *ied* (*carry, carried*). As formas irregulares dos verbos aparecem no dicionário em ordem alfabética, remetidas à forma infinitiva, e também, na lista de verbos no apêndice.

As pronúncias inglesa e portuguesa são dadas em acordo com o Alfabeto Fonético Internacional. A pronúncia é dada para todos os verbetes, assim como para aquelas palavras derivadas cuja pronúncia não seja facilmente deduzida a partir do verbete.

Proprietary terms

This dictionary includes some words which are, or are asserted to be, proprietary names or trade marks. Their inclusion does not imply that they have acquired for legal purposes a non-proprietary or general significance, nor is any other judgement implied concerning their legal status. In cases where the editor has some evidence that a word is used as a proprietary name or trade mark this is indicated by the label *propr*, but no judgement concerning the legal status of such words is made or implied thereby.

Nomes comerciais

Este dicionário inclui algumas palavras que são, ou acredita-se ser, nomes comerciais ou marcas registradas. A sua inclusão no dicionário não implica que elas tenham adquirido para fins legais um significado geral ou não-comercial, assim como não afeta em nenhum dos conceitos implícitos o seu status legal.

Nos casos em que o editor tenha prova suficiente de que uma palavra seja usada como um nome comercial ou marca registrada, este emprego é indicado pela etiqueta *propr*, mas nenhuma apreciação relativa ao status legal de tais palavras é feita ou sugerida por esta indicação.

Portuguese pronunciation

Vowels and Diphthongs

a, à, á, â	/ã/	cham*a*m, *a*mbos, *a*ntes	1) before *m* at the end of a word, or before *m* or *n* and another consonant, is nasalized
	/a/	*a*b*a*, *à*, *a*colá, desânimo	2) in other positions is like *a* in English r*a*ther
ã	/ã/	irm*ã*	is nasalized
e	/ẽ/	s*e*m, v*e*nda	1) before *m* at the end of a word, or before *m* or *n* and another consonant, is nasalized
	/i/	art*e*	2) at the end of a word is like *y* in English happ*y*
	/e/	m*e*nas	3) in other positions is like *e* in English th*e*y
é	/ɛ/	art*é*ria	is like *e* in English g*e*t
ê	/e/	f*ê*mur	is like *e* in English th*e*y
i	/ĩ/	s*i*m, v*i*ndo	1) before *m* at the end of a word, or before *m* or *n* and another consonant, is nasalized
	/i/	f*i*la	2) in other positions is like *ee* in English s*ee*
o	/õ/	c*o*m, s*o*mbra, *o*nda	1) before *m* at the end of a word, or before *m* or *n* and another consonant, is nasalized
	/u/	muit*o*	2) at the end of a word, unstressed, is like *u* in English r*u*le

	/o/	comover	3) in other positions, unstressed, is like *o* in English p*o*le
	/o/	bob*o*	4) stressed, is like *o* in English p*o*le or *o* in sh*o*p
	/ɔ/	l*o*ja	
ó	/ɔ/	*ó*pera	is like *o* in English p*o*le
ô	/o/	t*ô*nica	is like *o* in English p*o*le
u, ú		g*u*erra, g*u*isado, q*u*e, q*u*ilo	1) is silent in *gue*, and *gui*, *que*, *qui*
	/u/	m*u*la, p*ú*rp*u*ra	2) in other positions is like *u* in English r*u*le
ü gü	/gw/	ung*ü*ento	in the combinations *güe* and *güi* is like *g* in English *g*ot, followed by English *w*
	/kw/	tranq*üi*lo	in the combinations *qüe* and *qüi* is like *qu* in English *qu*een
ãe	/ãj/	m*ãe*, p*ãe*s, alem*ãe*s	is like *y* in English b*y*, but nasalized
ai	/aj/	v*ai*, p*ai*, s*ai*, c*ai*ta	is like *y* in English b*y*
ao, au	/aw/	*ao*s, *au*todefesa	is like *ow* in English h*ow*
ão	/ãw/	n*ão*	is like *ow* in English h*ow*, but nasalized
ei	/ej/	l*ei*	is like *ey* in English th*ey*
eu	/ew/	d*eu*s, fl*eu*gma	both vowels pronounced separately
oẽ	/õj/	eleiç*õe*s	is like *oi* in English c*oi*n, but nasalized
oi	/oj/	n*oi*te	is like *oi* in English c*oi*n
ou	/o/	p*ou*co	is like *o* in English p*o*le

Consonants

b	/b/	*b*anho	is like *b* in English *b*all
c	/s/	*c*inza, *c*em	1) before *e* or *i* is like *s* in English *s*it
	/k/	*c*asa	2) in other positions is like *c* in English *c*at
ç	/s/	esta*ç*ão	is like *s* in English *s*it
ch	/ʃ/	*ch*á	is like *sh* in English *sh*out
d	/dʒ/	*d*izer, *d*onde	1) before *i* or final unstressed *e* is like *j* in English *j*oin
	/d/	*d*ar	2) in other positions is like *d* in English *d*og
f	/f/	*f*alar	is like *f* in English *f*all
g	/ʒ/	a*g*ente, *g*iro	1) before *e* or *i* is like *s* in English vi*s*ion
	/g/	*g*ato	2) in other positions is like *g* in English *g*et
h		*h*aver	is silent in Portuguese, but see *ch*, *lh*, *nh*
j	/ʒ/	*j*unta	is like *s* in English vi*s*ion
k	/k/	*k*it	is like English *k* in *k*ey
l	/w/	fa*l*ta	1) between a vowel and a consonant, or following a vowel at the end of a word, is like *w* in English *w*ater
	/l/	*l*ata	2) in other positions is like *l* in English *l*ike
l	/ʎ/	ca*l*har	is like *lli* in English mi*lli*on
m		a*m*bas /ãbuʃ/ co*m* /kõ/	1) between a vowel and a consonant, or after a vowel at the end of a word, *m* nasalizes the preceding vowel

	/m/	*m*ato, *m*ão	2) in other positions is like *m* in English *m*other
n		ci*n*za /'sĩza/	1) between a vowel and a consonant, *n* nasalizes the preceding vowel
	/n/	be*n*ig*n*o	2) in other positions is like *n* in English *n*ear
nh	/ɲ/	ba*nh*o	is like *ni* in English opi*ni*on
p	/p/	*p*az	is like *p* in English *p*oor
q	/k/	*q*ue, in*q*uieto	1) *qu* before *e* or *i* is like English *k*
	/kw/	*q*uase, *q*uórum	2) *qu* before *a* or *o*, or *qü* before *e* or *i*, is like *qu* in English *qu*een
r	/r/	apa*r*ato, go*r*do	1) between two vowels, or between a vowel and a consonant, is trilled
	/x/	*r*ato, ga*rr*a, mel*r*o, gen*r*o, Is*r*ael	2) at the beginning of a word, or in *rr*, or after *l*, *n*, or *s*, is like *ch* in Scottish lo*ch*
s	/ʃ/	depoi*s*	at the end of a word is like *sh* in English *sh*oot
	/z/	a*s*a, de*s*de, abi*s*mo, I*s*rael	2) between two vowels, or before *b*, *d*, *g*, *l*, *m*, *n*, *r*, *v*, is like *z* in English *z*ebra
	/s/	*s*uave	3) in other positions is like *s* in English *s*it
t	/tʃ/	*t*io, an*t*es	1) before *i* or final unstressed *e* is like *ch* in English *ch*eese
	/tʃi/	ki*t*	2) at the end of a word is like *chy* in English it*chy*

	/t/	a*t*ar	3) in other positions is like *t* in English *t*ap
v	/v/	lu*v*a	is like *v* in English *v*ain
w	/u/	*w*att	is shorter than English *w*
x	/z/	e*x*ato, e*x*emplo	1) in the prefix *ex* before a vowel, is pronounced like *z* in *z*ero
	/ʃ/	*x*ícara, bai*x*o, pei*x*e, frou*x*o	2) at the beginning of a word or after *ai*, *ei* or *ou*, is pronounced like *sh* in *sh*ow
	/s/	e*x*plodir,	3) is like *s* in English auxiliar*s*it
	/ks/	a*x*ila, fi*x*o	4) is like *x* in English e*x*it 5) in the combination *xce*, *xci*, *x* is not pronounced in Portuguese e.g. e*x*celente, e*x*citar
z	/s/	fala*z*	1) at the end of a word, is like *s* in English *s*it
	/z/	di*z*er	2) in other positions, is like English *z*

Pronuncia Inglesa

Vogals e Ditongos

/iː/	*see*, *tea*	como *i* em g*i*ro
/ɪ/	s*i*t, happ*y*	é um som mais breve do que *i* em l*i*
/e/	s*e*t	como *e* em t*é*pido
/æ/	h*a*t	é um som mais breve do que *a* em *a*mor
/aː/	*a*rm, c*a*lm	como *a* em c*a*rtaz
/ɒ/	g*o*t	como *o* em ex*ó*tico
/ɔː/	s*aw*, m*o*re	como *o* em c*o*rte
/ʊ/	p*u*t, l*oo*k	como *u* em m*u*rro
/uː/	t*oo*, d*ue*	como *u* em d*u*ro
/ʌ/	c*u*p, s*o*me	como *a* em p*a*no
/ɜː/	f*ir*m, f*ur*	como *e* em enx*e*rto
/ə/	*a*go, weath*er*	como *e* no português europeu par*t*e
/eɪ/	p*a*ge, p*ai*n, p*ay*	como *ei* em l*ei*te
/əʊ/	h*o*me, r*oa*m	é um som mais longo do que *o* em c*o*ma
/aɪ/	f*i*ne, b*y*, g*uy*	como *ai* em s*ai*
/aɪə/	f*i*re, t*yre*	como *ai* em s*ai* seguido por /ə/
/aʊ/	n*ow*, sh*ou*t	como *au* em *au*la
/aʊə/	h*our*, fl*ower*	como *au* em *au*la seguido por /ə/
/ɔɪ/	j*oi*n, b*oy*	como *oi* em d*ói*
/ɪə/	d*ear*, h*ere*, b*eer*	como *ia* em d*ia*
/eə/	h*air*, c*are*, b*ear*, th*ere*	como *e* em et*é*reo
/ʊə/	p*oor*, d*ur*ing	como *ua* em s*ua*

Consoantes

/p/	sna*p*	como *p* em *p*ato
/b/	*b*ath	como *b* em *b*ala
/t/	*t*ap	como *t* em *t*ela
/d/	*d*ip	como *d* em *d*ar
/k/	*c*at, *k*ite, stoma*ch*, pi*que*	como *c* em *c*asa
/ks/	e*x*ercise	como *x* em a*x*ila
/g/	*g*ot	como *g* em *g*ato
/tʃ/	*ch*in	como *t* em *t*io
/dʒ/	*J*une, *g*eneral, *j*udge	como *d* em *d*izer
/f/	*f*all	como *f* em *f*aca
/v/	*v*ine, o*f*	como *v* em *v*aca
/θ/	*th*in, mo*th*	não tem equivalente, soa como um *s* entre os dentes
/ð/	*th*is	não tem equivalente, soa como um *z* entre os dentes
/s/	*s*o, voi*ce*	como *s* em *s*uave
/z/	*z*oo, ro*se*	como *z* em fa*z*er
/ʃ/	*sh*e, lun*ch*	como *ch* em *ch*egar
/ʒ/	mea*s*ure, vi*s*ion	como *j* em *j*amais
/h/	*h*ow	*h* aspirado
/m/	*m*an	como *m* em *m*ala
/n/	*n*one	como *n* em *n*ada
/ŋ/	si*ng*	como *n* em ci*n*to
/l/	*l*eg	como *l* em *l*uva
/r/	*r*ed, *wr*ite	como *r* em ca*r*a
/j/	*y*es, *y*oke	como *i* em *i*oga
/w/	*w*eather, s*w*itch	como *u* ég*u*a

European Portuguese

Brazilian Portuguese, which is used in this dictionary, differs in a number of respects from that used in Portugal and the rest of the Portuguese-speaking world. These differences affect both spelling and pronunciation. Spelling variations appear on the Portuguese–English side. In so far as they affect pronunciation, the main variants are:

Brazilian Portuguese often omits the letters *b*, *c*, *m*, and *p*, which are retained by European Portuguese:

	Brazilian	**European**
b	su*t*il	su*b*til
c	a*ç*ão	ac*ç*ão
	a*t*o	ac*t*o
	elé*t*rico	elé*c*trico
m	inde*n*izar	inde*m*nizar
p	ba*t*ismo	ba*p*tismo
	exce*ç*ão	exce*p*ção

Letters *c* and *p* in such variant forms are usually silent, hence acto /'atu/,ba'ptismo /batiʒmu/. However, *c* is pronounced in the combination *ect*, hence eléctrico /i'lektriku/.

The combinations *gü* and *qü* become *gu* and *qu*:

	Brazilian	**European**
	un*gü*ento	un*gu*ento
	tran*qü*ilo	tran*qu*ilo

However, they are still pronounced /gw/ and /kw/ respectively.

The other main differences in pronunciation are:

d	/d/	*d*ar, *d*izer, bal*d*e, *d*onde	1) at the beginning of a word, or after *l*, or *n*, is like *d* in English *d*og

/ð/		cidade, medroso	2) in other positions is a sound between *d* in English *d*og and *th* in English *th*is
e	/ə/	arte	at the end of a word, is like *e* in English quarr*e*l
r	/rr/	*r*ato, ga*rr*a, mel*r*o, gen*r*o, Is*r*ael, guel*r*a, ten*r*o, is*r*aelense	at the beginning of a word, or in *rr*, or after *l, n,* or *s,* is strongly trilled
s	/ʃ/	depoi*s*, a*s*co, ra*s*par, co*s*tura	1) at the end of a word, or before *c, f, p, qu,* or *t,* is like English *sh*
	/ʒ/	de*s*de, I*s*lā abi*s*mo, I*s*rael	2) before *b, d, g, l, m, n, r,* or *v* is like *s* in English vi*s*ion
t	/t/	a*t*ar, an*t*es, *t*io	is like *t* in English *t*ap
z	/ʃ/	fala*z*	at the end of a word, is like *sh* in English *sh*ake

Abbreviations/Abreviaturas

adjective	a	adjetivo
abbreviation	abbr/abr	abreviatura
something	aco	alguma coisa
adverb	adv	advérbio
somebody, someone	alg	algúem
article	art	artigo
American (English)	Amer	(inglês) americano
anatomy	anat	anatomia
architecture	arquit	arquitetura
astrology	astr/astrol	astrologia
motoring	auto	automobilismo
aviation	aviat	aviação
Brazilian Portuguese	B	português do Brasil
biology	biol	biologia
botany	bot	botânica
Brazilian Portuguese	Bras	português do Brasil
cinema	cine	cinema
colloquial	colloq	coloquial
commerce	comm/com	comércio
computing	comput	computação
conjunction	conj	conjunção
cookery	culin	cozinha
electricity	electr/eletr	eletricidade
feminine	f	feminina
familiar	fam	familiar
figurative	fig	figurativo
geography	geog	geografia

English	Abbreviation	Portuguese
grammar	gramm/gram	gramática
infinitive	inf	infinitivo
interjection	int	interjeição
interrogative	interr	interrogativo
invariable	invar	invariável
legal, law	jur/jurid	jurídico
language	lang	linguagem
literal	lit	literal
masculine	m	masculino
mathematics	mat	matemática
mechanics	mech	mecânica
medicine	med	medicina
military	mil	militar
music	mus	música
noun	n	substantivo
nautical	naut	náutico
negative	neg	negativo
oneself	o.s.	se, si mesmo
European Portuguese	P	português de Portugal
pejorative	pej	pejorativo
philosophy	phil	filosofia
plural	pl	plural
politics	pol	política
European Portuguese	Port	português de Portugal
past participle	pp	particípio passado
prefix	pref	prefixo
preposition	prep	preposição
present	pres	presente
present participle	pres p	particípio presente
pronoun	pron	pronome

psychology	psych/psic	psicologia
past tense	pt	pretérito
relative	rel	relativo
religion	relig	religião
somebody	sb	alguém
singular	sing	singular
slang	sl	gíria
someone	s.o.	alguém
something	sth	alguma coisa
subjunctive	subj	subjuntivo
technology	techn/tecn	tecnologia
theatre	theat/teat	teatro
television	TV	televisão
university	univ	universidade
auxiliary verb	v aux	verbo auxiliar
intransitive verb	vi	verbo intransitivo
pronominal verb	vpr	verbo pronominal
transitive verb	vt	verbo transitivo
transitive & intransitive verb	vt/i	verbo transitivo e intransitivo

PORTUGUÊS-INGLÊS

PORTUGUESE-ENGLISH

A

a¹ /a/ *artigo* the □ *pron* (*mulher*) her; (*coisa*) it; (*você*) you

a² /a/ *prep* (*para*) to; (*em*) at; às 3 horas at 3 o'clock; à noite at night; a lápis in pencil; a mão by hand

à /a/ = a² + a¹

aba /'aba/ *f* (*de chapéu*) brim; (*de camisa*) tail; (*de mesa*) flap

abacate /aba'katʃi/ *m* avocado (pear)

abacaxi /abaka'ʃi/ *m* pineapple; (*fam: problema*) pain, headache

aba|de /a'badʒi/ *m* abbot; ~dia *f* abbey

aba|fado /aba'fadu/ *a* (*tempo*) humid, close; (*quarto*) stuffy; ~far *vt* (*asfixiar*) stifle; muffle <*som*>; smother <*fogo*>; suppress <*informação*>; cover up <*escândalo, assunto*>

abagunçar /abagu'sar/ *vt* mess up

abaixar /aba'ʃar/ *vt* lower; turn down <*som, rádio*> □ *vi* ~-se *vpr* bend down

abaixo /a'baʃu/ *adv* down; ~ de below; mais ~ further down; ~-assinado *m* petition

abajur /aba'ʒur/ *m* (*quebra-luz*) lampshade; (*lâmpada*) (table) lamp

aba|lar /aba'lar/ *vt* shake; (*fig*) shock; ~lar-se *vpr* be shocked, be shaken; ~lo *m* shock

abanar /aba'nar/ *vt* shake, wave; wag <*rabo*>; (*com leque*) fan

abando|nar /abãdo'nar/ *vt* abandon; (*deixar*) leave; ~no /o/ *m* abandonment; (*estado*) neglect

abarcar /abar'kar/ *vt* comprise, cover

abarro|tado /abaxo'tadu/ *a* crammed full; (*lotado*) crowded, packed; ~tar *vt* cram full, stuff

abastado /abas'tadu/ *a* wealthy

abaste|cer /abaste'ser/ *vt* supply; fuel <*motor*>; fill up (with petrol) <*carro*>; refuel <*avião*>; ~cimento *m* supply; (*de carro, avião*) refuelling

aba|ter /aba'ter/ *vt* knock down; cut down, fell <*árvore*>; shoot down <*avião, ave*>; slaughter <*gado*>; knock down, cut <*preço*>; ~ter alg <*trabalho*> get s.o. down, wear s.o. out; <*má notícia*> sadden s.o.; <*doença*> lay s.o. low, knock the stuffing out of s.o.; ~tido *a* dispirited, dejected; <*cara*> haggard, worn;

~timento *m* dejection; (*de preço*) reduction

abaulado /abaw'ladu/ *a* convex; <*estrada*> cambered

abcesso /ab'sɛsu/ *m* (*Port*) *veja* abscesso

abdi|cação /abidʒika'sãw/ *f* abdication; ~car *vt/i* abdicate

abdômen /abi'domẽ/ *m* abdomen

abecedário /abese'dariu/ *m* alphabet, ABC

abeirar-se /abe'rarsi/ *vr* draw near

abe|lha /a'beʎa/ *f* bee; ~lhudo *a* inquisitive, nosy

abençoar /abẽso'ar/ *vt* bless

aber|to /a'bɛrtu/ *pp de* abrir □ *a* open; <*céu*> clear; <*gás, torneira*> on; <*sinal*> green; ~tura *f* opening; (*foto*) aperture; (*pol*) liberalization

abeto /a'betu/ *m* fir (tree)

abis|mado /abiz'madu/ *a* astonished; ~mo *m* abyss

abjeto /abi'ʒɛtu/ *a* abject

abóbada /a'bɔbada/ *f* vault

abobalhado /aboba'ʎadu/ *a* silly

abóbora /a'bɔbora/ *f* pumpkin

abobrinha /abo'briɲa/ *f* courgette, (*Amer*) zucchini

abo|lição /aboli'sãw/ *f* abolition; ~lir *vt* abolish

abomi|nação /abomina'sãw/ *f* abomination; ~nável (*pl* ~náveis) *a* abominable

abo|nar /abo'nar/ *vt* guarantee <*dívida*>; give a bonus to <*empregado*>; ~no /o/ *m* guarantee; (*no salário*) bonus; (*subsídio*) allowance, benefit; (*reforço*) endorsement

abor|dar /abor'dar/ *vt* approach <*pessoa*>; broach, tackle <*assunto*>; (*naut*) board

aborre|cer /aboxe'ser/ *vt* (*irritar*) annoy; (*entediar*) bore; ~cer-se *vpr* get annoyed; get bored; ~cido *a* annoyed; bored; ~cimento *m* annoyance; boredom

abor|tar /abor'tar/ *vi* miscarry, have a miscarriage □ *vt* abort; ~to /o/ *m* abortion; (*natural*) miscarriage

aboto|adura /abotoa'dura/ *f* cufflink; ~ar *vt* button (up) □ *vi* bud

abra|çar /abra'sar/ *vt* hug, embrace;

embrace <*causa*>; ~ço *m* hug, embrace

abrandar /abrã'dar/ *vt* ease <*dor*>; temper <*calor, frio*>; mollify, appease, placate <*povo*>; tone down, smooth over <*escândalo*> □ *vi* <*dor*> ease; <*calor, frio*> become less extreme; <*tempestade*> die down

abranger /abrã'ʒer/ *vt* cover; (*entender*) take in, grasp; ~ a extend to

abrasileirar /abrazile'rar/ *vt* Brazilianize

abre-|garrafas /abriga'xafas/ *m invar* (Port) bottle-opener; ~latas *m invar* (Port) can-opener

abreugrafia /abrewgra'fia/ *f* X-ray

abrevi|ar /abrevi'ar/ *vt* abbreviate <*palavra*>; abridge <*livro*>; ~atura *f* abbreviation

abridor /abri'dor/ *m* ~ (de lata) canopener; ~ de garrafa bottle-opener

abri|gar /abri'gar/ *vt* shelter; house <*sem-teto*>; ~gar-se *vpr* (take) shelter; ~go *m* shelter

abril /a'briw/ *m* April

abrir /a'brir/ *vt* open; (*a chave*) unlock; turn on <*gás, torneira*>; make <*buraco, exceção*> □ *vi* open; <*céu, tempo*> clear (up); <*sinal*> turn green; ~-se *vpr* open; (*desabafar*) open up

abrupto /a'bruptu/ *a* abrupt

abrutalhado /abruta'ʎadu/ *a* <*sapato*> heavy; <*pessoa*> coarse

abscesso /abi'sɛsu/ *m* abscess

absolu|tamente /absoluta'mẽtʃi/ *adv* absolutely; (*não*) not at all; ~to *a* absolute; em ~to not at all, absolutely not

absol|ver /abisow'ver/ *vt* absolve; (*jurid*) acquit; ~vição *f* absolution; (*jurid*) acquittal

absor|ção /abisor'sãw/ *f* absorption; ~to *a* absorbed; ~vente *a* <*tecido*> absorbent; <*livro*> absorbing; ~ver *vt* absorb; ~ver-se *vpr* get absorbed

abs|têmio /abis'temiu/ *a* abstemious; (*de álcool*) teetotal □ *m* teetotaller; ~tenção *f* abstention; ~tencionista *a* abstaining □ *m/f* abstainer; ~ter-se *vpr* abstain; ~ter-se de refrain from; ~tinência *f* abstinence

abstra|ção /abistra'sãw/ *f* abstraction; (*mental*) distraction; ~ir *vt* separate; ~to *a* abstract

absurdo /abi'surdu/ *a* absurd □ *m* nonsense

abun|dância /abũ'dãsia/ *f* abundance; ~dante *a* abundant; ~dar *vi* abound

abu|sar /abu'zar/ *vi* go too far; ~sar de abuse; (*aproveitar-se*) take advantage of; ~so *m* abuse

abutre /a'butri/ *m* vulture

aca|bado /aka'badu/ *a* finished; (*exausto*) exhausted; (*velho*) decrepit; ~bamento *m* finish; ~bar *vt* finish □ *vi* finish, end; (*esgotar-se*) run out; ~bar-se *vpr* end, be over; (*esgotar-se*) run out; ~bar com put an end to, end; (*abolir, matar*) do away with; split up with <*namorado*>; wipe out <*adversário*>; ~bou de chegar he has just arrived; ~bar fazendo *or* por fazer end up doing

acabrunhado /akabru'ɲadu/ *a* dejected

aca|demia /akade'mia/ *f* academy; (*de ginástica etc*) gym; ~dêmico *a & m* academic

açafrão /asa'frãw/ *m* saffron

acalentar /akalẽ'tar/ *vt* lull to sleep <*bebê*>; cherish <*esperanças*>; have in mind <*planos*>

acalmar /akaw'mar/ *vt* calm (down) □ *vi* <*vento*> drop; <*mar*> grow calm; ~-se *vpr* calm down

acam|pamento /akãpa'mẽtu/ *m* camp; (*ato*) camping; ~par *vi* camp

aca|nhado /aka'ɲadu/ *a* shy; ~nhamento *m* shyness; ~nhar-se *vpr* be shy

ação /a'sãw/ *f* action; (*jurid*) lawsuit; (*com*) share

acariciar /akarisi'ar/ *vt* (*com a mão*) caress, stroke; (*adular*) make a fuss of; cherish <*esperanças*>

acarretar /akaxe'tar/ *vt* bring, cause

acasalar /akaza'lar/ *vt* mate; ~-se *vpr* mate

acaso /a'kazu/ *m* chance; ao ~ at random; por ~ by chance

aca|tamento /akata'mẽtu/ *m* respect, deference; ~tar *vt* respect, defer to <*pessoa, opinião*>; obey, abide by <*leis, ordens*>; take in <*criança*>

acc-, acç- (Port) *veja* ac-, aç-

acautelar-se /akawte'larsi/ *vpr* be cautious

acei|tação /asejta'sãw/ *f* acceptance; ~tar *vt* accept; ~tável (*pl* ~táveis) *a* acceptable

acele|ração /aselera'sãw/ *f* acceleration; ~rador *m* accelerator; ~rar *vi* accelerate □ *vt* speed up

acenar /ase'nar/ *vi* signal; (*saudando*) wave; ~ com promise, offer

acender /asẽ'der/ *vt* light <*cigarro, fogo, vela*>; switch on <*luz*>; heat up <*debate*>

aceno /a'senu/ *m* signal; (*de saudação*) wave

acen|to /a'sẽtu/ *m* accent; ~tuar *vt* accentuate; accent <*letra*>

acepção /asep'sãw/ *f* sense

acepipes /ase'pipʃ/ *m pl* (Port) cocktail snacks

acerca /a'serka/ ~ de *prep* about, concerning

acercar-se /aser'karsi/ *vpr* ~ de approach

acertar /aser'tar/ *vt* find <*(com o) caminho, (a) casa*>; put right, set <*relógio*>; get right <*pergunta*>; guess (correctly) <*solução*>; hit <*alvo*>; make <*acordo, negócio*>; fix, arrange <*encontro*> □ *vi* (*ter razão*) be right; (*atingir o alvo*) hit the mark; ~ com find, happen upon; ~ em hit

acervo /a'servu/ *m* collection; (*jurid*) estate

aceso /a'sezu/ *pp de* acender □ *a* <*luz*> on; <*fogo*> alight

aces|sar /ase'sar/ *vt* access; ~sível (*pl* ~síveis) *a* accessible; affordable <*preço*>; ~so /ε/ *m* access; (*de raiva, tosse*) fit; (*de febre*) attack; ~sório *a* & *m* accessory

acetona /ase'tona/ *f* (*para unhas*) nail varnish remover

achado /a'ʃadu/ *m* find

achaque /a'ʃaki/ *m* ailment

achar /a'ʃar/ *vt* find; (*pensar*) think; ~-se *vpr* (*estar*) be; (*considerar-se*) think that one is; acho que sim/não I think so/I don't think so

achatar /aʃa'tar/ *vt* flatten; cut <*salário*>

aciden|tado /asidẽ'tadu/ *a* rough <*terreno*>; bumpy <*estrada*>; eventful <*viagem, vida*>; injured <*pessoa*>; ~tal (*pl* ~tais) *a* accidental; ~te *m* accident

acidez /asi'des/ *f* acidity

ácido /'asidu/ *a* & *m* acid

acima /a'sima/ *adv* above; ~ de above; mais ~ higher up

acio|nar /asio'nar/ *vt* operate; (*jurid*) sue; ~nista *m/f* shareholder

acirrado /asi'xadu/ *a* stiff, tough

acla|mação /aklama'sãw/ *f* acclaim; (*de rei*) acclamation; ~mar *vt* acclaim

aclarar /akla'rar/ *vt* clarify, clear up □ *vi* clear up; ~-se *vpr* become clear

aclimatar /aklima'tar/ *vt* acclimatize, (*Amer*) acclimate; ~-se *vpr* get acclimatized, (*Amer*) get acclimated

aço /'asu/ *m* steel; ~ inoxidável stainless steel

acocorar-se /akoko'rarsi/ *vpr* squat (down)

acolá /ako'la/ *adv* over there

acolcho|ado /akowʃo'adu/ *m* quilt; ~ar *vt* quilt; upholster <*móveis*>

aco|lhedor /akoʎe'dor/ *a* welcoming; ~lher *vt* welcome <*hóspede*>; take in <*criança, refugiado*>; accept <*decisão, convite*>; respond to <*pedido*>; ~lhida *f*, ~lhimento *m* welcome; (*abrigo*) refuge

acomodar /akomo'dar/ *vt* accommodate; (*ordenar*) arrange; (*tornar cô-*

modo) make comfortable; ~-se *vpr* make o.s. comfortable

acompa|nhamento /akõpaɲa'mẽtu/ *m* (*mus*) accompaniment; (*prato*) side dish; (*comitiva*) escort; ~nhante *m/f* companion; (*mus*) accompanist; ~nhar *vt* accompany, go with; watch <*jogo, progresso*>; keep up with <*eventos, caso*>; keep up with, follow <*aula, conversa*>; share <*política, opinião*>; (*mus*) accompany; a estrada ~nha o rio the road runs alongside the river

aconche|gante /akõʃe'gãtʃi/ *a* cosy, (*Amer*) cozy; ~gar *vt* (*chegar a si*) cuddle; (*agasalhar*) wrap up; (*na cama*) tuck up; (*tornar cômodo*) make comfortable; ~gar-se *vpr* ensconce o.s.; ~gar-se com snuggle up to; ~go /e/ *m* cosiness, (*Amer*) coziness; (*abraço*) cuddle

acondicionar /akõdʒisio'nar/ *vt* condition; pack, package <*mercadoria*>

aconse|lhar /akõse'ʎar/ *vt* advise; ~lhar-se *vpr* consult; ~lhar alg a advise s.o. to; ~lhar aco a alg recommend sth to s.o.; ~lhável (*pl* ~lháveis) *a* advisable

aconte|cer /akõte'ser/ *vi* happen; ~cimento *m* event

acordar /akor'dar/ *vt/i* wake up

acorde /a'kɔrdʒi/ *m* chord

acordeão /akordʒi'ãw/ *m* accordion

acordo /a'kordu/ *m* agreement; de ~ com in agreement with <*pessoa*>; in accordance with <*lei etc*>; estar de ~ agree

Açores /a'soris/ *m pl* Azores

açoriano /asori'ano/ *a* & *m* Azorean

acorrentar /akoxẽ'tar/ *vt* chain (up)

acossar /ako'sar/ *vt* hound, badger

acos|tamento /akosta'mẽtu/ *m* hard shoulder, (*Amer*) berm; ~tar-se *vpr* lean back

acostu|mado /akostu'madu/ *a* usual, customary; estar ~mado a be used to; ~mar *vt* accustom; ~mar-se a get used to

acotovelar /akotove'lar/ *vt* (*empurrar*) jostle; (*para avisar*) nudge

açou|gue /a'sogi/ *m* butcher's (shop); ~gueiro *m* butcher

acovardar /akovar'dar/ *vt* cow, intimidate

acre /'akri/ *a* <*gosto*> bitter; <*aroma*> acrid, pungent; <*tom*> harsh

acredi|tar /akredʒi'tar/ *vt* believe; accredit <*representante*>; ~tar em believe <*pessoa, história*>; believe in <*Deus, fantasmas*>; (*ter confiança*) have faith in; ~tável (*pl* ~táveis) *a* believable

acre-doce /akri'dosi/ *a* sweet and sour

acrescentar /akresẽ'tar/ vt add

acres|cer /akre'ser/ vt (juntar) add;
(aumentar) increase □ vi increase;
~cido de with the addition of; ~ce
que add to that the fact that

acréscimo /a'krɛsimu/ m addition;
(aumento) increase

acriançado /akriã'sadu/ a childish

acrílico /a'kriliku/ a acrylic

acroba|cia /akroba'sia/ f acrobatics;
~ta m/f acrobat

act- (Port) veja at-

acuar /aku'ar/ vt corner

açúcar /a'sukar/ m sugar

açuca|rar /asuka'rar/ vt sweeten;
sugar <café, chá>; ~reiro m
sugar bowl

açude /a'sudʒi/ m dam

acudir /aku'dʒir/ vt/i ~ (a) come to
the rescue (of)

acumular /akumu'lar/ vt accumulate; combine <cargos>

acupuntura /akupũ'tura/ f acupunc-
ture

acu|sação /akuza'sãw/ f accusation;
~sar vt accuse; (jurid) charge; (revelar) reveal, show up; acknowledge
<recebimento>

acústi|ca /a'kustʃika/ f acoustics;
~co a acoustic

adap|tação /adapta'sãw/ f ad-
aptation; ~tado a <criança> well-
adjusted; ~tar vt adapt; (para encaixar) tailor; ~tar-se vpr adapt;
~tável (pl ~táveis) a adaptable

adega /a'dɛga/ f wine cellar

adentro /a'dẽtru/ adv inside; selva
~ into the jungle

adepto /a'deptu/ m follower; (Port: de
equipa) supporter

ade|quado /ade'kwadu/ a appropri-
ate, suitable; ~quar vt adapt, tailor

adereços /ade'resus/ m pl props

ade|rente /ade'rẽtʃi/ m/f follower;
~rir vi (colar) stick; join <a partido,
causa>; follow <a moda>; ~são f ad-
hesion; (apoio) support; ~sivo a
sticky, adhesive □ m sticker

ades|trado /ades'tradu/ a skilled;
~trador m trainer; ~trar vt train;
break in <cavalo>

adeus /a'dews/ int goodbye □ m goodbye, farewell

adian|tado /adʒiã'tadu/ a advanced;
<relógio> fast; chegar ~tado be
early; ~tamento m progress; (pagamento) advance; ~tar vt advance
<dinheiro>; put forward <relógio>;
bring forward <data, reunião>; get
ahead with <trabalho> □ vi
<relógio> gain; (ter efeito) be of use;
~tar-se vpr progress, get ahead;
não ~ta (fazer) it's no use (doing);
~te adv ahead

adia|r /adʒi'ar/ vt postpone; adjourn
<sessão>; ~mento m postponement,
adjournment

adi|ção /adʒi'sãw/ f addition;
~cionar vt add; ~do m attaché

adivi|nhação /adʒivina'sãw/ f guess-
work; (por adivinho) fortune-telling;
~nhar vt guess; tell <futuro, sorte>;
read <pensamento>; ~nho m fortune-
teller

adjetivo /adʒe'tʃivu/ m adjective

adminis|tração /adʒiministra'sãw/ f
administration; (de empresas)
management; ~trador m adminis-
trator; manager; ~trar vt administer; manage <empresa>

admi|ração /adʒimira'sãw/ f admira-
tion; (assombro) wonder(ment);
~rado a admired; (surpreso) amazed,
surprised; ~rador m admirer □ a
admiring; ~rar vt admire; (assombrar) amaze; ~rar-se vpr be
amazed; (assombroso) amazing;
~rável (pl ~ráveis) a ad-
mirable; (assombroso) amazing

admis|são /adʒimi'sãw/ f admission;
(de escola) intake; ~sível (pl
~síveis) a admissible

admitir /adʒimi'tʃir/ vt admit; (permitir) permit, allow; (contratar) take
on

adoção /ado'sãw/ f adoption

ado|çar /ado'sar/ vt sweeten;
~cicado a slightly sweet

adoecer /adoe'ser/ vi fall ill □ vt make
ill

adoles|cência /adole'sẽsia/ f adoles-
cence; ~cente a & m adolescent

adopt- (Port) veja adot-

adorar /ado'rar/ vt (amar) adore;
worship <deus>; (fam: gostar de)
love

adorme|cer /adorme'ser/ vi fall
asleep; <perna> go to sleep, go
numb; ~cido a sleeping; <perna>
numb

ador|nar /ador'nar/ vt adorn; ~no
/o/ m adornment

ado|tar /ado'tar/ vt adopt; ~tivo a
adopted

adquirir /adʒiki'rir/ vt acquire

adu|bar /adu'bar/ vt fertilize; ~bo m
fertilizer

adu|lação /adula'sãw/ f flattery; (do
público) adulation; ~lar vt make a
fuss of; (com palavras) flatter

adulterar /aduwte'rar/ vt adulterate;
cook, doctor <contas> □ vi commit
adultery

adúltero /a'duwteru/ m adulterer (f
-ess) □ a adulterous

adul|tério /aduw'tɛriu/ m adultery;
~to a & m adult

advento /adʒi'vẽtu/ m advent

advérbio /adʒi'vɛrbiu/ m adverb

adver|sário /adʒiver'sariu/ *m* opponent; (*inimigo*) adversary; ~sidade *f* adversity; ~so *a* adverse; (*adversário*) opposed

adver|tência /adʒiver'tẽsia/ *f* warning; ~tir *vt* warn

advo|cacia /adʒivoka'sia/ *f* legal practice; ~gado *m* lawyer; ~gar *vt* advocate; (*jurid*) plead □ *vi* practise law

aéreo /a'ɛriu/ *a* air

aero|dinâmica /aerodʒi'namika/ *f* aerodynamics; ~dinâmico *a* aerodynamic; ~dromo *m* airfield; ~moça /o/ *f* air hostess; ~nauta *m* airman (*f* -woman); ~náutica *f* (*força*) air force; (*ciência*) aeronautics; ~nave *f* aircraft; ~porto /o/ *m* airport

aeros|sol /aero'sɔw/ (*pl* ~sóis) *m* aerosol

afabilidade /afabili'dadʒi/ *f* friendliness, kindness

afagar /afa'gar/ *vt* stroke

afamado /afa'madu/ *a* renowned, famed

afas|tado /afas'tadu/ *a* remote; <*parente*> distant; ~tado de (far) away from; ~tamento *m* removal; (*distância*) distance; (*de candidato*) rejection; ~tar *vt* move away; (*tirar*) remove; ward off <*perigo, ameaça*>; put out of one's mind <*idéia*>; ~tar-se *vpr* move away; (*distanciar-se*) distance o.s.; (*de cargo*) step down

afá|vel /a'favew/ (*pl* ~veis) *a* friendly, genial

afazeres /afa'zeris/ *m pl* business; ~ domésticos (household) chores

afect- (*Port*) veja afet-

Afeganistão /afeganis'tãw/ *m* Afghanistan

afe|gão /afe'gãw/ *a & m* (*f* ~gã) Afghan

afeição /afej'sãw/ *f* affection, fondness

afeiçoado /afejsu'adu/ *a* (*devoto*) devoted; (*amoroso*) fond

afeminado /afemi'nadu/ *a* effeminate

aferir /afe'rir/ *vt* check, inspect <*pesos, medidas*>; (*avaliar*) assess; (*cotejar*) compare

aferrar /afe'xar/ *vt* grasp; ~se-a cling to

afe|tação /afeta'sãw/ *f* affectation; ~tado *a* affected; ~tar *vt* affect; ~tivo *a* (*carinhoso*) affectionate; (*sentimental*) emotional; ~to /ɛ/ *m* affection; ~tuoso /o/ *a* affectionate

afi|ado /afi'adu/ *a* sharp; skilled <*pessoa*>; ~ar *vt* sharpen

aficionado /afisio'nadu/ *m* enthusiast

afilhado /afi'ʎadu/ *m* godson (*f* -daughter)

afili|ação /afilia'sãw/ *f* affiliation; ~ada *f* affiliate; ~ar *vt* affiliate

afim /a'fĩ/ *a* related, similar

afinado /afi'nadu/ *a* in tune

afinal /afi'naw/ *adv* ~ (de contas) (*por fim*) in the end; (*pensando bem*) after all

afinar /afi'nar/ *vt* tune □ *vi* taper

afinco /a'fĩku/ *m* perseverance, determination

afinidade /afini'dadʒi/ *f* affinity

afir|mação /afirma'sãw/ *f* assertion; ~mar *vt* claim, assert; ~mativo *a* affirmative

afivelar /afive'lar/ *vt* buckle

afixar /afik'sar/ *vt* stick, post

afli|ção /afli'sãw/ *f* (*física*) affliction; (*cuidado*) anxiety; ~gir *vt* <*doença*> afflict; (*inquietar*) trouble; ~gir-se *vpr* worry; ~to *a* troubled, worried

afluente /aflu'etʃi/ *m* tributary

afo|bação /afoba'sãw/ *f* fluster, flap; ~bado *a* in a flap, flustered; ~bar *vt* fluster; ~bar-se *vpr* get flustered, get in a flap

afo|gado /afo'gadu/ *a* drowned; morrer ~gado drown; ~gador *m* choke; ~gar *vt/i* drown; (*auto*) flood; ~gar-se *vpr* (*matar-se*) drown o.s.

afoito /a'fojtu/ *a* bold, daring

afora /a'fɔra/ *adv* pelo mundo ~ throughout the world

afortunado /afortu'nadu/ *a* fortunate

afresco /a'fresku/ *m* fresco

Africa /'afrika/ *f* Africa; ~ do Sul South Africa

africano /afri'kanu/ *a & m* African

afrodisíaco /afrodʒi'ziaku/ *a & m* aphrodisiac

afron|ta /a'frõta/ *f* affront, insult; ~tar *vt* affront, insult

afrouxar /afro'ʃar/ *vt/i* loosen; (*de rapidez*) slow down; (*de disciplina*) relax

afta /'afta/ *f* (*mouth*) ulcer

afugentar /afuʒẽ'tar/ *vt* drive away; rout <*inimigo*>

afundar /afũ'dar/ *vt* sink; ~se-se *vpr* sink

agachar /aga'ʃar/ *vi* ~se-se *vpr* bend down

agarrar /aga'xar/ *vt* grab, snatch; ~se-a *vpr* ~se-a cling to, hold on to

agasalhar /agaza'ʎar/ *vt* ~lhar-se *vpr* wrap up (warmly); ~lho *m* (*casaco*) coat; (*suéter*) sweater

agência /a'ʒẽsia/ *f* agency; ~ de correio post office; ~ de viagens travel agency

agenda /a'ʒẽda/ *f* diary

agente /a'ʒẽtʃi/ *m/f* agent

ágil /'aʒiw/ (*pl* ágeis) *a* <*pessoa*> agile; <*serviço*> quick, efficient

agili|dade /aʒili'dadʒi/ *f* agility; (*rapidez*) speed; ~zar *vt* speed up, streamline

ágio /'aʒiu/ *m* premium

agiota /aʒi'ɔta/ *m/f* loan shark

agir /a'ʒir/ *vi* act

agi|tado /aʒi'tadu/ *a* agitated; <*mar*> rough; ~tar *vt* wave <*braços*>; wag <*rabo*>; shake <*garrafa*>; (*perturbar*) agitate; ~tar-se *vpr* get agitated; <*mar*> get rough

aglome|ração /aglomera'sãw/ *f* collection; (*de pessoas*) crowd; ~rar collect; ~rar-se *vpr* gather

agonia /ago'nia/ *f* anguish; (*da morte*) death throes

agora /a'gora/ *adv* now; (*há pouco*) just now; ~ mesmo right now; de ~ em diante from now on; até ~ so far, up till now

agosto /a'gostu/ *m* August

agouro /a'goru/ *m* omen

agraciar /agrasi'ar/ *vt* decorate

agra|dar /agra'dar/ *vt* please; (*fazer agrados*) be nice to, fuss over □ *vi* be pleasing, please; (*cair no gosto*) go down well; ~dável (*pl* ~dáveis) *a* pleasant

agrade|cer /agrade'ser/ *vt* ~cer aco a alg, ~cer a alg por aco thank s.o. for sth □ *vi* say thank you; ~cido *a* grateful; ~cimento *m* gratitude; *pl* thanks

agrado /a'gradu/ *m* fazer ~s a be nice to, make a fuss of

agrafar /agra'far/ *vt* (*Port*) staple; ~dor *m* stapler

agrário /a'grariu/ *a* land, agrarian

agra|vante /agra'vãtʃi/ *a* aggravating □ *f* aggravating circumstance; ~var *vt* aggravate, make worse; ~var-se *vpr* get worse

agredir /agre'dʒir/ *vt* attack

agregado /agre'gadu/ *m* (*em casa*) lodger

agres|são /agre'sãw/ *f* aggression; (*ataque*) assault; ~sivo *a* aggressive; ~sor *m* aggressor

agreste /a'grɛstʃi/ *a* rural

agrião /agri'ãw/ *m* watercress

agrícola /a'grikola/ *a* agricultural

agricul|tor /agrikuw'tor/ *m* farmer; ~tura *f* agriculture, farming

agridoce /agri'dosi/ *a* bittersweet

agropecuá|ria /agropeku'aria/ *f* farming; ~rio *a* agricultural

agru|pamento /agrupa'mẽtu/ *m* grouping; ~par *vt* group; ~par-se *vpr* group (together)

água /'agwa/ *f* water; dar ~ na boca be mouthwatering; ir por ~ abaixo go down the drain; ~ benta holy water; ~ doce fresh water; ~ mineral mineral water; ~ salgada s▯ water; ~ sanitária household ▯▯h

ag▯▯iro /agwa'seru/ *m* downpo▯▯

água-de|-coco /agwadʒi'koku/ *f* coconut water; ~-colônia *f* eau de cologne

aguado /a'gwadu/ *a* watery

aguardar /agwar'dar/ *vt* wait for, await □ *vi* wait

aguardente /agwar'dẽtʃi/ *f* spirit

aguarrás /agwa'xas/ *m* turpentine

água-viva /agwa'viva/ *f* jellyfish

agu|çado /agu'sadu/ *a* pointed; <*sentidos*> acute; ~çar *vt* sharpen; ~deza *f* sharpness; (*mental*) perceptiveness; ~do *a* sharp; <*som*> shrill; (*fig*) acute

agüentar /agwẽ'tar/ *vt* stand, put up with; hold <*peso*> □ *vi* <*pessoa*> hold out; <*suporte*> hold

águia /'agia/ *f* eagle

agulha /a'guʎa/ *f* needle

ai /aj/ *m* sigh; (*de dor*) groan □ *int* ah!; (*de dor*) ouch!

aí /a'i/ *adv* there; (*então*) then

aidético /aj'dɛtʃiku/ *a* suffering from Aids □ *m* Aids sufferer

AIDS /'ajdʒis/ *f* Aids

ainda /a'ĩda/ *adv* still; melhor ~ even better; não ... ~ not ... yet; ~ assim even so; ~ bem just as well; ~ por cima moreover, in addition; ~ que even if

aipim /aj'pĩ/ *m* cassava

aipo /'ajpu/ *m* celery

ajeitar /aʒej'tar/ *vt* (*arrumar*) sort out; (*arranjar*) arrange; (*ajustar*) adjust; ~-se *vpr* adapt; (*dar certo*) turn out right, sort o.s. out

ajoe|lhado /aʒoe'ʎadu/ *a* kneeling (down); ~lhar *vi*, ~lhar-se *vpr* kneel (down)

aju|da /a'ʒuda/ *f* help; ~dante *m/f* helper; ~dar *vt* help

ajuizado /aʒui'zadu/ *a* sensible

ajus|tar /aʒus'tar/ *vt* adjust; settle <*disputa*>; take in <*roupa*>; ~tar-se *vpr* conform; ~tável (*pl* ~táveis) *a* adjustable; ~te *m* adjustment; (*acordo*) settlement

ala /'ala/ *f* wing

ala|gação /alaga'sãw/ *f* flooding; ~gadiço *a* marshy □ *m* marsh; ~gar *vt* flood

alameda /ala'meda/ *f* avenue

álamo /'alamu/ *m* poplar (tree)

alarde /a'lardʒi/ *m* fazer ~ de flaunt; make a big thing of <*notícia*>; ~ar *vt/i* flaunt

alargar /alar'gar/ *vt* widen; (*fig*) broaden, let out <*roupa*>

alarido /ala'ridu/ *m* outcry

alar|ma /a'larma/ *m* alarm; ~mante *a* alarming; ~mar *vt* alarm; ~me *m* alarm; ~mista *a & m* alarmist

alastrar /alas'trar/ *vt* scatter; (*disseminar*) spread □ *vi* spread alavanca /ala'vãka/ f lever; ~ de mudanças gear lever

alban|ês /awba'nes/ a & m (f ~esa) Albanian

Albânia /aw'bania/ f Albania

albergue /aw'bergi/ m hostel

álbum /'awbũ/ m album

alça /'awsa/ f handle; (de roupa) strap; (de fusil) sight

alcachofra /awka'ʃofra/ f artichoke

alçada /aw'sada/ f competence, power

álcali /'awkali/ m alkali

alcan|çar /awkã'sar/ vt reach; (conseguir) attain; (compreender) understand □ vi reach; ~çável (pl ~cáveis) a reachable; attainable; ~ce m reach; (de tiro) range; (importância) consequence; (compreensão) understanding

alcaparra /awka'paxa/ f caper

alcatra /aw'katra/ f rump steak

alcatrão /awka'trãw/ m tar

álcool /'awkɔw/ m alcohol

alcoó|latra /awko'ɔlatra/ m/f alcoholic; ~lico a & m alcoholic

alcunha /aw'kuɲa/ f nickname

aldeia /aw'deja/ f village

aleatório /alia'tɔriu/ a random, arbitrary

alecrim /ale'krĩ/ m rosemary

ale|gação /alega'sãw/ f allegation; ~gar vt allege

ale|goria /alego'ria/ f allegory; ~górico a allegorical

ale|grar /ale'grar/ vt cheer up; brighten up <casa>; ~grar-se vpr cheer up; ~gre /ɛ/ a cheerful; <cores> bright; ~gria f joy

alei|jado /ale'ʒadu/ a crippled □ m cripple; ~jar vt cripple

alei|tamento /alejta'mẽtu/ m breast-feeding; ~tar vt breast-feed

além /a'lẽj/ adv beyond; ~ de (ao lado de lá de) beyond; (mais de) over; (ademais de) apart from

Alemanha /ale'maɲa/ f Germany

alemão /ale'mãw/ (pl ~mães) a & m (f ~mã) German

alen|tador /alẽta'dor/ a encouraging; ~tar vt encourage; ~tar-se vpr cheer up; ~to m courage; (fôlego) breath

alergia /aler'ʒia/ f allergy

alérgico /a'lerʒiku/ a allergic (a to)

aler|ta /a'lerta/ a & m alert □ adv on the alert; ~tar vt alert

alfa|bético /awfa'bɛtʃiku/ a alphabetical; ~betização f literacy; ~betizar vt teach to read and write; ~beto m alphabet

alface /aw'fasi/ f lettuce

alfaiate /awfaj'atʃi/ m tailor

al|fândega /aw'fãdʒiga/ f customs;

~fandegário a customs □ m customs officer

alfine|tada /awfine'tada/ f prick; (dor) stabbing pain; (fig) dig; ~te /e/ m pin; ~te de segurança safety pin

alforreca /alfo'xeka/ f (Port) jellyfish

alga /'awga/ f seaweed

algarismo /awga'rizmu/ m numeral

algazarra /awga'zaxa/ f uproar, racket

alge|mar /awʒe'mar/ vt handcuff; ~mas /e/ f pl handcuffs

algibeira /alʒi'bejra/ f (Port) pocket

algo /'awgu/ pron something; (numa pergunta) anything □ adv somewhat

algodão /awgo'dãw/ m (-(doce) candy floss, (Amer) cotton candy; ~ (hidrófilo) cotton wool, (Amer) absorbent cotton

alguém /aw'gẽj/ pron somebody, someone; (numa pergunta) anybody, anyone

al|gum /aw'gũ/ (f ~guma) a some; (numa pergunta) any; (nenhum) no, not one □ pron pl some; ~guma coisa something

algures /aw'guris/ adv somewhere

alheio /a'ʎeju/ a (de outra pessoa) someone else's; (de outras pessoas) other people's; (a foreign to; (impróprio) irrelevant to; (desatento) unaware of; ~ de removed from

alho /'aʎu/ m garlic; ~-poró m leek

ali /a'li/ adv (over) there

ali|ado /ali'adu/ a allied □ m ally; ~ança f alliance; (anel) wedding ring; ~ar vt, ~ar-se vpr ally

aliás /a'ljaʃ/ adv (além disso) what's more, furthermore; (no entanto) however; (diga-se de passagem) by the way, incidentally; (senão) otherwise

álibi /'alibi/ m alibi

alicate /ali'katʃi/ m pliers; ~ de unhas nail clippers

alicerce /ali'sɛrsi/ m foundation; (fig) basis

alie|nado /alie'nadu/ a alienated; (demente) insane; ~nar vt alienate; transfer <bens>; ~nígena a & m/f alien

alimen|tação /alimẽta'sãw/ f (ato) feeding; (comida) food; (tecn) supply; ~tar a food; <hábitos> eating □ vt feed; (fig) nurture; ~tar-se de live on; ~tício a foodstuffs; ~to m food

ali|nhado /ali'ɲadu/ a aligned; <pessoa> smart, (Amer) sharp; ~nhar vt align

alíquota /a'likwota/ f (de imposto) bracket

alisar /ali'zar/ vt smooth (out); straighten <cabelo>

alistar /alis'tar/ vt recruit; ~-se vpr enlist

aliviar /alivi'ar/ vt relieve

alívio /a'liviu/ m relief

alma /'awma/ f soul

almanaque /awma'naki/ m yearbook

almejar /awme'ʒar/ vt long for

almirante /awmi'rãtʃi/ m admiral

almoç|ar /awmo'sar/ vi have lunch □ vt have for lunch; ~ço /o/ m lunch

almofada /awmo'fada/ f cushion; (Port: de cama) pillow

almôndega /aw'mõdʒiga/ f meatball

almoxarifado /awmoʃari'fadu/ m storeroom

alô /a'lo/ int hallo

alocar /alo'kar/ vt allocate

alo|jamento /aloʒa'mẽtu/ m accommodation, (Amer) accommodations; (habitação) housing; ~jar vt accommodate; house <sem-teto>; ~jar-se vpr stay

alongar /alõ'gar/ vt lengthen; extend, stretch out <braço>

alpendre /aw'pẽdri/ m shed; (pórtico) porch

Alpes /'awpis/ m pl Alps

alpinis|mo /awpi'nizmu/ m mountaineering; ~ta m/f mountaineer

alqueire /aw'keri/ m = 4.84 hectares, (in São Paulo = 2.42 hectares)

alquimi|a /awki'mia/ f alchemy; ~sta mf alchemist

alta /'awta/ f rise; dar ~ a discharge; ter ~ be discharged

altar /aw'tar/ m altar

alterar /awte'rar/ vt alter; (falsificar) falsify; ~-se vpr change; (zangar-se) get angry

alter|nado /awter'nadu/ a alternate; ~nar vt/i, ~nar-se vpr alternate; ~nativa f alternative; ~nativo a alternative; <corrente> alternating

al|teza /aw'teza/ f highness; ~titude f altitude

alti|vez /awtʃi'ves/ f arrogance; ~vo a arrogant; (elevado) majestic

alto /'awtu/ a high; <pessoa> tall; <barulho> loud □ adv high; <falar> loud(ly); <ler> aloud □ m top; os ~s e baixos the ups and downs □ int halt!; ~-falante m loudspeaker

altura /aw'tura/ f height; (momento) moment; ser à ~ de be up to

aluci|nação /alusina'sãw/ f hallucination; ~nante a mind-boggling, crazy

aludir /alu'dʒir/ vi allude (a to)

alu|gar /alu'gar/ vt let, rent out <casa>; hire, rent <carro>; <locador> let, rent out, hire out; ~guel (Port), ~guer /ɛ/ m rent; (ato) renting

alumiar /alumi'ar/ vt light (up)

alumínio /alu'miniu/ m aluminium, (Amer) aluminum

aluno /a'lunu/ m pupil

alusão /alu'zãw/ f allusion (a to)

alvará /awva'ra/ m permit, licence

alve|jante /awve'ʒãtʃi/ m bleach; ~jar vt bleach; (visar) aim at

alvenaria /awvena'ria/ f masonry

alvo /'awvu/ m target

alvorada /awvo'rada/ f dawn

alvoro|çar /awvoro'sar/ vt stir up, agitate; (entusiasmar) excite; ~ço /o/ m (tumulto) uproar; (entusiasmo) excitement

amabilidade /amabili'dadʒi/ f kindness

amaci|ante /amasi'ãtʃi/ m (de roupa) (fabric) conditioner; ~ar vt soften; run in <carro>

amador /ama'dor/ a & m amateur; ~ismo m amateurism; ~ístico a amateurish

amadurecer /amadure'ser/ vt/i <fruta> ripen; (fig) mature

âmago /'amagu/ m heart, core; (da questão) crux

amaldiçoar /amawdʒiso'ar/ vt curse

amamentar /amamẽ'tar/ vt breastfeed

amanhã /ama'ɲã/ m & adv tomorrow; depois de ~ the day after tomorrow

amanhecer /amaɲe'ser/ vi & m dawn

amansar /amã'sar/ vt tame; (fig) placate <pessoa>

a|mante /a'mãtʃi/ m/f lover; ~mar vt/i love

amarelo /ama'rɛlu/ a & m yellow

amar|go /a'margu/ a bitter; ~gura f bitterness; ~gurar vt embitter; (sofrer) endure

amarrar /ama'xar/ vt tie (up); (naut) moor; ~ a cara frown, scowl

amarrotar /amaxo'tar/ vt crease

amassar /ama'sar/ vt crush, squash; screw up <papel>; crease <roupa>; dent <carro>; knead <pão>; mash <batatas>

amá|vel /a'mavew/ (pl ~veis) a kind

Ama|zonas /ama'zonas/ m Amazon; ~zônia f Amazonia

âmbar /'ãbar/ m amber

ambi|ção /ãbi'sãw/ f ambition; ~cionar vt aspire to; ~cioso /o/ a ambitious

ambien|tal /ãbiẽ'taw/ (pl ~tais) a environmental; ~tar vt set <filme, livro>; set up <casa>; ~tar-se vpr settle in; ~te m environment; (atmosfera) atmosphere

am|bigüidade /ãbigwi'dadʒi/ f ambiguity; ~bíguo a ambiguous

âmbito /'ãbitu/ m scope, range

ambos /'ãbus/ a & pron both

ambu|lância /ăbu'lãsia/ f ambulance; ~lante a (que anda) walking; <músico> wandering; <venda> mobile; ~latório m out-patient clinic

amea|ça /ami'asa/ f threat; ~çadora a threatening; ~çar vt threaten

ameba /a'mɛba/ f amoeba

amedrontar /amedrõ'tar/ vt scare; ~-se vpr get scared

ameixa /a'meʃa/ f plum; (passa) prune

amém /a'mẽj/ int amen □ m agreement; dizer ~ a go along with

amêndoa /a'mẽdoa/ f almond

amendoim /amẽdo'ĩ/ m peanut

ame|nidade /ameni'dadʒi/ f pleasantness; pl pleasantries, small talk; ~nizar vt ease; calm <ânimos>; settle <disputa>; tone down <repreensão>; ~no /e/ a pleasant; mild <clima>

América /a'mɛrika/ f America; ~ do Norte/Sul North/South America

america|nizar /amerikani'zar/ vt Americanize; ~no a & m American

amestrar /ames'trar/ vt train

ametista /ame'tʃista/ f amethyst

amianto /ami'ãtu/ m asbestos

ami|gar-se /ami'garsi/ vpr make friends; ~gável (pl ~gáveis) a amicable

amígdala /a'migdala/ f tonsil

amigdalite /amigda'litʃi/ f tonsillitis

amigo /a'migu/ a friendly □ m friend; ~ da onça false friend

amistoso /amis'tozu/ a & m friendly

amiúde /ami'udʒi/ adv often

amizade /ami'zadʒi/ f friendship

amnésia /ami'nɛzia/ f amnesia

amnistia /amnis'tia/ f (Port) veja anistia

amo|lação /amola'sãw/ f annoyance; ~lante a annoying; ~lar vt annoy, bother; sharpen <faca>; ~lar-se vpr get annoyed

amolecer /amole'ser/ vt/i soften

amol|gadura /amowga'dura/ f dent; ~gar vt dent

amoníaco /amo'niaku/ m ammonia

amontoar /amõto'ar/ vt pile up; amass <riquezas>; ~-se vpr pile up

amor /a'mor/ m love; ~ próprio self-esteem

amora /a'mɔra/ f ~ preta, (Port) silvestre blackberry

amordaçar /amorda'sar/ vt gag

amoroso /amo'rozu/ adj loving

amor-perfeito /amorper'fejtu/ m pansy

amorte|cedor /amortese'dor/ m shock absorber; ~cer vt deaden; absorb <impacto>; break <queda> □ vi fade

amostra /a'mɔstra/ f sample

ampa|rar /ăpa'rar/ vt support; (fig) protect; ~rar-se vpr lean; ~ro m (apoio) support; (proteção) protection; (ajuda) aid

ampère /ă'pɛri/ m amp(ere)

ampli|ação /ăplia'sãw/ f (de foto) enlargement; (de casa) extension; ~ar vt enlarge <foto>; extend <casa>; broaden <conhecimentos>

amplifi|cador /ăplifika'dor/ m amplifier; ~car vt amplify

amplo /'ăplu/ a <sala> spacious; <roupa> full; <sentido, conhecimento> broad

ampola /ă'pola/ f ampoule

amputar /ăpu'tar/ vt amputate

Amsterdã /amister'dã/, (Port) Amsterdão /amiʃter'dăw/ f Amsterdam

amu|ado /amu'adu/ a in a sulk, sulky; ~ar vi sulk

amuleto /amu'leto/ m charm

amuo /a'muu/ m sulk

ana|crônico /ana'kroniku/ a anachronistic; ~cronismo m anachronism

anais /a'najs/ m pl annals

analfabeto /anawfa'bɛtu/ a & m illiterate

analisar /anali'zar/ vt analyse

análise /a'nalizi/ f analysis

ana|lista /ana'lista/ m/f analyst; ~lítico a analytical

analogia /analo'ʒia/ f analogy

análogo /a'nalogu/ a analogous

ananás /ana'naʃ/ m invar (Port) pineapple

anão /a'năw/ a & m (f anã) dwarf

anarquia /anar'kia/ f anarchy; (fig) chaos

anárquico /a'narkiku/ a anarchic

anarquista /anar'kista/ m/f anarchist

ana|tomia /anato'mia/ f anatomy; ~tômico a anatomical

anca /'ăka/ f (de pessoa) hip; (de animal) rump

anchova /ă'ʃova/ f anchovy

ancinho /ă'siɲu/ m rake

âncora /'ăkora/ f anchor

anco|radouro /ăkora'doru/ m anchorage; ~rar vt/i anchor

andaime /ă'dajmi/ m scaffolding

an|damento /ăda'mẽtu/ m (progresso) progress; (rumo) course; dar ~damento a set in motion; ~dar m (jeito de andar) gait, walk; (de prédio) floor; (Port: apartamento) flat, (Amer) apartment □ vi (ir a pé) walk; (de trem, ônibus) travel; (a cavalo, de bicicleta) ride; (funcionar, progredir) go; ele anda deprimido he's been depressed lately

Andes /ˈãdʒis/ m pl Andes

andorinha /ãdoˈriɲa/ f swallow

anedota /aneˈdɔta/ f anecdote

anel /aˈnɛw/ (pl anéis) m ring; (no cabelo) curl; ~ viário ringroad

anelado /aneˈladu/ a curly

anemia /aneˈmia/ f anaemia

anêmico /aˈnemiku/ a anaemic

anes|tesia /anesteˈzia/ f anaesthesia; (droga) anaesthetic; ~tesiar vt anaesthetize; ~tésico a & m anaesthetic; ~tesista m/f anaesthetist

ane|xar /anekˈsar/ vt annex <terras>; (em carta) enclose; (juntar) attach; ~xo /ε/ a attached; (em carta) enclosed □ m annexe; (em carta) enclosure

anfíbio /ãˈfibiu/ a amphibious □ m amphibian

anfiteatro /ãfitʃiˈatru/ m amphitheatre; (no teatro) dress circle

anfi|trião /ãfitriˈãw/ m (f ~triã) host (f -ess)

angariar /ãgariˈar/ vt raise <fundos>; canvass for <votos>; win <adeptos, simpatia>

angli|cano /ãgliˈkanu/ a & m Anglican; ~cismo m Anglicism

anglo-saxônico /ãglusakˈsoniku/ a Anglo-Saxon

Angola /ãˈgɔla/ f Angola

angolano /ãgoˈlanu/ a & m Angolan

angra /ˈãgra/ f inlet, cove

angular /ãguˈlar/ a angular

ângulo /ˈãgulu/ m angle

angústia /ãˈgustʃia/ f anguish, anxiety

angustiante /ãgustʃiˈãtʃi/ a distressing; <momento> anxious

ani|mado /aniˈmadu/ a (vivo) lively; (alegre) cheerful; (entusiasmado) enthusiastic; ~mador a encouraging □ m presenter; ~mal (pl ~mais) a & m animal; ~mar vt encourage; liven up <festa>; ~mar-se vpr cheer up; <festa> liven up

ânimo /ˈanimu/ m courage, spirit; pl tempers

animosidade /animoziˈdadʒi/ f animosity

aniquilar /anikiˈlar/ vt destroy; (prostrar) shatter

anis /aˈnis/ m aniseed

anistia /anisˈtʃia/ f amnesty

aniver|sariante /aniversariˈãtʃi/ m/f birthday boy (f girl); ~sário m birthday; (de casamento etc) anniversary

anjo /ˈãʒu/ m angel

ano /ˈanu/ m year; fazer ~s have a birthday; ~ bissexto leap year; ~ letivo academic year; ~-bom m New Year

anoite|cer /anojteˈser/ m nightfall □ vi ~ceu night fell

anomalia /anomaˈlia/ f anomaly

anônimato /anoniˈmatu/ m anonymity

anônimo /aˈnonimu/ a anonymous

anor|mal /anorˈmaw/ (pl ~mais) a abnormal

ano|tação /anotaˈsãw/ f note; ~tar vt note down, write down

ânsia /ˈãsia/ f anxiety; (desejo) longing; ~s de vômito nausea

ansi|ar /ãsiˈar/ vi ~ por long for; ~edade f anxiety; (desejo) eagerness; ~oso /o/ a anxious

antártico /ãˈtartʃiku/ a & m Antarctic

antebraço /ãtʃiˈbrasu/ m forearm

antece|dência /ãteseˈdẽsia/ f com ~dência in advance; ~dente a preceding; ~dentes m pl record, past

antecessor /ãteseˈsor/ m (f ~a) predecessor

anteci|pação /ãtʃisipaˈsãw/ f anticipation; com ~pação in advance; ~padamente adv in advance; ~pado a advance; ~par vt anticipate, forestall; (adiantar) bring forward; ~par-se vpr be previous

antena /ãˈtena/ f aerial, (Amer) antenna; (de inseto) feeler

anteontem /ãtʃiˈõtẽ/ adv the day before yesterday

antepassado /ãtʃipaˈsadu/ m ancestor

anterior /ãteriˈor/ a previous; (dianteiro) front

antes /ˈãtʃis/ adv before; (ao contrário) rather; ~ de/que before

ante-sala /ãtʃiˈsala/ f ante-room

anti|biótico /ãtʃibiˈɔtʃiku/ a & m antibiotic; ~caspa a anti-dandruff; ~concepcional (pl ~concepcionais) a & m contraceptive; ~congelante m antifreeze; ~corpo m antibody

antídoto /ãˈtʃidotu/ m antidote

antiético /ãtʃiˈɛtʃiku/ a unethical

antigamente /ãtʃigaˈmẽtʃi/ adv formerly

anti|go /ãˈtʃigu/ a old; (da antiguidade) ancient; <móveis etc> antique; (anterior) former; ~guidade f antiquity; (numa firma) seniority; pl (monumentos) antiquities; (móveis etc) antiques

anti-|higiênico /ãtʃiʒiˈeniku/ a unhygienic; ~histamínico a & m antihistamine; ~horário a anti-clockwise

antilhano /ãtʃiˈʎanu/ a & m West Indian

Antilhas /ãˈtʃiʎas/ f pl West Indies

anti|patia /ãtʃipaˈtʃia/ f dislike; ~pático a unpleasant, unfriendly

antiquado /ãtʃi'kwadu/ a antiquated, out-dated

anti-semitismo /ãtʃisemi'tʃizmu/ m anti-Semitism; ~séptico a & m antiseptic; ~social (pl ~sociais) a antisocial

antítese /ã'tʃitezi/ f antithesis

antologia /ãtolo'ʒia/ f anthology

antônimo /ã'tonimu/ m antonym

antro /'ãtru/ m cavern; (de animal) lair; (de ladrões) den

antro|pófago /ãtro'pɔfagu/ a man-eating; ~pologia f anthropology; ~pólogo m anthropologist

anu|al /anu'aw/ (pl ~ais) a annual, yearly

anu|lação /anula'sãw/ f cancellation; ~lar vt cancel; annull □ a (compensar) cancel out □ m ring finger

anunciar /anũsi'ar/ vt announce; advertise <produto>

anúncio /a'nũsiu/ m announcement; (propaganda, classificado) advert(ise-ment); (cartaz) notice

ânus /'anus/ m invar anus

an|zol /ã'zɔw/ (pl ~zóis) m fish-hook

aonde /a'õdʒi/ adv where

apadrinhar /apadri'ɲar/ vt be godfather to <afilhado>; be best man for <noivo>; (proteger) protect; (patrocinar) support

apa|gado /apa'gadu/ a <fogo> out; <luz, TV> off; (indistinto) faint; (pessoa) dull; ~gar vt put out <cigarro, fogo>; blow out <vela>; switch off <luz, TV>; rub out <erro>; clean <quadro-negro>; ~gar-se vpr <fogo, luz> go out; <lembrança> fade; (desmaiar) pass out; (fam: dormir) nod off

apaixo|nado /apaʃo'nadu/ a in love (por with); ~nante a captivating; ~nar-se vpr fall in love (por with)

apalpar /apaw'par/ vt touch, feel; <médico> examine

apanhar /apa'ɲar/ vt catch; (do chão) pick up; pick <flores, frutas>; (ir buscar) pick up; (alcançar) catch up □ vi be beaten

aparafusar /aparafu'zar/ vt screw

apa|ra-lápis /apara'lapiʃ/ m invar (Port) pencil sharpener; ~rar vt catch <bola>; parry <golpe>; trim <cabelo>; sharpen <lápis>

aparato /apa'ratu/ m pomp, ceremony

apare|cer /apare'ser/ vi appear; ~ça! do drop in!; ~cimento m appearance

apare|lhagem /apare'ʎaʒẽ/ f equipment; ~lhar vt equip; ~lho /e/ m apparatus; (máquina) machine; (de chá) set, service; (fone) phone

aparência /apa'rẽsia/ f appearance; na ~ apparently

aparen|tado /aparẽ'tadu/ a related; ~tar vt show; (fingir) feign; ~te a apparent

apar|tamento /aparta'mẽtu/ m flat, (Amer) apartment; ~tar vt, ~tar-se vpr separate; ~te m aside

apatia /apa'tʃia/ f apathy

apático /a'patʃiku/ a apathetic

apavo|rante /apavo'rãtʃi/ a terrifying; ~rar vt terrify; ~rar-se vpr be terrified

apaziguar /apazi'gwar/ vt appease

apear-se /api'arsi/ vpr (de cavalo) dismount; (de ônibus) alight

ape|gar-se /ape'garsi/ vpr become attached (a to); ~go /e/ m attachment

ape|lação /apela'sãw/ f appeal; (fig) exhibitionism; ~lar vi appeal (de against); ~lar para appeal to; (fig) resort to

apeli|dar /apeli'dar/ vt nickname; ~do m nickname

apelo /a'pelu/ m appeal

apenas /a'penas/ adv only

apêndice /a'pẽdʒisi/ m appendix

apendicite /apẽdʒi'sitʃi/ f appendicitis

aperceber-se /aperse'bersi/ vpr ~ (de) notice, realize

aperfeiçoar /aperfejso'ar/ vt perfect

aperitivo /aperi'tʃivu/ m aperitif

aper|tado /aper'tadu/ a tight; (sem dinheiro) hard-up; ~tar vt (segurar) hold tight; tighten <cinto>; press <botão>; squeeze <esponja>; take in <vestido>; fasten <cinto de segurança>; step up <vigilância>; cut down on <despesas>; break <coração>; (fig) pressurize <pessoa> □ vi <sapato> pinch; <chuva, frio> get worse; <estrada> narrow; ~tar-se vpr (gastar menos) tighten one's belt; (não ter dinheiro) feel the pinch; ~tar a mão de alg shake hands with s.o.; ~to /e/ m pressure; (de botão) press; (dificuldade) tight spot, jam; ~to de mãos handshake

apesar /ape'zar/ ~ de prep in spite of

apeti|te /ape'tʃitʃi/ m appetite; ~toso /o/ a appetizing

apetrechos /ape'treʃus/ m pl gear; (de pesca) tackle

apimentado /apimẽ'tadu/ a spicy, hot

apinhar /api'ɲar/ vt crowd, pack; ~-se vpr crowd

api|tar /api'tar/ vi whistle □ vt referee <jogo>; ~to m whistle

aplanar /apla'nar/ vt level <terreno>; (fig) smooth <caminho>; smooth over <problema>

aplau|dir /aplaw'dʒir/ vt applaud; ~so(s) m (pl) applause

apli|cação /aplika'sãw/ f application; (de dinheiro) investment; (de lei) enforcement; ~car vt apply; invest <dinheiro>; enforce <lei>; ~car-se vpr apply (a to); (ao estudo etc) apply o.s. (a to); ~que m hairpiece

apoderar-se /apode'rarsi/ vpr ~ de take possession of; <raiva> take hold of

apodrecer /apodre'ser/ vt/i rot

apoiar /apoj'ar/ vt lean; (fig) support; (basear) base; ~ar-se vpr ~ar-se em lean on; (fig) be based on, rest on; ~o m support

apólice /a'polisi/ f policy; (ação) bond

apontador /apõta'dor/ m pencil sharpener; ~tar vt (com o dedo) point at, point to; point out <erro, caso interessante>; aim <arma>; name <nomes>; put forward <razão>; (à sol, planta) come up; (com o dedo) point (para to)

apoquentar /apokē'tar/ vt annoy

aporrinhar /apoxi'ɲar/ vt annoy

após /a'pɔs/ adv after; loção ~-barba after-shave (lotion)

aposentado /apozē'tadu/ a retired □ m pensioner; ~tadoria f retirement; (pensão) pension; ~tar vt, ~tar-se vpr retire; ~to m room

após-guerra /apɔz'gɛxa/ m post-war period

aposta /a'pɔsta/ f bet; ~tar vt bet (em on); (fig) have faith (em in)

apostila /apos'tʃila/ f revision aid, book of key facts

apóstolo /a'pɔstolu/ m apostle

apóstrofo /a'pɔstrofu/ m apostrophe

apreciação /apresia'sãw/ f appreciation; ~ciar vt appreciate; think highly of <pessoa>; ~ciativo a appreciative; ~ciável (pl ~ciáveis) a appreciable; ~ço /e/ m regard

apreender /apriē'der/ vt seize <contrabando>; apprehend <criminoso>; grasp <sentido>; ~são f (de contrabando) seizure; ~sivo a apprehensive

apregoar /aprego'ar/ vt proclaim; cry <mercadoria>

aprender /aprē'der/ vt/i learn; ~diz m/f (de ofício) apprentice; (de direção) learner; ~dizado m, ~dizagem f (de ofício) apprenticeship; (de profissão) training; (escolar) learning

apresentação /aprezēta'sãw/ f presentation; (teatral etc) performance; (de pessoas) introduction; ~tador m presenter; ~tar vt present; introduce <pessoa>; ~tar-se vpr (identificar-se) introduce o.s.; <ocasião, problema> present o.s., arise; ~tar-se para report to <polícia etc>; go in for <exame>; stand for <eleição>; ~tável (pl ~táveis) a presentable

apressado /apre'sadu/ a hurried; ~sar vt hurry; ~sar-se vpr hurry (up)

aprimorar /aprimo'rar/ vt perfect, refine

aprofundar /aprofū'dar/ vt deepen; study carefully <questão>; ~se vpr get deeper; ~se em go deeper into

aprontar /aprõ'tar/ vt get ready; pick <briga> □ vi act up; ~se vpr get ready

apropriado /apropri'adu/ a appropriate, suitable

aprovação /aprova'sãw/ f approval; (num exame) pass; ~var vt approve of; approve <lei> □ vi make the grade; ser ~vado (num exame) pass

aproveitador /aprovejta'dor/ m opportunist; ~tamento m utilization; ~tar vt take advantage of; take <ocasião>; (utilizar) use □ vi make the most of it; (Port: adiantar) be of use; ~tar-se vpr take advantage (de of); ~te! (divirta-se) have a good time!

aproximação /aprosima'sãw/ f (chegada) approach; (estimativa) approximation; ~mado a <valor> approximate; ~mar vt move nearer; (aliar) bring together; ~mar-se vpr approach, get nearer (de to)

aptidão /aptʃi'dãw/ f aptitude, suitability; ~to a suitable

apunhalar /apuɲa'lar/ vt stab

apurado /apu'radu/ a refined; ~rar vt (aprimorar) refine; (descobrir) ascertain; investigate <caso>; collect <dinheiro>; count <votos>; ~rar-se vpr (com a roupa) dress smartly; ~ro m refinement; (no vestir) elegance; (dificuldade) difficulty; pl trouble

aquarela /akwa'rela/ f watercolour

aquariano /akwari'anu/ a & m Aquarian

aquário /a'kwariu/ m aquarium; Aquário Aquarius

aquartelar /akwarte'lar/ vt billet

aquático /a'kwatʃiku/ a aquatic, water

aquecedor /akese'dor/ m heater; ~cer vi heat □ vi, ~cer-se vpr heat up; ~cimento m heating

aqueduto /ake'dutu/ m aqueduct

aquele /a'keli/ a that; pl those □ pron that one; pl those; ~ que the one that

àquele = a²⁺ + aquele

aqui /a'ki/ adv here

aquilo /a'kilu/ pron that

àquilo = a²⁺ + aquilo

aquisição /akizi'sãw/ f acquisition; ~tivo a poder ~tivo purchasing power

ar /ar/ m air; (aspecto) look, air; (Port: no carro) choke; ao ~ livre in the open air; no ~ (*fig*) up in the air; (*TV*) on air; ~ condicionado air conditioning

árabe /'arabi/ *a & m* Arab; (*ling*) Arabic

Arábia /a'rabia/ *f* Arabia; ~ Saudita Saudi Arabia

arado /a'radu/ *m* plough, (*Amer*) plow

aragem /a'raʒẽ/ *f* breeze

arame /a'rami/ *m* wire; ~ farpado barbed wire

aranha /a'raɲa/ *f* spider

arar /a'rar/ *vt* plough, (*Amer*) plow

arara /a'rara/ *f* parrot

arbi|trar /arbi'trar/ *vt/i* referee <*jogo*>; arbitrate <*disputa*>; ~trário *a* arbitrary

arbítrio /ar'bitriu/ *m* judgement; livre ~ free will

árbitro /'arbitru/ *m* arbiter <*da moda etc*>; (*jurid*) arbitrator; (*de futebol*) referee; (*de tênis*) umpire

arborizado /arbori'zadu/ *a* wooded, green; <*rua*> tree-lined

arbusto /ar'bustu/ *m* shrub

ar|ca /'arka/ *f* ~ca de Noé Noah's Ark; ~cada *f* (*galeria*) arcade; (*arco*) arch

arcaico /ar'kajku/ *a* archaic

arcar /ar'kar/ *vt* ~ com deal with

arcebispo /arse'bispu/ *m* archbishop

arco /'arku/ *m* (*arquit*) arch; (*arma, mus*) bow; (*eletr; mat*) arc; ~da-velha *m* coisa do ~-da-velha amazing thing; ~-íris *m invar* rainbow

ar|dente /ar'dẽtʃi/ *a* burning; (*fig*) ardent; ~der *vi* burn; <*olhos, ferida*> sting

ar|dil /ar'dʒiw/ (*pl* ~dis) *m* trick, ruse

ardor /ar'dor/ *m* heat; (*fig*) ardour; com ~ ardently

árduo /'arduu/ *a* strenuous, arduous

área /'aria/ *f* area; (*grande*) ~ penalty area; ~ (*de serviço*) yard

arear /ari'ar/ *vt* scour <*panela*>

areia /a'reja/ *f* sand

arejar /are'ʒar/ *vt* air □ *vi*, ~-se *vpr* get some air; (*descansar*) have a breather

are|na /a'rena/ *f* arena; ~noso /o/ *a* sandy

arenque /a'rẽki/ *m* herring

argamassa /arga'masa/ *f* mortar

Argélia /ar'ʒɛlia/ *f* Algeria

argelino /arʒe'linu/ *a & m* Algerian

Argentina /arʒẽ'tʃina/ *f* Argentina

argentino /arʒẽ'tʃinu/ *a & m* Argentinian

argila /ar'ʒila/ *f* clay

argola /ar'gola/ *f* ring

argumen|tar /argumẽ'tar/ *vt/i* argue; ~to *m* argument; (*de filme etc*) subject-matter

ariano /ari'anu/ *a & m* (*do signo Aries*) Arian

árido /'aridu/ *a* arid; barren <*deserto*>; (*fig*) dull, dry

Aries /'aris/ *f* Aries

arisco /a'risku/ *a* timid

aristo|cracia /aristokra'sia/ *f* aristocracy; ~crata *m/f* aristocrat; ~crático *a* aristocratic

aritmética /aritʃ'mɛtʃika/ *f* arithmetic

arma /'arma/ *f* weapon; *pl* arms; ~ de fogo firearm

ar|mação /arma'sãw/ *f* frame; (*de óculos*) frames; (*naut*) rigging; ~madilha *f* trap; ~madura *f* suit of armour; (*armação*) framework; ~mar *vt* (*dar armas a*) arm; (*montar*) put up, assemble; set up <*máquina*>; set, lay <*armadilha*>; fit out <*navio*>;hatch <*plano, complô*>; cause <*briga*>; ~mar-se *vpr* arm o.s.

armarinho /arma'riɲu/ *m* haberdashery, (*Amer*) notions

armário /ar'mariu/ *m* cupboard; (*de roupa*) wardrobe

arma|zém /arma'zẽj/ *m* warehouse; (*loja*) general store; (*depósito*) storeroom; ~zenagem *f*, ~zenamento *m* storage; ~zenar *vt* store

Armênia /ar'menia/ *f* Armenia

armênio /ar'meniu/ *a & m* Armenian

aro /'aru/ *m* (*de roda, óculos*) rim; (*de porta*) frame

aro|ma /a'roma/ *f* aroma; (*perfume*) fragrance; ~mático *a* aromatic; fragrant

ar|pão /ar'pãw/ *m* harpoon; ~poar *vt* harpoon

arquear /arki'ar/ *vt* arch; ~-se *vpr* bend, bow

arque|ologia /arkiolo'ʒia/ *f* archaeology; ~ológico *a* archaeological; ~ólogo *m* archaeologist

arquétipo /ar'kɛtʃipu/ *m* archetype

arquibancada /arkibã'kada/ *f* terraces, (*Amer*) bleachers

arquipélago /arki'pɛlagu/ *m* archipelago

arquite|tar /arkite'tar/ *vt* think up; ~to /ɛ/ *m* architect; ~tônico *a* architectural; ~tura *f* architecture

arqui|var /arki'var/ *vt* file <*papéis*>; shelve <*plano, processo*>; ~vista *m/f* archivist; ~vo *m* file; (*conjunto*) files; (*móvel*) filing cabinet; *pl* (*do Estado etc*) archives

arran|cada /axã'kada/ *f* lurch; (*de atleta, fig*) spurt; ~car *vt* pull out <*cabelo etc*>; pull off <*botão etc*>; pull up <*erva daninha etc*>; take out <*dente*>; (*das mãos de alg*) wrench, snatch; extract <*confissão, dinheiro*> □ *vi* <*carro*> roar off; <*pessoa*> take off; (*dar solavanco*) lurch forward; ~car-se *vpr* take off; ~co *m* pull, tug; *veja* ~cada

arranha-céu /axaɲa'sɛw/ *m* skyscraper

arra|nhadura /axaɲa'dura/ *f* scratch; ~nhão *m* scratch; ~nhar *vt* scratch; have a smattering of <*língua*>

arran|jar /axã'ʒar/ *vt* arrange; (*achar*) get, find; (*resolver*) settle, sort out; ~jar-se *vpr* manage; ~jo *m* arrangement

arrasar /axa'zar/ *vt* devastate; raze, flatten <*casa, cidade*>; ~se *vpr* be devastated

arrastar /axas'tar/ *vt* drag; <*corrente, avalancha*> sweep away; (*atrair*) draw □ *vi* trail; ~se *vpr* crawl; <*tempo*> drag; <*processo*> drag out

arreba|tador /axebata'dor/ *a* entrancing; shocking <*notícia*>; ~tar *vt* (*enlevar*) entrance, send; (*chocar*) shock

arreben|tação /axebẽta'sãw/ *f* surf; ~tar *vi* <*bomba*> explode; <*corda*> snap, break; <*balão, pessoa*> burst; <*onda*> break □ *vt* snap, break <*corda*>; burst <*balão*>; break down <*porta*>

arrebitar /axebi'tar/ *vt* turn up <*nariz*>; prick up <*orelhas*>

arreca|dação /axekada'sãw/ *f* (*dinheiro*) tax revenue; ~dar *vt* collect

arredar /axe'dar/ *vt* não ~ pé stand one's ground

arredio /axe'dʒiu/ *a* withdrawn

arredondar /axedõ'dar/ *vt* round up <*quantia*>; round off <*ângulo*>

arredores /axe'doris/ *m pl* surroundings; (*de cidade*) outskirts

arrefecer /axefe'ser/ *vt/i* cool

arregaçar /axega'sar/ *vt* roll up

arrega|lado /axega'ladu/ *a* <*olhos*> wide; ~lar *vt* ~lar os olhos be wide-eyed with amazement

arreganhar /axega'ɲar/ *vt* bare <*dentes*>; ~se *vpr* grin

arremata|r /axema'tar/ *vt* finish off; (*no tricô*) cast off; ~te *m* conclusion; (*na costura*) finishing off; (*no futebol*) finishing

arremes|sar /axeme'sar/ *vt* hurl; ~so /e/ *m* throw

arrepen|der-se /axepẽ'dersi/ *vpr* be sorry; <*pecador*> repent; ~der-se de regret; <*pecador*> repentant; ~dimento *m* regret; (*de pecado, crime*) repentance

arrepia|do /axepi'adu/ *a* <*cabelo*> standing on end; <*pele, pessoa*> covered in goose pimples; ~ar *vt* (*dar calafrios*) make shudder; make stand on end <*cabelo*>; me ~a (a pele) it

gives me goose pimples; ~ar-se *vpr* (*estremecer*) shudder; <*cabelo*> stand on end; (*na pele*) get goose pimples; ~o *m* shudder; me dá ~os it makes me shudder

arris|cado /axis'kadu/ *a* risky; ~car *vt* risk; ~car-se *vpr* take a risk, risk it; ~car-se a fazer risk doing

arro|char /axo'ʃar/ *vt* tighten up □ *vi* be tough; ~cho /o/ *m* squeeze

arro|gância /axo'gãsia/ *f* arrogance; ~gante *a* arrogant

arro|jado /axo'ʒadu/ *a* bold; ~jar *vt* throw

arrombar /axõ'bar/ *vt* break down <*porta*>; break into <*casa*>; crack <*cofre*>

arro|tar /axo'tar/ *vi* burp, belch; ~to /o/ *m* burp

arroz /a'xoz/ *m* rice; ~ doce rice pudding; ~al (*pl* ~ais) *m* rice field

arrua|ça /axu'asa/ *f* riot; ~ceiro *m* rioter

arruela /axu'ɛla/ *f* washer

arruinar /axui'nar/ *vt* ruin; ~se *vpr* be ruined

arru|madeira /axuma'dera/ *f* (*de hotel*) chambermaid; ~mar *vt* tidy (up) <*casa*>; sort out <*papéis, vida*>; pack <*mala*>; (*achar*) find, get; make up <*desculpa*>; (*vestir*) dress up; ~mar-se *vpr* (*aprontar-se*) get ready; (*na vida*) sort o.s. out

arse|nal /arse'naw/ (*pl* ~nais) *m* arsenal

arsênio /ar'seniu/ *m* arsenic

arte /'artʃi/ *f* art; fazer ~ <*criança*> get up to mischief; ~fato *m* product, article

arteiro /ar'teru/ *a* mischievous

artéria /ar'tɛria/ *f* artery

artesa|nal /arteza'naw/ (*pl* ~nais) *a* craft; ~nato *m* craftwork

arte|são /arte'zãw/ (*pl* ~s) *m* (*f* ~sã) artisan, craftsman (*f* -woman)

ártico /'artʃiku/ *a & m* arctic

articu|lação /artʃikula'sãw/ *f* articulation; (*anat, tecn*) joint; ~lar *vt* articulate

arti|ficial /artʃifisi'aw/ (*pl* ~ficiais) *a* artificial; ~fício *m* trick

artigo /ar'tʃigu/ *m* article; (*com*) item

arti|lharia /artʃiʎa'ria/ *f* artillery; ~lheiro *m* (*mil*) gunner; (*no futebol*) striker

artimanha /artʃi'maɲa/ *f* trick; (*método*) clever way

ar|tista /ar'tʃista/ *m/f* artist; ~tístico *a* artistic

artrite /ar'tritʃi/ *f* arthritis

árvore /'arvori/ *f* tree

arvoredo /arvo'redu/ *m* grove

as /as/ *artigo & pron veja* a[1]

ás /as/ *m* ace

às = a² + as

asa /'aza/ *f* wing; (*de xícara*) handle; ~-delta *f* hang-glider

ascen|dência /asẽ'dẽsia/ *f* ancestry; (*superioridade*) ascendancy; ~dente *a* rising; ~der *vi* rise; ascend <*ao trono*>; ~são *f* rise; (*relig*) Ascension; em ~são rising; (*fig*) up and coming; ~sor *m* lift, (*Amer*) elevator; ~sorista *m/f* lift operator

asco /'asku/ *m* revulsion, disgust; dar ~ be revolting

asfalto /as'fawtu/ *m* asphalt

asfixi|ar /asfiksi'ar/ *vt/i* asphyxiate Asia /'azia/ *f* Asia

asiático /azi'atʃiku/ *a* & *m* Asian

asilo /a'zilu/ *m* (*refúgio*) asylum; (*de velhos, crianças*) home

as|ma /'azma/ *f* asthma; ~mático *a* & *m* asthmatic

asneira /az'nera/ *f* stupidity; (*uma*) stupid thing

aspas /'aspas/ *f pl* inverted commas

asparago /as'pargu/ *m* asparagus

aspecto /as'pɛktu/ *m* appearance, look; (*de um problema*) aspect

aspereza /aspe'reza/ *f* roughness; (*do clima, de um som*) harshness; (*fig*) rudeness

áspero /'asperu/ *a* rough; <*clima, som*> harsh; (*fig*) rude

aspi|ração /aspira'sãw/ *f* aspiration; (*med*) inhalation; ~rador *m* vacuum cleaner; ~rar *vt* inhale, breathe in <*ar, fumaça*>; suck up <*líquido*>; ~rar a aspire to

aspirina /aspi'rina/ *f* aspirin

asqueroso /aske'rozu/ *a* revolting, disgusting

assa|do /a'sadu/ *a* & *m* roast; ~dura *f* (*na pele*) sore patch

assalariado /asalari'adu/ *a* salaried □ *m* salaried worker

assal|tante /asaw'tãtʃi/ *m* robber; (*na rua*) mugger; (*de casa*) burglar; ~tar *vt* rob; burgle, (*Amer*) burglarize <*casa*>; ~to *m* (*roubo*) robbery; (*a uma casa*) burglary; (*ataque*) assault; (*no boxe*) round

assanhado /asa'ɲadu/ *a* worked up; <*criança*> excitable; (*erótico*) amorous

assar /a'sar/ *vt* roast

assassi|nar /asasi'nar/ *vt* murder; (*pol*) assassinate; ~nato *m* murder; (*pol*) assassination; ~no *m* murderer; (*pol*) assassin

asseado /asi'adu/ *a* well-groomed

as|sediar /asedʒi'ar/ *vt* besiege <*cidade*>; (*fig*) pester; ~sédio *m* siege; (*fig*) pestering

assegurar /asegu'rar/ *vt* (*tornar seguro*) secure; (*afirmar*) guarantee; ~ a alg aco/que assure s.o. of sth/

that; ~-se de/que make sure of/that

assembléia /asẽ'blɛja/ *f* (*pol*) assembly; (*com*) meeting

assemelhar /aseme'ʎar/ *vt* liken; ~-se *vpr* be alike; ~-se a resemble, be like

assen|tar /asẽ'tar/ *vt* (*estabelecer*) establish, define; settle <*povo*>; lay <*tijolo*> □ *vi* <*pó*> settle; ~tar-se *vpr* settle down; ~tar com go with; ~tar a <*roupa*> suit; ~to *m* seat; (*fig*) basis; tomar ~to take a seat; <*pó*> settle

assen|tir /asẽ'tʃir/ *vi* agree; ~timento *m* agreement

assessor /ase'sor/ *m* adviser; ~ar *vt* advise

assexuado /aseksu'adu/ *a* asexual

assidu|idade /asidui'dadʒi/ *f* (*à escola*) regular attendance; (*diligência*) diligence

assíduo /a'siduu/ *a* (*que freqüenta*) regular; (*diligente*) assiduous

assim /a'sĩ/ *adv* like this, like that; (*portanto*) therefore; e ~ por diante and so on; ~ como as well as; ~ que as soon as

assimétrico /asi'mɛtriku/ *a* asymmetrical

assimi|lar /asimi'lar/ *vt* assimilate; ~-se *vpr* be assimilated

assinalar /asina'lar/ *vt* (*marcar*) mark; (*distinguir*) distinguish; (*apontar*) point out

assi|nante /asi'nãtʃi/ *m/f* subscriber; ~nar *vt/i* sign; ~natura *f* (*nome*) signature; (*de revista*) subscription

assis|tência /asis'tẽsia/ *f* assistance; (*presença*) attendance; (*público*) audience; ~tente *a* assistant □ *m/f* assistant; ~tente social social worker; ~tir (a) *vt/i* (*ver*) watch; (*presenciar*) attend; assist <*doente*>

assoalho /aso'aʎu/ *m* floor

assoar /aso'ar/ *vt* ~ o nariz, (*Port*) ~-se blow one's nose

assobi|ar /asobi'ar/ *vt/i* whistle; ~o *m* whistle

associ|ação /asosia'sãw/ *f* association; ~ado *a* & *m* associate; ~ar *vt* associate (a with); ~ar-se *vpr* associate; (*com*) go into partnership (a with)

assolar /aso'lar/ *vt* devastate

assom|bração /asõbra'sãw/ *f* ghost; ~brar *vt* astonish, amaze; ~brar-se *vpr* be amazed; ~bro *m* amazement, astonishment; (*coisa*) marvel; ~broso /o/ *a* astonishing, amazing

assoprar /aso'prar/ *vi* blow □ *vt* blow; blow out <*vela*>

assovi- *veja* assobi-

assu|mido /asu'midu/ *a'* (*confesso*) confirmed, self-confessed; ~mir *vt* assume, take on; accept, admit <*defeito*> □ *vi* take office

assunto /a'sûtu/ *m* subject; (*negócio*) matter

assus|tador /asusta'dor/ *a* frightening; ~**tar** *vt* frighten, scare; ~**tar-se** *vpr* get frightened, get scared

asterisco /aste'risku/ *m* asterisk

as|tral /as'traw/ (*pl* ~**trais**) *m* (*fam*) state of mind; ~**tro** *m* star; ~**trologia** *f* astrology; ~**trólogo** *m* astrologer; ~**tronauta** *m/f* astronaut; ~**tronave** *f* spaceship; ~**tronomia** *f* astronomy; ~**tronômico** *a* astronomical; ~**trônomo** *m* astronomer

as|túcia /as'tusia/ *f* cunning; <*comerciante*> astute; ~**tuto** *a* cunning,

ata /'ata/ *f* minutes

ata|ca|dista /ataka'dʒista/ *m/f* wholesaler; ~**do** *m* por ~**do** wholesale

ata|cante /ata'kâtʃi/ *a* attacking □ *m/f* attacker; ~**car** *vt* attack; tackle <*problema*>

atadura /ata'dura/ *f* bandage

ata|lhar /ata'ʎar/ *vi* take a shortcut; ~**lho** *m* shortcut

ataque /a'taki/ *m* attack; (*de raiva, riso*) fit

atar /a'tar/ *vt* tie

atarantado /atarã'tadu/ *a* flustered, in a flap

atarefado /atare'fadu/ *a* busy

atarracado /ataxa'kadu/ *a* stocky

atarraxar /ataxa'ʃar/ *vt* screw

até /a'tɛ/ *prep* (up) to, as far as; (*tempo*) until □ *adv* even; ~ **logo** goodbye; ~ **que** until

atéia /a'tɛja/ *a* & *f* veja ateu

ateliê /ateli'e/ *m* studio

atemorizar /atemori'zar/ *vt* frighten

Atenas /a'tenas/ *f* Athens

aten|ção /atẽ'sãw/ *f* attention; *pl* (*bondade*) thoughtfulness; com ~**ção** attentively; ~**cioso** *a* thoughtful, considerate

aten|der /atẽ'der/ ~**der** (**a**) *vt/i* answer <*telefone, porta*>; answer to <*nome*>; serve <*freguês*>; see <*paciente, visitante*>; grant, meet <*pedido*>; heed <*conselho*>; ~**dimento** *m* service; (*de médico etc*) consultation

aten|tado /atẽ'tadu/ *m* murder attempt; (*pol*) assassination attempt; (*ataque*) attack (*contra* on); ~**tar** *vi* ~**tar contra** make an attempt on

atento /a'tẽtu/ *a* attentive; ~ **a** mindful of

aterrador /atexa'dor/ *a* terrifying

ater|ragem /ate'xaʒẽ/ *f* (*Port*) landing; ~**rar** *vi* (*Port*) land

aterris|sagem /atexi'saʒẽ/ *f* landing; ~**sar** *vi* land

ater-se /a'tersi/ *vpr* ~ **a** keep to, go by

ates|tado /ates'tadu/ *m* certificate; ~**tar** *vt* attest (to)

ateu /a'tew/ *a* & *m* (*f* atéia) atheist

atiçar /atʃi'sar/ *vt* poke <*fogo*>; stir up <*ódio, discórdia*>; arouse <*pessoa*>

atinar /atʃi'nar/ *vt* work out, guess; ~ **com** find; ~ **em** notice

atingir /atʃĩ'ʒir/ *vt* reach; hit <*alvo*>; (*conseguir*) attain; (*afetar*) affect

atirar /atʃi'rar/ *vt* throw □ *vi* shoot; ~ **em** fire at

atitude /atʃi'tudʒi/ *f* attitude; tomar uma ~ take action

ati|va /atʃi'va/ *f* active service; ~**var** *vt* activate; ~**vidade** *f* activity; ~**vo** *a* active □ *m* (*com*) assets

Atlântico /at'lâtʃiku/ *m* Atlantic

atlas /'atlas/ *m* atlas

at|leta /at'leta/ *m/f* athlete; ~**lético** *a* athletic; ~**letismo** *m* athletics

atmosfera /atʃimos'fera/ *f* atmosphere

ato /'atu/ *m* act; (*ação*) action; no ~ on the spot

ato|lar /ato'lar/ *vt* bog down; ~**lar-se** *vpr* get bogged down; ~**leiro** *m* bog; (*fig*) fix, spot of trouble

atômico /a'tomiku/ *a* atomic

atomizador /atomiza'dor/ *m* atomizer spray

átomo /'atomu/ *m* atom

atônito /a'tonitu/ *a* astonished, stunned

ator /a'tor/ *m* actor

atordoar /atordo'ar/ *vt* <*golpe, notícia*> stun; <*som*> deafen; (*alucinar*) bewilder

atormentar /atormẽ'tar/ *vt* plague, torment

atração /atra'sãw/ *f* attraction

atracar /atra'kar/ *vt/i* (*naut*) moor; ~**se** *vpr* grapple; (*fam*) neck

atractivo (*Port*) veja atrativo

atraente /atra'ẽtʃi/ *a* attractive

atraiçoar /atrajso'ar/ *vt* betray

atrair /atra'ir/ *vt* attract

atrapalhar /atrapa'ʎar/ *vt/i* (*confundir*) confuse; (*estorvar*) hinder; (*perturbar*) disturb; ~**se** *vpr* get mixed up

atrás /a'traʃ/ *adv* behind; (*no fundo*) at the back; ~ **de** behind; (*depois de, no encalço de*) after; um mês ~ a month ago; ficar ~ be left behind

atra|sado /atra'zadu/ *a* late; <*país, criança*> backward; <*relógio*> slow; <*pagamento*> overdue; <*idéias*> oldfashioned; ~**sar** *vt* delay; put back <*relógio*> □ *vi* be late; <*relógio*> lose; ~**sar-se** *vpr* be late; (*num trabalho*) get behind; (*no pagar*) get into arrears; ~**so** *m* delay; (*de país etc*) backwardness; *pl* (*com*) arrears; com ~**so** late atrativo /atra'tʃivu/ m attraction

através /atra'vɛs/ ~ de prep through; (de um lado ao outro) across

atravessado /atrave'sadu/ a <espinha> stuck; estar com alg ~ na garganta be fed up with s.o.

atravessar /atrave'sar/ vt go through; cross <rua, rio>

atrever-se /atre'versi/ vpr dare; ~ver-se a dare to; ~vido a daring; (insolente) impudent; ~vimento m daring, boldness; (insolência) impudence

atribuir /atribu'ir/ vt attribute (a to); confer <prêmio, poderes> (a on); attach <importância> (a to); ~to m attribute

atrito /a'tritu/ m friction; (desavença) disagreement

atriz /a'tris/ f actress

atrocidade /atrosi'dadʒi/ f atrocity

atropelar /atrope'lar/ vt run over, knock down <pedestre>; (empurrar) jostle; mix up <palavras>; ~lamento m (de pedestre) running over; ~lo /e/ m scramble

atroz /a'tros/ a awful, terrible; heinous <crime>; cruel <pessoa>

atuação /atua'sãw/ f (ação) action; (desempenho) performance

atual /atu'aw/ (pl ~ais) a current, present; <assunto, interesse> topical; <pessoa, carro> up-to-date; ~alidade f (presente) present (time); (de um livro) topicality; pl current affairs; ~alizado a up-to-date; ~alizar vt update; ~alizar-se vpr bring o.s. up to date; ~almente adv at present, currently

atum /a'tũ/ m tuna

aturdir /atur'dʒir/ vt veja atordoar

audácia /aw'dasia/ f boldness; (insolência) audacity

audição /awdʒi'sãw/ f hearing; (concerto) recital; ~ência f audience; (jurid) hearing

audiovisual /awdʒiovizu'aw/ (pl ~ais) a audiovisual

auditório /awdʒi'toriu/ m auditorium; programa de ~ variety show

auge /'awʒi/ m peak, height

aula /'awla/ f class, lesson; dar ~ teach

aumentar /awmẽ'tar/ vt increase; raise <preço, salário>; extend <casa>; (com lente) magnify; (acrescentar) add □ vi increase; <preço, salário> go up; ~to m increase; (de salário) rise, (Amer) raise

ausência /aw'zẽsia/ f absence; ~sente a absent □ m/f absentee

auspícios /aws'pisius/ m pl auspices; ~picioso /o/ a auspicious

austeridade /awsteri'dadʒi/ f austerity; ~ro /ɛ/ a austere

Austrália /aw'stralia/ f Australia

australiano /awstrali'anu/ a & m Australian

Áustria /'awstria/ f Austria

austríaco /aws'triaku/ a & m Austrian

autarquia /awtar'kia/ f public authority

autêntico /aw'tẽtʃiku/ a authentic; genuine <pessoa>; true <fato>

autobiografia /awtobiogra'fia/ f autobiography; ~gráfico a autobiographical

autocarro /awto'kaxu/ m (Port) bus

autocrata /awto'krata/ a autocratic

autodefesa /awtode'feza/ f self-defence

autodidata /awtodʒi'data/ a & m/f self-taught (person)

autódromo /aw'tɔdromu/ m race track

auto-escola /awtois'kɔla/ f driving school

auto-estrada /awtois'trada/ f motorway, (Amer) expressway

autógrafo /aw'tografu/ m autograph

automação /awtoma'sãw/ f automation; ~mático a automatic; ~matizar vt automate

automobilismo /awtomobi'lizmu/ m motoring; (esporte) motor racing; ~móvel (pl ~móveis) m motor car, (Amer) automobile

autonomia /awtono'mia/ f autonomy; ~tônomo a autonomous; <trabalhador> selfemployed

autopeça /awto'pesa/ f car spare

autópsia /aw'tɔpsia/ f autopsy

autor /aw'tor/ m (f ~a) author; (de crime) perpetrator; (jurid) plaintiff

auto-retrato /awtoxe'tratu/ m self-portrait

autoria /awto'ria/ f authorship; (de crime) responsibility (de for)

autoridade /awtori'dadʒi/ f authority; ~zação f authorization; ~zar vt authorize

autuar /awtu'ar/ vt sue

auxiliar /awsili'ar/ a auxiliary □ m/f assistant □ vt assist; ~ilio m assistance, aid

aval /a'vaw/ (pl avais) m endorsement; (com) guarantee

avaliação /avalia'sãw/ f (de preço) valuation; (fig) evaluation; ~ar vt value <quadro etc> (em at); assess <danos, riscos>; (fig) evaluate

avançar /avã'sar/ vt move forward □ vi move forward; (mil, fig) advance; ~çar a (montar) amount to; ~ço m advance

avareza /ava'reza/ f meanness; ~ento a mean

ava|ria /ava'ria/ f damage; (de máquina) breakdown; ~riado a damaged; <máquina> out of order; <carro> broken down; ~riar vt damage □ vi be damaged; <máquina> break down

ave /'avi/ f bird; ~ de rapina bird of prey

aveia /a'veja/ f oats

avelã /ave'lã/ f hazelnut

avenida /ave'nida/ f avenue

aven|tal /avē'taw/ (pl ~tais) m apron

aventu|ra /avē'tura/ f adventure; (amorosa) fling; ~rar vt venture; ~rar-se vpr venture (a to); ~reiro a adventurous □ m adventurer

averiguar /averi'gwar/ vt check out

avermelhado /averme'ʎadu/ a reddish

aver|são /aver'sãw/ f aversion; ~so a averse (a to)

aves|sas /a'vɛsas/ às ~sas the wrong way round; (de cabeça para baixo) upside down; ~so /e/ m ao ~so inside out

avestruz /aves'trus/ m ostrich

avi|ação /avia'sãw/ f aviation; ~ão m (aero)plane, (Amer) (air)plane; ~ão a jato jet

avi|dez /avi'des/ f (cobiça) greediness; ~do a greedy

avi|sar /avi'zar/ vt (informar) tell, let know; (advertir) warn; ~so m notice; (advertência) warning

avistar /avis'tar/ vt catch sight of

avo /'avu/ m um doze ~s one twelfth

avó /a'vɔ/ f grandmother; ~s m pl grandparents

avô /a'vo/ m grandfather

avoado /avo'adu/ a dizzy, scatterbrained

avulso /a'vuwsu/ a loose, odd

avultado /avuw'tadu/ a bulky

axila /ak'sila/ f armpit

azaléia /aza'lɛja/ f azalea

azar /a'zar/ m bad luck; ter ~ be unlucky; ~ado, ~ento a unlucky

aze|dar /aze'dar/ vt sour □ vi go sour; ~do /e/ a sour

azei|te /a'zejtʃi/ m oil; ~tona /o/ f olive

azevinho /aze'viɲu/ m holly

azia /a'zia/ f heartburn

azucrinar /azukri'nar/ vt annoy

azul /a'zuw/ (pl azuis) a blue

azulejo /azu'leʒu/ m (ceramic) tile

azul-marinho /azuwma'riɲu/ a invar navy blue

B

babá /ba'ba/ f nanny; ~ eletrônica baby alarm

ba|bado /ba'badu/ m frill; ~bador m

bib; ~bar vt/i, ~bar-se vpr drool (por over); <bebê> dribble; ~beiro (Port) m bib

baby-sitter /bejbi'siter/ (pl ~s) m/f babysitter

bacalhau /baka'ʎaw/ m cod

bacana /ba'kana/ (fam) a great

bacha|rel /baʃa'rɛw/ (pl ~réis) bachelor; ~relado m bachelor's degree; ~relar-se vpr graduate

bacia /ba'sia/ f basin; (da privada) bowl; (anat) pelvis

baço /'basu/ m spleen

bacon /'bejkõ/ m bacon

bactéria /bak'tɛria/ f bacterium; pl bacteria

bada|lado /bada'ladu/ a (fam) talked about; ~lar vt ring <sino> □ vi ring; (fam) go out and about; ~lativo a (fam) a fun-loving, gadabout

badejo /ba'deʒu/ m sea bass

baderna /ba'dɛrna/ f (tumulto) commotion; (desordem) mess

badulaque /badu'laki/ m trinket

bafafá /bafa'fa/ (fam) m to-do, kerfuffle

ba|fo /'bafu/ m bad breath; ~fômetro m Breathalyser; ~forada f puff

bagaço /ba'gasu/ m pulp; (Port: aguardente) brandy

baga|geiro /baga'ʒeru/ m (de carro) roofrack; (Port: homem) porter; ~gem f luggage; (cultural etc) baggage

bagatela /baga'tɛla/ f trifle

Bagdá /bagi'da/ f Baghdad

bago /'bagu/ m berry; (de chumbo) pellet

bagulho /ba'guʎu/ m piece of junk; pl junk; ele é um ~ he's as ugly as sin

bagun|ça /ba'gũsa/ f mess; ~çar vt mess up; ~ceiro a messy □ m messer

baía /ba'ia/ f bay

baiano /ba'janu/ a & m Bahian

baila /'bajla/ f trazer/vir à ~ bring/come up

bai|lar /baj'lar/ vt/i dance; ~larino m ballet dancer; ~le m dance; (de gala) ball

bainha /ba'iɲa/ f (de vestido) hem; (de arma) sheath

baioneta /bajo'neta/ f bayonet

bairro /'bajxu/ m neighbourhood, area

baixa /'baʃa/ f drop, fall; (de guerra) casualty; (dispensa) discharge; ~mar f low tide

baixar /ba'ʃar/ vt lower; issue <ordem>; pass <lei> □ vi drop, fall; (fam: pintar) turn up

baixaria /baʃa'ria/ f sordidness; (uma) sordid thing

baixela /ba'ʃɛla/ f set of cutlery

baixeza /ba'ʃeza/ f baseness

baixo /'baʃu/ *a* low; <*pessoa*> short; <*som*, *voz*> quiet, soft; <*cabeça*, *olhos*> lowered; (*vil*) sordid □ *adv* low; <*falar*> softly, quietly □ *m* bass; em ~ underneath; (*em casa*) downstairs; em ~ de under; para ~ down; (*em casa*) downstairs; por ~ de under(neath)

baju|lador /baʒula'dor/ *a* obsequious □ *m* sycophant; ~lar *vi* fawn on

bala /'bala/ *f* (*de revólver*) bullet; (*doce*) sweet

balada /ba'lada/ *f* ballad

balaio /ba'laju/ *m* linen basket

balan|ça /ba'lãsa/ *f* scales; Balança (*signo*) Libra; ~ça de pagamentos balance of payments; ~çar *vt/i* (*no ar*) swing; (*numa cadeira etc*) rock; <*carro*, *avião*> shake; <*navio*> roll; ~çar-se *vpr* swing; ~cete /e/ *m* trial balance; ~ço *m* (*com*) balance sheet; (*brinquedo*) swing; (*movimento no ar*) swinging; (*de carro*, *avião*) shaking; (*de navio*) rolling; (*de cadeira*) rocking; fazer um ~ço de (*fig*) take stock of

balangandã /balãgã'dã/ *m* bauble

balão /ba'lãw/ *m* balloon; soltar um ~de-ensaio (*fig*) put out feelers

balar /ba'lar/ *vi* bleat

balbu|ciar /bawbusi'ar/ *vt/i* babble; ~cio *m* babble, babbling

balbúrdia /baw'burdʒia/ *f* hubbub

bal|cão /baw'kãw/ *m* (*em loja*) counter; (*de informações*, *bilhetes*) desk; (*de cozinha*) worktop, (*Amer*) counter; (*no teatro*) circle; ~conista *m/f* shop assistant

balde /'bawdʒi/ *m* bucket

baldeação /bawdʒia'sãw/ *f* fazer ~ change (trains)

baldio /baw'dʒiu/ *a* fallow; terreno ~ (piece of) waste ground

balé /ba'lɛ/ *m* ballet

balear /bali'ar/ *vt* shoot

baleia /ba'leja/ *f* whale

balido /ba'lidu/ *m* bleat, bleating

balísti|ca /ba'listʃika/ *f* ballistics; ~co *a* ballistic

bali|za /ba'liza/ *f* marker; (*luminosa*) beacon; ~zar *vt* mark out

balneário /bawni'ariu/ *m* seaside resort

balofo /ba'lofu/ *a* fat, tubby

baloiço, balouço /ba'lojsu, ba'losu/ (*Port*) *m* (*de criança*) swing

balsa /'bawsa/ *f* (*de madeira etc*) raft; (*que vai e vem*) ferry

bálsamo /'bawsamu/ *m* balm

báltico /'bawtʃiku/ *a & m* Baltic

baluarte /balu'artʃi/ *m* bulwark

bambo /'bãbu/ *a* loose, slack; <*pernas*> limp; <*mesa*> wobbly

bambo|lê /bãbo'le/ *m* hula hoop;

~lear *vi* <*pessoa*> sway, totter; <*coisa*> wobble

bambu /bã'bu/ *m* bamboo

ba|nal /ba'naw/ (*pl* ~nais) *a* banal; ~nalidade *f* banality

bana|na /ba'nana/ *f* banana □ (*fam*) *m/f* wimp; ~nada *f* banana fudge; ~neira *f* banana tree; plantar ~neira do a handstand

banca /'bãka/ *f* (*de trabalho*) bench; (*de jornais*) newsstand; ~ examinadora examining board; ~da *f* (*pol*) bench

bancar /bã'kar/ *vt* (*custear*) finance; (*fazer papel de*) play; (*fingir*) pretend

bancário /bã'kariu/ *a* bank □ *m* bank employee

bancarrota /bãka'xota/ *f* bankruptcy; ir à ~ go bankrupt

banco /'bãku/ *m* (*com*) bank; (*no parque*) bench; (*na cozinha*, *num bar*) stool; (*de bicicleta*) saddle; (*de carro*) seat; ~ de areia sandbank; ~ de dados database

banda /'bãda/ *f* band; (*lado*) side; de ~ sideways on; nestas ~s in these parts; ~ desenhada (*Port*) cartoon

bandei|ra /bã'dera/ *f* flag; (*divisa*) banner; dar ~ra (*fam*) give o.s. away; ~rante *m/f* pioneer □ *f* girl guide; ~rinha *m* linesman

bandeja /bã'deʒa/ *f* tray

bandido /bã'dʒidu/ *m* bandit

bando /'bãdu/ *m* (*de pessoas*) band; (*de pássaros*) flock

bandolim /bãdo'lĩ/ *m* mandolin

bangalô /bãga'lo/ *m* bungalow

Bangcoc /bã'koki/ *f* Bangkok

bangue-bangue /bãgi'bãgi/ (*fam*) *m* western

banguela /bã'gɛla/ *a* toothless

banha /'bana/ *f* lard; *pl* (*no corpo*) flab

banhar /ba'nar/ *vt* (*molhar*) bathe; (*lavar*) bath; ~se *vpr* bathe

banhei|ra /ba'nera/ *f* bath, (*Amer*) bathtub; ~ro *m* bathroom; (*Port*) lifeguard

banhista /ba'nista/ *m/f* bather

banho /'banu/ *m* bath; (*no mar*) bathe, dip; tomar ~ have a bath; (*no chuveiro*) have a shower; tomar um ~ de loja/cultura go on a shopping/ cultural spree; ~ de sol sunbathing; ~-maria (*pl* ~s-maria) *m* bain marie

ba|nimento /bani'mẽtu/ *m* banishment; ~nir *vt* banish

banjo /'bãʒu/ *m* banjo

banqueiro /bã'keru/ *m* banker

banqueta /bã'keta/ *f* foot-stool

banque|te /bã'ketʃi/ *m* banquet; ~teiro *m* caterer

banzé /bã'zɛ/ (*fam*) *m* commotion, uproar

bapt- (*Port*) *veja* bat-

baque /'baki/ *m* thud, crash; (*revés*) blow; ~**ar** *vi* topple over □ *vt* hit hard, knock for six

bar /bar/ *m* bar

barafunda /bara'fũda/ *f* jumble; (*barulho*) racket

bara|lhada /bara'ʎada/ *f* jumble; ~**lho** *m* pack of cards, (*Amer*) deck of cards

barão /ba'rãw/ *m* baron

barata /ba'rata/ *f* cockroach

bara|tear /barat∫i'ar/ *vt* cheapen; ~**teiro** *a* cheap

baratinar /barat∫i'nar/ *vt* fluster; (*transtornar*) rattle, shake up

barato /ba'ratu/ *a* cheap □ *adv* cheaply □ (*fam*) *m* um ~ great; que ~! that's brilliant!

barba /'barba/ *f* beard; *pl* (*de gato etc*) whiskers; fazer a ~ shave; (*de* walkover) (*cavalo*) favourite; ~**do** *a* bearded

barbante /bar'bãt∫i/ *m* string

bar|baridade /barbari'dadʒi/ *f* barbarity; (*fam: muito dinheiro*) fortune; ~**bárie** *f*, ~**barismo** *m* barbarism

bárbaro /'barbaru/ *m* barbarian □ *a* barbaric; (*fam: forte, bom*) terrific

barbatana /barba'tana/ *f* fin

bar|beador /barbia'dor/ *m* shaver; ~**bear** *vt* shave; ~**bear-se** *vpr* shave; ~**bearia** *f* barber's shop; ~**beiragem** (*fam*) *f* bit of bad driving; ~**beiro** *m* barber; (*fam: motorista*) bad driver

bar|ca /'barka/ *f* barge; (*balsa*) ferry; ~**caça** *f* barge; ~**co** *m* boat; ~**co a motor** motorboat; ~**co a remo/vela** rowing/sailing boat, (*Amer*) rowboat/sailboat

barga|nha /bar'gaɲa/ *f* bargain; ~**nhar** *vt/i* bargain

barítono /ba'ritonu/ *m* baritone

barômetro /ba'rometru/ *m* barometer

baronesa /baro'neza/ *f* baroness

barra /'baxa/ *f* bar; (*sinal gráfico*) slash, stroke; (*fam: situação*) situation; segurar a ~ hold out; forçar a ~ force the issue

barra|ca /ba'xaka/ *f* (*de acampar*) tent; (*na feira*) stall; (*casinha*) hut; (*guarda-sol*) sunshade; ~**cão** *m* shed; ~**co** *m* shack, shanty

barragem /ba'xaʒẽ/ *f* (*represa*) dam

barra-pesada /baxape'zada/ (*fam*) *a invar* <*bairro*> rough; <*pessoa*> shady; (*difícil*) tough

bar|rar /ba'xar/ *vt* bar; ~**reira** *f* barrier; (*em corrida*) hurdle; (*em futebol*) wall

barrento /ba'xẽtu/ *a* muddy

barricada /baxi'kada/ *f* barricade

barri|ga /ba'xiga/ *f* stomach, (*Amer*) belly; ~**ga da perna** calf, (*Amer*) pot-bellied

barril /ba'xiw/ (*pl* ~**ris**) *m* barrel

barro /'baxu/ *m* (*argila*) clay; (*lama*) mud

barroco /ba'xoku/ *a & m* baroque

barrote /ba'xɔt∫i/ *m* beam, joist

baru|lheira /baru'ʎera/ *f* racket, din; ~**lhento** *a* noisy; ~**lho** *m* noise

base /'bazi/ *f* base; (*fig: fundamento*) basis; com ~ em on the basis of; na ~ de based on; ~**ado** *a* based; (*firme*) well-founded □ (*fam*) *m* joint; ~**ar** *vt* base; ~**ar-se em** be based on

básico /'baziku/ *a* basic

basquete /bas'ket∫i/ *m*, **basquetebol** /basket∫i'bɔw/ *m* basketball

bas|ta /'basta/ *m* dar um ~**ta em** call a halt to; ~**tante** *a* (*muito*) quite a lot of; (*suficiente*) enough □ *adv* (*com adjetivo, advérbio*) quite; (*com verbo*) quite a lot; (*suficientemente*) enough

bastão /bas'tãw/ *m* stick; (*num revezamento, de comando*) baton

bastar /bas'tar/ *vi* be enough

bastidores /bast∫i'doris/ *m pl* (*no teatro*) wings; nos ~ (*fig*) behind the scenes

bata /'bata/ *f* (*de mulher*) smock; (*de médico etc*) overall

bata|lha /ba'taʎa/ *f* battle; ~**lhador** *a* plucky, feisty □ *m* fighter; ~**lhão** *m* battalion; ~**lhar** *vi* battle; (*esforçar-se*) fight hard □ *vt* fight hard to get

batata /ba'tata/ *f* potato; ~ **doce** sweet potato; ~ **frita** chips, (*Amer*) French fries; (*salgadinhos*) crisps, (*Amer*) potato chips

bate-boca /bat∫i'boka/ *m* row, argument

bate|deira /bate'dera/ *f* whisk; (*de manteiga*) churn; ~**dor** *m* (*policial etc*) outrider; (*no criquete*) batsman; (*no beisebol*) batter; (*de caça*) beater; ~**dor de carteiras** pickpocket

batelada /bate'lada/ *f* batch; ~**s de** heaps of

batente /ba'tẽt∫i/ *m* (*de porta*) doorway; para o/no ~ (*fam: ao trabalho*) to/at work

bate-papo /bat∫i'papu/ *m* chat.

bater /ba'ter/ *vt* beat; stamp <*pé*>; slam <*porta*>; strike <*horas*>; take <*foto*>; flap <*asas*>; (*datilografar*) type; (*lavar*) wash; (*usar muito*) wear a lot <*roupa*>; (*fam*) pinch <*carteira*> □ *vi* <*coração*> beat; <*porta*> slam; <*janela*> bang; <*horas*> strike; <*sino*> ring; (*à porta*) knock; (*com o carro*) crash; ~**-se** *vpr* (*lutar*) fight; ~ **à máquina** type; ~ **à**

ou na porta knock at the door; ~ em hit; harp on <*assunto*>; <*luz, sol*> shine on; ~ com o carro crash one's car, have a crash; ~ com a cabeça bang one's head; ele batia os dentes de frio his teeth were chattering with cold; ele não bate bem (*fam*) he's not all there

bate|ria /bate'ria/ *f* (*eletr*) battery; (*mus*) drums; ~ria de cozinha kitchen utensils; ~rista *m/f* drummer

bati|da /ba'tʃida/ *f* beat; (*à porta*) knock; (*no carro*) crash; (*policial*) raid; (*bebida*) cocktail of rum, sugar and fruit juice; ~do *a* beaten; <*roupa*> well worn; <*assunto*> hackneyed □ *m* ~do de leite (*Port*) milkshake

batina /ba'tʃina/ *f* cassock

ba|tismo /ba'tʃizmu/ *m* baptism; ~tizado *m* christening; ~tizar *vt* baptize; (*pôr nome*) christen

batom /ba'tõ/ *m* lipstick

batu|cada /batu'kada/ *f* samba percussion group; ~car *vt/i* drum in a samba rhythm; ~que *m* samba rhythm

batuta /ba'tuta/ *f* baton; sob a ~ de under the direction of

baú /ba'u/ *m* trunk

baunilha /baw'niʎa/ *f* vanilla

bazar /ba'zar/ *m* bazaar; (*loja*) stationery and haberdashery shop

bê-a-bá /bea'ba/ *m* ABC

bea|titude /beatʃi'tudʒi/ *f* (*felicidade*) bliss; (*devoção*) piety, devoutness; ~to *a* (*devoto*) pious, devout; (*feliz*) blissful

bêbado /'bebadu/ *a* & *m* drunk

bebê /be'be/ *m* baby; ~ de proveta test-tube baby

bebe|deira /bebe'dera/ *f* (*estado*) drunkenness; (*ato*) drinking bout; ~dor *m* drinker; ~douro *m* drinking fountain

beber /be'ber/ *vt/i* drink

bebericar /beberi'kar/ *vt/i* sip

bebida /be'bida/ *f* drink

beca /'bɛka/ *f* gown

beça /'bɛsa/ *f* à ~ (*fam*) (*com substantivo*) loads of; (*com adjetivo*) really; (*com verbo*) a lot

beco /'beku/ *m* alley; ~ sem saída dead end

bedelho /be'deʎu/ *m* meter o ~ (em) stick one's oar in(to)

bege /'bɛʒi/ *a invar* beige

bei|cinho /bej'siɲu/ *m* fazer ~cinho pout; ~ço *m* lip; ~çudo *a* thick-lipped

beija-flor /bejʒa'flor/ *m* hummingbird

bei|jar /be'ʒar/ *vt* kiss; ~jo *m* kiss; ~joca /ɔ/ *f* peck

bei|ra /'bera/ *f* edge; (*fig: do desastre*

etc) verge, brink; à ~ra de at the edge of; (*fig*) on the verge of; ~rada *f* edge; ~ra-mar *f* seaside; ~rar *vt* (*ficar*) border (on); (*andar*) skirt; (*fig*) border on, verge on; ele está ~rando os 30 anos he's nearing thirty

beisebol /bejzi'bɔw/ *m* baseball

belas-artes /bɛlaʃ'artʃiʃ/ *f pl* fine arts

bel|dade /bew'dadʒi/ *f*, beleza /be'leza/ *f* beauty

belga /'bɛwga/ *a* & *m* Belgian

Bélgica /'bɛwʒika/ *f* Belgium

beliche /be'liʃi/ *m* bunk

bélico /'bɛliku/ *a* war

belicoso /beli'kozu/ *a* warlike

belis|cão /belis'kãw/ *m* pinch; ~car *vt* pinch; nibble <*comida*>

Belize /be'lizi/ *m* Belize

belo /'bɛlu/ *a* beautiful

beltrano /bew'tranu/ *m* such-and-such

bem /bẽj/ *adv* well; (*bastante*) quite; (*muito*) very □ *m* good; *pl* goods, property; está ~ (it's) fine, OK; fazer ~ a be good for; tudo ~? (*fam*) how's things?; se ~ que even though; ~ feito (por você) (*fam*) it serves you right; muito ~! well done!; de ~ com alg on good terms with s.o.; ~ como as well as

bem-apessoado /bẽjapeso'adu/ *a* nice-looking; ~-comportado *a* well-behaved; ~-disposto *a* keen, willing; ~-estar *m* well-being; ~-humorado *a* good-humoured; ~-intencionado *a* well-intentioned; ~-passado *a* <*carne*> well-done; ~-sucedido *a* successful; ~-vindo *a* welcome; ~-visto *a* well thought of

bênção /'bẽsãw/ (*pl* ~s) *f* blessing

bendito /bẽ'dʒitu/ *a* blessed

benefi|cência /benefi'sẽsia/ *f* (*bondade*) goodness, kindness; (*caridade*) charity; ~cente *a* <*associação*> charitable; <*concerto, feira*> charity; ~ciado *m* beneficiary; ~ciar *vt* benefit; ~ciar-se *vpr* benefit (de from)

benefício /bene'fisiu/ *m* benefit; em ~ de in aid of

benéfico /be'nɛfiku/ *a* beneficial (a to)

benevolência /benevo'lẽsia/ *f* benevolence

benévolo /be'nɛvolu/ *a* benevolent

benfeitor /bẽfej'tor/ *m* benefactor

bengala /bẽ'gala/ *f* walking stick; (*pão*) French stick

benigno /be'niginu/ *a* benign

ben|to /'bẽtu/ *a* blessed; <*água*> holy; ~zer *vt* bless; ~zer-se *vpr* cross o.s.

berço /'bersu/ *m* (*de embalar*) cradle; (*caminha*) cot; (*fig*) birthplace; ter ~ be from a good family

berimbau /beri'baw/ m Brazilian percussion instrument shaped like a bow

berinjela /beri'ʒɛla/ f aubergine, (Amer) eggplant

Berlim /ber'li/ f Berlin

berma /'berma/ (Port) f hard shoulder, (Amer) berm

bermuda /ber'muda/ f Bermuda shorts

Berna /'berna/ f Berne

ber|rante /be'xãtʃi/ a loud, flashy; ~rar vi <pessoa> shout; <criança> bawl; <boi> bellow; ~reiro m (gritaria) yelling, shouting; (choro) crying, bawling; ~ro /ɛ/ m yell, shout; (de boi) bellow; aos ~ros shouting

besouro /be'zoru/ m beetle

bes|ta /'besta/ a (idiota) stupid; (cheio de si) full of o.s.; (pedante) pretentious □ f (pessoa) dimwit, numbskull; ficar ~ta (fam) be taken aback; ~teira f stupidity; (uma) stupid thing; falar ~teira talk rubbish; ~tial (pl ~tiais) a bestial; ~tificar vt astound, dumbfound

besuntar /bezũ'tar/ vt coat; (sujar) smear

betão /be'tãw/ (Port) m concrete

beterraba /bete'xaba/ f beetroot

betoneira /beto'nera/ f cement mixer

bexiga /be'ʃiga/ f bladder

bezerro /be'zexu/ m calf

bibelô /bibe'lo/ m ornament

Bíblia /'biblia/ f Bible

bíblico /'bibliku/ a biblical

biblio|grafia /bibliogra'fia/ f bibliography; ~teca /ɛ/ f library; ~tecário m librarian □ a library

bica /'bika/ f tap; (Port: cafezinho) espresso; suar em ~s drip with sweat

bicama /bi'kama/ f truckle bed

bicar /bi'kar/ vt peck

biceps /'bisɛps/ m invar biceps

bicha /'biʃa/ f (Port: fila) queue; (Bras: fam) queer, fairy

bicheiro /bi'ʃeru/ m organizer of illegal numbers game, racketeer

bicho /'biʃu/ m animal; (inseto) insect, (Amer) bug; que ~ te mordeu? what's got into you?; ~-da-seda (pl ~s-da-seda) m silkworm; ~-de-sete-cabeças (fam) m big deal, big thing; ~-do-mato (pl ~s-do-mato) m very shy person

bicicleta /bisi'klɛta/ f bicycle, bike

bico /'biku/ m (de pássaro) beak; (de faca) point; (de sapato) toe; (de bule) spout; (de caneta) nib; (do seio) nipple; (de gás) jet; (fam) (emprego) odd job, sideline; (boca) mouth

bidê /bi'de/ m bidet

bidimensio|nal /bidʒimẽsio'naw/ (pl ~nais) a two-dimensional

biela /bi'ɛla/ f connecting rod

Bielo-Rússia /bielo'xusia/ f Byelorussia

bielo-russo /bielo'xusu/ a & m Byelorussian

bie|nal /bie'naw/ (pl ~nais) a biennial □ f biennial art exhibition

bife /'bifi/ m steak

bifo|cal /bifo'kaw/ (pl ~cais) a bifocal

bifur|cação /bifurka'sãw/ f fork; ~car-se vpr fork

bigamia /biga'mia/ f bigamy

bigamo /'bigamu/ a bigamous □ m bigamist

bigo|de /bi'godʒi/ m moustache; ~dudo a with a big moustache

bigorna /bi'gorna/ f anvil

bijuteria /biʒute'ria/ f costume jewellery

bila|teral /bilate'raw/ (pl ~rais) a bilateral

bilhão /bi'ʎãw/ m thousand million, (Amer) billion

bilhar /bi'ʎar/ m pool, billiards

bilhe|te /bi'ʎetʃi/ m ticket; (recado) note; ~te de ida e volta return ticket, (Amer) round-trip ticket; o ~te azul (fam) the sack; ~teria f, (Port) ~teira f (no cinema, teatro) box office; (na estação) ticket office

bilingue /bi'ligwi/ a bilingual

bilionário /bilio'nariu/ a & m billionaire

bílis /'bilis/ f bile

binário /bi'nariu/ a binary

bingo /'bigu/ m bingo

binóculo /bi'nɔkulu/ m binoculars

biodegradá|vel /biodegra'davew/ (pl ~veis) a biodegradable

bio|grafia /biogra'fia/ f biography; ~gráfico a biographical

biógrafo /bi'ɔgrafu/ m biographer

bio|logia /biolo'ʒia/ f biology; ~lógico a biological

biólogo /bi'ɔlogu/ m biologist

biombo /bi'õbu/ m screen

biônico /bi'oniku/ a bionic; (pol) unelected

biópsia /bi'ɔpsia/ f biopsy

bioquími|ca /bio'kimika/ f biochemistry; ~co a biochemical □ m biochemist

biquíni /bi'kini/ m bikini

birma|nês /birma'nes/ a & m (f ~nesa) Burmese

Birmânia /bir'mania/ f Burma

birô /bi'ro/ m bureau

bir|ra /'bixa/ f wilfulness; fazer ~ra have a tantrum; ~rento a wilful

biruta /bi'ruta/ (fam) a crazy □ f windsock

bis /bis/ int encore!, more! □ m invar encore

bisa|vó /biza'vɔ/ f great-grandmother; ~vós m pl great-grandparents; ~vô m great-grandfather

bisbilho|tar /biʒbiʎo'tar/ vt pry into □ vi pry; ~teiro a prying □ m busybody; ~tice f prying

bisca|te /bis'katʃi/ m odd job; ~teiro m odd-job man

biscoito /bis'kojtu/ m biscuit, (Amer) cookie

bisnaga /biz'naga/ f (pão) bridge roll; (tubo) tube

bisne|ta /biz'nɛta/ f great-granddaughter; ~to /ɛ/ m great-grandson; pl great-grandchildren

bis|pado /bis'padu/ m bishopric; ~po m bishop

bissexto /bi'sestu/ a occasional; ano ~ leap year

bissexu|al /biseksu'aw/ (pl ~ais) a & m/f bisexual

bisturi /bistu'ri/ m scalpel

bito|la /bi'tɔla/ f gauge; ~lado a narrow-minded

bizarro /bi'zaxu/ a bizarre

blablablá /blabla'bla/ (fam) m chit-chat

black /'blɛki/ m black market; ~-tie m evening dress

blas|femar /blasfe'mar/ vi blaspheme; ~fêmia f blasphemy; ~femo /e/ a blasphemous □ m blasphemer

blecaute /ble'kawtʃi/ m power cut

ble|far /ble'far/ vi bluff; ~fe /ɛ/ m bluff

blin|dado /blĩ'dadu/ a armoured; ~dagem f armour-plating

blitz /blits/ f invar police spot-check (on vehicles)

blo|co /'blɔku/ m block; (pol) bloc; (de papel) pad; (no carnaval) section; ~quear vt block; (mil) blockade; ~queio m blockage; (psic) mental block; (mil) blockade

blusa /'bluza/ f shirt; (de mulher) blouse; (de lã) sweater

boa /'boa/ f de bom; numa ~ (fam) well; (sem problemas) easily; estar numa ~ (fam) be doing fine; ~-gente (fam) a invar nice; ~-pinta (pl ~s-pintas) (fam) a nice-looking; ~-praça (pl ~s-praças) (fam) a friendly, sociable

boate /bo'atʃi/ f nightclub

boato /bo'atu/ m rumour

boa|-nova /boa'nɔva/ (pl ~s-novas) f good news; ~-vida (pl ~s-vidas) m/f good-for-nothing, waster; ~zinha a sweet, kind

bo|bagem /bo'baʒẽ/ f silliness; (uma) silly thing; ~beada f slip-up; ~bear vi slip up; ~beira f veja bobagem

bobe /'bɔbi/ m curler, roller

bobina /bo'bina/ f reel; (eletr) coil

bobo /'bobu/ a silly □ m fool; (da corte) jester; ~ca /ɔ/ (fam) a stupid □ m/f twit

bo|ca /'boka/ f mouth; (no fogão) ring; ~ca da noite nightfall; ~cado m (na boca) mouthful; (pedaço) piece, bit; ~cal (pl ~cais) m mouthpiece

boce|jar /bose'ʒar/ vi yawn; ~jo /e/ m yawn

boche|cha /bo'ʃeʃa/ f cheek; ~char vi rinse one's mouth; ~cho /e/ m mouthwash; ~chudo a with puffy cheeks

bodas /'bodas/ f pl wedding anniversary; ~ de prata/ouro silver/golden wedding

bode /'bɔdʒi/ m (billy) goat; ~ expiatório scapegoat

bodega /bo'dɛga/ f (de bebidas) off-licence, (Amer) liquor store; (de secos e molhados) grocer's shop, corner shop

boêmio /bo'emiu/ a & m Bohemian

bofe|tada /bofe'tada/ f, bofe|tão /bofe'tãw/ m slap; ~tear vt slap

boi /boj/ m bullock, (Amer) steer

bói /boj/ m office boy

bóia /'bɔja/ f (de balizamento) buoy; (de cortiça, isopor etc) float; (câmara de borracha) rubber ring; (de braço) armband, water wing; (na caixa-d'água) ballcock; (fam: comida) grub; ~ salva-vidas lifebelt; ~-fria (pl ~s-frias) m/f itinerant farm labourer

boiar /bo'jar/ vt/i float; (fam) be lost

boico|tar /bojko'tar/ vt boycott; ~te /ɔ/ m boycott

boiler /'bojler/ (pl ~s) m boiler

boina /'bojna/ f beret

bo|jo /'boʒu/ m bulge; ~judo a (cheio) bulging; (arredondado) bulbous

bola /'bɔla/ f ball; dar ~ para (fam) give attention to <pessoa>; care about <coisa>; ~ de gude marble; ~ de neve snowball

bolacha /bo'laʃa/ f (biscoito) biscuit, (Amer) cookie; (descanso) beermat; (fam: tapa) slap

bo|lada /bo'lada/ f large sum of money; ~lar vt think up, devise

boléia /bo'lɛja/ f cab; (Port: carona) lift

boletim /bole'tʃĩ/ m bulletin; (escolar) report

bolha /'boʎa/ f bubble; (na pele) blister □ (fam) m/f pain

boliche /bo'liʃi/ m skittles

Bolívia /bo'livia/ f Bolivia

boliviano /bolivi'anu/ a & m Bolivian

bolo /'bolu/ m cake

bo|lor /bo'lor/ m mould, mildew; ~lorento a mouldy

bolota /bo'lɔta/ f (*glande*) acorn; (*bolinha*) little ball

bol|sa /'bowsa/ f bag; ~sa (de estudo) scholarship; ~sa (de valores) stock exchange; ~sista m/f, (*Port*) ~seiro m scholarship student; ~so /o/ m pocket

bom /bõ/ a (f boa) good; (*de saúde*) well; <*comida*> nice; está ~ that's fine

bomba¹ /'bõba/ f (*explosiva*) bomb; (*doce*) eclair; (*fig*) bombshell; levar ~ (*fam*) fail

bomba² /'bõba/ f (*de bombear*) pump

Bombaim /bõba'ĩ/ f Bombay

bombar|dear /bõbardʒi'ar/ vt bombard; (*do ar*) bomb; ~deio m bombardment; (*do ar*) bombing

bomba-relógio /bõbaxe'lɔʒiu/ (pl ~s-relógio) f time bomb

bom|bear /bõbi'ar/ vt pump; ~beiro m fireman; (*encanador*) plumber

bombom /bõ'bõ/ m chocolate

bombordo /bõ'bordu/ m port

bondade /bõ'dadʒi/ f goodness

bonde /'bõdʒi/ m tram; (*teleférico*) cable car

bondoso /bõ'dozu/ a good(-hearted)

boné /bo'nɛ/ m cap

bone|ca /bo'nɛka/ f doll; ~co /ɛ/ m dummy

bonificação /bonifika'sãw/ f bonus

bonito /bo'nitu/ a <*mulher*> pretty; <*homem*> handsome; <*tempo, casa etc*> lovely

bônus /'bonus/ m invar bonus

boqui|aberto /bokia'bɛrtu/ a open-mouthed, flabbergasted; ~nha f snack

borboleta /borbo'leta/ f butterfly; (*roleta*) turnstile

borbotão /borbo'tãw/ m spurt

borbu|lha /bor'buʎa/ f bubble; ~lhar vi bubble

borda /'bɔrda/ f edge; ~do a edged; (à linha) embroidered □ m embroidery

bordão /bor'dãw/ m (*frase*) catch-phrase

bordar /bor'dar/ vt (à linha) embroider

bor|del /bor'dɛw/ (pl ~déis) m brothel

bordo /'bordu/ m a ~ aboard

borra /'boxa/ f dregs; (*de café*) grounds

borra|cha /bo'xaʃa/ f rubber; ~cheiro m tyre fitter

bor|rão /bo'xãw/ m (*de tinta*) blot; (*rascunho*) rough draft; ~rar vt (*sujar*) blot; (*riscar*) cross out; (*pintar*) daub

borrasca /bo'xaska/ f squall

borri|far /boxi'far/ vt sprinkle; ~fo m sprinkling

bosque /'bɔski/ m wood

bosta /'bɔsta/ f (*de animal*) dung; (*chulo*) crap

bota /'bɔta/ f boot

botâni|ca /bo'tanika/ f botany; ~co a botanical □ m botanist

bo|tão /bo'tãw/ m button; (*de flor*) bud; falar com os seus ~tões say to o.s.

botar /bo'tar/ vt put; put on <*roupa*>; set <*mesa, despertador*>; lay <*ovo*>; find <*defeito*>

bote¹ /'bɔtʃi/ m (*barco*) dinghy; ~ salva-vidas lifeboat; (*de borracha*) life-raft

bote² /'bɔtʃi/ m (*de animal etc*) lunge

botequim /butʃi'kĩ/ m bar

botoeira /boto'era/ f buttonhole

boxe /'bɔksi/ m boxing; ~ador m boxer

brabo /'brabu/ a <*animal*> ferocious; <*calor, sol*> fierce; <*doença*> bad; <*prova, experiência*> tough; (*zangado*) angry

bra|çada /bra'sada/ f armful; (*em natação*) stroke; ~çadeira (faixa) armband; (ferragem) bracket; (de atleta) sweatband; ~çal (pl ~çais) a manual; ~celete /e/ m bracelet; ~ço m arm; ~ço direito (fig: pessoa) right-hand man

bra|dar /bra'dar/ vi/t shout; ~do m shout

braguilha /bra'giʎa/ f fly, flies

braile /'brajli/ m Braille

bra|mido /bra'midu/ m roar; ~mir vi roar

branco /'brãku/ a white □ m (*homem*) white man; (*espaço*) blank; em ~ <*cheque etc*> blank; noite em ~ sleepless night

bran|do /'brãdu/ a gentle; <*doença*> mild; (*indulgente*) lenient, soft; ~dura f gentleness; (*indulgência*) softness, leniency

brasa /'braza/ f em ~ red-hot; mandar ~ (*fam*) go to town

brasão /bra'zãw/ m coat of arms

braseiro /bra'zeru/ m brasier

Brasil /bra'ziw/ m Brazil

brasi|leiro /brazi'leru/ a & m Brazilian; ~liense a & m/f (*person*) from Brasilia

bra|vata /bra'vata/ f bravado; ~vio a wild; <*mar*> rough; ~vo a (corajoso) brave; (*zangado*) angry; <*mar*> rough; ~vura f bravery

breca /'brɛka/ f levado da ~ very naughty

brecar /bre'kar/ vt stop <*carro*>; (*fig*) curb □ vi brake

brecha /'brɛʃa/ f gap; (*na lei*) loophole

bre|ga /'brɛga/ (*fam*) a tacky, naff; ~guice (*fam*) f tack, tackiness brejo /'brɛʒu/ *m* marsh; ir para o ∼ (*fig*) go down the drain

brenha /'brɛɲa/ *f* thicket

breque /'brɛki/ *m* brake

breu /'brew/ *m* tar, pitch

breve /'brɛvi/ *a* short, brief; em ∼ve soon, shortly; ∼vidade *f* shortness, brevity

briga /'briga/ *f* fight; (*bate-boca*) argument

brigada /bri'gada/ *f* brigade; ∼deiro *m* brigadier; (*doce*) chocolate truffle

brigão /bri'gãw/ *a* (*f* ∼gona) belligerent; (*na fala*) argumentative □ *m* (*f* ∼gona) troublemaker; ∼gar *vi* fight; (*com palavras*) argue; <*cores*> clash

brilhante /bri'ʎãtʃi/ *a* (*reluzente*) shiny; (*fig*) brilliant; ∼lhar *vi* shine; ∼lho *m* (*de sapatos etc*) shine; (*dos olhos, de metais*) gleam; (*das estrelas*) brightness; (*de uma cor*) brilliance; (*fig: esplendor*) splendour

brincadeira /brĩka'dera/ *f* (*piada*) joke; (*brinquedo, jogo*) game; de ∼ cadeira for fun; ∼calhão (*f* ∼calhona*) *a* playful □ *m* joker; ∼car *vi* (*divertir-se*) play; (*gracejar*) joke

brinco /'brĩku/ *m* earring

brindar /brĩ'dar/ *vt* (*saudar*) toast, drink to; (*presentear*) give a gift to; ∼dar alg com aco afford s.o. sth; (*de presente*) give s.o. sth as a gift; ∼de *m* (*saudação*) toast; (*presente*) free gift

brinquedo /brĩ'kedu/ *m* toy

brio /'briu/ *m* self-esteem, character; ∼so /o/ *a* self-confident

brisa /'briza/ *f* breeze

britadeira /brita'dera/ *f* pneumatic drill

britânico /bri'taniku/ *a* British □ *m* Briton; os ∼s the British

broca /'brɔka/ *f* drill

broche /'brɔʃi/ *m* brooch

brochura /bro'ʃura/ *f* livro de ∼ paperback

brócolis /'brɔkulis/ *m pl*, (*Port*) brócolos /'brɔkuluʃ/ *m pl* broccoli

bronca /'brõka/ (*fam*) *f* telling-off; dar uma ∼ca em alg tell s.o. off; ∼co *a* coarse, rough

bronquite /brõ'kitʃi/ *f* bronchitis

bronze /'brõzi/ *m* bronze; ∼ado *a* tanned, brown □ *m* (sun)tan; ∼ador *a* tanning □ *m* suntan lotion; ∼amento *m* tanning; ∼ar *vt* tan; ∼ar-se *vpr* go brown, tan

brotar /bro'tar/ *vt* sprout <*folhas, flores*> ; spout <*lágrimas, palavras*> □ *vi* <*planta*> sprout; <*água*> spout; <*idéias*> pop up; ∼tinho (*fam*) *m* youngster; ∼to /o/ *m* shoot; (*fam*) youngster

broxa /'brɔʃa/ *f* (large) paint brush □ (*fam*) *a* impotent

bruços /'brusus/ de ∼ face down

bruma /'bruma/ *f* mist; ∼moso /o/ *a* misty

brusco /'brusku/ *a* brusque, abrupt

brutal /bru'taw/ (*pl* ∼tais) *a* brutal; ∼talidade *f* brutality; ∼to *a* <*feições*> coarse; <*homem*> brutish; <*tom, comentário*> aggressive; <*petróleo*> crude; <*peso, lucro, salário*> gross □ *m* brute

bruxa /'bruʃa/ *f* witch; (*feia*) hag; ∼ria *f* witchcraft

Bruxelas /bru'ʃɛlas/ *f* Brussels

bruxo /'bruʃu/ *m* wizard

bruxulear /bruʃuli'ar/ *vi* flicker

bucha /'buʃa/ *f* (*tampão*) bung; (*para paredes*) rawlplug (R); acertar na ∼ (*fam*) hit the nail on the head

bucho /'buʃu/ *m* gut; ∼ de boi tripe

budismo /bu'dʒizmu/ *m* Buddhism; ∼ta *a* & *m/f* Buddhist

bueiro /bu'eru/ *m* storm drain

búfalo /'bufalu/ *m* buffalo

bufante /bu'fãtʃi/ *a* full, puffed; ∼far *vi* snort; (*reclamar*) grumble, moan

bufê /bu'fe/ *m* (*refeição*) buffet; (*serviço*) catering service; (*móvel*) sideboard

buginganga /buʒi'gãga/ *f* knickknack

bujão /bu'ʒãw/ *m* ∼ de gás gas cylinder

bula /'bula/ *f* (*de remédio*) directions; (*do Papa*) bull

bulbo /'buwbu/ *m* bulb

bule /'buli/ *m* (*de chá*) teapot; (*de café etc*) pot

Bulgária /buw'garia/ *f* Bulgaria

búlgaro /'buwgaru/ *a* & *m* Bulgarian

bulhufas /bu'ʎufas/ (*fam*) *pron* nothing

bulício /bu'lisiu/ *m* bustle

bumbum /bũ'bũ/ (*fam*) *m* bottom, bum

bunda /'bũda/ *f* bottom

buquê /bu'ke/ *m* bouquet

buraco /bu'raku/ *m* hole; (*de agulha*) eye; (*jogo de cartas*) rummy; ∼ da fechadura keyhole

burburinho /burbu'riɲu/ *m* (*de vozes*) hubbub

burguês /bur'ges/ *a* & *m* (*f* ∼guesa*) bourgeois; ∼guesia *f* bourgeoisie

burlar /bur'lar/ *vt* get round <*lei*> ; get past <*defesas, vigilância*>

burocracia /burokra'sia/ *f* bureaucracy; ∼crata *m/f* bureaucrat; ∼crático *a* bureaucratic; ∼cratizar *vt* make bureaucratic

burrice /bu'xisi/ *f* stupidity; (*uma*) stupid thing; ∼ro *a* stupid; (*ignorante*) dim □ *m* (*animal*) donkey; (*pessoa*) halfwit, dunce; ∼ro de carga (*fig*) workhorse bus|ca /'buska/ f search; dar ~ca em search; ~ca-pé m banger; ~car vt fetch; (de carro) pick up; mandar ~car send for

bússola /'busola/ f compass; (fig) guide

busto /'bustu/ m bust

butique /bu't∫iki/ f boutique

buzi|na /bu'zina/ f horn; ~nada f toot (of the horn); ~nar vi sound the horn, toot the horn

C

cá /ka/ adv here; o lado de ~ this side; para ~ here; de ~ para lá back and forth; de lá para ~ since then; ~ entre nós between you and me

ca|bal /ka'baw/ (pl ~bais) a complete, full; <prova> conclusive

cabana /ka'bana/ f hut; (casinha no campo) cottage

cabeça /ka'besa/ f head; (de lista) top; (pessoa inteligente) mind □ m/f (chefe) ringleader; (integrante mais inteligente) brains; de ~ <saber> off the top of one's head; <calcular> in one's head; de ~ para baixo upside down; deu-lhe na ~ de he took it into his head to; esquentar a ~ (fam) get worked up; fazer a ~ de alg convince s.o.; quebrar a ~ rack one's brains; subir à ~ go to s.o.'s head; ter a ~ no lugar have one's head screwed on; ~da f (no futebol) header; (pancada) head butt; dar uma ~da no teto bang one's head on the ceiling; ~de-porco (pl ~s-de-porco) f tenement; ~de-vento (pl ~s-de-vento) m/f scatterbrain, airhead; ~lho m heading

cabe|cear /kabesi'ar/ vt head <bola>; ~ceira f head; ~çudo a pigheaded

cabe|dal /kabe'daw/ (pl ~dais) m wealth

cabelei|ra /kabe'lera/ f head of hair; (peruca) wig; ~reiro m hairdresser

cabe|lo /ka'belu/ m hair; cortar o ~lo have one's hair cut; ~ludo a hairy; (difícil) complicated; <palavra, piada> dirty

caber /ka'ber/ vi fit; (ter cabimento) be fitting; ~ a <mérito, parte> be due to; <tarefa> fall to; cabe a você ir it is up to you to go; ~ em alg <roupa> fit s.o.

cabide /ka'bidʒi/ m (peça de madeira, arame etc) hanger; (móvel) hat stand; (na parede) coat rack

cabimento /kabi'mētu/ m ter ~ be fitting, be appropriate; não ter ~ be out of the question

cabine /ka'bini/ f cabin; (de avião) cockpit; (de loja) changing room; ~ telefônica phone box, (Amer) phone booth

cabisbaixo /kabiz'baʃu/ a crestfallen

cabí|vel /ka'bivew/ (pl ~veis) a appropriate, fitting

cabo¹ /'kabu/ m (militar) corporal; ao ~ de after; levar a ~ carry out; ~ eleitoral campaign worker

cabo² /'kabu/ m (fio) cable; (de panela etc) handle; TV por ~ cable TV; ~ de extensão extension lead; ~ de força tug of war

caboclo /ka'boklu/ a & m mestizo

ca|bra /'kabra/ f goat; ~brito m kid

ca|ça /'kasa/ f (atividade) hunting; (caçada) hunt; (animais) game □ m (avião) fighter; à ~ça de in pursuit of; ~ça das bruxas (fig) witch hunt; ~cador m hunter; ~ça-minas m invar minesweeper; ~ça-níqueis m invar slot machine; ~çar vt hunt <animais, criminoso etc>; (procurar) hunt for □ vi hunt

cacareco /kaka'rɛku/ m piece of junk; pl junk

cacare|jar /kakare'ʒar/ vi cluck; ~jo /e/ m clucking

caçarola /kasa'rɔla/ f saucepan

cacau /ka'kaw/ m cocoa

cace|tada /kase'tada/ f blow with a club; (fig) annoyance; ~te /e/ m club □ (fam) int damn

cachaça /ka'ʃasa/ f white rum

cachê /ka'ʃe/ m fee

cache|col /kaʃe'kɔw/ (pl ~cóis) m scarf

cachimbo /ka'ʃĩbu/ m pipe

cacho /'kaʃu/ m (de banana, uva) bunch; (de cabelo) lock; (fam: caso) affair

cachoeira /kaʃo'era/ f waterfall

cachor|rinho /kaʃo'xĩu/ m (nado) doggy paddle; ~ro /o/ m dog; (Port) puppy; (pessoa) scoundrel; ~ro-quente (pl ~ros-quentes) m hot dog

cacife /ka'sifi/ m (fig) pull

caci|que /ka'siki/ m (indio) chief; (político) boss; ~quia f leadership

caco /'kaku/ m shard; (pessoa) old crock

cacto /'kaktu/ m cactus

caçula /ka'sula/ m/f youngest child □ a youngest

cada /'kada/ a each; ~ duas horas every two hours; custam £5 ~ (um) they cost £5 each; ~ vez mais more and more; ~ vez mais fácil easier and easier; ele fala ~ coisa (fam) he says the most amazing things

cadafalso /kada'fawsu/ m gallows

cadarço /ka'darsu/ m shoelace

cadas|trar /kadas'trar/ vt register; ~tro m register; (ato) registration;

(*policial, bancário*) records, files; (*imobiliário*) land register

ca|dáver /ka'daver/ *m* (dead) body, corpse; ~davérico *a* cadaverous, corpse-like; <*exame*> post-mortem

cadê /ka'de/ (*fam*) *adv* where is/are...?

cadeado /kadʒi'adu/ *m* padlock

cadeia /ka'deja/ *f* (*de eventos, lojas etc*) chain; (*prisão*) prison; (*rádio, TV*) network

cadeira /ka'dera/ *f* (*móvel*) chair; (*no teatro*) stall; (*de político*) seat; (*função de professor*) chair; (*matéria*) subject; *pl* (*anat*) hips; ~ de balanço rocking chair; ~ de rodas wheelchair; ~ elétrica electric chair

ca|dência /ka'dẽsia/ *f* (*mus, da voz*) cadence; (*compasso*) rhythm; ~denciado *a* rhythmic; <*passos*> measured

cader|neta /kader'neta/ *f* notebook; (*de professor*) register; (*de banco*) passbook; ~neta de poupança savings account; ~no /ɛ/ *m* exercise book; (*pequeno*) notebook; (*no jornal*) section

cadete /ka'detʃi/ *m* cadet

cadu|car /kadu'kar/ *vi* <*pessoa*> become senile; <*contrato*> lapse; ~co *a* <*pessoa*> senile; <*contrato*> lapsed; ~quice *f* senility

cafajeste /kafa'ʒɛstʃi/ *m* swine

ca|fé /ka'fɛ/ *m* coffee; (*botequim*) café; ~fé da manhã breakfast; tomar ~fé have breakfast; ~fé-com-leite *a invar* coffee-coloured, light brown □ *m* white coffee; ~feeiro *a* coffee □ *m* coffee plant; ~feicultura *f* coffee-growing; ~feína *f* caffein(e)

cafetã /kafe'tã/ *m* caftan

cafetão /kafe'tãw/ *m* pimp

cafe|teira /kafe'tera/ *f* coffee pot; ~zal (*pl* ~zais) *m* coffee plantation; ~zinho *m* small black coffee

cafo|na /ka'fɔna/ (*fam*) a naff, tacky; ~nice *f* tackiness; (*coisa*) tacky thing

cágado /'kagadu/ *m* turtle

caiar /kaj'ar/ *vt* whitewash

cãibra /'kãjbra/ *f* cramp

cai|da /ka'ida/ *f* fall; *veja* queda; ~do *a* <*árvore etc*> fallen; <*beiços etc*> drooping; (*deprimido*) dejected; (*apaixonado*) smitten

caimento /kaj'mẽtu/ *m* fall

caipi|ra /kaj'pira/ *a* <*pessoa*> countrified; <*festa, música*> country; <*sotaque*> rural □ *m/f* country person; (*depreciativo*) country bumpkin; ~rinha *f* cachaça with limes, sugar and ice

cair /ka'ir/ *vi* fall; <*dente, cabelo*> fall out; <*botão etc*> fall off; <*comércio, trânsito etc*> fall off; <*tecido, cortina*>

hang; ~ bem/mal <*roupa*> go well/badly; <*ato, dito*> go down well, badly; estou caindo de sono I'm really sleepy

cais /kajs/ *m* quay; (*Port: na estação*) platform

caixa /'kaʃa/ *f* box; (*de lojas etc*) cash-desk □ *m/f* cashier; ~ de correio letter box; ~ de mudanças, (*Port*) ~ de velocidades gear box; ~ postal post office box, PO Box; ~-d'água (*pl* ~s-d'água) *f* water tank; ~-forte (*pl* ~s-fortes) *f* vault

cai|xão /ka'ʃãw/ *m* coffin; ~xeiro *m* (*em loja*) assistant; salesman; ~xilho *m* frame; ~xote /ɔ/ *m* crate

caju /ka'ʒu/ *m* cashew fruit; ~eiro *m* cashew tree

cal /kaw/ *f* lime

calado /ka'ladu/ *a* quiet

calafrio /kala'friu/ *m* shudder, shiver

calami|dade /kalami'dadʒi/ *f* calamity; ~toso /o/ *a* calamitous

calar /ka'lar/ *vi* be quiet □ *vt* keep quiet about <*segredo, sentimento*>; silence <*pessoa*>; ~-se *vpr* go quiet

calça /'kawsa/ *f* trousers, (*Amer*) pants

calça|da /kaw'sada/ *f* pavement, (*Amer*) sidewalk; (*Port: rua*) roadway; ~dão *m* pedestrian precinct; ~deira *f* shoe-horn; ~do *a* paved □ *m* shoe; *pl* footwear

calcanhar /kawka'ɲar/ *m* heel

calção /kaw'sãw/ *m* shorts; ~ de banho swimming trunks

calcar /kaw'kar/ *vt* (*pisar*) trample; (*comprimir*) press; ~ aco em (*fig*) base sth on, model sth on

calçar /kaw'sar/ *vt* put on <*sapatos, luvas*>; take <*número*>; pave <*rua*>; (*com calço*) wedge □ *vi* <*sapato*> fit; ~-se *vpr* put one's shoes on

calcário /kaw'kariu/ *m* limestone □ *a* <*água*> hard

calças /'kawsas/ *f pl veja* calça

calcinha /kaw'siɲa/ *f* knickers, (*Amer*) panties

cálcio /'kawsiu/ *m* calcium

calço /'kawsu/ *m* wedge

calcu|ladora /kawkula'dora/ *f* calculator; ~lar *vt/i* calculate; ~lista *a* calculating □ *m/f* opportunist

cálculo /'kawkulu/ *m* calculation; (*diferencial*) calculus; (*med*) stone

cal|da /'kawda/ *f* syrup; *pl* hot springs; ~deira *f* boiler; ~deirão *m* cauldron; ~do *m* (*sopa*) broth; (*suco*) juice; ~do de carne/galinha beef/chicken stock

calefação /kalefa'sãw/ *f* heating

caleidoscópio /kalejdos'kɔpiu/ *m* kaleidoscope

calejado /kale'ʒadu/ *a* <*mãos*> calloused; <*pessoa*> experienced
calendário /kalẽ'dariu/ *m* calendar
calha /'kaʎa/ *f* (*no telhado*) gutter; (*sulco*) gulley
calhamaço /kaʎa'masu/ *m* tome
calhambeque /kaʎã'bɛki/ (*fam*) *m* banger
calhar /ka'ʎar/ *vi* calhou que it so happened that; calhou pegar em o mesmo trem they happened to get the same train; ~ de happen to; vir a ~ come at the right time
cali|brado /kali'bradu/ *a* (*bêbado*) tipsy; ~**brar** *vt* calibrate; check (the pressure of) <*pneu*>; ~**bre** *m* calibre; coisas desse ~ things of this order
cálice /'kalisi/ *m* (*copo*) liqueur glass; (*na missa*) chalice
caligrafia /kaligra'fia/ *f* (*letra*) handwriting; (*arte*) calligraphy
calista /ka'lista/ *m/f* chiropodist, (*Amer*) podiatrist
cal|ma /'kawma/ *f* calm; com ~**ma** calmly □ *int* calm down; ~**mante** *m* tranquilizer; ~**mo** *a* calm
calo /'kalu/ *m* (*na mão*) callus; (*no pé*) corn
colombo /ka'lõbu/ *m* bump
calor /ka'lor/ *m* heat; (*agradável, fig*) warmth; estar com ~ be hot
calo|rento /kalo'rẽtu/ *a* <*pessoa*> sensitive to heat; <*lugar*> hot; ~**ria** *f* calorie; ~**roso** /o/ *a* warm; <*protesto*> lively
calota /ka'lɔta/ *f* hubcap
calo|te /ka'lɔtʃi/ *m* bad debt; ~**teiro** *m* bad risk
calouro /ka'loru/ *m* (*na faculdade*) freshman; (*em outros ramos*) novice
ca|lúnia /ka'lunia/ *f* slander; ~**luniar** *vt* slander; ~**lunioso** /o/ *a* slanderous
cal|vície /kaw'visi/ *f* baldness; ~**vo** *a* bald
cama /'kama/ *f* bed; ~ de casal/solteiro double/single bed; ~-**beliche** (*pl* ~s-**beliches**) *f* bunk bed
camada /ka'mada/ *f* layer; (*de tinta*) coat
câmara /'kamara/ *f* chamber; (*fotográfica*) camera; em ~ lenta in slow motion; ~ municipal town council; (*Port*) town hall
camarada /kama'rada/ *a* friendly □ *m/f* comrade; ~**gem** *f* comradeship; (*convivência agradável*) camaraderie
câmara-de-ar /kamaradʒi'ar/ (*pl* **câmaras-de-ar**) *f* inner tube
camarão /kama'rãw/ *m* shrimp; (*maior*) prawn
cama|reira /kama'rera/ *f* chambermaid; ~**rim** *m* dressing room;

cambada /kã'bada/ *f* gang, horde
cambalacho /kãba'laʃu/ *m* scam
camba|lear /kãbali'ar/ *vi* stagger; ~**lhota** *f* somersault
cambi|al /kãbi'aw/ (*pl* ~**ais**) *a* exchange; ~**ante** *m* shade; ~**ar** *vt* change
câmbio /'kãbiu/ *m* exchange; (*taxa*) rate of exchange; ~ oficial/paralelo official/black market exchange rate
cambista /kã'bista/ *m/f* (*de entradas*) ticket-tout, (*Amer*) scalper; (*de dinheiro*) money changer
Camboja /kã'bɔʒa/ *m* Cambodia
cambojano /kãbo'ʒanu/ *a & m* Cambodian
camburão /kãbu'rãw/ *m* police van
camélia /ka'mɛlia/ *f* camelia
camelo /ka'melu/ *m* camel
camelô /kame'lo/ *m* street vendor
camião /kami'ãw/ (*Port*) *m* veja caminhão
caminhada /kami'nada/ *f* walk
caminhão /kami'nãw/ *m* lorry, (*Amer*) truck
cami|nhar /kami'nar/ *vi* walk; (*fig*) advance, progress; ~**nho** *m* way; (*estrada*) road; (*trilho*) path; a ~ on the way; a meio ~**nho** halfway; ~**nho de ferro** (*Port*) railway, (*Amer*) railroad
caminho|neiro /kamiɲo'neru/ *m* lorry driver, (*Amer*) truck driver; ~**nete** /ɛ/ *m* van
camio|neta /kamio'neta/ *f* van; ~**nista** (*Port*) *m/f* veja caminhoneiro
cami|sa /ka'miza/ *f* shirt; ~**sa-de-força** (*pl* ~**sas-de-força**) *f* straitjacket; ~**sa-de-vênus** (*pl* ~**sas-de-vênus**) *f* condom; ~**seta** /e/ *f* T-shirt; (*de baixo*) vest; ~**sinha** (*fam*) *f* condom; ~**sola** /ɔ/ *f* nightdress; (*Port*) sweater
camomila /kamo'mila/ *f* camomile
campainha /kãpa'iɲa/ *f* bell; (*da porta*) doorbell
campanário /kãpa'nariu/ *m* belfry
campanha /kã'paɲa/ *f* campaign
campe|ão /kãpi'ãw/ *m* (*f* ~**ã**) champion; ~**onato** *m* championship
cam|pestre /kã'pɛstri/ *a* rural; ~**pina** *f* grassland
cam|ping /'kãpĩ/ *m* camping; (*lugar*) campsite; ~**pismo** (*Port*) *m* camping
campo /'kãpu/ *m* field; (*interior*) country; (*de futebol*) pitch; (*de golfe*) course; ~ de concentração concentration camp; ~**nês** *m* (*f* ~**nesa*) peasant
camu|flagem /kamu'flaʒẽ/ *f* camouflage; ~**flar** *vt* camouflage
camundongo /kamũ'dõgu/ *m* mouse

cana /'kana/ f cane; ~ de açúcar sugar cane

Canadá /kana'da/ m Canada

canadense /kana'dẽsi/ a & m Canadian

ca|nal /ka'naw/ (pl ~nais) m channel; (hidrovia) canal

canalha /ka'naʎa/ m/f scoundrel

canali|zação /kanaliza'sãw/ f piping; ~zador (Port) m plumber; ~zar vt channel < líquido, esforço, recursos>; canalize <rio>; pipe for water and drainage <cidade>

canário /ka'nariu/ m canary

canastrão /kanas'trãw/ m (f ~trona) ham actor (f actress)

canavi|al /kanavi'aw/ (pl ~ais) m cane field; ~eiro a sugar cane

canção /kã'sãw/ f song

cance|lamento /kãsela'mẽtu/ m cancellation; ~lar vt cancel; (riscar) cross out

câncer /'kãser/ m cancer; Câncer (signo) Cancer

cance|riano /kãseri'anu/ a & m Cancerian; ~rígeno a carcinogenic; ~roso /o/ a cancerous □ m person with cancer

cancro /'kãkru/ m (Port: câncer) cancer; (fig) canker

candango /kã'dãgu/ m person from Brasília

cande|eiro /kãdʒi'eru/ m (oil-)lamp; ~labro m candelabra

candida|tar-se /kãdʒida'tarsi/ vpr (a vaga) apply (a for); (à presidência etc) stand; (Amer) run (a for); ~to m candidate (a for); (a vaga) applicant (a for); ~tura f candidature; (a vaga) application (a for)

cândido /'kãdʒidu/ a innocent

candomblé /kãdõ'blɛ/ m Afro-Brazilian cult; (reunião) candomble meeting

candura /kã'dura/ f innocence

cane|ca /ka'nɛka/ f mug; ~co /ɛ/ m tankard

canela[1] /ka'nɛla/ f (condimento) cinnamon

canela[2] /ka'nɛla/ f (da perna) shin; ~da f dar uma ~da em alg kick s.o. in the shins; dar uma ~da em aco hit one's shins on sth

cane|ta /ka'neta/ f pen; ~ esferográfica ball-point pen; ~ta-tinteiro (pl ~tas-tinteiro) f fountain pen

cangote /kã'gɔtʃi/ m nape of the neck

canguru /kãgu'ru/ m kangaroo

canhão /ka'ɲãw/ m (arma) cannon; (vale) canyon

canhoto /ka'ɲotu/ a left-handed □ m (talão) stub

cani|bal /kani'baw/ (pl ~bais) m/f cannibal; ~balismo m cannibalism

caniço /ka'nisu/ m reed; (pessoa) skinny person

canícula /ka'nikula/ f heat wave

ca|nil /ka'niw/ (pl ~nis) m kennel

canivete /kani'vetʃi/ m penknife

canja /'kãʒa/ f chicken soup; (fam) piece of cake

canjica /kã'ʒika/ f corn porridge

cano /'kanu/ m pipe; (de bota) top; (de arma de fogo) barrel

cano|a /ka'noa/ f canoe; ~agem f canoeing; ~ista m/f canoeist

canonizar /kanoni'zar/ vt canonize

can|saço /kã'sasu/ m tiredness; ~sado a tired; ~sar vt tire; (aborrecer) bore □ vi, ~sar-se vpr get tired; ~sativo a tiring; (aborrecido) boring; ~seira f tiredness; (lida) toil

can|tada /kã'tada/ f (fam) chat-up; ~tar vt/i sing; (fam) chat up

cântaro /'kãtaru/ m chover a ~s pour down, bucket down

cantarolar /kãtaro'lar/ vt/i hum

cantei|ra /kã'tera/ f quarry; ~ro m (de flores) flowerbed; (artífice) stonemason; ~ro de obras site office

cantiga /kã'tʃiga/ f ballad

can|til /kã'tʃiw/ (pl ~tis) m canteen; ~tina f canteen

canto[1] /'kãtu/ m (ângulo) corner

canto[2] /'kãtu/ m (cantar) singing; ~tor m singer; ~toria f singing

canudo /ka'nudu/ m (de beber) straw; (tubo) tube; (fam: diploma) diploma

cão /kãw/ (pl cães) m dog

caolho /ka'oʎu/ a one-eyed

ca|os /kaws/ m chaos; ~ótico a chaotic

capa /'kapa/ f (de livro, revista) cover; (roupa sem mangas) cape; ~ de chuva raincoat

capacete /kapa'setʃi/ m helmet

capacho /ka'paʃu/ m doormat

capaci|dade /kapasi'dadʒi/ f capacity; (aptidão) ability; ~tar vt enable; (convencer) convince

capataz /kapa'tas/ m foreman

capaz /ka'pas/ a capable (de of); ser ~ de (poder) be able to; (ser provável) be likely to

cape|la /ka'pela/ f chapel; ~lão (pl ~lães) m chaplain

capen|ga /ka'pẽga/ a doddery; ~gar vt/i dodder

capeta /ka'peta/ m (diabo) devil; (criança) little devil

capilar /kapi'lar/ a hair

ca|pim /ka'pĩ/ m grass; ~pinar vt/i weed

capi|tal /kapi'taw/ (pl ~tais) a & m/f capital; ~talismo m capitalism; ~talista a & m/f capitalist; ~talizar vt (com) capitalize; (aproveitar) capitalize on

capi|tanear /kapitani'ar/ vt captain
<navio>; (fig) lead; ~tania f
captaincy; ~tania do porto port
authority; ~tão (pl ~tães) m captain

capitulação /kapitula'sãw/ f capit-
ulation, surrender

capítulo /ka'pitulu/ m chapter; (de
telenovela) episode

capô /ka'po/ m bonnet, (Amer) hood

capoeira /kapo'era/ f Brazilian kick-
boxing

capo|ta /ka'pɔta/ f roof; ~tar vi over-
turn

capote /ka'pɔtʃi/ m overcoat

capri|char /kapri'ʃar/ vi excel o.s.;
~cho m (esmero) care; (desejo) whim;
(teimosia) contrariness; ~choso /o/ a
(cheio de caprichos) capricious; (com
esmero) painstaking, meticulous

Capricórnio /kapri'kɔrniu/ m Capricorn

capricorniano /kaprikorni'anu/ a &
m Capricorn

cápsula /'kapsula/ f capsule

cap|tar /kap'tar/ vt pick up <emissão,
sinais>; tap <água>; catch, grasp
<sentido>; win <simpatia, admira-
ção>; ~tura f capture; ~turar vt
capture

capuz /ka'pus/ m hood

caquético /ka'kɛtʃiku/ a broken-
down, on one's last legs

caqui /ka'ki/ m persimmon

cáqui /'kaki/ a invar & m khaki

cara /'kara/ f face; (aparência) look;
(ousadia) cheek □ (fam) m guy; ~ a
~ face to face; de ~ straightaway;
dar de ~ com run into; está na ~
it's obvious; fechar a ~ frown; ~ de
pau cheek; ~ de tacho (fam) sheepish look

cara|col/kara'kɔw/(pl ~cóis) m snail

caracte|re /karak'tɛri/ m character;
~rística f characteristic, feature;
~rístico a characteristic; ~rizar vt
characterize; ~rizar-se vpr be char-
acterized

cara-de-pau /karadʒi'paw/ (pl caras-
de-pau) a cheeky, brazen

caramba /ka'rãba/ int (de espanto)
wow; (de desagrado) damn

caramelo /kara'mɛlu/ m caramel;
(bala) toffee

caramujo /kara'muʒu/ m water snail

caranguejo /karã'geʒu/ m crab

caratê /kara'te/ m karate

caráter /ka'rater/ m character

caravana /kara'vana/ f caravan

car|boidrato /karboi'dratu/ m
carbohydrate; ~bono /o/ m carbon

carbu|rador /karbura'dor/ m carbur-
ettor, (Amer) carburator; ~rante m
fuel

carcaça /kar'kasa/ f carcass; (de navio etc) frame

cárcere /'karseri/ m jail

carcereiro /karse'reru/ m jailer,
warder

carcomido /karko'midu/ a worm-
eaten; <rosto> pock-marked

cardápio /kar'dapiu/ m menu

carde|al /kard3i'aw/ (pl ~ais) a car-
dinal

cardíaco /kar'd3iaku/ a cardiac; ataque ~ heart attack

cardio|lógico /kard3io'lɔ3iku/ a
heart; ~logista m/f heart specialist,
cardiologist

cardume /kar'dumi/ m shoal

ca|recer /kare'ser/ ~recer de vt lack;
~rência f lack; (social) deprivation;
(afetiva) lack of affection; ~rente a
lacking; (socialmente) deprived; (afeti-
vamente) in need of affection

carestia /kares'tʃia/ f high cost; (geral) high cost of living; (escassez)
shortage

careta /ka'reta/ f grimace □ a (fam)
straight, square

car|ga /'karga/ f load; (mercadorias)
cargo; (elétrica) charge; (de cavalaria)
charge; (de caneta) refill; (fig)
burden; ~ga horária workload;
~go m (função) post, job; a ~go de
in the charge of; ~gueiro m (navio)
cargo ship, freighter

cariar /kari'ar/ vi decay

Caribe /ka'ribi/ m Caribbean

caricatu|ra /karika'tura/ f cari-
cature; ~rar vt caricature; ~rista
m/f caricaturist

carícia /ka'risia/ f (com a mão)
stroke, caress; (carinho) affection

cari|dade /kari'dad3i/ f charity; obra
de ~dade charity; ~doso /o/ a
charitable

cárie /'kari/ f tooth decay

carim|bar /karĩ'bar/ vt stamp; post-
mark <carta>; ~bo m stamp; (do correio) postmark

cari|nho /ka'riɲu/ m affection; (um)
caress; ~nhoso /o/ a affectionate

carioca /kari'ɔka/ a from Rio de Janeiro □ m/f person from Rio de Janeiro □ (Port) m weak coffee

caris|ma /ka'rizma/ m charisma;
~mático a charismatic

carna|val /karna'vaw/ (pl ~vais) m
carnival; ~valesco /e/ a carnival;
<roupa> over the top, overdone □ m
carnival organizer

car|ne /'karni/ f (humana etc) flesh;
(comida) meat; ~neiro m sheep; (macho) ram; (como comida) mutton;
~niça f carrion; ~nificina f

slaughter; ~ívoro *a* carnivorous □ *m* carnivore; ~nudo *a* fleshy

caro /'karu/ *a* expensive; (*querido*) dear □ *adv* <*custar, cobrar*> a lot; <*comprar, vender*> at a high price; pagar ~ pay a high price (for)

caroço /ka'rosu/ *m* (*de pêssego etc*) stone; (*de maçã*) core; (*em sopa, molho etc*) lump

carona /ka'rona/ *f* lift

carpete /kar'petʃi/ *m* fitted carpet

carpin|taria /karpĩta'ria/ *f* carpentry; ~teiro *m* carpenter

carran|ca /ka'xãka/ *f* scowl; ~cudo *a* <*cara*> scowling; <*pessoa*> sullen

carrapato /kaxa'patu/ *m* (*animal*) tick; (*fig*) hanger-on

carrasco /ka'xasku/ *m* executioner; (*fig*) butcher

carre|gado /kaxe'gadu/ *a* <*céu*> dark, black; <*cor*> dark; <*ambiente*> tense; ~gador *m* porter; ~gamento *m* loading; (*carga*) load; ~gar *vt* load <*navio, arma, máquina fotográfica*>; (*levar*) carry; charge <*bateria, pilha*>; ~gar em overdo; pronounce strongly <*letra*>; (*Port*) press

carreira /ka'xera/ *f* career

carre|tel /kaxe'tɛw/ (*pl* ~téis) *m* reel

car|ril /ka'xiw/ (*pl* ~ris) (*Port*) *m* rail

carrinho /ka'xiɲu/ *m* (*para bagagem, compras*) trolley; (*de criança*) pram; ~ de mão wheel-barrow

carro /'kaxu/ *m* car; (*de boi*) cart; ~ alegórico float; ~ esporte sports car; ~ fúnebre hearse; ~ça /a/ *f* cart; ~ceria *f* bodywork; ~-chefe (*pl* ~s-chefes) *m* (*no carnaval*) main float; (*fig*) centrepiece; ~-forte (*pl* ~s-fortes) *m* security van

carros|sel /kaxo'sɛw/ (*pl* ~séis) *m* merry-go-round

carruagem /kaxu'aʒẽ/ *f* carriage, coach

carta /'karta/ *f* letter; (*mapa*) chart; (*do baralho*) card; ~ branca (*fig*) carte blanche; ~ de condução (*Port*) driving licence, (*Amer*) driver's license; ~-bomba (*pl* ~s-bomba) *f* letter bomb; ~da *f* (*fig*) move

cartão /kar'tãw/ *m* card; (*Port: papelão*) cardboard; ~ de crédito credit card; ~ de visita visiting card; ~postal (*pl* cartões-postais) *m* postcard

car|taz /kar'tas/ *m* poster, (*Amer*) bill; em ~ showing, (*Amer*) playing; ~teira *f* (*para dinheiro*) wallet; (*cartão*) card; (*mesa*) desk; ~teira de identidade identity card; ~teira de motorista driving licence, (*Amer*) driver's license; ~teiro *m* postman

car|tel /kar'tɛw/ (*pl* ~téis) *m* cartel

cárter /'karter/ *m* sump

carto|la /kar'tɔla/ *f* top hat □ *m* director; ~lina *f* card; ~mante *m/f* tarot reader, fortune-teller

cartório /kar'tɔriu/ *m* registry office

cartucho /kar'tuʃu/ *m* cartridge; (*de dinamite*) stick; (*de amendoim etc*) bag

car|tum /kar'tũ/ *m* cartoon; ~tunista *m/f* cartoonist

caruncho /ka'rũʃu/ *m* woodcorm

carvalho /kar'vaʎu/ *m* oak

car|vão /kar'vãw/ *m* coal; (*de desenho*) charcoal; ~voeiro *a* coal

casa /'kaza/ *f* house; (*comercial*) firm; (*de tabuleiro*) square; (*de botão*) hole; em ~ at home; para ~ home; na ~ dos 30 anos in one's thirties; ~ da moeda mint; ~ de banho (*Port*) bathroom; ~ de campo country house; ~ de saúde private hospital; ~ decimal decimal place; ~ popular council house

casaco /ka'zaku/ *m* (*sobretudo*) coat; (*paletó*) jacket; (*de lã*) pullover

ca|sal /ka'zaw/ (*pl* ~sais) *m* couple; ~samento *m* marriage; (*cerimônia*) wedding; ~sar *vt* marry; (*fig*) combine □ *vi* get married; (*fig*) go together; ~sar-se *vpr* get married; (*fig*) combine; ~sar-se com marry

casarão /kaza'rãw/ *m* mansion

casca /'kaska/ *f* (*de árvore*) bark; (*de laranja, limão*) peel; (*de banana*) skin; (*de noz, ovo*) shell; (*de milho*) husk; (*de pão*) crust; (*de ferida*) scab

cascalho /kas'kaʎu/ *m* gravel

cascata /kas'kata/ *f* waterfall; (*fam*) fib

casca|vel /kaska'vew/ (*pl* ~véis) *m* (*cobra*) rattlesnake □ *f* (*mulher*) shrew

casco /'kasku/ *m* (*de cavalo etc*) hoof; (*de navio*) hull; (*garrafa vazia*) empty

ca|sebre /ka'zebri/ *m* hovel, shack; ~seiro *a* <*comida*> home-made; <*pessoa*> home-loving; <*vida*> home □ *m* housekeeper

caserna /ka'zɛrna/ *f* barracks

casmurro /kaz'muxu/ *a* sullen

caso /'kazu/ *m* case; (*amoroso*) affair; (*conto*) story □ *conj* in case; em todo ou qualquer ~ in any case; fazer ~ de take notice of; vir ao ~ be relevant; ~ contrário otherwise

casório /ka'zɔriu/ (*fam*) *m* wedding

caspa /'kaspa/ *f* dandruff

casquinha /kas'kiɲa/ *f* (*de sorvete*) cone, cornet

cassar /ka'sar/ *vt* revoke, withdraw <*direitos, autorização*>; ban <*político*>

cassete /ka'sɛtʃi/ *m* cassette

cassetete /kase'tɛtʃi/ *m* truncheon, (*Amer*) nightstick

cassino /ka'sinu/ *m* casino; ~ de oficiais officers' mess

casta|nha /kas'taɲa/ f chestnut; ~nha de caju cashew nut; ~nha-do-pará (pl ~nhas-do-pará) f Brazil nut; ~nheiro m chestnut tree; ~nho a chestnut(-coloured); ~nholas /ɔ/ f pl castanets

castelhano /kaste'ʎanu/ a & m Castilian

castelo /kas'tɛlu/ m castle

casti|çal /kastʃi'saw/ (pl ~çais) m candlestick

cas|tidade /kastʃi'dadʒi/ f chastity; ~tigar vt punish; ~tigo m punishment; ~to a chaste

castor /kas'tor/ m beaver

castrar /kas'trar/ vt castrate

casu|al /kazu'aw/ (pl ~ais) a chance; (fortuito) fortuitous; ~alidade f chance

casulo /ka'zulu/ m (de larva) cocoon

cata /'kata/ f à ~ de in search of

cata|lão /kata'lâw/ (pl ~lães) a & m (f ~lã) Catalan

catalisador /kataliza'dor/ m catalyst; (de carro) catalytic convertor

catalogar /katalo'gar/ vt catalogue

catálogo /ka'talogu/ m catalogue; (de telefones) phone book

Catalunha /kata'luɲa/ f Catalonia

catapora /kata'pora/ f chicken pox

catar /ka'tar/ vt (procurar) search for; (recolher) gather; (do chão) pick up; sort <arroz, café>

catarata /kata'rata/ f waterfall; (no olho) cataract

catarro /ka'taxu/ m catarrh

catástrofe /ka'tastrofi/ f catastrophe

catastrófico /katas'trɔfiku/ a catastrophic

catecismo /kate'sizmu/ m catechism

cátedra /'katedra/ f chair

cate|dral /kate'draw/ (pl ~drais) f cathedral; ~drático m professor

cate|goria /katego'ria/ f category; (social) class; (qualidade) quality; ~górico a categorical; ~gorizar vt categorize

catinga /ka'tʃĩga/ f body odour, stink

cati|vante /katʃi'vãtʃi/ a captivating; ~var vt captivate; ~veiro m captivity; ~vo a & m captive

catolicismo /katoli'sizmu/ m Catholicism

católico /ka'tɔliku/ a & m Catholic

catorze /ka'torzi/ a & m fourteen

cau|da /'kawda/ f tail; ~dal (pl ~dais) m torrent

caule /'kawli/ m stem

cau|sa /'kawza/ f cause; (jurid) case; por ~sa de because of; ~sar vt cause

caute|la /kaw'tɛla/ f caution; (documento) ticket; ~loso /o/ a cautious, careful

cava /'kava/ f armhole

cava|do /ka'vadu/ a <vestido> low-cut; <olhos> deep-set; ~dor a hardworking □ m hard worker

cava|laria /kavala'ria/ f cavalry; ~lariça f stable; ~leiro m horseman; (na Idade Média) knight

cavalete /kava'letʃi/ m easel

caval|gadura /kavawga'dura/ f mount; ~gar vt/i ride; sit astride <muro, banco>; (saltar) jump

cavalhei|resco /kavaʎe'resku/ a gallant, gentlemanly; ~ro m gentleman □ a gallant, gentlemanly

cavalo /ka'valu/ m horse; a ~ on horseback; ~-vapor (pl ~s-vapor) m horsepower

cavanhaque /kava'ɲaki/ m goatee

cavaquinho /kava'kiɲu/ m ukulele

cavar /ka'var/ vt dig; (fig) go all out for □ vi dig; (fig) go all out; ~ em (vasculhar) delve into; ~ a vida make a living

caveira /ka'vera/ f skull

caverna /ka'vɛrna/ f cavern

caviar /kavi'ar/ m caviar

cavidade /kavi'dadʒi/ f cavity

cavilha /ka'viʎa/ f peg

cavo /'kavu/ a hollow

cavoucar /kavo'kar/ vt excavate

caxemira /kaʃe'mira/ f cashmere

caxumba /ka'ʃũba/ f mumps

cear /si'ar/ vt have for supper □ vi have supper

cebo|la /se'bola/ f onion; ~linha f spring onion

ceder /se'der/ vt give up; (dar) give; (emprestar) lend □ vi (não resistir) give way; ~ a yield to

cedilha /se'dʒiʎa/ f cedilla

cedo /'sedu/ adv early; mais ~ ou mais tarde sooner or later

cedro /'sedru/ m cedar

cédula /'sɛdula/ f (de banco) note, (Amer) bill; (eleitoral) ballot paper

ce|gar /se'gar/ vt blind; blunt <faca>; ~go /ɛ/ a blind; <faca> blunt □ m blind man; às ~gas blindly

cegonha /se'goɲa/ f stork

cegueira /se'gera/ f blindness

ceia /'seja/ f supper

cei|fa /'sejfa/ f harvest; (massacre) slaughter; ~far vt reap; claim <vidas>; (matar) mow down

cela /'sɛla/ f cell

cele|bração /selebra'sâw/ f celebration; ~brar vt celebrate

célebre /'sɛlebri/ a celebrated

celebridade /selebri'dadʒi/ f celebrity

celeiro /se'leru/ m granary

célere /'sɛleri/ a swift, fast

celeste /se'lɛstʃi/ a celestial

celeuma /se'lewma/ f pandemonium

celibato /seli'batu/ m celibacy

celofane /selo'fani/ m cellophane

celta /'sɛwta/ a Celtic □ m/f Celt □ m (*língua*) Celtic

célula /'sɛlula/ f cell

celu|lar /selu'lar/ a cellular; ~lite f cellulite; ~lose /ɔ/ f cellulose

cem /sēj/ a & m hundred

cemitério /semi'tɛriu/ m cemetery; (*fig*) graveyard

cena /'sena/ f scene; (*palco*) stage; em ~ on stage

cenário /se'nariu/ m scenery; (*de crime etc*) scene

cênico /'seniku/ a stage

cenoura /se'nora/ f carrot

cen|so /'sēsu/ m census; ~sor censor; ~sura f (*de jornais etc*) censorship; (*órgão*) censor(s); (*condenação*) censure; ~surar vt censor <*jornal, filme etc*>; (*condenar*) censure

centavo /sē'tavu/ m cent

centeio /sē'teju/ m rye

centelha /sē'teʎa/ f spark; (*fig: de gênio etc*) flash

cente|na /sē'tena/ f hundred; uma ~na de about a hundred; às ~nas in their hundreds; ~nário m centenary

centésimo /sē'tɛzimu/ a hundredth

centi|grado /sē'tʃigradu/ m centigrade; ~litro m centilitre; ~metro m centimetre

cento /'sētu/ a & m hundred; por ~ per cent

cen|tral /sē'traw/ (*pl* ~trais) a central; ~tralizar vt centralize; ~trar vt centre; ~tro m centre

cepti- (*Port*) *veja* ceti-

cera /'sera/ f wax; fazer ~ waste time, faff about

cerâmi|ca /se'ramika/ f ceramics, pottery; ~co a ceramic

cer|ca /'serka/ f fence; ~ca viva hedge □ adv ~ca de around, about; ~cado m enclosure; (*para criança*) playpen; ~car vt surround; (*com muro, cerca*) enclose; (*assediar*) besiege

cercear /sersi'ar/ vt (*fig*) curtail, restrict

cerco /'serku/ m (*mil*) siege; (*policial*) dragnet

cere|al /seri'aw/ (*pl* ~ais) m cereal

cere|bral /sere'braw/ (*pl* ~brais) a cerebral

cérebro /'sɛrebru/ m brain; (*inteligência*) intellect

cere|ja /se're3a/ f cherry; ~jeira f cherry tree

cerimônia /seri'monia/ f ceremony; sem ~ unceremoniously; fazer ~ stand on ceremony

cerimoni|al /serimoni'aw/ (*pl* ~ais) a & m ceremonial; ~oso /o/ a ceremonious

cer|rado /se'xadu/ a <*barba, mata*> thick; <*punho, dentes*> clenched □ m scrubland; ~rar vt close; ~rar-se vpr close; <*noites, trevas*> close in

certeiro /ser'teru/ a well-aimed, accurate

certe|za /ser'teza/ f certainty; com ~ certainly; ter ~ be sure (de of; de que that)

certi|dão /sertʃi'dāw/ f certificate; ~ de nascimento birth certificate

certifi|cado /sertʃifi'kadu/ m certificate; ~car vt certify; ~car-se de make sure of

certo /'sɛrtu/ a (*correto*) right; (*seguro*) certain; (*algum*) a certain □ adv right; dar ~ work

cerveja /ser've3a/ f beer; ~ria f brewery; (*bar*) pub

cervo /'servu/ m deer

cer|zidura /serzi'dura/ f darning; ~zir vt darn

cesariana /sezari'ana/ f Caesarian

césio /'sɛziu/ m caesium

cessar /se'sar/ vt/i cease

ces|ta /'sesta/ f basket; (*de comida*) hamper; ~to /e/ m basket; ~to de lixo wastepaper basket

ceticismo /setʃi'sizmu/ m scepticism

cético /'sɛtʃiku/ a sceptical □ m sceptic

cetim /se'tʃī/ m satin

céu /sɛw/ m sky; (*na religião*) heaven; ~ da boca roof of the mouth

cevada /se'vada/ f barley

chá /ʃa/ m tea

chacal /ʃa'kaw/ (*pl* ~cais) m jackal

chácara /'ʃakara/ f smallholding; (*casa*) country cottage

chaci|na /ʃa'sina/ f slaughter; ~nar vt slaughter

chá|-de-bar /ʃadʒi'bar/ (*pl* ~s-de-bar) m bachelor party; ~-de-panela (*pl* ~s-de-panela) m hen night, (*Amer*) wedding shower

chafariz /ʃafa'ris/ m fountain

chaga /'ʃaga/ f sore

chaleira /ʃa'lera/ f kettle

chama /'ʃama/ f flame

cha|mada /ʃa'mada/ f call; (*dos presentes*) roll call; (*dos alunos*) register; ~mado m call □ a (*depois do substantivo*) called; (*antes do substantivo*) so-called; ~mar vt call; (*para sair lde*) ask, invite; attract <*atenção*> □ vi call; <*telefone*> ring; ~mar-se vpr be called; ~mariz m decoy; ~mativo a showy, flashy

chamejar /ʃame'3ar/ vi flare

chaminé /ʃami'nɛ/ f (*de casa, fábrica*) chimney; (*de navio, trem*) funnel champanhe /ʃãˈpaɲi/ *m* champagne

champu /ʃãˈpu/ (*Port*) *m* shampoo

chamuscar /ʃamusˈkar/ *vt* singe, scorch

chance /ˈʃãsi/ *f* chance

chanceler /ʃãseˈler/ *m* chancellor

chanchada /ʃãˈʃada/ *f* (*peça*) second-rate play; (*filme*) B movie

chantagear /ʃãtaʒiˈar/ *vt* blackmail; ~gem *f* blackmail; ~gista *m/f* blackmailer

chão /ˈʃãw/ (*pl* ~s) *m* ground; (*dentro de casa etc*) floor

chapa /ˈʃapa/ *f* sheet; (*foto*) plate; ~ eleitoral electoral list; ~ de matrícula (*Port*) number plate, (*Amer*) license plate □ (*fam*) *m* mate

chapéu /ʃaˈpɛw/ *m* hat

charada /ʃaˈrada/ *f* riddle

charge /ˈʃarʒi/ *f* (political) cartoon; ~gista *m/f* cartoonist

charlatanismo /ʃarlataˈnizmu/ *m* charlatanism; ~tão (*pl* ~tães) *m* (*f* ~tona) charlatan

charme /ˈʃarmi/ *m* charm; fazer ~me turn on the charm; ~moso /o/ *a* charming

charneca /ʃarˈnɛka/ *f* moor

charuto /ʃaˈrutu/ *m* cigar

chassi /ʃaˈsi/ *m* chassis

chata /ˈʃata/ *f* (*barca*) barge

chateação /ʃatʃiaˈsãw/ *f* annoyance; ~ar *vt* annoy; ~ar-se *vpr* get annoyed

chatice /ʃaˈtʃisi/ *f* nuisance; ~to *a* (*tedioso*) boring; (*irritante*) annoying; (*mal-educado*) rude; (*plano*) flat

chauvinismo /ʃoviˈnizmu/ *m* chauvinism; ~ta *m/f* chauvinist □ *a* chauvinistic

chavão /ʃaˈvãw/ *m* cliché; ~ve *f* key; (*ferramenta*) spanner; ~ve de fenda screwdriver; ~ve inglesa wrench; ~veiro *m* (*aro*) keyring; (*pessoa*) locksmith

chávena /ˈʃavena/ *f* soup bowl; (*Port*: *xícara*) cup

checar /ʃeˈkar/ *vt* check

chefe /ˈʃɛfi/ *m/f* (*patrão*) boss; (*gerente*) manager; (*dirigente*) leader; ~fia *f* leadership; (*de empresa*) management; (*sede*) headquarters; ~fiar *vt* lead; be in charge of <*trabalho*>

chegada /ʃeˈgada/ *f* arrival; ~gado *a* <*amigo, relação*> close; ~gar *vi* arrive; (*deslocar-se*) move up; (*ser suficiente*) be enough □ *vt* bring up <*prato, cadeira*>; ~gar a fazer go as far as doing; aonde você quer ~gar? what are you driving at?; ~gar lá (*fig*) make it

cheia /ˈʃeja/ *f* flood

cheio /ˈʃeju/ *a* full; (*fam*: *farto*) fed up

cheirar /ʃeˈrar/ *vt/i* smell (a of); ~roso /o/ *a* scented

cheque /ˈʃɛki/ *m* cheque, (*Amer*) check; ~ de viagem traveller's cheque; ~ em branco blank cheque

chiado /ˈʃiadu/ *m* (*de pneus, freios*) screech; (*de porta*) squeak; (*de vapor, numa fita*) hiss; ~ar *vi* <*porta*> squeak; <*pneus, freios*> screech; <*vapor, fita*> hiss; <*fritura*> sizzle; (*fam*: *reclamar*) grumble, moan

chiclete /ʃiˈklɛtʃi/ *m* chewing gum; ~ de bola bubble gum

chicotada /ʃikoˈtada/ *f* lash; ~te /ɔ/ *m* whip; ~tear *vt* whip

chifrar /ʃiˈfrar/ (*fam*) *vt* cheat on <*marido, esposa*>; two-time <*namorado, namorada*>; ~fre *m* horn; ~frudo *a* horned; (*fam*) cuckolded □ *m* cuckold

Chile /ˈʃili/ *m* Chile

chileno /ʃiˈlenu/ *a* & *m* Chilean

chilique /ʃiˈliki/ (*fam*) *m* funny turn

chilrear /ʃiwxiˈar/ *vi* chirp, twitter; ~reio *m* chirping, twittering

chimarrão /ʃimaˈxãw/ *m* unsweetened maté tea

chimpanzé /ʃĩpãˈzɛ/ *m* chimpanzee

China /ˈʃina/ *f* China

chinelo /ʃiˈnɛlu/ *m* slipper

chinês /ʃiˈnes/ *a* & *m* (*f* ~nesa) Chinese

chinfrim /ʃĩˈfrĩ/ *a* tatty, shoddy

chio /ˈʃiu/ *m* squeak; (*de pneus*) screech; (*de vapor*) hiss

chique /ˈʃiki/ *a* <*pessoa, aparência, roupa*> smart, (*Amer*) sharp; <*hotel, bairro, loja etc*> smart, up-market, posh

chiqueiro /ʃiˈkeru/ *m* pigsty

chispa /ˈʃispa/ *f* flash; ~pada *f* dash; ~par *vi* (*soltar chispas*) flash; (*correr*) dash

chocalhar /ʃokaˈʎar/ *vt/i* rattle; ~lho *m* rattle

chocante /ʃoˈkãtʃi/ *a* shocking; (*fam*) incredible; ~car *vt/i* hatch <*ovos*>; (*ultrajar*) shock; ~car-se *vpr* <*carros etc*> crash; <*teorias etc*> clash

chocho /ˈʃoʃu/ *a* dull, insipid

chocolate /ʃokoˈlatʃi/ *m* chocolate

chofer /ʃoˈfɛr/ *m* chauffeur

chope /ˈʃopi/ *m* draught lager

choque /ˈʃɔki/ *m* shock; (*colisão*) collision; (*conflito*) clash

choradeira /ʃoraˈdera/ *f* fit of crying; ~ramingar *vi* whine; ~ramingas *m/f* *invar* whiner; ~rão *m* (*salgueiro*) weeping willow □ *a* (~rona) tearful; ~rar *vi* cry; ~ro /o/ *m* crying; ~roso /o/ *a* tearful

chouriço /ʃoˈrisu/ *m* black pudding; (*Port*) sausage

chover /ʃo'ver/ *vi* rain

chuchu /ʃu'ʃu/ *m* chayote

chucrute /ʃu'krutʃi/ *m* sauerkraut

chumaço /ʃu'masu/ *m* wad

chum|bado /ʃũ'badu/ (*fam*) *a* knocked out; ~bar (*Port*) *vt* fail <*dente*>; fail <*aluno*> □ *vi* <*aluno*> fail; ~bo *m* lead; (*Port: obturação*) filling

chu|par /ʃu'par/ *vt* suck; <*esponja*> suck up; ~peta /e/ *f* dummy, (*Amer*) pacifier

churras|caria /ʃuxaska'ria/ *f* barbecue restaurant; ~co *m* barbecue; ~queira *f* barbecue; ~quinho *m* kebab

chu|tar /ʃu'tar/ *vt/i* kick; (*fam: adivinhar*) guess; ~te *m* kick; ~teira *f* football boot

chu|va /'ʃuva/ *f* rain; ~va de pedra hail; ~varada *f* torrential rainstorm; ~veiro *m* shower; ~viscar *vi* drizzle; ~visco *m* drizzle; ~voso /o/ *a* rainy

cica|triz /sika'tris/ *f* scar; ~trizar *vt* scar □ *vi* <*ferida*> heal

cic|lismo /si'klizmu/ *m* cycling; ~lista *m/f* cyclist; ~lo *m* cycle; ~lone /o/ *m* cyclone; ~lovia *f* cycle lane

cida|dania /sidada'nia/ *f* citizenship; ~dão /o/ *m* (*f* ~dã) citizen; ~de *f* town; (*grande*) city; ~dela /ɛ/ *f* citadel

ciência /si'ẽsia/ *f* science

cien|te /si'ẽtʃi/ *a* aware; ~tífico *a* scientific; ~tista *m/f* scientist

ci|fra /'sifra/ *f* figure; (*código*) cipher; ~frão *m* dollar sign; ~frar *vt* encode

cigano /si'ganu/ *a* & *m* gypsy

cigarra /si'gaxa/ *f* cicada; (*dispositivo*) buzzer

cigar|reira /siga'xera/ *f* cigarette case; ~ro *m* cigarette

cilada /si'lada/ *f* trap; (*estratagema*) trick

cilindrada /sili'drada/ *f* (engine) capacity

cilíndrico /si'lĩdriku/ *a* cylindrical

cilindro /si'lĩdru/ *m* cylinder; (*rolo*) roller

cílio /'siliu/ *m* eyelash

cima /'sima/ *f* em ~ on top; (*na casa*) upstairs; em ~ de on, on top of; para ~ up; (*na casa*) upstairs; por ~ over the top; por ~ de over; de ~ from above; ainda por ~ moreover

címbalo /'sĩbalu/ *m* cymbal

cimeira /si'mera/ *f* crest; (*Port: cúpula*) summit

cimen|tar /simẽ'tar/ *vt* cement; ~to *m* cement

cinco /'sĩku/ *a* & *m* five

cine|asta /sini'asta/ *m/f* film-maker; ~ma /e/ *m* cinema

Cingapura /sĩga'pura/ *f* Singapore

cínico /'siniku/ *a* cynical □ *m* cynic

cinismo /si'nizmu/ *m* cynicism

cinqüen|ta /sĩ'kwẽta/ *a* & *m* fifty; ~tão *a* & *m* (*f* ~tona) fifty-year-old

cinti|lante /sĩtʃi'lãtʃi/ *a* glittering; ~lar *vi* glitter

cin|to /'sĩtu/ *m* belt; ~to de segurança seatbelt; ~tura *f* waist; ~turão *m* belt

cin|za /'sĩza/ *f* ash □ *a invar* grey; ~zeiro *m* ashtray

cin|zel /sĩ'zɛw/ (*pl* ~zéis) *m* chisel; ~zelar *vt* carve

cinzento /sĩ'zẽtu/ *a* grey

cipó /si'pɔ/ *m* vine, liana; ~poal (*pl* ~poais) *m* jungle

cipreste /si'prestʃi/ *m* cypress

cipriota /sipri'ɔta/ *a* & *m* Cypriot

ciranda /si'rãda/ *f* (*fig*) merry-go-round

cir|cense /sir'sẽsi/ *a* circus; ~co *m* circus

circu|ito /sir'kuitu/ *m* circuit; ~lação *f* circulation; ~lar *a* & *f* circular □ *vt* circulate □ *vi* <*dinheiro, sangue*> circulate; <*carro*> drive; <*ônibus*> run; <*trânsito*> move; <*pessoa*> go round

círculo /'sirkulu/ *m* circle

circunci|dar /sirkũsi'dar/ *vt* circumcise; ~ção *f* circumcision

circun|dar /sirkũ'dar/ *vt* surround; ~ferência *f* circumference; ~flexo /ɛks/ *a* & *m* circumflex; ~scrição *f* district; ~scrição eleitoral constituency; ~specto /ɛ/ *a* circumspect; ~stância *f* circumstance; ~stanciado *a* detailed; ~stancial (*pl* ~stanciais) *a* circumstantial; ~stante *m/f* bystander

cirrose /si'xɔzi/ *f* cirrhosis

cirur|gia /sirur'ʒia/ *f* surgery; ~gião *m* (*f* ~giã) surgeon

cirúrgico /si'rurʒiku/ *a* surgical

cisão /si'zãw/ *f* split, division

cisco /'sisku/ *m* speck

cisma¹ /'sizma/ *m* schism

cis|ma² /'sizma/ *f* (*mania*) fixation; (*devaneio*) imagining, daydream; (*prevenção*) irrational dislike; (*de criança*) whim; ~mar *vt/i* be lost in thought; <*criança*> be insistent; ~mar em brood over; ~mar de ou em fazer insist on doing; ~mar que insist on thinking that; ~mar com alg take a dislike to s.o.

cisne /'sizni/ *m* swan

cistite /sis'tʃitʃi/ *f* cystitis

ci|tação /sita'sãw/ *f* quotation; (*jurid*) summons; ~tar *vt* quote; (*jurid*) summon

ciúme /si'umi/ *m* jealousy; ter ~s de be jealous of

ciu|meira /siu'mera/ *f* fit of jealousy; ~**mento** *a* jealous

cívico /'siviku/ *a* civic

ci|vil /si'viw/ (*pl* ~**vis**) *a* civil □ *m* civilian; ~**vilidade** *f* civility

civili|zação /siviliza'sãw/ *f* civilization; ~**zado** *a* civilized; ~**zar** *vt* civilize

civismo /si'vizmu/ *m* public spirit

cla|mar /kla'mar/ *vt/i* cry out, clamour (por for); ~**mor** *m* outcry; ~**moroso** /o/ *a* <*protesto*> loud, noisy; <*erro, injustiça*> blatant

clandestino /klãdes'tʃinu/ *a* clandestine

cla|ra /'klara/ *f* egg white; ~**rabóia** *f* skylight; ~**rão** *m* flash; ~**rear** *vt* brighten; clarify <*questão*> □ *vi* brighten up; (*fazer-se dia*) become light; ~**reira** *f* clearing; ~**reza** /e/ *f* clarity; ~**ridade** *f* brightness; (*do dia*) daylight

cla|rim /kla'rĩ/ *m* bugle; ~**rinete** /e/ *m* clarinet

clarividente /klarivi'dẽtʃi/ *m/f* clairvoyant

claro /'klaru/ *a* clear; <*luz*> bright; <*cor*> light □ *adv* clearly □ *int* of course; ~ que sim/não of course/of course not; às claras openly; noite em ~ sleepless night; já é dia ~ it's already daylight

classe /'klasi/ *f* class; ~ média middle class

clássico /'klasiku/ *a* classical; (*famoso, exemplar*) classic □ *m* classic

classifi|cação /klasifika'sãw/ *f* classification; (*numa competição esportiva*) placing, place; ~**cado** *a* classified; <*candidato*> successful; <*esportista, time*> qualified; ~**car** *vt* classify; (*considerar*) describe (de as); ~**car-se** *vpr* <*candidato, esportista*> qualify; (*chamar-se*) describe o.s. (de as); ~**catório** *a* qualifying

classudo /kla'sudu/ (*fam*) *a* classy

claustro|fobia /klawstrofo'bia/ *f* claustrophobia; ~**fóbico** *a* claustrophobic

cláusula /'klawzula/ *f* clause

cla|ve /'klavi/ *f* clef; ~**vícula** *f* collar bone

cle|mência /kle'mẽsia/ *f* clemency; ~**mente** <*pessoa*> lenient; <*tempo*> clement

cleptomaníaco /kleptoma'niaku/ *m* kleptomaniac

clérigo /'klɛrigu/ *m* cleric, clergyman

clero /'klɛru/ *m* clergy

clien|te /kli'ẽtʃi/ *m/f* (*de loja*) customer; (*de advogado, empresa*) client;

~**tela** /ɛ/ *f* (*de loja*) customers; (*de restaurante, empresa*) clientele

cli|ma /'klima/ *m* climate; ~**mático** *a* climatic

clímax /'klimaks/ *m invar* climax

clíni|ca /'klinika/ *f* clinic; ~**ca geral** general practice; ~**co** *a* clinical □ *m* ~**co geral** general practitioner, GP

clipe /'klipi/ *m* clip; (*para papéis*) paper clip

clone /'kloni/ *m* clone

cloro /'kloru/ *m* chlorine

close /'klozi/ *m* close-up

clube /'klubi/ *m* club

coação /koa'sãw/ *f* coercion

coadjuvante /koadʒu'vãtʃi/ *a* <*ator*> supporting □ *m/f* (*em peça, filme*) co-star; (*em crime*) accomplice

coador /koa'dor/ *m* strainer; (*de legumes*) colander; (*de café*) filter bag

coadunar /koadu'nar/ *vt* combine

coagir /koa'ʒir/ *vt* compel

coagular /koagu'lar/ *vt/i* clot; ~**-se** *vpr* clot

coágulo /ko'agulu/ *m* clot

coalhar /koa'ʎar/ *vt/i* curdle; ~**-se** *vpr* curdle

coalizão /koali'zãw/ *f* coalition

coar /ko'ar/ *vt* strain

coaxar /koa'ʃar/ *vi* croak □ *m* croaking

cobaia /ko'baja/ *f* guinea pig

cober|ta /ko'bɛrta/ *f* (*de cama*) bedcover; (*de navio*) deck; ~**to** /ɛ/ *a* covered □ *pp de* cobrir; ~**tor** *m* blanket; ~**tura** *f* (*revestimento*) covering; (*reportagem*) coverage; (*seguro*) cover; (*apartamento*) penthouse

cobi|ça /ko'bisa/ *f* greed, covetousness; ~**çar** *vt* covet; ~**çoso** /o/ *a* covetous

cobra /'kɔbra/ *f* snake

co|brador /kobra'dor/ *m* (*no ônibus*) conductor; ~**brança** *f* (*de dívida*) collection; (*de preço*) charging; (*de atitudes*) asking for something in return (de for); ~**brança de penalti/falta** penalty (kick)/free kick; ~**brar** *vt* collect <*dívida*>; ask for <*coisa prometida*>; take <*penalti*>; ~**brar aco a alg** (*em dinheiro*) charge s.o. for sth; (*fig*) make s.o. pay for sth; ~**brar uma falta** (*no futebol*) take a free kick

cobre /'kɔbri/ *m* copper

cobrir /ko'brir/ *vt* cover; ~**-se** *vpr* <*pessoa*> cover o.s. up; <*coisa*> be covered

cocaína /koka'ina/ *f* cocaine

coçar /ko'sar/ *vt* scratch □ *vi* (*esfregar-se*) scratch; (*comichar*) itch; ~**-se** *vpr* scratch o.s.

cócegas /'kɔsegas/ *f pl* fazer ~ em tickle; sentir ~ be ticklish

coceira /ko'sera/ f itch

cochichar /koʃi'ʃar/ vt/i whisper; ~cho m whisper

cochichlada /koʃi'lada/ f doze; ~lar vi doze; ~lo m snooze

coco /'koku/ m coconut

cócoras /'kɔkoras/ f pl de ~ squatting; ficar de ~ squat

côdea /'kodʒia/ f crust

codificlar /kodʒifi'kar/ vt encode <mensagem>; codify <leis>

código /'kɔdʒigu/ m code; ~ de barras bar code

codinome /kodʒi'nomi/ m codename

coeficiente /koefisi'ẽtʃi/ m coefficient; (fig: fator) factor

coelho /ko'eʎu/ m rabbit

coentro /ko'ẽtru/ m coriander

coerção /koer'sãw/ f coercion

coerência /koe'rẽsia/ f (lógica) coherence; (consequência) consistency; ~rente a (lógico) coherent; (consequente) consistent

coexistência /koezis'tẽsia/ f coexistence; ~tir vi coexist

cofre /'kɔfri/ m safe; (de dinheiro público) coffer

cogitlação /kodʒita'sãw/ f contemplation; fora de ~tação out of the question; ~tar vt/i contemplate

cogumelo /kogu'mɛlu/ m mushroom

coibir /koi'bir/ vt restrict; ~-se de keep o.s. from

coice /'kojsi/ m kick

coincidência /koĩsi'dẽsia/ f coincidence; ~dir vi coincide

coisa /'kojza/ f thing

coitado /koj'tadu/ m poor thing; ~ do pai poor father

cola /'kɔla/ f glue; (cópia) crib

colaborlação /kolabora'sãw/ f collaboration; (de escritor etc) contribution; ~rador m collaborator; (em jornal, livro) contributor; ~rar vi collaborate; (em jornal, livro) contribute (em to)

colagem /ko'laʒẽ/ f collage

colágeno /ko'laʒenu/ m collagen

colapso /ko'lapsu/ m collapse

colar¹ /ko'lar/ m necklace

colar² /ko'lar/ vt (grudar) stick; (copiar) crib □ vi stick; (copiar) crib; <desculpa etc> stand up, stick

colarinho /kola'riɲu/ m collar; (de cerveja) head

colatelral /kolate'raw/ (pl ~rais) a efeito ~ral side effect

colcha /'kowʃa/ f bedspread; ~chão m mattress

colchete /kow'ʃetʃi/ m fastener; (sinal de pontuação) square bracket; ~ de pressão press stud, popper

colchonete /kowʃo'nɛtʃi/ m (foldaway) mattress

coldre /'kɔwdri/ m holster

colleção /kole'sãw/ f collection; ~cionador m collector; ~cionar vt collect

colega /ko'lɛga/ m/f (amigo) friend; (de trabalho) colleague

colegilal /koleʒi'aw/ a (pl ~ais) a school □ m/f schoolboy (f -girl)

colégio /ko'lɛʒiu/ m secondary school, (Amer) high school

coleira /ko'lera/ f collar

cólera /'kɔlera/ f (doença) cholera; (raiva) fury

colérico /ko'lɛriku/ a (furioso) furious □ m (doente) cholera victim

colesterol /koleste'rɔw/ m cholesterol

colleta /ko'lɛta/ f collection; ~tânea f collection; ~tar vt collect

colete /ko'letʃi/ m waistcoat, (Amer) vest; ~ salva-vidas life-jacket, (Amer) life-preserver

coletivo /kole'tʃivu/ a collective; <transporte> public □ m bus

colheita /ko'ʎejta/ f harvest; (produtos colhidos) crop

colher¹ /ko'ʎɛr/ f spoon

colher² /ko'ʎer/ vt pick <flores, frutos>; gather <informações>

colherada /koʎe'rada/ f spoonful

colibri /koli'bri/ m hummingbird

cólica /'kɔlika/ f colic

colidir /koli'dʒir/ vi collide

colilgação /koliga'sãw/ f (pol) coalition; ~gado m (pol) coalition partner; ~gar vt bring together; ~gar-se vpr join forces; (pol) form a coalition

colina /ko'lina/ f hill

colírio /ko'liriu/ m eyewash

colisão /koli'zãw/ f collision

collant /ko'lã/ (pl ~s) m body; (de ginástica) leotard

colmeia /kow'meja/ f beehive

colo /'kɔlu/ f (regaço) lap; (pescoço) neck

collocação /koloka'sãw/ f placing; (emprego) position; (exposição de fatos) statement; (de aparelho, pneus, carpete etc) fitting; ~cado a placed; o primeiro ~cado (em ranking) person in first place; ~cador m fitter; ~car put; fit <aparelho, pneus, carpete etc>; put forward, state <opinião, idéias>; (empregar) get a job for

Colômbia /ko'lõbia/ f Colombia

colombiano /kolõbi'anu/ a & m Colombian

cólon /'kɔlõ/ m colon

colônia¹ /ko'lonia/ f (colonos) colony

colônia² /ko'lonia/ f (perfume) cologne

colonilal /koloni'aw/ (pl ~ais) a colonial; ~alismo m colonialism;

~alista a & m/f colonialist; ~zar vt colonize

colono /ko'lonu/ m settler, colonist; (lavrador) tenant farmer

coloqui|al /koloki'aw/ (pl ~ais) a colloquial

colóquio /ko'lɔkiu/ m (conversa) conversation; (congresso) conference

colo|rido /kolo'ridu/ a colourful □ m colouring; ~rir vt colour

colu|na /ko'luna/ f column; (vertebral) spine; ~nável (pl ~náveis) a famous □ m/f celebrity; ~nista m/f columnist

com /kõ/ prep with; o comentário foi comigo the comment was meant for me; você está ~ a chave? have you got the key?; ~ seis anos de idade at six years of age

coma /'koma/ f coma

comadre /ko'madri/ f (madrinha) godmother of one's child; (mãe do afilhado) mother of one's godchild; (urinol) bedpan

coman|dante /komã'dãtʃi/ m commander; ~dar vt lead; (ordenar) command; (elevar-se acima de) dominate; ~do m command; (grupo) commando group

comba|te /kõ'batʃi/ m combat; (a drogas, doença etc) fight (a against); ~ter vt/i fight; ~ter-se vpr fight

combi|nação /kõbina'sãw/ f combination; (acordo) arrangement; (plano) scheme; (roupa) petticoat; ~nar vt (juntar) combine; (ajustar) arrange □ vi go together, match; ~nar com go with, match; ~nar de sair arrange to go out; ~nar-se vpr (juntar-se) combine; (harmonizar-se) go together, match

comboio /kõ'boju/ m convoy; (Port: trem) train

combustí|vel /kõbus'tʃivew/ (pl ~veis) m fuel

come|çar /kome'sar/ vt/i start, begin; ~ço /e/ m beginning, start

comédia /ko'medʒia/ f comedy

comediante /komedʒi'ãtʃi/ m/f comedian (f comedienne)

comemo|ração /komemora'sãw/ f (celebração) celebration; (lembrança) commemoration; ~rar vt (festejar) celebrate; (lembrar) commemorate; ~rativo a commemorative

comen|tar /komẽ'tar/ vt comment on; (falar mal de) make comments about; ~tário m comment; (de texto, na TV etc) commentary; sem ~tários no comment; ~tarista m/f commentator

comer /ko'mer/ vt eat; <ferrugem etc> eat away; take <peça de xadrez> □ vi eat; ~-se vpr (de raiva etc) be

consumed (de with); dar de ~ a feed

comerci|al /komersi'aw/ (pl ~ais) a & m commercial; ~alizar vt market; ~ante m/f trader; ~ar vi do business, trade; ~ário m shopworker

comércio /ko'mersiu/ m (atividade) trade; (loja etc) business; (lojas) shops

comes /'komis/ m pl ~ e bebes (fam) food and drink; ~tíveis m pl foods, food; ~tível (pl ~tíveis) a edible

cometa /ko'meta/ m comet

cometer /kome'ter/ vt commit <crime>; make <erro>

comichão /komi'ʃãw/ f itch

comício /ko'misiu/ m rally

cômico /'komiku/ a (de comédia) comic; (engraçado) comical

comida /ko'mida/ f food; (uma) meal

comigo = com + mim

comi|lão /komi'lãw/ a (f ~lona) greedy □ m (f ~lona) glutton

cominho /ko'miɲu/ m cummin

comiserar-se /komize'rarsi/ vpr commiserate (de with)

comis|são /komi'sãw/ f commission; ~sário m commissioner; ~sário de bordo (aéreo) steward; (de navio) purser; ~sionar vt commission

comitê /komi'te/ m committee; ~tiva f group; (de uma pessoa) retinue

como /'komu/ adv (na condição de) as; (da mesma forma que) like; (de que maneira) how □ conj as; ~? (pedindo repetição) pardon?; ~ se as if; assim ~ as well as

cômoda /'komoda/ f chest of drawers, (Amer) bureau

como|didade /komodʒi'dadʒi/ f comfort; (conveniência) convenience; ~dismo m complacency; ~dista a complacent

cômodo /'komodu/ a comfortable; (conveniente) convenient □ m (aposento) room

como|vente /komo'vẽtʃi/ a moving; ~ver vt move □ vi be moving; ~ver-se vpr be moved

compacto /kõ'paktu/ a compact □ m single

compadecer-se /kõpade'sersi/ vpr feel pity (de for)

compadre /kõ'padri/ m (padrinho) godfather of one's child; (pai do afilhado) father of one's godchild

compaixão /kõpa'ʃãw/ f compassion

companhei|rismo /kõpaɲe'rizmu/ m companionship; ~ro m (de viagem etc) companion; (amigo) friend, mate

companhia /kõpa'ɲia/ f company; fazer ~ a alg keep s.o. company

compa|ração /kõpara'sãw/ f comparison; ~rar vt compare; ~rativo *a* comparative; ~rável (*pl* ~ráveis) *a* comparable

compare|cer /kõpare'ser/ *vi* appear; ~cer a attend; ~cimento *m* attendance

comparsa /kõ'parsa/ *m/f* (*ator*) bit player; (*cúmplice*) sidekick

comparti|lhar /kõpartʃi'ʎar/ *vt/i* share (de in); ~mento *m* compartment

compassado /kõpa'sadu/ *a* (*medido*) measured; (*ritmado*) regular

compassivo /kõpa'sivu/ *a* compassionate

compasso /kõ'pasu/ *m* (*mus*) beat, time; (*instrumento*) compass, pair of compasses

compatí|vel /kõpa'tʃivew/ (*pl* ~veis) *a* compatible

compatriota /kõpatri'ɔta/ *m/f* compatriot, fellow countryman (*f* -woman)

compelir /kõpe'lir/ *vt* compel

compene|tração /kõpenetra'sãw/ *f* conviction; ~trar *vt* convince; ~trar-se *vpr* convince o.s.

compen|sação /kõpẽsa'sãw/ *f* compensation; (*de cheques*) clearing; ~sar *vt* make up for <*defeitos, danos*>; offset <*peso, gastos*>; clear <*cheques*> □ *vi* <*crime*> pay

compe|tência /kõpe'tẽsia/ *f* competence; ~tente *a* competent

compe|tição /kõpetʃi'sãw/ *f* competition; ~tidor *m* competitor; ~tir *vi* compete; ~tir a be up to; ~tividade *f* competitiveness; ~titivo *a* competitive

compla|cência /kõpla'sẽsia/ *f* complaisance; ~cente *a* obliging

complemen|tar /kõplemẽ'tar/ *vt* complement □ *a* complementary; ~to *m* complement

comple|tar /kõple'tar/ *vt* complete; top up <*copo, tanque etc*>; ~tar 20 anos turn 20; ~to /ɛ/ *a* complete; (*cheio*) full up; por ~to completely; escrever por ~to write out in full

comple|xado /kõplek'sadu/ *a* with a complex; ~xidade *f* complexity; ~xo /ɛ/ *a & m* complex

compli|cação /kõplika'sãw/ *f* complication; ~cado *a* complicated; ~car *vt* complicate; ~car-se *vpr* get complicated

complô /kõ'plo/ *m* conspiracy, plot

com|ponente /kõpo'nẽtʃi/ *a & m* component; ~por *vt/i* compose; ~por-se *vpr* (*controlar-se*) compose o.s.; ~por-se de be composed of

compor|tamento /kõporta'mẽtu/ *m* behaviour; ~tar *vt* hold; bear <*dor, prejuízo*>; ~tar-se *vpr* behave

composi|ção /kõpozi'sãw/ *f* composi-

tion; (*acordo*) conciliation; ~tor *m* (*de música*) composer; (*gráfico*) compositor

compos|to /kõ'postu/ *pp de* compor □ *a* compound; <*pessoa*> level-headed □ *m* compound; ~to de made up of; ~tura *f* composure

compota /kõ'pɔta/ *f* fruit in syrup

com|pra /'kõpra/ *f* purchase; *pl* shopping; fazer ~pras go shopping; ~prador *m* buyer; ~prar *vt* buy; bribe <*oficial, juiz*>; pick <*briga*>

compreen|der /kõprië'der/ *vt* (*conter em si*) contain; (*estender-se a*) cover, take in; (*entender*) understand; ~são *f* understanding; ~sível (*pl* ~síveis) *a* understandable; ~sivo *a* understanding

compres|sa /kõ'presa/ *f* compress; ~são *f* compression; ~sor *m* compressor; rolo ~sor steamroller

compri|do /kõ'pridu/ *a* long; ~mento *m* length

compri|mido /kõpri'midu/ *m* pill, tablet □ *a* <*ar*> compressed; ~mir *vt* (*apertar*) press; (*reduzir o volume de*) compress

compromete|dor /kõpromete'dor/ *a* compromising; ~ter *vt* (*envolver*) involve; (*prejudicar*) compromise; ~ter alg a fazer commit s.o. to doing; ~ter-se *vpr* (*obrigar-se*) commit o.s.; (*prejudicar-se*) compromise o.s.; ~tido *a* (*ocupado*) busy; (*noivo*) spoken for

compromisso /kõpro'misu/ *m* commitment; (*encontro marcado*) appointment; sem ~ without obligation

compro|vação /kõprova'sãw/ *f* proof; ~vante *m* receipt; ~var *vt* prove

compul|são /kõpuw'sãw/ *f* compulsion; ~sivo *a* compulsive; ~sório *a* compulsory

compu|tação /kõputa'sãw/ *f* computation; (*matéria, ramo*) computing; ~tador *m* computer; ~tadorizar *vt* computerize; ~tar *vt* compute

comum /ko'mũ/ *a* common; (*não especial*) ordinary; fora do ~ out of the ordinary; em ~ <*trabalho*> joint; <*atuar*> jointly; ter muito em ~ have a lot in common

comungar /komũ'gar/ *vi* take communion

comunhão /komu'ɲãw/ *f* communion; (*relig*) (Holy) Communion

comuni|cação /komunika'sãw/ *f* communication; ~cação social/visual media studies/ graphic design; ~cado *m* notice; (*pol*) communiqué; ~car *vt* communicate; (*unir*) connect □ *vi*, ~car-se *vpr* communicate; ~cativo *a* communicative comu|nidade /komuni'dadʒi/ f community; ~nismo m communism; ~nista a & m/f communist; ~nitário a (da comunidade) community; (para todos juntos) communal

côncavo /'kõkavu/ a concave

conce|ber /kõse'ber/ vt conceive; (imaginar) conceive of □ vi conceive; ~bível (pl ~bíveis) a conceivable

conceder /kõse'der/ vt grant; ~ em accede to

concei|to /kõ'sejtu/ m concept; (opinião) opinion; (fama) reputation; ~tuado a highly thought of; ~tuar vt (imaginar) conceptualize; (avaliar) assess

concen|tração /kõsẽtra'sãw/ f concentration; (de jogadores) training camp; ~trar vt concentrate; ~trar-se vpr concentrate

concepção /kõsep'sãw/ f conception; (opinião) view

concernir /kõser'nir/ vt ~ a concern

concerto /kõ'sertu/ m concert

conces|são /kõse'sãw/ f concession; ~sionária f dealership; ~sionário m dealer

concha /'kõʃa/ f (de molusco) shell; (colher) ladle

concili|ação /kõsilia'sãw/ f conciliation; ~ador a conciliatory; ~ar vt reconcile

concílio /kõ'siliu/ m council

conci|são /kõsi'zãw/ f conciseness; ~so a concise

conclamar /kõkla'mar/ vt call <eleição, greve>; call upon <pessoa>

conclu|dente /kõklu'dẽtʃi/ a conclusive; ~ir vt/i conclude; ~são f conclusion; ~sivo a concluding

concor|dância /kõkor'dãsia/ f agreement; ~dante a consistent; ~dar vi agree (em to) □ vt bring into line; ~data f abrir ~data go into liquidation

concórdia /kõ'kordʒia/ f concord

concor|rência /kõko'xẽsia/ f competition (a for); ~rente a competing; ~rer vi compete (a for); ~rer para contribute to; ~rido a popular

concre|tizar /kõkretʃi'zar/ vt realize; ~tizar-se vpr be realized; ~to /ɛ/ a & m concrete

concurso /kõ'kursu/ m contest; (prova) competition

con|dado /kõ'dadu/ m county; ~de m count

condeco|ração /kõdekora'sãw/ f decoration; ~rar vt decorate

conde|nação /kõdena'sãw/ f condemnation; (jurid) conviction; ~nar vt condemn; (jurid) convict

conden|sação /kõdẽsa'sãw/ f condensation; ~sar vt condense; ~sar-se vpr condense

condescen|dência /kõdesẽ'dẽsia/ f acquiescence; ~dente a acquiescent; ~der vi acquiesce; ~der a comply with <pedido, desejo>; ~der a ir condescend to go

condessa /kõ'desa/ f countess

condi|ção /kõdʒi'sãw/ f condition; (qualidade) capacity; ter ~ção ou ~ções para be able to; em boas ~ções in good condition; ~cionado a conditioned; ~cional (pl ~cionais) a conditional; ~cionamento m conditioning

condimen|tar /kõdʒimẽ'tar/ vt season; ~to m seasoning

condoer-se /kõdo'ersi/ vpr ~ de feel sorry for

condolência /kõdo'lẽsia/ f sympathy; pl condolences

condomínio /kõdo'miniu/ m (taxa) service charge

condu|ção /kõdu'sãw/ f (de carro etc) driving; (transporte) transport; ~cente a conducive (a to); ~ta f conduct; ~to m conduit; ~tor m (de carro) driver; (eletr) conductor; ~zir vt lead; drive <carro>; (eletr) conduct □ vi (de carro) drive; (levar) lead (a to)

cone /'koni/ m cone

conectar /konek'tar/ vt connect

cone|xão /konek'sãw/ f connection; ~xo /ɛ/ a connected

confec|ção /kõfek'sãw/ f (roupa) off-the-peg outfit; (loja) clothes shop, boutique; (fábrica) clothes manufacturer; ~cionar vt make

confederação /kõfedera'sãw/ f confederation

confei|tar /kõfej'tar/ vt ice; ~taria f cake shop; ~teiro m confectioner

confe|rência /kõfe'rẽsia/ f conference; (palestra) lecture; ~rencista m/f speaker

conferir /kõfe'rir/ vt check (com against); (conceder) confer (a on) □ vi (controlar) check; (estar exato) tally

confes|sar /kõfe'sar/ vt/i confess; ~sar-se vpr confess; ~sionário m confessional; ~sor m confessor

confete /kõ'fɛtʃi/ m confetti

confi|ança /kõfi'ãsa/ f (convicção) confidence; (fé) trust; ~ante a confident (em of); ~ar vt (dar) entrust; ~ar em trust; ~ável (pl ~áveis) a reliable; ~dência f confidence; ~dencial (pl ~denciais) a confidential; ~denciar vt tell in confidence; ~dente m/f confidant (f confidante)

configu|ração /kõfigura'sãw/ f configuration; ~rar vt (representar) represent; (formar) shape; (comput) configure con|finar /kõfi'nar/ vi ~finar com border on; ~fins m pl borders

confir|mação /kõfirma'sãw/ f confirmation; ~mar vt confirm; ~mar-se vpr be confirmed

confis|car /kõfis'kar/ vt confiscate; ~co m confiscation

confissão /kõfi'sãw/ f confession

confla|gração /kõflagra'sãw/ f conflagration; ~grar vt set alight; (fig) throw into turmoil

confli|tante /kõfli'tãtʃi/ a conflicting; ~to m conflict

confor|mação /kõforma'sãw/ f resignation; ~mado a resigned (com to); ~mar vt adapt (a to); ~mar-se com conform to <regra, politica>; resign o.s. to, come to terms with <destino, evento>; ~me /ɔ/ prep according to □ conj depending on; ~me it depends; ~midade f conformity; ~mismo m conformism; ~mista a & m/f conformist

confor|tar /kõfor'tar/ vt comfort; ~tável (pl ~táveis) a comfortable; ~to /o/ m comfort

confraternizar /kõfraterni'zar/ vi fraternize

confron|tação /kõfrõta'sãw/ f confrontation; ~tar vt confront; (comparar) compare; ~to m confrontation; (comparação) comparison

con|fundir /kõfũ'dʒir/ vt confuse; ~fundir-se vpr get confused; ~fusão f confusion; (desordem) mess; (tumulto) commotion; ~fuso a (confundido) confused; (que confunde) confusing

conge|lador /kõʒela'dor/ m freezer; ~lamento m (de preços etc) freeze; ~lar vt freeze; ~lar-se vpr freeze

congênito /kõ'ʒenitu/ a congenital

congestão /kõʒes'tãw/ f congestion

congestio|nado /kõʒestʃio'nadu/ a <rua, cidade> congested; <pessoa, rosto> flushed; <olhos> bloodshot; ~namento m (de trânsito) traffic jam; ~nar vt congest; ~nar-se vpr <rua> get congested; <rosto> flush

conglomerado /kõglome'radu/ m conglomerate

congratular /kõgratu'lar/ vt congratulate (por on)

congre|gação /kõgrega'sãw/ f (na igreja) congregation; (reunião) gathering; ~gar vt bring together; ~gar-se vpr congregate

congresso /kõ'gresu/ m congress

conhaque /ko'ɲaki/ m brandy

conhe|cedor /koɲese'dor/ a knowing □ m connoisseur; ~cer vt know; (ser apresentado a) get to know; (visitar) go to, visit; ~cido a known; (famoso) well-known □ m acquaintance;

~cimento m knowledge; tomar ~cimento de learn of; travar ~cimento com alg make s.o.'s acquaintance, become acquainted with s.o.

cônico /'koniku/ a conical

coni|vência /koni'vẽsia/ f connivance; ~vente a conniving (em at)

conjetu|ra /kõʒe'tura/ f conjecture; ~rar vt/i conjecture

conju|gação /kõʒuga'sãw/ f (ling) conjugation; ~gar vt conjugate <verbo>

cônjuge /'kõʒuʒi/ m/f spouse

conjun|ção /kõʒũ'sãw/ f conjunction; ~tivo a & m subjunctive; ~to a joint □ m set; (roupa) outfit; (musical) group; o ~to de the body of; em ~to jointly; ~tura f state of affairs; (econômica) state of the economy

conosco = com + nós

cono|tação /konota'sãw/ f connotation; ~tar vt connote

conquanto /kõ'kwãtu/ conj although, even though

conquis|ta /kõ'kista/ f conquest; (proeza) achievement; ~tador m conqueror □ a conquering; ~tar vt conquer <terra, pais>; win <riqueza, independência>; win over <pessoa>

consa|gração /kõsagra'sãw/ f (de uma igreja) consecration; (dedicação) dedication; ~grado a <artista, expressão> established; ~grar vt consecrate <igreja>; establish <artista, estilo>; dedicate (a to); ~grar-se a dedicate o.s. to

consci|ência /kõsi'ẽsia/ f (moralidade) conscience; (sentidos) consciousness; (no trabalho) conscientiousness; (de um fato etc) awareness; ~encioso /o/ a conscientious; ~ente a conscious; ~entizar vt make aware (de of); ~entizar-se vpr become aware (de of)

consecutivo /kõseku'tʃivu/ a consecutive

conse|guinte /kõse'gĩtʃi/ a por ~guinte consequently; ~guir vt get; ~guir fazer manage to do □ vi succeed

conse|lheiro /kõse'ʎeru/ m counsellor, adviser; ~lho /e/ m piece of advice; pl advice; (órgão) council

consen|so /kõ'sẽsu/ m consensus; ~timento m consent; ~tir vt allow □ vi consent (em to)

conse|quência /kõse'kwẽsia/ f consequence; por ~quência consequently; ~quente a consequent; (coerente) consistent

conser|tar /kõser'tar/ vt repair; ~to /e/ m repair

conser|va /kõ'sɛrva/ f (em vidro) preserve; (em lata) tinned food; ~vação f preservation; ~vador a & m conservative; ~vadorismo m conservatism; ~vante a & m preservative; ~var vt preserve; (manter, guardar) keep; ~var-se vpr keep; ~vatório m conservatory

conside|ração /kõsidera'sãw/ f consideration; (estima) esteem; levar em ~ração take into consideration; ~rar vt consider; (estimar) think highly of □ vi consider; ~rar-se vpr consider o.s.; ~rável (pl ~ráveis) a considerable

consig|nação /kõsigna'sãw/ f consignment; ~nar vt consign

consigo = com + si

consis|tência /kõsis'tẽsia/ f consistency; ~tente a firm; ~tir vi consist (em in)

consoante /kõso'ãtʃi/ f consonant

conso|lação /kõsola'sãw/ f consolation; ~lador a consoling; ~lar vt console; ~lar-se vpr console o.s.

consolidar /kõsoli'dar/ vt consolidate; mend <fratura>

consolo /kõ'solu/ m consolation

consórcio /kõ'sɔrsiu/ m consortium

consorte /kõ'sɔrtʃi/ m/f consort

conspícuo /kõs'pikuu/ a conspicuous

conspi|ração /kõspira'sãw/ f conspiracy; ~rador m conspirator; ~rar vi conspire

cons|tância /kõs'tãsia/ f constancy; ~tante a & f constant; ~tar vi (em lista etc) appear; não me ~ta I am not aware; ~ta que it is said that; ~tar de consist of

consta|tação /kõstata'sãw/ f observation; ~tar vt note, notice; certify <óbito>

conste|lação /kõstela'sãw/ f constellation; ~lado a star-studded

conster|nação /kõsterna'sãw/ f consternation; ~nar vt dismay

consti|pação /kõstʃipa'sãw/ f (Port: resfriado) cold; ~pado a (resfriado) with a cold; (no intestino) constipated; ~par-se vpr (Port: resfriar-se) get a cold

constitu|cional /kõstʃitusio'naw/ (pl ~cionais) a constitutional; ~ição f constitution; ~inte a constituent □ f Constituinte Constituent Assembly; ~ir vt form <governo, sociedade>; (representar) constitute; (nomear) appoint

constran|gedor /kõstrãʒe'dor/ a embarrassing; ~ger vt embarrass; (coagir) constrain; ~ger-se vpr get embarrassed; ~gimento m (embaraço) embarrassment; (coação) constraint

constru|ção /kõstru'sãw/ f construction; (terreno) building site; ~ir vt build <casa, prédio>; (fig) construct; ~tivo a constructive; ~tor m builder; ~tora f building firm

cônsul /'kõsuw/ (pl ~es) m consul

consulado /kõsu'ladu/ m consulate

consul|ta /kõ'suwta/ f consultation; ~tar vt consult; ~tor m consultant; ~toria f consultancy; ~tório m (médico) surgery, (Amer) office

consu|mação /kõsuma'sãw/ f (taxa) minimum charge; ~mado a fato ~mado fait accompli; ~mar vt accomplish <projeto>; carry out <crime, sacrifício>; consummate <casamento>

consu|midor /kõsumi'dor/ a & m consumer; ~mir vt consume; take up <tempo>; ~mismo m consumerism; ~mista a & m/f consumerist; ~mo m consumption

conta /'kõta/ f (a pagar) bill; (bancária) account; (contagem) count; (de vidro etc) bead; pl (com) accounts; em ~ economical; por ~ de on account of; por ~ própria on one's own account; ajustar ~s settle up; dar ~ de (fig) be up to; dar ~ do recado (fam) deliver the goods; dar-se ~ de realize; fazer de ~ pretend; ficar por ~ de be left to; levar ou ter em ~ take into account; prestar ~s de account for; tomar ~ de take care of; ~ bancária bank account; ~ corrente current account

contabi|lidade /kõtabili'dadʒi/ f accountancy; (contas) accounts; (seção) accounts department; ~lista (Port) m/f accountant; ~lizar vt write up <quantia>; (fig) notch up

contact- (Port) veja contat-

conta|dor /kõta'dor/ m (pessoa) accountant; (de luz etc) meter; ~gem f counting; (de pontos num jogo) scoring; ~gem regressiva countdown

contagi|ante /kõtaʒi'ãtʃi/ a infectious; ~ar vt infect; ~ar-se vpr become infected

contágio /kõ'taʒiu/ m infection

contagioso /kõtaʒi'ozu/ a contagious

contami|nação /kõtamina'sãw/ f contamination; ~nar vt contaminate

contanto /kõ'tãtu/ adv ~ que provided that

contar /kõ'tar/ vt/i count; (narrar) tell; ~ com count on

conta|tar /kõta'tar/ vt contact; ~to m contact; entrar em ~to com get in touch with; tomar ~to com come into contact with

contem|plação /kõtẽpla'sãw/ f contemplation; ~plar vt (considerar) contemplate; (dizer respeito a) concern; ~plar alg com treat s.o. to □ vi ponder; ~plativo a contemplative

contemporâneo /kõtẽpo'raniu/ a & m contemporary

contenção /kõtẽ'sãw/ f containment

conten|cioso /kõtẽsi'ozu/ a contentious; ~da f dispute

conten|tamento /kõtẽta'mẽtu/ m contentment; ~tar vt satisfy; ~tar-se vpr be content; ~te a (feliz) happy; (satisfeito) content; ~to m a ~ to satisfactorily

conter /kõ'ter/ vt contain; ~-se vpr contain o.s.

conterrâneo /kõte'xaniu/ m fellow countryman (f -woman)

contestar /kõtes'tar/ vt question; (jurid) contest

conteúdo /kõte'udu/ m (de recipiente) contents; (fig: de carta etc) content

contexto /kõ'testu/ m context

contigo = com + ti

continência /kõtʃi'nẽsia/ f (mil) salute

continen|tal /kõtʃinẽ'taw/ (pl ~tais) a continental; ~te m continent

contin|gência /kõtʃĩ'ʒẽsia/ f contingency; ~gente a (eventual) possible; (incerto) contingent □ m contingent

continu|ação /kõtʃinua'sãw/ f continuation; ~ar vt/i continue; eles ~am ricos they are still rich; ~idade f continuity

contínuo /kõ'tʃinuu/ a continuous □ m office junior

con|tista /kõ'tʃista/ m/f (short) story writer; ~to m (short) story; ~to de fadas fairy tale; ~to-do-vigário (pl ~tos-do-vigário) m confidence trick, swindle

contorcer /kõtor'ser/ vt twist; ~-se vpr (de dor) writhe

contor|nar /kõtor'nar/ vt go round; (fig) get round <obstáculo, problema>; (cercar) surround; (delinear) outline; ~no /o/ m outline; (da paisagem) contour

contra /'kõtra/ prep against

contra-atacar /kõtrata'kar/ vt counterattack; ~-ataque m counter-attack

contrabaixo /kõtra'baʃu/ m double bass

contrabalançar /kõtrabalã'sar/ vt counterbalance

contraban|dear /kõtrabãdʒi'ar/ vt smuggle; ~dista m/f smuggler; ~do m (ato) smuggling; (artigos) contraband

contração /kõtra'sãw/ f contraction

contracenar /kõtrase'nar/ vi ~ com play up to

contraceptivo /kõtrasep't∫ivu/ a & m contraceptive

contracheque /kõtra'ʃɛki/ m pay slip

contradi|ção /kõtradʒi'sãw/ f contradiction; ~tório a contradictory; ~zer vt contradict; ~zer-se vpr <pessoa> contradict o.s.; <idéias etc> be contradictory

contragosto /kõtra'gostu/ m a ~ reluctantly

contrair /kõtra'ir/ vt contract; pick up <hábito, vício>; ~-se vpr contract

contramão /kõtra'mãw/ f opposite direction □ a invar one way

contramestre /kõtra'mɛstri/ m supervisor; (em navio) bosun

contra-ofensiva /kõtraofẽ'siva/ f counter-offensive

contrapartida /kõtrapar'tʃida/ f (fig) compensation; em ~ on the other hand

contraproducente /kõtraprodu-'sẽtʃi/ a counter-productive

contrari|ar /kõtrari'ar/ vt go against, run counter to; (aborrecer) annoy; ~edade f adversity; (aborrecimento) annoyance

contrário /kõ'trariu/ a opposite; (desfavorável) adverse; ~ a contrary to; <pessoa> opposed to □ m opposite; pelo ou ao ~ on the contrary; ao ~ de contrary to; em ~ to the contrary

contras|tante /kõtras'tãtʃi/ a contrasting; ~tar vt/i contrast; ~te m contrast

contra|tante /kõtra'tãtʃi/ m/f contractor; ~tar vt employ, take on <operários>

contratempo /kõtra'tẽpu/ m hitch

contra|to /kõ'tratu/ m contract; ~tual (pl ~tuais) a contractual

contraven|ção /kõtravẽ'sãw/ f contravention; ~tor m offender

contribu|ição /kõtribui'sãw/ f contribution; ~inte m/f contributor; (pagador de impostos) taxpayer; ~ir vt contribute □ vi contribute; (pagar impostos) pay tax

contrição /kõtri'sãw/ f contrition

contro|lar /kõtro'lar/ vt control; (fiscalizar) check; ~le /o/, (Port) ~lo /o/ m control; (fiscalização) check

contro|vérsia /kõtro'vɛrsia/ f controversy; ~verso /ɛ/ a controversial

contudo /kõ'tudu/ conj nevertheless

contun|dir /kõtũ'dʒir/ vt (dar hematoma em) bruise; injure <jogador>; ~-se vpr bruise o.s.; <jogador> get injured

conturbado /kõtur'badu/ a troubled

contu|são /kõtu'zãw/ f bruise; (de jogador) injury; ~so a bruised; <jogador> injured convales|cença /kõvale'sẽsa/ f convalescence; ~cer vi convalesce

convenção /kõvẽ'sãw/ f convention

conven|cer /kõvẽ'ser/ vt convince; ~cido a (convicto) convinced; (metido) conceited; ~cimento m (convicção) conviction; (imodéstia) conceitedness

convencio|nal /kõvẽsio'naw/ (pl ~nais) a conventional

conveni|ência /kõveni'ẽsia/ f convenience; ~ente a convenient; (cabível) appropriate

convênio /kõ'veniu/ m agreement

convento /kõ'vẽtu/ m convent

convergir /kõver'ʒir/ vi converge

conver|sa /kõ'versa/ f conversation; a ~sa dele the things he says; ~sa fiada idle talk; ~sação f conversation; ~sado a <pessoa> talkative; <assunto> talked about; ~sador a talkative

conversação /kõver'sãw/ f conversion

conversar /kõver'sar/ vi talk

conver|sível /kõver'sivew/ (pl ~síveis) a & m convertible; ~ter vt convert; ~ter-se vpr be converted; ~tido m convert

con|vés /kõ'vɛs/ (pl ~veses) m deck

convexo /kõ'veksu/ a convex

convic|ção /kõvik'sãw/ f conviction; ~to a (convencido) convinced; (ferrenho) confirmed; <criminoso> convicted

convi|dado /kõvi'dadu/ m guest; ~dar vt invite; ~dativo a inviting

convincente /kõvĩ'sẽtʃi/ a convincing

convir /kõ'vir/ vi (ficar bem) be appropriate; (concordar) agree (em on); ~ a suit, be convenient for; convém notar que one should note that

convite /kõ'vitʃi/ m invitation

convi|vência /kõvi'vẽsia/ f coexistence; (relação) close contact; ~ver vi coexist; (ter relações) associate (com with)

convívio /kõ'viviu/ m association (com with)

convocar /kõvo'kar/ vt call <eleições, greve>; call upon <pessoa> (a to); (ao serviço militar) call up

convosco = com + vós

convul|são /kõvuw'sãw/ f (do corpo) convulsion; (da sociedade etc) upheaval; ~sionar vt convulse <corpo>; (fig) churn up; ~sivo a convulsive

cooper /'kuper/ m jogging; fazer ~ go jogging

coope|ração /koopera'sãw/ f cooperation; ~rar vi cooperate; ~rativa f cooperative; ~rativo a cooperative

coorde|nação /koordena'sãw/ f coordination; ~nada f coordinate; ~nar vt coordinate

copa /'kɔpa/ f (de árvore) top; (aposento) breakfast room; (torneio) cup; pl (naipe) hearts; a Copa (do Mundo) the World Cup; ~-cozinha (pl ~s-cozinhas) f kitchen-diner

cópia /'kɔpia/ f copy

copiar /kopi'ar/ vt copy

co-piloto /kopi'lotu/ m co-pilot

copioso /kopi'ozu/ a ample; <refeição> substantial

copo /'kɔpu/ m glass

coque /'kɔki/ m (penteado) bun

coqueiro /ko'keru/ m coconut palm

coqueluche /koke'luʃi/ f (doença) whooping cough; (mania) fad

coque|tel /koke'tɛw/ (pl ~téis) m cocktail; (reunião) cocktail party

cor[1] /kor/ m de ~ by heart

cor[2] /kor/ f colour; TV a ~es colour TV; pessoa de ~ coloured person

coração /kora'sãw/ m heart

cora|gem /ko'raʒẽ/ f courage; ~joso /o/ a courageous

co|ral[1] /ko'raw/ (pl ~rais) m (animal) coral

co|ral[2] /ko'raw/ (pl ~rais) m (de cantores) choir □ a choral

co|rante /ko'rãtʃi/ a & m colouring; ~rar vt colour □ vi blush

cor|da /'kɔrda/ f rope; (mus) string; (para roupa lavada) clothes line; dar ~da em wind <relógio>; ~da bamba tightrope; ~das vocais vocal chords; ~dão m cord; (de sapatos) lace; (policial) cordon

cordeiro /kor'deru/ m lamb

cor|del /kor'dɛw/ (pl ~déis) (Port) m string; literatura de ~del trash

cor-de-rosa /kordʒi'rɔza/ a invar pink

cordi|al /kordʒi'aw/ (pl ~ais) a & m cordial; ~alidade f cordiality

cordilheira /kordʒi'ʎera/ f chain of mountains

coreano /kori'anu/ a & m Korean

Coréia /ko'rɛja/ f Korea

core|ografia /koriogra'fia/ f choreography; ~ógrafo m choreographer

coreto /ko'retu/ m bandstand

coriza /ko'riza/ f runny nose

corja /'kɔrʒa/ f pack; (de pessoas) rabble

córner /'kɔrner/ m corner

coro /'koru/ m chorus

coro|a /ko'roa/ f crown; (de flores etc) wreath □ (fam) m/f old man (f woman); ~ação f coronation; ~ar vt crown

coro|nel /koro'nɛw/ (pl ~néis) m colonel

coronha /ko'rona/ f butt

corpete /kor'petʃi/ m bodice

corpo /'kɔrpu/ m body; (físico de mulher) figure; (físico de homem) physique; ~ de bombeiros fire brigade; ~ diplomático diplomatic corps; ~ docente teaching staff, (*Amer*) faculty; ~-a-~ *m invar* pitched battle, (*Amer*) ~ral (*pl* ~rais) *a* physical; <*pena*> corporal

corpu|lência /korpu'lêsia/ *f* stoutness; ~lento *a* stout

correção /koxe'sãw/ *f* correction

corre-corre /koxi'kɔxi/ *m* (*debandada*) stampede; (*correria*) rush

correct- (*Port*) *veja* corret-

corre|diço /koxe'dʒisu/ *a* <*porta*> sliding; ~dor *m* (*atleta*) runner; (*passagem*) corridor

correia /ko'xeja/ *f* strap; (*peça de máquina*) belt; (*para cachorro*) lead, (*Amer*) leash

correio /ko'xeju/ *m* post, mail; (*repartição*) post office; pôr no ~ post, (*Amer*) mail; ~ aéreo air mail

correlação /koxela'sãw/ *f* correlation·

correligionário /koxeliʒio'nariu/ *m* party colleague

corrente /ko'xẽtʃi/ *a* <*água*> running; <*mês, conta*> current; <*estilo*> fluid; (*usual*) common □ *f* (*de água, eletricidade*) current; (*cadeia*) chain; ~ de ar draught; <*za* /e/ *f* current; (*de ar*) draught

cor|rer /ko'xer/ *vi* (à *pé*) run; (*de carro*) drive fast, speed; (*fazer rápido*) rush; <*água, sangue*> flow; <*tempo*> elapse; <*boato*> go round □ *vt* draw <*cortina*>; run <*risco*>; ~reria *f* rush

correspon|dência /koxespõ'dẽsia/ *f* correspondence; ~dente *a* corresponding □ *m/f* correspondent; (*equivalente*) equivalent; ~der *vi* ~der a correspond to; (*retribuir*) return; ~der-se *vpr* correspond (com with)

corre|tivo /koxe'tʃivu/ *a* corrective □ *m* punishment; ~to /ɛ/ *a* correct

corretor /koxe'tor/ *m* broker; ~ de imóveis estate agent, (*Amer*) realtor

corrida /ko'xida/ *f* (*prova*) race; (*ação de correr*) run; (*de taxi*) ride

corrigir /koxi'ʒir/ *vt* correct

corrimão /koxi'mãw/ (*pl* ~s) *m* handrail; (*de escada*) banister

corriqueiro /koxi'keru/ *a* ordinary, run-of-the-mill

corroborar /koxobo'rar/ *vt* corroborate

corroer /koxo'er/ *vt* corrode <*metal*>; (*fig*) erode; ~-se *vpr* corrode; (*fig*) erode

corromper /koxõ'per/ *vt* corrupt; ~-se *vpr* be corrupted

corro|são /koxo'zãw/ *f* (*de metal*) corrosion; (*fig*) erosion; ~sivo *a* corrosive

corrup|ção /koxup'sãw/ *f* corruption; ~to *a* corrupt

cor|tada /kor'tada/ *f* (*em tênis*) smash; (*em pessoa*) put-down; ~tante *a* cutting; ~tar *vt* cut; cut off <*luz, telefone, perna etc*>; cut down <*árvore*>; cut out <*efeito, vício*>; take away <*prazer*>; (*com o carro*) cut up; (*desprezar*) cut dead □ *vi* cut; ~tar o cabelo (*no cabeleireiro*) get one's hair cut; ~te¹ /ɔ/ *m* cut; (*gume*) blade; (*desenho*) cross-section; sem ~te <*faca*> blunt; ~te de cabelo haircut

cor|te² /'kortʃi/ *f* court; ~tejar *vt* court; ~tejo /e/ *m* (*séquito*) retinue; (*fúnebre*) cortège; ~tês *a* (*f* ~tesa) courteous, polite; ~tesão (*pl* ~tesãos) *m* courtier; ~tesia *f* courtesy

corti|ça /kor'tʃisa/ *f* cork; ~ço *m* (*casa popular*) slum tenement

cortina /kor'tʃina/ *f* curtain

cortisona /kortʃi'zona/ *f* cortisone

coruja /ko'ruʒa/ *f* owl □ *a* <*pai, mãe*> proud, doting

coruscar /korus'kar/ *vi* flash

corvo /'korvu/ *m* crow

cós /kɔs/ *m invar* waistband

coser /ko'zer/ *vt/i* sew

cosmético /koz'mɛtʃiku/ *a* & *m* cosmetic

cósmico /'kɔzmiku/ *a* cosmic

cosmo /'kɔzmu/ *m* cosmos; ~nauta *m/f* cosmonaut; ~polita *a* cosmopolitan □ *m/f* globetrotter

costa /'kɔsta/ *f* coast; *pl* (*dorso*) back; Costa do Marfim Ivory Coast; Costa Rica Costa Rica

costarriquenho /kostaxi'keɲu/ *a* & *m* Costa Rican

cos|teiro /kos'teru/ *a* coastal; ~tela /ɛ/ *f* rib; ~teleta /e/ *f* chop; *pl* (*suíças*) sideburns; ~telinha *f* (*de porco*) spare rib

costu|mar /kostu'mar/ *vt* ~ma fazer he usually does; ~mava fazer he used to do; ~me *m* (*uso*) custom; (*traje*) costume; de ~me usually; como de ~me as usual; ter o ~me de have a habit of; ~meiro *a* customary

costu|ra /kos'tura/ *f* sewing; ~rar *vt/i* sew; ~reira *f* (*mulher*) dressmaker; (*caixa*) needlework box

cota /'kɔta/ *f* quota; ~tação *f* (*preço*) rate; (*apreço*) rating; ~tado *a* <*ação*> quoted; (*conceituado*) highly rated; ~tar *vt* rate; quote <*ações*>

cotejar /kote'ʒar/ *vt* compare; ~jo /e/ *m* comparison

cotidiano /kotʃidʒi'anu/ *a* everyday □ *m* everyday life

cotonete /koto'nɛtʃi/ *m* cotton bud

cotove|lada /kotove'lada/ f (*para abrir caminho*) shove; (*para chamar atenção*) nudge; ~lo /e/ m elbow

coura|ça /ko'rasa/ f (*armadura*) breastplate; (*de navio, animal*) armour; ~çado (*Port*) m battleship

couro /'koru/ m leather; ~ cabeludo scalp

couve /'kovi/ f spring greens; ~-de-bruxelas (*pl* ~s-de-bruxelas) f Brussels sprout; ~-flor (*pl* ~s-flores*) f cauliflower

couvert /ku'vɛr/ (*pl* ~s) m cover charge

cova /'kɔva/ f (*buraco*) pit; (*sepultura*) grave

covar|de /ko'vardʒi/ m/f coward □ a cowardly; ~dia f cowardice

coveiro /ko'veru/ m gravedigger

covil /ko'viw/ (*pl* ~vis) m den, lair

covinha /ko'viɲa/ f dimple

co|xa /'koʃa/ f thigh; ~xear vi hobble

coxia /ko'ʃia/ f aisle

coxo /'koʃu/ a hobbling; ser ~ hobble

co|zer /ko'zer/ vt/i cook; ~zido m stew, casserole

cozi|nha /ko'ziɲa/ f (*aposento*) kitchen; (*comida, ação*) cooking; (*arte*) cookery; ~nhar vt/i cook; ~nheiro m cook

crachá /kra'ʃa/ m badge, (*Amer*) button

crânio /'kraniu/ m skull; (*pessoa*) genius

crápula /'krapula/ m/f scoundrel

craque /'kraki/ m (*de futebol*) soccer star; (*fam*) expert

crase /'krazi/ f contraction; a com ~ a grave (à)

crasso /'krasu/ a crass

cratera /kra'tɛra/ f crater

cravar /kra'var/ vt drive in <*prego*>; dig <*unha*>; stick <*estaca*>; ~ com os olhos stare at; ~-se vpr stick

cravejar /krave'ʒar/ vt nail; (*com balas*) spray, riddle

cravo¹ /'kravu/ m (*flor*) carnation; (*condimento*) clove

cravo² /'kravu/ m (*na pele*) blackhead; (*prego*) nail

cravo³ /'kravu/ m (*instrumento*) harpsichord

creche /'krɛʃi/ f crèche

credenci|ais /kredẽsi'ajs/ f pl credentials; ~ar vt qualify

credi|ário /kredʒi'ariu/ m hire purchase agreement, credit plan; ~bilidade f credibility; ~tar vt credit

crédito /'krɛdʒitu/ m credit; a ~ on credit

cre|do /'krɛdu/ m creed □ int heavens; ~dor m creditor □ a <*saldo*> credit

crédulo /'krɛdulu/ a gullible

cre|mação /krema'sãw/ f cremation; ~mar vt cremate; ~matório m crematorium

cre|me /'krɛmi/ a invar & m cream; ~me Chantilly whipped cream; ~me de leite (sterilized) cream; ~moso /o/ a creamy

cren|ça /'krẽsa/ f belief; ~dice f superstition; ~te m believer; (*protestante*) Protestant □ a religious; (*protestante*) Protestant; estar ~te que believe that

crepe /'krɛpi/ m crepe

crepitar /krepi'tar/ vi crackle

crepom /kre'põ/ m crepe; papel ~ tissue paper

crepúsculo /kre'puskulu/ m twilight

crer /krer/ vt/i believe (em in); creio que I think (that); ~-se vpr believe o.s. to be

cres|cendo /kre'sẽdu/ m crescendo; ~cente a growing □ m crescent; ~cer vi grow; <*bolo*> rise; ~cido a grown; ~cimento m growth

crespo /'krespu/ a <*cabelo*> frizzy; <*mar*> choppy

cretino /kre'tʃinu/ m cretin

cria /'kria/ f baby; pl young

criação /kria'sãw/ f creation; (*educação*) upbringing; (*de animais*) raising; (*gado*) livestock

criado /kri'adu/ m servant; ~-mudo (*pl* ~s-mudos) m bedside table

criador /kria'dor/ m creator; (*de animais*) farmer, breeder

crian|ça /kri'ãsa/ f child □ a childish; ~çada f kids; ~cice f childishness; (*uma*) childish thing

criar /kri'ar/ vt (*fazer*) create; bring up <*filhos*>; rear <*animais*>; grow <*planta*>; pluck up <*coragem*>; ~-se vpr be brought up, grow up

criati|vidade /kriatʃivi'dadʒi/ f creativity; ~vo a creative

criatura /kria'tura/ f creature

crime /'krimi/ m crime

crimi|nal /krimi'naw/ (*pl* ~nais) a criminal; ~nalidade f crime; ~noso m criminal

crina /'krina/ f mane

crioulo /kri'olu/ a & m creole; (*negro*) black

cripta /'kripta/ f crypt

crisálida /kri'zalida/ f chrysalis

crisântemo /kri'zãtemu/ m chrysanthemum

crise /'krizi/ f crisis

cris|ma /'krizma/ f confirmation; ~mar vt confirm; ~mar-se vpr get confirmed

crista /'krista/ f crest

cris|tal /kris'taw/ (*pl* ~tais) m crystal; (*vidro*) glass; ~talino a crystal-clear; ~talizar vt/i crystallize cris|tandade /kristã'dadʒi/ f Christendom; ~tão (pl ~tãos) a & m (f ~tã) Christian; ~tianismo m Christianity

Cristo /'kristu/ m Christ

cri|tério /kri'teriu/ m discretion; (norma) criterion; ~terioso a perceptive, discerning

crítica /'kritʃika/ f criticism; (análise) critique; (de filme, livro) review; (críticos) critics

criticar /kritʃi'kar/ vt criticize; review <filme, livro>

crítico /'kritʃiku/ a critical □ m critic

crivar /kri'var/ vt (furar) riddle

cri|vel /'krivew/ (pl ~veis) a credible

crivo /'krivu/ m sieve; (fig) scrutiny

crocante /kro'kãtʃi/ a crunchy

crochê /kro'ʃe/ m crochet

crocodilo /kroko'dʒilu/ m crocodile

cromo /'kromu/ m chrome

cromossomo /kromo'somu/ m chromosome

crôni|ca /'kronika/ f (histórica) chronicle; (no jornal) feature; (conto) short story; ~co a chronic

cronista /kro'nista/ m/f (de jornal) feature writer; (contista) short story writer; (historiador) chronicler

crono|grama /krono'grama/ m schedule; ~logia f chronology; ~lógico a chronological; ~metrar vt time

cronômetro /kro'nometru/ m stopwatch

croquete /kro'kɛtʃi/ m savoury meatball in breadcrumbs

croqui /kro'ki/ m sketch

crosta /'krosta/ f crust; (em ferida) scab

cru /kru/ a (f ~a) raw; <luz, tom, palavra> harsh; crude; <verdade> unvarnished, plain

cruci|al /krusi'aw/ (pl ~ais) a crucial

crucifi|cação /krusifika'sãw/ f crucifixion; ~car vt crucify; ~xo /ks/ m crucifix

cru|el /kru'ew/ (pl ~éis) a cruel; ~eldade f cruelty; ~ento a bloody

crupe /'krupi/ m croup

crustáceos /krus'tasius/ m pl shellfish

cruz /krus/ f cross

cruza|da /kru'zada/ f crusade; ~do¹ m (soldado) crusader

cru|zado² /kru'zadu/ m (moeda) cruzado; ~zador m cruiser; ~zamento m (de ruas) crossroads, junction, (Amer) intersection; (de raças) cross; ~zar vt/i cross □ vi <navio> cruise; ~zar com pass; ~zar-se vpr cross; <pessoas> pass each other;

~zeiro m (moeda) cruzeiro; (viagem) cruise; (cruz) cross

cu /ku/ m (chulo) arse, (Amer) ass

Cuba /'kuba/ f Cuba

cubano /ku'banu/ a & m Cuban

cúbico /'kubiku/ a cubic

cubículo /ku'bikulu/ m cubicle

cubis|mo /ku'bizmu/ m cubism; ~ta a & m/f cubist

cubo /'kubu/ m cube; (de roda) hub

cuca /'kuka/ (fam) f head

cuco /'kuku/ m cuckoo; (relógio) cuckoo clock

cu|-de-ferro /kudʒi'fɛxu/ (pl ~s-de-ferro) (fam) m swot

cueca /ku'ɛka/ f underpants; pl (Port: de mulher) knickers

cueiro /ku'eru/ m baby wrap

cuia /'kuia/ f gourd

cuidado /kui'dadu/ m care; com ~ carefully; ter ou tomar ~ be careful; ~so /o/ a careful

cuidar /kui'dar/ vi ~ de take care of; ~-se vpr look after o.s.

cujo /'kuʒu/ pron whose

culatra /ku'latra/ f breech; sair pela ~ (fig) backfire

culiná|ria /kuli'naria/ f cookery; ~ria a culinary

culmi|nância /kuwmi'nãsia/ f culmination; ~nante a culminating; ~nar vi culminate (em in)

cul|pa /'kuwpa/ f guilt; foi ~pa minha it was my fault; ter ~pa de be to blame for; ~pabilidade f guilt; ~pado a guilty □ m culprit; ~par vt blame (de for); (na justiça) find guilty (de of); ~par-se vpr take the blame (de for); ~pável (pl ~páveis) a culpable, guilty

culti|var /kuwtʃi'var/ vt cultivate; grow <plantas>; ~vo m cultivation; (de plantas) growing

cul|to /'kuwtu/ a cultured □ m cult; ~tura f culture; (de terra) cultivation; ~tural (pl ~turais) a cultural

cumbuca /kũ'buka/ f bowl

cume /'kumi/ m peak

cúmplice /'kũplisi/ m/f accomplice

cumplicidade /kũplisi'dadʒi/ f complicity

cumprimen|tar /kũprimẽ'tar/ vt/i (saudar) greet; (parabenizar) compliment; ~to m (saudação) greeting; (elogio) compliment; (de lei, ordem) compliance (de with); (de promessa, palavra) fulfilment

cumprir /kũ'prir/ vt keep <promessa, palavra>; comply with <lei, ordem>; do <dever>; carry out <obrigações>; serve <pena>; ~ com keep to □ vi cumpre-nos ir we should go; ~-se vpr be fulfilled cúmulo /'kumulu/ m height; é o ~! that's the limit!

cunha /'kuɲa/ f wedge

cunha|da /ku'ɲada/ f sister-in-law; ~do m brother-in-law

cunhar /ku'ɲar/ vt coin <palavra, expressão>; mint <moedas>

cunho /'kuɲu/ m hallmark

cupim /ku'pĩ/ m termite

cupom /ku'põ/ m coupon

cúpula /'kupula/ f (abóbada) dome; (de abajur) shade; (chefia) leadership; (reunião de) ~ summit (meeting)

cura /'kura/ f cure □ m curate, priest

curandeiro /kurã'deru/ m (religioso) faith-healer; (índio) medicine man; (charlatão) quack

curar /ku'rar/ vt cure; dress <ferida>; ~-se vpr be cured

curativo /kura'tʃivu/ m dressing

curá|vel /ku'ravew/ (pl ~veis) a curable

curin|ga /ku'rĩga/ m wild card; ~gão m joker

curio|sidade /kuriozi'dadʒi/ f curiosity; ~so /o/ a curious □ m (espectador) onlooker

cur|ral /ku'xaw/ (pl ~rais) m pen

currículo /ku'xikulu/ m curriculum; (resumo) curriculum vitae, CV

cur|sar /kur'sar/ vt attend <escola, aula>; study <matéria>; ~so m course; ~sor m cursor

curta-metragem /kurtame'traʒẽ/ (pl ~s-metragens) m short (film)

cur|tição /kurtʃi'sãw/ (fam) f enjoyment; ~tir vt (fam) enjoy; tan <couro>

curto /'kurtu/ a short; <conhecimento, inteligência> limited; ~-circuito (pl ~s-circuitos) m short circuit

cur|va /'kurva/ f curve; (de estrada, rio) bend; ~va fechada hairpin bend; ~var vt bend; ~var-se vpr bend; (fig) bow (a to); ~vo /o/ a curved; <estrada> winding

cus|parada /kuspa'rada/ f spit; ~pe m spit, spittle; ~pir vt/i spit

cus|ta /'kusta/ f à ~ta de at the expense of; ~tar vt cost □ vi (ser difícil) be hard; ~tar a fazer (ter dificuldade) find it hard to do; (demorar) take a long time to do; ~tear vt finance, fund; ~teio m funding; (relação de despesas) costing; ~to m cost; a ~to with difficulty

custódia /kus'tɔdʒia/ f custody

cutelo /ku'telu/ m cleaver

cutícula /ku'tʃikula/ f cuticle

cútis /'kutʃis/ f invar complexion

cutucar /kutu'kar/ vt (com o cotovelo, joelho) nudge; (com o dedo) poke; (com instrumento) prod

czar /zar/ m tsar

D

da = de + a

dádiva /'dadʒiva/ f gift; (donativo) donation

dado /'dadu/ m (de jogar) die, dice; (informação) fact, piece of information; pl data

daí /da'i/ adv (no espaço) from there; (no tempo) then; ~ por diante from then on; e ~? (fam) so what?

dali /da'li/ adv from over there

dália /'dalia/ f dahlia

dal|tônico /daw'toniku/ a colour-blind; ~tonismo m colour-blindness

dama /'dama/ f lady; (em jogos) queen; pl (jogo) draughts, (Amer) checkers; ~ de honra bridesmaid

da|nado /da'nadu/ a damned; (zangado) angry; (travesso) naughty; ~nar-se vpr get angry; ~ne-se! (fam) who cares?

dan|ça /'dãsa/ f dance; ~çar vt dance □ vi dance; (fam) miss out; <coisa> go by the board; <criminoso> get caught; ~çarino m dancer; ~ceteria f discotheque

da|nificar /danifi'kar/ vt damage; ~ninho a undesirable; ~no m (pl) damage; ~noso /o/ a damaging

dantes /'dãtʃis/ adv formerly

daquela(s), daquele(s) = de + aquela(s), aquele(s)

daqui /da'ki/ adv from here; ~ a 2 dias in 2 days' time); ~ a pouco in a minute; ~ por diante from now on

daquilo = de + aquilo

dar /dar/ vt give; have <dormida, lida etc>; do <pulo, cambalhota etc>; cause <problemas>; produce <frutas, leite>; deal <cartas>; (lecionar) teach □ vi (ser possível) be possible; (ser suficiente) be enough; ~ com come across; ~ em lead to; ele dá para ator he'd make a good actor; ~ por (considerar como) consider to be; (reparar em) notice; ~-se vpr <coisa> happen; <pessoa> get on

dardo /'dardu/ m dart; (no atletismo) javelin

das = de + as

da|ta /'data/ f date; de longa ~ long since; ~tar vt/i date

dati|lografar /datʃilogra'far/ vt/i type; ~lografia f typing; ~lógrafo m typist

de /dʒi/ prep of; (procedência) from; ~ carro by car; trabalho ~ repórter I work as a reporter

debaixo /dʒi'baʃu/ adv below; ~ **de** under

debalde /dʒi'bawdʒi/ adv in vain

debandada /debã'dada/ f stampede

deba|te /de'batʃi/ m debate; ~**ter** vt debate; ~**ter-se** vpr grapple

debelar /debe'lar/ vt overcome

dé|bil /'dɛbiw/ (pl ~**beis**) a feeble; ~**bil** mental retarded (person)

debili|dade /debili'dadʒi/ f debility; ~**tar** vt debilitate; ~**tar-se** vpr become debilitated

debitar /debi'tar/ vt debit

débito /'dɛbitu/ m debit

debo|chado /debo'ʃadu/ a sardonic; ~**char** vt mock; ~**che** /ɔ/ m jibe

debruar /debru'ar/ vt/i edge

debruçar-se /debru'sarsi/ vpr bend over; ~ **sobre** study

debrum /de'brũ/ m edging

debulhar /debu'ʎar/ vt thresh

debu|tante /debu'tãtʃi/ f debutante; ~**tar** vi debut, make one's debut

década /'dɛkada/ f decade; a ~ **dos 60** the sixties

deca|dência /deka'dẽsia/ f decadence; ~**dente** a decadent

decair /deka'ir/ vi decline; (degringolar) go downhill; <planta> wilt

decal|car /dekaw'kar/ vt trace; ~**que** m tracing

decapitar /dekapi'tar/ vt decapitate

decatlo /de'katlu/ m decathlon

de|cência /de'sẽsia/ f decency; ~**cente** a decent

decepar /dese'par/ vt cut off

decep|ção /desep'sãw/ f disappointment; ~**cionar** vt disappoint; ~**cionar-se** vpr be disappointed

decerto /dʒi'sɛrtu/ adv certainly

deci|dido /desi'dʒidu/ a <pessoa> determined; (sem vt/i decide; ~**dir-se** vpr make up one's mind; ~**dir-se por** decide on

decíduo /de'siduu/ a deciduous

decifrar /desi'frar/ vt decipher

deci|mal /desi'maw/ (pl ~**mais**) a & m decimal

décimo /'dɛsimu/ a & m tenth; ~ **primeiro** eleventh; ~ **segundo** twelfth; ~ **terceiro** thirteenth; ~ **quarto** fourteenth; ~ **quinto** fifteenth; ~ **sexto** sixteenth; ~ **sétimo** seventeenth; ~ **oitavo** eighteenth; ~ **nono** nineteenth

deci|são /desi'zãw/ f decision; ~**sivo** a decisive

decla|ração /deklara'sãw/ f declaration; ~**rado** a <inimigo> sworn; <crente> avowed; <ladrão> self-confessed; ~**rar** vt declare

decli|nação /deklina'sãw/ f declension; ~**nar** vt ~**nar (de)** decline □ vi decline; <sol> go down; <chão> slope down

declínio /de'kliniu/ m decline

declive /de'klivi/ m (downward) slope, incline

decodificar /dekodʒifi'kar/ vt decode

deco|lagem /deko'laʒẽ/ f take-off; ~**lar** vi take off; (fig) get off the ground

decom|por /dekõ'por/ vt break down; contort <feições>; ~**por-se** vpr break down; <cadáver> decompose; ~ **posição** f (de cadáver) decomposition

deco|ração /dekora'sãw/ f decoration; (aprendizagem) learning by heart; ~**rar** vt (adornar) decorate; (aprender) learn by heart, memorize; ~**rativo** a decorative; ~**reba** /ɛ/ (fam) f rote-learning; ~**ro** /o/ m decorum; ~**roso** /o/ a decorous

decor|rência /deko'xẽsia/ f consequence; ~**rente** a resulting (de from); ~**rer** vi <tempo> elapse; <acontecimento> pass off; (resultar) result (de from) □ m no ~**rer de** in the course of; com o ~**rer do tempo** in time, with the passing of time

deco|tado /deko'tadu/ a low-cut; ~**te** /ɔ/ m neckline

decrépito /de'krɛpitu/ a decrepit

decres|cente /dekre'sẽtʃi/ a decreasing; ~**cer** vi decrease

decre|tar /dekre'tar/ vt decree; declare <estado de sítio>; ~**to** /ɛ/ m decree; ~**to-lei** (pl ~**tos-leis**) m act

decurso /de'kursu/ m course

de|dal /de'daw/ (pl ~**dais**) m thimble; ~**dão** m (da mão) thumb; (do pé) big toe

dedetizar /dedetʃi'zar/ vt spray with insecticide

dedi|cação /dedʒika'sãw/ f dedication; ~**car** vt dedicate; devote <tempo>; ~**car-se** vpr dedicate o.s. (a to); ~**catória** f dedication

dedilhar /dedʒi'ʎar/ vt pluck

dedo /'dedu/ m finger; (do pé) toe; cheio de ~**s** all fingers and thumbs; (sem graça) awkward; ~**duro** (pl ~**s-duros**) m sneak; (político, criminoso) informer

dedução /dedu'sãw/ f deduction

dedurar /dedu'rar/ vt sneak on; (à polícia) inform on

dedu|tivo /dedu'tʃivu/ a deductive; ~**zir** vt (descontar) deduct; (concluir) deduce

defa|sado /defa'zadu/ a out of step; ~**sagem** f gap, lag

defecar /defe'kar/ vi defecate

defei|to /de'fejtu/ m defect; botar ~**to em** find fault with; ~**tuoso** /o/ a defective defen|der /defë'der/ vt defend; ~der-se vpr (virar-se) fend for o.s.; (contra-atacar) defend o.s. (de against); ~siva f na ~siva on the defensive; ~sor m defender; (advogado) defence counsel

defe|rência /defe'rēsia/ f deference; ~rente a deferential

defesa /de'feza/ f defence □ m defender

defici|ência /defisi'ēsia/ f deficiency; ~ente a deficient; (física ou mentalmente) handicapped □ m/f handicapped person

déficit /'dɛfisitʃi/ (pl ~s) m deficit

deficitário /defisitʃi'ariu/ a in deficit; <empresa> loss-making

definhar /defi'ɲar/ vi waste away; <planta> wither

defi|nição /defini'sãw/ f definition; ~nir vt define; ~nir-se vpr (descrever-se) define o.s.; (decidir-se) come to a decision; (explicar-se) make one's position clear; ~nitivo a definitive; ~nível (pl ~níveis) a definable

defla|ção /defla'sãw/ f deflation; ~cionário a deflationary

deflagrar /defla'grar/ vt set off □ vi break out

defor|mar /defor'mar/ vt misshape; deform <corpo>; distort <imagem>; ~midade f deformity

defraudar /defraw'dar/ vt defraud (de of)

defron|tar /defrõ'tar/ vt ~tar com face; ~te adv opposite; ~te de opposite

defumar /defu'mar/ vt smoke

defunto /de'fũtu/ a & m deceased

dege|lar /deʒe'lar/ vt/i thaw; ~lo /e/ m thaw

degeneração /deʒenera'sãw/ f degeneration

degenerar /deʒene'rar/ vi degenerate (em into)

degolar /dego'lar/ vt cut the throat of

degra|dação /degrada'sãw/ f degradation; ~dante a degrading; ~dar vt degrade

degrau /de'graw/ m step

degringolar /degrĩgo'lar/ vi deteriorate, go downhill

degustar /degus'tar/ vt taste

dei|tada /dej'tada/ f lie-down; ~tado a lying down; (dormindo) in bed; (fam: preguiçoso) idle; ~tar vt lay down; (na cama) put to bed; (pôr) put; (Port: jogar) throw □ vi, ~tar-se vpr lie down; (ir para cama) go to bed

dei|xa /'deʃa/ f cue; ~xar vt leave; (permitir) let; ~xar de (parar) stop; (omitir) fail; não pôde ~xar de rir he couldn't help laughing; ~xar alg

nervoso make s.o. annoyed; ~xar cair drop; ~xar a desejar leave a lot to be desired; ~xar (para lá) (fam) never mind, forget it

dela(s) = de + ela(s)

delatar /dela'tar/ vt report

delavé /dela've/ a invar faded

dele(s) = de + ele(s)

dele|gação /delega'sãw/ f delegation; ~gacia f police station; ~gado m delegate; ~gado de polícia police chief; ~gar vt delegate

delei|tar /delej'tar/ vt delight; ~tar-se vpr delight (com in); ~te m delight; ~toso /o/ a delightful

delgado /dew'gadu/ a slender

delibe|ração /delibera'sãw/ f deliberation; ~rar vt/i deliberate

delica|deza /delika'deza/ f delicacy; (cortesia) politeness; ~do a delicate; (cortês) polite

delícia /de'lisia/ f delight; ser uma ~ <comida> be delicious; <sol etc> be lovely

delici|ar /delisi'ar/ vt delight; ~ar-se delight (com in); ~oso /o/ a delightful, lovely; <comida> delicious

deline|ador /delinia'dor/ m eye-liner; ~ar vt outline

delin|qüência /delĩ'kwēsia/ f delinquency; ~qüente a & m delinquent

deli|rante /deli'rãtʃi/ a rapturous; (med) delirious; ~rar vi go into raptures; <doente> be delirious

delírio /de'liriu/ m (febre) delirium; (excitação) raptures

delito /de'litu/ m crime

delonga /de'lõga/ f delay

delta /'dɛwta/ f delta

dema|gogia /demago'ʒia/ f demagogy; ~gógico a demagogic; ~gogo /o/ m demagogue

demais /dʒi'majs/ a & adv (muito) very much; (em demasia) too much; os ~ the rest, the others; é ~! (fam) it's great!

deman|da /de'mãda/ f demand; (jurid) action; ~dar vt sue

demão /de'mãw/ f coat

demar|car /demar'kar/ vt demarcate; ~catório a demarcation

demasia /dema'zia/ f excess; em ~ too much, (much, many)

de|mência /de'mēsia/ f insanity; (med) dementia; ~mente a insane; (med) demented

demissão /demi'sãw/ f sacking, dismissal; pedir ~ resign

demitir /demi'tʃir/ vt sack, dismiss; ~-se vpr resign

demo|cracia /demokra'sia/ f democracy; ~crata m/f democrat; ~crático a democratic; ~cratizar *vt* democratize; ~grafia *f* demography; ~gráfico *a* demographic

demolição /demoli'sãw/ *f* demolition; ~lir *vt* demolish

demónio /de'moniu/ *m* demon

demonstração /demõstra'sãw/ *f* demonstration; ~trar *vt* demonstrate; ~trativo *a* demonstrative

demora /de'mɔra/ *f* delay; ~rado *a* lengthy; ~rar *vi* (levar) take; (tardar *a voltar, terminar etc*) be long; (levar *muito tempo*) take a long time □ *vt* delay

dendê /dẽ'de/ *m* (óleo) palm oil

denegrir /dene'grir/ *vt* denigrate

dengoso /dẽ'gozu/ *a* coy

dengue /'dẽgi/ *m* dengue

denominação /denomina'sãw/ *f* denomination; ~nar *vt* name

denotar /deno'tar/ *vt* denote

densidade /dẽsi'dadʒi/ *f* density; ~so *a* dense

dentado /dẽ'tadu/ *a* serrated; ~tadura *f* (set of) teeth; (postiça) dentures, false teeth; ~tal (pl ~tais) *a* dental; ~tário *a* dental; ~te *m* tooth; (de alho) clove; ~te do siso wisdom tooth; (dentadura) teeth; ~tifrício *m* toothpaste; ~tista *m/f* dentist

dentre = de + entre

dentro /'dẽtru/ *adv* inside; lá ~ in there; por ~ on the inside; ~ de inside; (tempo) within

dentuça /dẽ'tusa/ *f* buck teeth; ~ço *a* with buck teeth

denúncia /de'nũsia/ *f* (à polícia etc) report; (na imprensa etc) disclosure

denunciar /denũsi'ar/ *vt* (à polícia etc) report; (na imprensa etc) denounce

deparar /depa'rar/ *vi* ~ com come across

departamento /departa'mẽtu/ *m* department

depauperar /depawpe'rar/ *vt* impoverish

depenar /depe'nar/ *vt* pluck <aves>; (roubar) fleece

dependência /depẽ'dẽsia/ *f* dependence; *pl* premises; ~dente *a* dependent (de on) □ *m/f* dependant; ~der *vi* depend (de on)

depilação /depila'sãw/ *f* depilation; ~lar *vt* depilate; ~latório *m* depilatory cream

deplorar /deplo'rar/ *vt* deplore; ~rável (pl ~ráveis) *a* deplorable

depoente /depo'ẽtʃi/ *m/f* witness; ~poimento *m* (à polícia) statement; (na justiça, fig) testimony

depois /de'pojs/ *adv* after(wards); ~ de after; ~ que after

depor /de'por/ *vi* (na polícia) make a statement; (na justiça) give evidence, testify □ *vt* lay down <armas>; depose <rei, presidente>

deportação /deporta'sãw/ *f* deportation; ~tar *vt* deport

depositante /depozi'tãtʃi/ *m/f* depositor; ~tar *vt* deposit; cast <voto>; place <confiança>

depósito /de'pozitu/ *m* deposit; (armazém) warehouse

depravação /deprava'sãw/ *f* depravity; ~vado *a* depraved; ~var *vt* deprave

depreciação /depresia'sãw/ *f* (perda de valor) depreciation; (menosprezo) deprecation; ~ciar *vt* (desvalorizar) devalue; (menosprezar) deprecate; ~ciar-se *vpr* <bens> depreciate; <pessoa> deprecate o.s.; ~ciativo *a* deprecatory

depredação /depreda'sãw/ *f* depredation; ~dar *vt* wreck

depressa /dʒi'prɛsa/ *adv* fast, quickly

depressão /depre'sãw/ *f* depression; ~sivo *a* depressive

deprimente /depri'mẽtʃi/ *a* depressing; ~mido *a* depressed; ~mir *vt* depress; ~mir-se *vpr* get depressed

depurar /depu'rar/ *vt* purify

deputação /deputa'sãw/ *f* deputation; ~tado *m* deputy, MP, (Amer) congressman (f -woman); ~tar *vt* delegate

deque /'dɛki/ *m* (sun)deck

deriva /de'riva/ *f* à ~va adrift; andar à ~va drift; ~vação *f* derivation; ~var *vt/i* derive; (desviar) divert □ *vi*, ~var-se *vpr* derive, be derived (de from); <navio> drift

dermatologia /dermatolo'ʒia/ *f* dermatology; ~gista *m/f* dermatologist

derradeiro /dexa'deru/ *a* last, final

derramamento /dexama'mẽtu/ *m* spill, spillage; ~mamento de sangue bloodshed; ~mar *vt* spill; shed <lágrimas>; ~mar-se *vpr* spill; ~me *m* spill, spillage; ~me cerebral stroke

derrapagem /dexa'paʒẽ/ *f* skidding; (uma) skid; ~par *vi* skid

derreter /dexe'ter/ *vt* melt; ~-se *vpr* melt

derrota /de'xɔta/ *f* defeat; ~tar *vt* defeat; ~tismo *m* defeatism; ~tista *a & m/f* defeatist

derrubar /dexu'bar/ *vt* knock down; bring down <governo>

desabafar /dʒizaba'far/ *vi* speak one's mind; ~fo *m* outburst

desabamento /dʒizaba'mẽtu/ *m* collapse; ~bar *vi* collapse; <chuva> pour down desabotoar /dʒiaboto'ar/ vt unbutton

desabri|gado /dʒizabri'gadu/ a homeless; ~gar vt make homeless

desabrochar /dʒizabro'ʃar/ vi blossom, bloom

desaca|tar /dʒizaka'tar/ vt defy; ~to m (de pessoa) disrespect; (da lei etc) disregard

desacerto /dʒiza'sertu/ m mistake

desacompanhado /dʒizakõpa-'nadu/ a unaccompanied

desaconse|lhar /dʒizakõse'ʎar/ vt advise against; ~lhável (pl ~lháveis) a inadvisable

desacor|dado /dʒizakor'dadu/ a unconscious; ~do /o/ m disagreement

desacostu|mado /dʒizakostu'madu/ a unaccustomed; ~mar vt ~mar alg de break s.o. of the habit of; ~mar-se de get out of the habit of

desacreditar /dʒizakredʒi'tar/ vt discredit

desafeto /dʒiza'fɛtu/ m disaffection

desafi|ador /dʒizafia'dor/ a < tarefa> challenging; < pessoa> defiant; ~ar vt challenge; (fazer face a) defy < perigo, morte>

desafi|nado /dʒizafi'nadu/ a out of tune; ~nar vi (cantando) sing out of tune; (tocando) play out of tune □ vt put out of tune

desafio /dʒiza'fiu/ m challenge

desafivelar /dʒizafive'lar/ vt unbuckle

desafo|gar /dʒizafo'gar/ vt vent; (desapertar) relieve; ~gar-se vpr give vent to one's feelings; ~go /o/ m (alívio) relief

desafo|rado /dʒizafo'radu/ a cheeky; ~ro /o/ m cheek; (um) liberty

desafortunado /dʒizafortu'nadu/ a unfortunate

desagra|dar /dʒizagra'dar/ vt displease; ~dável (pl ~dáveis) a unpleasant; ~do m displeasure

desagravo m redress, amends

desagregar /dʒizagre'gar/ vt split up; ~se vpr split up

desaguar /dʒiza'gwar/ vt drain □ vi < rio> flow (em into)

desajeitado /dʒizaʒej'tadu/ a clumsy

desajuizado /dʒizaʒui'zadu/ a foolish

desajus|tado /dʒizaʒus'tadu/ a (psic) maladjusted; ~te m (psic) maladjustment

desalen|tar /dʒizalẽ'tar/ vt dishearten; ~tar-se vpr get disheartened; ~to m discouragement

desali|nhado /dʒizali'nadu/ a untidy; ~nho m untidiness

desalojar /dʒizalo'ʒar/ vt turn out < inquilino>; flush out < inimigo, ladrões>

desamarrar /dʒizama'xar/ vt untie □ vi cast off

desamarrotar /dʒizamaxo'tar/ vt smooth out

desamassar /dʒizama'sar/ vt smooth out

desambientado /dʒizãbiẽ'tadu/ a unsettled

desampa|rar /dʒizãpa'rar/ vt abandon; ~ro m abandonment

desandar /dʒizã'dar/ vi < molho> separate; ~ a start to

desa|nimar /dʒizani'mar/ vt discourage □ vi < pessoa> lose heart; < fato> discouraging; ~sânimo m discouragement

desapaixonado /dʒizapaʃo'nadu/ a dispassionate

desaparafusar /dʒizaparafu'zar/ vt unscrew

desapare|cer /dʒizapare'ser/ vi disappear; ~cimento m disappearance

desapego /dʒiza'pegu/ m detachment; (indiferença) indifference

desapercebido /dʒizaperse'bidu/ a unnoticed

desapertar /dʒizaper'tar/ vt loosen

desapon|tamento /dʒizapõta'mẽtu/ m disappointment; ~tar vt disappoint

desapropriar /dʒizapropri'ar/ vt expropriate

desapro|vação /dʒizaprova'sãw/ f disapproval; ~var vt disapprove of

desaproveitado /dʒizaprovej'tadu/ a wasted

desar|mamento /dʒizarma'mẽtu/ m disarmament; ~mar vt disarm; take down < barraca>

desarran|jar /dʒizaxã'ʒar/ vt mess up; upset < estômago>; ~jo m mess; (do estômago) upset

desarregaçar /dʒizaxega'sar/ vt roll down

desarru|mado /dʒizaxu'madu/ a untidy; ~mar vt untidy; unpack < mala>

desarticular /dʒizartʃiku'lar/ vt dislocate

desarvorado /dʒizarvo'radu/ a disoriented, at a loss

desassociar /dʒizasosi'ar/ vt disassociate; ~se vpr disassociate o.s.

desas|trado /dʒizas'tradu/ a accident-prone; ~tre m disaster; ~troso /o/ a disastrous

desatar /dʒiza'tar/ vt untie; ~ a chorar dissolve in tears

desatarraxar /dʒizataxa'ʃar/ vt unscrew

desaten|cioso /dʒizatẽsi'ozu/ a inattentive; ~to a oblivious (a to)

desati|nar /dʒizatʃi'nar/ vt bewilder □ vi not think straight; ~no m mental aberration, bewilderment; (um) folly desativar /dʒizatʃi'var/ vt deactivate; shut down <*fábrica*>

desatrelar /dʒizatre'lar/ vt unhitch

desatualizado /dʒizatuali'zadu/ a out-of-date

desavença /dʒiza'vẽsa/ f disagreement

desavergonhado /dʒizavergo'ɲadu/ a shameless

desbancar /dʒizbã'kar/ vt outdo

desbaratar /dʒizbara'tar/ vt (*desperdiçar*) waste

desbocado /dʒizbo'kadu/ a outspoken

desbotar /dʒizbo'tar/ vt/i fade

desbra|vador /dʒizbrava'dor/ m explorer; ~var vt explore

desbun|dante /dʒizbũ'dãtʃi/ (*fam*) a mind-blowing; ~dar (*fam*) vt blow the mind of □ vi flip, freak out; ~de (*fam*) m knockout

descabido /dʒiska'bidu/ a inappropriate

descalabro /dʒiska'labru/ m débâcle

descalço /dʒis'kawsu/ a barefoot

descambar /dʒiskã'bar/ vi deteriorate, degenerate

descan|sar /dʒiskã'sar/ vt/i rest; ~so m rest; (*de prato, copo*) mat

desca|rado /dʒiska'radu/ a blatant; ~ramento m cheek

descarga /dʒis'karga/ f (*eletr*) discharge; (*da privada*) flush; dar ~ flush (the toilet)

descarregar /dʒiskaxe'gar/ vt unload <*mercadorias*>; discharge <*poluentes*>; vent <*raiva*> □ vi <*bateria*> go flat; ~ em cima de alg take it out on s.o.

descarrilhar /dʒiskaxi'ʎar/ vt/i derail

descar|tar /dʒiskar'tar/ vt discard; ~tável (*pl* ~táveis) a disposable

descascar /dʒiskas'kar/ vt peel <*frutas, batatas*>; shell <*nozes*> □ vi <*pessoa, pele*> peel

descaso /dʒis'kazu/ m indifference

descen|dência /dʒisẽ'dẽsia/ f descent; ~dente a descended □ m/f descendant; ~der vi descend (de from)

descentralizar /dʒisẽtrali'zar/ vt decentralize

des|cer /de'ser/ vi go down; <*avião*> descend; (*de ônibus, trem*) get out (*de carro*) get out □ vt go down <*escada, ladeira*>; ~cida f descent

desclassificar /dʒisklasifi'kar/ vt disqualify

desco|berta /dʒisko'bɛrta/ f discovery; ~berto /ɛ/ a uncovered; <*conta*> overdrawn; a ~berto overdrawn; ~bridor m discoverer; ~brimento m discovery; ~brir vt discover; (*expor*) uncover

descolar /dʒisko'lar/ vt unstick; (*fam*) (*dar*) give; (*arranjar*) get hold of, rustle up; (*Port*) <*avião*> take off

descom|por /dʒiskõ'por/ vt (*censurar*) scold; ~-se vpr <*pessoa*> lose one's composure; ~postura f (*estado*) loss of composure; (*censura*) talking-to

descomprometido /dʒiskõprome-'tʃidu/ a free

descomu|nal /dʒiskomu'naw/ (*pl* ~nais) a extraordinary; (*grande*) huge

desconcentrar /dʒiskõsẽ'trar/ vt distract

desconcer|tante /dʒiskõser'tãtʃi/ a disconcerting; ~tar vt disconcert

desconexo /dʒisko'nɛksu/ a incoherent

desconfi|ado /dʒiskõfi'adu/ a suspicious; ~ança f mistrust; ~ar vi suspect

desconfor|tável /dʒiskõfor'tavew/ (*pl* ~táveis) a uncomfortable; ~to /o/ m discomfort

descongelar /dʒiskõʒe'lar/ vt defrost <*geladeira*>; thaw <*comida*>

descongestio|nante /dʒiskõʒestʃio-'nãtʃi/ a & m decongestant; ~nar vt decongest

desconhe|cer /dʒiskoɲe'ser/ vt not know; ~cido a unknown □ m stranger

desconsiderar /dʒiskõside'rar/ vt ignore

desconsolado /dʒiskõso'ladu/ a disconsolate

descontar /dʒiskõ'tar/ vt deduct; (*não levar em conta*) discount

desconten|tamento /dʒiskõtẽta-'mẽtu/ m discontent; ~te a discontent

desconto /dʒis'kõtu/ m discount; dar um ~ (*fig*) make allowances

descontra|ção /dʒiskõtra'sãw/ f informality; ~ído a informal, casual; ~ir vt relax; ~ir-se vpr relax

descontro|lar-se /dʒiskõtro'larsi/ vpr <*pessoa*> lose control; <*coisa*> go out of control; ~le /o/ m lack of control

desconversar /dʒiskõver'sar/ vi change the subject

descortesia /dʒiskorte'zia/ f rudeness

descostu|rar /dʒiskostu'rar/ vt unrip; ~rar-se vpr come undone

descrédito /dʒis'krɛdʒitu/ m discredit

descren|ça /dʒis'krẽsa/ f disbelief; ~te a sceptical, disbelieving

des|crever /dʒiskre'ver/ vt describe; ~crição f description; ~critivo a descriptive

descui|dado /dʒiskui'dadu/ a careless; ~dar vt neglect; ~do m carelessness; (*um*) oversight descul|pa /dʒisˈkuwpa/ f excuse; pedir ~pas apologize; ~par vt excuse; ~pe! sorry!; ~par-se vpr apologize; ~pável (pl ~páveis) a excusable

desde /ˈdezdʒi/ prep since; ~ que since

des|dém /dezˈdẽj/ m disdain; ~denhar vt disdain; ~nhoso /o/ a disdainful

desdentado /dʒizdẽˈtadu/ a toothless

desdita /dʒizˈdʒita/ f unhappiness

desdizer /dʒizdʒiˈzer/ vt take back, withdraw □ vi take back what one said

desdo|bramento /dʒizdobraˈmẽtu/ m implication; (de dados, contas) break down <dados, contas>; ~brar vt (abrir) unfold; break down <dados, contas>; ~brar-se vpr unfold; (empenhar-se) go to a lot of trouble, bend over backwards

dese|jar /dezeˈʒar/ vt want; (apaixonadamente) desire; ~jar aco a alg wish s.o. sth; ~jável (pl ~jáveis) a desirable; ~jo /e/ m wish; (forte) desire; ~joso /o/ a desirous

deselegante /dʒizeleˈgãtʃi/ a inelegant

desemaranhar /dʒizemaraˈɲar/ vt untangle

desembara|çado /dʒizĩbaraˈsadu/ a <pessoa> confident, nonchalant; ~çar-se vpr rid o.s. of); ~ço m confidence, ease

desembar|car /dʒizĩbarˈkar/ vt/i disembark; ~que m disembarkation; (seção do aeroporto) arrivals

desembocar /dʒizĩboˈkar/ vi flow

desembol|sar /dʒizĩbowˈsar/ vt spend, pay out; ~so /o/ m expenditure

desembrulhar /dʒizĩbruˈʎar/ vt unwrap

desembuchar /dʒizĩbuˈʃar/ (fam) vi (desabafar) get things off one's chest; (falar logo) spit it out

desempacotar /dʒizĩpakoˈtar/ vt unpack

desempatar /dʒizĩpaˈtar/ vt decide <jogo>

desempe|nhar /dʒizĩpeˈɲar/ vt perform; play <papel>; ~nho m performance

desempre|gado /dʒizĩpreˈgadu/ a unemployed; ~go /e/ m unemployment

desencadear /dʒizĩkadʒiˈar/ vt set off, trigger

desencaminhar /dʒizĩkamiˈɲar/ vt lead astray; embezzle <dinheiro>

desencantar /dʒizĩkãˈtar/ vt disenchant

desencon|trar-se /dʒizĩkõˈtrarsi/ vpr miss each other, fail to meet; ~tro m failure to meet

desencorajar /dʒizĩkoraˈʒar/ vt discourage

desenferrujar /dʒizĩfexuˈʒar/ vt derust <metal>; stretch <pernas>; brush up <língua>

desenfreado /dʒizĩfriˈadu/ a unbridled

desenganar /dʒizĩgaˈnar/ vt disabuse; declare incurable <doente>

desengonçado /dʒizĩgõˈsadu/ a <pessoa> ungainly

desengre|nado /dʒizĩgreˈnadu/ a <carro> in neutral; ~nar vt put in neutral <carro>; (tec) disengage

dese|nhar /dezeˈɲar/ vt draw; ~nhista m/f drawer; (industrial) designer; ~nho /e/ m drawing

desenlace /dʒizĩˈlasi/ m dénouement, outcome

desenredar /dʒizĩxeˈdar/ vt unravel

desenrolar /dʒizĩxoˈlar/ vt unroll <rolo>

desenten|der /dʒizĩtẽˈder/ vt misunderstand; ~der-se vpr (não se dar bem) not get on; ~dimento m misunderstanding

desenterrar /dʒizĩteˈxar/ vt dig up <cadáver>; unearth <informação>

desentortar /dʒizĩtorˈtar/ vt straighten out

desentupir /dʒizĩtuˈpir/ vt unblock

desenvol|to /dʒizĩˈvowtu/ a casual, nonchalant; ~tura f casualness, nonchalance; com ~tura nonchalantly; ~ver vt develop; ~ver-se vpr develop; ~vimento m development

desequi|librado a unbalanced; ~librar vt unbalance; ~librar-se vpr become unbalanced; ~líbrio m imbalance

deser|ção /dezerˈsãw/ f desertion; ~tar vt/i desert; ~to /ɛ/ a deserted; ilha ~ta desert island □ m desert; ~tor m deserter

desespe|rado /dʒizispeˈradu/ a desperate; ~rador a hopeless; ~rar vt (desesperançar) make despair □ vi, ~rar-se vpr despair; ~ro /e/ m despair

desestabilizar /dʒizistabiliˈzar/ vt destabilize

desestimular /dʒizistʃimuˈlar/ vt discourage

desfal|car /dʒisfawˈkar/ vt embezzle; ~que m embezzlement

desfal|ecer /dʒisfaleˈser/ vt (desmaiar) faint; ~ecimento m faint

desfavor /dʒisfaˈvor/ m disfavour

desfavo|rável /dʒisfavoˈravew/ (pl ~ráveis) a unfavourable; ~recer vt be unfavourable to; treat less favourably <minorias etc>

desfazer /dʒisfaˈzer/ vt undo; unpack <mala>; strip <cama>; break <contrato>; clear up <mistério>; ~-se *vpr* come undone; *<casamento>* break up; *<sonhos>* crumble; ~se em lágrimas dissolve into tears

desfe|char /dʒisfe'ʃar/ *vt* throw *<murro, olhar>*; ~**cho** /e/ *m* outcome, dénouement

desfeita /dʒis'fejta/ *f* slight, insult

desferir /dʒisfe'rir/ *vt* give *<pontapé>*; launch *<ataque>*; fire *<flecha>*

desfiar /dʒisfi'ar/ *vt* pick the meat off *<frango>*; ~**se** *vpr <tecido>* fray

desfigurar /dʒisfigu'rar/ *vt* disfigure; (*fig*) distort

desfi|ladeiro /dʒisfila'deru/ *m* pass; ~**lar** *vi* parade; ~**le** *m* parade; ~**le de modas** fashion show

desflorestamento /dʒisfloresta'mẽtu/ *m* deforestation

desforra /dʒis'fɔxa/ *f* revenge

desfraldar /dʒisfraw'dar/ *vt* unfurl

desfrutar /dʒisfru'tar/ *vt* enjoy

desgas|tante /dʒizgas'tãtʃi/ *a* wearing, stressful; ~**tar** *vt* wear out; ~**te** *m* (*de máquina etc*) wear and tear; (*de pessoa*) stress and strain

desgosto /dʒiz'gostu/ *m* sorrow

desgovernar-se /dʒizgover'narsi/ *vpr* go out of control

desgraça /dʒiz'grasa/ *f* misfortune; ~**do** *a* wretched □ *m* wretch

desgravar /dʒizgra'var/ *vt* erase

desgrenhado /dʒizgre'ɲadu/ *a* unkempt

desgrudar /dʒizgru'dar/ *vt* unstick; ~**se** *vpr <pessoa>* tear o.s. away

desidra|tação /dʒizidrata'sãw/ *f* dehydration; ~**tar** *vt* dehydrate

desig|nação /dezigna'sãw/ *f* designation; ~**nar** *vt* designate

desi|gual /dʒizi'gwaw/ (*pl* ~**guais**) *a* unequal; *<terreno>* uneven; ~**gualdade** *f* inequality; (*de terreno*) unevenness

desilu|dir /dʒizilu'dʒir/ *vt* disillusion; ~**são** /õ/ *f* disillusionment

desinfe|tante /dʒizĩfe'tãtʃi/ *a & m* disinfectant; ~**tar** *vt* disinfect

desinibido /dʒizini'bidu/ *a* uninhibited

desintegrar-se /dʒizĩte'grarsi/ *vpr* disintegrate

desinteres|sado /dʒizĩtere'sadu/ *a* uninterested; ~**sante** *a* uninteresting; ~**sar-se** *vpr* lose interest (de in); ~**se** /e/ *m* disinterest

desis|tência /dezis'tẽsia/ *f* giving up; ~**tir** *vt/i* ~**tir** (de) give up

desle|al /dʒizle'aw/ (*pl* ~**ais**) *a* disloyal; ~**aldade** *f* disloyalty

deslei|xado /dʒizle'ʃadu/ *a* sloppy; (*no vestir*) scruffy; ~**xo** *m* carelessness; (*no vestir*) scruffiness

desli|gado /dʒizli'gadu/ *a <luz, TV>* off; *<pessoa>* absent-minded; ~**gar** *vt*

turn off *<luz, TV, motor>*; hang up, put down *<telefone>* □ *vi* (*ao telefonar*) hang up, put the phone down

deslindar /dʒizlĩ'dar/ *vt* clear up, solve

desli|zante /dʒizli'zãtʃi/ *a* slippery; *<inflação>* creeping; ~**zar** *vi* slip; ~**zar-se** *vpr* creep; ~**ze** *m* slip; (*fig: erro*) slip-up

deslo|cado *a <membro>* dislocated; (*fig*) out of place; ~**car** *vt* move; (*med*) dislocate; ~**car-se** *vpr* move

deslum|brado /dʒizlũ'bradu/ *a* (*fig*) starry-eyed; ~**bramento** *m* (*fig*) wonderment; ~**brante** *a* dazzling; ~**brar** *vt* dazzle; ~**brar-se** *vpr* (*fig*) be dazzled

desmai|ado /dʒizmaj'adu/ *a* unconscious; ~**ar** *vi* faint; ~**o** *m* faint

desman|cha-prazeres /dʒizmãʃapra'zeris/ *m/f invar* spoilsport; ~**char** *vt* break up; break off *<noivado>*; shatter *<sonhos>*; ~**char-se** *vpr* break up; (*no ar, na água, em lágrimas*) dissolve

desmantelar /dʒizmãte'lar/ *vt* dismantle

desmarcar /dʒizmar'kar/ *vt* cancel *<encontro>*

desmascarar /dʒizmaske'rar/ *vt* unmask

desma|tamento /dʒizmata'mẽtu/ *m* deforestation; ~**tar** *vt* clear (of forest)

desmedido /dʒizme'didu/ *a* excessive

desmemoriado /dʒizmemori'adu/ *a* forgetful

desmen|tido /dʒizmẽ'tʃidu/ *m* denial; ~**tir** *vt* deny

desmiolado /dʒizmio'ladu/ *a* brainless

desmontar /dʒizmõ'tar/ *vt* dismantle

desmorali|zante /dʒizmorali'zãtʃi/ *a* demoralizing; ~**zar** *vt* demoralize

desmoro|namento /dʒizmorona'mẽtu/ *m* collapse; ~**nar** *vt* destroy; ~**nar-se** *vpr* collapse

desnatar /dʒizna'tar/ *vi* skim *<leite>*

desnecessário /dʒiznese'sariu/ *a* unnecessary

desní|vel /dʒiz'nivew/ (*pl* ~**veis**) *m* difference in height

desnortear /dʒiznortʃi'ar/ *vt* disorientate, (*Amer*) disorient

desnutrição /dʒiznutri'sãw/ *f* malnutrition

desobe|decer /dʒizobede'ser/ *vt/i* ~**decer** (a) disobey; ~**diência** *f* disobedience; ~**diente** *a* disobedient

desobrigar /dʒizobri'gar/ *vt* release (de from)

desobstruir /dʒizobstru'ir/ *vt* unblock; empty *<casa>*

desocupado /dʒizoku'padu/ a unoccupied

desodorante /dʒizodo'rãtʃi/ m, (Port) desodorizante /dʒizoduri'zãtʃi/ m deodorant

deso|lação /dezola'sãw/ f desolation; ~lado a < lugar > desolate; < pessoa > desolated; ~lar vt desolate

desones|tidade /dʒizonestʃi'dadʒi/ f dishonesty; ~to /ɛ/ a dishonest

deson|ra /dʒi'zõxa/ f dishonour; ~rar vt dishonour; ~roso /o/ a dishonourable

desor|deiro /dʒizor'deru/ a trouble-making □ m troublemaker; ~dem f disorder; ~denado a disorganized; < vida > disordered; ~denar vt disorganize

desorgani|zação /dʒizorganiza'sãw/ f disorganization; ~zar vt disorganize; ~zar-se vpr get disorganized

desorientar /dʒizoriẽ'tar/ vt disorientate, (Amer) disorient

desossar /dʒizo'sar/ vt bone

deso|va /dʒi'zova/ f roe; ~var vi spawn

despa|chado /dʒispa'ʃadu/ a efficient; ~chante m/f (de mercadorias) shipping agent; (de documentos) documentation agent; ~char vt deal with; dispatch, forward < mercadorias >; ~cho m dispatch

desparafusar /dʒisp.arafu'zar/ vt unscrew

despedaçar /dʒispeda'sar/ vt (rasgar) tear to pieces; (quebrar) smash; ~se vpr < vidro, vaso > smash; < papel, tecido > tear

despe|dida /dʒispe'dʒida/ f farewell; ~dida de solteiro stag night, (Amer) bachelor party; ~dir vt dismiss; sack < empregado >; ~dir-se vpr say goodbye (de to)

despei|to /dʒispej'tadu/ a spiteful; ~to m spite; a ~to de despite, in spite of

despe|jar /dʒispe'ʒar/ vt pour out < liquido >; empty < recipiente >; evict < inquilino >; ~jo /e/ m (de inquilino) eviction

despencar /dʒispẽ'kar/ vi plummet

despender /dʒispẽ'der/ vt spend < dinheiro >

despensa /dʒis'pẽsa/ f pantry, larder

despentear /dʒispẽtʃi'ar/ vt mess up < cabelo >; mess up the hair of < pessoa >

despercebido /dʒisperse'bidu/ a unnoticed

desper|diçar /dʒisperdʒi'sar/ vt waste; ~dício m waste

desper|tador /dʒisperta'dor/ m alarm clock; ~tar vt rouse < pessoa >;

(fig) arouse < interesse, suspeitas etc > □ vi awake

despesa /dʒis'peza/ f expense

des|pido /des'pidu/ a bare, stripped (de of); ~pir vt strip (de of); strip off < roupa >; ~pir-se vpr strip (off), get undressed

despo|jar /dʒispo'ʒar/ vt strip (de of); ~jar-se vpr divest o.s. (de of); ~jo /o/ m spoils, booty; ~jos mortais mortal remains

despontar /dʒispõ'tar/ vi emerge

despor|tista /diʃpur'tiʃta/ (Port) m/f sportsman (f -woman); ~tivo (Port) a sporting; ~to /o/ (Port) m sport; carro de ~to sports car

déspota /'dɛspota/ m/f despot

despótico /des'pɔtʃiku/ a despotic

despovoar /dʒispovo'ar/ vt depopulate

desprender /dʒisprẽ'der/ vt detach; (da parede) take down; ~se vpr come off; (fig) detach o.s.

despreocupado /dʒisprioku'padu/ a unconcerned

despreparado /dʒisprepa'radu/ a unprepared

despretensioso /dʒispretẽsi'ozu/ a unpretentious

desprestigiar /dʒisprestʃiʒi'ar/ vt discredit

desprevenido /dʒispreve'nidu/ a off one's guard, unprepared; apanhar ~ catch unawares

despre|zar /dʒispre'zar/ vt despise; (ignorar) ignore; ~zível (pl ~zíveis) a despicable; ~zo /e/ m contempt

desproporção /dʒispropor'sãw/ f disproportion

desproporcio|nado /dʒisproporsio'nadu/ a disproportionate; ~nal (pl ~nais) a disproportional

despropositado /dʒispropozi'tadu/ a (absurdo) preposterous

desprovido /dʒispro'vidu/ a ~ de without

desqualificar /dʒiskwalifi'kar/ vt disqualify

desqui|tar-se /dʒiski'tarsi/ vpr (legally) separate; ~te m (legal) separation

desrespei|tar /dʒizxespej'tar/ vt not respect; (ignorar) disregard; ~to m disrespect; ~toso /o/ a disrespectful

dessa(s), desse(s) = de + essa(s), esse(s)

desta = de + esta

desta|camento /dʒistaka'mẽtu/ m detachment; ~car vt detach; (ressaltar) bring out, make stand out; ~carse vpr (desprender-se) come off; < corredor > break away; (sobressair) stand out (sobre against); ~cável (pl

~cáveis) *a* detachable; <*caderno*> pull-out

destam|pado /dʒistãˈpadu/ *a* (*panela*) uncovered; ~par *vt* remove the lid of

destapar /dʒistaˈpar/ *vt* uncover

destaque /dʒisˈtaki/ *m* prominence; (*coisa, pessoa*) highlight; (*do notíciario*) headline

destas, deste = de + estas, este

destemido /dʒisteˈmidu/ *a* intrepid, courageous

desterrar /dʒisteˈxar/ *vt* (*exilar*) exile

destes = de + estes

destilar /destiˈlar/ *vt* distil; ~iaʃ*f* distillery

desti|nado /destʃiˈnadu/ *a* (*fadado*) destined; ~nar *vt* intend, mean (para for); ~natário *m* addressee; ~no *m* (*de viagem*) destination; (*sorte*) fate

destituir /destʃituˈir/ *vt* remove

deso|lante /dʒisoˈãtʃi/ *a* <*sons*> discordant; <*cores*> clashing; ~ar *vi* ~ar de clash with

destrancar /dʒistrãˈkar/ *vt* unlock

destreza /desˈtreza/ *f* skill

destrinchar /dʒistrĩˈʃar/ *vt* (*expor*) dissect; (*resolver*) sort out

destro /ˈdestru/ *a* skilful

destro|çar /dʒistroˈsar/ *vt* wreck; ~ços *m pl* wreckage

destronar /dʒistroˈnar/ *vt* depose

destroncar /dʒistrõˈkar/ *vt* rick

destru|ição /dʒistruiˈsãw/ *f* destruction; ~idor *a* destructive □ *m* destroyer; ~ir *vt* destroy

desumano /dʒizuˈmanu/ *a* inhuman; (*cruel*) inhumane

desunião /dʒizuniˈãw/ *f* disunity

desu|sado /dʒizuˈzadu/ *a* disused; ~so *m* disuse

desvairado /dʒizvajˈradu/ *a* delirious, raving

desvalori|zação /dʒizvalorizaˈsãw/ *f* devaluation; ~zar *vt* devalue

desvanta|gem /dʒizvãˈtaʒẽ/ *f* disadvantage; ~joso /o/ *a* disadvantageous

desve|lar /dʒizveˈlar/ *vt* unveil; uncover <*segredo*>; ~lar-se *vpr* go to a lot of trouble; ~lo /e/ *m* great care

desvencilhar /dʒizvẽsiˈʎar/ *vt* extricate, free

desvendar /dʒizvẽˈdar/ *vt* reveal <*segredo*>; solve <*mistério*>

desventura /dʒizvẽˈtura/ *f* misfortune; (*infelicidade*) unhappiness

desviar /dʒizviˈar/ *vt* divert <*trânsito, rio, atenção, dinheiro*>; avert <*golpe, suspeitas, olhos*>; ~se *vpr* deviate; <*do tema*> digress

desvincular /dʒizvĩkuˈlar/ *vt* free

desvio /dʒizˈviu/ *m* diversion; (*do trânsito*) diversion, (*Amer*) detour; (*linha ferroviária*) siding

desvirtuar /dʒizvirtuˈar/ *vt* misrepresent <*verdade*>

deta|lhado /detaˈʎadu/ *a* detailed; ~lhar *vt* detail; ~lhe *m* detail

detec|tar /deteˈktar/ *vt* detect; ~tive (*Port*) *m veja* detetive; ~tor *m* detector

de|tenção /detẽˈsãw/ *f* (*prisão*) detention; ~tentor *m* holder; ~ter *vt* (*ter*) hold; (*prender*) detain

detergente /deterˈʒẽtʃi/ *m* detergent

deterio|ração /deterioraˈsãw/ *f* deterioration; ~rar *vt* damage; ~rar-se *vpr* deteriorate

determi|nação /determinaˈsãw/ *f* determination; ~nado *a* (*certo*) certain; (*resoluto*) determined; ~nar *vt* determine

detestar /detesˈtar/ *vt* hate

detetive /deteˈtʃivi/ *m* detective

detido /deˈtʃidu/ *pp de* deter □ *a* thorough □ *m* detainee

detonar /detoˈnar/ *vt* detonate; (*fam: criticar*) pull to pieces □ *vi* detonate

detrás /deˈtraʃ/ *adv* behind □ *prep* ~ de behind

detrito /deˈtritu/ *m* detritus

deturpar /deturˈpar/ *vt* misrepresent, distort

deus /dews/ *m* (*f* deusa) god (*f* goddess); ~dará *m* ao ~dará at the mercy of chance

devagar /dʒivaˈgar/ *adv* slowly

deva|near /devaniˈar/ *vi* daydream; ~neio *m* daydream

devas|sar /devaˈsar/ *vt* expose; ~sidão *f* debauchery; ~so *a* debauched

devastar /devasˈtar/ *vt* devastate

de|vedor /deveˈdor/ *a* debit □ *m* debtor; ~ver *vt* owe □ *vaux* ~ve fazer (*obrigação*) he has to do; ~ve chegar (*probabilidade*) he should arrive; ~ve ser (*suposição*) he must be; ~ve ter sido he must have gone; ~v(er)ia fazer he ought to do; ~v(er)ia ter feito he ought to have done; ~vidamente *adv* duly; ~vido *a* due (a to)

devoção /devoˈsãw/ *f* devotion

de|volução /devoluˈsãw/ *f* return; ~volver *vt* return

devorar /devoˈrar/ *vt* devour

devo|tar /devoˈtar/ *vt* devote; ~tar-se *vpr* devote o.s. (a to); ~to /ɔ/ *a* devout

dez /dɛs/ *a & m* ten

dezanove /dzaˈnɔv/ (*Port*) *a & m* nineteen

dezas|seis /dzaˈsejʃ/ (*Port*) *a & .m* sixteen; ~sete /ɛ/ (*Port*) *a & m* seventeen

dezembro /deˈzẽbru/ *m* December

deze|na /de'zena/ *f* ten; uma ~ (de) about ten; ~nove /ɔ/ *a & m* nineteen; **dezes|seis** /dʒize'sejs/ *a & m* sixteen; ~sete /ɛ/ *a & m* seventeen

dezoito /dʒi'zojtu/ *a & m* eighteen

dia /'dʒia/ *m* day; de ~ by day; (no) ~ 20 de julho (on) July 20th; ~ de folga day off; ~ útil working day; ~a-~ *m* everyday life

dia|bete /dʒia'bɛtʃi/ *f* diabetes; ~bético *a & m* diabetic

dia|bo /dʒi'abu/ *m* devil; ~bólico *a* diabolical, devilish; ~brete /e/ *m* little devil; ~brura *f* (de criança) bit of mischief; *pl* mischief

diadema /dʒia'dema/ *m* tiara

diafragma /dʒia'fragima/ *m* diaphragm

dia|gnosticar /dʒiagnostʃi'kar/ *vt* diagnose; ~gnóstico *m* diagnosis □ *a* diagnostic

diago|nal /dʒiago'naw/ (*pl* ~nais) *a & f* diagonal

diagra|ma /dʒia'grama/ *m* diagram; ~mação *f* design; ~mador *m* designer; ~mar *vt* design < *livro, revista*>

dialect- (Port) veja dialet-

dia|lética /dʒia'lɛtʃika/ *f* dialectics; ~leto /ɛ/ *m* dialect

dialogar /dʒialo'gar/ *vi* talk; (pol) hold talks

diálogo /dʒi'alogu/ *m* dialogue

diamante /dʒia'mãtʃi/ *m* diamond

diâmetro /dʒi'ametru/ *m* diameter

dian|te /dʒi'ãtʃi/ *adv* de ~ em ~ te from ... on(wards); ~te de (enfrentando) faced with; (perante) before; ~teira *f* lead; ~teiro *a* front

diapasão /dʒiapa'zãw/ *m* tuning-fork

diapositivo /dʒiapozi'tʃivu/ *m* transparency

diá|ria /dʒi'aria/ *f* daily rate; ~rio *a* daily

diarista /dʒia'rista/ *m/f* day labourer; (faxineira) daily (help)

diarréia /dʒia'xeja/ *f* diarrhoea

dica /'dʒika/ *f* tip, hint

dicção /dʒik'sãw/ *f* diction

dicionário /dʒisio'nariu/ *m* dictionary

didáti|ca /dʒi'datʃika/ *f* teaching methodology; ~co *a* teaching; < *livro*> educational; < *estilo*> didactic

die|ta /dʒi'eta/ *f* diet; de ~ta on a diet; ~tista *m/f* dietician

difa|mação /dʒifama'sãw/ *f* defamation; ~mar *vt* defame; ~matório *a* defamatory

diferen|ça /dʒife'rẽsa/ *f* difference; ~cial (*pl* ~ciais) *a & f* differential; ~ciar *vt* differentiate; ~ciar-se *vpr* differ; ~te *a* different

dife|rimento /dʒiferi'mẽtu/ *m* deferment; ~rir *vt* defer □ *vi* differ

difí|cil /dʒi'fisiw/ (*pl* ~ceis) *a* difficult; (improvável) unlikely

dificilmente /dʒifisiw'mẽtʃi/ *adv* ~ poderá fazê-lo he's unlikely to be able to do it

dificul|dade /dʒifikuw'dadʒi/ *f* difficulty; ~tar *vt* make difficult

difteria /dʒifte'ria/ *f* diphtheria

difun|dir /dʒifũ'dʒir/ *vt* spread; (pela rádio) broadcast; diffuse < *luz, calor*>; ~dir-se *vpr* spread

difu|são /dʒifu'zãw/ *f* diffusion; ~so *a* diffuse

dige|rir /dʒiʒe'rir/ *vt* digest; ~rível (*pl* ~ríveis) *a* digestible

diges|tão /dʒiʒes'tãw/ *f* digestion; ~tivo *a* digestive

digi|tal /dʒiʒi'taw/ (*pl* ~tais) *a* digital; impressão ~tal fingerprint; ~tar *vt* key

dígito /'dʒiʒitu/ *m* digit

digladiar /dʒigladʒi'ar/ *vi* do battle

dig|nar-se /dʒig'narsi/ *vpr* deign (de to); ~nidade *f* dignity; ~nificar *vt* dignify; ~no *a* worthy (de of); (decoroso) dignified

dilace|rante /dʒilase'rãtʃi/ *a* < *dor*> excruciating; ~rar *vt* tear to pieces

dilapidar /dʒilapi'dar/ *vt* squander

dilatar /dʒila'tar/ *vt* expand; (med) dilate; ~-se *vpr* expand; (med) dilate

dilema /dʒi'lema/ *m* dilemma

diletante /dʒile'tãtʃi/ *a & m/f* dilettante

dili|gência /dʒili'ʒẽsia/ *f* diligence; (carruagem) stagecoach; ~gente *a* diligent, hard-working

diluir /dʒilu'ir/ *vt* dilute

dilúvio /dʒi'luviu/ *m* deluge

dimen|são /dʒimẽ'sãw/ *f* dimension; ~sionar *vt* size up

diminu|ição /dʒiminui'sãw/ *f* reduction; ~ir *vt* reduce □ *vi* lessen; < *carro, motorista*> slow down; ~tivo *a & m* diminutive; ~to *a* minute

Dinamarca /dʒina'marka/ *f* Denmark

dinamar|quês /dʒinamar'kes/ (*f* ~quesa) *a* Danish □ *m* Dane

dinâmi|ca /dʒi'namika/ *f* dynamics; ~co *a* dynamic

dina|mismo /dʒina'mizmu/ *m* dynamism; ~mite *f* dynamite

dínamo /'dʒinamu/ *m* dynamo

dinastia /dʒinas'tʃia/ *f* dynasty

dinda /'dʒida/ (fam) *f* godmother

dinheiro /dʒi'ɲeru/ *m* money

dinossauro /dʒino'sawru/ *m* dinosaur

diocese /dʒio'sɛzi/ *f* diocese

dióxido /dʒi'ɔksidu/ *m* dioxide; ~ de carbono carbon dioxide

diplo|ma /dʒi'ploma/ *m* diploma; ~macia *f* diplomacy; ~mar-se *vpr* take one's diploma; ~mata *m/f* diplomat □ *a* diplomatic; ~mático *a* diplomatic

direção /dʒire'sãw/ *f* (*sentido*) direction; (*de empresa*) management; (*condução de carro*) driving; (*manuseio do volante*) steering

direct- (*Port*) *veja* diret-

direi|ta /dʒi'rejta/ *f* right; ~tinho *adv* exactly right; ~tista *a* rightwing □ *m/f* rightwinger, rightist; ~to *a* right; (*ereto*) straight □ *adv* properly □ *m* right

dire|tas /dʒi'rɛtas/ *f pl* direct (presidential) elections; ~to *a* direct □ *adv* directly; ~tor *m* director; (*de escola*) headteacher; (*de jornal*) editor; ~torgerente managing director; ~toria *f* (*diretores*) board of directors; (*sala*) boardroom; ~tório *m* directory; ~triz *f* directive

diri|gente /dʒiri'ʒẽtʃi/ *a* leading □ *m/f* leader; ~gir *vt* direct; manage <*empresa*>; drive <*carro*>; ~gir-se *vpr* (*ir*) make one's way; ~gir-se a (*falar com*) address

dis|cagem /dʒis'kaʒẽ/ *f* dialling; ~car *vt/i* dial

discente /dʒi'sẽtʃi/ *a* corpo ~ student body

discer|nimento /dʒiserni'mẽtu/ *m* discernment; ~nir *vt* discern

disci|plina /dʒisi'plina/ *f* discipline; ~nador *a* disciplinary; ~nar *vt* discipline

discípulo /dʒi'sipulu/ *m* disciple

disc-jóquei /dʒisk'ʒɔkej/ *m* disc-jockey

disco /'dʒisku/ *m* disc; (*de música*) record; (*no atletismo*) discus □ (*fam*) *f* disco; ~ flexível/rígido floppy/hard disk; ~ laser CD, compact disc; ~ voador flying saucer

discor|dante /dʒiskor'dãtʃi/ *a* conflicting; ~dar *vi* disagree (*de* with)

discote|ca /dʒisko'tɛka/ *f* discotheque; ~cário *m* DJ

discre|pância /dʒiskre'pãsia/ *f* discrepancy; ~pante *a* inconsistent; ~par *vi* diverge (*de* from)

dis|creto /dʒis'krɛtu/ *a* discreet; ~crição *f* discretion

discrimi|nação /dʒiskrimina'sãw/ *f* discrimination; (*descrição*) description; ~nar *vt* discriminate; ~natório *a* discriminatory

discur|sar /dʒiskur'sar/ *vi* speak; ~so *m* speech

discussão /dʒisku'sãw/ *f* discussion; (*briga*) argument

discu|tir /dʒisku'tʃir/ *vt/i* discuss; (*brigar*) argue; ~tível (*pl* ~tíveis) *a* debatable

disenteria /dʒizẽte'ria/ *f* dysentery

disfar|çar /dʒisfar'sar/ *vt* disguise; ~çar-se *vpr* disguise o.s.; ~ce *m* disguise

dis|lético /dʒiz'lɛtʃiku/ *a* & *m* dyslexic; ~lexia *f* dyslexia; ~léxico *a* & *m* dyslexic

dispa|rada /dʒispa'rada/ *f* bolt; ~rado *adv* o melhor ~rado the best by a long way; ~rar *vt* fire <*arma*> □ *vi* (*com arma*) fire; <*preços, inflação*> shoot up; <*corredor*> surge ahead

disparate /dʒispa'ratʃi/ *m* piece of nonsense; *pl* nonsense

dis|pêndio /dʒis'pẽdʒiu/ *m* expenditure; ~pendioso /o/ *a* costly

dispen|sa /dʒis'pẽsa/ *f* exemption; ~sar *vt* (*distribuir*) dispense; (*isentar*) exempt (*de* from); (*prescindir de*) dispense with; ~sável (*pl* ~sáveis) *a* dispensable

dispersar /dʒisper'sar/ *vt* disperse; waste <*energias*> □ *vi*, ~-se *vpr* disperse

disperso /dʒis'pɛrsu/ *adj* scattered

dispo|nibilidade /dʒisponibili-'dadʒi/ *f* availability; ~nível (*pl* ~níveis) *a* available

dis|por /dʒis'por/ *vt* arrange □ *vi* ~por de have at one's disposal; ~por-se *vpr* form up □ *m* ao seu ~por at your disposal; ~posição *f* (*vontade*) willingness; (*arranjo*) arrangement; (*de espírito*) frame of mind; (*de testamento etc*) provision; à ~posição de alg at s.o.'s disposal; ~positivo *m* device; ~posto *a* prepared, willing (a to)

dispu|ta /dʒis'puta/ *f* dispute; ~tar *vt* dispute; (*tentar ganhar*) compete for

disquete /dʒis'ketʃi/ *m* diskette, floppy (disk)

dissabores /dʒisa'boris/ *m pl* troubles

disseminar /dʒisemi'nar/ *vt* disseminate

dissertação /dʒiserta'sãw/ *f* dissertation, lecture

dissi|dência /dʒisi'dẽsia/ *f* dissidence; ~dente *a* & *m* dissident

dissídio /dʒi'sidʒiu/ *m* dispute

dissimular /dʒisimu'lar/ *vt* hide □ *vi* dissimulate

disso = de + isso

dissipar /dʒisi'par/ *vt* clear <*nevoeiro*>; dispel <*dúvidas, suspeitas, ilusões*>; dissipate <*fortuna*>; ~-se *vpr* <*nevoeiro*> clear; <*dúvidas etc*> be dispelled

dissolu|ção /dʒisolu'sãw/ *f* dissolution; ~to *a* dissolute

dissolver /dʒisow'ver/ *vt* dissolve; ~-se *vpr* dissolve

dissuadir /dʒisua'dʒir/ *vt* dissuade (*de* from)

distância /dʒis'tãsia/ f distance

distanciar /dʒistãsi'ar/ vt distance; ~ciar-se vpr distance o.s.; ~te a distant

distender /dʒistẽ'der/ vt stretch <pernas>; relax <músculo>; ~der-se vpr relax; ~são f (med) pull; ~são muscular pulled muscle

distinção /dʒistʃĩ'sãw/ f distinction; ~guir vt distinguish (de from); ~guir-se vpr distinguish o.s.; ~tivo a distinctive □ m badge; ~to a distinct; <senhor> distinguished

disto = de + isto

distorção /dʒistor'sãw/ f distortion; ~cer vt distort

distração /dʒistra'sãw/ f distraction; ~ído a absent-minded; ~ir vt distract; (divertir) amuse; ~ir-se vpr be distracted; (divertir-se) amuse o.s.

distribuição /dʒistribui'sãw/ f distribution; ~idor m distributor; ~idora f distributor, distribution company; ~ir vt distribute

distrito /dʒis'tritu/ m district

distúrbio /dʒis'turbiu/ m trouble

ditado /dʒi'tadu/ m dictation; (provérbio) saying; ~tador m dictator; ~tadura f dictatorship; ~tame m dictate; ~tar vt dictate; ~tatorial (pl ~tatoriais) a dictatorial

dito /'dʒitu/ a ~ e feito no sooner said than done □ m remark

ditongo /dʒi'tõgu/ m diphthong

DIU /'dʒiu/ m IUD, coil

diurno /dʒi'urnu/ a day

divã /dʒi'vã/ m couch

divagar /dʒiva'gar/ vi digress

divergência /dʒiver'ʒẽsia/ a divergence; ~gente a divergent; ~gir vi diverge (de from); ~são f diversion; (divertimento) amusement; ~sidade f diversity; ~sificar vt/i diversify; ~so /ɛ/ a (diferente) diverse; pl (vários) several; ~tido a (engraçado) funny; (que se curte) enjoyable; ~timento m enjoyment, fun; (um) amusement; ~tir vt amuse; ~tir-se vpr enjoy o.s., have fun

dívida /'dʒivida/ f debt; ~ externa foreign debt

dividendo /dʒivi'dẽdu/ m dividend; ~dido a <pessoa> torn; ~dir vt divide; (compartilhar) share; ~dir-se vpr be divided

divindade /dʒivĩ'dadʒi/ f divinity

divino /dʒi'vinu/ a divine

divisa /dʒi'viza/ f (lema) motto; (galão) stripes; (fronteira) border; pl foreign currency; ~são f division; ~sória f partition; ~sório a dividing

divorciado /dʒivorsi'adu/ a divorced □ m divorcé (f divorcée); ~ar vt

divorce; ~ar-se vpr get divorced; ~ar-se de divorce

divórcio /dʒi'vorsiu/ m divorce

divulgado /dʒivuw'gadu/ a widespread; ~gar vt spread; publish <notícia>; divulge <segredo>; ~gar-se vpr be spread

dizer /dʒi'zer/ vt say; ~ a alg que tell sb that; ~ para alg fazer tell s.o. to do □ vi ~ com go with; ~-se vpr claim to be □ m saying

dizimar /dʒizi'mar/ vt decimate

do = de +o

dó /dɔ/ m pity; dar ~ be pitiful; ter ~ de feel sorry for

doação /doa'sãw/ f donation; ~ador m donor; ~ar vt donate

dobra /'dɔbra/ f fold; (de calça) turn-up, (Amer) cuff; ~bradiça f hinge; ~bradiço a pliable; ~brado a (duplo) double; ~brar vt (duplicar) double; (fazer dobra em) fold; (curvar) bend; go round <esquina>; ring <sinos> □ vi double; <sinos> ring; ~brar-se vpr bend; ~bro m double

doca /'dɔka/ f dock

doce /'dosi/ a sweet; <água> fresh □ m sweet; ~ de leite fudge

docente /do'sẽtʃi/ a teaching; corpo ~ teaching staff, (Amer) faculty

dócil /'dɔsiw/ (pl ~ceis) a docile

documentação /dokumẽta'sãw/ f documentation; ~tar vt document; ~tário a & m documentary; ~to m document

doçura /do'sura/ f sweetness

dodói /do'dɔj/ (fam) m ter ~ have a pain □ a poorly, ill

doença /do'ẽsa/ f illness; (infecciosa, fig) disease; ~te a ill; ~tio a <criança, aspecto> sickly; <interesse, curiosidade> morbid

doer /do'er/ vi hurt; <cabeça, músculo> ache

dogma /'dɔgima/ m dogma; ~mático a dogmatic

doido /'dojdu/ a crazy

dois /dojs/ a & m (f duas) two

dólar /'dɔlar/ m dollar

dolorido /dolo'ridu/ a sore; ~roso /o/ a painful

dom /dõ/ m gift

domador /doma'dor/ m tamer; ~mar vt tame

doméstica /do'mɛstʃika/ f housemaid

domesticar /domɛstʃi'kar/ vt domesticate

doméstico /do'mɛstʃiku/ a domestic

domiciliar /domisili'ar/ a home; ~cílio m home

dominação /domina'sãw/ f domination; ~nador a domineering; ~nante a dominant; ~nar vt dom-

inate; have a command of <*língua*>;
~nar-se *vpr* control o.s.
domin|go /do'mĩgu/ *m* Sunday;
~gueiro *a* Sunday
domini|cal /domini'kaw/ (*pl* ~cais)
a Sunday; ~cano *a* & *m* Dominican
domínio /do'miniu/ *m* command
dona /'dona/ *f* owner; Dona (*com
nome*) Miss; ~ de casa *f* housewife
donativo /dona'tʃivu/ *m* donation
donde /'dõdʒi/ *adv* from where; (*motivo*) from whence
dono /'donu/ *m* owner
donzela /dõ'zɛla/ *f* maiden
dopar /do'par/ *vt* drug
dor /dor/ *f* pain; (*menos aguda*) ache;
~ de cabeça headache
dor|mente /dor'mẽtʃi/ *a* numb □ *m*
sleeper; ~mida *f* sleep; ~minhoco
/o/ *m* sleepyhead; ~mir *vi* sleep;
~mitar *vi* doze; ~mitório *m* bedroom; (*comunitário*) dormitory
dorso /'dorsu/ *m* back; (*de livro*) spine
dos = de + os
do|sagem /do'zaʒẽ/ *f* dosage; ~sar *vt*
moderate; ~se /ɔ/ *f* dose; (*de uísque
etc*) shot, measure
dossiê /dosi'e/ *m* file
do|tação /dota'sãw/ *f* endowment;
~tado *a* gifted; ~tado de endowed
with; ~tar *vt* endow (de with); ~te
/ɔ/ *m* (*de noiva*) dowry; (*dom*) endow-
ment
dou|rado /do'radu/ *a* (*de cor*) golden;
(*revestido de ouro*) gilded, gilt □ *m* gilt;
~rar *vt* gild
dou|to /'dotu/ *a* learned; ~tor *m*
doctor; ~torado *m* doctorate, PhD;
~trina *f* doctrine; ~trinar *vt* indoc-
trinate
doze /'dozi/ *a* & *m* twelve
dragão /dra'gãw/ *m* dragon
dragar /dra'gar/ *vt* dredge
drágea /'draʒia/ *f* lozenge
dra|ma /'drama/ *m* drama; ~malhão
m melodrama; ~mático *a* dramatic;
~matizar *vt* dramatize; ~maturgo
m dramatist, playwright
drapeado /drapi'adu/ *a* draped
drástico /'drastʃiku/ *a* drastic
dre|nagem /dre'naʒẽ/ *f* drainage;
~nar *vt* drain; ~no /ɛ/ *m* drain
driblar /dri'blar/ *vt* (*em futebol*)
dribble round, beat; (*fig*) get round
drinque /'drĩki/ *m* drink
drive /'drajvi/ *m* disk drive
dro|ga /'drɔga/ *f* drug; (*fam*) (*coisa
sem valor*) dead loss; (*coisa chata*)
drag □ *int* damn; ~gado *a* on drugs
□ *m* drug addict; ~gar *vt* drug;
~gar-se *vpr* take drugs; ~garia *f*
dispensing chemist's, pharmacy
duas /'duas/ *veja* dois
dúbio /'dubiu/ *a* dubious

dub|lagem /du'blaʒẽ/ *f* dubbing;
~lar *vt* dub <*filme*>; mime
<*música*>; ~lê *m* double
ducentésimo /dusẽ'tɛzimu/ *a* two-
hundredth
ducha /'duʃa/ *f* shower
ducto /'duktu/ *m* duct
duelo /du'ɛlu/ *m* duel
duende /du'ẽdʒi/ *m* elf
dueto /du'etu/ *m* duet
duna /'duna/ *f* dune
duodécimo /duo'dɛsimu/ *a* twelfth
duodeno /duo'dɛnu/ *m* duodenum
dupla /'dupla/ *f* pair, duo; <*no tênis*>
doubles
duplex /du'plɛks/ *a invar* two-floor □
m invar two-floor apartment, (*Amer*)
duplex
dupli|car /dupli'kar/ *vt/i* double;
~cidade *f* duplicity; ~cata *f* duplicate
duplo /'duplu/ *a* double
duque /'duki/ duke; ~sa /e/ *f* duchess
du|ração /dura'sãw/ *f* duration;
~radouro *a* lasting; ~rante *prep*
during; ~rar *vi* last; ~rável (*pl*
~ráveis) *a* durable
durex /du'rɛks/ *m invar* sellotape
du|reza /du'reza/ *f* hardness; ~ro *a*
hard; (*fam: sem dinheiro*) hard up,
broke
dúvida /'duvida/ *f* doubt; (*pergunta*)
query
duvi|dar /duvi'dar/ *vt/i* doubt;
~doso /o/ *a* doubtful
duzentos /du'zẽtus/ *a* & *m* two hundred
dúzia /'duzia/ *f* dozen

E

e /i/ *conj* and
ébano /'ɛbanu/ *m* ebony
ébrio /'ɛbriu/ *a* drunk □ *m* drunkard
ebulição /ebuli'sãw/ *f* boiling
eclesiástico /eklezi'astʃiku/ *a* ecclesiastical
eclético /e'klɛtʃiku/ *a* eclectic
eclip|sar /eklip'sar/ *vt* eclipse; ~se *m*
eclipse
eclodir /eklo'dʒir/ *vi* emerge; (*esto-
urar*) break out; open
eco /'ɛku/ *m* echo; ter ~ have
repercussions; ~ar *vt/i* echo
eco|logia /ekolo'ʒia/ *f* ecology;
~lógico *a* ecological; ~logista *m/f*
ecologist
eco|nomia /ekono'mia/ *f* economy;
(*ciência*) economics; *pl* (*dinheiro poupado*) savings; ~nômico *a* economic;
(*rentável, barato*) economical; ~no-
mista *m/f* economist; ~nomizar *vt*
save □ *vi* economize

écran /ɛ'krã/ (Port) m screen

eczema /ek'zɛma/ m eczema

edição /edʒi'sãw/ f edition; (de filmes) editing

edificante /edʒifi'kãtʃi/ a edifying

edifício /edʒi'fisiu/ m building

Edimburgo /edʒi'burgu/ f Edinburgh

edi|tal /edʒi'taw/ (pl ~tais) m announcement; ~tar vt publish; (comput) edit; ~to m edict; ~tor m publisher; ~tora f publishing company; ~torial (pl ~toriais) a publishing □ m editorial

edredom /edre'dõ/ m, (Port) edredão /edre'dãw/ m quilt

educa|ção /eduka'sãw/ f (ensino) education; (polidez) good manners; é falta de ~ção it's rude; ~cional (pl ~cionais) a education

edu|cado /edu'kadu/ a polite; ~car vt educate; ~cativo a educational

efeito /e'fejtu/ m effect; fazer ~ have an effect; para todos os ~s to all intents and purposes; ~ colateral side effect; ~ estufa greenhouse effect

efêmero /e'fēmeru/ a ephemeral

efeminado /efemi'nadu/ a effeminate

efervescente /eferve'stʃi/ a effervescent

efe|tivar /efetʃi'var/ vt bring into effect; (contratar) make a permanent member of staff; ~tivo a real, effective; <cargo, empregado> permanent; ~tuar vt carry out, effect

eficácia /efi'kasia/ f effectiveness; ~caz a effective

efici|ência /efisi'ēsia/ f efficiency; ~ente a efficient

efígie /e'fiʒi/ f effigy

efusivo /efu'zivu/ a effusive

Egeu /e'ʒew/ a & m Aegean

égide /'ɛʒidʒi/ f aegis

egípcio /e'ʒipsiu/ a & m Egyptian

Egito /e'ʒitu/ m Egypt

ego /'ɛgu/ m ego; ~cêntrico a self-centred, egocentric; ~ismo m selfishness; ~ista a selfish □ m/f egoist □ m (de rádio etc) earplug

égua /'ɛgwa/ f mare

eis /ejs/ adv (aqui está) here is/are; (isso é) that is

eixo /'ejʃu/ m axle; (mat, entre cidades) axis; pôr nos ~s set straight

ela /'ɛla/ pron she; (coisa) it; (com preposição) her; (coisa) it

elaborar /elabo'rar/ vt (fazer) make, produce; (desenvolver) work out

elasticidade /elastʃisi'dadʒi/ f (de coisa) elasticity; (de pessoa) suppleness

elástico /e'lastʃiku/ a elastic □ m (de borracha) elastic band; (de calcinha etc) elastic

ele /'eli/ pron he; (coisa) it; (com preposição) him; (coisa) it

electr- (Port) veja eletr-

eléctrico /i'lɛktriku/ (Port) m tram, (Amer) streetcar □ a veja elétrico

elefante /ele'fãtʃi/ m elephant

ele|gância /ele'gãsia/ f elegance; ~gante a elegant

eleger /ele'ʒer/ vt elect; ~-se vpr get elected

elegia /ele'ʒia/ f elegy

elei|ção /elej'sãw/ f election; ~to a elected, elect; <povo> chosen; ~tor m voter; ~torado m electorate; ~toral (pl ~torais) a electoral

elemen|tar /elemē'tar/ a elementary; ~to m element

elenco /e'lēku/ m (de filme, peça) cast

eletri|cidade /eletrisi'dadʒi/ f electricity; ~cista m/f electrician

elétrico /e'lɛtriku/ a electric

eletri|ficar /eletrifi'kar/ vt electrify; ~zar vt electrify

eletro /e'lɛtru/ m ECG; ~cutar vt electrocute; ~do /o/ m electrode; ~domésticos m pl electrical appliances

eletrôni|ca /ele'tronika/ f electronics; ~co a electronic

ele|vação /eleva'sãw/ f elevation; (aumento) rise; ~vado a high; <sentimento, estilo> elevated; ~vador m lift, (Amer) elevator; ~var vt raise; (promover) elevate; ~var-se vpr rise

elimi|nar /elimi'nar/ vt eliminate; ~natória f heat; ~natório a eliminatory

elipse /e'lipsi/ f ellipse

elíptico /e'liptʃiku/ a elliptical

eli|te /e'litʃi/ f elite; ~tismo m elitism; ~tista a & m/f elitist

elmo /'ɛwmu/ m helmet

elo /'ɛlu/ m link

elo|giar /eloʒi'ar/ vt praise; ~giar alg por compliment s.o. on; ~gio m (louvor) praise; (um) compliment; ~gioso /o/ a complimentary

eloquência /elo'kwēsia/ f eloquence; ~quente a eloquent

eluci|dar /elusi'dar/ vt elucidate; ~dativo a elucidatory

em /j/ prep in; (sobre) on; ela está no Eduardo she's at Eduardo's (house); de casa ~ casa from house to house; aumentar ~ 10% increase by 10%

emagre|cer /emagre'ser/ vi lose weight, get thinner □ vt make thinner; ~cimento m slimming

emanar /ema'nar/ vi emanate (de from)

emanci|pação /emãsipa'sãw/ f emancipation; ~par vt emancipate; ~par-se vpr become emancipated

emara|nhado /emara'ɲadu/ a tangled □ m tangle; ~nhar vt tangle; (envolver) entangle; ~nhar-se vpr get tangled up; (*envolver-se*) become entangled (em in)

embaçar /ība'sar/, (*Port*) embaciar /ībasi'ar/ *vt* steam up <*vidro*> □ *vi* <*vidro*> steam up; <*olhos*> grow misty

embainhar /ībaj'ɲar/ *vt* hem <*vestido, calça*>

embaixa|da /ība'ʃada/ *f* embassy; ~dor *m* ambassador; ~triz *f* ambassador; (*esposa*) ambassador's wife

embaixo /ī'baʃu/ *adv* underneath; (*em casa*) downstairs; ~ de under

emba|lagem /ība'laʒē/ *f* packaging; ~lar¹ *vt* pack

emba|lar² /ība'lar/ *vt* rock <*criança*>; ~lo *m* (*fig*) excitement, thrill

embalsamar /ībawsa'mar/ *vt* embalm

embara|çar /ībara'sar/ *vt* embarrass; ~çar-se *vpr* get embarrassed (com by); ~ço *m* embarrassment; ~çoso /o/ *a* embarrassing

embaralhar /ībara'ʎar/ *vt* muddle up; shuffle <*cartas*>; ~se *vpr* get muddled up

embar|cação /ībarka'sãw/ *f* vessel; ~cadouro *m* wharf; ~car *vt/i* board, embark

embar|gado /ībar'gadu/ *a* <*voz*> faltering; ~go *m* embargo

embarque /ī'barki/ *m* boarding; (*seção do aeroporto*) departures

embasba|cado /ībazba'kadu/ *a* openmouthed; ~car-se *vpr* be left openmouthed

embate /ī'batʃi/ *m* (*de carros etc*) crash; (*fig*) clash

embebedar /ībebe'dar/ *vt* make drunk; ~se *vpr* get drunk

embeber /ībe'ber/ *vt* soak; ~se em soak up; ~se em absorbed in

embele|zador /ībeleza'dor/ *a* <*cirurgia*> cosmetic; ~zar *vt* embellish; spruce up <*casa*>; ~zar-se *vpr* make o.s. beautiful

embevecer /ībeve'ser/ *vt* captivate, engross; ~se *vpr* get engrossed, be captivated

emblema /ē'blema/ *m* emblem

embocadura / īboka'dura/ *f* (*de instrumento*) mouthpiece; (*de freio*) bit; (*de rio*) mouth; (*de rua*) entrance

êmbolo /'ēbulu/ *m* piston

embolsar /ībow'sar/ *vt* pocket; (*reembolsar*) reimburse

embora /ī'bora/ *adv* away □ *conj* although

emborcar /ībor'kar/ *vi* overturn; <*barco*> capsize

emboscada /ībos'kada/ *f* ambush

embrai|agem /ēbraj'aʒē/ (*Port*) *f* veja embreagem; ~ar (*Port*) *vi* veja embrear

embre|agem /ēbri'aʒē/ *f* clutch; ~ar *vi* let in the clutch

embria|gar /ēbria'gar/ *vt* intoxicate; ~gar-se *vpr* get drunk, become intoxicated; ~guez /e/ *f* drunkenness; ~guez no volante drunken driving

embri|ão /ēbri'ãw/ *m* embryo; ~onário *a* embryonic

embro|mação /ībroma'sãw/ *f* flannel; ~mar *vt* flannel, string along; (*enganar*) con □ *vi* stall, drag one's feet

embru|lhada /ībru'ʎada/ *f* muddle; ~lhar *vt* wrap up <*pacote*>; upset <*estômago*>; (*confundir*) muddle up; ~lhar-se *vpr* <*pessoa*> get muddled up; ~lho *m* parcel; (*fig*) mix-up

embur|rado /ību'xadu/ *a* sulky; ~rar *vi* sulk

embuste /ī'bustʃi/ *m* hoax, put-up job

embu|tido /ību'tʃidu/ *a* built-in, fitted; ~tir *vt* build in, fit

emen|da /e'mēda/ *f* correction, improvement; (*de lei*) amendment; ~dar *vt* correct; amend <*lei*>; ~dar-se *vpr* mend one's ways

ementa /i'mēta/ (*Port*) *f* menu

emer|gência /emer'ʒēsia/ *f* emergency; ~gente *a* emergent; ~gir *vi* surface

emi|gração /emigra'sãw/ *f* emigration; (*de aves etc*) migration; ~grado *a* & *m* émigré; ~grante *a* & *m/f* emigrant; ~grar *vi* emigrate; <*aves, animais*> migrate

emi|nência /emi'nēsia/ *f* eminence; ~nente *a* eminent

emis|são /emi'sãw/ *f* (*de ações etc*) issue; (*na rádio, TV*) transmission, broadcast; (*de som, gases*) emission; ~sário *m* emissary; ~sor *m* transmitter; ~sora (*de rádio*) radio station; (*de TV*) TV station

emitir /emi'tʃir/ *vt* issue <*ações, selos etc*>; emit <*sons*>; (*pela rádio, TV*) transmit, broadcast

emoção /emo'sãw/ *f* emotion; (*excitação*) excitement

emocio|nal /emosio'naw/ (*pl* ~nais) *a* emotional; ~nante *a* (*excitante*) exciting; (*comovente*) touching, emotional; ~nar *vt* (*excitar*) excite; (*comover*) move, touch; ~nar-se *vpr* get emotional

emoldurar /emowdu'rar/ *vt* frame

emotivo /emo'tʃivu/ *a* emotional

empa|car /īpa'kar/ *vi* <*cavalo*> baulk; <*negociações etc*> grind to a halt; <*orador*> dry up

empacotar /īpako'tar/ *vt* pack up; (*pôr em pacotes*) packet

empa|da /ē'pada/ *f* pie; ~dão *m* (large) pie

empalhar /īpa'ʎar/ *vt* stuff

empalidecer /īpalide'ser/ *vi* turn pale

empanar¹ /ēpa'nar/ vt tarnish, dull

empanar² /ēpa'nar/ vt cook in batter <carne etc>

empanturrar /ĩpãtu'xar/ vt stuff; ~-se vpr stuff o.s. (de with)

empapar /ĩpa'par/ vt soak

empa|tar /ẽpa'tar/ vt draw <jogo> □ vi <times> draw; <corredores> tie; ~te m (em jogo) draw; (em corrida, votação) tie; (em xadrez, fig) stalemate

empatia /ẽpa'tʃia/ f empathy

empecilho /ẽpe'siʎu/ m hindrance

empenar /ẽpe'nar/ vt/i warp

empe|nhar /ẽpe'ɲar/ vt (penhorar) pawn; (prometer) pledge; ~nhar-se vpr do one's utmost (em to); ~nho /e/ m (compromisso) pledge; (diligência) effort, commitment

emperrar /ĩpe'xar/ vt make stick □ vi stick

emperti|gado /ĩpertʃi'gadu/ a upright; ~gar-se vpr stand up straight

empilhar /ĩpi'ʎar/ vt pile up

empi|nado /ĩpi'nadu/ a erect; (ingreme) sheer, steep; <nariz> turned-up; (fig) stuck-up; ~nar vt stand upright; fly <pipa>; tip up <copo>

empírico /ẽ'piriku/ a empirical

emplacar /ĩpla'kar/ vt notch up <pontos, sucessos, anos>; license <carro>

emplastro /ĩ'plastru/ m surgical plaster; ~ de nicotina nicotine patch

empobre|cer /ĩpobre'ser/ vt impoverish; ~cimento m impoverishment

empoleirar /ĩpole'rar/ vt perch; ~-se vpr perch

empol|gação /ĩpowga'sãw/ f fascination; ~gante a fascinating; ~gar vt fascinate

empossar /ĩpo'sar/ vt swear in

empreen|dedor /ẽpriẽde'dor/ a enterprising □ m entrepreneur; ~der vt undertake; ~dimento m undertaking

empre|gada /ĩpre'gada/ f (doméstica) maid; ~gado m employee; ~gador m employer; ~gar vt employ; ~gar-se vpr get a job; ~gatício a vínculo ~gatício contract of employment; ~go /e/ m (trabalho) job; (uso) use; ~guismo m patronage

emprei|tada /ĩprej'tada/ f commission, contract; (empreendimento) venture; ~teira f contractor, firm of contractors; ~teiro m contractor

empre|sa /ĩ'preza/ f company; ~sariado m business community; ~sarial (pl ~sariais) a business; ~sário m businessman; (de cantor etc) manager

empres|tado /ĩpres'tadu/ a on loan; pedir ~tado (ask to) borrow; tomar ~tado borrow; ~tar vt lend

empréstimo /ĩ'prestʃimu/ m loan

empur|rão /ĩpu'xãw/ m push; ~rar vt push

emular /emu'lar/ vt emulate

enamorado /enamo'radu/ a (apaixonado) in love

encabeçar /ĩkabe'sar/ vt head

encabu|lado /ĩkabu'ladu/ a shy; ~lar vt embarrass; ~lar-se vpr be shy

encadear /ĩkade'ar/ vt chain ou link together

encader|nação /ĩkaderna'sãw/ f binding; ~nado a bound; (com capa dura) hardback; ~nar vt bind

encai|xar /ĩka'ʃar/ vt/i fit; ~xe m (cavidade) socket; (juntura) joint

encalço /ĩ'kawsu/ m pursuit; no ~ de in pursuit of

encalhar /ĩka'ʎar/ vi <barco> run aground; (fig) get bogged down; <mercadoria> not sell; (fam: ficar solteiro) be left on the shelf

encaminhar /ĩkami'ɲar/ vt (dirigir) steer, direct; (remeter) pass on; set in motion <processo>; ~-se vpr set out

encana|dor /ĩkana'dor/ m plumber; ~mento m plumbing

encan|tador /ĩkãta'dor/ a enchanting; ~tamento m enchantment; ~tar vt enchant; ~to m charm

encaraco|lado /ĩkarako'ladu/ a curly; ~lar vt curl; ~lar-se vpr curl up

encarar /ĩka'rar/ vt confront, face

encarcerar /ĩkarse'rar/ vt imprison

encardido /ĩkar'dʒidu/ a grimy

encarecidamente /ĩkaresida'mẽtʃi/ adv insistently

encargo /ĩ'kargu/ m task, responsibility

encar|nação /ĩkarna'sãw/ f (do espírito) incarnation; (de um personagem) embodiment; ~nar vt embody; play <papel>

encarre|gado /ĩkaxe'gadu/ a in charge (de of) □ m person in charge; (de operários) foreman; ~gado de negócios chargé d'affaires; ~gar vt ~gar alg de put s.o. in charge of; ~gar-se de undertake to

encarte /ĩ'kartʃi/ m insert

ence|nação /ĩsena'sãw/ f (de peça) production; (fingimento) playacting; ~nar vt put on □ vi put it on

ence|radeira /ĩsera'dera/ f floor polisher; ~rar vt wax

encer|rado /ĩse'xadu/ a closed; ~ramento m close; ~rar vt close; ~rar-se vpr close

encharcar /ĩʃar'kar/ vt soak

en|chente /ẽ'ʃẽtʃi/ f flood; ~cher vt fill; (fam) annoy □ (fam) vi be annoying; ~cher-se vpr fill up; (fam: fartar-se) get fed up (de with)

enciclopédia /ēsiklo'pɛdʒia/ f encyclo-
paedia

enco|berto /īko'bɛrtu/ a <céu, tem-
po> overcast; ~brir vt cover up □ vi
<tempo> become overcast

encolher /īko'ʎer/ vt shrug
<ombros>; pull up <pernas>; shrink
<roupa> □ vi <roupa> shrink; ~-se
vpr (de medo) shrink; (de frio) huddle;
(espremer-se) squeeze up

encomen|da /īko'mēda/ f order; de
ou sob ~da to order; ~dar vt order
(a from)

encon|trão /īkõ'trãw/ m bump; (em-
purrão) shove; ~trar vt (achar) find;
(ver) meet; ~trar com meet; ~trar-
se vpr (ver-se) meet; (estar) be; ~tro
m meeting; (mil) encounter; ir ao
~tro de go to meet; (fig) meet; ir
de ~tro a run into; (fig) go against

encorajar /īkora'ʒar/ vt encourage

encor|pado /īkor'padu/ a stocky;
<vinho> full-bodied; ~par vt/i fill
out

encos|ta /ī'kɔsta/ f slope; ~tar vt
(apoiar) lean; park <carro>; leave on
the latch <porta>; (pôr de lado) put
aside □ vi <carro> pull in; ~tar-se
vpr lean; ~to /o/ m back

encra|vado /īkra'vadu/ a <unha,
pêlo> ingrowing; ~var vt stick

encren|ca /ī'krēka/ f fix, jam; pl
trouble; ~car vt get into trouble
<pessoa>; complicate <situação> □
vi <situação> get complicated;
<carro> break down; ~car-se vpr
<pessoa> get into trouble; ~queiro
m troublemaker

encres|pado /īkres'padu/ a <mar>
choppy; ~par vt frizz <cabelo>;
~par-se vpr <cabelo> go frizzy;
<mar> get choppy

encruzilhada /īkruzi'ʎada/ f crossroads

encurralar /īkuxa'lar/ vt hem in, pen
in

encurtar /īkur'tar/ vt shorten

endere|çar /īdere'sar/ vt address;
~ço /e/ m address

endinheirado /īdʒiɲe'radu/ a well-
off

endireitar /īdʒirej'tar/ vt straighten;
~-se vpr straighten up

endivi|dado /īdʒivi'dadu/ a in debt;
~dar vt put into debt; ~dar-se vpr
get into debt

endoidecer /īdojde'ser/ vi get mad

endos|sar /īdo'sar/ vt endorse; ~so
/o/ m endorsement

endurecer /īdure'ser/ vt/i harden

ener|gético /ener'ʒɛtʃiku/ a energy;
~gia/ʒia/ f energy

enérgico /e'nɛrʒiku/ a vigorous;
<remédio, discurso> powerful

enevoado /enevu'adu/ a (com névoa)
misty; (com nuvens) cloudy

enfarte /ī'fartʃi/ m heart attack

ênfase /'ēfazi/ f emphasis; dar ~ a
emphasize

enfático /ē'fatʃiku/ a emphatic

enfatizar /ēfatʃi'zar/ vt emphasize

enfei|tar /īfej'tar/ vt decorate; ~tar-
se vpr dress up; ~te m decoration

enfeitiçar /īfejtʃi'sar/ vt bewitch

enfer|magem /īfer'maʒē/ f nursing;
~maria f ward; ~meira f nurse;
~meiro m male nurse; ~midade f
illness; ~mo a sick □ m patient

enferru|jado /īfexu'ʒadu/ a rusty;
~jar vt/i rust

enfezado /īfe'zadu/ a bad-tempered

enfiar /ī'fiar/ vt put; slip on <roupa>;
thread <agulha>; string <pérolas>

enfileirar /īfilej'rar/ vt line up; ~-se
vpr line up

enfim /ē'fĩ/ adv (finalmente) finally;
(resumindo) anyway

enfo|car /īfo'kar/ vt tackle; ~que m
approach

enfor|camento /īforka'mētu/ m
hanging; ~car vt hang; ~car-se vpr
hang o.s.

enfraquecer /īfrake'ser/ vt/i weaken

enfrentar /īfrē'tar/ vt face

enfumaçado /īfuma'sadu/ a smoky

enfurecer /īfure'ser/ vt infuriate; ~-
se vpr get furious

enga|jamento /īgaʒa'mētu/ m
commitment; ~jado a committed;
~jar-se vpr get involved (em in)

engalfinhar-se /īgawfi'ɲarsi/ vpr
grapple

enga|nado /īga'nadu/ a (errado)
mistaken; ~nar vt deceive; cheat on
<marido, esposa>; stave off <fome>;
~nar-se vpr be mistaken; ~no m
(erro) mistake; (desonestidade) deception

engarra|famento /īgaxafa'mētu/ m
traffic jam; ~far vt bottle <vinho
etc>; block <trânsito>

engas|gar /īgaz'gar/ vt choke □ vi
choke; <motor> backfire; ~go m
choking

engastar /īgaʃ'tar/ vt set <jóias>

engatar /īga'tar/ vt hitch <reboque
etc> (a to); engage <marcha>

engatinhar /īgatʃi'ɲar/ vi crawl;
(fig) start out

engave|tamento /īgaveta'mētu/ m
pile-up; ~tar vt shelve

engelhar /īʒe'ʎar/ vi (pele) wrinkle

enge|nharia /īʒeɲa'ria/ f engineer-
ing; ~nheiro m engineer; ~nho /e/
m (de pessoa) ingenuity; (de açúcar)
sugar mill; (máquina) device;
~nhoca /ɔ/ f gadget; ~nhoso a ingenious

engessar /ĩʒe'sar/ vt put in plaster

engodo /ĩ'godu/ m lure

engolir /ĩgo'lir/ vt/i swallow; ~ em seco gulp

engomar /ĩgo'mar/ vt press; (com goma) starch

engordar /ĩgor'dar/ vt make fat; fatten <animais> □ vi <pessoa> put on weight; <comida> be fattening

engraçado /ĩgra'sadu/ a funny

engradado /ĩgra'dadu/ m crate

engravidar /ĩgravi'dar/ vt make pregnant □ vi get pregnant

engraxar /ĩgra'ʃar/ vt polish

engrejnado /ĩgre'nadu/ a <carro> in gear; ~nagem f gear; (fig) mechanism; ~nar vt put into gear <carro>; strike up <conversa>; ~nar-se vpr mesh; (fig) <pessoas> get on

engrossar /ĩgro'sar/ vt thicken; raise <voz> □ vi thicken; <pessoa> turn nasty

enguia /ẽ'gia/ f eel

enguijçar /ẽgi'sar/ vi break down; ~ço m breakdown

enigma /e'nigima/ m enigma; ~mático a enigmatic

enjaular /ĩʒaw'lar/ vt cage

enjojar /ĩʒo'ar/ vt sicken □ vi, ~ar-se vpr get sick (de of); ~ativo a <comida> sickly; <livro etc> boring

enjôo /ĩ'ʒou/ m sickness

enlameado /ĩlami'adu/ a muddy

enlatado /ĩla'tadu/ a tinned, canned; ~s m pl tinned foods

enlejvar /ẽle'var/ vt enthral; ~vo /e/ m rapture

enlouquecer /ĩloke'ser/ vt drive mad □ vi go mad

enluarado /ĩlua'radu/ a moonlit

enorjme /e'nɔrmi/ a enormous; ~midade f enormity

enquadrar /ĩkwa'drar/ vt fit □ vi, ~-se vpr fit in

enquanto /ĩ'kwãtu/ conj while; ~ isso meanwhile; por ~ for the time being

enquête /ã'ketʃi/ f survey

enraivecer /ĩxajve'ser/ vt enrage

enredo /ẽ'redu/ m plot

enrijecer /ĩxiʒe'ser/ vt stiffen; ~-se vpr stiffen

enrique|cer /ĩxike'ser/ vt (dar dinheiro a) make rich; (fig) enrich □ vi get rich; ~cimento m enrichment

enro|lado /ĩxo'ladu/ a complicated; ~lar vt (envolver) roll up; (complicar) complicate; (enganar) cheat; ~lar-se vpr roll up; (confundir-se) get mixed up

enroscar /ĩxos'kar/ vt twist

enrouquecer /ĩxoke'ser/ vi go hoarse

enrugar /ĩxu'gar/ vt wrinkle <pele, tecido>; furrow <testa>

enrustido /ĩxus'tʃidu/ a repressed

ensaboar /ĩsabo'ar/ vt soap

ensajar /ĩsaj'ar/ vt (provar) try out; (repetir) rehearse; ~o m (prova) test; (repetição) rehearsal; (escrito) essay

ensangüentado /ĩsãgwẽ'tadu/ a bloody, bloodstained

enseada /ĩsi'ada/ f inlet

ensebado /ĩse'badu/ a greasy

ensimesmado /ĩsimez'madu/ a lost in thought

ensi|nar /ẽsi'nar/ vt/i teach (aco a alg s.o. sth); ~nar alg a nadar teach s.o. to swim; ~no m teaching; (em geral) education

ensolarado /ĩsola'radu/ a sunny

enso|pado /ĩso'padu/ a soaked □ m stew; ~par vt soak

ensurdecedor /ĩsurdese'dor/ a deafening; ~cer vt deafen □ vi go deaf

entabular /ĩtabu'lar/ vt open, start

entalar /ĩta'lar/ vt wedge, jam; (em apertos) get; ~-se vpr get wedged, get jammed; (em apertos) get caught up

entalhar /ĩta'ʎar/ vt carve

entanto /ĩ'tãtu/ m no ~ however

então /ĩ'tãw/ adv then; (nesse caso) so

entardecer /ĩtarde'ser/ m sunset

ente /'ẽtʃi/ m being

entejada /ẽtʃi'ada/ f stepdaughter; ~do m stepson

entedi|ante /ĩtedʒi'ãtʃi/ a boring; ~ar vt bore; ~ar-se vpr get bored

entenjder /ĩtẽ'der/ vt understand; ~der-se vpr (dar-se bem) get on (com with); dar a ~der give to understand; ~der de futebol know about football; ~dimento m understanding

enternecedor /ĩternese'dor/ a touching

entejrar /ĩte'xar/ vt bury; ~ro /e/ m burial; (cerimônia) funeral

entidade /ẽtʃi'dadʒi/ f entity; (órgão) body

entornar /ĩtor'nar/ vt tip over, spill

entorpejcente /ĩtorpe'sẽtʃi/ m drug, narcotic; ~cer vt numb

entortar /ĩtor'tar/ vt make crooked

entrada /ẽ'trada/ f entry; (onde se entra) entrance; (bilhete) ticket; (prato) starter; (pagamento) deposit; pl (no cabelo) receding hairline; dar ~ a enter; ~ proibida no entry

entranhas /ĩ'tranas/ f pl entrails

entrar /ẽ'trar/ vi go/come in; ~ com enter <dados>; put in <dinheiro>; ~ em detalhes go into details; ~ em vigor come into force

entravar /ẽtra'var/ vt hamper

entre /'ẽtri/ prep between; (em meio a) among

entreaberto /ẽtria'bertu/ a half-open

entrecortar /ẽtrikor'tar/ vt intersperse; (cruzar) intersect

entre|ga /ĩ'trɛga/ f delivery; (rendição) surrender; ~ga a domicílio home delivery; ~gar vt hand over; deliver <mercadorias, cartas>; hand in <caderno, trabalho escolar>; ~gar-se vpr give o.s. up (a to); ~gue pp de entregar

entrelaçar /ẽtrela'sar/ vt intertwine; clasp <mãos>

entrelinhas /ẽtri'liɲas/ f pl ler nas ~ read between the lines

entremear /ẽtrimi'ar/ vt intersperse

entreolhar-se /ẽtrio'ʎarsi/ vpr look at one another

entretanto /ẽtre'tãtu/ conj however

entre|tenimento /ẽtreteni'mẽtu/ m entertainment; ~ter vt entertain

entrever /ẽtre'ver/ vt glimpse

entrevis|ta /ẽtre'vista/ f interview; ~tador m interviewer; ~tar vt interview

entristecer /ĩtriste'ser/ vt sadden □ vi be saddened (com by)

entroncamento /ĩtrõka'mẽtu/ m junction

entrosar /ĩtro'zar/ vt/i integrate

entu|lhar /ĩtu'ʎar/ vt cram (de with); ~lho m rubble

entupir /ĩtu'pir/ vt block; ~pir-se vpr get blocked; (de comida) stuff o.s. (de with)

enturmar-se /ĩtur'marsi/ vpr mix in, fit in

entusias|mar /ĩtuziaz'mar/ vt fill with enthusiasm; ~mar-se vpr get enthusiastic (com about); ~mo m enthusiasm; ~ta m/f enthusiast □ a enthusiastic

entusiástico /ĩtuzi'astʃiku/ a enthusiastic

enumerar /enume'rar/ vt enumerate

envelope /ẽve'lɔpi/ m envelope

envelhecer /ĩveʎe'ser/ vt/i age

envenenar /ĩvene'nar/ vt poison; (fam) soup up <carro>

envergadura /ĩverga'dura/ f wing-span; (fig) scale

envergo|nhado /ĩvergo'ɲadu/ a ashamed; (constrangido) embarrassed; ~nhar vt disgrace; (constranger) embarrass; ~nhar-se vpr be ashamed; (acanhar-se) get embarrassed

envernizar /ĩverni'zar/ vt varnish

en|viado /ẽvi'adu/ m envoy; ~viar vt send; ~vio m (ato) sending; (remessa) consignment

envidraçar /ĩvidra'sar/ vt glaze

enviesado /ĩvie'zadu/ a (não vertical) slanting; (torto) crooked

envol|vente /ĩvow'vẽtʃi/ a compelling, gripping; ~ver vt (embrulhar) wrap; (enredar) involve; ~ver-se vpr (enrolar-se) wrap o.s.; (enredar-se) get involved; ~vimento m involvement

enxada /ẽ'ʃada/ f hoe

enxaguar /ẽʃa'gwar/ vt rinse

enxame /ẽ'ʃami/ m swarm

enxaqueca /ẽʃa'keka/ f migraine

enxergar /ĩʃer'gar/ vt/i see

enxer|tar /ĩʃer'tar/ vt graft; ~to /e/ m graft

enxotar /ĩʃo'tar/ vt drive away

enxofre /ẽ'ʃofri/ m sulphur

enxo|val /ẽʃo'vaw/ (pl ~vais) m (de noiva) trousseau; (de bebê) layette

enxugar /ĩʃu'gar/ vt dry; ~-se vpr dry o.s.

enxurrada /ĩʃu'xada/ f torrent; (fig) flood

enxuto /ĩ'ʃutu/ a dry; <corpo> shapely

enzima /ẽ'zima/ f enzyme

epicentro /epi'sẽtru/ m epicentre

épico /'ɛpiku/ a epic

epidemia /epide'mia/ f epidemic

epi|lepsia /epilep'sia/ f epilepsy; ~léptico a & m epileptic

epílogo /e'pilogu/ m epilogue

episódio /epi'zɔdʒiu/ m episode

epitáfio /epi'tafiu/ m epitaph

época /'ɛpoka/ f time; (da história) age, period; fazer ~ make history; móveis da ~ period furniture

epopéia /epo'pɛja/ f epic

equação /ekwa'sãw/ f equation

equador /ekwa'dor/ m equator; o Equador Ecuador

equatori|al /ekwatori'aw/ (pl ~ais) a equatorial; ~ano a & m Ecuadorian

equilibrar /ekili'brar/ vt balance; ~-se vpr balance

equilíbrio /eki'libriu/ m balance

equipa /e'kipa/ (Port) f team

equi|pamento /ekipa'mẽtu/ m equipment; ~par vt equip

equiparar /ekipa'rar/ vt equate (com with); ~-se vpr compare (a with)

equipe /e'kipi/ f team

equitação /ekita'sãw/ f riding

equiva|lência /ekiva'lẽsia/ f equivalence; ~lente a equivalent; ~ler vi be equivalent (a to)

equivo|cado /ekivo'kadu/ a mistaken; ~car-se vpr make a mistake

equívoco /e'kivoku/ a equivocal □ m mistake

era /'ɛra/ f era

erário /e'rariu/ m exchequer

ereção /ere'sãw/ f erection

eremita /ere'mita/ m/f hermit

ereto /e'rɛtu/ a erect

erguer /er'ger/ vt raise; erect <monumento etc>; ~-se vpr rise

eri|çado /eri'sadu/ a bristling; ~çar-se vpr bristle

ermo /'ermu/ a deserted □ m wilderness

erosão /ero'zãw/ f erosion

erótico /e'rɔtʃiku/ a erotic

erotismo /ero'tʃizmu/ m eroticism

er|rado /e'xadu/ a wrong; ~rante a wandering; ~rar vt (não fazer certo) get wrong; miss <alvo> □ vi (enganar-se) be wrong; (vaguear) wander; ~ro /e/ m mistake; fazer um ~ro make a mistake; ~rôneo a erroneous

erudi|ção /erudʒi'sãw/ f learning; ~to a learned; <música> classical □ m scholar

erupção /erup'sãw/ f (vulcânica) eruption; (cutânea) rash

erva /'ɛrva/ f herb; ~ daninha weed; ~-doce f aniseed

ervilha /er'viʎa/ f pea

esban|jador /izbãʒa'dor/ a extravagant □ m spendthrift; ~jar vt squander; burst with <saúde, imaginação, energia etc>

esbar|rão /izba'xãw/ m bump; ~rar vi ~rar com ou em bump into <pessoa>; come up against <problema>

esbelto /iz'bewtu/ a svelte

esbo|çar /izbo'sar/ vt sketch <desenho etc>; outline <plano etc>; ~çar um sorriso give a hint of a smile; ~ço /o/ m (desenho) sketch; (plano) outline; (de um sorriso) hint

esbofetear /izbofetʃi'ar/ vt slap

esborrachar /izboxa'ʃar/ vt squash; ~-se vpr crash

esbravejar /izbrave'ʒar/ vi rant, rail

esbura|cado /izbura'kadu/ a full of holes; ~car vt make holes in

esbugalhado /izbuga'ʎadu/ a <olhos> bulging; ~lhar-se vpr <olhos> pop out

escabroso /iska'brozu/ a (fig) difficult, tough

escada /is'kada/ f (dentro de casa) stairs; (na rua) steps; (de mão) ladder; ~ de incêndio fire escape; ~ rolante escalator; ~ria f staircase

escafan|drista /iskafã'drista/ m/f diver; ~dro m diving suit

escala /is'kala/ f scale; (de navio) port of call; (de avião) stopover; fazer ~ stop over; sem ~ <vôo> non-stop

esca|lada /iska'lada/ f (fig) escalation; ~lão m echelon, level; ~lar vt (subir a) scale; (designar) select

escaldar /iskaw'dar/ vt scald; blanch <vegetais>

escalfar /iskaw'far/ vt poach

escalonar /iskalo'nar/ vt schedule <pagamento>

escama /is'kama/ f scale

escanca|rado /iskãka'radu/ a wide open; ~rar vt open wide

escandalizar /iskãdali'zar/ vt scandalize; ~-se vpr be scandalized

escândalo /is'kãdalu/ m (vexame) scandal; (tumulto) fuss, uproar; fazer um ~ make a scene

escandaloso /iskãda'lozu/ a (chocante) scandalous; (espalhafatoso) outrageous, loud

Escandinávia /iskãdʒi'navia/ f Scandinavia

escandinavo /iskãdʒi'navu/ a & m Scandinavian

escanga|lhado /iskãga'ʎadu/ a broken; ~lhar vt break up; ~lhar-se vpr fall to pieces; ~lhar-se de rir split one's sides laughing

escaninho /iska'niɲu/ m pigeonhole

escanteio /iskã'teju/ m corner

esca|pada /iska'pada/ f (fuga) escape; (aventura) escapade; ~pamento m exhaust; o copo ~pou-me das mãos the glass slipped out of my hands; o nome me ~pa the name escapes me; ~par vi ~par de boa have a narrow escape; ~patória f way out; (desculpa) pretext; ~pe m escape; (de carro etc) exhaust; ~pulir vi escape (de from)

escaramuça /iskara'musa/ f skirmish

escaravelho /iskara'veʎu/ m beetle

escarcéu /iskar'sɛw/ m uproar, fuss

escarlate /iskar'latʃi/ a scarlet

escarnecer /iskarne'ser/ vt mock

escárnio /is'karniu/ m derision

escarpado /iskar'padu/ a steep

escarrado /iska'xadu/ m ele é o pai ~ he's the spitting image of his father

escarro /is'kaxu/ m phlegm

escas|sear /iskasi'ar/ vi run short; ~sez f shortage; ~so a (raro) scarce; (ralo) scant

esca|vadeira /iskava'dera/ f digger; ~var vt excavate

esclare|cer /isklare'ser/ vt explain <fatos>; enlighten <pessoa>; ~cer-se vpr <fato> be explained; <pessoa> find out; ~cimento m (de pessoas) enlightenment; (de fatos) explanation

esclerosado /isklero'zadu/ a senile

escoar /isko'ar/ vt/i drain

esco|cês /isko'ses/ a (f ~cesa) Scottish □ m (f ~cesa) Scot

Escócia /is'kɔsia/ f Scotland

esco|la /is'kɔla/ f school; ~la de samba samba school; ~lar a school □ m/f schoolchild; ~laridade f schooling

esco|lha /is'koʎa/ f choice; ~lher vt choose

escol|ta /is'kɔwta/ f escort; ~tar vt
escort

escombros /is'kõbrus/ m pl debris

escon|de-esconde /iskõdʒis'kõdʒi/ m
hide-and-seek; ~der vt hide; ~der-se
vpr hide; ~derijo m hiding place; (de
bandidos) hideout; ~didas f pl às
~didas secretly

esco|ra /is'kɔra/ f prop; ~rar vt prop
up; ~rar-se vpr <argumento etc> be
based (em on)

escore /is'kɔri/ m score

escória /is'kɔria/ f scum, dross

escori|ação /iskoria'sãw/ f graze,
abrasion; ~ar vt graze

escorpião /iskorpi'ãw/ m scorpion;
Escorpião Scorpio

escorredor /iskoxe'dor/ m drainer

escorrega /isko'xega/ m slide

escorre|gador /iskoxega'dor/ m
slide; ~gão m slip; ~gar vi slip

escor|rer /isko'xer/ vt drain □ vi
trickle; ~rido a <cabelo> straight

escoteiro /isko'teru/ m boy scout

escotilha /isko'tʃiʎa/ f hatch

esco|va /is'kova/ f brush; fazer ~va
no cabelo blow-dry one's hair; ~va
de dentes toothbrush; ~var vt
brush; ~vinha f cabelo à ~vinha
crew-cut

escra|chado /iskra'ʃadu/ (fam) a
outspoken; ~char (fam) vt tell off

escra|vatura /iskrava'tura/ f slavery;
~vidão f slavery; ~vizar vt enslave;
~vo m slave

escre|vente /iskre'vẽtʃi/ m/f clerk;
~ver vt/i write

escri|ta /is'krita/ f writing; ~to pp de
escrever □ a written; por ~to in
writing; ~tor m writer; ~tório m
office; (numa casa) study

escritu|ra /iskri'tura/ f (a Bíblia)
scripture; (contrato) deed; ~ração f
bookkeeping; ~rar vt keep, write up
<contas>; draw up <documento>

escri|vaninha /iskriva'niɲa/ f bur-
eau, writing desk; ~vão m (f ~vã)
registrar

escrúpulo /is'krupulu/ m scruple

escrupuloso /iskrupu'lozu/ a scrupulous

escrutínio /iskru'tʃiniu/ m ballot

escu|dar /isku'dar/ vt shield; ~deria
f team; ~do m shield; (moeda) escudo

escula|chado /iskula'ʃadu/ (fam) a
sloppy; ~char (fam) vt mess up
<coisa>; tell off <pessoa>; ~cho
(fam) m (bagunça) mess; (bronca)
telling-off

escul|pir /iskuw'pir/ vt sculpt; ~tor
m sculptor; ~tura f sculpture; ~tu-
ral (pl ~turais) a statuesque

escuma /is'kuma/ f scum; ~deira f
skimmer

escuna /is'kuna/ f schooner

escu|ras/is'kuras/ f pl às ~ras in the
dark; ~recer vt darken □ vi get dark;
~ridão f darkness; ~ro a & m dark

escuso /is'kuzu/ a shady

escu|ta /is'kuta/ f listening; estar à
~ta be listening; ~ta telefônica
phone tapping; ~tar vt (perceber)
hear; (prestar atenção a) listen to □
vi (poder ouvir) hear; (prestar atenção) listen

esdrúxulo /iz'druʃulu/ a weird

esfacelar /isfase'lar/ vt wreck

esfalfar /isfaw'far/ vt wear out; ~-se
vpr get worn out

esfaquear /isfaki'ar/ vt stab

esfarelar /isfare'lar/ vt crumble; ~-
se vpr crumble

esfarrapado /isfaxa'padu/ a ragged;
<desculpa> lame

es|fera /is'fɛra/ f sphere; ~férico a
spherical

esferográfi|co /isfero'grafiku/ a ca-
neta ~ca ball-point pen

esfiapar /isfia'par/ vt fray; ~-se vpr
fray

esfinge /is'fĩʒi/ f sphinx

esfolar /isfo'lar/ vt skin; (fig) overcharge

esfomeado /isfomi'adu/ a starving,
famished

esfor|çar-se /isfor'sarsi/ vpr make an
effort; ~ço /o/ m effort; fazer ~ço
make an effort

esfre|gaço /isfre'gasu/ m smear;
~gar vt rub; (para limpar) scrub

esfriar /isfri'ar/ vt cool □ vi cool
(down); (sentir frio) get cold

esfumaçado /isfuma'sadu/ a smoky

esfuziante /isfuzi'ãtʃi/ a irrepress-
ible, exuberant

esganar /izga'nar/ vt throttle

esganiçado /izgani'sadu/ a shrill

esgarçar /izgar'sar/ vt/i fray

esgo|tado /izgo'tadu/ a exhausted;
<estoque, lotação> sold out;
~tamento m exhaustion; ~tamento
nervoso nervous breakdown; ~tar
vt exhaust; (gastar) use up; ~tar-se
vpr <pessoa> become exhausted;
<estoque, lotação> sell out; <recursos,
provisões> run out; ~to /o/ m drain;
(de detritos) sewer

esgri|ma /iz'grima/ f fencing; ~mir
vt brandish □ vi fence; ~mista m/f
fencer

esgrouvinhado /izgrovi'ɲadu/ a
tousled, dishevelled

esgueirar-se /izge'rarsi/ vpr slip,
sneak

esguelha /iz'geʎa/ f de ~ askew;
<olhar> askance

esgui|char /izgi'ʃar/ vt/i spurt,
squirt; ~cho m jet, spurt

esguio /iz'gio/ a slender

eslavo /iz'lavu/ a Slavic □ m Slav

esmaecer /izmaj'ser/ vi fade

esma|gador /izmaga'dor/ a <vitória, maioria> overwhelming; <provas> incontrovertible; ~gar vt crush

esmalte /iz'mawtʃi/ m enamel; ~ de unhas nail varnish

esmeralda /izme'rawda/ f emerald

esme|rar-se /izme'rarsi/ vpr take great care (em over); ~ro /e/ m great care

esmigalhar /izmiga'ʎar/ vt crumble <pão etc>; shatter <vidro, copo>; ~-se vpr <pão etc> crumble; <vidro, copo> shatter

esmiuçar /izmiu'sar/ vt examine in detail

esmo /'ezmu/ m a ~ <escolher> at random; <andar> aimlessly; <falar> nonsense

esmola /iz'mɔla/ f donation; pl charity

esmorecer /izmore'ser/ vi flag

esmurrar /izmu'xar/ vt punch

esno|bar /izno'bar/ vt snub □ vi be snobbish; ~be /iz'nɔbi/ a snobbish □ m/f snob; ~bismo m snobbishness

esotérico /ezo'tɛriku/ a esoteric

espa|çar /ispa'sar/ vt space out; make less frequent <visitas, consultas etc>; ~cial (pl ~ciais) a space; ~ço m space; <cultural etc> venue; ~çoso /o/ a spacious

espada /is'pada/ f sword; pl (naipe) spades; ~chim m swordsman

espádua /is'padua/ f shoulder blade

espaguete /ispa'getʃi/ m spaghetti

espaire|cer /ispajre'ser/ vt amuse □ vi relax; (dar uma volta) go for a walk; ~cimento m recreation

espaldar /ispaw'dar/ m back

espalhafato /ispaʎa'fatu/ m (barulho) fuss, uproar; (de roupa etc) extravagance; ~so /o/ a (barulhento) noisy, rowdy; (ostentoso) extravagant

espalhar /ispa'ʎar/ vt scatter; spread <notícia, terror etc>; shed <luz>; ~-se vpr spread; <pessoas> spread out

espa|nador /ispana'dor/ m feather duster; ~nar vt dust

espan|camento /ispãka'mẽtu/ m beating; ~car vt beat up

Espanha /is'paɲa/ f Spain

espa|nhol /ispa'ɲɔw/ (pl ~nhóis) a (f ~nhola) Spanish □ m (f ~nhola) Spaniard; (língua) Spanish; os ~nhóis the Spanish

espan|talho /ispã'taʎu/ m scarecrow; ~tar vt (admirar) amaze; (assustar) scare; (afugentar) drive away; ~tar-se vpr (admirar-se) be amazed; (assustar-se) get scared; ~to m (susto) fright; (admiração) amazement; ~toso /o/ a amazing

esparadrapo /ispara'drapu/ m sticking plaster

espargo /is'pargu/ (Port) m asparagus

esparramar /ispaxa'mar/ vt scatter; ~-se vpr be scattered, spread

espartano /ispar'tanu/ a spartan

espartilho /ispar'tʃiʎu/ m corset

espas|mo /is'pazmu/ m spasm; ~módico a spasmodic

espatifar /ispatʃi'far/ vt smash; ~-se vpr smash; <carro, avião> crash

especi|al /ispesi'aw/ (pl ~ais) a special; ~alidade f speciality; ~alista m/f specialist

especiali|zado /ispesiali'zadu/ a specialized; <mão-de-obra> skilled; ~zar-se vpr specialize (em in)

especiaria /ispesia'ria/ f spice

espécie /is'pɛsi/ f sort, kind; (de animais) species

especifi|cação /ispesifika'sãw/ f specification; ~car vt specify

específico /ispe'sifiku/ a specific

espécime /is'pɛsimi/ m specimen

espectador /ispekta'dor/ m (de TV) viewer; (de jogo, espetáculo) spectator; (de acidente etc) onlooker

espectro /is'pɛktru/ m (fantasma) spectre; (de cores) spectrum

especu|lação /ispekula'sãw/ f speculation; ~lador m speculator; ~lar vi speculate (sobre on); ~lativo a speculative

espe|lhar /ispe'ʎar/ vt mirror; ~lhar-se vpr be mirrored; ~lho /e/ m mirror; ~lho retrovisor rearview mirror

espelunca /ispe'lũka/ (fam) f dive

espera /is'pera/ f wait; à ~ de waiting for

esperan|ça /ispe'rãsa/ f hope; ~çoso /o/ a hopeful

esperar /ispe'rar/ vt (aguardar) wait for; (desejar) hope for; (contar com) expect □ vi wait (por for); fazer alg ~ keep s.o. waiting; espero que ele venha I hope that he comes; espero que sim/não I hope so/not

esperma /is'pɛrma/ m sperm

espernear /isperni'ar/ vi kick; (fig: reclamar) kick up

esper|talhão /isperta'ʎãw/ m (f ~talhona) wise guy; ~teza /e/ f cleverness; (uma) clever move; ~to /e/ a clever

espes|so /is'pesu/ a thick; ~sura f thickness

espeta|cular /ispetaku'lar/ a spectacular; ~táculo m (no teatro etc) show; (cena impressionante) spectacle; ~taculoso /o/ a spectacular

espe|tar /ispe'tar/ vt (cravar) stick; (furar) skewer; ~tar-se vpr (cravarse) stick; (ferir-se) prick o.s.; ~tinho *m* skewer; (*de carne etc*) kebab; ∼to /e/ *m* spit

espevitado /iʃpevi'tadu/ *a* cheeky

espezinhar /iʃpezi'ɲar/ *vt* walk all over

espi|a /is'pia/ *m/f* spy; ∼ão *m* (*f* ∼ã) spy; ∼ada *f* peep; ∼ar *vt* (*observar*) spy on; (*aguardar*) watch for □ *vi* peer, peep

espicaçar /ispika'sar/ *vt* goad <*pessoa*>; excite <*imaginação, curiosidade*>

espichar /ispi'ʃar/ *vt* stretch □ *vi* shoot up; ∼-se *vpr* stretch out

espiga /is'piga/ *f* (*de trigo etc*) ear; (*de milho*) cob

espina|fração /ispinafra'sãw/ (*fam*) *f* telling-off; ∼frar (*fam*) *vt* tell off; ∼fre *m* spinach

espingarda /ispĩ'garda/ *f* rifle, shotgun

espinha /is'piɲa/ *f* (*de peixe*) bone; (*na pele*) spot; ∼ dorsal spine

espinho /is'piɲu/ *m* thorn; ∼so /o/ *a* thorny; (*fig*) difficult, tough

espio|nagem /ispio'naʒẽ/ *f* espionage, spying; ∼nar *vt* spy on □ *vi* spy

espiral /ispi'raw/ (*pl* ∼rais) *a* & *f* spiral

espirita /is'pirita/ *a* & *m/f* spiritualist

espiritismo /ispiri'tʃizmu/ *m* spiritualism

espírito /is'piritu/ *m* spirit; (*graça*) wit

espiritu|al /ispiritu'aw/ (*pl* ∼ais) *a* spiritual; ∼oso /o/ *a* witty

espir|rar /ispi'xar/ *vi* spurt □ *vi* <*pessoa*> sneeze; <*lama, tinta etc*> spatter; <*fogo, lenha, fritura etc*> spit; ∼ro *m* sneeze

esplêndido /is'plẽdʒidu/ *a* splendid

esplendor /isplẽ'dor/ *m* splendour

espoleta /ispo'leta/ *f* fuse

espoliar /ispoli'ar/ *vt* plunder, pillage

espólio /is'poliu/ *m* (*herdado*) estate; (*roubado*) spoils

espon|ja /is'põʒa/ *f* sponge; ∼joso /o/ *a* spongy

espon|taneidade /ispõtanej'dadʒi/ *f* spontaneity; ∼tâneo *a* spontaneous

espora /is'pora/ *f* spur

esporádico /ispo'radʒiku/ *a* sporadic

esporear /ispori'ar/ *vt* spur on

espor|te /is'portʃi/ *m* sport □ *a invar* <*roupa*> casual; carro ∼te sports car; ∼tista *m/f* sportsman (*f* -woman); ∼tiva *f* sense of humour; ∼tivo *a* sporting

espo|sa /is'poza/ *f* wife; ∼so *m* husband

espregui|çadeira /ispregisa'dera/ *f* (*tipo cadeira*) deckchair; (*tipo cama*) sun lounger; ∼çar-se *vpr* stretch

esprei|ta /is'prejta/ *f* ficar à ∼ta lie in wait; ∼tar *vt* stalk <*caça, vítima*>; spy on <*vizinhos, inimigos etc*>; look out for <*ocasião*> □ *vi* peep, spy

espre|medor /ispreme'dor/ *m* squeezer; ∼mer *vt* squeeze; wring out <*roupa*>; squash <*pessoa*>; ∼mer-se *vpr* squeeze up

espu|ma /is'puma/ *f* foam; ∼ma de borracha foam rubber; ∼mante *a* <*vinho*> sparkling; ∼mar *vi* foam, froth

espúrio /is'puriu/ *a* spurious

esqua|dra /is'kwadra/ *f* squad; ∼dra de polícia (*Port*) police station; ∼drão *m* squadron; ∼dria *f* doors and windows; ∼drinhar *vt* explore; ∼dro *m* set square

esqualidez /iskwali'deʃ/ *f* squalor

esquálido /is'kwalidu/ *a* squalid

esquartejar /iskwarte'ʒar/ *vt* chop up

esque|cer /iske'ser/ *vt/i* forget; ∼cer-se de forget; ∼cido *a* forgotten; (*com memória fraca*) forgetful; ∼cimento *m* oblivion; (*memória fraca*) forgetfulness

esque|lético /iske'letʃiku/ *a* skinny, skeleton-like; ∼leto /e/ *m* skeleton

esque|ma /is'kema/ *m* outline, draft; (*operação*) scheme; ∼ma de segurança security operation; ∼mático *a* schematic

esquentar /iskẽ'tar/ *vt* warm up □ *vi* warm up; <*roupa*> be warm; ∼-se *vpr* get annoyed; ∼ a cabeça (*fam*) get worked up

esquer|da /is'kerda/ *f* left; à ∼da (*posição*) on the left; (*direção*) to the left; ∼dista *a* left-wing □ *m/f* left-winger; ∼do /e/ *a* left

esqui /is'ki/ *m* ski; (*esporte*) skiing; ∼ aquático water skiing; ∼ador *m* skier; ∼ar *vi* ski

esquilo /is'kilu/ *m* squirrel

esquina /is'kina/ *f* corner

esquisi|tice /iskizi'tʃisi/ *f* strangeness; (*uma*) strange thing; ∼to *a* strange

esqui|var-se /iski'varsi/ *vpr* dodge out of the way; ∼var-se de dodge; ∼vo *a* elusive; <*pessoa*> aloof, antisocial

esquizofrenia /iskizofre'nia/ *f* schizophrenia; ∼frênico *a* & *m* schizophrenic

es|sa /'esa/ *pron* that (one); ∼sa é boa that's a good one; ∼sa não come off it; por ∼sas e outras for these and other reasons; ∼se /e/ *a* that; *pl* those; (*fam: este*) this; *pl* these □ *pron* that one; *pl* those; (*fam: este*) this one; *pl* these

essência /e'sẽsia/ *f* essence

essenci|al /esési'aw/ (*pl* ~ais) *a* essential; o ~al what is essential

estabele|cer /istabele'ser/ *vt* establish; ~cer-se *vpr* establish o.s.; ~cimento *m* establishment

estabili|dade /istabili'dadʒi/ *f* stability; ~zar *vt* stabilize; ~zar-se *vpr* stabilize

estábulo /is'tabulu/ *m* cowshed

estaca /is'taka/ *f* stake; (*de barraca*) peg; voltar à ~ zero go back to square one

estação /ista'sãw/ *f* (*do ano*) season; (*ferroviária etc*) station; ~ balneária seaside resort

estacar /ista'kar/ *vi* stop short

estacio|namento /istasiona'mẽtu/ *m* (*ação*) parking; (*lugar*) car park, (*Amer*) parking lot; ~nar *vt/i* park

estada /is'tada/ *f*, estadia /ista'dʒia/ *f* stay

estádio /is'tadʒiu/ *m* stadium

esta|dista /ista'dʒista/ *m/f* statesman (*f*-woman); ~do *m* state; ~do civil marital status; ~do de espírito state of mind; Estados Unidos da América United States of America; Estado-Maior *m* Staff; ~dual (*pl* ~duais) *a* state

esta|fa /is'tafa/ *f* exhaustion; ~fante *a* exhausting; ~far *vt* tire out; ~far-se *vpr* get tired out

estagi|ar /istaʒi'ar/ *vi* do a traineeship; ~ário *m* trainee

estágio /is'taʒiu/ *m* traineeship

estag|nado /istag'nadu/ *a* stagnant; ~nar *vi* stagnate

estalagem /ista'laʒẽ/ *f* inn

estalar /ista'lar/ *vt* (*quebrar*) crack; (*fazer barulho com*) click □ *vi* crack

estaleiro /ista'leru/ *m* shipyard

estalo /is'talu/ *m* crack; (*de dedos, língua*) click; me deu um ~ it clicked (in my mind)

estam|pa /is'tãpa/ *f* print; ~pado *a* <*tecido*> patterned □ *m* (*desenho*) pattern; (*tecido*) print; ~par *vt* print

estampido /istã'pidu/ *m* bang

estancar /istã'kar/ *vt* staunch; ~-se *vpr* dry up

estância /is'tãsia/ *f* ~ hidromineral spa

estandarte /istã'dartʃi/ *m* banner

estanho /is'taɲu/ *m* tin

estanque /is'tãki/ *a* watertight

estante /is'tãtʃi/ *f* bookcase

estapafúrdio /istapa'furdʒiu/ *a* weird, odd

estar /is'tar/ *vi* be; (~ em casa) be in; está chovendo, (*Port*) está a chover it's raining; ~ com have; ~ com calor/sono be hot/sleepy; ~ para terminar be about to finish; ele não está para ninguém he's not avail-

able to see anyone; o trabalho está por terminar the work is yet to be finished

estardalhaço /istarda'ʎasu/ *m* (*barulho*) fuss; (*ostentação*) extravagance

estarre|cedor /istaxese'dor/ *a* horrifying; ~cer *vt* horrify; ~cer-se *vpr* be horrified

esta|tal /ista'taw/ (*pl* ~tais) *a* stateowned □ *f* state company

estate|lado /istate'ladu/ *a* sprawling; ~lar *vt* knock down; ~lar-se *vpr* go sprawling

estático /is'tatʃiku/ *a* static

estatísti|ca /ista'tʃistʃika/ *f* statistics; ~co *a* statistical

estati|zação /istatʃiza'sãw/ *f* nationalization; ~zar *vt* nationalize

estátua /is'tatua/ *f* statue

estatueta /istatu'eta/ *f* statuette

estatura /ista'tura/ *f* stature

estatuto /ista'tutu/ *m* statute

está|vel /is'tavew/ (*pl* ~veis) *a* stable

este¹ /'estʃi/ *m a invar & m* east

este² /'estʃi/ *a* this; *pl* these □ *pron* this one; *pl* these; (*mencionado por último*) the latter

esteio /is'teju/ *m* prop; (*fig*) mainstay

esteira /is'tera/ *f* (*tapete*) mat; (*rastro*) wake

estelionato /istelio'natu/ *m* fraud

estender /istẽ'der/ *vt* (*desdobrar*) spread out; (*alongar*) stretch; (*ampliar*) extend; hold out <*mão*>; hang out <*roupa*>; roll out <*massa*>; draw out <*conversa*>; ~-se *vpr* (*deitar-se*) stretch out; (*ir longe*) stretch, extend; ~-se sobre dwell on

esteno|datilógrafo /istenodatʃi'lografu/ *m* shorthand typist; ~grafia *f* shorthand

estepe /is'tepi/ *m* spare wheel

esterco /is'terku/ *m* dung

estéreo /is'teriu/ *a invar* stereo

estere|otipado /isteriotʃi'padu/ *a* stereotypical; ~ótipo *m* stereotype

esté|ril /is'teriw/ (*pl* ~reis) *a* sterile

esterili|dade /isterili'dadʒi/ *f* sterility; ~zar *vt* sterilize

esterli|no /ister'lino/ *a* libra ~na pound sterling

esteróide /iste'rɔjdʒi/ *m* steroid

estepe /is'tepi/ spare wheel

estética /is'tɛtʃika/ *f* aesthetics

esteticista /istetʃi'sista/ *m/f* beautician

estético /is'tɛtʃiku/ *a* aesthetic

estetoscópio /istetos'kɔpiu/ *m* stethoscope

estiagem /istʃi'aʒẽ/ *f* dry spell

estibordo /istʃi'bordu/ *m* starboard

esti|cada /istʃi'kada/ *f* dar uma ~cada go on; ~car *vt* stretch □ (*fam*) *vi* go on; ~car-se *vpr* stretch out

estigma /is'tʃigima/ m stigma;
~tizar vt brand (de as)

estilha|çar /istʃiʎa'sar/ vt shatter;
~çar-se vpr shatter; ~ço m shard,
fragment

estilingue /istʃi'lĩgi/ m catapult

estilis|mo /istʃi'lizmu/ m fashion
design; ~ta m/f fashion designer

esti|lístico /istʃi'listʃiku/ a stylistic;
~lizar vt stylize; ~lo m style; ~lo
de vida lifestyle

esti|ma /es'tʃima/ f esteem; ~mação
f estimation; cachorro de ~mação
pet dog; ~mado a esteemed; Estima-
do Senhor Dear Sir; ~mar vt value
<bens, jóias etc> (em at); estimate
<valor, preço etc> (em at); think
highly of <pessoa>; ~mativa f estimate

estimu|lante /istʃimu'lãtʃi/ a stimu-
lating □ m stimulant; ~lar vt stimulate; (incentivar) encourage

estímulo /is'tʃimulu/ m stimulus; (incentivo) incentive

estio /is'tʃiu/ m summer

estipu|lação /istʃipula'sãw/ f stipu-
lation; ~lar vt stipulate

estirar /istʃi'rar/ vt stretch; ~-se vpr
stretch

estirpe /is'tʃirpi/ f stock, line

estivador /istʃiva'dor/ m docker

estocada /isto'kada/ f thrust

estocar /isto'kar/ vt stock □ vi stock
up

Estocolmo /isto'kɔwmu/ f Stockholm

esto|far /isto'far/ vt upholster
<móveis>; ~fo /o/ m upholstery

estóico /is'tɔjku/ a & m stoic

estojo /is'toʒu/ m case

estômago /is'tomagu/ m stomach

Estônia /is'tonia/ f Estonia

estonte|ante /istõtʃi'ãtʃi/ a stunning,
mind-boggling; ~ar vt stun

estopim /isto'pĩ/ m fuse; (fig) flash-
point

estoque /is'tɔki/ m stock

estore /is'tɔri/ m blind

estória /is'tɔria/ f story

estor|var /istor'var/ vt hinder; ob-
struct <entrada, trânsito>; ~vo /o/
m hindrance

estou|rado /isto'radu/ a <pessoa>
explosive; ~rar vi <bomba, escândalo, pessoa> blow up; <pneu> burst;
<guerra> break out; <moda, cantor
etc> make it big; ~ro m (de bomba,
moda etc) explosion; (de pessoa) outburst; (de pneu) blowout; (de guerra)
outbreak

estrábico /is'trabiku/ a <olhos>
squinty; <pessoa> squint-eyed

estrabismo /istra'bizmu/ m squint

estraçalhar /istrasa'ʎar/ vt tear to
pieces

estrada /is'trada/ f road; ~ de ferro
railway, (Amer) railroad; ~ de
rodagem highway; ~ de terra dirt
road

estrado /is'tradu/ m podium; (de
cama) base

estraga-prazeres /istragapra'zeris/
m/f invar spoilsport

estragão /istra'gãw/ m tarragon

estra|gar /istra'gar/ vt (tornar desa-
gradável) spoil; (acabar com) ruin □
vi (quebrar) break; (apodrecer) go off;
~go m damage; pl damage; (da guerra, do tempo) ravages

estrangeiro /istrã'ʒeru/ a foreign □
m foreigner; do ~ from abroad; para
o/no ~ abroad

estrangular /istrãgu'lar/ vt strangle

estra|nhar /istra'ɲar/ vt (achar es-
tranho) find strange; (não se adaptar
a) find it hard to get used to; (não se
sentir à vontade com) be shy with;
~nhar que find it strange that; estou te ~nhando that's not like you;
não é de se ~nhar it's not
surprising; ~nheza /e/ f (esquisitice)
strangeness; (surpresa) surprise;
~nho a strange □ m stranger

estratagema /istrata'ʒema/ m stratagem

estraté|gia /istra'teʒia/ f strategy;
~gico a strategic

estrato /is'tratu/ m (camada)
stratum; (nuvem) stratus; ~sfera f
stratosphere

estre|ante /istri'ãtʃi/ a new □ m/f
newcomer; ~ar vt première <peça,
filme>; embark on <carreira>; wear
for the first time <roupa> □ vi <pes-
soa> make one's début; <filme, peça>
open

estrebaria /istreba'ria/ f stable

estréia /is'treja/ f (de pessoa) début;
(de filme, peça) première

estrei|tar /istrej'tar/ vt narrow; take
in <vestido>; make closer <relações,
laços> □ vi narrow; ~tar-se vpr <re-
lações> become closer; ~to a narrow;
<relações, laços> close; <saia>
straight □ m strait

estre|la /is'trela/ f star; ~lado a
<céu> starry; <ovo> fried; ~lado
por <filme etc> starring; ~la-do-
mar (pl ~las-do-mar) f starfish;
~lar vt fry <ovo>; star in <filme,
peça>; ~lato m stardom; ~lismo m
star quality

estreme|cer /istreme'ser/ vt shake;
strain <relações, amizade> □ vi shudder; <relações, amizade> become
strained; ~cimento m shudder; (de
relações, amizade) strain

estrepar-se /istre'parsi/ (fam) vpr
come a cropper

estrépito /is'trɛpitu/ m noise; com ~ noisily

estrepitoso /istrepi'tozu/ a noisy; <sucesso etc> resounding

estressante /istre'sãtʃi/ a stressful; ~sar vt stress; ~se /ɛ/ m stress

estria /is'tria/ f streak; (no corpo) stretch mark

estribeira /istri'bera/ f stirrup; perder as ~s lose control

estribilho /istri'biʎu/ m chorus

estribo /is'tribu/ m stirrup

estridente /istri'dẽtʃi/ a strident

estripulia /istripu'lia/ f antic

estrito /is'tritu/ a strict

estrofe /is'trɔfi/ f stanza, verse

estrogonofe /istrogo'nɔfi/ m stroganoff

estrógeno /is'trɔʒenu/ m oestrogen

estrondo /is'trõdu/ m crash; ~doso /o/ a loud; <aplausos> thunderous; <sucesso, fracasso> resounding

estropiar /istropi'ar/ vt cripple <pessoa>; mangle <palavras>

estrume /is'trumi/ m manure

estrutura /istru'tura/ f structure; ~ral (pl ~rais) a structural; ~rar vt structure

estuário /istu'ariu/ m estuary

estudante /istu'dãtʃi/ m/f student; ~til (pl ~tis) a student

estudar /istu'dar/ vt/i study

estúdio /is'tudʒiu/ m studio

estudioso /istudʒi'ozu/ a studious □ m scholar; ~do m study

estufa /is'tufa/ f (para plantas) greenhouse; (de aquecimento) stove; ~do m stew

estupefato /istupe'fatu/ a dumbfounded

estupendo /iste'pẽdu/ a stupendous

estupidez /istupi'des/ f (grosseria) rudeness; (uma) rude thing; (burrice) stupidity; (uma) stupid thing

estúpido /is'tupidu/ a (grosso) rude, coarse; (burro) stupid □ m lout

estupor /istu'por/ m stupor

estuprador /istupra'dor/ m rapist; ~prar vt rape; ~pro m rape

esturricar /istuxi'kar/ vt parch

esvair-se /izva'irsi/ vpr fade; ~ em sangue bleed to death

esvaziar /izvazi'ar/ vt empty; ~se vpr empty

esverdeado /izverdʒi'adu/ a greenish

esvoaçante /izvoa'sãtʃi/ a <cabelo> fly-away; ~çar vi flutter

eta /'eta/ int what a

etapa /e'tapa/ f stage; (de corrida, turnê etc) leg

etário /e'tariu/ a age

éter /'ɛter/ m ether

etéreo /e'tɛriu/ a ethereal

eternidade /eterni'dadʒi/ f eternity; ~no /ɛ/ a eternal

ética /'ɛtʃika/ f ethics; ~co a ethical

etimologia /etʃimolo'ʒia/ f etymology; ~lógico a etymological

etíope /e'tʃiopi/ a & m/f Ethiopian

Etiópia /etʃi'ɔpia/ f Ethiopia

etiqueta /etʃi'keta/ f (rótulo) label; (bons modos) etiquette; ~tar vt label

étnico /'ɛtʃiniku/ a ethnic

eu /ew/ pron I □ m self; mais alto do que ~ taller than me; sou ~ it's me

EUA m pl USA

eucalipto /ewka'liptu/ m eucalyptus

eufemismo /ewfe'mizmu/ m euphemism

euforia /ewfo'ria/ f euphoria

Europa /ew'rɔpa/ f Europe

europeu /ewro'pew/ a & m (f ~péia) European

eutanásia /ewta'nazia/ f euthanasia

evacuação /evakua'sãw/ f evacuation; ~ar vt evacuate

evadir /eva'dʒir/ vt evade; ~se vpr escape (de from)

evangelho /evã'ʒeʎu/ m gospel; ~gélico a evangelical

evaporar /evapo'rar/ vt evaporate; ~se vpr evaporate

evasão /eva'zãw/ f escape; (fiscal etc) evasion; ~são escolar truancy; ~siva f excuse; ~sivo a evasive

evento /e'vẽtu/ m event; ~tual (pl ~tuais) a possible; ~tualidade f eventuality

evidência /evi'dẽsia/ f evidence; ~ciar /evidẽsi'ar/ vt show up; ~ciar-se vpr show up; ~te a obvious, evident

evitar /evi'tar/ vt avoid; ~tar de beber avoid drinking; ~tável (pl ~táveis) a avoidable

evocar /evo'kar/ vt call to mind, evoke <passado etc>; call up <espíritos etc>

evolução /evolu'sãw/ f evolution; ~ir vi evolve

exacerbar /ezaser'bar/ vt exacerbate

exagerado /ezaʒe'radu/ a over the top; ~rar vt (atribuir proporções irreais a) exaggerate; (fazer em excesso) overdo □ vi (ao falar) exaggerate; (exceder-se) overdo it; ~ro /e/ m exaggeration

exalação /ezala'sãw/ f fume; (agradável) scent; ~lar vt give off <perfume etc>

exaltação /ezawta'sãw/ f (excitação) agitation; (engrandecimento) exaltation; ~tar vt (excitar) agitate; (enfurecer) infuriate; (louvar) exalt; ~tar-se vpr (excitar-se) get agitated; (enfurecer-se) get furious

exame /e'zami/ m examination; (na escola) exam(ination); ~me de sangue blood test; ~minar *vt* examine

exaspe|ração /ezaspera'sãw/ *f* exasperation; ~rar *vt* exasperate; ~rar-se *vpr* get exasperated

exa|tidão /ezatʃi'dãw/ *f* exactness; ~to *a* exact

exaurir /ezaw'rir/ *vt* exhaust; ~-se *vpr* become exhausted

exaus|tivo /ezaws'tʃivu/ *a* <*estudo*> exhaustive; <*trabalho*> exhausting; ~to *a* exhausted

exceção /ese'sãw/ *f* exception; abrir ~ make an exception; com ~ de with the exception of

exce|dente /ese'dẽtʃi/ *a & m* excess, surplus; ~der *vt* exceed; ~der-se *vpr* overdo it

exce|lência /ese'lẽsia/ *f* excellence; (*tratamento*) excellency; ~lente *a* excellent

excentricidade /esẽtrisi'dadʒi/ *f* eccentricity

excêntrico /e'sẽtriku/ *a & m* eccentric

exce|pção /i∫se'sãw/ (*Port*) *f veja* exceção; ~cional (*pl* ~cionais) *a* exceptional; (*deficiente*) handicapped

exces|sivo /ese'sivu/ *a* excessive; ~so /ɛ/ *m* excess; ~so de bagagem excess baggage; ~so de velocidade speeding

exce|to /e'sɛtu/ *prep* except; ~tuar *vt* except

exci|tação /esita'sãw/ *f* excitement; ~tante *a* exciting; ~tar *vt* excite; ~tar-se *vpr* get excited

excla|mação /isklama'sãw/ *f* exclamation; ~mar *vt/i* exclaim

exclu|ir /isklu'ir/ *vt* exclude; ~são *f* exclusion; com ~são de with the exclusion of; ~sividade *f* exclusive rights; com ~sividade exclusively; ~sivo *a* exclusive; ~so *a* excluded

excomungar /iskomũ'gar/ *vt* excommunicate

excremento /iskre'mẽtu/ *m* excrement

excur|são /iskur'sãw/ *f* excursion; (*a pé*) hike, walk; ~sionista *m/f* day-tripper; (*a pé*) hiker, walker

execu|ção /ezeku'sãw/ *f* execution; ~tante *m/f* performer; ~tar *vt* carry out <*ordem, plano etc*>; perform <*papel, música*>; execute <*preso, criminoso etc*>; ~tivo *a & m* executive

exem|plar /ezẽ'plar/ *a* exemplary □ *m* (*de espécie*) example; (*de livro, jornal etc*) copy; ~plificar *vt* exemplify

exemplo /e'zẽplu/ *m* example; a ~ de following the example of; por ~ for example; dar o ~ set an example

exequível /eze'kwivew/ (*pl* ~veis) *a* feasible

exer|cer /ezer'ser/ *vt* exercise; exert <*pressão, influência*>; carry on <*profissão*>; ~cício *m* exercise; (*mil*) drill; (*de profissão*) practice; (*financeiro*) financial year; ~citar *vt* exercise; practise <*ofício*>; ~citar-se *vpr* train

exército /e'zɛrsitu/ *m* army

exibição /ezibi'sãw/ *f* (*de filme, passaporte etc*) showing; (*de talento, força, ostentação*) show

exibicionis|mo /ezibisio'nizmu/ *m* exhibitionism; ~ta *a & m/f* exhibitionist

exi|bido /ezi'bidu/ *a* <*pessoa*> pretentious □ *m* show-off; ~bir *vt* show; (*ostentar*) show off; ~bir-se *vpr* (*ostentar-se*) show off

exi|gência /ezi'ʒẽsia/ *f* demand; ~gente *a* demanding; ~gir *vt* demand

exíguo /e'zigwu/ *a* (*muito pequeno*) tiny; (*escasso*) minimal

exi|lado /ezi'lado/ *a* exiled □ *m* exile; ~lar *vt* exile; ~lar-se *vpr* go into exile

exílio /e'ziliu/ *m* exile

exímio /e'zimiu/ *a* distinguished

eximir /ezi'mir/ *vt* exempt (from); ~-se de get out of

exis|tência /ezis'tẽsia/ *f* existence; ~tencial (*pl* ~tenciais) *a* existential; ~tente *a* existing; ~tir *vi* exist

êxito /'ezitu/ *m* success; (*música, filme etc*) hit; ter ~ succeed

êxodo /'ezodu/ *m* exodus

exonerar /ezone'rar/ *vt* (*de cargo*) dismiss, sack; ~-se *vpr* resign

exorbitante /ezorbi'tãtʃi/ *a* exorbitant

exor|cismo /ezor'sizmu/ *m* exorcism; ~cista *m/f* exorcist; ~cizar *vt* exorcize

exótico /e'zɔtʃiku/ *a* exotic

expan|dir /ispã'dʒir/ *vt* spread; ~dir-se *vpr* spread; <*pessoa*> open up; ~dir-se sobre expand upon; ~são *f* expansion; ~sivo *a* expansive, open

expatri|ado /ispatri'ado/ *a & m* expatriate; ~ar-se *vpr* leave one's country

expectativa /ispekta'tʃiva/ *f* expectation; na ~ de expecting; estar na ~ wait to see what happens; ~ de vida life expectancy

expedi|ção /espedʒi'sãw/ *f* (*de encomendas, cartas*) dispatch; (*de passaporte, diploma etc*) issue; (*viagem*) expedition

expediente /ispedʒi'ẽtʃi/ *a* <*pessoa*> resourceful □ *m* (*horário*) working hours; (*meios*) expedient; meio ~ part-time

expe|dir /ispe'dʒir/ vt dispatch <encomendas, cartas>; issue <passaporte, diploma>; ~dito a prompt, quick
expelir /ispe'lir/ vt expel
experi|ência /isperi'ẽsia/ f experience; (teste, tentativa) experiment; ~ente a experienced
experimen|tação /isperimẽta'sãw/ f experimentation; ~tado a experienced; ~tar vt (provar) try out; try on <roupa>; try <comida>; (sentir, viver) experience; ~to m experiment
expi|ar /espi'ar/ vt atone for; ~atório a bode ~atório scapegoat
expi|ração /espira'sãw/ f (vencimento) expiry; (de ar) exhalation; ~rar vt exhale □ vi (morrer, vencer) expire; (expelir ar) breath out, exhale
expli|cação /isplika'sãw/ f explanation; ~car vt explain; ~car-se vpr explain o.s.; ~cável (pl ~cáveis) a explainable
explicitar /isplisi'tar/ vt set out
explícito /is'plisitu/ a explicit
explodir /isplo'dʒir/ vi explode □ vi explode; <ator etc> make it big
explo|ração /isplora'sãw/ f (uso, abuso) exploitation; (pesquisa) exploration; ~rar vt (tirar proveito de) exploit; (esquadrinhar) explore
explo|são /isplo'zãw/ f explosion; ~sivo a & m explosive
expor /es'por/ vt (sujeitar, arriscar) expose a to); display <mercadorias>; exhibit <obras de arte>; (explicar) expound; ~ a vida risk one's life; ~-se vpr expose o.s. (a to)
expor|tação /isporta'sãw/ f export; ~tador a exporting □ m exporter; ~tadora f export company; ~tar vt export
exposi|ção /ispozi'sãw/ f (de arte etc) exhibition; (de mercadorias) display; (de filme fotográfico) exposure; (explicação) exposition; ~tor m exhibitor
exposto /is'postu/ a exposed (a to); <mercadoria, obra de arte> on display
expres|são /ispre'sãw/ f expression; ~sar vt express; ~sar-se vpr express o.s.; ~sivo a expressive; <número, quantia> significant; ~so /ɛ/ a & m express
exprimir /ispri'mir/ vt express; ~-se vpr express o.s.
expropriar /ispropri'ar/ vt expropriate
expul|são /ispuw'sãw/ f expulsion; (de jogador) sending off; ~sar vt (de escola, partido, país etc) expel; (de clube, bar, festa etc) throw out; (de jogo) send off; ~so pp de expulsar
expur|gar /ispur'gar/ vt purge; expurgate <livro>; ~go m purge
êxtase /'estazi/ f ecstasy

extasiado /istazi'adu/ a ecstatic
exten|são /istẽ'sãw/ f extension; (tamanho, alcance, duração) extent; (de terreno) expanse; ~sivo a extensive; ~so a extensive; por ~so in full
extenu|ante /istenu'ãtʃi/ a wearing, tiring; ~ar vt tire out; ~ar-se vpr tire o.s. out
exterior /isteri'or/ a outside, exterior; <aparência> outward; <relações, comércio etc> foreign □ m outside, exterior; (de pessoa) exterior; o ~ (outros países) abroad; para o/no ~ abroad
exter|minar /istermi'nar/ vt exterminate; ~mínio m extermination
exter|nar /ister'nar/ vt show; ~na /ɛ/ f location shot; ~no /ɛ/ a external; <dívida etc> foreign □ m day-pupil
extin|ção /istʃĩ'sãw/ f extinction; ~guir vt extinguish <fogo>; wipe out <dívida, animal, povo>; ~guir-se vpr <fogo, luz> go out; <animal, planta> become extinct; ~to a extinct; <organização, pessoa> defunct; ~tor m fire extinguisher
extirpar /istʃir'par/ vt remove <tumor etc>; uproot <ervas daninhas>; eradicate <abusos>
extor|quir /istor'kir/ vt extort; ~são f extortion
extra /'ɛstra/ a & m/f extra; horas ~s overtime
extração /istra'sãw/ f extraction; (da loteria) draw
extraconju|gal /istrakõʒu'gaw/ (pl ~gais) a extramarital
extracurricular /istrakuxiku'lar/ a extracurricular
extradi|ção /istradʒi'sãw/ f extradition; ~tar vt extradite
extrair /istra'ir/ vt extract; draw <números da loteria>
extrajudici|al /estraʒudʒisi'aw/ (pl ~ais) a out-of-court; ~almente adv out of court
extraordinário /istraordʒi'nariu/ a extraordinary
extrapolar /istrapo'lar/ vt (exceder) overstep; (calcular) extrapolate □ vi overstep the mark, go too far
extra-sensori|al /istrasẽsori'aw/ (pl ~ais) a extra-sensory
extraterrestre /estrate'xestri/ a & m extraterrestrial
extrato /is'trato/ m extract; (de conta) statement
extrava|gância /istrava'gãsia/ f extravagance; ~gante a extravagant
extravasar /istrava'zar/ vt release, let out <emoções, sentimentos> □ vi overflow
extra|viado /istravi'adu/ a lost; ~viar vt lose, mislay <papéis, car-

ta>; lead astray <*pessoa*>; embezzle <*dinheiro*>; ~**viar-se** *vpr* go astray; <*carta*> get lost; ~**vio** *m* (*perda*) misplacement; (*de dinheiro*) embezzlement

extremidade /estremi'dadʒi/ *f* end; (*do corpo*) extremity; ~**mismo** *m* extremism; ~**mista** *a* & *m/f* extremist; ~**mo** /e/ *a* & *m* extreme; **o Extremo Oriente** the Far East; ~**moso** /o/ *a* doting

extrovertido /istrover'tʃido/ *a* & *m* extrovert

exuberância /ezube'rãsia/ *f* exuberance; ~**rante** *a* exuberant

exultar /ezuw'tar/ *vi* exult

exumar /ezu'mar/ *vt* exhume <*cadáver*>; dig up <*documentos etc*>

F

fã /fã/ *m/f* fan

fábrica /'fabrika/ *f* factory

fabricação /fabrika'sãw/ *f* manufacture; ~**cante** *m/f* manufacturer; ~**car** *vt* manufacture; (*inventar*) fabricate

fábula /'fabula/ *f* fable; (*fam: dinheirão*) fortune

fabuloso /fabu'lozu/ *a* fabulous

faca /'faka/ *f* knife; ~**da** *f* knife blow; **dar uma** ~**da em** (*fig*) get some money off

façanha /fa'saɲa/ *f* feat

facção /fak'sãw/ *f* faction

face /'fasi/ *f* face; (*do rosto*) cheek; ~**ta** /e/ *f* facet

fachada /fa'ʃada/ *f* façade

facho /'faʃu/ *m* beam

facial /fasi'aw/ (*pl* ~**ais**) *a* facial

fácil /'fasiw/ (*pl* ~**ceis**) *a* easy; <*pessoa*> easy-going

facilidade /fasili'dadʒi/ *f* ease; (*talento*) facility; ~**tar** *vt* facilitate

fã-clube /fã'klubi/ *m* fan club

fac-símile /fak'simili/ *m* facsimile; (*fax*) fax

fact- (*Port*) *veja* **fat-**

faculdade /fakuw'dadʒi/ *f* (*mental etc*) faculty; (*escola*) university, (*Amer*) college; **fazer** ~**dade** go to university; ~**tativo** *a* optional

fada /'fada/ *f* fairy; ~**do** *a* destined, doomed; ~-**madrinha** (*pl* ~**s-madrinhas**) *f* fairy godmother

fadiga /fa'dʒiga/ *f* fatigue

fadista /fa'dʒista/ *m/f* fado singer; ~**do** *m* fado

fagote /fa'gɔtʃi/ *m* bassoon

fagulha /fa'guʎa/ *f* spark

faia /'faja/ *f* beech

faisão /faj'zãw/ *m* pheasant

faísca /fa'iska/ *f* spark

faiscante /fajs'kãtʃi/ *a* sparkling; ~**car** *vi* spark; (*cintilar*) sparkle

faixa /'faʃa/ *f* strip; (*cinto*) sash; (*em karaté, judô*) belt; (*da estrada*) lane; (*para pedestres*) zebra crossing, (*Amer*) crosswalk; (*atadura*) bandage; (*de disco*) track; ~ **etária** age group

fajuto /fa'ʒutu/ (*fam*) *a* fake

fala /'fala/ *f* speech

falácia /fa'lasia/ *f* fallacy

falado /fa'ladu/ *a* <*língua*> spoken; <*caso, pessoa*> talked about; ~**lante** *a* talkative; ~**lar** *vt/i* speak; (*dizer*) say; ~**lar com tal** to; ~**lar de ou em** talk about; **por** ~**lar em** speaking of; **sem** ~**lar** not to mention; ~**lou!** (*fam*) OK!; ~**latório** *m* (*boatos*) talk; (*som de vozes*) talking

falaz /fa'las/ *a* fallacious

falcão /faw'kãw/ *m* falcon

falcatrua /fawka'trua/ *f* swindle

falecer /fale'ser/ *vi* die, pass away; ~**cido** *a* & *m* deceased; ~**cimento** *m* death

falência /fa'lẽsia/ *f* bankruptcy; **ir à** ~ go bankrupt

falésia /fa'lɛzia/ *f* cliff

falha /'faʎa/ *f* fault; (*omissão*) failure; ~**lhar** *vi* fail; ~**lho** *a* faulty

fálico /'faliku/ *a* phallic

falido /fa'lidu/ *a* & *m* bankrupt; ~**lir** *vi* go bankrupt; ~**lível** (*pl* ~**líveis**) *a* fallible

falo /'falu/ *m* phallus

falsário /faw'sariu/ *m* forger; ~**sear** *vt* falsify; ~**sete** *m* falsetto; ~**sidade** *f* falseness; (*mentira*) falsehood

falsificação /fawsifika'sãw/ *f* forgery; ~**cador** *m* forger; ~**car** *vt* falsify; forge <*documentos, notas*>

falso /'fawsu/ *a* false

falta /'fawta/ *f* lack; (*em futebol*) foul; **em** ~**ta at** fault; **por** ~**ta de** for lack of; **sem** ~**ta** without fail; **fazer** ~**ta** be needed; **sentir a** ~**ta de** miss; ~**tar** *vi* be missing; <*aluno*> be absent; ~**tam dois dias para** it's two days until; **me** ~**ta ...** I don't have ...; ~**tar a** miss <*aula etc*>; break <*palavra, promessa*>; ~**to a** short (**de** of)

fama /'fama/ *f* reputation; (*celebridade*) fame; ~**migerado** *a* notorious

família /fa'milia/ *f* family

familiar /famili'ar/ *a* familiar; (*de família*) family; ~**aridade** *f* familiarity; ~**arizar** *vt* familiarize; ~**arizar-se** *vpr* familiarize o.s.

faminto /fa'mĩtu/ *a* starving

famoso /fa'mozu/ *a* famous

fanático /fa'natʃiku/ *a* fanatical □ *m* fanatic

fanatismo /fana'tʃizmu/ *m* fanaticism

fanfarrão /fãfa'xãw/ *m* braggart

fanhoso /fa'ɲozu/ *a* nasal; ser ~ talk through one's nose

fanta|sia /fãta'zia/ *f* (*faculdade*) imagination; (*devaneio*) fantasy; (*roupa*) fancy dress; ~siar *vt* dream up □ *vi* fantasize; ~siar-se *vpr* dress up (de as); ~sioso /o/ *a* fanciful; <*pessoa*> imaginative; ~sista *a* imaginative

fantasma /fã'tazma/ *m* ghost; ~górico *a* ghostly

fantástico /fã'tastʃiku/ *a* fantastic

fantoche /fã'tɔʃi/ *m* puppet

faqueiro /fa'keru/ *m* canteen of cutlery

fara|ó /fara'ɔ/ *m* pharaoh; ~ônico *a* (*fig*) of epic proportions

farda /'farda/ *f* uniform; ~do *a* uniformed

fardo /'fardu/ *m* (*fig*) burden

fare|jador /fareʒa'dor/ *a* cão ~jador sniffer dog; ~jar *vt* sniff out □ *vi* sniff

farelo /fa'relu/ *m* bran; (de *pão*) crumb; (de *madeira*) sawdust

farfalhar /farfa'ʎar/ *vi* rustle

farináceo /fari'nasiu/ *a* starchy; ~s *m pl* starchy foods

farin|ge /fa'rĩʒi/ *f* pharynx; ~gite *f* pharyngitis

farinha /fa'riɲa/ *f* flour; ~ de rosca breadcrumbs

far|macêutico /farma'sewtʃiku/ *a* pharmaceutical □ *m* (*pessoa*) pharmacist; ~mácia *f* (*loja*) chemist's, (*Amer*) pharmacy; (*ciência*) pharmacy

faro /'faru/ *m* sense of smell; (*fig*) nose

faroeste /faro'estʃi/ *m* (*filme*) western; (*região*) wild west

faro|fa /fa'rɔfa/ *f* fried manioc flour; ~feiro (*fam*) *m* day-tripper

fa|rol /fa'rɔw/ (*pl* ~róis) *m* (de *carro*) headlight; (de *trânsito*) traffic light; (à *beira-mar*) lighthouse; ~rol alto full beam; ~rol baixo dipped beam; ~roleiro *a* boastful □ *m* bighead; ~rolete /e/ *m*, (*Port*) ~rolim *m* side-light; (*traseiro*) tail-light

farpa /'farpa/ *f* splinter; (de *metal*, *fig*) barb; ~do *a* arame ~do barbed wire

farra /'faxa/ (*fam*) partying; cair na ~ go out and party

farrapo /fa'xapu/ *m* rag

far|rear /faxi'ar/ (*fam*) *vi* party; ~rista (*fam*) *m/f* raver

far|sa /'farsa/ *f* (*peça*) farce; (*fingimento*) pretence; ~sante *m/f* (*brincalhão*) joker; (*pessoa sem seriedade*) unreliable character

far|tar /far'tar/ *vt* satiate; ~tar-se *vpr* (*saciar-se*) gorge o.s. (de with); (*cansar*) get fed up; ~to *a* (*abundante*) plentiful; (*cansado*) fed up (de with); ~tura *f* abundance

fascículo /fa'sikulu/ *m* instalment

fasci|nação /fasina'sãw/ *f* fascination; ~nante *a* fascinating; ~nar *vt* fascinate

fascínio /fa'siniu/ *m* fascination

fas|cismo /fa'sizmu/ *m* fascism; ~cista *a* & *m/f* fascist

fase /'fazi/ *f* phase

fa|tal /fa'taw/ (*pl* ~tais) *a* fatal; ~talismo *m* fatalism; ~talista *a* fatalistic □ *m/f* fatalist; ~talmente *adv* inevitably

fatia /fa'tʃia/ *f* slice

fatídico /fa'tʃidʒiku/ *a* fateful

fati|gante /fatʃi'gãtʃi/ *a* tiring; ~gar *vt* tire, fatigue

fato[1] /'fatu/ *m* fact; de ~ as a matter of fact, in fact; ~ consumado fait accompli

fato[2] /'fatu/ (*Port*) *m* suit

fator /fa'tor/ *m* factor

fátuo /'fatuu/ *a* fatuous

fatu|ra /fa'tura/ *f* invoice; ~ramento *m* turnover; ~rar *vt* invoice for <*encomenda*>; make <*dinheiro*>; (*fig*: *emplacar*) notch up □ *vi* (*fam*) rake it in

fauna /'fawna/ *f* fauna

fava /'fava/ *f* broad bean; mandar alg às ~s tell s.o. where to get off

favela /fa'vela/ *f* shanty town; ~do *m* shanty-dweller

favo /'favu/ *m* honeycomb

favor /fa'vor/ *m* favour; a ~ de in favour of; por ~ please; faça ~ please

favo|rável /favo'ravew/ (*pl* ~ráveis) *a* favourable; ~recer *vt* favour; ~ritismo *m* favouritism; ~rito *a* & *m* favourite

faxi|na /fa'ʃina/ *f* clean-up; ~neiro *m* cleaner

fazen|da /fa'zẽda/ *f* (de *café*, *gado etc*) farm; (*tecido*) fabric, material; (*pública*) treasury; ~deiro *m* farmer

fazer /fa'zer/ *vt* do; (*produzir*) make; ask <*pergunta*>; ~-se *vpr* (*tornar-se*) become; ~-se de make o.s. out to be; ~ anos have a birthday; ~ 20 anos be twenty; faz dois dias que ele está aqui he's been here for two days; faz dez anos que ele morreu it's ten years since he died; tanto faz it doesn't matter

faz-tudo /fas'tudu/ *m/f invar* jack of all trades

fé /fε/ *f* faith

fe|bre /'fεbri/ *f* fever; ~bre amarela yellow fever; ~bre do feno hay fever; ~bril (*pl* ~bris) *a* feverish

fe|chado /fe'ʃadu/ *a* closed; <*curva*> sharp; <*sinal*> red; <*torneira*> off; <*tempo*> overcast; <*cara*> stern; <*pessoa*> reserved; ~chadura *f* lock; ~chamento m closure; ~char vt close, shut; turn off < torneira >; do up < calça, casaco >; close < negócio >; □ vi close, shut; < sinal > go red; < tempo > cloud over; ~char à chave lock; ~char a cara frown; ~cho /e/ m fastener; ~cho ecler zip

fécula /'fɛkula/ f starch

fecun|dar /fekũ'dar/ vt fertilize; ~do a fertile

feder /fe'der/ vi stink

fede|ração /federa'sãw/ f federation; ~ral (pl ~rais) a federal; (fam) huge; ~rativo a federal

fedor /fe'dor/ m stink, stench; ~ento a stinking

feérico /feeriku/ a magical

feições /fej'sõjs/ f pl features

fei|jão /fe'ʒãw/ m bean; (coletivo) beans; ~joada f bean stew; ~joeiro m bean plant

feio /'feju/ a ugly; < palavra, situação, tempo> nasty; < olhar> dirty; ~so /o/ a plain

fei|ra /'fera/ f market; (industrial) trade fair; ~rante m/f market trader

feiti|caria /fejtʃi'sera/ f magic; ~ceira f witch; ~ceiro m wizard □ a bewitching; ~ço m spell

fei|tio /fej'tʃiu/ m (de pessoa) make-up; ~to pp de fazer □ m (ato) deed; (proeza) feat □ conj like; bem ~to por ele (it) serves him right; ~tura f making

feiúra /fej'ura/ f ugliness

feixe /'fejʃi/ m bundle

fel /fɛw/ f gall; (fig) bitterness

felicidade /felisi'dadʒi/ f happiness

felici|tações /felisita'sõjs/ f pl congratulations; ~tar vt congratulate (por on)

felino /fe'linu/ a feline

feliz /fe'lis/ a happy; ~ardo a lucky; ~mente adv fortunately

fel|pa /'fewpa/ f (de pano) nap; (penugem) down, fluff; ~pudo a fluffy

feltro /'fewtru/ m felt

fêmea /'femia/ a & f female

femi|nino /femi'ninu/ (pl ~nis) a feminine; ~nilidade f femininity; ~nino a female; < palavra> feminine; ~nismo m feminism; ~nista a & m/f feminist

fêmur /'femur/ m femur

fen|da /'fẽda/ f crack; ~der vt/i split, crack

feno /'fenu/ m hay

fenome|nal /fenome'naw/ (pl ~nais) a phenomenal

fenômeno /fe'nomenu/ m phenomenon

fera /'fɛra/ f wild beast; ficar uma ~ get really angry; ser ~ em (fam) be brilliant at

féretro /'fɛretru/ m coffin

feriado /feri'adu/ m public holiday

férias /'fɛrias/ f pl holiday(s), (Amer) vacation; de ~ on holiday; tirar ~ take a holiday

feri|da /fe'rida/ f injury; (com arma) wound; ~do a injured; (mil) wounded □ m injured person; os ~dos the injured; (mil) the wounded; ~r vt injure; (com arma) wound; (magoar) hurt

fermen|tar /fermē'tar/ vt/i ferment; ~to m yeast; (fig) ferment; ~to em pó baking powder

fe|rocidade /ferosi'dadʒi/ f ferocity; ~roz a ferocious

fer|rado /fe'xadu/ a estou ~rado (fam) I've had it; ~rado no sono fast asleep; ~radura f horseshoe; ~ragem f ironwork; pl hardware; ~ramenta f tool; (coletivo) tools; ~rão m (de abelha) sting; ~rar vt brand < gado>; shoe < cavalo>; ~rar-se (fam) come a cropper; ~reiro m blacksmith; ~renho a < partidário etc> staunch; < vontade> iron

férreo /'fɛxiu/ a iron

ferro /'fɛxu/ m iron; ~lho /o/ m bolt; ~-velho (pl ~s-velhos) m (pessoa) scrap-metal dealer; (lugar) scrap-metal yard; ~via f railway, (Amer) railroad; ~viário a railway □ m railway worker

ferrugem /fe'xuʒe/ f rust

fér|til /'fɛrtʃiw/ (pl ~teis) a fertile

fertili|dade /fertʃili'dadʒi/ f fertility; ~zante m fertilizer; ~zar vt fertilize

fer|vente /fer'vẽtʃi/ a boiling; ~ver vi boil; (de raiva) seethe; ~vilhar vi bubble; ~vilhar de swarm with; ~vor m fervour; ~vura f boiling

fes|ta /'fɛsta/ f party; (religiosa) festival; ~tejar vt/i celebrate; (acolher) fete; ~tejo /e/ m celebration; ~tim m feast; ~tival (pl ~tivais) m festival; ~tividade f festivity; ~tivo a festive

feti|che /fe'tʃiʃi/ m fetish; ~chismo m fetishism; ~chista m/f fetishist □ a fetishistic

fétido /'fɛtʃidu/ a fetid

feto[1] /'fɛtu/ m (no útero) foetus

feto[2] /'fɛtu/ (Port) m (planta) fern

feu|dal /few'daw/ (pl ~dais) a feudal; ~dalismo m feudalism

fevereiro /feve'reru/ m February

fezes /'fɛzis/ f pl faeces

fia|ção /fia'sãw/ f (eletr) wiring; (fábrica) mill

fia|do /fi'adu/ a < conversa> idle □ adv < comprar> on credit; ~dor m guarantor

fiambre /fi'ãbri/ m cooked ham

fiança /fi'ãsa/ f surety; (*jurid*) bail
fiapo /fi'apu/ m thread
fiar /fi'ar/ vt spin < *lã etc*>
fiasco /fi'asku/ m fiasco
fibra /'fibra/ f fibre
ficar /fi'kar/ vi (*tornar-se*) become; (*estar, ser*) be; (*manter-se*) stay; ~ fazendo keep (on) doing; ~ com keep; get < *impressão, vontade*>; ~ com medo get scared; ~ de fazer arrange to do; ~ para be left for; ~ bom turn out well; (*recuperar-se*) get better; ~ bem look good
ficção /fik'sãw/ f fiction; ~ção científica science fiction; ~cionista m/f fiction writer
ficha /'fiʃa/ f (*de telefone*) token; (*de jogo*) chip; (*da caixa*) ticket; (*de fichário*) file card; (*na polícia*) record; (*Port: tomada*) plug; ~chário m, (*Port*) ~cheiro m file; (*móvel*) filing cabinet
fictício /fik'tʃisiu/ a fictitious
fidalgo /fi'dalgu/ m nobleman
fide|digno /fide'dʒignu/ a trustworthy; ~lidade f fidelity
fiduciário /fidusi'ariu/ a fiduciary □ m trustee
fi|el /fi'ɛw/ (*pl* ~éis) a faithful □ m os ~éis (*na igreja*) the congregation
figa /'figa/ f talisman
fígado /'figadu/ m liver
fi|go /'figu/ m fig; ~gueira f fig tree
figu|ra /fi'gura/ f figure; (*carta de jogo*) face card; (*fam: pessoa*) character; fazer (má) ~ra make a (bad) impression; ~rado a figurative; ~rante m/f extra; ~rão m big shot; ~rar vi appear, figure; ~rativo a figurative; ~rinha f sticker; ~rino m fashion plate; (*de filme, peça*) costume design; (*fig*) model; como manda o ~rino as it should be
fila /'fila/ f line; (*de espera*) queue, (*Amer*) line; (*fileira*) row; fazer ~ queue up, (*Amer*) stand in line; ~ indiana single file
filamento /fila'mẽtu/ m filament
filante /fi'lãtʃi/ (*fam*) m/f sponger
filan|tropia /filãtro'pia/ f philanthropy; ~trópico a philanthropic; ~tropo /o/ m philanthropist
filão /fi'lãw/ m (*de ouro*) seam; (*fig*) money-spinner
filar /fi'lar/ (*fam*) vt sponge, cadge
filar|mônica /filar'monika/ f philharmonic (orchestra); ~mônico a philharmonic
filate|lia /filate'lia/ f philately; ~lista m/f philatelist
filé /fi'lɛ/ m fillet
fileira /fi'lera/ f row
filete /fi'letʃi/ m fillet
fi|lha /'fiʎa/ f daughter; ~lho m son; pl (*crianças*) children; ~lho da puta

(*chulo*) bastard, (*Amer*) son of a bitch; ~lho de criação foster child; ~lho único only child; ~lhote m (*de cão*) pup; (*de lobo etc*) cub; pl young
fili|ação /filia'sãw/ f affiliation; ~al (*pl* ~ais) a filial □ f branch
Filipinas /fili'pinas/ f pl Philippines
filipino /fili'pinu/ a & m Filipino
fil|madora /fiwma'dora/ f camcorder; ~magem f filming; ~mar vt/i film; ~me m film
fi|lologia /filolo'ʒia/ f philology; ~lólogo m philologist
filo|sofar /filozo'far/ vi philosophize; ~sofia f philosophy; ~sófico a philosophical
filósofo /fi'lozofu/ m philosopher
fil|trar /fiw'trar/ vt filter; ~tro m filter
fim /fĩ/ m end; a ~ de (*para*) in order to; estar a ~ de fancy; por ~ finally; sem ~ endless; ter ~ come to an end; ~ de semana weekend
fi|nado /fi'nadu/ a & m deceased, departed; ~nal (*pl* ~nais) a final □ m end □ f final; ~nalista m/f finalist; ~nalizar vt/i finish
finan|ças /fi'nãsas/ f pl finances; ~ceiro a financial □ m financier; ~ciamento m financing; (*um*) loan; ~ciar vt finance; ~cista m/f financier
fincar /fĩ'kar/ vt plant; ~ o pé (*fig*) dig one's heels in
findar /fĩ'dar/ vt/i end
fineza /fi'neza/ f finesse; (*favor*) kindness
fin|gido /fĩ'ʒidu/ a feigned; < *pessoa* > insincere; ~gimento m pretence; ~gir vt pretend; feign < *doença etc* > □ vi pretend; ~gir-se de pretend to be
finito /fi'nitu/ a finite
finlan|dês /fĩlã'des/ a (*f* ~desa) Finnish □ m (*f* ~desa) Finn; (*língua*) Finnish
Finlândia /fĩ'lãdʒia/ f Finland
fi|ninho /fi'niɲu/ adv sair de ~ninho slip away; ~no a (*não grosso*) thin; < *areia, pó etc* > fine; (*refinado*) refined; ~nório a crafty; ~nura f thinness; fineness
fio /'fiu/ m thread; (*elétrico*) wire; (*de sangue, água*) trickle; (*de luz, esperança*) glimmer; (*de navalha etc*) edge; horas a ~ hours on end
fir|ma /'firma/ f firm; (*assinatura*) signature; ~mamento m firmament; ~mar vt fix; (*basear*) base □ vi settle; ~mar-se vpr be based (em on); ~me a firm; < *tempo* > settled □ adv firmly; ~meza f firmness
fis|cal /fis'kaw/ (*pl* ~cais) m inspector; ~calização f inspection;

~calizar *vt* inspect; ~co *m* inland revenue, (*Amer*) internal revenue service

fis|gada /fiz'gada/ *f* stabbing pain; ~gar *vt* hook

físi|ca /'fizika/ *f* physics; ~co *a* physical □ *m* (*pessoa*) physicist; (*corpo*) physique

fisio|nomia /fizio'mia/ *f* face; ~nomista *m/f* ser ~nomista have a good memory for faces; ~terapeuta *m/f* physiotherapist; ~terapia *f* physiotherapy

fissura /fi'sura/ *f* fissure; (*fam*) craving; ~do *a* ~do em (*fam*) mad about

fita /'fita/ *f* tape; (*fam: encenação*) playacting; fazer ~ (*fam*) put on an act; ~ adesiva (*Port*) adhesive tape; ~ métrica tape measure

fitar /fi'tar/ *vt* stare at

fivela /fi'vɛla/ *f* buckle

fi|xador /fiksa'dor/ *m* (*de cabelo*) setting lotion; (*de fotos*) fixative; ~xar *vt* fix; stick up <*cartaz*>; ~xo *a* fixed

flácido /'flasidu/ *a* flabby

flagelo /fla'ʒɛlu/ *m* scourge

fla|grante /fla'grãtʃi/ *a* flagrant; apanhar em ~grante (*delito*) catch in the act; ~grar *vt* catch

flame|jante /flame'ʒãtʃi/ *a* blazing; ~jar *vi* blaze

flamengo /fla'mẽgu/ *a* Flemish □ *m* Fleming; (*língua*) Flemish

flamingo /fla'mĩgu/ *m* flamingo

flâmula /'flamula/ *f* pennant

flanco /'flãku/ *m* flank

flanela /fla'nɛla/ *f* flannel

flanquear /flãki'ar/ *vt* flank

flash /flɛʃ/ *m invar* flash

flau|ta /'flawta/ *f* flute; ~tista *m/f* flautist

flecha /'flɛʃa/ *f* arrow

fler|tar /fler'tar/ *vi* flirt; ~te *m* flirtation

fleuma /'flewma/ *f* phlegm

fle|xão /flek'sãw/ *f* press-up, (*Amer*) push-up; (*ling*) inflection; ~xibilidade *f* flexibility; ~xionar *vt/i* flex <*perna, braço*>; (*ling*) inflect; ~xível (*pl* ~xíveis) *a* flexible

fliperama /flipe'rama/ *m* pinball machine

floco /'flɔku/ *m* flake

flor /flor/ *f* flower; a fina ~ the cream; à ~ da pele (*fig*) on edge

flo|ra /'flɔra/ *f* flora; ~reado *a* full of flowers; (*fig*) florid; ~reio *m* clever turn of phrase; ~rescer *vi* flower; ~resta /ɛ/ *f* forest; ~restal (*pl* ~restais) *a* forest; ~rido *a* in flower; (*fig*) florid; ~rir *vi* flower

flotilha /flo'tʃiʎa/ *f* flotilla

flu|ência /flu'ẽsia/ *f* fluency; ~ente *a* fluent

flui|dez /flui'des/ *f* fluidity; ~do *a* & *m* fluid

fluir /flu'ir/ *vi* flow

fluminense /flumi'nẽsi/ *a* & *m* (person) from Rio de Janeiro state

fluorescente /fluore'sẽtʃi/ *a* fluorescent

flutu|ação /flutua'sãw/ *f* fluctuation; ~ante *a* floating; ~ar *vi* float; <*bandeira*> flutter; (*hesitar*) waver

fluvi|al /fluvi'aw/ (*pl* ~ais) *a* river

fluxo /'fluksu/ *m* flow; ~grama *m* flowchart

fobia /fo'bia/ *f* phobia

foca /'fɔka/ *f* seal

focalizar /fokali'zar/ *vt* focus on

focinho /fo'siɲu/ *m* snout

foco /'fɔku/ *m* focus; (*fig*) centre

fofo /'fofu/ *a* soft; <*pessoa*> cuddly

fofo|ca /fo'fɔka/ *f* piece of gossip; *pl* gossip; ~car *vi* gossip; ~queiro *m* gossip □ *a* gossipy

fo|gão /fo'gãw/ *m* stove; (*de cozinhar*) cooker; ~go /o/ *m* fire; tem ~go? have you got a light?; ser ~go (*fam*) (*ser chato*) be a pain in the neck; (*ser incrível*) be amazing; ~gos de artifício fireworks; ~goso /o/ *a* fiery; ~gueira *f* bonfire; ~guete /e/ *m* rocket

foice /'fojsi/ *f* scythe

fol|clore /fow'klɔri/ *m* folklore; ~clórico *a* folk

fole /'fɔli/ *m* bellows

fôlego /'folegu/ *m* breath; (*fig*) stamina

fol|ga /'fowga/ *f* rest, break; (*fam: cara-de-pau*) cheek; ~gado *a* <*roupa*> full, loose; <*vida*> leisurely; (*fam: atrevido*) cheeky; ~gar *vt* loosen □ *vi* have time off

fo|lha /'foʎa/ *f* leaf; (*de papel*) sheet; novo em ~lha brand new; ~lha de pagamento payroll; ~lhagem *f* foliage; ~lhear *vt* leaf through; ~lheto /e/ *m* pamphlet; ~lhinha *f* tear-off calendar; ~lhudo *a* leafy

foli|a /fo'lia/ *f* revelry; ~ão *m* (*f* ~ona) reveller

folículo /fo'likulu/ *m* follicle

fome /'fomi/ *f* hunger; estar com ~ be hungry

fomentar /fomẽ'tar/ *vt* foment

fone /'foni/ *m* (*do telefone*) receiver; (*de rádio etc*) headphones

fonema /fo'nema/ *m* phoneme

fonéti|ca /fo'nɛtʃika/ *f* phonetics; ~co *a* phonetic

fonologia /fonolo'ʒia/ *f* phonology

fonte /'fotʃi/ *f* (*de água*) spring; (*fig*) source

fora /'fɔra/ *adv* outside; (*não em casa*) out; (*viajando*) away □ *prep* except; dar um ~ drop a clanger; dar um

~ em alg cut s.o. dead; chuck <namorado>; por ~ on the outside; ~-de-lei m/f invar outlaw

foragido /fora'ʒidu/ a at large, on the run □ m fugitive

forasteiro /foras'teru/ m outsider

forca /'forka/ f gallows

for|ça /'forsa/ f (vigor) strength; (violência) force; (elétrica) power; dar uma ~ça a alg help s.o. out; fazer ~ça make an effort; ~ças armadas armed forces; ~çar vt force; ~ça-tarefa (pl ~ças-tarefa) f task force

fórceps /'forseps/ m invar forceps

forçoso /for'sozu/ a forced

for|ja /'forʒa/ f forge; ~jar vt forge

forma /'forma/ f form; (contorno) shape; (maneira) way; de qualquer ~ anyway; manter a ~ keep fit

fôrma /'forma/ f mould; (de cozinha) baking tin

for|mação /forma'sãw/ f formation; (educação) education; (profissionalizante) training; ~mado m graduate; ~mal (pl ~mais) a formal; ~malidade f formality; ~malizar vt formalize; ~mar vt form; (educar) educate; ~mar-se upr be formed; <estudante> graduate; ~mato m format; ~matura f graduation

formidá|vel /formi'davew/ (pl ~veis) a formidable; (muito bom) tremendous

formi|ga /for'miga/ f ant; ~gamento m pins and needles; ~gar vi swarm (de with); <perna, mão etc> tingle; ~gueiro m ants' nest

formosura /formo'zura/ f beauty

fórmula /'formula/ f formula

formu|lação /formula'sãw/ f formulation; ~lar vt formulate; ~lário m form

fornalha /for'naʎa/ f furnace

forne|cedor /fornese'dor/ m supplier; ~cer vt supply; ~cer aco a alg supply s.o. with sth; ~cimento m supply

forno /'fornu/ m oven; (para louça etc) kiln

foro /'foru/ m forum

forra /'foxa/ f ir à ~ get one's own back

for|ragem /fo'xaʒẽ/ f fodder; ~rar vt line <roupa, caixa etc>; cover <sofá etc>; carpet <assoalho, sala etc>; ~ro /o/ m (de roupa, caixa etc) lining; (de sofá etc) cover; (carpete) (fitted) carpet

forró /fo'xɔ/ m type of Brazilian dance

fortale|cer /fortale'ser/ vt strengthen; ~cimento m strengthening; ~za /e/ f fort-ress

for|te /'fortʃi/ a strong; <golpe> hard; <chuva> heavy; <físico> muscular □ adv strongly; <bater, chover> hard □

m (militar) fort; (habilidade) strong point, forte; ~tificação f fortification; ~tificar vt fortify

fortu|ito /for'tuitu/ a chance; ~na f fortune

fosco /'fosku/ a dull; <vidro> frosted

fosfato /fos'fatu/ m phosphate

fósforo /'fosforu/ m match; (elemento químico) phosphor

fossa /'fɔsa/ f pit; na ~ (fig) miserable, depressed

fós|sil /'fɔsiw/ (pl ~seis) m fossil

fosso /'fosu/ m ditch; (de castelo) moat

foto /'fɔtu/ f photo; ~cópia f photocopy; ~copiadora f photocopier; ~copiar vt photocopy; ~gênico a photogenic; ~grafar vt photograph; ~grafia f photography; ~gráfico a photographic

fotógrafo /fo'tɔgrafu/ m photographer

foz /fɔs/ f mouth

fração /fra'sãw/ f fraction

fracas|sado /fraka'sadu/ a failed □ m failure; ~sar vi fail; ~so m failure

fracionar /frasio'nar/ vt break up

fraco /'fraku/ a weak; <luz, som> faint; <mediocre> poor □ m weakness, weak spot

fract- (Port) veja frat-

frade /'fradʒi/ m friar

fragata /fra'gata/ f frigate

frá|gil /'fraʒiw/ (pl ~geis) a fragile; <pessoa> frail

fragilidade /fraʒili'dadʒi/ f fragility; (de pessoa) frailty

fragmen|tar /fragmẽ'tar/ vt fragment; ~tar-se upr fragment; ~to m fragment

fra|grância /fra'grãsia/ f fragrance; ~grante a fragrant

fralda /'frawda/ f nappy, (Amer) diaper

framboesa /frãbo'eza/ f raspberry

França /'frãsa/ f France

fran|cês /frã'ses/ a (f ~cesa) French □ m (f ~cesa) Frenchman (f -woman); (língua) French; os ~ceses the French

franco /'frãku/ a (honesto) frank; (óbvio) clear; (gratuito) free □ m franc; ~-atirador (pl ~-atiradores) m sniper; (fig) maverick

frangalho /frã'gaʎu/ m tatter

frango /'frãgu/ m chicken

franja /'frãʒa/ f fringe; (do cabelo) fringe, (Amer) bangs

fran|quear /frãki'ar/ vt frank <carta>; ~queza /e/ f frankness; ~quia f (de cartas) franking; (jur) franchise

fran|zino /frã'zinu/ a skinny; ~zir vt gather <tecido>; wrinkle <testa>

fraque /'fraki/ m morning suit

fraqueza /fra'keza/ f weakness; (de luz, som) faintness

frasco /'frasku/ m bottle

frase /'frazi/ f (oração) sentence; (locução) phrase; ~ado m phrasing

frasqueira /fras'kera/ f vanity case

frater|nal /frater'naw/ (pl ~nais) a fraternal; ~nidade f fraternity; ~nizar vi fraternize; ~no a fraternal

fratu|ra /fra'tura/ f fracture; ~rar vt fracture; ~rar-se vpr fracture

frau|dar /fraw'dar/ vt defraud; ~de f fraud; ~dulento a fraudulent

frear /fri'ar/ vt/i brake

freezer /'frizer/ m freezer

fre|guês /fre'ges/ m (f ~guesa) customer; ~guesia f (de loja etc) clientele; (paróquia) parish

frei /frej/ m brother

freio /'freju/ m brake; (de cavalo) bit

freira /'frera/ f nun

freixo /'frefu/ m ash

fremir /fre'mir/ vi shake

frêmito /'fremitu/ m wave

frenesi /frene'zi/ m frenzy

frenético /fre'netfiku/ a frantic

frente /'frētfi/ f front; em ~ a ou de in front of; para a ~ forward; pela ~ ahead; fazer ~ a face

freqüência /fre'kwēsia/ f frequency; (assiduidade) attendance; com muita ~ often

freqüen|tador /frekwēta'dor/ m regular visitor (de to); ~tar vt frequent; (cursar) attend; ~te a frequent

fres|cão /fres'kaw/ m air-conditioned coach; ~co /e/ a <comida etc> fresh; <vento, água, quarto> cool; (fam) (afetado) affected; (exigente) fussy; ~cobol m kind of racquetball; ~cor m freshness; ~cura f (fam) (afetação) affectation; (ser exigente) fussiness; (coisa sem importância) trifle

fresta /'fresta/ f slit

fre|tar /fre'tar/ vt charter <avião>; hire <caminhão>; ~te /ε/ m freight; (aluguel de avião) charter; (de caminhão) hire

frevo /'frevu/ m type of Brazilian dance

fria /'fria/ (fam) f difficult situation, spot; ~gem f chill

fric|ção /frik'saw/ f friction; ~cionar vt rub

fri|eira /fri'era/ f chilblain; ~eza /e/ f coldness

frigideira /friʒi'dera/ f frying pan

frígido /'friʒidu/ a frigid

frigorífico /frigo'rifiku/ m cold store, refrigerator, fridge

frincha /'frifa/ f chink

frio /'friu/ a & m cold; estar com ~ be cold; ~rento a sensitive to the cold

frisar /fri'zar/ vt (enfatizar) stress; crimp <cabelo>

friso /'frizu/ m frieze

fri|tada /fri'tada/ f fry-up; ~tar vt fry; ~tas f pl chips, (Amer) French fries; ~to a fried; está ~to (fam) he's had it; ~tura f fried food

frivolidade /frivoli'dadʒi/ f frivolity; frívolo a frivolous

fronha /'frona/ f pillowcase

fronte /'frõtʃi/ f forehead, brow

frontei|ra /frõ'tera/ f border; ~riço a border

frota /'frota/ f fleet

frou|xidão /froʃi'dãw/ f looseness; (moral) laxity; ~xo a loose; <regulamento> lax; <pessoa> lackadaisical

fru|gal /fru'gaw/ (pl ~gais) a frugal; ~galidade f frugality

frus|tração /frustra'sãw/ f frustration; ~trante a frustrating; ~trar vt frustrate

fru|ta /'fruta/ f fruit; ~ta-do-conde (pl ~tas-do-conde) f sweetsop; ~ta-pão (pl ~tas-pão) f breadfruit; ~teira f fruitbowl; ~tífero a (fig) fruitful; ~to m fruit

fubá /fu'ba/ m maize flour

fu|çar /fu'sar/ vi nose around; ~ças (fam) f pl face, chops

fu|ga /'fuga/ f escape; ~gaz a fleeting; ~gida f escape; ~gir vi run away; (soltar-se) escape; ~gir a avoid; ~gitivo a & m fugitive

fulano /fu'lanu/ m whatever his name is

fuleiro /fu'leru/ a down-market, cheap and cheerful

fulgor /fuw'gor/ m brightness; (fig) splendour

fuligem /fu'liʒẽ/ f soot

fulmi|nante /fuwmi'nãtʃi/ a devastating; ~nar vt strike down; (fig) devastate; ~nado por um raio struck by lightning □ vi (criticar) rail

fu|maça /fu'masa/ f smoke; ~maceira f cloud of smoke; ~mante (Port) ~mador m smoker; ~mar vt/i smoke; ~mê a invar smoked; ~megar vi smoke; ~mo m (tabaco) tobacco; (Port: fumaça) smoke; (fumar) smoking

função /fũ'sãw/ f function; em ~ de as a result of; fazer as funções de function as

funcho /'fũʃu/ m fennel

funcio|nal /fũsio'naw/ (pl ~nais) a functional; ~nalismo m civil service; ~namento m working; ~nar vi work; ~nário m employee; ~nário público civil servant

fun|dação /fũda'sãw/ f foundation; ~dador m founder □ a founding

fundamen|tal /fũdamẽ'taw/ (*pl* ~**tais**) *a* fundamental; ~**tar** *vt* (*basear*) base; (*justificar*) substantiate; ~**to** *m* foundation

fun|dar /fũ'dar/ *vt* (*criar*) found; (*basear*) base; ~**dar-se** *vpr* be based (em on); ~**dear** *vi* drop anchor, anchor; ~**dilho** *m* seat

fundir /fũ'dʒir/ *vt* melt <*ouro, ferro*>; cast <*sino, estátua*>; (*juntar*) merge; ~**-se** *vpr* <*ouro, ferro*> melt; (*juntar-se*) merge

fundo /'fũdu/ *a* deep □ *m* (*parte de baixo*) bottom; (*parte de trás*) back; (*de quadro, foto*) background; (*de dinheiro*) fund; no ~ basically; ~**s** *m pl* (*da casa etc*) back; (*recursos*) funds

fúnebre /'funebri/ *a* funereal

funerário /fune'rariu/ *a* funeral

funesto /fu'nestu/ *a* fatal

fungar /fũ'gar/ *vt/i* sniff

fungo /'fũgu/ *m* fungus

fu|nil /fu'niw/ (*pl* ~**nis**) *m* funnel; ~**nilaria** *f* panel-beating; (*oficina*) bodyshop

furacão /fura'kãw/ *m* hurricane

furado /fu'radu/ *a* papo ~ (*fam*) hot air

furão /fu'rãw/ *m* (*animal*) ferret

furar /fu'rar/ *vt* pierce <*orelha etc*>; puncture <*pneu*>; make a hole in <*roupa etc*>; jump <*fila*>; break <*greve*> □ *vi* <*roupa etc*> go into a hole; <*pneu*> puncture; (*fam*) <*programa*> fall through

fur|gão /fur'gãw/ *m* van; ~**goneta** /e/ (*Port*) *f* van

fúria /'furia/ *f* fury

furioso /furi'ozu/ *a* furious

furo /'furu/ *m* hole; (*de pneu*) puncture; (*jornalístico*) scoop; (*fam: gafe*) blunder, faux pas; dar um ~ put one's foot in it

furor /fu'ror/ *m* furore

fur|ta-cor /furta'kor/ *a invar* iridescent; ~**tar** *vt* steal; ~**tivo** *a* furtive; ~**to** *m* theft

furúnculo /fu'rũkulu/ *m* boil

fusão /fu'zãw/ *f* fusion; (*de empresas*) merger

fusca /'fuska/ *f* VW beetle

fuselagem /fuze'laʒẽ/ *f* fuselage

fusí|vel /fu'zivew/ (*pl* ~**veis**) *m* fuse

fuso /'fuzu/ *m* spindle; ~ **horário** time zone

fustigar /fustʃi'gar/ *vt* lash; (*fig: com palavras*) lash out at

futebol /futʃi'bɔw/ *m* football; ~**ístico** *a* football

fú|til /'futʃiw/ (*pl* ~**teis**) *a* frivolous, inane

futilidade /futʃili'dadʒi/ *f* frivolity, inanity; (*uma*) frivolous thing

futu|rismo /futu'rizmu/ *m* futurism;

~**rista** *a & m* futurist; ~**rístico** *a* futuristic; ~**ro** *a & m* future

fu|zil /fu'ziw/ (*pl* ~**zis**) *m* rifle; ~**zilamento** *m* shooting; ~**zilar** *vt* shoot □ *vi* flash; ~**zileiro** *m* rifleman; ~**zileiro naval** marine

fuzuê /fuzu'e/ *m* commotion

G

gabar-se /ga'barsi/ *vpr* boast (de of)

gabarito /gaba'ritu/ *m* calibre

gabinete /gabi'netʃi/ *m* (*em casa*) study; (*escritório*) office; (*ministros*) cabinet

gado /'gadu/ *m* livestock; (*bovino*) cattle

gaélico /ga'ɛliku/ *a & m* Gaelic

gafanhoto /gafa'ɲotu/ *m* (*pequeno*) grasshopper; (*grande*) locust

gafe /'gafi/ *f* faux pas, gaffe

gafieira /gafi'era/ *f* dance; (*salão*) dance hall

gagá /ga'ga/ *a* (*fam*) senile

ga|go /'gagu/ *a* stuttering □ *m* stutterer; ~**gueira** /ga'gera/ *f* stutter; ~**guejar** *vi* stutter

gaiato /gaj'atu/ *a* funny

gaiola /gaj'ɔla/ *f* cage

gaita /'gajta/ *f* ~ de foles bagpipes

gaivota /gaj'vota/ *f* seagull

gajo /'gaʒu/ *m* (*Port*) guy, bloke

gala /'gala/ *f* festa de ~ gala; roupa de ~ formal dress

galã /ga'lã/ *m* leading man

galan|tear /galãtʃi'ar/ *vt* woo; ~**teio** *m* wooing; (*um*) courtesy

galão /ga'lãw/ *m* (*enfeite*) braid; (*mil*) stripe; (*medida*) gallon; (*Port: café*) white coffee

galáxia /ga'laksia/ *f* galaxy

galé /ga'lɛ/ *f* galley

galego /ga'legu/ *a & m* Galician

galera /ga'lɛra/ *f* (*fam*) crowd

galeria /gale'ria/ *f* gallery

Gales /'galis/ *m* País de ~ Wales

ga|lês /ga'les/ *a* (*f* ~**lesa**) Welsh □ *m* (*f* ~**lesa**) Welshman (*f* -woman); (*língua*) Welsh

galeto /ga'letu/ *m* spring chicken

galgar /gaw'gar/ *vt* (*transpor*) jump over; climb <*escada*>

galgo /'gawgu/ *m* greyhound

galheteiro /gaʎe'teru/ *m* cruet stand

galho /'gaʎu/ *m* branch; quebrar um ~ (*fam*) help out

galináceos /gali'nasius/ *m pl* poultry

gali|nha /ga'liɲa/ *f* chicken; ~**nheiro** *m* chicken coop

galo /'galu/ *m* cock; (*inchação*) bump

galocha /ga'lɔʃa/ *f* Wellington boot

galo|pante /galo'pãtʃi/ *a* galloping; ~**par** *vi* gallop; ~**pe** /ɔ/ *m* gallop

galpão /gaw'pãw/ m shed

galvanizar /gawvani'zar/ vt galvanize

gama /'gama/ f (musical) scale; (fig) range

gamado /ga'madu/ a besotted (por with)

gamão /ga'mãw/ m backgammon

gamar /ga'mar/ vi fall in love (por with)

gana /'gana/ f desire

ganância /ga'nãsia/ f greed

ganancioso /ganãsi'ozu/ a greedy

gancho /'gãʃu/ m hook

gangorra /gã'goxa/ f seesaw

gangrena /gã'grena/ f gangrene

gangue /'gãgi/ m gang

ga|nhador /gaɲa'dor/ m winner □ a winning; ~nhar vt win <corrida, prêmio>; earn <salário>; get <presente>; gain <vantagem, tempo, amigo> □ vi win; ~nhar a vida earn a living; ~nha-pão m livelihood; ~nho m gain; pl (no jogo) winnings □ pp de ganhar

ga|nido m squeal; (de cachorro) yelp; ~nir vi squeal; <cachorro> yelp

ganso /'gãsu/ m goose

gara|gem /ga'raʒẽ/ f garage; ~gista m/f garage attendant

garanhão /gara'ɲãw/ m stallion

garan|tia /garã'tʃia/ f guarantee; ~tir vt guarantee

garatujar /garatu'ʒar/ vt scribble

gar|bo /'garbu/ m grace; ~boso a graceful

garça /'garsa/ f heron

gar|çom /gar'sõ/ m waiter; ~çonete /ɛ/ f waitress

gar|fada /gar'fada/ f forkful; ~fo m fork

gargalhada /garga'ʎada/ f gale of laughter; rir às ~s roar with laughter

gargalo /gar'galu/ m bottleneck; tomar no ~ drink out of the bottle

garganta /gar'gãta/ f throat

gargare|jar /gargare'ʒar/ vi gargle; ~jo /e/ m gargle

gari /ga'ri/ m/f (lixeiro) dustman, (Amer) garbage collector; (varredor de rua) roadsweeper, (Amer) streetsweeper

garim|par /garĩ'par/ vi prospect; ~peiro m prospector; ~po m mine

garo|a /ga'roa/ f drizzle; ~ar vi drizzle

garo|to /ga'rotu/ f girl; ~to /o/ m boy; (Port: café) coffee with milk

garoupa /ga'ropa/ f grouper

garra /'gaxa/ f claw; (fig) drive, determination; pl (poder) clutches

garra|fa /ga'xafa/ f bottle; ~fada f blow with a bottle; ~fão m flagon

garrancho /ga'xãʃu/ m scrawl

garrido /ga'xidu/ a (alegre) lively

garupa /ga'rupa/ f (de animal) rump; (de moto) pillion seat

gás /gas/ m gas; pl (intestinais) wind, (Amer) gas; ~ lacrimogêneo tear gas

gasóleo /ga'zɔliu/ m diesel oil

gasolina /gazo'lina/ f petrol

gaso|sa /ga'zɔza/ f fizzy lemonade, (Amer) soda; ~so a gaseous; <bebida> fizzy

gáspea /'gaspia/ f upper

gas|tador /gasta'dor/ a & m spendthrift; ~tar vt spend <dinheiro, tempo>; use up <energia>; wear out <roupa, sapatos>; ~to m expense; pl spending, expenditure; dar para o ~to do

gastrenterite /gastrẽte'ritʃi/ f gastroenteritis

gástrico /'gastriku/ a gastric

gastrite /gas'tritʃi/ f gastritis

gastronomia /gastrono'mia/ f gastronomy

ga|ta /'gata/ f cat; (fam) sexy woman; ~tão m (fam) hunk

gatilho /ga'tʃiʎu/ m trigger

ga|tinha /ga'tʃina/ f (fam) sexy woman; ~to m cat; (fam) hunk; fazer alg de ~to-sapato treat s.o. like a doormat

gatuno /ga'tunu/ m crook □ a crooked

gaúcho /ga'uʃu/ a & m (person) from Rio Grande do Sul

gaveta /ga'veta/ f drawer

gavião /gavi'ãw/ m hawk

gaze /'gazi/ f gauze

gazela /ga'zɛla/ f gazelle

gazeta /ga'zeta/ f gazette

geada /ʒi'ada/ f frost

ge|ladeira /ʒela'dera/ f fridge; ~lado a frozen; (muito frio) freezing □ m (Port) ice cream; ~lar vt/i freeze

gelati|na /ʒela'tʃina/ f (sobremesa) jelly; (pó) gelatine; ~noso /o/ a gooey

geléia /ʒe'lɛja/ f jam

ge|leira /ʒe'lera/ f glacier; ~lo /e/ m ice

gema /'ʒema/ f (de ovo) yolk; (pedra) gem; carioca da ~ carioca born and bred; ~da f egg yolk whisked with sugar

gêmeo /'ʒemiu/ a & m twin; Gêmeos (signo) Gemini

ge|mer /ʒe'mer/ vi moan, groan; ~mido m moan, groan

gene /'ʒeni/ m gene; ~alogia f genealogy; ~alógico a genealogical; árvore ~alógica family tree

Genebra /ʒe'nebra/ f Geneva

gene|ral /ʒene'raw/ (pl ~rais) m general; ~ralidade f generality; ~ralização f generalization;

~ralizar *vt/i* generalize; ~ralizar-se *upr* become generalized

genérico /ʒeˈnɛriku/ *a* generic

gênero /ˈʒeneru/ *m* type, kind; (*gramatical*) gender; (*literário*) genre; *pl* goods; ~s alimentícios foodstuffs; ela não faz o meu ~ she's not my type

generosidade /ʒeneroziˈdadʒi/ *f* generosity; ~roso /o/ *a* generous

genética /ʒeˈnɛtʃika/ *f* genetics; ~co *a* genetic

gengibre /ʒēˈʒibri/ *m* ginger

gengiva /ʒēˈʒiva/ *f* gum

genial /ʒeniˈaw/ (*pl* ~ais) *a* brilliant

gênio /ˈʒeniu/ *m* genius; (*temperamento*) temperament

genioso /ʒeniˈozu/ *a* temperamental

genital /ʒeniˈtaw/ (*pl* ~tais) *a* genital

genitivo /ʒeniˈtʃivu/ *a & m* genitive

genocídio /ʒenoˈsidʒiu/ *m* genocide

genro /ˈʒēxu/ *m* son-in-law

gente /ˈʒētʃi/ *f* people; (*fam*) folks; a ~ (*sujeito*) we; (*objeto*) us □ *interj* (*fam*) gosh

gentil /ʒēˈtʃiw/ (*pl* ~tis) *a* kind; ~tileza /e/ *f* kindness

genuíno /ʒenuˈinu/ *a* genuine

geografia /ʒeograˈfia/ *f* geography; ~gráfico *a* geographical

geógrafo /ʒeˈɔgrafu/ *m* geographer

geologia /ʒeoloˈʒia/ *f* geology; ~lógico *a* geological

geólogo /ʒeˈɔlogu/ *m* geologist

geometria /ʒeomeˈtria/ *f* geometry; ~métrico *a* geometrical; ~político *a* geopolitical

Geórgia /ʒiˈɔrʒia/ *f* Georgia

georgiano /ʒiorʒiˈanu/ *a & m* Georgian

geração /ʒeraˈsãw/ *f* generation; ~dor *m* generator

geral /ʒeˈraw/ (*pl* ~rais) *a* general □ *f* (*limpeza*) spring-clean; em ~ral in general

gerânio /ʒeˈraniu/ *m* geranium

gerar /ʒeˈrar/ *vt* create; generate < *eletricidade*>

gerência /ʒeˈrēsia/ *f* management

gerenciador /ʒerēsiaˈdor/ *m* manager; ~al (*pl* ~ais) *a* management; ~ar *vt* manage

gerente /ʒeˈrētʃi/ *m* manager □ *a* managing

gergelim /ʒerʒeˈlĩ/ *m* sesame

geriatria /ʒeriaˈtria/ *f* geriatrics; ~átrico *a* geriatric

geringonça /ʒerīˈgõsa/ *f* contraption

gerir /ʒeˈrir/ *vt* manage

germânico /ʒerˈmaniku/ *a* Germanic

germe /ˈʒermi/ *m* germ; ~me de trigo wheatgerm; ~minar *vi* germinate

gerúndio /ʒeˈrũdʒiu/ *m* gerund

gesso /ˈʒesu/ *m* plaster

gestação /ʒestaˈsãw/ *f* gestation; ~tante *f* pregnant woman

gestão /ʒesˈtãw/ *f* management

gesticular *vi* gesticulate; ~to /ˈʒestu/ *m* gesture

gibi /ʒiˈbi/ *m* (*fam*) comic

Gibraltar /ʒibrawˈtar/ *f* Gibraltar

gigante /ʒiˈgãtʃi/ *a & m* giant; ~tesco /e/ *a* gigantic

gilete /ʒiˈlɛtʃi/ *f* razor blade □ *a & m/f* (*fam*) bisexual

gim /ʒĩ/ *m* gin

ginásio /ʒiˈnaziu/ *m* (*escola*) secondary school; (*de ginástica*) gymnasium

ginasta /ʒiˈnasta/ *m/f* gymnast

ginástica /ʒiˈnastʃika/ *f* gymnastics; (*aeróbica*) aerobics; ~co *a* gymnastic

ginecologia /ʒinekoloˈʒia/ *f* gynaecology; ~gista *m/f* gynaecologist

gingar /ʒĩˈgar/ *vi* sway

gira-discos /ʒiraˈdʒiskuʃ/ *m invar* (*Port*) record player

girafa /ʒiˈrafa/ *f* giraffe

girar /ʒiˈrar/ *vt/i* spin, revolve; ~rassol (*pl* ~rassóis) *m* sunflower; ~ratório *a* revolving

gíria /ˈʒiria/ *f* slang; (*uma* ~) slang expression

giro /ˈʒiru/ *m* spin, turn □ *a* (*Port fam*) great

giz /ʒis/ *m* chalk

glacê /glaˈse/ *m* icing; ~cial (*pl* ~ciais) *a* icy

glamour /glaˈmur/ *m* glamour; ~oso /o/ *a* glamorous

glândula /ˈglãdula/ *f* gland

glandular /glãduˈlar/ *a* glandular

glicerina /gliseˈrina/ *f* glycerine

glicose /gliˈkɔzi/ *f* glucose

global /gloˈbaw/ (*pl* ~bais) *a* (*mundial*) global; < *preço etc*> overall; ~bo /o/ *m* globe; ~bo ocular eyeball

glóbulo /ˈglobulu/ *m* globule; (*do sangue*) corpuscle

glória /ˈgloria/ *f* glory

glorificar /glorifiˈkar/ *vt* glorify; ~oso /o/ *a* glorious

glossário /gloˈsariu/ *m* glossary

glutão /gluˈtãw/ *m* (*f* ~tona) glutton □ *a* (*f* ~tona) greedy

gnomo /ˈgnomu/ *m* gnome

godê /goˈde/ *a* flared

goela /goˈɛla/ *f* gullet

gogó /goˈgɔ/ *m* (*fam*) Adam's apple

goiaba /gojˈaba/ *f* guava; ~bada *f* guava jelly; ~beira *f* guava tree

gol /ˈgow/ (*pl* ~s) *m* goal

gola /ˈgola/ *f* collar

gole /ˈgoli/ *m* mouthful

goleiro /goliˈar/ *vt* thrash; ~leiro *m* goalkeeper

golfe /ˈgowfi/ *m* golf

golfinho /gowˈfiɲu/ *m* dolphin

golfista /gow'fista/ m/f golfer

golo /'golu/ m (Port) goal

golpe /'gowpi/ m blow; (manobra) trick; ~ (de estado) coup (d'état); ~ de mestre masterstroke; ~ de vento gust of wind; ~ de vista glance; ~ar vt hit

goma /'goma/ f gum; (para roupa) starch

gomo /'gomu/ m segment

gôndola /'gõdola/ f rack

gongo /'gõgu/ m gong

gonorréia /gono'xeja/ f gonorrhea

gonzo /'gõzu/ m hinge

gorar /go'rar/ vi go wrong, fail

gor|do /'gordu/ a fat; ~ducho a plump

gordu|ra /gor'dura/ f fat; ~rento a greasy; ~roso /u/ a fatty; <pele> greasy, oily

gorgolejar /gorgole'ʒar/ vi gurgle

gorila /go'rila/ m gorilla

gor|jear /gorʒi'ar/ vi twitter; ~jeio m twittering

gorjeta /gor'ʒeta/ f tip

gorro /'goxu/ m hat

gos|ma /'gɔzma/ f slime; ~mento a slimy

gos|tar /gos'tar/ vi ~tar de like; ~to /o/ m taste; (prazer) pleasure; para o meu ~to for my taste; ter ~to de taste of; ~toso a nice; <comida> nice, tasty; (fam) <pessoa> gorgeous

go|ta /'gota/ f drop; (que cai) drip; (doença) gout; foi a ~ta d'água (fig) it was the last straw; ~teira f (buraco) leak; (cano) gutter; ~tejar vi drip; <telhado> leak □ vt drip

gótico /'gɔtʃiku/ a Gothic

gotícula /go'tʃicula/ f droplet

gover|nador /governa'dor/ m governor; ~namental (pl ~namentais) a government; ~nanta f housekeeper; ~nante a ruling □ m/f ruler; ~nar vt govern; ~nista a governist □ m/f government supporter; ~no /e/ m government

go|zação /goza'sãw/ f joking; (uma) send-up; ~zado a funny; ~zar vt ~zar (de) enjoy; (fam: zombar de) make fun of □ vi (ter orgasmo) come; ~zo m (prazer) enjoyment; (posse) possession; (orgasmo) orgasm; ser um ~zo be funny

Grã-Bretanha /grãbre'taɲa/ f Great Britain

graça /'grasa/ f grace; (piada) joke; (humor) humour, funny side; (jur) pardon; de ~ for nothing; sem ~ (enfadonho) dull; (não engraçado) unfunny; (envergonhado) embarrassed; ser uma ~ be lovely; ter ~ be funny; não tem ~ sair sozinho it's no fun to go out alone; ~s a thanks to

grace|jar /grase'ʒar/ vi joke; ~jo /e/ m joke

graci|nha /gra'siɲa/ f ser uma ~nha be sweet; ~oso /o/ a gracious

grada|ção /grada'sãw/ f gradation; ~tivo a gradual

grade /'gradʒi/ f grille, grating; (cerca) railings; atrás das ~s behind bars; ~ado a <janela> barred

grado /'gradu/ m de bom/mau ~ willingly/unwillingly

gradu|ação /gradua'sãw/ f graduation; (mil) rank; (variação) gradation; ~ado a <escala> graduated; <estudante> graduate; <militar> high-ranking; (eminente) respected; ~al (pl ~ais) a gradual; ~ar vt graduate <escala>; (ordenar) grade; (regular) regulate; ~ar-se vpr <estudante> graduate

grafia /gra'fia/ f spelling

gráfi|ca /'grafika/ f (arte) graphics; (oficina) print shop; ~co a graphic □ m (pessoa) printer; (diagrama) graph; pl (de computador) graphics

grã-fino /grã'finu/ (fam) a posh, upper-class □ m posh person

grafite /gra'fitʃi/ f (mineral) graphite; (de lápis) lead; (pichação) piece of graffiti

grafologia /grafolo'ʒia/ f graphology; ~fólogo m graphologist

grama[1] /'grama/ m gramme

grama[2] /'grama/ f grass; ~do m lawn; (campo de futebol) field

gramática /gra'matʃika/ f grammar

gramati|cal /gramatʃi'kaw/ (pl ~cais) a grammatical

gram|peador /grãpia'dor/ m stapler; ~pear vt staple <papéis etc>; tap <telefone>; ~po m (de cabelo) hairclip; (para papéis etc) staple; (ferramenta) clamp

grana /'grana/ f (fam) cash

granada /gra'nada/ f (projétil) grenade; (pedra) garnet

gran|dalhão /grãda'ʎãw/ a (f ~dalhona) enormous; ~dão a (f ~dona) huge; ~de a big; (fig) <escritor, amor etc> great; ~deza / f greatness; (tamanho) magnitude; ~dioso /o/ a grand

granel /gra'nɛw/ m a ~ in bulk

granito /gra'nitu/ m granite

granizo /gra'nizu/ m hail

gran|ja /'grãʒa/ f farm; ~jear vt win, gain

granulado /granu'ladu/ a granulated

grânulo /'granulu/ m granule

grão /grãw/ (pl ~s) m grain; (de café) bean; ~-de-bico (pl ~s-de-bico) m chickpea

grasnar /graz'nar/ vi <pato> quack; <rã> croak; <corvo> caw

grati|dão /gratʃi'dãw/ f gratitude; ~ficação f (dinheiro a mais) gratuity; (recompensa) gratification; ~ficante a gratifying; ~ficar vt (dar dinheiro a) give a gratuity to; (recompensar) gratify

gratinado /gratʃi'nadu/ a & m gratin

grátis /'gratʃis/ adv free

grato /'gratu/ a grateful

gratuito /gra'tuito/ a (de graça) free; (sem motivo) gratuitous

grau /graw/ m degree; escola de 1º/ 2º ~ primary/secondary school

graúdo /gra'udu/ a big; (importante) important

gra|vação /grava'sãw/ f (de som) recording; (de desenhos etc) engraving; ~vador m (pessoa) engraver; (máquina) tape recorder; ~vadora f record company; ~var vt record <música, disco>; (fixar na memória) memorize; (estampar) engrave

gravata /gra'vata/ f tie; (golpe) stranglehold; ~ borboleta bowtie

grave /'gravi/ a serious; <voz, som> deep; <acento> grave

grávida /'gravida/ f pregnant

gravidade /gravi'dadʒi/ f gravity

gravidez /gravi'des/ f pregnancy

gravura /gra'vura/ f engraving; (em livro) illustration

graxa /'graʃa/ f (de sapatos) polish; (de lubrificar) grease

Grécia /'gresia/ f Greece

grego /'gregu/ a & m Greek

grei /grej/ f flock

grelha /'greʎa/ f grill; ~lhado a grilled □ m grill; ~lhar vt grill

grêmio /'gremiu/ m guild, association

grená /gre'na/ a & m dark red

greta /'greta/ f crack; ~tar vt/i crack

greve /'grevi/ f strike; entrar em ~ve go on strike; ~ve de fome hunger strike; ~vista m/f striker

gri|fado /gri'fadu/ a in italics; ~far vt italicize

griffe /grif/ f label, line

gri|lado /gri'ladu/ a (fam) hung-up; ~lar (fam) vt bug; ~lar-se vpr get hung-up (com about)

grilhão /gri'ʎãw/ m fetter

grilo /'grilu/ m (bicho) cricket; (fam) (preocupação) hang-up; (problema) hassle; (barulho) squeak

grinalda /gri'nawda/ f garland

gringo /'grĩgu/ (fam) a foreign □ m foreigner

gri|pado /gri'padu/ a estar/ficar ~pado have/get the flu; ~par-se vpr get the flu; ~pe f flu, influenza

grisalho /gri'zaʎu/ a grey

gri|tante /gri'tãtʃi/ a <erro> glaring, gross; <cor> loud, garish; ~tar vt/i shout; (de medo) scream; ~taria f shouting; ~to m shout; (de medo) scream; aos ~tos in a loud voice; no ~to (fam) by force

grogue /'grɔgi/ a groggy

grosa /'grɔza/ f gross

groselha /gro'zeʎa/ f (vermelha) redcurrant; (espinhosa) gooseberry; ~ negra blackcurrant

gros|seiro /gro'seru/ a rude; (tosco, malfeito) rough; ~seria f rudeness; (uma) rude thing; ~so /o/ a thick; <voz> deep; (fam) <pessoa, atitude> rude; ~sura f thickness; (fam: grosseria) rudeness

grotesco /gro'tesku/ a grotesque

grua /'grua/ f crane

gru|dado /gru'dadu/ a stuck; (fig) very attached (em to); ~dar vt/i stick; ~de m glue; ~dento a sticky

gru|nhido /gru'ɲidu/ m grunt; ~nhir vi grunt

grupo /'grupu/ m group

gruta /'gruta/ f cave

guaraná /gwara'na/ m guarana

guarani /gwara'ni/ a & m/f Guarani

guarda /'gwarda/ f guard □ m/f guard; (policial) policeman (f -woman); ~ costeira coastguard; ~-chuva m umbrella; ~-costas m invar bodyguard; ~-dor m parking attendant; ~-florestal (pl ~s-florestais) m/f forest ranger; ~-louça m china cupboard; ~ napo m napkin, serviette; ~-noturno (pl ~s-noturnos) m night watchman

guardar /gwar'dar/ vt (pôr no lugar) put away; (conservar) keep; (vigiar) guard; (não esquecer) remember; ~-se de guard against

guarda|-redes /'gwarda-'xedʃ/ m invar (Port) goalkeeper; ~-roupa m wardrobe; ~-sol (pl ~-sóis) m sunshade

guardi|ão /gwardʒi'ãw/ (pl ~ães ou ~ões) m (f ~ã) guardian

guarita /gwa'rita/ f sentry box

guar|necer /gwarne'ser/ vt (fortificar) garrison; (munir) equip; (enfeitar) garnish; ~nição f (mil) garrison; (enfeite) garnish

Guatemala /gwate'mala/ f Guatemala

guatemalteco /gwatemal'tɛku/ a & m Guatemalan

gude /'gudʒi/ m bola de ~ marble

guelra /'gɛwxa/ f gill

guer|ra /'gɛxa/ f war; ~reiro m warrior □ a warlike; ~rilha f guerrilla war; ~rilheiro a & m guerrilla

gueto /'getu/ m ghetto

guia /'gia/ m/f guide □ m guide(book) □ f delivery note

Guiana /gi'ana/ f Guyana

guianense /gia'nẽsi/ a & m/f Guyanan

guiar /gi'ar/ vt guide; drive <veículo> □ vi drive; ~-se vpr be guided

guichê /gi'ʃe/ m window

guidom /gi'dõ/, (Port) guidão /gi'dãw/ m handlebars

guilhotina /giʎo'tʃina/ f guillotine

guimba /'gĩba/ f butt

guinada /gi'nada/ f change of direction; dar uma ~ change direction

guinchar¹ /gĩ'ʃar/ vi squeal; <freios> screech

guinchar² /gĩ'ʃar/ vt tow <carro>; (içar) winch

guincho¹ /'gĩʃu/ m squeal; (de freios) screech

guincho² /'gĩʃu/ m (máquina) winch; (veículo) tow truck

guindar /gĩ'dar/ vt hoist; ~daste m crane

Guiné /gi'nɛ/ f Guinea

guisado /gi'zadu/ m stew; ~sar vt stew

guitarra /gi'taxa/ f (electric) guitar; ~rista m/f guitarist

guizo /'gizu/ m bell

gula /'gula/ f greed; ~lodice f greed; ~loseima f delicacy; ~loso /o/ a greedy

gume /'gumi/ m cutting edge

guri /gu'ri/ m boy; ~a f girl

guru /gu'ru/ m guru

gutural /gutu'raw/ (pl ~rais) a guttural

H

hábil /'abiw/ (pl ~beis) a clever, skilful

habilidade /abili'dadʒi/ f skill; ter ~dade com be good with; ~doso /o/ a skilful; ~tação f qualification; ~tar vt qualify

habitação /abita'sãw/ f housing; (casa) dwelling; ~tacional (pl ~tacionais) a housing; ~tante m/f inhabitant; ~tar vt inhabit □ vi live; ~tável (pl ~táveis) a habitable

hábito /'abitu/ m habit

habitual /abitu'aw/ (pl ~ais) a habitual; ~ar vt accustom (a to); ~ar-se vpr get accustomed (a to)

hadoque /a'dɔki/ m haddock

Haia /'aja/ f the Hague

Haiti /aj'tʃi/ m Haiti

haitiano /ajtʃi'anu/ a & m Haitian

hálito /'alitu/ m breath

halitose /ali'tɔzi/ f halitosis

hall /xɔw/ (pl ~s) m hall; (de hotel) foyer

haltere /aw'tɛri/ m dumbbell; ~rofilismo m weight lifting; ~rofilista m/f weight lifter

hambúrguer /ã'burger/ m hamburger

hangar /ã'gar/ m hangar

haras /'aras/ m invar stud farm

hardware /'xardwɛr/ m hardware

harmonia /armo'nia/ f harmony; ~nioso /o/ a harmonious; ~nizar vt harmonize; (conciliar) reconcile; ~nizar-se vpr (combinar) tone in; (concordar) coincide

harpa /'arpa/ f harp; ~pista m/f harpist

haste /'astʃi/ m pole; (de planta) stem, stalk; ~ar vt hoist, raise

Havaí /ava'i/ m Hawaii

havaiano /avaj'anu/ a & m Hawaiian

haver /a'ver/ m credit; pl possessions □ vt (auxiliar) have; (impessoal) há there is/are; ele tem havido there it had been; (impessoal) há there is/are; ele trabalha aqui há anos he's been working here for years; ela morreu há vinte anos (atrás) she died twenty years ago

haxixe /a'ʃiʃi/ m hashish

hebraico /e'brajku/ a & m Hebrew; ~breu a & m (f ~bréia) Hebrew

hectare /ek'tari/ m hectare

hediondo /edʒi'õdu/ a hideous

hein /ẽj/ int eh

hélice /'ɛlisi/ f propeller

helicóptero /eli'kɔpteru/ m helicopter

hélio /'ɛliu/ m helium

heliporto /eli'portu/ m heliport

hem /ẽj/ int eh

hematoma /ema'toma/ m bruise

hemisfério /emis'fɛriu/ m hemisphere; Hemisfério Norte/Sul Northern/Southern Hemisphere

hemofilia /emofi'lia/ f haemophilia; ~fílico a & m haemophiliac; ~globina f haemoglobin; ~grama m blood count

hemorragia /emoxa'ʒia/ f haemorrhage; ~róidas f pl haemorrhoids

henê /e'ne/ m henna

hepatite /epa'tʃitʃi/ f hepatitis

hera /'ɛra/ f ivy

heráldica /e'rawdʒika/ f heraldry; ~co a heraldic

herança /e'rãsa/ f inheritance; (de um povo etc) heritage

herbicida /erbi'sida/ m weedkiller; ~bívoro a herbivorous □ m herbivore

herdar /er'dar/ vt inherit; ~deiro m heir

hereditário /eredʒi'tariu/ a hereditary

herege /e'rɛʒi/ m/f heretic; ~sia f heresy

herético /e'rɛtʃiku/ a heretical

hermético /er'mɛtʃiku/ a airtight; (fig) obscure

hérnia /'ɛrnia/ f hernia

herói /e'rɔj/ m hero; ~co a heroic

hero|ína /ero'ina/ f (*mulher*) heroine; (*droga*) heroin; ~ismo m heroism

herpes /'ɛrpis/ m *invar* herpes; ~zoster m shingles

hesi|tação /ezita'sãw/ f hesitation; ~tante a hesitant; ~tar vi hesitate

hetero|doxo /etero'dɔksu/ a unorthodox; ~gêneo a heterogeneous

heterossexu|al /eteroseksu'aw/ (*pl* ~ais) a & m heterosexual

hexago|nal /eksago'naw/ (*pl* ~nais) a hexagonal

hexágono /ek'sagonu/ m hexagon

hiato /i'atu/ m hiatus

hiber|nação /iberna'sãw/ f hibernation; ~nar vi hibernate

híbrido /'ibridu/ a & m hybrid

hidrante /i'drãtʃi/ m fire hydrant

hidra|tante /idra'tãtʃi/ a moisturising □ m moisturizer; ~tar vt moisturize <*pele*>; ~to m ~to de carbono carbohydrate

hidráuli|ca /i'drawlika/ f hydraulics; ~co a hydraulic

hidrelétri|ca /idre'lɛtrika/ f hydroelectric power station; ~co a hydroelectric

hidro|avião /idroavi'ãw/ m seaplane; ~carboneto /e/ m hydrocarbon

hidrófilo /i'drɔfilu/ a absorbent; algodão ~ cotton wool, (*Amer*) absorbent cotton

hidrofobia /idrofo'bia/ f rabies

hidro|gênio /idro'ʒeniu/ m hydrogen; ~massagem f banheira de ~massagem jacuzzi; ~via f waterway

hiena /i'ena/ f hyena

hierarquia /ierar'kia/ f hierarchy

hieróglifo /ie'rɔglifu/ m hieroglyphic

hífen /'ifẽ/ m hyphen

higi|ene /iʒi'eni/ f hygiene; ~ênico a hygienic

hilari|ante /ilari'ãtʃi/ a hilarious; ~dade f hilarity

Himalaia /ima'laja/ m Himalayas

hin|di /ĩ'dʒi/ m Hindi; ~du a & m/f Hindu; ~duísmo m Hinduism; ~duísta a & m/f Hindu

hino /'inu/ m hymn; ~ nacional national anthem

hipermercado /ipermer'kadu/ m hypermarket

hipersensí|vel /ipersẽ'sivew/ (*pl* ~veis) a hypersensitive

hipertensão /ipertẽ'sãw/ f hypertension

hípico /'ipiku/ a horseriding

hipismo /i'pizmu/ m horseriding; (*corridas*) horseracing

hip|nose /ip'nɔzi/ f hypnosis; ~nótico a hypnotic; ~notismo m hypnotism; ~notizador m hypnotist; ~notizar vt hypnotize

hipocondríaco /ipokõ'driaku/ a & m hypochondriac

hipocrisia /ipokri'zia/ f hypocrisy

hipócrita /i'pɔkrita/ m/f hypocrite □ a hypocritical

hipódromo /i'pɔdromu/ m race course, (*Amer*) race track

hipopótamo /ipo'pɔtamu/ m hippopotamus

hipote|ca /ipo'tɛka/ f mortgage; ~car vt mortgage; ~cário a mortgage

hipotermia /ipoter'mia/ f hypothermia

hipótese /i'pɔtezi/ f hypothesis; na ~ de in the event of; na pior das ~s at worst

hipotético /ipo'tɛtʃiku/ a hypothetical

hirto /'irtu/ adj rigid, stiff

hispânico /is'paniku/ a Hispanic

histamina /ista'mina/ f histamine

his|terectomia /isterekto'mia/ f hysterectomy; ~teria f hysteria; ~térico a hysterical; ~terismo m hysteria

his|tória /is'tɔria/ f (*do passado*) history; (*conto*) story; *pl* (*amolação*) trouble; ~toriador m historian; ~tórico a historical; (*marcante*) historic □ m history

hoje /'oʒi/ adv today; ~ em dia nowadays; ~ de manhã this morning; ~ à noite tonight

Holanda /o'lãda/ f Holland

holan|dês /olã'des/ a (f ~desa) Dutch □ m (f ~desa) Dutchman (f -woman); (*língua*) Dutch; os ~deses the Dutch

holding /'xowdʒĩ/ (*pl* ~s) f holding company

holerite /ole'ritʃi/ m pay slip

holo|causto /olo'kawstu/ m holocaust; ~fote /ɔ/ m spotlight; ~grama m hologram

homem /'omẽ/ m man; ~ de negócios businessman; ~-rã (*pl* homens-rã) m frogman

homena|gear /omenaʒi'ar/ vt pay tribute to; ~gem f tribute; em ~gem a in honour of

homeo|pata /omio'pata/ m/f homoeopath; ~patia f homoeopathy; ~pático a homoeopathic

homérico /o'mɛriku/ a (*estrondoso*) booming; (*extraordinário*) phenomenal

homi|cida /omi'sida/ a homicidal □ m/f murderer; ~cídio m homicide; ~cídio involuntário manslaughter

homo|geneizado /omoʒeneȷ'zadu/ a <*leite*> homogenized; ~gêneo a homogeneous

homologar /omolo'gar/ vt ratify

homólogo /o'mɔlogu/ m opposite number □ a equivalent

homónimo /o'monimu/ m (xará) namesake; (vocábulo) homonym

homossexual /omoseksu'aw/ (pl ~ais) a & m homosexual; ~alismo m homosexuality

Honduras /õ'duras/ f Honduras

hondurenho /õdu'reɲu/ a & m Honduran

honestidade /onestʃi'dadʒi/ f honesty; ~to /ɛ/ a honest

honorário /ono'rariu/ a honorary; ~rários m pl fees; ~rífico a honorific

honra /'õxa/ f honour; ~radez f honesty, integrity; ~rado a honourable; ~rar vt honour; ~roso /o/ a honourable

hóquei /'ɔkej/ m (field) hockey; ~ sobre gelo ice hockey; ~ sobre patins roller hockey

hora /'ɔra/ f (unidade de tempo) hour; (ocasião) time; que ~s são? what's the time?; a que ~s? at what time?; às três ~s at three o'clock; dizer as ~s tell the time; tem ~s? do you have the time?; de ~ em ~ every hour; em cima da ~ at the last minute; na ~ (naquele momento) at the time; (no ato) on the spot; (a tempo) on time; está na ~ de ir it's time to go; na ~ H (no momento certo) at just the right moment; (no momento crítico) at the crucial moment; meia ~ half an hour; toda a ~ all the time; fazer ~ kill time; marcar ~ make an appointment; perder a ~ lose track of time; não tenho ~ my time is my own; não vejo a ~ de ir I can't wait to go; ~s extras overtime; ~s vagas spare time

horário /o'rariu/ a hourly; km ~s km per hour □ m (hora) time; (tabela) timetable; (de trabalho etc) hours; ~ nobre prime time

horda /'ɔrda/ f horde

horista /o'rista/ a paid by the hour □ m/f worker paid by the hour

horizontal /orizõ'taw/ (pl ~tais) a & f horizontal; ~te m horizon

hormonal /ormo'naw/ (pl ~nais) a hormonal; ~mônio m hormone

horóscopo /o'rɔskopu/ m horoscope

horrendo /o'xẽdu/ a horrid

horripilante /oxipi'lãtʃi/ a horrifying; ~lar vt horrify

horrível /o'xivew/ (pl ~veis) a horrible, awful

horror /o'xor/ m horror (a of); (coisa horrorosa) horrible thing; ser um ~ be awful; que ~! how awful!

horrorizar /oxori'zar/ vt/i horrify; ~rizar-se vpr be horrified; ~roso /o/ a horrible

horta /'ɔrta/ f vegetable plot; ~ comercial market garden, (Amer) truck farm; ~liça f vegetable

hortelã /orte'lã/ f mint; ~-pimenta peppermint

horti|cultor /ortʃikuw'tor/ m horticulturalist; ~cultura f horticulture; ~frutigranjeiros m pl fruit and vegetables; ~granjeiros m pl vegetables

horto /'ɔrtu/ m market garden; (viveiro) nursery

hospedagem /ospe'daʒẽ/ f accommodation; ~dar vt put up; ~dar-se vpr stay

hóspede /'ɔspidʒi/ m/f guest

hospedeira /ospe'dera/ f landlady; ~ra de bordo (Port) stewardess; ~ro m landlord

hospício /os'pisiu/ m (de loucos) asylum

hospital /ospi'taw/ (pl ~tais) m hospital; ~talar a hospital; ~taleiro a hospitable; ~talidade f hospitality; ~talizar vt hospitalize

hóstia /'ɔstʃia/ f Host, Communion wafer

hostil /os'tʃiw/ (pl ~tis) a hostile; ~tilidade f hostility; ~tilizar vt antagonize

hotel /o'tɛw/ (pl ~téis) m hotel; ~teleiro a hotel □ m hotelier

huma|nidade /umani'dadʒi/ f humanity; ~nismo m humanism; ~nista a & m/f humanist; ~nitário a & m humanitarian; ~nizar vt humanize; ~no a human; (compassivo) humane; ~nos m pl humans

húmido /'umidu/ adj (Port) humid

humil|dade /umiw'dadʒi/ f humility; ~de a humble

humi|lhação /umiʎa'sãw/ f humiliation; ~lhante a humiliating; ~lhar vt humiliate

humor /u'mor/ m humour; (disposição do espírito) mood; de bom/mau ~ in a good/bad mood

humo|rismo /umo'rizmu/ m humour; ~rista m/f (no palco) comedian; (escritor) humorist; ~rístico a humorous

húngaro /'ũgaru/ a & m Hungarian

Hungria /ũ'gria/ f Hungary

hurra /'uxa/ int hurrah □ m cheer

I

iate /i'atʃi/ m yacht; ~tismo m yachting; ~tista m/f yachtsman (f -woman)

ibérico /i'bɛriku/ a & m Iberian

ibope /i'bɔpi/ m dar ~ (fam) be popular

içar /i'sar/ vt hoist

iceberg /ajs'bɛrgi/ (pl ~s) m iceberg

ícone /'ikoni/ m icon

iconoclasta /ikono'klasta/ m/f iconoclast □ a iconoclastic

icterícia /ikte'risia/ f jaundice

ida /'ida/ f going; na ~ on the way there; ~ e volta return, (Amer) round trip

idade /i'dadʒi/ f age; meia ~ middle age; homem de meia ~ middle-aged man; senhor de ~ elderly man; Idade Média Middle Ages

ideal /ide'aw/ (pl ~ais) a & m ideal; ~alismo m idealism; ~alista m/f idealist □ a idealistic; ~alizar vt (criar) devise; (sublimar) idealize; ~ar vt devise; ~ário m ideas

idéia /i'deja/ f idea; mudar de ~ change one's mind

idem /'idẽ/ adv ditto

idêntico /i'dẽtʃiku/ a identical

identidade /idẽtʃi'dadʒi/ f identity; ~ficar vt identify; ~ficar-se vpr identify (com with)

ideologia /ideolo'ʒia/ f ideology; ~lógico a ideological

idílico /i'dʒiliku/ a idyllic

idílio /i'dʒiliu/ m idyll

idioma /idʒi'oma/ m language; ~mático a idiomatic

idiota /idʒi'ɔta/ m/f idiot □ a idiotic; ~tice f stupidity; (uma) stupid thing

idolatrar /idola'trar/ vt idolize; ~tria f idolatry

ídolo /'idulu/ m idol

idôneo /i'doniu/ a suitable

idoso /i'dozu/ a elderly

Iêmen /i'emẽ/ m Yemen

iemenita /ieme'nita/ a & m/f Yemeni

iene /i'ɛni/ m yen

iglu /i'glu/ m igloo

ignição /igni'sãw/ f ignition

ignomínia /igno'minia/ f ignominy

ignorância /igno'rãsia/ f ignorance; ~rante a ignorant; ~rar (desconsiderar) ignore; (desconhecer) not know

igreja /i'greʒa/ f church

igual /i'gwaw/ (pl ~ais) a equal; (em aparência) identical; (liso) even □ m/f equal; por ~al equally; ~alar vt equal; level <terreno>; ~alar(-se) a be equal to; ~aldade f equality; ~alitária a egalitarian; ~almente adv equally; (como resposta) the same to you; ~alzinho a exactly the same (a as)

iguaria /igwa'ria/ f delicacy

iídiche /i'idiʃi/ m Yiddish

ilegal /ile'gaw/ (pl ~gais) a illegal; ~galidade f illegality

ilegítimo /ile'ʒitʃimu/ a illegitimate

ilegível /ile'ʒivew/ (pl ~veis) a illegible

ileso /i'lɛzu/ a unhurt

iletrado /ile'tradu/ adj & m illiterate

ilha /'iʎa/ f island

ilharga /i'ʎarga/ f side

ilhéu /i'ʎɛw/ m (f ilhoa) islander

ilhós /i'ʎɔs/ m invar eyelet

ilhota /i'ʎɔta/ f small island

ilícito /i'lisitu/ a illicit

ilimitado /ilimi'tadu/ a unlimited

ilógico /i'lɔʒiku/ a illogical

iludir /ilu'dʒir/ vt delude; ~-se vpr delude o.s.

iluminação /ilumina'sãw/ f lighting; (inspiração) enlightenment; ~nar vt light up, illuminate; (inspirar) enlighten

ilusão /ilu'zãw/ f illusion; (sonho) delusion; ~sionista m/f illusionist; ~sório a illusory

ilustração /ilustra'sãw/ f illustration; (erudição) learning; ~trador m illustrator; ~trar vt illustrate; ~trativo a illustrative; ~tre a illustrious; ~tríssimo senhor Dear Sir

ímã /'imã/ m magnet

imaculado /imaku'ladu/ a immaculate

imagem /i'maʒẽ/ f image; (da TV) picture

imaginação /imaʒina'sãw/ f imagination; ~nar vt imagine; ~nário a imaginary; ~nativo a imaginative; ~nável (pl ~náveis) a imaginable; ~noso /o/ a imaginative

imaturidade /imaturi'dadʒi/ f immaturity; ~ro a immature

imbatível /ĩba'tʃivew/ (pl ~veis) a unbeatable

imbecil /ĩbe'siw/ (pl ~cis) a stupid □ m/f imbecile

imberbe /ĩ'bɛrbi/ adj (sem barba) beardless

imbricar /ĩbri'kar/ vt overlap; ~-se vpr overlap

imediações /imedʒia'sõjs/ f pl vicinity; ~tamente adv immediately; ~to a immediate

imemorial /imemori'aw/ (pl ~ais) a immemorial

imensidão /imẽsi'dãw/ f vastness; ~so a immense

imergir /imer'ʒir/ vt immerse

imigração /imigra'sãw/ f immigration; ~grante a & m/f immigrant; ~grar vi immigrate

iminência /imi'nẽsia/ f imminence; ~nente a imminent

imiscuir-se /imisku'irsi/ vpr interfere

imitação /imita'sãw/ f imitation; ~tador m imitator; ~tar vt imitate imobili|ária /imobili'aria/ *f* estate agent's, (*Amer*) realtor; ~ário *a* property; ~dade *f* immobility; ~zar *vt* immobilize

imo|ral /imo'raw/ (*pl* ~rais) *a* immoral; ~ralidade *f* immorality

imor|tal /imor'taw/ (*pl* ~tais) *a* immortal □ *m/f* member of the Brazilian Academy of Letters; ~talidade *f* immortality; ~talizar *vt* immortalize

imó|vel /i'mɔvew/ (*pl* ~veis) *a* motionless, immobile □ *m* building, property; real estate

impaci|ência /ipasi'ēsia/ *f* impatience; ~entar-se *vpr* get impatient; ~ente *a* impatient

impacto /i'paktu/, (*Port*) impacte /i'paktʃi/ *m* impact

impagá|vel /ipa'gavew/ (*pl* ~veis) *a* priceless

ímpar /'ipar/ *a* unique; <*número*> odd

imparci|al /iparsi'aw/ (*pl* ~ais) *a* impartial; ~alidade *f* impartiality

impasse /i'pasi/ *m* impasse

impassí|vel /ipa'sivew/ (*pl* ~veis) *a* impassive

impecá|vel /ipe'kavew/ (*pl* ~veis) *a* impeccable

impe|dido /ipe'dʒidu/ *a* <*rua*> blocked; (*Port: ocupado*) engaged, (*Amer*) busy; (*no futebol*) offside; ~dimento *m* prevention; (*estorvo*) obstruction; (*no futebol*) offside position; ~dir *vt* stop; (*estorvar*) hinder; block <*rua*>; ~dir alg de ir ou que alg vá stop s.o. going

impelir /ipe'lir/ *vt* drive

impenetrá|vel /ipene'travew/ (*pl* ~veis) *a* impenetrable

impensá|vel /ipe'savew/ (*pl* ~veis) *a* unthinkable

impe|rador /ipera'dor/ *m* emperor; ~rar *vi* reign, rule; ~rativo *a* & *m* imperative; ~ratriz *f* empress

impercepti|vel /ipersep'tʃivew/ (*pl* ~veis) *a* imperceptible

imperdi|vel /iper'dʒivew/ (*pl* ~veis) *a* unmissable

imperdoá|vel /iperdo'avew/ (*pl* ~veis) *a* unforgivable

imperfei|ção /iperfej'sãw/ *f* imperfection; ~to *a* & *m* imperfect

imperi|al /iperi'aw/ (*pl* ~ais) *a* imperial; ~alismo *m* imperialism; ~alista *a* & *m/f* imperialist

império /i'pɛriu/ *m* empire

imperioso /iperi'ozu/ *a* imperious; <*necessidade*> pressing

imperme|abilizar /ipermiabili'zar/ *vt* waterproof; ~ável (*pl* ~áveis) *a* waterproof; (*fig*) impervious (a to) □ *m* raincoat

imperti|nência /ipertʃi'nēsia/ *f* impertinence; ~nente *a* impertinent

impesso|al /ipeso'aw/ (*pl* ~ais) *a* impersonal

ímpeto /'ipetu/ *m* (*vontade*) urge, impulse; (*de emoção*) surge; (*movimento*) start; (*na física*) impetus

impetuo|sidade /ipetuozi'dadʒi/ *f* impetuosity; ~so /o/ *a* impetuous

impiedoso /ipie'dozu/ *a* merciless

impingir /ipī'ʒir/ *vt* foist (a on)

implacá|vel /ipla'kavew/ (*pl* ~veis) *a* implacable

implan|tar /iplã'tar/ *vt* introduce; (*no corpo*) implant; ~te *m* implant

implemen|tar /iplemē'tar/ *vt* implement; ~to *m* implement

impli|cação /iplika'sãw/ *f* implication; ~cância *f* (*ato*) harassment; (*antipatia*) grudge; estar de ~cância com have it in for; ~cante *a* troublesome □ *m/f* troublemaker; ~car *vt* (*comprometer*) implicate; ~car (em) (*dar a entender*) imply; (*acarretar, exigir*) involve; ~car com (*provocar*) pick on; (*antipatizar*) not get on with

implícito /i'plisitu/ *a* implicit

implorar /iplo'rar/ *vt* plead for (a from)

imponente /ipo'nētʃi/ *a* imposing

impopular /ipopu'lar/ *a* unpopular

impor /i'por/ *vt* impose (a on); command <*respeito*>; ~-se *vpr* assert o.s.

impor|tação /iporta'sãw/ *f* import; ~tador *m* importer; ~tadora *f* import company; ~tados *m pl* imported goods; ~tância *f* importance; (*quantia*) amount; ter ~tância be important; ~tante *a* important; ~tar *vt* import <*mercadorias*> □ *vi* matter; ~tar em (*montar a*) amount to; (*resultar em*) lead to; ~tar-se (com) mind

importu|nar /iportu'nar/ *vt* bother; ~no *a* annoying

imposição /ipozi'sãw/ *f* imposition

impossibili|dade /iposibili'dadʒi/ *f* impossibility; ~tar *vt* make impossible; ~tar alg de ir, ~tar a alg ir prevent s.o. from going, make it impossible for s.o. to go

impossí|vel /ipo'sivew/ (*pl* ~veis) *a* impossible

impos|to /i'postu/ *m* tax; ~to de renda income tax; ~to sobre o valor acrescentado (*Port*) VAT; ~tor *m* impostor; ~tura *f* deception

impo|tência /ipo'tēsia/ *f* impotence; ~tente *a* impotent

impreci|são /ipresi'zãw/ *f* imprecision; ~so *a* imprecise

impregnar /ipreg'nar/ *vt* impregnate

imprensa /i'prēsa/ *f* press; ~ marrom gutter press

imprescindí|vel /ĩpresĩ'dʒivew/ (pl ~veis) a essential

impres|são /ĩpre'sãw/ f impression; (no prelo) printing; ~são digital fingerprint; ~sionante a (imponente) impressive; (comovente) striking; ~sionar vt (causar admiração) impress; (comover) make an impression on; ~sionar-se vpr be impressed (com by); ~sionável (pl ~sionáveis) a impressionable; ~sionismo m impressionism; ~sionista a & m/f impressionist; ~so a printed □ m printed sheet; pl printed matter; ~sor m printer; ~sora f printer

impresta|vel /ĩpres'tavew/ (pl ~veis) a useless

impre|visível /ĩprevi'zivew/ (pl ~visíveis) a unpredictable; ~visto a unforeseen □ m unforeseen circumstance

imprimir /ĩpri'mir/ vt print

impropério /ĩpro'pεriu/ m term of abuse; pl abuse

impróprio /ĩ'prɔpriu/ a improper; (inadequado) unsuitable (para for)

imprová|vel /ĩpro'vavew/ (pl ~veis) a unlikely

improvi|sação /ĩproviza'sãw/ f improvisation; ~sar vt/i improvise; ~so m de ~so on the spur of the moment

impru|dência /ĩpru'dẽsia/ f recklessness; ~dente a reckless

impul|sionar /ĩpuwsio'nar/ vt drive; ~sivo a impulsive; ~so m impulse

impu|ne /ĩ'puni/ a unpunished; ~nidade f impunity

impu|reza /ĩpu'reza/ f impurity; ~ro a impure

imun|dície /imũ'dʒisi/ f filth; ~do a filthy

imu|ne /i'muni/ a immune (a to); ~nidade f immunity; ~nizar vt immunize

inabalá|vel /inaba'lavew/ (pl ~veis) a unshakeable

iná|bil /i'nabiw/ (pl ~bis) a (desafeitado) clumsy

inabitado /inabi'tadu/ a uninhabited

inacabado /inaka'badu/ a unfinished

inaceitá|vel /inasej'tavew/ (pl ~veis) a unacceptable

inacessí|vel /inase'sivew/ (pl ~veis) a inaccessible

inacreditá|vel /inakredʒi'tavew/ (pl ~veis) a unbelievable

inadequado /inade'kwadu/ a unsuitable

inadmissí|vel /inadʒimi'sivew/ (pl ~veis) a inadmissible

inadvertência /inadʒiver'tẽsia/ f oversight

inalar /ina'lar/ vt inhale

inalcançá|vel /inawkã'savew/ (pl ~veis) a unattainable

inalterá|vel /inawte'ravew/ (pl ~veis) a unchangeable

inanição /inani'sãw/ f starvation

inanimado /inani'madu/ a inanimate

inapto /i'naptu/ a (incapaz) unfit

inati|vidade /inatʃivi'dadʒi/ f inactivity; ~vo a inactive

inato /i'natu/ a innate

inaudito /inaw'dʒitu/ a unheard of

inaugu|ração /inawgura'sãw/ f inauguration; ~ral (pl ~rais) a inaugural; ~rar vt inaugurate

incabí|vel /ĩka'bivew/ (pl ~veis) a inappropriate

incalculá|vel /ĩkawku'lavew/ (pl ~veis) a incalculable

incandescente /ĩkãde'sẽtʃi/ a red-hot

incansá|vel /ĩkã'savew/ (pl ~veis) a tireless

incapaci|tado /ĩkapasi'tadu/ a <pessoa> disabled; ~tar vt incapacitate

incauto /ĩ'kawtu/ a reckless

incendi|ar /ĩsẽdʒi'ar/ vt set alight; ~ar-se vpr catch fire; ~ário a incendiary; (fig) <discurso> inflammatory □ m arsonist; (fig) agitator

incêndio /ĩ'sẽdʒiu/ m fire

incenso /ĩ'sẽsu/ m incense

incenti|var /ĩsẽtʃi'var/ vt encourage; ~vo m incentive

incer|teza /ĩser'teza/ f uncertainty; ~to /ε/ a uncertain

inces|to /ĩ'sestu/ m incest; ~tuoso /o/ a incestuous

incha|ção /ĩʃa'sãw/ f swelling; ~char vt/i swell

inci|dência /ĩsi'dẽsia/ f incidence; ~dente m incident; ~dir vi ~dir em <luz> shine on; <imposto> be payable on

incinerar /ĩsine'rar/ vt incinerate

inci|são /ĩsi'zãw/ f incision; ~sivo a incisive

incitar /ĩsi'tar/ vt incite

incli|nação /ĩklina'sãw/ f (do chão) incline; (da cabeça) nod; (propensão) inclination; ~nado a <chão> sloping; <edifício> leaning; (propenso) inclined (a to); ~nar vt tilt; nod <cabeça> □ vi <chão> slope; <edifício> lean; (tender) incline (para towards); ~nar-se vpr lean

inclu|ir /ĩklu'ir/ vt include; ~são f inclusion; ~sive prep including □ adv inclusive; (até) even; ~so a included

incoe|rência /ĩkoe'rẽsia/ f (falta de nexo) incoherence; (inconseqüência) inconsistency; ~rente a (sem nexo) incoherent; (inconseqüente) inconsistent incógni|ta /i'kɔgnita/ *f* unknown; ~to *adv* incognito

incolor /iko'lor/ *a* colourless

incólume /i'kɔlumi/ *a* unscathed

incomodar /ikomo'dar/ *vt* bother □ *vi* be a nuisance; ~-se *vpr* (*dar-se ao trabalho*) bother (em to); ~-se (com) be bothered (by), mind

incómodo /i'kɔmodu/ *a* (*desagradável*) tiresome; (*sem conforto*) uncomfortable □ *m* nuisance

incompa|rável /ikõpa'ravew/ (*pl* ~ráveis) *a* incomparable; ~tível (*pl* ~tíveis) *a* incompatible

incompe|tência /ikõpe'tẽsia/ *f* incompetence; ~tente *a* incompetent

incompleto /ikõ'plɛtu/ *a* incomplete

incompreen|sível /ikõprië'sivew/ (*pl* ~veis) *a* incomprehensible

inconcebí|vel /ikõse'bivew/ (*pl* ~veis) *a* inconceivable

incondicio|nal /ikõdʒisio'naw/ (*pl* ~nais) *a* unconditional; <*fé, partidário*> firm

inconformado /ikõfor'madu/ *a* un-reconciled (com to)

inconfundí|vel /ikõfũ'dʒivew/ (*pl* ~veis) *a* unmistakeable

inconsciente /ikõsi'ẽtʃi/ *a & m* unconscious

inconseqüente /ikõse'kwẽtʃi/ *a* inconsistent

incons|tância /ikõs'tãsia/ *f* changeability; ~tante *a* changeable

inconstitucio|nal /ikõstʃitusio'naw/ (*pl* ~nais) *a* unconstitutional

incontestá|vel /ikõtes'tavew/ (*pl* ~veis) *a* indisputable

inconveniente /ikõveni'ẽtʃi/ *a* (*difícil*) inconvenient; (*desagradável*) annoying, tiresome; (*indecente*) unseemly □ *m* drawback

incorporar /ikorpo'rar/ *vt* incorporate

incorrer /iko'xer/ *vi* ~ em <*multa etc*> incur

incorrigí|vel /ikoxi'ʒivew/ (*pl* ~veis) *a* incorrigible

incrédulo /i'krɛdulu/ *a* incredulous

incremen|tado /ikremẽ'tadu/ *a* (*fam*) stylish; ~tar *vt* build up; (*fam*) jazz up; ~to *m* development, growth

incriminar /ikrimi'nar/ *vt* incriminate

incrí|vel /i'krivew/ (*pl* ~veis) *a* incredible

incu|bação /ikuba'sãw/ *f* incubation; ~badora *f* incubator; ~bar *vt/i* incubate

inculto /i'kuwtu/ *a* <*pessoa*> uneducated; <*terreno*> uncultivated

incum|bência /ikũ'bẽsia/ *f* task; ~bir *vt* ~bir alg de aco/de ir as-

sign s.o. sth/to go □ *vi* ~bir a be up to; ~bir-se de take on

incurá|vel /iku'ravew/ (*pl* ~veis) *a* incurable

incursão /ikur'sãw/ *f* incursion

incutir /iku'tʃir/ *vt* instil (em in)

indagar /ida'gar/ *vt* inquire (into)

inde|cência /ide'sẽsia/ *f* indecency; ~cente *a* indecent

indecifrá|vel /idesi'fravew/ (*pl* ~veis) *a* indecipherable

indeciso /ide'sizu/ *a* undecided

indecoroso /ideko'rozu/ *a* indecorous

indefi|nido /idefi'nidu/ *a* indefinite; ~nível (*pl* ~níveis) *a* indefinable

indelé|vel /ide'lɛvew/ (*pl* ~veis) *a* indelible

indelica|deza /idelika'deza/ *f* impoliteness; (*uma*) impolite thing; ~do *a* impolite

indeni|zação /ideniza'sãw/ *f* compensation; ~zar *vt* compensate

indepen|dência /idepẽ'dẽsia/ *f* independence; ~dente *a* independent

indescriti|vel /idʒiskri'tʃivew/ (*pl* ~veis) *a* indescribable

indesculpá|vel /idʒiskuw'pavew/ (*pl* ~veis) *a* inexcusable

indesejá|vel /ideze'ʒavew/ (*pl* ~veis) *a* undesirable

indestruti|vel /idʒistru'tʃivew/ (*pl* ~veis) *a* indestructible

indeterminado /idetermi'nadu/ *a* indeterminate

indevido /ide'vidu/ *a* undue

indexar /idek'sar/ *vt* index; index-link <*salário, preços*>

Índia /'idʒia/ *f* India

indiano /idʒi'anu/ *a & m* Indian

indi|cação /idʒika'sãw/ *f* indication; (*do caminho*) directions; (*nomeação*) nomination; (*recomendação*) recommendation; ~cador *m* indicator; (*dedo*) index finger □ *a* indicative (de of); ~car *vt* indicate; (*para cargo, prêmio*) nominate (para for); (*recomendar*) recommend; ~cativo *a & m* indicative

índice /'idʒisi/ *m* (*taxa*) rate; (*em livro etc*) index; ~ de audiência ratings

indiciar /idʒisi'ar/ *vt* charge

indício /i'dʒisiu/ *m* sign, indication; (*de crime*) clue

indife|rença /idʒife'rẽsa/ *f* indifference; ~rente *a* indifferent

indígena /i'dʒiʒena/ *a* indigenous, native □ *m/f* native

indiges|tão /idʒiʒes'tãw/ *f* indigestion; ~to *a* indigestible; (*fig*) heavygoing

indig|nação /idʒigna'sãw/ *f* indignation; ~nado *a* indignant; ~nar *vt* make indignant; ~nar-se *vpr* get indignant (com about)

indig|nidade /idʒigni'dadʒi/ *f* indignity; ~no *a* <*pessoa*> unworthy; <*ato*> despicable

índio /'idʒiu/ *a & m* Indian

indire|ta /idʒi'rɛta/ *f* hint; ~to /ɛ/ *a* indirect

indis|creto /idʒis'krɛtu/ *a* indiscreet; ~crição *f* indiscretion

indiscriminado /idʒiskrimi'nadu/ *a* indiscriminate

indiscuti|vel /idʒisku'tʃivew/ (*pl* ~veis) *a* unquestionable

indispensá|vel /idʒispẽ'savew/ (*pl* ~veis) *a* indispensable

indisponí|vel /idʒispo'nivew/ (*pl* ~veis) *a* unavailable

indis|por /idʒis'por/ *vt* upset; ~por alg contra turn s.o. against; ~por-se *vpr* fall out (com with); ~posição *f* indisposition; ~posto *a* (*doente*) indisposed

indistinto /idʒis'tʃĩtu/ *a* indistinct

individu|al /idʒividu'aw/ (*pl* ~ais) *a* individual; ~alidade *f* individuality; ~alismo *m* individualism; ~alista *a & m/f* individualist

indivíduo /idʒi'viduu/ *m* individual

indizí|vel /idʒi'zivew/ (*pl* ~veis) *a* unspeakable

índole /'idoli/ *f* nature

indo|lência /ido'lẽsia/ *f* indolence; ~lente *a* indolent

indolor /ido'lor/ *a* painless

Indonésia /ido'nɛzia/ *f* Indonesia

indonésio /ido'nɛziu/ *a & m* Indonesian

indubitá|vel /idubi'tavew/ (*pl* ~veis) *a* undoubted

indul|gência /iduw'ʒẽsia/ *f* indulgence; ~gente *a* indulgent

indulto /i'duwtu/ *m* pardon

indumentária /idumẽ'taria/ *f* outfit

indústria /i'dustria/ *f* industry

industri|al /idustri'aw/ (*pl* ~ais) *a* industrial □ *m/f* industrialist; ~alizado *a* <*país*> industrialized; <*mercadoria*> manufactured; <*comida*> processed; ~alizar *vt* industrialize <*país, agricultura etc*>; process <*comida, lixo etc*>; ~oso /o/ *a* industrious

induzir /idu'zir/ *vt* (*persuadir*) induce; (*inferir*) infer (de from); ~ em erro lead astray, mislead s.o.

inebriante /inebri'ãtʃi/ *a* intoxicating

inédito /i'nɛdʒitu/ *a* unheard-of, unprecedented; (*não publicado*) unpublished

ineficaz /inefi'kas/ *a* ineffective

inefici|ência /inefisi'ẽsia/ *f* inefficiency; ~ente *a* inefficient

inegá|vel /ine'gavew/ (*pl* ~veis) *a* undeniable

inepcia /i'nɛpsia/ *f* ineptitude

inepto /i'nɛptu/ *a* inept

inequívoco /ine'kivoku/ *a* unmistakeable

inércia /i'nɛrsia/ *f* inertia

inerente /ine'rẽtʃi/ *a* inherent (a in)

inerte /i'nɛrtʃi/ *a* inert

inesgotá|vel /inezgo'tavew/ (*pl* ~veis) *a* inexhaustible

inesperado /inespe'radu/ *a* unexpected

inesquecí|vel /ineske'sivew/ (*pl* ~veis) *a* unforgettable

inevitá|vel /inevi'tavew/ (*pl* ~veis) *a* inevitable

inexato /ine'zatu/ *a* inaccurate

inexis|tência /inezis'tẽsia/ *f* lack; ~tente *a* non-existent

inexperi|ência /inisperi'ẽsia/ *f* inexperience; ~ente *a* inexperienced

inexpressivo /inespre'sivu/ *a* expressionless

infalí|vel /ifa'livew/ (*pl* ~veis) *a* infallible

infame /i'fami/ *a* despicable; (*péssimo*) dreadful

infâmia /i'famia/ *f* disgrace

infância /i'fãsia/ *f* childhood

infantaria /ifãta'ria/ *f* infantry

infan|til /ifã'tʃiw/ *a* <*roupa, livro*> children's; (*bobo*) childish; ~tilidade *f* childishness; (*uma*) childish thing

infarto /i'fartu/ *m* heart attack

infeliz /ife'lis/ *a* (*não contente*) unhappy; (*inconveniente*) unfortunate; (*desgraçado*) wretched □ *m* (*desgraçado*) wretch; ~mente *adv* unfortunately

inferi|or /iferi'or/ *a* lower; (*em qualidade*) inferior (a to); ~oridade *f* inferiority

inferir /ife'rir/ *vt* infer

infer|nal /ifer'naw/ (*pl* ~nais) *a* infernal; ~nizar *vt* ~nizar a vida dele make his life hell; ~no /ɛ/ *m* hell

infér|til /i'fɛrtʃiw/ (*pl* ~teis) *a* infertile

infertilidade /ifertʃili'dadʒi/ *f* infertility

infestar /ifes'tar/ *vt* infest

infetar /ife'tar/ *vt* infect

infidelidade /ifideli'dadʒi/ *f* infidelity

infi|el /ifi'ɛw/ (*pl* ~éis) *a* unfaithful

infiltrar /ifiw'trar/ *vt* infiltrate; ~-se em infiltrate

ínfimo /'ifimu/ *a* lowest; (*muito pequeno*) tiny

infindá|vel /ifĩ'davew/ (*pl* ~veis) *a* unending

infinidade /ĩfini'dadʒi/ f infinity; uma ∼ de an infinite number of

infini|tesimal /ĩfinitezi'maw/ (pl ∼tesimais) a infinitesimal; ∼tivo a & m infinitive; ∼to a infinite □ m infinity

infla|ção /ĩfla'sãw/ f inflation; ∼cionar vt inflate; ∼cionário a inflationary; ∼cionista a & m/f inflationist

infla|mação /ĩflama'sãw/ f inflammation; ∼mar vt inflame; ∼mar-se vpr become inflamed; ∼matório a inflammatory; ∼mável (pl ∼máveis) a inflammable

in|flar vt inflate; ∼flar-se vpr inflate; ∼flável (pl ∼fláveis) a inflatable

infle|xibilidade /ĩfleksibili'dadʒi/ f inflexibility; ∼xível (pl ∼xíveis) a inflexible

infligir /ĩfli'ʒir/ vt inflict (a on)

influência /ĩflu'ẽsia/ f influence

influen|ciar /ĩfluẽsi'ar/ vt ∼ciar (em) influence; ∼ciar-se vpr be influenced; ∼ciável (pl ∼ciáveis) a open to influence; ∼te a influential

influir /ĩflu'ir/ vi ∼ em ou sobre influence

informação /ĩforma'sãw/ f information; (uma) a piece of information; (mil) intelligence; pl information

infor|mal /ĩfor'maw/ (pl ∼mais) a informal; ∼malidade f informality

infor|mar /ĩfor'mar/ vt inform; ∼mar-se vpr find out (de about); ∼mática f information technology; ∼mativo a informative; ∼matizar vt computerize; ∼me m (mil) piece of intelligence

infortúnio /ĩfor'tuniu/ m misfortune

infração /ĩfra'sãw/ f infringement

infra-estrutura /ĩfraistru'tura/ f infrastructure

infrator /ĩfra'tor/ m offender

infravermelho /ĩfraver'meʎu/ a infrared

infringir /ĩfrĩ'ʒir/ vt infringe

infrutífero /ĩfru'tʃiferu/ a fruitless

infundado /ĩfũ'dadu/ a unfounded

infundir /ĩfũ'dʒir/ vt (insuflar) infuse; (incutir) instil

infusão /ĩfu'zãw/ f infusion

ingenuidade /ĩʒenui'dadʒi/ f naivety

ingênuo /ĩ'ʒenuu/ a naive

Inglaterra /ĩgla'tɛxa/ f England

ingerir /ĩʒe'rir/ vt ingest; (engolir) swallow

in|glês /ĩ'gles/ a (f ∼glesa) English □ m (f ∼glesa) Englishman (f -woman) (língua) English; os ∼gleses the English

ingra|tidão /ĩgratʃi'dãw/ f ingratitude; ∼to a ungrateful

ingrediente /ĩgredʒi'ẽtʃi/ m ingredient

íngreme /'ĩgrimi/ a steep

ingres|sar /ĩgre'sar/ vi ∼sar em join; ∼so m entry; (bilhete) ticket

inhame /i'ɲami/ m yam

ini|bição /inibi'sãw/ f inhibition; ∼bir vt inhibit

inici|ado /inisi'adu/ m initiate; ∼al (pl ∼ais) a & f initial; ∼ar vt (começar) begin; (em ciência, seita etc) initiate (em into) □ vi begin; ∼ativa f initiative

início /i'nisiu/ m beginning

inigualá|vel /inigwa'lavew/ (pl ∼veis) a unparalleled

inimaginá|vel /inimaʒi'navew/ (pl ∼veis) a unimaginable

inimi|go /ini'migu/ a & m enemy; ∼zade f enmity

ininterrupto /inĩte'xuptu/ a continuous

inje|ção /iʒe'sãw/ f injection; ∼tado a <olhos> bloodshot; ∼tar vt inject; ∼tável (pl ∼táveis) a <droga> intravenous

injúria /ĩ'ʒuria/ f insult

injuriar /ĩʒuri'ar/ vt insult

injus|tiça /ĩʒus'tʃisa/ f injustice; ∼tiçado a wronged; ∼to a unfair, unjust

ino|cência /ino'sẽsia/ f innocence; ∼centar vt clear (de of); ∼cente a innocent

inocular /inoku'lar/ vt inoculate

inócuo /i'nɔkuu/ a harmless

inodoro /ino'doru/ a odourless

inofensivo /inofẽ'sivu/ a harmless

inoportuno /inopor'tunu/ a inopportune

inorgânico /inor'ganiku/ a inorganic

inóspito /i'nɔspitu/ a inhospitable

ino|vação /inova'sãw/ f innovation; ∼var vt/i innovate

inoxidá|vel /inoksi'davew/ (pl ∼veis) a <aço> stainless

inquérito /ĩ'kɛritu/ m inquiry

inquie|tação /ĩkieta'sãw/ f concern; ∼tador, ∼tante a worrying; ∼tar vt worry; ∼tar-se vpr worry; ∼to /ɛ/ a uneasy

inquili|nato /ĩkili'natu/ m tenancy; ∼no m tenant

inquirir /ĩki'rir/ vt cross-examine <testemunha>

Inquisição /ĩkizi'sãw/ f a ∼ the Inquisition

insaciá|vel /ĩsasi'avew/ (pl ∼veis) a insatiable

insalubre /ĩsa'lubri/ a unhealthy

insatis|fação /ĩsatʃisfa'sãw/ f dissatisfaction; ∼fatório a unsatisfactory; ∼feito a dissatisfied ins|crever /iʃkre'ver/ vt (registrar) register; (gravar) inscribe; ~crever-se vpr register; (em escola etc) enrol; ~crição f (registro) registration; (em clube, escola) enrolment; (em monumento etc) inscription

insegu|rança /isegu'rãsa/ f insecurity; ~ro a insecure

insemi|nação /isemina'sãw/ f insemination; ~nar vt inseminate

insen|satez /isẽsa'tes/ f folly; ~sato a foolish; ~sibilidade f insensitivity; ~sível (pl ~síveis) a insensitive

insepará|vel /isepa'ravew/ (pl ~veis) a inseparable

inserção /iser'sãw/ f insertion

inserir /ise'rir/ vt insert; enter <dados>

inse|ticida /iseti'sida/ m insecticide; ~to /ɛ/ m insect

insígnia /i'signia/ f insignia

insignifi|cância /isignifi'kãsia/ f insignificance; ~cante a insignificant

insincero /isi'sɛru/ a insincere

insinu|ante /isinu'ãtʃi/ a suggestive; ~ar vt/i insinuate

insípido /i'sipidu/ a insipid

insis|tência /isis'tẽsia/ f insistence; ~tente a insistent; ~tir vt/i insist (em on)

insolação /isola'sãw/ f sunstroke

inso|lência /iso'lẽsia/ f insolence; ~lente a insolent

insólito /i'sɔlitu/ a unusual

insolú|vel /iso'luvew/ (pl ~veis) a insoluble

insone /i'soni/ a <noite> sleepless; <pessoa> insomniac □ m/f insomniac

insônia /i'sonia/ f insomnia

insosso /i'sosu/ a bland; (sem sabor) tasteless; (sem sal) unsalted

inspe|ção /iʃpe'sãw/ f inspection; ~cionar vt inspect; ~tor m inspector

inspi|ração /iʃpira'sãw/ f inspiration; ~rar vt inspire; ~rar-se vpr take inspiration (em from)

instabilidade /istabili'dadʒi/ f instability

insta|lação /istala'sãw/ f installation; ~lar vt install; ~lar-se vpr install o.s.

instan|tâneo /istã'taniu/ a instant; ~te m instant

instaurar /istaw'rar/ vt set up

instá|vel /i'stavew/ (pl ~veis) a unstable; <tempo> unsettled

insti|gação /istʃiga'sãw/ f instigation; ~gante a stimulating; ~gar vt incite

instin|tivo /istʃĩ'tʃivu/ a instinctive; ~to m instinct

institu|cional /istʃitusio'naw/ (pl ~cionais) a institutional; ~ição f

institution; ~ir vt set up; set <prazo>; ~to m institute

instru|ção /istru'sãw/ f instruction; ~ir vt instruct; train <recrutas>; (informar) advise (sobre of)

instrumen|tal /istrumẽ'taw/ (pl ~tais) a instrumental; ~tista m/f instrumentalist; ~to m instrument

instru|tivo /istru'tʃivu/ a instructive; ~tor m instructor

insubstituí|vel /isubistʃitui'vew/ (pl ~veis) a irreplaceable

insucesso /isu'sesu/ m failure

insufici|ência /isufisi'ẽsia/ f insufficiency; (dos órgãos) failure; ~ente a insufficient

insulina /isu'lina/ f insulin

insul|tar /isuw'tar/ vt insult; ~to m insult

insuperá|vel /isupe'ravew/ (pl ~veis) a <problema> insurmountable; <qualidade> unsurpassed

insuportá|vel /isupor'tavew/ (pl ~veis) a unbearable

insur|gente /isur'ʒẽtʃi/ a & m/f insurgent; ~gir-se vpr rise up, revolt; ~reição f insurrection

intato /i'tatu/ a intact

íntegra /'itegra/ f full text; na ~ in full

inte|gração /itegra'sãw/ f integration; ~gral (pl ~grais) a whole; arroz/pão ~gral brown rice/bread; ~grante a integral □ m/f member; ~grar vt make up, form; ~grar-se em become a part of; ~gridade f integrity

íntegro /'itegru/ a honest

intei|ramente /itera'mẽtʃi/ adv completely; ~rar vt (informar) fill in, inform (de about); ~rar-se vpr find out (de about); ~riço a in one piece; ~ro a whole

intelec|to /ite'lektu/ m intellect; ~tual (pl ~tuais) a & m/f intellectual

inteli|gência /iteli'ʒẽsia/ f intelligence; ~gente a clever, intelligent; ~gível (pl ~gíveis) a intelligible

intem|périe /itẽ'pɛri/ f bad weather; ~pestivo a ill-timed

inten|ção /itẽ'sãw/ f intention; segundas ~ções ulterior motives

intencio|nado /itẽsio'nadu/ a bem ~nado well-meaning; ~nal (pl ~nais) a intentional; ~nar vt intend

inten|sidade /itẽsi'dadʒi/ f intensity; ~sificar vt intensify; ~sificar-se vpr intensify; ~sivo a intensive; ~so a intense

intento /i'tẽtu/ m intention

intera|ção /itera'sãw/ f interaction; ~gir vi interact; ~tivo a interactive inter|calar /ĩterka'lar/ vt insert; ~câmbio m exchange/ ~ceptar vt intercept

intercontinen|tal /ĩterkõtʃinē'taw/ (pl ~tais) a intercontinental

interdepen|dência /ĩterdepē'dẽsia/ f interdependence; ~dente a interdependent

interdi|ção /ĩterdʒi'sãw/ f closure; (jurid) injunction; ~tar vt close <rua etc>; (proibir) ban

interes|sante /ĩtere'sãtʃi/ a interesting; ~sar vt interest □ vi be relevant; ~sar-se vpr be interested (em ou por in); ~se /e/ m interest; (próprio) self-interest; ~seiro a self-seeking

interestadu|al /ĩterestadu'aw/ (pl ~ais) a interstate

interface /ĩter'fasi/ f interface

interfe|rência /ĩterfe'rẽsia/ f interference; ~rir vi interfere

interfone /ĩter'foni/ m intercom

ínterim /'ĩteri/ m interim; nesse ~ in the interim

interino /ĩte'rinu/ a temporary

interior /ĩteri'or/ a inner; (dentro do país) internal, domestic □ m inside; (do país) country, interior

inter|jeição /ĩterʒej'sãw/ f interjection; ~ligar vt interconnect; ~locutor m interlocutor; ~mediário a & m intermediary

intermédio /ĩter'mɛdʒiu/ m por ~ de through

intermi|nável /ĩtermi'navew/ (pl ~veis) a interminable

intermitente /ĩtermi'tẽtʃi/ a intermittent

internacio|nal /ĩternasio'naw/ (pl ~nais) a international

inter|nar vt intern <preso>; admit to hospital <doente>; ~nato m boarding school; ~no a internal

interpelar /ĩterpe'lar/ vt question

interpor /ĩter'por/ vt interpose; ~-se vpr intervene

interpre|tação /ĩterpreta'sãw/ f interpretation; ~tar vt interpret; perform <papel, música>; intérprete m/f (de línguas) interpreter; (de teatro etc) performer

interro|gação /ĩtexoga'sãw/ f interrogation; ~gar vt interrogate, question; ~gativo a interrogative; ~gatório m interrogation

inter|romper /ĩtexõ'per/ vt interrupt; ~rupção f interruption; ~ruptor m switch

interurbano /ĩterur'banu/ a long-distance □ m trunk call

intervalo /ĩter'valu/ m interval

inter|venção /ĩtervẽ'sãw/ f intervention; ~vir vi intervene

intesti|nal /ĩtestʃi'naw/ (pl ~nais) a intestinal; ~no m intestine

inti|mação /ĩtʃima'sãw/ f (da justiça) summons; ~mar vt order; (à justiça) summon

intimidade /ĩtʃimi'dadʒi/ f intimacy; (entre amigos) closeness; (vida íntima) private life; ter ~ com be close to

intimidar /ĩtʃimi'dar/ vt intimidate; ~-se vpr be intimidated

íntimo /'ĩtʃimu/ a intimate; <amigo> close; <vida> private □ m close friend

intitular /ĩtʃitu'lar/ vt entitle

intocá|vel /ĩto'kavew/ (pl ~veis) a untouchable

intole|rância /ĩtole'rãsia/ f intolerance; ~rante a intolerant; ~rável (pl ~ráveis) a intolerable

intoxi|cação /ĩtoksika'sãw/ f poisoning; ~cação alimentar food poisoning; ~car vt poison

intragá|vel /ĩtra'gavew/ (pl ~veis) a <comida> inedible; <pessoa> unbearable

intransigente /ĩtrãzi'ʒẽtʃi/ a uncompromising

intransi|tável /ĩtrãzi'tavew/ (pl ~táveis) a impassable; ~tivo a intransitive

intratá|vel /ĩtra'tavew/ (pl ~veis) a <pessoa> difficult

intra-uterino /ĩtraute'rinu/ a dispositivo ~ intra-uterine device, IUD

intrépido /ĩ'trɛpidu/ a intrepid

intri|ga /ĩ'triga/ f intrigue; (enredo) plot; ~gante a intriguing; ~gar vt intrigue

intrincado /ĩtrĩ'kadu/ a intricate

intrínseco /ĩ'trĩsiku/ a intrinsic

introdu|ção /ĩtrodu'sãw/ f introduction; ~tório a introductory; ~zir vt introduce

introme|ter-se /ĩtrome'tersi/ vpr interfere; ~tido a interfering □ m busybody

introspec|ção /ĩtrospek'sãw/ f introspection; ~tivo a introspective

introvertido /ĩtrover'tʃidu/ a introverted □ m introvert

intruso /ĩ'truzu/ a intrusive □ m intruder

intu|ição /ĩtui'sãw/ f intuition; ~ir vt intuit; ~itivo a intuitive; ~to m purpose

inumano /inu'manu/ a inhuman

inumerá|vel /inume'ravew/ (pl ~veis) a innumerable

inúmero /i'numeru/ a countless

inun|dação /inũda'sãw/ f flood; ~dar vt/i flood

inusitado /inuzi'tadu/ a unusual

inú|til /i'nutʃiw/ (pl ~teis) a useless

inutilmente /inutʃiw'mẽtʃi/ adv in vain

inutilizar /inutʃili'zar/ vt render useless; damage <aparelho>; thwart <esforços>

invadir /ĩva'dʒir/ vt invade

invali|dar /ĩvali'dar/ vt invalidate; disable <pessoa>; ~dez /e/ f disability

inválido /ĩ'validu/ a & m invalid

invariá|vel /ĩvari'avew/ (pl ~veis) a invariable

inva|são /ĩva'zãw/ f invasion; ~sor m invader □ a invading

inve|ja /ĩ'vɛʒa/ f envy; ~jar vt envy; ~jável /o/-jáveis) a enviable; ~joso /o/ a envious

inven|ção /ĩvẽ'sãw/ f invention; ~tar vt invent; ~tário m inventory; ~tivo a inventive; ~tor m inventor

inver|nar /ĩver'nar/ vi winter, spend the winter; ~no /ɛ/ m winter

inverossí|mil /ĩvero'simiw/ (pl ~meis) a improbable

inver|são /ĩver'sãw/ f inversion; ~so a inverse; <ordem> reverse □ m reverse; ~ter vt reverse; (colocar de cabeça para baixo) invert

invertebrado /ĩverte'bradu/ a & m invertebrate

invés /ĩ'vɛs/ m ao ~ de instead of

investida /ĩves'tʃida/ f attack

investidura /ĩvestʃi'dura/ f investiture

investi|gação /ĩvestʃiga'sãw/ f investigation; ~gar vt investigate

inves|timento /ĩvestʃi'mẽtu/ m investment; ~tir vt/i invest; ~tir contra attack

inveterado /ĩvete'radu/ a inveterate

inviá|vel /ĩvi'avew/ (pl ~veis) a impracticable

invicto /ĩ'viktu/ a unbeaten

invisí|vel /ĩvi'zivew/ (pl ~veis) a invisible

invocar /ĩvo'kar/ vt invoke; (fam) pester

invólucro /ĩ'vɔlukru/ m covering

involuntário /ĩvolũ'tariu/ a involuntary

invulnerá|vel /ĩvuwne'ravew/ (pl ~veis) a invulnerable

iodo /i'odu/ m iodine

ioga /i'ɔga/ f yoga

iogurte /io'gurtʃi/ m yoghurt

ir /ir/ vi go; ~-se vpr go away; vou voltar I will come back; vou melhorando I am (gradually) getting better

ira /'ira/ f wrath

Irã /i'rã/ m Iran

iraniano /irani'anu/ a & m Iranian

Irão /i'rãw/ m (Port) Iran

Iraque /i'raki/ m Iraq

iraquiano /iraki'anu/ a & m Iraqui

Irlanda /ir'lãda/ f Ireland

irlan|dês /irlã'des/ a (f ~desa) Irish □ m (f ~desa) Irishman (f -woman); (língua) Irish; os ~deses the Irish

irmã /ir'mã/ f sister

irmandade /irmã'dadʒi/ f (associação) brotherhood

irmão /ir'mãw/ (pl ~s) m brother

ironia /iro'nia/ f irony

irônico /i'roniku/ a ironic

irracio|nal /ixasio'naw/ (pl ~nais) a irrational

irradiar /ixadʒi'ar/ vt radiate; (pelo rádio) broadcast □ vi shine; ~-se vpr spread, radiate

irre|al /ixe'aw/ (pl ~ais) a unreal

irreconheci|vel /ixekoɲe'sivew/ (pl ~veis) a unrecognizable

irrecuperá|vel /ixekupe'ravew/ (pl ~veis) a irretrievable

irrefletido /ixefle'tʃidu/ a rash

irregu|lar /ixegu'lar/ a irregular; (inconstante) erratic; ~laridade f irregularity

irrelevante /ixele'vãtʃi/ a irrelevant

irrepará|vel /ixepa'ravew/ (pl ~veis) a irreparable

irrepreensí|vel /ixepriẽ'sivew/ (pl ~veis) a irreproachable

irrequieto /ixeki'etu/ a restless

irresisti|vel /ixezis'tʃivew/ (pl ~veis) a irresistible

irresoluto /ixezo'lutu/ a <questão> unresolved; <pessoa> indecisive

irresponsá|vel /ixespõ'savew/ (pl ~veis) a irresponsible

irreverente /ixeve'rẽtʃi/ a irreverent

irri|gação /ixiga'sãw/ f irrigation; ~gar vt irrigate

irrisório /ixi'zɔriu/ a derisory

irri|tação /ixita'sãw/ f irritation; ~tadiço a irritable; ~tante a irritating; ~tar vt irritate; ~tar-se vpr get irritated

irromper /ixõ'per/ vi ~ em burst into

isca /'iska/ f bait

isen|ção /izẽ'sãw/ f exemption; ~tar vt exempt; ~to a exempt

Islã /iz'lã/ m Islam

islâmico /iz'lamiku/ a Islamic

isla|mismo /izla'mizmu/ m Islam; ~mita a & m/f Muslim

islan|dês /izlã'des/ a (f ~desa) Icelandic □ m (f ~desa) Icelander; (língua) Icelandic

Islândia /iz'lãdʒia/ f Iceland

iso|lamento /izola'mẽtu/ m isolation; (eletr) insulation; ~lante a insulating; ~lar vt isolate; (eletr) insulate □ vi (contra azar) touch wood, (Amer) knock on wood

isopor /izo'por/ m polystyrene

isqueiro /is'keru/ m lighter

Israel /izxa'ɛw/ m Israel

israe|lense /izraj'lẽsi/ a & m/f Israeli; ~lita a & m/f Israelite

isso /'isu/ pron that; por ~ therefore

isto /'istu/ pron this; ~ é that is

Itália /i'talia/ f Italy

italiano /itali'anu/ a & m Italian

itálico /i'taliku/ a & m italic

item /'itẽ/ m item

itine|rante /itʃine'rãtʃi/ a itinerant; ~rário m itinerary

Iugoslávia /iugoz'lavia/ f Yugoslavia

iugoslavo /iugoz'lavu/ a & m Yugoslavian

J

já /ʒa/ adv already; (agora) right away □ conj on the other hand; desde ~ from now on; ~ não no longer; ~ que since; ~, ~ in no time

jabuticaba /ʒabutʃi'kaba/ f jaboticaba

jaca /'ʒaka/ f jack fruit

jacaré /ʒaka'rɛ/ m alligator

jacinto /ʒa'sĩtu/ m hyacinth

jactância /ʒak'tãsia/ f boasting

jade /'ʒadʒi/ m jade

jaguar /ʒagu'ar/ m jaguar

jagunço /ʒa'gũsu/ m hired gunman

jamais /ʒa'majs/ adv never

Jamaica /ʒa'majka/ f Jamaica

jamaicano /ʒamaj'kanu/ a & m Jamaican

jamanta /ʒa'mãta/ f juggernaut

janeiro /ʒa'neru/ m January

janela /ʒa'nɛla/ f window

jangada /ʒã'gada/ f (fishing) raft

janta /'ʒãta/ f (fam) dinner

jantar /ʒã'tar/ m dinner □ vi have dinner □ vt have for dinner

Japão /ʒa'pãw/ m Japan

japo|na /ʒa'pona/ f pea jacket □ m/f (fam) Japanese; ~nês a & m (f ~nesa) Japanese

jaqueira /ʒa'kera/ f jack-fruit tree

jaqueta /ʒa'keta/ f jacket

jarda /'ʒarda/ f yard

jar|dim /ʒar'dʒĩ/ m garden; ~dim-de-infância (pl ~dins-de-infância) f kindergarten

jardi|nagem /ʒardʒi'naʒẽ/ f gardening; ~nar vi garden; ~neira /calça) dungarees pl; (vestido) pinafore dress, (Amer) jumper; (ônibus) open-sided bus; (para flores) flower stand; ~neiro m gardener

jargão /ʒar'gãw/ m jargon

jar|ra /'ʒaxa/ f pot; ~ro m jug

jasmim /ʒaz'mĩ/ m jasmine

jato /'ʒatu/ m jet

jaula /'ʒawla/ f cage

ja|zer /ʒa'zer/ vi lie; ~zida f deposit; ~zigo m grave

jazz /dʒaz/ m jazz; ~ista m/f jazz artist; ~ístico a jazzy

jeca /'ʒɛka/ m/f country bumpkin □ a countrified; (cafona) tacky; ~tatu m/f country bumpkin

jei|tão /ʒej'tãw/ m (fam) individual style; ~tinho m knack; ~to m way; (de pessoa) manner; (habilidade) skill; de qualquer ~to anyway; de ~to nenhum no way; pelo ~to by the looks of things; sem ~to awkward; dar um ~to find a way; dar um ~to em (arrumar) tidy up; (consertar) fix; (torcer) twist <pé etc>; ter ~to de look like; ter ou levar ~to para be good at; tomar ~to pull one's socks up; ~toso /o/ a skilful; (de aparência) elegant

je|juar /ʒeʒu'ar/ vi fast; ~jum m fast

Jeová /ʒio'va/ m testemunha de ~ Jehovah's witness

jérsei /'ʒersej/ m jersey

jesuíta /ʒezu'ita/ a & m/f Jesuit

Jesus /ʒe'zus/ m Jesus

jibóia /ʒi'bɔja/ f boa constrictor

jiboiar /ʒiboj'ar/ vi have a rest to let one's dinner go down

jiló /ʒi'lɔ/ m okra

jipe /'ʒipi/ m jeep

jiu-jitsu /ʒiu'ʒitsu/ m jiu-jitsu

joa|lheiro /ʒoa'ʎeru/ m jeweller; ~lheria f jeweller's (shop)

joaninha /ʒoa'niŋa/ f ladybird, (Amer) ladybug; (alfinete) safety pin

joão-ninguém /ʒoãwnĩ'gẽj/ (pl joões-ninguém) m nobody

jocoso /ʒo'kozu/ a jocular

joe|lhada /ʒoe'ʎada/ f blow with the knee; ~lheira f kneepad; ~lho /e/ m knee; de ~lhos kneeling

jo|gada /ʒo'gada/ f move; ~gado a <papéis, roupa etc> lying around; ~gador m player; (no cassino etc) gambler; ~gar vt play; (atirar) throw; (arriscar no jogo) gamble □ vi play; (no cassino etc) gamble; (balançar) toss; ~gar fora throw away; ~gatina f gambling

jogging /'ʒogĩ/ m (cooper) jogging; (roupa) track suit

jogo /'ʒogu/ m (partida) game; (ação de jogar) play; (jogatina) gambling; (conjunto) set; em ~ at stake; ~ de cintura (fig) flexibility, room to manoeuvre; ~ de luz lighting effects; ~ do bicho illegal numbers game; Jogos Olímpicos Olympic Games; ~da-velha f noughts and crosses

joguete /ʒo'getʃi/ m plaything

jóia /'ʒɔja/ f jewel; (propina) entry fee □ a (fam) great

joio /ˈʒoju/ m chaff; separar o ~ do trigo separate the wheat from the chaff

jóquei /ˈʒɔkej/ m (pessoa) jockey; (lugar) race course

Jordânia /ʒorˈdania/ f Jordan

jordaniano /ʒordaniˈanu/ a & m Jordanian

jor|nada /ʒorˈnada/ f (viagem) journey; ~nada de trabalho working day; ~nal (pl ~nais) m newspaper; (na TV) news

jornal|eco /ʒornaˈleku/ m rag, scandal sheet; ~leiro m (vendedor) newsagent, (Amer) newsdealer; (entregador) paperboy; ~lismo m journalism; ~lista m/f journalist; ~lístico a journalistic

jor|rar /ʒoˈxar/ vi gush, spurt; ~ro /ˈʒoxu/ m spurt

jota /ˈʒɔta/ m letter J

jovem /ˈʒovẽ/ a young; (criado por jovens) youth □ m/f young man (f -woman); pl young people

jovi|al /ʒoviˈaw/ (pl ~ais) a jovial

juba /ˈʒuba/ f mane

jubileu /ʒubiˈlew/ m jubilee

júbilo /ˈʒubilu/ m joy

ju|daico /ʒuˈdajku/ a Jewish; ~daísmo m Judaism; ~deu a (f ~dia) Jewish □ m (f ~dia) Jew; ~diação f ill-treatment; (uma) terrible thing; ~diar vi ~diar de ill-treat

judici|al /ʒudʒisiˈaw/ (pl ~ais) a judicial; ~ário a judicial □ m judiciary; ~oso /o/ a judicious

judô /ʒuˈdo/ m judo

judoca /ʒuˈdɔka/ m/f judo player

jugo /ˈʒugu/ m yoke

juiz /ʒuˈis/ m (f juíza) judge; (em jogos) referee

juizado /ʒuiˈzadu/ m court

juízo /ʒuˈizu/ m judgement; (tino) sense; (tribunal) court; perder o ~ lose one's head; ter ~ be sensible; tomar ou criar ~ come to one's senses

jujuba /ʒuˈʒuba/ f (bala) fruit jelly

jul|gamento /ʒuwgaˈmẽtu/ m judgement; ~gar vt judge; pass judgement on <réu>; (imaginar) think; ~gar-se vpr consider o.s.

julho /ˈʒuʎu/ m July

jumento /ʒuˈmẽtu/ m donkey

junção /ʒũˈsãw/ f join; (ação) joining

junco /ˈʒũku/ m reed

junho /ˈʒuɲu/ m June

juni|no /ʒuˈninu/ a festa ~na St John's Day festival

júnior /ˈʒunior/ a & m junior

jun|ta /ˈʒũta/ f board; (pol) junta; ~tar vt (acrescentar) add; (uma coisa a outra) join; (uma coisa com outra) combine; save up <dinheiro>; gather up <papéis, lixo etc> □ vi gather; ~tar-se vpr join together; <multidão> gather; <casal> live together; ~tar-se a join; ~to a together □ adv together; ~to a next to; ~to com together with

ju|ra /ˈʒura/ f vow; ~rado m juror; ~ramentado a accredited; ~ramento m oath; ~rar vt/i swear; ~ra? (fam) really?

júri /ˈʒuri/ m jury

jurídico /ʒuˈridʒiku/ a legal

juris|consulto /ʒuriskõˈsuwtu/ m legal advisor; ~dição f jurisdiction; ~prudência f jurisprudence; ~ta m/f jurist

juros /ˈʒurus/ m pl interest

jus /ʒus/ m fazer ~ a live up to

jusante /ʒuˈzãtʃi/ f a ~ downstream

justamente /ʒustaˈmẽtʃi/ adv exactly; (com justiça) fairly

justapor /ʒustaˈpor/ vt juxtapose

justi|ça /ʒusˈtʃisa/ f (perante a lei) justice; (para com outros) fairness; (tribunal) court; ~ceiro a fairminded □ m vigilante

justifi|cação /ʒustʃifikaˈsãw/ f justification; ~car vt justify; ~cativa f justification; ~cável (pl ~cáveis) a justifiable

justo /ˈʒustu/ a fair; (apertado) tight □ adv just

juve|nil /ʒuveˈniw/ (pl ~nis) a youthful; (para jovens) for young people; <time, torneio> junior □ m junior championship

juventude /ʒuvẽˈtudʒi/ f youth

K

karaokê /karaoˈke/ m karaoke

kart /ˈkartʃi/ (pl ~s) m go-kart

ketchup /keˈtʃupi/ m ketchup

kit /ˈkitʃi/ (pl ~s) m kit

kitchenette /kitʃeˈnɛtʃi/ f bedsitter

Kuwait /kuˈwajtʃi/ m Kuwait

kuwaitiano /kuwajtʃiˈanu/ a & m Kuwaiti

L

lá /la/ adv there; até ~ <ir> there; <esperar etc> until then; por ~ (naquela direção) that way; (naquele lugar) around there; ~ fora outside; sei ~ how should I know?

lã /lã/ f wool

labareda /labaˈreda/ f flame

lábia /ˈlabia/ f flannel; ter ~ have the gift of the gab

lábio /ˈlabio/ m lip

labirinto /labi'rītu/ *m* labyrinth

laboratório /labora'toriu/ *m* laboratory

laborioso /labori'ozu/ *a* hard-working

labu|ta /la'buta/ *f* drudgery; ~tar *vi* slog

laca /'laka/ *f* lacquer

laçada /la'sada/ *f* slipknot

lacaio /la'kaju/ *m* lackey

la|çar /la'sar/ *vt* lasso < *boi*>; ~ço *m* bow; (*de vaqueiro*) lasso; (*vínculo*) tie

lacônico /la'koniku/ *a* laconic

lacraia /la'kraja/ *f* centipede

la|crar /la'krar/ *vt* seal; ~cre *m* (*substância*) sealing wax; (*fechamento*) seal

lacri|mejar /lakrime'ʒar/ *vi* water; ~mogêneo *a* < *gás* > tear; < *filme* > tearjerking; ~moso /o/ *a* tearful

lácteo /'laktʃiu/ *a* milk; Via Láctea Milky Way

laticínio /laktʃi'siniu/ *m veja* laticínio

lacuna /la'kuna/ *f* gap

ladainha /lada'iɲa/ *f* litany

la|dear /ladʒi'ar/ *vt* flank; sidestep < *dificuldade* >; ~deira *f* slope

lado /'ladu/ *m* side; o ~ de cá/lá this/that side; ao ~ de beside; ~ a ~ side by side; para este ~ this way; por outro ~ on the other hand

la|drão /la'drãw/ *m* (*f* ~dra) thief; (*tubo*) overflow pipe □ *a* thieving

ladrar /la'drar/ *vi* bark

ladri|lhar /ladri'ʎar/ *vt* tile; ~lho *m* tile

ladroagem /ladro'aʒẽ/ *f* stealing

lagar|ta /la'garta/ *f* caterpillar; (*numa roda*) caterpillar track; ~tar *vi* bask in the sun; ~tixa *f* gecko; ~to *m* lizard

lago /'lagu/ *m* lake

lagoa /la'goa/ *f* lagoon

lagos|ta /la'gosta/ *f* lobster; ~tim *m* crayfish, (*Amer*) crawfish

lágrima /'lagrima/ *f* tear

laia /'laja/ *f* kind

laico /'lajku/ *adj* < *pessoa* > lay; < *ensino* > secular

laivos /'lajvus/ *m pl* traces

laje /'laʒi/ *m* flagstone; ~ar *vt* pave

lajota /la'ʒota/ *f* small paving stone

lama /'lama/ *f* mud; ~çal (*pl* ~çais) *m* bog; ~cento *a* muddy

lamba|da /lã'bada/ *f* lambada; ~teria *f* lambada club

lam|ber /lã'ber/ *vt* lick; ~bida *f* lick

lambreta /lã'breta/ *f* moped

lambris /lã'bris/ *m pl* panelling

lambuzar /lãbu'zar/ *vt* smear; ~-se *vpr* get sticky

lamen|tar/lamẽ'tar/ *vt* (*lastimar*) lament; (*sentir*) be sorry; ~tar-se de lament; ~tável (*pl* ~táveis) *a* lamentable; ~to *m* lament

lâmina /'lamina/ *f* blade; (*de persiana*) slat

laminar /lami'nar/ *vt* laminate

lâmpada /'lãpada/ *f* light bulb; (*abajur*) lamp

lampe|jar /lãpe'ʒar/ *vi* flash; ~jo /e/ *m* flash

lampião /lãpi'ãw/ *m* lantern

lamúria /la'muria/ *f* moaning

lamuriar-se /lamuri'arsi/ *vpr* moan (about)

lan|ça /'lãsa/ *f* spear; ~çamento *m* (*de navio, foguete, produto*) launch; (*de filme, disco*) release; (*novo produto*) new line; (*novo filme, disco*) release; (*novo livro*) new title; (*em livro comercial*) entry; ~çar *vt* (*atirar*) throw; launch < *navio, foguete, novo produto, livro* >; release < *filme, disco* >; (*em livro comercial*) enter; (*em leilão*) bid; ~çar mão de make use of; ~ce *m* (*num filme, jogo*) bit, moment; (*episódio*) episode; (*questão*) matter; (*jogada*) move; (*em leilão*) bid; (*de escada*) flight; (*de casas*) row

lancha /'lãʃa/ *f* launch

lan|char /lã'ʃar/ *vi* have a snack □ *vt* have a snack of; ~che *m* snack; ~chonete /ɛ/ *f* snack bar

lancinante /lãsi'nãtʃi/ *a* < *dor* > shooting; < *grito* > piercing

lânguido /'lãgidu/ *a* languid

lantejoula /lãte'ʒola/ *f* sequin

lanter|na /lã'tɛrna/ *f* lantern; (*de bolso*) torch, (*Amer*) flashlight; ~nagem *f* panel-beating; (*oficina*) body-shop; ~ninha *m/f* usher *f* usherette

lanugem /la'nuʒẽ/ *f* down

lapela /la'pɛla/ *f* lapel

lapi|dar /lapi'dar/ *vt* cut < *pedra preciosa* >; (*fig*) polish

lápide /'lapidʒi/ *f* tombstone

lápis /'lapis/ *m invar* pencil

lapiseira /lapi'zera/ *f* propelling pencil; (*caixa*) pencil box

Lapônia /la'ponia/ *f* Lappland

lapso /'lapsu/ *m* lapse

la|quê /la'ke/ *m* lacquer; ~quear *vt* lacquer

lar /lar/ *m* home

laran|ja /la'rãʒa/ *f* orange □ *a invar* orange; ~jada *f* orangeade; ~jeira *f* orange tree

lareira /la'rera/ *f* hearth, fireplace

lar|gada /lar'gada/ *f* start; dar a ~gada start off; ~gar *vt* (*soltar*) let go of; give up < *estudos, emprego etc* >; ~gar de fumar give up smoking; ~goa wide; < *roupa* > loose □ *m* (*praça*) square; ao ~go (*no alto-mar*) out at sea; ~gura *f* width

larin|ge /la'riʒi/ *f* larynx; ~gite *f* laryngitis

larva /'larva/ *f* larva

lasanha /la'zaɲa/ f lasagna

las|ca /'laska/ f chip; ~car vt/i chip; de ~car (fam) awful

lástima /'lastʃima/ f shame

lastro /'lastru/ m ballast

la|ta /'lata/ f (material) tin; (recipiente) tin, (Amer) can; ~ta de lixo dustbin, (Amer) trash can; ~tão m brass

late|jante /late'ʒātʃi/ a throbbing; ~jar vi throb

latente /la'tētʃi/ a latent

late|ral /late'raw/ (pl ~rais) a side, lateral

laticínio /latʃi'siniu/ m dairy product

latido /la'tʃidu/ m bark

lati|fundiário /latʃifūdʒi'ariu/ a landowning □ m landowner; ~fúndio m estate

latim /la'tʃĩ/ m Latin

latino /la'tʃinu/ a & m Latin; ~americano a & m Latin American

latir /la'tʃir/ vi bark

latitude /latʃi'tudʒi/ f latitude

lauda /'lawda/ f side

laudo /'lawdu/ m report, findings

lava /'lava/ f lava

lava|bo /la'vabu/ m toilet; ~dora f washing machine; ~gem f washing; ~gem a seco dry cleaning; ~gem cerebral brainwashing

lavanda /la'vāda/ f lavender

lavanderia /lavāde'ria/ f laundry

lavar /la'var/ vt wash; ~ a seco dry-clean; ~-se vpr wash

lavatório /lava'toriu/ m (Port) wash-basin

lavoura /la'vora/ f (agricultura) farming; (terreno) field

lav|rador /lavra'dor/ m farmhand; ~rar vt work; draw up <documento>

laxante /la'ʃātʃi/ a & m laxative

lazer /la'zer/ m leisure

le|al /le'aw/ (pl ~ais) a loyal; ~aldade f loyalty

leão /le'āw/ m lion; Leão (signo) Leo; ~-de-chácara (pl leões-de-chácara) m bouncer

lebre /'lɛbri/ f hare

lecionar /lesio'nar/ vt/i teach

le|gação /lega'sāw/ f legation; ~gado m (pessoa) legate; (herança) legacy

le|gal /le'gaw/ (pl ~gais) a legal; (fam) good; <pessoa> nice; tá ~gal OK; ~galidade f legality; ~galizar vt legalize

legar /le'gar/ vt bequeath

legenda /le'ʒēda/ f (de quadro) caption; (de filme) subtitle; (inscrição) inscription

legi|ão /leʒi'āw/ f legion; ~onário m (romano) legionary; (da legião estrangeira) legionnaire

legis|lação /leʒizla'sāw/ f legislation; ~lador m legislator; ~lar vi

legislate; ~lativo a legislative □ m legislature; ~latura f legislature; ~ta m/f legal expert

legiti|mar /leʒitʃi'mar/ vt legitimize; ~midade f legitimacy

legítimo /le'ʒitʃimu/ a legitimate

legí|vel /le'ʒivew/ (pl ~veis) a legible

légua /'lɛgwa/ f league

legume /le'gumi/ m vegetable

lei /lej/ f law

leigo /'lejgu/ a lay □ m layman

lei|lão /lej'lāw/ m auction; ~loar vt auction; ~loeiro m auctioneer

leitão /lej'tāw/ m sucking pig

lei|te /'lejtʃi/ m milk; ~te condensado/desnatado condensed/skimmed milk; ~teira f (jarro) milk jug; (panela) milk saucepan; ~teiro m milkman □ a <vaca> dairy

leito /'lejtu/ m bed

leitor /lej'tor/ m reader

leitoso /lej'tozu/ a milky

leitura /lej'tura/ f (ação) reading; (material) reading matter

lema /'lema/ m motto

lem|brança /lē'brāsa/ f memory; (presente) souvenir; ~brar vt/i remember; ~brar-se de remember; ~brar aco a alg remind s.o. of sth; ~brete /e/ m reminder

leme /'lemi/ m rudder

len|ço /'lēsu/ m (para o nariz) handkerchief; (para vestir) scarf; ~çol /ɔ/ (pl ~çóis) m sheet

len|da /'lēda/ f legend; ~dário a legendary

lenha /'leɲa/ f firewood; (uma) log; ~dor m woodcutter

lente /'lētʃi/ f lens; ~ de contato contact lens

lentidão /lētʃi'dāw/ f slowness

lentilha /lē'tʃiʎa/ f lentil

lento /'lētu/ a slow

leoa /le'oa/ f lioness

leopardo /lio'pardu/ m leopard

le|pra /'lɛpra/ f leprosy; ~proso /o/ a leprous □ m leper

leque /'lɛki/ m fan; (fig) array

ler /ler/ vt/i read

ler|deza /ler'deza/ f sluggishness; ~do /ɛ/ a sluggish

le|são /le'zāw/ f lesion, injury; ~sar vt damage

lésbi|ca /'lɛzbika/ f lesbian; ~co a lesbian

lesionar /lezio'nar/ vt injure

lesma /'lezma/ f slug

leste /'lɛstʃi/ m east

le|tal /le'taw/ (pl ~tais) a lethal

le|tão /le'tāw/ a & m (f ~tã) Latvian

letargia /letar'ʒia/ f lethargy

letivo /le'tʃivu/ a ano ~ academic year

Letônia /le'tonia/ f Latvia

letra /'letra/ f letter; (de música) lyrics, words; (caligrafia) writing; Letras Modern Languages; ao pé da ~ literally; com todas as ~s in no uncertain terms; tirar de ~ take in one's stride; ~ de fôrma block letter

letreiro /le'treru/ m sign

leucemia /lewse'mia/ f leukaemia

leva /ε/ f batch

levado /le'vadu/ a naughty

levan|tamento /levãta'mẽtu/ m (enquete) survey; (rebelião) uprising; ~tamento de pesos weightlifting; ~tar vt raise; lift <peso> □ vi get up; ~tar-se vpr get up; (revoltar-se) rise up

levante /le'vãtʃi/ m east

levar /le'var/ vt take; lead <vida>; get <tapa, susto etc> □ vi lead (a to)

leve /'levi/ a light; (não grave) slight; de ~ lightly

levedura /leve'dura/ f yeast

leveza /le'veza/ f lightness

levi|andade /leviã'dadʒi/ f frivolity; ~ano a frivolous

levitar /levi'tar/ vi levitate

lexi|cal /leksi'kaw/ (pl ~cais) a lexical

léxico /'leksiku/ m lexicon

lexicografia /leksikogra'fia/ f lexicography

lhe /ʎi/ pron (a ele) to him; (a ela) to her; (a você) to you; ~s pron to them; (a vocês) to you

liba|nês /liba'nes/ a & m (f ~nesa) Lebanese

Líbano /'libanu/ m Lebanon

libélula /li'belula/ f dragonfly

libe|ração /libera'sãw/ f release; ~ral (pl ~rais) a & m liberal; ~ralismo m liberalism; ~ralizar vt liberalize; ~rar vt release

liberdade /liber'dadʒi/ f freedom; pôr em ~ set free; ~ condicional probation

libero /'liberu/ m sweeper

liber|tação /liberta'sãw/ f liberation; ~tar vt free

Líbia /'libia/ f Libya

líbio /'libiu/ a & m Libyan

libi|dinoso /libidʒi'nozu/ a lecherous; ~do f libido

li|bra /'libra/ f pound; Libra (signo) Libra; ~briano a & m Libran

lição /li'sãw/ f lesson

licen|ça /li'sẽsa/ f leave; (documento) licence; com ~ça excuse me; de ~ça on leave; sob ~ça under licence; ~ciar vt (autorizar) license; (dar férias a) give leave to; ~ciar-se vpr (tirar férias) take leave; (formar-se) graduate; ~ciatura f degree; ~cioso /o/ a licentious

liceu /li'sew/ m (Port) secondary school, (Amer) high school

licor /li'kor/ m liqueur

lida /'lida/ f slog, grind; (leitura) read

lidar /li'dar/ vt/i ~ com deal with

lide /'lidʒi/ f (trabalho) work

líder /'lider/ m/f leader

lide|rança /lide'rãsa/ f (de partido etc) leadership; (em corrida, jogo etc) lead; ~rar vt lead

lido /'lidu/ a well-read

liga /'liga/ f (aliança) league; (tira) garter; (presilha) suspender; (de metais) alloy

li|gação /liga'sãw/ f connection; (telefônica) call; (amorosa) liaison; ~gada f call, ring; ~gado a <luz, TV> on; ~gado em attached to <pessoa>; hooked on <droga>; ~gamento m ligament; ~gar vt join, connect; switch on <luz, TV etc>; start up <carro>; bind <amigos> □ vi ring up, call; ~gar para (telefonar) ring, call; (dar importância) care about; (dar atenção) pay attention to; ~gar-se vpr join

ligeiro /li'ʒeru/ a light; <ferida, melhora> slight; (ágil) nimble

lilás /li'las/ m lilac □ a invar mauve

lima¹ /'lima/ f (ferramenta) file

lima² /'lima/ f (fruta) sweet orange

limão /li'mãw/ m lime; (amarelo) lemon

limar /li'mar/ vt file

limeira /li'mera/ f sweet orange tree

limiar /limi'ar/ m threshold

limi|tação /limita'sãw/ f limitation; ~tar vi limit; ~tar-se vpr limit o.s.; ~tar(-se) com border on; ~te m limit; (de terreno) boundary; passar dos ~tes go too far; ~te de velocidade speed limit

limo|eiro /limo'eru/ m lime tree; ~nada f lemonade

lim|pador /lĩpa'dor/ m ~pador de pára-brisas windscreen wiper; ~par vt clean; wipe <lágrimas, suor>; (fig) clean up <cidade, organização>; ~peza /e/ f (ato) cleaning; (qualidade) cleanness; (fig) clean-up; ~peza pública sanitation; ~po a clean; <céu, consciência> clear; <lucro> net, clear; (fig) pure; passar a ~po write <trabalho>; (fig) sort out <vida>; tirar a ~po get to the bottom of <caso>

limusine /limu'zini/ f limousine

lince /'lĩsi/ m lynx

lindo /'lĩdu/ a beautiful

linear /lini'ar/ a linear

lingote /'lĩgotʃi/ m ingot

língua /'lĩgwa/ f (na boca) tongue; (idioma) language; ~ materna mother tongue

linguado /lĩ'gwadu/ *m* sole

lingua|gem /lĩ'gwaʒẽ/ *f* language; ~**jar** *m* speech, dialect

lingüeta /lĩ'gweta/ *f* bolt

lingüiça /lĩ'gwisa/ *f* pork sausage

lin|güista /lĩ'gwi∫ta/ *m/f* linguist; ~**güística** *f* linguistics; ~**güístico** *a* linguistic

linha /'liɲa/ *f* line; (*fio*) thread; perder a ~ lose one's cool; ~ aérea airline; ~ de fogo firing line; ~ de montagem assembly line; ~**gem** *f* lineage

linho /'liɲu/ *m* linen; (*planta*) flax

linóleo /li'nɔliu/ *m* lino(leum)

lipoaspiração /lipoaspira'sãw/ *f* liposuction

liqui|dação /likida'sãw/ *f* liquidation; (*de loja*) clearance sale; (*de conta*) settlement; ~**dar** *vt* liquidate; settle <*conta*>; pay off <*dívida*>; sell off, clear <*mercadorias*>

liqüidificador /likwidʒifika'dor/ *m* liquidizer

líquido /'likidu/ *a* liquid; <*lucro, salário*> net □ *m* liquid

líri|ca /'lirika/ *f* (*mus*) lyrics; (*poesia*) lyric poetry; ~**co** *a* lyrical; <*poesia*> lyric

lírio /'liriu/ *m* lily

Lisboa /liz'boa/ *f* Lisbon

lisboeta /lizbo'eta/ *a & m/f* (person) from Lisbon

liso /'lizu/ *a* smooth; (*sem desenho*) plain; <*cabelo*> straight; (*fam: duro*) broke

lison|ja /li'zõʒa/ *f* flattery; ~**jear** *vt* flatter

lista /'li∫ta/ *f* list; (*listra*) stripe; ~ telefônica telephone directory

listra /'li∫tra/ *f* stripe; ~**do** *a* striped, stripey

lite|ral /lite'raw/ (*pl* ~**rais**) *a* literal; ~**rário** *a* literary; ~**ratura** *f* literature

litígio /li't∫iʒiu/ *m* dispute; (*jurid*) lawsuit

lito|ral /lito'raw/ (*pl* ~**rais**) *m* coastline; ~**râneo** *a* coastal

litro /'litru/ *m* litre

Lituânia /litu'ania/ *f* Lithuania

lituano /litu'anu/ *a & m* Lithuanian

living /'livĩ/ (*pl* ~**s**) *m* living room

livrar /li'vrar/ *vt* free; (*salvar*) save; ~-**se** *vpr* escape; ~-**se** *de* get rid of

livraria /livra'ria/ *f* bookshop

livre /'livri/ *a* free; ~ **de impostos** tax-free; ~-**arbítrio** *m* free will

liv|reiro /li'vreru/ *m* bookseller; ~**ro** *m* book; ~**ro de consulta** reference book; ~**ro de cozinha** cookery book; ~**ro de texto** text book

li|xa /'li∫a/ *f* (*de unhas*) emery board; (*para madeira etc*) sandpaper; ~**xar**

vt sand <*madeira*>; file <*unhas*>; estou me ~**xando** (*fam*) I couldn't care less

li|xeira /li'∫era/ *f* dustbin, (*Amer*) garbage can; ~**xeiro** *m* dustman, (*Amer*) garbage collector; ~**xo** rubbish, (*Amer*) garbage; (*atômico*) waste

lobisomem /lobi'zomẽ/ *m* werewolf

lobo /'lobu/ *m* wolf; ~-**marinho** (*pl* ~**s-marinhos**) *m* sea lion

lóbulo /'lɔbulu/ *m* lobe

lo|cação /loka'sãw/ *f* (*de imóvel*) lease; (*de carro*) rental; ~**cador** *m* (*de casa*) landlord; ~**cadora** *f* rental company; (*de vídeos*) video shop

lo|cal /lo'kaw/ (*pl* ~**cais**) *a* local □ *m* site; (*de um acidente etc*) scene; ~**calidade** *f* locality; ~**calização** *f* location; ~**calizar** *vt* locate; ~**calizar-se** *vpr* (*orientar-se*) get one's bearings

loção /lo'sãw/ *f* lotion; ~ **após-barba** aftershave lotion

locatário /loka'tariu/ *m* (*de imóvel*) tenant; (*de carro etc*) hirer

locomo|tiva /lokomo't∫iva/ *f* locomotive; ~**ver-se** *vpr* get around

locu|ção /loku'sãw/ *f* phrase; ~**tor** *m* announcer

lodo /'lodu/ *m* mud; ~**so** /o/ *a* muddy

logaritmo /loga'rit∫imu/ *m* logarithm

lógi|ca /'lɔʒika/ *f* logic; ~**co** *a* logical

logo /'lɔgu/ *adv* (*em seguida*) straightaway; (*em breve*) soon; (*justamente*) just; ~ **mais** later; ~ **antes/depois** just before/straight after; ~ **que** as soon as; **até** ~ goodbye

logotipo /logo't∫ipu/ *m* logo

logradouro /logra'doru/ *m* public place

loiro /'lojru/ *a veja* louro

lo|ja /'lɔʒa/ *f* shop, (*Amer*) store; ~**ja de departamentos** department store; ~**ja maçônica** masonic lodge; ~**jista** *m/f* shopkeeper

lom|bada /lõ'bada/ *f* (*de livro*) spine; (*na rua*) speed bump; ~**binho** *m* tenderloin; ~**bo** *m* back; (*carne*) loin

lona /'lona/ *f* canvas

Londres /'lõdris/ *f* London

londrino /lõ'drinu/ *a* London □ *m* Londoner

longa-metragem /lõgame'traʒẽ/ (*pl* **longas-metragens**) *m* feature film

longe /'lõʒi/ *adv* far, a long way; **de** ~ from a distance; (*por muito*) by far; ~ **disso** far from it

longevidade /lõʒevi'dadʒi/ *f* longevity

longínquo /lõ'ʒĩkwu/ *a* distant

longitude /lõʒi'tudʒi/ *f* longitude

longo /'lõgu/ *a* long □ *m* long dress; **ao** ~ **de** along; (*durante*) through, over

lontra /ˈlõtra/ f otter
lorde /ˈlɔrdʒi/ m lord
lorota /loˈrɔta/ (fam) f fib
losango /loˈzãgu/ m diamond
lo|tação /lotaˈsãw/ f capacity; (ônibus) bus; ~tação esgotada full house; ~tado a crowded; <teatro, ônibus> full; ~tar vt fill □ vi fill up
lote /ˈlɔtʃi/ m (quinhão) portion; (de terreno) plot, (Amer) lot; (em leilão) lot; (porção de coisas) batch
loteria /loteˈria/ f lottery
louça /ˈlosa/ f china; (pratos etc) crockery; lavar a ~ wash up, (Amer) do the dishes
lou|co /ˈloku/ a mad, crazy □ m madman; estou ~co para ir (fam) I'm dying to go; ~cura f madness; (uma) crazy thing
louro /ˈloru/ a blond □ m laurel; (condimento) bayleaf
lou|var /loˈvar/ vt praise; ~vável (pl ~váveis) a praiseworthy; ~vor /o/ m praise
lua /ˈlua/ f moon; ~-de-mel f honeymoon
lu|ar /luˈar/ m moonlight; ~arento a moonlit
lubrifi|cação /lubrifikaˈsãw/ f lubrication; ~cante a lubricating □ m lubricant; ~car vt lubricate
lucidez /lusiˈdes/ f lucidity
lúcido /ˈlusidu/ a lucid
lu|crar /luˈkrar/ vi profit (com by); ~cratividade f profitability; ~crativo a profitable, lucrative; ~cro m profit
ludibriar /ludʒibriˈar/ vt cheat
lúdico /ˈludʒiku/ a playful
lugar /luˈgar/ m place; (espaço) room; em ~ de in place of; em primeiro ~ in the first place; em algum ~ somewhere; em todo ~ everywhere; dar ~ a give rise to; ter ~ take place
lugarejo /lugaˈreʒu/ m village
lúgubre /ˈlugubri/ a gloomy, dismal
lula /ˈlula/ f squid
lume /ˈlumi/ m fire
luminária /lumiˈnaria/ f light, lamp; pl illuminations
luminoso /lumiˈnozu/ a luminous; <idéia> brilliant
lunar /luˈnar/ a lunar □ m mole
lupa /ˈlupa/ f magnifying glass
lusco-fusco /luskuˈfusku/ m twilight
lusitano /luziˈtanu/, **luso** /ˈluzu/ a & m Portuguese
lus|trar /lusˈtrar/ vt shine, polish; ~tre m shine; (fig) lustre; (luminária) light, lamp; ~troso /o/ a shiny
lu|ta /ˈluta/ f fight, struggle; ~ta livre wrestling; ~tador m fighter; (de luta livre) wrestler; ~tar vi fight □ vt do <judô etc>

luto /ˈlutu/ m mourning
luva /ˈluva/ f glove
luxação /luʃaˈsãw/ f dislocation
Luxemburgo /luʃẽˈburgu/ m Luxembourg
luxembur|guês /luʃẽburˈges/ a (f ~guesa) Luxemburg □ m (f ~guesa) Luxemburger; (língua) Luxemburgish
luxo /ˈluʃu/ m luxury; hotel de ~ luxury hotel; cheio de ~ (fam) fussy
luxuoso /luʃuˈozu/ a luxurious
luxúria /luˈʃuria/ f lust
luxuriante /luʃuriˈatʃi/ a lush
luz /lus/ f light; à ~ de by the light of <velas etc>; in the light of <fatos etc>; dar à ~ give birth to
luzidio /luziˈdʒio/ a shiny
luzir /luˈzir/ vi shine

M

maca /ˈmaka/ f stretcher
maçã /maˈsã/ f apple
macabro /maˈkabru/ a macabre
maca|cão /makaˈkãw/ m (de trabalho) overalls, (Amer) coveralls; (tipo de calça) dungarees; (roupa inteiriça) jumpsuit; (para bebê) romper suit; ~co m monkey; (aparelho) jack
maçada /maˈsada/ f bore
maçaneta /masaˈneta/ f doorknob
maçante /maˈsãtʃi/ a boring
macar|rão /makaˈxãw/ m pasta; (espaguete) spaghetti; ~ronada f pasta with tomato sauce and cheese
macarrônico /makaˈxoniku/ a broken
macete /maˈsetʃi/ m trick
machado /maˈʃadu/ m axe
ma|chão /maˈʃãw/ a tough □ m tough guy; ~chismo m machismo; ~chista a chauvinistic □ m male chauvinist; ~cho a male; <homem> macho □ m male
machu|cado /maʃuˈkadu/ m injury; (na pele) sore patch; ~car vt/i hurt; ~car-se vpr hurt o.s.
maciço /maˈsisu/ a solid; <dose etc> massive □ m massif
macieira /masiˈera/ f apple tree
maciez /masiˈes/ f softness
macilento /masiˈlẽtu/ a haggard
macio /maˈsiu/ a soft; <carne> tender
maço /ˈmasu/ m (de cigarros) packet; (de notas) bundle
ma|çom /maˈsõ/ m freemason; ~çonaria f freemasonry
maconha /maˈkoɲa/ f marijuana
maçônico /maˈsoniku/ a masonic
má-criação /makriaˈsãw/ f rudeness
macrobiótico /makrobiˈɔtʃiku/ a macrobiotic

macum|ba /ma'kũba/ f Afro-Brazilian cult; (*uma*) spell; ~beiro *m* follower of macumba □ *a* macumba

madame /ma'dami/ f lady

Madeira /ma'dera/ f Madeira

madeira /ma'dera/ f wood □ *m* (*vinho*) Madeira; ~ de lei hardwood

madeirense /made'rẽsi/ *a* & *m* Madeiran

madeixa /ma'deʃa/ f lock

madrasta /ma'drasta/ f stepmother

madrepérola /madre'perola/ f mother of pearl

madressilva /madre'siwva/ f honeysuckle

Madri /ma'dri/ f Madrid

madrinha /ma'driɲa/ f (*de batismo*) godmother; (*de casamento*) bridesmaid

madru|gada /madru'gada/ f early morning; ~gador *m* early riser; ~gar *vi* get up early

maduro /ma'duru/ *a* <*fruta*> ripe; <*pessoa*> mature

mãe /mãj/ f mother; ~-de-santo (*pl* ~s-de-santo) f macumba priestess

maes|tria /majs'tria/ f expertise; ~tro *m* conductor

máfia /'mafia/ f mafia

magazine /maga'zini/ *m* department store

magia /ma'ʒia/ f magic

mági|ca /'maʒika/ f magic; (*uma*) magic trick; ~co *a* magic □ *m* magician

magis|tério /maʒis'teriu/ *m* teaching; (*professores*) teachers; ~trado *m* magistrate

magnânimo /mag'nanimu/ *a* magnanimous

magnata /mag'nata/ *m* magnate

magnésio /mag'neziu/ *m* magnesium

mag|nético /mag'netʃiku/ *a* magnetic; ~netismo *m* magnetism; ~netizar *vt* magnetize; (*fig*) mesmerize

mag|nificência /magnifi'sẽsia/ f magnificence; ~nífico *a* magnificent

magnitude /magni'tudʒi/ f magnitude

mago /'magu/ *m* magician; os reis ~s the Three Wise Men

mágoa /'magoa/ f sorrow

magoar /mago'ar/ *vt/i* hurt; ~-se *vpr* be hurt

ma|gricela /magri'sɛla/ *a* skinny; ~gro *a* thin; <*leite*> skimmed; <*carne*> lean; (*fig*) meagre

maio /'maju/ *m* May

maiô /ma'jo/ *m* swimsuit

maionese /majo'nɛzi/ f mayonnaise

maior /ma'jɔr/ *a* bigger; <*escritor, amor etc*> greater; o ~ carro the biggest car; o ~ escritor the greatest writer; ~ de idade of age

Maiorca /ma'jɔrka/ f Majorca

maio|ria /majo'ria/ f majority; a ~ria dos brasileiros most Brazilians; ~ridade f majority, adulthood

mais /majs/ *adv* & *pron* more; ~ dois two more; dois dias a ~ two more days; não trabalho ~ I don't work any more; ~ ou menos more or less

maisena /maj'zena/ f cornflour, (*Amer*) cornstarch

maître /mɛtr/ *m* head waiter

maiúscula /ma'juskula/ f capital letter

majes|tade /maʒes'tadʒi/ f majesty; ~toso *a* majestic

major /ma'ʒɔr/ *m* major

majoritário /maʒori'tariu/ *a* majority

mal /maw/ *adv* badly; (*quase não*) hardly □ *conj* hardly □ *m* evil; (*doença*) sickness; não faz ~ never mind; levar a ~ take offence at; passar ~ be sick

mala /'mala/ f suitcase; (*do carro*) boot, (*Amer*) trunk; ~ aérea air courier

malabaris|mo /malaba'rizmu/ *m* juggling act; ~ta *m/f* juggler

malagradecido /malagrade'sidu/ *a* ungrateful

malagueta /mala'geta/ f chilli pepper

malaio /ma'laju/ *a* & *m* Malay

Malaísia /mala'izia/ f Malaysia

malaísio /mala'iziu/ *a* & *m* Malaysian

malan|dragem /malã'draʒẽ/ f hustling; (*uma*) clever trick; ~dro *a* cunning □ *m* hustler

malária /ma'laria/ f malaria

mal-assombrado /malaso'bradu/ *a* haunted

Malavi /mala'vi/ *m* Malawi

malcriado /mawkri'adu/ *a* rude

mal|dade /maw'dadʒi/ f wickedness; (*uma*) wicked thing; por ~dade out of spite; ~dição f curse; ~dito *a* cursed, damned; ~doso /o/ *a* wicked

maleá|vel /mali'avew/ (*pl* ~veis) *a* malleable

maledicência /maledi'sẽsia/ f malicious gossip

maléfico /ma'lɛfiku/ *a* evil; (*prejudicial*) harmful

mal-encarado /malĩka'radu/ *a* shady, dubious □ *m* shady character

mal-entendido /malĩtẽ'dʒidu/ *m* misunderstanding

mal-estar /malis'tar/ *m* (*doença*) ailment; (*constrangimento*) discomfort

maleta /ma'leta/ f overnight bag

malévolo /ma'lɛvolu/ *a* malevolent

malfei|to /maw'fejtu/ *a* badly done; <*roupa etc*> badly made; (*fig*) wrongful; ~tor *m* wrongdoer; ~toria f wrongdoing

malha /'maʎa/ f (*ponto*) stitch; (*tricô*) knitting; (*tecido*) jersey; (*casaco*) jumper, (*Amer*) sweater; (*para ginástica*) leotard; (*de rede*) mesh; fazer ~lha knit; ~lhado *a* <*animal*> dappled; <*roque*> heavy; ~lhar *vt* beat; thresh <*trigo etc*> □ *vi* (*fam*) work out

mal-humorado /malumo'radu/ *a* in a bad mood, grumpy

malícia /ma'lisia/ f (*má índole*) malice; (*astúcia*) guile; (*humor*) innuendo

malicioso /malisi'ozu/ *a* (*mau*) malicious; (*astuto*) crafty; (*que põe malícia*) dirty-minded

maligno /ma'liginu/ *a* malignant

malmequer /malme'ker/ *m* marigold

maloca /ma'lɔka/ f Indian village

malo|grar-se /malo'grarsi/ *vpr* go wrong, fail; ~gro /o/ *m* failure

mal-passado /mawpa'sadu/ *a* <*carne*> rare

Malta /'mawta/ f Malta

malte /'mawtʃi/ *m* malt

maltrapilho /mawtra'piʎu/ *a* scruffy

maltratar /mawtra'tar/ *vt* ill-treat, mistreat

malu|co /ma'luku/ *a* mad, crazy □ *m* madman; ~quice f madness; (*uma*) crazy thing

malvado /maw'vadu/ *a* wicked

malver|sação /mawversa'sãw/ f mismanagement; (*de fundos*) misappropriation; ~sar *vt* mismanage; misappropriate <*dinheiro*>

Malvinas /maw'vinas/ f pl Falklands

mamadeira /mama'dera/ f (baby's) bottle

mamãe /ma'mãj/ f mum

mamão /ma'mãw/ *m* papaya

ma|mar /ma'mar/ *vi* suckle; ~mata f (*fam*) fiddle

mamífero /ma'miferu/ *m* mammal

mamilo /ma'milu/ *m* nipple

mamoeiro /mamo'eru/ *m* papaya tree

manada /ma'nada/ f herd

manancial /manãsi'aw/ (*pl* ~ais) *m* spring; (*fig*) rich source

man|cada /mã'kada/ f blunder; ~car *vi* limp; ~car-se *vpr* (*fam*) take the hint, get the message

Mancha /'mãʃa/ f o canal da ~ the English Channel

man|cha /'mãʃa/ f stain; (*na pele*) mark; ~char *vt* stain

manchete /mã'ʃetʃi/ f headline

manco /'mãku/ *a* lame □ *m* cripple

mandachuva /mãda'ʃuva/ *m* (*fam*) bigwig; (*chefe*) boss

man|dado /mã'dadu/ *m* order; ~dado de busca search warrant; ~dado de prisão arrest warrant; ~damento *m* commandment; ~dante *m/f* person

in charge; ~dão *a* (f ~dona) bossy; ~dar *vt* (*pedir*) order; (*enviar*) send □ *vi* be in charge; ~dar-se *vpr* (*fam*) take off; ~dar buscar fetch; ~dar dizer send word; ~dar alg ir tell s.o. to go; ~dar ver (*fam*) go to town; ~dar em alg order s.o. about; ~dato *m* mandate

mandíbula /mã'dʒibula/ f (lower) jaw

mandioca /mãdʒi'ɔka/ f manioc

maneira /ma'nera/ f way; *pl* (*boas*) manners; desta ~ in this way; de qualquer ~ anyway

mane|jar /mane'ʒar/ *vt* handle; operate <*máquina*>; ~jável (*pl* ~jáveis) *a* manageable; ~jo /e/ *m* handling

manequim /mane'ki/ *m* (*boneco*) dummy; (*medida*) size □ *m/f* mannequin, model

maneta /ma'neta/ *a* one-armed □ *m/f* person with one arm

manga¹ /'mãga/ f (*de roupa*) sleeve

manga² /'mãga/ f (*fruta*) mango

manganês /mãga'nes/ *m* manganese

mangue /'mãgi/ *m* mangrove swamp

mangueira¹ /mã'gera/ f (*tubo*) hose

mangueira² /mã'gera/ f (*árvore*) mango tree

manha /'maɲa/ f tantrum

manhã /ma'ɲã/ f morning; de ~ in the morning

manhoso /ma'ɲozu/ *a* wilful

mania /ma'nia/ f (*moda*) craze; (*doença*) mania

maníaco /ma'niaku/ *a* manic □ *m* maniac; ~-depressivo *a* & *m* manic depressive

manicômio /mani'komiu/ *m* lunatic asylum

manicura /mani'kura/ f manicure; (*pessoa*) manicurist

manifes|tação /manifesta'sãw/ f manifestation; (*passeata*) demonstration; ~tante *m/f* demonstrator; ~tar *vt* manifest, demonstrate; ~tar-se *vpr* (*revelar-se*) manifest o.s.; (*exprimir-se*) express an opinion; ~to /ɛ/ *a* manifest, clear □ *m* manifesto

manipular /manipu'lar/ *vt* manipulate

manjedoura /mãʒe'dora/ f manger

manjericão /mãʒeri'kãw/ *m* basil

mano|bra /ma'nɔbra/ f manoeuvre; ~brar *vt* manoeuvre; ~brista *m/f* parking valet

mansão /mã'sãw/ f mansion

man|sidão /mãsi'dãw/ f gentleness; (*do mar*) calm; ~sinho *de* ~sinho (*devagar*) slowly; (*de leve*) gently; (*de fininho*) stealthily; ~so *a* gentle; <*mar*> calm; <*animal*> tame

manta /'mãta/ f blanket; (*casaco*) cloak

mantei|ga /mã'tejga/ f butter; ~gueira f butter dish

manter /mã'ter/ vt keep; ~-se vpr keep; (sustentar-se) keep o.s.

mantimentos /mãtʃi'mẽtus/ m pl provisions

manto /'mãtu/ m mantle

manu|al /manu'aw/ (pl ~ais) a & m manual; ~fatura f manufacture; (fábrica) factory; ~faturar vt manufacture

manuscrito /manus'kritu/ a hand-written □ m manuscript

manu|sear /manuzi'ar/ vt handle; ~seio m handling

manutenção /manutẽ'sãw/ f maintenance; (de prédio) upkeep

mão /mãw/ (pl ~s) f hand; (do trânsito) direction; (de tinta) coat; abrir ~ de give up; agüentar a ~ hang on; dar a ~ a alg hold s.o.'s hand; (cumprimentando) shake s.o.'s hand; deixar alg na ~ let s.o. down; enfiar ou meter a ~ em hit, slap; lançar ~ de make use of; escrito à ~ written by hand; ter à ~ have to hand; de ~s dadas hand in hand; em segunda ~ second-hand; fora de ~ out of the way; ~ única one way; ~-de-obra f labour

mapa /'mapa/ m map

maquete /ma'kɛtʃi/ f model

maqui|agem /maki'aʒẽ/ f make-up; ~ar vt make up; ~ar-se vpr put on make-up

maquiavélico /makia'veliku/ a Machiavellian

maqui|lagem, ~lar, (Port) ~lhagem, ~lhar veja maqui|agem, ~ar

máquina /'makina/ f machine; (ferroviária) engine; escrever à ~ type; ~ de costura sewing machine; ~ de escrever typewriter; ~ de lavar (roupa) washing machine; ~ de lavar pratos dishwasher; ~ fotográfica camera

maqui|nação /makina'sãw/ f machination; ~nal (pl ~nais) a mechanical; ~nar vt/i plot; ~naria f machinery; ~nista m/f (ferroviário) engine driver; (de navio) engineer

mar /mar/ m sea

maracu|já /maraku'ʒa/ m passion fruit; ~jazeiro m passion-fruit plant

marasmo /ma'razmu/ m stagnation

marato|na /mara'tona/ f marathon; ~nista m/f marathon runner

maravi|lha /mara'viʎa/ f marvel; às mil ~lhas wonderfully; ~lhar vt amaze; ~lhar-se vpr marvel (de at); ~lhoso /o/ a marvellous

mar|ca /'marka/ f (sinal) mark; (de carro, máquina) make; (de cigarro, sabão etc) brand; ~ca registrada registered trademark; ~cação f marking; (Port: discagem) dialling; ~cador m marker; (em livro) bookmark; (placar) scoreboard; (jogador) scorer; ~cante a outstanding; ~capasso m pacemaker; ~car vt mark; arrange <hora, encontro, jantar etc>; score <gol, ponto>; (Port: discar) dial; <relógio, termômetro> show; brand <gado>; (observar) keep a close eye on; (impressionar) leave one's mark on □ vi make one's mark; ~car época make history; ~car hora make an appointment; ~car o compasso beat time; ~car os pontos keep the score

marce|naria /marsena'ria/ f cabinet-making; (oficina) cabinet maker's workshop; ~neiro m cabinet maker

mar|cha /'marʃa/ f march; (de carro) gear; pôr-se em ~cha get going; ~cha à ré (Port) ~cha atrás reverse; ~char vi march

marci|al /marsi'aw/ (pl ~ais) a martial; ~ano a & m Martian

marco¹ /'marku/ m (sinal) landmark

marco² /'marku/ m (moeda) mark

março /'marsu/ m March

maré /ma'rɛ/ f tide

mare|chal /mare'ʃaw/ (pl ~chais) m marshal

maresia /mare'zia/ f smell of the sea

marfim /mar'fĩ/ m ivory

margarida /marga'rida/ f daisy; (para impressora) daisywheel

margarina /marga'rina/ f margarine

mar|gem /'marʒẽ/ f (de rio) bank; (de lago) shore; (parte em branco, fig) margin; ~ginal (pl ~ginais) a marginal; (delinqüente) delinquent □ m/f delinquent □ f (rua) riverside road; ~ginalidade f delinquency; ~ginalizar vt marginalize

marido /ma'ridu/ m husband

marimbondo /marĩ'bõdu/ m hornet

marina /ma'rina/ f marina

mari|nha /ma'rina/ f navy; ~nha mercante merchant navy; ~nheiro m sailor; ~nho a marine

marionete /mario'nɛtʃi/ f puppet

mariposa /mari'poza/ f moth

mariscos /ma'riskus/ m seafood

mari|tal /mari'taw/ (pl ~tais) a marital

marítimo /ma'ritʃimu/ a sea; <cidade> seaside

marmanjo /mar'mãʒu/ m grown-up

marme|lada /marme'lada/ f (fam) fix; ~lo /ɛ/ m quince

marmita /mar'mita/ f (de soldado) mess tin; (de trabalhador) lunchbox

mármore /'marmori/ m marble

marmóreo /mar'moriu/ a marble

marquise /mar'kizi/ f awning

marreco /ma'xɛku/ m wild duck

Marrocos /ma'xɔkus/ m Morocco

marrom /ma'xõ/ a & m brown

marroquino /maxo'kinu/ a & m Moroccan

Marte /'martʃi/ m Mars

martelada /marte'lada/ f hammer blow; ~lar vt/i hammer; ~lar em (fig) go on and on about; ~lo /ɛ/ m hammer

mártir /'martʃir/ m/f martyr

martírio /mar'tʃiriu/ m martyrdom; (fig) torture; ~tirizar vt martyr; (fig) torture

marujo /ma'ruʒu/ m sailor

marxismo /mark'sizmu/ m Marxism; ~xista a & m/f Marxist

mas /mas/ conj but

mascar /mas'kar/ vt chew

máscara /'maskara/ f mask; (tratamento facial) face-pack

mascarar /maska'rar/ vt mask

mascate /mas'katʃi/ m street vendor

mascavo /mas'kavu/ a açúcar ~ brown sugar

mascote /mas'kɔtʃi/ f mascot

masculino /masku'linu/ a male; (para homens) men's; <palavra> masculine □ m masculine

másculo /'maskulu/ a masculine

masmorra /maz'moxa/ f dungeon

masoquismo /mazo'kizmu/ m masochism; ~ta m/f masochist □ a masochistic

massa /'masa/ f mass; (de pão) dough; (de torta, empada) pastry; (macarrão etc) pasta; cultura de ~ mass culture; em ~ en masse; as ~s the masses

massacrante /masa'krãtʃi/ a gruelling; ~crar vt massacre; (fig: maçar) wear out; ~cre m massacre

massagear /masaʒi'ar/ vt massage; ~gem f massage; ~gista m/f masseur (f masseuse)

mastigar /mastʃi'gar/ vt chew; (ponderar) chew over

mastro /'mastru/ m mast; (de bandeira) flagpole

masturbação /masturba'sãw/ f masturbation; ~bar-se vpr masturbate

mata /'mata/ f forest

mata-borrão /matabo'xãw/ m blotting paper

matadouro /mata'doru/ m slaughterhouse

matagal /mata'gaw/ (pl ~gais) m thicket

mata-moscas /mata'moskas/ m invar fly spray

matança /ma'tãsa/ f slaughter; ~tar vt kill; satisfy <fome>; quench <sede>; guess <charada>; (fazer nas coxas) dash off; (fam) skive off <aula, serviço> □ vi kill

mate[1] /'matʃi/ m (chá) maté

mate[2] /'matʃi/ a invar matt

matemática /mate'matʃika/ f mathematics; ~co a mathematical □ m mathematician

matéria /ma'tɛria/ f (assunto, disciplina) subject; (no jornal) article; (substância) matter; (usada para fazer algo) material; em ~ de in the way of

material /materi'aw/ (pl ~ais) m materials □ a material; ~alismo m materialism; ~alista a materialistic □ m/f materialist; ~alizar-se vpr materialize

matéria-prima /matɛria'prima/ (pl matérias-primas) f raw material

maternal /mater'naw/ (pl ~nais) a maternal; ~nidade f maternity; (clínica) maternity hospital; ~no /ɛ/ a maternal; língua ~na mother tongue

matinal /matʃi'naw/ (pl ~nais) a morning; ~nê f matinée

matiz /ma'tʃis/ m shade; (político) colouring; (pontinha: de ironia etc) tinge

matizar /matʃi'zar/ vt tinge (de with)

mato /'matu/ m scrubland, bush

matraca /ma'traka/ f rattle; (tagarela) chatterbox

matreiro /ma'treru/ a cunning

matriarca /matri'arka/ f matriarch; ~cal (pl ~cais) a matriarchal

matrícula /ma'trikula/ f enrolment; (taxa) enrolment fee; (Port: de carro) number plate, (Amer) license plate

matricular /matriku'lar/ vt enrol; ~se vpr enrol

matrimonial /matrimoni'aw/ (pl ~moniais) a marriage; ~mônio m marriage

matriz /ma'tris/ f matrix; (útero) womb; (sede) head office

maturidade /maturi'dadʒi/ f maturity

matutino /matu'tʃinu/ a morning □ m morning paper

matuto /ma'tutu/ a countrified □ m country bumpkin

mau /maw/ a (f má) bad; ~-caráter m invar bad lot □ a invar no-good; ~-olhado m evil eye

mausoléu /mawzo'lɛw/ m mausoleum

maus-tratos /maws'tratus/ m pl ill-treatment

maxilar /maksi'lar/ m jaw

máxima /'masima/ f maxim

maximizar /masimi'zar/ vt maximize; (exagerar) play up

máximo /'masimu/ a (antes do substantivo) utmost, greatest; (depois do substantivo) maximum □ m maximum; o ~ (*fam*: o *melhor*) really something; ao ~ to the maximum; no ~ at most

maxixe /ma'ʃiʃi/ *m* gherkin

me /mi/ *pron* me; (*indireto*) (to) me; (*reflexivo*) myself

meada /mi'ada/ *f* skein; perder o fio da ~ lose one's thread

meados /mi'adus/ *m pl* ~ de maio mid-May

meandro /mi'ãdru/ *f* meander; *pl* (*fig*) twists and turns

mecâni|ca /me'kanika/ *f* mechanics; ~co *a* mechanical □ *m* mechanic

meca|nismo /meka'nizmu/ *m* mechanism; ~nizar *vt* mechanize

mecenas /me'sɛnas/ *m invar* patron

mecha /'mɛʃa/ *f* (*de vela*) wick; (*de bomba*) fuse; (*porção de cabelos*) lock; (*cabelo tingido*) highlight; ~do *a* highlighted

meda|lha /me'daʎa/ *f* medal; ~lhão *m* medallion; (*jóia*) locket

média /'mɛdʒia/ *f* average; (*café*) white coffee; em ~ on average

medi|ação /medʒia'sãw/ *f* mediation; ~ador *m* mediator; ~ante *prep* through, by; ~ar *vi* mediate

medica|ção /medʒika'sãw/ *f* medication; ~mento *m* medicine

medição /medʒi'sãw/ *f* measurement

medicar /medʒi'kar/ *vt* treat □ *vi* practise medicine; ~se *vpr* dose o.s. up

medici|na /medʒi'sina/ *f* medicine; ~na legal forensic medicine; ~nal (*pl* ~nais) *a* medicinal

médico /'mɛdʒiku/ *m* doctor □ *a* medical; ~-legal (*pl* ~-legais) *a* forensic; ~-legista (*pl* ~-s-legistas) *m/f* forensic scientist

medi|da /me'dʒida/ *f* measure; (*dimensão*) measurement; à ~da que as; sob ~da made to measure; tirar as ~das de alg take s.o.'s measurements; ~dor *m* meter

medie|val /medʒie'vaw/ (*pl* ~vais) *a* medieval

médio /'mɛdʒiu/ *a* (*típico*) average; <*tamanho, prazo*> medium; <*classe, dedo*> middle

mediocre /me'dʒiokri/ *a* mediocre

mediocridade /medʒiokri'dadʒi/ *f* mediocrity

medir /me'dʒir/ *vt* measure; weigh <*palavras*> □ *vi* measure; ~se *vpr* measure o.s.; quanto você mede? ·how tall are you?

medi|tação /medʒita'sãw/ *f* meditation; ~tar *vi* meditate

mediterrâneo /medʒite'xaniu/ *a* Mediterranean □ *m* o Mediterrâneo the Mediterranean

médium /'mɛdʒiũ/ *m/f* medium

medo /'medu/ *m* fear; ter ~ de be

afraid of; com ~ afraid; ~nho /o/ *a* frightful

medroso /me'drozu/ *a* fearful, timid

medula /me'dula/ *f* marrow

megalomania /megaloma'nia/ *f* megalomania

megalomaníaco /megaloma'niaku/ *a* megalomaniac

meia /'meja/ *f* (*comprida*) stocking; (*curta*) sock; (*seis*) six; ~calça (*pl* ~s-calças) *f* tights, (*Amer*) pantihose; ~idade *f* middle age; ~noite *f* midnight; ~volta (*pl* ~s-voltas) *f* about-turn

mei|go /'mejgu/ *a* sweet; ~guice *f* sweetness

meio /'meju/ *a* half □ *adv* rather □ *m* (*centro*) middle; (*ambiente*) environment; (*recurso*) means; ~ litro half a litre; dois meses e ~ two and a half months; em ~ a amid; por ~ de through; o ~ ambiente the environment; os ~s de comunicação the media; ~-dia *m* midday; ~-fio *m* kerb; ~-termo *m* (*acordo*) compromise

mel /mɛw/ *m* honey

mela|ço /me'lasu/ *m* molasses; ~do *a* sticky □ *m* treacle

melancia /melã'sia/ *f* watermelon

melan|colia /melãko'lia/ *f* melancholy; ~cólico *a* melancholy

melão /me'lãw/ *m* melon

melar /me'lar/ *vt* make sticky

melhor /me'ʎor/ *a* & *adv* better; o ~ the best

melho|ra /me'ʎora/ *f* improvement; ~ras! get well soon!; ~ramento *m* improvement; ~rar *vt* improve □ *vi* improve; <*doente*> get better

melin|drar /melĩ'drar/ *vt* hurt; ~drar-se *vpr* be hurt; ~droso /o/ *a* delicate; <*pessoa*> sensitive

melodi|a /melo'dʒia/ *f* melody; ~oso /o/ *a* melodious

melodra|ma /melo'drama/ *m* melodrama; ~mático *a* melodramatic

meloso /me'lozu/ *a* sickly sweet

melro /'mɛwxu/ *m* blackbird

membrana /mẽ'brana/ *f* membrane

membro /'mẽbru/ *m* member; (*braço, perna*) limb

memo|rando /memo'rãdu/ *m* memo; ~rável (*pl* ~ráveis) *a* memorable

memória /me'mɔria/ *f* memory; *pl* (*autobiografia*) memoirs

men|ção /mẽ'sãw/ *f* mention; fazer ~ção de mention; ~cionar *vt* mention

mendi|cância /mẽdʒi'kãsia/ *f* begging; ~gar *vi* beg; ~go *m* beggar

menina /me'nina/ *f* girl; a ~ dos olhos de alg the apple of s.o.'s eye

meningite /menĩ'ʒitʃi/ *f* meningitis

meni|nice /meni'nisi/ *f* (*idade*) childhood; ~no *m* boy

menopausa /meno'pawza/ f menopause

menor /me'nɔr/ a smaller □ m/f minor; o/a ~ the smallest; (mínimo) the slightest, the least

menos /'menos/ adv & pron less □ prep except; dois dias a ~ two days less; a ~ que unless; ao ou pelo ~ at least; o ~ bonito the least pretty; ~prezar vt look down upon; ~prezo /e/ m disdain

mensa|geiro /mẽsa'ʒeru/ m messenger; ~gem f message

men|sal /mẽ'saw/ (pl ~sais) a monthly; ~salidade f monthly payment; ~salmente adv monthly

menstru|ação /mẽstrua'sãw/ f menstruation; ~ada a estar ~ada be having one's period; ~al (pl ~ais) a menstrual; ~ar vi menstruate

menta /'mẽta/ f mint

men|tal /mẽ'taw/ (pl ~tais) a mental; ~talidade f mentality; ~te f mind

men|tir /mẽ'tʃir/ vi lie; ~tira f lie; ~tiroso /o/ a lying □ m liar

mentor /mẽ'tor/ m mentor

mercado /mer'kadu/ m market; ~ria f commodity; pl goods

mercan|te /mer'kãtʃi/ a merchant; ~til (pl ~tis) a mercantile; ~tilismo m commercialism

mercê /mer'se/ f à ~ de at the mercy of

merce|aria /mersia'ria/ f grocer's; ~eiro m grocer

mercenário /merse'nariu/ a & m mercenary

mercúrio /mer'kuriu/ m mercury; Mercúrio Mercury

merda /'mɛrda/ f (chulo) shit

mere|cedor /merese'dor/ a deserving; ~cer vt deserve □ vi be deserving; ~cimento m merit

merenda /me'rẽda/ f packed lunch; ~ escolar school dinner

mere|trício /mere'trisiu/ m prostitution; ~triz f prostitute

mergu|lhador /merguʎa'dor/ m diver; ~lhar vt dip (em into) □ vi (na água) dive; (no trabalho) bury o.s.; ~lho m dive; (esporte) diving; (banho de mar) dip

meridi|ano /meridʒi'anu/ m meridian; ~onal (pl ~onais) a southern

mérito /'mɛritu/ m merit

merluza /mer'luza/ f hake

mero /'mɛru/ a mere

mês /mes/ (pl meses) m month

mesa /'meza/ f table; (de trabalho) desk; ~ de centro coffee table; ~ de jantar dining table; ~ telefônica switchboard

mesada /me'zada/ f monthly allowance

mescla /'mɛskla/ f mixture, blend

mesmice /mez'misi/ f sameness

mesmo /'mezmu/ a same □ adv (até) even; (justamente) right; (de verdade) really; você ~ you yourself; hoje ~ this very day; ~ assim even so; ~ que even if; dá no ~ it comes to the same thing; fiquei na mesma I'm none the wiser

mesqui|nharia /meskiɲa'ria/ f meanness; (uma) mean thing; ~nho a mean

mesquita /mes'kita/ f mosque

Messias /me'sias/ m Messiah

mesti|çagem /mestʃi'saʒẽ/ f interbreeding; ~ço a <pessoa> of mixed race; <animal> crossbred □ m (pessoa) person of mixed race; (animal) mongrel

mes|trado /mes'tradu/ m master's degree; ~tre /ɛ/ m (f ~tra) master (f mistress); (de escola) teacher □ a main; <chave> master; ~tre-de-obras (pl ~tres-de-obras) m foreman; ~tre-sala (pl ~tres-salas) m master of ceremonies (in carnival procession); ~tria f expertise

meta /'mɛta/ f (de corrida) finishing post; (gol, fig) goal

meta|bólico /meta'bɔliku/ a metabolic; ~bolismo m metabolism

metade /me'tadʒi/ f half; pela ~ halfway

metafísi|ca /meta'fizika/ f metaphysics; ~co a metaphysical

metáfora /me'tafora/ f metaphor

metafórico /meta'fɔriku/ a metaphorical

me|tal /me'taw/ (pl ~tais) m metal; pl (numa orquestra) brass; ~tálico a metallic

meta|lurgia /metalur'ʒia/ f metallurgy; ~lúrgica f metal works; ~lúrgico a metallurgical □ m metalworker

metamorfose /metamor'fɔzi/ f metamorphosis

metano /me'tanu/ m methane

meteórico /mete'ɔriku/ a meteoric

meteoro /mete'ɔru/ m meteor; ~logia f meteorology; ~lógico a meteorological; ~logista m/f (cientista) meteorologist; (na TV) weather forecaster

meter /me'ter/ vt put; ~-se vpr (envolver-se) get (em into); (intrometer-se) meddle (em in); ~ medo be frightening

meticuloso /metʃiku'lozu/ a meticulous

metido /me'tʃidu/ a snobbish; ele é ~ a perito he thinks he's an expert

metódico /me'tɔdʒiku/ a methodical

metodista /meto'dʒista/ a & m/f Methodist

método /'mɛtodu/ m method

metra|lhadora /metraʎa'dora/ f machine gun; ~lhar vt machine-gun

métri|co /'mɛtriku/ a metric; fita ~ca tape measure

metro¹ /'mɛtru/ m metre

metro² /'mɛtru/ m (Port: metropolitano) underground, (Amer) subway

metrô /me'tro/ m underground, (Amer) subway

metrópole /me'trɔpoli/ f metropolis

metropolitano /metropoli'tanu/ a metropolitan □ m (Port) underground, (Amer) subway

meu /mew/ a (f minha) my □ pron (f minha) mine; um amigo ~ a friend of mine; fico na minha (fam) I keep myself to myself

mexer /me'ʃer/ vt move; (com colher etc) stir □ vi move; ~-se vpr move; (apressar-se) get a move on; ~ com (comover) affect, get to; (brincar com) tease; (trabalhar com) work with; ~ em touch

mexeri|ca /meʃe'rika/ f tangerine; ~car vi gossip; ~co m piece of gossip; pl gossip; ~queiro a gossiping □ m gossip

mexicano /meʃi'kanu/ a & m Mexican

México /'mɛʃiku/ m Mexico

mexido /me'ʃidu/ a ovos ~s scrambled eggs

mexilhão /meʃi'ʎãw/ m mussel

mi|ado /mi'adu/ m miaow; ~ar vi miaow

micróbio /mi'krɔbiu/ m microbe

micro|cosmo /mikro'kɔzmu/ m microcosm; ~empresa /e/ f small business; ~empresário m small businessman; ~filme m microfilm; ~fone m microphone; ~onda f microwave; (forno de) ~s m microwave (oven); ~ônibus m invar minibus; ~processador m microprocessor

microrganismo /mikrorga'nizmu/ m microorganism

microscó|pico /mikros'kɔpiku/ a microscopic; ~pio m microscope

mídia /'midʒia/ f media

migalha /mi'gaʎa/ f crumb

mi|gração /migra'sãw/ f migration; ~grar vi migrate; ~gratório a migratory

mijar /mi'ʒar/ vi (fam) pee; ~jar-se vpr wet o.s.; ~jo m (fam) pee

mil /miw/ a & m invar thousand; estar a ~ be on top form

mila|gre /mi'lagri/ m miracle; ~groso /o/ a miraculous

milênio /mi'leniu/ m millennium

milésimo /mi'lɛzimu/ a thousandth

milha /'miʎa/ f mile

milhão /mi'ʎãw/ m million; um ~ de dólares a million dollars

milhar /mi'ʎar/ m thousand; ~es de vezes thousands of times; aos ~es in their thousands

milho /'miʎo/ m maize, (Amer) corn

milico /mi'liku/ m (fam) military man; os ~s the military

mili|grama /mili'grama/ m milligram; ~litro m millilitre; ~metro /e/ m millimetre

milionário /milio'nariu/ a & m millionaire

mili|tante /mili'tãtʃi/ a & m militant; ~tar a military □ m soldier

mim /mĩ/ pron me

mimar /mi'mar/ vt spoil

mímica /'mimika/ f mime; (brincadeira) charades

mi|na /'mina/ f mine; ~nar vt mine; (fig: prejudicar) undermine

mindinho /mĩ'dʒiɲu/ m little finger, (Amer) pinkie

mineiro /mi'neru/ a mining; (de MG) from Minas Gerais □ m miner; (de MG) person from Minas Gerais

mine|ração /minera'sãw/ f mining; ~ral (pl ~rais) a & m mineral; ~rar vt/i mine

minério /mi'nɛriu/ m ore

mingau /mĩ'gaw/ m porridge

míngua /'mĩgwa/ f lack

minguante /mĩ'gwãtʃi/ a quarto ~ last quarter

minguar /mĩ'gwar/ vi dwindle

minha /'miɲa/ a & pron veja meu

minhoca /mi'ɲɔka/ f worm

miniatura /minia'tura/ f miniature

mini|malista /minima'lista/ a & m/f minimalist; ~mizar vt minimize; (subestimar) play down

mínimo /'minimu/ a (muito pequeno) tiny; (mais baixo) minimum □ m minimum; a mínima idéia the slightest idea; no ~ at least

minissaia /mini'saja/ f miniskirt

minis|terial /ministeri'aw/ (pl ~teriais) a ministerial; ~tério m ministry; Ministério do Interior Home Office, (Amer) Department of the Interior

minis|trar /minis'trar/ vt administer; ~tro m minister; primeiro ~tro prime minister

Minorca /mi'nɔrka/ f Menorca

mino|ritário /minori'tariu/ a minority; ~ria f minority

minúcia /mi'nusia/ f detail

minucioso /minusi'ozu/ a thorough

minúscu|la /mi'nuskula/ f small letter; ~lo a < letra> small; (muito pequeno) minuscule

minuta /mi'nuta/ f (rascunho) rough draft

minuto /mi'nutu/ *m* minute

miolo /mi'olu/ *f* (*de fruta*) flesh; (*de pão*) crumb; *pl* brains

míope /'miopi/ *a* short-sighted

miopia /mio'pia/ *f* myopia

mira /'mira/ *f* sight; ter em ∼ have one's sights on

mirabolante /mirabo'lãtʃi/ *a* amazing; <*idéias, plano*> grandiose

mi|ragem /mi'raʒẽ/ *f* mirage; ∼rante *m* lookout; ∼rar *vt* look at; ∼rar-se *vpr* look at o.s.

mirim /mi'rĩ/ *a* a little

miscelânea /mise'lania/ *f* miscellany

miscigenação /misiʒena'sãw/ *f* interbreeding

mise-en-plis /mizã'pli/ *m* shampoo and set

miserá|vel /mize'ravew/ (*pl* ∼veis) *a* miserable

miséria /mi'zɛria/ *f* misery; (*pobreza*) poverty; uma ∼ (*pouco dinheiro*) a pittance; chorar ∼ claim poverty

miseri|córdia /mizeri'kɔrdʒia/ *f* mercy; ∼cordioso *a* merciful

misógino /mi'zɔʒinu/ *m* misogynist □ *a* misogynous

miss /'misi/ *f* beauty queen

missa /'misa/ *f* mass

missão /mi'sãw/ *f* mission

mís|sil /'misiw/ (*pl* ∼seis) *m* missile; ∼sil de longo alcance long-range missile

missionário /misio'nariu/ *m* missionary

missiva /mi'siva/ *f* missive

mis|tério /mis'tɛriu/ *m* mystery; ∼terioso *a* mysterious; ∼ticismo *m* mysticism

místico /'mistʃiku/ *m* mystic □ *a* mystical

misto /'mistu/ *a* mixed □ *m* mix; ∼ quente toasted ham and cheese sandwich

mistu|ra /mis'tura/ *f* mixture; ∼rar *vt* mix; (*confundir*) mix up; ∼rar-se *vpr* mix (com with)

mítico /'mitʃiku/ *a* a mythical

mito /'mitu/ *m* myth; ∼logia *f* mythology; ∼lógico *a* mythological

miudezas /miu'dezas/ *f pl* odds and ends

miúdo /mi'udu/ *a* tiny, minute; <*chuva*> fine; <*despesas*> minor □ *m* (*criança*) child, little one; *pl* (*de galinha*) giblets; trocar em ∼s go into detail

mixaria /miʃa'ria/ *f* (*fam*) (*soma irrisória*) pittance

mixórdia /mi'ʃɔrdʒia/ *f* muddle

mnemônico /ne'moniku/ *a* mnemonic

mobilar /mobi'lar/ *vt* (*Port*) furnish

mobília /mo'bilia/ *f* furniture

mobili|ar /mobili'ar/ *vt* furnish; ∼ário *m* furniture

mobili|dade /mobili'dadʒi/ *f* mobility; ∼zar *vt* mobilize

moça /'mosa/ *f* girl

moçambicano /mosãbi'kanu/ *a & m* Mozambican

Moçambique /mosã'biki/ *m* Mozambique

moção /mo'sãw/ *f* motion

mochila /mo'ʃila/ *f* rucksack

moço /'mosu/ *a* young □ *m* boy, lad

moda /'mɔda/ *f* fashion; na ∼ fashionable

modalidade /modali'dadʒi/ *f* (*esporte*) event

mode|lagem /mode'laʒẽ/ *f* modelling; ∼lar *vt* model (a on); ∼lar-se *vpr* model o.s. (a on) □ *a* model; ∼lo /e/ *m* model

mode|ração /modera'sãw/ *f* moderation; ∼rado *a* moderate; ∼rar *vt* moderate; reduce <*velocidade, despesas*>; ∼rar-se *vpr* restrain oneself

moder|nidade /moderni'dadʒi/ *f* modernity; ∼nismo *m* modernism; ∼nista *a & m/f* modernist; ∼nizar *vt* modernize; ∼no /ɛ/ *a* modern

modess /'mɔdʒis/ *m invar* sanitary towel

modéstia /mo'dɛstʃia/ *f* modesty

modesto /mo'dɛstu/ *a* modest

módico /'mɔdʒiku/ *a* modest

modifi|cação /modʒifika'sãw/ *f* modification; ∼car *vt* modify

mo|dismo /mo'dʒizmu/ *m* idiom; ∼dista *f* dressmaker

modo /'mɔdu/ *m* way; (*ling*) mood; *pl* (*maneiras*) manners

modular /modu'lar/ *vt* modulate □ *a* modular

módulo /'mɔdulu/ *m* module

moeda /mo'ɛda/ *f* (*peça de metal*) coin; (*dinheiro*) currency

mo|edor /moe'dor/ *m* ∼edor de café coffee-grinder; ∼edor de carne mincer; ∼er *vt* grind <*café, trigo*>; squeeze <*cana*>; mince <*carne*>; (*bater*) beat

mo|fado /mo'fadu/ *a* mouldy; ∼far *vi* moulder; ∼fo /o/ *m* mould

mogno /'mɔgnu/ *m* mahogany

moinho /mo'iɲu/ *m* mill; ∼ de vento windmill

moisés /moj'zɛs/ *m invar* carry-cot

moita /'mojta/ *f* bush

mola /'mɔla/ *f* spring

mol|dar /mow'dar/ *vt* mould; cast <*metal*>; ∼de /ɔ/ *m* mould; (*para costura etc*) pattern

moldu|ra /mow'dura/ *f* frame; ∼rar *vt* frame

mole /'mɔli/ *a* soft; <*pessoa*> listless; (*fam*) (*fácil*) easy □ *adv* easily; é ~? (*fam*) can you believe it?

molécula /mo'lɛkula/ *f* molecule

moleque /mo'lɛki/ *m* (*menino*) lad; (*de rua*) urchin; (*homem*) scoundrel

molestar /moles'tar/ *vt* bother

moléstia /mo'lɛstʃia/ *f* disease

moletom /mole'tõ/ *m* (*tecido*) knitted cotton; (*blusa*) sweatshirt

moleza /mo'leza/ *f* softness; (*de pessoa*) laziness; viver na ~ lead a cushy life; ser ~ be easy

mo|lhado /mo'ʎadu/ *a* wet; ~lhar *vt* wet; ~lhar-se *vpr* get wet

molho¹ /'mɔʎu/ *m* (*de chaves*) bunch; (*de palha*) sheaf

molho² /'moʎu/ *m* sauce; (*para salada*) dressing; deixar de ~ leave in soak <*roupa*>; ~ inglês Worcester sauce

molusco /mo'lusku/ *m* mollusc

momen|tâneo /momē'taniu/ *a* momentary; ~to *m* moment; (*força*) momentum

Mônaco /'monaku/ *m* Monaco

monar|ca /mo'narka/ *m/f* monarch; ~quia *f* monarchy; ~quista *a* & *m/f* monarchist

monástico /mo'nastʃiku/ *a* monastic

monção /mõ'sãw/ *f* monsoon

mone|tário /mone'tariu/ *a* monetary; ~tarismo *m* monetarism; ~tarista *a* & *m/f* monetarist

monge /'mõʒi/ *m* monk

monitor /moni'tor/ *m* monitor; ~ de vídeo VDU

monitorar /monito'rar/ *vt* monitor

mono|cromo /mono'krɔmu/ *a* monochrome; ~gamia *f* monogamy

monógamo /mo'nɔgamu/ *a* monogamous

monograma /mono'grama/ *m* monogram

monólogo /mo'nɔlogu/ *m* monologue

mononucleose /mononukli'ɔzi/ *f* glandular fever

mono|pólio /mono'pɔliu/ *m* monopoly; ~polizar *vt* monopolize

monossilabo /mono'silabu/ *a* monosyllabic □ *m* monosyllable

monotonia /monoto'nia/ *f* monotony

monótono /mo'nɔtonu/ *a* monotonous

monóxido /mo'nɔksidu/ *m* ~ de carbono carbon monoxide

mons|tro /'mõstru/ *m* monster; ~truosidade *f* monstrosity; ~truoso /o/ *a* monstrous

monta|dor /mõta'dor/ *m* (*de cinema*) editor; ~dora *f* assembly company; ~gem *f* assembly; (*de filme*) editing; (*de peça teatral*) production

monta|nha /mõ'taɲa/ *f* mountain; ~nha-russa (*pl* ~nhas-russas) *f* roller coaster; ~nhismo *m* mountaineering; ~nhoso /o/ *a* mountainous

mon|tante /mõ'tãtʃi/ *m* amount □ *a* rising; a ~tante upstream; ~tão *m* heap; ~tar *vt* ride <*cavalo, bicicleta*>; assemble <*peças, máquina*>; put up <*barraca*>; set up <*empresa, escritório*>; mount <*guarda, diamante*>; put on <*espetáculo, peça*>; edit <*filme*> □ *vi* ride; ~tar a <*dividas etc*> amount to; ~tar em (*subir em*) mount; ~taria *f* mount; ~te *m* heap; um ~te de coisas (*fam*) loads of things; o Monte Branco Mont Blanc

Montevidéu /mõtʃivi'dɛw/ *f* Montevideo

montra /'mõtra/ *f* (*Port*) shop window

monumen|tal /monumē'taw/ (*pl* ~tais) *a* monumental; ~to *m* monument

mo|rada /mo'rada/ *f* dwelling; (*Port*) address; ~dia *f* dwelling; ~dor *m* resident

mo|ral /mo'raw/ (*pl* ~rais) *a* moral □ *f* (*ética*) morals; (*de uma história*) moral □ *m* (*ânimo*) morale; (*de pessoa*) moral sense; ~ralidade *f* morality; ~ralista *a* moralistic □ *m/f* moralist; ~ralizar *vi* moralize

morango /mo'rãgu/ *m* strawberry

morar /mo'rar/ *vi* live

moratória /mora'tɔria/ *f* moratorium

mórbido /'mɔrbidu/ *a* morbid

morcego /mor'segu/ *m* bat

mor|daça /mor'dasa/ *f* gag; (*para cão*) muzzle; ~daz *a* scathing; ~der *vt/i* bite; ~dida *f* bite

mordo|mia /mordo'mia/ *f* (*no emprego*) perk; (*de casa etc*) comfort; ~mo /o/ *m* butler

more|na /mo'rena/ *f* brunette; ~no *a* dark; (*bronzeado*) brown □ *m* dark person

morfina /mor'fina/ *f* morphine

moribundo /mori'bũdu/ *a* dying

moringa /mo'rĩga/ *f* water jug

morma|cento /morma'sẽtu/ *a* sultry; ~ço *m* sultry weather

morno /'mornu/ *a* lukewarm

moro|sidade /morozi'dadʒi/ *f* slowness; ~so /o/ *a* slow

morrer /mo'xer/ *vi* die; <*luz, dia, ardor, esperança etc*> fade; <*carro*> stall

morro /'moxu/ *m* hill; (*fig: favela*) slum

mortadela /morta'dɛla/ *f* mortadella, salami

mor|tal /mor'taw/ (*pl* ~tais) *a* & *m* mortal; ~talha *f* shroud; ~talidade *f* mortality; ~tandade *f* slaughter; ~te /ɔ/ *f* death; ~tifero *a* deadly; ~tificar *vt* mortify; ~to /o/ *a* dead mosaico /mo'zajku/ m mosaic

mosca /'moska/ f fly

Moscou /mos'ku/, (Port) Moscovo /mof'kovu/ f Moscow

mosquito /mos'kitu/ m mosquito

mostarda /mos'tarda/ f mustard

mosteiro /mos'teru/ m monastery

mos|tra /'mɔstra/ f display; dar ~tras de show signs of; pôr à ~tra show up; ~trador m face, dial; ~trar vt show; ~trar-se vpr (revelar-se) show o.s. to be; (exibir-se) show off; ~truário m display case

mo|tel /mo'tɛw/ (pl ~téis) m motel

motim /mo'tʃĩ/ m riot; (na marinha) mutiny

moti|vação /motʃiva'sãw/ f motivation; ~var vt (incentivar) motivate; (provocar) cause; ~vo m (razão) reason; (estímulo) motive; (na arte, música) motif; dar ~vo de give cause for

moto /'mɔtu/ f motorbike; ~ca /mo'tɔka/ f (fam) motorbike

motoci|cleta /motosi'klɛta/ f motorcycle; ~clismo m motorcycling; ~clista m/f motorcyclist

motoqueiro /moto'keru/ m (fam) biker

motor /mo'tor/ m (de carro, avião etc) engine; (elétrico) motor □ a (f motriz) <força> driving; (anat) motor; ~ de arranque starter motor; ~ de popa outboard motor

moto|rista /moto'rista/ m/f driver; ~rizado a motorized; ~rizar vt motorize

movedi|ço /move'dʒisu/ a unstable, moving; areia ~ça quicksand

mó|vel /'mɔvew/ (pl ~veis) a <peça, parte> moving; <tropas> mobile; <festa> movable □ m piece of furniture; pl furniture

mo|ver /mo'ver/ vt move; (impulsionar, fig) drive; ~ver-se vpr move; ~vido a driven; ~vido a álcool alcohol-powered

movimen|tação /movimẽta'sãw/ f bustle; ~tado a <rua, loja> busy; <música> up-beat, lively; <pessoa, sessão> lively; ~tar vt liven up; ~tar-se vpr move; ~to m movement; (tecn) motion; (na rua etc) activity

muam|ba /mu'ãba/ f contraband; ~beiro m smuggler

muco /'muku/ m mucus

muçulmano /musuw'manu/ a & m Muslim

mu|da /'muda/ f (planta) seedling; ~da de roupa change of clothes; ~dança f change; (de casa) move; (de carro) transmission; ~dar vt/i change; ~dar de assunto change the subject; ~dar (de casa) move (house); ~dar de cor change colour;

~dar de idéia change one's mind; ~dar de lugar change places; ~dar de roupa change (clothes); ~dar-se vpr move

mu|dez /mu'des/ f silence; ~do a silent; (deficiente) dumb; <telefone> dead □ m mute

mu|gido /mu'ʒidu/ m moo; ~gir vi moo

muito /'mũitu/ a a lot of; pl many □ pron a lot □ adv (com adjetivo, advérbio) very; (com verbo) a lot; ~ maior much bigger; ~ tempo a long time

mula /'mula/ f mule

mulato /mu'latu/ a & m mulatto

muleta /mu'leta/ f crutch

mulher /mu'ʎer/ f woman; (esposa) wife

mulherengo /muʎe'rẽgu/ a womanizing □ m womanizer, ladies' man

mul|ta /'muwta/ f fine; ~tar vt fine

multicolor /muwtʃiko'lor/ a multi-coloured

multidão /muwtʃi'dãw/ f crowd

multinacio|nal /muwtʃinasio'naw/ (pl ~nais) a & f multinational

multipli|cação /muwtʃiplika'sãw/ f multiplication; ~car vt multiply; ~car-se vpr multiply; ~cidade f multiplicity

múltiplo /'muwtʃiplu/ a & m multiple

multirraci|al /muwtʃixasi'aw/ (pl ~ais) a multiracial

múmia /'mumia/ f mummy

mun|dano /mũ'danu/ a <prazeres etc> worldly; <vida, mulher> society; ~dial (pl ~diais) a world □ m world championship; ~do m world; todo (o) ~do everybody

munição /muni'sãw/ f ammunition

muni|cipal /munisi'paw/ (pl ~cipais) a municipal; ~cípio m (lugar) borough, community; (prédio) town hall; (autoridade) local authority

munir /mu'nir/ vt provide (de with); ~-se vpr equip o.s. (de with)

mu|ral /mu'raw/ (pl ~rais) a & m mural; ~ralha f wall

mur|char /mur'ʃar/ vi <planta> wither, wilt; <salada> go limp; <beleza> fade □ vt wither, wilt <planta>; ~cho a <planta> wilting; <pessoa> broken

mur|murar /murmu'rar/ vi murmur; (queixar-se) mutter □ vt murmur; ~múrio m murmur

muro /'muru/ m wall

murro /'muxu/ m punch

musa /'muza/ f muse

muscu|lação /muskula'sãw/ f weight-training; ~lar a muscular; ~latura f musculature

músculo /'muskulu/ m muscle

musculoso /musku'lozu/ a muscular

museu /mu'zew/ m museum

musgo /'muzgu/ m moss

música /'muzika/ f music; (uma) song; ~ de câmara chamber music; ~ de fundo background music; ~ clássica ou erudita classical music

musi|cal /muzi'kaw/ (pl ~cais) a & m musical; ~car vt set to music

músico /'muziku/ m musician □ a musical

musse /'musi/ f mousse

mutilar /mutʃi'lar/ vt mutilate; maim <pessoa>

mutirão /mutʃi'rãw/ m joint effort

mútuo /'mutuu/ a mutual

muxoxo /mu'ʃoʃu/ m fazer ~ tut

N

na = em + a

nabo /'nabu/ m turnip

nação /na'sãw/ f nation

nacio|nal /nasio'naw/ (pl ~nais) a national; (brasileiro) home-produced; ~nalidade f nationality; ~nalismo m nationalism; ~nalista a & m/f nationalist; ~nalizar vt nationalize

naco /'naku/ m chunk

nada /'nada/ pron nothing □ adv not at all; de ~ (não há de quê) don't mention it; que ~!, ~ disso! no way!

na|dadeira /nada'dera/ f (de peixe) fin; (de mergulhador) flipper; ~dador m swimmer; ~dar vi swim

nádegas /'nadegas/ f pl buttocks

nado /'nadu/ m ~ borboleta butterfly stroke; ~ de costas backstroke; ~ de peito breaststroke; atravessar a ~ swim across

náilon /'najlõ/ m nylon

naipe /'najpi/ m (em jogo de cartas) suit

namo|rada /namo'rada/ f girlfriend; ~rado m boyfriend; ~rador a amorous □ m ladies' man; ~rar vt (ter relação com) go out with; (cobiçar) eye up □ vi (~casal) (ter relação) go out together; (beijar-se etc) kiss and cuddle; <homem> have a girlfriend; <mulher> have a boyfriend; ~ro /o/ m relationship

nanar /na'nar/ vi (col) sleep

nanico /na'niku/ a tiny

não /nãw/ adv not; (resposta) no □ m no; ~-alinhado a non-aligned; ~-conformista a & m/f non-conformist

naquela, naquele, naquilo = em + aquela, aquele, aquilo

narci|sismo /narsi'zizmu/ m narcissism; ~sista m/f narcissist □ a narcissistic; ~so m narcissus

narcótico /nar'kɔtʃiku/ a & m narcotic

nari|gudo /nari'gudu/ a with a big nose; ser ~gudo have a big nose; ~na f nostril

nariz /na'ris/ m nose

nar|ração /naxa'sãw/ f narration; ~rador m narrator; ~rar vt narrate; ~rativa f narrative; ~rativo a narrative

nas = em + as

na|sal /na'zaw/ (pl ~sais) a nasal; ~salizar vt nasalize

nas|cença /na'sẽsa/ f birth; ~cente f nascent □ f source; ~cer vi be born; <dente, espinha> grow; <planta> sprout; <sol, lua> rise; <dia> dawn; (fig) <empresa, projeto etc> come into being □ m o ~cer do sol sunrise; ~cimento m birth

nata /'nata/ f cream

natação /nata'sãw/ f swimming

Natal /na'taw/ m Christmas

na|tal /na'taw/ (pl ~tais) a <país, terra> native

nata|lício /nata'lisiu/ a & m birthday; ~lidade f índice de ~lidade birth rate; ~lino a Christmas

nati|vidade /natʃivi'dadʒi/ f nativity; ~vo a & m native

nato /'natu/ a born

natu|ral /natu'raw/ (pl ~rais) a natural; (oriundo) originating (de from) □ m native (de of)

natura|lidade /naturali'dadʒi/ f naturalness; com ~lidade matter-of-factly; de ~lidade carioca born in Rio de Janeiro; ~lismo m naturalism; ~lista a & m/f naturalist; ~lizar vt naturalize; ~lizar-se vpr become naturalized

natureza /natu'reza/ f nature; ~ morta still life

naturis|mo /natu'rizmu/ m naturism; ~ta m/f naturist

náuti|ca /'nawtʃika/ f navigation; ~co a nautical

na|val /na'vaw/ (pl ~vais) a naval; construção ~val shipbuilding

navalha /na'vaʎa/ f razor; ~da f cut with a razor

nave /'navi/ f nave; ~ espacial spaceship

nave|gação /navega'sãw/ f navigation; (tráfego) shipping; ~gador m navigator; ~gante m/f seafarer; ~gar vt navigate; sail <mar> □ vi sail; (traçar o rumo) navigate; ~gável (pl ~gáveis) a navigable

navio /na'viu/ m ship; ~ cargueiro cargo ship; ~ de guerra warship; ~ petroleiro oil tanker

nazista /na'zista/, (Port) nazi /na'zi/ a & m/f Nazi

neblina /ne'blina/ f mist

nebulo|sa /nebu'loza/ f nebula; ~sidade f cloud; ~so /o/ a cloudy; (fig) obscure

neces|saire /nese'ser/ m toilet bag; ~sário a necessary; ~sidade f necessity; (que se impõe) need; (pobreza) need; ~sitado a needy □ m person in need; ~sitar vt require; (tornar necessário) necessitate; ~sitar de need

necro|lógio /nekro'lɔʒiu/ m obituary column; ~tério m mortuary, (Amer) morgue

néctar /'nɛktar/ m nectar

nectarina /nekta'rina/ f nectarine

nefasto /ne'fastu/ a fatal

ne|gação /nega'sãw/ f denial; (ling) negation; ser uma ~gação em be hopeless at; ~gar vt deny; ~gar-se a refuse to; ~gativa f refusal; (ling) negative; ~gativo a & m negative

negli|gência /negli'ʒẽsia/ f negligence; ~genciar vt neglect; ~gente a negligent

negoci|ação /negosia'sãw/ f negotiation; ~ador m negotiator; ~ante m/f dealer (de in); ~ar vt/i negotiate; ~ar em deal in; ~ata f shady deal; ~ável (pl ~áveis) a negotiable

negócio /ne'gɔsiu/ m deal; (fam: coisa) thing, pl business; a ou de ~s <viajar> on business

negocista /nego'sista/ m wheeler-dealer □ a wheeler-dealing

ne|grito /ne'gritu/ m bold; ~gro /e/ a & m black; (de raça) Negro

nela, nele = em + ela, ele

nem /nẽj/ adv not even □ conj ~ ... ~ ... neither ... nor ...; ~ sempre not always; ~ todos not all; ~ que not even if; que ~ like; ~ eu nor do I; ~ um not a single one; ~ por isso not really; ~ por isso not for that reason; ~ que no matter how; ~ que no mistakes; erro ~ no mistakes at all, not a single mistake; ~ lugar nowhere

nenê /ne'ne/, neném /ne'nẽj/ m baby

nenhum /ne'nũ/ a (f nenhuma) no □ pron (f nenhuma) not one; ~ dos dois neither of them; ~ erro no mistakes; erro ~ no mistakes at all, not a single mistake; ~ lugar nowhere

nenúfar /ne'nufar/ f waterlily

neologismo /neolo'ʒizmu/ m neologism

néon /'neõ/ m neon

neozelan|dês /neozelã'des/ a (f ~desa) New Zealand □ m (f ~desa) New Zealander

Nepal /ne'paw/ m Nepal

nervo /'nervu/ m nerve; ~sismo m (chateação) annoyance; (medo) nerv-

ousness; ~so /o/ a <sistema, doença> nervous; (chateado) annoyed; (medroso) nervous; deixar alg ~so get on s.o.'s nerves

nessa(s), nesse(s) = em + essa(s), esse(s)

nesta(s), neste(s) = em + esta(s), este(s)

ne|ta /'nɛta/ f granddaughter; ~to /ɛ/ m grandson; pl grandchildren

neuro|logia /newrolo'ʒia/ f neurology; ~lógico a neurological; ~logista m/f neurologist

neu|rose /new'rɔzi/ f neurosis; ~rótico a neurotic

neutrali|dade /newtrali'dadʒi/ f neutrality; ~zar vt neutralize

neutrão /new'trãw/ m (Port) veja nêutron

neutro /'newtru/ a neutral

nêutron /'newtrõ/ m neutron

ne|vada /ne'vada/ f snowfall; ~vado a snow-covered; ~var vi snow; ~vasca f snowstorm; ~ve /ɛ/ f snow

névoa /'nevoa/ f haze

nevoeiro /nevo'eru/ m fog

nexo /'nɛksu/ m connection; sem ~ incoherent

Nicarágua /nika'ragwa/ f Nicaragua

nicaragüense /nikara'gwẽsi/ a & m/f Nicaraguan

nicho /'niʃu/ m niche

nicotina /niko'tʃina/ f nicotine

Niger /'niʒer/ m Niger

Nigéria /ni'ʒeria/ f Nigeria

nigeriano /niʒeri'anu/ a & m Nigerian

Nilo /'nilu/ m Nile

ninar /ni'nar/ vt lull to sleep

ninfa /'nĩfa/ f nymph

ninguém /nĩ'gẽj/ pron no-one, nobody

ninhada /ni'nada/ f brood

ninharia /nina'ria/ f trifle

ninho /'ninu/ m nest

níquel /'nikew/ m nickel

nisei /ni'sej/ a & m/f Japanese Brazilian

nisso = em + isso

nisto = em + isto

nitidez /nitʃi'des/ f (de imagem etc) sharpness

nítido /'nitʃidu/ a <imagem, foto> sharp; <diferença, melhora> distinct, clear

nitrogênio /nitro'ʒeniu/ m nitrogen

ní|vel /'nivew/ (pl ~veis) m level; a ~vel de in terms of

nivelamento /nivela'mẽtu/ m levelling

nivelar /nive'lar/ vt level

no = em + o

nó /nɔ/ m knot; dar um ~ tie a knot; ~ dos dedos knuckle; um ~ na garganta a lump in one's throat nobre /'nɔbri/ a noble; < *bairro*> exclusive □ m/f noble; ~za /e/ f nobility

noção /no'sãw/ f notion; pl (*rudimentos*) elements

nocaute /no'kawtʃi/ m knockout; pôr alg ~ knock s.o. out; ~ar vt knock out

nocivo /no'sivu/ a harmful

nódoa /'nodoa/ f (*Port*) stain

nogueira /no'gera/ f (*árvore*) walnut tree

noi|tada /noj'tada/ f night; ~te f night; (*antes de dormir*) evening; à ou de ~te at night; (*antes de dormir*) in the evening; hoje à ~te tonight; ontem à ~te last night; boa ~te (*ao chegar*) good evening; (*ao despedir-se*) good night; ~te em branco *ou* claro sleepless night

noi|vado /noj'vadu/ m engagement; ~va f fiancée; (*no casamento*) bride; ~vo m fiancé; (*no casamento*) bridegroom; os ~vos the engaged couple; (*no casamento*) the bride and groom; ficar ~vo get engaged

no|jento /no'ʒẽtu/ a disgusting; ~jo /o/ m disgust

nômade /'nomadʒi/ m/f nomad □ a nomadic

nome /'nomi/ m name; de ~ by name; em ~ de in the name of; ~ comercial trade name; ~ de batismo Christian name; ~ de guerra professional name

nome|ação /nomia'sãw/ f appointment; ~ar vt (*para cargo*) appoint; (*chamar pelo nome*) name

nomi|nal /nomi'naw/ (pl ~nais) a nominal

nonagésimo /nona'ʒezimu/ a ninetieth

nono /'nonu/ a & m ninth

nora /'nɔra/ f daughter-in-law

nordes|te /nor'dɛstʃi/ m northeast; ~tino a Northeastern □ m person from the Northeast (*of Brazil*)

nórdico /'nɔrdʒiku/ a Nordic

nor|ma /'nɔrma/ f norm; ~mal (pl ~mais) a normal

normali|dade /normali'dadʒi/ f normality; ~zar vt bring back to normal; normalize <*relações diplomáticas*>; ~zar-se vpr return to normal

noroeste /noro'ɛstʃi/ a & m northwest

norte /'nortʃi/ a & m north; ~africano a & m North African; ~americano a & m North American; ~coreano a & m North Korean

nortista /nor'tʃista/ a Northern □ m/f Northerner

Noruega /noru'ɛga/ f Norway

norue|guês /norue'ges/ a & m (f ~guesa) Norwegian

nos[1] = em + os

nos[2] /nus/ pron us; (*indireto*) (to) us; (*reflexivo*) ourselves

nós /nɔs/ pron we; (*depois de preposição*) us

nos|sa /'nɔsa/ int gosh; ~so /ɔ/ a our □ pron ours

nos|talgia /nostaw'ʒia/ f nostalgia; ~tálgico a nostalgic

nota /'nɔta/ f note; (*na escola etc*) mark; (*conta*) bill; custar uma ~ (preta) (*fam*) cost a bomb; tomar ~ take note (de of); ~ fiscal receipt

no|tação /nota'sãw/ f notation; ~tar vt notice, note; fazer ~tar point out; ~tável (pl ~táveis) a & m/f notable

notícia /no'tʃisia/ f piece of news; pl news

notici|ar /notʃi'sjar/ vt report; ~ário m (*na TV*) news; (*em jornal*) news section; ~arista m/f (*na TV*) newsreader; (*em jornal*) news reporter; ~oso /o/ a; agência ~osa news agency

notifi|cação /notʃifika'sãw/ f notification; ~car vt notify

noti|vago /no'tʃivagu/ a nocturnal □ m night person

notório /no'tɔriu/ a well-known

noturno /no'turnu/ a night; <*animal*> nocturnal

nova /'nɔva/ f piece of news; ~mente adv again

novato /no'vatu/ m novice

nove /'nɔvi/ a & m nine; ~centos a & m nine hundred

novela /no'vɛla/ f (*na TV*) soap opera; (*livro*) novella

novembro /no'vẽbru/ m November

noventa /no'vẽta/ a & m ninety

noviço /no'visu/ m novice

novidade /novi'dadʒi/ f novelty; (*notícia*) piece of news; pl (*notícias*) news

novilho /no'viʎu/ m calf

novo /'novu/ a new; (*jovem*) young; de ~ again; ~ em folha brand new

noz /nɔs/ f walnut; ~ moscada nutmeg

nu /nu/ a (f ~a) <*corpo, pessoa*> naked; <*braço, parede, quarto*> bare □ m nude; ~ em pêlo stark naked; a verdade ~a e crua the plain truth

nuança /nu'ãsa/ f nuance

nu|blado /nu'bladu/ a cloudy; ~blar vt cloud; ~blar-se vpr cloud over

nuca /'nuka/ f nape of the neck

nuclear /nukli'ar/ a nuclear

núcleo /'nukliu/ m nucleus

nu|dez /nu'des/ f nakedness; (*na TV etc*) nudity; (*da parede etc*) bareness; ~dismo m nudism; ~dista m/f nudist

nulo /'nulu/ a void

num, numa(s) = em + um, uma(s)

nume|ral /nume'raw/ (pl ~rais) a & m numeral; ~rar vt number

numérico /nu'mɛriku/ a numerical

número /'numeru/ m number; (de jornal, revista) issue; (de sapatos) size; (espetáculo) act; fazer ~ make up the numbers

numeroso /nume'rozu/ a numerous

nunca /'nũka/ adv never; ~ mais never again

nuns = em + uns

nupci|al /nupsi'aw/ (pl ~ais) a bridal

núpcias /'nupsias/ f pl marriage

nu|trição /nutri'sãw/ f nutrition; ~trir vt nourish; (fig) harbour <ódio, esperança>; ~tritivo a nourishing; <valor> nutritional

nuvem /'nuvẽ/ f cloud

O

o /u/ artigo the □ pron (homem) him; (coisa) it; (você) you; ~ que (a coisa que) what; (aquele que) the one that; ~ quê? what?; meu livro e ~ do João my book and John's (one)

ó /ɔ/ int (fam) look

ô /o/ int oh

oásis /o'azis/ m invar oasis

oba /'oba/ int great

obcecar /obise'kar/ vt obsess

obe|decer /obede'ser/ vt ~decer a obey; ~diência f obedience; ~diente a obedient

obe|sidade /obezi'dadʒi/ f obesity; ~so /e/ a obese

óbito /'ɔbitu/ m death

obituário /obitu'ariu/ m obituary

obje|ção /obiʒe'sãw/ f objection; ~tar vt/i object (a to)

obje|tiva /obiʒe'tʃiva/ f lens; ~tividade f objectivity; ~vo a & m objective

objeto /obi'ʒɛtu/ m object

oblíquo /o'blikwu/ a oblique; <olhar> sidelong

obliterar /oblite'rar/ vt obliterate

oblongo /o'blõgu/ a oblong

obo|é /obo'ɛ/ m oboe; ~ísta m/f oboist

obra /'ɔbra/ f work; em ~s being renovated; ~ de caridade work of art; ~ de caridade charity; ~-prima (pl ~s-primas) f masterpiece

obri|gação /obriga'sãw/ f obligation; (título) bond; ~gado int thank you; (não querendo) no thank you; ~gar vt force, oblige (a to); ~gar-se vpr undertake (a to); ~gatório a obligatory, compulsory

obsce|nidade /obiseni'dadʒi/ f obscenity; ~no /e/ a obscene

obscu|ridade /obiskuri'dadʒi/ f obscurity; ~ro a obscure

obséquio /obi'sɛkiu/ m favour

obsequioso /obiseki'ozu/ a obsequious

obser|vação /obiserva'sãw/ f observation; ~vador a observant □ m observer; ~vância f observance; ~var vt observe; ~vatório m observatory

obses|são /obise'sãw/ f obsession; ~sivo a obsessive

obsoleto /obiso'letu/ a obsolete

obstáculo /obis'takulu/ m obstacle

obstar /obis'tar/ vt stand in the way (a of)

obs|tetra /obis'tɛtra/ m/f obstetrician; ~tetrícia f obstetrics; ~tétrico a obstetric

obsti|nação /obistina'sãw/ f obstinacy; ~nado a obstinate; ~nar-se vpr insist (em on)

obstru|ção /obistru'sãw/ f obstruction; ~ir vt obstruct

ob|tenção /obitẽ'sãw/ f obtaining; ~ter vt obtain

obtu|ração /obitura'sãw/ f filling; ~rador m shutter; ~rar vt fill <dente>

obtuso /obi'tuzu/ a obtuse

óbvio /'ɔbviu/ a obvious

ocasi|ão /okazi'ãw/ f occasion; (oportunidade) opportunity; (compra) bargain; ~onal (pl ~onais) a chance; ~onar vt cause

Oceania /osia'nia/ f Oceania

oce|ânico /osi'aniku/ a ocean; ~ano m ocean

ociden|tal /osidẽ'taw/ (pl ~tais) a western □ m/f Westerner; ~te m West

ócio /'ɔsiu/ m (lazer) leisure; (falta de trabalho) idleness

ocioso /osi'ozu/ a idle □ m idler

oco /'oku/ a hollow; <cabeça> empty

ocor|rência /oko'xẽsia/ f occurrence; ~rer vi occur (a to)

ocu|lar /oku'lar/ a testemunha ~lar eye witness; ~lista m/f optician

óculos /'ɔkulus/ m pl glasses; ~ de sol sunglasses

ocul|tar /okuw'tar/ vt conceal; ~to a hidden; (sobrenatural) occult

ocu|pação /okupa'sãw/ f occupation; ~pado a <pessoa> busy; <cadeira> taken; <telefone> engaged, (Amer) busy; ~par vt occupy; take up <tempo, espaço>; hold <cargo>; ~par-se vpr keep busy; ~par-se com ou de be involved with <política, literatura etc>; take care of <cliente, doente, problema>; occupy one's time with <leitura, palavras cruzadas etc>

ode /'ɔdʒi/ f ode

odiar /oˈdʒiˈar/ vt hate

ódio /ˈɔdʒiu/ m hatred, hate; (raiva) anger

odioso /oˈdʒiˈozu/ a hateful

odontologia /odõtoloˈʒia/ f dentistry

odor /oˈdor/ m odour

oeste /oˈɛstʃi/ a & m west

ofe|gante /ofeˈgãtʃi/ a panting; ~gar vi pant

ofen|der /ofeˈder/ vt offend; ~der-se vpr take offence; ~sa f insult; ~siva f offensive; ~sivo a offensive

ofere|cer /ofereˈser/ vt offer; ~cer-se vpr <pessoa> offer o.s. (como as); <ocasião> arise; ~cer-se para ajudar offer to help; ~cimento m offer

oferenda /ofeˈrẽda/ f offering

oferta /oˈfɛrta/ f offer; em ~ on offer; a ~ e a demanda supply and demand

ofici|al /ofisiˈaw/ (pl ~ais) a official □ m officer; ~alizar vt make official; ~ar vi officiate

oficina /ofiˈsina/ f workshop; (para carros) garage, (Amer) shop

ofício /oˈfisiu/ m (profissão) trade; (na igreja) service

oficioso /ofisiˈozu/ a unofficial

ofus|cante /ofusˈkãtʃi/ a dazzling; ~car vt dazzle <pessoa>; obscure <sol etc>; (fig: eclipsar) outshine

oi /oj/ int (cumprimento) hi; (resposta) yes?

oi|tavo /oiˈtavu/ a & m eighth; ~tenta a & m eighty; ~to a & m eight; ~tocentos a & m eight hundred

olá /oˈla/ int hello

olaria /olaˈria/ f pottery

óleo /ˈɔliu/ m oil

oleo|duto /oliuˈdutu/ m oil pipeline; ~so /o/ a oily

olfato /owˈfatu/ m sense of smell

olhada /oˈʎada/ f look; dar uma ~ have a look

olhar /oˈʎar/ vt look at; (assistir) watch □ vi look □ m look; ~ para look at; ~ por look after; e olhe lá (fam) and that's pushing it

olheiras /oˈʎeras/ f pl dark rings under one's eyes

olho /ˈoʎu/ m eye; a ~ nu with the naked eye; custar os ~s da cara cost a fortune; ficar de ~ keep an eye out; ficar de ~ em keep an eye on; pôr alg no ~ da rua throw s.o. out; não pregar o ~ not sleep a wink; ~ gordo ou grande envy; ~ mágico peephole; ~ roxo black eye

Olimpíada /oliˈpiada/ f Olympic Games

olímpico /oˈlĩpiku/ a <jogos, vila> Olympic; (fig) blithe

oliveira /oliˈvera/ f olive tree

olmo /ˈowmu/ m elm

om|breira /õˈbrera/ f (para roupa) shoulder pad; ~bro m shoulder; dar de ~bros shrug one's shoulders

omelete /omeˈlɛtʃi/, (Port) omeleta /omeˈleta/ f omelette

omis|são /omiˈsãw/ f omission; ~so a negligent, remiss

omitir /omiˈtʃir/ vt omit

omni- (Port) veja oni-

omoplata /omoˈplata/ f shoulder blade

onça¹ /ˈõsa/ f (peso) ounce

onça² /ˈõsa/ f (animal) jaguar

onda /ˈõda/ f wave; pegar ~ (fam) surf

onde /ˈõdʒi/ adv where; por ~? which way?; ~ quer que wherever

ondu|lação /õdulaˈsãw/ f undulation; (do cabelo) wave; ~lado a wavy; ~lante a undulating; ~lar vt wave <cabelo> □ vi undulate

onerar /oneˈrar/ vt burden

ônibus /ˈonibus/ m invar bus; ~ espacial space shuttle

onipotente /onipoˈtẽtʃi/ a omnipotent

onírico /oˈniriku/ a dreamlike

onisciente /onisiˈẽtʃi/ a omniscient

onomatopéia /onomatoˈpeja/ f onomatopoeia

ontem /ˈõtẽ/ adv yesterday

onze /ˈõzi/ a & m eleven

opaco /oˈpaku/ a opaque

opala /oˈpala/ f opal

opção /opˈsãw/ f option

ópera /ˈɔpera/ f opera

ope|ração /operaˈsãw/ f operation; (bancária etc) transaction; ~rador m operator; ~rar vt operate; operate on <doente>; work <milagre> □ vi operate; ~rar-se vpr (acontecer) come about; (fazer operação) have an operation; ~rário a working □ m worker

opereta /opeˈreta/ f operetta

opinar /opiˈnar/ vt think □ vi express one's opinion

opinião /opiniˈãw/ f opinion; na minha ~ in my opinion; ~ pública public opinion

ópio /ˈɔpiu/ m opium

opor /oˈpor/ vt put up <resistência, argumento>; (pôr em contraste) contrast (a with); ~-se a (não aprovar) oppose; (ser diferente) contrast with

oportu|nidade /oportuniˈdadʒi/ f opportunity; ~nista a & m/f opportunist; ~no a opportune

oposi|ção /opoziˈsãw/ f opposition (a to); ~cionista a opposition □ m/f opposition politician

oposto /oˈpostu/ a & m opposite

opres|são /opre'sãw/ f oppression; (no peito) tightness; ~sivo a oppressive; ~sor m oppressor

oprimir /opri'mir/ vt oppress; (com trabalho) weigh down □ vi be oppressive

optar /opi'tar/ vi opt (por for); ~ por ir opt to go

óptica, óptico veja ótica, ótico

opu|lência /opu'lēsia/ f opulence; ~lento a opulent

ora /'ɔra/ adv & conj now □ int come; ~ essa! come now!; ~ ..., ~ ... first ..., then

oração /ora'sãw/ f (prece) prayer; (discurso) oration; (frase) clause

oráculo /o'rakulu/ m oracle

orador /ora'dor/ m orator

oral /o'raw/ (pl orais) a & f oral

orar /o'rar/ vi pray

órbita /'ɔrbita/ f orbit; (do olho) socket

orçamen|tário /orsamē'tariu/ a budgetary; ~to m (plano financeiro) budget; (previsão dos custos) estimate

orçar /or'sar/ vt estimate (em at)

ordeiro /or'deru/ a orderly

ordem /'ordẽ/ f order; por ~ alfabética in alphabetical order; ~ de pagamento banker's draft; ~ do dia agenda

orde|nação /ordena'sãw/ f ordering; (de padre) ordination; ~nado a ordered □ m wages; ~nar vt order; put in order <papéis, livros etc>; ordain <padre>

ordenhar /orde'ɲar/ vt milk

ordinário /ordʒi'nariu/ a (normal) ordinary; (grosseiro) vulgar; (de má qualidade) inferior; (sem caráter) rough

orégano /o'reganu/ m oregano

ore|lha /o're.ʎa/ f ear; ~lhão m phone booth; ~lhudo a with big ears; ser ~lhudo have big ears

orfanato /orfa'natu/ m orphanage

ór|fão /'ɔrfãw/ (pl ~fãos) a & m (f ~fã) orphan

orgânico /or'ganiku/ a organic

orga|nismo /orga'nizmu/ m organism; (do Estado etc) institution; ~nista m/f organist

organi|zação /organiza'sãw/ f organization; ~zador a organizing □ m organizer; ~zar vt organize

órgão /'ɔrgãw/ (pl ~s) m organ; (do Estado etc) body

orgasmo /or'gazmu/ m orgasm

orgia /or'ʒia/ f orgy

orgu|lhar /orgu'ʎar/ vt make proud; ~lhar-se vpr be proud (de of); ~lho m pride; ~lhoso a proud

orien|tação /oriẽta'sãw/ f orientation; (direção) direction; (vocacional etc) guidance; ~tador m advisor; ~tal (pl ~tais) a eastern; (da Ásia) oriental; ~tar vt direct; (aconselhar) advise; (situar) position; ~tar-se get one's bearings; ~tar-se por be guided by; ~te m east; Oriente Médio Middle East; Extremo Oriente Far East

orifício /ori'fisiu/ m opening; (no corpo) orifice

origem /o'riʒẽ/ f origin; dar ~ a give rise to; ter ~ originate

origi|nal /oriʒi'naw/ (pl ~nais) a & m original; ~nalidade f originality; ~nar vt give rise to; ~nar-se vpr originate; ~nário a <planta, animal> native (de to); <pessoa> originating (de from)

oriundo /o'rjũdu/ a originating (de from)

orla /'ɔrla/ f border; ~ marítima seafront

ornamen|tação /ornamēta'sãw/ f ornamentation; ~tal (pl ~tais) a ornamental; ~tar vt decorate; ~to m ornament

orques|tra /or'kɛstra/ f orchestra; ~tra sinfônica symphony orchestra; ~tral (pl ~trais) a orchestral; ~trar vt orchestrate

orquídea /or'kidʒia/ f orchid

ortodoxo /orto'dɔksu/ a orthodox

orto|grafia /ortogra'fia/ f spelling, orthography; ~gráfico a orthographic

orto|pedia /ortope'dʒia/ f orthopaedics; ~pédico a orthopaedic; ~pedista m/f orthopaedic surgeon

orvalho /or'vaʎu/ m dew

os /us/ artigo & pron veja o

oscilar /osi'lar/ vi oscillate

ósseo /'ɔsiu/ a bone

os|so /'osu/ m bone; ~sudo a bony

ostensivo /ostē'sivu/ a ostensible

osten|tação /ostēta'sãw/ f ostentation; ~tar vt show off; ~toso a showy, ostentatious

osteopata /ostʃio'pata/ m/f osteopath

ostra /'ostra/ f oyster

ostracismo /ostra'sizmu/ m ostracism

otário /o'tariu/ m (fam) fool

óti|ca /'ɔtʃika/ f (ciência) optics; (loja) optician's; (ponto de vista) viewpoint; ~co a optical

otimis|mo /otʃi'mizmu/ m optimism; ~ta m/f optimist □ a optimistic

ótimo /'ɔtʃimu/ a excellent

otorrino /oto'xinu/ m ear, nose and throat specialist

ou /o/ conj or; ~ ..., ~ ... either ... or ...; ~ seja in other words

ouriço /o'risu/ m hedgehog; ~-do-mar (pl ~s-do-mar) m sea urchin ouri|ves /o'rivis/ m/f invar jeweller; ~vesaria f (loja) jeweller's

ouro /'oru/ m gold; pl (naipe) diamonds; de ~ golden

ou|sadia /oza'dʒia/ f daring; (uma) daring step; ~sado a daring; ~sar vt/i dare

outdoor /'awtdor/ (pl ~s) m billboard

outo|nal /oto'naw/ (pl ~nais) a autumnal; ~no /o/ m autumn, (Amer) fall

outorgar /otor'gar/ vt grant

ou|trem /o'trẽj/ pron (outro) someone else; (outros) others; ~tro a other □ pron (um) another (one); pl others; ~tro copo another glass; ~tra coisa something else; ~tro dia the other day; no ~tro dia the next day; ~tra vez again; ~trora adv once upon a time; ~trossim adv equally

outubro /o'tubru/ m October

ou|vido /o'vidu/ m ear; de ~vido by ear; dar ~vidos a listen to; ~vinte m/f listener; ~vir vt hear; (atentamente) listen to □ vi hear; ~vir dizer que hear that; ~vir falar de hear of

ovação /ova'sãw/ f ovation

oval /o'vaw/ (pl ovais) a & f oval

ovário /o'variu/ m ovary

ovelha /o'veʎa/ f sheep

óvni /'ɔvni/ m UFO

ovo /'ovu/ m egg; ~ cozido/frito/mexido/pochê boiled/fried/scrambled/poached egg

oxi|genar /oksiʒe'nar/ vt bleach <cabelo>; ~gênio m oxygen

ozônio /o'zoniu/ m ozone

P

pá /pa/ f spade; (de hélice) blade; (de moinho) sail □ m (Port: fam) mate

pacato /pa'katu/ a quiet

paci|ência /pasi'ẽsia/ f patience; ~ente a & m/f patient

pacificar /pasifi'kar/ vt pacify

pacífico /pa'sifiku/ a peaceful; Oceano Pacífico Pacific Ocean; ponto ~ undisputed point

pacifis|mo /pasi'fizmu/ m pacifism; ~ta a & m/f pacifist

paço /'pasu/ m palace

pacote /pa'kɔtʃi/ m (de biscoitos etc) packet; (mandado pelo correio) parcel; (econômico, turístico, software) package

pacto /'paktu/ m pact

padaria /pada'ria/ f baker's (shop), bakery

padecer /pade'ser/ vt/i suffer

padeiro /pa'deru/ m baker

padiola /padʒi'ɔla/ f stretcher

padrão /pa'drãw/ m standard; (desenho) pattern

padrasto /pa'drastu/ m stepfather

padre /'padri/ m priest

padrinho /pa'drinu/ m (de batismo) godfather; (de casamento) best man

padroeiro /padro'eru/ m patron saint

padronizar /padroni'zar/ vt standardize

paetê /paj'te/ m sequin

paga /'paga/ f pay; ~mento m payment

pa|gão /pa'gãw/ (pl ~gãos) a & m (f ~gã) pagan

pagar /pa'gar/ vt pay for <compra, erro etc>; pay <dívida, conta, empregado etc>; pay back <empréstimo>; repay <gentileza etc> □ vi pay; eu pago para ver I'll believe it when I see it

página /'paʒina/ f page

pago /'pagu/ a paid □ pp de pagar

pagode /pa'gɔdʒi/ m (torre) pagoda; (fam) singalong

pai /paj/ m father; pl (pai e mãe) parents; ~-de-santo (pl ~s-de-santo) m macumba priest

pai|nel /paj'nɛw/ (pl ~néis) m panel; (de carro) dashboard

paio /'paju/ m pork sausage

pairar /paj'rar/ vi hover

país /pa'is/ m country; País de Gales Wales; Países Baixos Netherlands

paisa|gem /paj'zaʒẽ/ f landscape; ~gista m/f landscape gardener

paisana /paj'zana/ f à ~ <policial> in plain clothes; <soldado> in civilian clothes

paixão /pa'ʃãw/ f passion

pala /'pala/ f (de boné) peak; (de automóvel) sun visor

palácio /pa'lasiu/ m palace

paladar /pala'dar/ m palate, taste

palanque /pa'lãki/ m stand

palavra /pa'lavra/ f word; pedir a ~ ask to speak; ter ~ be reliable; tomar a ~ start to speak; sem ~ <pessoa> unreliable; ~ de ordem watchword; ~s cruzadas crossword

palavrão /pala'vrãw/ m swearword

palco /'pawku/ m stage

palestino /pales'tʃinu/ a & m Palestinian

palestra /pa'lɛstra/ f lecture

paleta /pa'leta/ f palette

paletó /pale'tɔ/ m jacket

palha /'paʎa/ f straw

palha|çada /paʎa'sada/ f joke; ~ço m clown

paliativo /palia'tʃivu/ a & m palliative

palidez /pali'des/ f paleness

pálido /'palidu/ a pale

pali|tar /pali'tar/ *vt* pick □ *vi* pick one's teeth; ~teiro *m* toothpick holder; ~to *m* (*para dentes*) toothpick; (*de fósforo*) matchstick; (*pessoa magra*) beanpole

pal|ma /'pawma/ *f* palm; *pl* (*aplauso*) clapping; bater ~mas clap; ~meira *f* palm tree; ~mito *m* palm heart; ~mo *m* span; ~mo a ~mo inch by inch

palpá|vel /paw'pavew/ (*pl* ~veis) *a* palpable

pálpebra /'pawpebra/ *f* eyelid

palpi|tação /pawpita'sãw/ *f* palpitation; ~tante *a* (*fig*) thrilling; ~tar *vi* <*coração*> flutter; <*pessoa*> tremble; (*dar palpite*) stick one's oar in; ~te *m* (*pressentimento*) hunch; (*no jogo etc*) tip; dar ~te stick one's oar in

panacéia /pana'seja/ *f* panacea

Panamá /pana'ma/ *m* Panama

panamenho /pana'meɲu/ *a* & *m* Panamanian

pan-americano /panameri'kanu/ *a* Pan-American

pança /'pãsa/ *f* paunch

pancada /pã'kada/ *f* blow; ~ d'água downpour; ~ria *f* fight, punch-up

pâncreas /'pãkrias/ *m invar* pancreas

pançudo /pã'sudu/ *a* paunchy

panda /'pãda/ *f* panda

pandarecos /pãda'rɛkus/ *m pl* aos ou em ~ battered

pandeiro /pã'deru/ *m* tambourine

pandemônio /pãde'moniu/ *m* pandemonium

pane /'pani/ *f* breakdown

panela /pa'nɛla/ *f* saucepan; ~ de pressão pressure cooker

panfleto /pã'fletu/ *m* pamphlet

pânico /'paniku/ *m* panic; em ~ in a panic; entrar em ~ panic

panifica|ção /panifika'sãw/ *f* bakery; ~dora *f* bakery

pano /'panu/ *m* cloth; ~ de fundo backdrop; ~ de pó duster; ~ de pratos tea towel

pano|rama /pano'rama/ *m* panorama; ~râmico *a* panoramic

panqueca /pã'kɛka/ *f* pancake

panta|nal /pãta'naw/ (*pl* ~nais) *m* marshland

pântano /'pãtanu/ *m* marsh

pantanoso /pãta'nozu/ *a* marshy

pantera /pã'tɛra/ *f* panther

pão /'pãw/ (*pl* pães) *m* bread; ~ de fôrma sliced loaf; ~ integral brown bread; ~-de-ló *m* sponge cake; ~-duro (*pl* pães-duros) (*fam*) *a* stingy, tight-fisted □ *m/f* skinflint; ~zinho *m* bread roll

Papa /'papa/ *m* Pope

papa /'papa/ *f* (*de nenem*) food; (*arroz etc*) mush

papagaio /papa'gaju/ *m* parrot

papai /pa'paj/ *m* dad, daddy; Papai Noël Father Christmas

papar /pa'par/ *vt/i* (*fam*) eat

papari|car /papari'kar/ *vt* pamper; ~cos *m pl* pampering

pa|pel /pa'pɛw/ (*pl* ~péis) *m* (*de escrever etc*) paper; (*um*) piece of paper; (*numa peça, filme*) part; (*fig: função*) role; de ~pel passado officially; ~pel de alumínio aluminium foil; ~pel higiênico toilet paper; ~pelada *f* paperwork; ~pelão *m* cardboard; ~pelaria *f* stationer's (shop); ~pelzinho *m* scrap of paper

papo /'papu/ *f* (*fam: conversa*) talk; (*do rosto*) double chin; bater um ~ (*fam*) have a chat; ~ furado idle talk

papoula /pa'pola/ *f* poppy

páprica /'paprika/ *f* paprika

paque|ra /pa'kɛra/ *f* (*fam*) pick-up; ~rador *a* flirtatious □ *m* flirt; ~rar *vt* flirt with <*pessoa*>; eye up <*vestido, carro etc*> □ *vi* flirt

paquista|nês /pakista'nes/ *a* & *m* (*f* ~nesa) Pakistani

Paquistão /pakis'tãw/ *m* Pakistan

par /par/ *a* even □ *m* pair; (*parceiro*) partner; a ~ de up to date with <*notícias etc*>; sem ~ unequalled

para /'para/ *prep* for; (*a*) to; ~ que so that; ~ quê? what for?; ~ casa home; estar ~ sair be about to leave; era ~ eu ir I was supposed to go

para|benizar /parabeni'zar/ *vt* congratulate (por on); ~béns *m pl* congratulations

parábola /pa'rabola/ *f* (*conto*) parable; (*curva*) parabola

parabóli|co /para'boliku/ *a* antena ~ca satellite dish

pára-|brisa /para'briza/ *m* windscreen, (*Amer*) windshield; ~choque *m* bumper

para|da /pa'rada/ *f* stop; (*interrupção*) stoppage; (*militar*) parade; (*fam: coisa difícil*) ordeal, challenge; ~da cardíaca cardiac arrest; ~deiro *m* whereabouts

paradisíaco /paradʒi'ziaku/ *a* idyllic

parado /pa'radu/ *a* <*trânsito, carro*> at a standstill, stopped; (*fig*) <*pessoa*> dull; ficar ~ <*pessoa*> stand still; <*trânsito*> come to a standstill; (*fig: deixar de trabalhar*) stop work

parado|xal /paradok'saw/ (*pl* ~xais) *a* paradoxical; ~xo /ɔ/ *m* paradox

parafina /para'fina/ *f* paraffin

paráfrase /pa'rafrazi/ *f* paraphrase

parafrasear /parafrazi'ar/ *vt* paraphrase

parafuso /para'fuzu/ f screw; entrar em ~ get into a state

para|gem /pa'raʒẽ/ f (Port: parada) stop; nestas ~gens in these parts

parágrafo /pa'ragrafu/ m paragraph

Paraguai /para'gwaj/ m Paraguay

paraguaio /para'gwaju/ a & m Paraguayan

paraíso /para'izu/ m paradise

pára-lama /para'lama/ m (de carro) wing, (Amer) fender; (de bicicleta) mudguard

parale|la /para'lɛla/ f parallel; pl (aparelho) parallel bars; ~lepípedo m paving stone; ~lo /ɛ/ a & m parallel

para|lisar /parali'zar/ vt paralyse; bring to a halt <fábrica, produção>; ~lisar-se vpr become paralysed; <fábrica, produção> grind to a halt; ~lisia f paralysis; ~lítico a & m paralytic

paranói|a /para'nɔja/ f paranoia; ~co a paranoid

parapeito /para'pejtu/ m (muro) parapet; (da janela) window-sill

pára-que|das /para'kɛdas/ m invar parachute; ~dista m/f parachutist; (militar) paratrooper

parar /pa'rar/ vt/i stop; ~ de fumar stop smoking; ir ~ end up

pára-raios /para'xajus/ m invar lightning conductor

parasita /para'zita/ a & m/f parasite

parceiro /par'seru/ m partner

parce|la /par'sɛla/ f (de terreno) plot; (prestação) instalment; ~lar vt spread <pagamento>

parceria /parse'ria/ f partnership

parci|al /parsi'aw/ (pl ~ais) a partial; (partidário) biased; ~alidade f bias

parco /'parku/ a frugal; <recursos> scant

par|dal /par'daw/ (pl ~dais) m sparrow; ~do a <papel> brown; <pessoa> mulatto

pare|cer /pare'ser/ vi (ter aparência de) seem; (ter semelhança com) be like; ~cer-se com look like, resemble □ m opinion; ~cido a similar (com to)

parede /pa'redʒi/ f wall

paren|te /pa'rẽtʃi/ m/f relative, relation; ~tesco /e/ m relationship

parêntese /pa'rẽtizi/ f parenthesis; pl (sinais) brackets, parentheses

paridade /pari'dadʒi/ f parity

parir /pa'rir/ vt give birth to □ vi give birth

parlamen|tar /parlamẽ'tar/ a parliamentary □ m/f member of parliament; ~tarismo m parliamentary system; ~to m parliament

parmesão /parme'zãw/ a & m (queijo) ~ Parmesan (cheese)

paródia /pa'rɔdʒia/ f parody

parodiar /parodʒi'ar/ vt parody

paróquia /pa'rɔkia/ f parish

parque /'parki/ m park

parte /'partʃi/ f part; (quinhão) share; (num litígio, contrato) party; a maior ~ de most of; à ~ (de lado) aside; (separadamente) separately; um erro da sua ~ a mistake on your part; em ~ in part; em alguma ~ somewhere; por toda ~ everywhere; por ~ do pai on one's father's side; fazer ~ de be part of; tomar ~ em take part in

parteira /par'tera/ f midwife

partici|pação /partʃisipa'sãw/ f participation; (numa empresa, nos lucros) share; ~pante a participating □ m/f participant; ~par vi take part (de ou em in)

particípio /partʃi'sipiu/ m participle

partícula /par'tʃikula/ f particle

particu|lar /partʃiku'lar/ a private; (especial) unusual □ m (pessoa) private individual; pl (detalhes) particulars; em ~lar (especialmente) in particular; (a sós) in private; ~laridade f peculiarity

partida /par'tʃida/ f (saída) departure; (de corrida) start; (de futebol, xadrez etc) match; dar ~ em start up

parti|dário /partʃi'dariu/ a partisan □ m supporter; ~tido a broken □ m (político) party; (casamento, par) match; tirar ~tido de benefit from; tomar o ~tido de side with; ~tilha f division; ~tir vi (sair) depart; <corredor> start □ vt break; ~tir-se vpr break; a ~tir de ... from ... onwards; ~tir para (fam) resort to; ~tir para outra do something different, change direction; ~titura f score

parto /'partu/ m birth

parvo /'parvu/ a (Port) stupid

Páscoa /'paskoa/ f Easter

pas|mar /paz'mar/ vt amaze; ~mar-se vpr be amazed (com at); ~mo □ m amazed □ m amazement

passa /'pasa/ f raisin

pas|sada /pa'sada/ f dar uma ~sada em call in at; ~sadeira f (mulher) woman who irons; (Port: faixa) zebra crossing, (Amer) crosswalk; ~sado a <ano, mês, semana> last; <tempo, particípio etc> past; <fruta, comida> off □ m past; são duas horas ~sadas it's gone two o'clock; bem/mal ~sado <bife> well done/rare

passa|geiro /pasa'ʒeru/ m passenger □ a passing; ~gem f passage; (bilhete) ticket; de ~gem <dizer etc> in passing; estar de ~gem be passing through; ~gem de ida e volta return ticket, (*Amer*) round trip ticket

passaporte /pasa'pɔrtʃi/ *m* passport

passar /pa'sar/ *vt* pass; spend *<tempo>*; cross *<ponte, rio>*; (*a ferro*) iron *<roupa etc>*; (*aplicar*) put on *<creme, batom etc>* □ *vi* pass; *<dor, medo, chuva etc>* go; (*ser aceitável*) be passable □ *m* passing; ~-se *vpr* happen; passou a beber muito he started to drink a lot; passei dos 30 anos I'm over thirty; não passa de um boato it's nothing more than a rumour; ~ por go through; go along *<rua>*; (*ser considerado*) be taken for; fazer-se ~ por pass o.s. off as; ~ por cima de (*fig*) overlook; ~ sem do without

passarela /pasa'rɛla/ *f* (*sobre rua*) footbridge; (*para desfile de moda*) catwalk

pássaro /'pasaru/ *m* bird

passatempo /pasa'tẽpu/ *m* pastime

passe /'pasi/ *m* pass

passear /pasi'ar/ *vi* go out and about; (*viajar*) travel around □ *vt* take for a walk; ~**seata** *f* protest march; ~**seio** *m* outing; (*volta a pé*) walk; (*volta de carro*) drive; dar um ~**seio** (*a pé*) go for a walk; (*de carro*) go for a drive

passional /pasio'naw/ (*pl* ~**nais**) *a* crime ~**nal** crime of passion

passista /pa'sista/ *m/f* dancer

passível /pa'sivew/ (*pl* ~**veis**) *a* ~**vel** de subject to

passividade /pasivi'dadʒi/ *f* passivity; ~**vo** *a* passive □ *m* (*com*) liabilities; (*ling*) passive

passo /'pasu/ *m* step; (*velocidade*) pace; (*barulho*) footstep; ~ **a** ~ step by step; a dois ~**s** de a stone's throw from; dar um ~ take a step

pasta /'pasta/ *f* (*matéria*) paste; (*bolsa*) briefcase; (*fichário*) folder; ministro sem ~ minister without portfolio; ~ de dentes toothpaste

pastagem /pas'taʒẽ/ *f* pasture; ~**tar** *vi* graze

pastel /pas'tɛw/ (*pl* ~**téis**) *m* (*para comer*) samosa; (*Port: doce*) pastry; (*para desenhar*) pastel; (*de comédia*) slapstick; ~**telaria** (*loja*) samosa vendor, (*Port*) pastry shop; (*Port: pastéis*) pastries

pasteurizado /pastewri'zadu/ *a* pasteurized

pastilha /pas'tʃiʎa/ *f* pastille

pasto /'pastu/ *m* (*erva*) fodder, feed; (*lugar*) pasture; ~**tor** *m* (*de gado*) shepherd; (*clérigo*) vicar; ~**tor** alemão (*cachorro*) Alsatian; ~**toral** (*pl* ~**torais**) *a* pastoral

pata /'pata/ *f* paw; ~**da** *f* kick

patamar /pata'mar/ *m* landing; (*fig*) level

patê /pa'te/ *m* pâté

patente /pa'tẽtʃi/ *a* obvious □ *f* (*mil*) rank; (*de invenção*) patent; ~**ar** *vt* patent *<produto, invenção>*

paternal /pater'naw/ (*pl* ~**nais**) *a* paternal; ~**nidade** *f* paternity; ~**no** /ɛ/ *a* paternal

pateta /pa'tɛta/ *a* daft, silly □ *m/f* fool; ~**tice** *f* stupidity; (*uma*) silly thing

patético /pa'tɛtʃiku/ *a* pathetic

patíbulo /pa'tʃibulu/ *m* gallows

patifaria /patʃifa'ria/ *f* roguishness; (*uma*) dirty trick; ~**fe** *m* scoundrel

patim /pa'tʃĩ/ *m* skate; ~ de rodas roller skate

patinação /patʃina'sãw/ *f* skating; (*rinque*) skating rink; ~**nador** *m* skater; ~**nar** *vi* skate; *<carro>* skid; ~**nete** /ɛ/ *m* skateboard

pátio /'patʃiu/ *m* courtyard; (*de escola*) playground

pato /'patu/ *m* duck

patologia /patolo'ʒia/ *f* pathology; ~**lógico** *a* pathological; ~**logista** *m/f* pathologist

patrão /pa'trãw/ *m* boss

pátria /'patria/ *f* homeland

patriarca /patri'arka/ *m* patriarch; ~**cal** (*pl* ~**cais**) *a* patriarchal

patrimônio /patri'moniu/ *m* (*bens*) estate, property; (*fig: herança*) heritage

patriota /patri'ɔta/ *m/f* patriot; ~**ótico** *a* patriotic; ~**otismo** *m* patriotism

patroa /pa'troa/ *f* boss; (*fam: esposa*) missus, wife

patrocinador /patrosina'dor/ *m* sponsor; ~**cinar** *vt* sponsor; ~**cínio** *m* sponsorship

patrulha /pa'truʎa/ *f* patrol; ~**lhar** *vt/i* patrol

pau /paw/ *m* stick; (*fam: cruzeiro*) cruzeiro; (*chulo: pênis*) prick; *pl* (*naipe*) clubs; a meio ~ at half mast; rachar ~ (*fam: brigar*) row, fight like cat and dog; ~**lada** *f* blow with a stick

paulista /paw'lista/ *a* & *m/f* (*person*) from the state of) São Paulo; ~**no** *a* & *m* (*person*) from the city of) São Paulo

pausa /'pawza/ *f* pause; ~**do** *a* slow

pauta /'pawta/ *f* (*em papel*) lines; (*de música*) stave; (*fig: de discussão etc*) agenda; ~**do** *a* *<papel>* lined

pavão /pa'vãw/ *m* peacock

pavilhão /pavi'ʎãw/ *m* pavilion; (*no jardim*) summerhouse

pavimentar /pavimẽ'tar/ *vt* pave; ~**to** *m* floor; (*de rua etc*) surface

pavio /pa'viu/ *m* wick

pavor /pa'vor/ *m* terror; ter ~ de be terrified of; ~**oso** /o/ *a* dreadful paz /pas/ *f* peace; fazer as ~es make up

pé /pɛ/ *m* foot; (*planta*) plant; (*de móvel*) leg; a ~ on foot; ao ~ da letra literally; estar de ~ <*festa etc*> be on; ficar de ~ stand up; em ~ standing (up); em ~ de igualdade on an equal footing

peão /pi'ãw/ *m* (*Port: pedestre*) pedestrian; (*no xadrez*) pawn

peça /'pɛsa/ *f* piece; (*de máquina, carro etc*) part; (*teatral*) play; pregar uma ~ em play a trick on; ~ de reposição spare part; ~ de vestuário item of clothing

pe|cado /pe'kadu/ *m* sin; ~cador *m* sinner; ~caminoso /o/ *a* sinful; ~car *vi* (*contra a religião*) sin; (*fig*) fall down

pechin|cha /pe'ʃiʃa/ *f* bargain; ~char *vi* bargain, haggle

peçonhento /peso'ɲẽtu/ *a* animais ~s vermin

pecu|ária /peku'aria/ *f* livestock-farming; ~ário *a* livestock; ~arista *m/f* livestock farmer

peculi|ar /pekuli'ar/ *a* peculiar; ~aridade *f* peculiarity

pecúlio /pe'kuliu/ *m* savings

pedaço /pe'dasu/ *m* piece; aos ~s in pieces; cair aos ~s fall to pieces

pedágio /pe'daʒiu/ *m* toll; (*cabine*) tollbooth

peda|gogia /pedago'ʒia/ *f* education; ~gógico *a* educational; ~gogo /o/ *m* educationalist

pe|dal /pe'daw/ (*pl* ~dais) *m* pedal; ~dalar *vt/i* pedal

pedante /pe'dãtʃi/ *a* pretentious □ *m/f* pseud

pé-de-atleta /pɛdʒiat'lɛta/ *m* athlete's foot; ~-de-meia (*pl* ~s-de-meia) *m* nest egg; ~-de-pato (*pl* ~s-de-pato) *m* flipper

pederneira /peder'nera/ *f* flint

pedes|tal /pedes'taw/ (*pl* ~tais) *m* pedestal

pedestre /pe'dɛstri/ *a* & *m/f* pedestrian

pé|-de-vento /pɛdʒi'vẽtu/ (*pl* ~s-de-vento) *m* gust of wind

pedia|tra /pedʒi'atra/ *m/f* paediatrician; ~tria *f* paediatrics

pedicuro /pedʒi'kuru/ *m* chiropodist, (*Amer*) podiatrist

pe|dido /pe'dʒidu/ *m* request; (*encomenda*) order; a ~dido de at the request of; ~dido de demissão resignation; ~dido de desculpa apology; ~dir *vt* ask for; (*num restaurante etc*) order □ *vi* ask; (*num restaurante etc*) order; ~dir aco a alg ask s.o. for sth; ~dir para alg ir ask s.o. to go; ~dir desculpa

apologize; ~dir em casamento propose to

pedinte /pe'dʒĩtʃi/ *m/f* beggar

pedra /'pedra/ *f* stone; ~ de gelo ice cube; chuva de ~ hail; ~ pomes pumice stone

pedregoso /pedre'gozu/ *a* stony

pedreiro /pe'dreru/ *m* builder

pegada /pe'gada/ *f* footprint; (*de goleiro*) save

pegajoso /pega'ʒozu/ *a* sticky

pegar /pe'gar/ *vt* get; catch <*bola, doença, ladrão, ônibus*>; (*segurar*) get hold of; pick up <*emissora, hábito, mania*> □ *vi* (*aderir*) stick; <*doença*> be catching; <*moda*> catch on; <*carro, motor*> start; <*mentira, desculpa*> stick; ~se *vpr* come to blows; bem/mal go down well/badly; ~ fogo catch fire; pega essa rua take that street; ~ em grab; ~ no sono get to sleep

pego /'pɛgu/ *pp de* pegar

pei|dar /pej'dar/ *vi* (*chulo*) fart; ~do *m* (*chulo*) fart

pei|to /'pejtu/ *m* chest; (*seio*) breast; (*fig: coragem*) guts; ~toril (*pl* ~toris) *m* window-sill; ~tudo *a* <*mulher*> busty; (*fig: corajoso*) gutsy

pei|xaria /pe'ʃaria/ *f* fishmonger's; ~xe *m* fish; Peixes (*signo*) Pisces; ~xeiro *m* fishmonger

pela = por + a

pelado /pe'ladu/ *a* (*nu*) naked, in the nude

pelan|ca /pe'lãka/ *f* roll of fat; *pl* flab; ~cudo *a* flabby

pelar /pe'lar/ *vt* peel <*fruta, batata*>; skin <*animal*>; (*fam: tomar dinheiro de*) fleece

pelas = por + as

pele /'pɛli/ *f* skin; (*como roupa*) fur; ~teiro *m* furrier; ~teria *f* furrier's

pelica /pe'lika/ *f* luvas de ~ kid gloves

pelicano /peli'kanu/ *m* pelican

película /pe'likula/ *f* skin

pelo = por + o

pêlo /'pelu/ *m* hair; (*de animal*) coat; nu em ~ stark naked; montar em ~ ride bareback

pelos = por + os

pelotão /pelo'tãw/ *m* platoon

pelúcia /pe'lusia/ *f* bicho de ~ soft toy, fluffy animal

peludo /pe'ludu/ *a* hairy

pena[1] /'pena/ *f* (*de ave*) feather; (*de caneta*) nib

pena[2] /'pena/ *f* (*castigo*) penalty; (*de amor etc*) pang; é uma ~ que it's a pity that; que ~! what a pity!; dar ~ be upsetting; estar com *ou* ter ~ de feel sorry for; (não) vale a ~ it's (not) worth it; vale a ~ tentar it's worth trying; ~ de morte death penalty

penada /pe'nada/ f stroke of the pen

pe|nal /pe'naw/ (pl ~nais) a penal; ~nalidade f penalty; ~nalizar vt penalize

pênalti /'penawtʃi/ m penalty

penar /pe'nar/ vi suffer

pen|dente /pẽ'dẽtʃi/ a hanging; (fig: causa) pending; ~der vi hang; (inclinar-se) slope; (tender) be inclined (a to); ~dor m inclination

pêndulo /'pẽdulu/ m pendulum

pendu|rado /pẽdu'radu/ a hanging; (fam: por fazer, pagar) outstanding; ~rar vt hang (up); (fam) put on the slate <compra> □ vi (fam) pay later; ~ricalho m pendant

penedo /pe'nedu/ m rock

penei|ra /pe'nera/ f sieve; ~rar vt sieve, sift □ vi drizzle

pene|tra /pe'nɛtra/ m/f (fam) gatecrasher; ~tração f penetration; (fig) perspicacity; ~trante a <som, olhar> piercing; <dor> sharp; <ferida> deep; <frio> biting; <análise, espírito> incisive, perceptive; ~trar vt penetrate □ vi ~trar em enter <casa>; (fig) penetrate

penhasco /pe'ɲasku/ m cliff

penhoar /peɲo'ar/ m dressing gown

penhor /pe'ɲor/ m pledge; casa de ~es pawnshop

penicilina /penisi'lina/ f penicillin

penico /pe'niku/ m potty

península /pe'nĩsula/ f peninsula

pênis /'penis/ m invar penis

penitência /peni'tẽsia/ f (arrependimento) penitence; (expiação) penance

penitenciá|ria /penitẽsi'aria/ f prison; ~rio a prison □ m prisoner

penoso /pe'nozu/ a <experiência, tarefa, assunto> painful; <trabalho, viagem> hard, difficult

pensa|dor /pẽsa'dor/ m thinker; ~mento m thought

pensão /pẽ'sãw/ f (renda) pension; (hotel) guesthouse; ~ (alimentícia) (paga por ex-marido) alimony; ~ completa full board

pen|sar /pẽ'sar/ vt/i think (em de ou about); ~sativo a thoughtful, pensive

pên|sil /'pẽsiw/ (pl ~seis) a ponte ~sil suspension bridge

penso /'pẽsu/ m (curativo) dressing

pentágono /pẽ'tagonu/ m pentagon

pentatlo /pẽ'tatlu/ m pentathlon

pente /'pẽtʃi/ m comb; ~adeira f dressing table; ~ado m hairstyle, hairdo; ~ar vt comb; ~ar-se vpr do one's hair; (com pente) comb one's hair

Pentecostes /pẽte'kɔstʃis/ m Whitsun

pente-fino /pẽtʃi'finu/ m passar a ~ go over with a fine-tooth comb

pente|lhar /pẽte'ʎar/ vt (fam) bother; ~lho /e/ m pubic hair; (fam: pessoa inconveniente) pain (in the neck)

penugem /pe'nuʒẽ/ f down

penúltimo /pe'nuwtʃimu/ a last but one, penultimate

penumbra /pe'nũbra/ f half-light

penúria /pe'nuria/ f penury, extreme poverty

pepino /pe'pinu/ m cucumber

pepita /pe'pita/ f nugget

peque|nez /peke'nes/ f smallness; (fig) pettiness; ~nininho a tiny; ~no /e/ a small; (mesquinho) petty

Pequim /pe'kĩ/ f Peking, Beijing

pequinês /peki'nes/ m Pekinese

pêra /'pera/ f pear

perambular /perãbu'lar/ vi wander

perante /pe'rãtʃi/ prep before

percalço /per'kawsu/ m pitfall

perceber /perse'ber/ vt realize; (Port: entender) understand; (psiqu) perceive

percen|tagem /persẽ'taʒẽ/ f percentage; ~tual (pl ~tuais) a & m percentage

percep|ção /persep'sãw/ f perception; ~tível (pl ~tíveis) a perceptible

percevejo /perse'veʒu/ m (bicho) bedbug; (tachinha) drawing pin, (Amer) thumbtack

per|correr /perko'xer/ vt cross; cover <distância>; (viajar por) travel through; ~curso m journey

percus|são /perku'sãw/ f percussion; ~sionista m/f percussionist

percutir /perku'tʃir/ vt strike

perda /'perda/ f loss; ~ de tempo waste of time

perdão /per'dãw/ f pardon

perder /per'der/ vt lose; (não chegar a ver, pegar) miss <ônibus, programa na TV etc>; waste <tempo> □ vi lose; ~se vpr get lost; ~se de alg lose s.o.; ~ aco de vista lose sight of sth

perdiz /per'dʒis/ f partridge

perdoar /perdo'ar/ vt forgive (aco a alg s.o. for sth)

perdulário /perdu'lariu/ a & m spendthrift

perdurar /perdu'rar/ vi endure; <coisa ruim> persist

pere|cer /pere'ser/ vi perish; ~cível (pl ~cíveis) a perishable

peregri|nação /peregrina'sãw/ f peregrination; (romaria) pilgrimage; ~nar vi roam; (por motivos religiosos) go on a pilgrimage; ~no m pilgrim

pereira /pe'rera/ f pear tree

peremptório /perẽp'toriu/ a peremptory

perene /pe'reni/ a perennial

perereca /pere'rɛka/ f tree frog

perfazer /perfa'zer/ *vt* make up

perfeccionis|mo /perfeksio'nizmu/ *m* perfectionism; ~ta *a* & *m/f* perfectionist

perfei|ção /perfej'sãw/ *f* perfection; ~to *a* & *m* perfect

per|fil /per'fiw/ (*pl* ~fis) *m* profile; ~filar *vt* line up; ~filar-se *vpr* line up

perfu|mado /perfu'madu/ *a* <*flor, ar*> fragrant; <*sabonete etc*> scented; <*pessoa*> with perfume on; ~mar *vt* perfume; ~mar-se *vpr* put perfume on; ~maria *f* perfumery; (*fam*) trimmings, frills; ~me *m* perfume

perfu|rador /perfura'dor/ *m* punch; ~rar *vt* punch <*papel, bilhete*>; drill through <*chão*>; perforate <*úlcera, pulmão etc*>; ~ratriz *f* drill

pergaminho /perga'miɲu/ *m* parchment

pergun|ta /per'gũta/ *f* question; fazer uma ~ta ask a question; ~tar *vt/i* ask; ~tar aco a alg ask s.o. sth; ~tar por ask after

perícia /pe'risia/ *f* (*mestria*) expertise; (*inspeção*) investigation; (*peritos*) experts

perici|al /perisi'aw/ (*pl* ~ais) *a* expert

periclitante /perikli'tãtʃi/ *a* precarious; ~tar *vi* be at risk

peri|feria /perife'ria/ *f* periphery; (*da cidade*) outskirts; ~férico *a* & *m* peripheral

perigo /pe'rigu/ *m* danger; ~so /o/ *a* dangerous

perímetro /pe'rimetru/ *m* perimeter

periódico /peri'ɔdʒiku/ *a* periodic □ *m* periodical

período /pe'riodu/ *m* period; trabalhar meio ~ work part-time

peripécias /peri'pɛsias/ *f pl* ups and downs, vicissitudes

periquito /peri'kitu/ *m* parakeet; (*de estimação*) budgerigar

periscópio /peris'kɔpiu/ *m* periscope

perito /pe'ritu/ *a* & *m* expert (em at)

per|jurar /perʒu'rar/ *vi* commit perjury; ~júrio *m* perjury; ~juro *m* perjurer

perma|necer /permane'ser/ *vi* remain; ~nência *f* permanence; (*estadia*) stay; ~nente *a* permanent □ *f* perm

permeá|vel /permi'avew/ (*pl* ~veis) *a* permeable

permis|são /permi'sãw/ *f* permission; ~sível (*pl* ~síveis) *a* permissible; ~sivo *a* permissive

permitir /permi'tʃir/ *vt* allow, permit; ~ a alg ir allow s.o. to go

permutar /permu'tar/ *vt* exchange

perna /'pɛrna/ *f* leg

pernicioso /pernisi'ozu/ *a* pernicious

per|nil /per'niw/ (*pl* ~nis) *m* leg

pernilongo /perni'lõgu/ *m* (large) mosquito

pernoi|tar /pernoj'tar/ *vi* spend the night; ~te *m* overnight stay

pérola /'pɛrola/ *f* pearl

perpendicular /perpẽdʒiku'lar/ *a* perpendicular

perpetrar /perpe'trar/ *vt* perpetrate

perpetu|ar /perpetu'ar/ *vt* perpetuate; ~idade *f* perpetuity

perpétu|o /per'pɛtuu/ *a* perpetual; prisão ~a life imprisonment

perple|xidade /perpleksi'dadʒi/ *f* puzzlement; ~xo /ɛ/ *a* puzzled

persa /'pɛrsa/ *a* & *m/f* Persian

perse|guição /persegi'sãw/ *f* pursuit; (*de minorias etc*) persecution; ~guidor *m* pursuer; (*de minorias etc*) persecutor; ~guir *vt* pursue; persecute <*minoria, seita etc*>

perseve|rança /perseve'rãsa/ *f* perseverance; ~rante *a* persevering; ~rar *vi* persevere

persiana /persi'ana/ *f* blind

pérsico /'pɛrsiku/ *a* Golfo Pérsico Persian Gulf

persignar-se /persig'narsi/ *vt* cross o.s.

persis|tência /persis'tẽsia/ *f* persistence; ~tente *a* persistent; ~tir *vi* persist

perso|nagem /perso'naʒẽ/ *m/f* (*pessoa famosa*) personality; (*em livro, filme etc*) character; ~nalidade *f* personality; ~nalizar *vt* personalize; ~nificar *vt* personify

perspectiva /perspek'tʃiva/ *f* (*na arte, ponto de vista*) perspective; (*possibilidade*) prospect

perspi|cácia /perspi'kasia/ *f* insight, perceptiveness; ~caz *a* perceptive

persua|dir /persua'dʒir/ *vt* persuade (alg a to); ~são *f* persuasion; ~sivo *a* persuasive

perten|cente /pertẽ'sẽtʃi/ *a* belonging (a to); (*que tem a ver com*) pertaining (a to); ~cer *vi* belong (a to); (*referir-se*) pertain (a to); ~ces *m pl* belongings

perto /'pɛrtu/ *adv* near (de to); aqui ~ near here, nearby; de ~ closely; <*ver*> close up

pertur|bação /perturba'sãw/ *f* disturbance; (*do espírito*) anxiety; ~bado *a* <*pessoa*> unsettled, troubled; ~bar *vt* disturb; ~bar-se *vpr* get upset, be perturbed

Peru /pe'ru/ *m* Peru

peru /pe'ru/ *m* turkey

perua /pe'rua/ *f* (*carro grande*) estate car, (*Amer*) station wagon; (*caminho-*

nete van; (*para escolares etc*) minibus; (*fam: mulher*) brassy woman
peruano /peru'ano/ *a* & *m* Peruvian
peruca /pe'ruka/ *f* wig
perver|são /perver'sãw/ *f* perversion; **~so** *a* perverse; **~ter** *vt* pervert
pesadelo /peza'delu/ *m* nightmare
pesado /pe'zadu/ *a* heavy; <*estilo, livro*> heavy-going □ *adv* heavily
pêsames /'pezamis/ *m pl* condolences
pesar[1] /pe'zar/ *vt* weigh; (*fig: avaliar*) weigh up □ *vi* weigh; (*influir*) carry weight; **~ sobre** <*ameaça etc*> hang over; **~-se** *vpr* weigh o.s.
pesar[2] /pe'zar/ *m* sorrow; **~oso** /o/ *a* sorry, sorrowful
pesca /'pɛska/ *f* fishing; **ir à ~ca** go fishing; **~cador** *m* fisherman; **~car** *vt* catch; (*retirar da água*) fish out □ *vi* fish; (*fam*) (*entender*) understand; (*cochilar*) nod off; **~car de** (*fam*) know all about
pescoço /pes'kosu/ *m* neck
peseta /pe'zeta/ *f* peseta
peso /'pezu/ *m* weight; *de ~* (*fig*) <*pessoa*> influential; <*livro, argumento*> authoritative
pesqueiro /pes'keru/ *a* fishing
pesqui|sa /pes'kiza/ *f* research; (*uma*) study; *pl* research; **~sa de mercado** market research; **~sador** *m* researcher; **~sar** *vt/i* research
pêssego /'pesigu/ *m* peach
pessegueiro /pesi'geru/ *m* peach tree
pessimis|mo /pesi'mizmu/ *m* pessimism; **~ta** *a* pessimistic □ *m/f* pessimist
péssimo /'pɛsimu/ *a* terrible, awful
pesso|a /pe'soa/ *f* person; *pl* people; **em ~a** in person; **~al** (*pl* **~ais**) *a* personal □ *m* staff; (*fam*) folks
pesta|na /pes'tana/ *f* eyelash; **tirar uma ~na** (*fam*) have a nap; **~nejar** *vi* blink; **sem ~nejar** (*fig*) without batting an eyelid
pes|te /'pɛstʃi/ *f* (*doença*) plague; (*criança etc*) pest; **~ticida** *m* pesticide
pétala /'pɛtala/ *f* petal
peteca /pe'tɛka/ *f* kind of shuttlecock; (*jogo*) kind of badminton played with the hand
peteleco /pete'lɛku/ *m* flick
petição /petʃi'sãw/ *f* petition
petisco /pe'tʃisku/ *m* savoury, titbit
petrificar /petrifi'kar/ *vt* petrify; (*de surpresa*) stun; **~-se** *vpr* be petrified; (*de surpresa*) be stunned
petroleiro /petro'leru/ *a* oil □ *m* oil tanker
petróleo /pe'trɔliu/ *m* oil, petroleum; **~ bruto** crude oil
petrolífero /petro'liferu/ *a* oil-producing

petroquími|ca /petro'kimika/ *f* petrochemicals; **~co** *a* petrochemical
petu|lância /petu'lãsia/ *f* cheek; **~lante** *a* cheeky
peúga /pi'uga/ *f* (*Port*) sock
pevide /pe'vidʒi/ *f* (*Port*) pip
pia /'pia/ *f* (*do banheiro*) washbasin; (*da cozinha*) sink; **~ batismal** font
piada /pi'ada/ *f* joke
pia|nista /pia'nista/ *m/f* pianist; **~no** *m* piano; **~no de cauda** grand piano
piar /pi'ar/ *vi* <*pinto*> cheep; <*coruja*> hoot
picada /pi'kada/ *f* (*de agulha, alfinete etc*) prick; (*de abelha, vespa*) sting; (*de mosquito, cobra*) bite; (*de heroína*) shot; (*de avião*) nosedive; **o fim da ~** (*fig*) the limit
picadeiro /pika'deru/ *m* ring
picante /pi'kãtʃi/ *a* <*comida*> hot, spicy; <*piada*> risqué; <*filme, livro*> raunchy
pica-pau /pika'paw/ *m* woodpecker
picar /pi'kar/ *vt* (*com agulha, alfinete etc*) prick; <*abelha, vespa, urtiga*> sting; <*mosquito, cobra*> bite; <*pássaro*> peck; chop <*carne, alho etc*>; shred <*papel*> □ *vi* <*peixe*> bite; <*lã, cobertor*> prickle
picareta /pika'reta/ *f* pickaxe
pi|chação /piʃa'sãw/ *f* piece of graffiti; *pl* graffiti; **~char** *vt* spray with graffiti <*muro, prédio*>; spray <*grafite, desenho*>; **~che** *m* pitch
picles /'piklis/ *m pl* pickles
pico /'piku/ *m* peak; **20 anos e ~** (*Port*) just over 20
picolé /piko'lɛ/ *m* ice lolly
pico|tar /piko'tar/ *vt* perforate; **~te** /ɔ/ *m* perforations
pie|dade /pie'dadʒi/ *f* (*religiosidade*) piety; (*compaixão*) pity; **~doso** /o/ *a* merciful, compassionate
pie|gas /pi'ɛgas/ *a invar* <*filme, livro*> sentimental, schmaltzy; <*pessoa*> soppy; **~guice** *f* sentimentality
pifar /pi'far/ *vi* (*fam*) break down, go wrong
pigar|rear /pigaxi'ar/ *vi* clear one's throat; **~ro** *m* frog in the throat
pigmento /pig'mẽtu/ *m* pigment
pig|meu /pig'mew/ *a* & *m* (*f* **~méia**) pygmy
pijama /pi'ʒama/ *m* pyjamas
pilantra /pi'lãtra/ *m/f* (*fam*) crook
pilão /pi'lãw/ *m* (*na cozinha*) pestle; (*na construção*) ram
pilar /pi'lar/ *m* pillar
pilastra /pi'lastra/ *f* pillar
pileque /pi'lɛki/ *m* drinking session; **tomar um ~** get drunk
pilha /'piʎa/ *f* (*monte*) pile; (*elétrica*) battery
pilhar /pi'ʎar/ *vt* pillage

pilhéria /pi'ʎɛria/ f joke

pilotar /pilo'tar/ vt fly, pilot <avião>; drive <carro>

pilotis /pilo'tʃis/ m pl pillars

piloto /pi'lotu/ m pilot; (de carro) driver; (de gás) pilot light □ a invar pilot

pilula /'pilula/ f pill

pimenta /pi'mẽta/ f pepper; ~ta de Caiena cayenne pepper; ~ta-do-reino f black pepper; ~ta-malagueta (pl ~tas-malaguetas) f chilli pepper; ~tão m (bell) pepper; ~teira f pepper pot

pinacoteca /pinako'tɛka/ f art gallery

pinça /'pĩsa/ (para tirar pêlos) tweezers; (para segurar) tongs; (de siri etc) pincer; ~çar vt pluck <sobrancelhas>

pincel /pĩ'sɛw/ (pl ~céis) m brush; ~celada f brush stroke; ~celar vt paint

pinga /'pĩga/ f Brazilian rum; ~gado a <café> with a dash of milk; ~gar vi drip; (começar a chover) spit (with rain) □ vt drip; ~gente m pendant; ~go m drop; (no i) dot

pingue-pongue /pĩgi'põgi/ m table tennis

pinguim /pĩ'gwĩ/ m penguin

pinha /'piɲa/ f pine cone; ~nheiro f pine tree; ~nho m pine

pino /'pinu/ m pin; (para trancar carro) lock; a ~ upright; bater ~ <carro> knock

pinta /'pĩta/ f (sinal) mole; (fam: aparência) look; ~tar vt paint; dye <cabelo>; put make-up on <rosto, olhos> □ vi paint; (fam) <pessoa> show up; <problema, oportunidade> crop up; ~tar-se vpr put on make-up

pintarroxo /pĩta'xoʃu/ m robin

pinto /'pĩtu/ m chick

pintor /pĩ'tor/ m painter; ~tura f painting

pio[1] /'piu/ m (de pinto) cheep; (de coruja) hoot

pio[2] /'piu/ a pious

piolho /pi'oʎu/ m louse

pioneiro /pio'neru/ m pioneer □ a pioneering

pior /pi'ɔr/ a & adv worse; o ~ the worst

piora /pi'ɔra/ f worsening; ~rar vt make worse, worsen □ vi get worse, worsen

pipa /'pipa/ f (que voa) kite; (de vinho) cask

pipilar /pipi'lar/ vi chirp

pipoca /pi'pɔka/ f popcorn; ~car vi spring up; ~queiro m popcorn seller

pique /'piki/ m (disposição) energy; a ~ vertically; ir a ~ <navio> sink

piquenique /piki'niki/ m picnic

piquete /pi'ketʃi/ m picket; ~teiro m picket

pirado /pi'radu/ a (fam) crazy

pirâmide /pi'ramidʒi/ f pyramid

piranha /pi'raɲa/ f piranha; (fam: mulher) maneater

pirar /pi'rar/ (fam) vi flip out, go mad

pirata /pi'rata/ a & m/f pirate; ~ria f piracy

pires /'piris/ m invar saucer

pirilampo /piri'lãpu/ m glow-worm

Pirineus /piri'news/ m pl Pyrenees

pirraça /pi'xasa/ f spiteful act; fazer ~ça be spiteful; ~cento a spiteful

pirueta /piru'eta/ f pirouette

pirulito /piru'litu/ m lollipop

pisada /pi'zada/ f step; (rastro) footprint; ~sar vt tread on; tread <uvas, palco>; (esmagar) trample on □ vi step; ~sar em step on; (entrar) set foot in

piscadela /piska'dɛla/ f wink; ~capisca m indicator; ~car vi (com o olho) wink; (pestanejar) blink; <estrela, luz> twinkle; <motorista> indicate □ m num ~car de olhos in a flash

piscicultura /pisikuw'tura/ f fish farming; (lugar) fish farm

piscina /pi'sina/ f swimming pool

piso /'pizu/ m floor

pisotear /pizotʃi'ar/ vt trample

pista /'pista/ f track; (da estrada) carriageway; (para aviões) runway; (de circo) ring; (dica) clue; ~ de dança dancefloor

pistache /pis'taʃi/ m, pistacho /pis'taʃu/ m pistachio (nut)

pistola /pis'tɔla/ f pistol; (para pintar) spray gun; ~lão m influential contact; ~leiro m gunman

pitada /pi'tada/ f pinch

piteira /pi'tera/ f cigarette-holder

pitoresco /pito'resku/ a picturesque

pitu /pi'tu/ m crayfish

pivete /pi'vetʃi/ m/f child thief

pivô /pi'vo/ m pivot

pixaim /piʃa'ĩ/ a frizzy

pizza /'pitsa/ f pizza; ~ria f pizzeria

placa /'plaka/ f plate; (de carro) number plate, (Amer) license plate; (comemorativa) plaque; (em computador) board; ~ de sinalização roadsign

placar /pla'kar/ m scoreboard; (escore) scoreline

plácido /'plasidu/ a placid

plagiário /plaʒi'ariu/ m plagiarist; ~ar vt plagiarize

plágio /'plaʒiu/ m plagiarism

plaina /'plajna/ f plane

planador /plana'dor/ m glider

planalto /pla'nawtu/ m plateau

planar /pla'nar/ vi glide

planeamento, planear (*Port*) *veja* planejamento, planejar

plane|jamento /planeʒa'mẽtu/ *m* planning; ~jamento familiar family planning; ~jar *vt* plan

planeta /pla'neta/ *m* planet

planície /pla'nisi/ *f* plain

planificar /planifi'kar/ *vt* (*programar*) plan (out)

planilha /pla'niʎa/ *f* spreadsheet

plano /'planu/ *a* flat □ *m* plan; (*superfície, nível*) plane; primeiro ~ foreground

planta /'plãta/ *f* plant; (*do pé*) sole; (*de edifício*) ground plan; ~ção *f* (*ato*) planting; (*terreno*) plantation; ~do *a* deixar alg ~do (*fam*) keep s.o. waiting around

plantão /plã'tãw/ *m* duty; (*noturno*) night duty; estar de ~ be on duty

plantar /plã'tar/ *vt* plant

plas|ma /'plazma/ *m* plasma; ~mar *vt* mould, shape

plásti|ca /'plastʃika/ *f* face-lift; ~co *a* & *m* plastic

plataforma /plata'fɔrma/ *f* platform

plátano /'platanu/ *m* plane tree

platéia /pla'tɛja/ *f* audience; (*parte do teatro*) stalls, (*Amer*) orchestra

platina /pla'tʃina/ *f* platinum; ~dos *m pl* points

platônico /pla'toniku/ *a* platonic

plausí|vel /plaw'zivew/ (*pl* ~veis) *a* plausible

ple|be /'plɛbi/ *f* common people; ~beu *a* (*f* ~béia) plebeian □ *m* (*f* ~béia) commoner; ~biscito *m* plebiscite

plei|tear /plejtʃi'ar/ *vt* contest; ~to *m* (*litígio*) case; (*eleitoral*) contest

ple|namente /plena'mẽtʃi/ *adv* fully; ~nário *a* plenary □ *m* plenary assembly; ~no *a* full; em ~no verão in the middle of summer

plissado /pli'sadu/ *a* pleated

pluma /'pluma/ *f* feather; ~gem *f* plumage

plu|ral /plu'raw/ (*pl* ~rais) *a* & *m* plural

plutônio /plu'toniu/ *m* plutonium

pluvi|al /pluvi'aw/ (*pl* ~ais) *a* rain

pneu /pi'new/ *m* tyre; ~mático *a* pneumatic □ *m* tyre

pneumonia /pineumo'nia/ *f* pneumonia

pó /pɔ/ *f* powder; (*poeira*) dust; leite em ~ powdered milk

pobre /'pɔbri/ *a* poor □ *m/f* poor man (*f* woman); os ~s the poor; ~za /e/ *f* poverty

poça /'posa/ *f* pool; (*deixada pela chuva*) puddle

poção /po'sãw/ *f* potion

pocilga /po'siwga/ *f* pigsty

poço /'posu/ *f* (*de água, petróleo*) well; (*de mina, elevador*) shaft

podar /po'dar/ *vt* prune

pó-de-arroz /pɔdʒia'xoz/ *m* (face) powder

poder /po'der/ *m* power □ *v aux* can, be able; (*eventualidade*) may; ele pode/podia/poderá vir he can/could/might come; ele pôde vir he was able to come; pode ser que it may be that; ~ com stand up to; em ~ de alg in sb's possession; estar no ~ be in power

pode|rio /pode'riu/ *m* might; ~roso /o/ *a* powerful

pódio /'pɔdʒiu/ *m* podium

podre /'podri/ *a* rotten; (*fam*) (*cansado*) exhausted; (*doente*) grotty; ~ de rico filthy rich; ~s *m pl* faults

poei|ra /po'era/ *f* dust; ~rento *a* dusty

poe|ma /po'ema/ *m* poem; ~sia *f* (*arte*) poetry; (*poema*) poem; ~ta *m* poet

poético /po'etʃiku/ *a* poetic

poetisa /poe'tʃiza/ *f* poetess

pois /pojs/ *conj* as, since; ~ é that's right; ~ não of course; ~ não? can I help you?; ~ sim certainly not

polaco /pu'laku/ (*Port*) *a* Polish □ *m* Pole; (*língua*) Polish

polar /po'lar/ *a* polar

polarizar /polari'zar/ *vt* polarize; ~se *vpr* polarize

pole|gada /pole'gada/ *f* inch; ~gar *m* thumb

poleiro /po'leru/ *m* perch

polêmi|ca /po'lemika/ *f* controversy, debate; ~co *a* controversial

pólen /'polẽ/ *m* pollen

polícia /po'lisia/ *f* police □ *m/f* policeman (*f* -woman)

polici|al /polisi'aw/ (*pl* ~ais) *a* < *carro, inquérito etc* > police; < *romance, filme* > detective □ *m/f* policeman (*f* -woman); ~amento *m* policing; ~ar *vt* police

poli|dez /poli'des/ *f* politeness; ~do *a* polite

poli|gamia /poliga'mia/ *f* polygamy; ~glota *a* & *m/f* polyglot

Polinésia /poli'nɛzia/ *f* Polynesia

polinésio /poli'nɛziu/ *a* & *m* Polynesian

pólio /'pɔliu/ *f* polio

polir /po'lir/ *vt* polish

polissílabo /poli'silabu/ *m* polysyllable

políti|ca /po'litʃika/ *f* politics; (*uma*) policy; ~co *a* political □ *m* politician

pólo[1] /'pɔlu/ *m* pole

pólo[2] /'pɔlu/ *m* (*jogo*) polo; ~ aquático water polo

polo|nês /polo'nes/ a (f ~nesa) Polish □ m (f ~nesa) Pole; (língua) Polish

Polônia /po'lonia/ f Poland

polpa /'powpa/ f pulp

poltrona /pow'trona/ f armchair

polu|ente /polu'ẽtʃi/ a & m pollutant; ~ição f pollution; ~ir vt pollute

polvilhar /powvi'ʎar/ vt sprinkle

polvo /'powvu/ m octopus

pólvora /'powvora/ f gunpowder

polvorosa /powvo'roza/ f uproar; em ~ in uproar; <pessoa> in a flap

pomada /po'mada/ f ointment

pomar /po'mar/ m orchard

pom|ba /'põba/ f dove; ~bo m pigeon

pomo-de-Adão /pomudʒia'dãw/ m Adam's apple

pom|pa /'põpa/ f pomp; ~poso /o/ a pompous

ponche /'põʃi/ m punch

ponderar /põde'rar/ vt/i ponder

pônei /'ponej/ m pony

ponta /'põta/ f end; (de faca, prego) point; (de nariz, dedo, língua) tip; (de sapato) toe; (Cin, Teat: papel curto) walk-on part; (no campo de futebol) wing; (jogador) winger; na ~ dos pés on tip-toe; uma ~ de a touch of <ironia etc>; agüentar as ~s (fam) hold on; ~cabeça /e/ f de ~-cabeça upside down

pontada /põ'tada/ f (dor) twinge

pontapé /põta'pɛ/ m kick; ~ inicial kick-off

pontaria /põta'ria/ f aim; fazer ~ take aim

ponte /'põtʃi/ f bridge; ~ aérea shuttle; (em tempo de guerra) airlift; ~ de safena heart bypass; ~ pênsil suspension bridge

ponteiro /põ'teru/ m pointer; (de relógio) hand

pontiagudo /põtʃia'gudu/ a sharp

pontilhado /põtʃi'ʎadu/ a dotted

ponto /'põtu/ m point; (de costura, tricô) stitch; (no final de uma frase) full stop, (Amer) period; (sinalzinho, no i) dot; (de ônibus) stop; (no teatro) prompter; a ~ de on the point of; ao ~ <carne> medium; até certo ~ to a certain extent; às duas em ~ at exactly two o'clock; dormir no ~ (fam) miss the boat; entregar os ~s (fam) give up; fazer ~ (fam) hang out; dois ~s colon; ~ de exclamação/interrogação exclamation/question mark; ~ de táxi taxi rank, (Amer) taxi stand; ~ de vista point of view; ~ morto neutral; ~-e-vírgula m semicolon

pontu|ação /põtua'sãw/ f punctuation; ~al (pl ~ais) a punctual; ~alidade f punctuality; ~ar vt punctuate

pontudo /põ'tudu/ a pointed

popa /'popa/ f stern

popu|lação /popula'sãw/ f population; ~lacional (pl ~lacionais) a population; ~lar a popular; ~laridade f popularity; ~larizar vt popularize; ~larizar-se vpr become popular

pôquer /'poker/ m poker

por /por/ prep for; (através de) through; (indicando meio, agente) by; (motivo) out of; ~ ano/mês/ etc per year/month/etc; ~ cento per cent; ~ aqui (nesta área) around here; (nesta direção) this way; ~ dentro/fora on the inside/outside; ~ isso for this reason; ~ sorte luckily; ~ que why; ~ mais caro que seja however expensive it may be; está ~ acontecer/fazer it is yet to happen/to be done

pôr /por/ vt put; put on <roupa, chapéu, óculos>; set <mesa, ovos> □ m o ~ do sol sunset; ~-se vpr <sol> set; ~-se a start to; ~-se a caminho set off

porão /po'rãw/ m (de prédio) basement; (de casa) cellar; (de navio) hold

porca /'porka/ f (de parafuso) nut; (animal) sow

porção /por'sãw/ f portion; uma ~ de (muitos) a lot of

porcaria /porka'ria/ f (sujeira) filth; (coisa malfeita) piece of trash; pl trash

porcelana /porse'lana/ f china

porcentagem /porsẽ'taʒẽ/ f percentage

porco /'porku/ a filthy □ m (animal, fig) pig; (carne) pork; ~-espinho (pl ~s-espinhos) m porcupine

porém /po'rẽj/ conj however

pormenor /porme'nor/ m detail

por|nô /por'no/ a porn □ m porn film; ~nografia f pornography; ~nográfico a pornographic

poro /'poru/ m pore; ~so /o/ a porous

por|quanto /por'kwãtu/ conj since; ~que /por'ki/ conj because; (Port: por quê?) why; ~quê /por'ke/ adv (Port) why □ m reason why

porquinho|-da-índia /porkiɲuda-'idʒia/ (pl ~s-da-índia) m guinea pig

porrada /po'xada/ f (fam) beating

porre /'poxi/ m (fam) drinking session, booze-up; de ~ drunk; tomar um ~ get drunk

porta /'porta/ f door

porta-aviões /portavi'õjs/ m invar aircraft carrier

portador /porta'dor/ m bearer

portagem /por'taʒẽ/ f (Port) toll

porta|chaves /porta'ʃavis/ m invar key-holder ou key-ring; ~-jóias m in-

var jewellery box; ~-lápis _m invar_ pencil holder; ~-luvas _m invar_ glove compartment; ~-malas _m invar_ boot, (_Amer_) trunk; ~-níqueis _m invar_ purse

portanto /por'tãtu/ _conj_ therefore

portão /por'tãw/ _m_ gate

portar /por'tar/ _vt_ carry; ~-se _vpr_ behave

porta-retrato /pɔrtaxe'tratu/ _m_ photo frame; ~-revistas _m invar_ magazine rack

portaria /porta'ria/ _f_ (_entrada_) entrance; (_decreto_) decree

portátil (_pl_ ~teis) _a_ portable

porta-toalhas /pɔrtato'aʎas/ _m invar_ towel rail; ~-voz _m/f_ spokesman (_f_ -woman)

porte /'pɔrtʃi/ _m_ (_frete_) carriage; (_de cartas etc_) postage; (_de pessoa_) bearing; (_dimensão_) scale; de grande/pequeno ~ large-/small-scale

porteiro /por'teru/ _m_ doorman; ~ eletrônico entryphone

porto /'portu/ _m_ port; o Porto Oporto; ~ de escala port of call; Porto Rico _m_ Puerto Rico; ~-riquenho /e/ _a & m_ Puertorican

portuense /portu'ẽsi/ _a & m/f_ (person) from Oporto

Portugal /portu'gaw/ _m_ Portugal

portu|guês /portu'ges/ _a & m_ (_f_ ~guesa) Portuguese

portuário /portu'ariu/ _a_ port □ _m_ dock worker, docker

po|sar /po'zar/ _vi_ pose; ~se /o/ _f_ pose; (_de filme_) exposure

pós-datar /pɔzda'tar/ _vt_ postdate

pós-escrito /pɔzis'kritu/ _m_ postscript

pós-gradua|ção /pɔzgradua'sãw/ _f_ postgraduation; ~do _a & m_ postgraduate

pós-guerra /pɔz'gɛxa/ _m_ post-war period; a Europa do ~ post-war Europe

posi|ção /pozi'sãw/ _f_ position; ~cionar _vt_ position; ~tivo _a & m_ positive

posologia /pozolo'ʒia/ _f_ dosage

pos|sante /po'sãtʃi/ _a_ powerful; ~se /ɔ/ _f_ (_de casa etc_) possession, ownership; (_do presidente etc_) swearing in; _pl_ (_pertences_) possessions; tomar ~se take office; tomar ~se de take possession of

posses|são /pose'sãw/ _f_ possession; ~sivo _a_ possessive; ~so /ɛ/ _a_ possessed; (_com raiva_) furious

possibili|dade /posibili'dadʒi/ _f_ possibility; ~tar _vt_ make possible

possí|vel /po'sivew/ (_pl_ ~veis) _a_ possible; fazer todo o ~vel do one's best

possuir /posu'ir/ _vt_ possess; (_ser dono de_) own

posta /'pɔsta/ _f_ (_de peixe_) steak

pos|tal /pos'taw/ (_pl_ ~tais) _a_ postal □ _m_ postcard

postar /pos'tar/ _vt_ place; ~-se _vpr_ position o.s.

poste /'pɔstʃi/ _m_ post

pôster /'poster/ _m_ poster

posteri|dade /posteri'dadʒi/ _f_ posterity; ~or _a (no tempo)_ subsequent, later; (_no espaço_) rear; ~ormente _adv_ subsequently

postiço /pos'tʃisu/ _a_ false

posto /'postu/ _m_ post; ~ de gasolina petrol station, (_Amer_) gas station; ~ de saúde health centre □ _pp de_ pôr; ~ que although

póstumo /'postumu/ _a_ posthumous

postura /pos'tura/ _f_ posture

potá|vel /po'tavew/ (_pl_ ~veis) _a_ água ~vel drinking water

pote /'pɔtʃi/ _m_ pot; (_de vidro_) jar

potência /po'tẽsia/ _f_ power

poten|cial /potẽsi'aw/ (_pl_ ~ciais) _a & m_ potential; ~te _a_ potent

potro /'potru/ _m_ foal

pouco /'poku/ _a & pron_ little; _pl_ few □ _adv_ not much □ _m_ um ~ a little; ~ a ~ little by little; aos ~s gradually; daqui a ~ shortly; por ~ almost; ~ tempo a short time

pou|pança /po'pãsa/ _f_ saving; (_conta_) savings account; ~par _vt_ save; spare <_vida_>

pouquinho /po'kiɲu/ _m_ um ~ (de) a little

pou|sada /po'zada/ _f_ inn; ~sar _vi_ land; ~so _m_ landing

po|vão /po'vãw/ _m_ common people; ~vo /o/ _m_ people

povo|ação /povoa'sãw/ _f_ settlement; ~ar _vt_ populate

poxa /'pɔʃa/ _int_ gosh

pra /pra/ _prep (fam) veja_ para

praça /'prasa/ _f_ (_largo_) square; (_mercado_) market □ _m_ (_soldado_) private

prado /'pradu/ _m_ meadow

pra-frente /pra'frẽtʃi/ _a invar (fam)_ with it, modern

praga /'praga/ _f_ curse; (_inseto, doença, pessoa_) pest

prag|mático /prag'matʃiku/ _a_ pragmatic; ~matismo _m_ pragmatism

praguejar /prage'ʒar/ _vt/i_ curse

praia /'praja/ _f_ beach

pran|cha /'prãʃa/ _f_ plank; (_de surfe_) board; ~cheta /e/ _f_ drawing board

pranto /'prãtu/ _m_ weeping

pra|ta /'prata/ _f_ silver; ~taria _f_ (_coisas de prata_) silverware; ~teado _a_ silver-plated; (_cor_) silver

prateleira /prate'lera/ _f_ shelf

prática /'pratʃika/ _f_ practice; na ~ in practice

prati|cante /pratʃi'kãtʃi/ a practising □ m/f apprentice; (de esporte etc) player; ~car vt practise; (cometer, executar) carry out □ vi practise; ~cável (pl ~cáveis) a practicable

prático /'pratʃiku/ a practical

prato /'pratu/ m (objeto) plate; (comida) dish; (parte de uma refeição) course; (do toca-discos) turntable; pl (instrumento) cymbals; ~ fundo dish; ~ principal main course

praxe /'praʃi/ f normal practice; de ~ usually

prazer /pra'zer/ m pleasure; muito ~ (em conhecê-lo) pleased to meet you; ~oso /o/ a pleasurable

prazo /'prazu/ m term, time; a ~ <compra etc> on credit; a curto/longo ~ in the short/long term; último ~ deadline

preâmbulo /pri'ãbulu/ m preamble

precário /pre'kariu/ a precarious

precaução /prekaw'sãw/ f precaution

preca|ver-se /preka'versi/ vpr take precautions (de against); ~vido a cautious

prece /'presi/ f prayer

prece|dência /prese'dẽsia/ f precedence; ~dente a preceding □ m precedent; ~der vt/i precede

preceito /pre'sejtu/ m precept

precioso /presi'ozu/ a precious

precipício /presi'pisiu/ m precipice

precipi|tação /presipita'sãw/ f haste; (chuva etc) precipitation; ~tado a <fuga> headlong; <decisão, ato> hasty, rash; ~tar vt (lançar) throw; (antecipar) hasten; ~tar-se vpr (lançar-se) throw o.s.; (apressar-se) rush; (agir sem pensar) act rashly

precisão /presi'zãw/ f precision, accuracy

precisamente /presiza'mẽtʃi/ adv precisely

preci|sar /presi'zar/ vt (necessitar) need; (indicar com exatidão) specify □ vi be necessary; ~sar de need; ~so ir I have to go; ~sa-se wanted; ~so a (exato) precise; (necessário) necessary

preço /'presu/ m price; ~ de custo cost price; ~ fixo set price

precoce /pre'kɔsi/ a <fruto> early; <velhice, calvície etc> premature; <criança> precocious

precon|cebido /prekõse'bidu/ a preconceived; ~ceito m prejudice; ~ceituoso a prejudiced

preconizar /prekoni'zar/ vt advocate

precursor /prekur'sor/ m forerunner

preda|dor /preda'dor/ m predator; ~tório a predatory

predecessor /predese'sor/ m predecessor

predestinar /predestʃi'nar/ vt predestine

predeterminar /predetermi'nar/ vt predetermine

predição /predʒi'sãw/ f prediction

predile|ção /predʒile'sãw/ f preference; ~to /ɛ/ a favourite

prédio /'predʒiu/ m building

predis|por /predʒis'por/ vt prepare (para for); (tornar parcial) prejudice (contra against); ~por-se vpr prepare o.s.; ~posto a predisposed; (contra) prejudiced

predizer /predʒi'zer/ vt predict, foretell

predomi|nância /predomi'nãsia/ f predominance; ~nante a predominant; ~nar vi predominate

predomínio /predo'miniu/ m predominance

preencher /priẽ'ʃer/ vt fill; fill in, (Amer) fill out <formulário>; meet <requisitos>

pré-|escola /preis'kɔla/ f infant school, (Amer) preschool; ~escolar a pre-school; ~estréia f preview; ~fabricado a prefabricated

prefácio /pre'fasiu/ m preface

prefei|to /pre'fejtu/ m mayor; ~tura f prefecture; (prédio) town hall

prefe|rência /prefe'rẽsia/ f preference; (direito no trânsito) right of way; de ~rência preferably; ~rencial (pl ~renciais) a preferential; <rua> main; ~rido a favourite; ~rir vt prefer (a to); ~rível (pl ~ríveis) a preferable

prefixo /pre'fiksu/ m prefix

prega /'prega/ f pleat

pregador¹ /prega'dor/ m (de roupa) peg

pre|gador² /prega'dor/ m (quem prega) preacher; ~gão m (de vendedor) cry; o ~gão (na bolsa de valores) trading; (em leilão) bidding

pregar¹ /pre'gar/ vt fix; (com prego) nail; sew on <botão>; não ~ olho not sleep a wink; ~ uma peça em play a trick on; ~ um susto em alg give s.o. a fright

pregar² /pre'gar/ vt/i preach

prego /'pregu/ m nail

pregui|ça /pre'gisa/ f laziness; (bicho) sloth; estou com ~ça de ir I can't be bothered to go; ~çoso a lazy

pré-histórico /preis'tɔriku/ a prehistoric

preia-mar /preja'mar/ f high tide

prejudi|car /preʒudʒi'kar/ vt harm; damage <saúde>; ~car-se vpr harm o.s.; ~cial (pl ~ciais) a harmful, damaging (a to) prejuízo /preʒu'izu/ *m* damage; (*financeiro*) loss; em ~ de to the detriment of

prejulgar /preʒuw'gar/ *vt* prejudge

preliminar /prelimi'nar/ *a* & *m/f* preliminary

prelo /'prɛlu/ *m* printing press; no ~ being printed

preludio /pre'ludʒiu/ *m* prelude

prematuro /prema'turu/ *a* premature

premeditar /premedʒi'tar/ *vt* premeditate

premente /pre'mētʃi/ *a* pressing

premi|ado /premi'adu/ *a* <*romance, atleta etc*> prize-winning; <*bilhete, número etc*> winning □ *m* prize-winner; ~ar *vt* award a prize to <*romance, atleta etc*>; reward <*honestidade, mérito*>

prêmio /'premiu/ *m* prize; (*de seguro*) premium; Grande Prêmio (*de F1*) Grand Prix

premissa /pre'misa/ *f* premiss

premonição /premoni'sãw/ *f* premonition

pré-na|tal /prɛna'taw/ (*pl* ~tais) *a* antenatal, (*Amer*) prenatal

prenda /'prɛda/ *f* (*Port*) present; ~s domésticas household chores; ~do *a* domesticated

pren|dedor /prẽde'dor/ *m* clip; ~dedor de roupa clothes peg; ~der *vt* (*pregar*) fix; (*capturar*) arrest; (*atar*) tie up <*cachorro*>; tie back <*cabelo*>; (*restringir*) restrict; (*ligar afetivamente*) bind; ~der (a atenção de) alg grab s.o.('s attention)

prenhe /'prɛɲi/ *a* pregnant

prenome /pre'nomi/ *m* first name

pren|sa /'prẽsa/ *f* press; ~sar *vt* press

preocu|pação /preokupa'sãw/ *f* concern; ~pante *a* worrying; ~par *vt* worry; ~par-se *vpr* worry (com about)

prepa|ração /prepara'sãw/ *f* preparation; ~rado *m* preparation; ~rar *vt* prepare; ~rar-se *vpr* prepare, get ready; ~rativos *m pl* preparations; ~ro *m* preparation; (*competência*) knowledge; ~ro físico physical fitness

preponderar /prepõde'rar/ *vi* prevail (sobre over)

preposição /prepozi'sãw/ *f* preposition

prerrogativa /prexoga'tʃiva/ *f* prerogative

presa /'preza/ *f* (*de caça*) prey; (*de cobra*) fang; (*de elefante*) tusk; ~ de guerra spoils of war

prescin|dir /presĩ'dʒir/ *vi* ~dir de dispense with; ~divel (*pl* ~diveis) *a* dispensable

pres|crever /preskre'ver/ *vt* prescribe; ~crição *f* prescription; (*norma*) rule

presen|ça /pre'zẽsa/ *f* presence; ~ça de espirito presence of mind; ~ciar *vt* (*estar presente a*) be present at; (*testemunhar*) witness; ~te *a* & *m* present; ~tear *vt* ~tear alg (com aco) give s.o. (sth as) a present

presépio /pre'zɛpiu/ *m* crib

preser|vação /prezerva'sãw/ *f* preservation; ~var *vt* preserve, protect; ~vativo *m* (*em comida*) preservative; (*camisinha*) condom

presi|dência /prezi'dẽsia/ *f* presidency; (*de uma reunião*) chair; ~dencial (*pl* ~denciais) *a* presidential; ~dencialismo *m* presidential system; ~dente *m* (*f* ~denta) president; (*de uma reunião*) chairperson

presidiário /prezidʒi'ariu/ *m* convict

presídio /pre'zidʒiu/ *m* prison

presidir /prezi'dʒir/ *vi* preside (a over)

presilha /pre'ziʎa/ *f* fastener; (*de cabelo*) slide

preso /'prezu/ *pp de* prender □ *m* prisoner; ficar ~ get stuck; <*saia, corda etc*> get caught

pressa /'prɛsa/ *f* hurry; às ~s in a hurry, hurriedly; estar com *ou* ter ~ be in a hurry

presságio /pre'saʒiu/ *m* omen

pressão /pre'sãw/ *f* pressure; fazer ~ sobre put pressure on; ~ arterial blood pressure

pressen|timento /presẽtʃi'mẽtu/ *m* premonition, feeling; ~tir *vt* sense

pressionar /presio'nar/ *vt* press <*botão*>; pressure <*pessoa*>

pressupor /presu'por/ *vt* <*pessoa*> presume; <*coisa*> presuppose

pressurizado /presuri'zadu/ *a* pressurized

pres|tação /presta'sãw/ *f* repayment, instalment; ~tar *vt* render <*contas, serviço*> □ *vi* be of use; não ~ta he/it is no good; ~tar atenção pay attention; ~tar juramento take an oath; ~tativo *a* helpful; ~tável (*pl* ~táveis) *a* serviceable

prestes /'prɛstʃis/ *a invar* ~ a about to

prestidigita|ção /prestʃidʒizita'sãw/ *f* conjuring; ~dor *m* conjurer

pres|tigiar /prestʃiʒi'ar/ *vt* give prestige to; ~tígio *m* prestige; ~tigioso /o/ *a* prestigious

préstimo /'prɛstʃimu/ *m* merit

presumir /prezu'mir/ *vt* presume

presun|ção /prezũ'sãw/ *f* presumption; ~çoso /o/ *a* presumptuous

presunto /pre'zũtu/ *m* ham

pretendente /pretẽˈdẽtʃi/ *m/f* (*candidato*) candidate, applicant

preten|der /pretẽˈder/ *vt* intend; ~são *f* pretension; ~sioso /o/ *a* pretentious

preterir /preteˈrir/ *vt* disregard

pretérito /preˈtɛritu/ *m* preterite

pretexto /preˈtestu/ *m* pretext

preto /ˈpretu/ *a & m* black; ~e-branco *a invar* black and white

prevalecer /prevaleˈser/ *vi* prevail

prevenção /prevẽˈsãw/ *f* (*impedimento*) prevention; (*parcialidade*) bias

prevenir /preveˈnir/ *vt* (*evitar*) prevent; (*avisar*) warn; ~se *vpr* take precautions

preventivo /prevẽˈtʃivu/ *a* preventive

prever /preˈver/ *vt* foresee, predict

previdência /previˈdẽsia/ *f* foresight; ~ social social security

prévio /ˈprɛviu/ *a* prior

previ|são /previˈzãw/ *f* prediction, forecast; ~são do tempo weather forecast; ~sível (*pl* ~síveis) *a* predictable

pre|zado /preˈzadu/ *a* esteemed; Prezado Senhor Dear Sir; ~zar *vt* think highly of; ~zar-se *vpr* have self-respect

prima /ˈprima/ *f* cousin

primário /priˈmariu/ *a* primary; (*fundamental*) basic

primata /priˈmata/ *m* primate

primave|ra /primaˈvera/ *f* spring; (*flor*) primrose; ~ril (*pl* ~ris) *a* spring

primazia /primaˈzia/ *f* primacy

primei|ra /priˈmera/ *f* (*marcha*) first (gear); de ~ra first-rate; <*carne*> prime; ~ra-dama (*pl* ~ras-damas) *f* first lady; ~ranista *m/f* first-year (student); ~ro *a & adv* first; no dia ~ro de maio on the first of May; em ~ro lugar (*para começar*) in the first place; (*numa corrida, competição*) in first place; ~ro de tudo first of all; ~ros socorros first aid; ~ro-ministro (*pl* ~ros-ministros) *m* (*f* ~ra-ministra) prime-minister

primitivo /primiˈtʃivu/ *a* primitive

primo /ˈprimu/ *m* cousin □ *a* número ~ prime number; ~gênito *a & m* first-born

primor /priˈmor/ *m* perfection

primordi|al /primordʒiˈaw/ (*pl* ~ais) *a* (*primitivo*) primordial; (*fundamental*) fundamental

primoroso /primoˈrozu/ *a* exquisite

princesa /prĩˈseza/ *f* princess

princi|pado /prĩsiˈpadu/ *m* principality; ~pal (*pl* ~pais) *a* main □ *m* principal

príncipe /ˈprĩsipi/ *m* prince

principiante /prĩsipiˈãtʃi/ *m/f* beginner

princípio /prĩˈsipiu/ *m* (*início*) beginning; (*regra*) principle; em ~ in principle; por ~ on principle

priori|dade /prioriˈdadʒi/ *f* priority; ~tário *a* priority

prisão /priˈzãw/ *f* (*ato de prender*) arrest; (*cadeia*) prison; (*encarceramento*) imprisonment; ~ perpétua life imprisonment; ~ de ventre constipation

prisioneiro /prizioˈneru/ *m* prisoner

prisma /ˈprizma/ *m* prism

privação /privaˈsãw/ *f* deprivation

privacidade /privasiˈdadʒi/ *f* privacy

pri|vada /priˈvada/ *f* toilet; ~vado *a* private; ~vado de deprived of; ~var *vt* deprive (de of); ~var-se *vpr* deprive o.s. (de of)

privati|vo /privaˈtʃivu/ *a* private; ~zar *vt* privatize

privi|legiado /privileʒiˈadu/ *a* privileged; <*tratamento*> preferential; ~legiar *vt* favour; ~légio *m* privilege

pro /pru/ (*fam*) = para + o

pró /prɔ/ *adv* for □ *m* os ~s e os contras the pros and cons

proa /ˈproa/ *f* bow, prow

probabilidade /probabiliˈdadʒi/ *f* probability

proble|ma /proˈblema/ *m* problem; ~mático *a* problematic

proce|dência /proseˈdẽsia/ *f* origin; ~dente *a* logical; ~dente de coming from; ~der *vi* proceed; (*comportar-se*) behave; (*na justiça*) take legal action; ~der de come from; ~dimento *m* procedure; (*comportamento*) behaviour; (*na justiça*) proceedings

proces|sador /prosesaˈdor/ *m* processor; ~sador de texto word processor; ~samento *m* processing; (*na justiça*) prosecution; ~samento de dados data processing; ~sar *vt* process; (*por crime*) prosecute; (*por causa civil*) sue; ~so /ɛ/ *m* process; (*criminal*) trial; (*civil*) lawsuit

procla|mação /proklamaˈsãw/ *f* proclamation; ~mar *vt* proclaim

procri|ação /prokriaˈsãw/ *f* procreation; ~ar *vt/i* procreate

procu|ra /proˈkura/ *f* search; (*de produto*) demand; à ~ra de in search of; ~ração *f* power of attorney; ~rado *a* sought after, in demand; ~rado pela polícia wanted by the police; ~rador *m* (*mandatário*) proxy; (*advogado*) public prosecutor; ~rar *vt* look for; (*contatar*) get in touch with; (*ir visitar*)lookup; ~rar saber try to find out

prodígio /proˈdʒiʒiu/ *m* wonder; (*pessoa*) prodigy

prodigioso /prodʒiʒi'ozu/ a prodigious

pródigo /'prɔdigu/ a lavish, extravagant

produ|ção /produ'sãw/ f production; ~tividade f productivity; ~tivo a productive; ~to m product; (renda) proceeds; ~to nacional bruto gross national product; ~tos agrícolas agricultural produce; ~tor m produtcer □ a país ~tor de trigo wheat-producing country; ~zido a (fam: arrumado) done up; ~zir vt produce

proeminente /proemi'nẽtʃi/ a prominent

proeza /pro'eza/ f achievement

profa|nar /profa'nar/ vt desecrate; ~no a profane

profecia /profe'sia/ f prophecy

proferir /profe'rir/ vt utter; give <discurso, palestra>; pass <sentença>

profes|sar /profe'sar/ vt profess; ~so /ɛ/ a professed; <político etc> seasoned; ~sor m teacher; ~sor catedrático professor

pro|feta /pro'fɛta/ m prophet; ~fético a prophetic; ~fetizar vt prophesy

profissão /profi'sãw/ f profession

profissio|nal /profisio'naw/ (pl ~nais) a & m/f professional; ~nalismo m professionalism; ~nalizante a vocational; ~nalizar-se vpr <esportista etc> turn professional

profun|didade /profũdʒi'dadʒi/ f depth; ~do a deep; <sentimento etc> profound

profusão /profu'zãw/ f profusion

prog|nosticar /prognostʃi'kar/ vt forecast; ~nóstico m forecast; (med) prognosis

progra|ma /pro'grama/ m programme; (de computador) program; (diversão) thing to do; ~mação f programming; ~mador m programmer; ~mar vt plan; program <computador etc>; ~mável (pl ~máveis) a programmable

progredir /progre'dʒir/ vi progress

progres|são /progre'sãw/ f progression; ~sista a & m/f progressive; ~sivo a progressive; ~so /ɛ/ m progress

proi|bição /proibi'sãw/ f ban (de on); ~bido a forbidden; ~bir vt forbid (alg de s.o. to); ban <livro, importações etc>; ~bitivo a prohibitive

proje|ção /proʒe'sãw/ f projection; ~tar vt plan <viagem, estrada etc>; design <casa, carro etc>; project <filme, luz>

projé|til /pro'ʒɛtʃiw/ (pl ~teis) m projectile

proje|tista /proʒe'tʃista/ m/f designer; ~to /ɛ/ m project; (de casa, carro) design; ~to de lei bill; ~tor m projector

prol /prɔw/ m em ~ de on behalf of

prole /'prɔli/ f offspring; ~tariado m proletariat; ~tário a & m proletarian

prolife|ração /prolifera'sãw/ f proliferation; ~rar vi proliferate

prolífico /pro'lifiku/ a prolific

prolixo /pro'liksu/ a verbose, long-winded

prólogo /'prologu/ m prologue

prolon|gado /prolõ'gadu/ a prolonged; ~gar vt prolong; ~gar-se vpr go on

promessa /pro'mɛsa/ f promise

prome|tedor /promete'dor/ a promising; ~ter vt promise □ vi (dar esperança) show promise; ~ter voltar promise to return

promíscuo /pro'miskuu/ a promiscuous

promis|sor /promi'sor/ a promising; ~sória f promissory note

promoção /promo'sãw/ f promotion

promontório /promõ'tɔriu/ m promontory

promo|tor /promo'tor/ m promoter; (advogado) prosecutor; ~ver vt promote

promulgar /promuw'gar/ vt promulgate

prono|me /pro'nomi/ m pronoun; ~minal (pl ~minais) a pronominal

pron|tidão /prõtʃi'dãw/ f readiness; com ~tidão promptly; estar de ~tidão be at the ready; ~tificar vt get ready; ~tificar-se vpr volunteer (a to; para for); ~to a ready; (rápido) prompt □ int that's that; ~to-socorro (pl ~tos-socorros) m casualty department; (Port: reboque) towtruck; ~tuário m (manual) manual, handbook; (médico) notes; (policial) record, file

pronúncia /pro'nũsia/ f pronunciation

pronunci|ado /pronũsi'adu/ a pronounced; ~amento m pronouncement; ~ar vt pronounce

propagar /propa'gar/ vt propagate <espécie>; spread <notícia, idéia, fé>; ~-se vpr spread; <espécie> propagate

propen|são /propẽ'sãw/ f propensity; ~so a inclined (a to)

pro|piciar /propisi'ar/ vt provide; ~pício a propitious

propina /pro'pina/ f bribe; (Port: escolar) fee

propor /pro'por/ vt propose; ~-se vpr set o.s. <objetivo>; ~-se a estudar set out to study

proporção /propor'sãw/ f proportion

proporcio|nado /proporsio'nadu/ a proportionate (a to); **bem ~nado** well proportioned; **~nal** (pl **~nais**) a proportional; **~nar** vt provide

proposi|ção /propozi'sãw/ f proposition; **~tado** a, **~tal** (pl **~tais**) a intentional

propósito /pro'pɔzitu/ m intention; a **~** by the way; a **~ de** on the subject of; **chegar a ~** arrive at the right time; **de ~** on purpose

proposta /pro'pɔsta/ f proposal

propriamente /propria'mẽtʃi/ adv strictly; **a casa ~ dita** the house proper

proprie|dade /proprie'dadʒi/ f property; (direito sobre bens) ownership; **~tário** m owner; (de casa alugada) landlord

próprio /'prɔpriu/ a (de si) own; <sentido> literal; <nome> proper; **meu ~ carro** my own car; **um carro ~ a** car of my own; **o ~ rei** the king himself; **~ a** peculiar to; **~ para** suited to

prorro|gação /proxoga'sãw/ f extension; (de dívida) deferment; (em futebol etc) extra time; **~gar** vt extend <prazo>; defer <pagamento>

pro|sa /'prɔza/ f prose; **~sador** m prose writer; **~saico** a prosaic

proscrever /proskre'ver/ vt proscribe

prospecto /pros'pɛktu/ m (livro) brochure; (folheto) leaflet

prospe|rar /prospe'rar/ vi prosper; **~ridade** f prosperity

próspero /'prɔsperu/ a prosperous

prosse|guimento /prosegi'mẽtu/ m continuation; **~guir** vt continue □ vi proceed, go on

prostitu|ição /prostʃitui'sãw/ f prostitution; **~ta** f prostitute

pros|tração /prostra'sãw/ f debility; **~trado** a prostrate; **~trar** vt prostrate; (enfraquecer) debilitate; **~trar-se** vpr prostrate o.s.

protago|nista /protago'nista/ m/f protagonist; **~nizar** vt be at the centre of <acontecimento>; feature in <peça, filme>

prote|ção /prote'sãw/ f protection; **~cionismo** m protectionism; **~cionista** a & m/f protectionist; **~ger** vt protect; **~gido** m protégé

proteína /prote'ina/ f protein

protelar /prote'lar/ vt put off

protes|tante /protes'tãtʃi/ a & m/f Protestant; **~tar** vt/i protest; **~to** /ɛ/ m protest

protetor /prote'tor/ m protector □ a protective

protocolo /proto'kɔlu/ m protocol; (registro) register

protótipo /pro'tɔtʃipu/ m prototype

protuberância /protube'rãsia/ f bulge

pro|va /'prɔva/ f (que comprova) proof; (teste) trial; (exame) exam; (esportiva) competition; (de livro etc) proof; pl (na justiça) evidence; **à ~ de bala** bulletproof; **pôr à ~va** put to the test; **~vado** a proven; **~var** vt try <comida>; try on <roupa>; try out <carro, novo sistema etc>; (comprovar) prove

prová|vel /pro'vavew/ (pl **~veis**) a probable

proveito /pro'vejtu/ m profit, advantage; **tirar ~ de** (beneficiar-se) profit from; (explorar) take advantage of; **~so** /o/ a useful

proveni|ência /proveni'ẽsia/ f origin; **~ente** a originating (de from)

proventos /pro'vẽtus/ m pl proceeds

prover /pro'ver/ vt provide (de with)

provérbio /pro'verbiu/ m proverb

proveta /pro'veta/ f test tube; **bebê de ~** test-tube baby

provi|dência /provi'dẽsia/ f (medida) measure, step; (divina) providence; **tomar ~dências** take steps, take action; **~denciar** vt (prover) get hold of, provide; (resolver) see to, take care of □ vi take action

província /pro'vĩsia/ f province; (longe da cidade) provinces

provinci|al /provĩsi'aw/ (pl **~ais**) a provincial; **~ano** a & m provincial

provir /pro'vir/ vi come (de from); (resultar) be due (de to)

provi|são /provi'zãw/ f provision; **~sório** a provisional

provo|cação /provoka'sãw/ f provocation; **~cador**, **~cante** a provocative; **~car** vt provoke; (ocasionar) cause

proximidade /prosimi'dadʒi/ f closeness; pl (imediações) vicinity

próximo /'prɔsimo/ a (no tempo) next; (perto) near, close (de to); <parente> close; <futuro> near □ m neighbour, fellow man

pru|dência /pru'dẽsia/ f prudence; **~dente** a prudent

prumo /'prumu/ m plumb line; **a ~** vertically

prurido /pru'ridu/ m itch

pseudônimo /pisew'donimu/ m pseudonym

psica|nálise /pisika'nalizi/ f psychoanalysis; **~nalista** m/f psychoanalyst

psi|cologia /pisikolo'ʒia/ f psychology; **~cológico** a psychological; **~cólogo** m psychologist

psico|pata /pisiko'pata/ m/f psychopath; **~se** /ɔ/ f psychosis; **~terapeuta** m/f psychotherapist; **~terapia** f psycho-therapy

psicótico /pisi'kɔtʃiku/ a & m psychotic

psique /pi'siki/ f psyche

psiqui|atra /pisiki'atra/ m/f psychiatrist; **~atria** f psychiatry; **~átrico** a psychiatric

psíquico /pi'sikiku/ a psychological

pua /'pua/ f bit

puber|dade /puber'dadʒi/ f puberty

publi|cação /publika'sãw/ f publication; **~car** vt publish

publici|dade /publisi'dadʒi/ f publicity; (reclame) advertising; **~tário** a publicity; (de reclame) advertising □ m advertising executive

público /'publiku/ a public □ m public; (platéia) audience; **em ~** in public; **o grande ~** the general public

pudera /pu'dera/ int no wonder!

pudico /pu'dʒiku/ a prudish

pudim /pu'dʒĩ/ m pudding

pudor /pu'dor/ m modesty, shame

pue|ril /pue'riw/ (pl **~ris**) a puerile

pugilis|mo /puʒi'lizmu/ m boxing; **~ta** m boxer

pu|ído /pu'idu/ a worn through; **~ir** vt wear through

pujan|ça /pu'ʒãsa/ f power; **~te** a powerful; (de saúde) robust

pular /pu'lar/ vt jump (over); (omitir) skip □ vi jump; **~ de contente** jump for joy; **~ carnaval** celebrate Carnival; **~ corda** skip

pulga /'puwga/ f flea

pulmão /puw'mãw/ m lung

pulo /'pulu/ m jump; **dar um ~ em** drop by; **dar ~s** jump up and down

pulôver /pu'lover/ m pullover

púlpito /'puwpitu/ m pulpit

pul|sar /puw'sar/ vi pulsate; **~seira** f bracelet; **~so** m (do braço) wrist; (batimento arterial) pulse

pulular /pulu'lar/ vi swarm (de with)

pulveri|zador /puwveriza'dor/ m spray; **~zar** vt spray <líquido>; (reduzir a pó, fig) pulverize

pun|gente /pũ'ʒẽtʃi/ a consuming; **~gir** vt afflict

pu|nhado /pu'ɲadu/ m handful; **~nhal** (pl **~nhais**) m dagger; **~nhalada** f stab wound; **~nho** m fist; (de camisa etc) cuff; (de espada) hilt

pu|nição /puni'sãw/ f punishment; **~nir** vt punish; **~nitivo** a punitive

pupila /pu'pila/ f pupil

purê /pu're/ m purée; **~ de batata** mashed potato

pureza /pu'reza/ f purity

pur|gante /pur'gãtʃi/ a & m purgative; **~gar** vt purge; **~gatório** m purgatory

purificar /purifi'kar/ vt purify

puritano /puri'tanu/ a & m puritan

puro /'puru/ a pure; <aguardente> neat; **~ e simples** pure and simple; **~-sangue** (pl **~s-sangues**) a & m thoroughbred

púrpura /'purpura/ a purple

purpurina /purpu'rina/ f glitter

purulento /puru'lẽtu/ a festering

pus /pus/ m pus

pusilânime /puzi'lanimi/ a fainthearted

pústula /'pustula/ f pimple

puta /'puta/ f whore □ a invar (fam) **um ~ carro** one hell of a car; **filho da ~** (chulo) bastard; **~ que (o) pariu!** (chulo) fucking hell!

puto /'putu/ a (fam) furious

putrefazer /putrefa'zer/ vi putrefy

puxa /'puʃa/ int gosh

pu|xado /pu'ʃadu/ a (fam) <exame> tough; <trabalho> hard; <aluguel, preço> steep; **~xador** m handle; **~xão** m pull, tug; **~xa-puxa** m toffee; **~xar** vt pull; strike up <conversa>; bring up <assunto>; **~xar de uma perna** limp; **~xar para** (parecer com) take after; **~xar por** (exigir muito de) push (hard); **~xa-saco** m (fam) creep

Q

QI /ke i/ m IQ

quadra /'kwadra/ f (de tênis etc) court; (quarteirão) block; **~do** a & m square

quadragésimo /kwadra'ʒɛzimu/ a fortieth

qua|dril /kwa'driw/ (pl **~dris**) m hip

quadrilha /kwa'driʎa/ f (bando) gang; (dança) square dance

quadrinho /kwa'drinu/ m frame; **história em ~s** comic strip

quadro /'kwadru/ m picture; (pintado) painting; (tabela) table; (pessoal) staff; (equipe) team; (de uma peça) scene; **~-negro** (pl **~s-negros**) m blackboard

quadruplicar /kwadrupli'kar/ vt/i quadruple

quádruplo /'kwadruplu/ a quadruple; **~s** m pl (crianças) quads

qual /kwaw/ (pl **quais**) pron which (one); **o/a ~** (coisa) that, which; (pessoa) that, who; **~ é o seu nome?** what's your name?; **seja ~ ~ for** a decisão whatever the decision may be

qualidade /kwali'dadʒi/ f quality; **na ~ de** in one's capacity as, as

qualifi|cação /kwalifika'sãw/ f qualification; **~car** vt qualify; (descrever) describe (de as); **~car-se** vpr qualify

qualitativo /kwalita'tʃivu/ a qualitativo

qualquer /kwaw'kɛr/ (pl quaisquer) a any; um livro ~ any old book; ~ um any one

quando /'kwãdu/ adv & conj when; ~ quer que whenever; ~ de at the time of; ~ muito at most

quantia /kwã'tʃia/ f amount

quanti|dade /kwãtʃi'dadʒi/ f quantity; uma ~dade de a lot of; em ~dade in large amounts; ~ficar vt quantify; ~tativo a quantitative

quanto /'kwãtu/ adv & pron how much; pl how many; ~ tempo? how long?; ~ mais barato melhor the cheaper the better; tão alto ~ eu as tall as me; ~ ri! how I laughed!; ~ a as for; ~ antes as soon as possible

quaren|ta /kwa'rẽta/ a & m forty; ~tão a & m (f ~tona) forty-year-old; ~tena /e/ f quarantine

quaresma /kwa'rezma/ f Lent

quarta /'kwarta/ f (dia) Wednesday; (marcha) fourth (gear); ~de-final (pl ~s-de-final) f quarter final; ~feira (pl ~s-feiras) f Wednesday

quartanista /kwarta'nista/ m/f fourth-year (student)

quarteirão /kwarte'rãw/ m block

quar|tel /kwar'tɛw/ (pl ~téis) m barracks; ~tel-general (pl ~téis-generais) m headquarters

quarteto /kwar'tetu/ m quartet; ~ de cordas string quartet

quarto /'kwartu/ a fourth □ m (parte) quarter; (aposento) bedroom; (guarda) watch; são três e/menos um ~ (Port) it's quarter past/to three; ~ de banho (Port) bathroom; ~ de hora quarter of an hour; ~ de hóspedes guest room

quartzo /'kwartzu/ m quartz

quase /'kwazi/ adv almost, nearly; ~ nada/nunca hardly anything/ever

quatro /'kwatru/ a & m four; de ~ (no chão) on all fours; ~centos a & m four hundred

que /ki/ a which, what; ~ dia é hoje? what's the date today?; ~ homem! what a man!; ~ triste! how sad! □ pron what; ~ é ~ é? what is it? □ pron rel (coisa) which, that; (pessoa) who, that; (interrogativo) what; o dia em ~ ... the day when/that ... □ conj that; (porque) because; espero ~ sim/não I hope so/not

quê /ke/ pron what □ m um ~ something; não tem de ~ don't mention it

quebra /'kɛbra/ f break; (de empresa, banco) crash; (de força) cut; de ~ in addition; ~cabeça m jigsaw (puzzle); (fig) puzzle; ~diço a breakable; ~do a broken; <carro> broken down;

~dos m pl small change; ~galho (fam) m stopgap; ~mar m breakwater; ~molas m invar speed bump; ~nozes m invar nutcrackers; ~pau (fam) m row; ~quebra m riot

quebrar /ke'brar/ vt break □ vi break; <carro etc> break down; <banco, empresa etc> crash, go bust; ~se vpr break

queda /'kɛda/ f fall; ter uma ~ por have a soft spot for; ~de-braço f arm wrestling

quei|jeira /ke'ʒera/ f cheese dish; ~jo m cheese; ~jo prato cheddar; ~jo-de-minas m Cheshire cheese

queima /'kejma/ f burning; ~da f forest fire; ~do a burnt; (bronzeado) tanned, brown; cheiro de ~do smell of burning

queimar /kej'mar/ vt burn; (bronzear) tan □ vi burn; <lâmpada> go; <fusível> blow; ~se vpr burn o.s.; (bronzear-se) go brown

queima-roupa /kejma'xopa/ f à ~ point-blank

quei|xa /'keʃa/ f complaint; ~xar-se vpr complain (de about)

queixo /'keʃu/ m chin; bater o ~ shiver

queixoso /ke'ʃozu/ a plaintive □ m plaintiff

quem /kẽj/ pron who; (a pessoa que) anyone who, he who; de ~ é este livro? whose is this book?; ~ quer que whoever; seja ~ for whoever it is; ~ falou isso fui eu it was me who said that; ~ me dera (que) ... I wish ..., if only

Quênia /'kenia/ m Kenya

queniano /keni'anu/ a & m Kenyan

quen|tão /kẽ'tãw/ m mulled wine; ~te a hot; (com calor agradável) warm; ~tura f heat

quepe /'kɛpi/ m cap

quer /kɛr/ conj ~ ... ~ ... whether ... or ...

querer /ke'rer/ vt/i want; quero ir I want to go; quero que você vá I want you to go; eu queria falar com o Sr X I'd like to speak to Mr X; vai ~ vir amanhã? do you want to come tomorrow?; vou ~ um cafezinho I'd like a coffee; se você quiser if you want; queira sentar do sit down; ~ dizer mean; quer dizer (isto é) that is to say, I mean

querido /ke'ridu/ a dear □ m darling

quermesse /ker'mɛsi/ f fête, fair

querosene /kero'zeni/ m kerosene

questão /kes'tãw/ m question; (assunto) matter; em ~ in question; fazer ~ de really want to; não faço ~ de ir I don't mind not going

questio|nar /kestʃio'nar/ *vt/i* question; ~nário *m* questionnaire; ~ná-vel (*pl* ~náveis) *a* questionable

quiabo /ki'abu/ *m* okra

quibe /'kibi/ *m* savoury meatball

quicar /ki'kar/ *vt/i* bounce

quiche /'kiʃi/ *f* quiche

quie|to /ki'etu/ *a* (*calado*) quiet; (*imóvel*) still; ~tude *f* quiet

quilate /ki'latʃi/ *m* carat; (*fig*) calibre

quilha /'kiʎa/ *f* keel

quilo /'kilo/ *m* kilo; ~grama *m* kilogram; ~metragem *f* mileage; ~métrico *a* mile-long

quilômetro /ki'lometru/ *m* kilometre

quimbanda /kĩ'bãda/ *m* Afro-Brazilian cult

qui|mera /ki'mera/ *f* fantasy; ~mérico *a* fanciful

quími|ca /'kimika/ *f* chemistry; ~co *a* chemical □ *m* chemist

quimioterapia /kimiotera'pia/ *f* chemotherapy

quimono /ki'mɔnu/ *m* kimono

quina /'kina/ *f* de ~ edgeways

quindim /kĩ'dʒĩ/ *m* sweet made of coconut, sugar and egg yolks

quinhão /ki'ɲãw/ *m* share

quinhentos /ki'ɲĩtus/ *a & m* five hundred

quinina /ki'nina/ *f* quinine

qüinquagésimo /kwĩkwa'ʒezimu/ *a* fiftieth

quinquilharias /kĩkiʎa'rias/ *f pl* knick-knacks

quinta¹ /'kĩta/ *f* (*fazenda*) farm

quinta² /'kĩta/ *f* (*dia*) Thursday; ~-feira (*pl* ~s-feiras) *f* Thursday

quin|tal /kĩ'taw/ (*pl* ~tais) *m* back yard

quinteiro /kĩ'tajru/ *m* (*Port*) farmer

quinteto /kĩ'tetu/ *m* quintet

quin|to /'kĩtu/ *a & m* fifth; ~tuplo *a* fivefold; ~tuplos *m pl* (*crianças*) quins

quinze /'kĩzi/ *a & m* fifteen; às dez e ~ at quarter past ten; são ~ para as dez it's quarter to ten; ~na /e/ *f* fortnight; ~nal (*pl* ~nais) *a* fortnightly; ~nalmente *adv* fortnightly

quiosque /ki'ɔski/ *m* (*banca*) kiosk; (*no jardim*) gazebo

quiro|mância /kiro'mãsia/ *f* palmistry; ~mante *m/f* palmist

quisto /'kistu/ *m* cyst

quitan|da /ki'tãda/ *f* grocer's (shop); ~deiro *m* grocer

qui|tar /ki'tar/ *vt* pay off <*dívida*>; ~te *a* estar ~te be quits

quociente /kwosi'ẽtʃi/ *m* quotient

quórum /'kwɔrũ/ *m* quorum

R

rã /xã/ *f* frog

rabanete /xaba'netʃi/ *m* radish

rabear /xabi'ar/ *vi* <*caminhão*> jack-knife

rabino /xa'binu/ *m* rabbi

rabis|car /xabis'kar/ *vt* scribble □ *vi* (*escrever mal*) scribble; (*fazer desenhos*) doodle; ~co *m* doodle

rabo /'xabu/ *m* (*de animal*) tail; com o ~ do olho out of the corner of one's eye; ~-de-cavalo (*pl* ~s-de-cavalo) *m* pony tail

rabugento /xabu'ʒẽtu/ *a* grumpy

raça /'xasa/ *f* (*de homens*) race; (*de animais*) breed

ração /xa'sãw/ *f* (*de comida*) ration; (*para animal*) food

racha /'xaʃa/ *f* crack; ~dura *f* crack

rachar /xa'ʃar/ *vt* (*dividir*) split; (*abrir fendas em*) crack; chop <*lenha*>; split <*despesas*> □ *vi* (*dividir-se*) split; (*apresentar fendas*) crack; (*ao pagar*) split the cost

raci|al /xasi'aw/ (*pl* ~ais) *a* racial

racio|cinar /xasiosi'nar/ *vi* reason; ~cínio *m* reasoning; ~nal (*pl* ~nais) *a* rational; ~nalizar *vt* rationalize

racio|namento /xasiona'mẽtu/ *m* rationing; ~nar *vt* ration

racis|mo /xa'sizmu/ *m* racism; ~ta *a & m/f* racist

radar /xa'dar/ *m* radar

radia|ção /xadʒia'sãw/ *f* radiation; ~dor *m* radiator

radialista /xadʒia'lista/ *m/f* radio announcer

radiante /xadʒi'ãtʃi/ *a* (*de alegria*) overjoyed

radi|cal /xadʒi'kaw/ (*pl* ~cais) *a & m* radical; ~car-se *vpr* settle

rádio¹ /'xadʒiu/ *m* radio □ *f* radio station

rádio² /'xadʒiu/ *m* (*elemento*) radium

radioati|vidade /xadʒioatʃivi'dadʒi/ *f* radioactivity; ~vo *a* radioactive

radiodifusão /xadʒiodʒifu'zãw/ *f* broadcasting

radiogra|far /xadʒiogra'far/ *vt* X-ray <*pulmões, osso etc*>; radio <*mensagem*>; ~fia *f* X-ray

radiolo|gia /xadʒiolo'ʒia/ *f* radiology; ~gista *m/f* radiologist

radio|novela /xadʒiono'vɛla/ *f* radio serial; ~patrulha *f* patrol car; ~táxi *m* radio taxi; ~terapia *f* radiotherapy, ray treatment

raia /'xaja/ *f* (*em corrida*) lane; (*peixe*) ray

rainha /xaˈiɲa/ f queen; ~-mãe f queen mother

raio /ˈxaju/ m (de luz etc) ray; (de círculo) radius; (de roda) spoke; (relâmpago) bolt of lightning; ~ de ação range

raiva /ˈxajva/ f rage; (doença) rabies; estar com ~va be furious (de with); ter ~va de alg have it in for s.o.; ~voso a furious; <cachorro> rabid

raiz /xaˈiz/ f root; ~ quadrada/cúbica square/cube root

rajada /xaˈʒada/ f (de vento) gust; (de tiros) burst

ra|lador /xalaˈdor/ m grater; ~lar vt grate

ralé /xaˈlɛ/ f rabble

ralhar /xaˈʎar/ vi scold

ralo[1] /ˈxalu/ m (ralador) grater; (de escoamento) drain

ralo[2] /ˈxalu/ a <cabelo> thinning; <sopa, tecido> thin; <vegetação> sparse; <café> weak

ra|mal /xaˈmaw/ (pl ~mais) m (telefone) extension; (de ferrovia) branch line

ramalhete /xamaˈʎetʃi/ m posy, bouquet

ramifi|cação /xamifikaˈsãw/ f branch; ~car-se vi branch off

ramo /ˈxamu/ m branch; (profissional etc) field; (buquê) bunch; Domingo de Ramos Palm Sunday

rampa /ˈxãpa/ f ramp

rancor /xãˈkor/ m resentment; ~oso /o/ a resentful

rançoso /xãˈsozu/ a rancid

ran|ger /xãˈʒer/ vt grind <dentes> □ vi creak; ~gido m creak

ranhura /xaˈɲura/ f groove; (para moedas) slot

ranzinza /xãˈzĩza/ a cantankerous

rapariga /xapaˈriga/ f (Port) girl

rapaz /xaˈpas/ m boy

rapé /xaˈpɛ/ m snuff

rapidez /xapiˈdes/ f speed

rápido /ˈxapidu/ a fast □ adv <fazer> quickly; <andar> fast

rapina /xaˈpina/ f ave de ~ bird of prey

rapo|sa /xaˈpoza/ f vixen; ~so m fox

rapsódia /xapˈsɔdʒia/ f rhapsody

rap|tar /xapˈtar/ vt abduct, kidnap <criança>; ~to m abduction, kidnapping (de criança)

raquete /xaˈkɛtʃi/ f, (Port) **raqueta** /xaˈketa/ f racquet

raquítico /xaˈkitʃiku/ a puny

ra|ramente /xaraˈmẽtʃi/ adv rarely; ~ridade f rarity; ~ro a rare □ adv rarely

rascunho /xasˈkuɲu/ m rough version, draft

ras|gado /xazˈgadu/ a torn; (fig)

<elogios etc> effusive; ~gão m tear; ~gar vt tear; (em pedaços) tear up □ vi, ~gar-se vpr tear; ~go m tear; (fig) burst

raso /ˈxazu/ a <água> shallow; <sapato> flat; <colher etc> level

ras|pão /xasˈpãw/ m graze; atingir de ~pão graze; ~par vt shave <cabeça, pêlos>; plane <madeira>; (para limpar) scrape; (tocar de leve) graze; ~par em scrape

ras|teiro /xasˈteru/ a <planta> creeping; <animal> crawling; ~tejante a crawling; <voz> slurred; ~tejar vi crawl

rasto /ˈxastu/ m veja rastro

ras|trear /xastriˈar/ vt track <satélite etc>; scan <céu, corpo etc>; ~tro m trail

ratear[1] /xatʃiˈar/ vi <motor> miss

ra|tear[2] /xatʃiˈar/ vt share; ~teio m sharing

ratifi|cação /xatʃifikaˈsãw/ f ratification; ~car vt ratify

rato /ˈxatu/ m rat; (camundongo) mouse; ~eira f mousetrap

ravina /xaˈvina/ f ravine

razão /xaˈzãw/ f reason; (proporção) ratio □ m ledger; à ~ de at the rate of; em ~ de on account of; ter ~ be right; não ter ~ be wrong

razoá|vel /xazoˈavew/ (pl ~veis) a reasonable

ré[1] /xɛ/ f (na justiça) defendant

ré[2] /xɛ/ f (marcha) reverse; dar ~ reverse

reabastecer /xeabasteˈser/ vt/i refuel

reabilitar /xeabiliˈtar/ vt rehabilitate

rea|ção /xeaˈsãw/ f reaction; ~ção em cadeia chain reaction; ~cionário a & m reactionary

readmitir /xeadʒimiˈtʃir/ vt reinstate <funcionário>

reagir /xeaˈʒir/ vi react; <doente> respond

reajus|tar /xeaʒusˈtar/ vt readjust; ~te m adjustment

re|al /xeˈaw/ (pl ~ais) a (verdadeiro) real; (da realeza) royal

real|çar /xeawˈsar/ vt highlight; ~ce m prominence

realejo /xeaˈleʒu/ m barrel organ

realeza /xeaˈleza/ f royalty

realidade /xealiˈdadʒi/ f reality

realimentação /xealimẽtaˈsãw/ f feedback

realis|mo /xeaˈlizmu/ m realism; ~ta a realistic □ m/f realist

reali|zado /xealiˈzadu/ a <pessoa> fulfilled; ~zar vt (fazer) carry out; (tornar real) realize <sonho, capital>; ~zar-se vpr <sonho> come true; <pessoa> fulfil o.s.; <casamento, reunião etc> take place realmente /xeaw'mētʃi/ adv really

reaparecer /xeapare'ser/ vi reappear

reativar /xeatʃi'var/ vt reactivate

reaver /xea'ver/ vt get back

reavivar /xeavi'var/ vt revive

rebaixar /xeba'ʃar/ vt lower <preço>; (fig) demean □ vi <preços> drop; ~-se vpr demean o.s.

rebanho /xe'banu/ m herd; (fiéis) flock

rebate /xe'batʃi/ m alarm; ~ter vt return <bola>; refute <acusação>; (à máquina) retype

rebelar-se /xebe'larsi/ vpr rebel

rebel|de /xe'bewdʒi/ a rebellious □ m/f rebel; ~dia f rebelliousness

rebelião /xebeli'ãw/ f rebellion

reben|tar /xebē'tar/ vt/i veja arrebentar; ~to m (de planta) shoot; (descendente) offspring

rebite /xe'bitʃi/ m rivet

rebobinar /xebobi'nar/ vt rewind

rebo|cador /xeboka'dor/ m tug; ~car vt (tirar) tow; (cobrir com reboco) plaster; ~co /o/ m plaster

rebolar /xebo'lar/ vi swing one's hips

reboque /xe'bɔki/ m towing; (veículo a ~) trailer; (com guindaste) tow-truck; a ~ on tow

rebuçado /xebu'sadu/ m (Port) sweet, (Amer) candy

rebuliço /xebu'lisu/ m commotion

rebuscado /xebus'kadu/ a recherché

recado /xe'kadu/ m message

reca|ída /xeka'ida/ f relapse; ~ir vi relapse; <acento, culpa> fall

recal|cado /xekaw'kadu/ a repressed; ~car vt repress

recanto /xe'kãtu/ m nook, recess

recapitular /xekapitu'lar/ vt review □ vi recap

reca|tado /xeka'tadu/ a reserved, withdrawn; ~to m reserve

recear /xese'ar/ vt/i fear (por for)

rece|ber /xese'ber/ vt receive; entertain <convidados> □ vi (~ber salário) get paid; (~ber convidados) entertain; ~bimento m receipt

receio /xe'seju/ m fear

recei|ta /xe'sejta/ f (de cozinha) recipe; (médica) prescription; (dinheiro) revenue; ~tar vt prescribe

recém-casados /xesējka'zadus/ m pl newly-weds; ~-chegado m newcomer; ~-nascido a newborn □ m newborn child, baby

recente /xe'sētʃi/ a recent; ~mente adv recently

receoso /xese'ozu/ a (apreensivo) afraid

recep|ção /xesep'sãw/ f reception; (Port: de carta) receipt; ~cionar vt receive; ~cionista m/f receptionist; ~táculo m receptacle; ~tivo a receptive; ~tor m receiver

reces|são /xese'sãw/ f recession; ~so /ɛ/ m recess

re|chear /xeʃi'ar/ vt stuff <frango, assado>; fill <empada>; ~cheio m (para frango etc) stuffing; (de empada etc) filling

rechonchudo /xeʃõ'ʃudu/ a plump

recibo /xe'sibu/ m receipt

reciclar /xesik'lar/ vt recycle

recife /xe'sifi/ m reef

recinto /xe'sĩtu/ m enclosure

recipiente /xesipi'ētʃi/ m container

reciprocar /xesipro'kar/ vt reciprocate

recíproco /xe'siproku/ a reciprocal; <sentimento> mutual

reci|tal /xesi'taw/ (pl ~tais) m recital; ~tar vt recite

recla|mação /xeklama'sãw/ f complaint; (no seguro) claim; ~mar vt claim □ vi complain (de about); (no seguro) claim; ~me m, (Port) ~mo m advertising

reclinar-se /xekli'narsi/ vpr recline

recluso /xe'kluzu/ a reclusive □ m recluse

recobrar /xeko'brar/ vt recover; ~-se vpr recover

recolher /xeko'ʎer/ vt collect; (retirar) withdraw; ~-se vpr retire

recomeçar /xekome'sar/ vt/i start again

recomen|dação /xekomēda'sãw/ f recommendation; ~dar vt recommend; ~dável (pl ~dáveis) a advisable

recompen|sa /xekõ'pēsa/ f reward; ~sar vt reward

reconcili|ação /xekõsilia'sãw/ f reconciliation; ~ar vt reconcile; ~ar-se vpr be reconciled

reconhe|cer /xekoɲe'ser/ vt recognize; (admitir) acknowledge; (mil) reconnoitre; identify <corpo>; ~cimento m recognition; (gratidão) gratitude; (mil) reconnaissance; (de corpo) identification; ~cível (pl ~cíveis) a recognizable

reconsiderar /xekõside'rar/ vt/i reconsider

reconstituinte /xekõstʃitu'ĩtʃi/ m tonic

reconstituir /xekõstʃitu'ir/ vt reform; reconstruct <crime, cena>

reconstruir /xekõstru'ir/ vt rebuild

recor|dação /xekorda'sãw/ f recollection; (objeto) memento; ~dar vt recollect; ~dar-se (de) recall

recor|de /xe'kɔrdʒi/ a invar & m record; ~dista a record-breaking □ m/f record-holder

recorrer /xeko'xer/ vi ~ a a turn to <médico, amigo>; resort to <violência, tática>; ~ de appeal against recor|tar /xekor'tar/ vt cut out; ~te /ɔ/ m cutting, (Amer) clipping

recostar /xekos'tar/ vt lean back; ~-se vpr lean back

recreio /xe'kreju/ m recreation; (na escola) break

recriar /xekri'ar/ vt recreate

recriminação /xekrimina'sāw/ f recrimination

recrudescer /xekrude'ser/ vi intensify

recru|ta /xe'kruta/ m/f recruit; ~tamento m recruitment; ~tar vt recruit

recu|ar /xeku'ar/ vi move back; <tropas> retreat; (no tempo) go back; (ceder) back down; (não cumprir) back out (de of) □ vt move back; ~o m retreat; (fig: de intento) climbdown

recupe|ração /xekupera'sāw/ f recovery; ~rar vt recover; make up <atraso, tempo perdido>; ~rar-se vpr recover (de from)

recurso /xe'kursu/ m resort; (coisa útil) resource; (na justiça) appeal; pl resources

recu|sa /xe'kuza/ f refusal; ~sar vt refuse; turn down <convite, oferta>; ~sar-se vpr refuse (a to)

reda|ção /xeda'sāw/ f (de livro, contrato) draft; (pessoal) editorial staff; (seção) editorial department; (na escola) composition; ~tor m editor

rede /'xedʒi/ f net; (para deitar) hammock; (fig: sistema) network

rédea /'xedʒia/ f rein

redemoinho /xedemo'iɲu/ m veja rodamoinho

reden|ção /xedē'sāw/ f redemption; ~tor a redeeming □ m redeemer

redigir /xedʒi'ʒir/ vt draw up <contrato>; write <artigo>; edit <dicionário>

redimir /xedʒi'mir/ vt redeem

redobrar /xedo'brar/ vt redouble

redon|deza /xedō'deza/ f roundness; pl vicinity; ~do a round

redor /xe'dɔr/ m ao ou em ~ de around

redução /xedu'sāw/ f reduction

redun|dante /xedū'dātʃi/ a redundant; ~dar vi ~dar em develop into

redu|zido /xedu'zidu/ a limited; (pequeno) small; ~zir vt reduce; ~zir-se vpr (ficar reduzido) be reduced (a to); (resumir-se) come down (a to)

reeleger /xeele'ʒer/ vt re-elect; ~-se vpr be re-elected

reeleição /xeelej'sāw/ f re-election

reembol|sar /xeēbow'sar/ vt reimburse <pessoa>; refund <dinheiro>; ~so /o/ m refund; ~so postal cash on delivery

reencarnação /xeēkarna'sāw/ f reincarnation

reentrância /xeē'trāsia/ f recess

reescalonar /xeeskalo'nar/ vt reschedule

reescrever /xeeskre'ver/ vt rewrite

refastelar-se /xefaste'larsi/ vpr stretch out

refazer /xefa'zer/ vt redo; rebuild <vida>; ~-se vpr recover (de from)

refei|ção /xefej'sāw/ f meal; ~tório m dining hall

refém /xe'fēj/ m hostage

referência /xefe'rēsia/ f reference; com ~ a with reference to

referendum /xefe'rēdū/ m referendum

refe|rente /xefe'rētʃi/ a ~rente a regarding; ~rir vt report; ~rir-se vpr refer (a to)

refestelar-se /xefeste'larsi/ vpr (Port) veja refastelar-se

re|fil /xe'fiw/ (pl ~fis) m refill

refi|nado /xefi'nadu/ a refined; ~namento m refinement; ~nar vt refine; ~naria f refinery

refle|tido /xefle'tʃidu/ a <decisão> well-thought-out; <pessoa> thoughtful; ~tir vt/i reflect; ~tir-se vpr be reflected; ~xão /ks/ f reflection; ~xivo /ks/ a reflexive; ~xo /eks/ a <luz> reflected; <ação> reflex □ m (de luz etc) reflection; (físico) reflex; (no cabelo) streak

refluxo /xe'fluksu/ m ebb

refo|gado /xefo'gadu/ m lightly fried mixture of onions and garlic; ~gar vt fry lightly

refor|çar /xefor'sar/ vt reinforce; ~ço /o/ m reinforcement

refor|ma /xe'forma/ f (da lei etc) reform; (na casa etc) renovation; (de militar) discharge; (pensão) pension; ~ma ministerial cabinet reshuffle; ~mado a reformed; (Port: aposentado) retired □ m (Port) pensioner; ~mar vt reform <lei, sistema etc>; renovate <casa, prédio>; (Port: aposentar) retire; ~mar-se vpr (Port: aposentar-se) retire; <criminoso> reform; ~matório m reform school; ~mista a & m/f reformist

refratário /xefra'tariu/ a <tigela etc> ovenproof, heatproof

refrear /xefri'ar/ vt rein in <cavalo>; (fig) curb, keep in check <paixões etc>; ~-se vpr restrain o.s.

refrega /xe'frega/ f clash, fight

refres|cante /xefres'kātʃi/ a refreshing; ~car vt freshen, cool <ar>; refresh <pessoa, memória etc> □ vi get cooler; ~car-se vpr refresh o.s.; ~co /e/ m (bebida) soft drink; pl refreshments refrige|rado /xefriʒe'radu/ a cooled; <casa etc> air-conditioned; (na geladeira) refrigerated; ~rador m refrigerator; ~rante m soft drink; ~rar vt keep cool; (na geladeira) refrigerate

refugi|ado /xefuʒi'adu/ m refugee; ~ar-se vpr take refuge

refúgio /xe'fuʒiu/ m refuge

refugo /xe'fugu/ m waste, refuse

refutar /xefu'tar/ vt refute

regaço /xe'gasu/ m lap

regador /xega'dor/ m watering can

regalia /xega'lia/ f privilege

regar /xe'gar/ vt water

regata /xe'gata/ f regatta

regatear /xegatʃi'ar/ vi bargain, haggle

re|gência /xe'ʒesia/ f (de verbo etc) government; ~gente m/f (de orquestra) conductor; ~ger vt govern □ vi rule

região /xeʒi'ãw/ f region; (de cidade etc) area

regi|me /xe'ʒimi/ m regime; (dieta) diet; fazer ~me diet; ~mento m (militar) regiment; (regulamento) regulations

régio /xeʒiu/ a regal

regio|nal /xeʒio'naw/ (pl ~nais) a regional

regis|trador /xeʒistra'dor/ a caixa ~tradora cash register; ~trar vt register; (anotar) record; ~tro m (lista) register; (de um fato, em banco de dados) record; (ato de ~trar) registration

rego /'xegu/ m (de arado) furrow; (de roda) rut; (para escoamento) ditch

regozi|jar /xegozi'ʒar/ vt delight; ~jar-se vpr be delighted; ~jo m delight

regra /'xegra/ f rule; pl (menstruações) periods; em ~ as a rule

regres|sar /xegre'sar/ vi return; ~sivo a regressive; contagem ~siva countdown; ~so /ɛ/ m return

régua /'xegwa/ f ruler

regu|lagem /xegu'laʒe/ f (de carro) tuning; ~lamento m regulations; ~lar a regular; <estatura, qualidade etc> average □ vt regulate; tune <carro, motor>; set <relógio> □ vi work; ~lar-se por go by, be guided by; ~laridade f regularity; ~larizar vt regularize

regurgitar /xegurʒi'tar/ vt bring up

rei /xej/ m king; ~nado m reign

reincidir /xeisi'dʒir/ vi <criminoso> reoffend

reino /'xejnu/ m kingdom; (fig: da fantasia etc) realm; Reino Unido United Kingdom

reiterar /xejte'rar/ vt reiterate

reitor /xej'tor/ m chancellor, (Amer) president

reivindi|cação /xejvĩdʒika'sãw/ f demand; ~car vt claim, demand

rejei|ção /xeʒej'sãw/ f rejection; ~tar vt reject

rejuvenescer /xeʒuvene'ser/ vt rejuvenate □ vi be rejuvenated

relação /xela'sãw/ f relationship; (relatório) account; (lista) list; pl relations; com ou em ~ a in relation to, regarding

relacio|namento /xelasiona'mẽtu/ m relationship; ~nar vt relate (com to); (listar) list; ~nar-se vpr relate (com to)

relações-públicas /xelasõjs'publikas/ m/f invar public-relations person

relâmpago /xe'lãpagu/ m flash of lightning; pl lightning □ a lightning; num ~ in a flash

relampejar /xelãpe'ʒar/ vi flash; relampejou there was a flash of lightning

relance /xe'lãsi/ m glance; olhar de ~ glance (at)

rela|tar /xela'tar/ vt relate; ~tivo a relative; ~to m account; ~tório m report

rela|xado /xela'ʃadu/ a relaxed; <disciplina> lax; <pessoa> lazy, complacent; ~xamento m (físico) relaxation; (de pessoa) complacency; ~xante a relaxing □ m tranquillizer; ~xar vt relax □ vi (descansar) relax; (tornar-se omisso) get complacent; ~xar-se vpr relax; ~xe m relaxation

reles /'xɛlis/ a invar <gente> common; <ação> despicable

rele|vância /xele'vãsia/ f relevance; ~vante a relevant; ~var vt emphasize; ~vo /e/ m relief; (importância) prominence

religi|ão /xeliʒi'ãw/ f religion; ~oso /o/ a religious

relin|char /xelĩ'ʃar/ vi neigh; ~cho m neighing

relíquia /xe'likia/ f relic

relógio /xe'lɔʒiu/ m clock; (de pulso) watch

relu|tância /xelu'tãsia/ f reluctance; ~tante a reluctant; ~tar vi be reluctant (em to)

reluzente /xelu'zẽtʃi/ a shining, gleaming

relva /'xewva/ f grass; ~do m lawn

remador /xema'dor/ m rower

remanescente /xemane'sẽtʃi/ a remaining □ m remainder

remar /xe'mar/ vt/i row

rema|tar /xema'tar/ vt finish off; ~te m finish; (adorno) finishing touch; (de piada) punch line remediar /xemedʒi'ar/ vt remedy

remédio /xe'medʒiu/ m (contra doença) medicine, drug; (a problema etc) remedy

remelento /xeme'lētu/ a bleary

remen|dar /xemē'dar/ vt mend; (com pedaço de pano) patch; ~do m mend; (pedaço de pano) patch

remessa /xe'mesa/ f (de mercadorias) shipment; (de dinheiro) remittance

reme|tente /xeme'tētʃi/ m/f sender; ~ter vt send <mercadorias, dinheiro etc>; refer <leitor> (a to)

remexer /xeme'ʃer/ vt shuffle <papéis>; stir up <poeira, lama>; wave <braços> □ vi rummage; ~se vpr move around

reminiscência /xemini'sēsia/ f reminiscence

remir /xe'mir/ vt redeem; ~se vpr redeem o.s.

remissão /xemi'sãw/ f (de pecados) redemption; (de doença, pena) remission; (num livro) cross-reference

remo /'xemu/ m oar; (esporte) rowing

remoção /xemo'sãw/ f removal

remoinho /xemo'iɲu/ m (Port) veja rodamoinho

remontar /xemõ'tar/ vi ~ a <coisa> date back to; <pessoa> think back to

remorso /xe'mɔrsu/ m remorse

remo|to /xe'mɔtu/ a remote; ~ver vt remove

remune|ração /xemunera'sãw/ f payment; ~rador a profitable; ~rar vt pay

rena /'xena/ f reindeer

re|nal /xe'naw/ (pl ~nais) a renal, kidney

Renascença /xena'sēsa/ f Renaissance

renas|cer /xena'ser/ vi be reborn; ~cimento m rebirth

renda¹ /'xēda/ f (tecido) lace

ren|da² /'xēda/ f income; (Port: aluguel) rent; ~der bring in, yield <lucro>; earn <juros>; fetch <preço>; bring <resultado> □ vi <investimento, trabalho, ação> pay off; <comida> go a long way; <produto comprado> give value for money; ~der-se vpr surrender; ~dição f surrender; ~dimento m (renda) income; (de investimento, terreno) yield; (de motor etc) output; (de produto comprado) value for money; ~doso /o/ a profitable

rene|gado /xene'gadu/ a & m renegade; ~gar vt renounce

renhido /xe'ɲidu/ a hard-fought

Reno /'xenu/ m Rhine

reno|mado /xeno'madu/ a renowned; ~me /o/ m renown

reno|vação /xenova'sãw/ f renewal; ~var vt renew

renque /'xēki/ m row

ren|tabilidade /xētabili'dadʒi/ f profitability; ~tável (pl ~táveis) a profitable

rente /'xētʃi/ adv ~ a close to □ a <cabelo> cropped

renúncia /xe'nūsia/ f renunciation (a of); (a cargo) resignation (a from)

renunciar /xenūsi'ar/ vi <presidente etc> resign; ~ a give up; waive <direito>

reorganizar /xeorgani'zar/ vt reorganize

repa|ração /xepara'sãw/ f reparation; (conserto) repair; ~rar vt (consertar) repair; make up for <ofensa, injustiça, erro>; make good <danos, prejuízo> □ vi ~rar (em) notice; ~ro m (conserto) repair

repar|tição /xepartʃi'sãw/ f division; (seção do governo) department; ~tir vt divide up

repassar /xepa'sar/ vt revise <matéria, lição>

repatriar /xepatri'ar/ vt repatriate

repe|lente /xepe'lētʃi/ a & m repellent; ~lir vt repel; reject <idéia, proposta etc>

repensar /xepē'sar/ vt/i rethink

repen|te /xe'pētʃi/ m de ~te suddenly; (fam: talvez) maybe; ~tino a sudden

reper|cussão /xeperku'sãw/ f repercussion; ~cutir vi <som> reverberate; (fig: ter efeito) have repercussions

repertório /xeper'tɔriu/ m (músico etc) repertoire; (lista) list

repe|tição /xepetʃi'sãw/ f repetition; ~tido a repeated; ~tidas vezes repeatedly; ~tir vt repeat □ vi (ao comer) have seconds; ~tir-se vpr <pessoa> repeat o.s.; <fato, acontecimento> recur; ~titivo a repetitive

repi|car /xepi'kar/ vt/i ring; ~que m ring

replay /xe'plej/ (pl ~s) m action replay

repleto /xe'plεtu/ a full up

réplica /'xεplika/ f reply; (cópia) replica

replicar /xepli'kar/ vt answer □ vi reply

repolho /xe'poʎu/ m cabbage

repor /xe'por/ vt (num lugar) put back; (substituir) replace

reportagem /xepor'taʒē/ f (uma) report; (ato) reporting

repórter /xe'pɔrter/ m/f reporter

reposição /xepozi'sãw/ f replacement

repou|sar /xepo'sar/ vt/i rest; ~so m rest

repreen|der /xepriē'der/ vt rebuke, reprimand; ~são f rebuke, reprimand; ~sível (*pl* ~síveis) *a* reprehensible

represa /xe'preza/ *f* dam

represália /xepre'zalia/ *f* reprisal

represen|tação /xeprezĕta'sãw/ *f* representation; (*espetáculo*) performance; (*ofício de ator*) acting; ~**tante** *m/f* representative; ~**tar** *vt* represent; (*no teatro*) perform <*peça*>; play <*papel, personagem*> □ *vi* <*ator*> act; ~**tativo** *a* representative

repres|são /xepre'sãw/ *f* repression; ~**sivo** *a* repressive

repri|mido /xepri'midu/ *a* repressed; ~**mir** *vt* repress

reprise /xe'prizi/ *f* (*na TV*) repeat; (*de filme*) rerun

reprodu|ção /xeprodu'sãw/ *f* reproduction; (*de atleta, mental*) endurance; (*de material, objeto*) strength; ~**zir** *vt* reproduce; ~**zir-se** *vpr* (*multiplicar-se*) reproduce; (*repetir-se*) recur

repro|vação /xeprova'sãw/ *f* disapproval; (*em exame*) failure; ~**var** *vt* (*rejeitar*) disapprove of; (*em exame*) fail; ser ~**vado** <*aluno*> fail

rép|til /'xɛptʃiw/ (*pl* ~**teis**) *m* reptile

república /xe'publika/ *f* republic; (*de estudantes*) hall of residence

republicano /xepubli'kanu/ *a* & *m* republican

repudiar /xepudʒi'ar/ *vt* disown; repudiate <*esposa*>

repug|nância /xepug'nãsia/ *f* repugnance; ~**nante** *a* repugnant

repul|sa /xe'puwsa/ *f* repulsion; (*recusa*) rejection; ~**sivo** *a* repulsive

reputação /xeputa'sãw/ *f* reputation

requebrar /xeke'brar/ *vt* swing; ~**se** *vpr* sway

requeijão /xeke'ʒãw/ *m* cheese spread, cottage cheese

reque|rer /xeke'rer/ *vt* (*pedir*) apply for; (*exigir*) require; ~**rimento** *m* application

requin|tado /xekĩ'tadu/ *a* refined; ~**tar** *vt* refine; ~**te** *m* refinement

requisi|ção /xekizi'sãw/ *f* requisition; ~**tar** *vt* requisition; ~**to** *m* requirement

rês /xes/ (*pl* **reses**) *m* head of cattle; *pl* cattle

rescindir /xesĩ'dʒir/ *vt* rescind

rés-do-chão /xɛzdu'ʃãw/ *m invar* (*Port*) ground floor, (*Amer*) first floor

rese|nha /xe'zeɲa/ *f* review; ~**nhar** *vt* review

reser|va /xe'zɛrva/ *f* reserve; (*em hotel, avião etc, ressalva*) reservation; ~**var** *vt* reserve; ~**vatório** *m* reservoir; ~**vista** *m/f* reservist

resfri|ado /xesfri'adu/ *a* estar ~**ado** have a cold □ *m* cold; ~**ar** *vt* cool □ *vi* get cold; (*tornar-se morno*) cool down; ~**ar-se** *vpr* catch a cold

resga|tar /xezga'tar/ *vt* (*salvar*) rescue; (*remir*) redeem; ~**te** *m* (*salvamento*) rescue; (*pago por refém*) ransom; (*remissão*) redemption

resguardar /xezgwar'dar/ *vt* protect; ~**se** *vpr* protect o.s. (*de* from)

residência /xezi'dĕsia/ *f* residence

residen|cial /xezidĕsi'aw/ (*pl* ~**ciais**) *a* <*bairro*> residential; <*telefone etc*> home; ~**te** *a* & *m/f* resident

residir /xezi'dʒir/ *vi* reside

resíduo /xe'ziduu/ *m* residue

resig|nação /xezigna'sãw/ *f* resignation; ~**nado** *a* resigned; ~**nar-se** *vpr* resign o.s. (*com* to)

resina /xe'zina/ *f* resin

resis|tência /xezis'tĕsia/ *f* resistance; (*de atleta, mental*) endurance; (*de material, objeto*) strength; ~**tente** *a* strong, tough; <*tecido, roupa*> hardwearing; <*planta*> hardy; ~**tente** *a* resistant to; ~**tir** *vi* (*opor* ~**tência**) resist; (*agüentar*) <*pessoa*> hold out; <*objeto*> hold; ~**tir** *a* (*combater*) resist; (*agüentar*) withstand; ~**tir ao tempo** stand the test of time

resmun|gar /xezmũ'gar/ *vi* grumble; ~**go** *m* grumbling

resolu|ção /xezolu'sãw/ *f* resolution; (*firmeza*) resolve; (*de problema*) solution; ~**to** *a* resolute; ~**to a** resolved to

resolver /xezow'ver/ *vt* (*esclarecer*) sort out; solve <*problema, enigma*>; (*decidir*) decide; ~**se** *vpr* make up one's mind (*a* to)

respaldo /xes'pawdu/ *m* (*de cadeira*) back; (*fig: apoio*) backing

respectivo /xespek'tʃivu/ *a* respective

respei|tabilidade /xespejtabili'dadʒi/ *f* respectability; ~**tador** *a* respectful; ~**tar** *vt* respect; ~**tável** (*pl* ~**táveis**) *a* respectable; ~**to** *m* respect (*por* for); a ~**to de** about; a este ~**to** in this respect; com ~**to a** with regard to; dizer ~**to a** concern; ~**toso** /o/ *a* respectful

respin|gar /xespĩ'gar/ *vt/i* splash; ~**go** *m* splash

respi|ração /xespira'sãw/ *f* breathing; ~**rador** *m* respirator; ~**rar** *vt/i* breathe; ~**ratório** *a* respiratory; ~**ro** *m* breath; (*descanso*) break, breather

resplande|cente /xesplãde'sẽtʃi/ *a* resplendent; ~**cer** *vi* shine

resplendor /xesplẽ'dor/ *m* brilliance; (*fig*) glory

respon|dão /xespõ'dãw/ *a* (*f* ~**dona**) cheeky; ~**der** *vt/i* answer; (*com insolência*) answer back; ~**der a** answer; ~**der por** answer for, take responsibility for

responsabili|dade /xespõsabili-
'dadʒi/ f responsibility; ~zar vt hold
responsible (por for); ~zar-se vpr
take responsibility (por for)

responsá|vel /xespõ'savew/ (pl
~veis) a responsible (por for)

resposta /xes'posta/ f answer

resquício /xes'kisiu/ m vestige, remnant

ressabiado /xesabi'adu/ a wary, suspicious

ressaca /xe'saka/ f (depois de beber)
hangover; (do mar) undertow

ressaltar /xesaw'tar/ vt emphasize □
vi stand out

ressalva /xe'sawva/ f reservation,
proviso; (proteção) safeguard

ressarcir /xesar'sir/ vt refund

resse|cado /xese'kadu/ a <terra>
parched; <pele> dry; ~car vt/i dry
up

ressen|tido /xesẽ'tʃidu/ a resentful;
~timento m resentment; ~tir-se de
(ofender-se) resent; (ser influenciado)
show the effects of

ressequido /xese'kidu/ a veja ressecado

resso|ar /xeso'ar/ vi resound; ~-
nância f resonance; ~nante a
resonant; ~nar vi (Port) snore

ressurgimento /xesurʒi'mẽtu/ m resurgence

ressurreição /xesuxej'sãw/ f resur-
rection

ressuscitar /xesusi'tar/ vt revive

restabele|cer /xestabele'ser/ vt re-
store; restore to health <doente>;
~cer-se vpr recover; ~cimento m
restoration; (de doente) recovery

res|tante /xes'tãtʃi/ a remaining □ m
remainder; ~tar vi remain; ~ta-me
dizer que ... it remains for me to say
that

restau|ração /xestawra'sãw/ f res-
toration; ~rante m restaurant;
~rar vt restore

restitu|ição /xestʃitui'sãw/ f return,
restitution; ~ir vt (devolver) return;
restore <forma, força etc>; reinstate
<funcionário>

resto /'xestu/ m rest; pl (de comida)
left-overs; (de cadáver) remains; de
~ besides

restrição /xestri'sãw/ f restriction

restringir /xestrĩ'ʒir/ vt restrict

restrito /xes'tritu/ a restricted

resul|tado /xezuw'tadu/ m result;
~tante a resulting (de from); ~tar
vi result (de from; em in)

resu|mir /xezu'mir/ vt (abreviar)
summarize; (conter em poucas palavras) sum up; ~mir-se (ser expresso em poucas palavras) be
summed up; ~mir-se em (ser

apenas) come down to; ~mo m
summary; em ~mo briefly

resvalar /xezva'lar/ vi (sem querer)
slip; (deslizar) slide

reta /'xɛta/ f (linha) straight line; (de
pista etc) straight; ~ final home
straight

retaguarda /xeta'gwarda/ f rear-
guard

retalho /xe'taʎu/ m scrap; a ~ (Port)
retail

retaliação /xetalia'sãw/ f retaliation

retangular /xetãgu'lar/ a rectangular

retângulo /xe'tãgulu/ m rectangle

retar|dado /xetar'dadu/ a retarded □
m retard; ~dar vt delay; ~datário m
latecomer

retenção /xetẽ'sãw/ f retention

reter /xe'ter/ vt keep <pessoa>; hold
back <águas, riso, lágrimas>; (na
memória) retain; ~-se vpr restrain
o.s.

rete|sado /xete'zadu/ a taut; ~sar vt
pull taut

reticência /xetʃi'sẽsia/ f reticence

reti|dão /xetʃi'dãw/ f rectitude;
~ficar vt rectify

reti|rada /xetʃi'rada/ f (de tropas) re-
treat; (de dinheiro) withdrawal;
~rado a secluded; ~rar vt withdraw; (afastar) move away; ~rar-se
vpr <tropas> retreat; (afastar-se)
withdraw; (de uma atividade) retire;
~ro m retreat

reto /'xɛtu/ a <linha etc> straight;
<pessoa> honest

retocar /xeto'kar/ vt touch up <dese-
nho, maquiagem etc>; alter <texto>

reto|mada /xeto'mada/ f (continua-
ção) resumption; (reconquista) re-
taking; ~mar vt (continuar com)
resume; (conquistar de novo) retake

retoque /xe'tɔki/ m finishing touch

retorcer /xetor'ser/ vt twist; ~-se vpr
writhe

retóri|ca /xe'tɔrika/ f rhetoric; ~co a
rhetorical

retor|nar /xetor'nar/ vi return; ~no
m return; (na estrada) turning place;
dar ~no do a U-turn

retrair /xetra'ir/ vt retract, withdraw; ~-se vpr (recuar) withdraw;
(encolher-se) retract

retrasa|do /xetra'zadu/ a a semana
~da the week before last

retratar[1] /xetra'tar/ vt (desdizer) retract

retra|tar[2] /xetra'tar/ vt (em quadro,
livro) portray, depict; ~to m portrait;
(foto) photo; (representação) por-
trayal; ~to falado identikit picture

retribuir /xetribu'ir/ vt return
<favor, visita>; repay <gentileza>

retroativo /xetroa'tʃivu/ a retroactive; <pagamento> backdated

retro|ceder /xetrose'der/ vi retreat; (desistir) back down; ~cesso /ɛ/ m retreat; (ao passado) regression

retrógrado /xe'trɔgradu/ a retrograde

retrospec|tiva /xetrospek'tʃiva/ f retrospective; ~tivo a retrospective; ~to /ɛ/ m look back; em ~to in retrospect

retrovisor /xetrovi'zor/ a & m (espelho) ~ rear-view mirror

retrucar /xetru'kar/ vt/i retort

retum|bante /xetũ'bãtʃi/ a resounding; ~bar vi resound

réu /'xɛw/ m (f ré) defendant

reumatismo /xewma'tʃizmu/ m rheumatism

reu|nião /xeuni'ãw/ f meeting; (descontraída) get-together; (de família) reunion; ~nião de cúpula summit meeting; ~nir vt bring together <pessoas>; combine <qualidades>; ~nir-se vpr meet; <amigos, familiares> get together; ~nir-se a join

revanche /xe'vãʃi/ f revenge; (jogo) return match

reveillon /xeve'jõ/ (pl ~s) m New Year's Eve

reve|lação /xevela'sãw/ f revelation; (de fotos) developing; (novo talento) promising newcomer; ~lar vt reveal; develop <filme, fotos>; ~lar-se vpr (vir a ser) turn out to be

revelia /xeve'lia/ f à ~ by default; à ~ de without the knowledge of

reven|dedor /xevẽde'dor/ m dealer; ~der vt resell

rever /xe'ver/ vt (ver de novo) see again; (revisar) revise; (examinar) check

reve|rência /xeve'rẽsia/ f reverence; (movimento do busto) bow; (dobrando os joelhos) curtsey; ~rente a reverent

reverso /xe'vɛrsu/ m reverse; o ~ da medalha the other side of the coin

revés /xe'vɛs/ (pl reveses) m setback

reves|timento /xevestʃi'mẽtu/ m covering; ~tir vt cover

reve|zamento /xeveza'mẽtu/ m alternation; ~zar vt/i alternate; ~zar-se vpr alternate

revi|dar /xevi'dar/ vt return <golpe, insulto>; refute <crítica>; (retrucar) retort □ vi hit back; ~de m response

revigorar /xevigo'rar/ vt strengthen □ vi, ~-se vpr regain one's strength

revi|rar /xevi'rar/ vt turn out <bolsos, gavetas>; turn over <terra>; turn inside out <roupa>; roll <olhos>; ~rar-se vpr toss and turn; ~ravolta /ɔ/ f (na política etc) about-face, about-turn; (da situação) turnabout, dramatic change

revi|são /xevi'zãw/ f (de lições etc) revision; (de máquina, motor) overhaul; (de carro) service; (de provas de provas) proofreading; ~sar vt revise <provas, lições>; service <carro>; ~sor m (de bilhetes) ticket inspector; ~sor de provas proofreader

revis|ta /xe'vista/ f (para ler) magazine; (teatral) revue; (de tropas etc) review; passar ~ta a review; ~tar vt search

reviver /xevi'ver/ vt relive □ vi revive

revogar /xevo'gar/ vt revoke <lei>; cancel <ordem>

revol|ta /xe'vɔwta/ f (rebelião) revolt; (indignação) disgust; ~tante a disgusting; ~tar vt disgust; ~tar-se vpr (rebelar-se) revolt; (indignar-se) be disgusted; ~to /o/ a <casa, gaveta> upside down; <cabelo> dishevelled; <mar> rough; <mundo, região> troubled; <anos> turbulent

revolu|ção /xevolu'sãw/ f revolution; ~cionar vt revolutionize; ~cionário a & m revolutionary

revolver /xevow'ver/ vt turn over <terra>; roll <olhos>; go through <gavetas, arquivos>

revólver /xe'vɔwver/ m revolver

re|za /'xeza/ f prayer; ~zar vi pray □ vt say <missa, oração>; (dizer) state

riacho /xi'aʃu/ m stream

ribalta /xi'bawta/ f footlights

ribanceira /xibã'sera/ f embankment

ribombar /xibõ'bar/ vi rumble

rico /'xiku/ a rich □ m rich man; os ~s the rich

ricochete /xiko'ʃetʃi/ m ricochet; ~ar vi ricochet

ricota /xi'kɔta/ f curd cheese, ricotta

ridicularizar /xidʒikulari'zar/ vt ridicule

ridículo /xi'dʒikulu/ a ridiculous

ri|fa /'xifa/ f raffle; ~far vt raffle

rifão /xi'fãw/ m saying

rifle /'xifli/ m rifle

rigidez /xiʒi'des/ f rigidity

rígido /'xiʒidu/ a rigid

rigor /xi'gor/ m severity; (meticulosidade) rigour; vestido a ~ evening dress; de ~ essential

rigoroso /xigo'rozu/ a strict; <inverno, pena> severe, harsh; <lógica, estudo> rigorous

rijo /'xiʒu/ a stiff; <músculos> firm

rim /xĩ/ m kidney; pl (parte das costas) small of the back

ri|ma /'xima/ f rhyme; ~mar vt/i rhyme

rí|mel /'ximew/ (pl ~meis) m mascara

ringue /'xĩgi/ m ring

rinoceronte /xinoseˈrõtʃi/ *m* rhinoceros

rinque /ˈxĩki/ *m* rink

rio /ˈxio/ *m* river

riqueza /xiˈkeza/ *f* wealth; (*qualidade*) richness; *pl* riches

rir /xir/ *vi* laugh (**de** at)

risada /xiˈzada/ *f* laugh, laughter; **dar ~ laugh**

ris|ca /ˈxiska/ *f* stroke; (*listra*) stripe; (*do cabelo*) parting; **à ~ca** to the letter; **~car** *vt* (*apagar*) cross out <*erro*>; strike <*fósforo*>; scratch <*mesa, carro etc*>; write off <*amigo etc*>; **~co¹** *m* (*na parede etc*) scratch; (*no papel*) line; (*esboço*) sketch

risco² /ˈxisku/ *m* risk

riso /ˈxizu/ *m* laugh; **~nho** /o/ *a* smiling

ríspido /ˈxispidu/ *a* harsh

rítmico /ˈxitʃmiku/ *a* rhythmic

ritmo /ˈxitʃimu/ *m* rhythm

rito /ˈxitu/ *m* rite

ritu|al /xituˈaw/ (*pl* ~ais) *a & m* ritual

ri|val /xiˈvaw/ (*pl* ~vais) *a & m/f* rival; **~validade** *f* rivalry; **~valizar** *vt* rival □ *vi* vie (**com** with)

rixa /ˈxiʃa/ *f* fight

robô /xoˈbo/ *m* robot

robusto /xoˈbustu/ *a* robust

roça /ˈxɔsa/ *f* (*campo*) country

rocambole /xokãˈbɔli/ *m* roll

roçar /xoˈsar/ *vt* graze; **~ em** brush against

ro|cha /ˈxɔʃa/ *f* rock; **~chedo** /e/ *m* cliff

roda /ˈxɔda/ *f* (*de carro etc*) wheel; (*de amigos etc*) circle; **~ dentada** cog; **~da** *f* round; **~do** *a* saia **~da** full skirt; **~-gigante** (*pl* ~**s-gigantes**) *f* big wheel, (*Amer*) ferris wheel; **~moinho** *m* (*de vento*) whirlwind; (*na água*) whirlpool; (*fig*) whirl, swirl; **~pé** *m* skirting board, (*Amer*) baseboard

rodar /xoˈdar/ *vt* (*fazer girar*) spin; (*viajar por*) go round; do <*quilometragem*>; shoot <*filme*>; run <*programa*> □ *vi* (*girar*) spin; (*de carro*) drive round

rodear /xodʒiˈar/ *vt* (*circundar*) surround; (*andar ao redor de*) go round

rodeio /xoˈdeju/ *m* (*ao falar*) circumlocution; (*de gado*) round-up; **falar sem ~s** talk straight

rodela /xoˈdɛla/ *f* (*de limão etc*) slice; (*peça de metal*) washer

rodízio /xoˈdʒiziu/ *m* rota

rodo /ˈxodu/ *m* rake

rodopiar /xodopiˈar/ *vi* spin round

rodovi|a /xodoˈvia/ *f* highway; **~ária** *f* bus station; **~ário** *a* road; **polícia ~ária** traffic police

ro|edor /xoeˈdor/ *m* rodent; **~er** *vt* gnaw; bite <*unhas*>; (*fig*) eat away

rogar /xoˈgar/ *vi* request

rojão /xoˈʒãw/ *m* rocket

rol /xɔw/ (*pl* **róis**) *m* roll

rolar /xoˈlar/ *vt* roll □ *vi* roll; (*fam*) (*acontecer*) happen

roldana /xowˈdana/ *f* pulley

roleta /xoˈleta/ *f* (*jogo*) roulette; (*borboleta*) turnstile

rolha /ˈxoʎa/ *f* cork

roliço /xoˈlisu/ *a* <*objeto*> cylindrical; <*pessoa*> plump

rolo /ˈxolu/ *m* (*de filme, tecido etc*) roll; (*máquina, bobe*) roller; **~ compressor** steamroller; **~ de massa** rolling pin

Roma /ˈxoma/ *f* Rome

romã /xoˈmã/ *f* pomegranate

roman|ce /xoˈmãsi/ *m* (*livro*) novel; (*caso*) romance; **~cista** *m/f* novelist

romano /xoˈmanu/ *a & m* Roman

romântico /xoˈmãtʃiku/ *a* romantic

romantismo /xomãˈtʃizmu/ *m* (*amor*) romance; (*idealismo*) romanticism

romaria /xomaˈria/ *f* pilgrimage

rombo /ˈxõbu/ *m* hole

Romênia /xoˈmenia/ *f* Romania

romeno /xoˈmenu/ *a & m* Romanian

rom|per /xõˈper/ *vt* break; break off <*relações*> □ *vi* <*dia*> break; <*sol*> rise; **~per com** break up with; **~pimento** *m* break; (*de relações*) breaking off

ron|car /xõˈkar/ *vi* (*ao dormir*) snore; <*estômago*> rumble; **~co** *m* snoring; (*um*) snore; (*de motor*) roar

ron|da /ˈxõda/ *f* round, patrol; (*de motor*) roar **~da** *f* round, patrol; **~dar** *vt* (*patrulhar*) patrol; (*espreitar*) prowl around □ *vi* <*vigia etc*> patrol; <*animal, ladrão*> prowl around

ronronar /xõxoˈnar/ *vi* purr

roque² /ˈxɔki/ *m* (*em xadrez*) rook

ro|que² /ˈxɔki/ *m* (*música*) rock; **~queiro** *m* rock musician

rosa /ˈxɔza/ *f* rose □ *a invar* pink; **~do** *a* rosy; <*vinho*> rosé

rosário /xoˈzariu/ *m* rosary

rosbife /xozˈbifi/ *m* roast beef

rosca /ˈxoska/ *f* (*de parafuso*) thread; (*biscoito*) rusk; **farinha de ~** breadcrumbs

roseira /xoˈzera/ *f* rosebush

roseta /xoˈzeta/ *f* rosette

rosnar /xozˈnar/ *vi* <*cachorro*> growl; <*pessoa*> snarl

rosto /ˈxostu/ *m* face

rota /ˈxɔta/ *f* route

rota|ção /xotaˈsãw/ *f* rotation; **~tividade** *f* turnround; **~tivo** *a* rotating

rotei|rista /xoteˈrista/ *m/f* scriptwriter; **~ro** *m* (*de viagem*) itinerary;

(de filme, peça) script; *(de discussão etc)* outline

rotina /xo'tʃina/ *f* routine; ~neiro *a* routine

rótula /'xɔtula/ *f* kneecap

rotular /xotu'lar/ *vt* label (de as)

rótulo /'xɔtulu/ *m* label

rou|bar /xo'bar/ *vt* steal <dinheiro, carro etc>; rob <pessoa, loja etc> □ *vi* steal; *(em jogo)* cheat; ~bo *m* theft, robbery

rouco /'xoku/ *a* hoarse; <voz> gravelly

rou|pa /'xopa/ *f* clothes; *(uma)* outfit; ~pa de baixo underwear; ~pa de cama bedclothes; ~pão *m* dressing gown

rouquidão /xoki'dãw/ *f* hoarseness

rouxi|nol /xoʃi'nɔw/ *(pl* ~nóis) *m* nightingale

roxo /'xoʃu/ *a* purple

rua /'xua/ *f* street

rubéola /xu'bɛola/ *f* German measles

rubi /xu'bi/ *m* ruby

rude /'xudʒi/ *a* rude

rudimentos /xudʒi'mẽtus/ *m pl* rudiments, basics

ruela /xu'ɛla/ *f* backstreet

rufar /xu'far/ *vi* <tambor> roll □ *m* roll

ruga /'xuga/ *f* *(na pele)* wrinkle; *(na roupa)* crease

ru|gido /xu'ʒidu/ *m* roar; ~gir *vi* roar

ruibarbo /xui'barbu/ *m* rhubarb

ruído /xu'idu/ *m* noise

ruidoso /xui'dozu/ *a* noisy

ruim /xu'ĩ/ *a* bad

ruína /xu'ina/ *f* ruin

ruivo /'xuivu/ *a* <cabelo> red; <pessoa> red-haired □ *m* redhead

rulê /xu'le/ *a* gola ~ roll-neck

rum /xũ/ *m* rum

ru|mar /xu'mar/ *vi* head (para for); ~mo *m* course; ~mo a heading for; sem ~mo <vida> aimless; <andar> aimlessly

rumor /xu'mor/ *m* *(da rua, de vozes)* hum; *(do trânsito)* rumble; *(boato)* rumour

ru|ral /xu'raw/ *(pl* ~rais) *a* rural

rusga /'xuzga/ *f* quarrel, disagreement

rush /xaʃ/ *m* rush hour

Rússia /'xusia/ *f* Russia

russo /'xusu/ *a & m* Russian

rústico /'xustʃiku/ *a* rustic

S

Saará /saa'ra/ *m* Sahara

sábado /'sabadu/ *m* Saturday

sabão /sa'bãw/ *m* soap; ~ em pó soap powder

sabatina /saba'tʃina/ *f* test

sabedoria /sabedo'ria/ *f* wisdom

saber /sa'ber/ *vt/i* know (de about); *(descobrir)* find out (de about) □ *m* knowledge; eu sei cantar I know how to sing, I can sing; sei lá I've no idea; que eu saiba as far as I know

sabiá /sabi'a/ *m* thrush

sabi|chão /sabi'ʃãw/ *a & m* *(f* ~chona) know-it-all

sábio /'sabiu/ *a* wise □ *m* wise man

sabone|te /sabo'netʃi/ *m* bar of soap; ~teira *f* soapdish

sabor /sa'bor/ *m* flavour; ao ~ de at the mercy of

sabo|rear /sabori'ar/ *vt* savour; ~roso *a* tasty

sabo|tador /sabota'dor/ *m* saboteur; ~tagem *f* sabotage; ~tar *vt* sabotage

saca /'saka/ *f* sack

sacada /sa'kada/ *f* balcony

sa|cal /sa'kaw/ *(pl* ~cais) *a* *(fam)* boring

saca|na /sa'kana/ *(fam)* *a* *(desonesto)* devious; *(lascivo)* dirty-minded, naughty □ *m/f* rogue; ~nagem *(fam)* *f* *(esperteza)* trickery; *(sexo)* sex; *(uma)* dirty trick; ~near *(fam)* *vt* *(enganar)* do the dirty on; *(amolar)* take the mickey out of

sacar /sa'kar/ *vt/i* withdraw <dinheiro>; draw <arma>; *(em tênis, vôlei etc)* serve; *(fam)* *(entender)* understand

saçaricar /sasari'kar/ *vi* play around

sacarina /saka'rina/ *f* saccharine

saca-rolhas /saka'xoʎas/ *m invar* corkscrew

sacer|dócio /saser'dɔsiu/ *m* priesthood; ~dote /ɔ/ *m* priest; ~dotisa *f* priestess

sachê /sa'ʃe/ *m* sachet

saciar /sasi'ar/ *vt* satisfy

saco /'saku/ *m* bag; que ~! *(fam)* what a pain!; estar de ~ cheio (de) *(fam)* be fed up (with), be sick (of); encher o ~ de alg *(fam)* get on s.o.'s nerves; puxar o ~ de alg *(fam)* suck up to s.o.; ~ de dormir sleeping bag; ~ la /ɔ/ *f* bag; ~lão *m* wholesale fruit and vegetable market; ~lejar *vt* shake

sacramento /sakra'mẽtu/ *m* sacrament

sacri|ficar /sakrifi'kar/ *vt* sacrifice; have put down <cachorro etc>; ~fício *m* sacrifice; ~légio *m* sacrilege

sacrílego /sa'krilegu/ *a* sacrilegious

sacro /'sakru/ *a* <música> religious

sacrossanto /sakro'sãtu/ *a* sacrosanct

sacu|dida /saku'dʒida/ *f* shake; ~dir *vt* shake

sádico /'sadʒiku/ a sadistic □ m sadist

sadio /sa'dʒiu/ a healthy

sadismo /sa'dʒizmu/ m sadism

safa|deza /safa'deza/ f (desonestidade) deviousness; (libertinagem) indecency; (uma) dirty trick; ~do a (desonesto) devious; (lascivo) dirty-minded; (esperto) quick; <criança> naughty

safena /sa'fɛna/ f ponte de ~ heart bypass; ~do m bypass patient

safira /sa'fira/ f sapphire

safra /'safra/ f crop

sagitariano /saʒitari'anu/ a & m Sagittarian

Sagitário /saʒi'tariu/ m Sagittarius

sagrado /sa'gradu/ a sacred

saguão /sa'gwãw/ m (de teatro, hotel) foyer, (Amer) lobby; (de estação, aeroporto) concourse

saia /'saja/ f skirt; ~-calça (pl ~s-calças) f culottes

saída /sa'ida/ f (partida) departure; (porta, fig) way out; de ~ at the outset; estar de ~ be on one's way out

sair /sa'ir/ vi (de dentro) go/come out; (partir) leave; (desprender-se) come off; <mancha> come out; (resultar) turn out; ~-se vpr fare; ~-se com (dizer) come out with; ~ mais barato work out cheaper

sal /saw/ (pl sais) m salt; ~ de frutas Epsom salts

sala /'sala/ f (numa casa) lounge; (num lugar público) hall; (classe) class; fazer ~ a entertain; ~ (de aula) classroom; ~ de embarque departure lounge; ~ de espera waiting room; ~ de jantar dining room; ~ de operação operating theatre

sala|da /sa'lada/ f salad; (fig) jumble, mishmash; ~da de frutas fruit salad; ~deira f salad bowl

sala-e-quarto /sali'kwartu/ m two-room flat

sala|me /sa'lami/ m salami; ~minho m pepperoni

salão /sa'lãw/ m hall; (de cabeleireiro) salon; (de carros) show; ~ de beleza beauty salon

salari|al /salari'aw/ (pl ~ais) a wage

salário /sa'lariu/ m salary

sal|dar /saw'dar/ vt settle; ~do m balance

saleiro /sa'leru/ m salt cellar

sal|gadinhos /sawga'dʒiɲus/ m pl snacks; ~gado a salty; <preço> exorbitant; ~gar vt salt

salgueiro /saw'geru/ m willow; ~chorão weeping willow

saliência /sali'ẽsia/ f projection

salien|tar /saliẽ'tar/ vt (deixar claro) point out; (acentuar) highlight; ~tar-se vpr distinguish o.s.; ~te a prominent

saliva /sa'liva/ f saliva

salmão /saw'mãw/ m salmon

salmo /'sawmu/ m psalm

salmonela /sawmo'nɛla/ f salmonella

salmoura /saw'mora/ f brine

salpicar /sawpi'kar/ vt sprinkle; (sem querer) spatter

salsa /'sawsa/ f parsley

salsicha /saw'siʃa/ f sausage

saltar /saw'tar/ vt (pular) jump; (omitir) skip □ vi jump; ~ à vista be obvious; ~ do ônibus get off the bus

saltear /sawtʃi'ar/ vt sauté <batatas etc>

saltitar /sawtʃi'tar/ vi hop

salto /'sawtu/ m (pulo) jump; (de sapato) heel; ~ com vara pole vault; ~ em altura high jump; ~ em distância long jump; ~-mortal (pl ~s-mortais) m somersault

salu|bre /sa'lubri/ a healthy; ~tar a salutary

salva[1] /'sawva/ f (de canhões) salvo; (bandeja) salver; ~ de palmas round of applause

salva[2] /'sawva/ f (erva) sage

salva|ção /sawva'sãw/ f salvation; ~dor m saviour

salvaguar|da /sawva'gwarda/ f safeguard; ~dar vt safeguard

sal|vamento /sawva'mẽtu/ m rescue; (de navio) salvage; ~var vt save; ~var-se vpr escape; ~va-vidas m invar (bóia) lifebelt □ m/f (pessoa) lifeguard □ a barco ~va-vidas lifeboat; ~vo a safe □ prep save; a ~vo safe

samambaia /samã'baja/ f fern

sam|ba /'sãba/ m samba; ~ba-canção (pl ~bas-canção) m slow samba □ a invar cueca ~ba-canção boxer shorts; ~ba-enredo (pl ~bas-enredo) m samba story; ~bar vi samba; ~bista m/f (dançarino) samba dancer; (compositor) composer of sambas; ~bódromo m Carnival parade ground

samovar /samo'var/ m tea urn

sanar /sa'nar/ vt cure

san|ção /sã'sãw/ f sanction; ~cionar vt sanction

sandália /sã'dalia/ f sandal

sandes /'sãdiʃ/ f invar (Port) sandwich

sanduíche /sãdu'iʃi/ m sandwich

sane|amento /sania'mẽtu/ m (esgotos) sanitation; (de finanças) rehabilitation; ~ar vt set straight <finanças>

sanfona /sã'fona/ f (instrumento) accordion; (tricô) ribbing; ~do a <porta> folding; <pulôver> ribbed

san|grar /sã'grar/ vt/i bleed; ~grento a bloody; <carne> rare;

~gria /f bloodshed; (de dinheiro) extortion

sangue /'sãgi/ m blood; ~ pisado bruise; ~-frio m cool, coolness

sanguessuga /sãgi'suga/ f leech

sanguinário /sãgi'nariu/ a bloodthirsty

sanguíneo /sã'giniu/ a blood

sanidade /sani'dadʒi/ f sanity

sanitário /sani'tariu/ a sanitary; ~s mpl toilets

sanitidade /sãtʃi'dadʒi/ f sanctity; ~tificar vt sanctify; ~to a holy □ m saint; todo ~to dia every single day; ~tuário m sanctuary

São /sãw/ a Saint

são /sãw/ (pl ~s) a (f sã) healthy; (mentalmente) sane; <conselho> sound

sapata /sa'pata/ f shoe; ~ria f shoe shop

sapateado /sapatʃi'adu/ m tap dancing; ~ador m tap dancer; ~ar vi tap one's feet; (dançar) tap-dance

sapateiro /sapa'teru/ f shoemaker; ~tilha f pump; ~tilha de balé ballet shoe; ~to m shoe

sapeca /sa'peka/ a saucy

sapinho /sa'piɲu/ m thrush; ~po m toad

saque[1] /'saki/ m (do banco) withdrawal; (em tênis, vôlei etc) serve

saque[2] /'saki/ m (de loja etc) looting; ~ar vt loot

saraiva /sa'rajva/ f hail; ~da f hailstorm; uma ~da de a hail of

sarampo /sa'rãpu/ m measles

sarar /sa'rar/ vt cure □ vi get better; <ferida> heal

sarcasmo /sar'kazmu/ m sarcasm; ~cástico a sarcastic

sarda /'sarda/ f freckle

Sardenha /sar'deɲa/ f Sardinia

sardento /sar'dẽtu/ a freckled

sardinha /sar'dʒiɲa/ f sardine

sardônico /sar'doniku/ a sardonic

sargento /sar'ʒẽtu/ m sergeant

sarjeta /sar'ʒeta/ f gutter

Satanás /sata'nas/ m Satan

satânico /sa'taniku/ a satanic

satélite /sa'tɛlitʃi/ a & m satellite

sátira /'satʃira/ f satire

satírico /sa'tʃiriku/ a satirical

satirizar /satʃiri'zar/ vt satirize

satisfação /satʃisfa'sãw/ f satisfaction; dar ~ções a answer to; ~tório a satisfactory; ~zer vt ~zer (a) satisfy □ vi be satisfactory; ~zer-se vpr be satisfied

satisfeito /satʃis'fejtu/ a satisfied; (contente) content; (de comida) full

saturar /satu'rar/ vt saturate

Saturno /sa'turnu/ m Saturn

saudação /sawda'sãw/ f greeting

saudade /saw'dadʒi/ f longing; (lembrança) nostalgia; estar com ~s de miss; matar ~s catch up

saudar /saw'dar/ vt greet

saudável /saw'davew/ (pl ~veis) a healthy

saúde /sa'udʒi/ f health □ int (ao beber) cheers; (ao espirrar) bless you

saudo|sismo /sawdo'zizmu/ m nostalgia; ~so /o/ a longing; estar ~so de miss; o nosso ~so amigo our much-missed friend

sauna /'sawna/ f sauna

saxofo|ne /sakso'foni/ m saxophone; ~nista m/f saxophonist

sazo|nado /sazo'nadu/ a seasoned; ~nal (pl ~nais) a seasonal

se[1] /si/ conj if; não sei ~ ... I don't know if/whether

se[2] /si/ pron (ele mesmo) himself; (ela mesma) herself; (você mesmo) yourself; (eles/elas) themselves; (vocês) yourselves; (um ao outro) each other; dorme-~ tarde no Brasil people go to bed late in Brazil; aqui ~ fala inglês English is spoken here

sebo /'sebu/ m (sujeira) grease; (livraria) secondhand bookshop; ~so /o/ a greasy; <pessoa> slimy

seca /'seka/ f drought; ~dor m ~dor de cabelo hairdryer; ~dora f tumble dryer

secar /se'kar/ vt/i dry

secção /sek'sãw/ f veja seção; ~cionar vt split up

seco /'seku/ a dry; <resposta, tom> curt; <pessoa, caráter> cold; <barulho, pancada> dull; estar ~ por I'm dying for

secretaria /sekreta'ria/ f (de empresa) general office; (ministério) department

secreta|ria /sekre'taria/ f secretary; ~ria eletrônica ansaphone; ~rio m secretary

secreto /se'krɛtu/ a secret

secular /seku'lar/ a (não religioso) secular; (antigo) age-old

século /'sekulu/ m century; pl (muito tempo) ages

secundário /sekũ'dariu/ a secondary

secura /se'kura/ f dryness; estar com uma ~ de be longing for/to

seda /'seda/ f silk

sedativo /seda'tʃivu/ a & m sedative

sede[1] /'sedʒi/ f headquarters; (local do governo) seat

sede[2] /'sedʒi/ f thirst (de for); estar com ~ be thirsty

sedentário /sedẽ'tariu/ a sedentary

sedento /se'dẽtu/ a thirsty (de for)

sediar /sedʒi'ar/ vt host

sedimen|tar /sedʒimẽ'tar/ vt consolidate; ~to m sediment

sedoso /se'dozu/ a silky

sedu|ção /sedu'sãw/ f seduction; ~tor a seductive; ~zir vt seduce

segmento /seg'mẽtu/ m segment

segredo /se'gredu/ m secret; (de cofre etc) combination

segregar /segre'gar/ vt segregate

segui|da /se'gida/ f em ~da (imediatamente) straight away; (depois) next; ~do a followed (de by); cinco horas ~das five hours running; ~dor m follower; ~mento m continuation; dar ~mento a go on with

se|guinte /se'gĩtʃi/ a following; < dia, semana etc> next; ~guir vt/i follow; (continuar) continue; ~guir-se vpr follow; ~guir em frente (ir embora) go; (indicação na rua) go straight ahead

segun|da /se'gũda/ f (dia) Monday; (marcha) second; de ~da secondrate; ~da-feira (pl ~das-feiras) f Monday; ~do a & m second □ adv secondly □ prep according to □ conj according to what; ~das intenções ulterior motives; de ~da mão second-hand

segu|rança /segu'rãsa/ f security; (estado de seguro) safety; (certeza) assurance □ m/f security guard; ~rar vt hold; ~rar-se vpr (controlar-se) control o.s.; ~rar-se em hold on to; ~ro a secure; (fora de perigo) safe; (com certeza) sure □ m insurance; estar no ~ro < bens> be insured; fazer ~ro de insure; ~ro-desemprego m unemployment benefit

seio /'seju/ m breast, bosom; no ~ de within

seis /sejs/ a & m six; ~centos a & m six hundred

seita /'sejta/ f sect

seixo /'sejʃu/ m pebble

sela /'sɛla/ f saddle

selar¹ /se'lar/ vt saddle < cavalo>

selar² /se'lar/ vt seal; (franquear) stamp

sele|ção /sele'sãw/ f selection; (time) team; ~cionar vt select; ~to /ɛ/ a select

selim /se'lĩ/ m saddle

selo /'selu/ m seal; (postal) stamp; (de discos) label

selva /'sɛwva/ f jungle; ~gem a wild; ~geria f savagery

sem /sẽj/ prep without; ~ eu saber without me knowing; ficar ~ dinheiro run out of money

semáforo /se'maforu/ m (na rua) traffic lights; (de ferrovia) signal

sema|na /se'mana/ f week; ~nal (pl ~nais) a weekly; ~nalmente adv weekly; ~nário m weekly

semear /semi'ar/ vt sow

semelhan|ça /seme'ʎãsa/ f similarity; ~te a similar; (tal) such

sêmen /'semẽ/ m semen

semente /se'mẽtʃi/ f seed; (em fruta) pip

semestre /se'mɛstri/ m six months; (da faculdade etc) term, (Amer) semester

semi|círculo /semi'sirkulu/ m semicircle; ~final (pl ~finais) f semifinal

seminário /semi'nariu/ m (aula) seminar; (colégio religioso) seminary

sem-número /sẽ'numeru/ m um ~ de innumerable

sempre /'sẽpri/ adv always; como ~ as usual; para ~ for ever; ~ que whenever

sem-|terra /sẽ'tɛxa/ m/f invar landless labourer; ~teto a homeless □ m/f homeless person; ~vergonha a invar brazen □ m/f invar scoundrel

sena|do /se'nadu/ m senate; ~dor m senator

senão /si'nãw/ conj otherwise; (mas antes) but rather □ m snag

senda /'sẽda/ f path

senha /'seɲa/ f (palavra) password; (número) code; (sinal) signal

senhor /se'ɲor/ m gentleman; (homem idoso) older man; (tratamento) sir (f ~a) mighty; Senhor (com nome) Mr; (Deus) Lord; o ~ (você) you

senho|ra /se'ɲora/ f lady; (mulher idosa) older woman; (tratamento) madam; Senhora (com nome) Mrs; a ~ra (você) you; nossa ~ra! (fam) gosh; ~ria f Vossa Senhoria you; ~rita f young lady; (tratamento) miss; Senhorita (com nome) Miss

se|nil (pl ~nis) a senile; ~nilidade f senility

sensação /sẽsa'sãw/ f sensation

sensacio|nal /sẽsasio'naw/ (pl ~nais) a sensational; ~nalismo m sensationalism; ~nalista a sensationalist

sen|sato /sẽ'satu/ a sensible; ~sibilidade f sensitivity; ~sível (pl ~síveis) a sensitive; (que se pode sentir) noticeable; ~so m sense; ~sual (pl ~suais) a sensual

sen|tado /sẽ'tadu/ a sitting; ~tar vt/i sit; ~tar-se vpr sit down

sentença /sẽ'tẽsa/ f sentence

sentido /sẽ'tʃidu/ m sense; (direção) direction □ a hurt; fazer ~ ou ter ~ make sense

sentimen|tal /sẽtʃimẽ'taw/ (pl ~tais) a sentimental; vida ~tal love life; ~to m feeling

sentinela /sẽtʃiˈnɛla/ f sentry

sentir /sẽˈtʃir/ vt feel; (notar) sense; smell <cheiro>; taste <gosto>; tell <diferença>; (ficar magoado por) be hurt by □ vi feel; ~-se vpr feel; sinto muito I'm very sorry

separação /separaˈsãw/ f separation; ~rado a separate; (casal) separated; ~rar vt separate; ~rar-se vpr separate

séptico /ˈsɛptʃiku/ a septic

sepultar /sepuwˈtar/ vt bury; ~tura f grave

sequência /seˈkwẽsia/ f sequence

sequer /seˈkɛr/ adv nem ~ not even

sequestrador /sekwestraˈdor/ m kidnapper; (de avião) hijacker; ~trar vt kidnap <pessoa>; hijack <avião>; sequestrate <bens>; ~tro /ɛ/ m (de pessoa) kidnapping; (de avião) hijack; (de bens) sequestration

ser /ser/ vi be □ m being; é (como resposta) yes; você gosta, não é? you like it, don't you?; ele foi morto he was killed; será que ele volta? I wonder if he's coming back; ou seja in other words; a não ~ except; a não ~ que unless; não sou de fofocar I'm not one to gossip

sereia /seˈreja/ f mermaid

serenata /sereˈnata/ f serenade

sereno /seˈrenu/ a serene; <tempo> fine

série /ˈsɛri/ f series; (na escola) grade; fora de ~ (fam) incredible

seriedade /serieˈdadʒi/ f seriousness

seringa /seˈrĩga/ f syringe; ~gueiro m rubber tapper

sério /ˈsɛriu/ a serious; (responsável) responsible; ~? really?; falar ~ be serious; levar a ~ take seriously

sermão /serˈmãw/ m sermon

serpente /serˈpẽtʃi/ f serpent; ~tear vi wind; ~tina f streamer

serra¹ /ˈsɛxa/ f (montanhas) mountain range

serra² /ˈsɛxa/ f (de serrar) saw; ~gem f sawdust; ~lheiro m locksmith

serrano /seˈxanu/ a mountain

serrar /seˈxar/ vt saw

sertanejo /sertaˈneʒu/ a from the backwoods □ m backwoodsman; ~tão m backwoods

servente /serˈvẽtʃi/ m/f labourer

Sérvia /ˈsɛrvia/ f Serbia

serviçal /serviˈsaw/ (pl ~çais) a helpful □ m/f servant; ~ço m service; (trabalho) work; (tarefa) job; estar de ~ço be on duty; ~dor m servant

servil /serˈviw/ (pl ~vis) a servile

sérvio /ˈsɛrviu/ a & m Serbian

servir /serˈvir/ vt serve □ vi serve; (ser adequado) do; (ser útil) be of use; <roupa, sapato etc> fit; ~-se

vpr (ao comer etc) help o.s. (de to); ~-se de make use of; ~ como ou de serve as; para que serve isso? what is this (used) for?

sessão /seˈsãw/ f session; (no cinema) showing, performance

sessenta /seˈsẽta/ a & m sixty

seta /ˈsɛta/ f arrow; (de carro) indicator

sete /ˈsɛtʃi/ a & m seven; ~centos a & m seven hundred

setembro /seˈtẽbru/ m September

setenta /seˈtẽta/ a & m seventy

sétimo /ˈsɛtʃimu/ a seventh

setor /seˈtor/ m sector

setuagésimo /setuaˈʒɛzimu/ a seventieth

seu /sew/ a (f sua) (dele) his; (dela) her; (de coisa) its; (deles) their; (de você, de vocês) your □ pron (dele) his; (dela) hers; (deles) theirs; (de você, de vocês) yours; ~ idiota! you idiot!; seu João Mr John

severidade /severiˈdadʒi/ f severity; ~ro /ɛ/ a severe

sexagésimo /seksaˈʒɛzimu/ a sixtieth

sexo /ˈsɛksu/ m sex; fazer ~ have sex

sexta /ˈsɛsta/ f Friday; ~ta-feira (pl ~tas-feiras) f Friday; Sexta-feira Santa Good Friday; ~to /e/ a & m sixth

sexual /seksuˈaw/ (pl ~ais) a sexual; vida ~al sex life

sexy /ˈsɛksi/ a invar sexy

shopping /ˈʃopi/ (pl ~s) m shopping centre, (Amer) mall

short /ˈʃortʃi/ m (pl ~s) shorts; um ~ a pair of shorts

show /ˈʃow/ m (pl ~s) m show; (de música) concert

si /si/ pron (ele) himself; (ela) herself; (coisa) itself; (você) yourself; (eles) themselves; (vocês) yourselves; (qualquer pessoa) oneself; em ~ in itself; fora de ~ beside o.s.; cheio de ~ full of o.s.; voltar a ~ come round

sibilar /sibiˈlar/ vi hiss

SIDA /ˈsida/ f (Port) AIDS

sideral /sideˈraw/ (pl ~rais) a espaço ~ral outer space.

siderurgia /siderurˈʒia/ f iron and steel industry

siderúrgica /sideˈrurʒika/ f steelworks; ~co a iron and steel □ m steelworker

sifão /siˈfãw/ m syphon

sífilis /ˈsifilis/ f syphilis

sigilo /siˈʒilu/ m secrecy; ~so /o/ a secret

sigla /ˈsigla/ f acronym

signatário /signaˈtariu/ m signatory

significação /signifikaˈsãw/ f significance; ~cado m meaning; ~car vt mean; ~cativo a significant

signo /'signu/ m sign
silaba /'silaba/ f syllable
silenciar /silẽsi'ar/ vt silence
silêncio /si'lẽsiu/ m silence
silencioso /silẽsi'ozu/ a silent □ m silencer, (Amer) muffler
silhueta /siʎu'eta/ f silhouette
silício /si'lisiu/ m silicon
silicone /sili'kɔni/ m silicone
silo /'silu/ m silo
silvar /siw'var/ vi hiss
sil|vestre /siw'vɛstri/ a wild; ~vicultura f forestry
sim /sĩ/ adv yes; acho que ~ I think so
simbólico /sĩ'bɔliku/ a symbolic
simbo|lismo /sĩbo'lizmu/ m symbolism; ~lizar vt symbolize
símbolo /'sĩbolu/ m symbol
si|metria /sime'tria/ f symmetry; ~métrico a symmetrical
similar /simi'lar/ a similar
sim|patia /sĩpa'tʃia/ f (qualidade) pleasantness; (afeto) fondness (por for); (compreensão, apoio) sympathy; pl sympathies; ter ~patia por be fond of; ~pático a nice
simpati|zante /sĩpatʃi'zãtʃi/ a sympathetic □ m/f sympathizer; ~zar vi ~zar com take a liking to <pessoa>; sympathize with <idéias, partido etc>
simples /'sĩplis/ a invar simple; (único) single □ f (no tênis etc) singles; ~mente adv simply
simpli|cidade /sĩplisi'dadʒi/ f simplicity; ~ficar vt simplify
simplório /sĩ'plɔriu/ a simple
simpósio /sĩ'pɔziu/ m symposium
simu|lação /simula'sãw/ f simulation; ~lar vt simulate
simultâneo /simuw'taniu/ a simultaneous
sina /'sina/ f fate
sinagoga /sina'gɔga/ f synagogue
si|nal /si'naw/ m (pl ~nais) m sign; (aviso, de rádio etc) signal; (de trânsito) traffic light; (no telefone) tone; (dinheiro) deposit; (na pele) mole; por ~nal as a matter of fact; ~nal de pontuação punctuation mark; ~naleira f traffic lights; ~nalização f (na rua) road signs; ~nalizar vt signal; signpost <rua, cidade>
since|ridade /sĩseri'dadʒi/ f sincerity; ~ro /ɛ/ a sincere
sincro|nia /sĩkro'nia/ f synchronization; ~nizar vt synchronize
sindi|cal /sĩdʒi'kaw/ (pl ~cais) a trade union; ~calismo m trade unionism; ~calista m/f trade unionist; ~calizar vt unionize; ~cato m trade union
síndico /'sĩdʒiku/ m house manager

síndrome /'sĩdromi/ f syndrome
sineta /si'neta/ f bell
sin|fonia /sĩfo'nia/ f symphony; ~fônica f symphony orchestra
singe|leza /sĩʒe'leza/ f simplicity; ~lo /ɛ/ a simple
singu|lar /sĩgu'lar/ a singular; (estranho) peculiar; ~larizar vt single out
sinis|trado /sinis'tradu/ a damaged; ~tro a sinister □ m accident
sino /'sinu/ m bell
sinônimo /si'nonimu/ a synonymous □ m synonym
sintaxe /sĩ'taksi/ f syntax
síntese /'sĩtezi/ f synthesis
sin|tético /sĩ'tɛtʃiku/ a (artificial) synthetic; (resumido) concise; ~tetizar vt summarize
sinto|ma /sĩ'toma/ m symptom; ~mático a symptomatic
sintoni|zador /sĩtoniza'dor/ m tuner; ~zar vt tune <rádio, TV>; tune in to <emissora> □ vi be in tune (com with)
sinuca /si'nuka/ f snooker
sinuoso /sinu'ozu/ a winding
sinusite /sinu'zitʃi/ f sinusitis
sirene /si'rɛni/ f siren
siri /si'ri/ m crab
Síria /'siria/ f Syria
sírio /'siriu/ a & m Syrian
siso /'sizu/ m good sense
siste|ma /sis'tema/ m system; ~mático a systematic
sisudo /si'zudu/ a serious
sítio /'sitʃiu/ m (chácara) farm; (Port: local) place; estado de ~ state of siege
situ|ação /situa'sãw/ f situation; (no governo) party in power; ~ar vt situate; ~ar-se vpr be situated; <pessoa> position o.s.
smoking /iz'mɔkĩ/ (pl ~s) m dinner jacket, (Amer) tuxedo
só /sɔ/ a alone; (sentindo solidão) lonely □ adv only; um ~ voto one single vote; ~ um carro only one car; a ~s alone; imagina ~ just imagine; ~ que except (that)
soalho /so'aʎu/ m floor
soar /so'ar/ vt/i sound
sob /'sobi/ prep under
sobera|nia /sobera'nia/ f sovereignty; ~no a & m sovereign
soberbo /so'berbu/ a <pessoa> haughty; (magnífico) splendid
sobra /'sobra/ f surplus; pl leftovers; tempo de ~ (muito) plenty of time; ficar de ~ be left over; ter aco de ~ (sobrando) have sth left over
sobraçar /sobra'sar/ vt carry under one's arm
sobrado /so'bradu/ m (casa) house; (andar) upper floor

sobrancelha /sobrã'seʎa/ f eyebrow

so|brar /so'brar/ vi be left; ~bram-me dois I have two left

sobre /'sobri/ prep (em cima de) on; (por cima de, acima de) over; (acerca de) about

sobreaviso /sobria'vizu/ m estar de ~ be on one's guard

sobrecapa /sobri'kapa/ f dust jacket

sobrecarregar /sobrikaxe'gar/ vt overload

sobreloja /sobri'lɔʒa/ f mezzanine

sobremesa /sobri'meza/ f dessert

sobrenatu|ral /sobrinatu'raw/ (pl ~rais) a supernatural

sobrenome /sobri'nomi/ m surname

sobrepor /sobri'por/ vt superimpose

sobrepujar /sobripu'ʒar/ vt (em altura) tower over; (em capacidade etc) surpass; overwhelm <adversário>; overcome <problemas>

sobrescritar /sobriskri'tar/ vt address

sobressair /sobrisa'ir/ vi stand out; ~-se vpr stand out

sobressalente /sobrisa'lẽtʃi/ a spare

sobressal|tar /sobrisaw'tar/ vt startle; ~tar-se vpr be startled; ~to m (movimento) start; (susto) fright

sobretaxa /sobri'taʃa/ f surcharge

sobretudo /sobri'tudu/ adv above all □ m overcoat

sobrevir /sobri'vir/ vi happen suddenly; (seguir) ensue; ~ a follow

sobrevi|vência /sobrivi'vẽsia/ f survival; ~vente a surviving □ m/f survivor; ~ver vt/i ~ver (a) survive

sobrevoar /sobrivo'ar/ vt fly over

sobri|nha /so'briɲa/ f niece; ~nho m nephew

sóbrio /'sɔbriu/ a sober

socar /so'kar/ vt (esmurrar) punch; (amassar) crush

soci|al /sosi'aw/ (pl ~ais) a social; camisa ~al dress shirt; ~alismo m socialism; ~alista a & m/f socialist; ~alite /-a'lajtʃi/ m/f socialite; ~ável (pl ~áveis) a sociable

sociedade /sosie'dadʒi/ f society; (parceria) partnership; ~ anônima limited company

sócio /'sɔsiu/ m (de empresa) partner; (de clube) member

socio-econômico /sosioeko'nomiku/ a socio-economic

soci|ologia /sosiolo'ʒia/ f sociology; ~ológico a sociological; ~ólogo m sociologist

soco /'soku/ m punch; dar um ~ em punch

socor|rer /soko'xer/ vt help; ~ro m aid □ int help; primeiros ~ros first aid

soda /'sɔda/ f (água) soda water; ~ cáustica caustic soda

sódio /'sɔdʒiu/ m sodium

sofá /so'fa/ m sofa; ~-cama (pl ~s-camas) m sofa-bed

sofisticado /sofistʃi'kadu/ a sophisticated

so|fredor /sofre'dor/ a martyred; ~frer vt suffer <dor, derrota, danos etc>; have <acidente>; undergo <operação, mudança etc> □ vi suffer; ~frer de suffer from <doença>; have trouble with <coração etc>; ~frido a long-suffering; ~frimento m suffering; ~frível (pl ~fríveis) a passable

soft /'sɔftʃi/ (pl ~s) m software package; ~ware m software; (um) software package

so|gra /'sɔgra/ f mother-in-law; ~gro /o/ m father-in-law; ~gros /ɔ/ m pl in-laws

soja /'sɔʒa/ f soya, (Amer) soy

sol /sɔw/ (pl sóis) m sun; faz ~ it's sunny

sola /'sɔla/ f sole; ~do a <bolo> flat

solapar /sola'par/ vt undermine

solar[1] /so'lar/ a solar

solar[2] /so'lar/ vt sole <sapato> □ vi <bolo> go flat

solavanco /sola'vãku/ m jolt; dar ~s jolt

soldado /sow'dadu/ m soldier

sol|dadura /sowda'dura/ f weld; ~dar vt weld

soldo /'sowdu/ m pay

soleira /so'lera/ f doorstep

sole|ne /so'leni/ a solemn; ~nidade f (cerimônia) ceremony; (qualidade) solemnity

soletrar /sole'trar/ vt spell

solici|tação /solisita'sãw/ f request (de for); (por escrito) application (de for); ~tante m/f applicant; ~tar vt request; (por escrito) apply for

solícito /so'lisitu/ a helpful

solidão /soli'dãw/ f loneliness

soli|dariedade /solidarie'dadʒi/ f solidarity; ~dário a supportive (com of)

soli|dez /soli'des/ f solidity; ~dificar vt solidify; ~dificar-se vpr solidify

sólido /'sɔlidu/ a & m solid

solista /so'lista/ m/f soloist

solitá|ria /soli'taria/ f (verme) tapeworm; (cela) solitary confinement; ~rio a solitary

solo[1] /'sɔlu/ m (terra) soil; (chão) ground

solo[2] /'sɔlu/ m solo

soltar /sow'tar/ vt let go <prisioneiros, animal etc>; let loose <cães>; (deixar de segurar) let go of; loosen <gravata, corda etc>; let down

<*cabelo*>; let out <*grito, suspiro etc*>; let off <*foguetes*>; tell <*piada*>; take off <*freio*>; ~-se *vpr* <*peça, parafuso*> come loose; (*pessoa*) let o.s. go

soltei|ra /sow'tera/ *f* single woman; ~rão *m* bachelor; ~ro a single □ *m* single man; ~rona *f* spinster

solto /'sowtu/ *a* (*livre*) free; <*cães*> loose; <*cabelo*> down; <*arroz*> fluffy; (*frouxo*) loose; (*à vontade*) relaxed; (*abandonado*) abandoned; correr ~ run wild

solução /solu'sãw/ *f* solution

soluçar /solu'sar/ *vi* (*ao chorar*) sob; (*engasgar*) hiccup

solucionar /solusio'nar/ *vt* solve

soluço /so'lusu/ *m* (*ao chorar*) sob; (*engasgo*) hiccup; estar com ~s have the hiccups

solú|vel /so'luvew/ (*pl* ~veis) *a* soluble

solvente /sow'vẽtʃi/ *a* & *m* solvent

som /sõ/ *m* sound; (*aparelho*) stereo; um ~ (*fam*) (*música*) a bit of music

so|ma /'soma/ *f* sum; ~mar *vt* add up <*números etc*>; (*ter como soma*) add up to

sombra /'sõbra/ *f* shadow; (*área abrigada do sol*) shade; à ~ de in the shade of; sem ~ de dúvida without a shadow of a doubt

sombre|ado /sõbri'adu/ *a* shady □ *m* shading; ~ar *vt* shade

sombrinha /sõ'briɲa/ *f* parasol

sombrio /sõ'briu/ *a* gloomy

somente /so'mẽtʃi/ *adv* only

sonâmbulo /so'nãbulu/ *m* sleepwalker

sonante /so'nãtʃi/ *a* moeda ~ hard cash

sonata /so'nata/ *f* sonata

son|da /'sõda/ *f* probe; ~dagem *f* (*no mar*) sounding; (*de terreno*) survey; ~dagem de opinião opinion poll; ~dar *vt* probe; sound <*profundeza*>; (*fig*) sound out <*pessoas, opiniões etc*>

soneca /so'nɛka/ *f* nap; tirar uma ~ have a nap

sone|gação /sonega'sãw/ *f* (*de impostos*) tax evasion; ~gador *m* tax dodger; ~gar *vt* withhold

soneto /so'netu/ *m* sonnet

so|nhador /soɲa'dor/ *a* dreamy □ *m* dreamer; ~nhar *vt/i* dream (com about); ~nho /'soɲu/ *m* dream; (*doce*) doughnut

sono /'sonu/ *m* sleep; estar com ~ be sleepy; pegar no ~ get to sleep; ~lento *a* sleepy

sono|plastia /sonoplas'tʃia/ *f* sound effects; ~ridade *f* sound quality; ~ro /ɔ/ *a* sound; <*voz*> sonorous; <*consoante*> voiced

sonso /'sõsu/ *a* devious

sopa /'sopa/ *f* soup

sopapo /so'papu/ *m* slap; dar um ~ em slap

sopé /so'pɛ/ *m* foot

sopeira /so'pera/ *f* soup tureen

soprano /so'pranu/ *m/f* soprano

so|prar /so'prar/ *vt* blow <*folhas etc*>; blow up <*balão*>; blow out <*vela*> □ *vi* blow; ~pro *m* blow; (*de vento*) puff; instrumento de ~pro wind instrument

soquete[1] /so'kɛtʃi/ *f* ankle sock

soquete[2] /so'ketʃi/ *m* socket

sordidez /sordʒi'des/ *f* sordidness; (*imundície*) squalor

sórdido /'sordʒidu/ *a* (*reles*) sordid; (*imundo*) squalid

soro /'soru/ *m* (*remédio*) serum; (*de leite*) whey

sorrateiro /soxa'teru/ *a* crafty

sor|ridente /soxi'dẽtʃi/ *a* smiling; ~rir *vi* smile; ~riso *m* smile

sorte /'sortʃi/ *f* luck; (*destino*) fate; pessoa de ~ lucky person; por ~ luckily; ter *ou* dar ~ be lucky; tive a ~ de conhecê-lo I was lucky enough to meet him; tirar a ~ draw lots; trazer *ou* dar ~ bring good luck

sor|tear /sortʃi'ar/ *vt* draw for <*prêmio*>; select in a draw <*pessoa*>; ~teio *m* draw

sorti|do /sor'tʃidu/ *a* assorted; ~mento *m* assortment

sorumbático /sorũ'batʃiku/ *a* sombre, gloomy

sorver /sor'ver/ *vt* sip <*bebida*>

sósia /'sɔzia/ *m/f* double

soslaio /soz'laju/ *m* de ~ sideways; <*olhar*> askance

sosse|gado /sose'gadu/ *a* <*vida*> quiet; ficar ~gado <*pessoa*> rest assured; ~gar *vt* reassure □ *vi* rest; ~go /e/ *m* peace

sótão /'sɔtãw/ (*pl* ~s) *m* attic, loft

sotaque /so'taki/ *m* accent

soterrar /sote'xar/ *vt* bury

soutien /suti'ã/ (*pl* ~s) *m* (*Port*) bra

sova|co /so'vaku/ *m* armpit; ~queira *f* BO, body odour

soviético /sovi'ɛtʃiku/ *a* & *m* Soviet

sovi|na /so'vina/ *a* stingy, mean, (*Amer*) cheap □ *m/f* cheapskate; ~nice *f* stinginess, meanness, (*Amer*) cheapness

sozinho /so'ziɲu/ *a* (*sem ninguém*) alone, on one's own; (*por si próprio*) by o.s.; falar ~ talk to o.s.

spray /is'prej/ (*pl* ~s) *m* spray

squash /is'kwɛʃ/ *m* squash

stand /is'tãdʒi/ (*pl* ~s) *m* stand

status /is'tatus/ *m* status

stripper /is'triper/ (*pl* ~s) *m/f* stripper

strip-tease /istripi'tʃizi/ m striptease

sua /'sua/ a & pron veja **seu**

su|ado /su'adu/ a <pessoa, roupa> sweaty; (fig) hard-earned; ~ar vt/i sweat; ~ar por/para (fig) work hard for/to; ~ar frio come out in a cold sweat

sua|ve /su'avi/ a <toque, subida> gentle; <gosto, cheiro, dor, inverno> mild; <música, voz> soft; <vinho> smooth; <trabalho> light; <prestações> easy; ~vidade f gentleness; mildness; softness; smoothness; veja **suave**; ~vizar vt soften; soothe <dor, pessoa>

subalterno /subaw'tɛrnu/ a & m subordinate

subconsciente /subikõsi'ẽtʃi/ a & m subconscious

subdesenvolvido /subidʒizĩvow'vidu/ a underdeveloped

súbdito /'subditu/ m (Port) veja **súdito**

subdividir /subidʒivi'dʒir/ vt subdivide

subemprego /subĩ'pregu/ m menial job

subemprei|tar /subĩprej'tar/ vt subcontract; ~teiro m subcontractor

subenten|der /subĩtẽ'der/ vt infer; ~dido a implied □ m insinuation

subestimar /subestʃi'mar/ vt underestimate

su|bida /su'bida/ f (ação) ascent; (ladeira) incline; (de preços etc, fig) rise; ~bir vi go up; <rio, águas> rise □ vt go up, climb; ~bir em climb <árvore>; get up onto <mesa>; get on <ônibus>

súbito /'subitu/ a sudden; (de) ~ suddenly

subjacente /subiʒa'sẽtʃi/ a underlying

subjeti|vidade /subiʒetʃivi'dadʒi/ f subjectivity; ~vo a subjective

subjugar /subiʒu'gar/ vt subjugate

subjuntivo /subiʒũ'tʃivu/ a & m subjunctive

sublevar-se /suble'varsi/ vpr rise up

sublime /su'blimi/ a sublime

subli|nhado /subli'nadu/ m underlining; ~nhar vt underline

sublocar /sublo'kar/ vt/i sublet

submarino /subima'rinu/ a underwater □ m submarine

submer|gir /subimer'ʒir/ vt submerge; ~gir-se vpr submerge; ~so a submerged

submeter /subime'ter/ vt subject (a to); put down, subdue <povo, rebeldes etc>; submit <projeto>; ~-se vpr (render-se) submit; ~-se a (sofrer) undergo

submis|são /subimi'sãw/ f submission; ~so a submissive

submundo /subi'mũdu/ m underworld

subnutrição /subinutri'sãw/ f malnutrition

subordi|nado /subordʒi'nadu/ a & m subordinate; ~nar vt subordinate (a to)

subor|nar /subor'nar/ vt bribe; ~no /o/ m bribe

subproduto /subipro'dutu/ m byproduct

subs|crever /subiskre'ver/ vt sign <carta etc>; subscribe to <opinião>; subscribe <dinheiro> (para to); ~crever-se vpr sign one's name; ~crição f subscription; ~crito pp de ~crever

subseqüente /subise'kwẽtʃi/ a subsequent

subserviente /subiservi'ẽtʃi/ a subservient

subsidiar /subisidʒi'ar/ vt subsidize

subsidiá|ria /subisidʒi'aria/ f subsidiary; ~rio a subsidiary

subsídio /subi'sidʒiu/ m subsidy

subsistência /subisis'tẽsia/ f subsistence

subsolo /subi'solu/ m (porão) basement

substância /subis'tãsia/ f substance

substan|cial /subistãsi'aw/ (pl ~ciais) a substantial; ~tivo m noun

substitu|ição /subistʃitui'sãw/ f replacement; substitution; ~ir vt (pôr B no lugar de A) replace (A por B A with B); (usar B em vez de A) substitute (A por B B for A); ~to a & m substitute

subterfúgio /subiter'fuʒiu/ m subterfuge

subterrâneo /subite'xaniu/ a underground

sub|til /sub'til/ (pl ~tis) a (Port) veja **sutil**

subtra|ção /subitra'sãw/ f subtraction; ~ir vt subtract <números>; (roubar) steal

suburbano /subur'banu/ a suburban

subúrbio /su'burbiu/ m suburbs

subven|ção /subivẽ'sãw/ f grant, subsidy; ~cionar vt subsidize

subver|são /subiver'sãw/ f subversion; ~sivo a subversive

suca|ta /su'kata/ f scrap metal; ~tear vt scrap

sucção /suk'sãw/ f suction

suce|der /suse'der/ vi (acontecer) happen □ vt ~der a succeed <rei etc>; (vir depois) follow; ~der-se vpr follow on from one another; ~dido a bem ~dido successful suces|são /suse'sãw/ f succession; ~sivo a successive; ~so /ε/ m success; (música) hit; fazer ou ter ~so be successful; ~sor m successor

sucinto /su'sĩtu/ a succinct

suco /'suku/ m juice

suculento /suku'lẽtu/ a juicy

sucumbir /sukũ'bir/ vi succumb (to)

sucur|sal /sukur'saw/ (pl ~sais) f branch

Sudão /su'dãw/ m Sudan

sudário /su'dariu/ m shroud

sudeste /su'dεstʃi/ a & m southeast; o Sudeste Asiático Southeast Asia

súdito /'sudʒitu/ m subject

sudoeste /sudo'εstʃi/ a & m southwest

Suécia /su'εsia/ f Sweden

sueco /su'εku/ a & m Swedish

suéter /su'εter/ m/f sweater

sufici|ência /sufisi'ẽsia/ f sufficiency; ~ente a enough, sufficient; o ~ente enough

sufixo /su'fiksu/ m suffix

suflê /su'fle/ m soufflé

sufo|cante /sufo'kãtʃi/ a stifling; ~car vt (asfixiar) suffocate; (fig) stifle □ vi suffocate; ~co /o/ m hassle; estar num ~co be having a tough time

sufrágio /su'fraʒiu/ m suffrage

sugar /su'gar/ vt suck

sugerir /suʒe'rir/ vt suggest

suges|tão /suʒes'tãw/ f suggestion; dar uma ~tão make a suggestion; ~tivo a suggestive

Suíça /su'isa/ f Switzerland

suíças /su'isas/ f pl sideburns

sui|cida /sui'sida/ a suicidal □ m/f suicide (victim); ~cidar-se vpr commit suicide; ~cídio m suicide

suíço /su'isu/ a & m Swiss

suíno /su'inu/ a & m pig

suíte /su'itʃi/ f suite

su|jar /su'ʒar/ vt dirty; (fig) sully <reputação etc> □ vi, ~jar-se vpr get dirty; ~jar-se com alg queer one's pitch with s.o.; ~jeira f dirt; (uma) dirty trick

suje|tar /suʒej'tar/ vt subject (to); ~tar-se vpr subject o.s. (to); ~to a subject (a to) □ m (de oração) subject; (pessoa) person

su|jidade /suʒi'dadʒi/ f (Port) dirt; ~jo a dirty

sul /suw/ a invar & m south; ~-africano a & m South African; ~-americano a & m South American; ~-coreano a & m South Korean

sul|car /suw'kar/ vt furrow <testa>; ~co m furrow

sulfúrico /suw'furiku/ a sulphuric

sulista /su'lista/ a southern □ m/f southerner

sultão /suw'tãw/ m sultan

sumário /su'mariu/ a <justiça> summary; <roupa> skimpy, brief

su|miço /su'misu/ m disappearance; dar ~miço em spirit away; tomar chá de ~miço disappear; ~mido a <cor, voz> faint; ele anda ~mido he's disappeared; ~mir vi disappear

sumo /'sumu/ m (Port) juice

sumptuoso /sũtu'ozu/ a (Port) veja suntuoso

sunga /'sũga/ f swimming trunks

suntuoso /sũtu'ozu/ a sumptuous

suor /su'or/ m sweat

superar /supe'rar/ vt overcome <dificuldade etc>; surpass <expectativa, pessoa>

superá|vel /supe'ravew/ (pl ~veis) a surmountable; ~vit (pl ~vits) m surplus

superestimar /superestʃi'mar/ vt overestimate

superestrutura /superistru'tura/ f superstructure

superfici|al /superfisi'aw/ (pl ~ais) a superficial

superfície /super'fisi/ f surface; (medida) area

supérfluo /su'pεrfluu/ a superfluous

superintendência /superitẽ'dẽsia/ f bureau

superi|or /superi'or/ a (de cima) upper; <ensino> higher; <número, temperatura etc> greater (a than); (melhor) superior (a to) □ m superior; ~oridade f superiority

superlativo /superla'tʃivu/ a & m superlative

superlota|ção /superlota'sãw/ f overcrowding; ~do a overcrowded

supermercado /supermer'kadu/ m supermarket

superpotência /superpo'tẽsia/ f superpower

superpovoado /superpovo'adu/ a overpopulated

supersecreto /superse'krεtu/ a top secret

supersensí|vel /supersẽ'sivew/ (pl ~veis) a oversensitive

supersônico /super'soniku/ a supersonic

supersti|ção /superstʃi'sãw/ f superstition; ~cioso /o/ a superstitious

supervi|são /supervi'zãw/ f supervision; ~sionar vt supervise; ~sor m supervisor

supetão /supe'tãw/ m de ~ all of a sudden

suplantar /suplã'tar/ vt supplant

suplemen|tar /suplemẽ'tar/ a supplementary □ vt supplement; ~to m supplement suplente /su'plētʃi/ a & m/f substitute

supletivo /suple'tʃivu/ a supplementary; ensino ∼ adult education

súplica /'suplika/ f plea; tom de ∼ pleading tone

suplicar /supli'kar/ vt plead for; (em juízo) petition for

suplício /su'plisiu/ m torture; (fig: aflição) torment

supor /su'por/ vt suppose

suportar /supor'tar/ vt (sustentar) support; (tolerar) stand, bear; ∼tável (pl ∼táveis) a bearable; ∼te /ɔ/ m support

suposição /supozi'sāw/ f supposition

supositório /supozi'toriu/ m suppository

supostamente /suposta'mētʃi/ adv supposedly; ∼to /o/ a supposed; ∼to que supposing that

supremacia /suprema'sia/ f supremacy; ∼mo /e/ a supreme

supressão /supre'sāw/ f (de lei, cargo, privilégio) abolition; (de jornal, informação, nomes) suppression; (de palavras, cláusula) deletion

suprimento /supri'mētu/ m supply

suprimir /supri'mir/ vt abolish <lei, cargo, privilégio>; suppress <jornal, informação, nomes>; delete <palavras, cláusula>

suprir /su'prir/ vt provide for <família, necessidades>; make up for <falta>; make up <quantia>; supply <o que falta>; (substituir) take the place of; ∼ alg de provide s.o. with; ∼ A por B substitute B for A

supurar /supu'rar/ vi turn septic

surdez /sur'des/ f deafness; ∼do a deaf; <consoante> voiceless □ m deaf person; os ∼dos the deaf; ∼do-mudo (pl ∼dos-mudos) a deaf and dumb □ m deaf-mute

surfe /'surfi/ m surfing; ∼fista m/f surfer

surgimento /surʒi'mētu/ m appearance; ∼gir vi arise; ∼gir à mente spring to mind

Suriname /suri'nami/ m Surinam

surpreendente /surprič'dētʃi/ a surprising; ∼der vt surprise □ vi be surprising; ∼der-se upr be surprised (de at)

surpresa /sur'preza/ f surprise; de ∼sa by surprise; ∼so /e/ a surprised

surra /'suxa/ f thrashing; ∼rado a <roupa> worn-out; ∼rar vt thrash <pessoa>; wear out <roupa>

surrealismo /suxea'lizmu/ m surrealism; ∼ta a & m/f surrealist

surtir /sur'tʃir/ vt produce; ∼ efeito be effective

surto /'surtu/ m outbreak

suscept- (Port) veja suscet-

susceptibilidade /susetʃibili'dadʒi/ f (de pessoa) sensitivity; ∼tível (pl ∼tíveis) a <pessoa> touchy, sensitive; ∼tível de open to

suscitar /susi'tar/ vt cause; raise <dúvida, suspeita>

suspeita /sus'pejta/ f suspicion; ∼tar vt/i ∼tar (de) suspect; ∼to a suspicious; (duvidoso) suspect □ m suspect; ∼toso /o/ a suspicious

suspender /suspē'der/ vt suspend; ∼são f suspension; ∼se m suspense; ∼so a suspended; ∼sórios m pl braces, (Amer) suspenders

suspirar /suspi'rar/ vi sigh; ∼rar por long for; ∼ro m sigh; (doce) meringue

sussurrar /susu'xar/ vt/i whisper; ∼ro m whisper

sustar /sus'tar/ vt/i stop

sustentáculo /sustē'takulu/ m mainstay; ∼tar vt support; (afirmar) maintain; ∼to m support; (ganha-pão) livelihood

susto /'sustu/ m fright

sutiã /sutʃi'ã/ m bra

sutil /su'tʃiw/ (pl ∼tis) a subtle; ∼tileza /e/ f subtlety

sutura /su'tura/ f suture; ∼rar vt suture

T

tá /ta/ int (fam) OK; veja estar

tabacaria /tabaka'ria/ f tobacconist's; ∼co m tobacco

tabefe /ta'bɛfi/ m slap

tabela /ta'bɛla/ f table; ∼lar vt tabulate

tablado /ta'bladu/ m platform

tabu /ta'bu/ a & m taboo

tábua /'tabua/ f board; ∼ de passar roupa ironing board

tabuleiro /tabu'leru/ m (de xadrez etc) board

tabuleta /tabu'leta/ f (letreiro) sign

taça /'tasa/ f (prêmio) cup; (de champanhe etc) glass

tacada /ta'kada/ f shot; de uma ∼cada in one go; ∼car vt hit <bola>; (fam) throw

tacha /'tasa/ f tack

tachar /ta'sar/ vt brand (de as)

tachinha /ta'sina/ f drawing pin, (Amer) thumbtack

tácito /'tasitu/ a tacit

taciturno /tasi'turnu/ a taciturn

taco /'taku/ m (de golfe) club; (de bilhar) cue; (de hóquei) stick

tact- (Port) veja tat-

tagarela /taga'rela/ a chatty, talkative □ m/f chatterbox; ∼larvi chatter

tailan|dês /tajlã'des/ *a & m* (*f* ~**desa**) Thai

Tailândia /taj'ladʒia/ *f* Thailand

tailleur /ta'jer/ (*pl* ~ s) *m* suit

Taiti /taj'tʃi/ *m* Tahiti

tal /taw/ (*pl* tais) *a* such; que ~? what do you think?, (*Port*) how are you?; que ~ uma cerveja? how about a beer?; ~ como such as; ~ qual just like; um ~ de João someone called John; e ~ and so on

tala /'tala/ *f* splint

talão /ta'lãw/ *m* stub; ~ de cheques chequebook

talco /'tawku/ *m* talc

talen|to /ta'lẽtu/ *m* talent; ~**toso** /o/ *a* talented

talhar /ta'ʎar/ *vt* slice < *dedo, carne*>; carve < *pedra, imagem*>

talharim /taʎa'rĩ/ *m* tagliatelle

talher /ta'ʎɛr/ *m* set of cutlery; *pl* cutlery

talho /'taʎu/ *m* (*Port*) butcher's

talismã /taliz'mã/ *m* charm, talisman

talo /'talu/ *m* stalk

talvez /taw'ves/ *adv* perhaps; ~ ele venha amanhã he may come tomorrow

tamanco /ta'mãku/ *m* clog

tamanho /ta'maɲu/ *m* size □ *adj* such

tâmara /'tamara/ *f* date

tamarindo /tama'rĩdu/ *m* tamarind

também /tã'bẽj/ *adv* also; ~ não not ... either, neither

tam|bor /tã'bor/ *m* drum; ~**borilar** *vi* < *dedos*> drum; < *chuva*> patter; ~**borim** *m* tambourine

Tâmisa /'tamiza/ *m* Thames

tam|pa /'tãpa/ *f* lid; ~**pão** *m* (*vaginal*) tampon; ~**par** *vt* put the lid on < *recipiente*>; (*tapar*) cover; ~**pinha** *f* top□ *m/f* (*fam*) shorthouse

tampouco /tã'poku/ *adv* nor, neither

tanga /'tãga/ *f* G-string; (*aventa*) loincloth

tangente /tã'ʒẽtʃi/ *f* tangent; pela ~ (*fig*) narrowly

tangerina /tãʒe'rina/ *f* tangerine

tango /'tãgu/ *m* tango

tanque /'tãki/ *m* tank; (*para lavar roupa*) sink

tanto /'tãtu/ *a & pron* so much; *pl* so many □ *adv* so much; ~ ... como ... both ... and ...; ~ (...) quanto as much (...) as; ~ melhor so much the better; ~ tempo so long; vinte e ~s anos twenty odd years; nem ~ not as much; um ~ difícil somewhat difficult; ~ que to the extent that

Tanzânia /tã'zania/ *f* Tanzania

tão /tãw/ *adv* so; ~ grande quanto as big as; ~-**somente** *adv* solely

tapa /'tapa/ *m ou f* slap; dar um ~ em slap

tapar /ta'par/ *vt* (*cobrir*) cover; block < *luz, vista*>; cork < *garrafa*>

tapeçaria /tapesa'ria/ *f* (*pano*) tapestry; (*loja*) carpet shop

tape|te /ta'petʃ/ *vt* carpet; ~**te** /e/ *m* carpet

tapioca /tapi'ɔka/ *f* tapioca

tapume /ta'pumi/ *m* fence

taquicardia /takikar'dʒia/ *f* palpitations

taquigra|far /takigra'far/ *vt/i* write in shorthand; ~**fia** *f* shorthand

tara /'tara/ *f* fetish; ~**do** *a* sex-crazed □ *m* sex maniac; ser ~**do** por be crazy about

tarefa /ta'rɛfa/ *f* task, job

tarifa /ta'rifa/ *f* tariff; ~ de embarque airport tax

tarimbado /tarĩ'badu/ *a* experienced

tarja /'tarʒa/ *f* strip

ta|rô /ta'ro/ *m* tarot; ~**rólogo** *m* tarot reader

tar|dar /tar'dar/ *vi* (*atrasar*) be late; (*demorar muito*) be long □ *vt* delay; ~**dar** a responder take a long time to answer, be a long time answering; o mais ~**dar** at the latest; sem mais ~**dar** without further delay; ~**de** *adv* late □ *f* afternoon; hoje à ~**de** this afternoon; à ~ da noite late at night; ~**dinha** *f* late afternoon; ~**dio** *a* late

tartamu|dear /tartamudʒi'ar/ *vi* stammer; ~**do** *a* stammering □ *m* stammerer

tártaro /'tartaru/ *m* tartar

tartaruga /tarta'ruga/ *f* (*bicho*) turtle; (*material*) tortoiseshell

tatear /tatʃi'ar/ *vt* feel □ *vi* feel one's way

táti|ca /'tatʃika/ *f* tactics; ~**co** *a* tactical

tá|til /'tatʃiw/ (*pl* ~**teis**) *a* tactile

tato /'tatu/ *m* (*sentido*) touch; (*diplomacia*) tact

tatu /ta'tu/ *m* armadillo

tatu|ador /tatua'dor/ *m* tattooist; ~**agem** *f* tattoo; ~**ar** *vt* tattoo

tauromaquia /tawroma'kia/ *f* bullfighting

taxa /'taʃa/ *f* (*a pagar*) charge; (*índice*) rate; ~ de câmbio exchange rate; ~ de juros interest rate; ~ rodoviária road tax

taxar /ta'ʃar/ *vt* tax

taxativo /taʃa'tʃivu/ *a* firm, categorical

táxi /'taksi/ *m* taxi

taxiar /taksi'ar/ *vi* taxi

taxímetro /tak'simetru/ *m* taxi meter

taxista /tak'sista/ *m/f* taxi driver

tchã /tʃã/ *m* (*fam*) special something

tchau /tʃaw/ *int* goodbye, bye

tcheco /'tʃɛku/ *a & m* Czech

Tchecoslováquia /tʃekoslo'vakia/ f Czechoslovakia

te /tʃi/ *pron* you; (*a ti*) to you

tear /tʃi'ar/ *m* loom

tea|tral /tʃia'traw/ (*pl* ~trais) *a* theatrical; <*grupo*> theatre; ~tro *m* theatre; ~trólogo *m* playwright

tece|lagem /tese'laʒẽ/ f (*trabalho*) weaving; (*fábrica*) textile factory; ~lão *m* (*f* ~lã) weaver

te|cer /te'ser/ *vt/i* weave; ~cido *m* cloth; (*no corpo*) tissue

te|cla /'tɛkla/ f key; ~cladista *m/f* (*músico*) keyboard player; (*de computador*) keyboard operator; ~clado *m* keyboard; ~clar *vt* key (in)

técni|ca /'tɛknika/ f technique; ~co a technical □ *m* specialist; (*de time*) manager; (*que mexe com máquinas*) technician

tecno|crata /tekno'krata/ *m/f* technocrat; ~logia f technology; ~lógico a technological

teco-teco /tɛku'tɛku/ *m* light aircraft

tecto /'tɛtu/ *m* (*Port*) *veja* teto

tédio /'tɛdʒiu/ *m* boredom

tedioso /tedʒi'ozu/ *a* boring, tedious

Teerã /tee'rã/ f Teheran

teia /'teja/ f web

tei|ma /'tejma/ f persistence; ~mar *vi* insist; ~mar em ir insist on going; ~mosia f stubbornness; ~moso /o/ *a* stubborn; <*ruido*> insistent

teixo /'tejʃu/ *m* yew

Tejo /'teʒu/ *m* Tagus

tela /'tɛla/ f (*de cinema, TV etc*) screen; (*tecido, pintura*) canvas

telecoman|dado /telekomã'dadu/ *a* remote-controlled; ~do *m* remote control

telecomunicação /telekomunika-'sãw/ f telecommunication

teleférico /tele'fɛriku/ *m* cable car

telefo|nar /telefo'nar/ *vi* telephone; ~nar para alg phone s.o.; ~ne /o/ *m* telephone; (*número*) phone number; ~ne celular cell phone; ~ne sem fio cordless phone; ~nema /e/ *m* phone call; ~nia f telephone technology

telefôni|co /tele'foniku/ *a* telephone; cabine ~ca phone box, (*Amer*) phone booth; mesa ~ca switchboard

telefonista /telefo'nista/ *m/f* (*da companhia telefônica*) operator; (*dentro de empresa etc*) telephonist

tele|grafar /telegra'far/ *vt/i* telegraph; ~gráfico *a* telegraphic

telégrafo /te'lɛgrafu/ *m* telegraph

tele|grama /tele'grama/ *m* telegram; ~guiado *a* remote-controlled

telejor|nal /teleʒor'naw/ (*pl* ~nais) *m* television news

tele|novela /teleno'vɛla/ f TV soap opera; ~objetiva f telephoto lens

tele|patia /telepa'tʃia/ f telepathy; ~pático *a* telepathic

telescó|pico /teles'kopiku/ *a* telescopic; ~pio *m* telescope

telespectador /telespekta'dor/ *m* television viewer □ *a* viewing

televi|são /televi'zãw/ f television; ~são a cabo cable television; ~sionar *vt* televise; ~sivo *a* television; ~sor *m* television set

telex /te'lɛks/ *m invar* telex

telha /'teʎa/ f tile; ~do *m* roof

te|ma /'tema/ *m* theme; ~mático *a* thematic

temer /te'mer/ *vt* fear □ *vi* be afraid; ~ por fear for

teme|rário /teme'rariu/ *a* reckless; ~ridade f recklessness; ~roso /o/ *a* fearful

te|mido /te'midu/ *a* feared; ~mível (*pl* ~míveis) *a* fearsome; ~mor *m* fear

tempão /tẽ'pãw/ *m* um ~ a long time

temperado /tẽpe'radu/ *a* <*clima*> temperate □ *pp de* temperar

temperamen|tal /tẽperamẽ'taw/ (*pl* ~tais) *a* temperamental; ~to *m* temperament

temperar /tẽpe'rar/ *vt* season <*comida*>; temper <*aço*>

temperatura /tẽpera'tura/ f temperature

tempero /tẽ'peru/ *m* seasoning

tempes|tade /tẽpes'tadʒi/ f storm; ~tuoso /o/ *a* stormy; (*fig*) tempestuous

templo /'tẽplu/ *m* temple

tempo /'tẽpu/ *m* (*período*) time; (*atmosférico*) weather; (*do verbo*) tense; (*de jogo*) half; ao mesmo ~ at the same time; nesse meio ~ in the meantime; o ~ todo all the time; de todos os ~s of all time; quanto ~ how long; muito/pouco ~ a long/ short time; ~ integral full time

têmpora /'tẽpora/ f temple

tempo|rada /tẽpo'rada/ f (*sazão*) season; (*tempo*) while; ~ral (*pl* ~rais) *a* temporal □ *m* storm; ~rário *a* temporary

te|nacidade /tenasi'dadʒi/ f tenacity; ~naz *a* tenacious □ f tongs

tenção /tẽ'sãw/ f intention

tencionar /tẽsio'nar/ *vt* intend

tenda /'tẽda/ f tent

tendão /tẽ'dãw/ *m* tendon; ~ de Aquiles Achilles tendon

tendência /tẽ'dẽsia/ f (*moda*) trend; (*propensão*) tendency

tendencioso /tẽdẽsi'ozu/ *a* tendentious

ten|der /tẽ'der/ *vi* tend (para towards); ~**de a engordar** he tends to get fat; **o tempo** ~**de a ficar bom the** weather is improving

tenebroso /tene'brozu/ *a* dark; (*fig: terrível*) dreadful

tenente /te'nẽtʃi/ *m/f* lieutenant

tênis /'tenis/ *m invar* (*jogo*) tennis; (*sapato*) trainer; **um** ~ (*par*) a pair of trainers; ~ **de mesa** table tennis

tenista /te'nista/ *m/f* tennis player

tenor /te'nor/ *m* tenor

tenro /'tẽxu/ *a* tender

ten|são /tẽ'sãw/ *f* tension; ~**são** (arterial) blood pressure; ~**so** *a* tense

tentação /tẽta'sãw/ *f* temptation

tentáculo /tẽ'takulu/ *m* tentacle

ten|tador /tẽta'dor/ *a* tempting; ~**tar** *vt* try; (*seduzir*) tempt □ *vi* try; ~**tativa** *f* attempt; ~**tativo** *a* tentative

tênue /'tenui/ *a* faint

teo|logia /teolo'ʒia/ *f* theology; ~**lógico** *a* theological

teólogo /te'ɔlogu/ *m* theologian

teor /te'or/ *m* (*de gordura etc*) content; (*de carta, discurso*) drift

teo|rema /teo'rema/ *m* theorem; ~**ria** *f* theory

teórico /te'ɔriku/ *a* theoretical

teorizar /teori'zar/ *vt* theorize

tépido /'tɛpidu/ *a* tepid

ter /ter/ *vt* have; **tenho vinte anos** I am twenty (years old); ~ **medo/sede** be afraid/thirsty; **tenho que** *ou* **de ir** I have to go; **tem** (*há*) **there is/are;** **não tem de quê** don't mention it; ~ **a ver com** have to do with

tera|peuta /tera'pewta/ *m/f* therapist; ~**pêutico** *a* therapeutic; ~**pia** *f* therapy

terça /'tersa/ *f* Tuesday; ~**-feira** (*pl* ~**s-feiras**) *f* Tuesday; **Terça-Feira Gorda** Shrove Tues- day

tercei|ra /ter'sera/ *f* (*marcha*) third; ~**ranista** *m/f* third-year; ~**ro** *a* third □ *m* third party

terço /'tersu/ *m* third

ter|col (*pl* ~**çóis**) *m* stye

tergal /ter'gaw/ *m* Terylene

térmi|co /'termiku/ *a* thermal; **garrafa** ~**ca** Thermos flask

termi|nal /termi'naw/ (*pl* ~**nais**) *a* & *m* terminal; ~**nal de vídeo** VDU; ~**nante** *a* definite; ~**nar** *vt* finish □ *vi* <*pessoa, coisa*> finish; <*coisa*> end; ~**nar com alg** (*cortar relação*) break up with s.o.

ter|minologia /terminolo'ʒia/ *f* terminology; ~**mo¹** /'termu/ *m* term; **pôr** ~**mo a** put an end to; **meio** ~**mo compromise**

termo² /'termu / *m* (*Port*) Thermos flask

ter|mômetro /ter'mometru/ *m* thermometer; ~**mostato** *m* thermostat

terno¹ /'ternu/ *m* suit

ter|no² /'ternu/ *a* tender; ~**nura** *f* tenderness

terra /'texa/ *f* land; (*solo, elétrico*) earth; (*chão*) ground; **a Terra Earth;** **por** ~ on the ground; ~ **natal** homeland

terraço /te'xasu/ *m* terrace

terra|cota /texa'kɔta/ *f* terracotta; ~**moto** /texa'mɔtu/ *m* (*Port*) earthquake; ~**plenagem** *f* earth moving

terreiro /te'xeru/ *m* meeting place for Afro-Brazilian cults

terremoto /texe'mɔtu/ *m* earthquake

terreno /te'xenu/ *a* earthly □ *m* ground; (*geog*) terrain; (*um*) piece of land; ~ **baldio** piece of waste ground

térreo /'tɛxiu/ *a* ground-floor; (*andar*) ~ ground floor; (*Amer*) first floor

terrestre /te'xɛstri/ *a* <*animal, batalha, forças*> land; (*da Terra*) of the Earth, the Earth's; <*alegrias etc*> earthly

terrificante /texifi'kãtʃi/ *a* terrifying

terrina /te'xina/ *f* tureen

territori|al /texitori'aw/ (*pl* ~**ais**) *a* territorial

território /texi'tɔriu/ *m* territory

terrí|vel /te'xivew/ (*pl* ~**veis**) *a* terrible

terror /te'xor/ *m* terror; **filme de** ~ horror film

terroris|mo /texo'rizmu/ *m* terrorism; ~**ta** *a* & *m/f* terrorist

tese /'tɛzi/ *f* theory; (*escrita*) thesis

teso /'tɛzu/ *a* (*apertado*) taut; (*rígido*) stiff

tesoura /te'zora/ *f* scissors; **uma** ~ a pair of scissors

tesou|reiro /tezo'reru/ *m* treasurer; ~**ro** *m* treasure; (*do Estado*) treasury

testa /'tɛsta/ *f* forehead; ~**-de-ferro** (*pl* ~**s-de-ferro**) *m* frontman

testamento /testa'mẽtu/ *m* will; (*na Bíblia*) testament

tes|tar /tes'tar/ *vt* test; ~**te** /ɛ/ *m* test

testemu|nha /teste'muɲa/ *f* witness; ~**nha ocular** eye witness; ~**nhar** *vt* bear witness to □ *vi* testify; ~**nho** *m* evidence, testimony

testículo /tes'tʃikulu/ *m* testicle

teta /'teta/ *f* teat

tétano /'tɛtanu/ *m* tetanus

teto /'tɛtu/ *m* ceiling; ~ **solar** sun roof

tétrico /'tɛtriku/ *a* (*triste*) dismal; (*medonho*) horrible

teu /tew/ (*f* **tua**) *a* your □ *pron* yours

têx|til /'testʃiw/ (*pl* ~**teis**) *m* textile

tex|to /'testu/ *m* text; ~**tura** *f* texture

texugo /te'ʃugu/ m badger

tez /tes/ f complexion

ti /tʃi/ pron you

tia /'tʃia/ f aunt; ~-avó (pl ~s-avós) f great aunt

tiara /tʃi'ara/ f tiara

tíbia /'tʃibia/ f shinbone

ticar /tʃi'kar/ vt tick

tico /'tʃiku/ m um ~ de a little bit of

tiete /tʃi'etʃi/ m/f fan

tifo /'tʃifu/ m typhoid

tigela /tʃi'ʒɛla/ f bowl; de meia ~ smalltime

tigre /'tʃigri/ m tiger; ~sa /e/ f tigress

tijolo /tʃi'ʒolu/ m brick

til /tʃiw/ (pl tis) m tilde

tilintar /tʃilĩ'tar/ vi jingle □ m jingling

timão /tʃi'mãw/ m tiller

timbre /'tʃibri/ m (insígnia) crest; (em papel) heading; (de som) tone; (de vogal) quality

time /'tʃimi/ m team

timidez /tʃimi'des/ f shyness

tímido /a tʃimidu/ a shy

tímpano /'tʃipanu/ m (tambor) kettledrum; (no ouvido) eardrum

tina /'tʃina/ f vat

tingir /tʃĩ'ʒir/ vt dye <tecido, cabelo>; (fig) tinge

ti'nido /tʃi'nidu/ m tinkling; ~nir vi tinkle; <ouvidos> ring; (tremer) tremble; estar ~nindo (fig) be in peak condition

tino /'tʃinu/ m sense, judgement; ter ~ para have a flair for

tin|ta /'tʃita/ f (para pintar) paint; (para escrever) ink; (para tingir) dye; ~teiro m inkwell

tintim /tʃĩ'tʃĩ/ m contar ~ por ~ give a blow-by-blow account of

tin|to /'tʃĩtu/ a dyed; <vinho> red; ~tura f dye; (fig) tinge; ~turaria f dry cleaner's

tio /'tʃiu/ m uncle; pl (~ e tia) uncle and aunt; ~-avô (pl ~s-avós) m great uncle

típico /'tʃipiku/ a typical

tipo /'tʃipu/ m type

tipóia /tʃi'pɔja/ f sling

tique /'tʃiki/ m (sinal) tick; (do rosto etc) twitch

tíquete /'tʃiketʃi/ m ticket

tiquinho /tʃi'kinu/ m um ~ de a tiny bit of

tira /'tʃira/ f strip □ m/f (fam) copper, (Amer) cop

tiracolo /tʃira'kɔlu/ m a ~ <bolsa> over one's shoulder; <pessoa> in tow

tiragem /tʃi'raʒẽ/ f (de jornal) circulation

tira|-gosto /tʃira'gostu/ m snack; ~manchas m invar stain remover

ti|rania /tʃira'nia/ f tyranny; ~rânico a tyrannical; ~rano m tyrant

tirar /tʃi'rar/ vt (afastar) take away; (de dentro) take out; take off <roupa, sapato, tampa>; take <foto, cópia, férias>; clear <mesa>; get <nota, diploma, salário>; get out <mancha>

tiritar /tʃiri'tar/ vi shiver

tiro /'tʃiru/ m shot; ~ ao alvo shooting; é ~ e queda (fam) it can't fail; ~teio m shoot-out

titânio /tʃi'taniu/ m titanium

títere /'tʃiteri/ m puppet

ti|tia /tʃi'tʃia/ f auntie; ~tio m uncle

titi|ti /tʃitʃi'tʃi/ m (fam) talk

titubear /tʃitubi'ar/ vi stagger, totter; (fig: hesitar) waver

titular /tʃitu'lar/ m/f title holder; (de time) captain □ vt title

título /'tʃitulu/ m title; (obrigação) bond; a ~ de on the basis of; a ~ pessoal on a personal basis

toa /'toa/ f à ~ (sem rumo) aimlessly; (ao acaso) at random; (sem motivo) without reason; (em vão) for nothing; (desocupado) at a loose end; (de repente) out of the blue

toada /to'ada/ f melody

toalete /toa'lɛtʃi/ m toilet

toalha /to'aʎa/ f towel; ~ de mesa tablecloth

tobogã /tobo'gã/ m (rampa) slide; (trenó) toboggan

toca /'tɔka/ f burrow

toca|-discos /tɔka'dʒiskus/ m invar record player; ~-fitas m invar tape player

tocaia /to'kaja/ f ambush

tocante /to'kãtʃi/ a (enternecedor) moving

tocar /to'kar/ vt touch; play <piano, música, disco etc>; ring <campainha> □ vi touch; <pianista, música, disco etc> play; <campainha, telefone, sino> ring; ~se vpr touch; (mancar-se) take the hint; ~ a (dizer respeito) concern; ~ em touch; touch on <assunto>

tocha /'tɔʃa/ f torch

toco /'toku/ m (de árvore) stump; (de cigarro) butt

toda /'toda/ f a ~ at full speed

todavia /toda'via/ conj however

todo /'todu/ a all; (cada) every; pl all; ~ o dinheiro all the money; ~ dia, ~s os dias every day; ~s os alunos all the pupils; o dia ~ all day; em ~ lugar everywhere; ~ mundo, ~s everyone; ~s nós all of us; ao ~ in all; ~-poderoso a almighty

tofe /'tɔfi/ m toffee

toga /'tɔga/ f gown; (de romano) toga

toicinho /toj'siɲu/ m bacon

toldo /'towdu/ m awning

tole|rância /tole'rãsia/ f tolerance; ~rante a tolerant; ~rar vt tolerate; ~rável (pl ~ráveis) a tolerable

to|lice /to'lisi/ f foolishness; (uma) foolish thing; ~lo /o/ a foolish □ m fool

tom /tõ/ m tone

to|mada /to'mada/ f (conquista) capture; (elétrica) plughole; (de filme) shot; ~mar vt take; (beber) drink; ~mar café have breakfast

tomara /to'mara/ int I hope so; ~ que let's hope that; ~-que-caia a invar <vestido> strapless

tomate /to'matʃi/ m tomato

tom|bar /tõ'bar/ vt (derrubar) knock down; list <edifício> □ vi fall over; ~bo m fall; levar um ~bo have a fall

tomilho /to'miʎu/ m thyme

tomo /'tomu/ m volume

tona /'tona/ f trazer à ~ bring up; vir à ~ emerge

tonalidade /tonali'dadʒi/ f (de música) key; (de cor) shade

to|nel /to'nɛw/ (pl ~néis) m cask; ~nelada f tonne

tôni|ca /'tonika/ f tonic; (fig: assunto) keynote; ~co a & m tonic

tonificar /tonifi'kar/ vt tone up

ton|tear /tõtʃi'ar/ vt ~tear alg make s.o.'s head spin; ~teira f dizziness; ~to a (zonzo) dizzy; (bobo) stupid; (atrapalhado) flustered; ~tura f dizziness

to|pada /to'pada/ f trip; dar uma ~pada em stub one's toe on; ~par vt agree to, accept; ~par com bump into <pessoa>; come across <coisa>

topázio /to'paziu/ m topaz

topete /to'petʃi/ m quiff

tópico /'topiku/ a topical □ m topic

topless /topi'lɛs/ a invar & adv topless

topo /'topu/ m top

topografia /topogra'fia/ f topography

topônimo /to'ponimu/ m place name

toque /'tɔki/ m touch; (da campainha, do telefone) ring; (de instrumento) playing; dar um ~ em (fam) have a word with

Tóquio /'tɔkiu/ f Tokyo

tora /'tɔra/ f log

toranja /to'rãʒa/ f grapefruit

tórax /'tɔraks/ m invar thorax

tor|ção /tor'sãw/ f (do braço etc) sprain; ~cedor m supporter; ~cer vt twist; (machucar) sprain; (espremer) wring <roupa>; (centrifugar) spin <roupa> □ vi (gritar) cheer (por for); (desejar sucesso) keep one's fingers crossed (por for; para que that); ~cer-se vpr twist about;

~cicolo /ɔ/ m stiff neck; ~cida f (torção) twist; (torcedores) supporters; (gritaria) cheering

tormen|ta /tor'mẽta/ f storm; ~to m torment; ~toso /o/ a stormy

tornado /tor'nadu/ m tornado

tornar /tor'nar/ vt make; ~-se vpr become

torne|ado /torni'adu/ a bem ~ado shapely; ~ar vt turn

torneio /tor'neju/ m tournament

torneira /tor'nera/ f tap, (Amer) faucet

torniquete /torni'ketʃi/ m (para ferido) tourniquet; (Port: de entrada) turnstile

torno /'tornu/ m lathe; (de ceramista) wheel; em ~ de around

tornozelo /torno'zelu/ m ankle

toró /to'rɔ/ m downpour

torpe /'tɔrpi/ a dirty

torpe|dear /torpedʒi'ar/ vt torpedo; ~do /e/ m torpedo

torpor /tor'por/ m torpor

torra|da /to'xada/ f piece of toast; pl toast; ~deira f toaster

torrão /to'xãw/ m (de terra) turf; (de açúcar) lump

torrar /to'xar/ vt toast <pão>; roast <café>; blow <dinheiro>; sell off <mercadorias>

torre /'toxi/ f tower; (em xadrez) rook; ~ de controle control tower; ~ão m turret

torrefação /toxefa'sãw/ f (ação) roasting; (fábrica) coffee-roasting plant

torren|cial /toxẽsi'aw/ (pl ~ciais) a torrential; ~te f torrent

torresmo /to'xezmu/ m crackling

tórrido /'tɔxidu/ a torrid

torrone /to'xoni/ m nougat

torso /'torsu/ m torso

torta /'tɔrta/ f pie, tart

tor|to /'tortu/ a crooked; a ~ e a direito left, right and centre; ~tuoso a winding

tortu|ra /tor'tura/ f torture; ~rador m torturer; ~rar vt torture

to|sa /'tɔza/ f (de cachorro) clipping; (de ovelhas) shearing; ~são m fleece; ~sar vt clip <cachorro>; shear <ovelhas>; crop <cabelo>

tosco /'tosku/ a rough, coarse

tosquiar /toski'ar/ vt shear <ovelha>

tos|se /'tɔsi/ f cough; ~se de cachorro whooping cough; ~sir vi cough

tostão /tos'tãw/ m penny

tostar /tos'tar/ vt brown <carne>; tan <pele, pessoa>; ~-se vpr (ao sol) go brown

to|tal /to'taw/ (pl ~tais) a & m total

totali|dade /totali'dadʒi/ f entirety; ~tário a totalitarian; ~zar vt total

touca /'toka/ f bonnet; (de freira) wimple; ~ de banho bathing cap; ~dor m dressing table

toupeira /to'pera/ f mole

tou|rada /to'rada/ f bullfight; ~reiro m bullfighter; ~ro m bull; Touro (signo) Taurus

tóxico /'toksiku/ a toxic □ m toxic substance

toxicômano /toksi'komanu/ m drug addict

toxina /tok'sina/ f toxin

traba|lhador /trabaʃa'dor/ a <pessoa> hard-working; <classe> working □ m worker; ~lhar vt work □ vi work; (numa peça, filme) act; ~lheira f big job; ~lhista a labour; ~lho m work; (um) job; (na escola) assignment; dar-se o ~lho de to the trouble of; ~lho de parto labour; ~lhos forçados hard labour; ~lhoso a laborious

traça /'trasa/ f moth

tração /tra'sãw/ f traction

tra|çar /tra'sar/ vt draw; draw up <plano>; set out <ordens>; ~ço m stroke; (entre frases) dash; (vestígio) trace; (característica) trait; pl (do rosto) features

tractor /tra'tor/ m (Port) veja trator

tradi|ção /tradʒi'sãw/ f tradition; ~cional (pl ~cionais) a traditional

tradu|ção /tradu'sãw/ f translation; ~tor m translator; ~zir vt/i translate (de from; para into)

trafe|gar /trafe'gar/ vi run; ~gável (pl ~gáveis) a open to traffic

tráfego /'trafegu/ m traffic

trafi|cância /trafi'kãsia/ f trafficking; ~cante m/f trafficker; ~car vt/i traffic (com in)

tráfico /'trafiku/ m traffic

tra|gada /tra'gada/ f (de bebida) swallow; (de cigarro) drag; ~gar vt swallow; inhale <fumaça>

tragédia /tra'ʒedʒia/ f tragedy

trágico /'traʒiku/ a tragic

trago /'tragu/ m (de bebida) swallow; (de cigarro) drag; de um ~ in one go

trai|ção /traj'sãw/ f (ato) betrayal; (deslealdade) treachery; (da pátria) treason; ~coeiro a treacherous; ~dor a treacherous □ m traitor

trailer /'trejler/ (pl ~s) m (de filme etc) trailer; (casa móvel) caravan, (Amer) trailer

traineira /traj'nera/ f trawler

training /'trejnĩ/ (pl ~s) m track suit

trair /tra'ir/ vt betray; be unfaithful to <marido, mulher>; ~-se vpr give o.s. away

tra|jar /tra'ʒar/ vt wear; ~jar-se vpr dress (de in); ~je m outfit; ~je a

rigor evening dress; ~je espacial space suit

traje|to /tra'ʒɛtu/ m (percurso) journey; (caminho) route; ~tória f trajectory; (fig) course

tralha /'traʎa/ f (trastes) junk

tra|ma /'trama/ f plot; ~mar vt/i plot

trambi|que /trã'biki/ (fam) m con; ~queiro (fam) m con artist

tramitar /trami'tar/ vi be processed

trâmites /'tramitʃis/ m pl channels

tramóia /tra'mɔja/ f scheme

trampolim /trãpo'lĩ/ m (de ginástica) trampoline; (de piscina, fig) springboard

tranca /'trãka/ f bolt; (em carro) lock

trança /'trãsa/ f (de cabelo) plait

tran|cafiar /trãkafi'ar/ vt lock up; ~car vt lock; cancel <matrícula>

trançar /trã'sar/ vt plait <cabelo>; weave <palha etc>

tranco /'trãku/ m jolt; aos ~s e barrancos in fits and starts

tranqueira /trã'kera/ f junk

tranqüi|lidade /trãkwili'dadʒi/ f tranquillity; ~lizador a reassuring; ~lizante m tranquillizer □ a reassuring; ~lizar vt reassure; ~lizar-se vpr be reassured; ~lo a <bairro, sono> peaceful; <pessoa, voz, mar> calm; <consciência> clear; <sucesso, lucro> sure-fire □ adv with no trouble

transa /'trãza/ f (fam) (negócio) deal; (caso) affair; ~ção f transaction; ~do a (fam) <roupa, pessoa, casa> stylish; <relação> healthy

Transamazônica /trãzama'zonika/ f trans-Amazonian highway

transar /trã'zar/ (fam) vt set up; do <drogas> □ vi (negociar) deal; (fazer sexo) have sex

transatlântico /trãzat'lãtʃiku/ a transatlantic □ m liner

transbordar /trãzbor'dar/ vi overflow

transcen|dental /trãsẽdẽ'taw/ (pl ~dentais) a transcendental; ~der vt/i ~der (a) transcend

trans|crever /trãskre'ver/ vt transcribe; ~crição f transcription; ~crito a transcribed □ m transcript

transe /'trãzi/ m trance

transeunte /trãzi'ũtʃi/ m/f passer-by

transfe|rência /trãsfe'rẽsia/ f transfer; ~ridor m protractor; ~rir vt transfer; ~rir-se vpr transfer

transfor|mação /trãsforma'sãw/ f transformation; ~mador m transformer; ~mar vt transform; ~mar-se vpr be transformed

trânsfuga /'trãsfuga/ m/f deserter; (de um país) defector

transfusão /trãsfu'zãw/ f transfusion

trans|gredir /trãzgre'dʒir/ vt infringe; ~gressão f infringement

transi|ção /trãzi'sãw/ f transition; ~cional (pl ~cionais) a transitional

transi|gente /trãzi'ʒẽtʃi/ a open to compromise; ~gir vi compromise

transis|tor /trãzis'tor/ m transistor; ~torizado a transistorized

transi|tar /trãzi'tar/ vi pass; ~tável (pl ~táveis) a passable; ~tivo a transitive

trânsito /'trãzitu/ m traffic; em ~ in transit

transitório /trãzi'toriu/ a transitory

translúcido /trãz'lusidu/ a translucent

transmis|são /trãzmi'sãw/ f transmission; ~sor m transmitter

transmitir /trãzmi'tʃir/ vt transmit <programa, calor, doença>; convey <notícia, ordens>; transfer <herança, direito>; ~-se vpr <doença> be transmitted

transpa|recer /trãspare'ser/ vi be visible; (fig) <emoção, verdade> come out; ~rência f transparency; ~rente a transparent

transpi|ração /trãspira'sãw/ f perspiration; ~rar vt exude □ vi (suar) perspire; <notícia> trickle through; <verdade> come out

transplan|tar /trãsplã'tar/ vt transplant; ~te m transplant

transpor /trãs'por/ vt cross <rio, fronteira>; get over <obstáculo, dificuldade>; transpose <letras, música>

transpor|tadora /trãsporta'dora/ f transport company; ~tar vt transport; (em contas) carry forward; ~te m transport; ~te coletivo public transport

transposto /trãs'postu/ pp de transpor

transtor|nar /trãstor'nar/ vt mess up <papéis, casa>; disrupt <rotina, ambiente>; disturb, upset <pessoa>; ~nar-se vpr <pessoa> be rattled; ~no /o/ m (de casa, rotina) disruption; (de pessoa) disturbance; (contratempo) upset

transver|sal /trãzver'saw/ (pl ~sais) a (rua) ~sal cross street; ~so /ɛ/ a transverse

transvi|ado /trãzvi'adu/ a wayward; ~ar vt lead astray

trapa|ça /tra'pasa/ f swindle; ~cear vi cheat; ~ceiro a crooked □ m cheat

trapa|lhada /trapa'ʎada/ f bungle; ~lhão a (f ~lhona) bungling □ m (f ~lhona) bungler

trapézio /tra'pɛziu/ m trapeze

trapezista /trape'zista/ m/f trapeze artist

trapo /'trapu/ m rag

traquéia /tra'kɛja/ f windpipe, trachea

traquejo /tra'keʒu/ m knack

traquinas /tra'kinas/ a invar mischievous

trás /tras/ adv de ~ from behind; a roda de ~ the back wheel; de ~ para frente back to front; para ~ backwards; deixar para ~ leave behind; por ~ de behind

traseiro /tra'zeru/ a rear, back □ m bottom

trasladar /trazla'dar/ vt transport

traspas|sado /traspa'sadu/ a <paletó> double-breasted; ~sar vt pierce

traste /'trastʃi/ m (pessoa) pain; (coisa) piece of junk

tra|tado /tra'tadu/ m (pacto) treaty; (estudo) treatise; ~tamento m treatment; (título) title; ~tar vt treat; negotiate <preço, venda> □ vi (manter relações) have dealings (com with); (combinar) negotiate (com with); ~tar de deal with; ~tar alg de ou por address s.o. as; ~tar de voltar (tentar) seek to return; (resolver) decide to return; ~tar-se de be a matter of; ~tável (pl ~táveis) a <doença> treatable; <pessoa> accommodating; ~tos m pl maus ~tos illtreatment

trator /tra'tor/ m tractor

trauma /'trawma/ m trauma; ~tizante a traumatic; ~tizar vt traumatize

tra|vão /tra'vãw/ m (Port) brake; ~var vt lock <rodas, músculos>; stop <carro>; block <passagem>; strike up <amizade, conversa>; wage <luta, combate> □ vi (Port) brake

trave /'travi/ f beam, joist; (do gol) crossbar

traves|sa /tra'vɛsa/ f (trave) crossbar; (rua) side street; (prato) dish; (pente) slide; ~são m dash; ~seiro m pillow; ~sia f crossing; ~so /e/ a <criança> naughty; ~sura f prank; pl mischief

travesti /traves'tʃi/ m transvestite; (artista) drag artist; ~do a in a drag

trazer /tra'zer/ vt bring; bear <nome, ferida>; wear <barba, chapéu, cabelo curto>

trecho /'treʃu/ m (de livro etc) passage; (de rua etc) stretch

treco /'treku/ m (fam) (coisa) thing; (ataque) turn

trégua /'trɛgwa/ f truce; (fig) respite

trei|nador /trejna'dor/ m trainer; ~namento m training; ~nar vt train <atleta, animal>; practise <língua etc> □ vi <atleta> train;

<pianista, principiante> practise;
~no *m* training; (*um*) training
session
trejeito /tre'ʒejtu/ *m* grimace
trela /'trɛla/ *f* lead, (*Amer*) leash
treliça /tre'lisa/ *f* trellis
trem /trẽj/ *m* train; ~ de aterrissagem undercarriage; ~ de carga
goods train, (*Amer*) freight train
trema /'trema/ *m* dieresis
treme|deira /treme'dera/ *f* shiver;
~licar *vi* tremble; ~luzir *vi* glimmer, flicker
tremendo /tre'mẽdu/ *a* tremendous
tre|mer /tre'mer/ *vi* tremble; <*terra*>
shake; ~mor *m* tremor; (*tremedeira*)
shiver; ~mular *vi* <*bandeira*> flutter; <*luz, estrela*> glimmer, flicker
trêmulo /'tremulu/ *a* trembling;
<*luz*> flickering
trena /'trena/ *f* tape measure
trenó /tre'nɔ/ *m* sledge, (*Amer*) sled;
(*puxado a cavalos etc*) sleigh
tre|padeira /trepa'dera/ *f* climbing
plant; ~par *vt* climb □ *vi* climb; (*chulo*) fuck
três /tres/ *a & m* three
tresloucado /trezlo'kadu/ *a* deranged
trevas /'trɛvas/ *f pl* darkness
trevo /'trevu/ *m* (*planta*) clover; (*rodoviário*) interchange
treze /'trezi/ *a & m* thirteen
trezentos /tre'zẽtus/ *a & m* three
hundred
triagem /tri'aʒẽ/ *f* (*escolha*) selection;
(*separação*) sorting; fazer uma ~ de
sort
tri|angular /triãgu'lar/ *a* triangular;
~ângulo *m* triangle
tri|bal /tri'baw/ (*pl* ~bais) *a* tribal;
~bo *f* tribe
tribu|na /tri'buna/ *f* rostrum; ~nal
(*pl* ~nais) *m* court
tribu|tação /tributa'sãw/ *f* taxation;
~tar *vt* tax; ~tário *a* tax □ *m*
tributary; ~to *m* tribute
tri|cô /tri'ko/ *m* knitting; artigos de
~cô knitwear; ~cotar *vt/i* knit
tridimensio|nal /tridʒimẽsio'naw/
(*pl* ~nais) *a* three- dimensional
trigêmeo /tri'ʒemiu/ *m* triplet
trigésimo /tri'ʒɛzimu/ *a* thirtieth
tri|go /'trigu/ *m* wheat; ~gueiro *a*
dark
trilha /'triʎa/ *f* path; (*pista, de disco*)
track; ~ sonora soundtrack
trilhão /tri'ʎãw/ *m* billion, (*Amer*)
trillion
trilho /'triʎu/ *m* track
trilogia /trilo'ʒia/ *f* trilogy
trimes|tral /trimes'traw/ (*pl* ~-
trais) *a* quarterly; ~tre /ɛ/ *m* quarter; (*do ano letivo*) term
trincar /trĩ'kar/ *vt/i* crack

trincheira /trĩ'ʃera/ *f* trench
trinco /'trĩku/ *m* latch
trindade /trĩ'dadʒi/ *f* trinity
trinta /'trĩta/ *a & m* thirty
trio /'triu/ *m* trio; ~ elétrico music
float
tripa /'tripa/ *f* gut
tripé /tri'pɛ/ *m* tripod
tripli|car /tripli'kar/ *vt/i*, ~car-se
vpr treble; ~cata *f* triplicate
triplo /'triplu/ *a & m* triple
tripu|lação /tripula'sãw/ *f* crew;
~lante *m/f* crew member; ~lar *vt*
man
triste /'tristʃi/ *a* sad; ~za /e/ *f* sad-
ness; é uma ~za (*fam*) it's pathetic
tritu|rador /tritura'dor/ *m* (*de papel*)
shredder; ~rador de lixo waste dis-
posal unit; ~rar *vt* shred <*legumes,
papel*>; grind up <*lixo*>
triun|fal /triũ'faw/ (*pl* ~fais) *a*
triumphal; ~fante *a* triumphant;
~far *vi* triumph; ~fo *m* triumph
trivi|al /trivi'aw/ (*pl* ~ais) *a* trivial;
~alidade *f* triviality; *pl* trivia
triz /tris/ *m* por um ~ narrowly, by a
hair's breadth; não foi atropelado
por um ~ he narrowly missed being
knocked down
tro|ca /'trɔka/ *f* exchange; em ~ca de
in exchange for; ~cadilho *m* pun;
~cado *m* change; ~cador *m*
conductor; ~car *vt* (*dar e receber*) exchange (por for); change <*dinheiro,
lençóis, lâmpada, lugares etc*>; (*transpor*) change round; (*confundir*) mix
up; ~car-se *vpr* change; ~car de
roupa/trem/lugar change clothes/
trains/places; ~ca-troca *m* swap;
~co /o/ *m* change; a ~co de quê?
what for?; dar o ~co em alg pay
s.o. back
troço /'trɔsu/ (*fam*) *m* (*coisa*) thing;
(*ataque*) turn; me deu um ~ I had a
funny turn
troféu /tro'fɛw/ *m* trophy
trólebus /'trɔlebus/ *m invar* trolley
bus
trom|ba /'trõba/ *f* (*de elefante*) trunk;
(*cara amarrada*) long face; ~bada *f*
crash; ~ba-d'água (*pl* ~bas-
d'água) *f* downpour; ~badinha *m*
bag snatcher; ~bar *vi* ~bar com
crash into <*poste, carro*>; bump into
<*pessoa*>
trombo|ne /trõ'boni/ *m* trombone;
~nista *m/f* trombonist
trompa /'trõpa/ *f* French horn; ~ de
Falópio fallopian tube
trompe|te /trõ'petʃi/ *m* trumpet;
~tista *m/f* trumpeter
tron|co /'trõku/ *m* trunk; ~cudo *a*
stocky
trono /'tronu/ *m* throne

tropa /'trɔpa/ f troop; (exército) army;
pl troops; ~ de choque riot police

trope|ção /trope'sãw/ m trip; (erro)
slip-up; ~çar vi trip; (errar) slip up;
~ço /e/ m stumbling block

trópego /'trɔpegu/ a unsteady

tropi|cal /tropi'kaw/ (pl ~cais) a
tropical

trópico /'trɔpiku/ m tropic

tro|tar /tro'tar/ vi trot; ~te /ɔ/ m (de
cavalo) trot; (de estudantes) practical
joke; (mentira) hoax

trouxa /'troʃa/ f (de roupa etc) bundle
□ m/f (fam) sucker □ a (fam) gullible

tro|vão /tro'vãw/ m clap of thunder; pl
thunder; ~vejar vi thunder; ~voada
f thunderstorm; ~voar vi thunder

trucidar /trusi'dar/ vt slaughter

trucu|lência /truku'lẽsia/ f bar-
barity; ~lento a (cruel) barbaric;
(brigão) belligerent

trufa /'trufa/ f truffle

trunfo /'trũfu/ m trump; (fig) trump
card

truque /'truki/ m trick

truta /'truta/ f trout

tu /tu/ pron you

tua /'tua/ veja teu

tuba /'tuba/ f tuba

tubarão /tuba'rãw/ m shark

tubá|rio /tu'bariu/ a gravidez ~ria
ectopic pregnancy

tuberculose /tubercu'lɔzi/ f tuberculosis

tubo /'tubu/ m tube; (no corpo) duct

tubulação /tubula'sãw/ f ducting

tucano /tu'kanu/ m toucan

tudo /'tudu/ pron everything; ~ bem?
(cumprimento) how are things?; ~ de
bom all the best; em ~ quanto é
lugar all over the place

tufão /tu'fãw/ m typhoon

tulipa /tu'lipa/ f tulip

tumba /'tũba/ f tomb

tumor /tu'mor/ m tumour; ~ cerebral brain tumour

túmulo /'tumulu/ m grave

tumul|to /tu'muwtu/ m commotion;
(motim) riot; ~tuado a disorderly,
rowdy; ~tuar vt disrupt □ vi cause
a commotion; ~tuoso a tumultuous

túnel /'tunew/ (pl ~neis) m tunnel

túnica /'tunika/ f tunic

Tunísia /tu'nizia/ f Tunisia

tupiniquim /tupini'kĩ/ a Brazilian

turbante /tur'bãtʃi/ m turban

turbilhão /turbi'ʎãw/ m whirlwind

turbina /tur'bina/ f turbine

turbu|lência /turbu'lẽsia/ f turbu-
lence; ~lento a turbulent

turco /'turku/ a & m Turkish

turfa /'turfa/ f peat

turfe /'turfe/ m horse-racing

turis|mo /tu'rizmu/ m tourism; fazer

~mo go sightseeing; ~ta m/f tourist

turístico /tu'ristʃiku/ a <ponto,
indústria> tourist; <viagem> sightseeing

turma /'turma/ f group; (na escola)
class

turnê /tur'ne/ f tour

turno /'turnu/ m (de trabalho) shift;
(de competição, eleição) round

turquesa /tur'keza/ m/f & a invar
turquoise

Turquia /tur'kia/ f Turkey

turra /'tuxa/ f às ~s com at loggerheads with

tur|var /tur'var/ vt cloud; ~vo a
cloudy

tutano /tu'tanu/ m marrow

tutela /tu'tɛla/ f guardianship

tutor /tu'tor/ m guardian

tutu /tu'tu/ m (vestido) tutu; (prato)
beans with bacon and manioc flour

TV /te've/ f TV

U

ubíquo /u'bikwu/ a ubiquitous

Ucrânia /u'krania/ f Ukraine

ucraniano /ukrani'anu/ a & m
Ukrainian

ué /u'ɛ/ int hang on

ufa /'ufa/ int phew

ufanis|mo /ufa'nizmu/ m chauvin-
ism; ~ta a & m/f chauvinist

Uganda /u'gãda/ m Uganda

ui /ui/ int (de dor) ouch; (de nojo) ugh;
(de espanto) oh

uísque /u'iski/ m whisky

ui|var /ui'var/ vi howl; ~vo m howl

úlcera /'uwsera/ f ulcer

ulterior /uwteri'or/ a further

ulti|mamente /uwtʃima'mẽtʃi/ adv
recently; ~mar vt finalize; ~mato
m ultimatum

último /'uwtʃimu/ a last; <moda,
notícia etc> latest; em ~ caso as a
last resort; nos ~s anos in recent
years; por ~ last

ultra|jante /uwtra'ʒãtʃi/ a offensive;
~jar vt offend; ~je m outrage

ultraleve /uwtra'lɛvi/ m microlite

ultra|mar /uwtra'mar/ m overseas;
~marino a overseas

ultrapas|sado /uwtrapa'sadu/ a out-
dated; ~sagem f overtaking, (Amer)
passing; ~sar vt (de carro) overtake,
(Amer) pass; (ser superior a) surpass;
(exceder) exceed; (extrapolar) go beyond □ vi overtake, (Amer) pass

ultra-sonografia /uwtrasonogra-
'fia/ f ultrasound scan

ultravioleta /uwtravio'leta/ a ultraviolet

ulu|lante /ulu'lãtʃi/ a (fig) blatant; ~**lar** vi wail

um /ũ/ (f uma; m pl uns, f pl umas) art a, an; pl some □ a & pron one; ~ **ao outro** one another; **vieram umas 20 pessoas** about 20 people came

umbanda /ũ'bãda/ m Afro-Brazilian cult

umbigo /ũ'bigu/ m navel

umbili|cal /ũbili'kaw/ (pl ~**cais**) a umbilical

umedecer /umede'ser/ vt moisten; ~**se** vpr moisten

umidade /umi'dadʒi/ f moisture; (*desagradável*) damp; (*do ar*) humidity

úmido /'umidu/ a moist; <*parede, roupa etc*> damp; <*ar, clima*> humid

unânime /u'nanimi/ a unanimous

unanimidade /unanimi'dadʒi/ f unanimity

undécimo /ũ'dɛsimu/ a eleventh

ungüento /ũ'gwẽtu/ m ointment

unha /'uɲa/ f nail; (*de animal, utensílio*) claw

unhar /u'ɲar/ vt claw

união /uni'ãw/ f union; (*concórdia*) unity; (*ato de unir*) joining

unicamente /unika'mẽtʃi/ adv only

único /'uniku/ a only; (*ímpar*) unique

uni|dade /uni'dadʒi/ f unit; ~**do a** united; <*família*> close

unifi|cação /unifika'sãw/ f unification; ~**car** vt unify

unifor|me /uni'fɔrmi/ a uniform; <*superfície*> even □ m uniform; ~**midade** f uniformity; ~**mizado a** <*policial etc*> uniformed; (*padronizado*) standardized; ~**zar** vt (*padronizar*) standardize

unilate|ral /unilate'raw/ (pl ~**rais**) a unilateral

unir /u'nir/ vt unite <*povo, nações, família etc*>; (*ligar, casar*) join; (*combinar*) combine (a ou com with); ~**se** vpr (*aliar-se*) unite (a with); (*juntarse*) join together; (*combinar-se*) combine (a ou com with)

unissex /uni'seks/ a invar unisex

uníssono /u'nisonu/ m em ~ in unison

univer|sal /univer'saw/ (pl ~**sais**) a universal

universi|dade /universi'dadʒi/ f university; ~**tário a** university □ m university student

universo /uni'versu/ m universe

untar /ũ'tar/ vt grease <*fôrma*>; spread <*pão*>; smear <*corpo, rosto etc*>

upa /'upa/ int (*incentivando*) upsadaisy; (*ao cair algo etc*) whoops

urânio /u'raniu/ m uranium

Urano /u'ranu/ m Uranus

urbanis|mo /urba'nizmu/ m town

planning; ~**ta** m/f town planner

urbani|zado /urbani'zadu/ a builtup; ~**zar** vt urbanize

urbano /ur'banu/ a (*da cidade*) urban; (*refinado*) urbane

urdir /ur'dʒir/ vt weave; (*maquinar*) hatch

urdu /ur'du/ m Urdu

ur|gência /ur'ʒẽsia/ f urgency; ~**gente a** urgent; ~**gir** vi be urgent; <*tempo*> press; ~**ge irmos** we must go urgently

uri|na /u'rina/ f urine; ~**nar** vt pass □ vi urinate; ~**nol** (pl ~**nóis**) m (*penico*) chamber pot; (*em banheiro*) urinal

urna /'urna/ f (*para cinzas*) urn; (*para votos*) ballot box; pl (*fig*) polls

ur|rar /u'xar/ vt/i roar; ~**ro** m roar

urso /'ursu/ m bear; ~**-branco** (pl ~**s-brancos**) m polar bear

urti|cária /urtʃi'karia/ f nettle rash; ~**ga** f nettle

urubu /uru'bu/ m black vulture

Uruguai /uru'gwaj/ m Uruguay

uruguaio /uru'gwaju/ a & m Uruguayan

urze /'urzi/ f heather

usado /u'zadu/ a used; <*roupa*> worn; (*palavra*) common

usar /u'zar/ vt wear <*roupa, óculos, barba etc*>; ~ (de) (*utilizar*) use

usina /u'zina/ f plant; ~ **termonuclear** nuclear power station

uso /'uzu/ m use; (*de palavras, linguagem*) usage; (*praxe*) practice

usu|al /uzu'aw/ (pl ~**ais**) a common; ~**ário** m user; ~**fruir** vt enjoy <*coisas boas*>; have the use of <*prédio, jardim etc*>; ~**fruto** m use

usurário /uzu'rariu/ a money-grubbing □ m money-lender

usurpar /uzur'par/ vt usurp

uten|sílio /utẽ'siliu/ m utensil; ~**te** m/f (Port) user

útero /'uteru/ m uterus, womb

UTI /ute'i/ f intensive care unit

útil /'utʃiw/ (pl **úteis**) a useful; **dia** ~ workday

utili|dade /utʃili'dadʒi/ f usefulness; (*uma*) utility; ~**tário a** utilitarian; ~**zar** vt (*empregar*) use; (*tornar útil*) utilize; ~**zável** (pl ~**záveis**) a usable

utopia /uto'pia/ f Utopia

utópico /u'tɔpiku/ a Utopian

uva /'uva/ f grape

úvula /'uvula/ f uvula

V

vaca /'vaka/ f cow

vaci|lante /vasi'lãtʃi/ a wavering; <*luz*> flickering; ~**lar** vi waver;

<luz> flicker; (*fam: bobear*) slip up

vaci|na /va'sina/ *f* vaccine; ~nação *f* vaccination; ~nar *vt* vaccinate

vácuo /'vakuu/ *m* vacuum

va|diar /vadʒi'ar/ *vi* (*viver ocioso*) laze around; (*fazer cera*) mess about; ~dio *a* idle □ *m* idler

vaga /'vaga/ *f* (*posto*) vacancy; (*para estacionar*) parking place

vagabun|dear /vagabũdʒi'ar/ *vi* (*perambular*) roam; (*vadiar*) laze around; ~do *a* <*pessoa, vida*> idle; <*produto, objeto*> shoddy □ *m* tramp; (*pessoa vadia*) bum

vaga-lume /vaga'lumi/ *m* glow-worm

va|gão /va'gãw/ *m* (*de passageiros*) carriage, (*Amer*) car; (*de carga*) wagon; ~gão-leito (*pl* ~gões-leitos) *m* sleeping car; ~gão-restaurante (*pl* ~gões-restaurantes) *m* dining car

vagar¹ /va'gar/ *vi* <*pessoa*> wander about; <*barco*> drift

vagar² /va'gar/ *vi* <*cargo, apartamento*> become vacant

vagaroso /vaga'rozu/ *a* slow

vagem /'vaʒẽ/ *f* green bean

vagi|na /va'ʒina/ *f* vagina; ~nal (*pl* ~nais) *a* vaginal

vago¹ /'vagu/ *a* (*indefinido*) vague

vago² /'vagu/ *a* (*desocupado*) vacant; <*tempo*> spare

vaguear /vagi'ar/ *vi* roam

vai|a /'vaja/ *f* boo; ~ar *vi* boo

vai|dade /vaj'dadʒi/ *f* vanity; ~doso *a* vain

vaivém /vaj'vẽj/ *m* comings and goings, toing and froing

vala /'vala/ *f* ditch; ~ comum mass grave

vale¹ /'vali/ *m* (*de rio etc*) valley

vale² /'vali/ *m* (*ficha*) voucher; ~ postal postal order

valen|tão /valẽ'tãw/ *a* (*f* ~tona) tough □ *m* tough guy; ~te *a* brave; ~tia *f* bravery; (*uma*) feat

valer /va'ler/ *vt* be worth □ *vi* be valid; ~ aco a alg earn s.o. sth; ~se de avail o.s. of; ~ a pena be worth it; vale a pena tentar it's worth trying; mais vale desistir it's better to give up; vale tudo anything goes; fazer ~ enforce <*lei*>; stand up for <*direitos*>; para ~ (*a sério*) for real; (*muito*) really

vale-refeição /valirefej'sãw/ (*pl* ~s-refeição) *m* luncheon voucher

valeta /va'leta/ *f* gutter

valete /va'letʃi/ *m* jack

valia /va'lia/ *f* value

validar /vali'dar/ *vt* validate

válido /'validu/ *a* valid

valioso /vali'ozu/ *a* valuable

valise /va'lizi/ *f* travelling bag

valor /va'lor/ *m* value; (*valentia*) valour; *pl* (*títulos*) securities; no ~ de to the value of; sem ~ worthless; objetos de ~ valuables; ~ nominal face value

valori|zação /valoriza'sãw/ *f* (*apreciação*) valuing; (*aumento no valor*) increase in value; ~zado *a* highly valued; ~zar *vt* (*apreciar*) value; (*aumentar o valor de*) increase the value of; ~zar-se *vt* <*coisa*> increase in value; <*pessoa*> value o.s.

val|sa /'vawsa/ *f* waltz; ~sar *vi* waltz

válvula /'vawvula/ *f* valve

vampiro /vã'piru/ *m* vampire

vandalismo /vãda'lizmu/ *m* vandalism

vândalo /'vãdalu/ *m* vandal

vangloriar-se /vãglori'arsi/ *vpr* brag (de about)

vanguarda /vã'gwarda/ *f* vanguard; (*de arte*) avant-garde

vanta|gem /vã'taʒẽ/ *f* advantage; contar ~gem boast; levar ~gem have the advantage (a over); tirar ~gem de take advantage of; ~joso /o/ *a* advantageous

vão /vãw/ (*pl* ~s) *a* (*f* vã) vain □ *m* gap; em ~ in vain

vapor /va'por/ *m* (*fumaça*) steam; (*gás*) vapour; (*barco*) steamer; máquina a ~ steam engine; a todo ~ at full blast

vaporizar /vapori'zar/ *vt* vaporize; (*com spray*) spray

vaqueiro /va'keru/ *m* cowboy

vaquinha /va'kiɲa/ *f* collection, whip-round

vara /'vara/ *f* rod; ~ cívil civil district; ~ mágica *ou* de condão magic wand

varanda /va'rãda/ *f* veranda

varão /va'rãw/ *m* male

varar /va'rar/ *vt* (*furar*) pierce; (*passar por*) sweep through

varejão /vare'ʒãw/ *m* wholesale store

varejeira /vare'ʒera/ *f* bluebottle

vare|jista /vare'ʒista/ *a* retail □ *m/f* retailer; ~jo /e/ *m* retail trade; vender a ~jo sell retail

vari|ação /varia'sãw/ *f* variation; ~ado *a* varied; ~ante *a & f* variant; ~ar *vt/i* vary; para ~ar for a change; ~ável (*pl* ~áveis) *a* variable; <*tempo*> changeable

varicela /vari'sela/ *f* chickenpox

variedade /varie'dadʒi/ *f* variety

vários /'varius/ *a pl* several

varíola /va'riola/ *f* smallpox

variz /va'ris/ *f* varicose vein

varo|nil /varo'niw/ (pl ~nis) a manly

var|rer /va'xer/ vt sweep; (fig) sweep away; ~rido a um doido ~rido a raving lunatic

Varsóvia /var'sɔviɑ/ f Warsaw

vascu|lhar /vasku'ʎar/ vt search through

vasectomia /vazekto'mia/ f vasectomy

vaselina /vaze'lina/ f vaseline

vasilha /va'ziʎɑ/ f jug

vaso /'vazu/ m pot; (para flores) vase; ~ sanguíneo blood vessel

vassoura /va'sora/ f broom

vas|tidão /vastʃi'dɐ̃w/ f vastness; ~to a vast

vatapá /vata'pa/ m spicy North-Eastern dish

Vaticano /vatʃi'kanu/ m Vatican

vati|cinar /vatʃisi'nar/ vt prophesy; ~cínio m prophecy

va|zamento /vaza'mẽtu/ m leak; ~zante f ebb tide; ~zão m outflow; dar ~zão a (fig) give vent to; ~zar vt/i leak

vazio /va'ziu/ a empty □ m emptiness; (um) void

veado /vi'adu/ m deer

ve|dação /veda'sɐ̃w/ f (de casa, janela) insulation; (em motor etc) gasket; ~dar vt seal <recipiente, abertura>; stanch <sangue>; seal off <saída, área>; ~dar aco (a alg) prohibit sth (for s.o.)

vedete /ve'dɛtɛ/ f star

vee|mência /vee'mẽsia/ f vehemence; ~mente a vehement

vege|tação /veʒeta'sɐ̃w/ f vegetation; ~tal (pl ~tais) a & m vegetable; ~tar vi vegetate; ~tariano a & m vegetarian

veia /'veja/ f vein

veicular /veiku'lar/ vt convey; place <anúncios>

veículo /ve'ikulu/ m vehicle; (de comunicação etc) medium

vela¹ /'vɛla/ f (de barco) sail; (esporte) sailing

vela² /'vɛla/ f candle; (em motor) spark plug; segurar a ~ (fam) play gooseberry

velar¹ /ve'lar/ vt (cobrir) veil

velar² /ve'lar/ vt watch over □ vi keep vigil

veleidade /velej'dadʒi/ f whim

ve|leiro /ve'leru/ m sailing boat; ~lejar vi sail

velhaco /ve'ʎaku/ a crooked □ m crook

ve|lharia /veʎa'ria/ f old thing; ~lhice f old age; ~lho /ɛ/ a old □ m old man; ~lhote /ɔ/ m old man

velocidade /velosi'dadʒi/ f speed;

(Port: marcha) gear; a toda ~ at full speed; ~ máxima speed limit

velocímetro /velo'simetru/ m speedometer

velocista /velo'sista/ m/f sprinter

velório /ve'lɔriu/ m wake

veloz /ve'lɔs/ a fast

veludo /ve'ludu/ m velvet; ~ cotelê corduroy

ven|cedor /vẽse'dor/ a winning □ m winner; ~cer vt win over <adversário etc>; win <partida, corrida, batalha> □ vi (triunfar) win; <prestação, aluguel, dívida> fall due; <contrato, passaporte, prazo> expire; <apólice> mature; ~cido a dar-se por ~cido give in; ~cimento m (de dívida, aluguel) due date; (de contrato, prazo) expiry date; (de alimento, remédio etc) best before date; (salário) payment; pl earnings

venda¹ /'vẽda/ f sale; (loja) general store; à ~ on sale; pôr à ~ put up for sale

ven|da² /'vẽda/ f blindfold; ~dar vt blindfold

venda|val /vẽda'vaw/ (pl ~vais) m gale, storm

ven|dável /vẽ'davew/ (pl ~dáveis) a saleable; ~dedor m (de loja) shop assistant; (em geral) seller; ~der vt/i sell; estar ~dendo saúde be bursting with health

vendeta /vẽ'deta/ f vendetta

veneno /ve'nenu/ m poison; (de cobra etc, malignidade) venom; ~so /o/ a poisonous; (maldoso) venomous

vene|ração /venera'sɐ̃w/ f reverence; (de Deus etc) worship; ~rar vt revere; worship <Deus etc>

venéreo /ve'nɛriu/ a doença ~rea venereal disease

Veneza /ve'neza/ f Venice

veneziana /venezi'ana/ f shutter

Venezuela /venezu'ɛla/ f Venezuela

venezuelano /venezue'lanu/ a & m Venezuelan

venta /'vẽta/ f nostril

ven|tania /vẽta'nia/ f gale; ~tar vi be windy; ~tarola /ɔ/ f fan

venti|lação /vẽtʃila'sɐ̃w/ f ventilation; ~lador m fan; ~lar vt ventilate; air <sala, roupa>

ven|to /'vẽtu/ m wind; de ~ to em popa smoothly; ~toinha f (cata-vento) weather vane; (Port: ventilador) fan; ~tosa /ɔ/ f sucker; ~toso /o/ a windy

ven|tre /'vẽtri/ m belly; ~tríloquo m ventriloquist

Vênus /'venus/ f Venus

ver /ver/ vt see; watch <televisão>; (resolver) see to □ vi see □ m a meu ~ in my view; ~-se vpr (no espelho *etc*) see o.s.; (*em estado, condição*) find o.s.; (*um ao outro*) see each other; ter a ~ com have to do with; vai ~ que ela não sabe (*fam*) I bet she doesn't know; vê se você não volta tarde see you don't get back late; viu? (*fam*) right?

veracidade /verasi'dadʒi/ f truthfulness

vera|near /verani'ar/ *vi* spend the summer; ~neio *m* summer holiday, (*Amer*) summer vacation; ~nista *m/f* holidaymaker, (*Amer*) vacationer

verão /ve'rãw/ *m* summer

veraz /ve'ras/ *a* truthful

verbas /'vɛrbas/ *f pl* funds

ver|bal /ver'baw/ (*pl* ~bais) *a* verbal; ~bete /e/ *m* entry; ~bo *m* verb; ~borragia *f* waffle; ~boso /o/ *a* verbose

verda|de /ver'dadʒi/ *f* truth; de ~ de <*coisa*> real; <*fazer*> really; na ~de actually; para falar a ~de to tell the truth; ~deiro *a* <*declaração, pessoa*> truthful; (*real*) true

verde /'verdʒi/ *a & m* green; jogar ~ para colher maduro fish for information; ~abacate *a invar* avocado; ~-amarelo *a* yellow and green; (*brasileiro*) Brazilian; (*nacionalista*) nationalistic; ~-esmeralda *a invar* emerald green; ~jar *vi* turn green

verdu|ra /ver'dura/ *f* (*para comer*) greens; (*da natureza*) greenery; ~reiro *m* greengrocer, (*Amer*) produce dealer

vereador /veria'dor/ *m* councillor

vereda /ve'reda/ *f* path

veredito /vere'dʒitu/ *m* verdict

vergar /ver'gar/ *vt/i* bend

vergo|nha /ver'goɲa/ *f* (*pudor*) shame; (*constrangimento*) embarrassment; (*timidez*) shyness; (*uma*) disgrace; ter ~nha be ashamed; be embarrassed; be shy; cria *ou* tome ~nha na cara! you should be ashamed of yourself!; ~nhoso *a* shameful

veridico /ve'ridʒiku/ *a* true

verificar /verifi'kar/ *vt* check, verify <*fatos, dados etc*>; ~ que ascertain that; ~ se check that; ~-se *vpr* <*previsão etc*> come true; <*acidente etc*> happen

verme /'vɛrmi/ *m* worm

verme|lhidão /vermeʎi'dãw/ *f* redness; ~lho /e/ *a & m* red; no ~lho (*endividado*) in the red

vernáculo /ver'nakulu/ *a & m* vernacular

verniz /ver'nis/ *f* varnish; (*couro*) patent leather

veros|símil /vero'simiw/ (*pl*

~símeis) *a* plausible; ~similhança *f* plausibility

verruga /ve'xuga/ *f* wart

ver|sado /ver'sadu/ *a* well-versed (em in); ~são *f* version; ~sar *vi* ~sar sobre concern; ~sátil (*pl* ~sáteis) *a* versatile; ~satilidade *f* versatility; ~sículo *m* (*da Bíblia*) verse; ~so¹ /ɛ/ *m* verse

verso² /ɛ/ *m* (*de página*) reverse, other side; vide ~ see over

vértebra /'vɛrtebra/ *f* vertebra

verte|brado /verte'bradu/ *a & m* vertebrate; ~bral (*pl* ~brais) *a* spinal

ver|tente /ver'tẽtʃi/ *f* slope; ~ter *vt* (*derramar*) pour; shed <*lágrimas, sangue*>; (*traduzir*) render (para into)

verti|cal /vertʃi'kaw/ (*pl* ~cais) *a & f* vertical; ~gem *f* dizziness; ~ginoso /o/ *a* dizzy

vesgo /'vezgu/ *a* cross-eyed

vesicula /ve'zikula/ *f* gall bladder

vespa /'vespa/ *f* wasp

véspera /'vespera/ *f* a ~ the day before; a ~ de the eve of; a ~ de Natal Christmas Eve; nas ~s de on the eve of

vespertino /vesper'tʃinu/ *a* evening

ves|te /'vestʃi/ *f* robe; ~tiário *m* (*para se trocar*) changing room; (*para guardar roupa*) cloakroom

vestibular /vestʃibu'lar/ *m* university entrance exam

vestíbulo /ves'tʃibulu/ *m* hall(way); (*do teatro*) foyer

vestido /ves'tʃidu/ *m* dress □ *a* dressed (de *m*)

vestígio /ves'tʃiʒiu/ *m* trace

ves|timenta /vestʃi'mẽta/ *f* (*de sacerdote*) vestments; ~tir *vt* (*pôr*) put on; (*usar*) wear; (*pôr roupa em*) dress; (*dar roupa a*) clothe; ~tir-se *vpr* dress; ~tir-se de branco/de padre dress in white/as a priest; ~tuário *m* clothing

vetar /ve'tar/ *vt* veto

veterano /vete'ranu/ *a & m* veteran

veterinária /veteri'nariu/ *a* veterinary □ *m* vet

veto /'vetu/ *m* veto

véu /vɛw/ *m* veil

vexa|me /ve'ʃami/ *m* disgrace; dar um ~me make a fool of o.s.; ~minoso /o/ *a* disgraceful

vexar /ve'ʃar/ *vt* shame; ~-se *vpr* be ashamed (de of)

vez /ves/ *f* (*ocasião*) time; (*turno*) turn; às ~es sometimes; cada ~ mais more and more; de ~ for good; desta ~ this time; de ~ em quando now and again, from time to time; de uma ~ (*ao mesmo tempo*) at once; (*de um golpe*) in one go; de uma ~ por todas once and for all; duas ~es twice; em ~ de instead of; fazer as ~es de take the place of; mais uma ~, outra ~ again; muitas ~es (*com muita frequência*) often; (*repetidamente*) many times; raras ~es seldom; repetidas ~es repeatedly; uma ~ ou duas ~ que since

via /'via/ *f* (*estrada*) road; (*rumo, meio*) way; (*exemplar*) copy; *pl* (*trâmites*) channels □ *prep* via; em ~s de on the point of; por ~ aérea/marítima by air/sea; por ~ das dúvidas just in case; por ~ de regra as a rule; Via Láctea Milky Way

viabili|dade /viabili'dadʒi/ *f* feasibility; ~zar *vt* make feasible

viação /via'sãw/ *f* (*transporte*) road transport; (*estradas*) road network; (*companhia*) bus company

viaduto /via'dutu/ *m* viaduct; (*rodoviário*) flyover, (*Amer*) overpass

via|gem /vi'aʒẽ/ *f* (*uma*) trip, journey; (*em geral*) travelling; *pl* (*de uma pessoa*) travels; (*em geral*) travel; boa ~gem! have a good trip!; ~gem de negócios business trip; ~jado *a* well-travelled; ~jante *a* travelling □ *m/f* traveller; ~jar *vi* travel; estar ~jando (*fam*) (*com o pensamento longe*) be miles away

viário /vi'ariu/ *a* road; anel ~ ring road

viatura /via'tura/ *f* vehicle

viá|vel /vi'avew/ (*pl* ~veis) *a* feasible

víbora /'vibora/ *f* viper

vi|bração /vibra'sãw/ *f* vibration; (*fig*) thrill; ~brante *a* vibrant; ~brar *vt* shake □ *vi* vibrate; (*fig*) be thrilled (com by)

vice /'visi/ *m/f* deputy

vice-cam|peão /visikãpi'ãw/ *m* (*f* ~peã) runner-up

vicejar /vise'ʒar/ *vi* flourish

vice-presiden|te /visiprezi'dẽtʃi/ *m* (*f* ~ta) vice-president

vice-rei /visi'xej/ *m* viceroy

vice-versa /visi'versa/ *adv* vice-versa

vici|ado /visi'adu/ *a* addicted (em to) □ *m* addict; um ~ado em drogas a drug addict; ~ar *vt* (*falsificar*) tamper with; (*estragar*) ruin □ *vi* <*droga*> be addictive; ~ar-se *vpr* get addicted (em to)

vício /'visiu/ *m* vice

vicioso /visi'ozu/ *a* círculo ~ vicious circle

vicissitudes /visisi'tudʒis/ *f pl* ups and downs

viço /'visu/ *m* (*de plantas*) exuberance; (*de pessoa, pele*) freshness; ~so /o/ *a* <*planta*> lush; <*pele, pessoa*> fresh

vida /'vida/ *f* life; sem ~ lifeless; dar ~ a liven up

videira /vi'dera/ *f* vine

vidente /vi'dẽtʃi/ *m/f* clairvoyant

vídeo /'vidʒiu/ *m* video; (*tela*) screen

video|cassete /vidʒiuka'setʃi/ *m* (*fita*) video tape; (*aparelho*) video, (*Amer*) VCR; ~clipe *m* video; ~clube *m* video club; ~game *m* videogame; ~teipe *m* video tape

vidra|ça /vi'drasa/ *f* window pane; ~caria *f* (*fábrica*) glassworks; (*vidraças*) glazing; ~ceiro *m* glazier

vi|drado /vi'dradu/ *a* glazed; estar ~drado em ou por (*fam*) love; ~drar *vt* glaze □ *vi* (*fam*) fall in love (em ou por with); ~dro *m* (*material*) glass; (*pote*) jar; (*janela*) window; ~dro fumê tinted glass

viela /vi'ɛla/ *f* alley

Viena /vi'ena/ *f* Vienna

Vietnã /vietʃi'nã/ *m*, (*Port*) Vietname /viet'nam/ *m* Vietnam

vietnamita /vietna'mita/ *a* & *m/f* Vietnamese

viga /'viga/ *f* joist

vigarice /viga'risi/ *f* swindle

vigário /vi'gariu/ *m* vicar

vigarista /viga'rista/ *m/f* swindler, con artist

vi|gência /vi'ʒẽsia/ *f* (*qualidade*) force; (*tempo*) period in force; ~gente *a* in force

vigésimo /vi'ʒɛzimu/ *a* twentieth

vigi|a /vi'ʒia/ *f* (*guarda*) watch; (*em navio*) porthole □ *m* night watchman; ~ar *vt* (*observar*) watch; (*cuidar de*) watch over; (*como sentinela*) guard □ *vi* keep watch

vigi|lância /viʒi'lãsia/ *f* vigilance; ~lante *a* vigilant

vigília /vi'ʒilia/ *f* vigil

vigor /vi'gor/ *m* vigour; em ~ in force

vigo|rar /vigo'rar/ *vi* be in force; ~roso *a* vigorous

vil /viw/ (*pl* vis) *a* base, despicable

vila /'vila/ *f* (*cidadezinha*) small town; (*casa elegante*) villa; (*conjunto de casas*) housing estate; ~ olímpica Olympic village

vi|lania /vila'nia/ *f* villainy; ~lão *m* (*f* ~lã) villain

vilarejo /vila'reʒu/ *m* village

vilipendiar /vilipẽdʒi'ar/ *vt* disparage

vime /'vimi/ *m* wicker

vina|gre /vi'nagri/ *m* vinegar; ~grete /ɛ/ *m* vinaigrette

vin|car /vĩ'kar/ *vt* crease; line <*rosto*>; ~co *m* crease; (*no rosto*) line

vincular /vĩku'lar/ *vt* bond, tie

vínculo /'vĩkulu/ *m* link, bond; ~ empregatício contract of employment vinda /'vĩda/ f coming; dar as boas ~s a welcome

vindicar /vĩdʒi'kar/ vt vindicate

vindima /vĩ'dʒima/ f vintage

vin|do /'vĩdu/ pp e pres de vir; ~douro a coming

vin|gança /vĩ'gãsa/ f vengeance, revenge; ~gar vt revenge □ vi <flores> thrive; <criança> survive; <plano, empreendimento> be successful; ~gar-se vpr take one's revenge (de for; em on); ~gativo a vindictive

vinha /'viɲa/ f vineyard

vinhedo /vi'ɲedu/ m vineyard

vinheta /vi'ɲeta/ f (na TV etc) sequence

vinho /'viɲu/ m wine □ a invar maroon; ~ do Porto port

vinícola /vi'nikola/ a wine-growing

vinicul|tor /vinikuw'tor/ m wine grower; ~tura f wine growing

vinil /vi'niw/ m vinyl

vinte /'vĩtʃi/ a & m twenty; ~na /e/ f score

viola /vi'ola/ f viola

violação /viola'sãw/ f violation

violão /vio'lãw/ m guitar

violar /vio'lar/ vt violate

vio|lência /vio'lẽsia/ f violence; (uma) act of violence; ~lentar vt rape <mulher>; ~lento a violent

violeta /vio'leta/ f violet □ a invar violet

violi|nista /violi'nista/ m/f violinist; ~no m violin

violonce|lista /violõse'lista/ m/f cellist; ~lo /ɛ/ m cello

vir /vir/ vi come; o ano que vem next year; venho lendo os jornais I have been reading the papers; vem cá come here; (fam) listen; isso não vem ao caso that's irrelevant; ~ a ser turn out to be; ~ com give <argumento etc>

virabrequim /virabre'kĩ/ m crankshaft

viração /vira'sãw/ f breeze

vira-casaca /viraka'zaka/ m/f turncoat

vira|da /vi'rada/ f turn; ~do a <roupa> inside out; (de cabeça para baixo) upside down; ~do para facing

vira-lata /vira'lata/ m mongrel

virar /vi'rar/ vt/i turn; turn over <disco, barco etc>; turn inside out <roupa>; turn out <bolsos>; tip <balde, água etc> □ vi turn; <barco> turn over; (tornar-se) become; ~-se vpr turn round; (na vida) get by, cope; ~-se para turn to; vira e mexe every so often

viravolta /vira'vɔwta/ f about-turn

virgem /'virʒẽ/ a <fita> blank; <floresta, noiva etc> virgin □ f virgin; Virgem (signo) Virgo

virgindade /virʒĩ'dadʒi/ f virginity

vírgula /'virgula/ f comma; (decimal) point

vi|ril /vi'riw/ (pl ~ris) a virile

virilha /vi'riʎa/ f groin

virilidade /virili'dadʒi/ f virility

virtu|al /virtu'aw/ (pl ~ais) a virtual

virtude /vir'tudʒi/ f virtue

virtuo|sismo /virtuo'zizmu/ m virtuosity; ~so /o/ a virtuous □ m virtuoso

virulento /viru'lẽtu/ a virulent

vírus /'virus/ m invar virus

visão /vi'zãw/ f vision; (aspecto, ponto de vista) view

visar /vi'zar/ vt aim at <caça, alvo>; ~ (a) aim for <objetivo>; <medida, ação> be aimed at

vísceras /'viseras/ f pl innards

viscon|de /vis'kõdʒi/ m viscount; ~dessa /e/ f viscountess

viscoso /vis'kozu/ a viscous

viseira /vi'zera/ f visor

visibilidade /vizibili'dadʒi/ f visibility

visionário /vizio'nariu/ a & m visionary

visi|ta /vi'zita/ f visit; (visitante) visitor; fazer uma ~ta a alg pay s.o. a visit; ~tante a visiting □ m/f visitor; ~tar vt visit

visí|vel /vi'zivew/ (pl ~veis) a visible

vislum|brar /vizlũ'brar/ vt (entrever) glimpse; (imaginar) envisage; ~bre m glimpse

visom /vi'zõ/ m mink

visor /vi'zor/ m viewfinder

vis|ta /'vista/ f sight; (dos olhos) eyesight; (panorama) view; à ~ta (visível) in view; (em dinheiro) in cash; à primeira ~ta at first sight; pôr à ~ta put on show; de ~ta <conhecer> by sight; em ~ta de in view of; ter em ~ta have in view; dar na ~ta attract attention; fazer ~ta look nice; fazer ~ta grossa turn a blind eye (a to); perder de ~ta lose sight of; a perder de ~ta as far as the eye can see; uma ~ta de olhos a quick look; ~to a seen □ m visa; pelo ~to by the looks of things; ~to que seeing that

visto|ria /visto'ria/ f inspection; ~riar vt inspect

vistoso /vis'tozu/ a eye-catching

visu|al /vizu'aw/ (pl ~ais) a visual □ m look; ~alizar vt visualize

vi|tal /vi'taw/ (pl ~tais) a vital; ~talício a for life; ~talidade f vitality vita|mina /vita'mina/ f vitamin; (bebida) liquidized fruit drink; ~minado a with added vitamins; ~mínico a vitamin

vitela /vi'tɛla/ f (carne) veal

viticultura /vitʃikuw'tura/ f viticulture

vítima /'vitʃima/ f victim

viti|mar /vitʃi'mar/ vt (matar) claim the life of; ser ~mado por fall victim to

vitória /vi'tɔria/ f victory

vitorioso /vitori'ozu/ a victorious

vi|tral /vi'traw/ (pl ~trais) m stained glass window

vitrine /vi'trini/ f shop window

vitrola /vi'trɔla/ f jukebox

viú|va /vi'uva/ f widow; ~vo a widowed □ m widower

viva /'viva/ f cheer □ int hurray; ~ a rainha long live the queen

vivacidade /vivasi'dadʒi/ f vivacity

vivalma /vi'vawma/ f não há ~ lá fora there's not a soul outside

vivar /vi'var/ vt/i cheer

vivaz /vi'vas/ a lively, vivacious; <planta> hardy

viveiro /vi'veru/ m (de plantas) nursery; (de peixes) fishpond; (de aves) aviary; (fig) breeding ground

vivência /vi'vēsia/ f experience

vívido /'vividu/ a vivid

viver /vi'ver/ vt/i live (de on) □ m life; ele vive reclamando he's always complaining

víveres /'viveris/ m pl provisions

vivissecção /vivisek'sãw/ f vivisection

vivo /'vivu/ a (que vive) living; (animado) lively; <cor> bright □ m os ~s the living; ao ~ live; estar ~ be alive; dinheiro ~ cash

vizi|nhança /vizi'ɲãsa/ f neighbourhood; ~nho a neighbouring □ m neighbour

vo|ador /voa'dor/ a flying; ~ar vi fly; (explodir) blow up; sair ~ando rush off

vocabulário /vokabu'lariu/ m vocabulary

vocábulo /vo'kabulu/ m word

voca|ção /voka'sãw/ f vocation; ~cional (pl ~cionais) a vocational; orientação ~cional careers guidance

vo|cal /vo'kaw/ (pl ~cais) a vocal

você /vo'se/ pron you; ~s pron you

vociferar /vosife'rar/ vi shout abuse

vodca /'vɔdʒka/ f vodka

voga /'vɔga/ f (moda) vogue

vo|gal /vo'gaw/ (pl ~gais) f vowel

volante /vo'lãtʃi/ m (de carro) steering wheel

volá|til /vo'latʃiw/ (pl ~teis) a volatile

vôlei /'volej/ m, voleibol /volej'bɔw/ m volleyball

volt /'vɔwtʃi/ (pl ~s) m volt

volta /'vɔwta/ f (retorno) return; (da pista) lap; (resposta) response; às ~s com tied up with; de ~ back; em ~ de around; na ~ on the way back; na ~ do correio by return of post; por ~ de around; dar a ~ ao mundo go round the world; dar a ~ por cima make a comeback; dar meia ~ turn round; dar uma ~ (a pé) go for a walk; (de carro) go for a drive; dar uma ~ em turn round; dar ~s spin round; ter ~ get a response; ~ e meia every so often; ~do a ~do para geared towards

voltagem /vow'taʒẽ/ f voltage

voltar /vow'tar/ vi go/come back, return □ vt rewind <fita>; ~-se vpr turn round; ~-se para/contra turn to/against; ~ a si come to; ~ a fazer do again; ~ atrás backtrack

volu|me /vo'lumi/ m volume; ~moso a sizeable; <som> loud

voluntário /volũ'tariu/ a & m volunteer

volúpia /vo'lupia/ f sensuality, lust

voluptuoso /voluptu'ozu/ a sensual; <mulher> voluptuous

volú|vel /vo'luvew/ (pl ~veis) a fickle

vomitar /vomi'tar/ vt/i vomit

vômito /'vomitu/ m vomit; pl vomiting

vontade /võ'tadʒi/ f will; à ~ (bem) at ease; (quanto quiser) as much as one likes; fique à ~ make yourself at home; tem comida à ~ there's plenty of food; estar com ~ de feel like; isso me dá ~ de chorar it makes me feel like crying; fazer a ~ de alg do what s.o. wants

vôo /'vou/ m flight; levantar ~ take off; ~ livre hang-gliding

voraz /vo'ras/ a voracious

vos /vus/ pron you; (a vocês) to you

vós /vɔs/ pron you

vosso /'vɔsu/ a your □ pron yours

vo|tação /vota'sãw/ f vote; ~tante m/ f voter; ~tar vt vote on <lei etc>; (dedicar) devote; (prometer) vow □ vi vote (em for)

voto /'vɔtu/ m (em votação) vote; (promessa) vow; pl (desejos) wishes

vo|vó /vo'vɔ/ f grandma; ~vô m grandpa

voz /vɔs/ f voice; dar ~ de prisão a alg place s.o. under arrest

vozeirão /voze'rãw/ m loud voice

vozerio /voze'riu/ m shouting

vul|cânico /vuw'kaniku/ a volcanic; ~cão m volcano

vul|gar /vuw'gar/ a ordinary; (baixo) vulgar; ~garizar vt popularize; (tornar baixo) vulgarize; ~go adv commonly known as

vulne|rabilidade /vuwnerabili-'dadʒi/ f vulnerability; ~rável (pl ~ráveis) a vulnerable

vul|to /'vuwtu/ m (figura) figure; (tamanho) bulk; (importância) importance; de ~to important; ~toso /o/ a bulky; (importante) important

W

walkie-talkie /uɔki'tɔki/ (pl ~s) m walkie-talkie

walkman /uɔk'mɛn/ m invar walkman

watt /u'ɔtʃi/ (pl ~s) m watt

windsur|fe /uĩ'surfi/ m windsurfing; ~fista m/f windsurfer

X

xadrez /ʃa'dres/ m (jogo) chess; (desenho) check; (fam: prisão) prison □ a invar check

xale /'ʃali/ m shawl

xampu /ʃã'pu/ m shampoo

xará /ʃa'ra/ m/f namesake

xarope /ʃa'rɔpi/ m syrup

xaxim /ʃa'ʃĩ/ m plant fibre

xenofobia /ʃenofo'bia/ f xenophobia

xenófobo /ʃe'nɔfobu/ a xenophobic □ m xenophobe

xepa /'ʃepa/ f scraps

xeque[1] /'ʃeki/ m (árabe) sheikh

xeque[2] /'ʃeki/ m (no xadrez) check; ~-mate m checkmate

xere|ta /ʃe'reta/ (fam) a nosy □ m/f nosy parker; ~tar (fam) vi nose around

xerez /ʃe'res/ m sherry

xerife /ʃe'rifi/ m sheriff

xerocar /ʃero'kar/ vt photocopy

xerox /ʃe'rɔks/ m invar photocopy

xexelento /ʃeʃe'lẽtu/ (fam) a scruffy □ m scruff

xícara /'ʃikara/ f cup

xiita /ʃi'ita/ a & m/f Shiite

xilofone /ʃilo'foni/ m xylophone

xingar /ʃĩ'gar/ vt swear at □ vi swear

xis /ʃis/ m invar letter X; o ~ do problema the crux of the problem

xixi /ʃi'ʃi/ (fam) m wee; fazer ~ do a wee

xô /ʃo/ int shoo

xucro /'ʃukru/ a ignorant

Z

zagueiro /za'geru/ m fullback

Zaire /'zajri/ m Zaire

Zâmbia /'zãbia/ f Zambia

zan|gado /zã'gadu/ a cross, annoyed; ~gar vt annoy; ~garse vpr get cross, get annoyed (com with)

zanzar /zã'zar/ vi wander

zarpar /zar'par/ vi set off; (de navio) set sail

zebra /'zebra/ f zebra; (pessoa) fool; (resultado) upset

ze|lador /zela'dor/ m caretaker, (Amer) janitor; ~lar (por) take care of; ~lo /e/ m zeal; ~lo por devotion to; ~loso /o/ a zealous

zero /'zɛru/ m zero; (em escores) nil; ~-quilômetro a invar brand new

ziguezague /zigi'zagi/ m zigzag; ~ar vi zigzag

Zimbábue /zĩ'babui/ m Zimbabwe

zinco /'zĩku/ m zinc

ziper /'ziper/ m zip, zipper

zodíaco /zo'dʒiaku/ m zodiac

zoeira /zo'era/ f din

zom|bador /zõba'dor/ a mocking; ~bar vi ~bar (de) mock; ~baria f mockery

zona /'zona/ f (área) zone; (de cidade) district; (desordem) mess; (tumulto) commotion; (bairro do meretrício) red-light district

zonzo /'zõzu/ a dizzy

zôo /'zou/ m zoo

zoo|logia /zoolo'ʒia/ f zoology; ~lógico a zoological

zoólogo /zo'ɔlogu/ m zoologist

zulu /zu'lu/ a & m/f Zulu

zum /zũ/ m zoom lens

zumbi /zũ'bi/ m zombie

zum|bido /zũ'bidu/ m buzz; (no ouvido) ringing; ~bir vi buzz

zu|nido /zu'nidu/ m (de vento, bala) whistle; (de inseto) buzz; ~nir vi <vento, bala> whistle; <inseto> buzz

zunzum /zũ'zũ/ m rumour

Zurique /zu'riki/ f Zurich

zurrar /zu'xar/ vi bray

ENGLISH-PORTUGUESE
INGLÊS-PORTUGUÊS

A

a /ə/; *emphatic* /eɪ/ (*before vowel* an /ən/; *emphatic* /æn/) *a um.* two pounds a metre duas libras o metro. sixty miles an hour sessenta milhas por hora, (P) à hora. once a year uma vez por ano

aback /ə'bæk/ *adv* taken ~ desconcertado, (P) surpreendido

abandon /ə'bændən/ *vt* abandonar □ *n* abandono *m*. ~ed *a* abandonado; (*behaviour*) livre, dissoluto. ~ment *n* abandono *m*

abashed /ə'bæʃt/ *a* confuso, (P) atrapalhado

abate /ə'beɪt/ *vt/i* abater, abrandar, diminuir. ~ment *n* abrandamento *m*, diminuição *f*

abattoir /'æbətwɑː(r)/ *n* matadouro *m*

abbey /'æbɪ/ *n* abadia *f*, mosteiro *m*

abbreviat|**e** /ə'briːvɪeɪt/ *vt* abreviar. ~ion /-'eɪʃn/ *n* abreviação *f*; (*short form*) abreviatura *f*

abdicat|**e** /'æbdɪkeɪt/ *vt/i* abdicar. ~ion /-'keɪʃn/ *n* abdicação *f*

abdom|**en** /'æbdəmən/ *n* abdómen *m*, (P) abdómen *m*. ~inal /-'dɒmɪnl/ *a* abdominal

abduct /æb'dʌkt/ *vt* raptar. ~ion /-ʃn/ *n* rapto *m*. ~or *n* raptor, -a *mf*

aberration /æbə'reɪʃn/ *n* aberração *f*

abet /ə'bet/ *vt* (*pt* abetted) (*jur*) instigar; (*aid*) auxiliar

abeyance /ə'beɪəns/ *n* in ~ (*matter*) em suspenso; (*custom*) em desuso

abhor /əb'hɔː(r)/ *vt* (*pt* abhorred) abominar, ter horror a. ~rence /-'hɒrəns/ *n* horror *m*. ~rent /-'hɒrənt/ *a* abominável, execrável

abide /ə'baɪd/ *vt* (*pt* abided) suportar, tolerar. ~ by (*promise*) manter; (*rules*) acatar

abiding /ə'baɪdɪŋ/ *a* eterno, perpétuo

ability /ə'bɪlətɪ/ *n* capacidade *f* (to do para or de fazer); (*cleverness*) habilidade *f*, esperteza *f*

abject /'æbdʒekt/ *vt* (*pt* abjected) abjecto

ablaze /ə'bleɪz/ *a* em chamas; (*fig*) aceso, (P) excitado

abl|**e** /'eɪbl/ *a* (~er, ~est) capaz (to de). be ~e to (*have power, opportunity*) ser capaz de, poder; (*know how*

to) ser capaz de, saber. ~y *adv* habilmente

ablutions /ə'bluːʃnz/ *npl* ablução *f*, abluções *fpl*

abnormal /æb'nɔːml/ *a* anormal. ~ity /-'mælətɪ/ *n* anormalidade *f*. ~ly *adv* (*unusually*) excepcionalmente

aboard /ə'bɔːd/ *adv* a bordo □ *prep* a bordo de

abode /ə'bəʊd/ *n* (*old use*) habitação *f*. place of ~ domicílio *m*

aboli|**sh** /ə'bɒlɪʃ/ *vt* abolir, extinguir. ~tion /æbə'lɪʃn/ *n* abolição *f*, extinção *f*

abominable /ə'bɒmɪnəbl/ *a* abominável, detestável

abominat|**e** /ə'bɒmɪneɪt/ *vt* abominar, detestar. ~ion /-'neɪʃn/ *n* abominação *f*

abort /ə'bɔːt/ *vt/i* (fazer) abortar. ~ive *a* (*attempt etc*) abortado, malogrado

abortion /ə'bɔːʃn/ *n* aborto *m*. have an ~ fazer um aborto, ter um aborto. ~ist *n* abortad/or, -eira *mf*

abound /ə'baʊnd/ *vi* abundar (in em)

about /ə'baʊt/ *adv* (*approximately*) aproximadamente, cerca de; (*here and there*) aqui e ali; (*all round*) por todos os lados, em roda, em volta; (*in existence*) por aí □ *prep* acerca de, sobre; (*round*) em torno de; (*somewhere in*) em, por. ~-face, ~-turn *ns* reviravolta *f*. ~ here por aqui. be ~ to estar prestes a. he was ~ to eat ia comer. how *or* what ~ leaving? e se nós fôssemos embora? know/talk ~ saber/falar sobre

above /ə'bʌv/ *adv* acima, por cima □ *prep* sobre. he's not ~ lying ele não éde mentir. ~ all sobretudo. ~-board *a* franco, honesto □ *adv* com lisura. ~-mentioned *a* acima, supracitado

abrasion /ə'breɪʒn/ *n* atrito *m*; (*injury*) escoriação *f*, esfoladura *f*

abrasive /ə'breɪsɪv/ *a* abrasivo; (*fig*) agressivo □ *n* abrasivo *m*

abreast /ə'brest/ *adv* lado a lado. keep ~ of manter-se a par de

abridge /ə'brɪdʒ/ *vt* abreviar. ~ment

n abreviação *f*, abreviatura *f*, redução *f*; (*abridged text*) resumo *m*

abroad /ə'brɔːd/ *adv* no estrangeiro; (*far and wide*) por todo o lado. go ~ ir para o estrangeiro

abrupt /ə'brʌpt/ *a* (*sudden, curt*) brusco; (*steep*) abrupto. ~ly *adv* (*suddenly*) bruscamente; (*curtly*) com brusquidão. ~ness *n* brusquidão *f*; (*steepness*) declive *m*

abscess /'æbsɪs/ *n* abscesso *m*, (*P*) abcesso *m*

abscond /əb'skɒnd/ *vi* evadir-se, andar fugido

absen|t[1] /'æbsənt/ *a* ausente; (*look etc*) distraído. ~ce *n* ausência *f*; (*lack*) falta *f*. ~t-minded *a* distraído. ~t-mindedness *n* distracção *f*, (*P*) distracção *f*

absent[2] /əb'sent/ *v refl* ~ o.s. ausentar-se

absentee /æbsen'tiː/ *n* ausente *mf*, (*P*) absentista *mf*. ~ism *n* absenteísmo *m*, (*P*) absentismo *m*

absolute /'æbsəluːt/ *a* absoluto; (*colloq: coward etc*) autêntico, (*P*) verdadeiro. ~ly *adv* absolutamente

absolution /æbsə'luːʃn/ *n* absolvição *f*

absolve /əb'zɒlv/ *vt* (*from sin*) absolver (from de); (*from vow*) desligar (from de)

absor|b /əb'sɔːb/ *vt* absorver. ~ption *n* absorção *f*

absorbent /əb'sɔːbənt/ *a* absorvente. ~ cotton (*Amer*) algodão hidrófilo *m*

abst|ain /əb'steɪn/ *vi* abster-se (from de). ~ention /-'stenʃn/ *n* abstenção *f*

abstemious /əb'stiːmɪəs/ *a* abstémio, (*P*) abstémio, sóbrio

abstinen|ce /'æbstɪnəns/ *n* abstinência *f*. ~t *a* abstinente

abstract[1] /'æbstrækt/ *a* abstrato, (*P*) abstracto

abstract[2] /əb'strækt/ *vt* (*take out*) extrair; (*separate*) abstrair. ~ed *a* distraído. ~ion /-ʃn/ *n* (*of mind*) distracção *f*, (*P*) distracção *f*; (*idea*) abstração *f*, (*P*) abstracção *f*

absurd /əb'sɜːd/ *a* absurdo. ~ity *n* absurdo *m*

abundan|t /ə'bʌndənt/ *a* abundante. ~ce *n* abundância *f*

abuse[1] /ə'bjuːz/ *vt* (*misuse*) abusar de; (*ill-treat*) maltratar; (*insult*) injuriar, insultar

abus|e[2] /ə'bjuːs/ *n* (*wrong use*) abuso *m* (of de); (*insults*) insultos *m pl.* ~ive *a* injurioso, ofensivo

abysmal /ə'bɪzməl/ *a* abismal; (*colloq: bad*) abissal

abyss /ə'bɪs/ *n* abismo *m*

academic /ækə'demɪk/ *a* académico, (*P*) académico, universitário; (*schol-arly*) intelectual; (*pej*) acadêmico, (*P*) teórico □ *n* universitário

academy /ə'kædəmɪ/ *n* academia *f*

accede /ək'siːd/ *vi* ~ to (*request*) aceder a; (*post*) assumir; (*throne*) ascender a, subir a

accelerat|e /ək'seləreɪt/ *vt* acelerar □ *vi* acelerar-se; (*auto*) acelerar. ~ion /-'reɪʃn/ *n* aceleração *f*

accelerator /ək'seləreɪtə(r)/ *n* (*auto*) acelerador *m*

accent[1] /'æksənt/ *n* acento *m*; (*local pronunciation*) sotaque *m*

accent[2] /æk'sent/ *vt* acentuar

accentuate /æk'sentʃʊeɪt/ *vt* acentuar

accept /ək'sept/ *vt* aceitar. ~able *a* aceitável. ~ance *n* aceitação *f*; (*approval*) aprovação *f*

access /'ækses/ *n* acesso *m* (to a). ~ible /ək'sesəbl/ *a* acessível

accessory /ək'sesərɪ/ *a* acessório □ *n* acessório *m*; (*jur: person*) cúmplice *m*

accident /'æksɪdənt/ *n* acidente *m*, desastre *m*; (*chance*) acaso *m*. ~al /-'dentl/ *a* acidental, fortuito. ~ally /-'dentlɪ/ *adv* acidentalmente, por acaso

acclaim /ə'kleɪm/ *vt* aclamar □ *n* aplauso *m*, aclamações *fpl*

acclimatiz|e /ə'klaɪmətaɪz/ *vt/i* aclimatar(-se). ~ation /-'zeɪʃn/ *n* aclimatação *f*

accommodat|e /ə'kɒmədeɪt/ *vt* acomodar; (*lodge*) alojar; (*adapt*) adaptar; (*supply*) fornecer; (*oblige*) fazer a vontade de. ~ing *a* obsequioso, amigo de fazer vontades. ~ion /-'deɪʃn/ *n* acomodação *f*, (*rooms*) alojamento *m*, quarto *m*

accompan|y /ə'kʌmpənɪ/ *vt* acompanhar. ~iment *n* acompanhamento *m*. ~ist *n* (*mus*) acompanhad/or, (*B*) -eira *mf*

accomplice /ə'kʌmplɪs/ *n* cúmplice *mf*

accomplish /ə'kʌmplɪʃ/ *vt* (*perform*) executar, realizar; (*achieve*) realizar, conseguir fazer. ~ed *a* acabado. ~ment *n* realização *f*, (*ability*) talento *m*, dote *m*

accord /ə'kɔːd/ *vi* concordar □ *vt* conceder □ *n* acordo *m.* of one's own ~ por vontade própria, espontaneamente. ~ance *n* in ~ance with em conformidade com, de acordo com

according /ə'kɔːdɪŋ/ *adv* ~ to conforme. ~ly *adv* (*therefore*) por conseguinte, por consequência; (*appropriately*) conformemente

accordion /ə'kɔːdɪən/ *n* acordeão *m*

accost /ə'kɒst/ *vt* abordar, abeirar-se de

account /ə'kaʊnt/ *n* (*comm*) conta *f*; (*description*) relato *m*; (*importance*)

importância *f* □ *vt* considerar. ~ for
dar contas de, explicar. on ~ of por
causa de. on no ~ em caso algum.
take into ~ ter *or* levar em conta.
~able /-əbl/ *a* responsável (for por).
~ability /-ə'bɪləti/ *n* responsabilidade *f*

accountant /ə'kaʊntənt/ *n* conta-
dor(a) *m/f*, (P) contabilista *mf*

accrue /ə'kru:/ *vi* acumular-se. ~ to
reverter em favor de

accumulat|e /ə'kju:mjʊleɪt/ *vt/i* acu-
mular(-se). ~ion /-'leɪʃn/ *n* acumulação *f*, acréscimo *m*

accumulator /ə'kju:mjʊleɪtə(r)/ *n*
(*electr*) acumulador *m*

accura|te /'ækjərət/ *a* exato, (P) exac-
to, preciso. ~cy *n* exatidão *f*, (P)
exactidão *f*, precisão *f*. ~tely *adv*
com exatidão, (P) exactidão

accuse /ə'kju:z/ *vt* acusar. the ~ed o
acusado. ~ation /ækju:'zeɪʃn/ *n*
acusação *f*

accustom /ə'kʌstəm/ *vt* acostumar,
habituar. ~ed *a* acostumado, habituado. get ~ed to acostumar-se a,
habituar-se a

ace /eɪs/ *n* ás *m*

ache /eɪk/ *n* dor *f* □ *vi* doer. my leg ~s
dói-me a perna, tenho dores na perna

achieve /ə'tʃi:v/ *vt* realizar, efetuar,
(*success*) alcançar. ~ment *n* realização *f*, (*feat*) feito *m*, façanha *f*,
sucesso *m*

acid /'æsɪd/ *a* ácido; (*wine*) azedo;
(*words*) áspero □ *n* ácido *m*. ~ity
/ə'sɪdəti/ *n* acidez *f*

acknowledge /ək'nɒlɪdʒ/ *vt* reconhecer. (*receipt of*) acusar a recepção de. ~ment *n* reconhecimen-
to *m*; (*letter etc*) acusação *f* de recebi-
mento, (P) aviso *m* de recepção

acne /'ækni/ *n* acne *mf*

acorn /'eɪkɔ:n/ *n* bolota *f*, glande *f*

acoustic /ə'ku:stɪk/ *a* acústico. ~s
npl acústica *f*

acquaint /ə'kweɪnt/ *vt* ~ s.o. with
sth pôr alg a par de alg coisa. be
~ed with (*person, fact*) conhecer.
~ance *n* (*knowledge, person*) conhecimento *m*; (*person*) conhecido *m*

acquiesce /ækwɪ'es/ *vi* consentir.
~nce *n* aquiescência *f*,
consentimento *m*

acqui|re /ə'kwaɪə(r)/ *vt* adquirir.
~sition /ækwɪ'zɪʃn/ *n* aquisição *f*

acquit /ə'kwɪt/ *vt* (*pt* acquitted)
absolver. ~ o.s. well sair-se bem.
~tal *n* absolvição *f*

acrid /'ækrɪd/ *a* acre

acrimon|ious /ækrɪ'məʊnɪəs/ *a*
acrimonioso. ~y /'ækrɪmənɪ/ *n* acrimónia *f*, (P) acrimónia *f*

acrobat /'ækrəbæt/ *n* acrobata *mf*.

~ic /-'bætɪk/ *a* acrobático. ~ics
/-'bætɪks/ *npl* acrobacia *f*

acronym /'ækrənɪm/ *n* sigla *f*

across /ə'krɒs/ *adv & prep* (*side to
side*) de lado a lado (de), de um lado
para o outro (de); (*on the other side*)
do outro lado (de); (*crosswise*) através
(de), de través. go *or* walk ~
atravessar. swim ~ atravessar a
nado

act /ækt/ *n* (*deed, theatr*) ato *m*, (P)
acto *m*; (*in variety show*) número *m*;
(*decree*) lei *f* □ *vi* agir, atuar, (P) actuar; (*theatr*) representar; (*function*)
funcionar; (*pretend*) fingir □ *vt* (*part,
role*) desempenhar. ~ as servir de.
~ing *a* interino □ *n* (*theatr*) desempenho *m*

action /'ækʃn/ *n* ação *f*, (P) acção *f*;
(*mil*) combate *m*. out of ~ fora de
combate; (*techn*) avariado. take ~
agir, atuar, (P) actuar

active /'æktɪv/ *a* ativo, (P) activo; (*interest*) vivo; (*volcano*) em atividade,
(P) actividade. ~ity /-'tɪvəti/ *n* atividade *f*, (P) actividade *f*

ac|tor /'æktə(r)/ *n* ator *m*, (P) actor *m*.
~tress *n* atriz *f*, (P) actriz *f*

actual /'æktʃʊəl/ *a* real, verdadeiro;
(*example*) concreto. the ~ pen which
a própria caneta que. ~ity /-'æləti/ *n*
realidade *f*. ~ly *adv* (*in fact*) na realidade

acumen /ə'kju:men/ *n* agudeza *f*,
perspicácia *f*

acupunctur|e /'ækjʊpʌŋktʃə(r)/ *n*
acupunctura *f*, (P) acupunctura *f*.
~ist *n* acupunturador *m*, (P) acu-
puncturista *mf*

acute /ə'kju:t/ *a* agudo; (*mind*) perspicaz; (*emotion*) intenso, vivo; (*shortage*) grande. ~ly *adv* vivamente

ad /æd/ *n* (*colloq*) anúncio *m*

AD *abbr* dC

adamant /'ædəmənt/ *a* inflexível

adapt /ə'dæpt/ *vt/i* adaptar(-se).
~ation /ædæp'teɪʃn/ *n* adaptação *f*.
~or (*electr*) *n* adaptador *m*

adaptab|le /ə'dæptəbl/ *a* adaptável.
~ility /-'bɪləti/ *n* adaptabilidade *f*

add /æd/ *vt/i* acrescentar. ~ (up)
somar. ~ up to (*total*) elevar-se a

adder /'ædə(r)/ *n* víbora *f*

addict /'ædɪkt/ *n* viciado *m*. drug ~
(*B*) viciado em droga, viciado na droga, (P) toxicodependente *mf*

addict|ed /ə'dɪktɪd/ *a* be ~ed to
(*drink, drugs; fig*) ter o vício de.
~ion /-ʃn/ *n* (*med*) dependência *f*;
(*fig*) vício *m*. ~ive *a* que produz dependência

addition /ə'dɪʃn/ *n* adição *f*. in ~
além disso. in ~ to além de. ~al
/-ʃənl/ *a* adicional, suplementar

address /ə'dres/ n endereço m; (speech) discurso m □ vt endereçar; (speak to) dirigir-se a

adenoids /'ædmɔɪdz/ npl adenóides mpl

adept /'ædept/ a & n especialista (mf), perito (m) (at em)

adequa|te /'ædɪkwət/ a adequado; (satisfactory) satisfatório. ~cy n adequação f; (of person) competência f. ~tely adv adequadamente

adhere /əd'hɪə(r)/ vi aderir (to a)

adhesive /əd'hi:sɪv/ a & n adesivo (m). ~ plaster esparadrapo m, (P) adesivo m

adjacent /ə'dʒeɪsnt/ a adjacente, contíguo (to a)

adjective /'ædʒektɪv/ n adjetivo m, (P) adjectivo m

adjoin /ə'dʒɔɪn/ vt confinar com, ficar contíguo a

adjourn /ə'dʒɜ:n/ vt adiar □ vi suspender a sessão. ~ to (go) passar a, ir para

adjudicate /ə'dʒu:dɪkeɪt/ vt/i julgar; (award) adjudicar

adjust /ə'dʒʌst/ vt/i (alter) ajustar, regular; (arrange) arranjar. ~ (o.s.) to adaptar-se a. ~able a regulável. ~ment n (techn) regulação f, afinação f; (of person) adaptação f

ad lib /æd'lɪb/ vi (pt ad libbed) (colloq) improvisar □ adv à vontade

administer /əd'mɪnɪstə(r)/ vt administrar

administrat|e /əd'mɪnɪstreɪt/ vt administrar, gerir. ~ion /-'streɪʃn/ n administração f. ~or n administrador m

administrative /əd'mɪnɪstrətɪv/ a administrativo

admirable /'ædmərəbl/ a admirável

admiral /'ædmərəl/ n almirante m

admir|e /əd'maɪə(r)/ vt admirar. ~ation /-mɪ'reɪʃn/ n admiração f. ~er /-'maɪərə(r)/ n admirador m

admission /əd'mɪʃn/ n admissão f; (to museum, theatre, etc) ingresso m, (P) entrada f; (confession) confissão f

admit /əd'mɪt/ vt (pt admitted) (let in) admitir, permitir a entrada a; (acknowledge) reconhecer, admitir. ~ to confessar. ~tance n admissão f

admoni|sh /əd'mɒnɪʃ/ vt admoestar. ~tion /-'nɪʃn/ n admoestação f

adolescen|t /ædə'lesnt/ a & n adolescente (mf). ~ce n adolescência f

adopt /ə'dɒpt/ vt adotar, (P) adoptar. ~ed child filho adotivo, (P) adoptivo. ~ion /-ʃn/ n adoção f, (P) adopção f

ador|e /ə'dɔ:(r)/ vt adorar. ~able a adorável. ~ation /ædə'reɪʃn/ n adoração f

adorn /ə'dɔ:n/ vt adornar, enfeitar

adrenalin /ə'drenəlɪn/ n adrenalina f

adrift /ə'drɪft/ a & adv à deriva

adult /'ædʌlt/ a & n adulto (m). ~hood n idade f adulta, (P) maioridade f

adulterat|e /ə'dʌltəreɪt/ vt adulterar. ~ion /'reɪʃn/ n adulteração f

adulter|y /ə'dʌltərɪ/ n adultério m. ~er, ~ess ns adúlter/o, -a mf. ~ous a adúltero

advance /əd'vɑ:ns/ vt/i avançar □ n avanço m; (payment) adiantamento m □ a (payment, booking) adiantado. in ~ com antecedência. ~d a avançado. ~ment n promoção f, ascensão f

advantage /əd'vɑ:ntɪdʒ/ n vantagem f. take ~ of aproveitar-se de, tirar partido de; (person) explorar. ~ous /ædvən'teɪdʒəs/ a vantajoso

adventur|e /əd'ventʃə(r)/ n aventura f. ~er n aventureiro m, explorador m. ~ous a aventuroso

adverb /'ædvɜ:b/ n advérbio m

adversary /'ædvəsərɪ/ n adversário m, antagonista mf

advers|e /'ædvɜ:s/ a (contrary) adverso; (unfavourable) desfavorável. ~ity /əd'vɜ:sətɪ/ n adversidade f

advert /'ædvɜ:t/ n (colloq) anúncio m

advertise /'ædvətaɪz/ vt/i anunciar, fazer publicidade (de); (sell) pôr um anúncio (para). ~ for procurar; ~r /-ə(r)/ n anunciante mf

advertisement /əd'vɜ:tɪsmənt/ n anúncio m; (advertising) publicidade f

advice /əd'vaɪs/ n conselho(s) mpl; (comm) aviso m

advis|e /əd'vaɪz/ vt aconselhar; (inform) avisar, informar. ~e against desaconselhar. ~able a aconselhável. ~er n conselheiro m; (in business) consultor m. ~ory a consultivo

advocate¹ /'ædvəkət/ n (jur) advogado m; (supporter) defensor(a) m/f

advocate² /'ædvəkeɪt/ vt advogar, defender

aerial /'eərɪəl/ a aéreo □ n antena f

aerobatics /eərə'bætɪks/ npl acrobacia f aérea

aerobics /eə'rəʊbɪks/ n ginástica f aeróbica

aerodynamic /eərəʊdaɪ'næmɪk/ a aerodinâmico

aeroplane /'eərəpleɪn/ n avião m

aerosol /'eərəsɒl/ n aerossol m

aesthetic /i:s'θetɪk/ a estético.

affair /ə'feə(r)/ n (business) negócio m; (romance) ligação f, aventura f; (matter) assunto m. love ~ paixão f

affect /ə'fekt/ vt afetar, (P) afectar. ~ation /æfek'teɪʃn/ n afetação f, (P) afectação f. ~ed a afetado, (P) afectado, pretencioso

affection /əˈfekʃn/ n afeição f, afeto m, (P) afecto m

affectionate /əˈfekʃənət/ a afetuoso, (P) afectuoso, carinhoso

affiliate /əˈfɪlɪeɪt/ vt afiliar. ~ed company filial f. ~ion /-ˈeɪʃn/ n afiliação f

affirm /əˈfɜːm/ vt afirmar. ~ation /æfəˈmeɪʃn/ n afirmação f

affirmative /əˈfɜːmətɪv/ a afirmativo □ n afirmativa f

afflict /əˈflɪkt/ vt afligir. ~ion /-ʃn/ n aflição f

affluen|t /ˈæfluənt/ a rico, afluente. ~ce n riqueza f, afluência f

afford /əˈfɔːd/ vt (have money for) permitir-se, ter meios (para). can you afford the time? você teria tempo? I can't afford a car eu não posso comprar um carro. we can't afford to lose não podemos perder

affront /əˈfrʌnt/ n afronta f □ vt insultar

afield /əˈfiːld/ adv far ~ longe

afloat /əˈfləʊt/ adv & a à tona, a flutuar; (at sea) no mar; (business) lançado, (P) sem dívidas

afraid /əˈfreɪd/ a be ~ ter medo (of, to de; that que); (be sorry) lamentar, ter muita pena. I'm ~ (that) (regret to say) lamento or tenho muita pena de dizer que

afresh /əˈfreʃ/ adv de novo

Africa /ˈæfrɪkə/ n África f. ~n a & n africano (m)

after /ˈɑːftə(r)/ adv depois □ prep depois de □ conj depois que. ~ all afinal de contas. ~ doing, depois de fazer. be ~ (seek) querer, pretender. ~-effect n sequela f, (P) sequela f, efeito m retardado (of drug) efeito m secundário

aftermath /ˈɑːftəmæθ/ n consequências fpl

afternoon /ˈɑːftəˈnuːn/ n tarde f

aftershave /ˈɑːftəʃeɪv/ n loção f após-barba, (P) loção f para a barba

afterthought /ˈɑːftəθɔːt/ n reflexão f posterior. as an ~ pensando melhor

afterwards /ˈɑːftəwədz/ adv depois, mais tarde

again /əˈɡen/ adv de novo, outra vez; (on the other hand) por outro lado. then ~ além disso

against /əˈɡenst/ prep contra

age /eɪdʒ/ n idade f; (period) época f, idade f □ vt/i (pres p ageing) envelhecer. ~s (colloq: very long time) há séculos mpl. of ~ (jur) maior. ten years of ~ com/de dez anos. under ~ menor. ~-group n faixa etária f. ~less a sempre jovem

aged[1] /eɪdʒd/ a ~ six de seis anos de idade

aged[2] /ˈeɪdʒɪd/ a idoso, velho

agen|cy /ˈeɪdʒənsɪ/ n agência f; (means) intermédio m. ~t n agente mf

agenda /əˈdʒendə/ n ordem f do dia

aggravat|e /ˈæɡrəveɪt/ vt agravar; (colloq: annoy) irritar. ~ion /-ˈeɪʃn/ n (worsening) agravamento m; (exasperation) irritação f; (colloq: trouble) aborrecimentos mpl

aggregate /ˈæɡrɪɡeɪt/ vt/i agregar (-se) □ a /ˈæɡrɪɡət/ total, global □ n (total, mass, materials) agregado m. in the ~ no todo

aggress|ive /əˈɡresɪv/ a agressivo; (weapons) ofensivo. ~ion /-ʃn/ n agressão f. ~iveness n agressividade f. ~or n agressor m

aggrieved /əˈɡriːvd/ a (having a grievance) lesado

agil|e /ˈædʒaɪl/ a ágil. ~ity /əˈdʒɪlətɪ/ n agilidade f

agitat|e /ˈædʒɪteɪt/ vt agitar. ~ion /-ˈteɪʃn/ n agitação f. ~or n agitador m

agnostic /æɡˈnɒstɪk/ a & n agnóstico (m)

ago /əˈɡəʊ/ adv há. a month ~ há um mês. long ~ há muito tempo

agony /ˈæɡənɪ/ n agonia f; (mental) angústia f. ~ize vi atormentar-se, torturar-se. ~izing a angustiante, (P) doloroso

agree /əˈɡriː/ vt/i concordar; (of figures) acertar. ~ that reconhecer que. ~ to do concordar em or aceitar fazer. ~ to sth concordar com alguma coisa. seafood doesn't ~ with me não me dou bem com mariscos. ~d a (time, place) combinado. be ~d estar de acordo

agreeable /əˈɡriːəbl/ a agradável. be ~ to estar de acordo com

agreement /əˈɡriːmənt/ n acordo m; (gramm) concordância f; (contract) contrato m. in ~ de acordo

agricultur|e /ˈæɡrɪkʌltʃə(r)/ n agricultura f. ~al /-ˈkʌltʃərəl/ a agrícola

aground /əˈɡraʊnd/ adv run ~ (of ship) encalhar

ahead /əˈhed/ adv à frente, adiante, (in advance) adiantado. ~ of sb diante de alguém, à frente de alguém. ~ of time antes da hora, adiantado. straight ~ sempre em frente

aid /eɪd/ vt ajudar □ n ajuda f. ~ and abet ser cúmplice de. in ~ of em auxílio de, a favor de

AIDS /eɪdz/ n (med) AIDS f, (P) sida m

ail /eɪl/ vt what ~s you? o que é que você tem? ~ing a doente. ~ment n doença f, achaque m aim /eɪm/ vt (gun) apontar; (efforts) dirigir; (send) atirar (at para) □ vi visar □ n alvo m. ~ at visar. ~ to aspirar a, tencionar. take ~ fazer pontaria. ~less a, ~lessly adv sem objectivo, (P) objectivo

air /eə(r)/ n ar m □ vt arejar; (views) expor □ a (base etc) aéreo. in the ~ (rumour) espalhado; (plans) no ar. on the ~ (radio) no ar. ~-conditioned a com ar condicionado. ~-conditioning n condicionamento m do ar, (P) ar m condicionado. ~-force Força f Aérea. ~-hostess aeromoça f, (P) hospedeira f de bordo. ~-raid ataque m aéreo

airborne /'eəbɔːn/ a (aviat: in flight) no ar; (diseases) levado pelo ar; (freight) por transporte aéreo

aircraft /'eəkrɑːft/ n (pl invar) avião m. ~-carrier n porta-aviões m

airfield /'eəfiːld/ n campo m de aviação

airgun /'eəgʌn/ n espingarda f de pressão

airlift /'eəlɪft/ n ponte f aérea □ vt transportar por ponte aérea

airline /'eəlaɪn/ n linha f aérea

airlock /'eəlɒk/ n câmara f de vácuo; (in pipe) bolha f de ar

airmail /'eəmeɪl/ n correio m aéreo. by ~ por avião

airport /'eəpɔːt/ n aeroporto m

airsick /'eəsɪk/ a enjoado. ~ness /-nɪs/ n enjôo m, (P) enjoo m

airstrip /'eəstrɪp/ n pista f de aterrissagem, (P) pista f de aterragem

airtight /'eətaɪt/ a hermético

airy /'eərɪ/ a (-ier, -iest) arejado; (manner) desenvolto

aisle /aɪl/ n (of church) nave f lateral; (gangway) coxia f

ajar /ə'dʒɑː(r)/ adv & a entreaberto

alabaster /'æləbɑːstə(r)/ n alabastro m

à la carte /ɑːlɑː'kɑːt/ adv & a à la carte, (P) à lista

alarm /ə'lɑːm/ n alarme m; (clock) campainha f □ vt alarmar. ~-clock n despertador m. ~-bell n campainha f de alarme. ~ing a alarmante. ~ist n alarmista mf

alas /ə'læs/ int ai! ai de mim!

albatross /'ælbətrɒs/ n albatroz m

album /'ælbəm/ n álbum m

alcohol /'ælkəhɒl/ n álcool m. ~ic /-'hɒlɪk/ a (person, drink) alcoólico □ n alcoólico m. ~ism n alcoolismo m

alcove /'ælkəʊv/ n recesso m, alcova f

ale /eɪl/ n cerveja f inglesa

alert /ə'lɜːt/ a (lively) vivo; (watchful) vigilante □ n alerta m □ vt alertar. be on the ~ estar alerta

algebra /'ældʒɪbrə/ n álgebra f. ~ic /-'breɪk/ a algébrico

Algeria /æl'dʒɪərɪə/ n Argélia f. ~n a & n argelino (m)

alias /'eɪlɪəs/ n (pl -ases) outro nome m, nome falso m, (P) pseudónimo m □ adv aliás

alibi /'ælɪbaɪ/ n (pl -is) álibi m, (P) alibi m

alien /'eɪlɪən/ n & a estrangeiro (m). ~ to (contrary) contrário a; (differing) alheio a, estranho a

alienate /'eɪlɪəneɪt/ vt alienar. ~ion /-'neɪʃn/ n alienação f

alight[1] /ə'laɪt/ vi descer; (bird) pousar

alight[2] /ə'laɪt/ a (on fire) em chamas; (lit up) aceso

align /ə'laɪn/ vt alinhar. ~ment n alinhamento m

alike /ə'laɪk/ a semelhante, parecido □ adv da mesma maneira. look or be ~ parecer-se

alimony /'ælɪmənɪ/ n pensão f alimentar, (P) de alimentos

alive /ə'laɪv/ a vivo. ~ to sensível a. ~ with fervilhando de, (P) a fervilhar de

alkali /'ælkəlaɪ/ n (pl -is) álcali m, (P) alcali m

all /ɔːl/ a & pron todo (f & pl -a, -os, -as) □ pron (everything) tudo □ adv completamente, de todo □ n tudo m. ~ the better/less/more/worse etc tanto melhor/menos/mais/pior etc. ~ (the) men todos os homens. ~ of us todos nós. ~ but quase, todos menos. ~ in (colloq: exhausted) estafado. ~ in a tudo incluído. ~ at a fundo, (P) completamente. ~-out a (effort) máximo. ~ over (in one's body) todo; (finished) acabado; (in all parts of) por todo. ~ right bem; (as a response) está bem. ~ round em tudo; (for all) para todos. ~-round a geral. ~ the same apesar de tudo. it's ~ the same to me (para mim) tanto faz

allay /ə'leɪ/ vt acalmar

allegation /ælɪ'geɪʃn/ n alegação f

allege /ə'ledʒ/ vt alegar. ~dly /-ɪdlɪ/ adv segundo dizem, alegadamente

allegiance /ə'liːdʒəns/ n fidelidade f, lealdade f

allegory /'ælɪgərɪ/ n alegoria f. ~ical /-'gɒrɪkl/ a alegórico

allergy /'ælədʒɪ/ n alergia f. ~ic /ə'lɜːdʒɪk/ a alérgico

alleviate /ə'liːvɪeɪt/ vt aliviar

alley /'ælɪ/ n (pl -eys) (street) viela f; (for bowling) pista f

alliance /ə'laɪəns/ n aliança f

allied /'ælaɪd/ a aliado

alligator /'ælɪgeɪtə(r)/ n jacaré m

allocate /'æləkeɪt/ vt (share out) distribuir; (assign) destinar. ~ion /-'keɪʃn/ n atribuição f allot /ə'lɒt/ vt (pt allotted) atribuir. ~ment n atribuição f; (share) distribuição f; (land) horta f alugada

allow /ə'laʊ/ vt permitir; (grant) conceder, dar; (reckon on) contar com; (agree) admitir, reconhecer. ~ sb to (+ inf) permitir a alg (+ inf or que + subj). ~ for levar em conta

allowance /ə'laʊəns/ n (for employees) ajudas fpl de custo; (monthly, for wife, child) benefício m; (tax) desconto m. make ~s for (person) levar em consideração, ser indulgente para com; (take into account) atender a, levar em consideração

alloy /ə'lɔɪ/ n liga f

allude /ə'lu:d/ vi ~ to aludir a

allure /ə'lʊə(r)/ vt seduzir, atrair

allusion /ə'lu:ʒn/ n alusão f

ally¹ /'ælaɪ/ n (pl -lies) aliado m

ally² /ə'laɪ/ vt aliar. ~ oneself with/ to aliar-se com/a

almanac /'ɔ:lmənæk/ n almanaque m

almighty /ɔ:l'maɪtɪ/ a todo-poderoso; (colloq) grande, formidável

almond /'a:mənd/ n amêndoa f. ~ paste maçapão m

almost /'ɔ:lməʊst/ adv quase

alone /ə'ləʊn/ a & adv só. leave ~ (abstain from interfering with) deixar em paz. let ~ (without considering) sem or para não falar de

along /ə'lɒŋ/ prep ao longo de □ adv (onward) para diante. all ~ durante todo o tempo. ~ with com. move ~, please ande, por favor

alongside /əlɒŋ'saɪd/ adv (naut) atracado. come ~ acostar □ prep ao lado de

aloof /ə'lu:f/ adv à parte □ a distante. ~ness n reserva f

aloud /ə'laʊd/ adv em voz alta

alphabet /'ælfəbet/ n alfabeto m. ~ical /-'betɪkl/ a alfabético

alpine /'ælpaɪn/ a alpino, alpestre

Alps /ælps/ npl the ~ os Alpes mpl

already /ɔ:l'redɪ/ adv já

also /'ɔ:lsəʊ/ adv também

altar /'ɔ:ltə(r)/ n altar m

alter /'ɔ:ltə(r)/ vt/i alterar(-se), modificar(-se). ~ation /-'reɪʃn/ n alteração f; (to garment) modificação f

alternate¹ /ɔ:l'tɜ:nət/ a alternado. ~ly adv alternadamente

alternate² /'ɔ:ltəneɪt/ vt/i alternar (-se). ~ing current (electr) corrente f alterna. ~or n (electr) alternador m

alternative /ɔ:l'tɜ:nətɪv/ a alternativo □ n alternativa f. ~ly adv em alternativa. or ~ly ou então

although /ɔ:l'ðəʊ/ conj embora, conquanto

altitude /'æltɪtju:d/ n altitude f

altogether /ɔ:ltə'geðə(r)/ adv (completely) completamente; (in total) ao todo; (on the whole) de modo geral

aluminium /æljʊ'mɪnɪəm/ (Amer aluminum /ə'lu:mɪnəm/) n alumínio m

always /'ɔ:lweɪz/ adv sempre

am /æm/ see be

a.m. /eɪ'em/ adv da manhã

amalgamate /ə'mælgəmeɪt/ vt/i amalgamar(-se); (comm) fundir

amass /ə'mæs/ vt amontoar, juntar

amateur /'æmətə(r)/ n & a amador (m). ~ish a (pej) de amador, (P) amadorístico

amaze /ə'meɪz/ vt assombrar, espantar. ~ed a espantado. ~ement n assombro m. ~ingly adv espantosamente

Amazon /'æməzən/ n the ~ o Amazonas

ambassador /æm'bæsədə(r)/ n embaixador m

amber /'æmbə(r)/ n âmbar m; (traffic light) luz f amarela

ambigu|ous /æm'bɪgjʊəs/ a ambíguo. ~ity /-'gju:ətɪ/ n ambigüidade f, (P) ambiguidade f

ambiti|on /æm'bɪʃn/ n ambição f. ~ous a ambicioso

ambivalen|t /æm'bɪvələnt/ a ambivalente. ~ce n ambivalência f

amble /'æmbl/ vi caminhar sem pressa

ambulance /'æmbjʊləns/ n ambulância f

ambush /'æmbʊʃ/ n emboscada f □ vt fazer uma emboscada para, (P) fazer uma emboscada a

amenable /ə'mi:nəbl/ a ~ to (responsive) sensível a

amend /ə'mend/ vt emendar, corrigir. ~ment n (to rule) emenda f. ~s n make ~s for reparar, compensar

amenities /ə'mi:nətɪz/ npl (pleasant features) atrativos mpl, (P) atractivos mpl; (facilities) confortos mpl, comodidades fpl

America /ə'merɪkə/ n América f. ~n a & n americano (m). ~nism /-nɪzəm/ n americanismo m. ~nize vt americanizar

amiable /'eɪmɪəbl/ a amável

amicable /'æmɪkəbl/ a amigável, amigo

amid(st) /ə'mɪd(st)/ prep entre, no meio de

amiss /ə'mɪs/ a & adv mal. sth ~ qq coisa que não está bem. take sth ~ levar qq coisa a mal

ammonia /ə'məʊnɪə/ n amoníaco m

ammunition /æmjʊ'nɪʃn/ n munições fpl

amnesia /æm'ni:zɪə/ n amnésia f

amnesty /ˈæmnəstɪ/ n anistia f, (P) amnistia f

amok /əˈmɒk/ adv run ~ enlouquecer; (crowd) correr desordenadamente

among(st) /əˈmʌŋ(st)/ prep entre, no meio de. ~ ourselves (aqui) entre nós

amoral /erˈmɒrəl/ a amoral

amorous /ˈæmərəs/ a amoroso

amount /əˈmaʊnt/ n quantidade f; (total) montante m; (sum of money) quantia f □ vi ~ to elevar-se a; (fig) equivaler a

amp /æmp/ n (colloq) ampère m

amphibia|n /æmˈfɪbɪən/ n anfíbio m. ~ous a anfíbio

ample /ˈæmpl/ a (-er, -est) (large, roomy) amplo; (enough) suficiente, bastante. ~y adv amplamente

amplif|y /ˈæmplɪfaɪ/ vt ampliar, amplificar. ~ier n amplificador m

amputat|e /ˈæmpjuteɪt/ vt amputar. ~ion /-ˈteɪʃn/ n amputação f

amus|e /əˈmjuːz/ vt divertir. ~ement n divertimento m. ~ing a divertido

an /ən, æn/ see a

anachronism /əˈnækrənɪzəm/ n anacronismo m

anaem|ia /əˈniːmɪə/ n anemia f. ~ic a anêmico, (P) anémico

anaesthetic /ænɪsˈθetɪk/ n anestético m, (P) anestésico m. give an ~ to anestesiar

anaesthetist /əˈniːsθətɪst/ n anestesista mf

anagram /ˈænəgræm/ n anagrama m

analog(ue) /ˈænəlɒg/ a análogo

analogy /əˈnælədʒɪ/ n analogia f

analys|e /ˈænəlaɪz/ vt analisar. ~t /-ɪst/ n analista mf

analysis /əˈnæləsɪs/ n (pl -yses /-əsiːz/) análise f

analytic(al) /ænəˈlɪtɪk(l)/ a analítico

anarch|y /ˈænəkɪ/ n anarquia f. ~ist n anarquista mf

anatom|y /əˈnætəmɪ/ n anatomia f. ~ical /ænəˈtɒmɪkl/ a anatômico, (P) anatómico

ancest|or /ˈænsestə(r)/ n antepassado m. ~ral /-ˈsestrəl/ a ancestral (pl -ais)

ancestry /ˈænsestrɪ/ n ascendência f, estirpe f

anchor /ˈæŋkə(r)/ n âncora f □ vt/i ancorar. ~age /-rɪdʒ/ n ancoradouro m

anchovy /ˈæntʃəvɪ/ n enchova f, (P) anchova f

ancient /ˈeɪnʃənt/ a antigo

ancillary /ænˈsɪlərɪ/ a ancilar, (P) subordinado

and /ənd/; emphatic /ænd/ conj e. go ~ see vá ver. better ~ better/ less ~ less etc cada vez melhor/menos etc

anecdote /ˈænɪkdəʊt/ n anedota f

angel /ˈeɪndʒl/ n anjo m. ~ic /ænˈdʒelɪk/ a angélico, angelical

anger /ˈæŋgə(r)/ n cólera f, zanga f □ vt irritar

angle[1] /ˈæŋgl/ n ângulo m

angle[2] /ˈæŋgl/ vi (fish) pescar (à linha). ~ for (fig: compliments, information) andar à procura de. ~r /-ə(r)/ n pescador m

anglicism /ˈæŋglɪsɪzəm/ n anglicismo m

Anglo- /ˈæŋgləʊ/ pref anglo-

Anglo-Saxon /ˈæŋgləʊˈsæksn/ a & n anglo-saxão (m)

angr|y /ˈæŋgrɪ/ a (-ier, -iest) zangado. get ~y zangar-se (with com). ~ily adv furiosamente

anguish /ˈæŋgwɪʃ/ n angústia f

angular /ˈæŋgjʊlə(r)/ a angular; (features) anguloso

animal /ˈænɪml/ a & n animal (m)

animate[1] /ˈænɪmət/ a animado

animat|e[2] /ˈænɪmeɪt/ vt animar. ~ion /-ˈmeɪʃn/ n animação f. ~ed cartoon filme m de bonecos animados, (P) de desenhos animados

animosity /ænɪˈmɒsətɪ/ n animosidade f

aniseed /ˈænɪsiːd/ n semente f de anis

ankle /ˈæŋkl/ n tornozelo m. ~ sock meia f soquete

annex /əˈneks/ vt anexar. ~ation /ænekˈseɪʃn/ n anexação f

annexe /ˈæneks/ n anexo m

annihilate /əˈnaɪəleɪt/ vt aniquilar

anniversary /ænɪˈvɜːsərɪ/ n aniversário m

announce /əˈnaʊns/ vt anunciar. ~ment n anúncio m. ~r /-ə(r)/ n (radio, TV) locutor m

annoy /əˈnɔɪ/ vt irritar, aborrecer. ~ance n aborrecimento m. ~ed a aborrecido (with com). get ~ed aborrecer-se. ~ing a irritante

annual /ˈænjʊəl/ a anual □ n (bot) planta f anual; (book) anuário m. ~ly adv anualmente

annuity /əˈnjuːətɪ/ n anuidade f

annul /əˈnʌl/ vt (pt annulled) anular. ~ment n anulação f

anomal|y /əˈnɒmalɪ/ n anomalia f. ~ous a anômalo, (P) anómalo

anonym|ous /əˈnɒnɪməs/ a anônimo, (P) anónimo. ~ity /ænəˈnɪmətɪ/ n anonimato m

anorak /ˈænəræk/ n anoraque m, anorak m

another /əˈnʌðə(r)/ a & pron (um) outro. ~ ten minutes mais dez minutos. to one ~ um ao outro, uns aos outros

answer /ˈɑːnsə(r)/ n resposta f; (solution) solução f □ vt responder a;

(*prayer*) atender a □ *vi* responder. ~ the door atender à porta. ~ **back** retrucar, (*P*) responder torto. ~ **for** responder por. ~**able** *a* responsável (for por; to perante). ~**ing machine** *n* secretária *f* eletrónica

ant /ænt/ *n* formiga *f*

antagonism /æn'tægənɪzəm/ *n* antagonismo *m*. ~**t** *n* antagonista *mf*. ~**tic** /-'nɪstɪk/ *a* antagónico, (*P*) antagónico, hostil

antagonize /æn'tægənaɪz/ *vt* antagonizar, hostilizar

Antarctic /æn'tɑːktɪk/ *n* Antártico, (*P*) Antárctico *m* □ *a* antártico, (*P*) antárctico

ante- /'æntɪ/ *pref* ante-

antecedent /æntɪ'siːdnt/ *a* & *n* antecedente (*m*)

antelope /'æntɪləʊp/ *n* antílope *m*

antenatal /æntɪ'neɪtl/ *a* pré-natal

antenna /æn'tenə/ *n* (*pl* -ae /-iː/) antena *f*

anthem /'ænθəm/ *n* cântico *m*. national ~ hino *m* nacional

anthology /æn'θɒlədʒɪ/ *n* antologia *f*

anthropology /ænθrə'pɒlədʒɪ/ *n* antropologia *f*. ~**ist** *n* antropólogo *m*

anti- /æntɪ/ *pref* anti-. ~**-aircraft** /-eəkrɑːft/ *a* antiaéreo

antibiotic /æntɪbaɪ'ɒtɪk/ *n* antibiótico *m*

antibody /'æntɪbɒdɪ/ *n* anticorpo *m*

anticipat|e /æn'tɪsɪpeɪt/ *vt* (*foresee*, *expect*) prever; (*forestall*) anteciparse a. ~**ion** /-'peɪʃn/ *n* antecipação *f*; (*expectation*) expectativa *f*. in ~**ion** of na previsão *or* expectativa de

anticlimax /æntɪ'klaɪmæks/ *n* anticlímax *m*; (*let-down*) decepção *f*. it was an ~ não correspondeu à expectativa

anticlockwise /æntɪ'klɒkwaɪz/ *adv* & *a* no sentido contrário ao dos ponteiros dum relógio

antics /'æntɪks/ *npl* (*of clown*) palhaçadas *fpl*; (*behaviour*) comportamento *m* bizarro

anticyclone /æntɪ'saɪkləʊn/ *n* anticiclone *m*

antidote /'æntɪdəʊt/ *n* antídoto *m*

antifreeze /'æntɪfriːz/ *n* anticongelante *m*

antihistamine /æntɪ'hɪstəmiːn/ *a* & *n* anti-histamínico (*m*)

antipathy /æn'tɪpəθɪ/ *n* antipatia *f*

antiquated /'æntɪkweɪtɪd/ *a* antiquado

antique /æn'tiːk/ *a* antigo □ *n* antiguidade *f*. ~ **dealer** antiquário *m*. ~ **shop** loja *f* de antiguidades, (*P*) antiquário *m*

antiquity /æn'tɪkwətɪ/ *n* antiguidade *f*

antiseptic /æntɪ'septɪk/ *a* & *n* anti-séptico (*m*)

antisocial /æntɪ'səʊʃl/ *a* anti-social; (*unsociable*) insociável

antithesis /æn'tɪθəsɪs/ *n* (*pl* -eses /-siːz/) antítese *f*.

antlers /'æntləz/ *npl* chifres *mpl*, esgalhos *mpl*

antonym /'æntənɪm/ *n* antónimo *m*, (*P*) antónimo *m*

anus /'eɪnəs/ *n* ânus *m*

anvil /'ænvɪl/ *n* bigorna *f*

anxiety /æŋ'zaɪətɪ/ *n* ansiedade *f*; (*eagerness*) ânsia *f*

anxious /'æŋkʃəs/ *a* (*worried*, *eager*) ansioso (to de, por). ~**ly** *adv* ansiosamente; (*eagerly*) impacientemente

any /'enɪ/ *a* & *pron* qualquer, quaisquer; (*in neg and interr sentences*) algum, alguns; (*in neg sentences*) nenhum, nenhuns; (*every*) todo. at ~ moment a qualquer momento. at ~ rate de qualquer modo, em todo o caso. in ~ case em todo o caso. have you ~ money/friends? você tem (algum) dinheiro/(alguns) amigos? I don't have ~ time não tenho nenhum tempo *or* tempo nenhum *or* tempo algum. has she ~? ela tem algum? she doesn't have ~ ela não tem nenhum □ *adv* (*at all*) de modo algum or nenhum; (*a little*) um pouco. ~ the less/the worse *etc* menos/pior *etc*

anybody /'enɪbɒdɪ/ *pron* qualquer pessoa; (*somebody*) alguém; (*after negative*) ninguém. he didn't see ~ ele não viu ninguém

anyhow /'enɪhaʊ/ *adv* (*no matter how*) de qualquer modo; (*badly*) de qualquer maneira, ao acaso; (*in any case*) em todo o caso. you can try, ~ em todo o caso, você pode tentar

anyone /'enɪwʌn/ *pron* = anybody

anything /'enɪθɪŋ/ *pron* (*something*) alguma coisa; (*no matter what*) qualquer coisa; (*after negative*) nada. he didn't say ~ não disse nada. it is ~ but cheap é tudo menos barato. ~ you do o que você fizer

anyway /'enɪweɪ/ *adv* de qualquer modo; (*in any case*) em todo o caso

anywhere /'enɪweə(r)/ *adv* (*somewhere*) em qualquer parte; (*after negative*) em parte alguma/nenhuma. ~ **else** em qualquer outro lado. ~ **you go** onde quer que você vá. he doesn't go ~ ele não vai a lado nenhum

apart /ə'pɑːt/ *adv* à parte; (*separated*) separado; (*into pieces*) aos bocados. ~ **from** à parte, além de. ten metres ~ a dez metros de distância entre si. come ~ desfazer-se. keep ~ manter separado. take ~ desmontar apartment /ə'pɑ:tmənt/ n (*Amer*) apartamento *m*. ~s aposentos *mpl*

apathy /'æpəθɪ/ n apatia *f*. ~etic /-'θetɪk/ a apático

ape /eɪp/ n macaco *m* □ *vt* macaquear

aperitif /ə'perətɪf/ n aperitivo *m*

aperture /'æpətʃə(r)/ n abertura *f*

apex /'eɪpeks/ n ápice *m*, cume *m*

apiece /ə'pi:s/ *adv* cada, por cabeça

apologetic /əpɒlə'dʒetɪk/ a (*tone etc*) apologético, de desculpas. be ~ desculpar-se. ~ally /-əlɪ/ *adv* desculpando-se

apologize /ə'pɒlədʒaɪz/ *vi* desculpar-se (for de, por; to junto de, perante), pedir desculpa (for, por; to, a)

apology /ə'pɒlədʒɪ/ n desculpa *f*; (*defence of belief*) apologia *f*

apostle /ə'pɒsl/ n apóstolo *m*

apostrophe /ə'pɒstrəfɪ/ n apóstrofe *f*

appal /ə'pɔ:l/ *vt* (*pt* appalled) estarrecer. ~ling a estarrecedor

apparatus /æpə'reɪtəs/ n aparelho *m*

apparent /ə'pærənt/ a aparente. ~ly *adv* aparentemente

apparition /æpə'rɪʃn/ n aparição *f*

appeal /ə'pi:l/ *vi* (*jur*) apelar (to para); (*attract*) atrair (to a); (*for funds*) angariar □ n apelo *m*; (*attractiveness*) atrativo *m*, (*P*) atractivo *m*; (*for funds*) angariação *f*. ~ to sb for sth pedir uma coisa a alg. ~ing a (*attractive*) atraente

appear /ə'pɪə(r)/ *vi* aparecer; (*seem*) parecer; (*in court, theatre*) apresentar-se. ~ance n aparição *f*; (*aspect*) aparência *f*; (*in court*) comparecimento *m*, (*P*) comparência *f*

appease /ə'pi:z/ *vt* apaziguar

appendage /ə'pendɪdʒ/ n apêndice *m*

appendicitis /əpendɪ'saɪtɪs/ n apendicite *f*

appendix /ə'pendɪks/ n (*pl* -ices /-si:z/) (*of book*) apêndice *m*; (*pl* -ixes /-ksɪz/) (*anat*) apêndice *m*

appetite /'æpɪtaɪt/ n apetite *m*

appetizer /'æpɪtaɪzə(r)/ n (*snack*) tiragosto *m*; (*drink*) aperitivo *m*

appetizing /'æpɪtaɪzɪŋ/ a apetitoso

applau|d /ə'plɔ:d/ *vt/i* aplaudir. ~se n aplauso(s) *m*(*pl*)

apple /'æpl/ n maçã *f*. ~ tree macieira *f*

appliance /ə'plaɪəns/ n aparelho *m*, instrumento *m*, utensílio *m*. household ~s utensílios *mpl* domésticos

applicable /'æplɪkəbl/ a aplicável

applicant /'æplɪkənt/ n candidato *m* (for a)

application /æplɪ'keɪʃn/ n aplicação *f*; (*request*) pedido *m*; (*form*) formulário *m*; (*for job*) candidatura *f*

apply /ə'plaɪ/ *vt* aplicar □ *vi* ~y to (*refer*) aplicar-se a; (*ask*) dirigir-se a.

~y for (*job, grant*) candidatar-se a. ~y o.s. to aplicar-se a. ~ied a aplicado

appoint /ə'pɔɪnt/ *vt* (*to post*) nomear; (*time, date*) marcar. well-~ed a bem equipado, bem provido. ~ment n nomeação *f*; (*meeting*) entrevista *f*; (*with friends*) encontro *m*; (*with doctor etc*) consulta *f*, (*P*) marcação *f*; (*job*) posto *m*

apprais|e /ə'preɪz/ *vt* avaliar. ~al n avaliação *f*

appreciable /ə'pri:ʃəbl/ a apreciável

appreciat|e /ə'pri:ʃɪeɪt/ *vt* (*value*) apreciar; (*understand*) compreender; (*be grateful for*) estar/ficar grato por □ *vi* encarecer. ~ion /-'eɪʃn/ n apreciação *f*; (*rise in value*) encarecimento *m*; (*gratitude*) reconhecimento *m*. ~ive /ə'pri:ʃɪətɪv/ a apreciador; (*grateful*) reconhecido

apprehen|d /æprɪ'hend/ *vt* (*seize, understand*) apreender; (*dread*) recear. ~sion n apreensão *f*

apprehensive /æprɪ'hensɪv/ a apreensivo

apprentice /ə'prentɪs/ n aprendiz, -a *mf* □ *vt* pôr como aprendiz (to de). ~ship n aprendizagem *f*

approach /ə'prəʊtʃ/ *vt* aproximar; (*with request or offer*) abordar □ *vi* aproximar-se □ n aproximação *f*. ~ to (*problem*) abordagem *f* de; (*place*) acesso *m* a; (*person*) diligência junto de. ~able a acessível

appropriate[1] /ə'prəʊprɪət/ a apropriado, próprio. ~ly *adv* apropriadamente, a propósito

appropriate[2] /ə'prəʊprɪeɪt/ *vt* apropriar-se de

approval /ə'pru:vl/ n aprovação *f*. on ~ (*comm*) sob condição, à aprovação

approv|e /ə'pru:v/ *vt/i* aprovar. ~e of aprovar. ~ingly *adv* com ar de aprovação

approximate[1] /ə'prɒksɪmət/ a aproximado. ~ly *adv* aproximadamente

approximat|e[2] /ə'prɒksɪmeɪt/ *vt/i* aproximar(-se) de. ~ion /-'meɪʃn/ n aproximação *f*

apricot /'eɪprɪkɒt/ n damasco *m*

April /'eɪprəl/ n Abril *m*. ~ Fool's Day o primeiro de Abril, o dia das mentiras. make an ~ fool of pregar uma mentira em, (*P*) pregar uma mentira a

apron /'eɪprən/ n avental *m*

apt /æpt/ a apto; (*pupil*) dotado. be ~ to ser propenso a. ~ly *adv* apropriadamente

aptitude /'æptɪtju:d/ n aptidão *f*, (*P*) aptitude *f*

aqualung /'ækwəlʌŋ/ n escafandro autónomo, (*P*) autónomo *m*

aquarium /ə'kweərɪəm/ n (pl -ums)
aquário m

Aquarius /ə'kweərɪəs/ n (astr)
Aquário m

aquatic /ə'kwætɪk/ a aquático; (sport)
náutico, aquático

aqueduct /'ækwɪdʌkt/ n aqueduto m

Arab /'ærəb/ a & n árabe (mf). ~ic a
& n (lang) árabe (m), arábico (m).
a~ic numerals algarismos mpl
árabes or arábicos

Arabian /ə'reɪbɪən/ a árabe

arable /'ærəbl/ a arável

arbitrary /'ɑ:bɪtrərɪ/ a arbitrário

arbitrat|e /'ɑ:bɪtreɪt/ vi arbitrar.
~ion /-'treɪʃn/ n arbitragem f. ~or
n árbitro m

arc /ɑ:k/ n arco m. ~ lamp lâmpada f
de arco. ~ welding soldadura f a
arco

arcade /ɑ:'keɪd/ n (shop) arcada f.
amusement ~ fliperama m

arch /ɑ:tʃ/ n arco m; (vault) abóbada f
□ vt/i arquear(-se)

arch- /ɑ:tʃ/ pref arqui-.

archaeolog|y /ɑ:kɪ'ɒlədʒɪ/ n arqueo-
logia f. ~ical /-ə'lɒdʒɪkl/ a arqueoló-
gico. ~ist n arqueólogo m

archaic /ɑ:'keɪɪk/ a arcaico

archbishop /ɑ:tʃ'bɪʃəp/ n arcebispo
m

arch-enemy /ɑ:tʃ'enəmɪ/ n inimigo m
número um

archer /'ɑ:tʃə(r)/ n arqueiro m. ~y n
tiro m ao arco

archetype /'ɑ:kɪtaɪp/ n arquétipo m

architect /'ɑ:kɪtekt/ n arquiteto m,
(P) arquitecto m

architectur|e /'ɑ:kɪtektʃə(r)/ n arqui-
tetura f, (P) arquitectura f. ~al
/-'tektʃərəl/ a arquitetónico, (P) ar-
quitectónico

archiv|es /'ɑ:kaɪvz/ npl arquivo m.
~ist /-ɪvɪst/ n arquivista mf

archway /'ɑ:tʃweɪ/ n arcada f

Arctic /'ɑ:ktɪk/ n ártico m, (P) árctico
m □ a ártico, (P) árctico. ~ weather
tempo m glacial

ardent /'ɑ:dnt/ a ardente. ~ly adv
ardentemente

ardour /'ɑ:də(r)/ n ardor m

arduous /'ɑ:djʊəs/ a árduo

are /ə(r)/; emphatic /ɑ:(r)/ see be

area /'eərɪə/ n área f

arena /ə'ri:nə/ n arena f

aren't /ɑ:nt/ = are not

Argentin|a /ɑ:dʒən'ti:nə/ n Argenti-
na f. ~ian /-'tɪnɪən/ a & n argentino
(m)

argu|e /'ɑ:gju:/ vi discutir; (reason)
argumentar, arguir □ vt (debate)
discutir. ~e that alegar que. ~able
a alegável. it's ~able that pode-se
sustentar que

argument /'ɑ:gjʊmənt/ n (dispute)
disputa f; (reasoning) argumento m.
~ative /-'mentətɪv/ a que gosta de
discutir, argumentativo

arid /'ærɪd/ a árido

Aries /'eəri:z/ n (astr) Áries m, Carneiro m

arise /ə'raɪz/ vi (pt arose, pp arisen)
surgir. ~ from resultar de

aristocracy /ærɪ'stɒkrəsɪ/ n aristocracia f

aristocrat /'ærɪstəkræt/ n aristocra-
ta mf. ~ic /-'krætɪk/ a aristocrático

arithmetic /ə'rɪθmətɪk/ n aritmética
f

ark /ɑ:k/ n Noah's ~ arca f de Noé

arm¹ /ɑ:m/ n braço m. ~ in ~ de
braço dado

arm² /ɑ:m/ vt armar □ n (mil) arma f.
~ed robbery assalto m à mão armada

armament /'ɑ:məmənt/ n armamen-
to m

armchair /'ɑ:mtʃeə(r)/ n cadeira f de
braços, poltrona f

armistice /'ɑ:mɪstɪs/ n armistício m

armour /'ɑ:mə(r)/ n armadura f; (on
tanks etc) blindagem f. ~ed a blindado

armoury /'ɑ:mərɪ/ n arsenal m

armpit /'ɑ:mpɪt/ n axila f, sovaco m

arms /ɑ:mz/ npl armas fpl. coat of ~
brasão m

army /'ɑ:mɪ/ n exército m

aroma /ə'rəʊmə/ n aroma m. ~tic
/ærə'mætɪk/ a aromático

arose /ə'rəʊz/ see arise

around /ə'raʊnd/ adv em redor, em
volta; (here and there) por aí □ prep
em redor de, em torno de, em volta de;
(approximately) aproximadamente. ~
here por aqui

arouse /ə'raʊz/ vt despertar; (excite)
excitar

arrange /ə'reɪndʒ/ vt arranjar; (time,
date) combinar. ~ to do sth combinar fazer alg coisa. ~ment n arranjo
m; (agreement) acordo m. make
~ments (for) (plans) tomar disposi-
ções (para); (preparations) fazer preparativos (para)

array /ə'reɪ/ vt revestir □ n an ~ of
(display) um leque de, uma série de

arrears /ə'rɪəz/ npl dívidas fpl em
atraso, atrasos mpl. in ~ em atraso

arrest /ə'rest/ vt (by law) deter,
prender; (process, movement) deter □
n captura f. under ~ sob prisão

arrival /ə'raɪvl/ n chegada f. new ~
recém-chegado m

arrive /ə'raɪv/ vi chegar

arrogan|t /'ærəgənt/ a arrogante.
~ce n arrogância f. ~tly adv com
arrogância

arrow /'ærəʊ/ n flecha f, seta f

arsenal /'ɑːsənl/ n arsenal m

arsenic /'ɑːsnɪk/ n arsènico m, (P) arsénico m

arson /'ɑːsn/ n fogo m posto. ~ist n incendiário m

art¹ /ɑːt/ n arte f. the ~s (univ) letras fpl. fine ~s belas-artes fpl. ~ gallery museu m (de arte); (private) galeria f de arte

artery /'ɑːtərɪ/ n artéria f

artful /'ɑːtfl/ a manhoso. ~ness n manha f

arthritis /ɑː'θraɪtɪs/ n artrite f

artichoke /'ɑːtɪtʃəʊk/ n alcachofra f. Jerusalem ~ topinambo m

article /'ɑːtɪkl/ n artigo m. ~d a (jur) em estágio, (P) a estagiar

articulate¹ /ɑː'tɪkjʊlət/ a que se exprime com clareza; (speech) bem articulado

articulat|e² /ɑː'tɪkjʊleɪt/ vt/i articular. ~ed lorry camião m articulado. ~ion /-'leɪʃn/ n articulação f

artifice /'ɑːtɪfɪs/ n artificio m

artificial /ɑːtɪ'fɪʃl/ a artificial

artillery /ɑː'tɪlərɪ/ n artilharia f

artisan /ɑːtɪ'zæn/ n artifice mf, artesão m, artesã f

artist /'ɑːtɪst/ n artista mf. ~ic /-'tɪstɪk/ a artístico. ~ry n arte f

artiste /ɑː'tiːst/ n artista mf

artless /'ɑːtlɪs/ a ingénuo, (P) ingénuo, simples

as /æz/; emphatic /æz/ adv & conj como; (while) enquanto; (when) quando. ~ a gift de presente. ~ tall as tão alto quanto, (P) tão alto como □ pron que. I ate the same ~ he comi o mesmo que ele. ~ for, ~ to quanto a. ~ from a partir de. ~ if como se. ~ much tanto, tantos. ~ many quanto, quantos. ~ soon as logo que. ~ well (also) também. ~ well as (in addition to) assim como

asbestos /æz'bestəs/ n asbesto m, amianto m

ascend /ə'send/ vt/i subir. ~ the throne ascender or subir ao trono

ascent /ə'sent/ n ascensão f; (slope) subida f, rampa f

ascertain /æsə'teɪn/ vt certificar-se de. ~ that certificar-se de que

ascribe /ə'skraɪb/ vt atribuir

ash¹ /æʃ/ n ~(-tree) freixo m

ash² /æʃ/ n cinza f. A~ Wednesday Quarta-feira f de Cinzas. ~en a pálido

ashamed /ə'ʃeɪmd/ a be ~ ter vergonha, ficar envergonhado (of de, por)

ashore /ə'ʃɔː(r)/ adv em terra. go ~ desembarcar

ashtray /'æʃtreɪ/ n cinzeiro m

Asia /'eɪʃə/ n ásia f. ~n a & n asiático (m)

aside /ə'saɪd/ adv de lado, de parte □ n (theat) aparte m. ~ from (Amer) à parte

ask /ɑːsk/ vt/i pedir; (a question) perguntar; (invite) convidar. ~ sb sth pedir uma coisa a alguém. ~ about informar-se de. ~ after sb pedir notícias de alg, perguntar por alg. ~ for pedir. ~ sb in mandar entrar alg. ~ sb to do sth pedir alguém para fazer alguma coisa

askew /ə'skjuː/ adv & a de través, de esguelha

asleep /ə'sliːp/ adv & a adormecido; (numb) dormente. fall ~ adormecer

asparagus /ə'spærəgəs/ n (plant) aspargo m, (P) espargo m; (culin) aspargos mpl, (P) espargos m

aspect /'æspekt/ n aspecto m; (direction) exposição f

aspersions /ə'spɜːʃnz/ npl cast ~ on caluniar

asphalt /'æsfælt/ n asfalto m □ vt asfaltar

asphyxiat|e /əs'fɪksɪeɪt/ vt/i asfixiar. ~ion /-'eɪʃn/ n asfixia f

aspir|e /ə'spaɪə(r)/ vi ~e to aspirar a. ~ation /æspə'reɪʃn/ n aspiração f

aspirin /'æsprɪn/ n aspirina f

ass /æs/ n burro m. make an ~ of o.s. fazer papel de palhaço, (P) fazer figura de parvo

assail /ə'seɪl/ vt assaltar, agredir. ~ant n assaltante mf, agressor m

assassin /ə'sæsɪn/ n assassino m

assassinat|e /ə'sæsɪneɪt/ vt assassinar. ~ion /-'eɪʃn/ n assassinato m

assault /ə'sɔːlt/ n assalto m □ vt assaltar, atacar

assemble /ə'sembl/ vt (people) reunir; (fit together) montar □ vi reunir-se

assembly /ə'semblɪ/ n assembléia f, (P) assembleia f. ~ line linha f de montagem

assent /ə'sent/ n assentimento m □ vi ~ to consentir em

assert /ə'sɜːt/ vt afirmar; (one's rights) reivindicar. ~ o.s. impor-se. ~ion /-ʃn/ n asserção f. ~ive a dogmático, peremptório. ~iveness n assertividade f, (P) firmeza f

assess /ə'ses/ vt avaliar; (payment) estabelecer o montante de. ~ment n avaliação f. ~or n (valuer) avaliador m

asset /'æset/ n (advantage) vantagem f. ~s (comm) ativo m, (P) activo m; (possessions) bens mpl

assiduous /ə'sɪdjʊəs/ a assíduo

assign /ə'saɪn/ vt atribuir, destinar;

(*jur*) transmitir. ~ **sb to** designar alg para

assignation /æsɪg'neɪʃn/ *n* combinação *f* (de hora e local) de encontro

assignment /ə'saɪnmənt/ *n* tarefa *f*, missão *f*; (*jur*) transmissão *f*

assimilat|e /ə'sɪmɪleɪt/ *vt/i* assimilar(-se). ~**ion** /-'eɪʃn/ *n* assimilação *f*

assist /ə'sɪst/ *vt/i* ajudar. ~**ance** *n* ajuda *f*, assistência *f*

assistant /ə'sɪstənt/ *n* (*helper*) assistente *mf*, auxiliar *mf*; (*in shop*) ajudante *mf*, empregado *m* □ *a* adjunto

associat|e[1] /ə'səʊʃɪeɪt/ *vt* associar □ *vi* ~**e with** conviver com. ~**ion** /-'eɪʃn/ *n* associação *f*

associate[2] /ə'səʊʃɪət/ *a & n* associado (*m*)

assort|ed /ə'sɔːtɪd/ *a* variados; (*foods*) sortidos. ~**ment** *n* sortimento *m*, (*P*) sortido *m*

assume /ə'sjuːm/ *vt* assumir; (*presume*) supor, presumir

assumption /ə'sʌmpʃn/ *n* suposição *f*

assurance /ə'ʃʊərəns/ *n* certeza *f*, garantia *f*; (*insurance*) seguro *m*; (*self-confidence*) segurança *f*, confiança *f*

assure /ə'ʃʊə(r)/ *vt* assegurar. ~**d** *a* certo, garantido. **rest** ~**d that** ficar certo que

asterisk /'æstərɪsk/ *n* asterisco *m*

asthma /'æsmə/ *n* asma *f*. ~**tic** /-'mætɪk/ *a & n* asmático (*m*)

astonish /ə'stɒnɪʃ/ *vt* espantar. ~**ingly** *adv* espantosamente. ~**ment** *n* espanto *m*

astound /ə'staʊnd/ *vt* assombrar

astray /ə'streɪ/ *adv & a* **go** ~ perder-se, extraviar-se. **lead** ~ desencaminhar

astride /ə'straɪd/ *adv & prep* escarranchado (em)

astringent /ə'strɪndʒənt/ *a & n* adstringente (*m*)

astrolog|y /ə'strɒlədʒɪ/ *n* astrologia *f*. ~**er** *n* astrólogo *m*

astronaut /'æstrənɔːt/ *n* astronauta *mf*

astronom|y /ə'strɒnəmɪ/ *n* astronomia *f*. ~**er** *n* astrónomo *m*, (*P*) astrónomo *m*. ~**ical** /æstrə'nɒmɪkl/ *a* astronómico, (*P*) astronómico

astute /ə'stjuːt/ *a* astuto, astucioso. ~**ness** *n* astúcia *f*

asylum /ə'saɪləm/ *n* asilo *m*

at /ət/; *emphatic* /æt/ *prep* a, em. ~ **home** em casa. ~ **night** à noite. ~ **once** imediatamente; (*simultaneously*) ao mesmo tempo. ~ **school** na escola. ~ **sea** no mar. ~ **the door** na porta. ~ **times** às vezes. **angry/surprised** ~ zangado/surpreendido

com. **not** ~ **all** de nada. **no wind** ~ **all** nenhum vento

ate /et/ *see* **eat**

atheis|t /'eɪθɪɪst/ *n* ateu *m*. ~**m** /-zəm/ *n* ateísmo *m*

athlet|e /'æθliːt/ *n* atleta *mf*. ~**ic** /-'letɪk/ *a* atlético. ~**ics** /-'letɪks/ *n*(*pl*) atletismo *m*

Atlantic /ət'læntɪk/ *a* atlântico □ *n* ~ (**Ocean**) Atlântico *m*

atlas /'ætləs/ *n* atlas *m*

atmospher|e /'ætməsfɪə(r)/ *n* atmosfera *f*. ~**ic** /-'ferɪk/ *a* atmosférico

atom /'ætəm/ *n* átomo *m*. ~**ic** /ə'tɒmɪk/ *a* atómico, (*P*) atómico. ~(**ic**) **bomb** bomba *f* atómica, (*P*) atómica

atomize /'ætəmaɪz/ *vt* atomizar, vaparizar, pulverizar. ~**r** /-ə(r)/ *n* pulverizador *m*, vaporizador *m*

atone /ə'təʊn/ *vi* ~ **for** expiar. ~**ment** *n* expiação *f*

atrocious /ə'trəʊʃəs/ *a* atroz

atrocity /ə'trɒsətɪ/ *n* atrocidade *f*

atrophy /'ætrəfɪ/ *n* atrofia *f* □ *vt/i* atrofiar(-se)

attach /ə'tætʃ/ *vt/i* (*affix*) ligar(-se), prender(-se); (*join*) juntar(-se). ~**ed** *a* (*document*) junto, anexo. **be** ~**ed to** (*like*) estar apegado a. ~**ment** *n* ligação *f*; (*affection*) apego *m*; (*accessory*) acessório *m*

attaché /ə'tæʃeɪ/ *n* (*pol*) adido *m*. ~ **case** pasta *f*

attack /ə'tæk/ *n* ataque *m* □ *vt/i* atacar. ~**er** *n* atacante *mf*

attain /ə'teɪn/ *vt* atingir. ~**able** *a* atingível. ~**ment** *n* consecução *f*. ~**ments** *npl* conhecimentos *mpl*, talentos *mpl* adquiridos

attempt /ə'tempt/ *vt* tentar □ *n* tentativa *f*

attend /ə'tend/ *vt/i* atender (**to** a); (*escort*) acompanhar; (*look after*) tratar; (*meeting*) comparecer a; (*school*) frequentar, (*P*) frequentar. ~**ance** *n* comparecimento *m*; (*times present*) frequência *f*, (*P*) frequência *f*; (*people*) assistência *f*

attendant /ə'tendənt/ *a* concomitante, que acompanha □ *n* empregado *m*; (*servant*) servidor *m*

attention /ə'tenʃn/ *n* atenção *f*. ~! (*mil*) sentido! **pay** ~ prestar atenção (**to** a)

attentive /ə'tentɪv/ *a* atento; (*considerate*) atencioso

attest /ə'test/ *vt/i* ~ (**to**) atestar. ~ **a signature** reconhecer uma assinatura. ~**ation** /ætə'steɪʃn/ *n* atestação *f*, prova *f*

attic /'ætɪk/ *n* sótão *m*, águafurtada *f*

attitude /'ætɪtjuːd/ *n* atitude *f*

attorney /əˈtɜːnɪ/ n (pl ~eys) procurador m; (Amer) advogado m

attract /əˈtrækt/ vt atrair. ~ion /-ʃn/ n atração f, (P) atracção f; (charm) atrativo m, (P) atractivo m

attractive /əˈtræktɪv/ a atraente. ~ly adv atraentemente, agradavelmente

attribute¹ /əˈtrɪbjuːt/ vt ~ to atribuir a

attribute² /ˈætrɪbjuːt/ n atributo m

attrition /əˈtrɪʃn/ n war of ~ guerra f de desgaste

aubergine /ˈəʊbəʒiːn/ n berinjela f

auburn /ˈɔːbən/ a cor de acaju, castanho-avermelhado

auction /ˈɔːkʃn/ n leilão □ vt leiloar. ~eer /-əˈnɪə(r)/ n leiloeiro m, (P) pregoeiro m

audaci|ous /ɔːˈdeɪʃəs/ a audacioso, audaz. ~ty /-ˈæsətɪ/ n audácia f

audible /ˈɔːdəbl/ a audível

audience /ˈɔːdɪəns/ n auditório m; (theat, radio; interview) audiência f

audiovisual /ɔːdɪəʊˈvɪʒʊəl/ a audiovisual

audit /ˈɔːdɪt/ n auditoria f □ vt fazer uma auditoria

audition /ɔːˈdɪʃn/ n audição f □ vt dar/fazer uma audição

auditor /ˈɔːdɪtə(r)/ n perito-contador m, (P) perito-contabilista m

auditorium /ɔːdɪˈtɔːrɪəm/ n auditório m

augment /ɔːɡˈment/ vt/i aumentar (-se)

augur /ˈɔːɡə(r)/ vi ~ well/ill ser de bom ou mau agouro

August /ˈɔːɡəst/ n Agosto m

aunt /ɑːnt/ n tia f

au pair /əʊˈpeə(r)/ n au pair f

aura /ˈɔːrə/ n aura f, emanação f

auspices /ˈɔːspɪsɪz/ npl under the ~ of sob os auspícios or o patrocínio de

auspicious /ɔːˈspɪʃəs/ a auspicioso

auster|e /ɒˈstɪə(r)/ a austero. ~ity /-erətɪ/ n austeridade f

Australia /ɒˈstreɪlɪə/ n Austrália f. ~n a & n australiano (m)

Austria /ˈɒstrɪə/ n áustria f. ~n a & n austríaco (m)

authentic /ɔːˈθentɪk/ a autêntico. ~ity /-ənˈtɪsətɪ/ n autenticidade f

authenticate /ɔːˈθentɪkeɪt/ vt autenticar

author /ˈɔːθə(r)/ n autor m, autora f. ~ship n (origin) autoria f

authoritarian /ɔːθɒrɪˈteərɪən/ a autoritário

authorit|y /ɔːˈθɒrətɪ/ n autoridade f; (permission) autorização f. ~ative /-ɪtətɪv/ a (trusted) autorizado; (manner) autoritário

authoriz|e /ˈɔːθəraɪz/ vt autorizar. ~ation /-ˈzeɪʃn/ n autorização f

autistic /ɔːˈtɪstɪk/ a autista, autístico

autobiography /ɔːtəˈbaɪɒɡrəfɪ/ n autobiografia f

autocrat /ˈɔːtəkræt/ n autocrata mf. ~ic /-ˈkrætɪk/ a autocrático

autograph /ˈɔːtəɡrɑːf/ n autógrafo m □ vt autografar

automat|e /ˈɔːtəmeɪt/ vt automatizar. ~ion /ɔːtəˈmeɪʃn/ n automação f

automatic /ɔːtəˈmætɪk/ a automático □ n (car) automático m. ~ally /-klɪ/ adv automaticamente

automobile /ˈɔːtəməbiːl/ n (Amer) automóvel m

autonom|y /ɔːˈtɒnəmɪ/ n autonomia f. ~ous a autónomo, (P) autónomo

autopsy /ˈɔːtɒpsɪ/ n autópsia f

autumn /ˈɔːtəm/ n outono m. ~al /-ˈtʌmnəl/ a outonal

auxiliary /ɔːɡˈzɪlɪərɪ/ a & n auxiliar (mf). ~ verb verbo m auxiliar

avail /əˈveɪl/ vt ~ o.s. of servir-se de □ vi (be of use) valer □ n of no ~ inútil. to no ~ sem resultado, em vão

availab|le /əˈveɪləbl/ a disponível. ~ility /-ˈbɪlətɪ/ n disponibilidade f

avalanche /ˈævəlɑːnʃ/ n avalanche f

avaric|e /ˈævərɪs/ n avareza f. ~ious /-ˈrɪʃəs/ a avarento

avenge /əˈvendʒ/ vt vingar

avenue /ˈævənjuː/ n avenida f; (fig: line of approach) via f

average /ˈævərɪdʒ/ n média f □ a médio □ vt tirar a média de; (produce, do) fazer em média □ vi ~ out at dar de média, dar uma média de. on ~ em média

avers|e /əˈvɜːs/ a be ~e to ser avesso a. ~ion /-ʃn/ n aversão f, repugnância f

avert /əˈvɜːt/ vt (turn away) desviar; (ward off) evitar

aviary /ˈeɪvɪərɪ/ n aviário m

aviation /eɪvɪˈeɪʃn/ n aviação f

avid /ˈævɪd/ a ávido

avocado /ævəˈkɑːdəʊ/ n (pl ~s) abacate m

avoid /əˈvɔɪd/ vt evitar. ~able a que se pode evitar, evitável. ~ance n evitação f

await /əˈweɪt/ vt aguardar

awake /əˈweɪk/ vt/i (pt awoke, pp awoken) acordar □ a be ~ estar acordado

awaken /əˈweɪkən/ vt/i despertar. ~ing n despertar m

award /əˈwɔːd/ vt atribuir, conferir; (jur) adjudicar □ n recompensa f, prêmio m, (P) prémio m; (scholarship) bolsa f

aware /əˈweə(r)/ a ciente, cônscio. be ~ of estar consciente de or ter conciência de. become ~ of tomar consciência de. make sb ~ of sensibilizar alg para. ~ness n consciência f

away /ə'weɪ/ adv (at a distance) longe; (to a distance) para longe; (absent) fora; (persistently) sem parar; (entirely) completamente. eight miles ~ a oito milhas (de distância). four days ~ daí a quatro dias □ a & n ~ (match) jogo m fora de casa

awe /ɔ:/ n assombro m, admiração f reverente, terror m respeitoso. ~some a assombroso. ~struck a assombrado, aterrado

awful /'ɔ:fl/ a terrível. ~ly adv muito, terrivelmente

awhile /ə'waɪl/ adv por algum tempo

awkward /'ɔ:kwəd/ a difícil; (clumsy, difficult to use) desajeitado; (inconvenient) inconveniente; (embarrassing) embaraçoso; (embarrassed) embaraçado. an ~ customer (colloq) um preguês perigoso or intratável

awning /'ɔ:nɪŋ/ n toldo m

awoke, awoken /ə'wəʊk, ə'wəʊkən/ see awake

awry /ə'raɪ/ adv torto. go ~ dar errado. be ~ estar torto

axe /æks/ n machado m □ vt (pres p axing) (reduce) cortar; (dismiss) despedir

axiom /'æksɪəm/ n axioma m

axis /'æksɪs/ n (pl axes /-i:z/) eixo m

axle /'æksl/ n eixo (de roda) m

Azores /ə'zɔ:z/ n Açores mpl

B

BA abbr see Bachelor of Arts

babble /'bæbl/ vi balbuciar; (baby) palrar; (stream) murmurar □ n balbucio m; (of baby) palrice f; (of stream) murmúrio m

baboon /bə'bu:n/ n babuíno m

baby /'beɪbɪ/ n bebê m, (P) bebé m. ~ carriage (Amer) carrinho m de bebê, (P) bebé. ~-sit vi tomar conta de crianças. ~-sitter n baby-sitter mf, babá f

babyish /'beɪbɪʃ/ a infantil

bachelor /'bætʃələ(r)/ n solteiro m. B~ of Arts/Science Bacharel m em Letras/Ciencias

back /bæk/ n (of person, hand, chair) costas fpl; (of animal) dorso m; (of car, train) parte f traseira; (of house, room) fundo m; (of coin) reverso m; (of page) verso m; (football) beque m; zagueiro m, (P) defesa m □ a traseiro, posterior; (taxes) em atraso □ adv atrás, para trás; (returned) de volta □ vt (support) apoiar; (horse) apos-

tar em; (car) (fazer) recuar □ vi recuar. at the ~ of beyond em casa do diabo, no fim do mundo. ~-bencher n (pol) deputado m sem pasta. ~ down desistir (from de). ~ number número m atrasado. ~ out (of an undertaking etc) fugir (ao combinado etc). ~ up (auto) fazer marcha à ré, (P) atrás; (comput) tirar um back-up de. ~-up n apoio m; (comput) back-up m; (Amer: traffic-jam) engarrafamento m □ a de reserva; (comput) back-up

backache /'bækeɪk/ n dor f nas costas

backbiting /'bækbaɪtɪŋ/ n maledicência f

backbone /'bækbəʊn/ n espinha f dorsal

backdate /bæk'deɪt/ vt antedatar

backer /'bækə(r)/ n (of horse) apostador m; (of cause) partidário m, apoiante mf; (comm) patrocinador m, financiador m

backfire /bæk'faɪə(r)/ vi (auto) dar explosões no tubo de escape; (fig) sair o tiro pela culatra

background /'bækgraʊnd/ n (of picture) fundo m, segundo-plano m; (context) contexto m; (environment) meio m; (experience) formação f

backhand /'bækhænd/ n (tennis) esquerda f. ~ed a com as costas da mão. ~ed compliment cumprimento m âmbeguo. ~er n (sl: bribe) suborno m, (P) luvas fpl (colloq)

backing /'bækɪŋ/ n apoio m; (comm) patrocínio m

backlash /'bæklæʃ/ n (fig) reação f violenta, repercussões fpl

backlog /'bæklɒg/ n acúmulo m (de trabalho etc)

backside /'bæksaɪd/ n (colloq: buttocks) traseiro m

backstage /bæk'steɪdʒ/ a & adv por detrás dos bastidores

backstroke /'bækstrəʊk/ n nado m de costas

backtrack /'bæktræk/ vi (fig) voltar atrás

backward /'bækwəd/ a retrógrado; (retarded) atrasado; (step, look, etc) para trás

backwards /'bækwədz/ adv para trás; (walk) para trás; (fall) de costas, para trás; (in reverse order) de trás para diante, às avessas. go ~ and forwards ir e vir, andar para trás e para a frente. know sth ~ saber alg coisa de trás para a frente

backwater /'bækwɔ:tə(r)/ n (pej: place) lugar m atrasado

bacon /'beɪkən/ n toucinho m defumado; (in rashers) bacon m bacteria /bæk'tɪərɪə/ npl bactérias *fpl*. ~l *a* bacteriano

bad /bæd/ *a* (worse, worst) mau; (*accident*) grave; (*food*) estragado; (*ill*) doente. feel ~ sentir-se mal. ~ language palavrões *mpl*. ~-mannered *a* mal educado. ~-tempered *a* mal humorado. ~ly *adv* mal; (*seriously*) gravemente. want ~ly (*desire*) desejar imensamente, ter grande vontade de; (*need*) precisar muito de

badge /bædʒ/ *n* emblema *m*; (*policeman's*) crachá *m*, (P) distintivo *m*

badger /'bædʒə(r)/ *n* texugo *m* □ *vt* atormentar; (*pester*) importunar

badminton /'bædmɪntən/ *n* badminton *m*

baffle /'bæfl/ *vt* atrapalhar, desconcertar

bag /bæg/ *n* saco *m*; (*handbag*) bolsa *f*, carteira *f*. ~s (*luggage*) malas *fpl* □ *vt* (*pt* bagged) ensacar; (*colloq*: *take*) embolsar

baggage /'bægɪdʒ/ *n* bagagem *f*

baggy /'bægɪ/ *a* (*clothes*) muito largo, bufante

bagpipes /'bægpaɪps/ *npl* gaita *f* de foles

Bahamas /bə'hɑːməz/ *npl* the ~ as Bahamas *fpl*

bail¹ /beɪl/ *n* fiança *f* □ *vt* pôr em liberdade sob fiança. be out on ~ estar solto sob fiança

bail² /beɪl/ *vt* ~ (out) (*naut*) esgotar, tirar água de

bailiff /'beɪlɪf/ *n* (*officer*) oficial *m* de diligências; (*of estate*) feitor *m*

bait /beɪt/ *n* isca *f* □ *vt* pôr isca; (*fig*) atormentar (com insultos), atazanar

bak|e /beɪk/ *vt/i* cozer (no forno); (*bread*, *cakes*, *etc*) assar; (*in the sun*) torrar. ~er *n* padeiro *m*; (*cakes*) doceiro *m*. ~ing *n* cozedura *f*; (*batch*) fornada *f*. ~ing-powder *n* fermento *m* em pó. ~ing-tin forma *f*

bakery /'beɪkərɪ/ *n* padaria *f*; (*cakes*) confeitaria *f*

balance /'bæləns/ *n* equilíbrio *m*; (*scales*) balança *f*; (*sum*) saldo *m*; (*comm*) balanço *m*. ~ of power equilíbrio *m* político. ~ of trade balança *f* comercial. ~-sheet *n* balanço *m* □ *vt* equilibrar; (*weigh up*) pesar; (*budget*) equilibrar □ *vi* equilibrar-se. ~d *a* equilibrado

balcony /'bælkənɪ/ *n* balcão *m*; (*in a house*) varanda *f*

bald /bɔːld/ *a* (-er, -est) calvo, careca; (*tyre*) careca. ~ing *a* be ~ing ficar calvo. ~ly *adv* a nu e cru, (P) secamente. ~ness *n* calvície *f*

bale¹ /beɪl/ *n* (*of straw*) fardo *m*; (*of cotton*) balote *m* □ *vt* enfardar

bale² /beɪl/ *vi* ~ out saltar em pára-quedas

balk /bɔːk/ *vt* frustrar, contrariar □ *vi* ~ at assustar-se com, recuar perante

ball¹ /bɔːl/ *n* bola *f*. ~-bearing *n* rolamento *m* de esferas. ~-cock *n* válvula *f* de depósito de água. ~-point *n* esferográfica *f*

ball² /bɔːl/ *n* (*dance*) baile *m*

ballad /'bæləd/ *n* balada *f*

ballast /'bæləst/ *n* lastro *m*

ballerina /bælə'riːnə/ *n* bailarina *f*

ballet /'bæleɪ/ *n* balé *m*, (P) ballet *m*, bailado *m*

balloon /bə'luːn/ *n* balão *m*

ballot /'bælət/ *n* escrutínio *m*. ~ (-paper) *n* cédula *f* eleitoral, (P) boletim *m* de voto. ~-box *n* urna *f* □ *vi* (*pt* balloted) (*pol*) votar □ *vt* (*members*) consultar por voto secreto

ballroom /'bɔːlruːm/ *n* salão *m* de baile

balm /bɑːm/ *n* bálsamo *m*. ~y *a* balsâmico; (*mild*) suave

balustrade /bælə'streɪd/ *n* balaustrada *f*

bamboo /bæm'buː/ *n* bambu *m*

ban /bæn/ *vt* (*pt* banned) banir. ~ from proibir de □ *n* proibição *f*

banal /bə'nɑːl/ *a* banal. ~ity /-'ælətɪ/ *n* banalidade *f*

banana /bə'nɑːnə/ *n* banana *f*

band /bænd/ *n* (*for fastening*) cinta *f*, faixa *f*; (*strip*) tira *f*, banda *f*; (*mus*: *mil*) banda *f*; (*mus*: *dance*, *jazz*) conjunto *m*; (*group*) bando *m* □ *vi* ~ together juntar-se

bandage /'bændɪdʒ/ *n* atadura *f*, (P) ligadura *f* □ *vt* ligar

bandit /'bændɪt/ *n* bandido *m*

bandstand /'bændstænd/ *n* coreto *m*

bandwagon /'bændwægən/ *n* climb on the ~ (*fig*) apanhar o trem

bandy /'bændɪ/ *vt* trocar. ~ a story about espalhar uma história

bandy-legged /'bændɪlegd/ *a* cambaio, de pernas tortas

bang /bæŋ/ *n* (*blow*) pancada *f*; (*loud noise*) estouro *m*, estrondo *m*; (*of gun*) detonação *f* □ *vt/i* (*hit*, *shut*) bater □ *vi* explodir □ *int* pum. ~ in the middle jogar no meio. shut the door with a ~ bater (com) a porta

banger /'bæŋə(r)/ *n* (*firework*) bomba *f*; (*sl*: *sausage*) salsicha *f*. (old) ~ (*sl*: *car*) calhambeque *m* (*colloq*)

bangle /'bæŋgl/ *n* pulseira *f*, bracelete *m*

banish /'bænɪʃ/ *vt* banir, desterrar

banisters /'bænɪstəz/ *npl* corrimão *m*

banjo /'bændʒəʊ/ *pl* (-os) banjo *m*

bank¹ /bæŋk/ *n* (*of river*) margem *f*; (*of earth*) talude *m*; (*of sand*) banco *m*

□ *vt* amontoar □ *vi* (*aviat*) inclinar-se numa curva

bank² /bæŋk/ *n* (*comm*) banco *m* □ *vt* depositar no banco. ~ account conta *f* bancária. ~ holiday feriado *m* nacional. ~ on contar com. ~ rate taxa *f* bancária. ~ with ter conta em

bank|er /'bæŋkə(r)/ *n* banqueiro *m*. ~ing /-ɪŋ/ *n* operações *fpl* bancárias; (*career*) carreira *f* bancária, banca *f*

banknote /'bæŋknəʊt/ *n* nota *f* de banco

bankrupt /'bæŋkrʌpt/ *a* & *n* falido (*m*). go ~ falir □ *vt* levar à falência. ~cy *n* falência *f*, bancarrota *f*

banner /'bænə(r)/ *n* bandeira *f*, estandarte *m*

banns /bænz/ *npl* proclamas *mpl*, (P) banhos *mpl*

banquet /'bæŋkwɪt/ *n* banquete *m*

banter /'bæntə(r)/ *n* gracejo *m*, brincadeira *f* □ *vi* gracejar, brincar

baptism /'bæptɪzəm/ *n* batismo *m*, (P) baptismo *m*

Baptist /'bæptɪst/ *n* batista *mf*, (P) baptista *mf*

baptize /bæp'taɪz/ *vt* batizar, (P) baptizar

bar /ba:(r)/ *n* (*of chocolate*) tablette *f*, barra *f*; (*of metal, soap, sand etc*) barra *f*; (*of door, window*) tranca *f*; (*in pub*) bar *m*; (*counter*) balcão *m*, bar *m*; (*mus*) barra *f* de compasso; (*fig: obstacle*) barreira *f*; (*in lawcourt*) teia *f*. the B~ a advocacia *f* □ *vt* (*pt* barred) (*obstruct*) barrar; (*prohibit*) proibir (from de); (*exclude*) excluir; (*door, window*) trancar □ *prep* salvo, exceto, (P) excepto ~ none sem exceção, (P) excepção. ~ code código *m* de barra. behind ~s na cadeia

Barbados /ba:'beɪdɒs/ *n* Barbados *mpl*

barbarian /ba:'beərɪən/ *n* bárbaro *m*

barbaric /ba:'bærɪk/ *a* bárbaro. ~ty /-ətɪ/ *n* barbaridade *f*

barbarous /'ba:bərəs/ *a* bárbaro

barbecue /'ba:bɪkju:/ *n* (*grill*) churrasqueira *f*; (*occasion, food*) churrasco *m* □ *vt* assar

barbed /ba:bd/ *a* ~ wire arame *m* farpado

barber /'ba:bə(r)/ *n* barbeiro *m*

barbiturate /ba:'bɪtjʊrət/ *n* barbitúrico *m*

bare /beə(r)/ *a* (-er, -est) nu; (*room*) vazio; (*mere*) mero □ *vt* pôr à mostra, pôr a nu, descobrir

bareback /'beəbæk/ *adv* em pêlo

barefaced /'beəfeɪst/ *a* descarado

barefoot /'beə(r)fʊt/ *adv* descalço

barely /'beəlɪ/ *adv* apenas, mal

bargain /'ba:gɪn/ *n* (*deal*) negócio *m*; (*good buy*) pechincha *f* □ *vi* negociar; (*haggle*) regatear. ~ esperar for

barge /ba:dʒ/ *n* barcaça *f* □ *vi* ~ in interromper (despropositadamente); (*into room*) irromper

bark¹ /ba:k/ *n* (*of tree*) casca *f*

bark² /ba:k/ *n* (*of dog*) latido *m* □ *vi* latir. his ~ is worse than his bite cão que ladra não morde

barley /'ba:lɪ/ *n* cevada *f*. ~ sugar açúcar *m* de cevada. ~ water *n* água *f* de cevada

barmaid /'ba:meɪd/ *n* empregada *f* de bar

barman /'ba:mən/ *n* (*pl* -men) barman *m*, empregado *m* de bar

barmy /'ba:mɪ/ *a* (*sl*) maluco

barn /ba:n/ *n* celeiro *m*

barometer /bə'rɒmɪtə(r)/ *n* barômetro *m*, (P) barómetro *m*

baron /'bærən/ *n* barão *m*. ~ess *n* baronesa *f*

baroque /bə'rɒk/ *a* & *n* barroco (*m*)

barracks /'bærəks/ *n* quartel *m*, caserna *f*

barrage /'bæra:ʒ/ *n* barragem *f*; (*fig*) enxurrada *f*; (*mil*) fogo *m* de barragem

barrel /'bærəl/ *n* (*of oil, wine*) barril *m*; (*of gun*) cano *m*. ~-organ *n* realejo *m*

barren /'bærən/ *a* estéril; (*soil*) árido, estéril

barricade /bærɪ'keɪd/ *n* barricada *f* □ *vt* barricar

barrier /'bærɪə(r)/ *n* barreira *f*; (*hindrance*) entrave *m*, barreira *f*

barring /'ba:rɪŋ/ *prep* salvo, exceto, (P) excepto

barrister /'bærɪstə(r)/ *n* advogado *m*

barrow /'bærəʊ/ *n* carrinho *m* de mão

barter /'ba:tə(r)/ *n* troca *f* □ *vt* trocar

base /beɪs/ *n* base *f* □ *vt* basear (on em) □ *a* baixo, ignóbil. ~less *a* infundado

baseball /'beɪsbɔ:l/ *n* beisebol *m*

basement /'beɪsmənt/ *n* porão *m*, (P) cave *f*

bash /bæʃ/ *vt* bater com violência □ *n* pancada *f* forte. have a ~ at (*sl*) experimentar

bashful /'bæʃfl/ *a* tímido

basic /'beɪsɪk/ *a* básico, elementar, fundamental. ~ally *adv* basicamente, no fundo

basil /'bæzl/ *n* mangericão *m*

basin /'beɪsn/ *n* bacia *f*; (*for food*) tigela *f*; (*naut*) ante-doca *f*; (*for washing*) pia *f*

basis /'beɪsɪs/ *n* (*pl* bases /-si:z/) base *f*

bask /ba:sk/ *vi* ~ in the sun apanhar sol

basket /'ba:skɪt/ *n* cesto *m*

basketball /'ba:skɪtbɔ:l/ n basquete(-bol) m

Basque /ba:sk/ a & n basco (m)

bass¹ /bæs/ n (pl bass) (fish) perca f

bass² /beɪs/ a (mus) grave □ n (pl basses) (mus) baixo m

bassoon /bə'su:n/ n fagote m

bastard /'ba:stəd/ n (illegitimate child) bastardo m; (sl: pej) safado (sl) m; (colloq: not pej) cara (colloq) m

baste /beɪst/ vt (culin) regar (com molho)

bastion /'bæstɪən/ n bastião m, baluarte m

bat¹ /bæt/ n (cricket) pá f; (baseball) bastão m; (table tennis) rafuete f □ vt/i (pt batted) bater (em). without ~ting an eyelid sem pestanejar

bat² /bæt/ n (zool) morcego m

batch /bætʃ/ n (loaves) fornada f; (people) monte m; (goods) remessa f; (papers, letters etc) batelada f, monte m

bated /'beɪtɪd/ a with ~ breath com a respiração em suspenso, com a respiração suspensa

bath /ba:θ/ n (pl -s /ba:ðz/) banho m; (tub) banheira f. ~s (washing) banho m público; (swimming) piscina f □ vt dar banho a □ vi tomar banho

bathe /beɪð/ vt dar banho em; (wound) limpar □ vi tomar banho (de mar) □ n banho m (de mar). ~r /-ə(r)/ n banhista mf

bathing /'beɪðɪŋ/ n banho m de mar. ~-costume/-suit n traje m de banho, (P) fato m de banho

bathrobe /'ba:rəʊb/ n (Amer) roupão m

bathroom /'ba:θru:m/ n banheiro m, (P) casa f de banho

baton /'bætən/ n (mus) batuta f; (policeman's) cassetete m; (mil) bastão m

battalion /bə'tælɪən/ n batalhão m

batter /'bætə(r)/ vt bater, espancar, maltratar □ n (culin: for cakes) massa f de bolos; (culin: for frying) massa f de empanar. ~ed a (car, pan) amassado; (child, wife) maltratado, espancado. ~ing n take a ~ing levar pancada or uma surra

battery /'bætərɪ/ n (mil, auto) bateria f; (electr) pilha f

battle /'bætl/ n batalha f; (fig) luta f □ vi combater, batalhar, lutar

battlefield /'bætlfi:ld/ n campo m de batalha

battlements /'bætlmənts/ npl ameias fpl

battleship /'bætlʃɪp/ n couraçado m

baulk /bɔ:lk/ vt/i = balk

bawdy /'bɔ:dɪ/ a (-ier -iest) obsceno, indecente

bawl /bɔ:l/ vt/i berrar

bay¹ /beɪ/ n (bot) loureiro m

bay² /beɪ/ n (geog) baía f. ~ window janela f saliente

bay³ /beɪ/ n (bark) latido m □ vi latir. at ~ (animal; fig) cercado, (P) em apuros. keep at ~ manter à distância

bayonet /'beɪənɪt/ n baioneta f

bazaar /bə'za:(r)/ n bazar m

BC abbr (before Christ) a C

be /bi:/ vi (pres am, are is; pt was, were; pp been) (permanent quality/ place) ser; (temporary place/state) estar; (become) ficar. ~ hot/right etc ter calor/razão etc. he's 30 (age) he tem 30 anos. it's fine/cold etc (weather) faz bom tempo/frio etc. how are you? (health) como está? I'm a doctor — are you? eu sou médico — é mesmo? it's pretty, isn't it? é bonito, não é? he is to come (must) ele deve vir. how much is it? (cost) quanto é? ~ reading eating etc estar lendo/comendo etc. the money was found o dinheiro foi encontrado. have been to ter ido a, ter estado em

beach /bi:tʃ/ n praia f

beacon /'bi:kən/ n farol m; (marker) baliza f

bead /bi:d/ n conta f. ~ of sweat gota f de suor

beak /bi:k/ n bico m

beaker /'bi:kə(r)/ n copo m de plástico com bico; (in lab) proveta f

beam /bi:m/ n (of wood) trave f, viga f; (of light) raio m; (of torch) feixe m de luz □ vt/i (radiate) irradiar; (fig) sorrir radiante. ~ing a radiante

bean /bi:n/ n feijão m. broad ~ fava f. coffee ~s café m em grão. runner ~ feijão m verde

bear¹ /beə(r)/ n urso m

bear² /beə(r)/ vt (pt bore pp borne) sustentar, suportar; (endure) agüentar, (P) aguentar; suportar; (child) dar à luz. ~ in mind ter em mente, lembrar. ~ left virar à esquerda. ~ on relacionar-se com, ter a ver com. ~ out confirmar. ~ up! coragem! ~able a tolerável, suportável. ~er n portador m

beard /bɪəd/ n barba f. ~ed a barbado, com barba

bearing /'beərɪŋ/ n (manner) porte m; (relevance) relação f; (naut) marcação f. get one's ~s orientar-se

beast /bi:st/ n (animal, person) besta f, animal m; (in fables) fera f. ~ of burden besta f de carga

beat /bi:t/ vt/i (pt beat pp beaten) bater □ n (med) batimento m; (mus) compasso m, ritmo m; (of drum) toque m; (of policeman) ronda f, (P) giro m. ~ about the bush estar com rodeios. ~ a retreat bater em retirada. ~ it (*sl: go away*) pôr-se a andar. it ~s me (*colloq*) não consigo entender. ~ up espancar. ~er *n* (*culin*) batedeira *f*. ~ing *n* sova *f*

beautician /bjuːˈtɪʃn/ *n* esteticista *mf*
beautiful /ˈbjuːtɪfl/ *a* belo, lindo. ~ly *adv* lindamente
beautify /ˈbjuːtɪfaɪ/ *vt* embelezar
beauty /ˈbjuːtɪ/ *n* beleza *f*. ~ parlour instituto *m* de beleza. ~ spot sinal *m* no rosto, mosca *f*; (*place*) local *m* pitoresco
beaver /ˈbiːvə(r)/ *n* castor *m*
became /brˈkeɪm/ *see* become
because /brˈkɒz/ *conj* porque □ *adv* ~ of por causa de
beckon /ˈbekən/ *vt/i* ~ (to) fazer sinal (para)
become /brˈkʌm/ *vt/i* (*pt* became, *pp* become) tornar-se; (*befit*) ficar bem a. what has ~ of her? que é feito dela?
becoming /brˈkʌmɪŋ/ *a* que fica bem, apropriado
bed /bed/ *n* cama *f*; (*layer*) camada *f*; (*of sea*) fundo *m*; (*of river*) leito *m*; (*of flowers*) canteiro *m* □ *vt/i* (*pt* bedded) ~ down in deitar-se. ~ in plantar. ~ and breakfast (b & b) quarto *m* com café da manhã. ~-sit(ter) *n* (*colloq*) misto *m* de quarto e sala. go to ~ ir para cama. in ~ na cama. ~ding *n* roupa *f* de cama
bedclothes /ˈbedkləʊðz/ *n* roupa *f* de cama
bedlam /ˈbedləm/ *n* confusão *f*, balbúrdia *f*
bedraggled /brˈdrægld/ *a* (*wet*) molhado; (*untidy*) desarrumado; (*dishevelled*) desgrenhado
bedridden /ˈbedrɪdn/ *a* preso ao leito, doente de cama
bedroom /ˈbedruːm/ *n* quarto *m* de dormir
bedside /ˈbedsaɪd/ *n* cabeceira *f*. ~ manner (*doctor's*) modos *mpl* que inspiram confiança
bedspread /ˈbedspred/ *n* colcha *f*
bedtime /ˈbedtaɪm/ *n* hora *f* de deitar, hora *f* de ir para a cama
bee /biː/ *n* abelha *f*. make a ~-line for ir direto a
beech /biːtʃ/ *n* faia *f*
beef /biːf/ *n* carne *f* de vaca
beefburger /ˈbiːfbɜːgə(r)/ *n* hambúrguer *m*
beehive /ˈbiːhaɪv/ *n* colméia *f*
been /biːn/ *see* be
beer /bɪə(r)/ *n* cerveja *f*
beet /biːt/ *n* beterraba *f*
beetle /ˈbiːtl/ *n* escaravelho *m*
beetroot /ˈbiːtruːt/ *n* (raiz de) beterraba *f*
before /brˈfɔː(r)/ *prep* (*time*) antes de; (*place*) em frente de □ *adv* antes; (*al-*

ready) já □ *conj* antes que. ~ leaving antes de partir. ~ he leaves antes que ele parta, antes de ele partir
beforehand /brˈfɔːhænd/ *adv* de antemão, antecipadamente
befriend /brˈfrend/ *vt* tornar-se amigo de; (*be helpful to*) auxiliar
beg /beg/ *vt/i* (*pt* begged) mendigar; (*entreat*) suplicar. ~ sb's pardon pedir desculpa a alg. ~ the question fazer uma petição de princípio. it's going ~ging está sobrando
began /brˈgæn/ *see* begin
beggar /ˈbegə(r)/ *n* mendigo *m*, pedinte *mf*; (*colloq: person*) cara (*colloq*) *m*
begin /brˈgɪn/ *vt/i* (*pt* began, *pp* begun, *pres p* beginning) começar, principiar. ~ner *n* principiante *mf*. ~ning *n* começo *m*, princípio *m*
begrudge /brˈgrʌdʒ/ *vt* ter inveja de; (*give*) dar de má vontade. ~ doing fazer de má vontade *or* a contragosto
beguile /brˈgaɪl/ *vt* enganar
begun /brˈgʌn/ *see* begin
behalf /brˈhɑːf/ *n* on ~ of em nome de; (*in the interest of*) em favor de
behave /brˈheɪv/ *vi* portar-se. ~ (o.s.) portar-se bem
behaviour /brˈheɪvjə(r)/ *n* conduta *f*, comportamento *m*
behead /brˈhed/ *vt* decapitar
behind /brˈhaɪnd/ *prep* atrás de □ *adv* atrás; (*late*) com atraso □ *n* (*colloq: buttocks*) traseiro (*colloq*) *m*. ~ the times antiquado, retrógrado. leave ~ deixar para trás
behold /brˈhəʊld/ *vt* (*pt* beheld) (*old use*) ver
beholden /brˈhəʊldən/ *a* em dívida (to para com)
beige /beɪʒ/ *a & n* bege (*m*), (*P*) beige (*m*)
being /ˈbiːɪŋ/ *n* ser *m*. bring into ~ criar. come into ~ nascer, originar-se
belated /brˈleɪtɪd/ *a* tardio, atrasado
belch /beltʃ/ *vi* arrotar □ *vt* ~ out (*smoke*) vomitar, lançar □ *n* arroto *m*
belfry /ˈbelfrɪ/ *n* campanário *m*
Belgium /ˈbeldʒəm/ *n* Bélgica *f*. ~an *a & n* belga (*mf*)
belief /brˈliːf/ *n* crença *f*; (*trust*) confiança *f*; (*opinion*) convicção *f*
believe /brˈliːv/ *vt/i* acreditar. ~e in acreditar em. ~able *a* crível. ~er /-ə(r)/ *n* crente *mf*
belittle /brˈlɪtl/ *vt* depreciar
bell /bel/ *n* sino *m*; (*small*) sineta *f*; (*on door, of phone*) campainha *f*; (*on cat, toy*) guizo *m*
belligerent /brˈlɪdʒərənt/ *a & n* beligerante (*mf*)

bellow /'beləʊ/ *vt/i* berrar, bramir. ~ out rugir

bellows /'beləʊz/ *npl* fole *m*

belly /'belɪ/ *n* barriga *f*, ventre *m*. ~-ache *n* dor *f* de barriga

bellyful /'belɪfʊl/ *n* have a ~ estar com a barriga cheia

belong /bɪ'lɒŋ/ *vi* ~ (to) pertencer (a); (*club*) ser sócio (de)

belongings /bɪ'lɒŋɪŋz/ *npl* pertences *mpl*. personal ~ objetos *mpl* de uso pessoal

beloved /bɪ'lʌvɪd/ *a & n* amado (*m*)

below /bɪ'ləʊ/ *prep* abaixo de, debaixo de □ *adv* abaixo, em baixo; (*on page*) abaixo

belt /belt/ *n* cinto *m*; (*techn*) correia *f*; (*fig*) zona *f* □ *vt* (*sl: hit*) zurzir □ *vi* (*sl: rush*) safar-se

bemused /bɪ'mjuːzd/ *a* estonteado, confuso; (*thoughtful*) pensativo

bench /bentʃ/ *n* banco *m*; (*seat, working-table*) bancada *f*. the ~ (*jur*) os magistrados (no tribunal)

bend /bend/ *vt/i* (*pt & pp* bent) curvar(-se); (*arm, leg*) dobrar; (*road, river*) fazer uma curva, virar □ *n* curva *f*. ~ over debruçar-se *or* inclinar-se sobre

beneath /bɪ'niːθ/ *prep* abaixo de, debaixo de; (*fig*) abaixo de □ *adv* debaixo, em baixo

benediction /benɪ'dɪkʃn/ *n* benção *f*

benefactor /'benɪfæktə(r)/ *n* benfeitor *m*

beneficial /benɪ'fɪʃl/ *a* benéfico, proveitoso

benefit /'benɪfɪt/ *n* (*advantage, performance*) beneficio *m*; (*profit*) proveito *m*; (*allowance*) subsidio *m* □ *vt/i* (*pt* benefited, *pres p* benefiting) (*be useful to*) beneficiar (by de); (*do good to*) beneficiar, fazer bem a; (*receive benefit*) lucrar, ganhar (by, from com)

beneficiary /benɪ'fɪʃərɪ/ *n* beneficiário *m*

benevolen|t /bɪ'nevələnt/ *a* benevolente. ~ce *n* benevolência *f*

benign /bɪ'naɪn/ *a* (*incl med*) benigno

bent /bent/ *see* **bend** □ *n* (for para) (*skill*) aptidão *f*, jeito *m*; (*liking*) queda *f* □ *a* curvado; (*twisted*) torcido; (*sl: dishonest*) desonesto. ~ on decidido a

bequeath /bɪ'kwiːð/ *vt* legar

bequest /bɪ'kwest/ *n* legado *m*

bereave|d /bɪ'riːvd/ *a* the ~d wife/ *etc* a esposa/*etc* do falecido. the ~d family a família enlutada. ~ment *n* luto *m*

bereft /bɪ'reft/ *a* ~ of privado de

beret /'bereɪ/ *n* boina *f*

Bermuda /bə'mjuːdə/ *n* Bermudas *fpl*

berry /'berɪ/ *n* baga *f*

berserk /bə'sɜːk/ *a* go a ~ ficar louco de raiva, perder a cabeça

berth /bɜːθ/ *n* (*in ship*) beliche *m*; (*in train*) couchette *f*; (*anchorage*) ancoradouro *m* □ *vi* atracar. give a wide ~ to passar ao largo, (*P*) de largo

beside /bɪ'saɪd/ *prep* ao lado de, junto de. ~ o.s. fora de si. be ~ the point não ter nada a ver com o assunto, não vir ao caso

besides /bɪ'saɪdz/ *prep* além de; (*except*) fora, salvo □ *adv* além disso

besiege /bɪ'siːdʒ/ *vt* sitiar, cercar. ~ with assediar

best /best/ *a & n* (the) ~ (o/a) melhor (*mf*) □ *adv* melhor. ~ man padrinho *m* de casamento. at (the) ~ na melhor das hipóteses. do one's ~ fazer o (melhor) que se pode. make the ~ of tirar o melhor partido de. the ~ part of a maior parte de. to the ~ of my knowledge que eu saiba

bestow /bɪ'stəʊ/ *vt* conferir. ~ praise fazer *or* tecer elogios

best-seller /best'selə(r)/ *n* best-seller *m*

bet /bet/ *n* aposta *f* □ *vt/i* (*pt* bet *or* betted) apostar (on em)

betray /bɪ'treɪ/ *vt* trair. ~al *n* traição *f*

better /'betə(r)/ *a & adv* melhor □ *vt* melhorar □ *n* our ~s os nossos superiores *mpl*. all the ~ tanto melhor. ~ off (*richer*) mais rico. he's ~ off at home é melhor para ele ficar em casa. I'd ~ go é melhor ir-me embora. the ~ part of it a maior parte disso. get ~ melhorar. get the ~ of sb levar a melhor em relação a alg

betting-shop /'betɪŋʃɒp/ *n* agência *f* de apostas

between /bɪ'twiːn/ *prep* entre □ *adv* in ~ no meio, no intervalo. ~ you and me aqui entre nós

beverage /'bevərɪdʒ/ *n* bebida *f*

beware /bɪ'weə(r)/ *vi* acautelar-se (of com), tomar cuidado (of com)

bewilder /bɪ'wɪldə(r)/ *vt* desorientar. ~ment *n* desorientação *f*, confusão *f*

bewitch /bɪ'wɪtʃ/ *vt* encantar, cativar

beyond /bɪ'jɒnd/ *prep* além de; (*doubt, reach*) fora de □ *adv* além. it's ~ me isso ultrapassame. he lives ~ his means ele vive acima dos seus meios

bias /'baɪəs/ *n* parcialidade *f*, (*pej: prejudice*) preconceito *m*; (*sewing*) viés *m* □ *vt* (*pt* biased) influenciar. ~ed *a* parcial. ~ed against de prevenção contra, (*P*) de pé atrás contra

bib /bɪb/ *n* babeiro *m*, babette *m*

Bible /'baɪbl/ *n* Bíblia *f*

biblical /'bɪblɪkl/ *a* bíblico

bibliography /bɪblɪˈɒgrəfɪ/ n bibliografia f

bicarbonate /baɪˈkɑːbənət/ n ~ of soda bicarbonato m de soda

biceps /ˈbaɪseps/ n bíceps m

bicker /ˈbɪkə(r)/ vi questionar, discutir

bicycle /ˈbaɪsɪkl/ n bicicleta f □ vi andar de bicicleta

bid /bɪd/ n oferta f, lance m; (attempt) tentativa f □ vt/i (pt bid, pres p bidding) fazer uma oferta, lançar, oferecer como lance. ~der n licitante mf. the highest ~der quem dá or oferece mais

bide /baɪd/ vt ~ one's time esperar pelo bom momento

bidet /ˈbiːdeɪ/ n bidê m, (P) bidé m

biennial /baɪˈenɪəl/ a bienal

bifocals /baɪˈfəʊklz/ npl óculos mpl bifocais

big /bɪg/ a (bigger, biggest) grande; (sl: generous) generoso □ adv (colloq) em grande. ~-headed a pretensioso, convencido. ~ shot (sl) manda-chuva m. talk ~ gabar-se (colloq). think ~ (colloq) ter grandes planos

bigam|y /ˈbɪgəmɪ/ n bigamia f. ~ist n bígamo m. ~ous a (colloq)

bigot /ˈbɪgət/ n fanático m, intolerante mf. ~ed a fanático, intolerante. ~ry n fanatismo m, intolerância f

bigwig /ˈbɪgwɪg/ n (colloq) manda-chuva m

bike /baɪk/ n (colloq) bicicleta f

bikini /bɪˈkiːnɪ/ n (pl -is) biquíni m

bilberry /ˈbɪlbərɪ/ n arando m

bile /baɪl/ n bílis f

bilingual /baɪˈlɪŋgwəl/ a bilíngüe

bilious /ˈbɪlɪəs/ a bilioso

bill¹ /bɪl/ n (invoice) fatura f, (P) factura f; (in restaurant) conta f; (pol) projeto m, (P) projecto m de lei; (Amer: banknote) nota f de banco; (poster) cartaz m □ vt faturar, (P) facturar; (theatre) anunciar, pôr no programa. ~ of exchange letra f de câmbio. ~ sb for apresentar a alg a conta de

bill² /bɪl/ n (of bird) bico m

billiards /ˈbɪljədz/ n bilhar m

billion /ˈbɪljən/ n (10⁹) mil milhões; (10¹²) um milhão de milhões

bin /bɪn/ n (for storage) caixa f, lata f; (for rubbish) lata f do lixo, (P) caixote m

bind /baɪnd/ vt (pt bound) (tie) atar; (book) encadernar; (jur) obrigar; (cover the edge of) debruar □ n (sl: bore) chatice f (sl). be ~ing on ser obrigatório para

binding /ˈbaɪndɪŋ/ n encadernação f; (braid) debrum m

binge /bɪndʒ/ n (sl) go on a ~ cair na farra; (overeat) empanturrar-se

bingo /ˈbɪŋgəʊ/ n bingo m □ int acertei!

binoculars /bɪˈnɒkjʊləz/ npl binóculo m

biochemistry /baɪəʊˈkemɪstrɪ/ n bioquímica f

biodegradable /baɪəʊdɪˈgreɪdəbl/ a biodegradável

biograph|y /baɪˈɒgrəfɪ/ n biografia f. ~er n biógrafo m

biolog|y /baɪˈɒlədʒɪ/ n biologia f. ~ical /-əˈlɒdʒɪkl/ a biológico. ~ist n biólogo m

biopsy /ˈbaɪɒpsɪ/ n biópsia f

birch /bɜːtʃ/ n (tree) bétula f; (whip) vara f de vidoeiro

bird /bɜːd/ n ave f, pássaro m; (sl: girl) garota f (colloq). ~ sanctuary refúgio m ornitológico. ~-watcher n ornitófilo m

Biro /ˈbaɪərəʊ/ n (pl -os) (caneta) esferográfica f, Bic f

birth /bɜːθ/ n nascimento m. ~ certificate certidão f de nascimento. ~-control/rate controle m/índice m de natalidade. ~-place n lugar m de nascimento. give ~ to dar à luz

birthday /ˈbɜːθdeɪ/ n aniversário m, (P) dia m de anos. his ~ is on 9 July ele faz anos no dia 9 de julho

birthmark /ˈbɜːθmɑːk/ n sinal m

biscuit /ˈbɪskɪt/ n biscoito m, bolacha f

bisect /baɪˈsekt/ vt dividir ao meio

bishop /ˈbɪʃəp/ n bispo m

bit¹ /bɪt/ n (small piece, short time) pedaço m, bocado m; (of bridle) freio m; (of tool) broca f. a ~ um pouco

bit² /bɪt/ see bite

bitch /bɪtʃ/ n cadela f; (sl: woman) peste f (fig), cadela f (sl) □ vt/i (colloq: criticize) malhar, (P) cortar (em) (colloq); (colloq: grumble) resmungar. ~y a (colloq) maldoso

bite /baɪt/ vt/i (pt bit, pp bitten) morder; (insect) picar □ n mordida f; (sting) picada f. have a ~ (to eat) comer qualquer coisa

biting /ˈbaɪtɪŋ/ a cortante

bitter /ˈbɪtə(r)/ a amargo; (weather) glacial. ~ly adv amargamente. it's ~ly cold está um frio de rachar. ~ness n amargura f; (resentment) ressentimento m

bizarre /bɪˈzɑː(r)/ a bizarro

black /blæk/ a (-er, -est) negro, preto □ n negro m, preto m. a B~ (person) um preto, um negro □ vt enegrecer; (goods) boicotar. ~ and blue coberto de nódoas negras. ~ coffee café m (sem leite). ~ eye olho m negro. ~-ice gelo m negro sobre o asfalto. ~-market mercado m negro. ~ spot (place) local m perigoso, ponto m negro

blackberry /'blækbərı/ *n* amora *f* silvestre

blackbird /'blækbɜ:d/ *n* melro *m*

blackboard /'blækbɔ:d/ *n* quadro *m* preto

blackcurrant /'blækkʌrənt/ *n* groselha *f* negra

blacken /'blækən/ *vt/i* escurecer. ~ sb's name difamar, denegrir

blackleg /'blækleg/ *n* fura-greves *m*

blacklist /'blæklɪst/ *n* lista *f* negra □ *vt* pôr na lista negra

blackmail /'blækmeɪl/ *n* chantagem *f* □ *vt* fazer chantagem. ~er *n* chantagista *mf*

blackout /'blækaʊt/ *n* (*wartime*) blecaute *m*; (*med*) desmaio *m*; (*electr*) falta *f* de corrente; (*theatr*) apagar *m* de luzes

blacksmith /'blæksmɪθ/ *n* ferreiro *m*

bladder /'blædə(r)/ *n* bexiga *f*

blade /bleɪd/ *n* lâmina *f*; (*of oar, propeller*) pá *f*; (*of grass*) ervinha *f*, folhinha *f* de erva

blame /bleɪm/ *vt* culpar □ *n* culpa *f*. be to ~ ser o culpado. ~less *a* irrepreensível; (*innocent*) inocente

bland /blænd/ *a* (-er, -est) (*of manner*) suave; (*mild*) brando; (*insipid*) insípido

blank /blæŋk/ *a* (*space, cheque*) em branco; (*look*) vago; (*wall*) nu □ *n* espaço *m* em branco; (*cartridge*) cartucho *m* sem bala

blanket /'blæŋkɪt/ *n* cobertor *m*; (*fig*) manto *m* □ *vt* (*pt* blanketed) cobrir com cobertor; (*cover thickly*) encobrir, recobrir. wet ~ desmancha-prazeres *mf*

blare /bleə(r)/ *vt/i* ressoar, atroar □ *n* clangor *m*; (*of horn*) buzinar *m*

blasé /'blɑ:zeɪ/ *a* blasé

blaspheme /blæs'fi:m/ *vt/i* blasfemar

blasphem|y /'blæsfəmɪ/ *n* blasfêmia *f*, (P) blasfémia *f*. ~ous *a* blasfemo

blast /blɑ:st/ *n* (*gust*) rajada *f*; (*sound*) som *m*; (*explosion*) explosão *f* □ *vt* dinamitar. ~! droga! ~ed *a* maldito. ~-furnace *n* alto forno *m*. ~-off *n* (*of missile*) lançamento *m*, início *m* de combustão

blatant /'bleɪtnt/ *a* flagrante; (*shameless*) descarado

blaze /bleɪz/ *n* chamas *fpl*; (*light*) clarão *m*; (*outburst*) explosão *f* □ *vi* arder; (*shine*) resplandecer, brilhar. ~ a trail abrir o caminho, ser pioneiro

blazer /'bleɪzə(r)/ *n* blazer *m*

bleach /bli:tʃ/ *n* descolorante, descorante *m*; (*household*) água *f* sanitária □ *vt/i* branquear; (*hair*) oxigenar

bleak /bli:k/ *a* (-er, -est) (*place*) desolado; (*chilly*) frio; (*fig*) desanimador

bleary-eyed /'blɪəraɪd/ *a* com olhos injetados

bleat /bli:t/ *n* balido *m* □ *vi* balir

bleed /bli:d/ *vt/i* (*pt* bled) sangrar

bleep /bli:p/ *n* bip *m*. ~er *n* bip *m*

blemish /'blemɪʃ/ *n* defeito *m*; (*on reputation*) mancha *f* □ *vt* manchar

blend /blend/ *vt/i* misturar(-se); (*go well together*) combinar-se □ *n* mistura *f*. ~er *n* (*culin*) liquidificador *m*

bless /bles/ *vt* abençoar. be ~ed with ter a felicidade de ter. ~ing *n* benção *f*; (*thing one is glad of*) felicidade *f*. it's a ~ing in disguise há males que vêm para bem

blessed /'blesɪd/ *a* bem-aventurado; (*colloq: cursed*) maldito

blew /blu:/ *see* blow

blight /blaɪt/ *n* doença *f* de plantas; (*fig*) influência *f* maligna □ *vt* arruinar, frustrar

blind /blaɪnd/ *a* cego □ *vt* cegar □ *n* (*on window*) persiana *f*; (*deception*) ardil *m*. ~ alley (*incl fig*) beco *m* sem saída. ~ man/woman cego *m*/cega *f*. be ~ to não ver. turn a ~ eye to fingir não ver, fechar os olhos a. ~ly *adv* às cegas. ~ness *n* cegueira *f*

blindfold /'blaɪndfəʊld/ *a* & *adv* de olhos vendados □ *n* venda *f* □ *vt* vendar os olhos a

blink /blɪŋk/ *vi* piscar

blinkers /'blɪŋkəz/ *npl* antolhos *mpl*

bliss /blɪs/ *n* felicidade *f*, beatitude *f*. ~ful *a* felicíssimo. ~fully *adv* maravilhosamente

blister /'blɪstə(r)/ *n* bolha *f*, empola *f* □ *vi* empolar

blizzard /'blɪzəd/ *n* tempestade *f* de neve, nevasca *f*

bloated /'bləʊtɪd/ *a* inchado

bloater /'bləʊtə(r)/ *n* arenque *m* salgado e defumado

blob /blɒb/ *n* pingo *m* grosso; (*stain*) mancha *f*

bloc /blɒk/ *n* bloco *m*

block /blɒk/ *n* bloco *m*; (*buildings*) quarteirão *m*; (*in pipe*) entupimento *m*. ~ (*of flats*) prédio *m* (de andares) □ *vt* bloquear, obstruir; (*pipe*) entupir. ~ letters maiúsculas *fpl*. ~age *n* obstrução *f*

blockade /blɒ'keɪd/ *n* bloqueio *m* □ *vt* bloquear

bloke /bləʊk/ *n* (*colloq*) sujeito *m* (*colloq*), cara *m* (*colloq*)

blond /blɒnd/ *a* & *n* louro (*m*)

blonde /blɒnd/ *a* & *n* loura (*f*)

blood /blʌd/ *n* sangue *m* □ *a* (*bank, donor, transfusion, etc*) de sangue; (*poisoning*) do sangue; (*group, vessel*) sangüíneo. ~-curdling *a* horrendo. ~ pressure tensão *f* arterial. ~ test exame *m* de sangue. ~less *a* (*fig*) pacifico

bloodhound /'blʌdhaʊnd/ *n* sabujo *m*

bloodshed /'blʌdʃed/ *n* derramamento *m* de sangue, carnificina *f*

bloodshot /'blʌdʃɒt/ *a* injetado *or* (*P*) injectado de sangue

bloodstream /'blʌdstri:m/ *n* sangue *m*, fluxo *m* sanguíneo

bloodthirsty /'blʌdθɜ:stɪ/ *a* sanguinário

bloody /'blʌdɪ/ *a* (-ier, -iest) ensangüentado; (*with much bloodshed*) sangrento; (*sl*) grande, maldito □ *adv* (*sl*) pra burro. ~-minded *a* (*colloq*) do contra (*colloq*), chato (*sl*)

bloom /blu:m/ *n* flor *f*; (*beauty*) frescura *f*, viço *m* □ *vi* florir; (*fig*) vicejar. in ~ em flor

blossom /'blɒsəm/ *n* flor *f*. in ~ em flor □ *vi* (*flower*) florir, desabrochar; (*develop, flourish*) florescer, desabrochar

blot /blɒt/ *n* mancha *f* □ *vt* (*pt* blotted) manchar; (*dry*) secar. ~ out apagar; (*hide*) tapar, toldar. ~ter, ~ting-paper *n* (papel) mata-borrão *m*

blotch /blɒtʃ/ *n* mancha *f*. ~y *a* manchado

blouse /blaʊz/ *n* blusa *f*; (*in uniform*) blusão *m*

blow[1] /bləʊ/ *vt/i* (*pt* blew, *pp* blown) soprar; (*fuse*) fundir-se, queimar; (*sl*: *squander*) esbanjar; (*trumpet etc*) tocar. ~ a whistle apitar. ~ away *or* off *vt* levar, soprar □ *vi* roar, ir pelos ares (fora). ~-dry *vt* (*hair*) fazer um brushing □ *n* brushing *m*. ~ one's nose assoar o nariz. ~ out (*candle*) apagar, soprar. ~ out (*colloq*: *of tyre*) rebentar *m*; (*colloq*: *large meal*) comilança *f* (*colloq*). ~ over passar. ~ up *vt* (*explode*) explodir; (*tyre*) encher; (*photograph*) ampliar □ *vi* (*explode*) explodir

blow[2] /bləʊ/ *n* pancada *f*; (*slap*) bofetada *f*; (*punch*) murro *m*; (*fig*) golpe *m*

blowlamp /'bləʊlæmp/ *n* maçarico *m*

blown /bləʊn/ *see* blow[1]

bludgeon /'blʌdʒən/ *n* moca *f* □ *vt* malhar em. ~ to death matar à pancada

blue /blu:/ *a* (-er, -est) azul; (*indecent*) indecente □ *n* azul *m*. come out of the ~ ser inesperado. ~s *n* (*mus*) blues. have the ~s estar deprimido (*colloq*)

bluebell /'blu:bel/ *n* jacinto *m* dos bosques

bluebottle /'blu:bɒtl/ *n* mosca *f* varejeira

blueprint /'blu:prɪnt/ *n* cópia *f* fotográfica de planta; (*fig*) projeto *m*, (*P*) projecto *m*

bluff /blʌf/ *vi* blefar, (*P*) fazer bluff □ *vt* enganar (fingindo), blefar □ *n* blefe *m*, (*P*) bluff *m*

blunder /'blʌndə(r)/ *vi* cometer um erro crasso; (*move*) avançar às cegas *or* tateando □ *n* erro *m* crasso, (*P*) bronca *f*

blunt /blʌnt/ *a* (-er, -est) embotado; (*person*) direto, (*P*) directo □ *vt* embotar. ~ly *adv* sem rodeios. ~ness *n* franqueza *f* rude

blur /blɜ:(r)/ *n* mancha *f* □ *vt* (*pt* blurred) (*smear*) manchar; (*make indistinct*) toldar

blurb /blɜ:b/ *n* contracapa *f*, sinopse *f* de um livro

blurt /blɜ:t/ *vt* ~ out deixar escapar

blush /blʌʃ/ *vi* corar □ *n* rubor *m*, vermelhidão *f*

bluster /'blʌstə(r)/ *vi* (*wind*) soprar em rajadas; (*swagger*) andar com ar fanfarrão. ~y *a* borrascoso

boar /bɔ:(r)/ *n* varrão *m*. wild ~ javali *m*

board /bɔ:d/ *n* tábua *f*; (*for notices*) quadro *m*, (*P*) placard *m*; (*food*) pensão *f*; (*admin*) conselho *m* □ *vt/i* cobrir com tábuas; (*aircraft, ship, train*) embarcar (em); (*bus, train*) subir (em). full ~ pensão *f* completa. half ~ meia-pensão *f*. on ~ a bordo. ~ up entaipar. ~ with ser pensionista em casa de. ~er *n* pensionista *mf*; (*at school*) interno *m*. ~ing-card *n* cartão *m* de embarque. ~ing-house *n* pensão *f*. ~ing-school *n* internato *m*

boast /bəʊst/ *vi* gabar-se □ *vt* orgulhar-se de □ *n* gabarolice *f*. ~er *n* gabola *mf*. ~ful *a* vaidoso. ~fully *adv* com vaidade, gabando-se

boat /bəʊt/ *n* barco *m*. in the same ~ nas mesmas circunstâncias. ~ing *n* passear de barco

bob /bɒb/ *vt/i* (*pt* bobbed) (*curtsy*) inclinar-se; (*hair*) cortar pelos ombros, (*P*) cortar à Joãozinho. ~ (up and down) andar para cima e para baixo

bobbin /'bɒbɪn/ *n* bobina *f*; (*sewing-machine*) canela *f*, bobina *f*

bob-sleigh /'bɒbsleɪ/ *n* trenó *m*

bode /bəʊd/ *vi* ~ well/ill ser de bom/mau agouro

bodice /'bɒdɪs/ *n* corpete *m*

bodily /'bɒdɪlɪ/ *a* corporal, físico. □ *adv* (*in person*) fisicamente, em pessoa; (*lift*) em peso

body /'bɒdɪ/ *n* corpo *m*; (*organization*) organismo *m*. ~(-work) *n* (*of car*) carroçaria *f*. in a ~ em massa. the main ~ of o grosso de. ~-building *n* body building *m*

bodyguard /'bɒdɪga:d/ n guarda-costas m; (escort) escolta f

bog /bɒg/ n pântano m □ vt get ~ged down atolar-se; (fig) ficar emperrado

boggle /'bɒgl/ vi the mind ~s não da para imaginar

bogus /'bəʊgəs/ a falso

boil[1] /bɔɪl/ n (med) furúnculo m

boil[2] /bɔɪl/ vt/i ferver. come to the ~ ferver. ~ down to resumir-se a. ~ over transbordar. ~ing hot fervendo. ~ing point ponto m de ebulição

boiler /'bɔɪlə(r)/ n caldeira f. ~ suit macacão m, (P) fato m de macaco

boisterous /'bɔɪstərəs/ a turbulento; (noisy and cheerful) animado

bold /bəʊld/ a (-er, -est) ousado; (of colours) vivo. ~ness n ousadia f

Bolivia /bə'lɪvɪə/ n Bolívia f. ~n a & n boliviano (m)

bollard /'bɒləd/ n (ship) abita f; (road) poste m

bolster /'bəʊlstə(r)/ n travesseiro m □ vt sustentar; ajudar. ~ one's spirits levantar o moral

bolt /bəʊlt/ n (on door etc) ferrolho m; (for nut) parafuso m; (lightning) relâmpago m □ vt aferrolhar; (food) engolir □ vi fugir, disparar. ~ upright reto como um fuso

bomb /bɒm/ n bomba f □ vt bombardear. ~er n (aircraft) bombardeiro m; (person) bombista mf

bombard /bɒm'ba:d/ vt bombardear. ~ment n bombardeamento m

bombastic /bɒm'bæstɪk/ a bombástico

bombshell /'bɒmʃel/ n granada f, (fig) bomba f

bond /bɒnd/ n (agreement) compromisso m; (link) laço m, vínculo m; (comm) obrigação f. in ~ em depósito na alfândega

bondage /'bɒndɪdʒ/ n escravidão f, servidão f

bone /bəʊn/ n osso m; (of fish) espinha f □ vt desossar. ~-dry a completamente seco, ressecado. ~ idle preguiçoso

bonfire /'bɒnfaɪə(r)/ n fogueira f

bonnet /'bɒnɪt/ n chapéu m; (auto) capô m do motor, (P) capot m

bonus /'bəʊnəs/ n bónus m, (P) bónus m

bony /'bəʊnɪ/ a (-ier, -iest) ossudo; (meat, fish) cheio de ossos/de espinhas

boo /bu:/ int fora □ vt/i vaiar □ n vaia f

boob /bu:b/ n (sl: mistake) asneira f, disparate m □ vi (sl) fazer asneira(s)

booby /'bu:bɪ/ n ~ prize prémio m de consolação. ~ trap bomba f armadilhada

book /bʊk/ n livro m. ~s (comm) contas fpl, escrita f □ vt (enter) averbar, registrar; (comm) escriturar; (reserve) marcar, reservar. ~ of matches carteira f de fósforos. ~ of tickets (bus, tube) caderneta f de módulos. be fully ~ed ter a lotação esgotada. ~ing office bilheteria f, (P) bilheteira f

bookcase /'bʊkkeɪs/ n estante f

bookkeep|er /'bʊkki:pə(r)/ n guarda-livros m. ~ing n contabilidade f, escrituração f

booklet /'bʊklɪt/ n brochura f

bookmaker /'bʊkmeɪkə(r)/ n book (maker) m

bookmark /'bʊkma:k/ n marca f de livro, marcador m de página

bookseller /'bʊkselə(r)/ n livreiro m

bookshop /'bʊkʃɒp/ n livraria f

bookstall /'bʊkstɔ:l/ n quiosque m

boom /bu:m/ vi ribombar; (of trade) prosperar □ n (sound) ribombo m; (comm) boom m, prosperidade f

boon /bu:n/ n benção f, vantagem f

boost /bu:st/ vt desenvolver, promover; (morale) levantar; (price) aumentar □ n força f (colloq). ~er n (med) dose suplementar f; (vaccine) revacinação f, (P) reforço m

boot /bu:t/ n bota f; (auto) portamala f □ vt ~ (up) (comput) to ~ (in addition) ainda por cima

booth /bu:ð/ n barraca f; (telephone, voting) cabine f

booty /'bu:tɪ/ n saque m, pilhagem f

booze /bu:z/ vi (colloq) embebedar-se (colloq), encharcar-se (colloq) □ n (colloq) pinga f (colloq)

border /'bɔ:də(r)/ n borda f, margem f; (frontier) fronteira f; (garden bed) canteiro m □ vi ~ on confinar com; (be almost the same as) atingir as raias de

borderline /'bɔ:dəlaɪn/ n linha f divisória. ~ case caso m limite

bore[1] /bɔ:(r)/ see **bear**[2]

bore[2] /bɔ:(r)/ vt/i (techn) furar, perfurar □ n (of gun barrel) calibre m

bore[3] /bɔ:(r)/ vt aborrecer, entediar □ n maçante m; (thing) chatice f. be ~d aborrecer-se, maçar-se. ~dom n tédio m. boring a tedioso, maçante

born /bɔ:n/ a nascido. be ~ nascer

borne /bɔ:n/ see **bear**[2]

borough /'bʌrə/ n município m

borrow /'bɒrəʊ/ vt pedir emprestado (from a)

bosom /'bʊzəm/ n peito m; (woman's; fig: midst) seio m. ~ friend amigo m íntimo

boss /bɒs/ n (colloq) patrão m, patroa f, manda-chuva (colloq) m □ vt mandar. ~ sb about (colloq) mandar em alg bossy /'bɒsɪ/ a mandão, autoritário

botan|y /'bɒtənɪ/ n botânica f. ~ical /bə'tænɪkl/ a botânico. ~ist /-ɪst/ n botânico m

botch /bɒtʃ/ vt atamancar; (spoil) estragar, escangalhar

both /bəʊθ/ a & pron ambos, os dois □ adv ~ ... and não só ... mas também, tanto ... como. ~ of us nós dois. ~ the books ambos os livros

bother /'bɒðə(r)/ vt/i incomodar(-se) □ n (inconvenience) incómodo m, (P) incômodo m, trabalho m; (effort) custo m, trabalho m; (worry) preocupação f. don't ~ não se incomode. I can't be ~ed não posso me dar o trabalho

bottle /'bɒtl/ n garrafa f; (small) frasco m; (for baby) mamadeira f, (P) biberão m □ vt engarrafar. ~-opener n sacarolhas m. ~ up reprimir

bottleneck /'bɒtlnek/ n (obstruction) entrave m; (traffic-jam) engarrafamento m

bottom /'bɒtəm/ n fundo m; (of hill) sopé m; (buttocks) traseiro m □ a inferior; (last) último. from top to ~ de alto a baixo. ~less a sem fundo

bough /baʊ/ n ramo m

bought /bɔːt/ see buy

boulder /'bəʊldə(r)/ n pedregulho m

bounce /baʊns/ vi saltar; (of person) pular, dar pulos; (sl: of cheque) ser devolvido □ vt fazer saltar □ n (of ball) salto m, (P) ressalto m

bound[1] /baʊnd/ vi pular; (move by jumping) ir aos pulos □ n pulo m

bound[2] /baʊnd/ see bind □ a be ~ to ir com destino a, ir para. be ~ to (obliged) ser obrigado a; (certain) haver de. she's ~ to like it ela há de gostar disso

boundary /'baʊndrɪ/ n limite m

bound|s /baʊndz/ npl limites mpl. out of ~s interdito. ~less a sem limites

bouquet /bʊ'keɪ/ n ramo m de flores; (wine) aroma m

bout /baʊt/ n período m; (med) ataque m; (boxing) combate m

boutique /buː'tiːk/ n boutique f

bow[1] /bəʊ/ n (weapon, mus) arco m; (knot) laço m. ~-legged a de pernas tortas. ~-tie n gravata borboleta f, (P) laço m

bow[2] /baʊ/ n vénia f, (P) vênia f □ vt/i inclinar(-se), curvar-se

bow[3] /baʊ/ n (naut) proa f

bowels /'baʊəlz/ npl intestinos mpl; (fig) entranhas fpl

bowl[1] /bəʊl/ n (basin) bacia f; (for food) tigela f; (of pipe) fornilho m

bowl[2] /bəʊl/ n (ball) boliche m, (P) bola f de madeira. ~s npl boliche m,

(P) jogo m com bolas de madeira □ vt (cricket) lançar. ~ over siderar, varar. ~ing n boliche m, (P) bowling m. ~ing-alley n pista f

bowler[1] /'bəʊlə(r)/ n (cricket) lançador m

bowler[2] /'bəʊlə(r)/ n ~ (hat) (chapéu de) coco m

box[1] /bɒks/ n caixa f; (theatr) camarote m □ vt pôr dentro duma caixa. ~ in fechar. ~ office n bilheteria f, (P) bilheteira f. Boxing Day feriado m no primeiro dia útil depois do Natal

box[2] /bɒks/ vt/i (sport) lutar boxe. ~ the ears of esbofetear. ~er n pugilista m, boxeur m. ~ing n boxe m, pugilismo m

boy /bɔɪ/ n rapaz m. ~friend n namorado m. ~hood n infância f. ~ish a de menino

boycott /'bɔɪkɒt/ vt boicotar □ n boicote m

bra /braː/ n soutien m

brace /breɪs/ n braçadeira f; (dental) aparelho m; (tool) berbequim m; (of birds) par m. ~s npl (for trousers) suspensórios mpl □ vt apoiar, firmar. ~ o.s. concentrar as energias, fazer força; (for blow) preparar-se

bracelet /'breɪslɪt/ n bracelete m, pulseira f

bracing /'breɪsɪŋ/ a tonificante, estimulante

bracken /'brækən/ n (bot) samambaia f, (P) feto m

bracket /'brækɪt/ n suporte m; (group) grupo m □ vt (pt bracketed) pôr entre parênteses; (put together) pôr em pé de igualdade, agrupar. age/income ~ faixa f etária/salarial. round ~s parênteses mpl. square ~s parênteses mpl, colchetes mpl

brag /bræg/ vi (pt bragged) gabar-se (about de)

braid /breɪd/ n galão m; (of hair) trança f

Braille /breɪl/ n braile m

brain /breɪn/ n cérebro m, miolos mpl (colloq); (fig) inteligência f. ~s (culin) miolos mpl. ~child n invenção f. ~less a estúpido

brainwash /'breɪnwɒʃ/ vt fazer uma lavagem cerebral

brainwave /'breɪnweɪv/ n idéia f, (P) ideia f genial

brainy /'breɪnɪ/ a (-ier, -iest) inteligente, esperto

braise /breɪz/ vt (culin) estufar

brake /breɪk/ n travão m □ vt/i travar. ~ light farol m do freio

bran /bræn/ n (husks) farelo m

branch /braːntʃ/ n ramo m; (of road) ramificação f; (of railway line) ramal *m*; (*comm*) sucursal *f*; (*of bank*) balcão *m* □ *vi* ~ (off) bifurcar-se, ramificar-se

brand /brænd/ *n* marca *f* □ *vt* marcar. ~ **name** marca *f* de fábrica. ~**new** *a* novo em folha. ~ **sb as** tachar alg de, (*P*) rotular alg de

brandish /'brændɪʃ/ *vt* brandir

brandy /'brændɪ/ *n* aguardente *f*, conhaque *m*

brass /brɑːs/ *n* latão *m*. the ~ (*mus*) os metais *mpl* □ *a* de cobre, de latão. **get down to** ~ **tacks** tratar das coisas sérias. **top** ~ (*sl*) os chefões (*colloq*)

brassière /'bræsɪə(r)/ *n* soutien *m*

brat /bræt/ *n* (*pej*) fedelho *m*

bravado /brə'vɑːdəʊ/ *n* bravata *f*

brave /breɪv/ *a* (-er, -est) bravo, valente □ *vt* arrostar. ~**ry** /-ərɪ/ *n* bravura *f*

brawl /brɔːl/ *n* briga *f*, rixa *f*, desordem *f* □ *vi* brigar

brawn /brɔːn/ *n* força *f* muscular, músculo *m*. ~**y** *a* musculoso

bray /breɪ/ *n* zurro *m* □ *vi* zurrar

brazen /'breɪzn/ *a* descarado

brazier /'breɪzɪə(r)/ *n* braseiro *m*

Brazil /brə'zɪl/ *n* Brasil *m*. ~**ian** *a* & *n* brasileiro (*m*). ~ **nut** castanha *f* do Pará

breach /briːtʃ/ *n* quebra *f*; (*gap*) brecha *f* □ *vt* abrir uma brecha em. ~ **of contract** quebra *f* de contrato. ~ **of the peace** perturbação *f* da ordem pública. ~ **of trust** abuso *m* de confiança

bread /bred/ *n* pão *m*. ~**-winner** *n* ganha-pão *m*

breadcrumbs /'bredkrʌmz/ *npl* migalhas *fpl*; (*culin*) farinha *f* de rosca

breadline /'bredlaɪn/ *n* on the ~ na miséria

breadth /bredθ/ *n* largura *f*; (*of mind, view*) abertura *f*

break /breɪk/ *vt* (*pt* **broke**, *pp* **broken**) partir, quebrar; (*vow, silence, etc*) quebrar; (*law*) transgredir; (*journey*) interromper; (*news*) dar; (*a record*) bater □ *vi* partir-se, quebrar-se; (*voice, weather*) mudar □ *n* quebra *f*, ruptura *f*; (*interval*) intervalo *m*; (*colloq: opportunity*) oportunidade *f*, chance *f*. ~ **one's arm/leg** quebrar o braço/a perna. ~ **down** *vt* analisar □ *vi* (*of person*) ir-se abaixo; (*of machine*) avariar-se. ~ **in** forçar uma entrada. ~ **off** *vt* quebrar □ *vi* desligar-se. ~ **out** rebentar. ~**up** *vt/i* terminar *vi* (*of schools*) entrar em férias. ~**able** *a* quebrável. ~**age** *n* quebra *f*

breakdown /'breɪkdaʊn/ *n* (*techn*) avaria *f*, pane *f*; (*med*) esgotamento *m* nervoso; (*of figures*) análise *f* □ *a*

(*auto*) de pronto-socorro. ~ **van** pronto-socorro *m*

breaker /'breɪkə(r)/ *n* vaga *f* de rebentação

breakfast /'brekfəst/ *n* café *m* da manhã

breakthrough /'breɪkθruː/ *n* descoberta *f* decisiva, avanço *m*

breakwater /'breɪkwɔːtə(r)/ *n* quebra-mar *m*

breast /brest/ *n* peito *m*. ~**-feed** *vt* (*pt* -fed) amamentar. ~**-stroke** *n* estilo *m* bruços

breath /breθ/ *n* respiração *f*. **bad** ~ mau hálito *m*. **out of** ~ sem fôlego. **under one's** ~ num murmúrio, baixo. ~**less** *a* ofegante

breathalyser /'breθəlaɪzə(r)/ *n* aparelho *m* para medir o nível de álcool no sangue, bafômetro *m* (*colloq*)

breath|e /briːð/ *vt/i* respirar. ~ **in** inspirar. ~ **out** expirar. ~**ing** *n* respiração *f*. ~**ing-space** *n* pausa *f*

breather /'briːðə(r)/ *n* pausa *f* de descanso, momento *m* para respirar

breathtaking /'breθteɪkɪŋ/ *a* assombroso, arrebatador

bred /bred/ *see* **breed**

breed /briːd/ *vt* (*pt* **bred**) criar □ *vi* reproduzir-se □ *n* raça *f*. ~**er** *n* criador *m*. ~**ing** *n* criação *f*; (*fig*) educação *f*

breeze /briːz/ *n* brisa *f*. ~**y** *a* fresco

brevity /'brevətɪ/ *n* brevidade *f*

brew /bruː/ *vt* (*beer*) fabricar; (*tea*) fazer; (*fig*) armar, tramar □ *vi* fermentar; (*tea*) preparar; (*fig*) armar-se, preparar-se □ *n* decocção *f*; (*tea*) infusão *f*. ~**er** *n* cervejeiro *m*. ~**ery** *n* cervejaria *f*

bribe /braɪb/ *n* suborno *m*, (*P*) peita *f* □ *vt* subornar. ~**ry** /-ərɪ/ *n* suborno *m*, corrupção *f*

brick /brɪk/ *n* tijolo *m*

bricklayer /'brɪkleɪə(r)/ *n* pedreiro *m*

bridal /'braɪdl/ *a* nupcial

bride /braɪd/ *n* noiva *f*

bridegroom /'braɪdgrʊm/ *n* noivo *m*

bridesmaid /'braɪdzmeɪd/ *n* dama *f* de honra, (*P*) honor

bridge[1] /brɪdʒ/ *n* ponte *f*; (*of nose*) cana *f* □ *vt* ~ **a gap** preencher uma lacuna

bridge[2] /brɪdʒ/ *n* (*cards*) bridge *m*

bridle /'braɪdl/ *n* cabeçada *f*, freio *m* □ *vt* refrear. ~**-path** *n* atalho *m*, carreiro *m*

brief[1] /briːf/ *a* (-er, -est) breve. ~**s** *npl* (*men's*) cueca *f*, (*P*) slip *m*; (*women's*) calcinhas *fpl*, (*P*) cuecas *fpl*. ~**ly** *adv* brevemente

brief[2] /briːf/ *n* (*jur*) sumário *m*; (*case*) causa *f*; (*instructions*) instruções *fpl* □ *vt* dar instruções a briefcase /'bri:fkeıs/ n pasta f

brigad|e /brı'geıd/ n brigada f. ~ier /-ə'dıə(r)/ n brigadeiro m

bright /braıt/ a (-er, -est) brilhante; (of colour) vivo; (of light) forte; (room) claro; (cheerful) alegre; (clever) inteligente. ~ness n (sheen) brilho m; (clarity) claridade f; (intelligence) inteligência m

brighten /'braıtn/ vt alegrar □ vi (of weather) clarear; (of face) animar-se, iluminar-se

brillian|t /'brıljənt/ a brilhante. ~ce n brilho m

brim /brım/ n borda f; (of hat) aba f □ vi (pt brimmed) ~ over transbordar, cair por fora

brine /braın/ n salmoura f

bring /brıŋ/ vt (pt brought) trazer. ~ about causar. ~ back trazer (de volta); (call to mind) relembrar. ~ down trazer para baixo; (bird, plane) abater; (prices) baixar. ~ forward adiantar, apresentar. ~ it off ser bem sucedido (em alg coisa). ~ out (take out) tirar; (show) revelar; (book) publicar. ~ round or to reanimar, fazer voltar a si. ~ to bear (pressure etc) exercer. ~ up educar; (med) vomitar; (question) levantar

brink /brıŋk/ n beira f, borda f

brisk /brısk/ a (-er, -est) (pace, movement) vivo, rápido; (business, demand) grande

bristl|e /'brısl/ n pêlo m. ~y a eriçado

Britain /'brıtən/ n Grã-Bretanha f

British /'brıtıʃ/ a britânico. the ~ o povo m britânico, os britânicos mpl

brittle /'brıtl/ a frágil

broach /brəʊtʃ/ vt abordar, entabular, encetar

broad /brɔ:d/ a (-er, -est) largo; (daylight) pleno. ~ bean fava f. ~-minded a tolerante, liberal. ~ly adv de modo geral

broadcast /'brɔ:dka:st/ vt/i (pt broadcast) transmitir, fazer uma transmissão; (person) cantar, falar etc na rádio or na TV □ n emissão f. ~ing a & n (de) rádiodifusão (f)

broaden /'brɔ:dn/ vt/i alargar(-se)

broccoli /'brɒkəlı/ n inv brócolis mpl, (P) brócolos mpl

brochure /'brəʊʃə(r)/ n brochura f

broke /brəʊk/ see break □ a (sl) depenado (sl), liso (sl), (P) teso (sl)

broken /'brəʊkən/ see break □ a ~ English inglês m estropeado. ~-hearted a com o coração despedaçado

broker /'brəʊkə(r)/ n corretor m, broker m

bronchitis /brɒŋ'kaıtıs/ n bronquite f

bronze /brɒnz/ n bronze m

brooch /brəʊtʃ/ n broche m

brood /bru:d/ n ninhada f □ vi chocar; (fig) cismar. ~y a (hen) choca; (fig) sorumbático, melancólico

brook /brʊk/ n regato m, ribeiro m

broom /bru:m/ n vassoura f; (bot) giesta f

broth /brɒθ/ n caldo m

brothel /'brɒθl/ n bordel m

brother /'brʌðə(r)/ n irmão m. ~-in-law n (pl ~s-in-law) cunhado m. ~hood n irmandade f, fraternidade f. ~ly a fraternal

brought /brɔ:t/ see bring

brow /braʊ/ n (forehead) testa f; (of hill) cume m; (eyebrow) sobrancelha f

browbeat /'braʊbi:t/ vt (pt -beat, pp -beaten) intimidar

brown /braʊn/ a (-er, -est) castanho □ n castanho m □ vt/i acastanhar; (in the sun) bronzear, tostar; (meat) alourar

browse /braʊz/ vi (through book) folhear; (of animal) pastar; (in a shop) olhar sem comprar

bruise /bru:z/ n hematoma m, contusão f □ vt causar um hematoma. ~d a coberto de hematomas, contuso; (fruit) machucado

brunette /bru:'net/ n morena f

brunt /brʌnt/ n the ~ of o maior peso de, o pior de

brush /brʌʃ/ n escova f; (painter's) pincel m; (skirmish) escaramuça f. ~ against roçar. ~ aside não fazer caso de. ~ off (colloq: reject) mandar passear (colloq). ~ up (on) aperfeiçoar

brusque /bru:sk/ a brusco

Brussels /'brʌslz/ n Bruxelas f. ~ sprouts couve-de-Bruxelas f

brutal /'bru:tl/ a brutal. ~ity /'tæləti/ n brutalidade f

brute /bru:t/ n & a (animal, person) bruto (m). by ~ force por força bruta

B Sc abbr see Bachelor of Science

bubb|le /'bʌbl/ n bolha f; (of soap) bola f de sabão □ vi borbulhar. ~le gum n chiclete m, (P) pastilha f elástica. ~le over transbordar. ~ly a efervescente

buck[1] /bʌk/ n macho m □ vi dar galões, (P) corcovear. ~ up (sl) animar(-se); (sl: rush) apressar-se, despachar-se

buck[2] /bʌk/ n (Amer sl) dólar m

buck[3] /bʌk/ n pass the ~ (sl) fazer o jogo do empurra

bucket /'bʌkıt/ n balde m

buckle /'bʌkl/ n fivela f □ vt/i afivelar(-se); (bend) torcer(-se), vergar. ~ down to empenhar-se

bud /bʌd/ n o botão m, rebento m □ vi (pt budded) rebentar. in ~ em botão

Buddhis|t /'bʊdɪst/ *a & n* budista (*mf*). ~m /-'zəm/ *n* budismo *m*

budding /'bʌdɪŋ/ *a* nascente, em botão, incipiente

budge /bʌdʒ/ *vt/i* mexer(-se)

budgerigar /'bʌdʒərɪgɑ:(r)/ *n* periquito *m*

budget /'bʌdʒɪt/ *n* orçamento *m* □ *vi* (*pt* budgeted) ~ for prever no orçamento *m*

buff /bʌf/ *n* (*colour*) côr *f* de camurça; (*colloq*) fanático *m*, entusiasta *mf* □ *vt* polir

buffalo /'bʌfələʊ/ *n* (*pl* -oes) búfalo *m*; (*Amer*) bisão *m*

buffer /'bʌfə(r)/ *n* pára-choque *m*

buffet[1] /'bʊfeɪ/ *n* (*meal, counter*) bufê *m*, bufete *m*

buffet[2] /'bʌfɪt/ *vt* (*pt* buffeted) esbofetear; (*by wind, rain; fig*) fustigar

buffoon /bə'fu:n/ *n* palhaço *m*

bug /bʌg/ *n* (*insect*) bicho *m*; (*bed-bug*) percevejo *m*; (*sl: germ*) virus *m*; (*sl: device*) microfone *m* de escuta; (*sl: defect*) defeito *m* □ *vt* (*pt* bugged) grampear; (*Amer sl: annoy*) chatear (*sl*)

bugbear /'bʌgbeə(r)/ *n* papão *m*

buggy /'bʌgɪ/ *n* (*for baby*) carrinho *m*

bugle /'bju:gl/ *n* clarim *m*, corneta *f*

build /bɪld/ *vt/i* (*pt* built) construir, edificar □ *n* físico *m*, compleição *f*. ~ up *vt/i* criar; (*increase*) aumentar; (*accumulate*) acumular(-se). ~-up *n* acumulação *f*; (*fig*) publicidade *f*. ~er *n* construtor *m*, empreiteiro *m*; (*workman*) operário *m*

building /'bɪldɪŋ/ *n* edifício *m*, prédio *m*. ~ site canteiro *m* de obras. ~ society sociedade *f* de investimentos imobiliários

built /bɪlt/ *see* build. ~-in *a* incorporado. ~-in wardrobe armário *m* embutido na parede. ~-up *a* urbanizado

bulb /bʌlb/ *n* bolbo *m*; (*electr*) lâmpada *f*. ~ous *a* bolboso

Bulgaria /bʌl'geərɪə/ *n* Bulgária *f*. ~n *a & n* búlgaro (*m*)

bulg|e /bʌldʒ/ *n* bojo *m*, saliência *f* □ *vi* inchar; (*jut out*) fazer uma saliência. ~ing *a* inchado; (*pocket etc*) cheio

bulk /bʌlk/ *n* quantidade *f*, volume *m*. in ~ por grosso; (*loose*) a granel. the ~ of a maior parte de. ~y *a* volumoso

bull /bʊl/ *n* touro *m*. ~'s-eye *n* (*of target*) centro *m* do alvo, mosca *f*

bulldog /'bʊldɒg/ *n* buldogue *m*

bulldoze /'bʊldəʊz/ *vt* terraplanar. ~r /-ə(r)/ *n* bulldozer *m*

bullet /'bʊlɪt/ *n* bala *f*. ~-proof *a* à prova de balas; (*vehicle*) blindado

bulletin /'bʊlətɪn/ *n* boletim *m*

bullfight /'bʊlfaɪt/ *n* tourada *f*, corrida *f* de touros. ~er *n* toureiro *m*. ~ing *n* tauromaquia *f*

bullring /'bʊlrɪŋ/ *n* arena *f*, (*P*) praça *f* de touros

bully /'bʊlɪ/ *n* mandão *m*, pessoa *f* prepotente; (*schol*) terror *m*, o mau □ *vt* intimidar; (*treat badly*) atormentar; (*coerce*) forçar (into a)

bum[1] /bʌm/ *n* (*sl: buttocks*) traseiro *m*, bunda *f* (*sl*)

bum[2] /bʌm/ *n* (*Amer sl*) vagabundo *m*

bump /bʌmp/ *n* choque *m*, embate *m*; (*swelling*) inchaço *m*; (*on head*) galo *m* □ *vt/i* bater, chocar. ~ into bater em, chocar com; (*meet*) esbarrar com, encontrar. ~y *a* (*surface*) irregular; (*ride*) aos solavancos

bumper /'bʌmpə(r)/ *n* pára-choques *m inv* □ *a* excepcional

bun /bʌn/ *n* pãozinho *m* doce com passas; (*hair*) coque *m*

bunch /bʌntʃ/ *n* (*of flowers*) ramo *m*; (*of keys*) molho *m*; (*of people*) grupo *m*; (*of grapes*) cacho *m*

bundle /'bʌndl/ *n* molho *m* □ *vt* atar num molho; (*push*) despachar

bung /bʌŋ/ *n* batoque *m*, rolha *f* □ *vt* rolhar; (*sl: throw*) atirar, deitar. ~ up entupir

bungalow /'bʌŋgələʊ/ *n* chalé *m*; (*outside Europe*) bungalô *m*, (*P*) bungalow *m*

bungle /'bʌŋgl/ *vt* fazer mal feito, estragar

bunion /'bʌnjən/ *n* (*med*) joanete *m*

bunk /bʌŋk/ *n* (*in train*) couchette *f*; (*in ship*) beliche *m*. ~-beds *npl* beliches *mpl*

bunker /'bʌŋkə(r)/ *n* (*mil*) abrigo *m*, casamata *f*, bunker *m*; (*golf*) obstáculo *m* em cova de areia

buoy /bɔɪ/ *n* bóia *f* □ *vt* ~ up animar

buoyan|t /'bɔɪənt/ *a* flutuante; (*fig*) alegre. ~cy *n* (*fig*) alegria *f*, exuberância *f*

burden /'bɜ:dn/ *n* fardo *m* □ *vt* collegar, sobrecarregar. ~some *a* pesado

bureau /'bjʊərəʊ/ *n* (*pl* -eaux) /-əʊz/ (*desk*) secretária *f*; (*office*) seção *f*, (*P*) secção *f*

bureaucracy /bjʊə'rɒkrəsɪ/ *n* burocracia *f*

bureaucrat /'bjʊərəkræt/ *n* burocrata *mf*. ~ic /-'krætɪk/ *a* burocrático

burger /'bɜ:gə(r)/ *n* hambúrguer *m*

burglar /'bɜ:glə(r)/ *n* ladrão *m*, assaltante *mf*. ~ alarm *n* alarme *m* contra ladrões. ~ize *vt* (*Amer*) assaltar. ~y *n* assalto *m*

burgle /'bɜ:gl/ *vt* assaltar

burial /'berɪəl/ *n* enterro *m*

burlesque /bɜ:'lesk/ *n* paródia *f*

burly /'bɜ:lɪ/ *a* (-ier, -iest) robusto e corpulento, forte

Burm|a /'bɜːmə/ n Birmânia f. ~ese
/-'miːz/ a & n birmanês (m)
burn /bɜːn/ vt (pt burned or burnt)
queimar □ vi queimar(-se), arder □ n
queimadura f. ~ down reduzir a
cinzas. ~er n (of stove) bico m de
gás. ~ing a (thirst, desire) ardente;
(topic) candente
burnish /'bɜːnɪʃ/ vt polir, brunir
burnt /bɜːnt/ see burn
burp /bɜːp/ n (colloq) arroto m □ vi
(colloq) arrotar
burrow /'bʌrəʊ/ n toca □ vi cavar,
fazer uma toca
burst /bɜːst/ vt/i (pt burst) arreben-
tar □ n estouro m, rebentar m; (of
anger, laughter) explosão f; (of firing)
rajada f; (of energy) acesso m. ~ into
(flames, room, etc) irromper em. ~
into tears desatar num choro, desfazer-se em lágrimas. ~ out laughing
desatar a rir
bury /'berɪ/ vt sepultar, enterrar;
(hide) esconder; (engross, thrust) mergulhar
bus /bʌs/ n (pl buses) ônibus m, (P)
autocarro m. ~-stop n paragem f
bush /bʊʃ/ n arbusto m; (land) mato
m. ~y a espesso
business /'bɪznɪs/ n (trade, shop,
affair) negócio m; (task) função f;
(occupation) ocupação f. have no
~ to não ter o direito de. it's no ~
of yours não é da sua conta. mind
your own ~ cuide da sua vida.
that's my ~ isso é meu problema.
~like a eficiente, sistemático.
~man n homem m de negócios, comerciante m
busker /'bʌskə(r)/ n músico m ambulante
bust¹ /bʌst/ n busto m
bust² /bʌst/ vt/i (pt busted or bust)
(sl) = burst, break □ a falido. ~-up n
(sl) discussão f, (P) bulha f. go ~ (sl)
falir
bustl|e /'bʌsl/ vi andar numa azáfa-
ma; (hurry) apressar-se □ n azáfama
f. ~ing a animado, movimentado
bus|y /'bɪzɪ/ a (-ier, -iest) ocupado;
(street) movimentado; (day) atarefado
□ vt ~ o.s. with ocupar-se com.
~ily adv ativamente, atarefadamente
busybody /'bɪzɪbɒdɪ/ n intrometido
m, pessoa f abelhuda
but /bʌt/ conj mas □ prep exceto, (p)
excepto, senão □ adv apenas, só. all
~ todos menos; (nearly) quaze, por
pouco não. ~ for sem, se não fosse.
last ~ one/two penúltimo/antepe-
núltimo. nobody ~ ninguém a não
ser
butcher /'bʊtʃə(r)/ n açougueiro m,
(P) homem m do talho; (fig) carrasco

m □ vt chacinar. the ~'s açougue m,
(P) talho m. ~y n chacina f
butler /'bʌtlə(r)/ n mordomo m
butt /bʌt/ n (of gun) coronha f; (of
cigarette) ponta f; (target) alvo m de
troça, de ridículo etc; (cask) barril m
□ vt/i dar cabeçada em. ~ in interromper
butter /'bʌtə(r)/ n manteiga f □ vt pôr
manteiga em. ~-bean n feijão m
branco
buttercup /'bʌtəkʌp/n botão-de-ouro m
butterfly /'bʌtəflaɪ/ n borboleta f
buttock /'bʌtək/ n nádega f
button /'bʌtn/ n botão m □ vt/i abo-
toar(-se)
buttonhole /'bʌtnhəʊl/ n casa f de
botão; (in lapel) botoeira f □ vt (fig)
obrigar a ouvir
buttress /'bʌtrɪs/ n contraforte m;
(fig) esteio m □ vt sustentar
buxom /'bʌksəm/ a roliço, rechonchudo
buy /baɪ/ vt (pt bought) comprar
(from a); (sl: believe) engolir (colloq)
□ n compra f. ~er n comprador m
buzz /bʌz/ n zumbido m □ vi zumbir.
~ off (sl) pôr-se a andar. ~er n campainha f
by /baɪ/ prep (near) junto de, perto de;
(along, past, means) por; (according
to) conforme; (before) antes de. ~
land/sea/air por terra/mar/ar. ~
bike/car etc de bicicleta/carro etc.
~ day/night de dia/noite. ~ the
kilo por quilo. ~ now a esta hora.
~ accident/mistake sem querer. ~
oneself sozinho □ adv (near) perto.
and ~ muito em breve. ~ and large
no conjunto. ~-election n eleição f
suplementar. ~-law n regulamento
m. ~-product n derivado m
bye(-bye) /'baɪ(baɪ)/ int (colloq) adeus,
adeusinho
bygone /'baɪgɒn/ a passado. let ~s be
~s o que passou, passou
bypass /'baɪpɑːs/ n (estrada) secundária f, desvio m; (med) by-pass m,
ponte f de safema □ vt fazer um desvio; (fig) contornar
bystander /'baɪstændə(r)/ n circunstante mf, espectador m
byte /baɪt/ n

C

cab /kæb/ n táxi m; (of lorry, train)
cabina f, cabine f
cabaret /'kæbəreɪ/ n variedades fpl,
cabaré m
cabbage /'kæbɪdʒ/ n couve f, repolho m
cabin /'kæbɪn/ n cabana f; (in plane)
cabina f; (in ship) camarote m

cabinet /'kæbɪnɪt/ n armário m. C~ (pol) gabinete m

cable /'keɪbl/ n cabo m. ~-car n funicular m, teleférico m. ~ railway funicular m. ~ television televisão f a cabo

cache /kæʃ/ n (esconderijo m de) tesouro m, armas fpl, provisões f pl

cackle /'kækl/ n cacarejo m □ vi cacarejar

cactus /'kæktəs/ n (pl ~es or cacti /-taɪ/) cacto m

caddie /'kædɪ/ n (golf) caddie m

caddy /'kædɪ/ n lata f para o chá

cadet /kə'det/ n cadete m

cadge /kædʒ/ vt/i filar, (P) cravar

Caesarean /sɪ'zeərɪən/ a ~ (section) cesariana f

café /'kæfeɪ/ n café m

cafeteria /kæfɪ'tɪərɪə/ n cafeteria f, restaurante m self-service

caffeine /'kæfiːn/ n cafeína f

cage /keɪdʒ/ n gaiola f

cagey /'keɪdʒɪ/ a (colloq: secretive) misterioso, reservado

cajole /kə'dʒəʊl/ vt ~ sb into doing sth convencer alguém (com lábia ou lisonjas) a fazer alg coisa

cake /keɪk/ n bolo m. ~d a empastado. his shoes were ~d with mud tinha os sapatos cobertos de lama. a piece of ~ (sl) canja f (sl)

calamity /kə'læmətɪ/ n calamidade f

calcium /'kælsɪəm/ n cálcio m

calculat|e /'kælkjʊleɪt/ vt/i calcular; (Amer: suppose) supor. ~ed a (action) deliberado, calculado. ~ing a calculista. ~ion /-'leɪʃn/ n cálculo m. ~or n calculador m, (P) maquina f de calcular

calendar /'kælɪndə(r)/ n calendário m

calf¹ /kɑːf/ n (pl calves) (young cow or bull) vitelo m, bezerro m; (of other animals) cria f

calf² /kɑːf/ n (pl calves) (of leg) barriga f da perna

calibrate /'kælɪbreɪt/ vt calibrar. ~ion /-'breɪʃn/ n calibragem f

calibre /'kælɪbə(r)/ n calibre m

calico /'kælɪkəʊ/ n pano m de algodão; (printed) chita f, algodão m

call /kɔːl/ vt/i chamar; (summon) convocar; (phone) telefonar. ~ (in or round) (visit) passar por casa de □ n chamada f; (bird's cry) canto m; (shout) brado m, grito m. be ~ed (named) chamar-se. be on ~ estar de serviço. ~ back (phone) tornar a telefonar; (visit) voltar. ~ for (demand) pedir, requerer; (fetch) ir buscar. ~ off cancelar. ~ on (visit) visitar, fazer uma visita a. ~ out (to) chamar. ~ up (mil) mobilizar, recrutar; (phone) telefonar. ~-box n

cabina f telefônica, (P) telefónica. ~er n visitante f, visita f; (phone) chamador m, (P) pessoa f que faz a chamada. ~ing n vocação f

callous /'kæləs/ a insensível. ~ly adv sem piedade

callow /'kæləʊ/ a (-er, -est) inexperiente, verde

calm /kɑːm/ a (-er, -est) calmo □ n calma f □ vt/i ~ (down) acalmar (-se). ~ness n calma f

calorie /'kælərɪ/ n caloria f

camber /'kæmbə(r)/ n (of road) abaulamento m

camcorder /'kæmkɔːdə(r)/ n câmera f de filmar

came /keɪm/ see come

camel /'kæml/ n camelo m

camera /'kæmərə/ n máquina f fotográfica; (cine, TV) câmera f. ~man n (pl -men) operador m

camouflage /'kæməflɑːʒ/ n camuflagem f □ vt camuflar

camp¹ /kæmp/ n acampamento m □ vi acampar. ~-bed n cama f de campanha. ~er n campista mf; (car) auto-caravana f. ~ing n campismo m

camp² /kæmp/ a afetado, efeminado

campaign /kæm'peɪn/ n campanha f □ vi fazer campanha

campsite /'kæmpsaɪt/ n área f de camping, (P) parque m de campismo

campus /'kæmpəs/ n (pl -puses /-pəsɪz/) campus m, (P) cidade f universitária

can¹ /kæn/ n vasilha f de lata; (for food) lata f (de conserva) □ vt (pt canned) enlatar. ~ned music música f em fita para locais públicos. ~-opener n abridor m de latas, (P) abrelatas m

can² /kæn/ v aux (be able to) poder, ser capaz de; (know how to) saber. I ~not/~'t go não posso ir

Canad|a /'kænədə/ n Canadá m. ~ian /kə'neɪdɪən/ a & n canadense (mf), (P) canadiano (m)

canal /kə'næl/ n canal m

canary /kə'neərɪ/ n canário m. C~ Islands npl as (Ilhas) Canárias

cancel /'kænsl/ vt (pt cancelled) cancelar; (cross out) riscar; (stamps) inutilizar. ~ out (fig) neutralizar-se mutuamente. ~lation /-'leɪʃn/ n cancelamento m

cancer /'kænsə(r)/ n câncer m, cancro m. C~ (astrol) Caranguejo m, Câncer m. ~ous a canceroso

candid /'kændɪd/ a franco. ~ly adv francamente

candida|te /'kændɪdeɪt/ n candidato m. ~cy /-əsɪ/ n candidatura f

candle /'kændl/ n vela f; (in church) vela f, círio m. ~-light n luz f de velas candlestick /'kændlstık/ n castiçal m

candour /'kændə(r)/ n franqueza f, candura f

candy /'kændı/ n bala f, (P) açúcar cândi; (Amer: sweet, sweets) doce(s) m (pl). ~-floss n algodão-doce m

cane /kem/ n cana f; (walking-stick) bengala f; (for baskets) verga f; (school: for punishment) vergasta f □ vt vergastar

canine /'kemam/ a & n canino (m)

canister /'kænıstə(r)/ n lata f

cannabis /'kænəbıs/ n cânhamo m, maconha f

cannibal /'kænıbl/ n canibal mf. ~ism /-zəm/ n canibalismo m

cannon /'kænən/ n inv canhão m. ~-ball n bala f de canhão

cannot /'kænət/ = can not

canny /'kænı/ a (-ier, -iest) astuto, manhoso

canoe /kə'nu:/ n canoa f □ vi andar de canoa. ~ing n (sport) canoagem f. ~ist n canoeiro m, (P) canoísta mf

canon /'kænən/ n cónego m, (P) cónego m; (rule) cânone m

canonize /'kænənaız/ vt canonizar

canopy /'kænəpı/ n dossel m; (over doorway) toldo m, marquise f; (fig) abóbada f

can't /ka:nt/ = can not

cantankerous /kæn'tæŋkərəs/ a irascível, intratável

canteen /kæn'ti:n/ n cantina f; (flask) cantil m; (for cutlery) estojo m

canter /'kæntə(r)/ n meio galope m, cânter m □ vi andar a meio galope

canton /'kæntɒn/ n cantão m

canvas /'kænvəs/ n lona f, (for painting or tapestry) tela f

canvass /'kænvəs/ vt/i angariar votos or fregueses

canyon /'kænjən/ n canhão m, (P) desfiladeiro m

cap /kæp/ n (with peak) boné m; (without peak) barrete m; (of nurse) touca f; (of bottle, pen, tube, etc) tampa f; (mech) tampa f, tampão m □ vt (pt capped) (bottle, pen, tube, etc) tapar, tampar; (rates) impor um limite a; (outdo) suplantar; (sport) seleccionar, (P) seleccionar. ~ped with encimado de, coroado de

capable /'keıpəbl/ a (person) capaz (of de); (things, situations) susceptível, (P) susceptível (of de). ~ility /-'bılətı/ n capacidade f. ~ly adv capazmente

capacity /kə'pæsətı/ n capacidade f. in one's ~ as na (sua) qualidade de

cape¹ /keıp/ n (cloak) capa f

cape² /keıp/ n (geog) cabo m

caper¹ /'keıpə(r)/ vi andar aos pinotes

caper² /'keıpə(r)/ n (culin) alcaparra f

capillary /kə'pılərı/ n (pl -ies) vaso m capilar

capital /'kæpıtl/ a capital □ n (town) capital f; (money) capital m. ~ (letter) maiúscula f. ~ punishment pena f de morte

capitalis|t /'kæpıtəlıst/ a & n capitalista (mf). ~m /-zəm/ n capitalismo m

capitalize /'kæpıtəlaız/ vi capitalizar; (finance) financiar; (writing) escrever com maiúscula. ~ on tirar partido de

capitulat|e /kə'pıtʃʊleıt/ vi capitular. ~ion /-'leıʃn/ n capitulação f

capricious /kə'prıʃəs/ a caprichoso

Capricorn /'kæprıkɔːn/ n (astrol) Capricórnio m

capsicum /'kæpsıkəm/ n pimento m

capsize /kæp'saız/ vt/i virar(-se)

capsule /'kæpsju:l/ n cápsula f

captain /'kæptın/ n capitão m; (navy) capitão-de-mar-e-guerra m □ vt capitanear, comandar

caption /'kæpʃn/ n legenda f; (heading) título m

captivate /'kæptıveıt/ vt cativar

captive /'kæptıv/ a & n cativo (m), prisioneiro (m). ~ity /-'tıvətı/ n cativeiro m

captor /'kæptə(r)/ n captor m

capture /'kæptʃə(r)/ vt capturar; (attention) prender □ n captura f

car /ka:(r)/ n carro m. ~ ferry barca f para carros. ~-park n (parque m de) estacionamento (m). ~ phone telefone m de carro. ~-wash n estação f de lavagem

carafe /kə'ræf/ n garrafa f para água ou vinho

caramel /'kærəmel/ n caramelo m.

carat /'kærət/ n quilate m

caravan /'kærəvæn/ n caravana f, reboque m

caraway /'kærəweı/ n ~ seed cariz f

carbohydrate /ka:bəʊ'haıdreıt/ n hidrato m de carbono

carbon /'ka:bən/ n carbono m. ~ copy cópia f em papel carbono, (P) químico. ~ monoxide óxido m de carbono. ~ paper papel m carbono, (P) químico

carburettor /ka:bjʊ'retə(r)/ n carburador m

carcass /'ka:kəs/ n carcaça f

card /ka:d/ n cartão m; (postcard) postal m; (playing-card) carta f. ~-game(s) n(pl) jogo(s) m(pl) de cartas. ~ index n fichário m, (P) ficheiro m

cardboard /'ka:dbɔːd/ n cartão m, papelão m

cardiac /'ka:dıæk/ a cardíaco

cardigan /'ka:dıgən/ n casaco m de lã

cardinal /'kɑ:dɪnl/ a cardeal, principal. ~ **number** numeral m cardinal □ n (relig) cardeal m

care /keə(r)/ n cuidado m; (concern) interesse m □ vi ~ **about** (be interested) estar interessado por; (be worried) estar preocupado com. ~ **for** (like) gostar de; (look after) tomar conta de. take ~ tomar cuidado. take ~ of cuidar de; (deal with) tratar de. he couldn't ~ less ele está pouco ligando, ele não dá a menor (colloq)

career /kə'rɪə(r)/ n carreira f □ vi ir a toda a velocidade, ir numa carreira

carefree /'keəfri:/ a despreocupado

careful /'keəfl/ a cuidadoso; (cautious) cauteloso. ~! cuidado! ~ly adv cuidadosamente; (cautiously) cautelosamente

careless /'keəlɪs/ a descuidado (about com). ~ly adv descuidadamente. ~ness n descuido m, negligência f

caress /kə'res/ n carícia f □ vt acariciar

caretaker /'keəteɪkə(r)/ n zelador m duma casa vizia; (janitor) zelador m, (P) porteiro m

cargo /'kɑ:gəʊ/ n (pl -oes) carregamento m, carga f

Caribbean /kærɪ'bi:ən/ a caraíba. the ~ as Caraíbas fpl

caricature /'kærɪkətjʊə(r)/ n caricatura f □ vt caricaturar

caring /'keərɪŋ/ a carinhoso, afetuoso, (P) afectuoso

carnage /'kɑ:nɪdʒ/ n carnificina f

carnation /kɑ:'neɪʃn/ n cravo m

carnival /'kɑ:nɪvl/ n carnaval m

carol /'kærəl/ n cântico m or canto m de Natal

carp[1] /kɑ:p/ n inv carpa f

carp[2] /kɑ:p/ vi ~ (at) criticar

carpenter /'kɑ:pɪntə(r)/ n carpinteiro m. ~ry n carpintaria f

carpet /'kɑ:pɪt/ n tapete m □ vt (pt carpeted) atapetar. with fitted ~s (estar) atapetado. be on the ~ (colloq) ser chamado à ordem. ~-sweeper n limpador m de tapetes

carport /'kɑ:pɔ:t/ n abrigo m, (P) telheiro m para automóveis

carriage /'kærɪdʒ/ n carruagem f; (of goods) frete m, transporte m; (cost, bearing) porte m

carriageway /'kærɪdʒweɪ/ n faixa f de rodagem, pista f

carrier /'kærɪə(r)/ n transportador m; (company) transportadora f; (med) portador m. ~ (bag) saco m de plástico

carrot /'kærət/ n cenoura f

carry /'kærɪ/ vt/i levar; (goods) transportar; (involve) acarretar; (have for

sale) ter à venda. be carried away entusiasmar-se, deixar-se levar. ~-cot n moisés m. ~ off levar à força; (prize) incluir. ~ it off sair-se bem (de). ~ on continuar; (colloq: flirt) flertar; (colloq: behave) portar-se (mal). ~ out executar; (duty) cumprir. ~ through levar a cabo

cart /kɑ:t/ n carroça f; carro m □ vt acarretar; (colloq) carregar com

cartilage /'kɑ:tɪlɪdʒ/ n cartilagem f

carton /'kɑ:tn/ n embalagem f de cartão or de plástico; (of yogurt) embalagem f, pote m; (of milk) pacote m

cartoon /kɑ:'tu:n/ n desenho m humorístico, caricatura f; (strip) estória f em quadrinhos, (P) banda f desenhada; (film) desenhos mpl animados. ~ist n caricaturista mf; (of strip, film) desenhador m

cartridge /'kɑ:trɪdʒ/ n cartucho m

carve /kɑ:v/ vt esculpir, talhar; (meat) trinchar. ~ing n obra f de talha; (on tree-trunk) incisão f. ~ing knife faca f de trinchar, trinchante m

cascade /kæs'keɪd/ n cascata f □ vi cair em cascata

case[1] /keɪs/ n caso m; (jur) causa f, processo m; (phil) argumentos mpl. in any ~ em todo caso. in ~ (of) no caso (de). in that ~ nesse caso

case[2] /keɪs/ n caixa f; (crate) caixa f, caixote m; (for camera, jewels, spectacles, etc) estojo m; (suitcase) mala f; (for cigarettes) cigarreira f

cash /kæʃ/ n dinheiro m, numerário m, cash m □ vt (obtain money for) cobrar, receber; (give money for) pagar. be short of ~ ter pouco dinheiro. ~ a cheque (receive/give) cobrar/descontar um cheque. ~ in receber. ~ in (on) aproveitar-se de. in ~ em dinheiro. pay ~ pagar em dinheiro. ~ desk caixa f. ~ dispenser caixa f electrónica. ~-flow n cash-flow m. ~ register caixa f registradora, (P) registadora f

cashew /kæ'ʃu:/ n caju m

cashier /kæ'ʃɪə(r)/ n caixa mf

cashmere /kæʃ'mɪə(r)/ n caxemira f

casino /kə'si:nəʊ/ n (pl -os) casino m

cask /kɑ:sk/ n casco m, barril m

casket /'kɑ:skɪt/ n pequeno cofre m; (Amer: coffin) caixão m

casserole /'kæsərəʊl/ n caçarola f; (stew) estufado m

cassette /kə'set/ n cassette f. ~ player gravador m. ~ recorder n gravador m

cast /kɑ:st/ vt (pt cast) lançar, arremessar; (shed) despojar-se de; (vote) dar; (metal) fundir; (shadow) projetar, (P) projectar □ n (theatr) elenco m; (mould) molde m; (med) aparelho *m* de gesso. ~ **iron** *n* ferro *m* fundido. ~-**iron** *a* de ferro fundido; (*fig*) muito forte. ~-**offs** *npl* roupa *f* velha

castanets /ˌkæstəˈnets/ *npl* castanholas *fpl*

castaway /ˈkɑːstəweɪ/ *n* náufrago *m*

caste /kɑːst/ *n* casta *f*

castigate /ˈkæstɪɡeɪt/ *vt* castigar

castle /ˈkɑːsl/ *n* castelo *m*; (*chess*) torre *f*

castor /ˈkɑːstə(r)/ *n* roda *f* de pé de móvel. ~ **sugar** açúcar *m* em pó

castrat|e /kæˈstreɪt/ *vt* castrar. ~**ion** /-ʃn/ *n* castração *f*

casual /ˈkæʒʊəl/ *a* (*chance: meeting*) casual; (*careless, unmethodical*) descuidado; (*informal*) informal. ~ **clothes** roupa *f* prática *or* de lazer. ~ **work** trabalho *m* ocasional. ~**ly** *adv* casualmente; (*carelessly*) sem cuidado

casualty /ˈkæʒʊəltɪ/ *n* (*dead*) morto *m*; (*death*) morte *f*; (*injured*) ferido *m*; (*victim*) vítima *f*; (*mil*) baixa *f*

cat /kæt/ *n* gato *m*. ~**'s-eyes** *npl* (P) reflectores *mpl*

Catalonia /kætəˈləʊnɪə/ *n* Catalunha *f*

catalogue /ˈkætəlɒɡ/ *n* catálogo *m* □ *vt* catalogar

catalyst /ˈkætəlɪst/ *n* catalisador *m*

catapult /ˈkætəpʌlt/ *n* (*child's*) atiradeira *f*, (P) fisga *f* □ *vt* catapultar

cataract /ˈkætərækt/ *f* (*waterfall & med*) catarata *f*

catarrh /kəˈtɑː(r)/ *n* catarro *m*

catastroph|e /kəˈtæstrəfɪ/ *n* catástrofe *f*. ~**ic** /kætəsˈtrɒfɪk/ *a* catastrófico

catch /kætʃ/ *vt* (*pt* caught) apanhar; (*grasp*) agarrar; (*hear*) perceber □ *vi* prender-se (in em); (*get stuck*) ficar preso □ *n* apanha *f*; (*of fish*) pesca *f*; (*trick*) ratoeira *f*; (*snag*) problema *m*; (*on door*) trinco *m*; (*fastener*) fecho *m*. ~ **fire** pegar fogo, (P) incendiar-se. ~ **on** (*colloq*) pegar, tornar-se popular. ~ **sb's eye** atrair a atenção de alg. ~ **sight of** avistar. ~ **up** (with) pôr-se a par (com); (*work*) pôr em dia. ~-**phrase** *n* cliché *m*

catching /ˈkætʃɪŋ/ *a* contagioso, infeccioso

catchment /ˈkætʃmənt/ *n* ~ **area** (*geog*) bacia *f* de captação; (*fig: of school, hospital*) área *f*

catchy /ˈkætʃɪ/ *a* (*tune*) que pega fácil

categorical /kætɪˈɡɒrɪkl/ *a* categórico

category /ˈkætɪɡərɪ/ *n* categoria *f*

cater /ˈkeɪtə(r)/ *vi* fornecer comida (para clubes, casamentos, etc.). ~ **for** (*pander to*) satisfazer; (*consumers*) dirigir-se a. ~**er** *n* fornecedor *m*. ~**ing** *n* catering *m*

caterpillar /ˈkætəpɪlə(r)/ *n* lagarta *f*

cathedral /kəˈθiːdrəl/ *n* catedral *f*

catholic /ˈkæθəlɪk/ *a* universal; (*eclectic*) eclético, (P) eclético. C~ *a* & *n* católico (*m*). C~**ism** /kəˈθɒlɪsɪzəm/ *n* catolicismo *m*

cattle /ˈkætl/ *npl* gado *m*

catty /ˈkætɪ/ *a* (dissimuladamente) maldoso, com perfídia

caught /kɔːt/ *see* catch

cauldron /ˈkɔːldrən/ *n* caldeirão *m*

cauliflower /ˈkɒlɪflaʊə/(r)/ *n* couve-flor *f*

cause /kɔːz/ *n* causa *f* □ *vt* causar. ~ **sth to grow/move** *etc* fazer crescer/ mexer *etc* alg coisa

causeway /ˈkɔːzweɪ/ *n* estrada *f* elevada, caminho *m* elevado

caustic /ˈkɔːstɪk/ *a* cáustico

cauti|on /ˈkɔːʃn/ *n* cautela *f*; (*warning*) aviso *m* □ *vt* avisar. ~**ous** /ˈkɔːʃəs/ *a* cauteloso. ~**ously** *adv* cautelosamente

cavalry /ˈkævəlrɪ/ *n* cavalaria *f*

cave /keɪv/ *n* caverna *f*, gruta *f* □ *vi* ~ **in** desabar, dar de si

caveman /ˈkeɪvmæn/ *n* (*pl* -men) troglodita *m*, homem *m* das cavernas; (*fig*) (tipo) primário *m*

cavern /ˈkævən/ *n* caverna *f*. ~**ous** *a* cavernoso

caviare /ˈkævɪɑː(r)/ *n* caviar *m*

caving /ˈkeɪvɪŋ/ *n* espeleologia *f*

cavity /ˈkævətɪ/ *n* cavidade *f*

cavort /kəˈvɔːt/ *vi* curvetear; (*person*) andar aos pinotes

CD /siːˈdiː/ *see* compact disc

cease /siːs/ *vt/i* cessar. ~-**fire** *n* cessar-fogo *m*. ~**less** *a* incessante

cedar /ˈsiːdə(r)/ *n* cedro *m*

cedilla /sɪˈdɪlə/ *n* cedilha *f*

ceiling /ˈsiːlɪŋ/ *n* (*lit & fig*) teto *m*, (P) tecto *m*

celebrat|e /ˈselɪbreɪt/ *vt/i* celebrar, festejar. ~**ion** /ˈbreɪʃn/ *n* celebração *f*, festejo *m*

celebrated /ˈselɪbreɪtɪd/ *a* célebre

celebrity /sɪˈlebrətɪ/ *n* celebridade *f*

celery /ˈselərɪ/ *n* aipo *m*

celiba|te /ˈselɪbət/ *a* celibatário. ~**cy** *n* celibato *m*

cell /sel/ *n* (*of prison, convent*) cela *f*; (*biol, pol, electr*) célula *f*

cellar /ˈselə(r)/ *n* porão *m*, cave *f*; (*for wine*) adega *f*, cave *f*

cell|o /ˈtʃeləʊ/ *n* (*pl* -os) violoncelo *m*. ~**ist** *n* violoncelista *mf*

Cellophane /ˈseləfeɪn/ *n* (*p*) celofane *m*

cellular /ˈseljʊlə(r)/ *a* celular

Celt /kelt/ *n* celta *mf*. ~**ic** *a* celta, céltico

cement /sɪˈment/ *n* cimento *m* □ *vt* cimentar. ~-**mixer** *n* betoneira *f* cemetery /'semətrɪ/ n cemitério m

censor /'sensə(r)/ n censor m □ vt censurar. ~ship n censura f

censure /'senʃə(r)/ n censura f, crítica f □ vt censurar, criticar

census /'sensəs/ n recenseamento m, censo m

cent /sent/ n cêntimo m

centenary /sen'tiːnərɪ/ n centenário m

centigrade /'sentɪgreɪd/ a centígrado

centilitre /'sentɪliːtə(r)/ n centilitro m

centimetre /'sentɪmiːtə(r)/ n centímetro m

centipede /'sentɪpiːd/ n centopéia f, (P) centopeia f

central /'sentrəl/ a central. ~ heating aquecimento m central. ~ize vt centralizar. ~ly adv no centro

centre /'sentə(r)/ n centro m □ vt (pt centred) centrar □ vi ~ on concentrar-se em, fixar-se em

centrifugal /sen'trɪfjʊgl/ a centrífugo

century /'sentʃərɪ/ n século m

ceramic /sɪ'ræmɪk/ a (object) em cerâmica. ~s n cerâmica f

cereal /'sɪərɪəl/ n cereal m

cerebral /'serɪbrəl/ a cerebral

ceremonial /serɪ'məʊnɪəl/ a de cerimônia □ n cerimonial m

ceremony /'serɪmənɪ/ n cerimônia f, (P) cerimónia f. ~ious /-'məʊnɪəs/ a cerimonioso

certain /'sɜːtn/ a certo. be ~ ter a certeza. for ~ com certeza, ao certo. make ~ confirmar, verificar. ~ly adv com certeza, certamente. ~ty n certeza f

certificate /sə'tɪfɪkət/ n certificado m; (birth, marriage) certidão f; (health) atestado m

certify /'sɜːtɪfaɪ/ vt/i certificar. ~ied a (as insane) declarado

cervical /sɜː'vaɪkl/ a cervical; (of cervix) do útero

cesspit, cesspool /'sespɪt, 'sespuːl/ ns fossa f sanitária

chafe /tʃeɪf/ vt/i esfregar; (make/become sore) esfolar/ficar esfolado; (fig) irritar(-se)

chaff /tʃɑːf/ vt brincar com □ n brincadeira f; (husk) casca f

chaffinch /'tʃæfɪntʃ/ n tentilhão m

chagrin /'ʃægrɪn/ n decepção f, desgosto m, aborrecimento m

chain /tʃeɪn/ n corrente f, cadeia f; (series) cadeia f □ vt acorrentar. ~ reaction reação f, (P) reacção f em cadeia. ~-smoke vi fumar cigarros um atrás do outro. ~ store loja f pertencente a uma cadeia

chair /tʃeə(r)/ n cadeira f; (position of chairman) presidência f; (univ) cátedra f □ vt presidir

chairman /'tʃeəmən/ n (pl -men) presidente mf

chalet /'ʃæleɪ/ n chalé m

chalk /tʃɔːk/ n greda f, cal f; (for writing) giz m □ vt traçar com giz

challeng|e /'tʃælɪndʒ/ n desafio m; (by sentry) interpelação f □ vt desafiar; (question truth of) contestar. ~er n (sport) pretendente mf (ao título). ~ing a estimulante, que constitui um desafio

chamber /'tʃeɪmbə(r)/ n (old use) aposento m. ~-maid n arrumadeira f. ~ music música f de câmara. C~ of Commerce Câmara f de Comércio

chamois /'ʃæmɪ/ n ~(-leather) camurça f

champagne /ʃæm'peɪn/ n champanhe m

champion /'tʃæmpɪən/ n campeão m, campeã f □ vt defender. ~ship n campeonato m

chance /tʃɑːns/ n acaso m; (luck) sorte f; (opportunity) oportunidade f, chance f; (likelihood) hipótese f, probabilidade f; (risk) risco m □ a casual, fortuito □ vi calhar □ vt arriscar. by ~ por acaso

chancellor /'tʃɑːnsələ(r)/ n chanceler m. C~ of the Exchequer Ministro m das Finanças

chancy /'tʃɑːnsɪ/ a arriscado

chandelier /ʃændə'lɪə(r)/ n lustre m

change /tʃeɪndʒ/ vt mudar; (exchange) trocar (for por); (clothes, house, trains, etc) mudar de □ vi mudar; (clothes) mudar-se, mudar de roupa □ n mudança f; (money) troco m. a ~ of clothes uma muda de roupa. ~ hands (ownership) mudar de dono. ~ into (a butterfly etc) transformar-se em; (evening dress etc) pôr. ~ one's mind mudar de idéia. ~-over passar, mudar (to para). ~-over n mudança f. ~able a variável

channel /'tʃænl/ n canal m □ vt (pt channelled) canalizar. the C~ Islands as Ilhas do Canal da Mancha. the (English) C~ o Canal da Mancha

chant /tʃɑːnt/ n cântico m; (of crowd etc) vt/i cantar, entoar

chao|s /'keɪɒs/ n caos m. ~tic /-'ɒtɪk/ a caótico

chap /tʃæp/ n (colloq) sujeito m, (B) cara m, (P) tipo m

chapel /'tʃæpl/ n capela f

chaperon /'ʃæpərəʊn/ n pau-de-cabeleira m, chaperon □ vt servir de pau-de-cabeleira or de chaperon

chaplain /'tʃæplɪn/ n capelão m. ~cy n capelania f

chapter /'tʃæptə(r)/ n capítulo m

char /tʃɑː(r)/ vt (pt charred) carbonizar

character /'kærəktə(r)/ *n* caráter *m*, (*P*) carácter *m*; (*in novel, play*) personagem *m*; (*reputation*) fama *f*; (*eccentric person*) excêntrico *m*; (*letter*) caractere *m*, (*P*) carácter *m*. ~ize *vt* caracterizar

characteristic /kærəktə'rıstık/ *a* característico □ *n* característica *f*. ~ally *adv* tipicamente

charade /ʃə'raːd/ *n* charada *f*

charcoal /'tʃaːkəʊl/ *n* carvão *m* de lenha

charge /tʃaːdʒ/ *n* preço *m*; (*electr, mil*) carga *f*; (*jur*) acusação *f*; (*task, custody*) cargo *m* □ *vt/i* (*price*) cobrar; (*enemy*) atacar; (*jur*) incriminar. be in ~ of ter a cargo. take ~ of encarregar-se de

chariot /'tʃærɪət/ *n* carro *m* de guerra *or* triunfal

charisma /kə'rızmə/ *n* carisma *m*. ~tic /kærız'mætık/ *a* carismático

charit|y /'tʃærətɪ/ *n* caridade *f*; (*society*) instituição *f* de caridade. ~able *a* caridoso

charlatan /'ʃaːlətən/ *n* charlatão *m*

charm /tʃaːm/ *n* encanto *m*, charme *m*; (*spell*) feitiço *m*; (*talisman*) amuleto *m* □ *vt* encantar. ~ing *a* encantador

chart /tʃaːt/ *n* (*naut*) carta *f*; (*table*) mapa *m*, gráfico *m*, tabela *f* □ *vt* fazer o mapa de

charter /'tʃaːtə(r)/ *n* carta *f*. ~ (*flight*) (*voo*) charter *m* □ *vt* fretar. ~ed accountant *n* perito *m* contador, (*P*) perito *m* de contabilidade

charwoman /'tʃaːwʊmən/ *n* (*pl* -women) faxineira *f*, (*P*) mulher *f* a dias

chase /tʃeɪs/ *vt* perseguir □ *vi* (*colloq*) correr (after atrás de) □ *n* caça *f*, perseguição *f*. ~ away *or* off afugentar, expulsar

chasm /'kæzm/ *n* abismo *m*

chassis /'ʃæsɪ/ *n* chassi *m*

chaste /tʃeɪst/ *a* casto

chastise /tʃæs'taɪz/ *vt* castigar

chastity /'tʃæstətɪ/ *n* castidade *f*

chat /tʃæt/ *n* conversa *f* □ *vi* (*pt* chatted) conversar, cavaquear. have a ~ bater um papo, (*P*) dar dois dedos de conversa. ~ty *a* conversador

chatter /'tʃætə(r)/ *vi* tagarelar. his teeth are ~ing seus dentes estão tiritando □ *n* tagarelice *f*

chauffeur /'ʃəʊfə(r)/ *n* motorista *m*, chofer (particular) *m*, chauffeur *m*

chauvinis|t /'ʃəʊvɪnɪst/ *n* chauvinista *mf*. male ~t (*pej*) machista *m*. ~m /-zəm/ *n* chauvinismo *m*

cheap /tʃiːp/ *a* (-er, -est) barato; (*fare, rate*) reduzido. ~(ly) *adv* barato. ~ness *n* barateza *f*

cheapen /'tʃiːpən/ *vt* depreciar

cheat /tʃiːt/ *vt* enganar, trapacear □ *vi* (*at games*) roubar, (*P*) fazer batota; (*in exams*) copiar □ *n* intrujão *m*; (*at games*) trapaceiro *m*, (*P*) batoteiro *m*

check¹ /tʃek/ *vt/i* (*examine*) verificar; (*tickets*) revisar; (*restrain*) controlar, refrear □ *n* verificação *f*; (*tickets*) controle *m*; (*curb*) freio *m*; (*chess*) xeque *m*; (*Amer: bill*) conta *f*; (*Amer: cheque*) cheque *m*. ~ in assinar o registro; (*at airport*) fazer o check-in. ~-in *n* check-in *m*. ~ out pagar a conta. ~-out *n* caixa *f*. ~-up *n* exame *m* médico, check-up *m*

check² /tʃek/ *n* (*pattern*) xadrez *m*. ~ed *a* de xadrez

checkmate /'tʃekmeɪt/ *n* xeque-mate *m*

cheek /tʃiːk/ *n* face *f*, (*fig*) descaramento *m*. ~y *a* descarado

cheer /tʃɪə(r)/ *n* alegria *f*; (*shout*) viva *m* □ *vt/i* aclamar, aplaudir. ~s! à sua, (*P*) vossa (saúde)!; (*thank you*) obrigadinho. ~ (up) animar(-se). ~ful *a* bem disposto; alegre

cheerio /tʃɪərɪ'əʊ/ *int* (*colloq*) até logo, (*P*) adeusinho

cheese /tʃiːz/ *n* queijo *m*

cheetah /'tʃiːtə/ *n* chita *f*, lobo-tigre *m*

chef /ʃef/ *n* cozinheiro-chefe *m*

chemical /'kemɪkl/ *a* químico □ *n* produto *m* químico

chemist /'kemɪst/ *n* farmacêutico *m*; (*scientist*) químico *m*. ~'s (shop) *n* farmácia *f*. ~ry *n* química *f*

cheque /tʃek/ *n* cheque *m*. ~-book *n* talão *m* de cheques. ~-card *n* cartão *m* de banco

cherish /'tʃerɪʃ/ *vt* estimar, querer; (*hope*) acalentar

cherry /'tʃerɪ/ *n* cereja *f*. ~-tree *n* cerejeira *f*

chess /tʃes/ *n* jogo *m* de xadrez. ~-board *n* tabuleiro *m* de xadrez

chest /tʃest/ *n* peito *m*; (*for money, jewels*) cofre *m*. ~ of drawers cômoda *f*, (*P*) cómoda *f*

chestnut /'tʃesnʌt/ *n* castanha *f*. ~-tree *n* castanheiro *m*

chew /tʃuː/ *vt* mastigar. ~ing-gum *n* chiclete *m*, (*P*) pastilha *f* elástica

chic /ʃiːk/ *a* chique

chick /tʃɪk/ *n* pinto *m*

chicken /'tʃɪkɪn/ *n* galinha *f* □ *vi* ~ out (*sl*) acovardar-se. ~-pox *n* catapora *f*, (*P*) varicela *f*

chicory /'tʃɪkərɪ/ *n* (*for coffee*) chicória *f*; (*for salad*) endívia *f*

chief /tʃiːf/ *n* chefe *m* □ *a* principal. ~ly *adv* principalmente

chilblain /'tʃɪlbleɪn/ *n* frieira *f*

child /tʃaɪld/ *n* (*pl* children /'tʃɪldrən/) criança *f*; (*son*) filho *m*;

(*daughter*) filha *f.* ~**hood** *n* infância *f.* meninice *f.* ~**ish** *a* infantil; (*immature*) acriançado, pueril. ~**less** *a* sem filhos. ~**like** *a* infantil. ~**-minder** *n* babá *f* que cuida de crianças em sua propria casa

childbirth /'tʃaɪldbɜːθ/ *n* parto *m*

Chile /'tʃɪlɪ/ *n* Chile *m*. ~**an** *a* & *n* chileno (*m*)

chill /tʃɪl/ *n* frio *m*; (*med*) resfriado *m*, (P) constipação *f* □ *vt/i* arrefecer; (*culin*) refrigerar. ~**y** *a* frio. be or feel ~**y** ter frio

chilli /'tʃɪlɪ/ *n* (*pl* -ies) malagueta *f*

chime /tʃaɪm/ *n* carrilhão *m*; (*sound*) música *m* de carrilhão □ *vt/i* tocar

chimney /'tʃɪmnɪ/ *n* (*pl* -eys) chaminé *f.* ~**-sweep** *n* limpador *m* de chaminés, (P) limpa-chaminés *m*

chimpanzee /tʃɪmpæn'ziː/ *n* chimpanzé *m*

chin /tʃɪn/ *n* queixo *m*

china /'tʃaɪnə/ *n* porcelana *f*, (*crockery*) louça *f*

China /'tʃaɪnə/ *n* China *f.* ~**ese** /-'niːz/ *a* & *n* chinês (*m*)

chink[1] /tʃɪŋk/ *n* (*crack*) fenda *f*, fresta *f*

chink[2] /tʃɪŋk/ *n* tinir *m* □ *vt/i* (fazer) tinir

chip /tʃɪp/ *n* (*broken piece*) bocado *m*; (*culin*) batata *f* frita em palitos; (*gambling*) ficha *f*, (*electronic*) chip *m*, circuito *m* integrado □ *vt/i* (*pt* chipped) lascar(-se)

chipboard /'tʃɪpbɔːd/ *n* compensado *m* (de madeira)

chiropodist /kɪ'rɒpədɪst/ *n* calista *mf*

chirp /tʃɜːp/ *n* pipilar *m*; (*of cricket*) cricri *m* □ *vi* pipilar; (*cricket*) cantar, fazer cricri

chisel /'tʃɪzl/ *n* cinzel *m*, escopro *m* □ *vt* (*pt* chiselled) talhar

chivalr|**y** /'ʃɪvlrɪ/ *n* cavalheirismo *m.* ~**ous** *a* cavalheiresco

chive /tʃaɪv/ *n* cebolinho *m*

chlorine /'klɔːriːn/ *n* cloro *m*

chocolate /'tʃɒklɪt/ *n* chocolate *m*

choice /tʃɔɪs/ *n* escolha *f* □ *a* escolhido, seleto, (P) seleccionado

choir /'kwaɪə(r)/ *n* coro *m*

choirboy /'kwaɪəbɔɪ/ *n* menino *m* de coro, corista *m*, (P) coralista *m*

choke /tʃəʊk/ *vt/i* sufocar; (*on food*) engasgar(-se) □ *n* (*auto*) afogador *m*, (P) botão *m* do ar (*colloq*)

cholesterol /kə'lestərɒl/ *n* colesterol *m*

choose /tʃuːz/ *vt/i* (*pt* chose, *pp* chosen) escolher; (*prefer*) preferir. ~ **to do** decidir fazer

choosy /'tʃuːzɪ/ *a* (*colloq*) exigente, difícil de contentar

chop /tʃɒp/ *vt/i* (*pt* chopped) cortar □

n (*wood*) machadada *f*; (*culin*) costeleta *f.* ~ **down** abater. ~**per** *n* cutelo *m*; (*sl*: *helicopter*) helicóptero *m*

choppy /'tʃɒpɪ/ *a* (*sea*) picado

chopstick /'tʃɒpstɪk/ *n* fachi *m*, pauzinho *m*

choral /'kɔːrəl/ *a* coral

chord /kɔːd/ *n* (*mus*) acorde *m*

chore /tʃɔː(r)/ *n* trabalho *m*; (*unpleasant task*) tarefa *f* maçante. **household** ~**s** afazeres *mpl* domésticos

choreograph|**er** /kɒrɪ'ɒgrəfə(r)/ *n* coreógrafo *m*. ~**y** *n* coreografia *f*

chortle /'tʃɔːtl/ *n* risada *f* □ *vi* rir alto

chorus /'kɔːrəs/ *n* coro *m*; (*of song*) refrão *m*, estribilho *m*

chose, chosen /tʃəʊz, 'tʃəʊzn/ *see* choose

Christ /kraɪst/ *n* Cristo *m*

christen /'krɪsn/ *vt* batizar, (P) baptizar. ~**ing** *n* batismo *m*, (P) baptismo *m*

Christian /'krɪstʃən/ *a* & *n* cristão (*m*). ~ **name** nome *m* de batismo, (P) baptismo. ~**ity** /-stɪ'ænətɪ/ *n* cristandade *f*

Christmas /'krɪsməs/ *n* Natal *m* □ *a* do Natal. ~ **card** cartão *m* de Boas Festas. ~ **Day/Eve** dia *m*/véspera *f* de Natal. ~ **tree** árvore *f* de Natal

chrome /krəʊm/ *n* cromo *m*

chromosome /'krəʊməsəʊm/ *n* cromossoma *m*

chronic /'krɒnɪk/ *a* crônico, (P) crónico

chronicle /'krɒnɪkl/ *n* crônica *f*

chronological /krɒnə'lɒdʒɪkl/ *a* cronológico

chrysanthemum /krɪ'sænθəməm/ *n* crisântemo *m*

chubby /'tʃʌbɪ/ *a* (-ier, -iest) gorducho, rechonchudo

chuck /tʃʌk/ *vt* (*colloq*) deitar, atirar. ~ **out** (*person*) expulsar; (*thing*) jogar fora, (P) deitar fora

chuckle /'tʃʌkl/ *n* riso *m* abafado □ *vi* rir sozinho

chum /tʃʌm/ *n* (*colloq*) amigo *m* intimo, camarada *mf.* ~**my** *a* amigável

chunk /tʃʌŋk/ *n* (grande) bocado *m*, naco *m*

church /tʃɜːtʃ/ *n* igreja *f*

churchyard /'tʃɜːtʃjɑːd/ *n* cemitério *m*

churlish /'tʃɜːlɪʃ/ *a* grosseiro, indelicado

churn /tʃɜːn/ *n* batedeira *f*; (*milk-can*) vasilha *f* de leite □ *vt* bater. ~ **out** produzir em série

chute /ʃuːt/ *n* calha *f*; (*for rubbish*) conduta *f* de lixo

chutney /'tʃʌtnɪ/ *n* (*pl*-eys) chutney *m*

cider /'saɪdə(r)/ *n* sidra *f*, (P) cidra *f*

cigar /sɪ'gɑː(r)/ *n* charuto *m*

cigarette /sɪgəˈret/ n cigarro m. ~-case n cigarreira f

cinder /ˈsɪndə(r)/ n brasa f. burnt to a ~ estorricado

cinema /ˈsɪnəmə/ n cinema m

cinnamon /ˈsɪnəmən/ n canela f

cipher /ˈsaɪfə(r)/ n cifra f

circle /ˈsɜːkl/ n círculo m; (theat) balcão m □ vt dar a volta a □ vi descrever círculos, voltear

circuit /ˈsɜːkɪt/ n circuito m

circuitous /sɜːˈkjuːɪtəs/ a indireto, tortuoso

circular /ˈsɜːkjʊlə(r)/ a circular

circulat|e /ˈsɜːkjʊleɪt/ vt/i (fazer) circular. ~ion /-ˈleɪʃn/ n circulação f; (sales of newspaper) tiragem f

circumcis|e /ˈsɜːkəmsaɪz/ vt circuncidar. ~ion /-ˈsɪʒn/ n circuncisão f

circumference /səˈkʌmfərəns/ n circunferência f

circumflex /ˈsɜːkəmfleks/ n circunflexo m

circumstance /ˈsɜːkəmstəns/ n circunstância f. ~s (means) situação f económica, (P) económica

circus /ˈsɜːkəs/ n circo m

cistern /ˈsɪstən/ n reservatório m; (of WC) autoclismo m

cit|e /saɪt/ vt citar. ~ation /-ˈteɪʃn/ n citação f

citizen /ˈsɪtɪzn/ n cidadão m, cidadã f; (of town) habitante mf. ~ship n cidadania f

citrus /ˈsɪtrəs/ n ~ fruit citrino m

city /ˈsɪtɪ/ n cidade f

civic /ˈsɪvɪk/ a cívico

civil /ˈsɪvl/ a civil; (rights) cívico; (polite) delicado. ~ servant funcionário m público. C~ Service Administração f Pública. ~ war guerra f civil. ~ity /-ˈvɪlətɪ/ n civilidade f, cortesia f

civilian /sɪˈvɪlɪən/ a & n civil (mf), paisano m

civiliz|e /ˈsɪvəlaɪz/ vt civilizar. ~ation /-ˈzeɪʃn/ n civilização f

claim /kleɪm/ vt reclamar; (assert) pretender □ vi (from insurance) reclamar □ n reivindicação f; (assertion) afirmação f; (right) direito m; (from insurance) reclamação f

clairvoyant /kleəˈvɔɪənt/ n vidente mf □ a clarividente

clam /klæm/ n molusco m

clamber /ˈklæmbə(r)/ vi trepar

clammy /ˈklæmɪ/ a (-ier, -iest) úmido, (P) húmido e pegajoso

clamour /ˈklæmə(r)/ n clamor m, vociferação f □ vi ~ for exigir aos gritos

clamp /klæmp/ n grampo m; (for car) bloqueador m □ vt prender com grampo; (a car) bloquear. ~ down on

apertar, suprimir; (colloq) cair em cima de (colloq)

clan /klæn/ n clã m

clandestine /klænˈdestɪn/ a clandestino

clang /klæŋ/ n tinir m

clap /klæp/ vt/i (pt clapped) aplaudir; (put) meter □ n aplauso m; (of thunder) ribombo m. ~ one's hands bater palmas

claptrap /ˈklæptræp/ n parlapatice f

claret /ˈklærət/ n clarete m

clarif|y /ˈklærɪfaɪ/ vt esclarecer. ~ication /-ˈkeɪʃn/ n esclarecimento m

clarinet /klærɪˈnet/ n clarinete m

clarity /ˈklærətɪ/ n claridade f

clash /klæʃ/ n choque m; (sound) estridor m; (fig) conflito m □ vt/i entrechocar(-se); (of colours) destoar

clasp /klɑːsp/ n (fastener) fecho m; (hold, grip) aperto m de mão □ vt apertar, serrar

class /klɑːs/ n classe f □ vt classificar

classic /ˈklæsɪk/ a & n clássico (m). ~s npl letras fpl clássicas, (P) estudos mpl clássicos. ~al a clássico

classif|y /ˈklæsɪfaɪ/ vt classificar. ~ication /-ˈkeɪʃn/ n classificação f. ~ied advertisement (anúncio m) classificado (m)

classroom /ˈklɑːsruːm/ n sala f de aulas

clatter /ˈklætə(r)/ n estardalhaço m □ vi fazer barulho

clause /klɔːz/ n cláusula f; (gram) oração f

claustrophob|ia /klɔːstrəˈfəʊbɪə/ n claustrofobia f. ~ic a claustrofóbico

claw /klɔː/ n garra f; (of lobster) tenaz f, pinça f □ vt (seize) agarrar; (scratch) arranhar; (tear) rasgar

clay /kleɪ/ n argila f, barro m

clean /kliːn/ a (-er, -est) limpo □ adv completamente □ vt limpar □ vi ~ up fazer a limpeza. ~-shaven a de cara rapada. ~er n faxineira f, (P) mulher f da limpeza; (of clothes) empregado m da tinturaria. ~ly adv com limpeza, como deve ser

cleans|e /klenz/ vt limpar; (fig) purificar. ~ing cream creme m de limpeza

clear /klɪə(r)/ a (-er, -est) claro; (glass) transparente; (without obstacles) livre; (profit) líquido; (sky) limpo □ adv claramente □ vt limpar; (snow, one's name, etc) limpar; (the table) tirar; (jump) transpor; (debt) saldar; (jur) absolver; (through customs) despachar □ vi (fog) dissipar-se; (sky) limpar. ~ of (away from) afastado de. ~ off or out (sl) sair andando, zarpar. ~ out (clean) fazer a limpeza. ~ up (tidy) arrumar; (mystery) desvendar; (of weather) clarear, limpar. ~ly adv claramente

clearance /'klɪərəns/ n autorização f; (for ship) despacho m; (space) espaço m livre. ~ sale liquidação f, saldos mpl

clearing /'klɪərɪŋ/ n clareira f

clearway /'klɪəweɪ/ n rodovia f de estacionamento proibido

cleavage /'kli:vɪdʒ/ n divisão f; (between breasts) rego m (of dress) decote m

cleaver /'kli:və(r)/ n cutelo m

clef /klef/ n (mus) clave f

cleft /kleft/ n fenda f

clench /klentʃ/ vt (teeth, fists) cerrar; (grasp) agarrar

clergy /'klɜ:dʒɪ/ n clero m. ~man (pl -men) clérigo m, sacerdote m

cleric /'klerɪk/ n clérigo m. ~al a (relig) clerical; (of clerks) de escritório

clerk /kla:k/ n auxiliar m de escritório

clever /'klevə(r)/ a (-er, -est) esperto, inteligente; (skilful) hábil, habilidoso. ~ly adv inteligentemente; (skilfully) habilmente, habilidosamente. ~ness n esperteza f, inteligência f

cliché /'kli:ʃeɪ/ n chavão m, lugar-comum m, cliché m

click /klɪk/ n estalido m, clique m □ vi dar um estalido

client /'klaɪənt/ n cliente mf

clientele /kli:ən'tel/ n clientela f

cliff /klɪf/ n penhasco m. ~s npl falésia f

climate /'klaɪmɪt/ n clima m. ~ic /'mætɪk/ a climático

climax /'klaɪmæks/ n clímax m, ponto m culminante

climb /klaɪm/ vt (stairs) subir; (tree, wall) subir em, trepar em; (mountain) escalar □ vi subir, trepar □ n subida f; (mountain) escalada f. ~ down descer; (fig) dar a mão à palmatória (fig). ~er n (sport) alpinista mf; (plant) trepadeira f

clinch /klɪntʃ/ vt (deal) fechar; (argument) resolver

cling /klɪŋ/ vi (pt clung) ~ (to) agarrar-se (a); (stick) colar-se (a)

clinic /'klɪnɪk/ n clínica f

clinical /'klɪnɪkl/ a clínico

clink /klɪŋk/ n tinido m □ vt/i (fazer) tilintar

clip¹ /klɪp/ n (for paper) clipe m; (for hair) grampo m, (P) gancho m; (for tube) braçadeira f □ vt (pt clipped) prender

clip² /klɪp/ vt (pt clipped) cortar; (trim) aparar □ n tosquia f; (colloq: blow) murro m. ~ping n recorte m

clique /kli:k/ n panelinha f, facção f, conventículo m

cloak /kləʊk/ n capa f, manto m

cloakroom /'kləʊkru:m/ n vestiário m; (toilet) toalete m, (P) lavabo m

clock /klɒk/ n relógio m □ vi ~in/out marcar o ponto (à entrada/à saída). ~ up (colloq: miles etc) fazer

clockwise /'klɒkwaɪz/ a & adv no sentido dos ponteiros do relógio

clockwork /'klɒkwɜ:k/ n mecanismo m. go like ~ ir às mil maravilhas

clog /klɒg/ n tamanco m, soco m □ vt/i (pt clogged) entupir(-se)

cloister /'klɔɪstə(r)/ n claustro m

close¹ /kləʊs/ a (-er, -est) próximo (to de); (link, collaboration) estreito; (friend) íntimo; (weather) abafado □ adv perto. ~ at hand, ~ by muito perto. ~ together (crowded) espremido. have a ~ shave (fig) escapar por um triz. ~up n grande plano m. ~ly adv de perto. ~ness n proximidade f

close² /kləʊz/ vt/i fechar(-se); (end) terminar; (of shop etc) fechar □ n fim m. ~d shop organização f que só admite trabalhadores sindicalizados

closet /'klɒzɪt/ n (Amer) armário m

closure /'kləʊʒə(r)/ n encerramento m

clot /klɒt/ n coágulo m □ vi (pt clotted) coagular

cloth /klɒθ/ n pano m; (tablecloth) toalha f de mesa

clothe /kləʊð/ vt vestir. ~ing n vestuário m, roupa f

clothes /kləʊðz/ npl roupa f, vestuário m. ~-line n varal m para roupa

cloud /klaʊd/ n nuvem f □ vt/i toldar (-se). ~y a nublado, toldado; (liquid) turvo

clout /klaʊt/ n cascudo m, (P) carolo m; (colloq: power) poder m efectivo □ vt (colloq) bater

clove /kləʊv/ n cravo m. ~ of garlic dente m de alho

clover /'kləʊvə(r)/ n trevo m

clown /klaʊn/ n palhaço m □ vi fazer palhaçadas

club /klʌb/ n clube m; (weapon) cacete m. ~s (cards) paus mpl □ vt/i (pt clubbed) dar bordoadas or cacetadas (em). ~ together (share costs) cotizar-se

cluck /klʌk/ vi cacarejar

clue /klu:/ n indício m, pista f; (in crossword) definição f. not have a ~ (colloq) não fazer a menor idéia

clump /klʌmp/ n maciço m, tufo m

clumsy /'klʌmzɪ/ a (-ier, -iest) desajeitado

clung /klʌŋ/ see cling

cluster /'klʌstə(r)/ n (pequeno) grupo m; (bot) cacho m □ vt/i agrupar(-se)

clutch /klʌtʃ/ vt agarrar (em), apertar □ vi agarrar-se (at a) □ n (auto) embreagem f, (P) embraiagem f. ~es npl garras fpl

clutter /'klʌtə(r)/ n barafunda f, desordem f □ vt atravancar

coach /kəʊtʃ/ n ònibus m, (P) camioneta f; (of train) carruagem f; (sport) treinador m □ vt (tutor) dar aulas a; (sport) treinar

coagulate /kəʊˈægjʊleɪt/ vt/i coagular(-se)

coal /kəʊl/ n carvão m

coalfield /'kəʊlfiːld/ n região f carbonífera

coalition /kəʊəˈlɪʃn/ n coligação f

coarse /kɔːs/ a (-er, -est) grosseiro

coast /kəʊst/ n costa f □ vi costear; (cycle) descer em roda-livre; (car) ir em ponto morto. ~al a costeiro

coastguard /'kəʊstgaːd/ n polícia f marítima

coastline /'kəʊstlaɪn/ n litoral m

coat /kəʊt/ n casaco m; (of animal) pêlo m; (of paint) camada f, demão f □ vt cobrir. ~ of arms brasão m. ~ing n camada f

coax /kəʊks/ vt levar com afagos ou lisonjas, convencer

cobble /'kɒbl/ n ~(-stone) n pedra f de calçada

cobweb /'kɒbweb/ n teia f de aranha

cocaine /kəʊˈkeɪn/ n cocaína f

cock /kɒk/ n (male bird) macho m; (rooster) galo m □ vt (gun) engatilhar; (ears) fitar. ~-eyed a (sl: askew) de esguelha

cockerel /'kɒkərəl/ n frango m, galo m novo

cockle /'kɒkl/ n berbigão m

cockney /'kɒknɪ/ n (pl -eys) (person) londrino m; (dialect) dialeto m do leste de Londres

cockpit /'kɒkpɪt/ n cabine f

cockroach /'kɒkrəʊtʃ/ n barata f

cocktail /'kɒkteɪl/ n cocktail m, coquetel m. fruit ~ salada f de fruta

cocky /'kɒkɪ/ a (-ier -iest) convencido (colloq)

cocoa /'kəʊkəʊ/ n cacau m

coconut /'kəʊkənʌt/ n coco m

cocoon /kəˈkuːn/ n casulo m

cod /kɒd/ n (pl invar) bacalhau m. ~-liver oil óleo m de fígado de bacalhau

code /kəʊd/ n código m □ vt codificar

coeducational /kəʊedʒʊˈkeɪʃənl/ a misto

coerc|e /kəʊˈɜːs/ vt coagir. ~ion /-ʃn/ n coação f, (P) coacção f

coexist /kəʊɪgˈzɪst/ vi coexistir. ~ence n coexistência f

coffee /'kɒfɪ/ n café m. ~ bar café m.

~-pot n cafeteira f. ~-table n mesa f baixa

coffin /'kɒfɪn/ n caixão m

cog /kɒg/ n dente m de roda. a ~ in the machine (fig) uma rodinha numa engrenagem

cogent /'kəʊdʒənt/ a convincente; (relevant) pertinente

cognac /'kɒnjæk/ n conhaque m

cohabit /kəʊˈhæbɪt/ vi coabitar

coherent /kəˈhɪərənt/ a coerente

coil /kɔɪl/ vt/i enrolar(-se) □ n rolo m; (electr) bobina f, (one ring) espiral f; (contraceptive) dispositivo m intrauterino, DIU

coin /kɔɪn/ n moeda f □ vt cunhar

coincide /kəʊɪnˈsaɪd/ vi coincidir

coinciden|ce /kəʊˈɪnsɪdəns/ n coincidência f. ~tal /dentl/ a que acontece por coincidência

colander /'kʌləndə(r)/ n peneira f, (P) coador m

cold /kəʊld/ a (-er, -est) frio □ n frio m; (med) resfriado m, constipação f. be or feel ~ estar com frio. it's ~ está frio. ~-blooded a (person) insensível; (deed) a sangue frio. ~ cream creme m para a pele. ~ness n frio m; (of feeling) frieza f

coleslaw /'kəʊlslɔː/ n salada f de repolho cru

colic /'kɒlɪk/ n cólica(s) f (pl)

collaborat|e /kəˈlæbəreɪt/ vi colaborar. ~ion /-'reɪʃn/ n colaboração f. ~or n colaborador m

collapse /kəˈlæps/ vi desabar; (med) ter um colapso □ n colapso m

collapsible /kəˈlæpsəbl/ a desmontável, dobrável

collar /'kɒlə(r)/ n gola f; (of shirt) colarinho m; (of dog) coleira f □ vt (colloq) pôr a mão a. ~-bone n clavícula f

colleague /'kɒliːg/ n colega mf

collect /kəˈlekt/ vt (gather) juntar; (fetch) ir/vir buscar; (money, rent) cobrar; (as hobby) colecionar □ vi juntar-se. call ~ (Amer) chamar a cobrar. ~ion /-ʃn/ n coleção f, (P) colecção f; (in church) coleta f, (P) colecta f; (of mail) tiragem f, coleta f, (P) abertura f. ~or n (as hobby) colecionador m, (P) coleccionador m

collective /kəˈlektɪv/ a coletivo, (P) colectivo

college /'kɒlɪdʒ/ n colégio m

collide /kəˈlaɪd/ vi colidir

colliery /'kɒlɪərɪ/ n mina f de carvão

collision /kəˈlɪʒn/ n colisão f, choque m; (fig) conflito m

colloquial /kəˈləʊkwɪəl/ a coloquial. ~ism n expressão f coloquial

collusion /kəˈluːʒn/ n conluio m

colon /'kəʊlən/ n (gram) dois pontos mpl; (anat) cólon m

colonel /'kɜ:nl/ n coronel m

colonize /'kɒlənaɪz/ vt colonizar

colon|y /'kɒlənɪ/ n colônia f, (P) colónia f. ~ial /kə'ləʊnɪəl/ a & n colonial (mf)

colossal /kə'lɒsl/ a colossal

colour /'kʌlə(r)/ n cor f □ a (photo, TV, etc) a cores; (film) colorido □ vt colorir, dar cor a □ vi (blush) corar. ~-blind a daltónico, (P) daltónico. ~ful a colorido. ~ing n (of skin) cor f; (in food) corante m. ~less a descolorido

coloured /'kʌləd/ a (pencil, person) de cor □ n pessoa f de cor

column /'kɒləm/ n coluna f

columnist /'kɒləmnɪst/ n colunista mf

coma /'kəʊmə/ n coma m

comb /kəʊm/ n pente m □ vt pentear; (search) vasculhar. ~ one's hair pentear-se

combat /'kɒmbæt/ n combate m □ vt (pt combated) combater

combination /kɒmbɪ'neɪʃn/ n combinação f

combine /kəm'baɪn/ vt/i combinar (-se), juntar(-se), reunir(-se)

combustion /kəm'bʌstʃən/ n combustão f

come /kʌm/ vi (pt came, pp come) vir; (arrive) chegar; (occur) suceder. ~ about acontecer. ~ across encontrar, dar com. ~ away or off soltar-se. ~ back voltar. ~-back n regresso m; (retort) réplica f. ~ by obter. ~down descer; (price) baixar. ~-down n humilhação f. ~ from vir de. ~ in entrar. ~ into (money) herdar. ~ off (succeed) ter êxito; (fare) sair-se. ~ on! vamos! ~ out sair. ~ round (after fainting) voltar a si; (be converted) deixar-se convencer. ~ to (amount to) montar a. ~ up subir; (seeds) despontar; (fig) surgir. ~ up with (idea) vir com, propor. ~-uppance n castigo m merecido

comedian /kə'mi:dɪən/ n comediante mf

comedy /'kɒmədɪ/ n comédia f

comet /'kɒmɪt/ n cometa m

comfort /'kʌmfət/ n conforto m □ vt confortar, consolar. ~able a confortável

comic /'kɒmɪk/ a cómico, (P) cómico □ n cómico m; (periodical) estórias fpl em quadrinhos, (P) revista f de banda desenhada. ~ strip estória f em quadrinhos, (p) banda f desenhada. ~al a cómico, (P) cómico

coming /'kʌmɪŋ/ n vinda f □ a próximo. ~s and goings idas e vindas fpl

comma /'kɒmə/ n vírgula f

command /kə'mɑ:nd/ n (mil) comando m; (order) ordem f; (mastery) domínio m □ vt comandar; (respect) inspirar, impor. ~er n comandante m. ~ing a imponente

commandeer /kɒmən'dɪə(r)/ vt requisitar

commandment /kə'mɑ:ndmənt/ n mandamento m

commemorat|e /kə'meməreɪt/ vt comemorar. ~ion /-'reɪʃn/ n comemoração f. ~ive a comemorativo

commence /kə'mens/ vt/i começar. ~ment n começo m

commend /kə'mend/ vt louvar; (entrust) confiar. ~able a louvável. ~ation /kɒmen'deɪʃn/ n louvor m

comment /'kɒment/ n comentário m □ vi comentar. ~ on comentar, fazer comentários

commentary /'kɒməntrɪ/ n comentário m; (radio, TV) relato m

commentat|e /'kɒmənteɪt/ vi fazer um relato. ~or n (radio, TV) comentarista mf, (P) comentador m

commerce /'kɒmɜ:s/ n comércio m

commercial /kə'mɜ:ʃl/ a comercial □ n publicidade (comercial) f. ~ize vt comercializar

commiserat|e /kə'mɪzəreɪt/ vi ~ with compadecer-se de. ~ion /-'reɪʃn/ n comiseração f, pesar m

commission /kə'mɪʃn/ n comissão f; (order for work) encomenda f □ vt encomendar; (mil) nomear. ~ to do encarregar de fazer. out of ~ fora de serviço activo, (P) activo. ~er n comissário m; (police) chefe m

commit /kə'mɪt/ vt (pt committed) cometer; (entrust) confiar. ~ o.s. comprometer-se, empenhar-se. ~ suicide suicidar-se. ~ to memory decorar. ~ment n compromisso m

committee /kə'mɪtɪ/ n comissão f, comité m, (P) comité m

commodity /kə'mɒdətɪ/ n artigo m, mercadoria f

common /'kɒmən/ a (-er, -est) comum; (usual) usual, corrente; (pej: ill-bred) ordinário □ n prado m público, (P) baldio m. ~ law direito m consuetudinário. C~ Market Mercado m Comum. ~-room n sala f dos professores. ~ sense bom senso m, senso m comum. House of C~s Câmara f dos Comuns. in ~ em comum. ~ly adv mais comum

commoner /'kɒmənə(r)/ n plebeu m

commonplace /'kɒmənpleɪs/ a banal □ n lugar-comum m

commotion /kə'məʊʃn/ n agitação f, confusão f, barulheira f

communal /'kɒmjʊnl/ a (of a commune) comunal; (shared) comum commune /'kɒmjuːn/ n comuna f

communicat|e /kə'mjuːnɪkeɪt/ vt/i comunicar. ~ion /-'keɪʃn/ n comunicação f. ~ion cord sinal m de alarme. ~ive /-ətɪv/ a comunicativo

communion /kə'mjuːnɪən/ n comunhão f

communis|t /'kɒmjʊnɪst/ n comunista mf □ a comunista. ~m /-zəm/ n comunismo m

community /kə'mjuːnətɪ/ n comunidade f. ~ centre centro m comunitário

commute /kə'mjuːt/ vi viajar diariamente para o trabalho. ~r /-ə(r)/ n pessoa f que viaja diariamente para o trabalho

compact¹ /kəm'pækt/ a compacto. ~ disc /'kɒmpækt/ cd m

compact² /'kɒmpækt/ n estojo m de pó-de-arroz, (P) caixa f

companion /kəm'pænɪən/ n companheiro m. ~ship n companhia f, convívio m

company /'kʌmpənɪ/ n companhia f; (guests) visitas fpl. keep sb ~ fazer companhia a alg

comparable /'kɒmpərəbl/ a comparável

compar|e /kəm'peə(r)/ vt/i comparar(-se) (to, with com). ~ative /'pærətɪv/ a comparativo; (comfort etc) relativo

comparison /kəm'pærɪsn/ n comparação f

compartment /kəm'paːtmənt/ n compartimento m

compass /'kʌmpəs/ n bússola f. ~es npl compasso m

compassion /kəm'pæʃn/ n compaixão f. ~ate a compassivo

compatib|le /kəm'pætəbl/ a compatível. ~ility /-'bɪlətɪ/ n compatibilidade f

compel /kəm'pel/ vt (pt compelled) compelir, forçar. ~ling a irresistível, convincente

compensat|e /'kɒmpənseɪt/ vt/i compensar. ~ion /-'seɪʃn/ n compensação f; (financial) indenização f, (P) indemnização f

compete /kəm'piːt/ vi competir. ~ with rivalizar com

competen|t /'kɒmpɪtənt/ a competente. ~ce n competência f

competition /kɒmpə'tɪʃn/ n competição f; (comm) concorrência f

competitive /kəm'petɪtɪv/ a (sport, prices) competitivo. ~ examination concurso m

competitor /kəm'petɪtə(r)/ n competidor m, concorrente mf

compile /kəm'paɪl/ vt compilar, coligir. ~r /-ə(r)/ n compilador m

complacen|t /kəm'pleɪsnt/ a satisfeito consigo mesmo, (P) complacente. ~cy n (auto-)satisfação f, (P) complacência f

complain /kəm'pleɪn/ vi queixar-se (about, of de)

complaint /kəm'pleɪnt/ n queixa f; (in shop) reclamação f; (med) doença f, achaque m

complement /'kɒmplɪmənt/ n complemento m □ vt completar, complementar. ~ary /-'mentrɪ/ a complementar

complet|e /kəm'pliːt/ a completo; (finished) acabado; (downright) perfeito □ vt completar; (a form) preencher. ~ely adv completamente. ~ion /-ʃn/ n conclusão f, feitura f, realização f

complex /'kɒmpleks/ a complexo □ n complexo m. ~ity /kəm'pleksətɪ/ n complexidade f

complexion /kəm'plekʃn/ n cor f da tez; (fig) caráter m, (P) carácter m, aspecto m

compliance /kəm'plaɪəns/ n docilidade f; (agreement) conformidade f. in ~ with em conformidade com

complicat|e /'kɒmplɪkeɪt/ vt complicar. ~ed a complicado. ~ion /-'keɪʃn/ n complicação f

compliment /'kɒmplɪmənt/ n cumprimento m □ vt /'kɒmplɪment/ cumprimentar

complimentary /kɒmplɪ'mentrɪ/ a amável, elogioso. ~ copy oferta f. ~ ticket bilhete m grátis

comply /kəm'plaɪ/ vi ~ with agir em conformidade com

component /kəm'pəʊnənt/ n componente m; (of machine) peça f □ a componente, constituinte

compose /kəm'pəʊz/ vt compor. ~ o.s. acalmar-se, dominar-se. ~d a calmo, senhor de si. ~r /-ə(r)/ n compositor m

composition /kɒmpə'zɪʃn/ n composição f

compost /'kɒmpɒst/ n húmus m, adubo m

composure /kəm'pəʊʒə(r)/ n calma f, domínio m de si mesmo

compound /'kɒmpaʊnd/ n composto m; (enclosure) cercado m, recinto m □ a composto. ~ fracture fratura f, (P) fractura f exposta

comprehen|d /kɒmprɪ'hend/ vt compreender. ~sion n compreensão f

comprehensive /kɒmprɪ'hensɪv/ a compreensivo, vasto; (insurance) contra todos os riscos. ~ school escola f de ensino secundário técnico e académico, (P) académico

compress /kəm'pres/ vt comprimir. ~ion /-ʃn/ n compressão f

comprise /kəm'praɪz/ vt compreender, abranger

compromise /'kɒmprəmaɪz/ n compromisso m □ vt comprometer □ vi chegar a um meio-termo

compulsion /kəm'pʌlʃn/ n (constraint) coação f; (psych) desejo m irresistível

compulsive /kəm'pʌlsɪv/ a (psych) compulsivo; (liar, smoker etc) inveterado

compulsory /kəm'pʌlsərɪ/ a obrigatório, compulsório

computer /kəm'pju:tə(r)/ n computador m. ~ science informática f. ~ize vt computerizar

comrade /'kɒmreɪd/ n camarada mf. ~ship n camaradagem f

con¹ /kɒn/ vt (pt conned) (sl) enganar □ n (sl) intrujice f, vigarice f, burla f. ~ man (sl) intrujão m, vigarista m, burlão m

con² /kɒn/ see pro

concave /'kɒŋkeɪv/ a côncavo

conceal /kən'si:l/ vt ocultar, esconder. ~ment n encobrimento m

concede /kən'si:d/ vt conceder, admitir; (in a game etc) ceder

conceit /kən'si:t/ n presunção f. ~ed a presunçoso, presumido, cheio de si

conceivable /kən'si:vəbl/ a concebível. ~y adv possivelmente

conceive /kən'si:v/ vt/i conceber

concentrate /'kɒnsntreɪt/ vt/i concentrar(-se). ~ion /-'treɪʃn/ n concentração f

concept /'kɒnsept/ n conceito m

conception /kən'sepʃn/ n concepção f

concern /kən'sɜ:n/ n (worry) preocupação f; (business) negócio m □ vt dizer respeito a, respeitar. ~ o.s. with, be ~ed with interessar-se por, ocupar-se de; (regard) dizer respeito a. it's no ~ of mine não me diz respeito. ~ing prep sobre, respeitante a

concerned /kən'sɜ:nd/ a inquieto, preocupado (about com)

concert /'kɒnsət/ n concerto m

concerted /kən'sɜ:tɪd/ a concertado

concession /kən'seʃn/ n concessão f

concise /kən'saɪs/ a conciso. ~ly adv concisamente

conclude /kən'klu:d/ vt concluir □ vi terminar. ~ding a final. ~sion n conclusão f

conclusive /kən'klu:sɪv/ a conclusivo. ~ly adv de forma conclusiva

concoct /kən'kɒkt/ vt preparar por mistura; (fig: invent) fabricar. ~ion /-ʃn/ n mistura f; (fig) invenção f, mentira f

concrete /'kɒŋkri:t/ n concreto m, (P) cimento m □ a concreto □ vt concretar, (P) cimentar

concur /kən'kɜ:(r)/ vi (pt concurred) concordar; (of circumstances) concorrer

concussion /kən'kʌʃn/ n comoção f cerebral

condemn /kən'dem/ vt condenar. ~ation /kɒndem'neɪʃn/ n condenação f

condens|e /kən'dens/ vt/i condensar(-se). ~ation /kɒnden'seɪʃn/ n condensação f

condescend /kɒndɪ'send/ vi condescender; (lower o.s.) rebaixar-se

condition /kən'dɪʃn/ n condição f □ vt condicionar. on ~ that com a condição de que. ~al a condicional. ~er n (for hair) condicionador m, creme m rinse

condolences /kən'dəʊlənsɪz/ npl condolências fpl, pêsames mpl, sentimentos mpl

condom /'kɒndəm/ n preservativo m

condone /kən'dəʊn/ vt desculpar, fechar os olhos a

conducive /kən'dju:sɪv/ a be ~ to contribuir para, ser propício a

conduct¹ /kən'dʌkt/ vt conduzir, dirigir; (orchestra) reger

conduct² /'kɒndʌkt/ n conduta f

conductor /kən'dʌktə(r)/ n maestro m; (electr; of bus) condutor m

cone /kəʊn/ n cone m; (bot) pinha f; (for ice-cream) casquinha f, (P) cone m

confectioner /kən'fekʃnə(r)/ n confeiteiro m, (P) pasteleiro m. ~y n confeitaria f, (P) pastelaria f

confederation /kənfedə'reɪʃn/ n confederação f

confer /kən'fɜ:(r)/ (pt conferred) vt conferir, outorgar □ vi conferenciar

conference /'kɒnfərəns/ n conferência f. in ~ em reunião f

confess /kən'fes/ vt/i confessar; (relig) confessar(-se). ~ion /-ʃn/ n confissão f. ~ional n confessionário m. ~or n confessor m

confetti /kən'fetɪ/ n confetes mpl, (P) confetti mpl

confide /kən'faɪd/ vt confiar □ vi ~ in confiar em

confiden|t /'kɒnfɪdənt/ a confiante, confiado. ~ce n confiança f; (boldness) confiança f em si; (secret) confidência f. ~ce trick vigarice f. in ~ce em confidência

confidential /kɒnfɪ'denʃl/ a confidencial

confine /kən'faɪn/ vt fechar; (limit) limitar (to a). ~ment n detenção f; (med) parto m confirm /kən'fɜ:m/ vt confirmar. ~ation /kɒnfə'meɪʃn/ n confirmação f. ~ed a (bachelor) inveterado

confiscat|e /'kɒnfɪskeɪt/ vt confiscar. ~ion /-'keɪʃn/ n confiscação f

conflict[1] /'kɒnflɪkt/ n conflito m

conflict[2] /kən'flɪkt/ vi estar em contradição. ~ing a contraditório

conform /kən'fɔ:m/ vt/i conformar (-se)

confound /kən'faʊnd/ vt confundir. ~ed a (colloq) maldito

confront /kən'frʌnt/ vt confrontar, defrontar, enfrentar. ~ with confrontar-se com. ~ation /kɒnfrʌn'teɪʃn/ n confrontação f

confus|e /kən'fju:z/ vt confundir. ~ed a confuso. ~ing a que faz confusão. ~ion /-ʒn/ n confusão f

congeal /kən'dʒi:l/ vt/i congelar, solidificar

congenial /kən'dʒi:nɪəl/ a (agreeable) simpático

congenital /kən'dʒenɪtl/ a congénito, (P) congénito

congest|ed /kən'dʒestɪd/ a congestionado. ~ion /-tʃn/ n (traffic) congestionamento m; (med) congestão f

congratulat|e /kən'grætjʊleɪt/ vt felicitar, dar os parabéns (on por). ~ions /-'leɪʃnz/ npl felicitações fpl, parabéns mpl

congregat|e /'kɒŋgrɪgeɪt/ vi reunirse. ~ion /-'geɪʃn/ n (in church) congregação f, fiéis mpl

congress /'kɒŋgres/ n congresso m. C~ (Amer) Congresso m

conjecture /kən'dʒektʃə(r)/ n conjetura f, (P) conjectura f □ vt/i conjeturar, (P) conjecturar

conjugal /'kɒndʒʊgl/ a conjugal

conjugat|e /'kɒndʒʊgeɪt/ vt conjugar. ~ion /-'geɪʃn/ n conjugação f

conjunction /kən'dʒʌŋkʃn/ n conjunção f

conjur|e /'kʌndʒə(r)/ vi fazer truques mágicos □ vt ~e up fazer aparecer. ~or n mágico m, prestidigitador m

connect /kə'nekt/ vt/i ligar(-se), (of train) fazer ligação. ~ed a ligado. be ~ed with estar relacionado com

connection /kə'nekʃn/ n ligação f, (rail; phone call) ligação f, (electr) contacto m

connoisseur /kɒnə'sɜ:(r)/ n conhecedor m, apreciador m

connotation /kɒnə'teɪʃn/ n conotação f

conquer /'kɒŋkə(r)/ vt vencer; (country) conquistar. ~or n conquistador m

conquest /'kɒŋkwest/ n conquista f

conscience /'kɒnʃəns/ n consciência f

conscientious /kɒnʃɪ'enʃəs/ a consciencioso

conscious /'kɒnʃəs/ a consciente. ~ly adv conscientemente. ~ness n consciência f

conscript[1] /kən'skrɪpt/ vt recrutar. ~ion /-ʃn/ n serviço m militar obrigatório

conscript[2] /'kɒnskrɪpt/ n recruta m

consecrate /'kɒnsɪkreɪt/ vt consagrar

consecutive /kən'sekjʊtɪv/ a consecutivo, seguido

consensus /kən'sensəs/ n consenso m

consent /kən'sent/ vi consentir (to em) □ n consentimento m

consequence /'kɒnsɪkwəns/ n consequência f, (P) consequência f

consequent /'kɒnsɪkwənt/ a resultante (on, upon de). ~ly adv por consequência, (P) consequência, por consequinte

conservation /kɒnsə'veɪʃn/ n conservação f

conservative /kən'sɜ:vətɪv/ a conservador; (estimate) moderado. C~ a & n conservador (m)

conservatory /kən'sɜ:vətrɪ/ n (greenhouse) estufa f, (house extension) jardim m de inverno

conserve /kən'sɜ:v/ vt conservar

consider /kən'sɪdə(r)/ vt considerar; (allow for) levar em consideração. ~ation /-'reɪʃn/ n consideração f. ~ing prep em vista de, tendo em conta

considerabl|e /kən'sɪdərəbl/ a considerável; (much) muito. ~y adv consideravelmente

considerate /kən'sɪdərət/ a atencioso, delicado

consign /kən'saɪn/ vt consignar. ~ment n consignação f

consist /kən'sɪst/ vi consistir (of, in, em)

consisten|t /kən'sɪstənt/ a (unchanging) constante; (not contradictory) coerente. ~t with conforme com. ~cy n consistência f; (fig) coerência f. ~tly adv regularmente

consol|e /kən'səʊl/ vt consolar. ~ation /kɒnsə'leɪʃn/ n consolação f. ~ation prize prémio m de consolação

consolidat|e /kən'sɒlɪdeɪt/ vt/i consolidar(-se). ~ion /-'deɪʃn/ n consolidação f

consonant /'kɒnsənənt/ n consoante f

consortium /kən'sɔ:tɪəm/ n (pl -tia) consórcio m

conspicuous /kən'spɪkjʊəs/ a conspícuo, visível; (striking) notável. make o.s. ~ fazer-se notar, chamar a atenção conspira|cy /kən'spɪrəsɪ/ n conspiração f. ~tor n conspirador m

conspire /kən'spaɪə(r)/ vi conspirar

constable /'kʌnstəbl/ n policia m

constant /'kɒnstənt/ a constante. ~ly adv constantemente

constellation /kɒnstə'leɪʃn/ n constelação f

consternation /kɒnstə'neɪʃn/ n consternação f

constipation /kɒnstɪ'peɪʃn/ n prisão f de ventre

constituency /kən'stɪtjʊənsɪ/ n (pl -cies) círculo m eleitoral

constituent /kən'stɪtjʊənt/ a & n constituinte (m)

constitut|e /'kɒnstɪtjuːt/ vt constituir. ~ion /-'tjuːʃn/ n constituição f. ~ional /-'tjuːʃənl/ a constitucional

constrain /kən'streɪn/ vt constranger

constraint /kən'streɪnt/ n constrangimento m

constrict /kən'strɪkt/ vt constringir, apertar. ~ion /-ʃn/ n constrição f

construct /kən'strʌkt/ vt construir. ~ion /-ʃn/ n construção f. under ~ion em construção

constructive /kən'strʌktɪv/ a construtivo

consul /'kɒnsl/ n cônsul m

consulate /'kɒnsjʊlət/ n consulado m

consult /kən'sʌlt/ vt consultar. ~ation /kɒnsl'teɪʃn/ n consulta f

consultant /kən'sʌltənt/ n consultor m; (med) especialista mf

consume /kən'sjuːm/ vt consumir. ~r /-ə(r)/ n consumidor m

consumption /kən'sʌmpʃn/ n consumo m

contact /'kɒntækt/ n contacto m; (person) relação f. ~ lenses lentes fpl de contacto □ vt contactar

contagious /kən'teɪdʒəs/ a contagioso

contain /kən'teɪn/ vt conter. ~ o.s. conter-se. ~er n recipiente m; (for transport) contentor m

contaminat|e /kən'tæmɪneɪt/ vt contaminar. ~ion /-'neɪʃn/ n contaminação f

contemplat|e /'kɒntempleɪt/ vt contemplar; (intend) ter em vista; (consider) esperar, pensar em. ~ion /-'pleɪʃn/ n contemplação f

contemporary /kən'temprərɪ/ a & n contemporâneo (m)

contempt /kən'tempt/ n desprezo m. ~ible a desprezível. ~uous /-tʃʊəs/ a desdenhoso

contend /kən'tend/ vt afirmar, sustentar □ vi ~ with lutar contra. ~er n adversário m, contendor m

content[1] /kən'tent/ a satisfeito, contente □ vt contentar. ~ed a satisfeito, contente. ~ment n contentamento m, satisfação f

content[2] /'kɒntent/ n conteúdo m. (table of) ~s índice m

contention /kən'tenʃn/ n disputa f, contenda f; (assertion) argumento m

contest[1] /'kɒntest/ n competição f; (struggle) luta f

contest[2] /kən'test/ vt contestar; (compete for) disputar. ~ant n concorrente mf

context /'kɒntekst/ n contexto m

continent /'kɒntɪnənt/ n continente m. the C~ a Europa (continental) f. ~al /-'nentl/ a continental; (of mainland Europe) europeu ~al breakfast café m da manhã europeu, (P) pequeno almoço m europeu. ~al quilt edredom m, (P) edredão m

contingen|t /kən'tɪndʒənt/ a & n contingente (m). ~cy n contingência f. ~cy plan plano m de emergência

continual /kən'tɪnjʊəl/ a contínuo. ~ly adv continuamente

continu|e /kən'tɪnjuː/ vt/i continuar. ~ation /-tɪnjʊ'eɪʃn/ n continuação f.

continuity /kɒntɪ'njuːətɪ/ n continuidade f

continuous /kən'tɪnjʊəs/ a contínuo. ~ly adv continuamente

contort /kən'tɔːt/ vt contorcer; (fig) distorcer. ~ion /-ʃn/ n contorção f

contour /'kɒntʊə(r)/ n contorno m

contraband /'kɒntrəbænd/ n contrabando m

contraception /kɒntrə'sepʃn/ n contracepção f

contraceptive /kɒntrə'septɪv/ a & n contraceptivo (m)

contract[1] /'kɒntrækt/ n contrato m

contract[2] /kən'trækt/ vt/i contrair (-se); (make a contract) contratar. ~ion /-ʃn/ n contração f, (P) contracção f

contractor /kən'træktə(r)/ n empreiteiro m; (firm) firma f empreiteira de serviços, (P) recrutadora f de mão de obra temporária

contradict /kɒntrə'dɪkt/ vt contradizer. ~ion /-ʃn/ n contradição f. ~ory a contraditório

contraflow /'kɒntrəfləʊ/ n fluxo m em sentido contrário

contrary[1] /'kɒntrərɪ/ a & n (opposite) contrário (m) □ adv ~ to contrariamente a. on the ~ ao ou pelo contrário

contrary[2] /kən'treərɪ/ a (perverse) do contra, embirrento

contrast[1] /'kɒntrɑːst/ n contraste m

contrast[2] /kən'trɑːst/ vt/i contrastar. ~ing a contrastante

contraven|e /kɒntrə'viːn/ vt infringir. ~tion /-'venʃn/ n contravenção f contribut|e /kən'trɪbjuːt/ *vt/i* contribuir (to para); (*to newspaper etc*) colaborar (to em). ~ion /-'bjuːʃn/ *n* contribuição *f*. ~or /-'trɪbjuːtə(r)/ *n* contribuinte *mf*; (*to newspaper*) colaborador *m*

contrivance /kən'traɪvəns/ *n* (*invention*) engenho *m*; (*device*) engenhoca *f*; (*trick*) maquinação *f*

contrive /kən'traɪv/ *vt* imaginar, inventar. ~ to do conseguir fazer

control /kən'trəʊl/ *vt* (*pt* controlled) (*check, restrain*) controlar; (*firm etc*) dirigir □ *n* controle *m*; (*management*) direção *f*, (*P*) direcção *f*. ~s (*of car, plane*) comandos *mpl*; (*knobs*) botões *mpl*. be in ~ of dirigir. under ~ sob controle

controversial /kɒntrə'vɜːʃl/ *a* controverso, discutível

controversy /'kɒntrəvɜːsɪ/ *n* controvérsia *f*

convalesce /kɒnvə'les/ *vi* convalescer. ~nce *n* convalescença *f*. ~nt /-nt/ *a* & *n* convalescente (*mf*). ~nt home casa *f* de repouso

convene /kən'viːn/ *vt* convocar □ *vi* reunir-se

convenience /kən'viːnɪəns/ *n* conveniência *f*. ~s (*appliances*) comodidades *fpl*; (*lavatory*) privada *f*, (*P*) casa *f* de banho. at your ~ quando (e como) lhe convier. ~ foods alimentos *mpl* semiprontos

convenient /kən'viːnɪənt/ *a* conveniente. be ~ for convir a. ~ly *adv* sem inconveniente; (*situated*) bem; (*arrive*) a propósito

convent /'kɒnvənt/ *n* convento *m*. ~ school colégio *m* de freiras

convention /kən'venʃn/ *n* convenção *f*; (*custom*) uso *m*, costume *m*. ~al *a* convencional

converge /kən'vɜːdʒ/ *vi* convergir

conversant /kən'vɜːsnt/ *a* be ~ with conhecer; (*fact*) saber; (*machinery*) estar familiarizado com

conversation /kɒnvə'seɪʃn/ *n* conversa *f*. ~al *a* de conversa, coloquial

converse¹ /kən'vɜːs/ *vi* conversar

converse² /'kɒnvɜːs/ *a* & *n* inverso (*m*). ~ly /kən'vɜːslɪ/ *adv* ao invés, inversamente

conver|t¹ /kən'vɜːt/ *vt* converter; (*house*) transformar. ~sion /-ʃn/ *n* conversão *f*; (*house*) transformação *f*. ~tible *a* convertível, conversível □ *n* (*auto*) conversível *m*

convert² /'kɒnvɜːt/ *n* convertido *m*, converso *m*

convex /'kɒnveks/ *a* convexo

convey /kən'veɪ/ *vt* transmitir; (*goods*) transportar; (*idea, feeling*) comunicar. ~ance *n* transporte *m*.

~or belt tapete *m* rolante, correia *f* transportadora

convict¹ /kən'vɪkt/ *vt* declarar culpado. ~ion /-ʃn/ *n* condenação *f*; (*opinion*) convicção *f*

convict² /'kɒnvɪkt/ *n* condenado *m*

convinc|e /kən'vɪns/ *vt* convencer. ~ing *a* convincente

convoluted /'kɒnvəluːtɪd/ *a* retorcido; (*fig*) complicado; (*bot*) convoluto

convoy /'kɒnvɔɪ/ *n* escolta *f*

convuls|e /kən'vʌls/ *vt* convulsionar; (*fig*) abalar. be ~ed with laughter torcer-se de riso. ~ion /-ʃn/ *n* convulsão *f*

coo /kuː/ *vi* (*pt* cooed) arrulhar □ *n* arrulho *m*

cook /kʊk/ *vt/i* cozinhar □ *n* cozinheira *f*, cozinheiro *m*. ~ up (*colloq*) cozinhar (*fig*), fabricar

cooker /'kʊkə(r)/ *n* fogão *m*

cookery /'kʊkərɪ/ *n* cozinha *f*. ~ book livro *m* de culinária

cookie /'kʊkɪ/ *n* (*Amer*) biscoito *m*

cool /kuːl/ *a* (-er, -est) fresco; (*calm*) calmo; (*unfriendly*) frio □ *n* frescura *f*; (*sl: composure*) sangue-frio *m* □ *vt/i* arrefecer. ~-box *n* geladeira *f* portátil. in the ~ no fresco. ~ly /kuːllɪ/ *adv* calmamente; (*fig*) friamente. ~ness *n* frescura *f*; (*fig*) frieza *f*

coop /kuːp/ *n* galinheiro *m* □ *vt* ~ up engaislar, fechar

co-operat|e /kəʊ'ɒpəreɪt/ *vi* cooperar. ~ion /-'reɪʃn/ *n* cooperação *f*

cooperative /kəʊ'ɒpərətɪv/ *a* cooperativo □ *n* cooperativa *f*

coordinat|e /kəʊ'ɔːdɪneɪt/ *vt* coordenar. ~ion /-'neɪʃn/ *n* coordenação *f*

cop /kɒp/ *n* (*sl*) porco *m* (*sl*), (*P*) xui *m* (*sl*)

cope /kəʊp/ *vi* aguentar-se, arranjar-se. ~ with poder com, dar conta de

copious /'kəʊpɪəs/ *a* copioso

copper¹ /'kɒpə(r)/ *n* cobre *m* □ *a* de cobre

copper² /'kɒpə(r)/ *n* (*sl*) porco *m* (*sl*), (*P*) xui *m* (*sl*)

coppice /'kɒpɪs/, copse /kɒps/ *ns* mata *f* de corte

copulat|e /'kɒpjʊleɪt/ *vi* copular. ~ion /-'leɪʃn/ *n* cópula *f*

copy /'kɒpɪ/ *n* cópia *f*; (*of book*) exemplar *m*; (*of newspaper*) número *m* □ *vt/i* copiar

copyright /'kɒpɪraɪt/ *n* direitos *mpl* autorais

coral /'kɒrəl/ *n* coral *m*

cord /kɔːd/ *n* cordão *m*; (*electr*) fio *m*

cordial /'kɔːdɪəl/ *a* & *n* cordial (*m*)

cordon /'kɔːdn/ *n* cordão *m* □ *vt* ~ off fechar (com um cordão de isolamento)

corduroy /'kɔːdərɔɪ/ *n* veludo *m* cotelé

core /kɔː(r)/ n âmago m; (of apple, pear) coração m

cork /kɔːk/ n cortiça f; (for bottle) rolha f □ vt rolhar

corkscrew /'kɔːkskruː/ n sacarolhas m

corn¹ /kɔːn/ n trigo m; (Amer: maize) milho m; (seed) grão m. ~ on the cob espiga f de milho

corn² /kɔːn/ n (hard skin) calo m

corned /kɔːnd/ a ~ beef carne f de vaca enlatada

corner /'kɔːnə(r)/ n canto m; (of street) esquina f; (bend in road) curva f □ vt encurralar; (market) monopolizar □ vi dar uma curva, virar

cornet /'kɔːnɪt/ n (mus) cornetim m; (for ice-cream) casquinha f, (P) cone m

cornflakes /'kɔːnfleɪks/ npl cornflakes mpl, cereais mpl

cornflour /'kɔːnflaʊə(r)/ n fécula f de milho, maisena f

Corn|wall /'kɔːnwəl/ n Cornualha f. ~ish a da Cornualha

corny /'kɔːnɪ/ a (colloq) batido, (P) estafado

coronary /'kɒrənrɪ/ n ~ (thrombosis) infarto m, enfarte m

coronation /kɒrə'neɪʃn/ n coroação f

coroner /'kɒrənə(r)/ n magistrado m que investiga os casos de morte suspeita

corporal¹ /'kɔːpərəl/ n (mil) cabo m

corporal² /'kɔːpərəl/ a ~ punishment castigo m corporal

corporate /'kɔːpərət/ a coletivo, (P) colectivo; (body) corporativo

corporation /kɔːpə'reɪʃn/ n corporação f; (of town) municipalidade f

corps /kɔː(r)/ n (pl corps /kɔːz/) corpo m

corpse /kɔːps/ n cadáver m

corpuscle /'kɔːpʌsl/ n corpúsculo m

correct /kə'rekt/ a correto, (P) correcto. the ~ time a hora certa. you are ~ você tem razão □ vt corrigir. ~ion /-ʃn/ n correção f, (P) correcção f, emenda f

correlat|e /'kɒrəleɪt/ vt/i correlacionar(-se). ~ion /-'leɪʃn/ n correlação f

correspond /kɒrɪ'spɒnd/ vi corresponder (to, with, a); (write letters) corresponder-se (with, com). ~ence n correspondência f. ~ent n correspondente mf. ~ing a correspondente

corridor /'kɒrɪdɔː(r)/ n corredor m

corroborate /kə'rɒbəreɪt/ vt corroborar

corro|de /kə'rəʊd/ vt/i corroer(-se). ~sion n corrosão f

corrugated /'kɒrəgeɪtɪd/ a corru-

gado. ~ cardboard cartão m canelado. ~ iron chapa f ondulada

corrupt /kə'rʌpt/ a corrupto □ vt corromper. ~ion /-ʃn/ n corrupção f

corset /'kɔːsɪt/ n espartilho m; (elasticated) cinta f elástica

Corsica /'kɔːsɪkə/ n Córsega f

cosmetic /kɒz'metɪk/ n cosmético m □ a cosmético; (fig) superficial

cosmonaut /'kɒzmənɔːt/ n cosmonauta mf

cosmopolitan /kɒzmə'pɒlɪtən/ a & n cosmopolita (mf)

cosset /'kɒsɪt/ vt (pt cosseted) proteger

cost /kɒst/ vt (pt cost) custar; (pt costed) fixar o preço de □ n custo m. ~s (jur) custos mpl. at all ~s custo o que custar. to one's ~ à sua custa. ~ of living custo m de vida

costly /'kɒstlɪ/ a (-ier, -iest) a caro; (valuable) precioso

costume /'kɒstjuːm/ n traje m

cos|y /'kəʊzɪ/ a (-ier, -iest) confortável, íntimo □ n abafador m (do bule do chá). ~iness n conforto m

cot /kɒt/ n cama f de bebê, berço m

cottage /'kɒtɪdʒ/ n pequena casa f de campo. ~ cheese requeijão m, ricota f. ~ industry artesanato m. ~ pie empada f de carne picada

cotton /'kɒtn/ n algodão m; (thread) fio m, linha f. ~ wool algodão m hidrófilo

couch /kaʊtʃ/ n divã m

couchette /kuː'ʃet/ n couchette f

cough /kɒf/ vi tossir □ n tosse f

could /kʊd, kəd/ pt of can²

couldn't /'kʊdnt/ = could not

council /'kaʊnsl/ n conselho m. ~ house casa f de bairro popular

councillor /'kaʊnsələ(r)/ n vereador m

counsel /'kaʊnsl/ n conselho m; (pl invar) (jur) advogado m. ~lor n conselheiro m

count¹ /kaʊnt/ vt/i contar □ n conta f. ~-down n (rocket) contagem f regressiva. ~ on contar com

count² /kaʊnt/ n (nobleman) conde m

counter¹ /'kaʊntə(r)/ n (in shop) balcão m; (in game) ficha f, (P) tento m

counter² /'kaʊntə(r)/ adv ~ to contrário a; (in the opposite direction) em sentido contrário a □ a oposto □ vt (oppose); (blow) aparar □ vi ripostar

counter- /'kaʊntə(r)/ pref contra-

counteract /kaʊntər'ækt/ vt neutralizar, frustrar

counter-attack /'kaʊntərətæk/ n contra-ataque m □ vt/i contra-atacar

counterbalance /'kaʊntəbæləns/ n contrapeso m □ vt contrabalançar counterfeit /'kaʊntəfɪt/ a falsificado, falso □ n falsificação f □ vt falsificar

counterfoil /'kaʊntəfɔɪl/ n talão m, canhoto m

counterpart /'kaʊntəpa:t/ n equivalente m; (person) homólogo m

counter-productive /'kaʊntəprə-dʌktɪv/ a contraproducente

countersign /'kaʊntəsaɪn/ vt subscrever documento já assinado; (cheque) contrassinar

countess /'kaʊntɪs/ n condessa f

countless /'kaʊntlɪs/ a sem conta, incontável, inúmero

country /'kʌntrɪ/ n país m; (homeland) pátria f; (countryside) campo m

countryside /'kʌntrɪsaɪd/ n campo m

county /'kaʊntɪ/ n condado m

coup /ku:/ n ~ (d'état) golpe m (de estado)

couple /'kʌpl/ n par m, casal m □ vt/i unir(-se), ligar(-se); (techn) acoplar. a ~ of um par de

coupon /'ku:pɒn/ n cupão m

courage /'kʌrɪdʒ/ n coragem f. ~ous /kə'reɪdʒəs/ a corajoso

courgette /kʊə'ʒet/ n abobrinha f

courier /'kʊrɪə(r)/ n correio m; (for tourists) guia mf; (for parcels, mail) estafeta m

course /kɔːs/ n curso m; (series) série f; (culin) prato m; (for golf) campo m; (fig) caminho m. in due ~ na altura devida, oportunamente. in the ~ of durante. of ~ está claro, com certeza

court /kɔːt/ n (of monarch) corte f; (courtyard) pátio m; (tennis) court m, quadra f, (P) campo m; (jur) tribunal m □ vt cortejar; (danger) provocar. ~ martial (pl courts martial) conselho m de guerra

courteous /'kɜːtɪəs/ a cortês, delicado

courtesy /'kɜːtəsɪ/ n cortesia f

courtship /'kɔːtʃɪp/ n namoro m, corte f

courtyard /'kɔːtjaːd/ n pátio m

cousin /'kʌzn/ n primo m. first/second ~ primo m em primeiro/segundo grau

cove /kəʊv/ n angra f, enseada f

covenant /'kʌvənənt/ n convenção f, convénio m; (jur) contrato m; (relig) aliança f

cover /'kʌvə(r)/ vt cobrir □ n cobertura f; (for bed) colcha f; (for book, furniture) capa f; (lid) tampa f; (shelter) abrigo m. ~ charge serviço m. ~ up tapar; (fig) encobrir. ~-up n (fig) encobrimento m. take ~ abrigar-se. under separate ~ em separado. ~ing n cobertura f. ~ing letter carta f (que acompanha um documento)

coverage /'kʌvərɪdʒ/ n (of events) reportagem f, cobertura f

covet /'kʌvɪt/ vt cobiçar

cow /kaʊ/ n vaca f

coward /'kaʊəd/ n covarde mf. ~ly a covarde

cowardice /'kaʊədɪs/ n covardia f

cowboy /'kaʊbɔɪ/ n cowboy m, vaqueiro m

cower /'kaʊə(r)/ vi encolher-se (de medo)

cowshed /'kaʊʃed/ n estábulo m

coy /kɔɪ/ a (-er, -est) (falsamente) tímido

crab /kræb/ n caranguejo m

crack /kræk/ n fenda f; (in glass) rachadura f; (noise) estalo m; (sl: joke) piada f; (drug) crack m □ a (colloq) de élite □ vt/i estalar; (nut) quebrar; (joke) contar; (problem) resolver; (voice) mudar. ~ down on (colloq) cair em cima de, arrochar. get ~ing (colloq) pôr mãos à obra

cracker /'krækə(r)/ n busca-pé m, bomba f de estalo; (culin) bolacha f de água e sal

crackers /'krækəz/ a (sl) desmiolado, maluco

crackle /'krækl/ vi crepitar □ n crepitação f

crackpot /'krækpɒt/ n (sl) desmiolado, maluco

cradle /'kreɪdl/ n berço m □ vt embalar

craft¹ /kra:ft/ n ofício m; (technique) arte f; (cunning) manha f, astúcia f

craft² /kra:ft/ n (invar) (boat) embarcação f

craftsman /'kra:ftsmən/ n (pl -men) artífice mf. ~ship n arte f

crafty /'kra:ftɪ/ a (-ier, -iest) manhoso, astucioso

crag /kræg/ n penhasco m. ~gy a escarpado, íngreme

cram /kræm/ vt (pt crammed) ~ (for an exam) decorar, (P) empinar. ~ into/with entulhar com

cramp /kræmp/ n cãibra f □ vt restringir, tolher. ~ed a apertado

crane /kreɪn/ n grua f; (bird) grou m □ vt (neck) esticar

crank¹ /kræŋk/ n (techn) manivela f. ~shaft n (techn) cambota f

crank² /kræŋk/ n excêntrico m. ~y a excêntrico

crash /kræʃ/ n acidente m; (noise) estrondo m; (comm) falência f; (financial) colapso m, crash m □ vt/i (fall/strike) cair/bater com estrondo; (two cars) chocar, bater; (comm) abrir falência; (plane) cair □ a (course, programme) intensivo. ~-helmet n capacete m. ~-land vi fazer uma aterrissagem forçada crate /kreɪt/ n engradado m

crater /'kreɪtə(r)/ n cratera f

crav|e /kreɪv/ vt/i ~e (for) ansiar por. ~ing n desejo m irresistível, ânsia f

crawl /krɔːl/ vi rastejar; (of baby) engatinhar, (P) andar de gatas; (of car) mover-se lentamente □ n rastejo m; (swimming) crawl m. be ~ing with fervilhar de, estar cheio de

crayfish /'kreɪfɪʃ/ n (pl invar) lagostim m

crayon /'kreɪən/ n crayon m, lápis m de pastel

craze /kreɪz/ n moda f, febre f

craz|y /'kreɪzɪ/ a (-ier, -iest) doido, louco (about por). ~iness n loucura f

creak /kriːk/ n rangido m □ vi ranger

cream /kriːm/ n (milk fat; fig) nata f; (cosmetic; culin) creme m □ a creme invar □ vt desnatar. ~ cheese queijo-creme m. ~y a cremoso

crease /kriːs/ n vinco m □ vt/i amarrotar(-se)

creat|e /kriːˈeɪt/ vt criar. ~ion /-ʃn/ n criação f. ~ive a criador. ~or n criador m

creature /ˈkriːtʃə(r)/ n criatura f

crèche /kreɪʃ/ n creche f

credentials /krɪˈdenʃlz/ npl credenciais fpl; (of competence etc) referências fpl

credib|le /ˈkredəbl/ a crível, verosímil, (P) verossímil. ~ility /-ˈbɪlətɪ/ n credibilidade f

credit /ˈkredɪt/ n crédito m; (honour) honra f. ~s (cinema) créditos mpl □ vt (pt credited) acreditar em; (comm) creditar. ~ card cartão m de crédito. ~ sb with atribuir a alg. ~or n credor m

creditable /ˈkredɪtəbl/ a louvável, honroso

credulous /ˈkredjʊləs/ a crédulo

creed /kriːd/ n credo m

creek /kriːk/ n enseada f estreita. be up the ~ (sl) estar frito (sl)

creep /kriːp/ vi (pt crept) rastejar; (move stealthily) mover-se furtivamente □ n (sl) cara m nojento. give sb the ~s dar arrepios a alg. ~er n (planta) f trepadeira (f). ~y a arrepiante

cremat|e /krɪˈmeɪt/ vt cremar. ~ion /-ʃn/ n cremação f

crematorium /ˌkreməˈtɔːrɪəm/ n (pl -ia) crematório m

crêpe /kreɪp/ n crepe m. ~ paper papel m crepom, (P) plissado

crept /krept/ see creep

crescent /ˈkresnt/ n crescente m; (street) rua f em semicírculo

cress /kres/ n agrião m

crest /krest/ n (of bird, hill) crista f; (on coat of arms) timbre m

Crete /kriːt/ n Creta f

crevasse /krɪˈvæs/ n fenda f (em geleira)

crevice /ˈkrevɪs/ n racha f, fenda f

crew¹ /kruː/ see crow

crew² /kruː/ n tripulação f; (gang) bando m. ~-cut n corte m à escovinha. ~-neck n gola f redonda e um pouco subida

crib¹ /krɪb/ n berço m; (Christmas) presépio m

crib² /krɪb/ vt/i (pt cribbed) (colloq) colar (sl), (P) cabular (sl) □ n cópia f, plágio m; (translation) burro m (sl)

cricket¹ /ˈkrɪkɪt/ n críquete m. ~er n jogador m de críquete

cricket² /ˈkrɪkɪt/ n (insect) grilo m

crime /kraɪm/ n crime m; (minor) delito m; (collectively) criminalidade f

criminal /ˈkrɪmɪnl/ a & n criminoso (m)

crimp /krɪmp/ vt preguear; (hair) frisar

crimson /ˈkrɪmzn/ a & n carmesim (m)

cring|e /krɪndʒ/ vi encolher-se. ~ing a servil

crinkle /ˈkrɪŋkl/ vt/i enrugar(-se) □ n vinco m, ruga f

cripple /ˈkrɪpl/ n aleijado m, coxo m □ vt estropiar; (fig) paralisar

crisis /ˈkraɪsɪs/ n (pl crises /-siːz/) crise f

crisp /krɪsp/ a (-er, est) (culin) crocante; (air) fresco; (manners, reply) decidido. ~s npl batatas fpl fritas redondas

criterion /kraɪˈtɪərɪən/ n (pl -ia) critério m

critic /ˈkrɪtɪk/ n crítico m. ~al a crítico. ~ally adv de forma crítica; (ill) gravemente

criticism /ˈkrɪtɪsɪzəm/ n crítica f

criticize /ˈkrɪtɪsaɪz/ vt/i criticar

croak /krəʊk/ n (frog) coaxar m; (raven) crocitar m, crocito m □ vi (frog) coaxar; (raven) crocitar

crochet /ˈkrəʊʃeɪ/ n crochê m □ vt fazer em crochê

crockery /ˈkrɒkərɪ/ n louça f

crocodile /ˈkrɒkədaɪl/ n crocodilo m

crocus /ˈkrəʊkəs/ n (pl -uses /-sɪz/) croco m

crony /ˈkrəʊnɪ/ n camarada mf, amigão m, parceiro m

crook /krʊk/ n (colloq: criminal) vigarista mf; (stick) cajado m

crooked /ˈkrʊkɪd/ a torcido; (winding) tortuoso; (askew) torto; (colloq: dishonest) desonesto. ~ly adv de través

crop /krɒp/ n colheita f; (fig) quantidade f; (haircut) corte m rente □ vt (pt cropped) cortar □ *vi* ~ up aparecer, surgir

croquet /'krəʊkeɪ/ *n* croquet *m*, croqué *m*

cross /krɒs/ *n* cruz *f* □ *vt/i* cruzar; (*cheque*) cruzar, (P) barrar; (*oppose*) contrariar; (*of paths*) cruzar-se □ *a* zangado. ~ off *or* out riscar. ~ o.s. benzer-se. ~ sb's mind passar pela cabeça *or* pelo espírito de alg, ocorrer a alg. talk at ~ purposes falar sem se entender. ~-country *a* & *adv* a corta-mato. ~-examine *vt* fazer o contra-interrogatório (de testemunhas). ~-eyed *a* vesgo, estrábico. ~-fire *n* fogo *m* cruzado. ~-reference *n* nota *f* remissiva. ~-section *n* corte *m* transversal; (*fig*) grupo *m or* sector *m* representativo. ~ly *adv* irritadamente

crossbar /'krɒsbɑ:(r)/ *n* barra *f* transversal *f*; (*of bicycle*) travessão *m*

crossing /'krɒsɪŋ/ *n* cruzamento *m*; (*by boat*) travessia *f*; (*on road*) passagem *f*

crossroads /'krɒsrəʊdz/ *n* encruzilhada *f*, cruzamento *m*

crossword /'krɒswɜ:d/ *n* palavras *fpl* cruzadas

crotch /krɒtʃ/ *n* entrepernas *fpl*

crotchet /'krɒtʃɪt/ *n* (*mus*) semínima *f*

crouch /kraʊtʃ/ *vi* agachar-se

crow /krəʊ/ *n* corvo *m* □ *vi* (*cock*) (*pt* crew) cantar; (*fig*) rejubilar-se (*over* com). as the ~ flies em linha reta, (P) recta

crowbar /'krəʊbɑ:(r)/ *n* alavanca *f*, pé-de-cabra *m*

crowd /kraʊd/ *n* multidão *f* □ *vi* afluir □ *vt* encher. ~ into apinhar-se em. ~ed *a* cheio, apinhado

crown /kraʊn/ *n* coroa *f*; (*of hill*) topo *m*, cume *m* □ *vt* coroar; (*tooth*) pôr uma coroa em

crucial /'kru:ʃl/ *a* crucial

crucifix /'kru:sɪfɪks/ *n* crucifixo *m*

crucif|y /'kru:sɪfaɪ/ *vt* crucificar. ~ixion /-'fɪkʃn/ *n* crucificação *f*

crude /kru:d/ *a* (-er -est) (*raw*) bruto; (*rough, vulgar*) grosseiro. ~ oil petróleo *m* bruto

cruel /krʊəl/ *a* (crueller, cruellest) cruel. ~ty *n* crueldade *f*

cruis|e /kru:z/ *n* cruzeiro *m* □ *vi* cruzar; (*of tourists*) fazer um cruzeiro; (*of car*) ir a velocidade de cruzeiro. ~er *n* cruzador *m*. ~ing speed velocidade *f* de cruzeiro

crumb /krʌm/ *n* migalha *f*, farelo *m*

crumble /'krʌmbl/ *vt/i* desfazer(-se); (*bread*) esmigalhar(-se); (*collapse*) desmoronar-se

crumple /'krʌmpl/ *vt/i* amarrotar(-se)

crunch /krʌntʃ/ *vt* trincar; (*under one's feet*) fazer ranger

crusade /kru:'seɪd/ *n* cruzada *f*. ~r /-ə(r)/ *n* cruzado *m*; (*fig*) militante *mf*

crush /krʌʃ/ *vt* esmagar; (*clothes, papers*) amassar, amarrotar □ *n* aperto *m*. a ~ on (*sl*) uma paixonite, (P) paixoneta por.

crust /krʌst/ *n* côdea *f*, crosta *f*. ~y *a* crocante

crutch /krʌtʃ/ *n* muleta *f*; (*crotch*) entrepernas *fpl*

crux /krʌks/ *n* (*pl* cruxes) o ponto crucial

cry /kraɪ/ *n* grito *m* □ *vi* (*weep*) chorar; (*call out*) gritar. a far ~ from muito diferente de.

crying /'kraɪɪŋ/ *a* a ~ shame uma grande vergonha

crypt /krɪpt/ *n* cripta *f*

cryptic /'krɪptɪk/ *a* críptico, enigmático

crystal /'krɪstl/ *n* cristal *m*. ~lize *vt/i* cristalizar(-se)

cub /kʌb/ *n* cria *f*, filhote *m*. C~ (Scout) lobito *m*

Cuba /'kju:bə/ *n* Cuba *f*. ~n *a* & *n* cubano (*m*)

cubby-hole /'kʌbɪhəʊl/ *n* cochicho *m*; (*snug place*) cantinho *m*

cub|e /kju:b/ *n* cubo *m*. ~ic *a* cúbico

cubicle /'kju:bɪkl/ *n* cubículo *m*, compartimento *m*; (*at swimming-pool*) cabine *f*

cuckoo /'kʊku:/ *n* cuco *m*

cucumber /'kju:kʌmbə(r)/ *n* pepino *m*

cuddl|e /'kʌdl/ *vt/i* abraçar com carinho; (*nestle*) aninhar(-se) □ *n* abracinho *m*, festinha *f*. ~y *a* fofo, aconchegante

cudgel /'kʌdʒl/ *n* cacete *m*, moca *f* □ *vt* (*pt* cudgelled) dar cacetadas em

cue¹ /kju:/ *n* (*theat*) deixa *f*; (*hint*) sugestão *f*, sinal *m*

cue² /kju:/ *n* (*billiards*) taco *m*

cuff /kʌf/ *n* punho *m*; (*blow*) sopapo *m* □ *vt* dar um sopapo. ~-link *n* botão *m* de punho. off the ~ de improviso

cul-de-sac /'kʌldəsæk/ *n* (*pl* culs-de-sac) beco *m* sem saída

culinary /'kʌlɪnərɪ/ *a* culinário

cull /kʌl/ *vt* (*select*) escolher; (*kill*) abater seletivamente, (P) selectivamente □ *n* abate *m*

culminat|e /'kʌlmɪneɪt/ *vi* ~e in acabar em. ~ion /-'neɪʃn/ *n* auge *m*, ponto *m* culminante

culprit /'kʌlprɪt/ *n* culpado *m*

cult /kʌlt/ *n* culto *m*

cultivat|e /'kʌltɪveɪt/ *vt* cultivar. ~ion /-'veɪʃn/ *n* cultivo *m*, cultivação *f* cultural /'kʌltʃərəl/ a cultural

culture /'kʌltʃə(r)/ n cultura f. ~d a culto

cumbersome /'kʌmbəsəm/ a (un-wieldy) pesado, incómodo, (P) incómodo

cumulative /'kju:mjʊlətɪv/ a cumulativo

cunning /'kʌnɪŋ/ a astuto, manhoso □ n astúcia f, manha f

cup /kʌp/ n xícara f, (P) chávena f; (prize) taça f. C~ Final Final de Campeonato f

cupboard /'kʌbəd/ n armário m

cupful /'kʌpfʊl/ n xícara f cheia, (P) chávena f (cheia)

curable /'kjʊərəbl/ a curável

curator /kjʊə'reɪtə(r)/ n (museum) conservador m; (jur) curador m

curb /kɜ:b/ n freio m □ vt refrear; (price increase etc) sustar

curdle /'kɜ:dl/ vt/i coalhar

cure /kjʊə(r)/ vt curar □ n cura f

curfew /'kɜ:fju:/ n toque m de recolher

curio /'kjʊərɪəʊ/ n (pl -os) curiosidade f

curi|ous /'kjʊərɪəs/ a curioso. ~osity /-'ɒsətɪ/ n curiosidade f

curl /kɜ:l/ vt/i encaracolar(-se) □ n caracol m. ~ up enroscar(-se)

curler /'kɜ:lə(r)/ n rolo m

curly /'kɜ:lɪ/ a (-ier, -iest) encaracolado, crespo

currant /'kʌrənt/ n passa f de Corinto

currency /'kʌrənsɪ/ n moeda f corrente; (general use) circulação f. foreign ~ moeda f estrangeira

current /'kʌrənt/ a (common) corrente; (event, price, etc) atual, (P) actual □ n corrente f. ~ account conta f corrente. ~ affairs atualidades fpl, (P) actualidades fpl. ~ly adv atualmente, (P) actualmente

curriculum /kə'rɪkjʊləm/ n (pl -la) currículo m, programa m de estudos. ~ vitae n curriculum vitae m

curry¹ /'kʌrɪ/ n caril m

curry² /'kʌrɪ/ vt ~ favour with procurar agradar a

curse /kɜ:s/ n maldição f, praga f; (bad language) palavrão m □ vt amaldiçoar, praguejar contra □ vi praguejar; (swear) dizer palavrões

cursor /'kɜ:sə(r)/ n cursor m

cursory /'kɜ:sərɪ/ a apressado, superficial. a ~ look uma olhada superficial

curt /kɜ:t/ a brusco

curtail /kɜ:'teɪl/ vt abreviar; (expenses etc) reduzir

curtain /'kɜ:tn/ n cortina f; (theat) pano m

curtsy /'kɜ:tsɪ/ n reverência f □ vi fazer uma reverência

curve /kɜ:v/ n curva f □ vt/i curvar (-se); (of road) fazer uma curva

cushion /'kʊʃn/ n almofada f □ vt (a blow) amortecer; (fig) proteger

cushy /'kʊʃɪ/ a (-ier, -iest) (colloq) fácil, agradável. ~ job sinecura f, boca f (fig)

custard /'kʌstəd/ n creme m

custodian /kʌ'stəʊdɪən/ n guarda m

custody /'kʌstədɪ/ n (safe keeping) custódia f; (jur) detenção f; (of child) tutela f

custom /'kʌstəm/ n costume m; (comm) freguesia f, clientela f. ~ary a habitual

customer /'kʌstəmə(r)/ n freguês m, cliente mf

customs /'kʌstəmz/ npl alfândega f □ a alfandegário. ~ clearance desembaraço m alfandegário. ~ officer funcionário m da alfândega

cut /kʌt/ vt/i (pt cut, pres p cutting) cortar; (prices etc) reduzir □ n corte m, golpe m; (of clothes, hair) corte m; (piece) pedaço m; (prices etc) redução f, corte m; (sl: share) comissão f, (P) talhada f (sl). ~ back or down (on) reduzir. ~-back n corte m. ~ in intrometer-se; (auto) cortar. ~ off cortar; (fig) isolar. ~ out recortar; (leave out) suprimir. ~-out n figura f para recortar. ~-price a a preço(s) reduzido(s). ~ short encurtar, (P) atalhar

cute /kju:t/ a (-er, -est) (colloq: clever) esperto; (attractive) bonito, (P) giro (colloq)

cuticle /'kju:tɪkl/ n cutícula f

cutlery /'kʌtlərɪ/ n talheres mpl

cutlet /'kʌtlɪt/ n costeleta f

cutting /'kʌtɪŋ/ a cortante □ n (from newspaper) recorte m; (plant) estaca f. ~ edge gume m

CV abbr see curriculum vitae

cyanide /'saɪənaɪd/ n cianeto m

cycl|e /'saɪkl/ n ciclo m; (bicycle) bicicleta f □ vi andar de bicicleta. ~ing n ciclismo m. ~ist n ciclista mf

cyclone /'saɪkləʊn/ n ciclone m

cylind|er /'sɪlɪndə(r)/ n cilindro m. ~rical /-'lɪndrɪkl/ a cilíndrico

cymbals /'sɪmblz/ npl (mus) pratos mpl

cynic /'sɪnɪk/ n cínico m. ~al a cínico. ~ism /-sɪzəm/ n cinismo m

Cypr|us /'saɪprəs/ n Chipre m. ~iot /'sɪprɪət/ a & n cipriota (mf)

cyst /sɪst/ n quisto m

Czech /tʃek/ a & n tcheco (m), (P) checo (m)

D

dab /dæb/ vt (pt **dabbed**) aplicar levemente □ n a ~ of uma aplicaçãozinha de. ~ sth on aplicar qq coisa em gestos leves

dabble /'dæbl/ vi ~ in interessar-se por, fazer um pouco de (como amador). ~r /-ə(r)/ n amador m

dad /dæd/ n (colloq) paizinho m. ~dy n (children's use) papai m, (P) papá m. ~dy-long-legs n pernilongo m

daffodil /'dæfədɪl/ n narciso m

daft /dɑːft/ a (-er, -est) doido, maluco

dagger /'dægə(r)/ n punhal m. at ~s drawn prestes a lutar (with com)

daily /'deɪlɪ/ a diário, quotidiano □ adv diariamente, todos os dias □ n (newspaper) diário m; (colloq: charwoman) faxineira f, (P) mulher f a dias

dainty /'deɪntɪ/ a (-ier -iest) delicado; (pretty, neat) gracioso

dairy /'deərɪ/ n leiteria f. ~ products laticínios mpl

daisy /'deɪzɪ/ n margarida f

dam /dæm/ n barragem f, represa f □ vt (pt **dammed**) represar

damage /'dæmɪdʒ/ n estrago(s) mpl. ~es (Jur) perdas fpl e danos mpl □ vt estragar, danificar; (fig) prejudicar. ~ing a prejudicial

dame /deɪm/ n (old use) dama f; (Amer sl) mulher f

damn /dæm/ vt (relig) condenar aõ inferno; (swear at) amaldiçoar, maldizer; (fig: condemn) condenar □ int raios!, bolas! □ n not care a ~ (colloq) estar pouco ligando (colloq), (P) estar-se marimbando (colloq) □ a (colloq) do diabo, danado □ adv (colloq) muitíssimo. I'll be ~ed if que um raio me atinja se. ~ation /-'neɪʃn/ n danação f, condenação f. ~ing a comprometedor, condenatório

damp /dæmp/ n umidade f, (P) humidade f □ a (-er, -est) úmido, (P) húmido □ vt umedecer, (P) humedecer. ~en vt = damp. ~ness n umidade f, (P) humidade f

dance /dɑːns/ vt/i dançar □ n dança f. ~ hall sala f de baile. ~r /-ə(r)/ n dançarino m; (professional) bailarino m

dandelion /'dændɪlaɪən/ n dente-de-leão m

dandruff /'dændrʌf/ n caspa f

Dane /deɪn/ n dinamarquês m

danger /'deɪndʒə(r)/ n perigo m. be in ~ of correr o risco de. ~ous a perigoso

dangle /'dæŋgl/ vi oscilar, pender □ vt

ter or trazer dependurado; (hold) balançar; (fig: hopes, etc) acenar com

Danish /'deɪnɪʃ/ a dinamarquês □ n (lang) dinamarquês m

dank /dæŋk/ a (-er -est) frio e úmido, (P) húmido

dare /deə(r)/ vt ~ to do ousar fazer. ~ sb to do desafiar alg a fazer □ n desafio m. I ~ say creio

daredevil /'deədevl/ n louco m, temerário m

daring /'deərɪŋ/ a audacioso □ n audácia f

dark /dɑːk/ a (-er, -est) escuro, sombrio; (gloomy) sombrio; (of colour) escuro; (of skin) moreno □ n escuridão f, escuro m; (nightfall) anoitecer m, cair m da noite. ~ horse concorrente mf que é uma incógnita. ~-room n câmara f escura. be in the ~ about (fig) ignorar. ~ness n escuridão f

darken /'dɑːkən/ vt/i escurecer

darling /'dɑːlɪŋ/ a & n querido (m)

darn /dɑːn/ vt serzir, remendar

dart /dɑːt/ n dardo m, flecha f. ~s (game) jogo m de dardos □ vi lançar-se

dartboard /'dɑːtbɔːd/ n alvo m

dash /dæʃ/ vi precipitar-se □ vt arremessar; (hopes) destruir □ n corrida f; (stroke) travessão m; (Morse) traço m. a ~ of um pouco de. ~ off partir a toda a velocidade; (letter) escrever às pressas

dashboard /'dæʃbɔːd/ n painel m de instrumentos, quadro m de bordo

data /'deɪtə/ npl dados mpl. ~ capture aquisição f de informações, recolha f de dados. ~base n base f de dados. ~ processing processamento m or tratamento m de dados

date[1] /deɪt/ n data f; (colloq) encontro m marcado □ vt/i datar; (colloq) andar com. out of ~ desatualizado, (P) desactualizado. to ~ até a data. up to ~ (style) moderno; (information etc) em dia. ~d a antiquado

date[2] /deɪt/ n (fruit) tâmara f

daub /dɔːb/ vt borrar, pintar toscamente

daughter /'dɔːtə(r)/ n filha f. ~-in-law n (pl ~s-in-law) nora f

daunt /dɔːnt/ vt assustar, intimidar, desencorajar

dawdle /'dɔːdl/ vi perder tempo

dawn /dɔːn/ n madrugada f □ vi madrugar, amanhecer. ~ on (fig) fazer-se luz no espírito de, começar a perceber

day /deɪ/ n dia m; (period) época f, tempo m. ~-dream n devaneio m □ vi devanear. the ~ before a véspera

daybreak /'deɪbreɪk/ n romper m do dia, aurora f, amanhecer m daylight /'deɪlaɪt/ n luz f do dia. ~ robbery roubar descaradamente

daytime /'deɪtaɪm/ n dia m, dia m claro

daze /deɪz/ vt aturdir □ n in a ~ aturdido

dazzle /'dæzl/ vt deslumbrar; (with headlights) ofuscar

dead /ded/ a morto; (numb) dormente □ adv completamente, de todo □ n in the ~ of the night a horas mortas, na calada da noite. the ~ os mortos. in the ~ centre bem no meio. stop ~ estacar. ~ beat a (colloq) morto de cansaço. ~ end beco m sem saída. ~ pan a inexpressivo

deaden /'dedn/ vt (sound, blow) amortecer; (pain) aliviar

deadline /'dedlaɪn/ n prazo m final

deadlock /'dedlɒk/ n impasse m

deadly /'dedlɪ/ a (-ier, -iest) mortal; (weapon) mortífero

deaf /def/ a (-er, -est) surdo. turn a ~ ear fingir que não ouve. ~ mute surdo-mudo m. ~ness n surdez f

deafen /'defn/ vt ensurdecer. ~ing a ensurdecedor

deal /di:l/ vt (pt dealt) distribuir; (a blow, cards) dar □ vi negociar □ n negócio m; (cards) vez de dar f. a great ~ muito (vale of de). ~ in negociar em. ~ with (person) tratar (com); (affair) tratar de. ~er n comerciante m; (agent) concessionário m; representante m

dealings /'di:lɪŋz/ npl relações fpl; (comm) negócios mpl

dealt /delt/ see deal

dean /di:n/ n decano m

dear /dɪə(r)/ a (-er, -est) (cherished) caro, querido; (expensive) caro □ n amor m □ adv caro □ int oh ~! meu Deus! ~ly adv (very much) muito; (pay) caro

dearth /dɜ:θ/ n escassez f

death /deθ/ n morte f. ~ certificate certidão f de óbito. ~ penalty pena f de morte. ~ rate taxa f de mortalidade. ~-trap n lugar m perigoso, ratoeira f. ~ly a de morte, mortal

debase /dɪ'beɪs/ vt degradar

debate /dɪ'beɪt/ n debate m □ vt debater. ~able a discutível

debauchery /dɪ'bɔ:tʃərɪ/ n deboche m, devassidão f

debility /dɪ'bɪlətɪ/ n debilidade f

debit /'debɪt/ n débito m □ vt (pt debited) debitar

debris /'debri:/ n destroços mpl

debt /det/ n dívida f. in ~ endividado. ~or n devedor m

debunk /di:'bʌŋk/ vt (colloq) desmitificar

début /'deɪbju:/ n (of actor, play etc) estreia f

decade /'dekeɪd/ n década f

decadent /'dekədənt/ a decadente. ~ce n decadência f

decaffeinated /di:'kæfi:meɪtɪd/ a sem cafeína

decanter /dɪ'kæntə(r)/ n garrafa f para vinho, de vidro ou cristal

decapitate /dɪ'kæpɪteɪt/ vt decapitar

decay /dɪ'keɪ/ vi apodrecer, estragar-se; (food, fig) deteriorar-se; (building) degradar-se □ n apodrecimento m; (of tooth) cárie f; (fig) declínio m, decadência f

deceased /dɪ'si:st/ a & n falecido (m), defunto m

deceit /dɪ'si:t/ n engano m. ~ful a enganador

deceive /dɪ'si:v/ vt enganar, iludir

December /dɪ'sembə(r)/ n dezembro m

decent /'di:snt/ a decente; (colloq: good) (bastante) bom; (colloq: likeable) simpático. ~cy n decência f

decentralize /di:'sentrəlaɪz/ vt descentralizar

deceptive /dɪ'septɪv/ a enganador, ilusório. ~ion /-ʃn/ n engano m

decibel /'desɪbel/ n decibel m

decide /dɪ'saɪd/ vt/i decidir. ~ on decidir-se por. ~ to do decidir fazer. ~d /-ɪd/ a decidido; (clear) definido, nítido. ~dly /-ɪdlɪ/ adv decididamente

decimal /'desɪml/ a decimal □ n (fração f, (P) fracção f) decimal m. ~ point vírgula f decimal

decipher /dɪ'saɪfə(r)/ vt decifrar

decision /dɪ'sɪʒn/ n decisão f

decisive /dɪ'saɪsɪv/ a decisivo; (manner) decidido. ~ly adv decisivamente

deck /dek/ n (of ship) convés m; (of cards) baralho m. ~-chair n espreguiçadeira f

declare /dɪ'kleə(r)/ vt declarar. ~ation /deklə'reɪʃn/ n declaração f

decline /dɪ'klaɪn/ vt (refuse) declinar, recusar delicadamente; (gram) declinar □ vi (deteriorate) declinar; (fall) baixar □ n declínio m; (fall) abaixamento m

decode /di:'kəʊd/ vt decifrar

decompose /di:kəm'pəʊz/ vt/i decompor(-se). ~ition /-ɒmpə'zɪʃn/ n decomposição f

décor /'deɪkɔ:(r)/ n decoração f

decorate /'dekəreɪt/ vt decorar, enfeitar; (paint) pintar; (paper) pôr papel em. ~ion /-'reɪʃn/ n decoração f; (medal etc) condecoração f. ~ive /-ətɪv/ a decorativo

decorum /dɪ'kɔ:rəm/ n decoro m

decoy¹ /'di:kɔɪ/ n chamariz m, engodo m; (trap) armadilha f

decoy² /dɪˈkɔɪ/ vt atrair, apanhar

decrease¹ /dɪˈkriːs/ vt/i diminuir

decrease² /ˈdiːkriːs/ n diminuição f

decree /dɪˈkriː/ n decreto m; (jur) decisão f judicial □ vt decretar

decrepit /dɪˈkrepɪt/ a decrépito

dedicat|e /ˈdedɪkeɪt/ vt dedicar. ~ed a dedicado. ~ion /-ˈkeɪʃn/ n dedicação f; (in book) dedicatória f

deduce /dɪˈdjuːs/ vt deduzir

deduct /dɪˈdʌkt/ vt deduzir; (from pay) descontar

deduction /dɪˈdʌkʃn/ n dedução f; (from pay) desconto m

deed /diːd/ n ato m; (jur) contrato m

deem /diːm/ vt julgar, considerar

deep /diːp/ a (-er, -est) profundo □ adv profundamente. ~-freeze n congelador m □ vt congelar. take a ~ breath respirar fundo. ~ly adv profundamente

deepen /ˈdiːpən/ vt/i aprofundar(-se); (mystery, night) adensar-se

deer /dɪə(r)/ n (pl invar) veado m

deface /dɪˈfeɪs/ vt danificar, degradar

defamation /defəˈmeɪʃn/ n difamação f

default /dɪˈfɔːlt/ vi faltar □ n by ~ à revelia. win by ~ (sport) ganhar por não comparecimento, (P) comparência □ a (comput) default m

defeat /dɪˈfiːt/ vt derrotar; (thwart) malograr □ n derrota f; (of plan, etc) malogro m

defect¹ /ˈdiːfekt/ n defeito m. ~ive /dɪˈfektɪv/ a defeituoso

defect² /dɪˈfekt/ vi desertar. ~ion n defecção m. ~or n trânsfuga mf, dissidente mf; (political) asilado m político

defence /dɪˈfens/ n defesa f. ~less a indefeso

defend /dɪˈfend/ vt defender. ~ant n (jur) réu m, acusado m. ~er n advogado m de defesa, defensor m

defensive /dɪˈfensɪv/ a defensivo □ n on the ~ na defensiva f; (person, sport) na retranca f (colloq)

defer /dɪˈfɜː(r)/ vt (pt deferred) adiar, diferir □ vi ~ to ceder, deferir

deferen|ce /ˈdefərəns/ n deferência f. ~tial /-ˈrenʃl/ a deferente

defian|ce /dɪˈfaɪəns/ n desafio m. in ~ of sem respeito por. ~t a de desafio. ~tly adv com ar de desafio

deficien|t /dɪˈfɪʃnt/ a deficiente. be ~t in ter falta de. ~cy n deficiência f

deficit /ˈdefɪsɪt/ n déficit m

define /dɪˈfaɪn/ vt definir

definite /ˈdefɪnɪt/ a definido; (clear) categórico, claro; (certain) certo. ~ly adv decididamente; (clearly) claramente

definition /defɪˈnɪʃn/ n definição f

definitive /dɪˈfɪnətɪv/ a definitivo

deflat|e /dɪˈfleɪt/ vt esvaziar; (person) desemproar, desinchar. ~ion /-ʃn/ n esvaziamento m; (econ) deflação f

deflect /dɪˈflekt/ vt/i desviar(-se)

deform /dɪˈfɔːm/ vt deformar. ~ed a deformado, disforme. ~ity n deformidade f

defraud /dɪˈfrɔːd/ vt defraudar

defrost /diːˈfrɒst/ vt descongelar

deft /deft/ a (-er, -est) hábil

defunct /dɪˈfʌŋkt/ a (law etc) caduco, extinto

defuse /diːˈfjuːz/ vt (a bomb) desativar, (P) desactivar; (a situation) acalmar

defy /dɪˈfaɪ/ vt desafiar; (attempts) resistir a; (the law) desobedecer a; (public opinion) opor-se a

degenerate /dɪˈdʒenəreɪt/ vi degenerar (into em)

degrad|e /dɪˈgreɪd/ vt degradar. ~ation /degrəˈdeɪʃn/ n degradação f

degree /dɪˈgriː/ n grau m; (univ) diploma m. to a ~ ao mais alto grau, muito

dehydrate /diːˈhaɪdreɪt/ vt/i desidratar(-se)

de-ice /diːˈaɪs/ vt descongelar, degelar; (windscreen) tirar o gelo de

deign /deɪn/ vt ~ to do dignar-se (a) fazer

deity /ˈdiːɪtɪ/ n divindade f

dejected /dɪˈdʒektɪd/ a abatido

delay /dɪˈleɪ/ vt atrasar; (postpone) retardar □ vi atrasar-se □ n atraso m, demora f

delegate¹ /ˈdelɪgət/ n delegado m

delegat|e² /ˈdelɪgeɪt/ vt delegar. ~ion /-ˈgeɪʃn/ n delegação f

delet|e /dɪˈliːt/ vt riscar. ~ion /-ʃn/ n rasura f

deliberate¹ /dɪˈlɪbərət/ a deliberado; (steps etc) compassado. ~ly adv deliberadamente, de propósito

deliberat|e² /dɪˈlɪbəreɪt/ vt/i deliberar. ~ion /-ˈreɪʃn/ n deliberação f

delica|te /ˈdelɪkət/ a delicado. ~cy n delicadeza f; (food) guloseima f, iguaria f, (P) acepipe m

delicatessen /delɪkəˈtesn/ n (shop) mercearias fpl finas

delicious /dɪˈlɪʃəs/ a delicioso

delight /dɪˈlaɪt/ n grande prazer m, delícia f; (thing) delícia f, encanto m □ vt deliciar □ vi ~ in deliciar-se com. ~ed a deliciado, encantado. ~ful a delicioso, encantador

delinquen|t /dɪˈlɪŋkwənt/ a & n delinquente mf, (P) delinquente mf. ~cy n delinquência f, (P) delinquência f

delir|ious /dɪˈlɪrɪəs/ a delirante. be ~ous delirar. ~um /-əm/ n delírio m

deliver /dɪˈlɪvə(r)/ vt entregar;

delude /dɪ'lu:d/ *vt* enganar. ~de o.s. ter ilusões. ~sion /-ʒn/ *n* ilusão *f*

deluge /'delju:dʒ/ *n* dilúvio *m* □ *vt* inundar

de luxe /də'lʌks/ *a* de luxo

delve /delv/ *vi* ~ into pesquisar, rebuscar

demand /dɪ'mɑ:nd/ *vt* exigir; (*ask to be told*) perguntar □ *n* exigência *f*; (*comm*) procura *f*; (*claim*) reivindicação *f*. in ~ procurado. ~ing *a* exigente; (*work*) puxado, custoso

demean /dɪ'mi:n/ *vt* ~ o.s. rebaixar-se

demeanour /dɪ'mi:nə(r)/ *n* comportamento *m*, conduta *f*

demented /dɪ'mentɪd/ *a* louco, demente. become ~ enlouquecer

demo /'deməʊ/ *n* (*pl* -os) (*colloq*) manifestação *f*, (*P*) manif *f*

democracy /dɪ'mɒkrəsɪ/ *n* democracia *f*

democrat /'deməkræt/ *n* democrata *mf*. ~ic /-'krætɪk/ *a* democrático

demolish /dɪ'mɒlɪʃ/ *vt* demolir. ~tion /demə'lɪʃn/ *n* demolição *f*

demon /'di:mən/ *n* demônio *m*

demonstrat|**e** /'demənstreɪt/ *vt* demonstrar □ *vi* (*pol*) fazer uma manifestação, manifestar-se. ~ion /-'streɪʃn/ *n* demonstração *f*; (*pol*) manifestação *f*. ~or *n* (*pol*) manifestante *mf*

demonstrative /dɪ'mɒnstrətɪv/ *a* demonstrativo

demoralize /dɪ'mɒrəlaɪz/ *vt* desmoralizar

demote /dɪ'məʊt/ *vt* fazer baixar de posto, rebaixar

demure /dɪ'mjʊə(r)/ *a* recatado, modesto

den /den/ *n* antro *m*, covil *m*; (*room*) cantinho *m*, recanto *m*

denial /dɪ'naɪəl/ *n* negação *f*; (*refusal*) recusa *f*; (*statement*) desmentido *m*

denigrate /'denɪgreɪt/ *vt* denegrir

denim /'denɪm/ *n* brim *m*. ~s (*jeans*) blue-jeans *mpl*

Denmark /'denmɑ:k/ *n* Dinamarca *f*

denomination /dɪnɒmɪ'neɪʃn/ *n* denominação *f*; (*relig*) confissão *f*, seita *f*; (*money*) valor *m*

denote /dɪ'nəʊt/ *vt* denotar

denounce /dɪ'naʊns/ *vt* denunciar

dens|**e** /dens/ *a* (-er, -est) denso; (*colloq: person*) obtuso. ~ely *adv* (*packed etc*) muito. ~ity *n* densidade *f*

dent /dent/ *n* mossa *f*, depressão *f* □ *vt* dentear

dental /'dentl/ *a* dentário, dental

dentist /'dentɪst/ *n* dentista *mf*. ~ry *n* odontologia *f*

denture /'dentʃə(r)/ *n* dentadura *f* (postiça)

denunciation /dɪnʌnsɪ'eɪʃn/ *n* denúncia *f*

deny /dɪ'naɪ/ *vt* negar; (*rumour*) desmentir; (*disown*) renegar; (*refuse*) recusar

deodorant /di:'əʊdərənt/ *n* & *a* desodorante (*m*), (*P*) desodorizante (*m*)

depart /dɪ'pɑ:t/ *vi* partir. ~ from (*deviate*) afastar-se de, desviar-se de

department /dɪ'pɑ:tmənt/ *n* departamento *m*; (*in shop, office*) seção *f*, (*P*) secção *f*; (*government*) repartição *f*. ~ store loja *f* de departamentos, (*P*) grande armazém *m*

departure /dɪ'pɑ:tʃə(r)/ *n* partida *f*. a ~ from (*custom, diet etc*) uma mudança de. a new ~ uma nova orientação

depend /dɪ'pend/ *vi* ~ on depender de; (*trust*) contar com. ~able *a* de confiança. ~ence *n* dependência *f*. ~ent (on) *a* dependente (de)

dependant /dɪ'pendənt/ *n* dependente *mf*

depict /dɪ'pɪkt/ *vt* descrever; (*in pictures*) representar

deplete /dɪ'pli:t/ *vt* reduzir; (*use up*) esgotar

deplor|**e** /dɪ'plɔ:(r)/ *vt* deplorar. ~able *a* deplorável

deport /dɪ'pɔ:t/ *vt* deportar. ~ation /di:pɔ:'teɪʃn/ *n* deportação *f*

depose /dɪ'pəʊz/ *vt* depor

deposit /dɪ'pɒzɪt/ *vt* (*pt* deposited) depositar □ *n* depósito *m*. ~ account conta *f* de depósito a prazo. ~or *n* depositante *mf*

depot /'depəʊ/ *n* (*mil*) depósito *m*; (*buses*) garagem *f*; (*Amer: station*) rodoviária *f*, estação *f* de trem, (*P*) de comboio

deprav|**e** /dɪ'preɪv/ *vt* depravar. ~ity /-'prævətɪ/ *n* depravação *f*

depreciat|**e** /dɪ'pri:ʃɪeɪt/ *vt/i* depreciar(-se). ~ion /-'eɪʃn/ *n* depreciação *f*

depress /dɪ'pres/ *vt* deprimir; (*press down*) carregar em. ~ion /-ʃn/ *n* depressão *f*

deprivation /deprɪ'veɪʃn/ *n* privação *f*

deprive /dɪ'praɪv/ *vt* ~ of privar de. ~d *a* privado; (*underprivileged*) deserdado (da sorte), destituído; (*child*) carente

depth /depθ/ *n* profundidade *f*. be out of one's ~ perder o pé; não ter pé; (*fig*) ficar desnorteado, estar perdido. in the ~(s) of no mais fundo de, nas profundezas de deputation /depjʊ'teɪʃn/ n delegação f

deputy /'depjʊtɪ/ n (pl -ies) delegado m □ a adjunto. ~ chairman vice-presidente m

derail /dɪ'reɪl/ vt descarrilhar. be ~ed descarrilhar. ~ment n descarrilhamento m

deranged /dɪ'reɪndʒd/ a (mind) transtornado, louco

derelict /'derəlɪkt/ a abandonado

deri|de /dɪ'raɪd/ vt escarnecer de. ~sion /-'rɪʒn/ n escárnio m. ~sive a escarninho. ~sory a escarninho; (offer etc) irrisório

derivative /dɪ'rɪvətɪv/ a derivado; (work) pouco original □ n derivado m

deriv|e /dɪ'raɪv/ vt ~e from tirar de □ vi ~e from derivar de. ~ation /derɪ'veɪʃn/ n derivação f

derogatory /dɪ'rɒɡətrɪ/ a pejorativo; (remark) depreciativo

derv /dɜːv/ n gasóleo m

descend /dɪ'send/ vt/i descer, descender. be ~ed from descender de. ~ant n descendente mf

descent /dɪ'sent/ n descida f; (lineage) descendência f, origem f

descri|be /dɪs'kraɪb/ vt descrever. ~ption /-'krɪpʃn/ n descrição f; ~ptive /-'krɪptɪv/ a descritivo

desecrat|e /'desɪkreɪt/ vt profanar. ~ion /-'kreɪʃn/ n profanação f

desert¹ /'dezət/ a & n deserto (m). ~ island ilha f deserta

desert² /dɪ'zɜːt/ vt/i desertar. ~ed a abandonado. ~er n desertor m. ~ion /-ʃn/ n deserção f

deserv|e /dɪ'zɜːv/ vt merecer. ~edly /dɪ'zɜːvɪdlɪ/ adv merecidamente, a justo título. ~ing a (person) merecedor; (action) meritório

design /dɪ'zaɪn/ n desenho m; (artistic) design m; (style of dress) modelo m; (pattern) padrão m, motivo m □ vt desenhar; (devise) conceber. ~er n desenhador m; (of dresses) costureiro m; (of machine) inventor m

designat|e /'dezɪɡneɪt/ vt designar. ~ion /-'neɪʃn/ n designação f

desir|e /dɪ'zaɪə(r)/ n desejo m □ vt desejar. ~able a desejável, atraente

desk /desk/ n secretária f; (of pupil) carteira f; (in hotel) recepção f; (in bank) caixa f

desolat|e /'desələt/ a desolado. ~ion /-'leɪʃn/ n desolação f

despair /dɪ'speə(r)/ n desespero m □ vi desesperar (of de)

desperate /'despərət/ a desesperado; (criminal) capaz de tudo. be ~ for ter uma vontade doida de. ~ly adv desesperadamente

desperation /despə'reɪʃn/ n desespero m

despicable /dɪ'spɪkəbl/ a desprezível

despise /dɪ'spaɪz/ vt desprezar

despite /dɪ'spaɪt/ prep apesar de, a despeito de, mau grado

despondent /dɪ'spɒndənt/ a desanimado. ~cy n desânimo m

despot /'despɒt/ n déspota mf

dessert /dɪ'zɜːt/ n sobremesa f. ~-spoon n colher f de sobremesa

destination /destɪ'neɪʃn/ n destino m, destinação f

destine /'destɪn/ vt destinar

destiny /'destɪnɪ/ n destino m

destitute /'destɪtjuːt/ a destituído, indigente

destr|oy /dɪ'strɔɪ/ vt destruir. ~uction /-'strʌkʃn/ n destruição f. ~uctive a destrutivo, destruidor

detach /dɪ'tætʃ/ vt separar, arrancar. ~able a separável; (lining etc) solto. ~ed a separado; (impartial) imparcial; (unemotional) desprendido. ~ed house casa f sem parede-meia com outra

detachment /dɪ'tætʃmənt/ n separação f; (indifference) desprendimento m; (mil) destacamento m; (impartiality) imparcialidade f

detail /'diːteɪl/ n pormenor m, detalhe m □ vt detalhar; (troops) destacar. ~ed a detalhado

detain /dɪ'teɪn/ vt reter; (in prison) deter. ~ee /diːteɪ'niː/ n detido m

detect /dɪ'tekt/ vt detectar. ~ion /-ʃn/ n detecção f. ~or n detector m

detective /dɪ'tektɪv/ n detective m. ~ story romance m policial

detention /dɪ'tenʃn/ n detenção f. be given a ~ (school) ficar de castigo na escola

deter /dɪ'tɜː(r)/ vt (pt deterred) dissuadir; (hinder) impedir

detergent /dɪ'tɜːdʒənt/ a & n detergente (m)

deteriorat|e /dɪ'tɪərɪəreɪt/ vi deteriorar(-se). ~ion /-'reɪʃn/ n deterioração f

determin|e /dɪ'tɜːmɪn/ vt determinar. ~e to do decidir fazer. ~ation /-'neɪʃn/ n determinação f. ~ed a determinado. ~ed to do decidido a fazer

deterrent /dɪ'terənt/ n dissuasivo m

detest /dɪ'test/ vt detestar. ~able a detestável

detonat|e /'detəneɪt/ vt/i detonar. ~ion /-'neɪʃn/ n detonação f. ~or n espoleta f, detonador m

detour /'diːtʊə(r)/ n desvio m

detract /dɪ'trækt/ vi ~ from depreciar, menosprezar

detriment /'detrɪmənt/ n detrimento m. ~al /-'mentl/ a prejudicial

devalu|e /di:ˈvælju:/ vt desvalorizar. ~ation /-ˈeɪʃn/ n desvalorização f

devastat|e /ˈdevəsteɪt/ vt devastar; (fig: overwhelm) arrasar. ~ing a devastador; (criticism) de arrasar

develop /dɪˈveləp/ vt/i (pt developed) desenvolver(-se); (get) contrair; (build on) urbanizar; (film) revelar. ~ into tornar-se. ~ing country pais m subdesenvolvido. ~ment n desenvolvimento m; (film) revelação f; (of land) urbanização f

deviat|e /ˈdi:vɪeɪt/ vi desviar-se. ~ion /-ˈeɪʃn/ n desvio m

device /dɪˈvaɪs/ n dispositivo m; (scheme) processo m. left to one's own ~s entregue a si mesmo

devil /ˈdevl/ n diabo m

devious /ˈdi:vɪəs/ a tortuoso; (fig: means) escuso; (fig: person) pouco franco

devise /dɪˈvaɪz/ vt imaginar, inventar

devoid /dɪˈvɔɪd/ a ~ of desprovido de, destituído de

devot|e /dɪˈvəʊt/ vt dedicar, devotar. ~ed a dedicado, devotado. ~ion /-ʃn/ n devoção f

devotee /devəˈti:/ n ~ of adepto m de, entusiasta mf de

devour /dɪˈvaʊə(r)/ vt devorar

devout /dɪˈvaʊt/ a devota; (prayer) fervoroso

dew /dju:/ n orvalho m

dexter|ity /dekˈsterəti/ n destreza f, jeito m. ~rous /ˈdekstrəs/ a destro, hábil

diabet|es /daɪəˈbi:ti:z/ n diabetes f. ~ic /-ˈbetɪk/ a & n diabético (m)

diabolical /daɪəˈbɒlɪkl/ a diabólico

diagnose /ˈdaɪəgnəʊz/ vt diagnosticar

diagnosis /daɪəgˈnəʊsɪs/ n (pl -oses /-si:z/) diagnóstico m

diagonal /daɪˈægənl/ a & n diagonal (f)

diagram /ˈdaɪəgræm/ n diagrama m, esquema m

dial /ˈdaɪəl/ n mostrador m □ vt (pt dialled) (number) marcar, discar. ~ling code código m de discagem. ~ling tone sinal m de discar

dialect /ˈdaɪəlekt/ n dialeto m, (P) dialecto m

dialogue /ˈdaɪəlɒg/ n diálogo m

diameter /daɪˈæmɪtə(r)/ n diâmetro m

diamond /ˈdaɪəmənd/ n diamante m, brilhante m; (shape) losango m. ~s (cards) ouros mpl

diaper /ˈdaɪəpə(r)/ n (Amer) fralda f

diaphragm /ˈdaɪəfræm/ n diafragma m

diarrhoea /daɪəˈrɪə/ n diarréia f, (P) diarreia f

diary /ˈdaɪərɪ/ n agenda f; (record) diário m

dice /daɪs/ n (pl invar) dado m

dictat|e /dɪkˈteɪt/ vt/i ditar. ~ion /-ʃn/ n ditado m

dictator /dɪkˈteɪtə(r)/ n ditador m. ~ship n ditadura f

diction /ˈdɪkʃn/ n dicção f

dictionary /ˈdɪkʃənrɪ/ n dicionário m

did /dɪd/ see do

diddle /ˈdɪdl/ vt (colloq) trapacear, enganar

didn't /ˈdɪdnt/ = did not

die /daɪ/ vi (pres p dying) morrer. be dying to estar doido para. ~ down diminuir, baixar. ~ out desaparecer, extinguir-se

diesel /ˈdi:zl/ n diesel m. ~ engine motor m diesel

diet /ˈdaɪət/ n dieta f □ vi fazer dieta, estar de dieta

differ /ˈdɪfə(r)/ vi diferir; (disagree) discordar

differen|t /ˈdɪfrənt/ a diferente. ~ce n diferença f; (disagreement) desacordo m. ~ly adv diferentemente

differentiate /dɪfəˈrenʃɪeɪt/ vt/i diferençar(-se), diferenciar(-se)

difficult /ˈdɪfɪkəlt/ a difícil. ~y n dificuldade f

diffiden|t /ˈdɪfɪdənt/ a acanhado, inseguro. ~ce n acanhamento m, insegurança f

diffuse[1] /dɪˈfju:s/ a difuso

diffus|e[2] /dɪˈfju:z/ vt difundir. ~ion /-ʒn/ n difusão f

dig /dɪg/ vt/i (pt dug, pres p digging) cavar; (thrust) espetar □ n (with elbow) cotovelada f; (with finger) cutucada f, (P) espetadela f; (remark) ferroada f, (archaeol) escavação f. ~s (colloq) quarto m alugado. ~ up desenterrar

digest /dɪˈdʒest/ vt/i digerir. ~ible a digerível, digestível. ~ion /-ʃn/ n digestão f

digestive /dɪˈdʒestɪv/ a digestivo

digit /ˈdɪdʒɪt/ n dígito m

digital /ˈdɪdʒɪtl/ a digital. ~ clock relógio m digital

dignif|y /ˈdɪgnɪfaɪ/ vt dignificar. ~ied a digno

dignitary /ˈdɪgnɪtərɪ/ n dignitário m

dignity /ˈdɪgnətɪ/ n dignidade f

digress /daɪˈgres/ vi digressar, divagar. ~ from desviar-se de. ~ion /-ʃn/ n digressão f

dike /daɪk/ n dique m

dilapidated /dɪˈlæpɪdeɪtɪd/ a (house) arruinado, degradado; (car) estragado

dilat|e /daɪˈleɪt/ vt/i dilatar(-se). ~ion /-ʃn/ n dilatação f

dilemma /dɪˈlemə/ n dilema m

diligen|t /ˈdɪlɪdʒənt/ a diligente, aplicado. ~ce n diligência f, aplicação f

dilute /dar'lju:t/ vt diluir □ a diluído

dim /dɪm/ a (dimmer, dimmest) (weak) fraco; (dark) sombrio; (indistinct) vago; (colloq: stupid) burro (colloq) □ vt/i (pt dimmed) (light) baixar. ~ly adv (shine) fracamente; (remember) vagamente

dime /daɪm/ n (Amer) moeda f de dez centavos

dimension /dar'menʃn/ n dimensão f

diminish /dr'mɪnɪʃ/ vt/i diminuir

diminutive /dr'mɪnjʊtɪv/ a diminuto □ n diminutivo m

dimple /'dɪmpl/ n covinha f

din /dɪn/ n barulheira f, (P) chinfrim m

dine /daɪn/ vi jantar. ~r /-ə(r)/ n (person) comensal m; (rail) vagãorestaurante m; (Amer: restaurant) lanchonete f

dinghy /'dɪŋgɪ/ n (pl -ghies) bote m; (inflatable) bote m de borracha, (P) barco m de borracha

dingy /'dɪndʒɪ/ a (-ier, -iest) com ar sujo, esquálido

dining-room /'daɪnɪŋru:m/ n sala f de jantar

dinner /'dɪnə(r)/ n jantar m; (lunch) almoço m. ~-jacket n smoking m

dinosaur /'daɪnəsɔ:(r)/ n dinossauro m

dip /dɪp/ vt/i (pt dipped) mergulhar; (lower) baixar □ n mergulho m; (bathe) banho m rápido, mergulho m; (slope) descida f; (culin) molho m. ~ into (book) folhear. ~ one's headlights baixar luzes para médios

diphtheria /dɪf'θɪərɪə/ n difteria f

diphthong /'dɪfθɒŋ/ n ditongo m

diploma /dɪ'pləʊmə/ n diploma m

diplomacy /dɪ'pləʊməsɪ/ n diplomacia f

diplomat /'dɪpləmæt/ n diplomata mf. ~ic /-'mætɪk/ a diplomático

dire /daɪə(r)/ a (-er, -est) terrível; (need, poverty) extremo

direct /dɪ'rekt/ a direto, (P) directo □ adv diretamente, (P) directamente □ vt dirigir. ~ sb to indicar a alg o caminho para

direction /dɪ'rekʃn/ n direção f, (P) direcção f, sentido m. ~s instruções fpl. ~s for use modo m de emprego

directly /dɪ'rektlɪ/ adv diretamente, (P) directamente, (at once) imediatamente, logo

director /dɪ'rektə(r)/ n diretor m, (P) director m

directory /dɪ'rektərɪ/ n (telephone) ~ lista f telefônica, (P) telefónica

dirt /dɜ:t/ n sujeira f. ~ cheap (colloq) baratíssimo

dirty /'dɜ:tɪ/ a (-ier, -iest) sujo; (word) obsceno □ vt/i sujar(-se). ~ trick golpe m baixo, (P) boa partida f

disability /dɪsə'bɪlətɪ/ n deficiência f

disable /dɪs'eɪbl/ vt incapacitar. ~d a inválido, deficiente

disadvantage /dɪsəd'va:ntɪdʒ/ n desvantagem f

disagree /dɪsə'gri:/ vi discordar (with de). ~ with (food, climate) não fazer bem. ~ment n desacordo m; (quarrel) desintendimento m

disagreeable /dɪsə'gri:əbl/ a desagradável

disappear /dɪsə'pɪə(r)/ vi desaparecer. ~ance n desaparecimento m

disappoint /dɪsə'pɔɪnt/ vt desapontar, decepcionar. ~ment n desapontamento m, decepção f

disapprov|e /dɪsə'pru:v/ vi ~e (of) desaprovar. ~al n desaprovação f

disarm /dɪs'ɑ:m/ vt/i desarmar. ~ament n desarmamento m

disast|er /dɪ'zɑ:stə(r)/ n desastre m. ~rous a desastroso

disband /dɪs'bænd/ vt/i debandar; (troops) dispersar

disbelief /dɪsbɪ'li:f/ n incredulidade f

disc /dɪsk/ n disco m. ~ jockey disc(o) jockey m

discard /dɪs'kɑ:d/ vt pôr de lado, descartar(-se) de; (old clothes etc) desfazer-se de

discern /dɪ'sɜ:n/ vt discernir. ~ible a perceptível. ~ing a perspicaz. ~ment n discernimento m, perspicácia f

discharge¹ /dɪs'tʃɑ:dʒ/ vt descarregar; (dismiss) despedir, mandar embora; (duty) cumprir; (liquid) vazar, (P) deitar; (patient) dar alta a; (prisoner) absolver, pôr em liberdade; (pus) purgar, (P) deitar

discharge² /'dɪstʃɑ:dʒ/ n descarga f; (dismissal) despedimento m; (of patient) alta f; (of prisoner) absolvição f; (med) secreção f

disciple /dɪ'saɪpl/ n discípulo m

disciplin|e /'dɪsɪplɪn/ n disciplina f □ vt disciplinar; (punish) castigar. ~ary a disciplinar

disclaim /dɪs'kleɪm/ vt (jur) repudiar; (deny) negar. ~er n desmentido m

disclos|e /dɪs'kləʊz/ vt revelar. ~ure /-ʒə(r)/ n revelação f

disco /'dɪskəʊ/ n (pl -os) (colloq) discoteca f

discolour /dɪs'kʌlə(r)/ vt/i descolorir(-se); (in sunlight) desbotar(-se)

discomfort /dɪs'kʌmfət/ n malestar m; (lack of comfort) desconforto m

disconcert /dɪskən'sɜ:t/ vt desconcertar. ~ing a desconcertante

disconnect /dɪskə'nekt/ vt desligar

discontent /dɪskən'tent/ n descontentamento m. ~ed a descontente discontinue /dɪskən'tɪnjuː/ *vt* descontinuar, suspender

discord /'dɪskɔːd/ *n* discórdia *f*. ~ant /-'skɔːdənt/ *a* discordante

discothèque /'dɪskətek/ *n* discoteca *f*

discount[1] /'dɪskaʊnt/ *n* desconto *m*

discount[2] /dɪs'kaʊnt/ *vt* descontar; (*disregard*) dar o desconto a

discourage /dɪs'kʌrɪdʒ/ *vt* desencorajar

discourte|ous /dɪs'kɜːtɪəs/ *a* indelicado. ~sy /-'sɪ/ *n* indelicadeza *f*

discover /dɪs'kʌvə(r)/ *vt* descobrir. ~y *n* descoberta *f*; (*of island etc*) descobrimento *m*

discredit /dɪs'kredɪt/ *vt* (*pt* discredited) desacreditar □ *n* descrédito *m*

discreet /dɪs'kriːt/ *a* discreto

discrepancy /dɪs'krepənsɪ/ *n* discrepância *f*

discretion /dɪs'kreʃn/ *n* discrição *f*; (*prudence*) prudência *f*

discriminat|e /dɪs'krɪmɪneɪt/ *vt/i* discriminar. ~e against tomar partido contra, fazer discriminação contra. ~ing *a* discriminador; (*having good taste*) com discernimento. ~ion /-'neɪʃn/ *n* discernimento *m*; (*bias*) discriminação *f*

discus /'dɪskəs/ *n* disco *m*

discuss /dɪs'kʌs/ *vt* discutir. ~ion /-ʃn/ *n* discussão *f*

disdain /dɪs'deɪn/ *n* desdém *m* □ *vt* desdenhar. ~ful *a* desdenhoso

disease /dɪ'ziːz/ *n* doença *f*. ~d *a* (*plant*) atacado por doença; (*person, animal*) doente

disembark /dɪsɪm'baːk/ *vt/i* desembarcar

disembodied /dɪsɪm'bɒdɪd/ *a* desencarnado

disenchant /dɪsɪn'tʃaːnt/ *vt* desencantar. ~ment *n* desencantamento *m*

disengage /dɪsɪn'geɪdʒ/ *vt* desprender, soltar; (*mech*) desengatar

disentangle /dɪsɪn'tæŋgl/ *vt* desembaraçar, desenredar

disfavour /dɪs'feɪvə(r)/ *n* desfavor *m*, desgraça *f*

disfigure /dɪs'fɪgə(r)/ *vt* desfigurar

disgrace /dɪs'greɪs/ *n* vergonha *f*; (*disfavour*) desgraça *f* □ *vt* desonrar. ~ful *a* vergonhoso

disgruntled /dɪs'grʌntld/ *a* descontente

disguise /dɪs'gaɪz/ *vt* disfarçar □ *n* disfarce *m*. in ~ disfarçado

disgust /dɪs'gʌst/ *n* repugnância *f* □ *vt* repugnar. ~ing *a* repugnante

dish /dɪʃ/ *n* prato *m* □ *vt* ~ out (*colloq*) distribuir. ~ up servir. the ~es (*crockery*) a louça *f*

dishcloth /'dɪʃklɒθ/ *n* pano *m* de prato

dishearten /dɪs'haːtn/ *vt* desencorajar, desalentar

dishevelled /dɪ'ʃevld/ *a* desgrenhado

dishonest /dɪs'ɒnɪst/ *a* desonesto. ~y *n* desonestidade *f*

dishonour /dɪs'ɒnə(r)/ *n* desonra *f* □ *vt* desonrar. ~able *a* desonroso

dishwasher /'dɪʃwɒʃə(r)/ *n* lavadora *f* de pratos, (*P*) máquina *f* de lavar a louça

disillusion /dɪsɪ'luːʒn/ *vt* desiludir. ~ment *n* desilusão *f*

disinfect /dɪsɪn'fekt/ *vt* desinfetar, (*P*) desinfectar. ~ant *n* desinfetante *m*, (*P*) desinfectante *f*

disinherit /dɪsɪn'herɪt/ *vt* deserdar

disintegrate /dɪs'ɪntɪgreɪt/ *vt/i* desintegrar(-se)

disinterested /dɪs'ɪntrəstɪd/ *a* desinteressado

disjointed /dɪs'dʒɔɪntɪd/ *a* (*talk*) descosido, desconexo

disk /dɪsk/ *n* (*comput*) disco *m*; (*Amer*) = disc. ~ drive unidade *f* de disco

dislike /dɪs'laɪk/ *n* aversão *f*, antipatia *f* □ *vt* não gostar de, antipatizar com

dislocat|e /'dɪsləkeɪt/ *vt* (*limb*) deslocar. ~ion /-'keɪʃn/ *n* deslocação *f*

dislodge /dɪs'lɒdʒ/ *vt* desalojar

disloyal /dɪs'lɔɪəl/ *a* desleal. ~ty *n* deslealdade *f*

dismal /'dɪzməl/ *a* tristonho

dismantle /dɪs'mæntl/ *vt* desmantelar

dismay /dɪs'meɪ/ *n* consternação *f* □ *vt* consternar

dismiss /dɪs'mɪs/ *vt* despedir; (*from mind*) afastar, pôr de lado. ~al *n* despedimento *m*

dismount /dɪs'maʊnt/ *vi* desmontar

disobedien|t /dɪsə'biːdɪənt/ *a* desobediente. ~ce *n* desobediência *f*

disobey /dɪsə'beɪ/ *vt/i* desobedecer (a)

disorder /dɪs'ɔːdə(r)/ *n* desordem *f*; (*med*) perturbações *fpl*, disfunção *f*. ~ly *a* desordenado; (*riotous*) desordeiro

disorganize /dɪs'ɔːgənaɪz/ *vt* desorganizar

disorientate /dɪs'ɔːrɪənteɪt/ *vt* desorientar

disown /dɪs'əʊn/ *vt* repudiar

disparaging /dɪ'spærɪdʒɪŋ/ *a* depreciativo

disparity /dɪ'spærətɪ/ *n* disparidade *f*

dispatch /dɪ'spætʃ/ *vt* despachar □ *n* despacho *m*

dispel /dɪs'pel/ *vt* (*pt* dispelled) dissipar

dispensary /dɪ'spensərɪ/ *n* dispensário *m*, farmácia *f*

dispense /dɪ'spens/ *vt* dispensar □ *vi*

~ with dispensar, passar sem. ~r /-ə(r)/ n (*container*) distribuidor *m*

disperse /dɪˈspɜːs/ *vt/i* dispersar (-se). ~al *n* dispersão *f*

dispirited /dɪˈspɪrɪtɪd/ *a* desanimado

displace /dɪsˈpleɪs/ *vt* deslocar; (*take the place of*) substituir. ~d person deslocado *m* de guerra

display /dɪsˈpleɪ/ *vt* exibir, mostrar; (*feeling*) manifestar, dar mostras de □ *n* exposição *f*; (*of computer*) apresentação *f* visual; (*comm*) objetos *mpl* expostos

displease /dɪsˈpliːz/ *vt* desagradar a. ~ed with descontente com. ~ure /ˈpleʒə(r)/ *n* desagrado *m*

disposable /dɪˈspəʊzəbl/ *a* descartável

dispose /dɪˈspəʊz/ *vt* dispor □ *vi* ~e of desfazer-se de. well ~ed towards bem disposto para com. ~al *n* (*of waste*) eliminação *f*. at sb's ~al à disposição de alg

disposition /dɪspəˈzɪʃn/ *n* disposição *f*; (*character*) índole *f*

disproportionate /dɪsprəˈpɔːʃənət/ *a* desproporcionado

disprove /dɪsˈpruːv/ *vt* refutar

dispute /dɪsˈpjuːt/ *vt* contestar; (*fight for, quarrel*) disputar □ *n* disputa *f*; (*industrial, pol*) conflito *m*. in ~ em questão

disqualif|y /dɪsˈkwɒlɪfaɪ/ *vt* tornar inapto; (*sport*) desqualificar. ~y from driving apreender a carteira de motorista. ~ication /-ɪˈkeɪʃn/ *n* desqualificação *f*

disregard /dɪsrɪˈɡɑːd/ *vt* não fazer caso de □ *n* indiferença *f* (*for* por)

disrepair /dɪsrɪˈpeə(r)/ *n* mau estado *m*, abandono *m*, degradação *f*

disreputable /dɪsˈrepjʊtəbl/ *a* pouco recomendável; (*in appearance*) com mau aspecto; (*in reputation*) vergonhoso, de má fama

disrepute /dɪsrɪˈpjuːt/ *n* descrédito *m*

disrespect /dɪsrɪˈspekt/ *n* falta *f* de respeito. ~ful *a* desrespeitoso, irreverente

disrupt /dɪsˈrʌpt/ *vt* perturbar; (*plans*) transtornar; (*break up*) dividir. ~ion /-ʃn/ *n* perturbação *f*. ~ive *a* perturbador

dissatisf|ied /dɪˈsætɪsfaɪd/ *a* descontente. ~action /dɪsætɪsˈfækʃn/ *n* descontentamento *m*

dissect /dɪˈsekt/ *vt* dissecar. ~ion /-ʃn/ *n* dissecação *f*

dissent /dɪˈsent/ *vi* dissentir, discordar □ *n* dissensão *f*, desacordo *m*

dissertation /dɪsəˈteɪʃn/ *n* dissertação *f*

disservice /dɪsˈsɜːvɪs/ *n* do sb a ~ prejudicar alg

dissident /ˈdɪsɪdənt/ *a* & *n* dissidente (*mf*)

dissimilar /dɪˈsɪmɪlə(r)/ *a* diferente

dissipate /ˈdɪsɪpeɪt/ *vt* dissipar; (*efforts, time*) desperdiçar. ~d *a* dissoluto

dissociate /dɪˈsəʊʃɪeɪt/ *vt* dissociar, desassociar

dissolution /dɪsəˈluːʃn/ *n* dissolução *f*

dissolve /dɪˈzɒlv/ *vt/i* dissolver(-se)

dissuade /dɪˈsweɪd/ *vt* dissuadir

distance /ˈdɪstəns/ *n* distância *f*. from a ~ de longe. in the ~ ao longe, à distância

distant /ˈdɪstənt/ *a* distante; (*relative*) afastado

distaste /dɪsˈteɪst/ *n* aversão *f*. ~ful *a* desagradável

distemper /dɪsˈtempə(r)/ *n* pintura *f* a têmpera; (*animal disease*) cinomose *f* □ *vt* pintar a têmpera

distend /dɪsˈtend/ *vt/i* distender(-se)

distil /dɪsˈtɪl/ *vt* (*pt* distilled) destilar. ~lation /ˈleɪʃn/ *n* destilação *f*

distillery /dɪsˈtɪlərɪ/ *n* destilaria *f*

distinct /dɪsˈtɪŋkt/ *a* distinto; (*marked*) claro, nítido. ~ion /-ʃn/ *n* distinção *f*. ~ive *a* distintivo, característico. ~ly *adv* distintamente; (*markedly*) claramente

distinguish /dɪsˈtɪŋɡwɪʃ/ *vt/i* distinguir. ~ed *a* distinto

distort /dɪsˈtɔːt/ *vt* distorcer; (*misrepresent*) deturpar. ~ion /-ʃn/ *n* distorção *f*; (*misrepresentation*) deturpação *f*

distract /dɪsˈtrækt/ *vt* distrair. ~ed *a* (*distraught*) desesperado, fora de si. ~ing *a* enlouquecedor. ~ion /-ʃn/ *n* distração *f*; (*P*) distracção *f*

distraught /dɪsˈtrɔːt/ *a* desesperado, fora de si

distress /dɪsˈtres/ *n* (*physical*) dor *f*; (*anguish*) aflição *f*; (*poverty*) miséria *f*; (*danger*) perigo *m* □ *vt* afligir. ~ing *a* aflitivo, doloroso

distribut|e /dɪsˈtrɪbjuːt/ *vt* distribuir. ~ion /-ˈbjuːʃn/ *n* distribuição *f*. ~or *n* distribuidor *m*

district /ˈdɪstrɪkt/ *n* região *f*; (*of town*) zona *f*

distrust /dɪsˈtrʌst/ *n* desconfiança *f* □ *vt* desconfiar de

disturb /dɪsˈtɜːb/ *vt* perturbar; (*move*) desarrumar; (*bother*) incomodar. ~ance *n* (*noise, disorder*) distúrbio *m*. ~ed *a* perturbado. ~ing *a* perturbador

disused /dɪsˈjuːzd/ *a* fora de uso, desusado, em desuso

ditch /dɪtʃ/ *n* fosso *m* □ *vt* (*sl: abandon*) abandonar, largar

dither /ˈdɪðə(r)/ *vi* hesitar

ditto /'dɪtəʊ/ adv idem

div|e /daɪv/ vi mergulhar; (rush) precipitar-se □ n mergulho m; (of plane) picada f; (sl: place) espelunca f. ~er n mergulhador m. ~ing-board n prancha f de saltos. ~ing-suit n escafandro m

diverge /daɪ'vɜːdʒ/ vi divergir

divergent /daɪ'vɜːdʒənt/ a divergente

diverse /daɪ'vɜːs/ a diverso

diversify /daɪ'vɜːsɪfaɪ/ vt diversificar

diversity /daɪ'vɜːsətɪ/ n diversidade f

diver|t /daɪ'vɜːt/ vt desviar; (entertain) divertir. ~sion /-ʃn/ n diversão f; (traffic) desvio m

divide /dɪ'vaɪd/ vt/i dividir(-se). ~ in two (branch, river, road) bifurcar-se

dividend /'dɪvɪdend/ n dividendo m

divine /dɪ'vaɪn/ a divino

divinity /dɪ'vɪnətɪ/ n divindade f; (theology) teologia f

division /dɪ'vɪʒn/ n divisão f

divorce /dɪ'vɔːs/ n divórcio m □ vt/i divorciar(-se) de. ~d a divorciado

divorcee /dɪvɔː'siː/ n divorciado m

divulge /daɪ'vʌldʒ/ vt divulgar

DIY see do-it-yourself

dizz|y /'dɪzɪ/ a (-ier, -iest) tonto. be or feel ~y ter tonturas, sentir-se tonto. ~iness n tontura f, vertigem f

do /duː/ vt/i (3 sing pres does, pt did, pp done) fazer; (be suitable) servir; (be enough) bastar (a); (sl: swindle) enganar, levar (colloq). how ~ you ~? como vai? well done muito bem!, (P) bravo!; (culin) bem passado. done for (colloq) liquidado (colloq), (P) anumado (colloq) □ v aux ~ you see? vê?; I ~ not smoke não fumo. don't you?, doesn't he? etc não é? □ n (pl dos or do's) festa f. ~-it-yourself a faça-você-mesmo. ~ away with eliminar, suprimir. ~ in (sl) matar, liquidar (colloq). ~ out limpar. ~ up (fasten) fechar; (house) renovar. I could ~ with a cup of tea apetecia-me uma xícara de chá. it could ~ with a wash precisa de uma lavagem

docile /'dəʊsaɪl/ a dócil

dock[1] /dɒk/ n doca f □ vt levar à doca □ vi entrar na doca. ~er n estivador m

dock[2] /dɒk/ n (jur) banco m dos réus

dockyard /'dɒkjɑːd/ n estaleiro m

doctor /'dɒktə(r)/ n médico m, doutor m; (univ) doutor m □ vt (cat) capar; (fig) adulterar; falsificar

doctorate /'dɒktərət/ n doutorado m, (P) doutoramento m

doctrine /'dɒktrɪn/ n doutrina f

document /'dɒkjʊmənt/ n documento m □ vt documentar. ~ary /-'mentrɪ/ a documental □ n documentário m

dodge /dɒdʒ/ vt/i esquivar(-se), furtar(-se) a □ n (colloq) truque m

dodgy /'dɒdʒɪ/ a (-ier, -iest) (colloq) delicado, difícil, embaraçoso

does /dʌz/ see do

doesn't /'dʌznt/ = does not

dog /dɒg/ n cão m □ vt (pt dogged) ir no encalço de, perseguir. ~-eared a com os cantos dobrados

dogged /'dɒgɪd/ a obstinado, persistente

dogma /'dɒgmə/ n dogma m. ~tic /-'mætɪk/ a dogmático

dogsbody /'dɒgzbɒdɪ/ n (colloq) paupara-toda-obra m (colloq), factótum m

doldrums /'dɒldrəmz/ npl be in the ~ estar com a neura; (business) estar parado

dole /dəʊl/ vt ~ out distribuir □ n (colloq) auxílio m desemprego. on the ~ (colloq) desempregado (titular de auxílio)

doleful /'dəʊlfl/ a tristonho, melancólico

doll /dɒl/ n boneca f □ vt/i ~ up (colloq) embonecar(-se)

dollar /'dɒlə(r)/ n dólar m

dolphin /'dɒlfɪn/ n golfinho m

domain /də'meɪn/ n domínio m

dome /dəʊm/ n cúpula f; (vault) abóbada f

domestic /də'mestɪk/ a (of home, animal, flights) doméstico; (trade) interno; (news) nacional. ~ated /-keɪtɪd/ a (animal) domesticado; (person) que gosta de trabalhos caseiros

dominant /'dɒmɪnənt/ a dominante

dominat|e /'dɒmɪneɪt/ vt/i dominar. ~ion /-'neɪʃn/ n dominação f, domínio m

domineer|ing /dɒmɪ'nɪə(r)/ vi ~ over mandar (em), ser autocrático (para com). ~ing a mandão, autocrático

dominion /də'mɪnjən/ n domínio m

domino /'dɒmɪnəʊ/ n (pl -oes) dominó m

donat|e /dəʊ'neɪt/ vt fazer doação de, doar, dar. ~ion /-ʃn/ n donativo m

done /dʌn/ see do

donkey /'dɒŋkɪ/ n burro m

donor /'dəʊnə(r)/ n (of blood) doador m, (P) dador m

don't /dəʊnt/ = do not

doodle /'duːdl/ vi rabiscar

doom /duːm/ n ruína f; (fate) destino m. be ~ed to ser/estar condenado a. ~ed (to failure) condenado ao fracasso

door /dɔː(r)/ n porta f

doorman /'dɔːmən/ n (pl -men) porteiro m

doormat /'dɔːmæt/ n capacho m

doorstep /'dɔːstep/ n degrau m da porta

doorway /'dɔːweɪ/ n vão m da porta, (P) entrada f

dope /dəʊp/ n (colloq) droga f; (sl: idiot) imbecil mf □ vt dopar, drogar

dormant /'dɔːmənt/ a dormente; (inactive) inativo, (P) inactivo; (latent) latente

dormitory /'dɔːmɪtrɪ/ n dormitório m; (Amer univ) residência f

dormouse /'dɔːmaʊs/ n (pl -mice) arganaz m

dos|e /dəʊs/ n dose f □ vt medicar. ~age n dosagem f; (on label) posologia f

doss /dɒs/ vi ~ (down) dormir sem conforto. ~house n pensão f miserável, asilo m noturno, (P) nocturno. ~er n vagabundo m

dot /dɒt/ n ponto m. on the ~ no momento preciso □ vt be ~ted with estar semeado de. ~ted line linha f pontilhada

dote /dəʊt/ vi ~ on ser louco por, adorar

double /'dʌbl/ a duplo; (room, bed) de casal □ adv duas vezes mais □ n dobro m. ~s (tennis) dupla f, (P) pares mpl □ vt/i dobrar, duplicar; (fold) dobrar em dois. at the ~ a passo acelerado. ~bass n contrabaixo m. ~chin papada f. ~cross vt enganar. ~dealing n jogo m duplo. ~decker n ônibus m, (P) autocarro m de dois andares. ~ Dutch algaraviada f, fala f incompreensível. ~ glazing (janela f de) vidro (m) duplo. doubly adv duplamente

doubt /daʊt/ n dúvida f □ vt duvidar de. ~ if or that duvidar que. ~ful a duvidoso; (hesitant) que tem dúvidas. ~less adv sem dúvida, indubitavelmente

dough /dəʊ/ n massa f

doughnut /'dəʊnʌt/ n sonho n, (P) bola f de Berlim

dove /dʌv/ n pomba f

dowdy /'daʊdɪ/ a (-ier, -iest) sem graça, sem gosto

down[1] /daʊn/ n (feathers, hair) penugem f

down[2] /daʊn/ adv (to lower place) abaixo, para baixo; (in lower place) em baixo. be ~ (level, price) descer; (sun) estar posto □ prep por (+n) (n+) abaixo. ~ the hill/street etc pelo monte/pela rua etc abaixo □ vt (colloq: knock down) jogar abaixo; (colloq: drink) esvaziar. come or go ~ descer. ~and-out n marginal m. ~hearted a desencorajado, desanimado. ~to-earth a terra-a-terra invar. ~ under na Austrália. ~ with abaixo

downcast /'daʊnkɑːst/ a abatido, deprimido, desmoralizado

downfall /'daʊnfɔːl/ n queda f, ruína f

downhill /daʊn'hɪl/ adv go ~ descer; (fig) ir abaixo □ a /'daʊnhɪl/ a descer, descendente

downpour /'daʊnpɔː(r)/ n aguaceiro m forte, (P) chuvada f

downright /'daʊnraɪt/ a franco; (utter) autêntico, verdadeiro □ adv positivamente

downstairs /daʊn'steəz/ adv (at/to) em/para baixo, no/para o andar de baixo □ a /'daʊnsteəz/ (flat etc) de baixo, do andar de baixo

downstream /'daʊnstriːm/ adv rio abaixo

downtown /'daʊntaʊn/ a & adv (de, em, para) o centro da cidade. ~ Boston o centro de Boston

downtrodden /'daʊntrɒdn/ a espezinhado, oprimido

downward /'daʊnwəd/ a descendente. ~(s) adv para baixo

dowry /'daʊərɪ/ n dote m

doze /dəʊz/ vi dormitar. ~ off cochilar □ n soneca f, cochilo m

dozen /'dʌzn/ n dúzia f. ~s of (colloq) dezenas de, dúzias de

Dr abbr (Doctor) Dr

drab /dræb/ a insípido; (of colour) morto, apagado

draft[1] /drɑːft/ n rascunho m; (comm) ordem f de pagamento □ vt fazer o rascunho de; (draw up) redigir. the ~ (Amer: mil) recrutamento m

draft[2] /drɑːft/ n (Amer) = draught

drag /dræg/ vt/i (pt dragged) arrastar(-se); (river) dragar; (pull away) arrancar □ n (colloq: task) chatice f (sl); (colloq: person) estorvo m; (sl: clothes) travesti m

dragon /'drægən/ n dragão m

dragonfly /'drægənflaɪ/ n libélula f

drain /dreɪn/ vt drenar; (vegetables) escorrer; (glass, tank) esvaziar; (use up) esgotar □ vi ~ (off) escoar-se □ n cano m. ~s npl (sewers) esgotos mpl. ~age n drenagem f. ~(-pipe) cano m de esgoto. ~ing-board n escorredouro m

drama /'drɑːmə/ n arte f dramática; (play, event) drama m. ~tic /drə'mætɪk/ a dramático. ~tist /'dræmətɪst/ n dramaturgo m. ~tize /'dræmətaɪz/ vt dramatizar

drank /dræŋk/ see **drink**

drape /dreɪp/ vt ~ round/over dispor (tecido) em pregas à volta de or sobre. ~s npl (Amer) cortinas fpl

drastic /'dræstɪk/ a drástico, violento

draught /drɑːft/ n corrente f de ar; (naut) calado m. ~s (game) (jogo m das) damas fpl. ~ beer chope m, (P) cerveja *f* à caneca, imperial *f* (*colloq*). ~y *a* com correntes de ar, ventoso

draughtsman /'drɑ:ftsmən/ *n* (*pl* -men) desenhista *m*, (*P*) desenhador *m*

draw /drɔ:/ *vt* (*pt* drew, *pp* drawn) puxar; (*attract*) atrair; (*picture*) desenhar; (*in lottery*) tirar à sorte; (*line*) traçar; (*open curtains*) abrir; (*close curtains*) fechar □ *vi* desenhar; (*sport*) empatar; (*come*) vir □ *n* (*sport*) empate *m*; (*lottery*) sorteio *m*. ~ back recuar. ~ in (*of days*) diminuir. ~ near aproximar-se. ~ out (*money*) levantar. ~ up deter-se, parar; (*document*) redigir; (*chair*) aproximar, chegar

drawback /'drɔ:bæk/ *n* inconveniente *m*, desvantagem *f*

drawer /drɔ:(r)/ *n* gaveta *f*

drawing /'drɔ:ɪŋ/ *n* desenho *m*. ~-board *n* prancheta *f*. ~-pin *n* percevejo *m*

drawl /drɔ:l/ *n* fala *f* arrastada

drawn /drɔ:n/ *see* draw

dread /dred/ *n* terror *m* □ *vt* temer

dreadful /'dredfl/ *a* medonho, terrível. ~ly *adv* terrivelmente

dream /dri:m/ *n* sonho *m* □ *vt/i* (*pt* dreamed *or* dreamt) sonhar (of com) □ *a* (*ideal*) dos seus sonhos. ~ up imaginar. ~er *n* sonhador *m*. ~y *a* sonhador; (*music*) romântico

dreary /'drɪərɪ/ *a* (-ier, -iest) tristonho; (*boring*) aborrecido

dredge /dredʒ/ *n* draga *f* □ *vt/i* dragar. ~r *-ə(r)/ *n* draga *f*; (*for sugar*) polvilhador *m*

dregs /dregz/ *npl* depósito *m*, sedimento *m*; (*fig*) escória *f*

drench /drentʃ/ *vt* encharcar

dress /dres/ *n* vestido *m*; (*clothing*) roupa *f* □ *vt/i* vestir(-se); (*food*) temperar; (*wound*) fazer curativo, (*P*) pensar, (*P*) tratar. ~ rehearsal ensaio *m* geral. ~ up as fantasiar-se de. get ~ed vestir-se

dresser /'dresə(r)/ *n* (*furniture*) guarda-louça *m*

dressing /'dresɪŋ/ *n* (*sauce*) tempero *m*; (*bandage*) curativo *m*, (*P*) penso *m*. ~-gown *n* roupão *m*. ~-room *n* (*sport*) vestiário *m*; (*theat*) camarim *m*. ~-table *n* toucador *m*

dressmak|er /'dresmeɪkə(r)/ *n* costureira *f*, modista *f*. ~ing *n* costura *f*

dressy /'dresɪ/ *a* (-ier, -iest) elegante, chique *invar*

drew /dru:/ *see* draw

dribble /'drɪbl/ *vi* pingar; (*person*) babar-se; (*football*) driblar

dried /draɪd/ *a* (*fruit etc*) seco

drier /'draɪə(r)/ *n* secador *m*

drift /drɪft/ *vi* ir à deriva; (*pile up*) amontoar-se □ *n* força *f* da corrente;

(*pile*) monte *m*; (*of events*) rumo *m*; (*meaning*) sentido *m*. ~er *n* pessoa *f* sem rumo

drill /drɪl/ *n* (*tool*) broca *f*; (*training*) exercício *m*, treino *m*; (*routine procedure*) exercícios *mpl* □ *vt* furar, perfurar; (*train*) treinar; (*tooth*) abrir □ *vi* treinar-se

drink /drɪŋk/ *vt/i* (*pt* drank, *pp* drunk) beber □ *n* bebida *f*. a ~ of water um copo de água. ~able *a* potável; (*palatable*) bebível. ~er *n* bebedor *m*. ~ing water água *f* potável

drip /drɪp/ *vi* (*pt* dripped) pingar □ *n* pingar *m*; (*sl: person*) banana *mf* (*colloq*). ~-dry *vt* deixar escorrer □ *a* que não precisa passar

dripping /'drɪpɪŋ/ *n* gordura *f* do assado

drive /draɪv/ *vt* (*pt* drove, *pp* driven /'drɪvn/) empurrar, impelir, levar; (*car, animal*) dirigir, conduzir, (*P*) guiar; (*machine*) acionar, (*P*) accionar □ *vi* dirigir, conduzir, (*P*) guiar □ *n* passeio *m* de carro; (*private road*) entrada *f* para veículos; (*fig*) energia *f*; (*psych*) drive *m*, compulsão *f*, impulso *m*; (*campaign*) campanha *f*. ~ at chegar a. ~ away (*car*) partir. ~ in (*force in*) enterrar. ~-in *n* (*bank, cinema etc*) banco *m*, cinema *m etc* em que se é atendido no carro, drive-in *m*. ~ mad (fazer) enlouquecer, pôr fora de si

drivel /'drɪvl/ *n* baboseira *f*, bobagem *f*

driver /'draɪvə(r)/ *n* condutor *m*; (*of taxi, bus*) chofer *m*, motorista *mf*

driving /'draɪvɪŋ/ *n* condução *f*. ~-licence *n* carteira *f* de motorista, (*P*) carta *f* de condução. ~ school auto-escola *f*, (*P*) escola *f* de condução. ~ test exame *m* de motorista, (*P*) de condução

drizzle /'drɪzl/ *n* chuvisco *m* □ *vi* chuviscar

drone /drəʊn/ *n* zumbido *m*; (*male bee*) zangão *m* □ *vi* zumbir; (*fig*) falar monotonamente

drool /dru:l/ *vi* babar(-se)

droop /dru:p/ *vi* pender, curvar-se

drop /drɒp/ *n* gota *f*; (*fall*) queda *f*; (*distance*) altura *f* de queda □ *vt/i* (*pt* dropped) (deixar) cair; (*fall, lower*) baixar. ~ (*off*) (*person from car*) deixar, largar. ~ a line escrever duas linhas (to a). ~ in passar por (on em casa de). ~ off (*doze*) adormecer. ~ out (*withdraw*) retirar-se; (*of student*) abandonar. ~-out *n* marginal *mf*, marginalizado *m*

droppings /'drɒpɪŋz/ *npl* excrementos *mpl* de animal; (*of birds*) cocô *m* (*colloq*), porcaria *f* (*colloq*)

dross /drɒs/ n escória f; (refuse) lixo m

drought /draut/ n seca f

drove /drəʊv/ see drive

drown /draʊn/ vt/i afogar(-se)

drowsy /'draʊzɪ/ a sonolento. be or feel ~ ter vontade de dormir

drudge /drʌdʒ/ n mouro m de trabalho. ~ry /-ərɪ/ n trabalho m penoso e monótono, estafa f

drug /drʌg/ n droga f; (med) medicamento m, remédio m □ vt (pt drugged) drogar. ~ addict drogado m, tóxico-dependente m

drugstore /'drʌgstɔː(r)/ n (Amer) farmácia f que vende também sorvetes etc

drum /drʌm/ n (mus) tambor m; (for oil) barril m, tambor m. ~s (mus) bateria f □ vi (pt drummed) tocar tambor; (with one's fingers) tamborilar □ vt ~ into sb fazer entrar na cabeça de alg. ~ up (support) conseguir obter; (business) criar. ~mer n tambor m; (in pop group etc) baterista m, (P) bateria f

drunk /drʌŋk/ see drink □ a embriagado, bêbedo. get ~ embebedar-se, embriagar-se □ n bêbedo m. ~ard n alcoólico m, bêbedo m. ~en a embriagado, bêbedo; (habitually) bêbedo

dry /draɪ/ a (drier, driest) seco; (day) sem chuva □ vt/i secar. be or feel ~ ter sede. ~-clean vt limpar a seco. ~-cleaner's n (loja de) lavagem f a seco, lavandaria f. ~ up (dishes) secar a louça f; (of supplies) esgotar-se. ~ness n secura f

dual /'djuːəl/ a duplo. ~ carriageway estrada f dividida por faixa central. ~-purpose a com fim duplo

dub /dʌb/ vt (pt dubbed) (film) dobrar; (nickname) apelidar de

dubious /'djuːbɪəs/ a duvidoso; (character, compliment) dúbio. feel ~ about ter dúvidas quanto a

duchess /'dʌtʃɪs/ n duquesa f

duck /dʌk/ n pato m □ vi abaixar-se rapidamente □ vt (head) baixar; (person) batizar, pregar uma amona em. ~ling n patinho m

duct /dʌkt/ n canal m, tubo m

dud /dʌd/ a (sl: thing) que não presta ou não funciona; (sl: coin) falso; (sl: cheque) sem fundos, (P) careca (sl)

due /djuː/ a devido; (expected) esperado □ adv ~ east/etc exatamente, (P) exactamente a leste/etc □ n devido m. ~s direitos mpl; (of club) cota f. ~ to devido a, por causa de. in ~ course no tempo devido

duel /'djuːəl/ n duelo m

duet /dju:'et/ n dueto m

duffel /'dʌfl/ a ~ bag saco m de lona. ~-coat n casaco m de tecido de lã

dug /dʌg/ see dig

duke /djuːk/ n duque m

dull /dʌl/ a (-er, -est) (boring) enfadonho; (colour) morto; (mirror) embaçado; (weather) encoberto; (sound) surdo; (stupid) burro

duly /'djuːlɪ/ adv devidamente; (in due time) no tempo devido

dumb /dʌm/ a (-er, -est) mudo; (colloq: stupid) bronco, burro

dumbfound /dʌm'faʊnd/ vt pasmar

dummy /'dʌmɪ/ n imitação f, coisa f simulada; (of tailor) manequim m; (of baby) chupeta f

dump /dʌmp/ vt (rubbish) jogar fora; (put down) deixar cair; (colloq: abandon) largar □ n monte m de lixo; (tip) lixeira f; (mil) depósito m; (colloq) buraco m

dunce /dʌns/ n burro m. ~'s cap orelhas fpl de burro

dune /djuːn/ n duna f

dung /dʌŋ/ n esterco m; (manure) estrume m

dungarees /dʌŋgə'riːz/ npl macacão m, (P) fato m de macaco

dungeon /'dʌndʒən/ n calabouço m, masmorra f

dupe /djuːp/ vt enganar □ n trouxa m

duplicate[1] /'djuːplɪkət/ n duplicado m □ a idêntico

duplicate[2] /'djuːplɪkeɪt/ vt duplicar, fazer em duplicado; (on machine) fotocopiar

duplicity /djuː'plɪsətɪ/ n duplicidade f

durable /'djʊərəbl/ a resistente; (enduring) duradouro, durável

duration /djʊ'reɪʃn/ n duração f

duress /djʊ'res/ n under ~ sob coação f, (P) coacção f

during /'djʊərɪŋ/ prep durante

dusk /dʌsk/ n crepúsculo m, anoitecer m

dusky /'dʌskɪ/ a (-ier, -iest) escuro, sombrio

dust /dʌst/ n pó m, poeira f □ vt limpar o pó de; (sprinkle) polvilhar. ~-jacket n sobrecapa f de livro

dustbin /'dʌstbɪn/ n lata f do lixo, (P) caixote m

duster /'dʌstə(r)/ n pano m do pó

dustman /'dʌstmən/ n (pl -men) lixeiro m, (P) homem m do lixo

dusty /'dʌstɪ/ a (-ier, -iest) poeirento, empoeirado

Dutch /dʌtʃ/ a holandês □ n (lang) holandês m. ~man n holandês m. ~woman n holandesa f. go ~ pagar cada um a sua despesa

dutiful /'djuːtɪfl/ a cumpridor; (showing respect) respeitador dut|y /'dju:tɪ/ n dever m; (tax) impostos mpl. ~ies (of official etc) funções fpl. off ~y de folga. on ~y de serviço. ~y-free a isento de impostos. ~y-free shop free shop m

duvet /'dju:veɪ/ n edredom m, (P) edredão m de penas

dwarf /dwɔːf/ n (pl -fs) anão m

dwell /dwel/ vi (pt dwelt) morar. ~ on alongar-se sobre. ~er n habitante. ~ing n habitação f

dwindle /'dwɪndl/ vi diminuir, reduzir-se

dye /daɪ/ vt (pres p dyeing) tingir □ n tinta f

dying /'daɪɪŋ/ see die

dynamic /daɪ'næmɪk/ a dinâmico

dynamite /'daɪnəmaɪt/ n dinamite f □ vt dinamitar

dynamo /'daɪnəməʊ/ n (pl -os) dínamo m

dynasty /'dɪnəstɪ/ n dinastia f

dysentery /'dɪsəntrɪ/ n disenteria f

dyslex|ia /dɪs'leksɪə/ n dislexia f. ~ic a disléxico

E

each /iːtʃ/ a & pron cada. ~ one cada um. ~ other um ao outro, uns aos outros. they like ~ other gostam um do outro/uns dos outros. know/love/etc ~ other conhecer-se/amar-se/etc

eager /'iːgə(r)/ a ansioso (to por), desejoso (for de); (supporter) entusiástico. be ~ to ter vontade de. ~ly adv com impaciência, ansiosamente; (keenly) com entusiasmo. ~ness n ansiedade f, desejo m; (keenness) entusiasmo m

eagle /'iːgl/ n águia f

ear /ɪə(r)/ n ouvido m; (external part) orelha f. ~-drum n tímpano m. ~-ring n brinco m

earache /'ɪəreɪk/ n dor f de ouvidos

earl /ɜːl/ n conde m

early /'ɜːlɪ/ (-ier, -iest) adv cedo □ a primeiro; (hour) matinal; (fruit) temporão; (retirement) antecipado. have an ~ dinner jantar cedo. in ~ summer no princípio do verão

earmark /'ɪəmɑːk/ vt destinar, reservar (for para)

earn /ɜːn/ vt ganhar; (deserve) merecer

earnest /'ɜːnɪst/ a sério. in ~ a sério

earnings /'ɜːnɪŋz/ npl salário m; (profits) ganhos mpl, lucros mpl

earshot /'ɪəʃɒt/ n within ~ ao alcance da voz

earth /ɜːθ/ n terra f □ vt (electr) ligar à terra. why on ~? por que diabo?, por que cargas d'água? ~ly a terrestre, terreno

earthenware /'ɜːθənweə(r)/ n louça f de barro, faiança f

earthquake /'ɜːθkweɪk/ n tremor m de terra, terremoto m

earthy /'ɜːθɪ/ a terroso, térreo; (coarse) grosseiro

earwig /'ɪəwɪg/ n lacrainha f, (P) bicha-cadela f

ease /iːz/ n facilidade f; (comfort) bem-estar m □ vt/i (from pain, anxiety) acalmar(-se); (slow down) afrouxar; (slide) deslizar. at ~ à vontade; (mil) descansar. ill at ~ pouco à vontade. with ~ facilmente. ~ in/out fazer entrar/sair com cuidado

easel /'iːzl/ n cavalete m

east /iːst/ n este m, leste m, pas-cente m, oriente m. the E~ o Oriente □ a este, (de) leste, oriental □ adv a/para leste. ~ of para o leste de ~erly a oriental, leste, a/de leste ~ward a, ~ward(s) adv para leste

Easter /'iːstə(r)/ n Páscoa f. ~ egg ovo m de Páscoa

eastern /'iːstən/ a oriental, leste

easy /'iːzɪ/ a (-ier, -iest) fácil; (relaxed) natural, descontraído. take it ~ levar as coisas com calma. ~ chair poltrona f. ~-going a bonacheirão. easily adv facilmente

eat /iːt/ vt/i (pt ate, pp eaten) comer. ~ into corroer. ~able a comestível

eaves /iːvz/ npl beiral m

eavesdrop /'iːvzdrɒp/ vi (pt -dropped) escutar por detrás da porta

ebb /eb/ n vazante f, baixa-mar m □ vi vazar; (fig) declinar

EC /iː'siː/ n (abbr of European Community) CE f

eccentric /ɪk'sentrɪk/ a & n excêntrico (m). ~ity /eksen'trɪsətɪ/ n excentricidade f

ecclesiastical /ɪkliːzɪ'æstɪkl/ a eclesiástico

echo /'ekəʊ/ n (pl -oes) eco m □ vt/i (pt echoed, pres p echoing) ecoar; (fig) repetir

eclipse /ɪ'klɪps/ n eclipse m □ vt eclipsar

ecolog|y /iː'kɒlədʒɪ/ n ecologia f. ~ical /iːkə'lɒdʒɪkl/ a ecológico

economic /iːkə'nɒmɪk/ a econômico, (P) económico; (profitable) rentável. ~al a econômico, (P) económico. ~s n economia f política

economist /ɪ'kɒnəmɪst/ n economista mf

econom|y /ɪ'kɒnəmɪ/ n economia f. ~ize vi/t economizar

ecstasy /'ekstəsɪ/ n êxtase m

ecstatic /ɪk'stætɪk/ a extático, extasiado

ecu /'eɪkjuː/ n unidade f monetária européia

eczema /'eksmə/ n eczema m

edge /edʒ/ n borda f, beira f; (of town) periferia f, limite m; (of knife) fio m □ vt debruar □ vi (move) avançar pouco a pouco

edging /'edʒɪŋ/ n borda f, (P) bordadura f

edgy /'edʒɪ/ a irritadiço, nervoso

edible /'edɪbl/ a comestível

edict /'iːdɪkt/ n édito m

edifice /'edɪfɪs/ n edifício m

edit /'edɪt/ vt (pt edited) (newspaper) dirigir; (text) editar

edition /ɪ'dɪʃn/ n edição f

editor /'edɪtə(r)/ n (of newspaper) diretor m, (P) director m, editor m responsável; (of text) organizador m de texto. the ~ (in chief) redatorchefe m, (P) redactor-chefe m. ~ial /edɪ'tɔːrɪəl/ a & n editorial (m)

educat|e /'edʒʊkeɪt/ vt instruir; (mind, public) educar. ~ed a instruído; educado. ~ion /-'keɪʃn/ n educação f; (schooling) ensino m. ~ional /'keɪʃənl/ a educativo, pedagógico

EEC /iːiːˈsiː/ n (abbr of European Economic Community) CEE f

eel /iːl/ n enguia f

eerie /'ɪərɪ/ a (-ier, -iest) arrepiante, misterioso

effect /ɪ'fekt/ n efeito m □ vt efetuar, (P) efectuar. come into ~ entrar em vigor. in ~ na realidade. take ~ ter efeito

effective /ɪ'fektɪv/ a eficaz, eficiente; (striking) sensacional; (actual) efetivo, (P) efectivo. ~ly adv (efficiently) eficazmente; (strikingly) de forma sensacional; (actually) efetivamente, (P) efectivamente. ~ness n eficácia f

effeminate /ɪ'femɪnət/ a efeminado, afeminado

effervescent /efə'vesnt/ a efervescente

efficien|t /ɪ'fɪʃnt/ a eficiente, eficaz. ~cy n eficiência f. ~tly adv eficientemente

effigy /'efɪdʒɪ/ n efígie f

effort /'efət/ n esforço m. ~less a fácil, sem esforço

effrontery /ɪ'frʌntərɪ/ n desfaçatez f

effusive /ɪ'fjuːsɪv/ a efusivo, expansivo

e.g. /iːˈdʒiː/ abbr por ex

egg /eg/ n ovo m. ~-cup n copinho m para ovo quente, oveiro m. ~-plant n beringela f

egg² /eg/ vt ~ on (colloq) incitar

eggshell /'egʃel/ n casca f de ovo

ego /'egəʊ/ n (pl -os) ego m, eu m. ~ism n egoísmo m. ~ist n egoísta mf. ~tism n egotismo m. ~tist n egotista mf

Egypt /'iːdʒɪpt/ n Egito m. ~ian /ɪ'dʒɪpʃn/ a & n egípcio (m)

eh /eɪ/ int (colloq) hã?

eiderdown /'aɪdədaʊn/ n edredão m, edredom m

eight /eɪt/ a & n oito (m). eighth /eɪtθ/ a & n oitavo (m)

eighteen /eɪ'tiːn/ a & n dezoito (m). ~th a & n décimo-oitavo (m)

eight|y /'eɪtɪ/ a & n oitenta (m). ~ieth a & n octogésimo (m)

either /'aɪðə(r)/ a & pron um e outro; (with negative) nem um nem outro; (each) cada □ adv também não □ conj ~ ... or ou ... ou; (with negative) nem ... nem

ejaculate /ɪ'dʒækjʊleɪt/ vt/i ejacular; (exclaim) exclamar

eject /ɪ'dʒekt/ vt expelir; (expel) expulsar, despejar

elaborate¹ /ɪ'læbərət/ a elaborado, rebuscado, minucioso

elaborate² /ɪ'læbəreɪt/ vt elaborar □ vi entrar em pormenores. ~ on estender-se sobre

elapse /ɪ'læps/ vi decorrer

elastic /ɪ'læstɪk/ a & n elástico (m). ~ band elástico m

elat|ed /ɪ'leɪtɪd/ a radiante, exultante. ~ion n exultação f

elbow /'elbəʊ/ n cotovelo m

elder¹ /'eldə(r)/ a mais velho. ~s npl pessoas fpl mais velhas

elder² /'eldə(r)/ n (tree) sabugueiro m

elderly /'eldəlɪ/ a idoso. the ~ as pessoas fpl de idade

eldest /'eldɪst/ a & n o mais velho (m)

elect /ɪ'lekt/ vt eleger □ a eleito. ~ion /-kʃn/ n eleição f

electric /ɪ'lektrɪk/ a elétrico, (P) eléctrico. ~al a elétrico, (P) eléctrico

electrician /ɪlek'trɪʃn/ n eletricista m, (P) electricista m

electricity /ɪlek'trɪsətɪ/ n eletricidade f, (P) electricidade f

electrify /ɪ'lektrɪfaɪ/ vt eletrificar, (P) electrificar; (fig: excite) eletrizar, (P) electrizar

electrocute /ɪ'lektrəkjuːt/ vt eletrocutar, (P) electrocutar

electronic /ɪlek'trɒnɪk/ a eletrônico, (P) electrónico. ~s n eletrónica f, (P) electrónica f

elegan|t /'elɪgənt/ a elegante. ~ce n elegância f. ~tly adv elegantemente, com elegância

element /'elɪmənt/ n elemento m; (of heater etc) resistência f. ~ary /-'mentrɪ/ a elementar; (school) primário

elephant /'elɪfənt/ n elefante m

elevat|e /'elɪveɪt/ vt elevar. ~ion n elevação f

elevator /'elɪveɪtə(r)/ n (Amer: lift) elevador m, ascensor m eleven /ɪˈlevn/ a & n onze (m). ~th a & n décimo primeiro (m). at the ~th hour à última hora

elf /elf/ n (pl elves) elfo m, duende m

elicit /ɪˈlɪsɪt/ vt extrair, obter

eligible /ˈelɪdʒəbl/ a (for office) idóneo, (P) idóneo (for para); (desirable) aceitável. be ~ for (entitled to) ter direito a

eliminate /ɪˈlɪmɪneɪt/ vt eliminar. ~ion /-ˈneɪʃn/ n eliminação f

élite /erˈliːt/ n elite f

ellipse /ɪˈlɪps/ n elipse f. ~tical a elíptico

elm /elm/ n olmo m, ulmeiro m

elocution /eləˈkjuːʃn/ n elocução f

elongate /ˈiːlɒŋgert/ vt alongar

elope /ɪˈləʊp/ vi fugir. ~ment n fuga f (de amantes), (P) (de amorosos)

eloquent /ˈeləkwənt/ a eloquente, (P) eloquente. ~ce n eloquência f, (P) eloquência f

else /els/ adv mais. everybody ~ todos os outros. nobody ~ mais ninguém. nothing ~ nada mais. or ~ ou então, senão. somewhere ~ noutro lado qualquer. ~where adv noutro lado

elude /ɪˈluːd/ vt escapar a; (a question) evadir

elusive /ɪˈluːsɪv/ a (person) esquivo, difícil de apanhar; (answer) evasivo

emaciated /ɪˈmeɪʃɪertɪd/ a emaciado, macilento

emancipate /ɪˈmænsɪpert/ vt emancipar. ~ion /-ˈpeɪʃn/ n emancipação f

embalm /ɪmˈbaːm/ vt embalsamar

embankment /ɪmˈbæŋkmənt/ n (of river) dique m; (of railway) terrapleno m, talude m, (P) aterro m

embargo /ɪmˈbaːgəʊ/ n (pl -oes) embargo m

embark /ɪmˈbaːk/ vt/i embarcar. ~ on (business etc) embarcar em, meter-se em (collog); (journey) começar

embarrass /ɪmˈbærəs/ vt embaraçar, confundir. ~ment n embaraço m, atrapalhação f

embassy /ˈembəsɪ/ n embaixada f

embellish /ɪmˈbelɪʃ/ vt embelezar, enfeitar. ~ment n embelezamento m, enfeite m

embezzle /ɪmˈbezl/ vt desviar (fundos). ~ment n desfalque m

embitter /ɪmˈbɪtə(r)/ vt (person) amargurar; (situation) azedar

emblem /ˈembləm/ n emblema m

embody /ɪmˈbɒdɪ/ vt encarnar; (include) incorporar, incluir. ~iment n personificação f

emboss /ɪmˈbɒs/ vt (metal) gravar em relevo; (paper) gofrar

embrace /ɪmˈbreɪs/ vt/i abraçar(-se); (offer, opportunity) acolher □ n abraço m

embroider /ɪmˈbrɔɪdə(r)/ vt bordar. ~y n bordado m

embryo /ˈembrɪəʊ/ n (pl -os) embrião m. ~nic /-ˈɒnɪk/ a embrionário

emerald /ˈemərəld/ n esmeralda f

emerge /ɪˈmɜːdʒ/ vi emergir, surgir

emergency /ɪˈmɜːdʒənsɪ/ n emergência f; (urgent case) urgência f. ~ exit saída f de emergência. in an ~ em caso de urgência

emigrant /ˈemɪgrənt/ n emigrante mf

emigrate /ˈemɪgreɪt/ vi emigrar. ~ion /ˈgreɪʃn/ n emigração f

eminent /ˈemɪnənt/ a eminente. ~tly adv eminentemente

emit /ɪˈmɪt/ vt (pt emitted) emitir. ~ssion /-ʃn/ n emissão f

emotion /ɪˈməʊʃn/ n emoção f. ~al a (person, shock) emotivo; (speech, scene) emocionante

emperor /ˈempərə(r)/ n imperador m

emphasis /ˈemfəsɪs/ n ênfase f. lay ~ on pôr em relevo

emphasize /ˈemfəsaɪz/ vt enfatizar, sublinhar; (syllable, word) acentuar

emphatic /ɪmˈfætɪk/ a enfático; (manner) enérgico. ~ally adv enfaticamente

empire /ˈempaɪə(r)/ n império m

employ /ɪmˈplɔɪ/ vt empregar. ~ee /emplɔɪˈiː/ n empregado m. ~er n patrão m. ~ment n emprego m. ~ment agency agência f de empregos

empower /ɪmˈpaʊə(r)/ vt autorizar (to do a fazer)

empress /ˈemprɪs/ n imperatriz f

empty /ˈemptɪ/ a vazio; (promise) falso □ vt/i esvaziar(-se). on an ~y stomach com o estômago vazio, em jejum. ~ies npl garrafas fpl vazias. ~iness n vazio m

emulate /ˈemjʊleɪt/ vt imitar, rivalizar com, emular com

emulsion /ɪˈmʌlʃn/ n emulsão f

enable /ɪˈneɪbl/ vt ~ sb to do permitir a alg fazer

enact /ɪˈnækt/ vt (jur) decretar; (theat) representar

enamel /ɪˈnæml/ n esmalte m □ vt (pt enamelled) esmaltar

enamoured /ɪˈnæməd/ a ~ of enamorado de, apaixonado por

encase /ɪnˈkeɪs/ vt encerrar (in em); (cover) revestir (in de)

enchant /ɪnˈtʃaːnt/ vt encantar. ~ing a encantador. ~ment n encantamento m

encircle /ɪnˈsɜːkl/ vt cercar, rodear

enclose /ɪnˈkləʊz/ vt (land) cercar; (with letter) enviar incluso/junto. ~d a (space) fechado; (with letter) anexo, incluso, junto enclosure /ɪnˈkləʊʒə(r)/ n cercado m, recinto m; (with letter) documento m anexo

encompass /ɪnˈkʌmpəs/ vt abranger

encore /ɒŋˈkɔː(r)/ int & n bis (m)

encounter /ɪnˈkaʊntə(r)/ vt encontrar, deparar com □ n encontro m

encourage /ɪnˈkʌrɪdʒ/ vt encorajar. ~ment n encorajamento m

encroach /ɪnˈkrəʊtʃ/ vi ~ on (land) invadir; (time) abusar de

encumber /ɪnˈkʌmbə(r)/ vt estorvar; (burden) sobrecarregar. ~rance n estorvo m, empecilho m; (burden) ónus m, (P) ónus m, encargo m

encyclopedia /ɪnsaɪkləˈpiːdɪə/ n enciclopédia f. ~ic a enciclopédico

end /end/ n fim m; (farthest part) extremo m, ponta f □ vt/i acabar, terminar. ~ up (arrive finally) ir parar (in a/em). ~ up doing acabar por fazer. in the ~ por fim. no ~ of (colloq) muito, enorme, imenso. on ~ (upright) em pé; (consecutive) a fio, de seguida

endanger /ɪnˈdeɪndʒə(r)/ vt pôr em perigo

endearing /ɪnˈdɪərɪŋ/ a cativante. ~ment n palavra f meiga; (act) carinho m

endeavour /ɪnˈdevə(r)/ n esforço m □ vi esforçar-se (to por)

ending /ˈendɪŋ/ n fim m; (of word) terminação f

endless /ˈendlɪs/ a interminável; (times) sem conta; (patience) infinito

endorse /ɪnˈdɔːs/ vt (document) endossar; (action) aprovar. ~ment n (auto) averbamento m

endow /ɪnˈdaʊ/ vt doar. ~ment n doação f

endure /ɪnˈdjʊə(r)/ vt suportar □ vi durar. ~able a suportável. ~ance n resistência f

enemy /ˈenəmɪ/ n & a inimigo (m)

energetic /enəˈdʒetɪk/ a enérgico

energy /ˈenədʒɪ/ n energia f

enforce /ɪnˈfɔːs/ vt aplicar

engage /ɪnˈɡeɪdʒ/ vt (staff) contratar; (mech) engrenar □ vi ~ in envolver-se em, lançar-se em. ~d a noivo; (busy) ocupado. ~ment n noivado m; (undertaking, appointment) compromisso m; (mil) combate m

engender /ɪnˈdʒendə(r)/ vt engendrar, produzir, causar

engine /ˈendʒɪn/ n motor m; (of train) locomotiva f

engineer /endʒɪˈnɪə(r)/ n engenheiro m □ vt engenhar. ~ing n engenharia f

England /ˈɪŋɡlənd/ n Inglaterra f

English /ˈɪŋɡlɪʃ/ a inglês □ n (lang) inglês m. the ~ os ingleses mpl.

~man n inglês m. ~-speaking a de língua inglesa f. ~woman n inglesa f

engrave /ɪnˈɡreɪv/ vt gravar. ~-ing n gravura f

engrossed /ɪnˈɡrəʊst/ a absorto (in em)

engulf /ɪnˈɡʌlf/ vt engolfar, tragar

enhance /ɪnˈhɑːns/ vt aumentar; (heighten) realçar

enigma /ɪˈnɪɡmə/ n enigma m. ~tic /enɪɡˈmætɪk/ a enigmático

enjoy /ɪnˈdʒɔɪ/ vt gostar de; (benefit from) gozar de. ~ o.s. divertir-se. ~able a agradável. ~ment n prazer m

enlarge /ɪnˈlɑːdʒ/ vt/i aumentar. ~ upon alargar-se sobre. ~ment n ampliação f

enlighten /ɪnˈlaɪtn/ vt esclarecer. ~ment n esclarecimento m, elucidação f

enlist /ɪnˈlɪst/ vt recrutar; (fig) aliciar, granjear □ vi alistar-se

enliven /ɪnˈlaɪvn/ vt animar

enmity /ˈenmətɪ/ n inimizade f

enormous /ɪˈnɔːməs/ a enorme

enough /ɪˈnʌf/ a, adv & n bastante (m), suficiente (m) □ int basta!, chega! have ~ of estar farto de

enquire /ɪnˈkwaɪə(r)/ vt/i perguntar, indagar. ~e about informar-se de, pedir informações sobre. ~y n pedido m de informações

enrage /ɪnˈreɪdʒ/ vt enfurecer, enraivecer

enrich /ɪnˈrɪtʃ/ vt enriquecer

enrol /ɪnˈrəʊl/ vt/i (pt enrolled) inscrever(-se); (schol) matricular(-se). ~ment n inscrição f, (schol) matrícula f

ensemble /ɒnˈsɒmbl/ n conjunto m

ensign /ˈensən/ n pavilhão m; (officer) guarda-marinha m

ensue /ɪnˈsjuː/ vi seguir-se. ~ing a decorrente

ensure /ɪnˈʃʊə(r)/ vt assegurar. ~ that assegurar-se de que

entail /ɪnˈteɪl/ vt acarretar

entangle /ɪnˈtæŋɡl/ vt emaranhar, enredar

enter /ˈentə(r)/ vt (room, club etc) entrar em; (register) registar; (data) entrar com □ vi entrar (into em). ~ for inscrever-se em

enterprise /ˈentəpraɪz/ n empresa f, empreendimento m; (fig) iniciativa f

enterprising /ˈentəpraɪzɪŋ/ a empreendedor

entertain /entəˈteɪn/ vt entreter; (guests) receber; (ideas) alimentar, nutrir. ~er n artista mf. ~ment n entretenimento m; (performance) espetáculo m, (P) espectáculo m enthral /ɪnˈθrɔːl/ vt (pt enthralled) fascinar

enthuse /ɪnˈθjuːz/ vi ~ over entusiasmar-se por

enthusias|m /ɪnˈθjuːzɪæzm/ n entusiasmo m. ~t n entusiasta mf. ~tic /-ˈæstɪk/ a entusiástico. ~tically /-ˈæstɪkəlɪ/ adv entusiasticamente

entice /ɪnˈtaɪs/ vt atrair. ~ to do induzir a fazer. ~ment n tentação f, engodo m

entire /ɪnˈtaɪə(r)/ a inteiro. ~ly adv inteiramente

entirety /ɪnˈtaɪərətɪ/ n in its ~ por inteiro, na (sua) totalidade

entitle /ɪnˈtaɪtl/ vt dar direito. ~d a (book) intitulado. be ~d to ter direito a qq coisa. ~ment n direito m

entity /ˈentɪtɪ/ n entidade f

entrance /ˈentrəns/ n entrada f (to para); (right to enter) admissão f

entrant /ˈentrənt/ n (sport) concorrente mf; (in exam) candidato m

entreat /ɪnˈtriːt/ vt rogar, suplicar. ~y n rogo m, súplica f

entrench /ɪnˈtrentʃ/ vt (mil) entrincheirar; (fig) fincar

entrust /ɪnˈtrʌst/ vt confiar

entry /ˈentrɪ/ n entrada f; (on list) item m; (in dictionary) verbete m. ~form ficha f de inscrição, (P) boletim m de inscrição. no ~ entrada proibida

enumerate /ɪˈnjuːməreɪt/ vt enumerar

envelop /ɪnˈveləp/ vt (pt enveloped) envolver

envelope /ˈenvələʊp/ n envelope m, sobrescrito m

enviable /ˈenvɪəbl/ a invejável

envious /ˈenvɪəs/ a invejoso. be ~ of ter inveja de. ~ly adv invejosamente, com inveja

environment /ɪnˈvaɪərənmənt/ n meio m; (ecological) meio-ambiente m. ~al /-ˈmentl/ a do meio; (ecological) do ambiente

envisage /ɪnˈvɪzɪdʒ/ vt encarar; (foresee) prever

envoy /ˈenvɔɪ/ n enviado m

envy /ˈenvɪ/ n inveja f □ vt invejar, ter inveja de

enzyme /ˈenzaɪm/ n enzima f

epic /ˈepɪk/ n epopéia f □ a épico

epidemic /epɪˈdemɪk/ n epidemia f

epilep|sy /ˈepɪlepsɪ/ n epilepsia f. ~tic /-ˈleptɪk/ a & n epiléptico (m)

episode /ˈepɪsəʊd/ n episódio m

epitaph /ˈepɪtɑːf/ n epitáfio m

epithet /ˈepɪθet/ n epíteto m

epitom|e /ɪˈpɪtəmɪ/ n (summary) epítome m; (embodiment) modelo m. ~ize vt (fig) representar, encarnar; (summarize) resumir

epoch /ˈiːpɒk/ n época f. ~-making a que marca uma época

equal /ˈiːkwəl/ a & n igual (m) □ vt (pt equalled) igualar, ser igual a. ~ to (task) à altura de. ~ity /iːˈkwɒlətɪ/ n igualdade f. ~ly adv igualmente; (similarly) de igual modo

equalize /ˈiːkwəlaɪz/ vt/i igualar; (sport) empatar

equanimity /ekwəˈnɪmətɪ/ n equanimidade f, serenidade f

equate /ɪˈkweɪt/ vt equacionar (with com); (treat as equal) equiparar (with a)

equation /ɪˈkweɪʒn/ n equação f

equator /ɪˈkweɪtə(r)/ n equador m. ~ial /ekwəˈtɔːrɪəl/ a equatorial

equilibrium /iːkwɪˈlɪbrɪəm/ n equilíbrio m

equip /ɪˈkwɪp/ vt (pt equipped) equipar (with com), munir (with de). ~ment n equipamento m

equitable /ˈekwɪtəbl/ a eqüitativo, (P) equitativo

equity /ˈekwɪtɪ/ n eqüidade f, (P) equidade f

equivalent /ɪˈkwɪvələnt/ a & n eqüivalente (m), (P) equivalente (m)

equivocal /ɪˈkwɪvəkl/ a equívoco

era /ˈɪərə/ n era f, época f

eradicate /ɪˈrædɪkeɪt/ vt erradicar, suprimir

erase /ɪˈreɪz/ vt apagar. ~r /-ə(r)/ n borracha f (de apagar)

erect /ɪˈrekt/ a ereto, (P) erecto □ vt erigir. ~ion /-ʃn/ n ereção f, (P) erecção f; (building) construção f, edifício m

ero|de /ɪˈrəʊd/ vt corroer. ~sion /ˈrəʊʒn/ n erosão f

erotic /ɪˈrɒtɪk/ a erótico

err /ɜː(r)/ vi (pt erred) errar

errand /ˈerənd/ n recado m

erratic /ɪˈrætɪk/ a errático, irregular; (person) variável, imprevisível

erroneous /ɪˈrəʊnɪəs/ a erróneo, (P) errôneo, errado

error /ˈerə(r)/ n erro m

erudit|e /ˈeruːdaɪt/ a erudito. ~ion /-ˈdɪʃn/ n erudição f

erupt /ɪˈrʌpt/ vi (war, fire) irromper; (volcano) entrar em erupção. ~ion /-ʃn/ n erupção f

escalat|e /ˈeskəleɪt/ vt/i intensificar (-se); (of prices) subir em espiral. ~ion /ˈleɪʃn/ n escalada f

escalator /ˈeskəleɪtə(r)/ n escada f rolante

escapade /eskəˈpeɪd/ n peripécia f

escape /ɪˈskeɪp/ vi escapar-se □ vt escapar a □ n fuga f, (of prisoner) evasão f, fuga f. ~ from sb escapar de alguém. ~ to fugir para. have a lucky or narrow ~ escapar por um triz escapism /ɪˈskeɪpɪzəm/ n escapismo m

escort[1] /ˈeskɔːt/ n escolta f; (of woman) cavalheiro m, acompanhante m

escort[2] /ɪˈskɔːt/ vt escoltar; (accompany) acompanhar

escudo /esˈkjuːdəʊ/ n (pl -os) escudo m

Eskimo /ˈeskɪməʊ/ n (pl -os) esquimó mf

especial /ɪˈspeʃl/ a especial. ~ly adv especialmente

espionage /ˈespɪənɑːʒ/ n espionagem f

espouse /ɪˈspaʊz/ vt (a cause etc) abraçar

espresso /eˈspresəʊ/ n (pl -os) (coffee) expresso m

essay /ˈeseɪ/ n ensaio m; (schol) redação f, (P) redacção f

essence /ˈesns/ n essência f

essential /ɪˈsenʃl/ a essencial □ n the ~s o essencial m. ~ly adv essencialmente

establish /ɪˈstæblɪʃ/ vt estabelecer; (business, state) fundar; (prove) provar, apurar. ~ment n estabelecimento m; (institution) instituição f. the E~ment o Establishment m, a classe f dirigente

estate /ɪˈsteɪt/ n propriedade f; (possessions) bens mpl; (inheritance) herança f. ~ agent agente m imobiliário. (housing) ~ conjunto m habitacional. ~ car perua f

esteem /ɪˈstiːm/ vt estimar □ n estima f

estimate[1] /ˈestɪmət/ n cálculo m, avaliação f; (comm) orçamento m, estimativa f

estimat|e[2] /ˈestɪmeɪt/ vt calcular, estimar. ~ion /-ˈmeɪʃn/ n opinião f

estuary /ˈestʃʊərɪ/ n estuário m

etc abbr = et cetera /ɪtˈsetərə/ etc

etching /ˈetʃɪŋ/ n água-forte f

eternal /ɪˈtɜːnl/ a eterno

eternity /ɪˈtɜːnətɪ/ n eternidade f

ethic /ˈeθɪk/ n ética f. ~s ética f. ~al a ético

ethnic /ˈeθnɪk/ a étnico

etiquette /ˈetɪket/ n etiqueta f

etymology /etɪˈmɒlədʒɪ/ n etimologia f

eulogy /ˈjuːlədʒɪ/ n elogio m

euphemism /ˈjuːfəmɪzəm/ n eufemismo m

euphoria /juːˈfɔːrɪə/ n euforia f

Europe /ˈjʊərəp/ n Europa f. ~an /-ˈpɪən/ a & n europeu (m)

euthanasia /juːθəˈneɪzɪə/ n eutanásia f

evacuat|e /ɪˈvækjʊeɪt/ vt evacuar. ~ion /-ˈeɪʃn/ n evacuação f

evade /ɪˈveɪd/ vt evadir, esquivar-se a

evaluate /ɪˈvæljʊeɪt/ vt avaliar

evangelical /iːvænˈdʒelɪkl/ a evangélico

evaporat|e /ɪˈvæpəreɪt/ vt/i evaporar(-se). ~ed milk leite m evaporado. ~ion /-ˈreɪʃn/ n evaporação f

evasion /ɪˈveɪʒn/ n evasão f

evasive /ɪˈveɪsɪv/ a evasivo

eve /iːv/ n véspera f

even /ˈiːvn/ a regular; (surface) liso, plano; (amounts) igual; (number) par □ vt/i ~ up igualar(-se), acertar □ adv mesmo. ~ better ainda melhor. get ~ with ajustar contas com. ~ly adv uniformemente; (amounts) em partes iguais

evening /ˈiːvnɪŋ/ n entardecer m, anoitecer m; (whole evening) serão m. ~ class aula f à noite (para adultos). ~ dress traje m de cerimónia, (P) trajo m de cerimónia or de rigor; (woman's) vestido m de noite

event /ɪˈvent/ n acontecimento m. in the ~ of no caso de. ~ful a movimentado, memorável

eventual /ɪˈventʃʊəl/ a final. ~ity /-ˈælətɪ/ n eventualidade f. ~ly adv por fim; (in future) eventualmente

ever /ˈevə(r)/ adv jamais; (at all times) sempre. do you ~ go? você já foi alguma vez?, vais alguma vez? the best I ~ saw o melhor que já vi. ~ since adv desde então □ prep desde □ conj desde que. ~ so (colloq) muitíssimo, tão. hardly ~ quase nunca

evergreen /ˈevəgriːn/ n sempre-verde f, planta f de folhas persistentes □ a persistente

everlasting /ˈevəlɑːstɪŋ/ a eterno

every /ˈevrɪ/ a cada. ~ now and then de vez em quando, volta e meia. ~ one cada um. ~ other day dia sim dia não, de dois em dois dias. ~ three days de três em três dias

everybody /ˈevrɪbɒdɪ/ pron todo mundo, todos

everyday /ˈevrɪdeɪ/ a cotidiano, (P) quotidiano, diário; (common) do dia a dia, vulgar

everyone /ˈevrɪwʌn/ pron todo mundo, todos

everything /ˈevrɪθɪŋ/ pron tudo

everywhere /ˈevrɪweə(r)/ adv (position) em todo lugar, em toda parte; (direction) a todo lugar, a toda parte

evict /ɪˈvɪkt/ vt expulsar, despejar. ~ion /-ʃn/ n despejo m

evidence /ˈevɪdns/ n evidência f; (proof) prova f; (testimony) testemunho m, depoimento m. ~ of sinal de. give ~ testemunhar. in ~ em evidência

evident /ˈevɪdənt/ a evidente. ~ly adv evidentemente

evil /'i:vl/ a mau □ n mal m

evo|ke /ɪ'vəʊk/ vt evocar. ~cative /ɪ'vɒkətɪv/ a evocativo

evolution /i:və'lu:ʃn/ n evolução f

evolve /ɪ'vɒlv/ vi evolucionar, evoluir □ vt desenvolver, produzir

ex- /eks/ pref ex-

exacerbate /ɪg'zæsəbeɪt/ vt exacerbar

exact /ɪg'zækt/ a exato, (P) exacto □ vt exigir (from de). ~ing a exigente; (task) difícil. ~ly adv exatamente, (P) exactamente

exaggerat|e /ɪg'zædʒəreɪt/ vt/i exagerar. ~ion /-'reɪʃn/ n exagero m

exam /ɪg'zæm/ n (colloq) exame m

examination /ɪgzæmɪ'neɪʃn/ n exame m; (jur) interrogatório m

examine /ɪg'zæmɪn/ vt examinar; (witness etc) interrogar. ~r /-ə(r)/ n examinador m

example /ɪg'za:mpl/ n exemplo m. for ~ por exemplo. make an ~ of castigar para servir de exemplo

exasperat|e /ɪg'zæspəreɪt/ vt exasperar. ~ion /-'reɪʃn/ n exaspero m

excavat|e /'ekskəveɪt/ vt escavar; (uncover) desenterrar. ~ion /-'veɪʃn/ n escavação f

exceed /ɪk'si:d/ vt exceder; (speed limit) ultrapassar, exceder

excel /ɪk'sel/ vi (pt excelled) distinguir-se □ vt superar, ultrapassar

excellen|t /'eksələnt/ a excelente. ~ce n excelência f. ~tly adv excelentemente

except /ɪk'sept/ prep exceto, (P) excepto, fora □ vt excetuar, (P) exceptuar. ~ for a não ser, menos, salvo. ~ing prep à exceção de, (P) à excepção de. ~ion /-ʃn/ n exceção f, (P) excepção f. take ~ion to (object to) achar inaceitável; (be offended by) achar ofensivo

exceptional /ɪk'sepʃənl/ a excepcional. ~ly adv excepcionalmente

excerpt /'eksɜ:pt/ n trecho m, excerto m

excess[1] /ɪk'ses/ n excesso m

excess[2] /'ekses/ a excedente, em excesso. ~ fare excesso m, suplemento m. ~ luggage excesso m de peso

excessive /ɪk'sesɪv/ a excessivo. ~ly adv excessivamente

exchange /ɪks'tʃeɪndʒ/ vt trocar □ n troca f; (of currency) câmbio m. (telephone) ~ central f telefônica, (P) telefónica. ~ rate taxa f de câmbio

excise /'eksaɪz/ n imposto m (indireto, (P) indirecto)

excit|e /ɪk'saɪt/ vt excitar; (rouse) despertar; (enthuse) entusiasmar. ~able a excitável. get ~ed a excitado, excitar-se, entusiasmar-se. ~ement n excitação f. ~ing a excitante, emocionante

exclaim /ɪk'skleɪm/ vi exclamar

exclamation /eksklə'meɪʃn/ n exclamação f. ~ mark ponto m de exclamação

exclu|de /ɪk'sklu:d/ vt excluir. ~ding prep excluído. ~sion /ɪk'sklu:ʒn/ n exclusão f

exclusive /ɪk'sklu:sɪv/ a (rights etc) exclusivo; (club etc) seleto, (P) selecto; (news item) (em) exclusivo. ~ of sem incluir. ~ly adv exclusivamente

excruciating /ɪk'skru:ʃɪeɪtɪŋ/ a excruciante, atroz

excursion /ɪk'skɜ:ʃn/ n excursão f

excus|e[1] /ɪk'skju:z/ vt desculpar. ~e me! desculpe!, com licença! ~e from (exempt) dispensar de. ~able a desculpável

excuse[2] /ɪk'skju:s/ n desculpa f

ex-directory /eksdɪ'rektərɪ/ a que não vem no anuário, (P) na lista

execute /'eksɪkju:t/ vt executar

execution /eksɪ'kju:ʃn/ n execução f

executive /ɪg'zekjʊtɪv/ a & n executivo (m)

exemplary /ɪg'zemplərɪ/ a exemplar

exemplify /ɪg'zemplɪfaɪ/ vt exemplificar, ilustrar

exempt /ɪg'zempt/ a isento (from de) □ vt dispensar, eximir. ~ion /-ʃn/ n isenção f

exercise /'eksəsaɪz/ n exercício m □ vt (powers, restraint etc) exercer; (dog) levar para passear □ vi fazer exercício. ~ book caderno m

exert /ɪg'zɜ:t/ vt empregar, exercer. ~ o.s. esforçar-se, fazer um esforço. ~ion /-ʃn/ n esforço m

exhaust /ɪg'zɔ:st/ vt esgotar □ n (auto) (tubo de) escape m. ~ed a esgotado, exausto. ~ion /-stʃən/ n esgotamento m, exaustão f

exhaustive /ɪg'zɔ:stɪv/ a exaustivo, completo

exhibit /ɪg'zɪbɪt/ vt exibir, mostrar; (thing, collection) expor □ n objeto m, (P) objecto m exposto

exhibition /eksɪ'bɪʃn/ n exposição f; (act of showing) demonstração f

exhilarat|e /ɪg'zɪləreɪt/ vt regozijar; (invigorate) animar, estimular. ~ion /-'reɪʃn/ n animação f, alegria f

exhort /ɪg'zɔ:t/ vt exortar

exile /'eksaɪl/ n exílio m; (person) exilado m □ vt exilar, desterrar

exist /ɪg'zɪst/ vi existir. ~ence n existência f. be in ~ence existir

exit /'eksɪt/ n saída f

exonerate /ɪg'zɒnəreɪt/ vt exonerar

exorbitant /ɪg'zɔ:bɪtənt/ a exorbitante

exorcize /'eksɔ:saɪz/ vt esconjurar, exorcisar

exotic /ɪg'zɒtɪk/ a exótico

expan|d /ɪk'spænd/ vt/i expandir(-se); (extend) estender(-se), alargar(-se); (gas, liquid, metal) dilatar(-se). ~sion /ɪk'spænʃn/ n expansão f; (extension) alargamento m; (of gas etc) dilatação f

expanse /ɪk'spæns/ n extensão f

expatriate /eks'pætrɪət/ a & n expatriado (m)

expect /ɪk'spekt/ vt esperar; (suppose) crer, supor; (require) contar com, esperar; (baby) esperar. ~ to do contar fazer. ~ation /ekspek'teɪʃn/ n expectativa f

expectan|t /ɪk'spektənt/ a ~t mother gestante f. ~cy n expectativa f

expedient /ɪk'spiːdɪənt/ a oportuno □ n expediente m

expedition /ekspɪ'dɪʃn/ n expedição f

expel /ɪk'spel/ vt (pt expelled) expulsar; (gas, poison etc) expelir

expend /ɪk'spend/ vt despender. ~able a descartável

expenditure /ɪk'spendɪtʃə(r)/ n despesa f, gasto m

expense /ɪk'spens/ n despesa f; (cost) custo m. at sb's ~ à custa de alg. at the ~ of (fig) à custa de

expensive /ɪk'spensɪv/ a caro, dispendioso; (tastes, habits) de luxo

experience /ɪk'spɪərɪəns/ n experiência f □ vt experimentar; (feel) sentir. ~d a experiente

experiment /ɪk'sperɪmənt/ n experiência f □ vi /ɪk'sperɪment/ fazer uma experiência. ~al /-'mentl/ a experimental

expert /'ekspɜːt/ a & n perito (m). ~ly adv com perícia, habilmente

expertise /ekspɜː'tiːz/ n perícia f, competência f

expir|e /ɪk'spaɪə(r)/ vi expirar. ~y n fim m de prazo, expiração f

expl|ain /ɪk'spleɪn/ vt/i explicar. ~anation /eksplə'neɪʃn/ n explicação f. ~anatory /ɪk'splænətrɪ/ a explicativo

expletive /ɪk'spliːtɪv/ n imprecação f, praga f

explicit /ɪk'splɪsɪt/ a explícito

explo|de /ɪk'spləʊd/ vt/i (fazer) explodir. ~sion /ɪk'spləʊʒn/ n explosão f. ~sive a & n explosivo (m)

exploit¹ /'eksplɔɪt/ n façanha f

exploit² /ɪk'splɔɪt/ vt explorar. ~ation /eksplɔː'teɪʃn/ n exploração f

exploratory /ɪk'splɒrətrɪ/ a exploratório; (talks) preliminar

explor|e /ɪk'splɔː(r)/ vt explorar; (fig) examinar. ~ation /eksplə'reɪʃn/ n exploração f. ~er n explorador m

exponent /ɪk'spəʊnənt/ n (person) expoente mf; (math) expoente m

export¹ /ɪk'spɔːt/ vt exportar. ~er n exportador m

export² /'ekspɔːt/ n exportação f. ~s npl exportações fpl

expos|e /ɪk'spəʊz/ vt expor; (disclose) revelar; (unmask) desmascarar. ~ure /-ʒə(r)/ n exposição f; (cold) frio m

expound /ɪk'spaʊnd/ vt explanar, expor

express¹ /ɪk'spres/ a expresso, categórico □ adv (por) expresso □ n (train) rápido m, expresso m. ~ly adv expressamente

express² /ɪk'spres/ vt exprimir. ~ion /-ʃn/ n expressão f. ~ive a expressivo

expulsion /ɪk'spʌlʃn/ n expulsão f

exquisite /'ekskwɪzɪt/ a requintado

extempore /ek'stempərɪ/ a improvisado □ adv de improviso, sem preparação prévia

exten|d /ɪk'stend/ vt (stretch) estender; (enlarge) aumentar, ampliar; (prolong) prolongar; (grant) oferecer □ vi (stretch) estender-se; (in time) prolongar-se. ~sion /ɪk'stenʃn/ n (incl phone) extensão f; (of deadline) prorrogação f; (building) anexo m

extensive /ɪk'stensɪv/ a extenso; (damage, study) vasto. ~ly adv muito

extent /ɪk'stent/ n extensão f; (degree) medida f. to some ~ até certo ponto, em certa medida. to such an ~ that a tal ponto que

exterior /ɪk'stɪərɪə(r)/ a & n exterior (m)

exterminat|e /ɪk'stɜːmɪneɪt/ vt exterminar. ~ion /-'neɪʃn/ n exterminação f, extermínio m

external /ɪk'stɜːnl/ a externo. ~ly adv exteriormente

extinct /ɪk'stɪŋkt/ a extinto. ~ion /-ʃn/ n extinção f

extinguish /ɪk'stɪŋgwɪʃ/ vt extinguir, apagar. ~er n extintor m

extol /ɪk'stəʊl/ vt (pt extolled) exaltar, elogiar, louvar

extort /ɪk'stɔːt/ vt extorquir (from a). ~ion /-ʃn/ n extorsão f

extortionate /ɪk'stɔːʃənət/ a exorbitante

extra /'ekstrə/ a extra, adicional □ adv extra, excepcionalmente. ~ strong extra-forte □ n extra m; (cine, theat) extra mf, figurante mf. ~ time (football) prorrogação f

extra- /'ekstrə/ pref extra-

extract¹ /ɪk'strækt/ vt extrair; (promise, tooth) arrancar; (fig) obter. ~ion /-ʃn/ n extracção f, (P) extracção f; (descent) origem f

extract² /'ekstrækt/ n extrato m, (P) extracto m

extradit|e /'ekstrədaɪt/ vt extraditar. ~ion /-'dɪʃn/ n extradição f

extramarital /ekstrə'mærɪtl/ a extraconjugal, extramatrimonial

extraordinary /ɪk'strɔ:dnrɪ/ a extraordinário

extravagan|t /ɪk'strævəgənt/ a extravagante; (wasteful) esbanjador. ~ce n extravagância f; (wastefulness) esbanjamento m

extrem|e /ɪk'stri:m/ a & n extremo (m). ~ely adv extremamente. ~ist n extremista mf

extremity /ɪk'stremətɪ/ n extremidade f

extricate /'ekstrɪkeɪt/ vt desembaraçar, livrar

extrovert /'ekstrəvɜ:t/ n extrovertido m

exuberan|t /ɪg'zju:bərənt/ a exuberante. ~ce n exuberância f

exude /ɪg'zju:d/ vt (charm etc) destilar, ressumar (P) transpirar

exult /ɪg'zʌlt/ vi exultar

eye /aɪ/ n olho m □ vt (pt eyed, pres p eyeing) olhar. keep an ~ on vigiar. see ~ to ~ concordar inteiramente. ~-opener n revelação f. ~-shadow n sombra f

eyeball /'aɪbɔ:l/ n globo m ocular

eyebrow /'aɪbraʊ/ n sobrancelha f

eyelash /'aɪlæʃ/ n pestana f

eyelid /'aɪlɪd/ n pálpebra f

eyesight /'aɪsaɪt/ n vista f

eyesore /'aɪsɔ:(r)/ n monstruosidade f, horror m

eyewitness /'aɪwɪtnɪs/ n testemunha f ocular

F

fable /'feɪbl/ n fábula f

fabric /'fæbrɪk/ n tecido m; (structure) edifício m

fabricat|e /'fæbrɪkeɪt/ vt fabricar; (invent) urdir, inventar. ~ion /-'keɪʃn/ n fabrico m; (invention) invenção f

fabulous /'fæbjʊləs/ a fabuloso

façade /fə'sɑ:d/ n fachada f

face /feɪs/ n face f, cara f, rosto m; (expression) face f; (grimace) careta f; (of clock) mostrador m □ vt (look towards) encarar; (confront) enfrentar □ vi (be opposite) estar de frente para. ~ up to enfrentar. ~ to face cara a cara, frente a frente. in the ~ of em vista de. on the ~ of it a julgar pelas aparências. pull ~s fazer caretas. ~-cloth n toalha f de rosto, (P) toalhete m de rosto. ~-lift n cirurgia f plástica do rosto. ~-pack n máscara de beleza f

faceless /'feɪslɪs/ a (fig) anónimo, (P) anónimo

facet /'fæsɪt/ n faceta f

facetious /fə'si:ʃəs/ a faceto; (pej) engraçadinho (colloq pej)

facial /'feɪʃl/ a facial

facile /'fæsaɪl/ a fácil; (superficial) superficial

facilitate /fə'sɪlɪteɪt/ vt facilitar

facilit|y /fə'sɪlətɪ/ n facilidade f. ~ies (means) facilidades fpl; (installations) instalações fpl

facing /'feɪsɪŋ/ n revestimento m

facsimile /fæk'sɪmɪlɪ/ n fac-simile m

fact /fækt/ n fato m, (P) facto m. in ~, as a matter of ~ na realidade

faction /'fækʃn/ n facção f

factor /'fæktə(r)/ n fator m, (P) factor m

factory /'fæktərɪ/ n fábrica f

factual /'fæktʃʊəl/ a concreto, real

faculty /'fækltɪ/ n faculdade f

fad /fæd/ n capricho m, mania f; (craze) moda f

fade /feɪd/ vt/i (colour) desbotar; (sound) diminuir; (disappear) apagar(-se)

fag /fæg/ n (colloq: chore) estafa f; (sl: cigarette) cigarro m. ~ged a estafado

fail /feɪl/ vt/i falhar; (in an examination) reprovar; (omit, neglect) deixar de; (comm) falir □ n without ~ sem falta

failing /'feɪlɪŋ/ n deficiência f □ prep na falta de, à falta de

failure /'feɪljə(r)/ n fracasso m, (P) falhanço m; (of engine) falha f; (of electricity) falta f; (person) fracassado m

faint /feɪnt/ a (-er, -est) (indistinct) apagado; (weak) fraco; (giddy) tonto □ vi desmaiar □ n desmaio m. ~-hearted a tímido. ~ly adv vagamente. ~ness n debilidade f; (indistinctness) apagado m

fair¹ /feə(r)/ n feira f. ~-ground n parque m de diversões, (P) largo m de feira

fair² /feə(r)/ a (-er, -est) (of hair) louro; (weather) bom; (moderate quality) razoável; (just) justo. ~ play jogo m limpo, fair-play m. ~ly adv razoavelmente. ~ness n justiça f

fairy /'feərɪ/ n fada f. ~-story, ~-tale conto m de fadas

faith /feɪθ/ n fé f; (religion) religião f; (loyalty) lealdade f. in good ~ de boa fé, (P) à boa fé. ~-healer n curandeiro m

faithful /'feɪθfl/ a fiel. ~ly adv fielmente. yours ~ly atenciosamente. ~ness n fidelidade f

fake /feɪk/ n (thing) imitação f; (person) impostor m □ a falsificado □ vt falsificar; (pretend) simular, fingir

falcon /'fɔlkən/ n falcão m

fall /fɔ:l/ vi (pt fell, pp fallen) cair □ n quedas f; (Amer: autumn) outono m.

~s npl (waterfall) queda-d'água f. ~
back bater em retirada. ~ back
on recorrer a. ~ behind atrasar-se
(with em). ~ down or off cair. ~ flat
falhar, não resultar. ~ flat on one's
face estatelar-se. ~ for (a trick) cair
em, deixar-se levar por; (colloq: a person) apaixonar-se por, ficar caído por
(colloq). ~ in (roof) ruir; (mil) ali-
nhar-se, pôr-se em forma. ~ out brigar, (P) zangar-se (with com). ~-out
n poeira f radioactiva, (P) radioactiva.
~ through (of plans) falhar

fallac|y /'fæləsɪ/ n falácia f, engano m.
~ious /fə'leɪʃəs/ a errôneo

fallen /'fɔːlən/ see fall

fallible /'fæləbl/ a falível

fallow /'fæləʊ/ a (of ground) de pou-
sio; (uncultivated) inculto

false /fɔːls/ a falso. ~ teeth~ly adv
falsamente. ~ness n falsidade f

falsehood /'fɔːlshʊd/ n falsidade f,
mentira f

falsify /'fɔːlsɪfaɪ/ vt (pt -fied) falsificar; (a story) deturpar

falter /'fɔːltə(r)/ vi vacilar; (of the
voice) hesitar

fame /feɪm/ n fama f. ~d a afamado

familiar /fə'mɪlɪə(r)/ a familiar; (intimate) íntimo. be ~ with estar familiarizado com

familiarity /fəmɪlɪˈærɪtɪ/ n familiari-
dade f

familiarize /fə'mɪlɪəraɪz/ vt familia-
rizar (with/to com); (make well
known) tornar conhecido

family /'fæmɪlɪ/ n família f. ~ doctor
médico m da família. ~ tree árvore f
genealógica

famine /'fæmɪn/ n fome f

famished /'fæmɪʃt/ a esfomeado,
faminto. be ~ (colloq) estar morren-
do de fome, (P) estar a morrer de
fome

famous /'feɪməs/ a famoso

fan[1] /fæn/ n (in the hand) leque m;
(mechanical) ventilador m, (P)
ventoínha f. ~ vt (pt fanned) abanar;
(a fire; fig) atiçar □ vi. ~ out abrir-se
em leque. ~ belt correia f da ventoí-
nhas

fan[2] /fæn/ n (colloq) fã mf. ~ mail
correio m de fãs

fanatic /fə'nætɪk/ n fanático m. ~al a
fanático. ~ism /-sɪzəm/ n fanatismo
m

fanciful /'fænsɪfl/ a fantasioso, fantasista

fancy /'fænsɪ/ n fantasia f; (liking)
gosto m □ a extravagante, fantástico;
(of buttons etc) de fantasia; (of prices)
exorbitante □ vt imaginar; (colloq:
like) gostar de; (colloq: want)
apetecer. it took my ~ gostei disso,

(P) deu-me no gosto. a passing ~ um
entusiasmo passageiro. ~ dress traje
m fantasia, (P) trajo m de fantasia

fanfare /'fænfeə(r)/ n fanfarra f

fang /fæŋ/ n presa f, dente m canino

fantastic /fæn'tæstɪk/ a fantástico

fantas|y /'fæntəsɪ/ n fantasia f. ~ize
vt fantasiar, imaginar

far /fɑː(r)/ adv longe; (much, very)
muito □ a distante, longínquo; (end,
side) outro. ~ away ~ off ao longe.
as ~ as (up to) até. as ~ as I know
tanto quanto saiba. the F~ East o
Extremo-Oriente m. ~-away a distante, longínquo. ~-fetched a forçado; (unconvincing) pouco plausível.
~-reaching a de grande alcance

farce /fɑːs/ n farsa f. ~ical a de farsa;
ridículo

fare /feə(r)/ n preço m da passagem;
(in taxi) tarifa f, preço m da corrida;
(passenger) passageiro m; (food) comida f □ vi (get on) dar-se

farewell /feə'wel/ int & n adeus (m)

farm /fɑːm/ n quinta f, fazenda f □ vt
cultivar □ vi ser fazendeiro, (P)
lavrador. ~ out (of work) delegar a
tarefeiros. ~-hand n trabalhador m
rural. ~er n fazendeiro m, (P) lavrador m. ~ing n agricultura f, lavoura
f

farmhouse /'fɑːmhaʊs/ n casa f da
fazenda, (P) quinta

farmyard /'fɑːmjɑːd/ n quintal de fazenda m, (P) pátio m de quinta

farth|er /'fɑːðə(r)/ adv mais longe □ a
mais distante. ~est adv mais longe □
a o mais distante

fascinat|e /'fæsɪneɪt/ vt fascinar.
~ion /-'neɪʃn/ n fascínio m, fas-
cinação f

fascis|t /'fæʃɪst/ n fascista mf. ~m
/-zəm/ n fascismo m

fashion /'fæʃn/ n moda f; (manner)
maneira f □ vt amoldar; (P) moldar.
~able a na moda, (P) à moda.
~ably adv na moda, (P) à moda

fast[1] /fɑːst/ a (-er, -est) rápido; (colour)
fixo, que não desbota □ adv depressa;
(firmly) firmemente. be ~ (of clock)
adiantar-se, estar adiantado. ~
asleep profundamente adormecido,
ferrado no sono. ~ food n fast-food f

fast[2] /fɑːst/ vi jejuar □ n jejum m

fasten /'fɑːsn/ vt/i prender; (door, window) fechar(-se); (seat-belt) apertar.
~en- ~ing ns fecho m

fastidious /fə'stɪdɪəs/ a exigente

fat /fæt/ n gordura f □ a (fatter, fat-
test) gordo. ~ness n gordura f

fatal /'feɪtl/ a fatal. ~ injuries feri-
mentos mpl mortais. ~ity /fə'tælətɪ/
n fatalidade f. ~ly adv fatalmente,
mortalmente

fate /feɪt/ n (*destiny*) destino m; (*one's lot*) destino m, sorte f. ~ful a fatídico

fated /'feɪtɪd/ a predestinado; (*doomed*) condenado (to, a)

father /'faːðə(r)/ n pai m □ vt gerar. ~-in-law n (pl ~s-in-law) sogro m. ~ly a paternal

fathom /'fæðəm/ n braça f □ vt ~ (out) (*comprehend*) compreender

fatigue /fə'tiːg/ n fadiga f □ vt fatigar

fatten /'fætn/ vt/i engordar. ~ing a que engorda

fatty /'fæti/ a (-ier, -iest) gorduroso; (*tissue*) adiposo

fault /fɔːlt/ n defeito m, falha f; (*blame*) falta f, culpa f; (*geol*) falha f. at ~ culpado.it's your ~ é culpa sua. ~less a impecável. ~y a defeituoso

favour /'feɪvə(r)/ n favor m □ vt favorecer; (*prefer*) preferir. do sb a ~ fazer um favor a alg. ~able a favorável. ~ably adv favoravelmente

favourite /'feɪvərɪt/ a & n favorito (m). ~ism /-ɪzəm/ n favoritismo m

fawn¹ /fɔːn/ n cervo m novo □ a (*colour*) castanho claro

fawn² /fɔːn/ vi ~ on adular, bajular

fax /fæks/ n fax m, fac-símile m □ vt mandar um fax. ~ machine fax m

fear /fɪə(r)/ n medo m, receio m, temor m; (*likelihood*) perigo m □ vt recear, ter medo de. for ~ of/that com medo de/que. ~ful a (*terrible*) medonho; (*timid*) medroso, receoso. ~less a destemido, intrépido

feasib|le /'fiːzəbl/ a factível, praticável; (*likely*) plausível. ~ility /-'bɪlətɪ/ n possibilidade f, (*plausibility*) plausibilidade f

feast /fiːst/ n festim m; (*relig; fig*) festa f □ vt/i festejar; (*eat and drink*) banquetear-se. ~ on regalar-se com

feat /fiːt/ n feito m, façanha f

feather /'feðə(r)/ n pena f, pluma f

feature /'fiːtʃə(r)/ n feição f, traço m; (*quality*) característica f; (*film*) longa metragem f; (*article*) artigo m em destaque □ vt representar; (*film*) ter como protagonista □ vi figurar

February /'febrʊərɪ/ n Fevereiro m

fed /fed/ see feed □ a be ~ up estar farto (*colloq*) (with de)

federa|l /'fedərəl/ a federal. ~tion /-'reɪʃn/ n federação f

fee /fiː/ n preço m. ~(s) (*of doctor, lawyer etc*) honorários mpl; (*member's subscription*) quota f; (*univ*) (P) propinas fpl. (errolment/registration) matrícula f school ~s mensalidades fpl escolares, (P) mensalidades fpl

feeble /'fiːbl/ a (-er, -est) débil, fraco. ~-minded a débil mental, (P) deficiente

feed /fiːd/ vt (pt fed) alimentar, dar de comer a; (*suckle*) alimentar; (*supply*) alimentar, abostecer □ vi alimentar-se □ n comida f; (*breast-feeding*) mamada f; (*mech*) alimentação f

feedback /'fiːdbæk/ n reação f, (P) reacção f; (*electr*) regeneração f

feel /fiːl/ vt (pt felt) sentir; (*touch*) apalpar, tatear □ vi (*tired, lonely etc*) sentir-se. ~ hot/thirsty ter calor/sede. ~ as if ter a impressão (de) que. ~ like ter vontade de

feeler /'fiːlə(r)/ n antena f

feeling /'fiːlɪŋ/ n sentimento m; (*physical*) sensação f

feet /fiːt/ see foot

feign /feɪn/ vt fingir

feline /'fiːlaɪn/ a felino

fell¹ /fel/ vt abater, derrubar

fell² /fel/ see fall

fellow /'feləʊ/ n companheiro m, camarada m; (*of society, college*) membro m; (*colloq*) cara m, (P) tipo m (*colloq*). ~-traveller n companheiro m de viagem. ~-ship n companheirismo m, camaradagem f; (*group*) associação f

felt¹ /felt/ n feltro m

felt² /felt/ see feel

female /'fiːmeɪl/ a (*animal etc*) fêmea f; (*voice, sex etc*) feminino □ n mulher f; (*animal*) fêmea f

feminin|e /'femənɪn/ a & n feminino (m). ~ity /-'nɪnətɪ/ n feminilidade f

feminist /'femɪnɪst/ n feminista mf

fenc|e /fens/ n tapume m, cerca f □ vt cercar □ vi esgrimir. ~er n esgrimista mf. ~ing n esgrima f; (*fences*) tapume m

fend /fend/ vi ~ for o.s. defender-se, virar-se (*colloq*), governar-se □ vt ~ off defender-se de

fender /'fendə(r)/ n guarda-fogo m; (*Amer: mudguard*) pára-lama m, guarda-lama m, (P) pára-choques m

fennel /'fenl/ n (*herb*) funcho m, erva-doce f

ferment¹ /fə'ment/ vt/i fermentar; (*excite*) excitar. ~ation /fɜːmen'teɪʃn/ n fermentação f

ferment² /'fɜːment/ n fermento m; (*fig*) efervescência f

fern /fɜːn/ n feto m

feroci|ous /fə'rəʊʃəs/ a feroz. ~ity /-'rɒsətɪ/ n ferocidade f

ferret /'ferɪt/ n furão m □ vi (pt ferreted) caçar com furões □ vt ~ out desenterrar

ferry /'ferɪ/ n barco m de travessia, ferry(-boat) m □ vt transportar

fertile /'fɜːtaɪl/ a fértil, fecundo. ~ity /fə'tɪlətɪ/ n fertilidade f, fecundidade f. ~ize /-əlaɪz/ vt fertilizar, fecundar

fertilizer /'fɜːtəlaɪzə(r)/ n adubo m, fertilizante m

fervent /'fɜ:vənt/ a fervoroso
fervour /'fɜ:və(r)/ n fervor m, ardor m
fester /'festə(r)/ vt/i infectar; (fig) envenenar
festival /'festɪvl/ n festival m; (relig) festa f
festive /'festɪv/ a festivo. ~e season periodo m das festas. ~ity /fes'tɪvəti/ n festividade f, regozijo m. ~ities festas fpl, festividades fpl
festoon /fe'stu:n/ vt engrinaldar
fetch /fetʃ/ vt (go for) ir buscar; (bring) trazer; (be sold for) vender-se por, render
fetching /'fetʃɪŋ/ a atraente
fête /feɪt/ n festa f or feira f de caridade ao ar livre □ vt festejar
fetish /'fetɪʃ/ n fetiche m, idolo m; (obsession) mania f
fetter /'fetə(r)/ vt agrilhoar. ~s npl ferros mpl, grilhões mpl, grilhetas fpl
feud /fju:d/ n discórdia f, inimizade f. ~al a feudal
fever /'fi:və(r)/ n febre f. ~ish a febril
few /fju:/ a & n poucos (mpl). ~ books poucos livros. they are ~ são poucos. a ~ a & n alguns (mpl). a good ~, quite a ~ bastantes. ~er a & n menos (de). they were ~er eram menos numerosos. ~est a & n o menor número (de)
fiancé /fɪ'ɑnseɪ/ n noivo m. ~e n noiva f
fiasco /fɪ'æskəʊ/ n (pl -os) fiasco m
fib /fɪb/ n lorota f, cascata f, peta f, (P) mentira f □ vi (pt fibbed) mentir
fibre /'faɪbə(r)/ n fibra f
fibreglass /'faɪbəglɑ:s/ n fibra f de vidro
fickle /'fɪkl/ a leviano, inconstante
fiction /'fɪkʃn/ n ficção f. (works of) ~ romances mpl, obras fpl de ficção. ~al a de ficção, fictício
fictitious /fɪk'tɪʃəs/ a fictício
fiddle /'fɪdl/ n (colloq) violino m; (sl: swindle) trapaça f □ vi (sl) trapacear (sl) □ vt (sl: falsify) falsificar, cozinhar (sl). ~ with (colloq) brincar com, remexer em, (P) estar a brincar com, estar a remexer em. ~r /-ə(r)/ n (colloq) violinista m/f
fidelity /fɪ'delətɪ/ n fidelidade f
fidget /'fɪdʒɪt/ vi (pt fidgeted) estar irrequieto, remexer-se. ~ with remexer em. ~y a irrequieto; (impatient) impaciente
field /fi:ld/ n campo m □ vt/i (cricket) (estar pronto para) apanhar ou interceptar a bola. ~-day n grande dia m. ~-glasses npl binóculo m. F~ Marshal marechal-de-campo m
fieldwork /'fi:ldwɜ:k/ n trabalho m de campo; (mil) fortificação f de campanha

fiend /fi:nd/ n diabo m, demônio m, (P) demônio m. ~ish a diabólico
fierce /fɪəs/ a (-er, -est) feroz; (storm, attack) violento; (heat) intenso, abrasador. ~ness n ferocidade f; (of storm, attack) violência f; (of heat) intensidade f
fiery /'faɪərɪ/ a (-ier, -iest) ardente; (temper, speech) inflamado
fifteen /fɪf'ti:n/ a & n quinze (m). ~th a & n décimo quinto (m)
fifth /fɪfθ/ a & n quinto (m)
fifty /'fɪftɪ/ a & n cinquenta (m), (P) cinquenta (m). ~y-~y a meias. ~ieth a & n qüinquagésimo (m), quinquagésimo (m)
fig /fɪg/ n figo m. ~-tree n figueira f
fight /faɪt/ vi (pt fought) lutar, combater □ vt lutar contra, combater □ n luta f; (quarrel, brawl) briga f. ~ over sth lutar por alg coisa. ~ shy of esquivar-se de, fugir de. ~er n lutador m; (mil) combatente m/f; (plane) caça m. ~ing n combate m
figment /'fɪgmənt/ n ~ of the imagination fruto m or produto m da imaginação
figurative /'fɪgjərətɪv/ a figurado. ~ly adv em sentido figurado
figure /'fɪgə(r)/ n (number) algarismo m; (diagram, body) figura f. ~s npl (arithmetic) contas fpl, aritmética f □ vt imaginar, supor □ vi (appear) figurar (in em). ~ of speech figura f de retórica. ~ out compreender. ~-head n figura f de proa; (pej: person) testa-de-ferro m, chefe m nominal
filament /'fɪləmənt/ n filamento m
file¹ /faɪl/ n (tool) lixa f, lima f □ vt lixar, limar. ~ings npl limalha f
file² /faɪl/ n fichário m, (P) dossier m; (box, drawer) fichário m, (P) ficheiro m; (comput) arquivo m (line) fila f □ vt arquivar □ vi ~e (past) desfilar, marchar em fila. ~e in/out entrar/sair em fila. (in) single ~e (past) em fila indiana. ~ing cabinet fichário m, (P) ficheiro m
fill /fɪl/ vt/i encher(-se); (vacancy) preencher □ n eat one's ~ comer o que quiser. have one's ~ estar farto. ~ in (form) preencher. ~ out (get fat) engordar. ~ up encher até cima; (auto) encher o tanque
fillet /'fɪlɪt/ n (meat, fish) filé m, (P) filete m □ vt (pt filleted) (meat, fish) cortar em filés, (P) filetes
filling /'fɪlɪŋ/ n recheio m; (of tooth) obturação f, (P) chumbo m. ~ station posto m de gasolina
film /fɪlm/ n filme m □ vt/i filmar. ~ star estrela f or vedete f or (P) vedeta f de cinema, astro m
filter /'fɪltə(r)/ n filtro m □ vt/i filtrar

(-se). ~ coffee café m filtro. ~-tip n cigarro m com filtro

filth /filθ/ n imundície f; (fig) obscenidade f. ~y a imundo; (fig) obsceno

fin /fin/ n barbatana f

final /'faɪnl/ a final; (conclusive) decisivo □ n (sport) final f. ~s npl (exams) finais fpl. ~ist n finalista mf. ~ly adv finalmente, por fim; (once and for all) definitivamente

finale /fɪ'nɑːlɪ/ n final m

finalize /'faɪnəlaɪz/ vt finalizar

financ|e /'faɪnæns/ n finança(s) f (pl) □ a financeiro □ vt financiar. ~ier /-'nænsɪə(r)/ n financeiro m

financial /faɪ'nænʃl/ a financeiro. ~ly adv financeiramente

find /faɪnd/ vt (pt found) (sth lost) achar, encontrar; (think) achar; (discover) descobrir; (jur) declarar □ n achado m. ~ out vt apurar, descobrir □ vi informar-se (about sobre)

fine[1] /faɪn/ n multa f □ vt multar

fine[2] /faɪn/ a (-er, -est) fino; (splendid) belo, lindo □ adv (muito) bem; (small) fino, fininho. ~ arts belas artes fpl. ~ weather bom tempo. ~ly adv lindamente; (cut) fininho, aos bocadinhos

finesse /fɪ'nes/ n finura f, sutileza f

finger /'fɪŋgə(r)/ n dedo m □ vt apalpar. ~-mark n dedada f. ~-nail n unha f

fingerprint /'fɪŋgəprɪnt/ n impressão f digital

fingertip /'fɪŋgətɪp/ n ponta f do dedo

finicky /'fɪnɪkɪ/ a meticuloso, miudinho

finish /'fɪnɪʃ/ vt/i acabar, terminar □ n fim m; (of race) chegada f; (on wood, clothes) acabamento m. ~ doing acabar de fazer. ~ up doing acabar por fazer. ~ up in ir parar a, acabar em

finite /'faɪnaɪt/ a finito

Fin|land /'fɪnlənd/ n Finlândia f. ~n n finlandês m. ~nish a & n (lang) finlandês (m)

fir /fɜː(r)/ n abeto m

fire /'faɪə(r)/ n fogo m; (conflagration) incêndio m; (heater) aquecedor m □ vt (bullet, gun, etc) disparar; (dismiss) despedir; (fig: stimulate) inflamar □ vi atirar, fazer fogo (at sobre). on ~ em chamas. set ~ to pôr fogo em. ~-alarm n alarme m de incêndio. ~-brigade n bombeiros mpl. ~-engine n carro m de bombeiro, (P) da bomba. ~-escape n saída f de incêndio. ~-extinguisher n extintor m de incêndio. ~-station n quartel m dos bombeiros

firearm /'faɪərɑːm/ n arma f de fogo

fireman /'faɪəmən/ n (pl -men) bombeiro m

fireplace /'faɪəpleɪs/ n chaminé f, lareira f

firewood /'faɪəwʊd/ n lenha f

firework /'faɪəwɜːk/ n fogo m de artifício

firing-squad /'faɪərɪŋskwɒd/ n pelotão m de execução

firm[1] /fɜːm/ n firma f comercial

firm[2] /fɜːm/ a (-er, -est) firme; (belief) firme, inabalável. ~ly adv firmemente. ~ness n firmeza f

first /fɜːst/ a & n primeiro (m); (auto) primeira (f) □ adv primeiro, em primeiro lugar. at ~ a princípio, no início. ~ of all antes de mais nada. for the ~ time pela primeira vez. ~ aid primeiros socorros mpl. ~-class a de primeira classe. ~ name nome de batismo m, (P) baptismo m. ~-rate a excelente. ~ly adv primeiramente, em primeiro lugar

fiscal /'fɪskl/ a fiscal

fish /fɪʃ/ n (pl usually invar) peixe m □ vt/i pescar. ~ out (colloq) tirar. ~ing n pesca f. go ~ing ir pescar, (P) ir à pesca. ~ing-rod n vara f de pescar. ~y a de peixe; (fig: dubious) suspeito

fisherman /'fɪʃəmən/ n (pl -men) pescador m

fishmonger /'fɪʃmʌŋgə(r)/ n dono m/ empregado m de peixaria. ~'s (shop) peixaria f

fission /'fɪʃn/ n fissão f, cisão f

fist /fɪst/ n punho m, mão f fechada, (P) punho m

fit[1] /fɪt/ n acesso m, ataque m; (of generosity) rasgo m

fit[2] /fɪt/ a (fitter, fittest) de boa saúde, em forma; (proper) próprio; (good enough) em condições; (able) capaz □ vt/i (pt fitted) (clothes) assentar, ficar bem (a); (into space) (match) ajustar (-se) (a); (install) instalar □ n be a good ~ assentar bem. be a tight ~ estar justo. ~ out equipar. ~ted carpet carpete m, (P) alcatifa f. ~ness n saúde f, (P) condição f física

fitful /'fɪtfl/ a intermitente

fitment /'fɪtmənt/ n móvel m de parede

fitting /'fɪtɪŋ/ a apropriado □ n (clothes) prova f. ~s npl (fitments) instalações fpl; (fitments) mobiliário m. ~ room cabine f

five /faɪv/ a & n cinco (m)

fix /fɪks/ vt fixar; (mend, prepare) arranjar □ n in a ~ em apuros, (P) numa alhada. ~ sb up with sth conseguir alg coisa para alguém. ~ed a fixo

fixation /fɪk'seɪʃn/ n fixação f; (obsession) obsessão f

fixture /'fɪkstʃə(r)/ n equipamento m,

instalação f; (sport) (data f marcada para) competição f

fizz /fɪz/ vi efervescer, borbulhar □ n efervescência f. ~y a gasoso

fizzle /fɪzl/ vi ~ out (plan etc) acabar em nada or (P) em águas de bacalhau (colloq)

flab /flæb/ n (colloq) gordura f, banha f (colloq). ~by a flácido

flabbergasted /ˈflæbəgɑːstɪd/ a (colloq) espantado, pasmado (colloq)

flag¹ /flæg/ n bandeira f □ vt (pt flagged) fazer sinal. ~ down fazer sinal para parar. ~-pole n mastro m (de bandeira)

flag² /flæg/ vi (pt flagged) (droop) cair, pender, tombar; (of person) esmorecer

flagrant /ˈfleɪgrənt/ a flagrante

flagstone /ˈflægstəʊn/ n laje f

flair /fleə(r)/ n jeito m, habilidade f

flake /fleɪk/ n floco m; (paint) lasca f □ vi descamar-se, lascar-se. ~y a (paint) descamado, lascado

flamboyant /flæmˈbɔɪənt/ a flamejante; (showy) flamante, vistoso; (of manner) extravagante

flame /fleɪm/ n chama f, labareda f □ vi flamejar. burst into ~s incendiar-se

flamingo /fləˈmɪŋgəʊ/ n (pl -os) flamingo m

flammable /ˈflæməbl/ a inflamável

flan /flæn/ n torta f, (P) tarte f

flank /flæŋk/ n flanco m □ vt flanquear

flannel /ˈflænl/ n flanela f; (for face) toalha f, (P) toalhete m de rosto

flap /flæp/ vi (pt flapped) bater □ vt ~ its wings bater as asas □ n (of table, pocket) aba f; (sl: panic) pânico m

flare /fleə(r)/ vi ~ up irromper em chamas; (of war) rebentar; (fig: of person) enfurecer-se □ n chamejar m; (dazzling light) clarão m; (signal) foguete m de sinalização. ~d a (skirt) évasé

flash /flæʃ/ vi brilhar subitamente; (on and off) piscar; (auto) fazer sinal com o pisca-pisca □ vt fazer brilhar; (send) lançar, dardejar; (flaunt) fazer alarde de, ostentar □ n clarão m, lampejo m; (photo) flash m. ~ past passar como uma bala, (P) passar como um bólide

flashback /ˈflæʃbæk/ n cena f retrospectiva, flashback m

flashlight /ˈflæʃlaɪt/ n lanterna f elétrica, (P) eléctrica

flashy /ˈflæʃɪ/ a espalhafatoso, que dá na vista

flask /flɑːsk/ n frasco m; (vacuum flask) garrafa f térmica, (P) garrafa f termos

flat /flæt/ a (flatter, flattest) plano, chato; (tyre) arriado, vazio; (battery) fraco; (refusal) categórico; (fare, rate) fixo; (monotonous) monótono; (mus) bemol; (out of tune) desafinado □ n apartamento m; (colloq: tyre) furo m no pneu; (mus) bemol m. ~ out (drive); (work) a dar tudo por tudo. ~ly adv categoricamente

flatter /ˈflætə(r)/ vt lisonjear, adular. ~er n lisonjeiro m, adulador m. ~ing a lisonjeiro, adulador. ~y n lisonja f

flatulence /ˈflætjʊləns/ n flatulência f

flaunt /flɔːnt/ vt/i pavonear(-se), ostentar

flavour /ˈfleɪvə(r)/ n sabor m (of a) □ vt dar sabor a, temperar. ~ing n aroma m sintético; (seasoning) tempero m

flaw /flɔː/ n falha f, imperfeição f. ~ed a imperfeito. ~less a perfeito

flea /fliː/ n pulga f

fled /fled/ see flee

fledged /fledʒd/ a fully-~ (fig) treinado, experiente

flee /fliː/ vi (pt fled) fugir □ vt fugir de

fleece /fliːs/ n lã f de carneiro, velo m □ vt (fig) esfolar, roubar

fleet /fliːt/ n (of warships) esquadra f; (of merchant ships, vehicles) frota f

fleeting /ˈfliːtɪŋ/ a curto, fugaz

Flemish /ˈflemɪʃ/ a & n (lang) flamengo (m)

flesh /fleʃ/ n carne f; (of fruit) polpa f. ~y a carnudo

flew /fluː/ see fly²

flex¹ /fleks/ vt flexionar

flex² /fleks/ n (electr) fio f flexível

flexible /ˈfleksəbl/ a flexível. ~ility /-ˈbɪlətɪ/ n flexibilidade f

flexitime /ˈfleksɪtaɪm/ n horário m flexível

flick /flɪk/ n (light blow) safanão m; (with fingertip) piparote m □ vt dar um safanão em; (with fingertip) dar um piparote a. ~-knife n navalha f de ponta e mola. ~ through folhear

flicker /ˈflɪkə(r)/ vi vacilar, oscilar, tremular □ n oscilação f, tremular m; (light) luz f oscilante

flier /ˈflaɪə(r)/ n = flyer

flies /flaɪz/ npl (of trousers) braguilha f

flight¹ /flaɪt/ n (flying) voo m. ~ of stairs lance m, (P) lanço m de escada. ~-deck n cabine f, (P) cabina f

flight² /flaɪt/ n (fleeing) fuga f. put to ~ pôr em fuga. take ~ pôr-se em fuga

flimsy /ˈflɪmzɪ/ a (-ier, -iest) (material) fino; (object) frágil; (excuse etc) fraco, esfarrapado flinch /flɪntʃ/ vi (wince) retrair-se; (draw back) recuar; (hesitate) hesitar

fling /flɪŋ/ vt/i (pt flung) atirar(-se), arremessar(-se); (rush) precipitar-se

flint /flɪnt/ n silex m; (for lighter) pedra f

flip /flɪp/ vt (pt flipped) fazer girar com o dedo e o polegar □ n pancadinha f. ~ through folhear

flippant /'flɪpənt/ a irreverente, petulante

flipper /'flɪpə(r)/ n (of seal) nadadeira f; (of swimmer) pé-de-pato m

flirt /flɜːt/ vi namoriscar, flertar, (P) flartar □ n namorador m, namoradeira f. ~ation /-'teɪʃn/ n namorico m, flerte m, (P) flirt m. ~atious a namorador m, namoradeira f

flit /flɪt/ vi (pt flitted) esvoaçar

float /fləʊt/ vt/i (fazer) flutuar; (company) lançar □ n bóia f; (low cart) carro m de alegórico

flock /flɒk/ n (of sheep; congregation) rebanho m; (of birds) bando m; (crowd) multidão f □ vi afluir, juntar-se

flog /flɒg/ vt (pt flogged) açoitar; (sl: sell) vender

flood /flʌd/ n inundação f, cheia f; (of tears) dilúvio m □ vt inundar, alagar □ vi estar inundado; (river) transbordar; (fig: people) afluir

floodlight /'flʌdlaɪt/ n projetor m, (P) projector m, holofote m □ vt (pt floodlit) iluminar

floor /flɔː(r)/ n chão m, soalho m; (for dancing) pista f; (storey) andar m □ vt assoalhar; (baffle) desconcertar, embatucar

flop /flɒp/ vi (pt flopped) (drop) (deixar-se) cair; (move helplessly) debater-se; (sl: fail) ser um fiasco □ n (sl) fiasco m. ~py a mole, tombado. ~py (disk) disquete m

floral /'flɔːrəl/ a floral

florid /'flɒrɪd/ a florido

florist /'flɒrɪst/ n florista mf

flounce /flaʊns/ n babado m, debrum f

flounder /'flaʊndə(r)/ vi esbracejar, debater-se; (fig) meter os pés pelas mãos

flour /'flaʊə(r)/ n farinha f. ~y a farinhento

flourish /'flʌrɪʃ/ vi florescer, prosperar □ vt brandir □ n floreado m; (movement) gesto m elegante. ~ing a próspero

flout /flaʊt/ vt escarnecer (de)

flow /fləʊ/ vi correr, fluir; (traffic) mover-se; (hang loosely) flutuar; (gush) jorrar □ n corrente f; (of tide; fig) enchente f. ~ into (of river) desaguar em. ~ chart organograma m, (P) organigrama m

flower /'flaʊə(r)/ n flor f □ vi florir, florescer. ~-bed n canteiro m. ~ed a de flores, (P) florido, às flores. ~y a florido

flown /fləʊn/ see fly²

flu /fluː/ n (colloq) gripe f

fluctuate /'flʌktʃʊeɪt/ vi flutuar, oscilar. ~ion /-'eɪʃn/ n flutuação f, oscilação f

flue /fluː/ n cano m de chaminé

fluen|t /'fluːənt/ a fluente. be ~t (in a language) falar correntemente (uma língua). ~cy n fluência f. ~tly adv fluentemente

fluff /flʌf/ n cotão m; (down) penugem f □ vt (colloq: bungle) estender-se em (sl), executar mal. ~y a penugento, fofo

fluid /'fluːɪd/ a & n fluido (m)

fluke /fluːk/ n bambúrrio (colloq) m, golpe m de sorte

flung /flʌŋ/ see fling

flunk /flʌŋk/ vt/i (Amer colloq) levar pau (colloq), (P) chumbar (colloq)

fluorescent /flʊə'resnt/ a fluorescente

fluoride /'flʊəraɪd/ n flúor m, fluor m

flurry /'flʌrɪ/ n rajada f, rabanada f, lufada f; (fig) atrapalhação f, agitação f

flush¹ /flʌʃ/ vi corar, ruborizar-se □ vt lavar com água, (P) lavar a jorros de água □ n rubor m, vermelhidão f; (fig) excitação f; (of water) jorro m □ a ~ with ao nível de, rente a. ~ the toilet dar descarga

flush² /flʌʃ/ vt ~ out desalojar

fluster /'flʌstə(r)/ vt atarantar, perturbar, enervar

flute /fluːt/ n flauta f

flutter /'flʌtə(r)/ vi esvoaçar; (wings) bater; (heart) palpitar □ vt bater. ~ one's eyelashes pestanejar □ n (of wings) batimento m; (fig) agitação f

flux /flʌks/ n in a state of ~ em mudança f contínua

fly¹ /flaɪ/ n mosca f

fly² /flaɪ/ vi (pt flew, pp flown) voar; (passengers) ir de/viajar de avião; (rush) correr □ vt pilotar; (passengers, goods) transportar por avião; (flag) hastear, (P) arvorar □ n (of trousers) braguilha f

flyer /'flaɪə(r)/ n aviador m; (Amer: circular) prospecto m

flying /'flaɪɪŋ/ a voador. with ~ colours com grande êxito, esplendidamente. ~ saucer disco m voador. ~ start bom arranque m. ~ visit visita f de médico

flyleaf /'flaɪliːf/ n (pl -leaves) guarda f, folha f em branco

flyover /'flaɪəʊvə(r)/ n viaduto m

foal /fəʊl/ n potro m

foam /fəʊm/ n espuma f □ vi espumar.
~ (rubber) n espuma f de borracha

fob /fob/ vt (pt fobbed) ~ off iludir,
entreter com artifícios. ~ off on impingir a

focus /'fəʊkəs/ n (pl -cuses or -ci
/-saɪ/) foco m □ vt/i (pt focused) focar; (fig) concentrar(-se). in ~ focado, em foco. out of ~ desfocado

fodder /'fodə(r)/ n forragem f

foetus /'fi:təs/ n (pl -tuses) feto m

fog /fog/ n nevoeiro m □ vt/i (pt
fogged) enevoar(-se). ~-horn n sereia f de nevoeiro. ~gy a enevoado,
brumoso. it is ~gy está nevoento

foible /'fɔɪbl/ n fraqueza f, ponto m
fraco

foil¹ /fɔɪl/ n papel m de alumínio; (fig)
contraste m

foil² /fɔɪl/ vt frustrar

foist /fɔɪst/ vt impingir (on a)

fold /fəʊld/ vt/i dobrar(-se); (arms)
cruzar; (colloq: fail) falir □ n dobra f.
~er n pasta f; (leaflet) prospecto m
(desdobrável). ~ing a dobrável, dobradiço

foliage /'fəʊlɪdʒ/ n folhagem f

folk /fəʊk/ n povo m. ~s n (family, people) gente f (colloq) □ a folclórico,
popular. ~lore n folclore m

follow /'foləʊ/ vt/i seguir. it ~s that
quer dizer que. ~ suit (cards) servir
o naipe jogado; (fig) seguir o exemplo, fazer o mesmo. ~ up (letter etc)
dar seguimento a. ~er n partidário
m, seguidor m. ~ing n partidários
mpl □ a seguinte □ prep em seguimento a

folly /'folɪ/ n loucura f

fond /fond/ a (-er -est) carinhoso;
(hope) caro. be ~ of gostar de, ser
amigo de. ~ness n (for people)
afeição f; (for thing) gosto m

fondle /'fondl/ vt acariciar

font /font/ n pia f batismal, (P) baptismal

food /fu:d/ n alimentação f, comida f;
(nutrient) alimento m □ a alimentar.
~ poisoning envenenamento m alimentar

fool /fu:l/ n idiota mf, parvo m □ vt
enganar □ vi ~ around andar sem
fazer nada

foolhardy /'fu:lha:dɪ/ a imprudente,
atrevido

foolish /'fu:lɪʃ/ a idiota, parvo. ~ly
adv parvamente. ~ness n idiotice f,
parvoíce f

foolproof /'fu:lpru:f/ a infalível

foot /fʊt/ n (pl feet) (of person, bed,
stairs) pé m; (of animal) pata f;
(measure) pé m (= 30,48 cm) □ vt ~
the bill pagar a conta. on ~ a pé. on
or to one's feet de pé. put one's ~

in it fazer uma gafe. to be under sb's
feet atrapalhar alg. ~-bridge n passarela f

football /'fʊtbɔ:l/ n bola f de futebol;
(game) futebol m. ~ pools loteria f
esportiva, (P) totobola m. ~er n futebolista mf, jogador m de futebol

foothills /'fʊthɪlz/ npl contrafortes
mpl

foothold /'fʊthəʊld/ n ponto m de
apoio

footing /'fʊtɪŋ/ n: firm ~ stor. on an
equal ~ em pé de igualdade

footlights /'fʊtlaɪts/ npl ribalta f

footnote /'fʊtnəʊt/ n nota f de rodapé

footpath /'fʊtpɑ:θ/ n (pavement) calçada f, (P) passeio m; (in open country) atalho m, caminho m

footprint /'fʊtprɪnt/ n pegada f

footstep /'fʊtstep/ n passo m

footwear /'fʊtweə(r)/ n calçado m

for /fə(r)/; emphatic /fɔ:(r)/ prep para;
(in favour of; in place of) por; (during) durante □ conj porque, visto
que. a liking ~ gosto por. he has
been away ~ two years há dois anos
que ele está fora. ~ éver para sempre

forage /'forɪdʒ/ vi forragear; (rummage) remexer à procura (de) □ n forragem f

forbade /fə'bæd/ see forbid

forbear /fɔ:'beə(r)/ vt/i (pt forbore,
pp forborne) abster-se (from de).
~ance n paciência f, tolerância f

forbid /fə'bɪd/ vt (pt forbade, pp forbidden) proibir. you are ~den to
smoke você está proibido de fumar,
(P) estás proibido de fumar. ~ding a
severo, intimidatório

force /fɔ:s/ n força f □ vt forçar. ~
into fazer entrar à força. ~ on impor
a. come into ~ entrar em vigor. the
~s as Forças Armadas. ~d a
forçado. ~ful a enérgico

force-feed /'fɔ:sfi:d/ vt (pt -fed) alimentar à força

forceps /'fɔ:seps/ n (pl invar) fórceps
m

forcible /'fɔ:səbl/ a convincente;
(done by force) à força. ~y adv à força

ford /fɔ:d/ n vau m □ vt passar a vau,
vadear

fore /fɔ:(r)/ a dianteiro □ n to the ~
em evidência

forearm /'fɔ:ra:m/ n antebraço m

foreboding /fɔ:'bəʊdɪŋ/ n pressentimento m

forecast /'fɔ:ka:st/ vt (pt forecast)
prever □ n previsão f. weather ~
boletim m meteorológico, previsão f
do tempo

forecourt /'fɔ:kɔ:t/ n pátio m de entrada; (of garage) área f das bombas
de gasolina

forefinger /'fɔːfɪŋgə(r)/ n (dedo) indicador m

forefront /'fɔːfrʌnt/ n vanguarda f

foregone /'fɔːgɒn/ a ∼ conclusion resultado m previsto

foreground /'fɔːgraʊnd/ n primeiro plano m

forehead /'fɒrɪd/ n testa f

foreign /'fɒrən/ a estrangeiro; (trade) externo; (travel) ao/no estrangeiro. F ∼ Office Ministério m dos Negócios Estrangeiros. ∼er n estrangeiro m.

foreman /'fɔːmən/ n (pl foremen) contramestre m; (of jury) primeiro jurado m

foremost /'fɔːməʊst/ a principal, primeiro □ adv first and ∼ antes de mais nada, em primeiro lugar

forename /'fɔːneɪm/ n nome m

forensic /fə'rensɪk/ a forense. ∼ medicine medicina f legal

forerunner /'fɔːrʌnə(r)/ n precursor m

foresee /fɔː'siː/ vt (pt -saw, pp -seen) prever. ∼able a previsível

foreshadow /fɔː'ʃædəʊ/ vt prefigurar, pressagiar

foresight /'fɔːsaɪt/ n previsão f, previdência f

forest /'fɒrɪst/ n floresta f

forestall /fɔː'stɔːl/ vt (do first) antecipar-se a; (prevent) prevenir; (anticipate) antecipar

forestry /'fɒrɪstrɪ/ n silvicultura f

foretell /fɔː'tel/ vt (pt foretold) predizer, profetizar

forever /fə'revə(r)/ adv (endlessly) constantemente

foreword /'fɔːwɜːd/ n prefácio m

forfeit /'fɔːfɪt/ n penalidade f, preço m; (in game) prenda f □ vt perder

forgave /fə'geɪv/ see forgive

forge[1] /fɔːdʒ/ vi ∼ ahead tomar a dianteira, avançar

forge[2] /fɔːdʒ/ n forja f □ vt (metal, friendship) forjar; (counterfeit) falsificar, forjar. ∼r /-ə(r)/ n falsificador m, forjador m. ∼ry /-ərɪ/ n falsificação f

forget /fə'get/ vt/i (pt forgot, pp forgotten) esquecer. ∼ o.s. portar-se com menos dignidade, esquecer-se de quem é. ∼-me-not n miosótis m. ∼ful a esquecido. ∼fulness n esquecimento m

forgive /fə'gɪv/ vt (pt forgave, pp forgiven) perdoar (sb for sth alg coisa a alg). ∼ness n perdão m

forgo /fɔː'gəʊ/ vt (pt forwent, pp forgone) renunciar a

fork /fɔːk/ n garfo m; (for digging etc) forquilha f; (in road) bifurcação f □ vi bifurcar. ∼ out (sl) desembolsar. ∼-lift truck empilhadeira f. ∼ed a bifurcado; (lightning) em zigzag

forlorn /fə'lɔːn/ a abandonado, desolado

form /fɔːm/ n forma f; (document) impresso m, formulário m; (schol) classe f □ vt/i formar(-se)

formal /'fɔːml/ a formal; (dress) de cerimónia, (P) cerimónia. ∼ity /-'mælətɪ/ n formalidade f. ∼ly adv formalmente

format /'fɔːmæt/ n formato m □ vt (pl formatted) (disk) formatar

formation /fɔː'meɪʃn/ n formação f

former /'fɔːmə(r)/ a antigo; (first of two) primeiro. the ∼ aquele. ∼ly adv antigamente

formidable /'fɔːmɪdəbl/ a formidável, tremendo

formula /'fɔːmjʊlə/ n (pl -ae /-iː/ or -as) fórmula f

formulate /'fɔːmjʊleɪt/ vt formular

forsake /fə'seɪk/ vt (pt forsook, pp forsaken) abandonar

fort /fɔːt/ n (mil) forte m

forth /fɔːθ/ adv adiante, para a frente. and so ∼ e assim por diante, etcetera. go back and ∼ andar de trás para diante.

forthcoming /fɔː'θkʌmɪŋ/ a que está para vir, próximo; (communicative) comunicativo, receptivo; (book) no prelo

forthright /'fɔːθraɪt/ a franco, direto, (P) direito

fortify /'fɔːtɪfaɪ/ vt fortificar. ∼ication /-ɪ'keɪʃn/ n fortificação f

fortitude /'fɔːtɪtjuːd/ n fortitude f, fortaleza f

fortnight /'fɔːtnaɪt/ n quinze dias mpl, (P) quinzena f. ∼ly a quinzenal □ adv de quinze em quinze dias

fortress /'fɔːtrɪs/ n fortaleza f

fortuitous /fɔː'tjuːɪtəs/ a fortuito, acidental

fortunate /'fɔːtʃənət/ a feliz, afortunado. be ∼ ter sorte. ∼ly adv felizmente

fortune /'fɔːtʃən/ n sorte f; (wealth) fortuna f. have the good ∼ to ter a sorte de. ∼-teller n cartomante mf

forty /'fɔːtɪ/ a & n quarenta (m). ∼ieth a &n quadragésimo (m)

forum /'fɔːrəm/ n fórum m, foro m

forward /'fɔːwəd/ a (in front) dianteiro; (towards the front) para a frente; (advanced) adiantado; (pert) atrevido □ n (sport) atacante m, (P) avançado m □ adv ∼(s) para a frente, para diante □ vt (letter) remeter; (goods) expedir; (fig: help) favorecer. come ∼ apresentar-se. go ∼ avançar. ∼ness n adiantamento m; (pertness) atrevimento m

fossil /'fɒsl/ a & n fóssil (m)

foster /'fɒstə(r)/ vt fomentar; (child)

criar. ~-child n filho m adotivo, (P) adoptivo. ~-mother n mãe f adotiva, (P) adoptiva

fought /fɔ:t/ see fight

foul /faʊl/ a (-er, -est) infecto; (language) obsceno; (weather) mau □ n (football) falta f □ vt sujar, emporcalhar. ~-mouthed a de linguagem obscena. ~ play jogo m desleal; (crime) crime m

found¹ /faʊnd/ see find

found² /faʊnd/ vt fundar. ~ation /-'deɪʃn/ n fundação f; (basis) fundamento m. ~ations npl (of building) alicerces mpl

founder¹ /'faʊndə(r)/ n fundador m

founder² /'faʊndə(r)/ vi afundar-se

foundry /'faʊndrɪ/ n fundição f

fountain /'faʊntɪn/ n fonte f. ~-pen n caneta-tinteiro f, (P) caneta f de tinta permanente

four /fɔ:(r)/ a & n quatro (m). ~fold a quádruplo □ adv quadruplamente. ~th a & n quarto (m)

foursome /'fɔ:səm/ n grupo m de quatro pessoas

fourteen /fɔ:'ti:n/ a & n catorze (m). ~th a & n décimo quarto (m)

fowl /faʊl/ n ave f de capoeira

fox /fɒks/ n raposa f □ vt (colloq) mistificar, enganar. be ~ed ficar perplexo

foyer /'fɔɪeɪ/ n foyer m

fraction /'frækʃn/ n fração f, (P) fracção f; (small bit) bocadinho m, particula f

fracture /'fræktʃə(r)/ n fratura f, (P) fractura f □ vt/i fraturar(-se), (P) fracturar(-se)

fragile /'frædʒaɪl/ a frágil

fragment /'frægmənt/ n fragmento m. ~ary /'frægməntrɪ/ a fragmentário

fragran|t /'freɪgrənt/ a fragrante, perfumado. ~ce n fragrância f, perfume m

frail /freɪl/ a (-er, -est) frágil

frame /freɪm/ n (techn; of spectacles) armação f; (of picture) moldura f; (of window) caixilho m; (body) corpo m, (P) estrutura f □ vt colocar a armação em; (picture) emoldurar; (fig) formular; (sl) incriminar falsamente, tramar. ~ of mind estado m de espirito

framework /'freɪmwɜ:k/ n estrutura f; (context) quadro m, esquema m

France /frɑ:ns/ n França f

franchise /'fræntʃaɪz/ n (pol) direito m de voto; (comm) concessão f, franchise f

frank¹ /fræŋk/ a franco. ~ly adv francamente. ~ness n franqueza f

frank² /fræŋk/ vt franquear

frantic /'fræntɪk/ a frenético

fraternal /frə'tɜ:nl/ a fraternal

fraternize /'frætənaɪz/ vi confraternizar

fraud /frɔ:d/ n fraude f; (person) impostor m. ~ulent /'frɔ:djʊlənt/ a fraudulento

fraught /frɔ:t/ a ~ with cheio de

fray¹ /freɪ/ n rixa f

fray² /freɪ/ vt/i desfiar(-se), puir, esgarçar(-se)

freak /fri:k/ n aberração f, anomalia f □ a anormal. ~ of nature aborto m da natureza. ~ish a anormal

freckle /'frekl/ n sarda f. ~d a sardento

free /fri:/ a (freer, freest) livre; (gratis) grátis; (lavish) liberal □ vt (pt freed) libertar (from de); (rid) livrar (of de). ~ of charge grátis, de graça. a ~ hand carta f branca. ~lance a independente, free-lance. ~-range a (egg) de galinha criada em galinheiro. ~ly adv livremente

freedom /'fri:dəm/ n liberdade f

freez|e /fri:z/ vt/i (pt froze, pp frozen) gelar; (culin; finance) congelar (-se) □ n gelo m; (culin; finance) congelamento m. ~er n congelador m. ~ing a gélido, glacial. below ~ing abaixo de zero

freight /freɪt/ n frete m

French /frentʃ/ a francês □ n (lang) francês m. the ~ os franceses. ~man n francês m. ~-speaking a francófono. ~ window porta f envidraçada. ~woman n francesa f

frenz|y /'frenzɪ/ n frenesi m. ~ied a frenético

frequen|t¹ /'fri:kwənt/ a freqüente, (P) frequente. ~cy n freqüência f, (P) frequência f. ~tly adv freqüentemente, (P) frequentemente

frequent² /frɪ'kwent/ vt freqüentar, (P) frequentar

fresh /freʃ/ a (-er, -est) fresco; (different, additional) novo; (colloq: cheeky) descarado, atrevido. ~ly adv recentemente. ~ness n frescura f

freshen /'freʃn/ vt/i refrescar. ~ up refrescar-se

fret /fret/ vt/i (pt fretted) ralar(-se). ~ful a rabugento

friar /'fraɪə(r)/ n frade m; (before name) frei m

friction /'frɪkʃn/ n fricção f

Friday /'fraɪdɪ/ n sexta-feira f. Good ~ sexta-feira f santa

fridge /frɪdʒ/ n (colloq) geladeira f, (P) frigorífico m

fried /fraɪd/ see fry □ a frito

friend /frend/ n amigo m. ~ship n amizade f

friendl|y /'frendlɪ/ a (-ier, -iest)

amigável, amigo, simpático. ~iness *n*
simpatia *f*, gentileza *f*

frieze /friːz/ *n* friso *m*

frigate /ˈfrɪɡət/ *n* fragata *f*

fright /fraɪt/ *n* medo *m*, susto *m*. give
sb a ~ pregar um susto em alguém.
~ful *a* medonho, assustador

frighten /ˈfraɪtn/ *vt* assustar. ~ off
afugentar. ~ed *a* assustado. be ~ed
(of) ter medo (de)

frigid /ˈfrɪdʒɪd/ *a* frígido. ~ity
/-ˈdʒɪdətɪ/ *n* frigidez *f*, frieza *f*; (*psych*)
frigidez *f*

frill /frɪl/ *n* babado *m*, (*P*) folho *m*

fringe /frɪndʒ/ *n* franja *f*; (*of area*)
borda *f*; (*of society*) margem *f*. ~ be-
nefits (*work*) regalias *fpl* extras. ~
theatre teatro *m* alternativo, teatro
m de vanguarda

frisk /frɪsk/ *vi* pular, brincar □ *vt* revistar

fritter[1] /ˈfrɪtə(r)/ *n* bolinho *m* frito,
(*P*) frito *m*

fritter[2] /ˈfrɪtə(r)/ *vt* ~ away desperdiçar

frivol|ous /ˈfrɪvələs/ *a* frívolo. ~ity
/-ˈvɒlətɪ/ *n* frivolidade *f*

fro /frəʊ/ *see* to and fro

frock /frɒk/ *n* vestido *m*

frog /frɒɡ/ *n* rã *f*

frogman /ˈfrɒɡmən/ *n* (*pl* -men)
homem-rã *m*

frolic /ˈfrɒlɪk/ *vi* (*pt* frolicked) brincar, fazer travessuras □ *n* brincadeira
f, travessura *f*

from /frəm/; *emphatic* /frɒm/ *prep* de;
(*with time, prices etc*) de, a partir de;
(*according to*) por, a julgar por

front /frʌnt/ *n* (*meteo, mil, pol*; *of car,
train*) frente *f*; (*of shirt*) peitilho *m*; (*of
building*; *fig*) fachada *f*; (*promenade*)
calçada *f* à beira-mar □ *a* da frente;
(*first*) primeiro. in ~ (of) em frente
(de). ~ door porta *f* da rua. ~-wheel
drive tracção *f*, (*P*) tracção *f* dianteira.
~age *n* frontaria *f*. ~al *a* frontal

frontier /ˈfrʌntɪə(r)/ *n* fronteira *f*

frost /frɒst/ *n* gelo *m*, temperatura *f*
abaixo de zero; (*on ground, plants etc*)
geada *f* □ *vt/i* cobrir(-se) de geada. ~-
bite *n* queimadura *f* de frio. ~-bitten
a queimado pelo frio. ~ed *a* (*glass*)
fosco. ~y *a* glacial

froth /frɒθ/ *n* espuma *f* □ *vi* espumar,
fazer espuma. ~y *a* espumoso

frown /fraʊn/ *vi* franzir as sobrancelhas □ *n* franzir *m* de sobrancelhas. ~
on desaprovar

froze, frozen /frəʊz, ˈfrəʊzn/ *see*
freeze

frugal /ˈfruːɡl/ *a* poupado; (*meal*)
frugal. ~ly *adv* frugalmente

fruit /fruːt/ *n* fruto *m*; (*collectively*)
fruta *f*. ~ machine caça-níqueis *ms*/

pl. ~ salad salada *f* de frutas. ~y *a*
que tem gosto *or* cheiro de fruta

fruit|ful /ˈfruːtfl/ *a* frutífero, pro-
dutivo. ~less *a* infrutífero

fruition /fruːˈɪʃn/ *n* come to ~ realizar-se

frustrat|e /frʌˈstreɪt/ *vt* frustrar.
~ion /-ʃn/ *n* frustração *f*

fry /fraɪ/ *vt/i* (*pt* fried) fritar. ~ing-
pan *n* frigideira *f*

fudge /fʌdʒ/ *n* (*culin*) doce *m* de leite,
(*P*) doce *m* acaramelado □ *vt/i* ~ (the
issue) lançar a confusão

fuel /ˈfjuːəl/ *n* combustível *m*; (*for
car*) carburante *m* □ *vt* (*pt* fuelled)
abastecer de combustível; (*fig*) atear

fugitive /ˈfjuːdʒətɪv/ *a* & *n* fugitivo
(*m*)

fulfil /fʊlˈfɪl/ *vt* (*pt* fulfilled) cumprir,
realizar; (*condition*) satisfazer. ~ o.s.
realizar-se. ~ling *a* satisfatório.
~ment *n* realização *f*; (*of condition*)
satisfação *f*

full /fʊl/ *a* (-er, -est) cheio; (*meal*)
completo; (*price*) total, por inteiro;
(*skirt*) rodado □ *adv* in ~
integralmente □ *a* speed a toda
velocidade. to the ~ ao máximo. be
~ up (*colloq*: *after eating*) estar cheio
(*colloq*). ~ moon lua *f* cheia. ~-scale
a em grande. ~-size *a* em tamanho
natural. ~ stop ponto *m* final. ~-
time *a* & *adv* a tempo integral, full-
time. ~y *adv* completamente

fulsome /ˈfʊlsəm/ *a* excessivo

fumble /ˈfʌmbl/ *vi* tatear, (*P*) tactear;
(*in the dark*) andar tateando. ~ with
estar atrapalhado com, andar às voltas com

fume /fjuːm/ *vi* defumar, (*P*) deitar
fumo, fumegar; (*with anger*) ferver.
~s *npl* gases *mpl*

fumigate /ˈfjuːmɪɡeɪt/ *vt* fumigar

fun /fʌn/ *n* divertimento *m*. for ~ de
brincadeira. make ~ of zombar de,
fazer troça de. ~-fair *n* parque *m* de
diversões, (*P*) feira *f* de diversões, (*P*)
feira *f* popular

function /ˈfʌŋkʃn/ *n* função *f* □ *vi*
funcionar. ~al *a* funcional

fund /fʌnd/ *n* fundos *mpl* □ *vt* financiar

fundamental /fʌndəˈmentl/ *a* fundamental

funeral /ˈfjuːnərəl/ *n* enterro *m*, funeral *m* □ *a* fúnebre

fungus /ˈfʌŋɡəs/ *n* (*pl* -gi /-gaɪ/) fungo
m

funnel /ˈfʌnl/ *n* funil *m*; (*of ship*)
chaminé *f*

funn|y /ˈfʌnɪ/ *a* (-ier, -iest) engraçado,
divertido; (*odd*) esquisito. ~ily *adv*
comicamente; (*oddly*) estranhamente.
~ily enough por incrível que pareça

fur /fɜː(r)/ n pêlo m; (for clothing) pele f; (in kettle) depósito m, crosta f. ~ coat casaco m de pele

furious /'fjʊərɪəs/ a furioso. ~ly adv furiosamente

furnace /'fɜːnɪs/ n fornalha f

furnish /'fɜːnɪʃ/ vt mobiliar, (P) mobilar; (supply) prover (with de). ~ings npl mobiliário m e equipamento m

furniture /'fɜːnɪtʃə(r)/ n mobilia f

furrow /'fʌrəʊ/ n sulco m; (wrinkle) ruga f □ vt sulcar; (wrinkle) enrugar

furry /'fɜːrɪ/ a (-ier, -iest) peludo; (toy) de pelúcia

further /'fɜːðə(r)/ a mais distante; (additional) adicional, suplementar □ adv mais longe; (more) mais □ vt promover. ~er education ensino m supletivo, cursos mpl livres, (P) educação f superior. ~est a o mais distante □ adv mais longe

furthermore /fɜːðə'mɔː(r)/ adv além disso

furtive /'fɜːtɪv/ a furtivo

fury /'fjʊərɪ/ n fúria f, furor m

fuse /fjuːz/ vt/i fundir(-se); (fig) amalgamar □ n fusível m. the lights ~d os fusíveis queimaram

fuse /fjuːz/ n (of bomb) espoleta f

fuselage /'fjuːzəlɑːʒ/ n fuselagem f

fusion /'fjuːʒn/ n fusão f

fuss /fʌs/ n história(s) f(pl), escarcéu m □ vi preocupar-se com ninharias. make a ~ of ligar demasiado para, criar caso com, fazer um espalhafato com. ~y a exigente, complicado

futile /'fjuːtaɪl/ a fútil

future /'fjuːtʃə(r)/ a & n futuro (m). in ~ no futuro, de agora em diante

futuristic /fjuːtʃə'rɪstɪk/ a futurista, futurístico

fuzz /fʌz/ n penugem f; (hair) cabelo m frisado

fuzzy /'fʌzɪ/ a (hair) frisado; (photo) pouco nítido, desfocado

G

gab /gæb/ n (colloq) have the gift of the ~ ter o dom da palavra

gabble /'gæbl/ vt/i tagarelar, falar, ler muito depressa □ n tagarelice f, algaravia f

gable /'geɪbl/ n empena f, oitão m

gad /gæd/ vi (pt gadded) ~ about (colloq) badalar

gadget /'gædʒɪt/ n pequeno utensílio m; (fitting) dispositivo m; (device) engenhoca f (colloq)

Gaelic /'geɪlɪk/ n galês m

gaffe /gæf/ n gafe f

gag /gæg/ n mordaça f; (joke) gag m, piada f □ vt (pt gagged) amordaçar

gaiety /'geɪətɪ/ n alegria f

gaily /'geɪlɪ/ adv alegremente

gain /geɪn/ vt ganhar □ vi (of clock) adiantar-se. ~ weight aumentar de peso. ~ on (get closer to) aproximar-se de □ n ganho m; (increase) aumento m. ~ful a lucrativo, proveitoso

gait /geɪt/ n (modo de) andar m

gala /'gɑːlə/ n gala m; (sport) festival m

galaxy /'gæləksɪ/ n galáxia f

gale /geɪl/ n vento m forte

gall /gɔːl/ n bílis f; (fig) fel m; (sl: impudence) descaramento m, desplante m, (P) lata f (sl). ~-bladder n vesícula f biliar. ~-stone n cálculo m biliar

gallant /'gælənt/ a galhardo, valente; (chivalrous) galante, cortês. ~ry n galhardia f, valentia f; (chivalry) galanteria f, cortesia f

gallery /'gælərɪ/ n galeria f

galley /'gælɪ/ n (pl -eys) galera f; (ship's kitchen) cozinha f

gallivant /gælɪ'vænt/ vi (colloq) vadiar, (P) andar na paródia

gallon /'gælən/ n galão m (= 4,546 litros; Amer = 3.785 litros)

gallop /'gæləp/ n galope m □ vi (pt galloped) galopar

gallows /'gæləʊz/ npl forca f

galore /gə'lɔː(r)/ adv a beça, em abundância

galvanize /'gælvənaɪz/ vt galvanizar

gambit /'gæmbɪt/ n gambito m

gamble /'gæmbl/ vt/i jogar □ n jogo (de azar) m; (fig) risco m. ~e on apostar em. ~er n jogador m. ~ing n jogo m (de azar)

game /geɪm/ n jogo m; (football) desafio m; (animals) caça f □ a bravo. ~ for pronto para

gamekeeper /'geɪmkiːpə(r)/ n guarda-florestal m

gammon /'gæmən/ n presunto m defumado

gamut /'gæmət/ n gama f

gang /gæŋ/ n bando m, gang m; (of workmen) turma f, (P) grupo m □ vi ~ up ligar-se (on contra)

gangling /'gæŋglɪŋ/ a desengonçado

gangrene /'gæŋgriːn/ n gangrena f

gangster /'gæŋstə(r)/ n gângster m, bandido m

gangway /'gæŋweɪ/ n passagem f; (aisle) coxia f; (on ship) portaló m; (from ship to shore) passadiço m

gaol /dʒeɪl/ n & vt = jail

gap /gæp/ n abertura f, brecha f; (in time) intervalo m; (deficiency) lacuna f

gape /geɪp/ vi ficar boquiaberto or embasbacado. ~ing a escancarado

garage /'gærɑːʒ/ n garagem f; (service station) posto m de gasolina, (P) estação f de serviço □ vt pôr na garagem

garbage /'ga:bɪdʒ/ n lixo m. ~ can (Amer) lata f do lixo, (P) caixote m do lixo

garble /'ga:bl/ vt deturpar

garden /'ga:dn/ n jardim m □ vi jardinar. ~er n jardineiro m. ~ing n jardinagem f

gargle /'ga:gl/ vi gargarejar □ n gargarejo m

gargoyle /'ga:gɔɪl/ n gárgula f

garish /'geərɪʃ/ a berrante, espalhafatoso

garland /'ga:lənd/ n grinalda f

garlic /'ga:lɪk/ n alho m

garment /'ga:mənt/ n peça f de vestuário, roupa f

garnish /'ga:nɪʃ/ vt enfeitar, guarnecer □ n guarnição f

garrison /'gærɪsn/ n guarnição f □ vt guarnecer

garrulous /'gærələs/ a tagarela

garter /'ga:tə(r)/ n liga f. ~-belt n (Amer) cinta f de ligas

gas /gæs/ n (pl gases) gás m; (med) anestésico m; (Amer colloq: petrol) gasolina f □ vt (pt gassed) asfixiar; (mil) gasear □ vi (colloq) fazer conversa fiada. ~ fire aquecedor m a gás. ~ mask máscara f anti-gás. ~ meter medidor m do gás

gash /gæʃ/ n corte m, lanho m □ vt cortar

gasket /'gæskɪt/ n junta f

gasoline /'gæsəli:n/ n (Amer) gasolina f

gasp /ga:sp/ vi arfar, arquejar; (fig: with rage, surprise) ficar sem ar □ n arquejo m

gassy /'gæsɪ/ a gasoso; (full of gas) cheio de gás

gastric /'gæstrɪk/ a gástrico

gastronomy /gæ'strɒnəmɪ/ n gastronomia f

gate /geɪt/ n portão m; (of wood) cancela f; (barrier) barreira f; (airport) porta f

gateau /'gætəʊ/ n (pl ~x /-təʊz/) bolo m grande com creme

gatecrash /'geɪtkræʃ/ vt/i entrar (numa festa) sem convite

gateway /'geɪtweɪ/ n (porta de) entrada f

gather /'gæðə(r)/ vt reunir, juntar; (pick up, collect) apanhar; (amass, pile up) acumular, juntar; (conclude) deduzir; (cloth) franzir □ vi reunir-se; (pile up) acumular-se. ~ speed ganhar velocidade. ~ing n reunião f

gaudy /'gɔ:dɪ/ a (-ier, -iest) (bright) berrante; (showy) espalhafatoso

gauge /geɪdʒ/ n medida f padrão; (device) indicador m; (railway) bitola f □ vt medir, avaliar

gaunt /gɔ:nt/ a emagrecido, macilento; (grim) lúgubre, desolado

gauntlet /'gɔ:ntlɪt/ n run the ~ of (fig) expor-se a. throw down the ~ lançar um desafio, (P) atirar a luva

gauze /gɔ:z/ n gaze f

gave /geɪv/ see give

gawky /'gɔ:kɪ/ a (-ier, -iest) desajeitado

gay /geɪ/ a (-er, -est) alegre; (colloq: homosexual) homosexual, gay

gaze /geɪz/ vi ~ (at) olhar fixamente (para) □ n contemplação f

gazelle /gə'zel/ n gazela f

GB abbr of Great Britain

gear /gɪə(r)/ n equipamento m; (techn) engrenagem f; (auto) velocidade f □ vt equipar; (adapt) adaptar. in ~ engrenado. out of ~ em ponto morto. ~-lever n alavanca f de mudanças

gearbox /'gɪəbɒks/ n caixa f de mudança, caixa f de transmissão, (P) caixa f de velocidades

geese /gi:s/ see goose

gel /dʒel/ n geléia f, (P) geleia f

gelatine /'dʒeləti:n/ n gelatina f

gelignite /'dʒelɪgnaɪt/ n gelignite f

gem /dʒem/ n gema f, pedra f preciosa

Gemini /'dʒemɪnaɪ/ n (astr) Gémeos mpl, (P) Gémeos mpl

gender /'dʒendə(r)/ n género m, (P) género m

gene /dʒi:n/ n gene m

genealogy /dʒi:nɪ'ælədʒɪ/ n genealogia f

general /'dʒenrəl/ a geral □ n general m. ~ election eleições fpl legislativas. ~ practitioner n clínico-geral m, (P) médico m de família. in ~ em geral. ~ly adv geralmente

generaliz|e /'dʒenrəlaɪz/ vt/i generalizar. ~ation /-'zeɪʃn/ n generalização f

generate /'dʒenəreɪt/ vt gerar, produzir

generation /dʒenə'reɪʃn/ n geração f

generator /'dʒenəreɪtə(r)/ n gerador m

gener|ous /'dʒenərəs/ a generoso; (plentiful) abundante. ~osity /-'rɒsətɪ/ n generosidade f

genetic /dʒɪ'netɪk/ a genético. ~s n genética f

genial /'dʒi:nɪəl/ a agradável

genital /'dʒenɪtl/ a genital. ~s npl órgãos mpl genitais

genius /'dʒi:nɪəs/ n (pl -uses) gênio m, (P) génio m

genocide /'dʒenəsaɪd/ n genocídio m

gent /dʒent/ n the G~s (colloq) banheiros mpl de homens, (P) lavabos mpl para homens

genteel /dʒen'tiːl/ a elegante, fino, refinado

gentl|e /'dʒentl/ a (~er, ~est) bran-
do, suave. ~eness n brandura f, suavidade f. ~y adv brandamente,
suavemente

gentleman /'dʒentlmən/ n (pl -men)
senhor m; (well-bred) cavalheiro m

genuine /'dʒenjuɪn/ a genuíno, verdadeiro; (belief) sincero

geograph|y /dʒɪ'ɒgrəfɪ/ n geografia f.
~er n geógrafo m. ~ical /dʒɪə-
'græfɪkl/ a geográfico

geolog|y /dʒɪ'ɒlədʒɪ/ n geologia f.
~ical /dʒɪə'lɒdʒɪkl/ a geológico.
~ist n geólogo m

geometr|y /dʒɪ'ɒmətrɪ/ n geometria
f. ~ic(al) /dʒɪə'metrɪk(l)/ a geomé-
trico

geranium /dʒə'remiəm/ n gerânio m

geriatric /dʒerɪ'ætrɪk/ a geriátrico

germ /dʒɜːm/ n germe m, micróbio m

German /'dʒɜːmən/ a & n alemão (m),
alemã (f); (lang) alemão (m). ~
measles rubéola f. ~ic /dʒə'mænɪk/
a germânico. ~y n Alemanha f

germinate /'dʒɜːmɪneɪt/ vi germinar

gestation /dʒe'steɪʃn/ n gestação f

gesticulate /dʒe'stɪkjʊleɪt/ vi gesticular

gesture /'dʒestʃə(r)/ n gesto m

get /get/ vt (pt got, pres p getting)
(have) ter; (receive) receber; (catch)
apanhar; (earn, win) ganhar; (fetch)
ir buscar; (find) achar; (colloq: understand) entender. ~ sb to do sth
fazer com que alguém faça alg coisa
□ vi ir, chegar; (become) ficar. ~ mar-
ried/ready casar-se/aprontar-se. ~
about andar dum lado para o outro. ~
across atravessar. ~ along or by
(manage) ir indo. ~ along or on
with entender-se com. ~ at (reach)
chegar a; (attack) atacar; (imply)
insinuar. ~ away ir-se embora; (escape) fugir. ~ back vi voltar □ vt
recuperar. ~ by (pass) passar, escapar; (manage) aguentar-se. ~ down
descer. ~ in entrar. ~ off vi descer;
(leave) partir; (jur) ser absolvido □ vt
(remove) tirar. ~ on (succeed) fazer
progressos, ir; (be on good terms)
dar-se bem. ~ out sair. ~ out of
(fig) fugir de. ~ over (illness) restabelecer-se de. ~ round (person) convencer; (rule) contornar. ~ up vi
levantar-se □ vt (mount) montar. ~-
up n (colloq) apresentação f

getaway /'getəweɪ/ n fuga f

geyser /'giːzə(r)/ n aquecedor m;
(geol) géiser m, (P) gêiser m

Ghana /'gɑːnə/ n Gana m

ghastly /'gɑːstlɪ/ a (-ier, -iest) horrível; (pale) lívido

gherkin /'gɜːkɪn/ n pepino m pequeno
para conservas, cornichão m

ghetto /'getəʊ/ n (pl -os) gueto m,
ghetto m

ghost /gəʊst/ n fantasma m, espectro
m. ~ly a fantasmagórico, espectral

giant /'dʒaɪənt/ a & n gigante (m)

gibberish /'dʒɪbərɪʃ/ n algaravia f,
linguagem f incompreensível

gibe /dʒaɪb/ n zombaria f □ vi ~ (at)
zombar (de)

giblets /'dʒɪblɪts/ npl miúdos mpl,
miudezas fpl

giddy /'gɪdɪ/ a (-ier, -iest) estonteante,
vertiginoso. be or feel ~ ter tonturas
or vertigens

gift /gɪft/ n presente m, dádiva f; (ability) dom m, dote m. ~-wrap vt (pt
-wrapped) fazer um embrulho de presente

gifted /'gɪftɪd/ a dotado

gig /gɪg/ n (colloq) show m, sessão f de
jazz etc

gigantic /dʒaɪ'gæntɪk/ a gigantesco

giggle /'gɪgl/ vi dar risadinhas nervo-
sas □ n risinho m nervoso

gild /gɪld/ vt dourar

gills /gɪlz/ npl guelras fpl

gilt /gɪlt/ a & n dourado (m). ~-edged
a de toda a confiança

gimmick /'gɪmɪk/ n truque m,
artifício m

gin /dʒɪn/ n gin m, genebra f

ginger /'dʒɪndʒə(r)/ n gengibre m □ a
louro-avermelhado, ruivo. ~ ale, ~
beer cerveja f de gengibre, (P) ginger
ale m

gingerbread /'dʒɪndʒəbred/ n pão m
de gengibre

gingerly /'dʒɪndʒəlɪ/ adv cautelosamente

gipsy /'dʒɪpsɪ/ n = gypsy

giraffe /dʒɪ'rɑːf/ n girafa f

girder /'gɜːdə(r)/ n trave f, viga f

girdle /'gɜːdl/ n cinto m; (corset) cinta
f □ vt rodear

girl /gɜːl/ n (child) menina f; (young
woman) moça f, (P) rapariga f. ~-
friend n amiga f; (of boy) namorada
f. ~hood n (of child) meninice f;
(youth) juventude f

giro /'dʒaɪrəʊ/ n sistema m de trans-
ferência de crédito entre bancos;
(cheque) cheque m pago pelo governo
a desempregados ou doentes

girth /gɜːθ/ n circunferência f,
perímetro m

gist /dʒɪst/ n essencial m

give /gɪv/ vt/i (pt gave, pp given) dar;
(bend, yield) ceder. ~ away dar; (secret) revelar, trair. ~ back devolver.
~ in dar-se por vencido, render-se. ~
off emitir. ~ out vt anunciar □ vi
esgotar-se. ~ up vt/i desistir (de),

renunciar (a). ~ o.s. up entregar-se. ~ way ceder; (traffic) dar prioridade; (collapse) dar de si

given /'gɪvn/ see give □ a dado. ~ name nome m de batismo, (P) baptismo

glacier /'glæsɪə(r)/ n glaciar m, geleira f

glad /glæd/ a contente. ~ly adv com (todo o) prazer

gladden /'glædn/ vt alegrar

glam|our /'glæmə(r)/ n fascinação f, encanto m. ~orize vt tornar fascinante. ~orous a fascinante, sedutor

glance /glɑːns/ n relance m, olhar m □ vi ~ at dar uma olhada a. at first ~ à primeira vista

gland /glænd/ n glândula f

glar|e /gleə(r)/ vi brilhar intensamente, faiscar □ n luz f crua; (fig) olhar m feroz. ~e at olhar ferozmente para. ~ing a brilhante; (obvious) flagrante

glass /glɑːs/ n vidro m; (vessel, its contents) copo m; (mirror) espelho m. ~es óculos mpl. ~y a vitreo

glaze /gleɪz/ vt (door etc) envidraçar; (pottery) vidrar □ n vidrado m

gleam /gliːm/ n raio m de luz frouxa; (fig) vislumbre m □ vi luzir, brilhar

glean /gliːn/ vt catar

glee /gliː/ n alegria f. ~ful a cheio de alegria

glib /glɪb/ a que tem a palavra fácil, verboso. ~ly adv fluentemente, sem hesitação. ~ness n verbosidade f

glide /glaɪd/ vi deslizar; (bird, plane) planar. ~r /-ə(r)/ n planador m

glimmer /'glɪmə(r)/ n luz f trêmula □ vi tremular

glimpse /glɪmps/ n vislumbre m. catch a ~ of entrever, ver de relance

glint /glɪnt/ n brilho m, reflexo m □ vi brilhar, cintilar

glisten /'glɪsn/ vi reluzir

glitter /'glɪtə(r)/ vi luzir, resplandecer □ n esplendor m, cintilação f

gloat /gləʊt/ vi ~ over ter um prazer maligno em, exultar com

global /'gləʊbl/ a global

globe /gləʊb/ n globo m

gloom /gluːm/ n obscuridade f; (fig) tristeza f. ~y a sombrio; (sad) triste; (pessimistic) pessimista

glorif|y /'glɔːrɪfaɪ/ vt glorificar. a ~ied waitress/etc pouco mais que uma garçonete/etc

glorious /'glɔːrɪəs/ a glorioso

glory /'glɔːrɪ/ n glória f; (beauty) esplendor m □ vi ~ in orgulhar-se de

gloss /glɒs/ n brilho m □ a brilhante □ vt ~ over minimizar, encobrir. ~y a brilhante

glossary /'glɒsərɪ/ n (pl -ries) glossário m

glove /glʌv/ n luva f. ~ compartment porta-luvas m. ~d a enluvado

glow /gləʊ/ vi arder; (person) resplandecer; (eyes) brilhar □ n brasa f. ~ing a (fig) entusiástico

glucose /'gluːkəʊs/ n glucose f

glue /gluː/ n cola f □ vt (pres p gluing) colar

glum /glʌm/ a (glummer, glummest) sorumbático; (dejected) abatido

glut /glʌt/ n superabundância f

glutton /'glʌtn/ n glutão m. ~ous a glutão. ~y n gula f

gnarled /naːld/ a nodoso

gnash /næʃ/ vt ~ one's teeth ranger os dentes

gnat /næt/ n mosquito m

gnaw /nɔː/ vt/i roer

gnome /nəʊm/ n gnomo m

go /gəʊ/ vi (pt went, pp gone) ir; (leave) ir-se, ir-se; (mech) andar, funcionar; (become) ficar; (be sold) vender-se; (vanish) ir-se, desaparecer □ n (pl goes) (energy) dinamismo m; (try) tentativa f; (success) sucesso m; (turn) vez f. ~ riding ir andar or montar a cavalo. ~ shopping ir às compras. be ~ing to do ir fazer. ~ ahead ir para diante. ~ away ir-se embora. ~ back voltar atrás (on com). ~ bad estragar-se. ~ by (pass) passar. ~ down descer; (sun) pôr-se; (ship) afundar-se. ~ for ir buscar; (like) gostar de; (sl: attack) atirar-se a, ir-se a (colloq). ~ in entrar. ~ in for (exam) apresentar-se a. ~ off ir-se; (explode) rebentar; (sound) soar; (decay) estragar-se. ~ on continuar; (happen) acontecer. ~ out sair; (light) apagar-se. ~ over or through verificar, examinar. ~ round (be enough) chegar. ~ under ir abaixo. ~ up subir. ~ without passar sem. on the ~ em grande atividade, (P) actividade. ~-ahead n luz f verde □ a dinâmico, empreendedor. ~-between n intermediário m. ~-kart n kart m. ~-slow n operação f tartaruga, (P) greve f de zelo

goad /gəʊd/ vt aguilhoar, espicaçar

goal /gəʊl/ n meta f; (area) baliza f; (score) gol m, (P) golo m. ~-post n trave f

goalkeeper /'gəʊlkiːpə(r)/ n goleiro m, (P) guarda-redes m

goat /gəʊt/ n cabra f

gobble /'gɒbl/ vt comer com sofreguidão, devorar

goblet /'gɒblɪt/ n taça f, cálice m

goblin /'gɒblɪn/ n duende m

God /gɒd/ n Deus m. ~-forsaken a miserável, abandonado

god /gɒd/ n deus m. ~-daughter n afilhada f. ~-dess n deusa f. ~-father n padrinho m. ~-ly a devoto. ~-mother n madrinha f. ~-son n afilhado m

godsend /'gɒdsend/ n achado m, dádiva f do céu

goggles /'gɒglz/ npl óculos mpl de protecção, (P) protecção

going /'gəʊŋ/ n it is slow/hard ~ é demorado/difícil □ a (price, rate) corrente, atual, (P) actual. ~s-on npl acontecimentos mpl estranhos

gold /gəʊld/ n ouro m □ a de/em ouro. ~-mine n mina f de ouro

golden /'gəʊldən/ a de ouro; (like gold) dourado; (opportunity) único. ~ wedding bodas fpl de ouro

goldfish /'gəʊldfɪʃ/ n peixe m dourado/vermelho

goldsmith /'gəʊldsmɪθ/ n ourives m inv

golf /gɒlf/ n golfe m. ~ club clube m de golfe, associação f de golfe; (stick) taco m. ~-course n campo m de golfe. ~er n jogador m de golfe

gone /gɒn/ see go □ a ido, passado. ~ six o'clock depois das seis

gong /gɒŋ/ n gongo m

good /gʊd/ a (better, best) bom □ n bem m. as ~ as praticamente. for ~ para sempre. it is no ~ não adianta. it is no ~ shouting/etc não adianta gritar/etc. ~ afternoon int boa(s) tarde(s). ~ evening/night int boa(s) noite(s). G~ Friday Sexta-feira f Santa. ~-looking a bonito. ~ morning int bom dia. ~ name bom nome m

goodbye /gʊd'baɪ/ int & n adeus (m)

goodness /'gʊdnɪs/ n bondade f. my ~ness! meu Deus!

goods /gʊdz/ npl (comm) mercadorias fpl. ~ train trem m de carga, (P) comboio m de mercadorias

goodwill /gʊd'wɪl/ n boa vontade f

goose /guːs/ n (pl geese) ganso m. ~-flesh, ~-pimples ns pele f de galinha

gooseberry /'gʊzbərɪ/ n (fruit) groselha f; (bush) groselheira f

gore¹ /gɔː(r)/ n sangue m coagulado

gore² /gɔː(r)/ vt perfurar

gorge /gɔːdʒ/ n desfiladeiro m, garganta f □ vt ~ o.s. empanturrar-se

gorgeous /'gɔːdʒəs/ a magnífico, maravilhoso

gorilla /gə'rɪlə/ n gorila m

gormless /'gɔːmlɪs/ a (sl) estúpido

gorse /gɔːs/ n giesta f, tojo m, urze f

gory /'gɔːrɪ/ a (-ier, -iest) sangrento

gosh /gɒʃ/ int puxa!, (P) caramba!

gospel /'gɒspl/ n evangelho m

gossip /'gɒsɪp/ n bisbilhotice f, fofoca f; (person) bisbilhoteiro m, fofoqueiro m □ vi (pt gossiped) bisbilhotar. ~y a bisbilhoteiro, fofoqueiro

got /gɒt/ see get. have ~ ter. have ~ to do ter de or que fazer

Gothic /'gɒθɪk/ a gótico

gouge /gaʊdʒ/ vt ~ out arrancar

gourmet /'gʊəmeɪ/ n gastrônomo m, (P) gastrónomo m, gourmet m

gout /gaʊt/ n gota f

govern /'gʌvn/ vt/i governar. ~ess n preceptora f. ~or n governador m; (of school, hospital etc) diretor m, (P) director m

government /'gʌvənmənt/ n governo m. ~al /-'mentl/ a governamental

gown /gaʊn/ n vestido m; (of judge, teacher) toga f

GP abbr see general practitioner

grab /græb/ vt (pt grabbed) agarrar, apanhar

grace /greɪs/ n graça f □ vt honrar; (adorn) ornar. say ~ dar graças. ~ful a gracioso

gracious /'greɪʃəs/ a gracioso; (kind) amável, afável

grade /greɪd/ n categoria f; (of goods) classe f, qualidade f; (on scale) grau m; (school mark) nota f □ vt classificar

gradient /'greɪdɪənt/ n gradiente m, declive m

gradual /'grædʒʊəl/ a gradual, progressivo. ~ly adv gradualmente

graduate¹ /'grædʒʊət/ n diplomado m, graduado m, licenciado m

graduate|e² /'grædʒʊeɪt/ vt/i formar (-se). ~ion /-'eɪʃn/ n colação f de grau, (P) formatura f

graffiti /grə'fiːtiː/ npl graffiti mpl

graft /grɑːft/ n (med, bot) enxerto m; (work) batalha f □ vt enxertar; (work) batalhar

grain /greɪn/ n grão m; (collectively) cereais mpl; (in wood) veio m. against the ~ (fig) contra a maneira de ser

gram /græm/ n grama m

gramm|ar /'græmə(r)/ n gramática f. ~atical /grə'mætɪkl/ a gramatical

grand /grænd/ a (-er, -est) grandioso, magnífico; (duke, master) grão. ~ piano piano m de cauda

grand|child /'græntʃaɪld/ n (pl -children) neto m. ~-daughter n neta f. ~-father n avô m. ~-mother n avó f. ~-parents npl avós mpl. ~-son n neto m

grandeur /'grændʒə(r)/ n grandeza f

grandiose /'grændɪəʊs/ a grandioso

grandstand /'grændstænd/ n tribuna f principal

granite /'grænɪt/ n granito m

grant /grɑːnt/ vt conceder; (a request) ceder a; (admit) admitir (that que) □ n subsídio m; (univ) bolsa f. take for

~ed ter como coisa garantida, contar com

grape /greɪp/ *n* uva *f*

grapefruit /'greɪpfruːt/ *n inv* grapefruit *m*, toranja *f*

graph /grɑːf/ *n* gráfico *m*

graphic /'græfɪk/ *a* gráfico; (*fig*) vívido. ~**s** *npl* (*comput*) gráficos *mpl*

grapple /'græpl/ *vi* ~ with estar engalfinhado com; (*fig*) estar às voltas com

grasp /grɑːsp/ *vt* agarrar; (*understand*) compreender □ *n* domínio *m*; (*reach*) alcance *m*; (*fig: understanding*) compreensão *f*

grasping /'grɑːspɪŋ/ *a* ganancioso

grass /grɑːs/ *n* erva *f*, (*lawn*) grama *f*, (*P*) relva *f*; (*pasture*) pastagem *f*; (*sl: informer*) delator *m* □ *vt* cobrir com grama; (*sl: betray*) delatar. ~ **roots** (*pol*) bases *fpl*. ~**y** *a* coberto de erva

grasshopper /'grɑːshɒpə(r)/ *n* gafanhoto *m*

grate[1] /greɪt/ *n* (*fireplace*) lareira *f*; (*frame*) grelha *f*

grate[2] /greɪt/ *vt* ralar □ *vi* ranger. ~ one's teeth ranger os dentes. ~**r** /-ə(r)/ *n* ralador *m*

grateful /'greɪtfl/ *a* grato, agradecido. ~**ly** *adv* com reconhecimento, com gratidão

gratify /'grætɪfaɪ/ *vt* (*pt* -fied) contentar, satisfazer. ~**ing** *a* gratificante

grating /'greɪtɪŋ/ *n* grade *f*

gratis /'greɪtɪs/ *a* & *adv* grátis (*invar*), de graça

gratitude /'grætɪtjuːd/ *n* gratidão *f*, reconhecimento *m*

gratuitous /grə'tjuːɪtəs/ *a* gratuito; (*uncalled-for*) sem motivo

gratuity /grə'tjuːətɪ/ *n* gratificação *f*, gorjeta *f*

grave[1] /greɪv/ *n* cova *f*, sepultura *f*, túmulo *m*

grave[2] /greɪv/ *a* (-er, -est) grave, sério. ~**ly** *adv* gravemente

grave[3] /grɑːv/ *a* ~ accent acento *m* grave

gravel /'grævl/ *n* cascalho *m* miúdo, saibro *m*

gravestone /'greɪvstəʊn/ *n* lápide *f*, campa *f*

graveyard /'greɪvjɑːd/ *n* cemitério *m*

gravity /'grævətɪ/ *n* gravidade *f*

gravy /'greɪvɪ/ *n* molho *m* (de carne)

graze[1] /greɪz/ *vt/i* pastar

graze[2] /greɪz/ *vt* roçar; (*scrape*) esfolar □ *n* esfoladura *f*, (*P*) esfoladela *f*

greas|**e** /griːs/ *n* gordura *f* □ *vt* engordurar; (*culin*) untar; (*mech*) lubrificar. ~**e-proof paper** papel *m* vegetal. ~**y** *a* gorduroso

great /greɪt/ *a* (-er, -est) grande; (*colloq: splendid*) esplêndido. G~ Brit-

ain Grã-Bretanha *f*. ~**-grandfather** *n* bisavô *m*. ~**-grandmother** *f* bisavó *f*. ~**ly** *adv* grandemente, muito. ~**ness** *n* grandeza *f*

Great Britain /greɪt'brɪtn/ *n* Grã-Bretanha *f*

Greece /griːs/ *n* Grécia *f*

greed /griːd/ *n* cobiça *f*, ganância *f*; (*for food*) gula *f*. ~**y** *a* cobiçoso, ganancioso; (*for food*) guloso

Greek /griːk/ *a* & *n* grego (*m*)

green /griːn/ *a* (-er, -est) verde □ *n* verde *m*; (*grass*) gramado *m*, (*P*) relvado *m*. ~**s** hortaliças *fpl*. ~ **belt** zona *f* verde, paisagem *f* protegida. ~ **light** luz *f* verde. ~**ery** *n* verdura *f*

greengrocer /'griːngrəʊsə(r)/ *n* quitandeiro *m*, (*P*) vendedor *m* de hortaliças

greenhouse /'griːnhaʊs/ *n* estufa *f*. ~ **effect** efeito estufa

Greenland /'griːnlənd/ *n* Groenlândia *f*

greet /griːt/ *vt* acolher. ~**ing** *n* saudação *f*; (*welcome*) acolhimento *m*. ~**ings** *npl* cumprimentos *mpl*; (*Christmas etc*) votos *mpl*, desejos *mpl*

gregarious /grɪ'geərɪəs/ *a* gregário; (*person*) sociável

grenade /grɪ'neɪd/ *n* granada *f*

grew /gruː/ *see* grow

grey /greɪ/ *a* (-er, -est) cinzento; (*of hair*) grisalho □ *n* cinzento *m*

greyhound /'greɪhaʊnd/ *n* galgo *m*

grid /grɪd/ *n* (*grating*) gradeamento *m*, grade *f*; (*electr*) rede *f*

grief /griːf/ *n* dor *f*. come to ~ acabar mal

grievance /'griːvns/ *n* razão *f* de queixa

grieve /griːv/ *vt* sofrer, afligir □ *vi* sofrer. ~ **for** chorar por

grill /grɪl/ *n* grelha *f*; (*food*) grelhado *m*; (*place*) grill *m* □ *vt* grelhar; (*question*) submeter a interrogatório cerrado, apertar com perguntas □ *vi* grelhar

grille /grɪl/ *n* grade *f*; (*of car*) grelha *f*

grim /grɪm/ *a* (grimmer, grimmest) sinistro; (*without mercy*) implacável

grimace /grɪ'meɪs/ *n* careta *f* □ *vi* fazer careta(s)

grim|**e** /graɪm/ *n* sujeira *f*, (*P*) encardido, sujo

grin /grɪn/ *vi* (*pt* grinned) sorrir abertamente, dar um sorriso largo □ *n* sorriso *m* aberto

grind /graɪnd/ *vt* (*pt* ground) triturar; (*coffee*) moer; (*sharpen*) amolar, afiar. ~ one's teeth ranger os dentes. ~ **to a halt** parar freando lentamente

grip /grɪp/ *vt* (*pt* gripped) agarrar;

(*interest*) prender □ *n* (*of hands*)
aperto *m*; (*control*) controle *m*,
domínio *m*. come to ~s with arcar
com. ~ping *a* apaixonante

grisly /'grɪzlɪ/ *a* (-ier, -iest) macabro,
horrível

gristle /'grɪsl/ *n* cartilagem *f*

grit /grɪt/ *n* areia *f*, grão *m* de areia;
(*fig: pluck*) coragem *f*, fortaleza *f* □ *vt*
(*pt* gritted) (*road*) jogar areia em;
(*teeth*) cerrar

groan /grəʊn/ *vi* gemer □ *n* gemido *m*

grocer /'grəʊsə(r)/ *n* dono/a *m/f* de
mercearia. ~ies *npl* artigos *mpl* de
mercearia. ~y *n* (*shop*) mercearia *f*

groggy /'grɒgɪ/ *a* (-ier, -iest) grogue,
fraco das pernas

groin /grɔɪn/ *n* virilha *f*

groom /gru:m/ *n* noivo *m*; (*for
horses*) moço *m* de estrebaria □ *vt*
(*horse*) tratar de; (*fig*) preparar

groove /gru:v/ *n* ranhura *f*; (*for door,
window*) calha *f*; (*in record*) estria *f*;
(*fig*) rotina *f*

grope /grəʊp/ *vi* tatear. ~ for procurar às cegas

gross /grəʊs/ *a* (-er, -est) (*vulgar*)
grosseiro; (*flagrant*) flagrante; (*of
error*) crasso; (*of weight, figure etc*)
bruto □ *n* (*pl invar*) grosa *f*. ~ly *adv*
grosseiramente; (*very*) extremamente

grotesque /grəʊ'tesk/ *a* grotesco

grotty /'grɒtɪ/ *a* (*sl*) sórdido

grouch /graʊtʃ/ *vi* (*colloq*) ralhar. ~y
a (*colloq*) rabugento

ground¹ /graʊnd/ *n* chão *m*, solo *m*;
(*area*) terreno *m*; (*reason*) razão *f*,
motivo *m*. ~s jardins *mpl*; (*of coffee*)
borra(s) *f* (*pl*) □ *vt/i* (*naut*) encalhar;
(*plane*) reter em terra. ~ floor térreo
m, (*P*) rés-do-chão *m*. ~less *a* infundado, sem fundamento

ground² /graʊnd/ *see* grind

grounding /'graʊndɪŋ/ *n* bases *fpl*,
conhecimentos *mpl* básicos

groundsheet /'graʊndʃi:t/ *n* impermeável *m* para o chão

groundwork /'graʊndwɜːk/ *n* trabalhos *mpl* de base *or* preliminares

group /gru:p/ *n* grupo *m* □ *vt/i* agru-
par(-se)

grouse¹ /graʊs/ *n* (*pl invar*) galo *m*
silvestre

grouse² /graʊs/ *vi* (*colloq: grumble*)
resmungar; (*colloq: complain*) queixar-se

grovel /'grɒvl/ *vi* (*pt* grovelled) hu-
milhar-se; (*fig*) rebaixar-se

grow /grəʊ/ *vi* (*pt* grew *pp* grown)
crescer; (*become*) tornar-se □ *vt*
cultivar. ~ old envelhecer. ~ up
crescer, tornar-se adulto. ~er *n* culti-
vador *m*, produtor *m*. ~ing *a* crescente

growl /graʊl/ *vi* rosnar □ *n* rosnadela
f

grown /grəʊn/ *see* grow □ *a* ~ man
homem feito. ~-up *a* adulto □ (*increase*) aumento *m*; (*med*) tumor *m*

grub /grʌb/ *n* larva *f*; (*sl: food*)
papança *f* (*collog*) (*B*) bóia (*sl*) *f*, (*P*)
alimento *m*

grubby /'grʌbɪ/ *a* (-ier, -iest) sujo,
porco

grudge /grʌdʒ/ *vt* dar/reconhecer de
má vontade □ *n* má vontade *f*. ~
doing fazer de má vontade. ~ sb sth
dar alg a alguém má vontade. have a
~ against ter ressentimento contra.
grudgingly *adv* relutantemente

gruelling /'gru:əlɪŋ/ *a* estafante, ex-
tenuante

gruesome /'gru:səm/ *a* macabro

gruff /grʌf/ *a* (-er, -est) carrancudo,
rude

grumble /'grʌmbl/ *vi* resmungar (at
contra, por)

grumpy /'grʌmpɪ/ *a* (-ier, -iest) mal-
humorado, rabugento

grunt /grʌnt/ *vi* grunhir □ *n* grunhi-
do *m*

guarantee /gærən'ti:/ *n* garantia *f* □
vt garantir

guard /gɑːd/ *vt* guardar, proteger □ *vi*
~ against precaver-se contra □ *n*
guarda *f*; (*person*) guarda *m*; (*on
train*) condutor *m*. ~ian *n* guar-
dião *m*, defensor *m*; (*of orphan*) tutor
m

guarded /'gɑːdɪd/ *a* cauteloso, cir-
cunspeto, (*P*) circunspecto

guerrilla /gə'rɪlə/ *n* guerrilheiro *m*,
(*P*) guerrilha *m*. ~ warfare guerrilha *f*, guerra *f* de guerrilhas

guess /ges/ *vt/i* adivinhar; (*suppose*)
supor □ *n* suposição *f*, conjetura *f*,
(*P*) conjectura *f*

guesswork /'geswɜːk/ *n* suposição *f*,
conjetura(s) *f* (*pl*), (*P*) conjectura(s)
f (*pl*)

guest /gest/ *n* convidado *m*; (*in hotel*)
hóspede *mf*. ~-house *n* pensão *f*

guffaw /gə'fɔː/ *n* gargalhada *f* □ *vi* rir
à(s) gargalhada(s)

guidance /'gaɪdns/ *n* orientação *f*,
direção *f*, (*P*) direcção *f*

guide /gaɪd/ *n* guia *mf* □ *vt* guiar. ~d
missile míssil *m* guiado; (*remote-
control*) míssil *m* teleguiado. ~-dog
n cão *m* de cego, cão-guia *m*. ~-
lines *npl* diretrizes *fpl*, (*P*) directrizes
fpl

Guide /gaɪd/ *n* Guia *f*

guidebook /'gaɪdbʊk/ *n* guia *m* (turístico)

guild /gɪld/ *n* corporação *f*

guile /gaɪl/ *n* astúcia *f*, manha *f*

guilt /gɪlt/ *n* culpa *f*. ~y *a* culpado

guinea-pig /'gɪnɪpɪg/ n cobaia f, porquinho-da-India m

guitar /gɪ'ta:(r)/ n guitarra f, violão m, (P) viola f. ~ist n guitarrista mf, tocador m de violão, (P) de viola

gulf /gʌlf/ n golfo m; (hollow) abismo m

gull /gʌl/ n gaivota f

gullible /'gʌləbl/ a crédulo

gully /'gʌlɪ/ n barranco m; (drain) sarjeta f

gulp /gʌlp/ vt engolir, devorar □ vi engolir em seco □ n trago m

gum¹ /gʌm/ n (anat) gengiva f

gum² /gʌm/ n goma f; (chewing-gum) chiclete m, goma f elástica, (P) pastilha f □ vt (pt gummed) colar

gumboot /'gʌmbu:t/ n bota f de borracha

gumption /'gʌmpʃn/ n (colloq) iniciativa f e bom senso m, cabeça f, juizo m

gun /gʌn/ n (pistol) pistola f; (rifle) espingarda f; (cannon) canhão m □ vt (pt gunned) ~ down abater a tiro

gunfire /'gʌnfaɪə(r)/ n tiroteio m

gunman /'gʌnmən/ n (pl -men) bandido m armado

gunpowder /'gʌnpaʊdə(r)/ n pólvora f

gunshot /'gʌnʃɒt/ n tiro m

gurgle /'gɜ:gl/ n gorgolejo m □ vi gorgolejar

gush /gʌʃ/ vi jorrar □ n jorro m. ~ing a efusivo, derretido

gust /gʌst/ n (of wind) rajada f; (of smoke) nuvem f. ~y a ventoso

gusto /'gʌstəʊ/ n gosto m, entusiasmo m

gut /gʌt/ n tripa f. ~s (belly) barriga f; (colloq: courage) coragem f □ vt (pt gutted) estripar; (fish) limpar; (fire) destruir o interior de

gutter /'gʌtə(r)/ n calha f, canaleta f; (in street) sarjeta f, valeta f

guy /gaɪ/ n (sl: man) cara m, (P) tipo m (colloq)

guzzle /'gʌzl/ vt/i comer/beber com sofreguidão, encher-se (de)

gym /dʒɪm/ n (colloq: gymnasium) ginásio m; (colloq: gymnastics) ginástica f. ~-slip n uniforme m escolar

gymnasium /dʒɪm'neɪzɪəm/ n ginásio m. ~nast /'dʒɪmnæst/ n ginasta mf. ~nastics /-'næstɪks/ npl ginástica f

gynaecolog|y /gaɪnɪ'kɒlədʒɪ/ n ginecologia f. ~ist n ginecologista mf

gypsy /'dʒɪpsɪ/ n cigano m

gyrate /dʒaɪ'reɪt/ vi girar

H

haberdashery /'hæbədæʃərɪ/ n armarinho m, (P) retrosaria f

habit /'hæbɪt/ n hábito m, costume m; (costume) hábito m. be in/get into the ~ of ter/apanhar o hábito de

habit|able /'hæbɪtəbl/ a habitável. ~ation /-'teɪʃn/ n habitação f

habitat /'hæbɪtæt/ n habitat m

habitual /hə'bɪtʃʊəl/ a habitual, costumeiro; (smoker, liar) inveterado. ~ly adv habitualmente

hack¹ /hæk/ n (horse) cavalo m de aluguel; (writer) escrevinhador (pej) m

hack² /hæk/ vt cortar, despedaçar. ~ to pieces cortar em pedaços

hackneyed /'hæknɪd/ a banal, batido

had /hæd/ see have

haddock /'hædək/ n invar hadoque m, eglefim m. smoked ~ hadoque m fumado

haemorrhage /'hemərɪdʒ/ n hemorragia f

haemorrhoids /'hemərɔɪdz/ npl hemorróidas fpl

haggard /'hægəd/ a desfigurado, com o rosto desfeito, magro e macilento

haggle /'hægl/ vi ~ (over) regatear

hail¹ /heɪl/ vt saudar; (taxi) fazer sinal para, chamar □ vi ~ from vir de

hail² /heɪl/ n granizo m, (P) saraiva f, (P) chuva f de pedra □ vi chover granizo, (P) saraivar

hailstone /'heɪlstəʊn/ n pedra f de granizo

hair /heə(r)/ n (on head) cabelo(s) m(pl); (on body) pêlos mpl; (single strand) cabelo m; (of animal) pêlo m. ~-do n (colloq) penteado m. ~-dryer n secador m de cabelo. ~-raising a horripilante, de pôr os cabelos em pé. ~-style n estilo m de penteado

hairbrush /'heəbrʌʃ/ n escova f para o cabelo

haircut /'heəkʌt/ n corte m de cabelo

hairdresser /'heədresə(r)/ n cabeleireiro m, cabeleireira f

hairpin /'heəpɪn/ n grampo m, (P) gancho m para o cabelo. ~ bend curva f techada, quase em W

hairy /'heərɪ/ a (-ier, -iest) peludo, cabeludo; (sl: terrifying) de pôr os cabelos em pé, horripilante

hake /heɪk/ n (pl invar) abrótea f

half /ha:f/ n (pl halves /ha:vz/) metade f, meio m □ a meio □ adv ao meio. ~ a dozen meia dúzia. ~ an hour meia hora. ~-caste n mestiço m. ~-hearted a sem grande entusiasmo. ~-term n férias fpl no meio do trimestre. ~-time n meio-tempo m. ~-way a & adv a meio caminho. ~-wit n idiota mf. go halves dividir as despesas

halibut /'hælɪbət/ n (pl invar) halibute m

hall /hɔːl/ n sala f; (entrance) vestíbulo m, entrada f; (mansion) solar m. ~ of residence residência f de estudantes

hallmark /'hɔːlmaːk/ n (on gold etc) marca f do contraste; (fig) cunho m, selo m

hallo /hə'ləʊ/ int & n (greeting, surprise) olá; (on phone) está

hallow /'hæləʊ/ vt consagrar, santificar

Halloween /hæləʊ'iːn/ n véspera f do Dia de Todos os Santos

hallucination /həluːsɪ'neɪʃn/ n alucinação f

halo /'heɪləʊ/ n (pl -oes) halo m, auréola f

halt /hɔːlt/ n parada f, (P) paragem f □ vt deter, fazer parar □ vi fazer alto, parar

halve /haːv/ vt dividir ao meio; (time etc) reduzir à metade

ham /hæm/ n presunto m

hamburger /'hæmbɜːɡə(r)/ n hambúrguer m, (P) hamburgo m

hamlet /'hæmlɪt/ n aldeola f, lugarejo m

hammer /'hæmə(r)/ n martelo m □ vt/i martelar; (fig) bater com força

hammock /'hæmək/ n rede f (de dormir)

hamper¹ /'hæmpə(r)/ n cesto m, (P) cabaz m

hamper² /'hæmpə(r)/ vt dificultar, atrapalhar

hamster /'hæmstə(r)/ n hamster m

hand /hænd/ n mão f; (of clock) ponteiro m; (writing) letra f; (worker) trabalhador m; (cards) mão f, (measure) palmo m. (helping) ~ ajuda f, mão f □ vt dar, entregar. at ~ à mão. ~-baggage n bagagem f de mão. ~ in or over entregar. ~ out distribuir. ~-out n impresso m, folheto m; (money) esmola f, donativo m. on the one ~... on the other ~ por um lado ... por outro. out of ~ incontrolável. to ~ à mão

handbag /'hændbæɡ/ n carteira f, bolsa de mão f, mala de mão f

handbook /'hændbʊk/ n manual m

handbrake /'hændbreɪk/ n freio m de mão, (P) travão m de mão

handcuffs /'hændkʌfs/ npl algemas fpl

handful /'hændfʊl/ n mão-cheia f, punhado m; (a few) punhado m; (diffi-cult task) mão-de-obra f. she's a ~ (colloq) ela é danada

handicap /'hændɪkæp/ n (in competition) handicap m; (disadvantage) desvantagem f □ vt (pt handicapped) prejudicar. ~ped a deficiente. mentally ~ped deficiente mental

handicraft /'hændɪkraːft/ n artesanato m, trabalho m manual

handiwork /'hændɪwɜːk/ n obra f, trabalho m

handkerchief /'hæŋkətʃɪf/ n lenço m

handle /'hændl/ n (of door etc) maçaneta f, puxador m; (of cup etc) asa f; (of implement) cabo m; (of pan etc) alça f, (P) pega f □ vt (touch) manusear, tocar; (operate with hands) manejar; (deal in) negociar em; (deal with) tratar de; (person) lidar com. fly off the ~ (colloq) perder as estribeiras

handlebar /'hændlbaː(r)/ n guidão m, (P) guiador m

handmade /'hændmeɪd/ a feito à mão

handshake /'hændʃeɪk/ n aperto m de mão

handsome /'hænsəm/ a bonito; (fig) generoso

handwriting /'hændraɪtɪŋ/ n letra f, caligrafia f

handy /'hændɪ/ a (-ier, -iest) a (convenient, useful) útil, prático; (person) jeitoso; (near) à mão

handyman /'hændɪmæn/ n (pl -men) faz-tudo m

hang /hæŋ/ vt (pt hung) pendurar, suspender; (head) baixar; (pt hanged) (criminal) enforcar □ vi estar dependurado, pender; (criminal) ser enforcado. get the ~ of (colloq) pegar o jeito de, (P) apanhar. ~ about andar por aí. ~ back hesitar. ~-gliding n asa f delta. ~ on (wait) aguardar. ~ on to (hold tightly) agarrar-se a. ~ out (sl: live) morar. ~ up (phone) desligar. ~-up n (sl) complexo m

hangar /'hæŋə(r)/ n hangar m

hanger /'hæŋə(r)/ n (for clothes) cabide m. ~-on n parasita mf

hangover /'hæŋəʊvə(r)/ n (from drinking) ressaca f

hanker /'hæŋkə(r)/ vi ~ after ansiar por, suspirar por

haphazard /hæp'hæzəd/ a ~ly adv ao acaso, à sorte

happen /'hæpən/ vi acontecer, suceder. he ~s to be out por acaso ele não está. ~ing n acontecimento m

happ|y /'hæpɪ/ a (-ier, -iest) feliz. be ~y with estar contente com. ~y-go-lucky a despreocupado. ~ily adv com satisfação; (fortunately) felizmente. she smiled ~ily ela sorriu feliz. ~iness n felicidade f

harass /'hærəs/ vt amofinar, atormentar, perseguir. ~ment n amofinação f, perseguição f. sexual ~ment assédio m sexual

harbour /'ha:bə(r)/ n porto m; (shelter) abrigo m □ vt abrigar, dar asilo a; (fig: in the mind) ocultar, obrigar

hard /ha:d/ a (-er, -est) duro; (difficult) difícil □ adv muito, intensamente; (look) fixamente; (pull) com força; (think) a fundo, a sério. ~back n livro m encadernado. ~ boiled egg ovo m cozido. ~ by muito perto. ~ disk disco m rígido. ~-headed a realista, prático. ~ of hearing meio surdo. ~ shoulder acostamento m, (P) berma f alcatroada. ~ up (colloq) sem dinheiro, teso (sl), liso (sl). ~ water água f dura

hardboard /'ha:dbɔ:d/ n madeira f compensada, madeira f prensada, (P) tabopan m

harden /'ha:dn/ vt/i endurecer. ~ed a (callous) calejado; (robust) enrijado

hardly /'ha:dlɪ/ adv mal, dificilmente, a custo. ~ ever quase nunca

hardship /'ha:dʃɪp/ n provação f, adversidade f; (suffering) sofrimento m; (financial) privação f

hardware /'ha:dweə(r)/ n ferragens fpl; (comput) hardware m

hardy /'ha:dɪ/ a (-ier, -iest) resistente

hare /heə(r)/ n lebre f

hark /ha:k/ vi ~ back to voltar a, recordar

harm /ha:m/ n mal m □ vt prejudicar, fazer mal a. ~ful a prejudicial, nocivo. ~less a inofensivo. out of ~'s way a salvo. there's no ~ in não há mal em

harmonica /ha:'mɒnɪkə/ n gaita f de boca, (P) beiços

harmony /'ha:mənɪ/ n harmonia f. ~ious /-'məʊnɪəs/ a harmonioso. ~ize vt/i harmonizar(-se)

harness /'ha:nɪs/ n arreios mpl □ vt arrear; (fig: use) aproveitar, utilizar

harp /ha:p/ n harpa f □ vi ~ on (about) repisar. ~ist n harpista mf

harpoon /ha:'pu:n/ n arpão m

harpsichord /'ha:psɪkɔ:d/ n cravo m

harrowing /'hærəʊɪŋ/ a dilacerante, lancinante

harsh /ha:ʃ/ a (-er, -est) duro, severo; (texture, voice) áspero; (light) cru; (colour) gritante; (climate) rigoroso. ~ly adv duramente. ~ness n dureza f

harvest /'ha:vɪst/ n colheita f, ceifa f □ vt colher, ceifar

has /hæz/ see have

hash /hæʃ/ n picadinho m, carne f cozida; (fig: jumble) bagunça f. make a ~ of fazer uma bagunça

hashish /'hæʃiːʃ/ n haxixe m

hassle /'hæsl/ n (colloq: quarrel) discussão f, (colloq: struggle) dificuldade f □ vt (colloq) aborrecer

haste /heɪst/ n pressa f. make ~ apressar-se

hasten /'heɪsn/ vt/i apressar(-se)

hasty /'heɪstɪ/ a (-ier, -iest) apressado; (too quick) precipitado. ~ily adv às pressas, precipitadamente

hat /hæt/ n chapéu m

hatch¹ /hætʃ/ n (for food) postigo m; (naut) escotilha f

hatch² /hætʃ/ vt/i chocar; (a plot etc) tramar, urdir

hatchback /'hætʃbæk/ n carro m de três ou cinco portas

hatchet /'hætʃɪt/ n machadinha f

hate /heɪt/ n ódio m □ vt odiar, detestar. ~ful a odioso, detestável

hatred /'heɪtrɪd/ n ódio m

haughty /'hɔ:tɪ/ a (-ier, -iest) altivo, soberbo, arrogante

haul /hɔ:l/ vt arrastar, puxar; (goods) transportar em camião □ n (booty) presa f; (fish caught) apanha f; (distance) percurso m. ~age n transporte m de cargas. ~ier n (firm) transportadora f rodoviária; (person) fretador m

haunt /hɔ:nt/ vt rondar, freqüentar; (P) frequentar; (ghost) assombrar; (thought) obcecar □ n lugar m favorito. ~ed house casa f malassombrada

have /hæv/ vt (3 sing pres has, pt had) ter; (bath etc) tomar; (meal) fazer; (walk) dar □ v aux ter. ~ done ter feito. ~ it out (with) pôr a coisa em pratos limpos, pedir uma explicação (para). ~ sth done mandar fazer alg coisa

haven /'heɪvn/ n porto m; (refuge) refúgio m

haversack /'hævəsæk/ n mochila f

havoc /'hævək/ n estragos mpl. play ~ with causar estragos em

hawk¹ /hɔ:k/ n falcão m

hawk² /hɔ:k/ vt vender de porta em porta. ~er n vendedor m ambulante

hawthorn /'hɔ:θɔ:n/ n pilriteiro m, estrepeiro m

hay /heɪ/ n feno m. ~ fever febre f do feno

haystack /'heɪstæk/ n palheiro m, (P) meda f de feno

haywire /'heɪwaɪə(r)/ a go ~ (colloq) ficar transtornado

hazard /'hæzəd/ n risco m □ vt arriscar. ~ warning lights pisca-alerta m. ~ous a arriscado haze /heiz/ n bruma f, neblina f, cerração f

hazel /'heizl/ n aveleira f. ~-nut n avelã f

hazy /'heizi/ a (-ier, -iest) brumoso, encoberto; (fig: vague) vago

he /hi:/ pron ele □ n macho m

head /hed/ n cabeça f; (chief) chefe m; (of beer) espuma f □ a principal □ vt encabeçar, estar à frente de □ vi ~ for dirigir-se para. ~-dress n toucador m. ~ first de cabeça. ~-on a frontal □ adv de frente. ~s or tails? cara ou coroa? ~ waiter chefe de garçons m, (P) dos criados. ~er n (football) cabeçada f

headache /'hedeik/ n dor f de cabeça

heading /'hediŋ/ n cabeçalho m, título m; (subject category) rubrica f

headlamp /'hedlæmp/ n farol m

headland /'hedlənd/ n promontório m

headlight /'hedlait/ n farol m

headline /'hedlain/ n título m, cabeçalho m

headlong /'hedloŋ/ a de cabeça; (rash) precipitado □ adv de cabeça; (rashly) precipitadamente

head|master /hed'ma:stə(r)/ n diretor m, (P) director m. ~mistress n diretora f, (P) directora f

headphone /'hedfəun/ n fone m de cabeça, (P) auscultador m

headquarters /hed'kwɔ:təz/ npl sede f; (mil) quartel m general

headrest /'hedrest/ n apoio m para a cabeça

headroom /'hedru:m/ n (auto) espaço m para a cabeça; (bridge) limite m de altura, altura f máxima

headstrong /'hedstroŋ/ a teimoso

headway /'hedwei/ n progresso m. make ~ fazer progressos

heady /'hedi/ a (-ier, -iest) empolgante

heal /hi:l/ vt/i curar(-se), sarar; (wound) cicatrizar

health /helθ/ n saúde f. ~ centre posto m de saúde. ~ foods alimentos mpl naturais. ~y a saudável, sadio

heap /hi:p/ n monte m, pilha f □ vt amontoar, empilhar. ~s of money (colloq) dinheiro aos montes (colloq)

hear /hiə(r)/ vt/i (pt heard /hɜ:d/) ouvir. ~, hear! apoiado! ~ from ter notícias de. ~ of or about ouvir falar de. I won't ~ of it nem quero ouvir falar nisso. ~ing n ouvido m, audição f; (jur) audiência f. ~ing-aid n aparelho m de audição

hearsay /'hiəsei/ n boato m. it's only ~ é só por ouvir dizer

hearse /hɜ:s/ n carro m funerário

heart /ha:t/ n coração m. ~s (cards) copas fpl. at ~ no fundo. by ~ de cor. ~ attack ataque m de coração. ~-beat n pulsação f, batida f. ~-breaking a de cortar o coração. ~-broken a com o coração partido, desfeito. ~-to-heart a com o coração nas mãos. lose ~ perder a coragem, desanimar

heartburn /'ha:tbɜ:n/ n azia f

hearten /'ha:tn/ vt animar, encorajar

heartfelt /'ha:tfelt/ a sincero, sentido

hearth /ha:θ/ n lareira f

heartless /'ha:tlis/ a insensível, desalmado, cruel

heart|y /'ha:ti/ a (-ier, -iest) caloroso; (meal) abundante. ~ily adv calorosamente; (eat, laugh) com vontade

heat /hi:t/ n calor m; (fig) ardor m; (contest) eliminatória f □ vt/i aquecer. ~stroke n insolação f. ~-wave n onda f de calor. ~er n aquecedor m. ~ing n aquecimento m

heated /'hi:tid/ a (fig) acalorado, aceso

heathen /'hi:ðn/ n pagão m, pagã f

heather /'heðə(r)/ n urze f

heave /hi:v/ vt/i (lift) içar; (a sigh) soltar; (retch) ter náuseas; (colloq: throw) atirar

heaven /'hevn/ n céu m. ~ly a celestial; (colloq) divino

heav|y /'hevi/ a (-ier, -iest) pesado; (blow, rain) forte; (cold, drinker) grande; (traffic) intenso. ~ily adv pesadamente; (drink, smoke etc) inveterado

heavyweight /'heviweit/ n (boxing) peso-pesado m

Hebrew /'hi:bru:/ a hebreu, hebraico □ n (lang) hebreu m

heckle /'hekl/ vt interromper, interpelar

hectic /'hektik/ a muito agitado, febril

hedge /hedʒ/ n sebe f □ vt cercar □ vi (in answering) usar de evasivas. ~ one's bets (fig) resguardar-se

hedgehog /'hedʒhog/ n ouriço-cacheiro m

heed /hi:d/ vt prestar atenção a, escutar □ n pay ~ to prestar atenção a, dar ouvidos a. ~less a ~less of indiferente a, sem prestar atenção a

heel /hi:l/ n calcanhar m; (of shoe) salto m; (sl) canalha m

hefty /'hefti/ a (-ier, -iest) robusto e corpulento

height /hait/ n altura f; (of mountain, plane) altitude f; (fig) auge m, cúmulo m

heighten /'haitn/ vt/i aumentar, elevar(-se)

heir /eə(r)/ n herdeiro m. ~ess n herdeira f

heirloom /ˈeəluːm/ n peça f de família, (P) relíquia f de família

held /held/ see hold[1]

helicopter /ˈhelɪkɒptə(r)/ n helicóptero m

hell /hel/ n inferno m. for the ~ of it só por gozo. ~-bent a decidido a todo o custo (on a). ~ish a infernal

hello /həˈləʊ/ int & n = hallo

helm /helm/ n leme m

helmet /ˈhelmɪt/ n capacete m

help /help/ vt/i ajudar □ n ajuda f. home ~ empregada f, faxineira f, (P) mulher f a dias. ~ o.s. to servir-se de. he cannot ~ laughing ele não pode conter o riso. it can't be ~ed não há remédio. ~er n ajudante mf. ~ful a útil; (serviceable) de grande ajuda. ~less a impotente

helping /ˈhelpɪŋ/ n porção f, dose f

hem /hem/ n bainha f □ vt (pt hemmed) fazer a bainha. ~ in cercar, encurralar

hemisphere /ˈhemɪsfɪə(r)/ n hemisfério m

hemp /hemp/ n cânhamo m

hen /hen/ n galinha f

hence /hens/ adv (from now) a partir desta altura; (for this reason) daí, por isso. a week ~ daqui a uma semana. ~forth adv de agora em diante, doravante

henpecked /ˈhenpekt/ a mandado, (P) dominado pela mulher

her /hɜː(r)/ pron a (a ela); (after prep) ela. (to) ~ lhe. I know ~ conheço-a □ a seu(s), sua(s); dela

herald /ˈherəld/ vt anunciar

heraldry /ˈherəldrɪ/ n heráldica f

herb /hɜːb/ n erva f culinária or medicinal

herd /hɜːd/ n manada f; (of pigs) vara f □ vi ~ together juntar-se em rebanho

here /hɪə(r)/ adv aqui □ int tome; aqui está. to/from ~ para aqui/daqui

hereafter /hɪərˈɑːftə(r)/ adv de/para o futuro, daqui em diante □ n the ~ a vida de além-túmulo, (P) a vida futura

hereby /hɪəˈbaɪ/ adv (jur) pelo presente ato ou decreto, etc, (P) pelo presente acto ou decreto, etc

hereditary /hɪˈredɪtrɪ/ a hereditário

heredity /hɪˈredətɪ/ n hereditariedade f

here|sy /ˈherəsɪ/ n heresia f. ~tic n herege mf. ~tical /hɪˈretɪkl/ a herético

heritage /ˈherɪtɪdʒ/ n herança f, património m, (P) património m

hermit /ˈhɜːmɪt/ n eremita m

hernia /ˈhɜːnɪə/ n hérnia f

hero /ˈhɪərəʊ/ n (pl -oes) herói m

heroic /hɪˈrəʊɪk/ a heróico

heroin /ˈherəʊɪn/ n heroína f

heroine /ˈherəʊɪn/ n heroína f

heroism /ˈherəʊɪzəm/ n heroísmo m

heron /ˈherən/ n garça f

herring /ˈherɪŋ/ n arenque m

hers /hɜːz/ poss pron o(s) seu(s), a(s) sua(s), o(s) dela, a(s) dela. it is ~ é o (o) dela or o seu

herself /hɜːˈself/ pron ela mesma; (reflexive) se. by ~ sozinha. for ~ para si mesma. to ~ a/para si mesma. Mary ~ said so foi a própria Maria que o disse

hesitant /ˈhezɪtənt/ a hesitante

hesitat|e /ˈhezɪteɪt/ vt hesitar. ~ion /-ˈteɪʃn/ n hesitação f

heterosexual /hetərəʊˈseksjʊəl/ a & n heterossexual (mf)

hexagon /ˈheksəgən/ n hexágono m. ~al /-ˈægənl/ a hexagonal

hey /heɪ/ int eh, olá

heyday /ˈheɪdeɪ/ n auge m, apogeu m

hi /haɪ/ int olá, viva

hibernat|e /ˈhaɪbəneɪt/ vi hibernar. ~ion /-ˈneɪʃn/ n hibernação f

hiccup /ˈhɪkʌp/ n soluço m □ vi soluçar, estar com soluços

hide[1] /haɪd/ vt/i (pt hid, pp hidden) esconder(-se) (from de). ~-and-seek n (game) esconde-esconde m. ~-out n (colloq) esconderijo m

hide[2] /haɪd/ n pele f, couro m

hideous /ˈhɪdɪəs/ a horrendo, medonho

hiding /ˈhaɪdɪŋ/ n (colloq: thrashing) sova f, surra f. go into ~ esconder-se. ~-place n esconderijo m

hierarchy /ˈhaɪərɑːkɪ/ n hierarquia f

hi-fi /ˈhaɪfaɪ/ a & n (de) alta fidelidade (f)

high /haɪ/ a (-er, -est) alto; (price, number) elevado; (voice, pitch) agudo □ n alta f □ adv alto. two metres ~ com dois metros de altura. ~ chair cadeira f alta para crianças. ~-handed a autoritário, prepotente. ~-jump salto m em altura. ~-rise building edifício m alto, (P) torre f. ~ school escola f secundária. in the ~ season em plena estação. ~-speed a ultra-rápido. ~-spirited a animado, vivo. ~ spot (sl) ponto m culminante. ~ street rua f principal. ~ tide maré f alta. ~er education ensino m superior

highbrow /ˈhaɪbraʊ/ a & n (colloq) intelectual m

highlight /ˈhaɪlaɪt/ n (fig) ponto m alto □ vt salientar, pôr em relevo, realçar

highly /ˈhaɪlɪ/ adv altamente, extremamente. ~-strung a muito sensível, nervoso, tenso. speak ~ of falar bem de

Highness /'haɪnɪs/ n Alteza f

highway /'haɪweɪ/ n estrada f, rodovia f. H~ Code Código m Nacional de Trânsito

hijack /'haɪdʒæk/ vt seqüestrar, (P) sequestrar □ n seqüestro m, (P) sequestro m. ~er n (of plane) pirata m (do ar)

hike /haɪk/ n caminhada no campo f □ vi fazer uma caminhada. ~r /-ə(r)/ n excursionista mf, caminhante mf

hilarious /hɪ'leərɪəs/ a divertido, desopilante

hill /hɪl/ n colina f, monte m; (slope) ladeira f, subida f. ~y a acidentado

hillside /'hɪlsaɪd/ n encosta f, vertente f

hilt /hɪlt/ n punho m. to the ~ completamente, inteiramente

him /hɪm/ pron o (a ele); (after prep) ele. (to) ~ lhe. I know ~ conheço-o

himself /hɪm'self/ pron ele mesmo; (reflexive) se. by ~ sozinho. for ~ para si mesmo. to ~ a/para si mesmo. Peter ~ saw it foi o próprio Pedro que o viu

hind /haɪnd/ a traseiro, posterior

hind|er /'hɪndə(r)/ vt empatar, estorvar; (prevent) impedir. ~rance n estorvo m

hindsight /'haɪndsaɪt/ n with ~ em retrospecto

Hindu /hɪn'duː/ n & a hindu (mf). ~ism /-ɪzəm/ n hinduísmo m

hinge /hɪndʒ/ n dobradiça f □ vi ~ on depender de

hint /hɪnt/ n insinuação f, indireta f, (P) indirecta f; (advice) sugestão f, dica f (colloq) □ vt dar a entender, insinuar □ vi ~ at fazer alusão a

hip /hɪp/ n quadril m

hippie /'hɪpɪ/ n hippie mf

hippopotamus /hɪpə'pɒtəməs/ n (pl -muses) hipopótamo m

hire /'haɪə(r)/ vt alugar; (person) contratar □ n aluguel m, (P) aluguer m. ~-purchase n compra f a prestações, (P) crediário m

hirsute /'hɜːsjuːt/ a hirsuto

his /hɪz/ a seu(s), sua(s), dele □ poss pron o(s) seu(s), a(s) sua(s), o(s) dele, a(s) dele. it is ~ é (o) dele or o seu

Hispanic /hɪs'pænɪk/ a hispânico

hiss /hɪs/ n silvo m; (for disapproval) assobio m, vaia f □ vt/i sibilar; (for disapproval) assobiar, vaiar

historian /hɪ'stɔːrɪən/ n historiador m

histor|y /'hɪstərɪ/ n história f. ~ic(al) /hɪ'stɒrɪk(l)/ a histórico

hit /hɪt/ vt (pt hit, pres p hitting) atingir, bater em; (knock against, collide with) chocar com, ir de encontro a; (strike a target) acertar em; (find)

descobrir; (affect) atingir □ vi ~ on dar com □ n pancada f; (fig: success) sucesso m. ~ it off dar-se bem (with com). ~-and-run a (driver) que foge depois do desastre. ~-or-miss a ao acaso

hitch /hɪtʃ/ vt atar, prender; (to a hook) enganchar □ n sacão m; (snag) problema m. ~ a lift, ~-hike viajar de carona, (P) boleia. ~-hiker n o que viaja de carona, boleia. ~ up puxar para cima

hive /haɪv/ n colméia f □ vt ~ off separar e tornar independente

hoard /hɔːd/ vt juntar, açambarcar □ n provisão f; (of valuables) tesouro m

hoarding /'hɔːdɪŋ/ n tapume m, outdoor m

hoarse /hɔːs/ a (-er, -est) rouco. ~ness n rouquidão f

hoax /həʊks/ n (malicious) logro m, embuste m; (humorous) trote m □ vt (malicious) enganer, lograr; passar um trote, pregar uma peça

hob /hɒb/ n placa f de aquecimento (do fogão)

hobble /'hɒbl/ vi coxear □ vt pear

hobby /'hɒbɪ/ n passatempo m favorito. ~-horse n (fig) tópico m favorito

hock /hɒk/ n vinho m branco do Reno

hockey /'hɒkɪ/ n hóquei m

hoe /həʊ/ n enxada f □ vt trabalhar com enxada

hog /hɒg/ n porco m; (greedy person) glutão m □ vt (pt hogged) (colloq) açambarcar

hoist /hɔɪst/ vt içar □ n guindaste m, (P) monta-cargas m

hold[^1] /həʊld/ vt (pt held) segurar; (contain) levar; (possess) ter, possuir; (occupy) ocupar; (keep, maintain) conservar, manter; (affirm) manter □ vi (of rope etc) agüentar(-se), (P) aguentar(-se) □ n (influence) domínio m. get ~ of pôr as mãos em; (fig) apanhar. ~ back reter. ~ on (colloq) esperar. ~ on to guardar; (cling to) agarrar-se a. ~ one's breath suster a respiração. ~ one's tongue calar-se. ~ the line não desligar. ~ out resistir. ~ up (support) sustentar; (delay) demorar; (rob) assaltar. ~-up n atraso m; (auto) engarrafamento m; (robbery) assalto m. ~ with agüentar, (P) aguentar. ~er n detentor m; (of post, title etc) titular mf; (for object) suporte m

hold[^2] /həʊld/ n (of ship, plane) porão m

holdall /'həʊldɔːl/ n saco m de viagem

holding /'həʊldɪŋ/ n (land) propriedade f; (comm) ações fpl, (P) acções fpl, valores mpl, holding m hole /həʊl/ n buraco m □ vt abrir buraco(s) em, esburacar

holiday /ˈhɒlədeɪ/ n férias fpl; (day off: public) feriado m □ vi passar férias. ~-maker n pessoa f em férias; (in summer) veranista mf, (P) veraneante mf

holiness /ˈhəʊlɪnɪs/ n santidade f

Holland /ˈhɒlənd/ n Holanda f

hollow /ˈhɒləʊ/ a oco, vazio; (fig) falso; (cheeks) fundo; (sound) surdo □ n (in the ground) cavidade f; (in the hand) cova f

holly /ˈhɒlɪ/ n azevinho m

holster /ˈhəʊlstə(r)/ n coldre m

holy /ˈhəʊlɪ/ a (-ier -iest) santo, sagrado; (water) benta. H~ Ghost, H~ Spirit Espírito m Santo

homage /ˈhɒmɪdʒ/ n homenagem f. pay ~ to prestar homenagem a

home /həʊm/ n casa f, lar m; (institution) lar m, asilo m; (country) país m natal □ a caseiro, doméstico; (of family) de família; (pol) nacional, interno; (football match) em casa □ adv (at) ~ em casa. come/go ~ vir/ir para casa. make oneself at ~ não fazer cerimónia, (P) cerimónia. ~-made a caseiro. H~ Office Ministério m do Interior. ~ town cidade f or terra f natal. ~ truth dura verdade f, verdade(s) f (pl) amarga(s). ~less a sem casa, desabrigado

homeland /ˈhəʊmlænd/ n pátria f

homely /ˈhəʊmlɪ/ a (-ier -iest) (simple) simples; (Amer: ugly) sem graça

homesick /ˈhəʊmsɪk/ a be ~ ter saudades

homeward /ˈhəʊmwəd/ a (journey) de regresso

homework /ˈhəʊmwɜːk/ n trabalho m de casa, dever m de casa

homicide /ˈhɒmɪsaɪd/ n homicídio m; (person) homicida mf

homoeopath|y /ˌhəʊmɪˈɒpəθɪ/ n homeopatia f. ~ic a homeopático

homosexual /ˌhɒməˈsekʃʊəl/ a & n homossexual (mf)

honest /ˈɒnɪst/ a honesto; (frank) franco. ~ly adv honestamente; (frankly) francamente. ~y n honestidade f

honey /ˈhʌnɪ/ n mel m; (colloq: darling) querido m, querida f, meu bem m

honeycomb /ˈhʌnɪkəʊm/ n favo m de mel

honeymoon /ˈhʌnɪmuːn/ n lua de mel f

honorary /ˈɒnərərɪ/ a honorário

honour /ˈɒnə(r)/ n honra f □ vt honrar. ~able a honrado, honroso

hood /hʊd/ n capuz m; (car roof) capota f, (P) tejadilho m; (Amer: bonnet)

hoodwink /ˈhʊdwɪŋk/ vt enganar

hoof /huːf/ n (pl -fs) casco m

hook /hʊk/ n gancho m; (on garment) colchete m; (for fishing) anzol m □ vt engancha; (fish) apanhar, pescar. off the ~ livre de dificuldades; (phone) desligado

hooked /hʊkt/ a be ~ on (sl) ter o vício de, estar viciado em

hookey /ˈhʊkɪ/ n play ~ (Amer sl) fazer gazeta

hooligan /ˈhuːlɪgən/ n desordeiro m

hoop /huːp/ n arco m; (of cask) cinta f

hooray /huːˈreɪ/ int & n = hurrah

hoot /huːt/ n (of owl) pio m de mocho; (of horn) buzinada f; (jeer) apupo m □ vi (of owl) piar; (of horn) buzinar; (jeer) apupar. ~er n buzina f; (of factory) sereia f

Hoover /ˈhuːvə(r)/ n aspirador de pó m, (P) aspirador m □ vt passar o aspirador

hop[1] /hɒp/ vi (pt hopped) saltar num pé só, (P) ao pé coxinho □ n salto m. ~ in (colloq) subir, saltar (colloq). ~ it (sl) pôr-se a andar (colloq). ~ out (colloq) descer, saltar (colloq)

hop[2] /hɒp/ n (plant) lúpulo m. ~s espigas fpl de lúpulo

hope /həʊp/ n esperança f □ vt/i esperar. ~ for esperar (ter). ~ful a esperançoso; (promising) promissor. be ~ful (that) ter esperança (que), confiar (em que). ~fully adv esperançosamente; (it is hoped that) é de esperar que. ~less a desesperado, sem esperança; (incompetent) incapaz

horde /hɔːd/ n horda f

horizon /həˈraɪzn/ n horizonte m

horizontal /ˌhɒrɪˈzɒntl/ a horizontal

hormone /ˈhɔːməʊn/ n hormónio m, (P) hormona f

horn /hɔːn/ n chifre m, corno m; (of car) buzina f; (mus) trompa f. ~y a caloso, calejado

hornet /ˈhɔːnɪt/ n vespão m

horoscope /ˈhɒrəskəʊp/ n horóscopo m, (P) horoscópio m

horrible /ˈhɒrəbl/ a horrível, horroroso

horrid /ˈhɒrɪd/ a horrível, horripilante

horrific /həˈrɪfɪk/ a horrífico

horror /ˈhɒrə(r)/ n horror m □ a (film etc) de terror. ~ify vt horrorizar, horripilar

horse /hɔːs/ n cavalo m. ~-chestnut n castanha f da Índia. ~-racing n corrida f de cavalos, hipismo m. ~-radish n rábano m

horseback /ˈhɔːsbæk/ n on ~ a cavalo

horseplay /'hɔ:spleɪ/ n brincadeira f grosseira, abrutalhada f

horsepower /'hɔ:spaʊə(r)/ n cavalo-vapor m

horseshoe /'hɔ:ʃu:/ n ferradura f

horticultur|e /'hɔ:tɪkʌltʃə(r)/ n horticultura f. ~al /-'kʌltʃərəl/ a hortícola

hose /həʊz/ n ~(-pipe) mangueira f □ vt regar com a mangueira

hospice /'hɒspɪs/ n hospício m; (for travellers) hospedaria f

hospit|able /həˈspɪtəbl/ a hospitaleiro. ~ality /-'tælətɪ/ n hospitalidade f

hospital /'hɒspɪtl/ n hospital m

host¹ /həʊst/ n anfitrião m, dono m da casa. ~ess n anfitriã f, dona f da casa

host² /həʊst/ n a ~ of uma multidão de, um grande número de

host³ /həʊst/ n (relig) hóstia f

hostage /'hɒstɪdʒ/ n refém m

hostel /'hɒstl/ n residência f de estudantes etc

hostile /'hɒstaɪl/ a hostil. ~ity /hɒ'stɪlətɪ/ n hostilidade f

hot /hɒt/ a (hotter, hottest) quente; (culin) picante. be or feel ~ estar com or ter calor. it is ~ está or faz calor □ vt/i (pt hotted) ~ up (colloq) aquecer. ~ dog cachorro-quente m. ~ line linha direta f, (P) directa esp entre chefes de estado. ~-water bottle saco m de água quente

hotbed /'hɒtbed/ n (fig) foco m

hotchpotch /'hɒtʃpɒtʃ/ n misturada f, (P) salgalhada f

hotel /həʊ'tel/ n hotel m. ~ier /-ɪə(r)/ n hoteleiro m

hound /haʊnd/ n cão m de caça e de corrida, sabujo m □ vt acossar, perseguir

hour /'aʊə(r)/ n hora f. ~ly adv de hora em hora □ a de hora em hora. ~ly pay retribuição f horária. paid ~ly pago por hora

house¹ /haʊs/ n (pl ~s /'haʊzɪz/) n casa f; (pol) câmara f. on the ~ por conta da casa. ~-warming n inauguração f da casa

house² /haʊz/ vt alojar; (store) arrecadar, guardar

houseboat /'haʊsbəʊt/ n casa f flutuante

household /'haʊshəʊld/ n família f, agregado m familiar. ~er n ocupante mf; (owner) proprietário m

housekeep|er /'haʊski:pə(r)/ n governanta f. ~ing n (work) tarefas fpl domésticas

housewife /'haʊswaɪf/ n (pl -wives) dona f de casa

housework /'haʊswɜ:k/ n tarefas fpl domésticas

housing /'haʊzɪŋ/ n alojamento m. ~ estate zona f residencial

hovel /'hɒvl/ n casebre m, tugúrio m

hover /'hɒvə(r)/ vi pairar; (linger) deixar-se ficar, demorar-se

hovercraft /'hɒvəkra:ft/ n invar aerobarco m, hovercraft m

how /haʊ/ adv como. ~ long/old is...? que comprimento/idade tem...? ~ far? a que distância? ~ many? quantos? ~ much? quanto? ~ often? com que freqüência, (P) frequência? ~ pretty it is como é lindo. ~ about a walk? e se fôssemos dar uma volta? ~ are you? como vai? ~ do you do? muito prazer! and ~! oh se é!

however /haʊ'evə(r)/ adv de qualquer maneira; (though) contudo, no entanto, todavia. ~ small it may be por menor que seja

howl /haʊl/ n uivo m □ vi uivar

HP abbr see hire-purchase

hp abbr see horsepower

hub /hʌb/ n cubo m da roda; (fig) centro m. ~-cap n calota f, (P) tampão m da roda

hubbub /'hʌbʌb/ n chinfrim m

huddle /'hʌdl/ vt/i apinhar(-se). ~ together aconchegar-se

hue¹ /hju:/ n matiz f, tom m

hue² /hju:/ n ~ and cry clamor m, alarido m

huff /hʌf/ n in a ~ com raiva, zangado

hug /hʌg/ vt (pt hugged) abraçar, apertar nos braços; (keep close to) chegar-se a □ n abraço m

huge /hju:dʒ/ a enorme

hulk /hʌlk/ n casco (esp de navio desmantelado) m. ~ing a (colloq) desajeitadão (colloq)

hull /hʌl/ n (of ship) casco m

hullo /hə'ləʊ/ int & n = hallo

hum /hʌm/ vt/i (pt hummed) cantar com a boca fechada; (of insect, engine) zumbir □ n zumbido m

human /'hju:mən/ a humano □ n ~ (being) ser m humano

humane /hju:'meɪn/ a humano, compassivo

humanitarian /hju:mænɪ'teərɪən/ a humanitário

humanity /hju:'mænətɪ/ n humanidade f

humbl|e /'hʌmbl/ a (-er, -est) humilde □ vt humilhar. ~y adv humildemente

humdrum /'hʌmdrʌm/ a monótono, rotineiro

humid /'hju:mɪd/ a úmido, (P) húmido. ~ity /-'mɪdətɪ/ n umidade f, (P) humidade f

humiliat|e /hju:'mɪlɪeɪt/ vt humilhar. ~ion /-'eɪʃn/ n humilhação f humility /hjuːˈmɪlətɪ/ n humildade f

humorist /ˈhjuːmərɪst/ n humorista mf

hum|our /ˈhjuːmə(r)/ n humor m ▫ vt fazer a vontade de. ~orous a humorístico; (person) divertido, espirituoso

hump /hʌmp/ n corcova f; (of the back) corcunda f ▫ vt corcovar, arquear. the ~ (sl) a neura (colloq)

hunch¹ /hʌntʃ/ vt curvar. ~ed up curvado

hunch² /hʌntʃ/ n (colloq) palpite m

hunchback /ˈhʌntʃbæk/ n corcunda mf

hundred /ˈhʌndrəd/ a cem ▫ n centena f, cento m. ~s of centenas de. ~fold a cêntuplo ▫ adv cem vezes mais. ~th a & n centésimo (m)

hundredweight /ˈhʌndrədweɪt/ n quintal m (= 50,8 kg; Amer 45,36 kg)

hung /hʌŋ/ see hang

Hungar|y /ˈhʌŋɡərɪ/ n Hungria f. ~ian /-ˈɡeərɪən/ a & n húngaro (m)

hunger /ˈhʌŋɡə(r)/ n fome f ▫ vi ~ for ter fome de; (fig) desejar vivamente, ansiar por

hungr|y /ˈhʌŋɡrɪ/ a (-ier -iest) esfomeado, faminto. be ~y ter fome, estar com fome. ~ily adv avidamente

hunk /hʌŋk/ n grande naco m

hunt /hʌnt/ vt/i caçar ▫ n caça f. ~ for andar à caça de, andar à procura de. ~er n caçador m. ~ing n caça f, caçada f

hurdle /ˈhɜːdl/ n obstáculo m

hurl /hɜːl/ vt arremessar, lançar com força

hurrah, hurray /huˈrɑː, huˈreɪ/ int & n hurra (m), viva (m)

hurricane /ˈhʌrɪkən/ n furacão m

hurried /ˈhʌrɪd/ a apressado. ~ly adv apressadamente, às pressas

hurry /ˈhʌrɪ/ vt/i apressar(-se), despachar(-se) ▫ n pressa f. be in a ~ estar com ar ter pressa. do sth in a ~ fazer alg coisa às pressas. ~ up! ande logo

hurt /hɜːt/ vt (pt hurt) fazer mal a; (injure, offend) magoar, ferir ▫ vi doer ▫ a magoado, ferido ▫ n mal m; (feelings) mágoa f. ~ful a prejudicial; (remark etc) que magoa

hurtle /ˈhɜːtl/ vi despenhar-se; (move rapidly) precipitar-se ▫ vt arremessar

husband /ˈhʌzbənd/ n marido m, esposo m

hush /hʌʃ/ vt (fazer) calar. ~! silencio! ▫ vi calar-se ▫ n silêncio m. ~hush a (colloq) muito em segredo. ~ up abafar, encobrir

husk /hʌsk/ n casca f

husky /ˈhʌskɪ/ a (-ier -iest) (hoarse) rouco, enrouquecido; (burly) corpulento ▫ n cão m esquimó

hustle /ˈhʌsl/ vt empurrar, dar encontrões a ▫ n empurrão m. ~ and bustle grande movimento m

hut /hʌt/ n cabana f, barraca f de madeira

hutch /hʌtʃ/ n coelheira f

hyacinth /ˈhaɪəsɪnθ/ n jacinto m

hybrid /ˈhaɪbrɪd/ a & n híbrido (m)

hydrant /ˈhaɪdrənt/ n hidrante m

hydraulic /harˈdrɔːlɪk/ a hidráulico

hydroelectric /haɪdrəʊˈlektrɪk/ a hidrelétrico, (P) hidroeléctrico

hydrofoil /ˈhaɪdrəʊfɔɪl/ n hidrofoil m

hydrogen /ˈhaɪdrədʒən/ n hidrogênio m, (P) hidrogénio m

hyena /harˈiːnə/ n hiena f

hygiene /ˈhaɪdʒiːn/ n higiene f

hygienic /harˈdʒiːnɪk/ a higiénico, (P) higiénico

hymn /hɪm/ n hino m, cântico m

hyper- /ˈhaɪpə(r)/ pref hiper-

hypermarket /ˈhaɪpəmɑːkɪt/ n hipermercado m

hyphen /ˈhaɪfn/ n hífen m, traço-de-união m. ~ate vt unir com hífen

hypno|sis /hɪpˈnəʊsɪs/ n hipnose f. ~tic /-ˈnɒtɪk/ a hipnótico

hypnot|ize /ˈhɪpnətaɪz/ vt hipnotizar. ~ism /-ɪzəm/ n hipnotismo m

hypochondriac /haɪpəˈkɒndrɪæk/ n hipocondríaco m

hypocrisy /hɪˈpɒkrəsɪ/ n hipocrisia f

hypocrite /ˈhɪpəkrɪt/ n hipócrita mf. ~ical /-ˈkrɪtɪkl/ a hipócrita

hypodermic /haɪpəˈdɜːmɪk/ a hipodérmico ▫ n seringa f

hypothe|sis /harˈpɒθəsɪs/ n (pl -theses /-siːz/) hipótese f. ~tical /-əˈθetɪkl/ a hipotético

hyster|ia /hɪˈstɪərɪə/ n histeria f. ~ical /hɪˈsterɪkl/ a histérico

I

I /aɪ/ pron eu

Iberian /arˈbɪərɪən/ a ibérico ▫ n íbero m

ice /aɪs/ n gelo m ▫ vt/i gelar; (cake) cobrir com glacê ▫ vi ~ up gelar. ~box n (Amer) geladeira f, (P) frigorífico m. ~(-cream) n sorvete m, (P) gelado m. ~-cube n cubo m or pedra f de gelo. ~ hockey hóquei m sobre o gelo. ~ lolly picolé m. ~pack n saco m de gelo. ~rink n rinque m de patinação, (P) patinagem f no gelo. ~ skating n patinação f, (P) patinagem f no gelo

iceberg /ˈaɪsbɜːɡ/ n iceberg m; (fig) pedaço m de gelo

Iceland /ˈaɪslənd/ n Islândia f. ~er n islandês m. ~ic /-ˈlændɪk/ a & n islandês (m)

icicle /ˈaɪsɪkl/ n pingente m de gelo

icing /'aɪsɪŋ/ n (*culin*) cobertura f de açúcar, glacê m

icy /'aɪsɪ/ a (-ier, -iest) gelado, gélido, glacial; (*road*) com gelo

idea /aɪ'dɪə/ n ideia f, (P) ideia f

ideal /aɪ'dɪəl/ a & n ideal (m). ~ize vt idealizar. ~ly adv idealmente

idealis|t /aɪ'dɪəlɪst/ n idealista mf. ~m /-zəm/ n idealismo m. ~tic /-'lɪstɪk/ a idealista

identical /aɪ'dentɪkl/ a idêntico

identify /aɪ'dentɪfaɪ/ vt identificar □ vi ~y with identificar-se com. ~ication /-ɪ'keɪʃn/ n identificação f; (*papers*) documentos mpl de identificação

identity /aɪ'dentətɪ/ n identidade f. ~ card carteira f de identidade

ideology /aɪdɪ'blɒdʒɪ/ n ideologia f. ~ical a /-ɪə'lɒdʒɪkl/ ideológico

idiom /'ɪdɪəm/ n idioma m; (*phrase*) expressão f idiomática. ~atic /-'mætɪk/ a idiomático

idiosyncrasy /ɪdɪə'sɪŋkrəsɪ/ n idiossincrasia f, peculiaridade f

idiot /'ɪdɪət/ n idiota mf. ~ic /-'ɒtɪk/ a idiota

idl|e /'aɪdl/ a (-er, -est) (*not active*; *lazy*) ocioso; (*unemployed*) sem trabalho; (*of machines*) parado; (*fig: useless*) inútil □ vt/i (*of engine*) estar em ponto morto, P estar no ralenti. ~eness n ociosidade f. ~y adv ociosamente

idol /'aɪdl/ n ídolo m. ~ize vt idolatrar

idyllic /ɪ'dɪlɪk/ a idílico

i.e. abbr isto é, quer dizer

if /ɪf/ conj se

igloo /'ɪɡluː/ n iglu m

ignite /ɪɡ'naɪt/ vt/i inflamar(-se), acender; (*catch fire*) pegar fogo; (*set fire to*) atear fogo a, (P) deitar fogo a

ignition /ɪɡ'nɪʃn/ n (*auto*) ignição f. ~ (key) chave f de ignição

ignoran|t /'ɪɡnərənt/ a ignorante. ~ce n ignorância f. be ~t of ignorar

ignore /ɪɡ'nɔː(r)/ vt não fazer caso de, passar por cima de; (*person in the street etc*) fingir não ver

ill /ɪl/ a (*sick*) doente; (*bad*) mau □ adv mal □ n mal m. ~-advised a pouco aconselhável. ~ at ease pouco à vontade. ~-bred a mal educado. ~-fated a malfadado. ~-treat vt maltratar. ~ will má vontade f, animosidade f

illegal /ɪ'liːɡl/ a ilegal

illegible /ɪ'ledʒəbl/ a ilegível

illegitima|te /ɪlɪ'dʒɪtɪmət/ a ilegítimo. ~cy n ilegitimidade f

illitera|te /ɪ'lɪtərət/ a analfabeto; (*uneducated*) iletrado. ~cy n analfabetismo m

illness /'ɪlnɪs/ n doença f

illogical /ɪ'lɒdʒɪkl/ a ilógico

illuminat|e /ɪ'luːmɪneɪt/ vt iluminar; (*explain*) esclarecer. ~ion /-'neɪʃn/ n iluminação f. ~ions npl luminárias fpl

illusion /ɪ'luːʒn/ n ilusão f

illusory /ɪ'luːsərɪ/ a ilusório

illustrat|e /'ɪləstreɪt/ vt ilustrar. ~ion /-'streɪʃn/ n ilustração f. ~ive /-ətɪv/ a ilustrativo

illustrious /ɪ'lʌstrɪəs/ a ilustre

image /'ɪmɪdʒ/ n imagem f. (public) ~ imagem f pública

imaginary /ɪ'mædʒɪnərɪ/ a imaginário

imaginat|ion /ɪmædʒɪ'neɪʃn/ n imaginação f. ~ive /ɪ'mædʒɪnətɪv/ a imaginativo

imagin|e /ɪ'mædʒɪn/ vt imaginar. ~able a imaginável

imbalance /ɪm'bæləns/ n desequilíbrio m

imbecile /'ɪmbəsiːl/ a & n imbecil (mf)

imbue /ɪm'bjuː/ vt imbuir, impregnar

imitat|e /'ɪmɪteɪt/ vt imitar. ~ion /-'teɪʃn/ n imitação f

immaculate /ɪ'mækjʊlət/ a imaculado; (*impeccable*) impecável

immaterial /ɪmə'tɪərɪəl/ a (*of no importance*) irrelevante. that's ~ to me para mim tanto faz

immature /ɪmə'tjʊə(r)/ a imaturo

immediate /ɪ'miːdɪət/ a imediato. ~ly adv imediatamente □ conj logo que, assim que

immens|e /ɪ'mens/ a imenso. ~ely /-slɪ/ adv imensamente. ~ity n imensidade f

immers|e /ɪ'mɜːs/ vt mergulhar, imergir. be ~ed in (*fig*) estar imerso em. ~ion /-ʃn/ n imersão f. ~ion heater aquecedor m de água elétrico, (P) eléctrico

immigr|ate /'ɪmɪɡreɪt/ vi imigrar. ~ant n & a imigrante (mf), imigrado (m). ~ation /-'ɡreɪʃn/ n imigração f

imminen|t /'ɪmɪnənt/ a iminente. ~ce n iminência f

immobil|e /ɪ'məʊbaɪl/ a imóvel. ~ize /-aɪz/ vt imobilizar

immoderate /ɪ'mɒdərət/ a imoderado, descomedido

immoral /ɪ'mɒrəl/ a imoral. ~ity /ɪmə'rælətɪ/ n imoralidade f

immortal /ɪ'mɔːtl/ a imortal. ~ity /-'tælətɪ/ n imortalidade f. ~ize vt imortalizar

immun|e /ɪ'mjuːn/ a imune, imunizado (from, to contra). ~ity n imunidade f

imp /ɪmp/ n diabrete m

impact /'ɪmpækt/ n impacto m

impair /ɪm'peə(r)/ vt deteriorar; (*damage*) prejudicar

impale /ɪm'peɪl/ vt empalar

impart /ɪm'pɑ:t/ vt comunicar, transmitir (to a)

impartial /ɪm'pɑ:ʃl/ a imparcial. ~ity /-ʃɪ'ælətɪ/ n imparcialidade f

impassable /ɪm'pɑ:səbl/ a (*road, river*) impraticável, intransitável; (*barrier etc*) intransponível

impasse /'æmpɑ:s/ n impasse m

impatien|t /ɪm'peɪʃənt/ a impaciente. ~ce n impaciência f. ~tly adv impacientemente

impeach /ɪm'pi:tʃ/ vt incriminar, acusar

impeccable /ɪm'pekəbl/ a impecável

impede /ɪm'pi:d/ vt impedir, estorvar

impediment /ɪm'pedɪmənt/ n impedimento m, obstáculo m. (speech) ~ defeito m (na fala)

impel /ɪm'pel/ vt (pt impelled) impelir, forçar (to do a fazer)

impending /ɪm'pendɪŋ/ a iminente

impenetrable /ɪm'penɪtrəbl/ a impenetrável

imperative /ɪm'perətɪv/ a imperativo; (*need etc*) imperioso □ n imperativo m

imperceptible /ɪmpə'septəbl/ a imperceptível

imperfect /ɪm'pɜ:fɪkt/ a imperfeito. ~ion /-ə'fekʃn/ n imperfeição f

imperial /ɪm'pɪərɪəl/ a imperial; (*of measures*) legal (*na GB*). ~ism /-lɪzəm/ n imperialismo m

imperious /ɪm'pɪərɪəs/ a imperioso

impersonal /ɪm'pɜ:sənl/ a impessoal

impersonat|e /ɪm'pɜ:səneɪt/ vt fazer-se passar por; (*theat*) fazer or representar (o papel) de. ~ion /neɪʃn/ n imitação f

impertinen|t /ɪm'pɜ:tɪnənt/ a impertinente. ~ce n impertinência f. ~tly adv com impertinência

impervious /ɪm'pɜ:vɪəs/ a ~ to (*water*) impermeável a; (*fig*) insensível a

impetuous /ɪm'petʃʊəs/ a impetuoso

impetus /'ɪmpɪtəs/ n ímpeto m

impinge /ɪm'pɪndʒ/ vi ~ on afetar, P afectar; (*encroach*) infringir

impish /'ɪmpɪʃ/ a travesso, malicioso

implacable /ɪm'plækəbl/ a implacável

implant /ɪm'plɑ:nt/ vt implantar

implement[1] /'ɪmplɪmənt/ n instrumento m, utensílio m

implement[2] /'ɪmplɪment/ vt implementar, executar

implicat|e /'ɪmplɪkeɪt/ vt implicar. ~ion /-'keɪʃn/ n implicação f

implicit /ɪm'plɪsɪt/ a implícito; (*unquestioning*) absoluto, incondicional

implore /ɪm'plɔ:(r)/ vt implorar, suplicar, rogar

imply /ɪm'plaɪ/ vt implicar; (*hint*) sugerir, dar a entender, insinuar

impolite /ɪmpə'laɪt/ a indelicado, incorreto, (P) incorrecto

import[1] /ɪm'pɔ:t/ vt importar. ~ation /-'teɪʃn/ n importação f. ~er n importador m

import[2] /'ɪmpɔ:t/ n importação f; (*meaning*) significado m; (*importance*) importância f

importan|t /ɪm'pɔ:tnt/ a importante. ~ce n importância f

impos|e /ɪm'pəʊz/ vt impôr; (*inflict*) infligir □ vi ~e on abusar de. ~ition /-ə'zɪʃn/ n imposição f; (*unfair burden*) abuso m

imposing /ɪm'pəʊzɪŋ/ a imponente

impossib|le /ɪm'pɒsəbl/ a impossível. ~ility /-'bɪlətɪ/ n impossibilidade f

impostor /ɪm'pɒstə(r)/ n impostor m

impoten|t /'ɪmpətənt/ a impotente. ~ce n impotência f

impound /ɪm'paʊnd/ vt apreender, confiscar

impoverish /ɪm'pɒvərɪʃ/ vt empobrecer

impracticable /ɪm'præktɪkəbl/ a impraticável

impractical /ɪm'præktɪkl/ a pouco prático

imprecise /ɪmprɪ'saɪs/ a impreciso

impregnable /ɪm'pregnəbl/ a inexpugnável; (*fig*) inabalável, irrefutável

impregnate /'ɪmpregneɪt/ vt impregnar (with de)

impresario /ɪmprɪ'sɑ:rɪəʊ/ n (pl -os) empresário m

impress /ɪm'pres/ vt impressionar, causar impressão a; (*imprint*) imprimir. ~ on s.o. inculcar algo em alguém

impression /ɪm'preʃn/ n impressão f. ~able a impressionável. ~ist n impressionista mf

impressive /ɪm'presɪv/ a impressionante, imponente

imprint[1] /'ɪmprɪnt/ n impressão f, marca f

imprint[2] /ɪm'prɪnt/ vt imprimir

imprison /ɪm'prɪzn/ vt prender, aprisionar. ~ment n aprisionamento m, prisão f

improbab|le /ɪm'prɒbəbl/ a improvável. ~ility /-'bɪlətɪ/ n improbabilidade f

impromptu /ɪm'prɒmptju:/ a & adv de improviso □ n impromptu m

improper /ɪm'prɒpə(r)/ a impróprio; (*indecent*) indecente, pouco decente; (*wrong*) incorreto, (P) incorrecto

improve /ɪm'pru:v/ vt/i melhorar. ~ on aperfeiçoar. ~ment n melhoria f;

(*in house etc*) melhoramento *m*; (*in health*) melhoras *fpl*

improvise /ˈɪmprəvaɪz/ *vt/i* improvisar. ~**ation** /-ˈzeɪʃn/ *n* improvisação *f*

imprudent /ɪmˈpruːdnt/ *a* imprudente

impuden|t /ˈɪmpjʊdənt/ *a* descarado, insolente. ~**ce** *n* descaramento *m*, insolência *f*

impulse /ˈɪmpʌls/ *n* impulso *m*

impulsive /ɪmˈpʌlsɪv/ *a* impulsivo

impur|e /ɪmˈpjʊə(r)/ *a* impuro. ~**ity** *n* impureza *f*

in /ɪn/ *prep* em, dentro de □ *adv* dentro; (*at home*) em casa; (*in fashion*) na moda. ~ Lisbon/English em Lisboa/inglês. ~ winter no inverno. ~ an hour (*at end of, within*) numa hora. ~ the rain na chuva. ~ doing ao fazer. ~ the evening à tardinha. the best ~ o melhor em. we are ~ for vamos ter. ~-**laws** *npl* (*colloq*) sogros *mpl*. ~-**patient** *n* doente *m* internado. the ~s and outs meandros *mpl*

inability /ɪnəˈbɪlətɪ/ *n* incapacidade *f* (to do para fazer)

inaccessible /mækˈsesəbl/ *a* inacessível

inaccura|te /ɪnˈækjərət/ *a* inexato, (*P*) inexacto. ~**cy** *n* inexatidão *f*, (*P*) inexactidão *f*, falta *f* de rigor

inaction /ɪnˈækʃn/ *n* inação *f*, (*P*) inacção *f*

inactiv|e /ɪnˈæktɪv/ *a* inativo, (*P*) inactivo. ~**ity** /-ˈtɪvətɪ/ *n* inação *f*, (*P*) inacção *f*

inadequa|te /ɪnˈædɪkwət/ *a* inadequado, impróprio; (*insufficient*) insuficiente. ~**cy** *n* inadequação *f*; (*insufficiency*) insuficiência *f*

inadmissible /məˈdmɪsəbl/ *a* inadmissível

inadvertently /məˈdvɜːtəntlɪ/ *adv* inadvertidamente; (*unintentionally*) sem querer, sem ser por mal

inadvisable /məˈdvaɪzəbl/ *a* desaconselhável, não aconselhável

inane /ɪˈneɪn/ *a* tolo, oco

inanimate /ɪnˈænɪmət/ *a* inanimado

inappropriate /məˈprəʊprɪət/ *a* impróprio, inadequado

inarticulate /maːˈtɪkjʊlət/ *a* inarticulado; (*of person*) incapaz de se exprimir claramente

inattentive /məˈtentɪv/ *a* desatento

inaugural /ɪˈnɔːgjʊrəl/ *a* inaugural

inaugura|te /ɪˈnɔːgjʊreɪt/ *vt* inaugurar. ~**ion** /-ˈreɪʃn/ *n* inauguração *f*

inauspicious /mɔːˈspɪʃəs/ *a* pouco auspicioso

inborn /ɪnˈbɔːn/ *a* inato

inbred /ɪnˈbred/ *a* inato, congênito, (*P*) congénito

incalculable /ɪnˈkælkjʊləbl/ *a* incalculável

incapable /ɪnˈkeɪpəbl/ *a* incapaz

incapacit|y /ɪnkəˈpæsətɪ/ *n* incapacidade *f*. ~**ate** *vt* incapacitar

incarnat|e /ɪnˈkaːneɪt/ *a* encarnado. the devil ~e o diabo em pessoa. ~**ion** /-ˈneɪʃn/ *n* encarnação *f*

incendiary /ɪnˈsendɪərɪ/ *a* incendiário □ *n* bomba *f* incendiária

incense[1] /ˈɪnsens/ *n* incenso *m*

incense[2] /ɪnˈsens/ *vt* exasperar, enfurecer

incentive /ɪnˈsentɪv/ *n* incentivo, estímulo

incessant /ɪnˈsesnt/ *a* incessante. ~**ly** *adv* incessantemente, sem cessar

incest /ˈɪnsest/ *n* incesto *m*. ~**uous** /ɪnˈsestjʊəs/ *a* incestuoso

inch /ɪntʃ/ *n* polegada *f* (= 2.54 cm) □ *vt/i* avançar aos palmos *or* pouco a pouco. within an ~ of a um passo de

incidence /ˈɪnsɪdəns/ *n* incidência *f*; (*rate*) percentagem *f*

incident /ˈɪnsɪdənt/ *n* incidente *m*

incidental /ɪnsɪˈdentl/ *a* incidental, acessório; (*casual*) acidental; (*expenses*) eventuais; (*music*) de cena, incidental. ~**ly** *adv* incidentalmente; (*by the way*) a propósito

incinerat|e /ɪnˈsɪnəreɪt/ *vt* incinerar. ~**or** *n* incinerador *m*

incision /ɪnˈsɪʒn/ *n* incisão *f*

incisive /ɪnˈsaɪsɪv/ *a* incisivo

incite /ɪnˈsaɪt/ *vt* incitar, instigar. ~**ment** *n* incitamento *m*

inclination /mklɪˈneɪʃn/ *n* inclinação *f*, tendência *f*

incline[1] /ɪnˈklaɪn/ *vt/i* inclinar(-se). be ~**d** to inclinar-se para; (*have tendency*) ter tendência para

incline[2] /ˈɪnklaɪn/ *n* inclinação *f*, declive *m*

inclu|de /ɪnˈkluːd/ *vt* incluir; (*in letter*) enviar junto *or* em anexo. ~**ding** *prep* inclusive. ~**sion** *n* inclusão *f*

inclusive /ɪnˈkluːsɪv/ *a & adv* inclusive. be ~ of incluir

incognito /ɪnkɒgˈniːtəʊ/ *a & adv* incógnito

incoherent /mkəˈhɪərənt/ *a* incoerente

income /ˈɪŋkʌm/ *n* rendimento *m*. ~ tax imposto sobre a renda, (*P*) sobre o rendimento

incoming /ˈɪnkʌmɪŋ/ *a* (*tide*) enchente; (*tenant etc*) novo

incomparable /ɪnˈkɒmpərəbl/ *a* incomparável

incompatible /mkəmˈpætəbl/ *a* incompatível

incompeten|t /ɪnˈkɒmpɪtənt/ *a* incompetente. ~**ce** *n* incompetência *f* incomplete /ɪnkəmˈpliːt/ a incompleto

incomprehensible /ɪnkɒmprɪˈhensəbl/ a incompreensível

inconceivable /ɪnkənˈsiːvəbl/ a inconcebível

inconclusive /ɪnkənˈkluːsɪv/ a inconcludente

incongruous /ɪnˈkɒŋgruəs/ a incongruente; (absurd) absurdo

inconsequential /ɪnkɒnsɪˈkwenʃl/ a sem importância

inconsiderate /ɪnkənˈsɪdərət/ a impensado, inconsiderado; (lacking in regard) pouco atencioso, sem consideração (pelos sentimentos etc de outrem)

inconsisten|t /ɪnkənˈsɪstənt/ a incoerente; (at variance) contraditório. ∼t with incompatível com. ∼cy n incoerência f. ∼cies npl contradições fpl

inconspicuous /ɪnkənˈspɪkjuəs/ a que não dá nas vistas, que não chama a atenção

incontinen|t /ɪnˈkɒntɪnənt/ a incontinente. ∼ce n incontinência f

inconvenien|t /ɪnkənˈviːnɪənt/ a inconveniente, incômodo. ∼ce n inconveniência f; (drawback) inconveniente m □ vt incomodar

incorporate /ɪnˈkɔːpəreɪt/ vt incorporar; (include) incluir

incorrect /ɪnkəˈrekt/ a incorreto, (P) incorrecto

incorrigible /ɪnˈkɒrɪdʒəbl/ a incorrigível

increas|e¹ /ɪnˈkriːs/ vt/i aumentar. ∼ing a crescente. ∼ingly adv cada vez mais

increase² /ˈɪnkriːs/ n aumento m. on the ∼ aumentando, crescendo

incredible /ɪnˈkredəbl/ a incrível

incredulous /ɪnˈkredjʊləs/ a incrédulo

increment /ˈɪŋkrəmənt/ n incremento m, aumento m

incriminat|e /ɪnˈkrɪmɪneɪt/ vt incriminar. ∼ing a comprometedor

incubat|e /ˈɪnkjʊbeɪt/ vt incubar. ∼ion /-ˈbeɪʃn/ n incubação f. ∼or n incubadora f

inculcate /ˈɪnkʌlkeɪt/ vt inculcar

incumbent /ɪnˈkʌmbənt/ n (pol, relig) titular mf □ a be ∼ on incumbir a, caber a

incur /ɪnˈkɜː/ vt (pt incurred) (displeasure, expense etc) incorrer em; (debts) contrair

incurable /ɪnˈkjʊərəbl/ a incurável, que não tem cura

indebted /ɪnˈdetɪd/ a ∼ to s.o. em dívida (para) com alg (for por)

indecen|t /ɪnˈdiːsnt/ a indecente. ∼t assault atentado m contra o pudor. ∼cy n indecência f

indecision /ɪndɪˈsɪʒn/ n indecisão f

indecisive /ɪndɪˈsaɪsɪv/ a inconcludente, não decisivo; (hesitating) indeciso

indeed /ɪnˈdiːd/ adv realmente, deveras, mesmo; (in fact) de fato, (P) facto. very much ∼ muitíssimo

indefinite /ɪnˈdefɪnət/ a indefinido; (time) indeterminado. ∼ly adv indefinidamente

indelible /ɪnˈdeləbl/ a indelével

indemnify /ɪnˈdemnɪfaɪ/ vt indenizar, (P) indemnizar (for de); (safeguard) garantir (against contra)

indemnity /ɪnˈdemnətɪ/ n (legal exemption) isenção f, (compensation) indenização f, (P) indemnização f; (safeguard) garantia f

indent /ɪnˈdent/ vt (notch) recortar; (typ) entrar. ∼ation /-ˈteɪʃn/ n recorte m; (typ) entrada f

independen|t /ɪndɪˈpendənt/ a independente. ∼ce n independência f. ∼tly adv independentemente

indescribable /ɪndɪˈskraɪbəbl/ a indescritível

indestructible /ɪndɪˈstrʌktəbl/ a indestrutível

indeterminate /ɪndɪˈtɜːmɪnət/ a indeterminado

index /ˈɪndeks/ n (pl indexes) n (in book) índice m; (in library) catálogo m □ vt indexar. ∼ card ficha f (de fichário). ∼ finger index m, (dedo) indicador m. ∼-linked a ligado ao índice de inflação

India /ˈɪndɪə/ n índia f. ∼n a & n (of India) indiano (m); (American) índio (m)

indicat|e /ˈɪndɪkeɪt/ vt indicar. ∼ion /-ˈkeɪʃn/ n indicação f. ∼or n indicador m; (auto) pisca-pisca m; (board) quadro m

indicative /ɪnˈdɪkətɪv/ a & n indicativo (m)

indict /ɪnˈdaɪt/ vt acusar. ∼ment n acusação f

indifferen|t /ɪnˈdɪfrənt/ a indiferente; (not good) medíocre. ∼ce n indiferença f

indigenous /ɪnˈdɪdʒɪnəs/ a indígena, natural, nativo (to de)

indigestion /ɪndɪˈdʒestʃən/ n indigestão f. ∼ible /-təbl/ a indigesto

indign|ant /ɪnˈdɪgnənt/ a indignado. ∼ation /-ˈneɪʃn/ n indignação f

indirect /ɪndɪˈrekt/ a indireto, (P) indirecto. ∼ly adv indiretamente, (P) indirectamente

indiscr|eet /ɪndɪˈskriːt/ a indiscreto; (not wary) imprudente. ∼etion

/-'eʃn/ n indiscrição f; (action, remark etc) deslize m

indiscriminate /ɪndɪ'skrɪmmət/ a que tem falta de discernimento; (random) indiscriminado. ~ly adv sem discernimento; (at random) indiscriminadamente, ao acaso

indispensable /ɪndɪ'spensəbl/ a indispensável

indispos|ed /ɪndɪ'spəʊzd/ a indisposto. ~ition /-ə'zɪʃn/ n indisposição f

indisputable /ɪndɪ'spjuːtəbl/ a indisputável, incontestável

indistinct /ɪndɪ'stɪŋkt/ a indistinto

indistinguishable /ɪndɪ'stɪŋgwɪʃəbl/ a indistinguível, imperceptível; (identical) indiferenciável

individual /ɪndɪ'vɪdʒʊəl/ a individual □ n indivíduo m. ~ity /-'ælətɪ/ n individualidade f. ~ly adv individualmente

indivisible /ɪndɪ'vɪzəbl/ a indivisível

indoctrinat|e /ɪn'dɒktrɪneɪt/ vt (en) doutrinar. ~ion /-'neɪʃn/ n (en) doutrinação f

indolen|t /'ɪndələnt/ a indolente. ~ce n indolência f

indoor /'ɪndɔː(r)/ a (de) interior, interno; (under cover) coberto; (games) de salão. ~s /ɪn'dɔːz/ adv dentro de casa, no interior

induce /ɪn'djuːs/ vt induzir, levar; (cause) causar, provocar. ~ment n incentivo m, encorajamento m

indulge /ɪn'dʌldʒ/ vt satisfazer; (spoil) fazer a(s) vontade(s) de □ vi ~ in entregar-se a

indulgen|t /ɪn'dʌldʒənt/ a indulgente. ~ce n (leniency) indulgência f; (desire) satisfação f

industrial /ɪn'dʌstrɪəl/ a industrial; (unrest etc) trabalhista; (action) reivindicativo. ~ estate zona f industrial. ~ist n industrial m. ~ized a industrializado

industrious /ɪn'dʌstrɪəs/ a trabalhador, aplicado

industry /'ɪndəstrɪ/ n indústria f; (zeal) aplicação f, diligência f, zelo m

inebriated /ɪ'niːbrɪeɪtɪd/ a embriagado, ébrio

inedible /ɪ'nedɪbl/ a não comestível

ineffective /ɪnɪ'fektɪv/ a ineficaz; (person) ineficiente, incapaz

ineffectual /ɪnɪ'fektʃʊəl/ a ineficaz, improfícuo

inefficien|t /ɪnɪ'fɪʃnt/ a ineficiente. ~cy n ineficiência f

ineligible /ɪn'elɪdʒəbl/ a inelegível; (undesirable) indesejável. be ~ for não ter direito a

inept /ɪ'nept/ a inepto

inequality /ɪnɪ'kwɒlətɪ/ n desigualdade f

inert /ɪ'nɜːt/ a inerte. ~ia /-ʃə/ n inércia f

inevitable /ɪn'evɪtəbl/ a inevitável, fatal

inexcusable /ɪnɪk'skjuːzəbl/ a indesculpável, imperdoável

inexhaustible /ɪnɪg'zɔːstəbl/ a inesgotável, inexaurível

inexorable /ɪn'eksərəbl/ a inexorável

inexpensive /ɪnɪk'spensɪv/ a barato, em conta

inexperience /ɪnɪk'spɪərɪəns/ n inexperiência f, falta de experiência f. ~d a inexperiente

inexplicable /ɪn'eksplɪkəbl/ a inexplicável

inextricable /ɪn'ekstrɪkəbl/ a inextricável

infallib|le /ɪn'fæləbl/ a infalível. ~ility /-'bɪlətɪ/ n infalibilidade f

infam|ous /'ɪnfəməs/ a infame. ~y n infâmia f

infan|t /'ɪnfənt/ n bebé m, (P) bebê m; (child) criança f. ~cy n infância f; (babyhood) primeira infância f

infantile /'ɪnfəntaɪl/ a infantil

infantry /'ɪnfəntrɪ/ n infantaria f

infatuat|ed /ɪn'fætʃʊeɪtɪd/ a ~ed with cego or perdido por. ~ion /-'eɪʃn/ n cegueira f, paixão f

infect /ɪn'fekt/ vt infectar. ~ s.o. with contagiar or contaminar alg com. ~ion /-ʃn/ n infecção f, contágio m. ~ious /-ʃəs/ a infeccioso, contagioso

infer /ɪn'fɜː(r)/ vt (pt inferred) inferir, deduzir. ~ence /'ɪnfərəns/ n inferência f

inferior /ɪn'fɪərɪə(r)/ a inferior; (work etc) de qualidade inferior □ n inferior m f; (in rank) subalterno m. ~ity /-'ɒrətɪ/ n inferioridade f

infernal /ɪn'fɜːnl/ a infernal

infertil|e /ɪn'fɜːtaɪl/ a infértil, estéril. ~ity /-ə'tɪlətɪ/ n infertilidade f, esterilidade f

infest /ɪn'fest/ vt infestar (with de). ~ation n infestação f

infidelity /ɪnfɪ'delətɪ/ n infidelidade f

infiltrat|e /'ɪnfɪltreɪt/ vt/i infiltrar (-se). ~ion /-'treɪʃn/ n infiltração f

infinite /'ɪnfɪnət/ a & n infinito (m). ~ly adv infinitamente

infinitesimal /ɪnfɪnɪ'tesɪml/ a infinitesimal, infinitésimo

infinitive /ɪn'fɪnətɪv/ n infinitivo m

infinity /ɪn'fɪnətɪ/ n infinidade f, infinito m

infirm /ɪn'fɜːm/ a débil, fraco. ~ity n (illness) enfermidade f; (weakness) fraqueza f

inflam|e /ɪn'fleɪm/ vt inflamar. ~mable /-æməbl/ a inflamável. ~mation /-ə'meɪʃn/ n inflamação f inflate /ɪnˈfleɪt/ vt (balloon etc) encher de ar; (prices) causar inflação de

inflation /ɪnˈfleɪʃn/ n inflação f. ∼ary a inflacionário

inflection /ɪnˈflekʃn/ n inflexão f; (gram) flexão f, desinência f

inflexible /ɪnˈfleksəbl/ a inflexível

inflict /ɪnˈflɪkt/ vt infligir, impor (on a)

influence /ˈɪnfluəns/ n influência f □ vt influenciar, influir sobre

influential /ɪnfluˈenʃl/ a influente

influenza /ɪnfluˈenzə/ n gripe f

influx /ˈɪnflʌks/ n afluência f, influxo m

inform /ɪnˈfɔːm/ vt informar. ∼ against or on denunciar. keep ∼ed manter ao corrente or a par. ∼ant n informante mf. ∼er n delator m, denunciante mf

informal /ɪnˈfɔːml/ a informal; (simple) simples, sem cerimónia, (P) cerimónia; (unofficial) oficioso; (colloquial) familiar; (dress) de passeio, à vontade; (dinner, gathering) íntimo. ∼ity /-ˈmæləti/ n informalidade f; (simplicity) simplicidade f, (intimacy) intimidade f. ∼ly adv informalmente, sem cerimónia, (P) cerimónia, à vontade

information /ɪnfəˈmeɪʃn/ n informação f; (facts, data) informações fpl. ∼ technology tecnologia f da informação

informative /ɪnˈfɔːmətɪv/ a informativo

infra-red /ɪnfrəˈred/ a infravermelho

infrequent /ɪnˈfriːkwənt/ a pouco frequente, (P) frequente. ∼ly adv raramente

infringe /ɪnˈfrɪndʒ/ vt infringir. ∼ on transgredir; (rights) violar. ∼ment n infração f, (P) infracção f; (rights) violação f

infuriate /ɪnˈfjʊərɪeɪt/ vt enfurecer, enraivecer. ∼ing a enfurecedor, de enfurecer, de dar raiva

infuse /ɪnˈfjuːz/ vt infundir, incutir; (herbs, tea) pôr de infusão. ∼ion /-ʒn/ n infusão f

ingenious /ɪnˈdʒiːnɪəs/ a engenhoso, bem pensado. ∼uity /-ɪˈnjuːəti/ n engenho m, habilidade f, imaginação f

ingenuous /ɪnˈdʒenjuəs/ a cândido, ingénuo, (P) ingénuo

ingot /ˈɪŋɡət/ n barra f, lingote m

ingrained /ɪnˈɡreɪnd/ a arraigado, enraizado; (dirt) entranhado

ingratiate /ɪnˈɡreɪʃɪeɪt/ vt ∼ o.s. with insinuar-se junto de, cair nas or ganhar as boas graças de

ingratitude /ɪnˈɡrætɪtjuːd/ n ingratidão f

ingredient /ɪnˈɡriːdɪənt/ n ingrediente m

inhabit /ɪnˈhæbɪt/ vt habitar. ∼able a habitável. ∼ant n habitante mf

inhale /ɪnˈheɪl/ vt inalar, aspirar. ∼r /-ə(r)/ n inalador m

inherent /ɪnˈhɪərənt/ a inerente. ∼ly adv inerentemente, em si

inherit /ɪnˈherɪt/ vt herdar (from de). ∼ance n herança f

inhibit /ɪnˈhɪbɪt/ vt inibir; (prevent) impedir. be ∼ed ser (um) inibido. ∼ion /-ˈbɪʃn/ n inibição f

inhospitable /ɪnˈhɒsprɪtəbl/ a inóspito; (of person) inospitaleiro, pouco nada hospitaleiro

inhuman /ɪnˈhjuːmən/ a desumano. ∼ity /-ˈmænəti/ n desumanidade f

inhumane /ɪnhjuːˈmeɪn/ a inumano, cruel

inimitable /ɪˈnɪmɪtəbl/ a inimitável

iniquitous /ɪˈnɪkwɪtəs/ a iníquo

initial /ɪˈnɪʃl/ a & n inicial (f) □ vt (pt initialled) assinar com as iniciais, rubricar. ∼ly adv inicialmente

initiate /ɪˈnɪʃɪeɪt/ vt iniciar (into em); (scheme) lançar. ∼ion /-ˈeɪʃn/ n iniciação f; (start) início m

initiative /ɪˈnɪʃətɪv/ n iniciativa f

inject /ɪnˈdʒekt/ vt injetar, (P) injectar; (fig) insuflar. ∼ion /-ʃn/ n injeção f, (P) injecção f

injure /ˈɪndʒə(r)/ vt (harm) fazer mal a, prejudicar, lesar; (hurt) ferir

injury /ˈɪndʒərɪ/ n ferimento m, lesão f; (wrong) mal m

injustice /ɪnˈdʒʌstɪs/ n injustiça f

ink /ɪŋk/ n tinta f. ∼-well n tinteiro m. ∼y a sujo de tinta

inkling /ˈɪŋklɪŋ/ n idéia f, (P) ideia f, suspeita f

inlaid /ɪnˈleɪd/ see inlay[1]

inland /ˈɪnlənd/ a interior □ adv /ɪnˈlænd/ no interior, para o interior. the I∼ Revenue o Fisco, a Receita Federal

inlay[1] /ɪnˈleɪ/ vt (pt inlaid) embutir, incrustar

inlay[2] /ˈɪnleɪ/ n incrustação f, obturação f

inlet /ˈɪnlet/ n braço m de mar, enseada f; (techn) admissão f

inmate /ˈɪnmeɪt/ n residente mf; (in hospital) internado m; (in prison) presidiário m

inn /ɪn/ n estalagem f

innards /ˈɪnədz/ npl (colloq) tripas (colloq) fpl

innate /ɪˈneɪt/ a inato

inner /ˈɪnə(r)/ a interior, interno; (fig) íntimo. ∼ city centro m da cidade. ∼most a mais profundo, mais íntimo. ∼ tube n câmara f de ar innings /'mɪŋz/ n (cricket) vez f de bater; (pol) período m no poder

innocen|t /'ɪnəsnt/ a & n inocente (mf). ~ce n inocência f

innocuous /ɪ'nɒkjʊəs/ a inócuo, inofensivo

innovat|e /'ɪnəveɪt/ vi inovar. ~ion /-'veɪʃn/ n inovação f. ~or n inovador m

innuendo /ɪnju:'endəʊ/ n (pl -oes) insinuação f, indireta f, (P) indirecta f

innumerable /ɪ'nju:mərəbl/ a inumerável

inoculat|e /ɪ'nɒkjʊleɪt/ vt inocular. ~ion /-'leɪʃn/ n inoculação f, vacina f

inoffensive /ɪnə'fensɪv/ a inofensivo

inoperative /ɪn'ɒpərətɪv/ a inoperante, ineficaz

inopportune /ɪn'ɒpətju:n/ a inoportuno

inordinate /ɪ'nɔ:dɪnət/ a excessivo, desmedido. ~ly adv excessivamente, desmedidamente

input /'ɪmpʊt/ n (data) dados mpl; (electr: power) energia f; (computer process) entrada f, dados mpl

inquest /'ɪnkwest/ n inquérito m

inquir|e /ɪn'kwaɪə(r)/ vi informar-se □ vt perguntar, indagar, inquirir. ~ about procurar informações sobre, indagar. ~e into inquirir, indagar. ~ing a (look) interrogativo; (mind) inquisitivo. ~y n (question) pergunta f; (jur) inquérito m; (investigation) investigação f

inquisition /ɪnkwɪ'zɪʃn/ n inquisição f

inquisitive /ɪn'kwɪzətɪv/ a curioso, inquisitivo; (prying) intrometido, bisbilhoteiro

insan|e /ɪn'seɪn/ a louco, doido. ~ity /ɪn'sænətɪ/ n loucura f, demência f

insanitary /ɪn'sænɪtrɪ/ a insalubre, anti-higiénico, (P) anti-higiénico

insatiable /ɪn'seɪʃəbl/ a insaciável

inscri|be /ɪn'skraɪb/ vt inscrever; (book) dedicar. ~ption /-ɪpʃn/ n inscrição f; (in book) dedicatória f

inscrutable /ɪn'skru:təbl/ a impenetrável, misterioso

insect /'ɪnsekt/ n inseto m, (P) insecto m

insecur|e /ɪnsɪ'kjʊə(r)/ a (not firm) inseguro, mal seguro; (unsafe; psych) inseguro. ~ity n insegurança f, falta f de segurança

insensible /ɪn'sensəbl/ a insensível; (unconscious) inconsciente

insensitive /ɪn'sensətɪv/ a insensível

inseparable /ɪn'seprəbl/ a inseparável

insert[1] /ɪn'sɜ:t/ vt inserir; (key) meter, colocar; (add) pôr, inserir. ~ion /-ʃn/ n inserção f

insert[2] /'ɪnsɜ:t/ n coisa f inserida

inside /ɪn'saɪd/ n interior m. ~s fpl (colloq) tripas fpl (colloq) □ a interior, interno □ adv no interior, dentro, por dentro □ prep dentro de; (of time) em menos de. ~ out de dentro para fora, do avesso; (thoroughly) por dentro e por fora, a fundo

insidious /ɪn'sɪdɪəs/ a insidioso

insight /'ɪnsaɪt/ n penetração f, perspicácia f; (glimpse) vislumbre m

insignificant /ɪnsɪg'nɪfɪkənt/ a insignificante

insincer|e /ɪnsɪn'sɪə(r)/ a insincero. ~ity /-'serətɪ/ n insinceridade f, falta f de sinceridade

insinuat|e /ɪn'sɪnjʊeɪt/ vt insinuar. ~ion /-'eɪʃn/ n (act) insinuação f; (hint) indireta f, (P) indirecta f, insinuação f

insipid /ɪn'sɪpɪd/ a insípido, sem sabor

insist /ɪn'sɪst/ vt/i ~ (on/that) insistir (em/em que)

insisten|t /ɪn'sɪstənt/ a insistente. ~ce n insistência f. ~tly adv insistentemente

insolen|t /'ɪnsələnt/ a insolente. ~ce n insolência f

insoluble /ɪn'sɒljʊbl/ a insolúvel

insolvent /ɪn'sɒlvənt/ a insolvente

insomnia /ɪn'sɒmnɪə/ n insónia f, (P) insónia f

inspect /ɪn'spekt/ vt inspecionar, (P) inspeccionar, examinar; (tickets) fiscalizar; (passport) controlar; (troops) passar revista a. ~ion /-ʃn/ n inspeção f, (P) inspecção f, exame m; (ticket) fiscalização f; (troops) revista f. ~or n inspetor m, (P) inspector m; (on train) fiscal m

inspir|e /ɪn'spaɪə(r)/ vt inspirar. ~ation /-ə'reɪʃn/ n inspiração f

instability /ɪnstə'bɪlətɪ/ n instabilidade f

install /ɪn'stɔ:l/ vt instalar; (heater etc) montar, instalar. ~ation /-ə'leɪʃn/ n instalação f

instalment /ɪn'stɔ:lmənt/ n prestação f; (of serial) episódio m

instance /'ɪnstəns/ n exemplo m, caso m. for ~ por exemplo. in the first ~ em primeiro lugar

instant /'ɪnstənt/ a imediato; (food) instantâneo □ n instante m. ~ly adv imediatamente, logo

instantaneous /ɪnstən'teɪnɪəs/ a instantâneo

instead /ɪn'sted/ adv em vez disso, em lugar disso. ~ of em vez de, em lugar de

instigat|e /'ɪnstɪgeɪt/ vt instigar, incitar. ~ion /-'geɪʃn/ n instigação f. ~or n instigador m instil /ɪn'stɪl/ vt (pt instilled) instilar, insuflar

instinct /'ɪnstɪŋkt/ n instinto m. ~ive /ɪn'stɪŋktɪv/ a instintivo

institutle /'ɪnstɪtjuːt/ n instituto m □ vt instituir; (legal proceedings) intentar; (inquiry) ordenar. ~ion /-'tjuːʃn/ n instituição f; (school) estabelecimento m de ensino; (hospital) estabelecimento m hospitalar

instruct /ɪn'strʌkt/ vt instruir; (order) mandar, ordenar; (a solicitor etc) dar instruções a. ~ s.o. in sth ensinar alg coisa a alguém. ~ion /-ʃn/ n instrução f. ~ions /-ʃnz/ npl instruções fpl, modo m de emprego; (orders) ordens fpl. ~ive a instrutivo. ~or n instrutor m

instrument /'ɪnstrʊmənt/ n instrumento m. ~ panel painel m de instrumentos

instrumental /ɪnstrʊ'mentl/ a instrumental. be ~ in ter um papel decisivo em. ~ist n instrumentalista mf

insubordinatle /ɪnsə'bɔːdɪnət/ a insubordinado. ~ion /-'neɪʃn/ n insubordinação f

insufferable /ɪn'sʌfrəbl/ a intolerável, insuportável

insufficient /ɪnsə'fɪʃnt/ a insuficiente

insular /'ɪnsjʊlə(r)/ a insular; (fig: narrow-minded) bitolado, limitado, (P) tacanho

insulatle /'ɪnsjʊleɪt/ vt isolar. ~ing tape fita f isolante. ~ion /-'leɪʃn/ n isolamento m

insulin /'ɪnsjʊlɪn/ n insulina f

insult[1] /ɪn'sʌlt/ vt insultar, injuriar. ~ing a insultante, injurioso

insult[2] /'ɪnsʌlt/ n insulto m, injúria f

insurle /ɪn'ʃʊə(r)/ vt segurar, pôr no seguro; (Amer) = ensure. ~ance n seguro m. ~ance policy apólice f de seguro

insurmountable /ɪnsə'maʊntəbl/ a insuperável

intact /ɪn'tækt/ a intato, (P) intacto

intake /'ɪnteɪk/ n admissão f; (techn) admissão f, entrada f; (of food) ingestão f

intangible /ɪn'tændʒəbl/ a intangível

integral /'ɪntɪɡrəl/ a integral. be an ~ part of ser parte integrante de

integratle /'ɪntɪɡreɪt/ vt/i integrar (-se). ~ed circuit circuito m integrado. ~ion /-'greɪʃn/ n integração f

integrity /ɪn'teɡrətɪ/ n integridade f

intellect /'ɪntəlekt/ n intelecto m, inteligência f. ~ual /-'lektʃʊəl/ a & n intelectual (mf)

intelligen|t /ɪn'telɪdʒənt/ a inteligente. ~ce n inteligência f; (mil) informações fpl. ~tly adv inteligentemente

intelligible /ɪn'telɪdʒəbl/ a inteligível

intend /ɪn'tend/ vt tencionar; (destine) reservar, destinar. ~ed a intencional, propositado

intensle /ɪn'tens/ a intenso; (person) emotivo. ~ely adv intensamente; (very) extremamente. ~ity n intensidade f

intensif|y /ɪn'tensɪfaɪ/ vt intensificar. ~ication /-ɪ'keɪʃn/ n intensificação f

intensive /ɪn'tensɪv/ a intensivo. ~ care tratamento m intensivo

intent /ɪn'tent/ n intento m, desígnio m, propósito m □ a atento, concentrado. ~ on absorto em; (intending to) decidido a. ~ly adv atentamente

intention /ɪn'tenʃn/ n intenção f. ~al a intencional. ~ally adv de propósito

inter /ɪn'tɜː(r)/ vt (pt interred) enterrar

inter- /'ɪntə(r)/ pref inter-

interact /ɪntə'rækt/ vi agir uns sobre os outros. ~ion /-ʃn/ n interação f, (P) interacção f

intercede /ɪntə'siːd/ vi interceder

intercept /ɪntə'sept/ vt interceptar

interchange[1] /ɪntə'tʃeɪndʒ/ vt permutar, trocar. ~able a permutável

interchange[2] /'ɪntətʃeɪndʒ/ n permuta f, intercâmbio m; (road junction) trevo m de trânsito, (P) nó m

intercom /'ɪntəkɒm/ n interfone m, (P) intercomunicador m

interconnected /ɪntəkə'nektɪd/ a (facts, events etc) ligado, relacionado

intercourse /'ɪntəkɔːs/ n (sexual) relações fpl sexuais

interest /'ɪntrəst/ n interesse m; (legal share) título m; (in finance) juro(s) m(pl). rate of ~ taxa f de juros □ vt interessar. ~ed a interessado. be ~ed in interessar-se por. ~ing a interessante

interface /'ɪntəfeɪs/ n interface f

interfer|e /ɪntə'fɪə(r)/ vi interferir, intrometer-se (in em); (meddle, hinder) interferir (with com); (tamper) mexer indevidamente (with em). ~ence n interferência f

interim /'ɪntərɪm/ n in the ~ nesse/neste interim m, (P) interim m □ a interino, provisório

interior /ɪn'tɪərɪə(r)/ a & n interior (m)

interjection /ɪntə'dʒekʃn/ n interjeição f

interlock /ɪntə'lɒk/ vt/i entrelaçar; (pieces of puzzle etc) encaixar(-se); (mech: wheels) engrenar, engatar

interloper /'ɪntələʊpə(r)/ n intruso m

intermarr|iage /ɪntə'mærɪdʒ/ n casamento m entre membros de diferentes famílias, raças etc; (*between near relations*) casamento m consangüíneo, (P) consanguíneo. ~y *vi* ligar-se por casamento

intermediary /ɪntə'miːdɪərɪ/ a & n intermediário (m)

intermediate /ɪntə'miːdɪət/ a intermédio, intermediário

interminable /ɪn'tɜːmɪnəbl/ a interminável, infindável

intermission /ɪntə'mɪʃn/ n intervalo m

intermittent /ɪntə'mɪtnt/ a intermitente. ~ly *adv* intermitentemente

intern /ɪn'tɜːn/ *vt* internar. ~ee /-'niː/ n internado m. ~ment n internamento m

internal /ɪn'tɜːnl/ a interno, interior. ~ly *adv* internamente, interiormente

international /ɪntə'næʃnəl/ a & n internacional (*mf*)

interpolate /ɪn'tɜːpəleɪt/ *vt* interpolar

interpret /ɪn'tɜːprɪt/ *vt/i* interpretar. ~ation /-'teɪʃn/ n interpretação f. ~er n intérprete *mf*

interrelated /ɪntərɪ'leɪtɪd/ a inter-relacionado, correlacionado

interrogate /ɪn'terəgeɪt/ *vt* interrogar. ~ion /-'geɪʃn/ n interrogação f; (*of police etc*) interrogatório m

interrogative /ɪntə'rɒgətɪv/ a interrogativo □ n (*pronoun*) pronome m interrogativo

interrupt /ɪntə'rʌpt/ *vt* interromper. ~ion /-ʃn/ n interrupção f

intersect /ɪntə'sekt/ *vt/i* intersectar (-se); (*roads*) cruzar-se. ~ion /-ʃn/ n intersecção f; (*crossroads*) cruzamento m

intersperse /ɪntə'spɜːs/ *vt* entremear, intercalar; (*scatter*) espalhar

interval /'ɪntəvl/ n intervalo m. at ~s a intervalos

interven|e /ɪntə'viːn/ *vi* (*interfere*) intervir; (*of time*) passar-se, decorrer; (*occur*) sobrevir, intervir. ~tion /-'venʃn/ n intervenção f

interview /'ɪntəvjuː/ n entrevista f □ *vt* entrevistar. ~ee n entrevistado m. ~er n entrevistador m

intestin|e /ɪn'testɪn/ n intestino m. ~al a intestinal

intima|te[1] /'ɪntɪmət/ a íntimo; (*detailed*) profundo. ~cy n intimidade f. ~tely *adv* intimamente

intimate[2] /'ɪntɪmeɪt/ *vt* (*announce*) dar a conhecer, fazer saber; (*imply*) dar a entender

intimidat|e /ɪn'tɪmɪdeɪt/ *vt* intimidar. ~ion /-'deɪʃn/ n intimidação f

into /'ɪntə/; *emphatic* /'ɪntuː/ *prep* para dentro de. divide ~ three dividir em três. ~ pieces aos bocados. translate ~ traduzir para

intolerable /ɪn'tɒlərəbl/ a intolerável, insuportável

intoleran|t /ɪn'tɒlərənt/ a intolerante. ~ce n intolerância f

intonation /ɪntə'neɪʃn/ n entonação f, entoação f, inflexão f

intoxicat|ed /ɪn'tɒksɪkeɪtɪd/ a embriagado, etilizado. ~ion /-'keɪʃn/ n embriaguez f

intra- /ɪntrə/ *pref* intra

intractable /ɪn'træktəbl/ a intratável, difícil

intransigent /ɪn'trænsɪdʒənt/ a intransigente

intransitive /ɪn'trænsətɪv/ a (*verb*) intransitivo

intravenous /ɪntrə'viːnəs/ a intravenoso

intrepid /ɪn'trepɪd/ a intrépido, arrojado

intrica|te /'ɪntrɪkət/ a intrincado, complexo. ~cy n complexidade f

intrigu|e /ɪn'triːg/ *vt/i* intrigar □ n intriga f. ~ing a intrigante, curioso

intrinsic /ɪn'trɪnsɪk/ a intrínseco. ~ally /-klɪ/ *adv* intrinsecamente

introduce /ɪntrə'djuːs/ *vt* (*programme, question*) apresentar; (*bring in, insert*) introduzir; (*initiate*) iniciar. ~ sb to sb (*person*) apresentar alg a alguém

introduct|ion /ɪntrə'dʌkʃn/ n introdução f; (*of/to person*) apresentação f. ~ory /-tərɪ/ a introdutório, de introdução; (*letter, words*) de apresentação

introspective /ɪntrə'spektɪv/ a introspectivo

introvert /'ɪntrəvɜːt/ n & a introvertido (m)

intru|de /ɪn'truːd/ *vi* intrometer-se, ser a mais. ~der n intruso m. ~sion n intrusão f. ~sive a intruso

intuit|ion /ɪntjuː'ɪʃn/ n intuição f. ~ive /ɪn'tjuːɪtɪv/ a intuitivo

inundate /'ɪnʌndeɪt/ *vt* inundar (with de)

invade /ɪn'veɪd/ *vt* invadir. ~r /-ə(r)/ n invasor m

invalid[1] /'ɪnvəlɪd/ n inválido m

invalid[2] /ɪn'vælɪd/ a inválido. ~ate *vt* invalidar

invaluable /ɪn'væljʊəbl/ a inestimável

invariab|le /ɪn'veərɪəbl/ a invariável. ~y *adv* invariavelmente

invasion /ɪn'veɪʒn/ n invasão f

invective /ɪn'vektɪv/ n invectiva f

invent /ɪn'vent/ vt inventar. ~ion n invenção f. ~ive a inventivo. ~or n inventor m

inventory /'ɪnvəntrɪ/ n inventário m

inverse /ɪn'vɜːs/ a & n inverso (m). ~ly adv inversamente

inver|t /ɪn'vɜːt/ vt inverter. ~ted commas aspas fpl. ~sion n inversão f

invest /ɪn'vest/ vt investir; (time, effort) dedicar □ vi fazer um investimento. ~ in (colloq: buy) gastar dinheiro em. ~ment n investimento m. ~or n investidor m, financiador m

investigat|e /ɪn'vestɪɡeɪt/ vt investigar. ~ion /-'ɡeɪʃn/ n investigação f. under ~ion em estudo. ~or n investigador m

inveterate /ɪn'vetərət/ a inveterado

invidious /ɪn'vɪdɪəs/ a antipático, odioso

invigorate /ɪn'vɪɡəreɪt/ vt revigorar; (encourage) estimular

invincible /ɪn'vɪnsəbl/ a invencível

invisible /ɪn'vɪzəbl/ a invisível

invit|e /ɪn'vaɪt/ vt convidar; (bring on) pedir, provocar. ~ation /ɪnvɪ'teɪʃn/ n convite m. ~ing a (tempting) tentador; (pleasant) acolhedor, convidativo

invoice /'ɪnvɔɪs/ n fatura f, (P) factura f □ vt faturar, (P) facturar

invoke /ɪn'vəʊk/ vt invocar

involuntary /ɪn'vɒləntrɪ/ a involuntário

involve /ɪn'vɒlv/ vt implicar, envolver. ~d a (complex) complicado; (at stake) em jogo; (emotionally) envolvido. ~d in implicado em. ~ment n envolvimento m, participação f

invulnerable /ɪn'vʌlnərəbl/ a invulnerável

inward /'ɪnwəd/ a interior; (thought etc) íntimo. ~(s) adv para dentro, para o interior. ~ly adv interiormente, intimamente

iodine /'aɪədiːn/ n iodo m; (antiseptic) tintura f de iodo

IOU /aɪəʊ'juː/ n abbr vale m

IQ /aɪ'kjuː/ abbr (intelligence quotient) QI m

Iran /ɪ'rɑːn/ n Irã m. ~ian /ɪ'reɪnɪən/ a & n iraniano (m)

Iraq /ɪ'rɑːk/ n Iraque m. ~i a & n iraquiano (m)

irascible /ɪ'ræsəbl/ a irascível

irate /aɪ'reɪt/ a irado, enraivecido

Ireland /'aɪələnd/ n Irlanda f

iris /'aɪərɪs/ n (anat, bot) íris f

Irish /'aɪərɪʃ/ a & n (language) irlandês (m). ~man n irlandês m. ~woman n irlandesa f

irk /ɜːk/ vt aborrecer,ncomodar. ~some a aborrecido

iron /'aɪən/ n ferro m; (appliance) ferro m de engomar □ a de ferro □ vt passar a ferro. ~ out fazer desaparecer; (fig) aplanar, resolver. ~ing n do the ~ing passar a roupa. ~ing-board n tábua f de passar roupa, (P) tábua f de engomar

ironic(al) /aɪ'rɒnɪk(l)/ a irônico, (P) irónico

ironmonger /'aɪənmʌŋɡə(r)/ n ferreiro m, (P) ferrageiro m. ~'s n (shop) loja f de ferragens

irony /'aɪərənɪ/ n ironia f

irrational /ɪ'ræʃənl/ a irracional; (person) ilógico, que não raciocina

irreconcilable /ɪrekən'saɪləbl/ a irreconciliável

irrefutable /ɪrɪ'fjuːtəbl/ a irrefutável

irregular /ɪ'reɡjʊlə(r)/ a irregular. ~ity /-'lærətɪ/ n irregularidade f

irrelevant /ɪ'reləvənt/ a irrelevante, que não é pertinente

irreparable /ɪ'repərəbl/ a irreparável, irremediável

irreplaceable /ɪrɪ'pleɪsəbl/ a insubstituível

irresistible /ɪrɪ'zɪstəbl/ a irresistível

irresolute /ɪ'rezəluːt/ a irresoluto

irrespective /ɪrɪ'spektɪv/ a ~ of sem levar em conta, independente de

irresponsible /ɪrɪ'spɒnsəbl/ a irresponsável

irretrievable /ɪrɪ'triːvəbl/ a irreparável

irreverent /ɪ'revərənt/ a irreverente

irreversible /ɪrɪ'vɜːsəbl/ a irreversível; (decision) irrevogável

irrigat|e /'ɪrɪɡeɪt/ vt irrigar. ~ion /-'ɡeɪʃn/ n irrigação f

irritable /'ɪrɪtəbl/ a irritável, irascível

irritat|e /'ɪrɪteɪt/ vt irritar. ~ion /-'teɪʃn/ n irritação f

is /ɪz/ see be

Islam /'ɪzlɑːm/ n Islã m. ~ic /ɪz'læmɪk/ a islâmico

island /'aɪlənd/ n ilha f. traffic ~ abrigo m de pedestres, (P) placa f de refugio

isolat|e /'aɪsəleɪt/ vt isolar. ~ion /-'leɪʃn/ n isolamento m

Israel /'ɪzreɪl/ n Israel m. ~i /ɪz'reɪlɪ/ a & n israelense (mf), (P) israelita (mf)

issue /'ɪʃuː/ n questão f; (outcome) resultado m; (of magazine etc) número m; (of stamps, money etc) emissão f □ vt distribuir, dar; (stamps, money etc) emitir; (orders) dar □ vi ~ from sair de. at ~ em questão. take ~ with entrar em discussão com, discutir com it /ɪt/ pron (subject) ele, ela; (object) o, a; (non-specific) isto, isso, aquilo. ~ is cold está or faz frio. ~ is the 6th of May hoje é seis de maio. that's ~ é isso. take ~ leva isso. who is ~? quem é?

italic /ɪ'tælɪk/ a itálico. ~s npl itálico m

Ital|y /'ɪtəlɪ/ n Itália f. ~ian /ɪ'tælɪən/ a & n (person, lang) italiano (m)

itch /ɪtʃ/ n coceira f, (P) comichão f, (fig: desire) desejo m ardente □ vi coçar, sentir comichão, comichar. my arm ~es estou com coceira no braço. I am ~ing to estou morto por (colloq). ~y a que dá coceira

item /'aɪtəm/ n item m, artigo m; (on programme) número m; (on agenda) ponto m. news ~ notícia f. ~ize /-aɪz/ vt discriminar, especificar

itinerant /aɪ'tɪnərənt/ a itinerante; (musician, actor) ambulante

itinerary /aɪ'tɪnərərɪ/ n itinerário m

its /ɪts/ a seu, sua, seus, suas

it's /ɪts/ = it is, it has

itself /ɪt'self/ pron ele mesmo, ele próprio, ela mesma, ela própria; (reflexive) se; (after prep) si mesmo, si próprio, si mesma, si própria. by ~ sozinho, por si

ivory /'aɪvərɪ/ n marfim m

ivy /'aɪvɪ/ n hera f

J

jab /dʒæb/ vt (pt jabbed) espetar □ n espetadela f; (colloq: injection) picada f

jabber /'dʒæbə(r)/ vi tagarelar; (indistinctly) falar confusamente □ n tagarelice f; (indistinct speech) algaravia f, (indistinct voices) algaraviada f

jack /dʒæk/ n (techn) macaco m; (cards) valete m □ vt ~ up levantar com macaco. the Union J~ a bandeira f inglesa

jackal /'dʒækl/ n chacal m

jackdaw /'dʒækdɔ:/ n gralha f

jacket /'dʒækɪt/ n casaco (curto) m, (of book) sobrecapa f, (of potato) casca f

jack-knife /'dʒæknaɪf/ vi (lorry) perder o controle

jackpot /'dʒækpɒt/ n sorte f grande. hit the ~ ganhar a sorte grande

Jacuzzi /dʒə'ku:zi:/ n (P) jacuzzi m, banheira f de hidromassagem

jade /dʒeɪd/ n (stone) jade m

jaded /'dʒeɪdɪd/ a (tired) estafado; (bored) enfastiado

jagged /'dʒægɪd/ a recortado, denteado; (sharp) pontiagudo

jail /dʒeɪl/ n prisão f □ vt prender,

colocar na cadeia. ~er n carcereiro m

jam¹ /dʒæm/ n geléia f, compota f

jam² /dʒæm/ vt/i (pt jammed) (wedge) entalar; (become wedged) entalar-se; (crowd) apinhar(-se); (mech) bloquear; (radio) provocar interferências □ n (crush) aperto m; (traffic) engarrafamento m; (colloq: difficulty) apuro m, aperto m. ~ one's brakes on (colloq) pôr o pé no freio, (P) no travão subitamente, apertar o freio subitamente. ~-packed a (colloq) abarrotado (with de)

Jamaica /dʒə'meɪkə/ n Jamaica f

jangle /'dʒæŋgl/ n som m estridente □ vi retinir

janitor /'dʒænɪtə(r)/ n porteiro m; (caretaker) zelador m

January /'dʒænjʊərɪ/ n Janeiro m

Japan /dʒə'pæn/ n Japão m. ~ese /dʒæpə'ni:z/ a & n japonês (m)

jar¹ /dʒɑ:(r)/ n pote m. jam-~ n frasco m de geléia

jar² /dʒɑ:(r)/ vt/i (pt jarred) ressoar, bater ruidosamente (against contra); (of colours) destoar; (disagree) discordar (with de) □ n (shock) choque m. ~ring a dissonante

jargon /'dʒɑ:gən/ n jargão m, gíria f profissional

jaundice /'dʒɔ:ndɪs/ n icterícia f. ~d a (fig) invejoso, despeitado

jaunt /dʒɔ:nt/ n (trip) passeata f

jaunty /'dʒɔ:ntɪ/ a (-ier, -iest) (cheerful) alegre, jovial; (sprightly) desenvolto

javelin /'dʒævlɪn/ n dardo m

jaw /dʒɔ:/ n maxilar m, mandíbula f

jay /dʒeɪ/ n gaio m. ~-walker n pedestre m imprudente, (P) peão m indisciplinado

jazz /dʒæz/ n jazz m □ vt ~ up animar. ~y a (colloq) espalhafatoso

jealous /'dʒeləs/ a ciumento; (envious) invejoso. ~y n ciúme m; (envy) inveja f

jeans /dʒi:nz/ npl (blue-)jeans mpl, calça f de zuarte, (P) calças fpl de ganga

jeep /dʒi:p/ n jipe m

jeer /dʒɪə(r)/ vt/i ~ at (laugh) fazer troça de; (scorn) escarnecer de; (boo) vaiar □ n (mockery) troça f; (booing) vaia f

jell /dʒel/ vi tomar consistência, gelatinizar-se

jelly /'dʒelɪ/ n gelatina f.

jellyfish /'dʒelɪfɪʃ/ n água-viva f

jeopard|y /'dʒepədɪ/ n perigo m. ~ize vt comprometer, pôr em perigo

jerk /dʒɜ:k/ n solavanco m, (P) sacão m; (sl: fool) idiota mf □ vt/i sacudir; (move) mover-se aos solavancos, (P) mover(-se) aos sacões. ~y *a* sacudido

jersey /'dʒɜːzɪ/ *n* (*pl* -eys) camisola *f*, pulóver *m*, suéter *m*; (*fabric*) jérsei *m*

jest /dʒest/ *n* gracejo *m*, graça *f* □ *vi* gracejar, brincar

Jesus /'dʒiːzəs/ *n* Jesus *m*

jet[1] /dʒet/ *n* azeviche *m*. ~-black *a* negro de azeviche

jet[2] /dʒet/ *n* jato *m*, (P) jacto *m*; (*plane*) (avião a) jato *m*, (P) jacto *m*. ~ lag cansaço *m* provocado pela diferença de fuso horário. ~-propelled *a* de propulsão a jato, (P) jacto

jettison /'dʒetɪsn/ *vt* alijar; (*discard*) desfazer-se de; (*fig*) abandonar

jetty /'dʒetɪ/ *n* (*breakwater*) quebra-mar *m*; (*landing-stage*) desembarcadouro *m*, cais *m*

Jew /dʒuː/ *n* judeu *m*

jewel /'dʒuːəl/ *n* jóia *f*. ~ler *n* joalheiro *m*. ~ler's (*shop*) joalheria *f*. ~lery *n* jóias *fpl*

Jewish /'dʒuːɪʃ/ *a* judeu

jib /dʒɪb/ *vi* (*pt* jibbed) recusar-se a avançar; (*of a horse*) empacar. ~ at (*fig*) opor-se a, ter relutância em □ *n* (*sail*) bujarrona *f*

jig /dʒɪg/ *n* jiga *f*

jiggle /'dʒɪgl/ *vt* (*rock*) balançar; (*jerk*) sacolejar

jigsaw /'dʒɪgsɔː/ *n* ~(-puzzle) puzzle *m*, quebra-cabeça *m*, (P) quebra-cabeças *m*

jilt /dʒɪlt/ *vt* deixar, abandonar, dar um fora em (*colloq*), (P) mandar passear (*colloq*)

jingle /'dʒɪŋgl/ *vt/i* tilintar, tinir □ *n* tilintar *m*, tinido *m*; (*advertising etc*) música *f* de anúncio

jinx /dʒɪŋks/ *n* (*colloq*) pessoa *f* or coisa *f* azarenta; (*fig: spell*) azar *m*

jitter|**s** /'dʒɪtəz/ *npl* the ~s (*colloq*) nervos *mpl*. ~y /-ərɪ/ *a* be ~y (*colloq*) estar nervoso, ter os nervos a flor da pele (*colloq*)

job /dʒɒb/ *n* trabalho *m*; (*post*) emprego *m*. have a ~ doing ter dificuldade em fazer. it is a good ~ that felizmente que. ~less *a* desempregado

jobcentre /'dʒɒbsentə(r)/ *n* posto *m* de desemprego

jockey /'dʒɒkɪ/ *n* (*pl* -eys) jóquei *m*

jocular /'dʒɒkjʊlə(r)/ *a* jocoso, galhofeiro, brincalhão

jog /dʒɒg/ *vt* (*pt* jogged) dar um leve empurrão em, tocar em; (*memory*) refrescar □ *vi* (*sport*) fazer jogging. ~ging *n* jogging *m*

join /dʒɔɪn/ *vt* juntar, unir; (*become member*) fazer-se sócio de, entrar para. ~ sb juntar-se a alg □ *vi* (*of roads*) juntar-se, entroncar-se; (*of rivers*) confluir □ *n* junção *f*, junta *f*.

~ in *vt/i* participar (em). ~ up alistar-se

joiner /'dʒɔɪnə(r)/ *n* marceneiro *m*

joint /dʒɔɪnt/ *a* comum, conjunto; (*effort*) conjunto □ *n* junta *f*, junção *f*; (*anat*) articulação *f*; (*culin*) quarto *m*; (*roast meat*) carne *f* assada; (*sl: place*) espelunca *f*. ~ author co-autor *m*. ~ly *adv* conjuntamente

joist /dʒɔɪst/ *n* trave *f*, barrote *m*

jok|**e** /dʒəʊk/ *n* piada *f*, gracejo *m* □ *vi* gracejar. ~er *n* brincalhão *m*; (*cards*) curinga *f* de baralho, (P) diabo *m*. ~ingly *adv* brincadeira

joll|**y** /'dʒɒlɪ/ *a* (-ier, -iest) alegre, bem disposto □ *adv* (*colloq*) muito. ~ity *n* festança *f*, pândega *f*

jolt /dʒəʊlt/ *vt* sacudir, sacolejar □ *vi* ir aos solavancos □ *n* solavanco *m*; (*shock*) choque *m*, sobressalto *m*

jostle /'dʒɒsl/ *vt* dar um encontrão or encontrões em, empurrar □ *vi* empurrar, acotovelar-se

jot /dʒɒt/ *n* (not a) ~ nada □ *vt* (*pt* jotted) ~ (down) apontar, tomar nota de. ~ter *n* (*pad*) bloco *m* de notas

journal /'dʒɜːnl/ *n* diário *m*; (*newspaper*) jornal *m*; (*periodical*) periódico *m*, revista *f*. ~ism *n* jornalismo *m*. ~ist *n* jornalista *mf*

journey /'dʒɜːnɪ/ *n* (*pl* -eys) viagem *f*; (*distance*) trajeto *m*, (P) trajecto *m* □ *vi* viajar

jovial /'dʒəʊvɪəl/ *a* jovial

joy /dʒɔɪ/ *n* alegria *f*. ~-ride *n* passeio *m* em carro roubado. ~ful, ~ous *adjs* alegre

jubil|**ant** /'dʒuːbɪlənt/ *a* cheio de alegria, jubiloso. ~ation /-leɪʃn/ *n* júbilo *m*, regozijo *m*

jubilee /'dʒuːbɪliː/ *n* jubileu *m*

Judaism /'dʒuːdeɪɪzəm/ *n* judaísmo *m*

judder /'dʒʌdə(r)/ *vi* trepidar, vibrar □ *n* trepidação *f*, vibração *f*

judge /dʒʌdʒ/ *n* juiz *m* □ *vt* julgar. ~ment (*judging*) julgamento *m*, juizo *m*; (*opinion*) juizo *m*; (*decision*) julgamento *m*

judic|**iary** /dʒuː'dɪʃərɪ/ *n* magistratura *f*; (*system*) judiciário *m*. ~ial *a* judiciário

judicious /dʒuː'dɪʃəs/ *a* judicioso

judo /'dʒuːdəʊ/ *n* judô *m*, (P) judo *m*

jug /dʒʌg/ *n* (*tall*) jarro *m*; (*round*) botija *f*; milk-~ *n* leiteira *f*

juggernaut /'dʒʌgənɔːt/ *n* (*lorry*) jainanta *f*, (P) camião *m* TIR

juggle /'dʒʌgl/ *vt/i* fazer malabarismos (with com). ~r /-ə(r)/ *n* malabarista *mf*

juic|**e** /dʒuːs/ *n* suco *m*, (P) sumo *m*. ~y *a* suculento; (*colloq: story etc*) picante

juke-box /'dʒuːkbɒks/ n juke-box m,
(P) máquina f de música
July /dʒu'laɪ/ n julho m
jumble /'dʒʌmbl/ vt misturar □ n mistura f. ~ sale venda f de caridade de
objetos usados
jumbo /'dʒʌmbəʊ/ a ~ jet (avião)
jumbo m
jump /dʒʌmp/ vt/i saltar; (start) so-
bressaltar(-se); (of prices etc) subir repentinamente □ n salto m; (start)
sobressalto m; (of prices) alta f. ~ at
aceitar imediatamente. ~ the gun
agir prematuramente. ~ the queue
furar a fila. ~ to conclusions tirar
conclusões apressadas
jumper /'dʒʌmpə(r)/ n pulôver m,
suéter m, (P) camisola f de lã
jumpy /'dʒʌmpɪ/ a nervoso
junction /'dʒʌŋkʃn/ n junção f; (of
roads etc) entroncamento m
June /dʒuːn/ n junho m
jungle /'dʒʌŋgl/ n selva f, floresta f
junior /'dʒuːnɪə(r)/ a júnior; (in age)
mais novo (to que); (in rank) subalterno; (school) primária □ n o mais novo
m; (sport) júnior mf. ~ to (in rank)
abaixo de
junk /dʒʌŋk/ n ferro-velho m, velha-
rias fpl; (rubbish) lixo m. ~ food comida f sem valor nutritivo. ~ mail
material m impresso, enviado por
correio, sem ter sido solicitado. ~
shop loja f de ferro-velho, bricabra-
que m
junkie /'dʒʌŋkɪ/ n (sl) drogado m
jurisdiction /dʒʊərɪs'dɪkʃn/ n juris-
dição f
juror /'dʒʊərə(r)/ n jurado m
jury /'dʒʊərɪ/ n júri m
just /dʒʌst/ a justo □ adv justamente,
exatamente, (P) exactamente; (only)
só. he has ~ left ele acabou de sair.
~ listen! escuta só! ~ as assim
como; (with time) assim que. ~ as
tall as exatamente, (P) exactamente
tão alto quanto. ~ as well that ainda
bem que. ~ before um momento
antes (de). ~ly adv com justiça, justamente
justice /'dʒʌstɪs/ n justiça f. J~ of
the Peace juiz m de paz
justifiabl|e /'dʒʌstɪfaɪəbl/ a justi-
ficável. ~y adv com razão, justificadamente
justif|y /'dʒʌstɪfaɪ/ vt justificar.
~ication /-ɪ'keɪʃn/ n justificação f
jut /dʒʌt/ vi (pt jutted) ~ out fazer
saliência, sobressair
juvenile /'dʒuːvənaɪl/ a (youthful) juvenil; (childish) pueril; (delinquent)
jovem; (court) de menores □ n jovem
mf
juxtapose /dʒʌkstə'pəʊz/ vt justapor

K

kaleidoscope /kə'laɪdəskəʊp/ n
caleidoscópio m
kangaroo /kæŋgə'ruː/ n canguru m
karate /kə'rɑːtɪ/ n klaratê m
kebab /kə'bæb/ n churrasquinho m,
espetinho m
keel /kiːl/ n quilha f □ vi ~ over virar-se
keen /kiːn/ a (-er, -est) (sharp) agudo;
(eager) entusiástico; (of appetite) de-
vorador; (of intelligence) vivo; (of
wind) cortante. ~ly adv vivamente,
(eagerly) com entusiasmo. ~ness n
vivacidade f; (enthusiasm) entusiasmo m
keep /kiːp/ (pt kept) vt guardar; (family) sustentar; (animals) ter, criar;
(celebrate) festejar; (conceal) esconder; (delay) demorar; (prevent) impedir (from de); (promise) cumprir;
(shop) ter □ vi manter-se, conservar-
se; (remain) ficar. ~ (on) continuar
(doing fazendo) □ n sustento m; (of
castle) torre f de menagem. ~ back
vt (withhold) reter □ vi manter-se
afastado. ~ in/out impedir de en-
trar/de sair. ~ up conservar. ~ up
(with) acompanhar. ~er n guarda mf
keeping /'kiːpɪŋ/ n guarda f, cuidado
m. in ~ with em harmonia com, (P)
de harmonia com
keepsake /'kiːpseɪk/ n (thing) lembrança f, recordação f
keg /keg/ n barril m pequeno
kennel /'kenl/ n casota f (de cão). ~s
npl canil m
kept /kept/ see keep
kerb /kɜːb/ n meio fio m, (P) borda f
do passeio
kernel /'kɜːnl/ n (of nut) miolo m
kerosene /'kerəsiːn/ n (paraffin)
querosene m, (P) petróleo m; (aviation fuel) gasolina f
ketchup /'ketʃəp/ n molho m de tomate, ketchup m
kettle /'ketl/ n chaleira f
key /kiː/ n chave f; (of piano etc) tecla
f; (mus) clave f □ a chave. ~-ring n
chaveiro m, porta-chaves m invar □ vt
~ in digitar, bater. ~ed up tenso
keyboard /'kiːbɔːd/ n teclado m
keyhole /'kiːhəʊl/ n buraco m da fechadura
khaki /'kɑːkɪ/ a & n cáqui (invar m),
(P) caqui (invar m)
kick /kɪk/ vt/i dar um pontapé or pon-
tapés (a, em); (ball) chutar (em); (of
horse) dar um coice or coices, escoi-
cear □ n pontapé m; (of gun, horse)
coice m; (colloq: thrill) excitação f,

prazer *m*. ~-off *n* chute *m* inicial, kick-off *m*. ~ out (*colloq*) pôr na rua. ~ up (*colloq: fuss, racket*) fazer

kid /kɪd/ *n* (*goat*) cabrito *m*; (*sl: child*) garoto *m*; (*leather*) pelica *f* □ *vt/i* (*pt kidded*) (*colloq*) brincar (com)

kidnap /'kɪdnæp/ *vt* (*pt kidnapped*) raptar. ~ping *n* rapto *m*

kidney /'kɪdnɪ/ *n* rim *m*

kill /kɪl/ *vt* matar; (*fig: put an end to*) acabar com □ *n* matança *f*. ~er *n* assassino *m*. ~ing *n* matança *f*, massacre *m*; (*of game*) caçada *f* □ *a* (*colloq: funny*) de morrer de rir; (*colloq: exhausting*) de morte

killjoy /'kɪldʒɔɪ/ *n* desmancha-prazeres *mf*

kiln /kɪln/ *n* forno *m*

kilo /'ki:ləʊ/ *n* (*pl* -os) quilo *m*

kilogram /'kɪləgræm/ *n* quilograma *m*

kilometre /'kɪləmi:tə(r)/ *n* quilómetro *m*, (*P*) quilómetro *m*

kilowatt /'kɪləwɒt/ *n* quilowatt *m*, (*P*) quilovate *m*

kilt /kɪlt/ *n* kilt *m*, saiote *m* escocês

kin /kɪn/ *n* família *f*, parentes *mpl*. next of ~ os parentes mais próximos

kind¹ /kaɪnd/ *n* espécie *f*, género *m*, (*P*) género *m*, natureza *f*. in ~ em géneros, (*P*) géneros; (*fig: in the same form*) na mesma moeda. ~ of (*colloq: somewhat*) de certo modo, um pouco

kind² /kaɪnd/ *a* (-er, -est) (*good*) bom; (*friendly*) gentil, amável. ~-hearted *a* bom, bondoso. ~ness *n* bondade *f*

kindergarten /'kɪndəga:tn/ *n* jardim de infância *m*, (*P*) infantil

kindle /'kɪndl/ *vt/i* acender(-se), atear(-se)

kindly /'kaɪndlɪ/ *a* (-ier, -iest) benévolo, bondoso □ *adv* bondosamente, gentilmente, com simpatia. ~ wait tenha a bondade de esperar

kindred /'kɪndrɪd/ *a* aparentado; (*fig: connected*) afim. ~ spirit espírito *m* congénere, alma *f* gémea

kinetic /kɪ'netɪk/ *a* cinético

king /kɪŋ/ *n* rei *m*. ~-size(d) *a* de tamanho grande

kingdom /'kɪŋdəm/ *n* reino *m*

kingfisher /'kɪŋfɪʃə(r)/ *n* pica-peixe *m*, martim-pescador *m*

kink /kɪŋk/ *n* (*in rope*) volta *f*, nó *m*; (*fig*) perversão *f*. ~y *a* (*colloq*) excêntrico, pervertido; (*of hair*) encarapinhado

kiosk /'ki:ɒsk/ *n* quiosque *m*. telephone ~ cabine telefónica, (*P*) telefónica

kip /kɪp/ *n* (*sl*) sono *m* □ *vi* (*pt kipped*) (*sl*) dormir

kipper /'kɪpə(r)/ *n* arenque *m* defumado

kiss /kɪs/ *n* beijo *m* □ *vt/i* beijar(-se)

kit /kɪt/ *n* equipamento *m*; (*set of tools*) ferramenta *f*; (*for assembly*) kit *m* □ *vt* (*pt kitted*) ~ out equipar

kitbag /'kɪtbæg/ *n* mochila *f* (de soldado etc); saco *m* de viagem

kitchen /'kɪtʃɪn/ *n* cozinha *f*. ~ garden horta *f*. ~ sink pia *f*, (*P*) lava-louças *m*

kite /kaɪt/ *n* (*toy*) pipa *f*, (*P*) papagaio *m* de papel

kith /kɪθ/ *n* ~ and kin parentes e amigos *mpl*

kitten /'kɪtn/ *n* gatinho *m*

kitty /'kɪtɪ/ *n* (*fund*) fundo *m* comum, vaquinha *f*; (*cards*) bolo *m*

knack /næk/ *n* jeito *m*

knapsack /'næpsæk/ *n* mochila *f*

knead /ni:d/ *vt* amassar

knee /ni:/ *n* joelho *m*

kneecap /'ni:kæp/ *n* rótula *f*

kneel /ni:l/ *vi* (*pt knelt*) ~ (down) ajoelhar(-se)

knelt /nelt/ *see* kneel

knew /nju:/ *see* know

knickers /'nɪkəz/ *npl* calcinhas (de senhora) *fpl*

knife /naɪf/ *n* (*pl* knives) faca *f* □ *vt* esfaquear, apunhalar

knight /naɪt/ *n* cavaleiro *m*; (*chess*) cavalo *m*. ~hood *n* grau *m* de cavaleiro

knit /nɪt/ *vt* (*pt knitted or* knit) tricotar □ *vi* tricotar, fazer tricô; (*fig: unite*) unir-se; (*of bones*) soldar-se. ~ one's brow franzir as sobrancelhas. ~ting *n* malha *f*, tricô *m*

knitwear /'nɪtweə(r)/ *n* roupa *f* de malha, malhas *fpl*

knob /nɒb/ *n* (*of door*) maçaneta *f*; (*of drawer*) puxador *m*; (*of radio, TV etc*) botão *m*; (*of butter*) noz *f*. ~bly *a* nodoso

knock /nɒk/ *vt/i* bater (em); (*sl: criticize*) desancar (em). ~ about *vt* tratar mal □ *vi* (*wander*) andar a esmo. ~ down (*chair, pedestrian*) deitar no chão, derrubar; (*demolish*) jogar abaixo; (*colloq: reduce*) baixar, reduzir; (*at auction*) adjudicar (to a). ~-down *a* (*price*) muito baixo. ~-kneed *a* de pernas de tesoura. ~ off *vt* (*colloq: complete quickly*) despachar; (*sl: steal*) roubar □ *vi* (*colloq*) parar de trabalhar, fechar a loja (*colloq*). ~ out pôr fora de combate, eliminar; (*stun*) assombrar. ~-out *n* (*boxing*) nocaute *m*, KO *m*. ~ over entornar. ~ up (*meal etc*) arranjar às pressas. ~er *n* aldrava *f*

knot /nɒt/ *n* nó *m* □ *vt* (*pt knotted*) atar com nó, dar nó *or* nós em

knotty /'nɒtɪ/ *a* (-ier, -iest) nodoso, cheio de nós; (*difficult*) complicado, espinhoso know /nəʊ/ vt/i (pt knew, pp known) saber (that que); (person, place) conhecer □ n in the ~ (colloq) por dentro. ~ about (cars etc) saber sobre, saber de. ~-all n sabe-tudo m (colloq). ~-how n know-how m, conhecimentos mpl técnicos, culturais etc. ~ of ter conhecimento de, ter ouvido falar de. ~ingly adv com ar conhecedor; (consciously) conscientemente

knowledge /'nɒlɪdʒ/ n conhecimento m; (learning) saber m. ~able a conhecedor, entendido, versado

known /nəʊn/ see know □ a conhecido

knuckle /'nʌkl/ n nó m dos dedos □ vi ~ under ceder, submeter-se

Koran /kə'ra:n/ n Alcorão m, Corão m

Korea /kə'rɪə/ n Coréia f

kosher /'kəʊʃə(r)/ a aprovado pela lei judaica; (colloq) como deve ser

kowtow /kaʊ'taʊ/ vi prosternar-se (to diante de); (act obsequiously) bajular

L

lab /læb/ n (colloq) laboratório m

label /'leɪbl/ n (on bottle etc) rótulo m; (on clothes, luggage) etiqueta f □ vt (pt labelled) rotular; etiquetar, pôr etiqueta em

laboratory /lə'bɒrətrɪ/ n laboratório m

laborious /lə'bɔːrɪəs/ a laborioso, trabalhoso

labour /'leɪbə(r)/ n trabalho m, labuta f; (workers) mão-de-obra f □ vi trabalhar; (try hard) esforçar-se □ vt alongar-se sobre, insistir em. in ~ em trabalho de parto. ~ed a (writing) laborioso, sem espontaneidade; (breathing, movement) difícil. ~-saving a que poupa trabalho

Labour /'leɪbə(r)/ n (party) Partido m Trabalhista, os trabalhistas □ a trabalhista

labourer /'leɪbərə(r)/ n trabalhador m; (on farm) trabalhador m rural

labyrinth /'læbərɪnθ/ n labirinto m

lace /leɪs/ n renda f; (of shoe) cordão m de sapato, (P) atacador m □ vt atar; (drink) juntar um pouco (de aguardente, rum etc)

lacerate /'læsəreɪt/ vt lacerar, rasgar

lack /læk/ n falta f □ vt faltar (a), não ter. be ~ing faltar. be ~ing in carecer de

lackadaisical /lækə'deɪzɪkl/ a lânguido, apático, desinteressado

laconic /lə'kɒnɪk/ a lacônico, (P) lacónico

lacquer /'lækə(r)/ n laca f

lad /læd/ n rapaz m, moço m

ladder /'lædə(r)/ n escada de mão f, (P) escadote m; (in stocking) fio m corrido, (P) malha f caída □ vi deixar correr um fio, (P) cair uma malha □ vt fazer malhas em

laden /'leɪdn/ a carregado (with de)

ladle /'leɪdl/ n concha f (de sopa) f

lady /'leɪdɪ/ n senhora f; (title) Lady f. ~-in-waiting n dama f de companhia, (P) dama f de honor. young ~ jovem f. ~-like a senhoril, elegante. Ladies n (toilets) toalete m das Senhoras

ladybird /'leɪdɪbɜːd/ n joaninha f

lag¹ /læg/ vi (pt lagged) atrasar-se, ficar para trás □ n atraso m

lag² /læg/ vt (pt lagged) (pipes etc) revestir com isolante térmico

lager /'la:gə(r)/ n cerveja f leve e clara, "loura" (P (sl)

lagoon /lə'gu:n/ n lagoa f

laid /leɪd/ see lay²

lain /leɪn/ see lie²

lair /leə(r)/ n toca f, covil m

laity /'leɪətɪ/ n leigos mpl

lake /leɪk/ n lago m

lamb /læm/ n cordeiro m, carneiro m; (meat) carneiro m

lambswool /'læmzwʊl/ n lã f

lame /leɪm/ a (-er, -est) coxo; (fig: unconvincing) fraco. ~ness n claudicação f, coxeadura f

lament /lə'ment/ n lamento m, lamentação f □ vt/i lamentar(-se) (de). ~able a lamentável

laminated /'læmɪneɪtɪd/ a laminado

lamp /læmp/ n lâmpada f

lamppost /'læmppəʊst/ n poste m (do candeeiro) (de iluminação pública)

lampshade /'læmpʃeɪd/ n abajur m, quebra-luz m

lance /la:ns/ n lança f □ vt lancetar

lancet /'la:nsɪt/ n bisturi m, (P) lanceta f

land /lænd/ n terra f; (country) país m; (plot) terreno m; (property) terras fpl □ a de terra, terrestre; (policy etc) agrário □ vt/i desembarcar; (aviat) aterrissar, (P) aterrar; (fall) ir parar (on em); (colloq: obtain) arranjar; (a blow) aplicar, mandar. ~-locked a rodeado de terra

landing /'lændɪŋ/ n desembarque m; (aviat) aterrissagem f, (P) aterragem f; (top of stairs) patamar m. ~-stage n cais m flutuante

landlady /'lændleɪdɪ/ n (of rented house) senhoria f, proprietária f; (who lets rooms) dona f da casa; (of boarding-house) dona f da pensão; (of inn etc) proprietária f, estalajadeira f. ~lord n (of rented house) senhorio *m*, proprietário *m*; (*of inn etc*) proprietário *m*, estalajadeiro *m*

landmark /'lændmɑ:k/ *n* (*conspicuous feature*) ponto *m* de referência; (*fig*) marco *m*

landscape /'lændskeɪp/ *n* paisagem *f* □ *vt* projetar, (*P*) projectar paisagisticamente

landslide /'lændslaɪd/ *n* desabamento *m* or desmoronamento *m* de terras; (*fig: pol*) vitória *f* esmagadora

lane /leɪn/ *n* senda *f*, caminho *m*; (*in country*) estrada *f* pequena; (*in town*) viela *f*, ruela *f*; (*of road*) faixa *f*, pista *f*; (*of traffic*) fila *f*; (*aviat*) corredor *m*; (*naut*) rota *f*

language /'læŋgwɪdʒ/ *n* língua *f*; (*speech, style*) linguagem *f*. bad ∼ linguagem *f* grosseira. ∼ lab laboratório *m* de línguas

languid /'læŋgwɪd/ *a* lânguido

languish /'læŋgwɪʃ/ *vi* elanguescer

lank /læŋk/ *a* (*of hair*) escorrido, liso

lanky /'læŋkɪ/ *a* (-ier, -iest) desengonçado, escanifrado

lantern /'læntən/ *n* lanterna *f*

lap[1] /læp/ *n* colo *m*; (*sport*) volta *f* completa. ∼-dog *n* cãozinho *m* de estimação

lap[2] /læp/ *vt* up beber lambendo □ *vi* marulhar

lapel /lə'pel/ *n* lapela *f*

lapse /læps/ *vi* decair, degenerar-se; (*expire*) caducar □ *n* lapso *m*; (*jur*) prescrição *f*. ∼ into (*thought*) mergulhar em; (*bad habit*) adquirir

larceny /'lɑ:sənɪ/ *n* furto *m*

lard /lɑ:d/ *n* banha de porco *f*

larder /'lɑ:də(r)/ *n* despensa *f*

large /lɑ:dʒ/ *a* (-er, -est) grande. at ∼ à solta, em liberdade. by and ∼ em geral. ∼ly *adv* largamente, em grande parte. ∼ness *n* grandeza *f*

lark[1] /lɑ:k/ *n* (*bird*) cotovia *f*

lark[2] /lɑ:k/ *n* (*colloq*) pândega *f*, brincadeira *f* □ *vi* ∼ about (*colloq*) fazer travessuras, brincar

larva /'lɑ:və/ *n* (*pl* -vae /-vi:/) larva *f*

laryngitis /lærɪn'dʒaɪtɪs/ *n* laringite *f*

larynx /'lærɪŋks/ *n* laringe *f*

lascivious /lə'sɪvɪəs/ *a* lascivo, sensual

laser /'leɪzə(r)/ *n* laser *m*. ∼ printer impressora *f* a laser

lash /læʃ/ *vt* chicotear, açoitar; (*rain*) fustigar □ *n* chicote *m*; (*stroke*) chicotada *f*; (*eyelash*) pestana *f*, cílio *m*. ∼ out atacar, atirar-se a; (*colloq: spend*) esbanjar dinheiro em algo

lashings /'læʃɪŋz/ *npl* ∼ of (*sl*) montes de (*colloq*)

lasso /læ'su:/ *n* (*pl* -os) laço *m* □ *vt* laçar

last[1] /lɑ:st/ *a* último □ *adv* no fim, em

último lugar; (*most recently*) a última vez □ *n* último *m*. at (long) ∼ por fim, finalmente. ∼-minute *a* de última hora. ∼ night ontem à noite, a noite passada. the ∼ straw a gota d'água. to the ∼ até o fim. ∼ly *adv* finalmente, em último lugar

last[2] /lɑ:st/ *vt/i* durar, continuar. ∼ing *a* duradouro, durável

latch /lætʃ/ *n* trinco *m*

late /leɪt/ *a* (-er, -est) atrasado; (*recent*) recente; (*former*) antigo, ex-, anterior; (*hour, fruit etc*) tardio; (*deceased*) falecido □ *adv* tarde. in ∼ July no fim de julho. of ∼ ultimamente. at the ∼st o mais tardar. ∼ness *n* atraso *m*

lately /'leɪtlɪ/ *adv* nos últimos tempos, ultimamente

latent /'leɪtnt/ *a* latente

lateral /'lætərəl/ *a* lateral

lathe /leɪð/ *n* torno *m*

lather /'lɑ:ðə(r)/ *n* espuma *f* de sabão □ *vt* ensaboar □ *vi* fazer espuma

Latin /'lætɪn/ *n* (*lang*) latim *m* □ *a* latino. ∼ America *n* América *f* Latina. ∼ American *a* & *n* latino-americano (*m*)

latitude /'lætɪtjuːd/ *n* latitude *f*

latter /'lætə(r)/ *a* último, mais recente □ *n* the ∼ este, esta. ∼ly *adv* recentemente

lattice /'lætɪs/ *n* treliça *f*, (*P*) gradeamento *m* de ripas

laudable /'lɔ:dəbl/ *a* louvável

laugh /lɑ:f/ *vi* rir (at de). ∼ off disfarçar com uma piada □ *n* riso *m*. ∼able *a* irrisório, ridículo. ∼ing-stock *n* objeto *m*, (*P*) objecto *m* de troça

laughter /'lɑ:ftə(r)/ *n* riso *m*, risada *f*

launch[1] /lɔ:ntʃ/ *vt* lançar □ *n* lançamento *m*. ∼ into → into lançar-se or meter-se em. ∼ing pad plataforma *f* de lançamento

launch[2] /lɔ:ntʃ/ *n* (*boat*) lancha *f*

launder /'lɔ:ndə(r)/ *vt* lavar e passar

launderette /lɔ:n'dret/ *n* lavandaria *f* automática

laundry /'lɔ:ndrɪ/ *n* lavandaria *f*; (*clothes*) roupa *f*. do the ∼ lavar a roupa

laurel /'lɒrəl/ *n* loureiro *m*, louro *m*

lava /'lɑ:və/ *n* lava *f*

lavatory /'lævətrɪ/ *n* privada *f*, (*P*) retrete *f*; (*room*) lavabo *m*, (*P*) lavabo *m*

lavender /'lævəndə(r)/ *n* alfazema *f*, lavanda *f*

lavish /'lævɪʃ/ *a* pródigo; (*plentiful*) copioso, generoso; (*lush*) suntuoso □ *vt* ser pródigo em, encher de. ∼ly *adv* prodigamente, copiosamente; suntuosamente

law /lɔ:/ *n* lei *f*; (*profession, study*) direito *m*. ∼-abiding *a* cumpridor da lei, respeitador da lei. ~ and order ordem *f* pública. ~-breaker *n* transgressor *m* da lei. ~-ful *a* legal, legítimo. ~fully *adv* legalmente. ~less *a* sem lei; (*act*) ilegal; (*person*) rebelde

lawcourt /'lɔːkɔːt/ *n* tribunal *m*

lawn /lɔːn/ *n* gramado *m*, (*P*) relvado *m*. ~-mower *n* cortador *m* de grama, (*P*) máquina *f* de cortar a relva

lawsuit /'lɔːsuːt/ *n* processo *m*, ação *f*, (*P*) acção *f* judicial

lawyer /'lɔːjə(r)/ *n* advogado *m*

lax /læks/ *a* negligente; (*discipline*) frouxo; (*morals*) relaxado. ~ity *n* negligência *f*; (*of discipline*) frouxidão *f*; (*of morals*) relaxamento *m*

laxative /'læksətɪv/ *n* laxante *m*, laxativo *m*

lay¹ /leɪ/ *a* leigo. ~ opinion opinião *f* de um leigo

lay² /leɪ/ *vt* (*pt* laid) pôr, colocar; (*trap*) preparar, pôr; (*eggs, table, siege*) pôr; (*plan*) fazer □ *vi* pôr (ovos). ~ aside pôr de lado. ~ down pousar; (*condition, law, rule*) impôr; (*arms*) depor; (*one's life*) oferecer; (*policy*) ditar. ~ hold of agarrar-(se a). ~ off *vt* (*worker*) suspender do trabalho □ *vi* (*colloq*) parar, desistir. ~-off *n* suspensão *f* temporária. ~ on (*gas, water etc*) instalar, ligar; (*entertainment etc*) organizar, providenciar; (*food*) servir. ~ out (*design*) traçar, planejar; (*spread out*) estender, espalhar; (*money*) gastar. ~ up *vt* (*store*) juntar; (*ship, car*) pôr fora de serviço

lay³ /leɪ/ *see* lie

layabout /'leɪəbaʊt/ *n* (*sl*) vadio *m*

lay-by /'leɪbaɪ/ *n* acostamento *m*, (*P*) berma *f*

layer /'leɪə(r)/ *n* camada *f*

layman /'leɪmən/ *n* (*pl* -men) leigo *m*

layout /'leɪaʊt/ *n* disposição *f*; (*typ*) composição *f*

laze /leɪz/ *vi* descansar, vadiar

laz|y /'leɪzɪ/ *a* (-ier, -iest) preguiçoso. ~iness *n* preguiça *f*. ~y-bones *n* (*colloq*) vadio *m*, vagabundo *m*

lead¹ /liːd/ *vt/i* (*pt* led) conduzir, guiar, levar; (*team etc*) chefiar, liderar; (*life*) levar; (*choir, band etc*) dirigir □ *n* (*distance*) avanço *m*; (*first place*) dianteira *f*; (*clue*) indício *m*, pista *f*; (*leash*) coleira *f*; (*electr*) cabo *m*; (*theatr*) papel *m* principal; (*example*) exemplo *m*. in the ~ na frente. ~ away levar. ~ on (*fig*) encorajar. ~ the way ir na frente. ~ up to conduzir a

lead² /led/ *n* chumbo *m*; (*of pencil*) grafite *f*. ~en *a* de chumbo; (*of colour*) plúmbeo

leader /'liːdə(r)/ *n* chefe *m*, líder *m*; (*of country, club, union etc*) dirigente *mf*; (*pol*) líder; (*of orchestra*) regente *mf*, maestro *m*; (*in newspaper*) editorial *m*. ~ship *n* direção *f*, (*P*) direcção *f*, liderança *f*

leading /'liːdɪŋ/ *a* principal. ~ article artigo *m* de fundo, editorial *m*

leaf /liːf/ *n* (*pl* leaves) folha *f*; (*flap of table*) aba □ *vi* ~ through folhear. ~y *a* frondoso

leaflet /'liːflɪt/ *n* prospecto *m*, folheto *m* informativo

league /liːg/ *n* liga *f*; (*sport*) campeonato *m* da Liga. in ~ with de coligação com, em conluio com

leak /liːk/ *n* (*escape*) fuga *f*; (*hole*) buraco *m* □ *vt/i* (*roof, container*) pingar; (*eletr gas*) ter um escapamento, (*P*) ter uma fuga; (*naut*) fazer água. ~ (*out*) (*fig: divulge*) divulgar; (*fig: become known*) transpirar, divulgar-se. ~age *n* vazamento *m*. ~y *a* que tem um vazamento

lean¹ /liːn/ *a* (-er, -est) magro. ~ness *n* magreza *f*

lean² /liːn/ *vt/i* (*pt* leaned *or* leant /lent/) encostar(-se), apoiar-se (on em); (*be slanting*) inclinar(-se). ~ back/forward *or* over inclinar-se para trás/para a frente. ~ on (*colloq*) pressionar. ~ to *n* alpendre *m*

leaning /'liːnɪŋ/ *a* inclinado □ *n* inclinação *f*

leap /liːp/ *vt* (*pt* leaped *or* leapt/ lept/) galgar, saltar por cima de □ *vi* saltar □ *n* salto *m*, pulo *m*. ~-frog *n* eixo-badeixo *m*, (*P*) jogo *m* do eixo. ~ year ano *m* bissexto

learn /lɜːn/ *vt/i* (*pt* learned *or* learnt) aprender; (*be told*) vir a saber, ouvir dizer. ~er *n* principiante *mf*, aprendiz *m*

learn|ed /'lɜːnɪd/ *a* erudito. ~ing *n* saber *m*, erudição *f*

lease /liːs/ *n* arrendamento *m*, aluguel *m*, (*P*) aluguer *m* □ *vt* arrendar, (*P*) alugar

leash /liːʃ/ *n* coleira *f*

least /liːst/ *a* o menor □ *n* o mínimo *m*, o menos □ *adv* o menos. at ~ pelo menos. not in the ~ de maneira alguma

leather /'leðə(r)/ *n* couro *m*, cabedal *m*

leave /liːv/ *vt/i* (*pt* left) deixar; (*depart from*) sair/partir (de), ir-se (de) □ *n* licença *f*, permissão *f*. be left (*over*) restar, sobrar. ~ alone deixar em paz, não tocar. ~ out omitir. ~ of absence licença *f*. on ~ (*mil*) de licença. take one's ~ despedir-se (of de)

leavings /'liːvɪŋz/ *npl* restos *mpl*

Lebanon /'lebənən/ n Líbano m.
~ese /'ni:z/ a & n libanês (m)

lecherous /'letʃərəs/ a lascivo

lectern /'lektən/ n estante f (de coro de igreja)

lecture /'lektʃə(r)/ n conferência f; (univ) aula f teórica; (fig) sermão m □ vi dar uma conferência; (univ) dar aula(s) □ vt pregar um sermão a alg (colloq). ~r /-ə(r)/ n conferente mf, conferencista mf; (univ) professor m

led /led/ see lead¹

ledge /ledʒ/ n rebordo m, saliência f; (of window) peitoril m

ledger /'ledʒə(r)/ n livro-mestre m, razão m

leech /li:tʃ/ n sanguessuga f

leek /li:k/ n alho-poró m, (P) alho-porro m

leer /lɪə(r)/ vi ~ (at) olhar de modo malicioso or manhoso (para) □ n olhar m malicioso or manhoso

leeway /'li:weɪ/ n (naut) deriva f; (fig) liberdade f de ação, (P) acção, margem f (colloq)

left¹ /left/ see leave· ~ luggage (office) depósito m de bagagens. ~overs npl restos mpl, sobras fpl

left² /left/ a esquerdo; (pol) de esquerda □ n esquerda f □ adv à/para à esquerda. ~-hand a da esquerda; (position) à esquerda. ~-handed a canhoto. ~-wing a (pol) de esquerda

leg /leg/ n perna f; (of table) pé m, perna f; (of journey) etapa f. pull sb's ~ brincar or mexer com alg. stretch one's ~s esticar as pernas. ~-room n espaço m para as pernas

legacy /'legəsɪ/ n legado m

legal /'li:gl/ a legal; (affairs etc) jurídico. ~ adviser advogado m. ~ity /li:'gælətɪ/ n legalidade f. ~ly adv legalmente

legalize /'li:gəlaɪz/ vt legalizar

legend /'ledʒənd/ n lenda f. ~ary /'ledʒəndrɪ/ a lendário

leggings /'legɪŋz/ npl perneiras fpl; (women's) legging m

legib|le /'ledʒəbl/ a legível. ~ility /-'bɪlətɪ/ n legibilidade f

legion /'li:dʒən/ n legião f

legislat|e /'ledʒɪsleɪt/ vi legislar. ~ion /-'leɪʃn/ n legislação f

legislat|ive /'ledʒɪslətɪv/ a legislativo. ~ure /-eɪtʃə(r)/ n corpo m legislativo

legitima|te /lɪ'dʒɪtɪmət/ a legítimo. ~cy n legitimidade f

leisure /'leʒə(r)/ n lazer m, tempo livre m. at one's ~ ao bel prazer, (P) a seu belo prazer. ~ centre centro m de lazer. ~ly a pausado, compassado □ adv sem pressa, devagar

lemon /'lemən/ n limão m

lemonade /lemə'neɪd/ n limonada f

lend /lend/ vt (pt lent) emprestar; (contribute) dar. ~ a hand to (help) ajudar. ~ itself to prestar-se a. ~er n pessoa f que empresta. ~ing n empréstimo m

length /leŋθ/ n comprimento m; (in time) período m; (of cloth) corte m. at ~ extensamente; (at last) por fim, finalmente. ~y a longo, demorado

lengthen /'leŋθən/ vt/i alongar(-se)

lengthways /'leŋθweɪz/ adv ao comprido, em comprimento, longitudinalmente

lenien|t /'li:nɪənt/ a indulgente, clemente. ~cy n indulgência f, clemência f

lens /lenz/ n (of spectacles) lente f; (photo) objetiva f, (P) objectiva f

lent /lent/ see lend

Lent /lent/ n Quaresma f

lentil /'lentl/ n lentilha f

Leo /'li:əʊ/ n (astr) Leão m

leopard /'lepəd/ n leopardo m

leotard /'li:əʊtɑːd/ n collant(s) m (pl), (P) maillot m de ginástica ou dança

leper /'lepə(r)/ n leproso m

leprosy /'leprəsɪ/ n lepra f

lesbian /'lezbɪən/ a lésbico □ n lésbica f

less /les/ a (in number) menor (than que); (in quantity) menos (than que) □ n, adv & prep menos. ~ and ~ cada vez menos

lessen /'lesn/ vt/i diminuir

lesser /'lesə(r)/ a menor. to a ~ degree em menor grau

lesson /'lesn/ n lição f

let /let/ vt (pt let, pres p letting) deixar, permitir; (lease) alugar, arrendar □ v aux ~'s go vamos. ~ him do it que o faça ele. ~ me know diga-me, avise-me □ n aluguel m, (P) aluguer m. ~ alone deixar em paz; (not to mention) sem falar em, para não falar em. ~ down baixar; (deflate) esvaziar; (disappoint) desapontar; (fail to help) deixar na mão. ~-down n desapontamento m. ~ go vt/i soltar. ~ in deixar entrar. ~ o.s. in for (task, trouble) meter-se em. ~ off (gun) disparar; (firework) soltar, (P) deitar; (excuse) desculpar. ~ on (colloq) vt revelar (that que) □ vi descoser-se (colloq), (P) descair-se (colloq). ~ out deixar sair. ~ through deixar passar. ~ up (colloq) abrandar, diminuir. ~up n (colloq) pausa f, trégua f

lethal /'li:θl/ a fatal, mortal

letharg|y /'leθədʒɪ/ n letargia f, apatia f. ~ic /lɪ'θɑːdʒɪk/ a letárgico, apático

letter /'letə(r)/ n (symbol) letra f; (message) carta f. ~-bomb n carta-bomba f. ~-box n caixa f do correio. ~ing n letras fpl lettuce /'letɪs/ n alface f

leukaemia /lu:'ki:mɪə/ n leucemia f

level /'levl/ n plano; (*on surface*) horizontal; (*in height*) no mesmo nível (with que); (*spoonful etc*) raso □ *n* nível *m* □ *vt* (*pt* levelled) nivelar; (*gun, missile*) apontar; (*accusation*) dirigir. on the ~ (*colloq*) franco, sincero. ~ crossing passagem *f* de nível. ~-headed *a* equilibrado, sensato

lever /'li:və(r)/ *n* alavanca *f* □ *vt* ~ up levantar com alavanca

leverage /'li:vərɪdʒ/ *n* influência *f*

levity /'levətɪ/ *n* frivolidade *f*, leviandade *f*

levy /'levɪ/ *vt* (*tax*) cobrar □ *n* imposto *m*

lewd /lu:d/ *a* (-er, -est) libidinoso, obsceno

liability /laɪə'bɪlətɪ/ *n* responsabilidade *f*; (*colloq: handicap*) desvantagem *f*. ~ies *as* dividas *fpl*

liable /'laɪəbl/ *a* ~ to do suscetível, (*P*) susceptível de fazer; ~ to (*illness etc*) suscetível, (*P*) susceptível a; (*fine*) sujeito a. ~ for responsável por

liaise /lɪ'eɪz/ *vi* (*colloq*) servir de intermediário (between entre), fazer a ligação (with com)

liaison /lɪ'eɪzn/ *n* ligação *f*

liar /'laɪə(r)/ *n* mentiroso *m*

libel /'laɪbl/ *n* difamação *f* □ *vt* (*pt* libelled) difamar

liberal /'lɪbərəl/ *a* liberal. ~ly *adv* liberalmente

Liberal /'lɪbərəl/ *a* & *n* liberal (*mf*)

liberat|e /'lɪbəreɪt/ *vt* libertar. ~ion /-'reɪʃn/ *n* libertação *f*; (*of women*) emancipação *f*

libert|y /'lɪbətɪ/ *n* liberdade *f*. at ~y to livre de. take ~ies tomar liberdades

libido /lɪ'bi:dəʊ/ *n* (*pl* -os) libido *m*

Libra /'li:brə/ *n* (*astr*) Balança *f*, Libra *f*

librar|y /'laɪbrərɪ/ *n* biblioteca *f*. ~ian /-'breərɪən/ *n* bibliotecário *m*

Libya /'lɪbɪə/ *n* Líbia *f*. ~n *a* & *n* líbio (*m*)

lice /laɪs/ *n see* louse

licence /'laɪsns/ *n* licença *f*; d (*for TV*) taxa *f*; (*for driving*) carteira *f*, (*P*) carta *f*; (*behaviour*) libertinagem *f*

license /'laɪsns/ *vt* dar licença para, autorizar □ *n* (*Amer*) = licence. ~ plate placa *f* do carro, (*P*) placa *f* de matrícula

licentious /laɪ'senʃəs/ *a* licencioso

lichen /'laɪkən/ *n* líquen *m*

lick /lɪk/ *vt* lamber; (*sl: defeat*) bater (*colloq*), dar uma surra em (*colloq*) □ *n* lambidela *f*. a ~ of paint uma mão de pintura

lid /lɪd/ *n* tampa *f*

lido /'li:dəʊ/ *n* (*pl* ~os) piscina *f* pública ao ar livre

lie¹ /laɪ/ *n* mentira *f* □ *vi* (*pt* lied, *pres p* lying) mentir. give the ~ to desmentir

lie² /laɪ/ *vi* (*pt* lay, *pp* lain, *pres p* lying) estar deitado; (*remain*) ficar; (*be situated*) estar, encontrar-se; (*in grave, on ground*) jazer. ~ down descansar. ~ in, have a ~-in dormir até tarde. ~ low (*colloq: hide*) andar escondido

lieu /lu:/ *n* in ~ of em vez de

lieutenant /lef'tenənt/ *n* (*army*) tenente *m*; (*navy*) 1° tenente *m*

life /laɪf/ *n* (*pl* lives) vida *f*. ~ cycle ciclo *m* vital. ~ expectancy probabilidade *f* de vida. ~-guard *n* salvavidas *m*. ~ insurance seguro *m* de vida. ~-jacket *n* colete *m* salva-vidas. ~-size(d) *a* (de) tamanho natural invar

lifebelt /'laɪfbelt/ *n* cinto *m* salvavidas, (*P*) cinto *m* de salvação

lifeboat /'laɪfbəʊt/ *n* barco *m* salvavidas

lifebuoy /'laɪfbɔɪ/ *n* bóia *f* salva-vidas, (*P*) bóia *f* de salvação

lifeless /'laɪflɪs/ *a* sem vida

lifelike /'laɪflaɪk/ *a* natural, real; (*of portrait*) muito parecido

lifelong /'laɪflɒŋ/ *a* de toda a vida, perpétuo

lifestyle /'laɪfstaɪl/ *n* estilo *m* de vida

lifetime /'laɪftaɪm/ *n* vida *f*. the chance of a ~ uma oportunidade única

lift /lɪft/ *vt/i* levantar(-se), erguer(-se); (*colloq: steal*) roubar, surripiar (*colloq*); (*of fog*) levantar, dispersar-se □ *n* ascensor *m*, elevador *m*; (*P*) boleia *f* (*colloq*). ~ off *n* decolagem *f*, (*P*) descolagem *f*

ligament /'lɪgəmənt/ *n* ligamento *m*

light¹ /laɪt/ *n* luz *f*; (*lamp*) lâmpada *f*; (*on vehicle*) farol *m*; (*spark*) lume *m* □ *a* claro □ *vt* (*pt* lit *or* lighted) (*ignite*) acender; (*illuminate*) iluminar. bring to ~ trazer à luz, revelar. come to ~ vir à luz. ~ up iluminar(-se), acender(-se). ~-year *n* ano-luz *m*

light² /laɪt/ *a* & *adv* (-er, -est) leve. ~-headed *a* (*dizzy*) estonteado, tonto; (*frivolous*) leviano. ~-hearted *a* alegre, despreocupado. ~ly *adv* de leve, levemente, ligeiramente. ~ness *n* leveza *f*

lighten¹ /'laɪtn/ *vt/i* iluminar(-se); (*make brighter*) clarear

lighten² /'laɪtn/ *vt/i* (*load etc*) aligerar(-se), tornar mais leve

lighter /'laɪtə(r)/ *n* isqueiro *m*

lighthouse /'laɪthaʊs/ *n* farol *m*

lighting /'laɪtɪŋ/ n iluminação f

lightning /'laɪtnɪŋ/ n relâmpago m; (thunderbolt) raio m □ a muito rápido. like ~ como um relâmpago

lightweight /'laɪtweɪt/ a leve

like[1] /laɪk/ a semelhante (a), parecido (com) □ prep como □ conj (colloq) como □ n igual m, coisa f parecida. ~-minded a da mesma opinião. the ~s of você(s).

like[2] /laɪk/ vt gostar (de). ~s npl gostos mpl. I would ~ gostaria (de), queria. if you ~ se quiser. would you ~? gostaria?, queria? ~able a simpático

likely /'laɪklɪ/ a (-ier, -iest) provável □ adv provavelmente. he is ~ly to come é provável que ele venha. not ~ly! (colloq) nem morto, nem por sonhos. ~lihood n probabilidade f

liken /'laɪkn/ vt comparar (to com)

likeness /'laɪknɪs/ n semelhança f

likewise /'laɪkwaɪz/ adv também; (in the same way) da mesma maneira

liking /'laɪkɪŋ/ n gosto m, inclinação f; (for person) afeição f. take a ~ to (thing) tomar gosto por; (person) simpatizar com

lilac /'laɪlək/ n lilás m □ a lilás invar

lily /'lɪlɪ/ n lírio m, lis m. ~ of the valley lírio m do vale

limb /lɪm/ n membro m

limber /'lɪmbə(r)/ vi ~ up fazer exercícios para desenferrujar (colloq)

lime[1] /laɪm/ n cal f

lime[2] /laɪm/ n (fruit) limão m

lime[3] /laɪm/ n ~(-tree) tília f

limelight /'laɪmlaɪt/ n be in the ~ estar em evidência

limerick /'lɪmərɪk/ n poema m humorístico (de cinco versos)

limit /'lɪmɪt/ n limite m □ vt limitar. ~ation /-'teɪʃn/ n limitação f. ~ed company sociedade f anônima, (P) anónima de responsabilidade limitada

limousine /'lɪməziːn/ n limusine f

limp[1] /lɪmp/ vi mancar, coxear □ n have a ~ coxear

limp[2] /lɪmp/ a (-er, -est) mole, frouxo

line[1] /laɪn/ n linha f; (string) fio m; (rope) corda f; (row) fila f; (of poem) verso m; (wrinkle) ruga f; (of business) ramo m; (of goods) linha f; (Amer: queue) fila f, (P) bicha f □ vt marcar com linhas; (streets etc) ladear, enfileirar-se ao longo de. ~d paper papel m pautado. in ~ with de acordo com. ~ up alinhar(-se), enfileirar(-se); (in queue) pôr(-se) em fila, (P) bicha. ~ up n (players) formação f

line[2] /laɪn/ vt (garment) forrar (with de)

lineage /'lɪnɪdʒ/ n linhagem f

linear /'lɪnɪə(r)/ a linear

linen /'lɪnɪn/ n (sheets etc) roupa f (branca) de cama; (material) linho m

liner /'laɪnə(r)/ n navio m de linha regular, (P) paquete m

linesman /'laɪnzmən/ n (football, tennis) juiz m de linha

linger /'lɪŋgə(r)/ vi demorar-se, deixar-se ficar; (of smells etc) persistir

lingerie /'lænʒərɪ/ n roupa f de baixo (de senhora), lingerie f

linguist /'lɪŋgwɪst/ n lingüista mf, (P) linguista mf

linguistic /lɪŋ'gwɪstɪk/ a lingüístico, (P) linguístico. ~s n lingüística f, (P) linguística f

lining /'laɪnɪŋ/ n forro m

link /lɪŋk/ n laço m; (of chain; fig) elo m □ vt unir, ligar; (relate) ligar; (arm) enfiar. ~ up (of roads) juntar-se (with a). ~age n ligação f

lino, linoleum /'laɪnəʊ, lɪ'nəʊlɪəm/ n linóleo m

lint /lɪnt/ n (med) curativo m de fibra de algodão; (fluff) cotão m

lion /'laɪən/ n leão m. ~ess n leoa f

lip /lɪp/ n lábio m, beiço m; (edge) borda f; (of jug etc) bico m. ~-read vt/i entender pelos movimentos dos lábios. pay ~-service to fingir pena, admiração etc

lipstick /'lɪpstɪk/ n batom m, (P) báton m

liquefy /'lɪkwɪfaɪ/ vt/i liquefazer(-se)

liqueur /lɪ'kjʊə(r)/ n licor m

liquid /'lɪkwɪd/ n & a líquido (m). ~ize vt liqüidificar, (P) liquidificar. ~izer n liqüidificador m, (P) liquidificador m

liquidat|e /'lɪkwɪdeɪt/ vt liquidar. ~ion /-'deɪʃn/ n liquidação f

liquor /'lɪkə(r)/ n bebida f alcoólica

liquorice /'lɪkərɪs/ n alcaçuz m

Lisbon /'lɪzbən/ n Lisboa f

lisp /lɪsp/ n ceceio m □ vi cecear

list[1] /lɪst/ n lista f □ vt fazer uma lista de; (enter) pôr na lista

list[2] /lɪst/ vi (of ship) adernar □ n adernamento m

listen /'lɪsn/ vi escutar, prestar atenção. ~ to, ~ in (to) escutar, pôr-se à escuta. ~er n ouvinte mf

listless /'lɪstlɪs/ a sem energia, apático

lit /lɪt/ see light[1]

literal /'lɪtərəl/ a literal. ~ly adv literalmente

litera|te /'lɪtərət/ a alfabetizado. ~cy n alfabetização f, instrução f

literature /'lɪtrətʃə(r)/ n literatura f; (colloq: leaflets etc) folhetos mpl

lithe /laɪð/ a ágil, flexível

litigation /lɪtɪ'geɪʃn/ n litígio m

litre /'liːtə(r)/ n litro m

litter /'lɪtə(r)/ n lixo m; (animals) ninhada f □ vt cobrir de lixo. ~ed with coberto de. ~-bin n lata f, (P) caixote m do lixo

little /'lɪtl/ a pequeno; (not much) pouco ▢ n pouco m ▢ adv pouco, mal, nem. a ~ um pouco (de). he ~ knows ele mal/nem sabe. ~ by ~ pouco a pouco

liturgy /'lɪtədʒɪ/ n liturgia f

live[1] /laɪv/ a vivo; (wire) eletrizado; (broadcast) em direto, (P) directo, ao vivo

live[2] /lɪv/ vt/i viver; (reside) habitar, morar, viver. ~ down fazer esquecer. ~ it up cair na farra. ~ on viver de; (continue) continuar a viver. ~ up to mostrar-se à altura de; (fulfil) cumprir

livelihood /'laɪvlɪhʊd/ n modo m de vida

lively /'laɪvlɪ/ a (-ier, -iest) vivo, animado. ~iness n vivacidade f, animação f

liven /'laɪvn/ vt/i ~ up animar(-se)

liver /'lɪvə(r)/ n fígado m

livery /'lɪvərɪ/ n libré f

livestock /'laɪvstɒk/ n gado m

livid /'lɪvɪd/ a lívido; (colloq: furious) furioso

living /'lɪvɪŋ/ a vivo ▢ n vida f; (livelihood) modo de vida m, sustento m. **earn** or **make a** ~ ganhar a vida. **standard of** ~ nível m de vida. ~-room n sala f de estar

lizard /'lɪzəd/ n lagarto m

llama /'lɑːmə/ n lama m

load /ləʊd/ n carga f; (of lorry, ship) carga f, carregamento m; (weight, strain) peso m. ~s of (colloq) montes de (colloq) ▢ vt carregar. ~ed a (dice) viciado; (sl: rich) cheio da nota

loaf[1] /ləʊf/ n (pl loaves) pão m

loaf[2] /ləʊf/ vi vadiar. ~er n preguiçoso m, vagabundo m

loan /ləʊn/ n empréstimo m ▢ vt emprestar. **on** ~ emprestado

loath /ləʊθ/ a sem vontade de, pouco disposto a, relutante em

loathe /ləʊð/ vt detestar. ~ing n repugnância f, aversão f. ~some a repugnante

lobby /'lɒbɪ/ n entrada f, vestíbulo m; (pol) lobby m, grupo m de pressão ▢ vt fazer pressão sobre

lobe /ləʊb/ n lóbulo m

lobster /'lɒbstə(r)/ n lagosta f

local /'ləʊkl/ a local; (shops etc) do bairro ▢ n pessoa f do lugar; (colloq: pub) taberna f/pub m do bairro. ~ **government** administração f municipal. ~**ly** adv localmente; (nearby) na vizinhança

locale /ləʊˈkɑːl/ n local m

locality /ləʊˈkælətɪ/ n localidade f; (position) lugar m

localized /'ləʊkəlaɪzd/ a localizado

locat|**e** /ləʊˈkeɪt/ vt localizar; (situate) situar. ~**ion** /-ˈʃn/ n localização f. **on** ~**ion** (cinema) em external, (P) no exterior

lock[1] /lɒk/ n (hair) mecha f de cabelo

lock[2] /lɒk/ n (on door etc) fecho m, fechadura f; (on canal) comporta f ▢ vt/i fechar à chave; (auto: wheels) imobilizar(-se). ~ **in** fechar à chave, encerrar. ~ **out** fechar a porta para, deixar na rua. ~-**out** n lockout m. ~ **up** fechar a casa. **under** ~ **and key** a sete chaves

locker /'lɒkə(r)/ n compartimento m com chave

locket /'lɒkɪt/ n medalhão m

locksmith /'lɒksmɪθ/ n serralheiro m, chaveiro m

locomotion /ləʊkəˈməʊʃn/ n locomoção f

locomotive /'ləʊkəməʊtɪv/ n locomotiva f

locum /'ləʊkəm/ n (med) substituto m

locust /'ləʊkəst/ n gafanhoto m

lodge /lɒdʒ/ n casa f do guarda numa propriedade; (of porter) portaria f ▢ vt alojar; (money) depositar. ~ **a complaint** apresentar uma queixa ▢ vi estar alojado (with em casa de); (become fixed) alojar-se. ~**r** /-ə(r)/ n hóspede mf

lodgings /'lɒdʒɪŋz/ n quarto m mobiliado; (flat) apartamento m

loft /lɒft/ n sótão m

lofty /'lɒftɪ/ a (-ier, -iest) elevado; (haughty) altivo

log /lɒg/ n tronco m, toro m. ~-(book) n (naut) diário m de bordo; (aviat) diário m de vôo. **sleep like a** ~ dormir como uma pedra ▢ vt (pt logged) (naut/aviat) lançar no diário de bordo. ~ **off** acabar de usar. ~ **on** começar a usar

loggerheads /'lɒgəhedz/ npl **at** ~ às turras (with com)

logic /'lɒdʒɪk/ a lógico. ~**al** a lógico. ~**ally** adv logicamente

logistics /ləˈdʒɪstɪks/ n logística f

logo /'ləʊgəʊ/ n (pl -os) (colloq) emblema m, logotipo m, (P) logótipo m

loin /lɔɪn/ n (culin) lombo m, alcatra f

loiter /'lɔɪtə(r)/ vi andar vagarosamente; (stand about) rondar

loll /lɒl/ vi refestelar-se

loll|**ipop** /'lɒlɪpɒp/ n pirulito m, (P) chupa-chupa m. ~**y** n (colloq) pirulito m, (P) chupa-chupa m; (sl: money) grana f

London /'lʌndən/ n Londres

lone /ləʊn/ a solitário. ~**r** /-ə(r)/ n solitário m. ~**some** a solitário

lonely /'ləʊnlɪ/ a (-ier, -iest) solitário; (person) só, solitário

long¹ /lɒŋ/ a (-er, -est) longo, comprido □ adv muito tempo, longamente. how ~ is...? (in size) qual é o comprimento de...? how ~? (in time) quanto tempo? he will not be ~ ele não vai demorar. a ~ time muito tempo. a ~ way longe. as or so ~ as contanto que, desde que. ~ ago há muito tempo. before ~ (future) daqui a pouco, dentro em pouco; (past) pouco (tempo) depois. in the ~ run no fim de contas. ~ before muito (tempo) antes. ~-distance a (flight) de longa distância; (phone call) interurbano. ~ face cara f triste. ~ jump salto m em distância. ~-playing record LP m. ~-range a de longo alcance; (forecast) a longo prazo. ~-sighted a que emxerga mal à distância. ~-standing a de longa data. ~-suffering a com paciência exemplar/de santo. ~-term a a longo prazo. ~ wave ondas fpl longas. ~-winded a prolixo. so ~! (colloq) até logo!

long² /lɒŋ/ vi ~ for ansiar por, ter grande desejo de. ~ to desejar. ~ing n desejo m ardente

longevity /lɒn'dʒevatɪ/ n longevidade f, vida f longa

longhand /'lɒŋhænd/ n escrita f à mão

longitude /'lɒndʒɪtjuːd/ n longitude f

loo /luː/ n (colloq) banheiro m, (P) casa f de banho

look /lʊk/ vt/i olhar; (seem) parecer □ n olhar m; (appearance) ar m, aspecto m. (good) ~s beleza f. ~ after tomar conta de, olhar por. ~ at olhar para. ~ down on desprezar. ~ for procurar. ~ forward to aguardar com impaciência. ~ in on visitar. ~ into examinar, investigar. ~ like parecer-se com, ter ar de. ~ on (as spectator) ver, assistir; (regard as) considerar. ~ out ter cautela. ~ out for procurar; (watch) estar à espreita de. ~-out n (mil) posto m de observação; (watcher) vigia m. ~ round olhar em redor. ~ up (word) procurar; (visit) ir ver. ~ up to respeitar

loom¹ /luːm/ n tear m

loom² /luːm/ vi surgir indistintamente; (fig) ameaçar

loony /'luːnɪ/ n & a (sl) maluco (m), doido (m)

loop /luːp/ n laçada f; (curve) volta f, arco m; (aviat) loop m □ vt dar uma laçada

loophole /'luːphəʊl/ n (in rule) saída f, furo m

loose /luːs/ a (-er, -est) (knot etc) frouxo; (page etc) solto; (clothes) folgado; (not packed) a granel; (inexact) vago; (morals) dissoluto, imoral. at a ~ end sem saber o que fazer, sem ocupação definida. break ~ soltar-se. ~ly adv sem apertar; (roughly) vagamente

loosen /'luːsn/ vt (slacken) soltar, desapertar; (untie) desfazer, desatar

loot /luːt/ n saque m □ vt pilhar, saquear. ~er n assaltante mf. ~ing n pilhagem f, saque m

lop /lɒp/ vt (pt lopped) ~ off cortar, podar

lop-sided /lɒp'saɪdɪd/ a torto, inclinado para um lado

lord /lɔːd/ n o senhor m; (title) lord m. the L~ o Senhor. the L~'s Prayer o Pai-Nosso. (good) L~! meu Deus! ~ly a magnífico, nobre; (haughty) altivo, arrogante

lorry /'lɒrɪ/ n camião m, caminhão m

lose /luːz/ vt/i (pt lost) perder. get lost perder-se. get lost! vai passear! (colloq). ~r /-ə(r)/ n perdedor m

loss /lɒs/ n perda f. be at a ~ estar perplexo. at a ~ for words sem saber o que dizer

lost /lɒst/ see lose □ a perdido. ~ property objetos mpl, (P) objectos mpl perdidos (e achados)

lot¹ /lɒt/ n sorte f; (at auction, land) lote m. draw ~s tirar à sorte

lot² /lɒt/ n the ~ tudo; (people) todos mpl. a ~ (of), ~s (of) (colloq) uma porção (de) (colloq). quite a ~ (of) (colloq) uma boa porção (de) (colloq)

lotion /'ləʊʃn/ n loção f

lottery /'lɒtərɪ/ n loteria f, (P) lotaria f

loud /laʊd/ a (-er, -est) alto, barulhento, ruidoso; (of colours) berrante □ adv alto. ~hailer n megafone m. out ~ em voz alta. ~ly adv alto

loudspeaker /laʊd'spiːkə(r)/ n alto-falante m

lounge /laʊndʒ/ vi recostar-se preguiçosamente □ n sala f, salão m

louse /laʊs/ n (pl lice) piolho m

lousy /'laʊzɪ/ a (-ier, -iest) piolhento; (sl: very bad) péssimo

lout /laʊt/ n pessoa f grosseira, arruaceiro m

lovable /'lʌvəbl/ a amoroso, adorável

love /lʌv/ n amor m; (tennis) zero m, nada m □ vt amar, estar apaixonado por; (like greatly) gostar muito de. in ~ apaixonado (with por). ~ affair aventura f amorosa. she sends you her ~ ela lhe manda lembranças

lovely /'lʌvlɪ/ a (-ier, -iest) lindo; (colloq: delightful) encantador, delicioso

lover /'lʌvə(r)/ n namorado m, apaixonado m; (illicit) amante m; (devotee) admirador m, apreciador m

lovesick /'lʌvsɪk/ a perdido de amor

loving /'lʌvɪŋ/ a amoroso, terno, extremoso

low /ləʊ/ a (-er, -est) baixo □ adv baixo □ n baixa f; (low pressure) área de baixa pressão f. ~-cut a decotado. ~-down a baixo, reles □ n (colloq) a verdade autêntica, (P) a verdade nua e crua. ~-fat a de baixo teor de gordura. ~-key a (fig) moderado, discreto

lower /ˈləʊə(r)/ a & adv see low □ vt baixar. ~ o.s. (re)baixar-se (to a)

lowlands /ˈləʊləndz/ npl planície(s) f (pl)

lowly /ˈləʊlɪ/ a (-ier, -iest) humilde, modesto

loyal /ˈlɔɪəl/ a leal. ~ly adv lealmente. ~ty n lealdade f

lozenge /ˈlɒzɪndʒ/ n (shape) losango m; (tablet) pastilha f

LP abbr see long-playing record

lubric|ate /ˈluːbrɪkeɪt/ vt lubrificar. ~ant n lubrificante m. ~ation /-ˈkeɪ/ n lubrificação f

lucid /ˈluːsɪd/ a lúcido. ~ity /luːˈsɪdətɪ/ n lucidez f

luck /lʌk/ n sorte f. bad ~ pouca sorte f. for ~ para dar sorte. good ~!

luck|y /ˈlʌkɪ/ a (-ier, -iest) sortudo, com sorte; (event etc) feliz; (number etc) que dá sorte. ~ily adv felizmente

lucrative /ˈluːkrətɪv/ a lucrativo, rentável

ludicrous /ˈluːdɪkrəs/ a ridículo, absurdo

lug /lʌg/ vt (pt lugged) arrastar

luggage /ˈlʌgɪdʒ/ n bagagem f. ~-rack n porta-bagagem m. ~-van n furgão m

lukewarm /ˈluːkwɔːm/ a morno; (fig) sem entusiasmo, indiferente

lull /lʌl/ vt (send to sleep) embalar; (suspicions) acalmar □ n calmaria f, (P) acalmia f

lullaby /ˈlʌləbaɪ/ n canção f de embalar

lumbago /lʌmˈbeɪgəʊ/ n lumbago m

lumber /ˈlʌmbə(r)/ n trastes mpl velhos; (wood) madeira f cortada □ vt ~ sb with

luminous /ˈluːmɪnəs/ a luminoso

lump /lʌmp/ n bocado m; (swelling) caroço m; (in the throat) nó m; (in liquid) grumo m; (of sugar) torrão m □ vt ~ together amontoar, juntar indiscriminadamente. ~ sum quantia f total; (payment) pagamento m de uma vez. ~y a grumoso, encaroçado

lunacy /ˈluːnəsɪ/ n loucura f

lunar /ˈluːnə(r)/ a lunar

lunatic /ˈluːnətɪk/ n lunático m. ~ asylum manicómio m, (P) manicómio m

lunch /lʌntʃ/ n almoço m □ vi almoçar. ~-time n hora f do almoço

luncheon /ˈlʌntʃən/ n (formal) almoço m. ~ meat carne f enlatada, (P) 'merenda' f. ~ voucher senha f de almoço

lung /lʌŋ/ n pulmão m

lunge /lʌndʒ/ n mergulho m, movimento m súbito para a frente; (thrust) arremetida f □ vi mergulhar, arremessar-se (at para cima de, contra)

lurch¹ /lɜːtʃ/ n leave sb in the ~ deixar alg em apuros

lurch² /lɜːtʃ/ vi ir aos ziguezagues, dar guinadas; (stagger) cambalear

lure /lʊə(r)/ vt atrair, tentar □ n chamariz m, engodo m. the ~ of the sea a atração, (P) atracção do mar

lurid /ˈlʊərɪd/ a berrante; (fig: sensational) sensacional; (fig: shocking) horrífico

lurk /lɜːk/ vi esconder-se à espreita; (prowl) rondar; (be latent) estar latente

luscious /ˈlʌʃəs/ a apetitoso; (voluptuous) desejável

lush /lʌʃ/ a viçoso, luxuriante

Lusitanian /lusɪˈteɪniən/ a & n lusitano (m)

lust /lʌst/ n luxúria f, sensualidade f; (fig) cobiça f, desejo m ardente □ vi ~ after cobiçar, desejar ardentemente. ~ful a sensual

lustre /ˈlʌstə(r)/ n lustre m; (fig) prestígio m

lusty /ˈlʌstɪ/ a (-ier, -iest) robusto, vigoroso

lute /luːt/ n alaúde m

Luxemburg /ˈlʌksəmbɜːg/ n Luxemburgo m

luxuriant /lʌgˈʒʊərɪənt/ a luxuriante

luxurious /lʌgˈʒʊərɪəs/ a luxuoso

luxury /ˈlʌkʃərɪ/ n luxo m □ a de luxo

lying /ˈlaɪɪŋ/ see lie¹, lie²

lynch /lɪntʃ/ vt linchar

lynx /lɪŋks/ n lince m

lyre /ˈlaɪə(r)/ n lira f

lyric /ˈlɪrɪk/ a lírico. ~s npl (mus) letra f. ~al a lírico

M

MA abbr see Master of Arts

mac /mæk/ n (colloq) impermeável m, gabardine f

macabre /məˈkɑːbrə/ a macabro

macaroni /mækəˈrəʊnɪ/ n macarrão m

macaroon /mækəˈruːn/ n bolinho m seco de amêndoa ralada

mace¹ /meɪs/ n (staff) maça f

mace² /meɪs/ n (spice) macis m

machination /mækɪ'neɪʃn/ n maquinação f

machine /mə'ʃi:n/ n máquina f □ vt fazer à máquina; (sewing) coser à máquina. ~-gun n metralhadora f. ~-readable a em linguagem de máquina. ~ tool máquina-ferramenta f

machinery /mə'ʃi:nərɪ/ n maquinaria f; (working parts; fig) mecanismo m

machinist /mə'ʃi:nɪst/ n maquinista m

macho /'mætʃəʊ/ a machista

mackerel /'mækrəl/ n (pl invar) cavala f

mackintosh /'mækɪntɒʃ/ n impermeável m, gabardine f

mad /mæd/ a (madder, maddest) doido, louco; (dog) raivoso; (colloq: angry) furioso (colloq). be ~ about ser doido por. like ~ como (um) doido. ~ly adv loucamente; (frantically) enlouquecidamente. ~ness n loucura f

Madagascar /mædə'gæskə(r)/ n Madagáscar m

madam /'mædəm/ n senhora f. no, ~ não senhora

madden /'mædn/ vt endoidecer, enlouquecer. it's ~ing é de enlouquecer

made /meɪd/ see make. ~ to measure feito sob medida

Madeira /mə'dɪərə/ n Madeira f; (wine) Madeira m

madman /'mædmən/ n (pl -men) doido m

madrigal /'mædrɪgl/ n madrigal m

Mafia /'mæfɪə/ n Máfia f

magazine /mægə'zi:n/ n revista f, magazine m; (of gun) carregador m

magenta /mə'dʒentə/ a & n magenta (m), carmin (m)

maggot /'mægət/ n larva f. ~y a bichento

Magi /'meɪdʒaɪ/ npl the ~ os Reis mpl Magos

magic /'mædʒɪk/ n magia f □ a mágico. ~al a mágico

magician /mə'dʒɪʃn/ n (conjuror) prestidigitador m; (wizard) feiticeiro m

magistrate /'mædʒɪstreɪt/ n magistrado m

magnanim|ous /mæg'nænɪməs/ a magnânimo. ~ity /-ə'nɪmətɪ/ n magnanimidade f

magnate /'mægneɪt/ n magnata m

magnet /'mægnɪt/ n íman m, (P) íman m. ~ic /-'netɪk/ a magnético. ~ism /-ɪzəm/ n magnetismo m. ~ize vt magnetizar

magnificen|t /mæg'nɪfɪsnt/ a magnífico. ~ce n magnificência f

magnify /'mægnɪfaɪ/ vt aumentar; (sound) ampliar, amplificar. ~ication /-ɪ'keɪʃn/ n aumento m, ampliação f. ~ying glass lupa f

magnitude /'mægnɪtjuːd/ n magnitude f

magpie /'mægpaɪ/ n pega f

mahogany /mə'hɒgənɪ/ n mogno m

maid /meɪd/ n criada f, empregada f. old ~ solteirona f

maiden /'meɪdn/ n (old use) donzela f □ a (aunt) solteira; (speech, voyage) inaugural. ~ name nome m de solteira

mail¹ /meɪl/ n correio m; (letters) correio m, correspondência f □ a postal □ vt postar, pôr no correio; (send by mail) mandar pelo correio. ~-bag n mala f postal. ~-box n (Amer) caixa f do correio. ~ing-list n lista f de endereços. ~ order n encomenda f por correspondência, (P) por correio

mail² /meɪl/ n (armour) cota f de malha

mailman /'meɪlmæn/ n (pl -men) (Amer) carteiro m

maim /meɪm/ vt mutilar, aleijar

main¹ /meɪn/ a principal □ n in the ~ em geral, essencialmente. ~ road estrada f principal. ~ly adv principalmente, sobretudo

main² /meɪn/ n (water/gas) ~ cano m de água/gás. the ~s (electr) a rede f eléctrica

mainland /'meɪnlənd/ n continente m

mainstay /'meɪnsteɪ/ n (fig) esteio m

mainstream /'meɪnstriːm/ n tendência f dominante, linha f principal

maintain /meɪn'teɪn/ vt manter, sustentar; (rights) defender, manter

maintenance /'meɪntənəns/ n (care, continuation) manutenção f; (allowance) pensão f

maisonette /meɪzə'net/ n dúplex m

maize /meɪz/ n milho m

majestic /mə'dʒestɪk/ a majestoso. ~ally adv majestosamente

majesty /'mædʒəstɪ/ n majestade f

major /'meɪdʒə(r)/ a maior; (very important) de vulto □ n major m □ vi ~ in (Amer: univ) especializar-se em. ~ road estrada f principal

Majorca /mə'dʒɔːkə/ n Maiorca f

majority /mə'dʒɒrətɪ/ n maioria f; (age) maioridade f □ a majoritário, (P) maioritário. the ~ of people a maioria or a maior parte das pessoas

make /meɪk/ vt/i (pt made) fazer; (decision) tomar; (destination) chegar a; (cause to) fazer (+ inf) or (com) que (+ subj). you ~ me angry você me aborrece □ n (brand) marca f. on the ~ (sl) oportunista. be made of ser feito de. ~ o.s. at home estar à vontade/

como em sua casa. ~ it chegar; (*succeed*) triunfar. I ~ it two o'clock são duas pelo meu relógio. ~ as if to fazer *ou* fingir que. ~ believe fingir. ~-believe *a* fingido □ *n* fantasia *f*. ~ do with arranjar-se com, contentar-se com. ~ for dirigir-se para; (*contribute to*) ajudar a. ~ good *vi* triunfar □ *vt* compensar; (*repair*) reparar. ~ off fugir (with com). ~ out avistar, distinguir; (*understand*) entender; (*claim*) pretender; (*a cheque*) passar, emitir. ~ over ceder, transferir. ~ up *vt* fazer, compor; (*story*) inventar; (*deficit*) suprir □ *vi* fazer as pazes. ~ up (one's face) maquilar-se, (P) maquilhar-se. ~-up *n* maquilagem *f*, (P) maquilhagem *f*; (*of object*) composição *f*; (*psych*) maneira *f* de ser, natureza *f*. ~ up for compensar. ~ up one's mind decidir-se

maker /'meɪkə(r)/ *n* fabricante *mf*

makeshift /'meɪkʃɪft/ *n* solução *f* temporária □ *a* provisório

making /'meɪkɪŋ/ *n* be the ~ of fazer, ser a causa do sucesso de. in the ~ em formação. he has the ~s of ele tem as qualidades essenciais de

maladjusted /mælə'dʒʌstɪd/ *a* desajustado, inadaptado

maladministration /mælədmɪnɪ'streɪʃn/ *n* mau governo *m*, má gestão *f*

malaise /mæ'leɪz/ *n* mal-estar *m*

malaria /mə'leərɪə/ *n* malária *f*

Malay /mə'leɪ/ *a* & *n* malaio (*m*). ~sia /-ʒə/ *n* Malásia *f*

male /meɪl/ *a* (*voice, sex*) masculino; (*biol, techn*) macho □ *n* (*human*) homem *m*, indivíduo *m* do sexo masculino; (*arrival*) macho *m*

malevolen|t /mə'levələnt/ *a* malévolo. ~ce *n* malevolência *f*, má vontade *f*

malformation /mælfɔː'meɪʃn/ *n* malformação *f*, deformidade *f*. ~ed *a* deformado

malfunction /mæl'fʌŋkʃn/ *n* mau funcionamento *m* □ *vi* funcionar mal

malice /'mælɪs/ *n* maldade *f*, malícia *f*. bear sb ~ guardar rancor a alg

malicious /mə'lɪʃəs/ *a* maldoso, malicioso. ~ly *adv* maldosamente, maliciosamente

malign /mə'laɪn/ *vt* caluniar, difamar

malignan|t /mə'lɪgnənt/ *a* (*tumour*) maligno; (*malevolent*) malévolo. ~cy *n* malignidade *f*; malevolência *f*

malinger /mə'lɪŋgə(r)/ *vi* fingir-se doente. ~er *n* pessoa *f* que se finge doente

mallet /'mælɪt/ *n* maço *m*

malnutrition /mælnjuː'trɪʃn/ *n* desnutrição *f*, subalimentação *f*

malpractice /mæl'præktɪs/ *n* abuso *m*; (*incompetence*) incompetência *f* profissional, negligência *f*

malt /mɔːlt/ *n* malte *m*

Malt|a /'mɔːltə/ *n* Malta *f*. ~ese /-'tiːz/ *a* & *n* maltês (*m*)

maltreat /mæl'triːt/ *vt* maltratar. ~ment *n* mau(s) trato(s) *m* (*pl*)

mammal /'mæml/ *n* mamífero *m*

mammoth /'mæməθ/ *n* mamute *m* □ *a* gigantesco, colossal

man /mæn/ *n* (*pl* men) homem *m*; (*in sports team*) jogador *m*; (*chess*) peça *f* □ *vt* (*pt* manned) prover de pessoal; (*mil*) guarnecer; (*naut*) guarnecer, equipar, tripular; (*be on duty at*) estar de serviço em. ~ in the street o homem da rua. ~-hour *n* hora *f* de trabalho por capita, homem-hora *f*. ~-hunt *n* caça *f* ao homem. ~-made *a* artificial. ~ to man de homem para homem

manage /'mænɪdʒ/ *vt* (*household*) governar; (*tool*) manejar; (*boat, affair, crowd*) manobrar; (*shop*) dirigir, gerir. I could ~ another drink (*colloq*) até que tomaria mais um drinque (*colloq*) □ *vi* arranjar-se. ~ to do conseguir fazer. ~able *a* manejável; (*easily controlled*) controlável. ~ment *n* gerência *f*, direção *f*, (P) direcção *f*. managing director director *m*, (P) director *m* geral

manager /'mænɪdʒə(r)/ *n* diretor *m*, (P) director *m*; (*of bank, shop*) gerente *m*; (*of actor*) empresário *m*; (*sport*) treinador *m*. ~ess /-'res/ *n* diretora *f*, (P) directora *f*; gerente *f*. ~ial /-'dʒɪərɪəl/ *a* diretivo, (P) directivo, administrativo. ~ial staff gestores *mpl*

mandarin /'mændərɪn/ *n* mandarim *m*. ~ (orange) mandarina *f*, tangerina *f*

mandate /'mændeɪt/ *n* mandato *m*

mandatory /'mændətrɪ/ *a* obrigatório

mane /meɪn/ *n* crina *f*; (*of lion*) juba *f*

mangle[1] /'mæŋgl/ *n* calandra *f* □ *vt* espremer (com a calandra)

mangle[2] /'mæŋgl/ *vt* (*mutilate*) mutilar, estropiar

mango /'mæŋgəʊ/ *n* (*pl* -oes) manga *f*

manhandle /'mænhændl/ *vt* mover à força de braço; (*treat roughly*) tratar com brutalidade

manhole /'mænhəʊl/ *n* poço *m* de inspeção, (P) inspecção *f*

manhood /'mænhʊd/ *n* idade adulta *f*; (*quality*) virilidade *f*

mania /'meɪnɪə/ *n* mania *f*. ~c /-ɪæk/ *n* maníaco *m*

manicur|e /'mænɪkjʊə(r)/ *n* manicure *f* □ *vt* fazer. ~ist *n* manicure *m* manifest /'mænɪfest/ a manifes to □ vt manifestar. ~ation /-'steɪʃn/ n manifestação f

manifesto /mænɪ'festəʊ/ n (pl -os) manifesto m

manipulat|e /mə'nɪpjʊleɪt/ vt manipular. ~ion /'leɪʃn/ n manipulação f

mankind /mæn'kaɪnd/ n humanidade f, género m, (P) género m humano

manly /'mænlɪ/ a viril, másculo

manner /'mænə(r)/ n maneira f, modo m; (attitude) modo(s) m (pl); (kind) espécie f. ~s maneiras fpl. bad ~s má-criação f, falta f de educação. good ~s (boa) educação f. ~ed a afetado

mannerism /'mænərɪzəm/ n maneirismo m

manoeuvre /mə'nu:və(r)/ n manobra f □ vt/i manobrar

manor /'mænə(r)/ n solar m

manpower /'mænpaʊə(r)/ n mão-de-obra f

mansion /'mænʃn/ n mansão f

manslaughter /'mænslɔ:tə(r)/ n homicídio m involuntário

mantelpiece /'mæntlpi:s/ n (shelf) consolo m da lareira, (P) prateleira f da chaminé

manual /'mænjʊəl/ a manual □ n manual m

manufacture /mænjʊ'fæktʃə(r)/ vt fabricar □ n fabrico m, fabricação f. ~r /-ə(r)/ n fabricante m

manure /mə'njʊə(r)/ n estrume m

manuscript /'mænjʊskrɪpt/ n manuscrito m

many /'menɪ/ a (more, most) muitos □ n muitos; (many people) muita gente f. a great ~ muitíssimos. a ~ man/tear/etc muitos homens/muitas lágrimas/etc. you may take as ~ as you want você pode levar quantos quiser. ~ of us/them/you muitos de nós/deles/de vocês. how ~? quantos? one too ~ um a mais

map /mæp/ n mapa m □ vt (pt mapped) fazer mapa de. ~ out planear em pormenor; (route) traçar

maple /'meɪpl/ n bordo m

mar /ma:(r)/ vt (pt marred) estragar; (beauty) desfigurar

marathon /'mærəθən/ n maratona f

marble /'ma:bl/ n mármore m; (for game) bola f de gude, (P) berlinde f

March /ma:tʃ/ n março m

march /ma:tʃ/ vi marchar □ vt ~ off fazer marchar, conduzir à força. he was ~ed off to prison fizeram-no marchar para a prisão □ n marcha f. ~-past n desfile m em revista militar

mare /meə(r)/ n égua f

margarine /ma:dʒə'ri:n/ n margarina f

margin /'ma:dʒɪn/ n margem f. ~al a marginal. ~al seat (pol) lugar m ganho com pequena maioria. ~ally adv por uma pequena margem, muito pouco

marigold /'mærɪgəʊld/ n cravo-de-defunto m, (P) malmequer m

marijuana /mærɪ'wa:nə/ n maconha f

marina /mə'ri:nə/ n marina f

marinade /mærɪ'neɪd/ n vinha d'alho, escalabeche m □ vt pôr na vinha d'alho

marine /mə'ri:n/ a marinho; (of ship, trade etc) marítimo □ n (shipping) marinha f; (sailor) fuzileiro m naval

marionette /mærɪə'net/ n fantoche m, marionete f

marital /'mærɪtl/ a marital, conjugal, matrimonial. ~ status estado m civil

maritime /'mærɪtaɪm/ a marítimo

mark¹ /ma:k/ n (currency) marco m

mark² /ma:k/ n marca f; (trace) marca f, sinal m; (stain) mancha f; (schol) nota f, (target) alvo m □ vt marcar; (exam etc) marcar, classificar. ~ out marcar. ~ out for escolher para, designar para. ~ time marcar passo. make one's ~ ganhar nome. ~er n marcador m. ~ing n marcas fpl, marcação f

marked /ma:kt/ a marcado. ~ly /-ɪdlɪ/ adv manifesto, visivelmente

market /'ma:kɪt/ n mercado m □ vt vender; (launch) comercializar, lançar. ~ garden horta f de legumes para venda. ~-place n mercado m. ~ research pesquisa f de mercado. on the ~ à venda. ~ing n marketing m

marksman /'ma:ksmən/ n (pl -men) atirador m especial

marmalade /'ma:məleɪd/ n compota f de laranja

maroon /mə'ru:n/ a & n bordô (m), (P) bordeaux (m)

marooned /mə'ru:nd/ a abandonado em ilha, costa deserta etc; (fig: stranded) encalhado (fig)

marquee /ma:'ki:/ n barraca f ou tenda f grande; (Amer: awning) toldo m

marriage /'mærɪdʒ/ n casamento m, matrimónio m, (P) matrimónio m. ~ certificate certidão f de casamento. ~able a casadouro

marrow /'mærəʊ/ n (of bone) tutano m, medula f; (vegetable) abóbora f. chilled to the ~ gelado até os ossos

marr|y /'mærɪ/ vt casar(-se) com; (give or unite in marriage) casar □ vi casar-se. ~ied a casado; (life) de casado, conjugal. get ~ied casar-se

Mars /ma:z/ n Marte m

marsh /maːʃ/ n pântano m. ~y a pantanoso

marshal /'maːʃl/ n (mil) marechal m; (steward) mestre m de cerimónias, (P) cerimónias ▫ vt (pt marshalled) dispor em ordem, ordenar; (usher) conduzir, escoltar

marshmallow /maːʃ'mæləʊ/ n marshmallow m

martial /'maːʃl/ a marcial. ~ law lei f marcial

martyr /'maːtə(r)/ n mártir mf ▫ vt martirizar. ~dom n martírio m

marvel /'maːvl/ n maravilha f, prodígio m ▫ vi (pt marvelled) (feel wonder) maravilhar-se (at com); (be astonished) pasmar (at com)

marvellous /'maːvələs/ a maravilhoso

Marxis|t /'maːksɪst/ a & n marxista (mf). ~m n /-zəm/ n marxismo m

marzipan /'maːzɪpæn/ n maçapão m

mascara /mæ'skaːrə/ n rímel m

mascot /'mæskət/ n mascote f

masculin|e /'mæskjʊlɪn/ a masculino ▫ n masculino m. ~ity n /'lɪnəti/ n masculinidade f

mash /mæʃ/ n (pulp) papa f ▫ vt esmagar. ~ed potatoes puré m de batata(s)

mask /maːsk/ n máscara f ▫ vt mascarar

masochis|t /'mæsəkɪst/ n masoquista mf. ~m n /-zəm/ n masoquismo m

mason /'meɪsn/ n maçom m; (building) pedreiro m. ~ry n maçonaria f, (building) alvenaria f

Mason /'meɪsn/ n Maçónico m, (P) Maçónico m. ~ic /mə'sɒnɪk/ a Maçónico, (P) Maçónico

masquerade /mæːskə'reɪd/ n mascarada f ▫ vi ~ as mascarar-se de, disfarçar-se de

mass¹ /mæs/ n (relig) missa f

mass² /mæs/ n massa f; (heap) montão m ▫ vt/i aglomerar(-se), reunir(-se) em massa. ~-produce vt produzir em série. the ~es as massas, a grande massa

massacre /'mæsəkə(r)/ n massacre m ▫ vt massacrar

massage /'mæsaːʒ/ n massagem f ▫ vt massagear, fazer massagens em, (P) dar massagens a

masseu|r /mæ'sɜː(r)/ n massagista m. ~se /mæ'sɜːz/ n massagista f

massive /'mæsɪv/ a (heavy) maciço; (huge) enorme

mast /maːst/ n mastro m; (for radio etc) antena f

master /'maːstə(r)/ n (in school) professor m, mestre m; (expert) mestre m; (boss) patrão m; (owner) dono m. M~ (boy) menino m ▫ vt dominar. ~-key

n chave-mestra f. ~-mind n (of scheme etc) cérebro m ▫ vt planejar, dirigir. M~ of Arts/etc Licenciado m em Letras/etc. ~-stroke n golpe m de mestre. ~y n domínio m (over sobre); (knowledge) conhecimento m; (skill) perícia f

masterly /'maːstəli/ a magistral

masterpiece /'maːstəpiːs/ n obra-prima f

masturbat|e /'mæstəbeɪt/ vi masturbar-se. ~ion /'beɪʃn/ n masturbação f

mat /mæt/ n tapete m pequeno; (at door) capacho m. (table-)~ n (of cloth) paninho m de mesa; (for hot dishes) descanso m para pratos

match¹ /mætʃ/ n fósforo m

match² /mætʃ/ n (contest) competição f, torneio m; (game) partida f; (equal) par m, parceiro m, igual mf; (fig: marriage) casamento m; (marriage partner) partido m ▫ vt/i (set against) contrapor (against a); (equal) igualar; (go with) condizer; (be alike) ir com, emparceirar com. her shoes ~ed her bag os sapatos dela combinavam com a bolsa. ~ing a condizente, a condizer

matchbox /'mætʃbɒks/ n caixa f de fósforos

mat|e¹ /meɪt/ n companheiro m, camarada mf; (of birds, animals) macho m, fêmea f; (assistant) ajudante mf ▫ vt/i acasalar(-se) (with com). ~ing season n época f de cio

mate² /meɪt/ n (chess) mate m, xeque-mate m

material /mə'tɪərɪəl/ n material m; (fabric) tecido m; (equipment) apetrechos mpl ▫ a material; (significant) importante

materialis|m /mə'tɪərɪəlɪzəm/ n materialismo m. ~tic /'lɪstɪk/ a materialista

materialize /mə'tɪərɪəlaɪz/ vi realizar-se, concretizar-se; (appear) aparecer

maternal /mə'tɜːnəl/ a maternal

maternity /mə'tɜːnəti/ n maternidade f ▫ a (clothes) de grávida. ~ hospital maternidade f. ~ leave licença f de maternidade

mathematic|s /mæθə'mætɪks/ n matemática f. ~al a matemático. ~ian /-ə'tɪʃn/ n matemático m

maths /mæθs/ n (colloq) matemática f

matinée /'mætɪneɪ/ n matinê f, (P) matinée f

matrimon|y /'mætrɪməni/ n matrimónio m, (P) matrimónio m. ~ial /'məʊnɪəl/ a matrimonial, conjugal

matrix /'meɪtrɪks/ n (pl matrices /-siːz/) matriz f

matron /'meɪtrən/ n matrona f; (in school) inspetora f; (former use: senior nursing officer) enfermeira-chefe f. ~ly a respeitável, muito digno

matt /mæt/ a fosco, sem brilho

matted /'mætɪd/ a emaranhado

matter /'mætə(r)/ n (substance) matéria f; (affair) assunto m, caso m, questão f; (pus) pus m □ vi importar. as a ~ of fact na verdade. it does not ~ não importa. ~-of-fact a prosaico, terra-a-terra. no ~ what happens não importa o que acontecer. what is the ~? o que é que há? what is the ~ with you? o que é que você tem?

mattress /'mætrɪs/ n colchão m

matur|e /mə'tjʊə(r)/ a maduro, amadurecido □ vt/i amadurecer; (comm) vencer-se. ~ity n madureza f, maturidade f; (comm) vencimento m

maul /mɔːl/ vt maltratar, atacar

Mauritius /mə'rɪʃəs/ n Ilha f Maurícia

mausoleum /mɔːsə'lɪəm/ n mausoléu m

mauve /məʊv/ a & n lilás (m)

maxim /'mæksɪm/ n máxima f

maxim|um /'mæksɪməm/ a & n (pl -ima) máximo (m). ~ize vt aumentar ao máximo, maximizar

may /meɪ/ v aux (pt might) poder. he ~/might come talvez venha/viesse. you might have podia ter. you ~ leave pode ir. ~ I smoke? posso fumar?, dá licença que eu fume? ~ he be happy que ele seja feliz. I ~ or might as well go talvez seja or fosse melhor eu ir

May /meɪ/ n maio n. ~ Day o primeiro de maio

maybe /'meɪbɪ/ adv talvez

mayhem /'meɪhem/ n (disorder) distúrbios mpl violentos; (havoc) estragos mpl

mayonnaise /meɪə'neɪz/ n maionese f

mayor /meə(r)/ n prefeito m. ~ess n prefeita f; (mayor's wife) mulher f do prefeito

maze /meɪz/ n labirinto m

me /miː/ pron me; (after prep) mim. with ~ comigo. he knows ~ ele me conhece. it's ~ sou eu

meadow /'medəʊ/ n prado m, campina f

meagre /'miːgə(r)/ a (thin) magro; (scanty) escasso

meal¹ /miːl/ n refeição f

meal² /miːl/ n (grain) farinha f grossa

mean¹ /miːn/ a (-er, -est) mesquinho; (unkind) mau. ~ness n mesquinhez f

mean² /miːn/ a médio □ n média f. Greenwich ~ time tempo m médio de Greenwich

mean³ /miːn/ vt (pt meant) (intend) tencionar or ter (a) intenção (to de); (signify) querer dizer, significar; (entail) dar em resultado, resultar provavelmente em; (refer to) referir-se a. be meant for destinar-se a. I didn't ~ it desculpe, foi sem querer. he ~s what he says ele está falando sério

meander /mɪ'ændə(r)/ vi serpentear; (wander) perambular

meaning /'miːnɪŋ/ n sentido m, significado m. ~ful a significativo. ~less a sem sentido

means /miːnz/ n meio(s) m(pl) □ npl meios mpl pecuniários, recursos mpl. by all ~ com certeza. by ~ of por meio de, através de. by no ~ de modo nenhum

meant /ment/ see mean³

mean|time /'miːntaɪm/ adv (in the) ~time entretanto, while /-waɪl/ adv entretanto

measles /'miːzlz/ n sarampo m. German ~ rubéola f

measly /'miːzlɪ/ a (sl) miserável, ínfimo

measurable /'meʒərəbl/ a mensurável

measure /'meʒə(r)/ n medida f □ vt/i medir. made to ~ feito sob medida. ~ up to mostrar-se à altura de. ~d a medido, calculado. ~ment n medida f

meat /miːt/ n carne f. ~y a carnudo; (fig: substantial) substancial

mechanic /mɪ'kænɪk/ n mecânico m

mechanic|al /mɪ'kænɪkl/ a mecânico. ~s n mecânica f; npl mecanismo m

mechan|ism /'mekənɪzəm/ n mecanismo m. ~ize vt mecanizar

medal /'medl/ n medalha f. ~list n condecorado m. be a gold ~list ser medalha de ouro

medallion /mɪ'dælɪən/ n medalhão m

meddle /'medl/ vi (interfere) imiscuir-se, intrometer-se (in em); (tinker) mexer (with em). ~some a intrometido, abelhudo

media /'miːdɪə/ see medium □ npl the ~ a média, os meios de comunicação social or de massa

mediat|e /'miːdɪeɪt/ vi servir de intermediário, mediar. ~ion /-'eɪʃn/ n mediação f. ~or n mediador m, intermediário m

medical /'medɪkl/ a médico □ n (colloq: examination) exame m médico

medicat|ed /'medɪkeɪtɪd/ a medicinal. ~ion /-'keɪʃn/ n medicamentação f

medicinal /mɪ'dɪsɪnl/ a medicinal

medicine /'medsn/ n medicina f; (substance) remédio m, medicamento m

medieval /medɪ'iːvl/ a medieval

mediocr|e /miːdɪ'əʊkə(r)/ a medíocre. ~ity /-'ɒkrətɪ/ n mediocridade f

meditat|e /'mediteit/ vt/i meditar.
~ion /-'teiʃn/ n meditação f

Mediterranean /medita'reinian/ a
mediterráneo □ the ~ o Mediterrâneo

medium /'mi:diəm/ n (pl media)
meio m; (pl mediums) (person)
médium mf □ a médio. ~ wave
(radio) onda f média. the happy ~
o meio-termo

medley /'medli/ n (pl -eys) miscelânea f

meek /mi:k/ a (-er, -est) manso, submisso, sofrido

meet /mi:t/ vt (pt met) encontrar; (in-
tentionally) encontrar-se com, ir ter
com; (at station etc) ir esperar, ir buscar; (make the acquaintance of) conhecer; (conform with) ir ao encontro
de, satisfazer; (opponent, obligation
etc) fazer face a; (bill, expenses) pagar
□ vi encontrar-se; (get acquainted) fa-
miliarizar-se; (in session) reunir-se. ~
with encontrar; (accident, misfortune) sofrer, ter

meeting /'mi:tɪŋ/ n reunião f, encontro m; (between two people) encontro
m. ~-place n ponto m de encontro

megalomania /megələʊ'meinɪə/ n
megalomania f, mania f de grandezas

megaphone /'megəfəʊn/ n megafone
m, porta-voz m

melancholy /'melənkɒlɪ/ n melanco-
lia f □ a melancólico

mellow /'meləʊ/ a (-er, -est) (fruit,
person) amadurecido, maduro;
(sound, colour) quente, suave □ vt/i
amadurecer; (soften) suavizar

melodious /mɪ'ləʊdɪəs/ a melodioso

melodrama /'melədra:mə/ n melodrama m. ~tic /-ə'mætɪk/ a melodra-
mático

melod|y /'melədɪ/ n melodia f. ~ic
/mɪ'lɒdɪk/ a melódico

melon /'melən/ n melão m

melt /melt/ vt/i (metals) fundir(-se);
(butter, snow etc) derreter (-se); (fade
away) desvanecer (-se). ~ing-pot n
cadinho m

member /'membə(r)/ n membro m;
(of club etc) sócio m. M~ of Parliament deputado m. ~ship n qualidade f de sócio; (members) número m
de sócios; (fee) cota f. ~ship
card carteira f, (P) cartão m de sócio

membrane /'membreɪn/ n membrana
f

memento /mɪ'mentəʊ/ n (pl -oes)
lembrança f, recordação f

memo /'meməʊ/ n (pl -os) (colloq)
nota f, apontamento m, lembrete m

memoir /'memwa:(r)/ n (record, essay) memória f, memorial m; ~s npl
(autobiography) memórias fpl

memorable /'memərəbl/ a memorável

memorandum /memə'rændəm/ n
(pl -da or -dums) nota f, lembrete m;
(diplomatic) memorando m

memorial /mɪ'mɔ:rɪəl/ n monumento
m comemorativo □ a comemorativo

memorize /'meməraɪz/ vt decorar,
memorizar, aprender de cor

memory /'memərɪ/ n memória f.
from ~ de memória, de cor. in ~ of
em memória de

men /men/ see man

menace /'menəs/ n ameaça f; (nuisance) praga f, chaga f □ vt ameaçar.
~ingly adv ameaçadoramente, de
modo ameaçador

menagerie /mɪ'nædʒərɪ/ n coleção f,
(P) colecção f de animais ferozes em
jaulas

mend /mend/ vt consertar, reparar;
(darn) remendar □ n conserto m;
(darn) remendo m. ~ one's ways
corrigir-se, emendar-se. on the ~ melhorando

menial /'mi:nɪəl/ a humilde

meningitis /menɪn'dʒaɪtɪs/ n meningite f

menopause /'menəpɔ:z/ n menopausa f

menstruation /menstrʊ'eɪʃn/ n
menstruação f

mental /'mentl/ a mental; (hospital)
de doentes mentais, psiquiátrico

mentality /men'tælətɪ/ n mentali-
dade f

mention /'menʃn/ vt mencionar □ n
menção f. don't ~ it! não tem de quê,
de nada

menu /'menju:/ n (pl -us) menu m, (P)
ementa f

mercenary /'mɜ:sɪnərɪ/ a & n mercenário (m)

merchandise /'mɜ:tʃəndaɪz/ n mercadorias fpl □ vt/i negociar

merchant /'mɜ:tʃənt/ n mercador m
□ a (ship, navy) mercante. ~ bank
banco m comercial

merciful /'mɜ:sɪfl/ a misericordioso

merciless /'mɜ:sɪlɪs/ a impiedoso,
sem dó

mercury /'mɜ:kjʊrɪ/ n mercúrio m

mercy /'mɜ:sɪ/ n piedade f, miseri-
córdia f. at the ~ of à mercê de

mere /mɪə(r)/ a mero, simples. ~ly
adv meramente, simplesmente, apenas

merge /mɜ:dʒ/ vt/i fundir(-se), amal-
gamar(-se); (comm: companies) fun-
dir(-se). ~r /-ə(r)/ n fusão f

meringue /mə'ræŋ/ n merengue m,
suspiro m

merit /'merɪt/ n mérito m □ vt (pt
merited) merecer

mermaid /'mɜːmeɪd/ n sereia f
merriment /'merɪmənt/ n divertimento m, alegria f, folguedo m
merry /'merɪ/ a (-ier, -iest) alegre,
divertido. ~ Christmas Feliz Natal.
~-go-round n carrossel m. ~-
making n festa f, divertimento m.
merrily adv alegremente
mesh /meʃ/ n malha f. ~es npl (network; fig) malhas fpl
mesmerize /'mezməraɪz/ vt hipnoti-
zar
mess /mes/ n (disorder) desordem f,
trapalhada f; (trouble) embrulhada f,
trapalhada f; (dirt) porcaria f; (mil:
place) cantina f; (mil: food) rancho m
□ vt ~ up (make untidy) desarrumar;
(make dirty) sujar; (confuse) atrapalhar, estragar □ vi ~ about with
tempo; (behave foolishly) fazer
asneiras. ~ about with (tinker with)
entreter-se com, andar às voltas com.
make a ~ of estragar
message /'mesɪdʒ/ n mensagem f; (informal) recado m
messenger /'mesɪndʒə(r)/ n mensa-
geiro m
Messiah /mɪ'saɪə/ n Messias m
messy /'mesɪ/ a (-ier, -iest) desarrumado, bagunçado; (dirty) sujo, porco
met /met/ see meet
metabolism /mɪ'tæbəlɪzm/ n metabo-
lismo m
metal /'metl/ n metal m □ a de metal.
~lic /mɪ'tælɪk/ a metálico; (paint,
colour) metalizado
metamorphosis /metə'mɔːfəsɪs/ n
(pl -phoses /-siːz/) metamorfose f
metaphor /'metəfə(r)/ n metáfora f.
~ical /'fɒrɪkl/ a metafórico
meteor /'miːtɪə(r)/ n meteoro m
meteorolog|y /miːtɪə'rɒlədʒɪ/ n me-
teorologia f. ~ical /-ə'lɒdʒɪkl/ a meteorológico
meter[1] /'miːtə(r)/ n contador m
meter[2] /'miːtə(r)/ n (Amer) = metre
method /'meθəd/ n método m
methodical /mɪ'θɒdɪkl/ a metódico
Methodist /'meθədɪst/ n metodista mf
methylated /'meθɪleɪtɪd/ a ~ spirit
álcool m metílico
meticulous /mɪ'tɪkjʊləs/ a meticuloso
metre /'miːtə(r)/ n metro m
metric /'metrɪk/ a métrico. ~ation
/-'keɪʃn/ n conversão f para o sistema
métrico
metropol|is /mə'trɒpəlɪs/ n metró-
pole f. ~itan /metrə'pɒlɪtən/ a metropolitano
mettle /'metl/ n têmpera f, caráter m,
(P) carácter m; (spirit) brio m
mew /mjuː/ n miado m □ vi miar
Mexic|o /'meksɪkəʊ/ n México m.
~an a & n mexicano (m)

miaow /miː'aʊ/ n & vi = mew
mice /maɪs/ see mouse
mickey /'mɪkɪ/ n take the ~ out of
(sl) fazer troça de, gozar (colloq)
micro- /'maɪkrəʊ/ pref micro-
microbe /'maɪkrəʊb/ n micróbio m
microchip /'maɪkrəʊtʃɪp/ n microchip m
microcomputer /'maɪkrəʊkəmpju:-
tə(r)/ n microcomputador m
microfilm /'maɪkrəʊfɪlm/ n micro-
filme m
microlight /'maɪkrəʊlaɪt/ n (aviat)
ultraleve m
microphone /'maɪkrəfəʊn/ n microfone m
microprocessor /maɪkrəʊ'prəʊse-
sə(r)/ n microprocessador m
microscop|e /'maɪkrəskəʊp/ n
microscópio m. ~ic /'skɒpɪk/ a mi-
croscópico
microwave /'maɪkrəʊweɪv/ n micro-
onda f. ~ oven forno m de microon-
das
mid /mɪd/ a em ~-air no ar, em
pleno vôo. in ~-March em meados de
março
midday /'mɪddeɪ/ n meio-dia m
middle /'mɪdl/ a médio, meio; (quality) médio, mediano □ n meio m. in
the ~ of no meio de. ~-aged a de
meia idade. M~ Ages Idade f Média.
~ class classe f média. ~-class a
burguês. M~ East Médio Oriente m.
~ name segundo nome m
middleman /'mɪdlmæn/ n (pl -men)
intermediário m
midge /mɪdʒ/ n mosquito m
midget /'mɪdʒɪt/ n anão m □ a minúsculo
Midlands /'mɪdləndz/ npl região f do
centro da Inglaterra
midnight /'mɪdnaɪt/ n meia-noite f
midriff /'mɪdrɪf/ n diafragma m; (abdomen) ventre m
midst /mɪdst/ n in the ~ of no meio
de
midsummer /mɪd'sʌmə(r)/ n pleno
verão m; (solstice) solstício m do verão
midway /mɪd'weɪ/ adv a meio caminho
midwife /'mɪdwaɪf/ n (pl -wives) parteira f
might[1] /maɪt/ n potência f; (strength)
força f. ~y a poderoso; (fig: great)
imenso □ adv (colloq) muito
might[2] /maɪt/ see may
migraine /'miːɡreɪn/ n enxaqueca f
migrant /'maɪɡrənt/ a migratório □ n
(person) migrante mf, emigrante mf
migrat|e /maɪ'ɡreɪt/ vi migrar. ~ion
/-ʃn/ n migração f
mike /maɪk/ n (colloq) microfone m

mild /maɪld/ a (-er, -est) brando, manso; (*illness, taste*) leve; (*climate*) temperado; (*weather*) ameno. ~ly adv brandamente, mansamente. to put it ~ly para não dizer coisa pior. ~ness n brandura f

mildew /ˈmɪldjuː/ n bolor m, mofo m; (*in plants*) míldio m

mile /maɪl/ n milha f (= 1.6 km). ~s too big/etc (*colloq*) grande demais. ~age n (*loosely*) quilometragem f

milestone /ˈmaɪlstəʊn/ n marco m miliário; (*fig*) data f or acontecimento m importante

militant /ˈmɪlɪtənt/ a & n militante (mf)

military /ˈmɪlɪtrɪ/ a militar

militate /ˈmɪlɪteɪt/ vi militar. ~ against militar contra

milk /mɪlk/ n leite m □ a (*product*) lácteo □ vt ordenhar; (*fig: exploit*) explorar. ~-shake n milk-shake m, leite m batido. ~y a (*like milk*) leitoso; (*tea etc*) com muito leite. M~ Way Via f Láctea

milkman /ˈmɪlkmən/ n (pl -men) leiteiro m

mill /mɪl/ n moinho m; (*factory*) fábrica f □ vt moer □ vi ~ around aglomerar-se; (*crowd*) apinhar-se, (P) agitar-se. ~er n moleiro m. pepper-~ n moedor m de pimenta

millennium /mɪˈlenɪəm/ n (pl -iums or -ia) milénio m, (P) milénio m

millet /ˈmɪlɪt/ n painço m, milhete m

milli- /ˈmɪlɪ/ pref mili-

milligram /ˈmɪlɪɡræm/ n miligrama m

millilitre /ˈmɪlɪliːtə(r)/ n mililitro m

millimetre /ˈmɪlɪmiːtə(r)/ n milímetro m

million /ˈmɪljən/ n milhão m. a ~ pounds um milhão de libras. ~aire /-ˈneə(r)/ n milionário m

millstone /ˈmɪlstəʊn/ n mó f. a ~ round one's neck um peso nos ombros

mime /maɪm/ n mímica f; (*actor*) mímico m □ vt/i exprimir por mímica, mimar

mimic /ˈmɪmɪk/ vt (pt mimicked) imitar □ n imitador m, parodiante mf. ~ry n imitação f

mince /mɪns/ vt picar □ n carne f moída, (P) carne f picada. ~-pie n pastel m recheado com massa de passas, amêndoas, especiarias etc. ~r n máquina f de moer

mincemeat /ˈmɪnsmiːt/ n massa f de passas, amêndoas, especiarias etc usada para recheio. make ~ of (*colloq*) arrasar, aniquilar

mind n espírito m, mente f; (*intellect*) intelecto m; (*sanity*) razão f □ vt (*look after*) tomar conta de, tratar de; (*heed*) prestar atenção a; (*object to*) importar-se com, incomodar-se com. do you ~ if I smoke? você se incomoda que eu fume? do you ~ helping me? quer fazer o favor de me ajudar? never ~ não se importe, não tem importância. to be out of one's ~ estar fora de si. have a good ~ to estar disposto a. make up one's ~ decidir-se. presence of ~ presença f de espírito. to my ~ a meu ver. ~ful of atento a, consciente de. ~less a insensato

minder /ˈmaɪndə(r)/ n pessoa f que toma conta mf; (*bodyguard*) guarda-costa mf, (P) guarda-costas mf

mine¹ /maɪn/ poss pron o(s) meu(s), a(s) minha(s). it is ~ é o(o) meu or (a) minha

mine² /maɪn/ n mina f □ vt escavar, explorar; (*extract*) extrair; (*mil*) minar. ~er n mineiro m. ~ing n exploração f mineira □ a mineiro

minefield /ˈmaɪnfiːld/ n campo m minado

mineral /ˈmɪnərəl/ n mineral m; (*soft drink*) bebida f gasosa. ~ water água f mineral

minesweeper /ˈmaɪnswiːpə(r)/ n caça-minas m

mingle /ˈmɪŋɡl/ vt/i misturar(-se) (with com)

mingy /ˈmɪndʒɪ/ a (-ier, -iest) (*colloq*) sovina, unha(s)-de-fome (*colloq*)

mini- /ˈmɪnɪ/ pref mini-

miniature /ˈmɪnɪtʃə(r)/ n miniatura f □ a miniatural

minibus /ˈmɪnɪbʌs/ n (*public*) microónibus m, (P) autocarro m pequeno

minim /ˈmɪnɪm/ n (*mus*) mínima f

minim|um /ˈmɪnɪməm/ a & n (pl -ma) mínimo (m). ~al a mínimo. ~ize vt minimizar, dar pouca importância a

miniskirt /ˈmɪnɪskɜːt/ n minissaia f

minist|er /ˈmɪnɪstə(r)/ n ministro m; (*relig*) pastor m. ~erial /-ˈstɪərɪəl/ a ministerial. ~ry n ministério m

mink /mɪŋk/ n (*fur*) marta f, visão m

minor /ˈmaɪnə(r)/ a & n menor (mf)

minority /maɪˈnɒrətɪ/ n minoria f □ a minoritário

mint¹ /mɪnt/ n the M~ a Casa da Moeda. a ~ uma fortuna □ vt cunhar. in ~ condition em perfeito estado, como novo, impecável

mint² /mɪnt/ n (*plant*) hortelã f; (*sweet*) pastilha f de hortelã

minus /ˈmaɪnəs/ prep menos; (*colloq: without*) sem □ n menos m

minute¹ /ˈmɪnɪt/ n minuto m. ~s (*of meeting*) ata f, (P) acta f

minute² /maɪˈnjuːt/ a diminuto, minúsculo; (*detailed*) minucioso

miracle /ˈmɪrəkl/ n milagre m. ~**ulous** /mɪˈrækjʊləs/ a milagroso, miraculoso

mirage /ˈmɪrɑːʒ/ n miragem f

mire /ˈmaɪə(r)/ n lodo m, lama f

mirror /ˈmɪrə(r)/ n espelho m; (*in car*) retrovisor m □ vt refletir, (P) reflectir, espelhar

mirth /mɜːθ/ n alegria f, hilaridade f

misadventure /mɪsədˈventʃə(r)/ n desgraça f. **death by** ~ morte f acidental

misanthropist /mɪˈsænθrəpɪst/ n misantropo m

misapprehension /mɪsæprɪˈhenʃn/ n mal-entendido m

misbehav|e /mɪsbɪˈheɪv/ vi portar-se mal, proceder mal. ~**iour** /-ˈheɪvɪə(r)/ n mau comportamento m, má conduta f

miscalculat|e /mɪsˈkælkjʊleɪt/ vi calcular mal, enganar-se. ~**ion** /-ˈleɪʃn/ n erro m de cálculo

miscarr|y /mɪsˈkærɪ/ vi abortar, ter um aborto; (*fail*) falhar, malograr-se. ~**iage** /-ɪdʒ/ n aborto m. ~**iage of justice** erro m judiciário

miscellaneous /mɪsəˈleɪnɪəs/ a variado, diverso

mischief /ˈmɪstʃɪf/ n (*of children*) diabrura f, travessura f; (*harm*) mal m, dano m. **get into** ~ fazer disparates. **make** ~ criar or semear discórdias

mischievous /ˈmɪstʃɪvəs/ a endiabrado, travesso

misconception /mɪskənˈsepʃn/ n idéia f errada, falso conceito m

misconduct /mɪsˈkɒndʌkt/ n conduta f imprópria

misconstrue /mɪskənˈstruː/ vt interpretar mal

misdeed /mɪsˈdiːd/ n má ação f, (P) acção f; (*crime*) crime m

misdemeanour /mɪsdɪˈmiːnə(r)/ n delito m

miser /ˈmaɪzə(r)/ n avarento m, sovina mf. ~**ly** a avarento, sovina

miserable /ˈmɪzrəbl/ a infeliz; (*wretched, mean*) desgraçado, miserável

misery /ˈmɪzərɪ/ n infelicidade f

misfire /mɪsˈfaɪə(r)/ vi (*plan, gun, engine*) falhar

misfit /ˈmɪsfɪt/ n inadaptado m

misfortune /mɪsˈfɔːtʃən/ n desgraça f, infelicidade f, pouca sorte f

misgiving(s) /mɪsˈɡɪvɪŋ(z)/ n(pl) dúvida(s) f(pl), receio(s) m(pl)

misguided /mɪsˈɡaɪdɪd/ a (*mistaken*) desencaminhado; (*misled*) mal aconselhado, enganado

mishap /ˈmɪshæp/ n contratempo m, desastre m

misinform /mɪsɪnˈfɔːm/ vt informar mal

misinterpret /mɪsɪnˈtɜːprɪt/ vt interpretar mal

misjudge /mɪsˈdʒʌdʒ/ vt julgar mal

mislay /mɪsˈleɪ/ vt (pt **mislaid**) perder, extraviar

mislead /mɪsˈliːd/ vt (pt **misled**) induzir em erro, enganar. ~**ing** a enganador

mismanage /mɪsˈmænɪdʒ/ vt dirigir mal. ~**ment** n má gestão f, desgoverno m

misnomer /mɪsˈnəʊmə(r)/ n termo m impróprio

misogynist /mɪˈsɒdʒɪnɪst/ n misógino m

misprint /ˈmɪsprɪnt/ n erro m tipográfico

mispronounce /mɪsprəˈnaʊns/ vt pronunciar mal

misquote /mɪsˈkwəʊt/ vt citar incorretamente

misread /mɪsˈriːd/ vt (pt **misread** /-ˈred/) ler or interpretar mal

misrepresent /mɪsreprɪˈzent/ vt deturpar, desvirtuar

miss /mɪs/ vt/i (*chance, bus etc*) perder; (*target*) errar, falhar; (*notice the loss of*) dar pela falta de; (*regret the absence of*) sentir a falta de, ter saudades de. **he** ~**es her/Portugal**/*etc* ele sente a falta or tem saudades dela/de Portugal/*etc* □ n falha f. **it was a near** ~ foi or escapou por um triz. ~ **out** omitir. ~ **the point** não compreender

Miss /mɪs/ n (pl **Misses**) Senhorita f, (P) Senhora f

misshapen /mɪsˈʃeɪpn/ a disforme

missile /ˈmɪsaɪl/ n míssil m; (*object thrown*) projétil m, (P) projéctil m

missing /ˈmɪsɪŋ/ a que falta; (*lost*) perdido; (*person*) desaparecido. **a book with a page** ~ um livro com uma página a menos

mission /ˈmɪʃn/ n missão f

missionary /ˈmɪʃənrɪ/ n missionário m

misspell /mɪsˈspel/ vt (pt **misspelt** or **misspelled**) escrever mal

mist /mɪst/ n neblina f, névoa f, bruma f; (*fig*) névoa f □ vt/i enevoar(-se); (*window*) embaçar(-se)

mistake /mɪsˈteɪk/ n engano m, erro m □ vt (pt **mistook**, pp **mistaken**) compreender mal; (*choose wrongly*) enganar-se em. ~ **for** confundir com, tomar por. ~**n** a errado. **be** ~**n** enganar-se. ~**nly** /-ənlɪ/ adv por engano

mistletoe /ˈmɪsltəʊ/ n visco m

mistreat /mɪsˈtriːt/ vt maltratar. ~**ment** n mau trato m mistress /'mɪstrɪs/ n senhora f, dona f; (*teacher*) professora f; (*lover*) amante f

mistrust /mɪs'trʌst/ vt desconfiar de, duvidar de □ n desconfiança f

misty /'mɪstɪ/ a (-ier, -iest) enevoado, brumoso; (*window*) embaçado; (*indistinct*) indistinto

misunderstand /mɪsʌndə'stænd/ vt (pt -stood) compreender mal. ~ing n mal-entendido m

misuse[1] /mɪs'juːz/ vt empregar mal; (*power etc*) abusar de

misuse[2] /mɪs'juːs/ n mau uso m; (*abuse*) abuso m; (*of funds*) desvio m

mitigat|e /'mɪtɪgeɪt/ vt atenuar, mitigar. ~ing circumstances circunstâncias fpl atenuantes

mitten /'mɪtn/ n luva f com uma única divisão entre o polegar e os dedos

mix /mɪks/ vt/i misturar(-se) □ n mistura f. ~ up misturar bem; (*fig: confuse*) confundir. ~-up n trapalhada f, confusão f. ~ with associar-se com. ~er n (*culin*) batedeira f

mixed /mɪkst/ a (*school etc*) misto; (*assorted*) sortido. be ~ up (*colloq*) estar confuso

mixture /'mɪkstʃə(r)/ n mistura f. cough ~ xarope m para a tosse

moan /məʊn/ n gemido m □ vi gemer; (*complain*) queixar-se, lastimar-se (about de). ~er n pessoa f lamurienta

moat /məʊt/ n fosso m

mob /mɒb/ n multidão f; (*tumultuous*) turba f; (*sl: gang*) bando m □ vt (pt mobbed) cercar, assediar

mobil|e /'məʊbaɪl/ a móvel. ~e home caravana f, trailer m. ~ity /-'bɪlətɪ/ n mobilidade f

mobiliz|e /'məʊbɪlaɪz/ vt/i mobilizar. ~ation /-'zeɪʃn/ n mobilização f

moccasin /'mɒkəsɪn/ n mocassim m

mock /mɒk/ vt/i zombar de, gozar □ a falso. ~-up n modelo m, maqueta f

mockery /'mɒkərɪ/ n troça f, gozação f. a ~ of uma gozação de

mode /məʊd/ n modo m; (*fashion*) moda f

model /'mɒdl/ n modelo m □ a modelo; (*exemplary*) exemplar; (*toy*) em miniatura □ vt (pt modelled) modelar; (*clothes*) apresentar □ vi ser or trabalhar como modelo

modem /'məʊdem/ n modem m

moderate[1] /'mɒdərət/ a & n moderado (m). ~ly adv moderadamente. ~ly good sofrível

moderat|e[2] /'mɒdəreɪt/ vt/i moderar(-se). ~ion /-'reɪʃn/ n moderação f. in ~ion com moderação

modern /'mɒdn/ a moderno. ~ languages línguas fpl vivas. ~ize vt modernizar

modest /'mɒdɪst/ a modesto. ~y n modéstia f. ~ly adv modestamente

modicum /'mɒdɪkəm/ n a ~ of um pouco de

modif|y /'mɒdɪfaɪ/ vt modificar. ~ication /-ɪ'keɪʃn/ n modificação f

modulat|e /'mɒdjʊleɪt/ vt/i modular. ~ion /-'leɪʃn/ n modulação f

module /'mɒdjuːl/ n módulo m

mohair /'məʊheə(r)/ n mohair m

moist /mɔɪst/ a (-er, -est) úmido, (P) húmido. ~ure /'mɔɪstʃə(r)/ n umidade f, (P) humidade f. ~urizer /-tʃəraɪzə(r)/ n creme m hidratante

moisten /'mɔɪsn/ vt/i umedecer, (P) humedecer

molasses /mə'læsɪz/ n melaço m

mole[1] /məʊl/ n (*on skin*) sinal na pele m

mole[2] /məʊl/ n (*animal*) toupeira f

molecule /'mɒlɪkjuːl/ n molécula f

molest /mə'lest/ vt meter-se com, molestar

mollusc /'mɒləsk/ n molusco m

mollycoddle /'mɒlɪkɒdl/ vt mimar

molten /'məʊltən/ a fundido

moment /'məʊmənt/ n momento m

momentar|y /'məʊməntrɪ/ a momentâneo. ~ily /'məʊməntrəlɪ/ adv momentâneamente

momentous /mə'mentəs/ a grave, importante

momentum /mə'mentəm/ n ímpeto m, velocidade f adquirida

Monaco /'mɒnəkəʊ/ n Mônaco m

monarch /'mɒnək/ n monarca mf. ~y n monarquia f

monast|ery /'mɒnəstrɪ/ n mosteiro m, convento m. ~ic /mə'næstɪk/ a monástico

Monday /'mʌndɪ/ n segunda-feira f

monetary /'mʌnɪtrɪ/ a monetário

money /'mʌnɪ/ n dinheiro m. ~-box n cofre m. ~-lender n agiota mf. ~ order vale m postal

mongrel /'mʌŋgrəl/ n (cão) vira-lata m, (P) rafeiro m

monitor /'mɒnɪtə(r)/ n chefe m de turma; (*techn*) monitor m □ vt controlar; (*a broadcast*) monitorar (a transmissão)

monk /mʌŋk/ n monge m, frade m

monkey /'mʌŋkɪ/ n (pl -eys) macaco m. ~-nut n amendoim m. ~-wrench n chave f inglesa

mono /'mɒnəʊ/ n (pl -os) gravação f mono □ a mono invar

monocle /'mɒnəkl/ n monóculo m

monogram /'mɒnəgræm/ n monograma m

monologue /'mɒnəlɒg/ n monólogo m

monopol|y /mə'nɒpəlɪ/ n monopólio m. ~ize vt monopolizar

monosyllab|le /'mɒnəsɪləbl/   n

monossilabo *m.* ~ic /-'læbɪk/ *a* monossilábico

monotone /'mɒnətəʊn/ *n* tom *m* uniforme

monoton|ous /mə'nɒtənəs/ *a* monótono. ~y *n* monotonia *f*

monsoon /mɒn'su:n/ *n* monção *f*

monst|er /'mɒnstə(r)/ *n* monstro *m*. ~rous *a* monstruoso

monstrosity /mɒn'strɒsətɪ/ *n* monstruosidade *f*

month /mʌnθ/ *n* mês *m*

monthly /'mʌnθlɪ/ *a* mensal □ *adv* mensalmente □ *n* (*periodical*) revista *f* mensal

monument /'mɒnjʊmənt/ *n* monumento *m*. ~al /-'mentl/ *a* monumental

moo /mu:/ *n* mugido *m* □ *vi* mugir

mood /mu:d/ *n* humor *m*, disposição *f*. in a good/bad ~ de bom/mau humor. ~y *a* de humor instável; (*sullen*) carrancudo

moon /mu:n/ *n* lua *f*

moon|light /'mu:nlaɪt/ *n* luar *m*. ~lit *a* iluminado pela lua, enluarado

moonlighting /'mu:nlaɪtɪŋ/ *n* (*colloq*) segundo emprego *m*, esp à noite

moor¹ /mʊə(r)/ *n* charneca *f*

moor² /mʊə(r)/ *vt* amarrar, atracar. ~ings *npl* amarras *fpl*; (*place*) amarradouro *m*, fundeadouro *m*

moose /mu:s/ *n* (*pl invar*) alce *m*

moot /mu:t/ *a* discutível □ *vt* levantar

mop /mɒp/ *n* esfregão *m* □ *vt* (*pt* mopped) ~ (up) limpar. ~ of hair trunfa *f*

mope /məʊp/ *vi* estar *or* andar abatido e triste

moped /'məʊped/ *n* (bicicleta) motorizada *f*

moral /'mɒrəl/ *a* moral □ *n* moral *f*. ~s *mpl* (*morals*) bons costumes *mpl*. ~ize *vi* moralizar. ~ly *adv* moralmente

morale /mə'rɑ:l/ *n* moral *m*

morality /mə'rælətɪ/ *n* moralidade *f*

morass /mə'ræs/ *n* pântano *m*

morbid /'mɔ:bɪd/ *a* mórbido

more /mɔ:(r)/ *a* & *adv* mais (than (do) que) □ *n* mais *m.* (some) ~ tea/pens/*etc* mais chá/canetas/*etc*. there is no ~ bread não há mais pão. ~ or less mais ou menos

moreover /mɔ:'rəʊvə(r)/ *adv* além disso, de mais a mais

morgue /mɔ:g/ *n* morgue *f*, necrotério *m*

moribund /'mɒrɪbʌnd/ *a* moribundo, agonizante

morning /'mɔ:nɪŋ/ *n* manhã *f*. in the ~ de manhã

Morocc|o /mə'rɒkəʊ/ *n* Marrocos *m.* ~an *a* & *n* marroquino (*m*)

moron /'mɔ:rɒn/ *n* idiota *mf*

morose /mə'rəʊs/ *a* taciturno e insociável, carrancudo

morphine /'mɔ:fi:n/ *n* morfina *f*

Morse /mɔ:s/ *n* ~ (code) (alfabeto) Morse *m*

morsel /'mɔ:sl/ *n* bocado *m* (esp de comida)

mortal /'mɔ:tl/ *a* & *n* mortal (*mf*). ~ity /mɔ:'tælətɪ/ *n* mortalidade *f*

mortar /'mɔ:tə(r)/ *n* argamassa *f*; (*bowl*) almofariz *m*; (*mil*) morteiro *m*

mortgage /'mɔ:gɪdʒ/ *n* hipoteca *f* □ *vt* hipotecar

mortify /'mɔ:tɪfaɪ/ *vt* mortificar

mortuary /'mɔ:tʃərɪ/ *n* casa *f* mortuária

mosaic /məʊ'zeɪk/ *n* mosaico *m*

Moscow /'mɒskəʊ/ *n* Moscou *m*, (*P*) Moscovo *m*

mosque /mɒsk/ *n* mesquita *f*

mosquito /mə'ski:təʊ/ *n* (*pl* -oes) mosquito *m*

moss /mɒs/ *n* musgo *m*. ~y *a* musgoso

most /məʊst/ *a* o mais, o maior; (*majority*) a maioria de, a maior parte de □ *n* mais *m*; (*majority*) a maioria, a maior parte, o máximo □ *adv* o mais; (*very*) muito. at ~ no máximo. for the ~ part na maior parte, na grande maioria. make the ~ of aproveitar ao máximo, tirar o melhor partido de. ~ly *adv* sobretudo

motel /məʊ'tel/ *n* motel *m*

moth /mɒθ/ *n* mariposa *f*, (*P*) borboleta *f* nocturna. (clothes-)~ *n* traça *f*. ~-ball *n* bola *f* de naftalina. ~-eaten *a* roído por traças

mother /'mʌðə(r)/ *n* mãe *f* □ *vt* tratar como a um filho. ~hood *n* maternidade *f*. ~-in-law *n* (*pl* ~s-in-law) sogra *f*. ~-of-pearl *n* madrepérola *f*. M~'s Day o Dia das Mães. ~-to-be *n* futura mãe *f*. ~ly *a* maternal

motif /məʊ'ti:f/ *n* tema *m*

motion /'məʊʃn/ *n* movimento *m*; (*proposal*) moção *f* □ *vt/i* ~ (to) sb to fazer sinal a alg para. ~less *a* imóvel

motivat|e /'məʊtɪveɪt/ *vt* motivar. ~ion /-'veɪʃn/ *n* motivação *f*

motive /'məʊtɪv/ *n* motivo *m*

motor /'məʊtə(r)/ *n* motor *m*; (*car*) automóvel *m* □ *a* (*anat*) motor; (*boat*) a motor □ *vi* ir de automóvel. ~ bike (*colloq*) moto *f* (*colloq*). ~ car carro *m.* ~ cycle motocicleta *f*. ~ cyclist *n* motociclista *mf*. ~ vehicle veículo *m* automóvel. ~ing *n* automobilismo *m*. ~ized *a* motorizado

motorist /'məʊtərɪst/ *n* motorista *mf*, automobilista *mf*

motorway /'məʊtəweɪ/ *n* autoestrada *f*

mottled /'mɒtld/ a sarapintado, pintalgado

motto /'mɒtəʊ/ n (pl -oes) divisa f, lema f

mould¹ /məʊld/ n (container) forma f, molde m; (culin) forma f □ vt moldar. ~ing n (archit) moldura f

mould² /məʊld/ n (fungi) bolor m, mofo m. ~y a bolorento

moult /məʊlt/ vi estar na muda

mound /maʊnd/ n monte m de terra or de pedras; (small hill) montículo m

mount /maʊnt/ vt/i montar □ n (support) engaste m; (for gem etc) engaste m. ~ up aumentar, subir

mountain /'maʊntɪn/ n montanha f. ~ bike mountain bike f. ~ous a montanhoso

mountaineer /maʊntɪ'nɪə(r)/ n alpinista mf. ~ing n alpinismo m

mourn /mɔːn/ vt/i ~ (for) chorar (a morte de). ~ (over) sofrer (por). ~er n pessoa f que acompanha o enterro. ~ing n luto m. in ~ing de luto

mournful /'mɔːnfl/ a triste; (sorrowful) pesaroso

mouse /maʊs/ n (pl mice) camundongo m

mousetrap /'maʊstræp/ n ratoeira f

mousse /muːs/ n mousse f

moustache /mə'staːʃ/ n bigode m

mouth¹ /maʊθ/ n boca f. ~-organ n gaita f de boca, (P) beiços

mouth² /maʊð/ vt/i declamar; (silently) articular sem som

mouthful /'maʊθfʊl/ n bocado m

mouthpiece /'maʊθpiːs/ n (mus) bocal m, boquilha f; (fig: person) porta-voz f

mouthwash /'maʊθwɒʃ/ n líquido m para bochecho

movable /'muːvəbl/ a móvel

move /muːv/ vt/i mover(-se), mexer (-se), deslocar(-se); (emotionally) comover; (incite) convencer, levar a; (act) agir; (propose) propor; (depart) ir, partir; (go forward) avançar. ~ (out) mudar-se, sair □ n movimento m; (in game) jogada f; (player's turn) vez f; (house change) mudança f. ~ back recuar. ~ forward avançar. ~ in mudar-se para. ~ on! circulem! ~ over, please chegue-se para lá, por favor. on the ~ em marcha

movement /'muːvmənt/ n movimento m

movie /'muːvɪ/ n (Amer) filme m. the ~s o cinema

moving /'muːvɪŋ/ a (touching) comovente; (movable) móvil; (in motion) em movimento

mow /məʊ/ vt (pp mowed or mown) ceifar; (lawn) cortar a grama, (P) relva. ~ down ceifar. ~er n (for

lawn) máquina f de cortar a grama, (P) relva

MP abbr see Member of Parliament

Mr /'mɪstə(r)/ n (pl Messrs) Senhor m. ~ Smith o Sr Smith

Mrs /'mɪsɪz/ n Senhora f. ~ Smith a Sra Smith. Mr and ~ Smith o Sr Smith e a mulher

Ms /mɪz/ n Senhora D f

much /mʌtʃ/ (more, most) a, adv & n muito (m). very ~ muito, muitíssimo. you may have as ~ as you need você pode levar o que precisar. ~ of it muito or grande parte dele. so ~ the better/worse tanto melhor/pior. how ~? quanto? not ~ não muito. too ~ demasiado, demais. he's not ~ of a gardener não é lá grande jardineiro

muck /mʌk/ n estrume m; (colloq: dirt) porcaria f □ vi ~ about (sl) entreter-se, perder tempo. ~ in (sl) ajudar, dar uma mão □ vt ~ up (sl) estragar. ~y a sujo

mucus /'mjuːkəs/ n muco m

mud /mʌd/ n lama f. ~dy a lamacento, enlameado

muddle /'mʌdl/ vt baralhar, atrapalhar, confundir □ vi ~ through sair-se bem, desenrascar-se (sl) □ n desordem f; (mix-up) confusão f, trapalhada f

mudguard /'mʌdgaːd/ n para-lama m

muff /mʌf/ n (for hands) regalo m

muffle /'mʌfl/ vt abafar. ~ (up) agasalhar(-se). ~d sounds sons mpl abafados. ~r /-ə(r)/ n cachecol m

mug /mʌg/ n caneca f; (sl: face) cara f; (sl: fool) trouxa mf (colloq) □ vt (pt mugged) assaltar, agredir. ~ger n assaltante mf. ~ging n assalto m

muggy /'mʌgɪ/ a abafado

mule /mjuːl/ n mulo m; (female) mula f

mull /mʌl/ vt ~ over ruminar; (fig) matutar em

multi- /'mʌltɪ/ pref mult(i)-

multicoloured /'mʌltɪkʌləd/ a multicolor

multinational /mʌltɪ'næʃnəl/ a & n multinacional (f)

multiple /'mʌltɪpl/ a & n múltiplo (m)

multiply /'mʌltɪplaɪ/ vt/i multiplicar(-se). ~ication /-ɪ'keɪʃn/ n multiplicação f

multi-storey /mʌltɪ'stɔːrɪ/ a (car park) em vários níveis

multitude /'mʌltɪtjuːd/ n multidão f

mum¹ /mʌm/ a keep ~ (colloq) ficar calado

mum² /mʌm/ (B) mamãe f (colloq) n (collog) (P) mamã

mumble /'mʌmbl/ vt/i resmungar, resmonear

mummy¹ /'mʌmɪ/ n (body) múmia f

mummy² /'mʌmɪ/ n (esp child's lang) mamã (B) mamãe f (colloq) mãezinha f (colloq), (P)

mumps /mʌmps/ n parotidite f, papeira f

munch /mʌntʃ/ vt mastigar

mundane /mʌn'deɪn/ a banal; (worldly) mundano

municipal /mju:'nɪsɪpl/ a municipal. ~ity /-'pæləti/ n municipalidade f

munitions /mju:'nɪʃnz/ npl munições fpl

mural /'mjʊərəl/ a & n mural (m)

murder /'mɜːdə(r)/ n assassínio m, assassinato m □ vt assassinar. ~er n assassino m, assassina f. ~ous a assassino, sanguinário; (of weapon) mortífero

murky /'mɜːkɪ/ a (-ier, -iest) escuro, sombrio

murmur /'mɜːmə(r)/ n murmúrio m □ vt/i murmurar

muscle /'mʌsl/ n músculo m □ vi ~ in (colloq) impor-se, intrometer-se

muscular /'mʌskjʊlə(r)/ a muscular; (brawny) musculoso

muse /mju:z/ vi meditar, cismar

museum /mju:'zɪəm/ n museu m

mush /mʌʃ/ n papa f de farinha de milho. ~y a mole; (sentimental) piegas inv

mushroom /'mʌʃrʊm/ n cogumelo m □ vi pulular, multiplicar-se com rapidez

music /'mju:zɪk/ n música f. ~al a musical □ n (show) comédia f musical, musical m. ~al box n caixa f de música. ~-stand n estante f de música

musician /mju:'zɪʃn/ n músico m

musk /mʌsk/ n almíscar m

Muslim /'mʊzlɪm/ a & n muçulmano (m)

muslin /'mʌzlɪn/ n musselina f

mussel /'mʌsl/ n mexilhão m

must /mʌst/ v aux dever. you ~ go é necessário que você parta. he ~ be old ele deve ser velho. I ~ have done it eu devo tê-lo feito □ n be a ~ (colloq) ser imprescindível

mustard /'mʌstəd/ n mostarda f

muster /'mʌstə(r)/ vt/i juntar(-se), reunir(-se). pass ~ ser aceitável

musty /'mʌstɪ/ a (-ier, -iest) mofado, bolorento

mutation /mju:'teɪʃn/ n mutação f

mute /mju:t/ a & n mudo (m)

muted /'mju:tɪd/ a (sound) em surdina; (colour) suave

mutilate /'mju:tɪleɪt/ vt mutilar. ~ion /-'leɪʃn/ n mutilação f

mutiny /'mju:tɪnɪ/ n motim f □ vi amotinar-se. ~ous a amotinado

mutter /'mʌtə(r)/ vt/i resmungar

mutton /'mʌtn/ n (carne de) carneiro m

mutual /'mju:tʃʊəl/ a mútuo; (colloq: common) comum. ~ly adv mutuamente

muzzle /'mʌzl/ n focinho m; (device) focinheira f; (of gun) boca f □ vt amordaçar; (dog) pôr focinheira em

my /maɪ/ a meu(s), minha(s)

myself /maɪ'self/ pron eu mesmo, eu próprio; (reflexive) me; (after prep) mim (próprio, mesmo). by ~ sozinho

mysterious /mɪ'stɪərɪəs/ a misterioso

mystery /'mɪstərɪ/ n mistério m

mystic /'mɪstɪk/ a & n místico (m). ~al a místico. ~ism /-sɪzəm/ n misticismo m

mystify /'mɪstɪfaɪ/ vt deixar perplexo

mystique /mɪ'sti:k/ n mística f

myth /mɪθ/ n mito m. ~ical a mítico

mythology /mɪ'θɒlədʒɪ/ n mitologia f. ~ical /mɪθə'lɒdʒɪkl/ a mitológico

N

nab /næb/ vt (pt nabbed) (sl) apanhar em flagrante, apanhar com a boca na botija (colloq), pilhar

nag /næg/ vt/i (pt nagged) implicar (com), criticar constantemente; (pester) apoquentar

nagging /'nægɪŋ/ a implicante; (pain) constante, contínuo

nail /neɪl/ n prego m; (of finger, toe) unha f □ vt pregar. ~-brush n escova f de unhas. ~-file n lixa f de unhas. ~-polish esmalte m, (P) verniz m para as unhas. hit the ~ on the head acertar em cheio. on the ~ sem demora

naïve /naɪ'i:v/ a ingênuo, (P) ingénuo

naked /'neɪkɪd/ a nu. to the ~ eye a olho nu, à vista desarmada. ~ness f nudez f

name /neɪm/ n nome m; (fig) reputação f, fama f □ vt (mention; appoint) nomear; (give a name to) chamar, dar o nome de; (a date) marcar. be ~d after ter o nome de. ~less a sem nome, anónimo, (P) anónimo

namely /'neɪmlɪ/ adv a saber

namesake /'neɪmseɪk/ n homônimo m (P) homónimo m

nanny /'nænɪ/ n ama f, babá f

nap¹ /næp/ n soneca f □ vi (pt napped) dormitar, tirar um cochilo. catch ~ping apanhar desprevenido

nap² /næp/ n (of material) felpa f

nape /neɪp/ n nuca f

napkin /'næpkɪn/ n guardanapo m; (for baby) fralda f

nappy /'næpɪ/ n fralda f. ~-**rash** n assadura f

narcotic /na:'kɒtɪk/ a & n narcótico(m)

narrat|e /nə'reɪt/ vt narrar. ~**ion** /-ʃn/ n narrativa f. ~**or** n narrador m

narrative /'nærətɪv/ n narrativa f □ a narrativo

narrow /'nærəʊ/ a (-er -est) estreito; (fig) restrito □ vt/i estreitar(-se); (limit) limitar(-se). ~**ly** adv (only just) por pouco; (closely, carefully) de perto, com cuidado. ~-**minded** ·a bitolado, de visão limitada. ~**ness** n estreiteza f

nasal /'neɪzl/ a nasal

nast|y /'nɑ:stɪ/ a (-ier -iest) (malicious, of weather) mau; (unpleasant) desagradável, intragável; (rude) grosseiro. ~**ily** adv maldosamente; (unpleasantly) desagradavelmente. ~**iness** f (malice) maldade f; (rudeness) grosseria f

nation /'neɪʃn/ n nação f. ~-**wide** a em todo o país, em escala or a nível nacional

national /'næʃnəl/ a nacional □ n natural mf. ~ **anthem** hino m nacional. ~**ism** n nacionalismo m. ~**ize** vt nacionalizar. ~**ly** adv em escala nacional

nationality /næʃə'nælətɪ/ n nacionalidade f

native /'neɪtɪv/ n natural mf, nativo m □ a nativo; (country) natal; (inborn) inato. **be a** ~ **of** ser natural de. ~ **language** língua f materna. ~ **speaker of Portuguese** pessoa f de língua portuguesa, falante m nativo de Português

Nativity /nə'tɪvətɪ/ n **the** ~ a Natividade f

natter /'nætə(r)/ vi fazer conversa fiada, falar à toa, tagarelar

natural /'nætʃrəl/ a natural. ~ **history** história f natural. ~**ist** n naturalista mf. ~**ly** adv naturalmente; (by nature) por natureza

naturaliz|e /'nætʃrəlaɪz/ vt/i naturalizar(-se); (animal, plant) aclimatar (-se). ~**ation** /-'zeɪʃn/ n naturalização f

nature /'neɪtʃə(r)/ n natureza f; (kind) género m, (P) género m; (of person) indole f

naughty /'nɔ:tɪ/ a (-ier -iest) (child) levado; (indecent) picante

nause|a /'nɔ:sɪə/ n náusea f. ~**ate** /'nɔ:sɪeɪt/ vt nausear. ~**ating**, ~**ous** a nauseabundo, repugnante

nautical /'nɔ:tɪkl/ a náutico. ~ **mile** milha f marítima

naval /'neɪvl/ a naval; (officer) de marinha

nave /neɪv/ n nave f

navel /'neɪvl/ n umbigo m

navigable /'nævɪgəbl/ a navegável

navigat|e /'nævɪgeɪt/ vt (sea etc) navegar; (ship) pilotar □ vi navegar. ~**ion** /-'geɪʃn/ n navegação f. ~**or** n navegador m

navy /'neɪvɪ/ n marinha f de guerra. ~ (**blue**) azul-marinho m invar

near /nɪə(r)/ adv perto, quase □ prep perto de □ a próximo □ vt aproximarse de, chegar-se a. **draw** ~ aproximar(-se) (**to** de). ~ **by** adv perto, próximo. **N**~ **East** Oriente m Próximo. ~ **to** perto de. ~**ness** n proximidade f

nearby /'nɪəbaɪ/ a & adv próximo, perto

nearly /'nɪəlɪ/ adv quase, por pouco. **not** ~ **as pretty/etc as** longe de ser tão bonita/etc como

neat /ni:t/ a (-er -est) (bem) cuidado; (room) bem arrumado; (spirits) puro, sem gelo. ~**ly** adv (with care) com cuidado; (cleverly) habilmente. ~**ness** n aspecto m cuidado

nebulous /'nebjʊləs/ a nebuloso; (vague) vago, confuso

necessar|y /'nesəsərɪ/ a necessário. ~**ily** adv necessariamente

necessitate /nɪ'sesɪteɪt/ vt exigir, obrigar a, tornar necessário

necessity /nɪ'sesətɪ/ n necessidade f; (thing) coisa f indispensável, artigo m de primeira necessidade

neck /nek/ n pescoço m; (of dress) gola f. ~ **and neck** emparelhados

necklace /'neklɪs/ n colar m

neckline /'neklaɪn/ n decote m

nectarine /'nektərɪn/ n pêssego m

née /neɪ/ a em solteira. **Ann Jones** ~ **Drewe** Ann Jones cujo nome de solteira era Drewe

need /ni:d/ n necessidade f □ vt precisar de, necessitar de. **you** ~ **not come** não temde or não precisa vir. ~**less** a inútil, desnecessário. ~**lessly** adv inutilmente, sem necessidade

needle /'ni:dl/ n agulha f □ vt (colloq: provoke) provocar

needlework /'ni:dlwɜ:k/ n costura f; (embroidery) bordado m

needy /'ni:dɪ/ a (-ier -iest) necessitado, carenciado

negation /nɪ'geɪʃn/ n negação f

negative /'negətɪv/ a negativo □ n negativa f, negação f; (photo) negativo m. **in the** ~ (answer) na negativa; (gram) na forma negativa. ~**ly** adv negativamente

neglect /nɪ'glekt/ vt descuidar; (opportunity) desprezar; (family) não cuidar de, abandonar; (duty) não cumprir □ n falta f de cuidado(s), descuido m. (**state of**) ~ abandono *m.* ~ **to** (*omit to*) esquecer-se de. ~**ful** *a* negligente

negligen|t /'neglɪdʒənt/ *a* negligente. ~**ce** *n* negligência *f*, desleixo *m*

negligible /'neglɪdʒəbl/ *a* insignificante, ínfimo

negotiable /nɪ'gəʊʃəbl/ *a* negociável

negotiat|e /nɪ'gəʊʃɪeɪt/ *vt/i* negociar; (*obstacle*) transpor; (*difficulty*) vencer. ~**ion** /-ʃɪ'eɪʃn/ *n* negociação *f*. ~**or** *n* negociador *m*

Negro /'niːgrəʊ/ *a* & *n* (*pl* ~**oes**) negro (*m*), preto (*m*)

neigh /neɪ/ *n* relincho *m* □ *vi* relinchar

neighbour /'neɪbə(r)/ *n* vizinho *m*. ~**hood** *f* vizinhança *f*. ~**ing** *a* vizinho. ~**ly** *a* de boa vizinhança

neither /'naɪðə(r)/ *a* & *pron* nenhum(a) (de dois *ou* duas), nem um nem outro, nem uma nem outra □ *adv* tampouco, também não □ *conj* nem. ~ **big nor small** nem grande nem pequeno. ~ **am I** nem eu

neon /'niːɒn/ *n* néon *m* □ *a* (*lamp etc*) de néon

nephew /'nevjuː/ *n* sobrinho *m*

nerve /nɜːv/ *n* nervo *m*; (*fig: courage*) coragem *f*; (*colloq: impudence*) descaramento *m*, (*P*) lata *f* (*colloq*). **get on sb's nerves** irritar, dar nos nervos de alg. ~**-racking** *a* de arrasar os nervos, enervante

nervous /'nɜːvəs/ *a* nervoso. **be** *ou* **feel** ~ (*afraid*) ter receio/um certo medo. ~ **breakdown** esgotamento *m* nervoso. ~**ly** *adv* nervosamente. ~**ness** *n* nervosismo *m*; (*fear*) receio *m*

nest /nest/ *n* ninho *m* □ *vi* aninhar-se, fazer *ou* ter ninho. ~**-egg** *n* pé-de-meia *m*

nestle /'nesl/ *vi* aninhar-se

net[1] /net/ *n* rede *f* □ *vt* (*pt* netted) apanhar na rede. ~**ting** *n* rede *f*. **wire** ~**ting** rede *f* de arame

net[2] /net/ *a* (*weight etc*) líquido

Netherlands /'neðələndz/ *npl* **the** ~ os Países Baixos

nettle /'netl/ *n* urtiga *f*

network /'netwɜːk/ *n* rede *f*, cadeia *f*

neuro|sis /njʊə'rəʊsɪs/ *n* (*pl* -**oses** /-siːz/) neurose *f*. ~**tic** /-'rɒtɪk/ *a* & *n* neurótico (*m*)

neuter /'njuːtə(r)/ *a* & *n* neutro (*m*) □ *vt* castrar, capar

neutral /'njuːtrəl/ *a* neutro. ~ (**gear**) ponto *m* morto. ~**ity** /-'trælətɪ/ *n* neutralidade *f*

never /'nevə(r)/ *adv* nunca; (*colloq: not*) não. **he** ~ **refuses** ele nunca recusa. **I** ~ **saw him** (*colloq*) nunca o vi. ~ **mind** não faz mal, deixe para lá. ~**-ending** *a* interminável

nevertheless /nevəðə'les/ *adv* & *conj* contudo, no entanto

new /njuː/ *a* (-**er**, -**est**) novo. ~**-born** *a* recém-nascido. ~ **moon** lua *f* nova. ~ **year** ano *m* novo. **N~ Year's Day** dia *m* de Ano Novo. **N~ Year's Eve** véspera *f* de Ano Novo. **N~ Zealand** Nova Zelândia *f*. **N~ Zealander** neo-zelandês *m*. ~**ness** *n* novidade *f*

newcomer /'njuːkʌmə(r)/ *n* recém-chegado *m*, (*P*) recém-vindo *m*

newfangled /'njuː'fæŋgld/ *a* (*pej*) moderno

newly /'njuːlɪ/ *adv* há pouco, recentemente. ~**-weds** *npl* recém-casados *mpl*

news /njuːz/ *n* notícia(s) *f(pl)*; (*radio*) noticiário *m*, notícias *fpl*; (*TV*) telejornal *m*. ~**-caster**, ~**-reader** *n* locutor *m*. ~**-flash** *n* notícia *f* de última hora

newsagent /'njuːzeɪdʒənt/ *n* jornaleiro *m*

newsletter /'njuːzletə(r)/ *n* boletim *m* informativo

newspaper /'njuːzpeɪpə(r)/ *n* jornal *m*

newsreel /'njuːzriːl/ *n* atualidades *fpl*, (*P*) actualidades *fpl*

newt /njuːt/ *n* tritão *m*

next /nekst/ *a* próximo; (*adjoining*) pegado, ao lado, contíguo; (*following*) seguinte □ *adv* a seguir □ *n* seguinte *mf*. ~**-door** *a* do lado. ~ **of kin** parente *m* mais próximo. ~ **to** ao lado de. ~ **to nothing** quase nada

nib /nɪb/ *n* bico *m*, (*P*) aparo *m*

nibble /'nɪbl/ *vt* mordiscar, dar dentadinhas em

nice /naɪs/ *a* (-**er**, -**est**) agradável, bom; (*kind*) simpático, gentil; (*pretty*) bonito; (*respectable*) bem educado, correto, (*P*) correcto; (*subtle*) fino, subtil. ~**ly** *adv* agradavelmente; (*well*) bem

nicety /'naɪsətɪ/ *n* sutileza *f*, (*P*) subtileza *f*

niche /nɪtʃ/ *n* nicho *m*; (*fig*) bom lugar *m*

nick /nɪk/ *n* corte *m*, chanfradura *f*; (*sl: prison*) cadeia *f* □ *vt* dar um corte em; (*sl: steal*) roubar, limpar (*colloq*); (*sl: arrest*) apanhar, pôr a mão em (*colloq*). **in good** ~ (*colloq*) em boa forma, em bom estado. **in the** ~ **of time** mesmo a tempo

nickel /'nɪkl/ *n* níquel *m*; (*Amer*) moeda *f* de cinco cêntimos

nickname /'nɪkneɪm/ *n* apelido *m*, (*P*) alcunha *f*; (*short form*) diminutivo *m* □ *vt* apelidar de

nicotine /'nɪkətiːn/ *n* nicotina *f*

niece /niːs/ *n* sobrinha *f*

Nigeria /naɪ'dʒɪərɪə/ *n* Nigéria *f*. ~**n** *a* & *n* nigeriano (*m*)

niggardly /'nɪgədlɪ/ a miserável
night /naɪt/ n noite f □ a de noite, noturno, (P) nocturno. at ~ à/de noite. by ~ de noite. ~-cap n (drink) bebida f na hora de deitar. ~-club n boate f, (P) boite f. ~-dress, ~-gown ns camisola f de dormir, (P) camisa f de noite. ~-life n vida f noturna, (P) nocturna. ~-school n escola f noturna, (P) nocturna. ~-time n noite f. ~-watchman n guarda-noturno m, (P) guarda-nocturno m
nightfall /'naɪtfɔːl/ n anoitecer m
nightingale /'naɪtɪŋgeɪl/ n rouxinol m
nightly /'naɪtlɪ/ a noturno, (P) nocturno □ adv de noite, à noite, todas as noites
nightmare /'naɪtmeə(r)/ n pesadelo m
nil /nɪl/ n nada m; (sport) zero m □ a nulo
nimble /'nɪmbl/ a (-er, -est) ágil, ligeiro
nin|e /naɪn/ a & n nove (m). ~th a & n nono (m)
nineteen /naɪn'tiːn/ a & n dezenove (m), (P) dezanove (m). ~th a & n décimo nono (m)
ninet|y /'naɪntɪ/ a & n noventa (m). ~ieth a & n nonagésimo (m)
nip /nɪp/ vt/i (pt nipped) apertar, beliscar; (colloq: rush) ir correndo, ir num pulo (colloq) □ n aperto m, beliscão m; (drink) gole m, trago m. a ~ in the air um frio cortante. ~ in the bud cortar pela raiz
nipple /'nɪpl/ n mamilo m
nippy /'nɪpɪ/ a (-ier, -iest) (colloq: quick) rápido; (colloq: chilly) cortante
nitrogen /'naɪtrədʒən/ n azoto m, nitrogênio m, (P) nitrogénio m
nitwit /'nɪtwɪt/ n (colloq) imbecil m
no /nəʊ/ a nenhum □ adv não □ n (pl noes) não m. ~ entry entrada f proibida. ~ money/time/etc nenhum dinheiro/tempo/etc. ~ man's land terra f de ninguém. ~ one = nobody. ~ smoking é proibido fumar. ~ way! (colloq) de modo nenhum!
nob|le /'nəʊbl/ a (-er, -est) nobre. ~ility /-'bɪlətɪ/ n nobreza f
nobleman /'nəʊblmən/ n (pl -men) nobre m, fidalgo m
nobody /'nəʊbədɪ/ pron ninguém □ n nulidade f. he knows ~ ele não conhece ninguém. ~ is there não tem ninguém lá
nocturnal /nɒk'tɜːnl/ a noturno, (P) nocturno
nod /nɒd/ vt/i (pt nodded) ~ (one's head) acenar (com) a cabeça; ~ (off) cabecear □ n aceno m com a cabeça

(para dizer que sim or para cumprimentar)
noise /nɔɪz/ n ruído m, barulho m. ~less a silencioso
nois|y /'nɔɪzɪ/ a (-ier, -iest) ruidoso, barulhento. ~ily adv ruidosamente
nomad /'nəʊmæd/ n nômade mf, (P) nómade mf. ~ic /-'mædɪk/ a nômade, (P) nómade
nominal /'nɒmɪnl/ a nominal; (fee, sum) simbólico
nominat|e /'nɒmɪneɪt/ vt (appoint) nomear; (put forward) propor. ~ion /-'neɪʃn/ n nomeação f
non- /nɒn/ pref não, sem, in-, a-, anti-, des-. ~-skid a antiderrapante. ~-stick a não-aderente
nonchalant /'nɒnʃələnt/ a indiferente, desinteressado
non-commissioned /nɒnkə'mɪʃnd/ a ~ officer sargento m, cabo m
non-committal /nɒnkə'mɪtl/ a evasivo
nondescript /'nɒndɪskrɪpt/ a insignificante, medíocre, indefinível
none /nʌn/ pron (person) nenhum, ninguém; (thing) nenhum, nada. ~ of us nenhum de nós. I have ~ não tenho nenhum. ~ of that! nada disso! □ adv ~ too não muito. he is ~ the happier nem por isso ele é mais feliz. ~ the less contudo, no entanto, apesar disso
nonentity /nɒ'nentətɪ/ n nulidade f, zero m à esquerda, João Ninguém m
non-existent /nɒnɪg'zɪstənt/ a inexistente
nonplussed /nɒn'plʌst/ a perplexo, pasmado
nonsens|e /'nɒnsns/ n absurdo m, disparate m. ~ical /-'sensɪkl/ a absurdo, disparatado
non-smoker /nɒn'sməʊkə(r)/ n não-fumante m, (P) não-fumador m
non-stop /nɒn'stɒp/ a ininterrupto, contínuo; (train) direto, (P) directo; (flight) sem escala □ adv sem parar
noodles /'nuːdlz/ npl talharim m, (P) macarronete m
nook /nʊk/ n (re)canto m
noon /nuːn/ n meio-dia m
noose /nuːs/ n laço m corrediço
nor /nɔː(r)/ conj & adv nem, também não. ~ do I nem eu
norm /nɔːm/ n norma f
normal /'nɔːml/ a & n normal (m). above/below ~ acima/abaixo do normal. ~ity /nɔː'mælətɪ/ n normalidade f. ~ly adv normalmente
north /nɔːθ/ n norte m □ a norte, do norte; (of country, people etc) setentrional □ adv a, ao/para o norte. ~ America América f do Norte. N~ American a & n norte-americano

(m). ~-east n nordeste m. ~erly
/'nɔːðəlɪ/ a do norte. ~ward a ao
norte. ~ward(s) adv para o norte.
~-west n noroeste m
northern /'nɔːðən/ a do norte
Norw|ay /'nɔːweɪ/ n Noruega f.
~egian /nɔː'wiːdʒən/ a & n norue-
guês (m)
nose /nəʊz/ n nariz m; (of animal)
focinho m □ vi ~ about farejar. pay
through the ~ pagar um preço exorbitante
nosebleed /'nəʊzbliːd/ n hemorragia
f nasal or pelo nariz
nosedive /'nəʊzdaɪv/ n vôo m picado
nostalg|ia /nɒ'stældʒə/ n nostalgia f.
~ic a nostálgico
nostril /'nɒstrəl/ n narina f; (of horse)
venta f (usually pl)
nosy /'nəʊzɪ/ a (-ier, -iest) (colloq) bisbilhoteiro
not /nɒt/ adv não. ~ at all nada, de
modo nenhum; (reply to thanks) de
nada. he is ~ at all bored ele não
está nem um pouco entediado. ~
yet ainda não. I suppose ~ creio
que não
notable /'nəʊtəbl/ a notável □ n no-
tabilidade f
notably /'nəʊtəblɪ/ adv notavelmente.
(particularly) especialmente
notch /nɒtʃ/ n corte m em V □ vt marcar com cortes. ~ up (score etc) marcar
note /nəʊt/ n nota f; (banknote) nota
(de banco) f; (short letter) bilhete m □
vt notar
notebook /'nəʊtbʊk/ n livrinho m de
notas, (P) bloco-notas m
noted /'nəʊtɪd/ a conhecido, famoso
notepaper /'nəʊtpeɪpə(r)/ n papel m
de carta
noteworthy /'nəʊtwɜːðɪ/ a notável
nothing /'nʌθɪŋ/ n nada m; (person)
nulidade f, zero m □ adv nada, de
modo algum or nenhum, de maneira
alguma or nenhuma. he eats ~ ele
não come nada. ~ big/etc nada (de)
grande/etc. ~ else nada mais. ~
much pouca coisa. for ~ (free) de
graça; (in vain) em vão
notice /'nəʊtɪs/ n anúncio m, notícia f;
(in street, on wall) letreiro m; (warning) aviso m; (attention) atenção f.
(advance) ~ pré-aviso m □ vt notar,
reparar. at short ~ num prazo curto.
a week's ~ o prazo de uma semana.
~-board n quadro m para afixar
anúncios etc. hand in one's ~ pedir
demissão. take ~ reparar (of em).
take no ~ não fazer caso (of de)
noticeabl|e /'nəʊtɪsəbl/ a visível. ~y
adv visivelmente
notif|y /'nəʊtɪfaɪ/ vt participar, noti-

ficar. ~ication /-ɪ'keɪʃn/ n participação f, notificação f
notion /'nəʊʃn/ n noção f
notor|ious /nəʊ'tɔːrɪəs/ a notório.
~iety /-ə'raɪətɪ/ n fama f
notwithstanding /ˌnɒtwɪθ'stændɪŋ/
prep apesar de, não obstante □ adv
mesmo assim, ainda assim □ conj embora, conquanto, apesar de que
nougat /'nuːgɑː/ n nugá m, torrone m
nought /nɔːt/ n zero m
noun /naʊn/ n substantivo m, nome m
nourish /'nʌrɪʃ/ vt alimentar, nutrir.
~ing a alimentício, nutritivo.
~ment n alimento m, sustento m
novel /'nɒvl/ n romance m □ a novo,
original. ~ist n romancista mf. ~ty
n novidade f
November /nəʊ'vembə(r)/ n novembro m
novice /'nɒvɪs/ n (beginner) noviço m,
novato m; (relig) noviço m
now /naʊ/ adv agora □ conj ~ (that)
agora que. by ~ a estas horas, por
esta altura. from ~ on de agora em
diante. ~ and again, ~ and then de
vez em quando. right ~ já
nowadays /'naʊədeɪz/ adv hoje em
dia, presentemente, atualmente, (P)
actualmente
nowhere /'nəʊweə(r)/ adv (position)
em lugar nenhum, em lado nenhum;
(direction) a lado nenhum, a parte alguma or nenhuma
nozzle /'nɒzl/ n bico m, bocal m; (of
hose) agulheta f
nuance /'njuːɑːns/ n nuance f, matiz
m
nuclear /'njuːklɪə(r)/ a nuclear
nucleus /'njuːklɪəs/ n (pl -lei /-lɪaɪ/)
núcleo m
nud|e /njuːd/ a & n nu (m). in the ~e
nu. ~ity n nudez f
nudge /nʌdʒ/ vt tocar com o cotovelo,
cutucar □ n ligeira cotovelada f, cutucada f
nudis|t /'njuːdɪst/ n nudista mf. ~m
/-zəm/ n nudismo m
nuisance /'njuːsns/ n aborrecimento
m, chatice f (sl); (person) chato m (sl)
null /nʌl/ a nulo. ~ and void (jur)
írrito e nulo. ~ify vt anular, invalidar
numb /nʌm/ a entorpecido, dormente
□ vt entorpecer, adormecer
number /'nʌmbə(r)/ n número m;
(numeral) algarismo m □ vt numerar;
(amount to) ser em número de; (count)
contar, incluir. ~-plate n chapa (do
carro) f
numeral /'njuːmərəl/ n número m,
algarismo m
numerate /'njuːmərət/ a que tem conhecimentos básicos de matemática

numerical /nju:'merɪkl/ a numérico
numerous /'nju:mərəs/ a numeroso
nun /nʌn/ n freira f, religiosa f
nurs|e /nɜ:s/ n enfermeira f, enfermeiro m; (nanny) ama(-seca) f, babá f □ vt cuidar de, tratar de; (hopes etc) alimentar, acalentar. ~ing e enfermagem f. ~ing home clínica f de repouso
nursery /'nɜ:sərɪ/ n quarto m de crianças; (for plants) viveiro m. (day) ~ creche f. ~ rhyme poema m or canção f infantil. ~ school jardim m de infância
nurture /'nɜ:tʃə(r)/ vt educar
nut /nʌt/ n (bot) noz f; (techn) porca f de parafuso
nutcrackers /'nʌtkrækəz/ npl quebra-nozes m invar
nutmeg /'nʌtmeg/ n noz-moscada f
nutrient /'nju:trɪənt/ n substância f nutritiva, nutriente m
nutrit|ion /nju:'trɪʃn/ n nutrição f. ~ious a nutritivo
nutshell /'nʌtʃel/ n casca f de noz. in a ~ em poucas palavras
nuzzle /'nʌzl/ vt esfregar com o focinho
nylon /'naɪlɒn/ n nylon m. ~s meias fpl de nylon

O

oaf /əʊf/ n (pl oafs) imbecil m, idiota m
oak /əʊk/ n carvalho m
OAP abbr see old-age pensioner
oar /ɔ:(r)/ n remo m
oasis /əʊ'eɪsɪs/ n (pl oases /-si:z/) oásis m
oath /əʊθ/ n juramento m; (swear-word) praga f
oatmeal /'əʊtmi:l/ n farinha f de aveia; (porridge) papa f de aveia
oats /əʊts/ npl aveia f
obedien|t /ə'bi:dɪənt/ a obediente. ~ce n obediência f. ~tly adv obedientemente
obes|e /əʊ'bi:s/ a obeso. ~ity n obesidade f
obey /ə'beɪ/ vt/i obedecer (a)
obituary /ə'bɪtʃʊərɪ/ n necrológio m, (P) necrologia f
object¹ /'ɒbdʒɪkt/ n objeto m, (P) objecto m; (aim) objetivo m, (P) objectivo m; (gram) complemento m
object² /əb'dʒekt/ vt/i objetar, (P) objectar (que). ~ to opor-se a, discordar de. ~ion /-ʃn/ n objeção f, (P) objecção f
objectionable /əb'dʒekʃnəbl/ a censurável; (unpleasant) desagradável
objective /əb'dʒektɪv/ a objetivo, (P)

objectivo. ~ity /-'tɪvətɪ/ n objetividade f, (P) objectividade f
obligation /ɒblɪ'geɪʃn/ n obrigação f. be under an ~ to sb dever favores a alg
obligatory /ə'blɪgətrɪ/ a obrigatório
oblig|e /ə'blaɪdʒ/ vt obrigar; (do a favour) fazer um favor a, obsequiar. ~ed a obrigado (to a). ~ed to sb em dívida (para) com alg. ~ing a prestável, amável. ~ingly adv amavelmente
oblique /ə'bli:k/ a oblíquo
obliterat|e /ə'blɪtəreɪt/ vt obliterar. ~ion /-'reɪʃn/ n obliteração f
oblivion /ə'blɪvɪən/ n esquecimento m
oblivious /ə'blɪvɪəs/ a esquecido, sem consciência (of/to de)
oblong /'ɒblɒŋ/ a oblongo □ n retângulo m, (P) rectângulo m
obnoxious /əb'nɒkʃəs/ a ofensivo, detestável
oboe /'əʊbəʊ/ n oboé m
obscen|e /əb'si:n/ a obsceno. ~ity /-'enətɪ/ n obscenidade f
obscur|e /əb'skjʊə(r)/ a obscuro □ vt obscurecer; (conceal) encobrir. ~ity n obscuridade f
obsequious /əb'si:kwɪəs/ a demasiado obsequioso, subserviente
observ|ant /əb'zɜ:vənt/ a observador. ~ce n observância f, cumprimento m
observatory /əb'zɜ:vətrɪ/ n observatório m
observ|e /əb'zɜ:v/ vt observar. ~ation /ɒbzə'veɪʃn/ n observação f. keep under ~ation vigiar. ~er n observador m
obsess /əb'ses/ vt obcecar. ~ion /-ʃn/ n obsessão f. ~ive a obsessivo
obsolete /'ɒbsəli:t/ a obsoleto, antiguado
obstacle /'ɒbstəkl/ n obstáculo m
obstetric|s /əb'stetrɪks/ n obstetrícia f. ~ian /ɒbstɪ'trɪʃn/ n obstetra mf
obstina|te /'ɒbstɪnət/ a obstinado. ~cy n obstinação f
obstruct /əb'strʌkt/ vt obstruir, bloquear; (hinder) estorvar, obstruir. ~ion /-ʃn/ n obstrução f; (thing) obstáculo m
obtain /əb'teɪn/ vt obter □ vi prevalecer, estar em vigor. ~able a que se pode obter
obtrusive /əb'tru:sɪv/ a importuno; (thing) demasiadamente em evidência, que dá muito na vista (colloq)
obvious /'ɒbvɪəs/ a óbvio, evidente. ~ly adv obviamente
occasion /ə'keɪʒn/ n ocasião f; (event) acontecimento m □ vt ocasionar. on ~ de vez em quando, ocasionalmente
occasional /ə'keɪʒənl/ a ocasional.

~ly *adv* de vez em quando, ocasionalmente

occult /ɒ'kʌlt/ *a* oculto

occupation /ɒkjʊ'peɪʃn/ *n* ocupação *f*. ~al *a* profissional; (*therapy*) ocupacional

occup|y /'ɒkjʊpaɪ/ *vt* ocupar. ~ant, ~ier *ns* ocupante *mf*

occur /ə'kɜ:(r)/ *vi* (*pt* occurred) ocorrer, acontecer, dar-se; (*arise*) apresentar-se, aparecer. ~ to sb ocorrer a alg

occurrence /ə'kʌrəns/ *n* acontecimento *m*, ocorrência *f*

ocean /'əʊʃn/ *n* oceano *m*

o'clock /ə'klɒk/ *adv* it is one ~ é uma hora. it is six ~ são seis horas

octagon /'ɒktəgən/ *n* octógono *m*. ~al /-'tægənl/ *a* octogonal

octave /'ɒktɪv/ *n* oitava *f*

October /ɒk'təʊbə(r)/ *n* outubro *m*

octopus /'ɒktəpəs/ *n* (*pl* -puses) polvo *m*

odd /ɒd/ *a* (-er, -est) estranho, singular; (*number*) ímpar; (*left over*) de sobra; (*not of set*) desemparelhado; (*occasional*) ocasional. ~ jobs (*paid*) biscates *mpl*; (*in garden etc*) trabalhos *mpl* diversos. twenty ~ vinte e tantos. ~ity *n* singularidade *f*; (*thing*) curiosidade *f*. ~ly *adv* de modo estranho

oddment /'ɒdmənt/ *n* resto *m*, artigo *m* avulso

odds /ɒdz/ *npl* probabilidades *fpl*, (*in betting*) ganhos *mpl* líquidos. at ~ em desacordo; (*quarrelling*) de mal, brigado. it makes no ~ não faz diferença. ~ and ends artigos *mpl* avulsos, coisas *fpl* pequenas

odious /'əʊdɪəs/ *a* odioso

odour /'əʊdə(r)/ *n* odor *m*. ~less *a* inodoro

of /əv/; *emphatic* /ɒv/ *prep* de. a friend ~ mine um amigo meu. the fifth ~ June (no dia) cinco de junho. take six ~ them leve seis deles

off /ɒf/ *adv* embora, fora; (*switched off*) apagado, desligado; (*taken off*) tirado, desligado; (*cancelled*) cancelado; (*food*) estragado □ *prep* (fora) de; (*distant from*) a alguma distância de. be ~ (*depart*) ir-se embora, partir. be well ~ estar abastado. be better/worse ~ estar em melhor/pior situação. a day ~ um dia de folga. 20% ~ redução de 20%. on the ~ chance that no caso de. ~ colour indisposto, adoentado. ~licence *n* loja *f* de bebidas alcoólicas. ~load *vt* descarregar. ~putting *a* desconcertante. ~stage *adv* fora de cena. ~white *a* branco-sujo

offal /'ɒfl/ *n* miudezas *fpl*, fressura *f*

offence /ə'fens/ *n* (*feeling*) ofensa *f*; (*crime*) delito *m*, transgressão *f*. give ~ to ofender. take ~ ofender-se (at com)

offend /ə'fend/ *vt* ofender. be ~ed ofender-se (at com). ~er *n* delinquente *mf*, (*P*) delinquente *mf*

offensive /ə'fensɪv/ *a* ofensivo; (*disgusting*) repugnante □ *n* ofensiva *f*

offer /'ɒfə(r)/ *vt* (*pt* offered) oferecer □ *n* oferta *f*. on ~ em promoção. ~ing *n* oferenda *f*

offhand /ɒf'hænd/ *a* espontâneo; (*curt*) seco □ *adv* de improviso, sem pensar

office /'ɒfɪs/ *n* escritório *m*; (*post*) cargo *m*; (*branch*) filial *f*. ~ hours horas *fpl* de expediente. in ~ no poder. take ~ assumir o cargo

officer /'ɒfɪsə(r)/ *n* oficial *m*; (*policeman*) agente *m*

official /ə'fɪʃl/ *a* oficial □ *n* funcionário *m*. ~ly *adv* oficialmente

officiate /ə'fɪʃɪeɪt/ *vi* (*relig*) oficiar. ~ as presidir, exercer as funções de

officious /ə'fɪʃəs/ *a* intrometido

offing /'ɒfɪŋ/ *n* in the ~ (*fig*) em perspectiva

offset /'ɒfset/ *vt* (*pt* -set, *pres p* -setting) compensar, contrabalançar

offshoot /'ɒfʃu:t/ *n* rebento *m*; (*fig*) efeito *m* secundário

offshore /'ɒfʃɔ:(r)/ *a* ao largo da costa

offside /ɒf'saɪd/ *a* & *adv* offside, em impedimento, (*P*) fora de jogo

offspring /'ɒfsprɪŋ/ *n* (*pl invar*) descendência *f*, prole *f*

often /'ɒfn/ *adv* muitas vezes, frequentemente, (*P*) frequentemente. every so ~ de vez em quando. how ~? quantas vezes?

oh /əʊ/ *int* oh, ah

oil /ɔɪl/ *n* óleo *m*; (*petroleum*) petróleo *m* □ *vt* lubrificar. ~painting *n* pintura *f* a óleo. ~ rig plataforma *f* de poço de petróleo. ~ well poço *m* de petróleo. ~y *a* oleoso; (*food*) gorduroso

oilfield /'ɔɪlfi:ld/ *n* campo *m* petrolífero

oilskins /'ɔɪlskɪnz/ *npl* roupa *f* de oleado

ointment /'ɔɪntmənt/ *n* pomada *f*

OK /əʊ'keɪ/ *a* & *adv* (*collog*) (está) bem, (está) certo, (está) legal

old /əʊld/ *a* (-er, -est) velho; (*person*) velho, idoso; (*former*) antigo. how ~ is he? que idade tem ele? he is eight years ~ ele tem oito anos (de idade). of ~ (d)antes, antigamente. ~ age velhice *f*. ~-age pensioner reformado *m*, aposentado *m*, pessoa *f* de terceira idade. ~ boy antigo aluno *m*. ~-fashioned *a* fora de moda. ~ girl antiga aluna *f*. ~ maid solteirona *f*.

~ man homem *m* idoso, velho *m*. ~
-time *a* antigo. ~ woman mulher *f*
idosa, velha *f*
olive /'ɒlɪv/ *n* azeitona *f* □ *a* de
azeitona. ~ oil azeite *m*
Olympic /ə'lɪmpɪk/ *a* olímpico. ~s
npl Olimpíadas *fpl*. ~ Games Jogos
mpl Olímpicos
omelette /'ɒmlɪt/ *n* omelete *f*
omen /'əʊmən/ *n* agouro *m*, presságio
m
ominous /'ɒmɪnəs/ *a* agourento; (*fig:
threatening*) ameaçador
omit|t /ə'mɪt/ *vt* (*pt* omitted) omitir.
~ssion /-ʃn/ *n* omissão *f*
on /ɒn/ *prep* sobre, em cima de, de, em
□ *adv* para diante, para a frente;
(*switched on*) aceso, ligado; (*tap*) aberto; (*machine*) em funcionamento; (*put
on*) posto; (*happening*) em curso. ~
arrival na chegada, ao chegar. ~
foot *etc* a pé *etc.* ~ doing ao fazer. ~
time na hora, dentro do horário. ~
Tuesday na terça-feira. ~ Tuesdays
às terças-feiras. walk/*etc* ~ continuar a andar/*etc.* be ~ at (*film, TV*)
estar levando *or* passando. ~ and off
de vez em quando. ~ and ~ sem
parar
once /wʌns/ *adv* uma vez; (*formerly*)
noutro(s) tempo(s) □ *conj* uma vez
que, desde que. all at ~ de repente;
(*simultaneously*) todos ao mesmo
tempo. just this ~ só esta vez. ~
(and) for all para sempre. ~ upon
a time era uma vez. ~-over
n (*colloq*) vista *f* de olhos
oncoming /'ɒnkʌmɪŋ/ *a* que se apro-
xima, próximo. the ~ traffic o trânsito que vem do sentido oposto, (*P*) no
sentido contrário
one /wʌn/ *a* um(a); (*sole*) único □ *n*
um(a) *mf* □ *pron* um(a) *mf*; (*impersonal*) se. ~ by ~ um a um. a big/
red/*etc* ~ um grande/vermelho/*etc.*
this/that ~ este/esse. ~ another
um ao outro, uns aos outros. ~-
sided *a* parcial. ~-way *a* (*street*)
mão única; (*ticket*) simples
oneself /wʌn'self/ *pron* si, si mesmo/
próprio; (*reflexive*) se. by ~ sozinho
onion /'ʌnɪən/ *n* cebola *f*
onlooker /'ɒnlʊkə(r)/ *n* espectador *m*,
circunstante *mf*
only /'əʊnlɪ/ *a* único □ *adv* apenas,
só, somente □ *conj* só que. an ~
child um filho único. he ~ has six
ele só tem seis. not ~ ... but also não
só ... mas também. ~ too muito, mais
que
onset /'ɒnset/ *n* começo *m*; (*attack*)
ataque *m*
onslaught /'ɒnslɔːt/ *n* ataque *m* violento, assalto *m*

onward(s) /'ɒnwəd(z)/ *adv* para a
frente/diante
ooze /uːz/ *vt/i* escorrer, verter
opal /'əʊpl/ *n* opala *f*
opaque /əʊ'peɪk/ *a* opaco, tosco
open /'əʊpən/ *a* aberto; (*view*) aberto,
amplo; (*free to all*) aberto ao público;
(*attempt*) franco □ *vt/i* abrir(-se); (*of
shop, play*) abrir. in the ~ air ao ar
livre. keep ~ house receber muito,
abrir a porta para todos. ~ on to dar
para. ~ out *or* up abrir(-se). ~-heart
a (*of surgery*) de coração aberto. ~-
minded *a* imparcial. ~-plan *a* sem
divisórias. ~ secret segredo *m* de
polichinelo. ~ sea mar *m* alto.
~ness *n* abertura *f*; (*frankness*) franqueza *f*
opener /'əʊpənə(r)/ *n* (*tins*) abridor *m*
de latas; (*bottles*) saca-rolhas *m invar*
opening /'əʊpənɪŋ/ *n* abertura *f*; (*beginning*) começo *m*; (*opportunity*)
oportunidade *f*; (*job*) vaga *f*
openly /'əʊpənlɪ/ *adv* abertamente
opera /'ɒprə/ *n* ópera *f*. ~-glasses *npl*
binóculo (de teatro) *m*, (*P*) binóculos
mpl. ~tic /ɒpə'rætɪk/ *a* de ópera
operat|e /'ɒpəreɪt/ *vt/i* operar; (*techn*)
(pôr a) funcionar. ~e on (*med*)
operar. ~ing-theatre *n* (*med*) anfiteatro *m*, sala *f* de operações. ~ion
/-'reɪʃn/ *n* operação *f*. in ~ion em
vigor; (*techn*) em funcionamento.
~ional /'ɒpə'reɪʃənl/ *a* operacional. ~or
n operador *m*; (*telephonist*) telefonista
mf
operative /'ɒpərətɪv/ *a* (*surgical*)
operatório; (*law etc*) em vigor
opinion /ə'pmɪən/ *n* opinião *f*, parecer *m*. in my ~ a meu ver. ~ poll *n*
sondagem (de opinião) *f*. ~ated
/-eɪtɪd/ *a* dogmático
opium /'əʊpɪəm/ *n* ópio *m*
Oporto /ə'pɔːtəʊ/ *n* Porto *m*
opponent /ə'pəʊnənt/ *n* adversário *m*,
antagonista *mf*, oponente *mf*
opportune /'ɒpətjuːn/ *a* oportuno
opportunity /ɒpə'tjuːnətɪ/ *n* oportunidade *f*
oppos|e /ə'pəʊz/ *vt* opor-se a. ~ed to
oposto a. ~ing *a* oposto
opposite /'ɒpəzɪt/ *a & n* oposto (*m*),
contrário (*m*) □ *adv* em frente □ *prep*
~ (to) em frente de
opposition /ɒpə'zɪʃn/ *n* oposição *f*
oppress /ə'pres/ *vt* oprimir. ~ion
/-ʃn/ *n* opressão *f*. ~ive *a* opressivo.
~or *n* opressor *m*
opt /ɒpt/ *vi* ~ for optar por. ~ out
recusar-se a participar (of de). ~ to
do escolher fazer
optical /'ɒptɪkl/ *a* óptico. ~ illusion
ilusão *f* óptica
optician /ɒp'tɪʃn/ *n* oculista *mf*

optimis|t /'ɒptɪmɪst/ n otimista mf.
(P) optimista mf. ~m /-zəm/ n otimismo m, (P) optimismo m. ~tic /-'mɪstɪk/ a otimista, (P) optimista. ~tically /-'mɪstɪklɪ/ adv com otimismo, (P) optimismo

optimum /'ɒptɪməm/ a & n (pl -ima) ótimo (m), (P) óptimo (m)

option /'ɒpʃn/ n escolha f, opção f. have no ~ (but) não ter outro remédio (senão)

optional /'ɒpʃənl/ a opcional, facultativo

opulen|t /'ɒpjʊlənt/ a opulento. ~ce n opulência f

or /ɔː(r)/ conj ou; (with negative) nem. ~ else senão

oracle /'ɒrəkl/ n oráculo m

oral /'ɔːrəl/ a oral

orange /'ɒrɪndʒ/ n laranja f; (colour) laranja m, cor f de laranja □ a de laranja; (colour) alaranjado, cor de laranja

orator /'ɒrətə(r)/ n orador m. ~y n oratória f

orbit /'ɔːbɪt/ n órbita f □ vt (pt orbited) gravitar em torno de

orchard /'ɔːtʃəd/ n pomar m

orchestra /'ɔːkɪstrə/ n orquestra f. ~l /'kestrəl/ a orquestral

orchestrate /'ɔːkɪstreɪt/ vt orquestrar

orchid /'ɔːkɪd/ n orquídea f

ordain /ɔː'deɪn/ vt decretar; (relig) ordenar

ordeal /ɔː'diːl/ n prova f, provação f

order /'ɔːdə(r)/ n ordem f, (comm) encomenda f, pedido m □ vt ordenar; (goods etc) encomendar. in ~ that para que. in ~ to para

orderly /'ɔːdəlɪ/ a ordenado, em ordem; (not unruly) ordeiro □ n (mil) ordenança f; (med) servente m de hospital

ordinary /'ɔːdɪnrɪ/ a normal, ordinário, vulgar. out of the ~ fora do comum

ordination /ɔːdɪ'neɪʃn/ n (relig) ordenação f

ore /ɔː(r)/ n minério m

organ /'ɔːgən/ n órgão m. ~ist n organista mf

organic /ɔː'gænɪk/ a orgânico

organism /'ɔːgənɪzəm/ n organismo m

organiz|e /'ɔːgənaɪz/ vt organizar. ~ation /-'zeɪʃn/ n organização f. ~er n organizador m

orgasm /'ɔːgæzəm/ n orgasmo m

orgy /'ɔːdʒɪ/ n orgia f

Orient /'ɔːrɪənt/ n the ~ o Oriente m. ~al /-'entl/ a & n oriental (mf)

orientat|e /'ɔːrɪənteɪt/ vt orientar. ~ion /-'teɪʃn/ n orientação f

orifice /'ɒrɪfɪs/ n orifício m

origin /'ɒrɪdʒɪn/ n origem f

original /ə'rɪdʒənl/ a original; (not copied) original. ~ity /-'nælətɪ/ n originalidade f. ~ly adv originalmente; (in the beginning) originariamente

originat|e /ə'rɪdʒəneɪt/ vt/i originar (-se). ~e from provir de. ~or n iniciador m, criador m, autor m

ornament /'ɔːnəmənt/ n ornamento m; (object) peça f decorativa. ~al /-'mentl/ a ornamental. ~ation /-ən'teɪʃn/ n ornamentação f

ornate /ɔː'neɪt/ a florido, floreado

ornitholog|y /ɔːnɪ'θɒlədʒɪ/ n ornitologia f. ~ist n ornitólogo m

orphan /'ɔːfn/ n órfão(o) f(m) □ vt deixar órfão. ~age n orfanato m

orthodox /'ɔːθədɒks/ a ortodoxo

orthopaedic /ɔːθə'piːdɪk/ a ortopédico

oscillate /'ɒsɪleɪt/ vi oscilar, vacilar

ostensibl|e /ɒs'tensəbl/ a aparente, pretenso; ~y adv aparentemente

ostentati|on /ɒsten'teɪʃn/ n ostentação f. ~ous /-'teɪʃəs/ a ostentoso, ostensivo

osteopath /'ɒstɪəpæθ/ n osteopata mf

ostracize /'ɒstrəsaɪz/ vt pôr de lado, marginalizar

ostrich /'ɒstrɪtʃ/ n avestruz mf

other /'ʌðə(r)/ a, n & pron outro (m) □ adv ~ than diferente de, senão. (some) ~s outros. the ~ day no outro dia. the ~ one o outro

otherwise /'ʌðəwaɪz/ adv de outro modo □ conj senão, caso contrário

otter /'ɒtə(r)/ n lontra f

ouch /aʊtʃ/ int ai!, ui!

ought /ɔːt/ v aux (pt ought) dever. you ~ to stay devia ficar. he ~ to succeed ele deve vencer. I ~ to have done it eu devia tê-lo feito

ounce /aʊns/ n onça f (= 28,35g)

our /'aʊə(r)/ a nosso(s), nossa(s)

ours /'aʊəz/ poss pron o(s) nosso(s), a(s) nossa(s)

ourselves /aʊə'selvz/ pron nós mesmos/próprios; (reflexive) nos. by ~ sozinhos

oust /aʊst/ vt expulsar, obrigar a sair

out /aʊt/ adv fora; (of light, fire) apagado; (in blossom) aberto, desabrochado; (of tide) baixo. be ~ não estar em casa, estar fora (de casa); (wrong) enganar-se. be ~ to estar resolvido a. run/etc ~ sair correndo/etc. ~-and-~ a completo, rematado. ~ of fora de; (without) sem. ~ of pity/etc por pena/etc. made ~ of feito de or em. take ~ of tirar de. 5 ~ of 6 5 (de) entre 6. ~ of date fora de moda; (not valid) fora do prazo. ~ of doors ao ar livre. ~ of one's mind doido. ~ of order quebrado. ~ of place deslocado. ~ of the way afastado. ~-patient n doente mf de consulta externa

outboard /'autbɔːd/ a ~ motor motor m de popa

outbreak /'autbreik/ n (of flu etc) surto m, epidemia f; (of war) deflagração f

outburst /'autbɜːst/ n explosão f

outcast /'autkɑːst/ n pária m

outcome /'autkʌm/ n resultado m

outcry /'autkraɪ/ n clamor m; (protest) protesto m

outdated /aut'deitid/ a fora da moda, ultrapassado

outdo /aut'duː/ vt (pt -did, pp -done) ultrapassar, superar

outdoor /'autdɔː(r)/ a ao ar livre. ~s /-'dɔːz/ adv fora de casa, ao ar livre

outer /'autə(r)/ a exterior. ~ space espaço (cósmico) m

outfit /'autfit/ n equipamento m; (clothes) roupa f

outgoing /'autgəuɪŋ/ a que vai sair; (of minister etc) demissionário; (fig) sociável. ~s npl despesas fpl

outgrow /aut'grəu/ vt (pt -grew, pp -grown) crescer mais do que; (clothes) já não caber em

outhouse /'authaus/ n anexo m, dependência f

outing /'autɪŋ/ n saída f, passeio m

outlandish /aut'lændɪʃ/ a exótico, estranho

outlaw /'autlɔː/ n fora-da-lei mf, bandido m □ vt banir, proscrever

outlay /'autleɪ/ n despesa(s) f(pl)

outlet /'autlet/ n saída f, escoadouro m; (for goods) mercado m, saída f; (for feelings) escape m, vazão m; (electr) tomada f

outline /'autlaɪn/ n contorno m; (summary) plano m geral, esquema m, esboço m □ vt contornar; (summarize) descrever em linhas gerais

outlive /aut'lɪv/ vt sobreviver a

outlook /'autluk/ n (view) vista f; (mental attitude) visão f; (future prospects) perspectiva(s) f(pl)

outlying /'autlaɪɪŋ/ a afastado, remoto

outnumber /aut'nʌmbə(r)/ vt ultrapassar em número

outpost /'autpəust/ n posto m avançado

output /'autput/ n rendimento m; (of computer) saída f, output m

outrage /'autreidʒ/ n atrocidade f, crime m; (scandal) escândalo m □ vt ultrajar

outrageous /aut'reidʒəs/ a (shocking) escandaloso; (very cruel) atroz

outright /'autraɪt/ adv completamente; (at once) imediatamente;

(frankly) abertamente □ a completo; (refusal) claro

outset /'autset/ n início m, começo m, princípio m

outside¹ /aut'saɪd/ n exterior m □ adv (lá) (por) fora □ prep (para) fora de, além de; (in front of) diante de. at the ~ no máximo

outside² /'autsaɪd/ a exterior

outsider /aut'saɪdə(r)/ n estranho m; (in race) cavalo m com poucas probabilidades, azarão m

outsize /'autsaɪz/ a tamanho extra invar

outskirts /'autskɜːts/ npl arredores mpl, subúrbios mpl

outspoken /aut'spəukn/ a franco

outstanding /aut'stændɪŋ/ a saliente, proeminente; (debt) por saldar; (very good) notável, destacado

outstretched /aut'stretʃt/ a (arm) estendido, esticado

outstrip /aut'strɪp/ vt (pt -stripped) ultrapassar, passar à frente de

outward /'autwəd/ a para o exterior; (sign etc) exterior; (journey) de ida. ~ly adv exteriormente. ~s adv para o exterior

outwit /aut'wɪt/ vt (pt -witted) ser mais esperto que, enganar

oval /'əuvl/ n & a oval (m)

ovary /'əuvərɪ/ n ovário m

ovation /əu'veɪʃn/ n ovação f

oven /'ʌvn/ n forno m

over /'əuvə(r)/ prep sobre, acima de, por cima de; (across) de para o/do outro lado de; (during) durante, em; (more than) mais de □ adv por cima; (too) demais, demasiadamente; (ended) acabado. the film is ~ o filme já acabou. jump/etc ~ saltar/ etc por cima. he has some ~ ele tem uns de sobra. all ~ the country em/ por todo o país. all ~ the table por toda a mesa. ~ and above (besides, in addition to) (para) além de. ~ and ~ repetidas vezes. ~ there ali, lá, acolá

over- /'əuvə(r)/ pref sobre-, super-; (excessively) demais, demasiado

overall¹ /'əuvərɔːl/ n bata f. ~s macacão m, (P) fato-macaco m

overall² /'əuvərɔːl/ a global; (length etc) total □ adv globalmente

overawe /əuvə'ɔː/ vt intimidar

overbalance /əuvə'bæləns/ vt/i (fazer) perder o equilíbrio

overbearing /əuvə'beərɪŋ/ a autoritário, despótico; (arrogant) arrogante

overboard /'əuvəbɔːd/ adv (pela) borda fora

overcast /əuvə'kɑːst/ a encoberto, nublado

overcharge /əuvə'tʃɑːdʒ/ vt ~ sb (for) cobrar demais a alg (por) overcoat /'əʊvəkəʊt/ n casacão m; (for men) sobretudo m

overcome /əʊvə'kʌm/ vt (pt -came, pp -come) superar, vencer. ~ by sucumbindo a, dominado or vencido por

overcrowded /əʊvə'kraʊdɪd/ a apinhado, superlotado; (country) superpovoado

overdo /əʊvə'du:/ vt (pt -did, pp -done) exagerar, levar longe demais. ~ne (culin) cozinhado demais

overdose /'əʊvədəʊs/ n dose f excessiva

overdraft /'əʊvədra:ft/ n saldo m negativo

overdraw /əʊvə'drɔ:/ vt (pt -drew, -drawn) sacar a descoberto

overdue /əʊvə'dju:/ a em atraso, atrasado; (belated) tardio

overestimate /əʊvər'estɪmeɪt/ vt sobreestimar, atribuir valor excessivo a

overexpose /əʊvərɪk'spəʊz/ vt expor demais

overflow¹ /əʊvə'fləʊ/ vt/i extravasar, transbordar (with de)

overflow² /'əʊvəfləʊ/ n (outlet) descarga f; (excess) excesso m

overgrown /əʊvə'grəʊn/ a que cresceu demais; (garden etc) invadido pela vegetação

overhang /əʊvə'hæŋ/ vt (pt -hung) estar sobranceiro a, pairar sobre □ vi projetar-se, (P) projectar-se para fora □ n saliência f

overhaul¹ /əʊvə'hɔ:l/ vt fazer uma revisão em

overhaul² /'əʊvəhɔ:l/ n revisão f

overhead¹ /əʊvə'hed/ adv em or por cima, ao or no alto

overhead² /'əʊvəhed/ a aéreo. ~s npl despesas fpl gerais

overhear /əʊvə'hɪə(r)/ vt (pt -heard) (eavesdrop) ouvir sem conhecimento do falante; (hear by chance) ouvir por acaso

overjoyed /əʊvə'dʒɔɪd/ a radiante, felicíssimo

overlap /əʊvə'læp/ vt/i (pt -lapped) sobrepor(-se) parcialmente, (fig) coincidir

overleaf /əʊvə'li:f/ adv no verso

overload /əʊvə'ləʊd/ vt sobrecarregar

overlook /əʊvə'lʊk/ vt deixar passar; (of window) dar para; (of building) dominar

overnight /əʊvə'naɪt/ adv durante a noite; (fig) dum dia para o outro □ a (train) da noite; (stay, journey, etc) noite, noturno; (fig) súbito

overpass /əʊvə'pɑ:s/ n passagem f superior

overpay /əʊvə'peɪ/ vt (pt -paid) pagar em excesso

overpower /əʊvə'paʊə(r)/ vt dominar, subjugar; (fig) esmagar. ~ing a esmagador; (heat) sufocante, insuportável

overpriced /əʊvə'praɪst/ a muito caro

overrate /əʊvə'reɪt/ vt sobreestimar, exagerar o valor de

override /əʊvə'raɪd/ vt (pt -rode, pp -ridden) prevalecer sobre, passar por cima de. ~ing a primordial, preponderante; (importance) maior

overripe /'əʊvəraɪp/ a demasiado maduro

overrule /əʊvə'ru:l/ vt anular, rejeitar; (claim) indeferir

overrun /əʊvə'rʌn/ vt (pt -ran, pp -run, pres p -running) invadir; (a limit) exceder, ultrapassar

overseas /əʊvə'si:z/ a ultramarino; (abroad) estrangeiro □ adv no ultramar, no estrangeiro

oversee /əʊvə'si:/ vt (pt -saw pp -seen) supervisionar. ~r /'əʊvəsɪə(r)/ n capataz m

overshadow /əʊvə'ʃædəʊ/ vt (fig) eclipsar, ofuscar

oversight /'əʊvəsaɪt/ n lapso m

oversleep /əʊvə'sli:p/ vi (pt -slept) acordar tarde, dormir demais

overt /'əʊvɜ:t/ a manifesto, claro, patente

overtake /əʊvə'teɪk/ vt/i (pt -took, pp -taken) ultrapassar

overthrow /əʊvə'θrəʊ/ vt (pt -threw, pp -thrown) derrubar □ n /'əʊvəθrəʊ/ (pol) derrubada f

overtime /'əʊvətaɪm/ n horas fpl extras

overtones /'əʊvətəʊnz/ npl (fig) tom m, implicação f

overture /'əʊvətjʊə(r)/ n (mus) abertura f; (fig) proposta f, abordagem f

overturn /əʊvə'tɜ:n/ vt/i virar(-se); (car, plane) capotar, virar-se

overweight /əʊvə'weɪt/ a be ~ ter excesso de peso

overwhelm /əʊvə'welm/ vt oprimir; (defeat) esmagar; (amaze) assoberbar. ~ing a esmagador; (urge) irresistível

overwork /əʊvə'wɜ:k/ vt/i sobrecarregar(-se) com trabalho □ n excesso m de trabalho

overwrought /əʊvə'rɔ:t/ a muito agitado, superexcitado

ow|e /əʊ/ vt dever. ~ing a devido. ~ing to devido a

owl /aʊl/ n coruja f

own¹ /əʊn/ a próprio. a house/etc of one's ~ uma casa/etc própria. get one's ~ back (colloq) ir à forra, (P) desforrar-se. hold one's ~ agüentar-se, (P) aguentar-se. on one's ~ sozinho

own² /əʊn/ vt possuir. ~ up (to) (colloq) confessar. ~er n proprietário m, dono m. ~ership n posse f, propriedade f

ox /ɒks/ n (pl oxen) boi m

oxygen /'ɒksɪdʒən/ n oxigénio m, (P) oxigénio m

oyster /'ɔɪstə(r)/ n ostra f

ozone /'əʊzəʊn/ n ozónio m, (P) ozono m. ~ layer camada f de ozónio, (P) ozono m

P

pace /peɪs/ n passo m; (fig) ritmo m □ vt percorrer passo a passo □ vi ~ up and down andar de um lado para o outro. keep ~ with acompanhar, manter-se a par de

pacemaker /'peɪsmeɪkə(r)/ n (med) marcapasso m, (P) pacemaker m

Pacific /pə'sɪfɪk/ a pacífico □ n ~ (Ocean) (Oceano) Pacifico m

pacifist /'pæsɪfɪst/ n pacifista mf

pacify /'pæsɪfaɪ/ vt pacificar, apaziguar

pack /pæk/ n pacote m; (mil) mochila f; (of hounds) matilha f; (of lies) porção f; (of cards) baralho m □ vt empacotar; (suitcase) fazer; (box, room) encher; (press down) atulhar; enher até não caber mais □ vi fazer as malas. ~ into (cram) apinhar em, comprimir em. send ~ing pôr a andar, mandar passear. ~ed a apinhado. ~ed lunch merenda f

package /'pækɪdʒ/ n pacote m, embrulho m □ vt embalar. ~ deal pacote m de propostas. ~ holiday pacote m turístico, (P) viagem f organizada

packet /'pækɪt/ n pacote m; (of cigarettes) maço m

pact /pækt/ n pacto m

pad /pæd/ n (in clothing) chumaço m; (for writing) bloco m de papel/de notas; (for ink) almofada f (de carimbo) f. (launching) ~ rampa f de lançamento □ vt (pt padded) enchumaçar, acolchoar; (fig: essay etc) encher linguiça. ~ding n chumaço m; (fig) linguiça f

paddle¹ /'pædl/ n remo m de canoa. ~-steamer n vapor m movido a rodas

paddle² /'pædl/ vi chapinhar, molhar os pés. ~ing pool piscina f de plástico para crianças

paddock /'pædək/ n cercado m; (at racecourse) paddock m

padlock /'pædlɒk/ n cadeado m □ vt fechar com cadeado

paediatrician /pi:dɪə'trɪʃn/ n pediatra mf

pagan /'peɪgən/ a & n pagão (m), pagã (f)

page¹ /peɪdʒ/ n (of book etc) página f

page² /peɪdʒ/ vt mandar chamar

pageant /'pædʒənt/ n espetáculo m, (P) espectáculo m (histórico); (procession) cortejo m. ~ry n pompa f

pagoda /pə'gəʊdə/ n pagode m

paid /peɪd/ see pay □ a put ~ to (colloq: end) pôr fim a

pail /peɪl/ n balde m

pain /peɪn/ n dor f. ~s esforços mpl □ vt magoar. be in ~ sofrer, ter dores. ~-killer n analgésico m. take ~s to esforçar-se por. ~ful a doloroso; (grievous, laborious) penoso. ~less a sem dor, indolor

painstaking /'peɪnzteɪkɪŋ/ a cuidadoso, esmerado, meticuloso

paint /peɪnt/ n tinta f. ~s (in box) tintas fpl □ vt/i pintar. ~er n pintor m. ~ing n pintura f

paintbrush /'peɪntbrʌʃ/ n pincel m

pair /peə(r)/ n par m. a ~ of scissors uma tesoura. a ~ of trousers um par de calças. in ~s aos pares □ vi ~ off formar pares

Pakistan /pa:kɪ'sta:n/ n Paquistão m. ~i a & n paquistanês (m)

pal /pæl/ n (colloq) colega mf, amigo m

palace /'pælɪs/ n palácio m

palat|e /'pælət/ n palato m. ~able a saboroso, gostoso; (fig) agradável

palatial /pə'leɪʃl/ a suntuoso, (P) sumptuoso

pale /peɪl/ a (-er, -est) pálido; (colour) claro □ vi empalidecer. ~ness n palidez f

Palestin|e /'pælɪstaɪn/ n Palestina f. ~ian /-'stɪnɪən/ a & n palestino (m)

palette /'pælɪt/ n paleta f. ~-knife n espátula f

pall /pɔ:l/ vi tornar-se enfadonho, perder o interesse (on para)

pallid /'pælɪd/ a pálido

palm /pa:m/ n (of hand) palma f; (tree) palmeira f □ vt ~ off impingir (on a). P~ Sunday Domingo m de Ramos

palpable /'pælpəbl/ a palpável

palpitat|e /'pælpɪtett/ vi palpitar. ~ion /-'teɪʃn/ n palpitação f

paltry /'pɔ:ltrɪ/ a (-ier, -iest) irrisório

pamper /'pæmpə(r)/ vt mimar, paparicar

pamphlet /'pæmflɪt/ n panfleto m, folheto m

pan /pæn/ n panela f; (for frying) frigideira f □ vt (pt panned) (colloq) criticar severamente

panacea /pænə'sɪə/ n panacéia f

panache /pæ'næʃ/ n brio m, estilo m, panache m

pancake /'pænkeɪk/ n crepe m, panqueca f

pancreas /'pæŋkrɪəs/ n pâncreas m

panda /'pændə/ n panda m

pandemonium /pændɪ'məʊnɪəm/ n pandemónio m, (P) pandemónio m, caos m

pander /'pændə(r)/ vi ~ to prestar-se a servir, ir ao encontro de, fazer concessões a

pane /peɪn/ n vidraça f

panel /'pænl/ n painel m; (jury) júri m; (speakers) convidados mpl. (instrument) ~ painel m de instrumentos, (P) de bordo. ~led a apainelado. ~ling n apainelamento m. ~list n convidado m

pang /pæŋ/ n pontada f, dor f aguda e súbita. ~s (of hunger) ataques mpl de fome. ~s of conscience remorsos mpl

panic /'pænɪk/ n pânico m □ vt/i (pt panicked) desorientar(-se), (fazer) entrar em pânico. ~-stricken a tomado de pânico

panoram|a /pænə'ra:mə/ n panorama m. ~ic /-'ræmɪk/ a panorâmico

pansy /'pænzɪ/ n amor-perfeito m

pant /pænt/ vi ofegar, arquejar

panther /'pænθə(r)/ n pantera f

panties /'pæntɪz/ npl (collog) calcinhas fpl

pantomime /'pæntəmaɪm/ n pantomima f

pantry /'pæntrɪ/ n despensa f

pants /pænts/ npl (collog: underwear) cuecas fpl; (collog: trousers) calças fpl

papal /'peɪpl/ a papal

paper /'peɪpə(r)/ n papel m; (newspaper) jornal m; (exam) prova f escrita; (essay) comunicação f. ~s npl (for identification) documentos mpl □ vt forrar com papel. on ~ por escrito. ~-clip n clipe m

paperback /'peɪpəbæk/ a & n ~ (book) livro m de capa mole

paperweight /'peɪpəweɪt/ n pesapapéis m invar, (P) pisa-papéis m invar

paperwork /'peɪpəwɜːk/ n trabalho m de secretária; (pej) papelada f

paprika /'pæprɪkə/ n páprica f, pimentão m doce

par /pa:(r)/ n be below ~ estar abaixo do padrão desejado. on a ~ with em igualdade com

parable /'pærəbl/ n parábola f

parachut|e /'pærəʃu:t/ n pára-quedas m invar □ vi descer de pára-quedas. ~ist n pára-quedista mf

parade /pə'reɪd/ n (mil) parada f militar; (procession) procissão f □ vi desfilar □ vt alardear, exibir

paradise /'pærədaɪs/ n paraíso m

paradox /'pærədɒks/ n paradoxo m. ~ical /-'dɒksɪkl/ a paradoxal

paraffin /'pærəfɪn/ n querosene m, (P) petróleo m

paragon /'pærəgən/ n modelo m de perfeição

paragraph /'pærəgra:f/ n parágrafo m

parallel /'pærəlel/ a & n paralelo (m) □ vt (pt parelleled) comparar(-se)

paralyse /'pærəlaɪz/ vt paralisar

paraly|sis /pə'ræləsɪs/ n paralisia f. ~tic /-'lɪtɪk/ a & n paralítico (m)

parameter /pə'ræmɪtə(r)/ n parâmetro m

paramount /'pærəmaʊnt/ a supremo, primordial

parapet /'pærəpɪt/ n parapeito m

paraphernalia /pærəfə'neɪlɪə/ n equipamento m, tralha f (collog)

paraphrase /'pærəfreɪz/ n paráfrase f □ vt parafrasear

paraplegic /pærə'pli:dʒɪk/ n paraplégico m

parasite /'pærəsaɪt/ n parasita mf

parasol /'pærəsɒl/ n sombrinha f; (on table) pára-sol m, guarda-sol m

parcel /'pa:sl/ n embrulho m; (for post) encomenda f

parch /pa:tʃ/ vt ressecar. be ~ed estar com muita sede

parchment /'pa:tʃmənt/ n pergaminho m

pardon /'pa:dn/ n perdão m; (jur) perdão m, indulto m □ vt (pt pardoned) perdoar. I beg your ~ perdão, desculpe. (I beg your) ~? como?

pare /peə(r)/ vt aparar, cortar; (peel) descascar

parent /'peərənt/ n pai m, mãe f. ~s npl pais mpl. ~al /pə'rentl/ a dos pais, paterno, materno

parenthesis /pə'renθəsɪs/ n (pl -theses) /-si:z/ parêntese m, parêntesis m

Paris /'pærɪs/ n Paris m

parish /'pærɪʃ/ n paróquia f; (municipal) freguesia f. ~ioner /pə-'rɪʃənə(r)/ n paroquiano m

parity /'pærətɪ/ n paridade f

park /pa:k/ n parque m □ vt estacionar. ~ing n estacionamento m. no ~ing estacionamento proibido. ~ing-meter n parquímetro m

parliament /'pa:ləmənt/ n parlamento m, assembleia f. ~ary /-'mentrɪ/ a parlamentar

parochial /pə'rəʊkɪəl/ a paroquial; (fig) provinciano, tacanho

parody /'pærədɪ/ n paródia f □ vt parodiar

parole /pə'rəʊl/ n on ~ em liberdade condicional □ vt pôr em liberdade condicional

parquet /'pa:keɪ/ n parquê m, parquete m

parrot /'pærət/ n papagaio m

parry /'pærɪ/ vt (a)parar □ n parada f

parsimonious /pa:sɪ'məʊnɪəs/ a parco; (mean) avarento

parsley /'pa:slɪ/ n salsa f

parsnip /'pa:snɪp/ n cherovia f, pastinaga f

parson /'pa:sn/ n pároco m, pastor m

part /pa:t/ n parte f; (of serial) episódio m; (of machine) peça f; (theatre) papel m; (side in dispute) partido m □ a parcial □ adv em parte □ vt/i separar (-se) (from de). in ~ em parte. on the ~ of da parte de. ~ exchange n troca f parcial. ~ of speech categoria f gramatical. ~time a & adv a tempo parcial, part-time. take ~ in tomar parte em. these ~s estas partes

partial /'pa:ʃl/ a (incomplete, biased) parcial. be ~ to gostar de. ~ity /-ɪ'ælətɪ/ n parcialidade f; (liking) predileção f, (P) predilecção f (for por). ~ly adv parcialmente

participate /pa:'tɪsɪpeɪt/ vi participar (in em). ~ant n /-ənt/ participante mf. ~ation /-'peɪʃn/ n participação f

participle /'pa:tɪsɪpl/ n particípio m

particle /'pa:tɪkl/ n partícula f; (of dust) grão m; (fig) mínimo m

particular /pə'tɪkjʊlə(r)/ a especial, particular; (fussy) exigente; (careful) escrupuloso. ~s npl pormenores mpl. in ~ adv em especial, particularmente. ~ly adv particularmente

parting /'pa:tɪŋ/ n separação f; (in hair) risca f □ a de despedida

partisan /pa:tɪ'zæn/ n partidário m; (mil) guerrilheiro m

partition /pa:'tɪʃn/ n (of room) tabique m, divisória f, (pol: division) partilha f, divisão f □ vt dividir, repartir. ~ off dividir por meio de tabique

partly /'pa:tlɪ/ adv em parte

partner /'pa:tnə(r)/ n sócio m; (cards, sport) parceiro m; (dancing) par m. ~ship n associação f; (comm) sociedade f

partridge /'pa:trɪdʒ/ n perdiz f

party /'pa:tɪ/ n festa f, reunião f; (group) grupo m; (pol) partido m; (jur) parte f. ~ line (telephone) linha f coletiva, (P) colectiva

pass /pa:s/ vt/i (pt passed) passar; (overtake) ultrapassar; (exam) passar; (approve) passar; (law) aprovar. ~ (by) passar por □ n (permit, sport) passe m; (geog) desfiladeiro m, garganta f; (in exam) aprovação f. make a ~ at (colloq) atirar-se para (colloq). ~ away falecer. ~ out or round distribuir. ~ out (colloq: faint) perder os sentidos, desmaiar. ~ over (disre-

gard, overlook) passar por cima de. ~ up (colloq: forgo) deixar perder

passable /'pa:səbl/ a passável; (road) transitável

passage /'pæsɪdʒ/ n passagem f; (voyage) travessia f; (corridor) corredor m, passagem f

passenger /'pæsɪndʒə(r)/ n passageiro m

passer-by /pa:sə'baɪ/ n (pl passersby) transeunte mf

passion /'pæʃn/ n paixão f. ~ate a apaixonado, exaltado

passive /'pæsɪv/ a passivo. ~ness n passividade f

Passover /'pa:səʊvə(r)/ n Páscoa f dos judeus

passport /'pa:spɔ:t/ n passaporte m

password /'pa:swɜ:d/ n senha f

past /pa:st/ a passado; (former) antigo □ n passado □ prep para além de; (in time) mais de; (in front of) diante de □ adv em frente de. ~ it já não ser capaz. it's five ~ eleven são cinco e cinco. these ~ months estes últimos meses

pasta /'pæstə/ n prato m de massa(s)

paste /peɪst/ n cola f; (culin) massa(s) f(pl); (dough) massa f; (jewellery) strass m □ vt colar

pastel /'pæstl/ n pastel m □ a pastel invar

pasteurize /'pæstʃəraɪz/ vt pasteurizar

pastille /'pæstɪl/ n pastilha f

pastime /'pa:staɪm/ n passatempo m

pastoral /'pa:stərəl/ a & n pastoral (f)

pastry /'peɪstrɪ/ n massa f (de pastelaria); (tart) pastel m

pasture /'pa:stʃə(r)/ n pastagem f

pasty[1] /'pæstɪ/ n empadinha f

pasty[2] /'peɪstɪ/ a pastoso

pat /pæt/ vt (pt patted) (hit gently) dar pancadinhas em; (caress) fazer festinhas a □ n pancadinha f; (caress) festinha f □ adv a propósito; (readily) prontamente □ a preparado, pronto

patch /pætʃ/ n remendo m; (over eye) tapa-olho m; (spot) mancha f; (small area) pedaço m; (of vegetables) canteiro m, (P) leira f □ vt ~ up remendar. ~ up a quarrel fazer as pazes. bad ~ mau bocado m. not be a ~ on não chegar aos pés de. ~work n obra f de retalhos. ~y a desigual

pâté /'pæteɪ/ n patê m

patent /'peɪtnt/ a & n patente (f) □ vt patentear. ~ leather verniz m, polimento m. ~ly adv claramente

paternal /pə'tɜ:nl/ a paternal; (relative) paterno

paternity /pə'tɜ:nətɪ/ n paternidade f

path /pa:θ/ n (pl -s /pa:ðz/) caminho m, trilha f; (in park) aléia f; (of rocket) trajetória f, (P) trajectória f

pathetic /pə'θetɪk/ a patético; (colloq: contemptible) desgraçado (colloq)

patholog|y /pə'θɒlədʒɪ/ n patologia f. ~ist n patologista mf

pathos /'peɪθɒs/ n patos m, patético m

patience /'peɪʃns/ n paciência f

patient /'peɪʃnt/ a paciente □ n doente mf, paciente mf. ~ly adv pacientemente

patio /'pætɪəʊ/ n (pl -os) pátio m

patriot /'pætrɪət/ n patriota mf. ~ic /-'ɒtɪk/ a patriótico. ~ism /-ɪzəm/ n patriotismo m

patrol /pə'trəʊl/ n patrulha f □ vt/i patrulhar. ~ car carro m de patrulha

patron /'peɪtrən/ n (of the arts etc) patrocinador m, protetor m, (P) protector m; (of charity) benfeitor m; (customer) freguês m, cliente mf. ~ saint padroeiro m, patrono m

patron|age /'pætrənɪdʒ/ n freguesia f, clientela f; (support) patrocínio m. ~ize vt ser cliente de; (support) patrocinar; (condescend) tratar com ares de superioridade

patter¹ /'pætə(r)/ n (of rain) tamborilar m, rufo m. ~ of steps som m leve de passos miúdos, corridinha f leve

patter² /'pætə(r)/ n (of class, profession) gíria f, jargão m; (chatter) conversa f fiada

pattern /'pætn/ n padrão m; (for sewing) molde m; (example) modelo m

paunch /pɔ:ntʃ/ n pança f

pause /pɔ:z/ n pausa f □ vi pausar, fazer (uma) pausa

pav|e /peɪv/ vt pavimentar. ~e the way preparar o caminho (for para). ~ing-stone n paralelepípedo m, laje f

pavement /'peɪvmənt/ n passeio m

pavilion /pə'vɪlɪən/ n pavilhão m

paw /pɔ:/ n pata f □ vt dar patadas em; (horse) escarvar; (colloq: person) pôr as patas em cima de

pawn¹ /pɔ:n/ n (chess) peão m; (fig) joguete m

pawn² /pɔ:n/ vt empenhar. ~-shop casa f de penhores, prego m (colloq)

pawnbroker /'pɔ:nbrəʊkə(r)/ n penhorista mf, dono m de casa de penhores, agiota mf

pay /peɪ/ vt/i (pt paid) pagar; (interest) render; (visit, compliment) fazer □ n pagamento m; (wages) vencimento m, ordenado m, salário m. in the ~ of em pagamento de. ~ attention prestar atenção. ~ back restituir. ~ for pagar. ~ homage prestar homenagem. ~ in depositar. ~-slip n contracheque m, (P) folha f de pagamento

payable /'peɪəbl/ a pagável

payment /'peɪmənt/ n pagamento m; (fig: reward) recompensa f

payroll /'peɪrəʊl/ n folha f de pagamentos. be on the ~ fazer parte da folha de pagamento de uma firma

pea /pi:/ n ervilha f

peace /pi:s/ n paz f. disturb the ~ perturbar a ordem pública. ~able a pacífico

peaceful /'pi:sfl/ a pacífico; (calm) calmo, sereno

peacemaker /'pi:smeɪkə(r)/ n mediador m, pacificador m

peach /pi:tʃ/ n pêssego m

peacock /'pi:kɒk/ n pavão m

peak /pi:k/ n pico m, cume m, cimo m; (of cap) pala f; (maximum) máximo m. ~ hours horas fpl de ponta; (electr) horas fpl de carga máxima. ~ed cap boné m de pala

peaky /'pi:kɪ/ a com ar doentio

peal /pi:l/ n (of bells) repique m; (of laughter) gargalhada f, risada f

peanut /'pi:nʌt/ n amendoim m. ~s (sl: small sum) uma bagatela f

pear /peə(r)/ n pera f

pearl /pɜ:l/ n pérola f. ~y a nacarado

peasant /'peznt/ n camponês m, aldeão m

peat /pi:t/ n turfa f

pebble /'pebl/ n seixo m, calhau m

peck /pek/ vt/i bicar; (attack) dar bicadas (em) □ n bicada f; (colloq: kiss) beijo m seco. ~ing order hierarquia f, ordem f de importância

peckish /'pekɪʃ/ a be ~ (colloq) ter vontade de comer

peculiar /pɪ'kju:lɪə(r)/ a bizarro, singular; (special) peculiar (to a), característico (to de). ~ity /-'ærətɪ/ n singularidade f; (feature) peculiaridade f

pedal /'pedl/ n pedal m □ vi (pt pedalled) pedalar

pedantic /pɪ'dæntɪk/ a pedante

peddle /'pedl/ vt vender de porta em porta; (drugs) fazer tráfico de

pedestal /'pedɪstl/ n pedestal m

pedestrian /pɪ'destrɪən/ n pedestre mf, (P) peão m □ a pedestre; (fig) prosaico. ~ crossing faixa f para pedestres, (P) passadeira f

pedigree /'pedɪgri:/ n estirpe f, linhagem f; (of animal) raça f □ a de raça

pedlar /'pedlə(r)/ n vendedor m ambulante

peek /pi:k/ vi espreitar □ n espreitadela f

peel /pi:l/ n casca f □ vt descascar □ vi (skin) pelar; (paint) escamar-se, descascar; (wallpaper) descolar-se. ~ings npl cascas fpl

peep /pi:p/ vi espreitar □ n espreitadela *f*. ~-hole *n* vigia *f*; (*in door*) olho *m* mágico

peer¹ /pɪə(r)/ *vi* ~ at/into (*searchingly*) perscrutar; (*with difficulty*) esforçar-se por ver

peer² /pɪə(r)/ *n* (*equal, noble*) par *m*. ~age *n* pariato *m*

peeved /piːvd/ *a* (*sl*) irritado, chateado (*sl*)

peevish /ˈpiːvɪʃ/ *a* irritável

peg /peg/ *n* cavilha *f*; (*for washing*) pregador *m* de roupa, (*P*) mola *f*; (*for coats etc*) cabide *m*; (*for tent*) □ *vt* (*pt* pegged) prender com estacas. off the ~ prêt-à-porter

pejorative /prɪˈdʒɒrətɪv/ *a* pejorativo

pelican /ˈpelɪkən/ *n* pelicano *m*. ~ crossing passagem *f* com sinais manobrados pelos pedestres

pellet /ˈpelɪt/ *n* bolinha *f*; (*for gun*) grão *m* de chumbo

pelt¹ /pelt/ *n* pele *f*

pelt² /pelt/ *vt* bombardear (with com) □ *vi* chover a cântaros; (*run fast*) correr em disparada

pelvis /ˈpelvɪs/ *n* (*anat*) pélvis *m*, bacia *f*

pen¹ /pen/ *n* (*enclosure*) cercado *m*. play-~ *n* cercado *m*, (*P*) pargue *m* □ *vt* (*pt* penned) encurralar

pen² /pen/ *n* caneta *f* □ *vt* (*pt* penned) escrever; ~-friend *n* correspondente *mf*. ~-name *n* pseudónimo *m*, (*P*) pseudónimo *m*

penal /ˈpiːnl/ *a* penal. ~ize *vt* impôr uma penalidadea; (*sport*) penalizar

penalty /ˈpenltɪ/ *n* pena *f*; (*fine*) multa *f*; (*sport*) penalidade *f*. ~ kick pênalti *m*, (*P*) grande penalidade *f*

penance /ˈpenəns/ *n* penitência *f*

pence /pens/ *see* penny

pencil /ˈpensl/ *n* lápis *m* □ *vt* (*pt* pencilled) escrever *or* desenhar a lápis. ~-sharpener *n* apontador *m*, (*P*) apara-lápis *m invar*

pendant /ˈpendənt/ *n* berloque *m*

pending /ˈpendɪŋ/ *a* pendente □ *prep* (*during*) durante; (*until*) até

pendulum /ˈpendjʊləm/ *n* pêndulo *m*

penetrat|e /ˈpenɪtreɪt/ *vt/i* penetrar (em). ~ing *a* penetrante. ~ion /-ˈtreɪʃn/ *n* penetração *f*

penguin /ˈpeŋgwɪn/ *n* pingüim *m*, (*P*) pinguim *m*

penicillin /penɪˈsɪlɪn/ *n* penicilina *f*

peninsula /pəˈnɪnsjʊlə/ *n* península *f*

penis /ˈpiːnɪs/ *n* pênis *m*, (*P*) pénis *m*

peniten|t /ˈpenɪtənt/ *a* & *n* penitente (*mf*). ~ce *n* /-əns/ contrição *f*, penitência *f*

penitentiary /penɪˈtenʃərɪ/ *n* (*Amer*) penitenciária *f*, cadeia *f*

penknife /ˈpennaɪf/ *n* (*pl* -knives) canivete *m*

penniless /ˈpenɪlɪs/ *a* sem vintém, sem um tostão

penny /ˈpenɪ/ *n* (*pl* pennies *or* pence) péni *m*, (*P*) péni *m*; (*fig*) centavo *m*, vintém *m*

pension /ˈpenʃn/ *n* pensão *f*; (*in retirement*) aposentadoria *f*, (*P*) reforma *f* □ *vt* ~ off reformar, aposentar. ~er *n* (*old-age*) ~er reformado *m*

pensive /ˈpensɪv/ *a* pensativo

Pentecost /ˈpentɪkɒst/ *n* Pentecostes *m*

penthouse /ˈpenthaʊs/ *n* cobertura *f*, (*P*) apartamento *m* de luxo (no último andar)

pent-up /ˈpentʌp/ *a* reprimido

penultimate /penˈʌltɪmət/ *a* penúltimo

people /ˈpiːpl/ *npl* pessoas *fpl* □ *n* gente *f*, povo *m* □ *vt* povoar. the Portuguese ~ os portugueses *mpl*. ~ say dizem, diz-se

pep /pep/ *n* vigor *m* □ *vt* ~ up animar. ~ talk discurso *m* de encorajamento

pepper /ˈpepə(r)/ *n* pimenta *f*; (*vegetable*) pimentão *m*, (*P*) pimento *m* □ *vt* apimentar. ~y *a* apimentado, picante

peppermint /ˈpepəmɪnt/ *n* hortelã-pimenta *f*; (*sweet*) bala *f*, (*P*) pastilha *f* de hortelã-pimenta

per /pɜː(r)/ *prep* por. ~ annum por ano. ~ cent por cento. ~ kilo/etc o quilo/etc

perceive /pəˈsiːv/ *vt* perceber; (*notice*) aperceber-se de

percentage /pəˈsentɪdʒ/ *n* percentagem *f*

perceptible /pəˈseptəbl/ *a* perceptível

percept|ion /pəˈsepʃn/ *n* percepção *f*. ~ive /-tɪv/ *a* perceptivo, penetrante, perspicaz

perch¹ /pɜːtʃ/ *n* poleiro *m* □ *vi* empoleirar-se, pousar

perch² /pɜːtʃ/ *n* (*fish*) perca *f*

percolat|e /ˈpɜːkəleɪt/ *vt/i* filtrar(-se), passar. ~or *n* máquina *f* de café com filtro, cafeteira *f*

percussion /pəˈkʌʃn/ *n* percussão *f*

peremptory /pəˈremptərɪ/ *a* peremptório, decisivo

perennial /pəˈrenɪəl/ *a* perene; (*plant*) perene

perfect¹ /ˈpɜːfɪkt/ *a* perfeito. ~ly *adv* perfeitamente

perfect² /pəˈfekt/ *vt* aperfeiçoar. ~ion /-ʃn/ *n* perfeição *f*. ~ionist *n* perfeccionista *mf*

perforat|e /ˈpɜːfəreɪt/ *vt* perfurar. ~ion /ˈreɪʃn/ *n* perfuração *f*; (*line of holes*) pontilhado *m*, picotado *m*

perform /pəˈfɔːm/ *vt* (*a task; mus*) executar; (*a function; theat*) desempenhar □ *vi* representar; (*function*) funcionar. ~ance *n* (*of task; mus*) execução f; (of function; theat) desempenho m; (of car) performance f, comportamento m, rendimento m; (colloq: fuss) drama m, cena f. ~er n artista mf

perfume /'pɜːfjuːm/ n perfume m

perfunctory /pəˈfʌŋktəri/ a superficial, negligente

perhaps /pəˈhæps/ adv talvez

peril /'perəl/ n perigo m. ~ous a perigoso

perimeter /pəˈrɪmɪtə(r)/ n perímetro m

period /'pɪərɪəd/ n período m, época f; (era) época f; (lesson) hora f de aula, período m letivo, (P) lectivo; (med) período m; (full stop) ponto (final) m □ a (of novel) de costumes; (of furniture) de estilo. ~ic /-ˈɒdɪk/ a periódico. ~ical /-ˈɒdɪkl/ n periódico m. ~ically /-ˈɒdɪklɪ/ adv periodicamente

peripher|y /pəˈrɪfərɪ/ n periferia f. ~al a periférico; (fig) marginal, à margem

perish /'perɪʃ/ vi morrer, perecer; (rot) estragar-se, deteriorar-se. ~able a (of goods) deteriorável

perjur|e /'pɜːdʒə(r)/ vpr ~e o.s. jurar falso, perjurar. ~y n perjúrio m

perk[1] /pɜːk/ vt/i ~ up (colloq) arrebitar(-se). ~y a (colloq) vivo, animado

perk[2] /pɜːk/ n (colloq) regalia f, extra m

perm /pɜːm/ n permanente f □ vt have one's hair ~ed fazer uma permanente

permanen|t /'pɜːmənənt/ a permanente. ~ce n permanência f. ~tly adv permanentemente, a título permanente

permeable /'pɜːmɪəbl/ a permeável

permeate /'pɜːmɪeɪt/ vt/i permear, penetrar

permissible /pəˈmɪsəbl/ a permissível, admissível

permission /pəˈmɪʃn/ n permissão f, licença f

permissive /pəˈmɪsɪv/ a permissivo. ~ society sociedade f permissiva. ~ness n permissividade f

permit[1] /pəˈmɪt/ vt (pt permitted) permitir, consentir (sb to a alguém que)

permit[2] /'pɜːmɪt/ n licença f; (pass) passe m

permutation /pɜːmjuːˈteɪʃn/ n permutação f

pernicious /pəˈnɪʃəs/ a pernicioso, prejudicial

perpendicular /pɜːpənˈdɪkjʊlə(r)/ a & n perpendicular (f)

perpetrat|e /'pɜːpɪtreɪt/ vt perpetrar. ~or n autor m

perpetual /pəˈpetʃʊəl/ a perpétuo

perpetuate /pəˈpetʃʊeɪt/ vt perpetuar

perplex /pəˈpleks/ vt deixar perplexo. ~ed a perplexo. ~ing a confuso. ~ity n perplexidade f

persecut|e /'pɜːsɪkjuːt/ vt perseguir. ~ion n /-ˈkjuːʃn/ n perseguição f

persever|e /pɜːsɪˈvɪə(r)/ vi perseverar. ~ance n perseverança f

Persian /'pɜːʃn/ a & n (lang) persa (m)

persist /pəˈsɪst/ vi persistir (in doing em fazer). ~ence n persistência f. ~ent a persistente; (obstinate) teimoso; (continual) contínuo, constante. ~ently adv persistentemente

person /'pɜːsn/ n pessoa f. in ~ em pessoa

personal /'pɜːsənl/ a pessoal; (secretary) particular. ~ stereo estereo m pessoal. ~ly adv pessoalmente

personality /pɜːsəˈnælətɪ/ n personalidade f; (on TV) vedete f

personify /pəˈsɒnɪfaɪ/ vt personificar

personnel /pɜːsəˈnel/ n pessoal m

perspective /pəˈspektɪv/ n perspectiva f

perspir|e /pəˈspaɪə(r)/ vi transpirar. ~ation /-ˈreɪʃn/ n transpiração f

persua|de /pəˈsweɪd/ vt persuadir (to a). ~sion n /-ˈsweɪʒn/ n persuasão f; (belief) crença f, convicção f. ~sive /-ˈsweɪsɪv/ a persuasivo

pert /pɜːt/ a (saucy) atrevido, descarado; (lively) vivo

pertain /pəˈteɪn/ vi ~ to pertencer a; (be relevant) ser pertinente a, (P) ser próprio de

pertinent /'pɜːtɪnənt/ a pertinente

perturb /pəˈtɜːb/ vt perturbar, transtornar

Peru /pəˈruː/ n Peru m. ~vian a & n peruano (m), (P) peruviano (m)

peruse /pəˈruːz/ vt ler com atenção

perva|de /pəˈveɪd/ vt espalhar-se por, invadir. ~sive a penetrante

perverse /pəˈvɜːs/ a que insiste no erro; (wicked) perverso; (wayward) caprichoso. ~ity n obstinação f; (wickedness) perversidade f; (waywardness) capricho m, birra f

pervert[1] /pəˈvɜːt/ vt perverter. ~sion n perversão f

pervert[2] /'pɜːvɜːt/ n pervertido m

peseta /pəˈseɪtə/ n peseta f

pessimis|t /'pesɪmɪst/ n pessimista mf. ~m /-zəm/ n pessimismo m. ~tic /-ˈmɪstɪk/ a pessimista

pest /pest/ n inseto m, (P) insecto m nocivo; (animal) animal m daninho; (person) peste f

pester /'pestə(r)/ vt incomodar (colloq)

pesticide /'pestɪsaɪd/ n pesticida m

pet /pet/ n animal m de estimação; (*favourite*) preferido m, querido m □ a (*rabbit etc*) de estimação □ vt (*pt petted*) acariciar. ~ name nome m usado em família

petal /'petl/ n pétala f

peter /'pi:tə(r)/ vi ~ out extinguir-se, acabar pouco a pouco, morrer (*fig*)

petition /pɪ'tɪʃn/ n petição f □ vt requerer

petrify /'petrɪfaɪ/ vt petrificar

petrol /'petrəl/ n gasolina f. ~ pump bomba f de gasolina. ~ station posto m de gasolina. ~ tank tanque m de gasolina

petroleum /pɪ'trəʊliəm/ n petróleo m

petticoat /'petɪkəʊt/ n combinação f, anágua f

petty /'petɪ/ a (-ier, -iest) pequeno, insignificante; (*mean*) mesquinho. ~ cash fundo m para pequenas despesas, caixa f pequena

petulan|t /'petjʊlənt/ a irritável. ~ce n irritabilidade f

pew /pju:/ n banco (de igreja) m

pewter /'pju:tə(r)/ n estanho m

phallic /'fælɪk/ a fálico

phantom /'fæntəm/ n fantasma m

pharmaceutical /fɑ:mə'sju:tɪkl/ a farmacêutico

pharmac|y /'fa:məsɪ/ n farmácia f. ~ist n farmacêutico m

phase /feɪz/ n fase f □ vt ~ in/out introduzir/retirar progressivamente

PhD abbr of Doctor of Philosophy n doutorado m

pheasant /'feznt/ n faisão m

phenomen|on /fɪ'nɒmɪnən/ n (*pl* -ena*) fenômeno m, (*P*) fenómeno m. ~al a fenomenal

philanthrop|ist /fɪ'lænθrəpɪst/ n filantropo m. ~ic /-ən'θrɒpɪk/ a filantrópico

Philippines /'fɪlɪpi:nz/ npl the ~ as Filipinas fpl

philistine /'fɪlɪstaɪn/ n filisteu m

philosoph|y /fɪ'lɒsəfɪ/ n filosofia f. ~er n filósofo m. ~ical /-ə'sɒfɪkl/ a filosófico

phlegm /flem/ n (*med*) catarro m, fleuma f

phobia /'fəʊbɪə/ n fobia f

phone /fəʊn/ n (*colloq*) telefone m □ vt/i (*colloq*) telefonar (para). on the ~ no telefone. ~ back voltar a telefonar, ligar de volta. ~ book lista f telefónica, (*P*) telefónica. ~ box cabine f telefónica, (*P*) telefónica. ~ call chamada f, telefonema m. ~-in n programa m de rádio ou tv com participação dos ouvintes

phonecard /'fəʊnka:d/ n cartão m para uso em telefone público

phonetic /fə'netɪk/ a fonetico. ~s n fonética f

phoney /'fəʊnɪ/ a (-ier, -iest) (*sl*) falso, fingido □ n (*sl: person*) fingido m; (*sl: thing*) falso m, (*P*) falsificação f

phosphate /'fɒsfeɪt/ n fosfato m

phosphorus /'fɒsfərəs/ n fósforo m

photo /'fəʊtəʊ/ n (*pl* -os) (*colloq*) retrato m, foto f

photocop|y /'fəʊtəʊkɒpɪ/ n fotocópia f □ vt fotocopiar. ~ier n fotocopiadora f

photogenic /fəʊtəʊ'dʒenɪk/ a fotogénico, (*P*) fotogénico

photograph /'fəʊtəgra:f/ n fotografia f □ vt fotografar. ~er /fə'tɒgrəfə(r)/ n fotógrafo m. ~ic /-ə'græfɪk/ a fotográfico. ~y /fə'tɒgrəfɪ/ n fotografia f

phrase /freɪz/ n expressão f, frase f; (*gram*) locução f, frase f elíptica □ vt exprimir. ~-book n livro m de expressões idiomáticas

physical /'fɪzɪkl/ a físico

physician /fɪ'zɪʃn/ n médico m

physicist /'fɪzɪsɪst/ n físico m

physics /'fɪzɪks/ n física f

physiology /fɪzɪ'ɒlədʒɪ/ n fisiologia f

physiotherap|y /fɪzɪəʊ'θerəpɪ/ n fisioterapia f. ~ist n fisioterapeuta mf

physique /fɪ'zi:k/ n físico m

pian|o /pɪ'ænəʊ/ n (*pl* -os) piano m. ~ist /'pɪənɪst/ n pianista mf

pick¹ /pɪk/ n (*tool*) picareta f

pick² /pɪk/ n escolher; (*flowers, fruit etc*) colher; (*lock*) forçar; (*teeth*) palitar □ n escolha f; (*best*) o/a melhor. ~ a quarrel with puxar uma briga com. ~ holes in an argument descobrir os pontos fracos dum argumento. ~ sb's pocket bater a carteira de alg. ~ off tirar, arrancar. ~ on implicar com. ~ out escolher; (*identify*) identificar, reconhecer. ~ up vt apanhar; (*speed*) ganhar. take one's ~ escolher livremente

pickaxe /'pɪkæks/ n picareta f

picket /'pɪkɪt/ n piquete m; (*single striker*) grevista mf de piquete □ vt (*pt picketed*) colocar um piquete em □ vi fazer piquete

pickings /'pɪkɪŋz/ npl restos mpl

pickle /'pɪkl/ n vinagre m. ~s picles mpl, (*P*) pickles mpl □ vt conservar em vinagre. in a ~ (*colloq*) numa encrenca (*colloq*)

pickpocket /'pɪkpɒkɪt/ n batedor m de carteiras, (*P*) carteirista m

picnic /'pɪknɪk/ n piquenique m □ vi (*pt picnicked*) piquenicar, (*P*) fazer um piquenique

pictorial /pɪk'tɔ:rɪəl/ a ilustrado

picture /'pɪktʃə(r)/ n imagem f; (*illustration*) estampa f, ilustração f; (*painting*) quadro m, pintura f;

(*photo*) fotografia *f*, retrato *m*; (*draw-ing*) desenho *m*; (*fig*) descrição *f*, quadro *m* □ *vt* imaginar; (*describe*) pintar, descrever. **the ~s** o cinema

picturesque /pɪktʃəˈresk/ *a* pitoresco

pidgin /ˈpɪdʒɪn/ *a* ~ **English** inglês *m* estropiado

pie /paɪ/ *n* torta *f*, (P) tarte *f*; (*of meat*) empada *f*

piece /piːs/ *n* pedaço *m*, bocado *m*; (*of machine, in game*) peça *f*; (*of currency*) moeda *f* □ *vt* ~ **together** juntar, montar. **a ~ of advice/furniture/** *etc* um conselho/um móvel/*etc*. ~ **work** *n* trabalho *m* por, (P) a peça por, (P) a tarefa. **take to ~s** desmontar

piecemeal /ˈpiːsmiːl/ *a* aos poucos, pouco a pouco

pier /pɪə(r)/ *n* molhe *m*

pierc|**e** /pɪəs/ *vt* furar, penetrar. ~**ing** *a* penetrante; (*of scream, pain*) lancinante

piety /ˈpaɪətɪ/ *n* piedade *f*, devoção *f*

pig /pɪg/ *n* porco *m*. ~-**headed** *a* cabeçudo, teimoso

pigeon /ˈpɪdʒɪn/ *n* pombo *m*. ~-**hole** *n* escaninho *m*

piggy /ˈpɪgɪ/ *a* como um porco. ~-**back** adv às costas. ~ **bank** cofre *m* de criança

pigment /ˈpɪgmənt/ *n* pigmento *m*. ~**ation** /-ˈteɪʃn/ *n* pigmentação *f*

pigsty /ˈpɪgstaɪ/ *n* pocilga *f*, chiqueiro *m*

pigtail /ˈpɪgteɪl/ *n* trança *f*

pike /paɪk/ *n* (*pl invar*) (*fish*) lúcio *m*

pilchard /ˈpɪltʃəd/ *n* peixe *m* pequeno da família do arenque, sardinha *f* européia

pile /paɪl/ *n* pilha *f*; (*of carpet*) pêlo *m* □ *vt/i* amontoar(-se), empilhar(-se) (**into** em). **a ~ of** (*colloq*) um monte de (*colloq*). ~ **up** acumular(-se). ~-**up** *n* choque *m* em cadeia

piles /paɪlz/ *npl* hemorróidas *fpl*

pilfer /ˈpɪlfə(r)/ *vt* furtar. ~**age** *n* furto *m* (*de coisas pequenas or* em pequenas quantidades)

pilgrim /ˈpɪlgrɪm/ *n* peregrino *m*, romeiro *m*. ~**age** *n* peregrinação *f*, romaria *f*

pill /pɪl/ *n* pílula *f*, comprimido *m*

pillage /ˈpɪlɪdʒ/ *n* pilhagem *f*, saque *m* □ *vt* pilhar, saquear

pillar /ˈpɪlə(r)/ *n* pilar *m*. ~-**box** *n* marco *m* do correio

pillion /ˈpɪlɪən/ *n* assento *m* traseiro de motorizada. **ride ~** ir no assento de trás

pillow /ˈpɪləʊ/ *n* travesseiro *m*

pillowcase /ˈpɪləʊkeɪs/ *n* fronha *f*

pilot /ˈpaɪlət/ *n* piloto *m* □ *vt* (*pt piloted*) pilotar. ~-**light** *n* piloto *m*;

(*electr*) lâmpada *f* testemunho; (*gas*) piloto *m*

pimento /pɪˈmentəʊ/ *n* (*pl* -**os**) pimentão *m* vermelho

pimple /ˈpɪmpl/ *n* borbulha *f*, espinha *f*

pin /pɪn/ *n* alfinete *m*; (*techn*) cavilha *f* □ *vt* (*pt pinned*) pregar *or* prender com alfinete(s); (*hold down*) prender, segurar. **have ~s and needles** estar com cãibra. ~ **sb down** (*fig*) obrigar alg a definir-se, apertar alg (*fig*). ~-**point** *vt* localizar com precisão. ~-**stripe** *a* de listras finas. ~ **up** pregar. ~-**up** *n* (*colloq*) pin-up *f*

pinafore /ˈpɪnəfɔː(r)/ *n* avental *m*. ~ **dress** veste *f*

pincers /ˈpɪnsəz/ *npl* (*tool*) torquês *f*, (P) alicate *m*; (*med*) pinça *f*; (*zool*) pinça(s) *f*(*pl*), tenaz(es) *f* (*pl*)

pinch /pɪntʃ/ *vt* apertar; (*sl: steal*) surripiar (*colloq*) □ *n* aperto *m*; (*tweak*) beliscão *m*; (*small amount*) pitada *f*. **at a ~** em caso de necessidade

pine¹ /paɪn/ *n* (*tree*) pinheiro *m*; (*wood*) pinho *m*

pine² /paɪn/ *vi* ~ **away** definhar, consumir-se. ~ **for** suspirar por

pineapple /ˈpaɪnæpl/ *n* abacaxi *m*, (P) ananás *m*

ping-pong /ˈpɪŋpɒŋ/ *n* pingue-pongue *m*

pink /pɪŋk/ *a & n* rosa (*m*)

pinnacle /ˈpɪnəkl/ *n* pináculo *m*

pint /paɪnt/ *n* quartilho *m* (= *0,57l*; *Amer = 0,47l*)

pioneer /paɪəˈnɪə(r)/ *n* pioneiro *m* □ *vt* ser o pioneiro em, preparar o caminho para

pious /ˈpaɪəs/ *a* piedoso, devoto

pip /pɪp/ *n* (*seed*) pevide *f*

pipe /paɪp/ *n* cano *m*, tubo *m*; (*of smoker*) cachimbo *m* □ *vt* encanar, canalizar ~ **down** calar a boca

pipeline /ˈpaɪplaɪn/ *n* (*for oil*) oleoduto *m*; (*for gas*) gaseoduto *m*, (P) gasoduto *m*. **in the ~** (*fig*) encaminhado

piping /ˈpaɪpɪŋ/ *n* tubagem *f*. ~ **hot** muito quente

piquant /ˈpiːkənt/ *a* picante

pira|**te** /ˈpaɪərət/ *n* pirata *m*. ~**cy** *n* pirataria *f*

Pisces /ˈpaɪsiːz/ *n* (*astr*) Peixe *m*, (P) Pisces *m*

pistol /ˈpɪstl/ *n* pistola *f*

piston /ˈpɪstən/ *n* êmbolo *m*, pistão *m*

pit /pɪt/ *n* (*hole*) cova *f*, fosso *m*; (*mine*) poço *m*; (*quarry*) pedreira *f* □ *vt* (*pt pitted*) picar, esburacar; (*fig*) opor. ~ **o.s. against** (*struggle*) medir-se com

pitch¹ /pɪtʃ/ *n* breu *m*. ~-**black** *a* escuro como breu

pitch² /pɪtʃ/ vt (throw) lançar; (tent) armar □ vi cair □ n (slope) declive m; (of sound) som m; (of voice) altura f; (sport) campo m

pitchfork /ˈpɪtʃfɔːk/ n forcado m

pitfall /ˈpɪtfɔːl/ n (fig) cilada f, perigo m inesperado

pith /pɪθ/ n (of orange) parte f branca da casca, mesocarpo m; (fig: essential part) cerne m, âmago m

pithy /ˈpɪθɪ/ a (-ier, -iest) preciso, conciso

piti|ful /ˈpɪtɪfl/ a lastimoso; (contemptible) miserável. ~less a impiedoso

pittance /ˈpɪtns/ n salário m miserável, miséria f

pity /ˈpɪtɪ/ n dó m, pena f, piedade f □ vt compadecer-se de. it's a ~ é uma pena. take ~ on ter pena de. what a ~! que pena!

pivot /ˈpɪvət/ n eixo m □ vt (pt pivoted) girar em torno de

placard /ˈplækɑːd/ n (poster) cartaz m

placate /pləˈkeɪt/ vt apaziguar, aplacar

place /pleɪs/ n lugar m, sítio m; (house) casa f; (seat, rank etc) lugar m □ vt colocar, pôr. ~ an order fazer uma encomenda. at/to my ~ em a or na minha casa. ~-mat n pano m de mesa individual, (P) napperon m à americana

placid /ˈplæsɪd/ a plácido

plagiar|ize /ˈpleɪdʒəraɪz/ vt plagiar. ~ism n plágio m

plague /pleɪg/ n peste f; (of insects) praga f □ vt atormentar, atazanar

plaice /pleɪs/ n (pl invar) solha f

plain /pleɪn/ a (-er, -est) claro; (candid) franco; (simple) simples; (not pretty) sem beleza; (not patterned) liso □ adv com franqueza □ n planície f. in ~ clothes à paisana. ~ly adv claramente; (candidly) francamente

plaintiff /ˈpleɪntɪf/ n queixoso m

plaintive /ˈpleɪntɪv/ a queixoso

plait /plæt/ vt entrançar □ n trança f

plan /plæn/ n plano m, projeto m, (P) projecto m; (of a house, city etc) plano m, planta f □ vt (pt planned) planear, planejar □ vi fazer planos. ~ to do ter a intenção de fazer

plane¹ /pleɪn/ n (level) plano m; (aeroplane) avião m □ a plano

plane² /pleɪn/ n (tool) plaina f □ vt aplainar

planet /ˈplænɪt/ n planeta m

plank /plæŋk/ n prancha f

planning /ˈplænɪŋ/ n planeamento m, planejamento m. ~ permission permissão f para construir

plant /plɑːnt/ n planta f; (techn) aparelhagem f; (factory) fábrica f □ vt

plantar. ~ a bomb colocar uma bomba. ~ation /-ˈteɪʃn/ n plantação f

plaque /plɑːk/ n placa f; (on teeth) tártaro m, pedra f

plaster /ˈplɑːstə(r)/ n reboco m; (adhesive) esparadrapo m, band-aid m □ vt rebocar; (cover) cobrir (with com, de). in ~ engessado. ~ of Paris gesso m. ~er n rebocador m, caiador m

plastic /ˈplæstɪk/ a plástico □ n plástica f. ~ surgery cirurgia f plástica

plate /pleɪt/ n prato m; (in book) gravura f □ vt revestir de metal

plateau /ˈplætəʊ/ n (pl -eaux /-əʊz/) planalto m, platô m

platform /ˈplætfɔːm/ n estrado m; (for speaking) tribuna f; (rail) plataforma f, cais m; (fig) programa m de partido político. ~ ticket bilhete m de gare

platinum /ˈplætɪnəm/ n platina f

platitude /ˈplætɪtjuːd/ n banalidade f, lugar-comum m

platonic /pləˈtɒnɪk/ a platónico, (P) platónico

plausible /ˈplɔːzəbl/ a plausível; (person) convincente

play /pleɪ/ vt/i (for amusement) brincar; (instrument) tocar; (cards, game) jogar; (opponent) jogar contra; (match) disputar □ n jogo m; (theatre) peça f; (movement) folga f, margem f. ~ down minimizar. ~ on (take advantage of) aproveitar-se de. ~ safe jogar pelo seguro. ~ up (colloq) dar problemas (a). ~-group n jardim m de infância, (P) jardim m infantil. ~-pen n cercado m para crianças

playboy /ˈpleɪbɔɪ/ n play-boy m

player /ˈpleɪə(r)/ n jogador m; (theat) artista mf; (mus) artista mf, executante mf, instrumentista f

playful /ˈpleɪfl/ a brincalhão m

playground /ˈpleɪgraʊnd/ n pátio m de recreio

playing /ˈpleɪŋ/ n atuação f, (P) actuação f. ~-card n carta f de jogar. ~-field n campo m de jogos

playwright /ˈpleɪraɪt/ n dramaturgo m

plc abbr (of public limited company) SARL

plea /pliː/ n súplica f; (reason) pretexto m, desculpa f; (jur) alegação f da defesa

plead /pliːd/ vt/i pleitear; (as excuse) alegar. ~ guilty confessar-se culpado. ~ with implorar

pleasant /ˈpleznt/ a agradável

pleas|e /pliːz/ vt/i agradar (a), dar prazer (a) □ adv por favor, (P) se faz favor. they ~e themselves, they do as they ~e eles fazem como bem entendem. ~ed *a* contente, satisfeito (with com). ~ing *a* agradável

pleasur|e /'pleʒə(r)/ *n* prazer *m*. ~able *a* agradável

pleat /pliːt/ *n* prega *f* □ *vt* preguear

pledge /pledʒ/ *n* penhor *m*, garantia *f*; (*fig*) promessa *f* □ *vt* prometer; (*pawn*) empenhar

plentiful /'plentɪfl/ *a* abundante

plenty /'plentɪ/ *n* abundância *f*, fartura *f*. ~ (of) muito (de); (*enough*) bastante (de)

pliable /'plaɪəbl/ *a* flexível

pliers /'plaɪəz/ *npl* alicate *m*

plight /plaɪt/ *n* triste situação *f*

plimsoll /'plɪmsəl/ *n* alpargata *f*, tênis *m*, (*P*) ténis *m*

plinth /plɪnθ/ *n* plinto *m*

plod /plɒd/ *vi* (*pt* plodded) caminhar lentamente; (*work*) trabalhar, marrar (*sl*). ~der *n* trabalhador *m* lento mas perseverante. ~ding *a* lento

plonk /plɒŋk/ *n* (*sl*) vinho *m* ordinário, (*P*) carrascão *m*

plot /plɒt/ *n* complô *m*, conspiração *f*; (*of novel etc*) trama *f*; (*of land*) lote *m* □ *vt/i* (*pt* plotted) conspirar; (*mark out*) traçar

plough /plaʊ/ *n* arado *m* □ *vt/i* arar. ~ back reinvestir. ~ into colidir. ~ through abrir caminho por

ploy /plɒɪ/ *n* (*colloq*) estratagema *m*

pluck /plʌk/ *vt* apanhar; (*bird*) depenar; (*eyebrows*) depilar; (*mus*) tanger □ *n* coragem *f*. ~ up courage ganhar coragem. ~y *a* corajoso

plug /plʌg/ *n* tampão *m*; (*electr*) tomada *f*, (*P*) ficha *f* □ *vt* (*pt* plugged) tapar com tampão; (*colloq: publicize*) fazer grande propaganda de □ *vi* ~ away (*colloq*) trabalhar com afinco. ~ in (*electr*) ligar. ~-hole *n* buraco *m* do cano

plum /plʌm/ *n* ameixa *f*

plumb /plʌm/ *adv* exatamente, (*P*) exactamente, mesmo □ *vt* sondar. ~-line *n* fio *m* de prumo

plumb|er /'plʌmə(r)/ *n* bombeiro *m*, encanador *m*, (*P*) canalizador *m*. ~ing *n* encanamento *m*, (*P*) canalização *f*

plummet /'plʌmɪt/ *vi* (*pt* plummeted) despencar

plump /plʌmp/ *a* (-er, -est) rechonchudo, roliço □ *vi* ~ for optar por. ~ness *n* gordura *f*

plunder /'plʌndə(r)/ *vt* pilhar, saquear □ *n* pilhagem *f*, saque *m*; (*goods*) despojo *m*

plunge /plʌndʒ/ *vt/i* mergulhar, atirar(-se), afundar(-se) □ *n* mergulho *m*. take the ~ (*fig*) decidir-se, dar o salto (*fig*)

plunger /'plʌndʒə(r)/ *n* (*of pump*)

êmbolo *m*, pistão *m*; (*for sink etc*) desentupidor *m*

pluperfect /pluː'pɜːfɪkt/ *n* mais-que-perfeito *m*

plural /'plʊərəl/ *a* plural; (*noun*) no plural □ *n* plural *m*

plus /plʌs/ *prep* mais □ *a* positivo □ *n* sinal +; (*fig*) qualidade *f* positiva

plush /plʌʃ/ *n* pelúcia *f* □ *a* de pelúcia; (*colloq*) de luxo

ply /plaɪ/ *vt* (*tool*) manejar; (*trade*) exercer □ *vi* (*ship, bus*) fazer carreira entre dois lugares. ~ sb with drink encher alguém de bebidas

plywood /'plaɪwʊd/ *n* madeira *f* compensada

p.m. /piː'em/ *adv* da tarde, da noite

pneumatic /njuː'mætɪk/ *a* pneumático. ~ drill broca *f* pneumática

pneumonia /njuː'məʊnɪə/ *n* pneumonia *f*

PO *abbr see* Post Office

poach /pəʊtʃ/ *vt/i* (*steal*) caçar/pescar em propriedade alheia; (*culin*) fazer poché, (*P*) escalfar. ~ed eggs ovos *mpl* pochês, (*P*) ovos *mpl* escalfados

pocket /'pɒkɪt/ *n* bolso *m*, algibeira *f* □ *a* de algibeira □ *vt* meter no bolso. ~-book *n* (*notebook*) livro *m* de apontamentos; (*Amer: handbag*) carteira *f*. ~-money *n* (*monthly*) mesada *f*, (*weekly*) semanada *f*, dinheiro *m* para pequenas despesas

pod /pɒd/ *n* vagem *f*

poem /'pəʊɪm/ *n* poema *m*

poet /'pəʊɪt/ *n* poeta *m*, poetisa *f*. ~ic /-'etɪk/ *a* poético

poetry /'pəʊɪtrɪ/ *n* poesia *f*

poignant /'pɔɪnjənt/ *a* pungente, doloroso

point /pɔɪnt/ *n* ponto *m*; (*tip*) ponta *f*; (*decimal point*) vírgula *f*; (*meaning*) sentido *m*, razão *f*; (*electr*) tomada *f*. ~s (*rail*) agulhas *fpl* □ *vt/i* (*aim*) apontar (at para); (*show*) apontar, indicar (at/to para). on the ~ of prestes a, quase a. ~-blank *a* & *adv* à queima-roupa; (*fig*) categórico. ~ of view ponto *m* de vista. ~ out apontar, fazer ver. that is a good ~ (*remark*) é uma boa observação. to the ~ a propósito. what is the ~? de que adianta?

pointed /'pɔɪntɪd/ *a* ponteagudo; (*of remark*) intencional, contundente

pointer /'pɔɪntə(r)/ *n* ponteiro *m*; (*colloq: hint*) sugestão *f*

pointless /'pɔɪntlɪs/ *a* inútil, sem sentido

poise /pɔɪz/ *n* equilíbrio *m*; (*carriage*) porte *m*; (*fig: self-possession*) presença *f*, segurança *f*. ~d *a* equilibrado; (*person*) seguro de si poison /'pɔɪzn/ n veneno m, peçonha f □ vt envenenar. blood-~ing n envenenamento m do sangue. food-~ing n intoxicação f alimentar. ~ous a venenoso

poke /pəʊk/ vt/i espetar; (with elbow) acotovelar; (fire) atiçar □ n espetadela f; (with elbow) cotovelada f. ~ about esgaravatar, remexer, procurar. ~ fun at fazer troça/pouco de. ~ out (head) enfiar

poker¹ /'pəʊkə(r)/ n atiçador m

poker² /'pəʊkə(r)/ n (cards) póquer m, (P) póquer m

poky /'pəʊkɪ/ a (-ier, -iest) acanhado, apertado

Poland /'pəʊlənd/ n Polónia f, (P) Polónia f

polar /'pəʊlə(r)/ a polar. ~ bear urso m branco

polarize /'pəʊləraɪz/ vt polarizar

pole¹ /pəʊl/ n vara f; (for flag) mastro m; (post) poste m

pole² /pəʊl/ n (geog) pólo m

Pole /pəʊl/ n polaco m

polemic /pə'lemɪk/ n polémica f, (P) polémica f

police /pə'li:s/ n polícia f □ vt policiar. ~ state estado m policial. ~ station distrito m, delegacia f, (P) esquadra f de polícia

police|man /pə'li:smən/ n (pl -men) polícial m, (P) polícia m, guarda m, agente m de polícia. ~-woman (pl -women) n polícia f feminina, (P) mulher-polícia f

policy¹ /'pɒlɪsɪ/ n (plan of action) política f

policy² /'pɒlɪsɪ/ n (insurance) apólice f de seguro

polio /'pəʊlɪəʊ/ n polio f

polish /'pɒlɪʃ/ vt polir, dar lustro em; (shoes) engraxar; (floor) encerar □ n (for shoes) graxa f; (for floor) cera f; (for nails) esmalte m, (P) verniz m; (shine) polimento m; (fig) requinte m. ~ off acabar (rapidamente). ~ up (language) aperfeiçoar. ~ed a requintado, elegante

Polish /'pəʊlɪʃ/ a & n polonês (m), (P) polaco (m)

polite /pə'laɪt/ a polido, educado, delicado. ~ly adv delicadamente. ~ness n delicadeza f, cortesia f

political /pə'lɪtɪkl/ a político

politician /pɒlɪ'tɪʃn/ n político m

politics /'pɒlətɪks/ n política f

polka /'pɒlkə/ n polca f. ~ dots bolas fpl

poll /pəʊl/ n votação f; (survey) sondagem f, pesquisa f □ vt (votes) obter. go to the ~s votar, ir às urnas. ~ing-booth n cabine f de voto

pollen /'pɒlən/ n pólen m

pollut|e /pə'lu:t/ vt poluir. ~ion /-ʃn/ n poluição f

polo /'pəʊləʊ/ n pólo m. ~ neck gola f rolê

polyester /pɒlɪ'estə/ n poliéster m

polytechnic /pɒlɪ'teknɪk/ n politécnica f

polythene /'pɒlɪθi:n/ n politeno m. ~ bag n saco m de plástico

pomegranate /'pɒmɪgrænɪt/ n romã f

pomp /pɒmp/ n pompa f

pompon /'pɒmpɒn/ n pompom m

pomp|ous /'pɒmpəs/ a pomposo. ~osity /-'pɒsətɪ/ n imponência f

pond /pɒnd/ n lagoa f, lago m; (artificial) tanque m, lago m

ponder /'pɒndə(r)/ vt/i ponderar, meditar (over sobre)

pong /pɒŋ/ n (sl) pivete m □ vi (sl) cheirar mal, tresandar

pony /'pəʊnɪ/ n pônei m, (P) pónei m. ~-tail n rabo m de cavalo. ~-trekking n passeio m de pônei, (P) pónei

poodle /'pu:dl/ n cão m de água, caniche m

pool¹ /pu:l/ n (puddle) charco m, poça f; (for swimming) piscina f

pool² /pu:l/ n (fund) fundo m comum; (econ, comm) pool m; (game) forma f de bilhar. ~s loteca f, (P) totobola m □ vt pôr num fundo comum

poor /pʊə(r)/ a (-er, -est) pobre; (not good) medíocre. ~ly adv mal □ a doente

pop¹ /pɒp/ n estalido m, ruído m seco □ vt/i (pt popped) dar um estalido, estalar; (of cork) saltar. ~ in/out/off entrar/sair/ir-se embora. ~ up aparecer de repente, saltar

pop² /pɒp/ n música f pop □ a pop invar

popcorn /'pɒpkɔ:n/ n pipoca f

pope /pəʊp/ n papa m

poplar /'pɒplə(r)/ n choupo m, álamo m

poppy /'pɒpɪ/ n papoula f

popular /'pɒpjʊlə(r)/ a popular; (in fashion) em voga, na moda. be ~ with ser popular entre. ~ity /-'lærətɪ/ n popularidade f. ~ize vt popularizar, vulgarizar

populat|e /'pɒpjʊleɪt/ vt povoar. ~ion /-'leɪʃn/ n população f

populous /'pɒpjʊləs/ a populoso

porcelain /'pɔ:slɪn/ n porcelana f

porch /pɔ:tʃ/ n alpendre m; (Amer) varanda f

porcupine /'pɔ:kjʊpaɪn/ n porco-espinho m

pore¹ /pɔ:(r)/ n poro m

pore² /pɔ:(r)/ vi ~ over examinar, estudar

pork /pɔ:k/ n carne f de porco

pornograph|y /pɔːˈnɒɡrəfɪ/ n pornografia f. **~ic** /-əˈɡræfɪk/ a pornográfico

porous /ˈpɔːrəs/ a poroso

porpoise /ˈpɔːpəs/ n toninha f, (P) golfinho m

porridge /ˈpɒrɪdʒ/ n (papa f de) flocos mpl de aveia

port¹ /pɔːt/ n (harbour) porto m

port² /pɔːt/ n (wine) (vinho do) Porto m

portable /ˈpɔːtəbl/ a portátil

porter¹ /ˈpɔːtə(r)/ n (carrier) carregador m

porter² /ˈpɔːtə(r)/ n (doorkeeper) porteiro m

portfolio /pɔːtˈfəʊlɪəʊ/ n (pl -os) (case, post) pasta f; (securities) carteira f de investimentos

porthole /ˈpɔːthəʊl/ n vigia f

portion /ˈpɔːʃn/ n (share, helping) porção f; (part) parte f

portly /ˈpɔːtlɪ/ a (-ier, -iest) corpulento e digno

portrait /ˈpɔːtrɪt/ n retrato m

portray /pɔːˈtreɪ/ vt retratar, pintar; (fig) descrever. **~al** n retrato m

Portugal /ˈpɔːtjʊɡl/ n Portugal m. **~uese** /-ˈɡiːz/ a & n invar português (m)

pose /pəʊz/ vt/i (fazer) posar; (question) fazer □ n pose f, postura f. **~ as** fazer-se passar por

poser /ˈpəʊzə(r)/ n quebra-cabeças m

posh /pɒʃ/ a (sl) chique invar

position /pəˈzɪʃn/ n posição f; (job) lugar m, colocação f; (state) situação f □ vt colocar

positive /ˈpɒzətɪv/ a positivo; (definite) categórico, definitivo; (colloq: downright) autêntico. **she's ~ that** ela tem certeza que. **~ly** adv positivamente; (absolutely) completamente

possess /pəˈzes/ vt possuir. **~ion** /-ʃn/ n posse f; (thing possessed) possessão f. **~or** n possuidor m

possessive /pəˈzesɪv/ a possessivo

possib|le /ˈpɒsəbl/ a possível. **~ility** /-ˈbɪlətɪ/ n possibilidade f

possibly /ˈpɒsəblɪ/ adv possivelmente, talvez. **if I ~ can** se me fôr possível. **I cannot ~ leave** estou impossibilitado de partir

post¹ /pəʊst/ n (pole) poste m □ vt (notice) afixar, pregar

post² /pəʊst/ n (station, job) posto m □ vt colocar; (appoint) colocar

post³ /pəʊst/ n (mail) correio m □ a postal □ vt mandar pelo correio. **keep ~ed** manter informado. **~-code** n código m postal. **P~ Office** agência f dos correios, (P) estação f dos correios; (corporation) Departamento m dos Correios e Telégrafos, (P) Correios, Telégrafos e Telefones mpl (CTT)

post- /pəʊst/ pref pós-

postage /ˈpəʊstɪdʒ/ n porte m

postal /ˈpəʊstl/ a postal. **~ order** vale m postal

postcard /ˈpəʊstkɑːd/ n cartão-postal m, (P) (bilhete) postal m

poster /ˈpəʊstə(r)/ n cartaz m

posterity /pɒˈsterətɪ/ n posteridade f

postgraduate /pəʊstˈɡrædʒʊət/ n pós-graduado m

posthumous /ˈpɒstjʊməs/ a póstumo. **~ly** adv a título póstumo

postman /ˈpəʊstmən/ n (pl -men) carteiro m

postmark /ˈpəʊstmɑːk/ n carimbo m do correio

post-mortem /pəʊstˈmɔːtəm/ n autópsia f

postpone /pəˈspəʊn/ vt adiar. **~ment** n adiamento m

postscript /ˈpəʊsskrɪpt/ n post scriptum m

postulate /ˈpɒstjʊleɪt/ vt postular

posture /ˈpɒstʃə(r)/ n postura f, posição f □ vi posar

post-war /ˈpəʊstwɔː(r)/ a de após-guerra

posy /ˈpəʊzɪ/ n raminho m de flores

pot /pɒt/ n pote m; (for cooking) panela f; (for plants) vaso m; (sl: marijuana) maconha f □ vt (pt potted) **~ (up)** plantar em vaso. **go to ~** (sl: business) arruinar, degringolar (colloq); (sl: person) estar arruinado or liquidado. **~-belly** n pança f, barriga f. **take ~ luck** aceitar o que houver. **take a ~-shot** dar um tiro de perto (at em); (at random) dar um tiro a esmo (at em)

potato /pəˈteɪtəʊ/ n (pl -oes) batata f

poten|t /ˈpəʊtnt/ a potente, poderoso; (drink) forte. **~cy** n potência f

potential /pəˈtenʃl/ a & n potencial (m). **~ly** adv potencialmente

pothol|e /ˈpɒthəʊl/ n caverna f, caldeirão m; (in road) buraco m. **~ing** n espeleologia f

potion /ˈpəʊʃn/ n poção f

potted /ˈpɒtɪd/ a (of plant) de vaso; (preserved) de conserva

potter¹ /ˈpɒtə(r)/ n oleiro m, ceramista mf. **~y** n olaria f, cerâmica f

potter² /ˈpɒtə(r)/ vi entreter-se com isto ou aquilo

potty¹ /ˈpɒtɪ/ a (-ier, -iest) (sl) doido, pirado (sl), (P) chanfrado (colloq)

potty² /ˈpɒtɪ/ n (pl -ties) (colloq) penico m de criança

pouch /paʊtʃ/ n bolsa f; (for tobacco) tabaqueira f

poultice /ˈpəʊltɪs/ n cataplasma f

poultry /'pəʊltrɪ/ n aves fpl domésticas

pounce /paʊns/ vi atirar-se (**on** sobre, para cima de) □ n salto m

pound[1] /paʊnd/ n (weight) libra f (= 453 g); (money) libra f

pound[2] /paʊnd/ n (for dogs) canil municipal m; (for cars) parque de viaturas rebocadas m

pound[3] /paʊnd/ vt/i (crush) esmagar, pisar; (of heart) bater com força; (bombard) bombardear; (on piano etc) martelar

pour /pɔː(r)/ vt deitar □ vi correr; (rain) chover torrencialmente. ~ **in/ out** (of people) afluir/sair em massa. ~ **off** or **out** esvaziar, vazar. ~**ing rain** chuva f torrencial

pout /paʊt/ vt/i ~ (**one's lips**) (sulk) fazer beicinho; (in annoyance) ficar de trombas □ n beicinho m

poverty /'pɒvatɪ/ n pobreza f, miséria f. ~**-stricken** a pobre

powder /'paʊdə(r)/ n pó m; (for face) pó-de-arroz m □ vt polvilhar; (face) empoar. ~**ed** a em pó. ~**-room** n toalete m, toucador m. ~**y** a como pó

power /'paʊə(r)/ n poder m; (maths, mech) potência f; (energy) energia f; (electr) corrente f. ~ **cut** corte m de energia, blecaute m. ~ **station** central f elétrica, (P) eléctrica. ~**ful** a poderoso; (mech) potente. ~**less** a impotente

practicable /'præktɪkəbl/ a viável

practical /'præktɪkl/ a prático. ~ **joke** brincadeira f de mau gosto

practically /'præktɪklɪ/ adv praticamente

practice /'præktɪs/ n prática f; (of law etc) exercício m; (sport) treino m; (clients) clientela f. **in** ~ (in fact) na prática; (well-trained) em forma. **out of** ~ destreinado, sem prática. **put into** ~ pôr em prática

practis|**e** /'præktɪs/ vt/i (skill, sport) praticar, exercitar-se em; (profession) exercer; (put into practice) pôr em prática. ~**ed** a experimentado, experiente. ~**ing** a (Catholic etc) praticante

practitioner /præk'tɪʃənə(r)/ n praticante mf. **general** ~ médico m de clínica geral or de família

pragmatic /præg'mætɪk/ a pragmático

prairie /'preərɪ/ n pradaria f

praise /preɪz/ vt louvar, elogiar □ n elogio(s) m(pl), louvor(es) m(pl)

praiseworthy /'preɪzwɜːðɪ/ a louvável, digno de louvor

pram /præm/ n carrinho m de bebê, (P) bebé

prance /prɑːns/ vi (of horse) curvetear, empinar-se; (of person) pavonear-se

prank /præŋk/ n brincadeira f de mau gosto

prattle /'prætl/ vi tagarelar

prawn /prɔːn/ n camarão m grande, (P) gamba f

pray /preɪ/ vi rezar, orar

prayer /preə(r)/ n oração f. **the Lord's P**~ o Padre-Nosso. ~**-book** n missal m

pre- /priː/ pref pré-

preach /priːtʃ/ vt/i pregar (**at, to** a). ~**er** n pregador m

preamble /priː'æmbl/ n preâmbulo m

prearrange /priːə'reɪndʒ/ vt combinar or arranjar de antemão

precarious /prɪ'keərɪəs/ a precário; (of position) instável, inseguro

precaution /prɪ'kɔːʃn/ n precaução f. ~**ary** a de precaução

preced|**e** /prɪ'siːd/ vt preceder. ~**ing** a precedente

precedent /'presɪdənt/ n precedente m

precinct /'priːsɪŋkt/ n precinto m; (Amer: district) circunscrição f. (**pedestrian**) ~ área f de pedestres, (P) zona f para peões

precious /'preʃəs/ a precioso

precipice /'presɪpɪs/ n precipício m

precipitat|**e** /prɪ'sɪpɪteɪt/ vt precipitar □ a /-ɪtət/ precipitado. ~**ion** /-'teɪʃn/ n precipitação f

precis|**e** /prɪ'saɪs/ a preciso; (careful) meticuloso. ~**ely** adv precisamente. ~**ion** /-'sɪʒn/ n precisão f

preclude /prɪ'kluːd/ vt evitar, excluir, impedir

precocious /prɪ'kəʊʃəs/ a precoce

preconc|**eived** /priːkən'siːvd/ a preconcebido. ~**eption** /priːkən'sepʃn/ n idéia f preconcebida

precursor /priː'kɜːsə(r)/ n precursor m

predator /'predətə(r)/ n animal m de rapina, predador m. ~**y** a predatório

predecessor /'priːdɪsesə(r)/ n predecessor m

predicament /prɪ'dɪkəmənt/ n situação f difícil

predict /prɪ'dɪkt/ vt predizer, prognosticar. ~**able** a previsível. ~**ion** /-ʃn/ n predição f, prognóstico m

predominant /prɪ'dɒmɪnənt/ a predominante, preponderante. ~**ly** adv predominantemente, preponderantemente

predominate /prɪ'dɒmɪneɪt/ vi predominar

pre-eminent /priː'emɪnənt/ a preeminente, superior

pre-empt /priː'empt/ vt adquirir por

preempção. ~ive *a* antecipado; (*mil*) preventivo

preen /pri:n/ *vt* alisar. ~ o.s. enfeitar-se

prefab /'pri:fæb/ *n* (*colloq*) casa *f* pré-fabricada. ~ricated /-'fæbrɪkeɪtɪd/ *a* pré-fabricado

preface /'prefɪs/ *n* prefácio *m*

prefect /'pri:fekt/ *n* aluno *m* autorizado a disciplinar outros; (*official*) prefeito *m*

prefer /prɪ'fɜ:(r)/ *vt* (*pt* preferred) preferir. ~able /'prefrəbl/ *a* preferível

preferen|ce /'prefrəns/ *n* preferência *f*. ~tial /-ə'renʃl/ *a* preferencial, privilegiado

prefix /'pri:fɪks/ *n* (*pl* -ixes) prefixo *m*

pregnan|t /'pregnənt/ *a* (*woman*) grávida; (*animal*) prenhe. ~cy *n* gravidez *f*

prehistoric /pri:hɪ'stɒrɪk/ *a* pré-histórico

prejudice /'predʒʊdɪs/ *n* preconceito *m*, idéia *f* preconcebida, prejuízo *m*; (*harm*) prejuízo *m* □ *vt* influenciar. ~d *a* com preconceitos

prelimina|ry /prɪ'lɪmɪnərɪ/ *a* preliminar. ~ies *npl* preliminares *mpl*, preâmbulos *mpl*

prelude /'prelju:d/ *n* prelúdio *m*

premarital /pri:'mærɪtl/ *a* antes do casamento, pré-marital

premature /'premətjʊə(r)/ *a* prematuro

premeditated /pri:'medɪteɪtɪd/ *a* premeditado

premier /'premɪə(r)/ *a* primeiro □ *n* (*pol*) primeiro-ministro *m*

premises /'premɪsɪz/ *npl* local *m*, edifício *m*. on the ~ neste estabelecimento, no local

premium /'pri:mɪəm/ *n* prêmio *m*, (*P*) prémio *m*. at a ~ a peso de ouro

premonition /pri:mə'nɪʃn/ *n* pressentimento *m*

preoccup|ation /pri:ɒkjʊ'peɪʃn/ *n* preocupação *f*. ~ied /-'ɒkjʊpaɪd/ *a* preocupado

preparation /prepə'reɪʃn/ *n* preparação *f*. ~s preparativos *mpl*

preparatory /prɪ'pærətrɪ/ *a* preparatório. ~ school escola *f* primária particular

prepare /prɪ'peə(r)/ *vt/i* preparar(-se) (for para). ~d to pronto a, preparado para

preposition /prepə'zɪʃn/ *n* preposição *f*

preposterous /prɪ'pɒstərəs/ *a* absurdo, disparatado, ridículo

prerequisite /pri:'rekwɪzɪt/ *n* condição *f* prévia

prerogative /prɪ'rɒgətɪv/ *n* prerrogativa *f*

Presbyterian /prezbɪ'tɪərɪən/ *a* & *n* presbiteriano (*m*)

prescri|be /prɪ'skraɪb/ *vt* prescrever; (*med*) receitar, prescrever. ~ption /-ɪpʃn/ *n* prescrição *f*; (*med*) receita *f*

presence /'prezns/ *n* presença *f*. ~ of mind presença *f* de espírito

present[1] /'preznt/ *a* & *n* presente (*mf*). at ~ no momento, presentemente

present[2] /'preznt/ *n* (*gift*) presente *m*

present[3] /prɪ'zent/ *vt* apresentar; (*film etc*) dar. ~ sb with oferecer a alg. ~able *a* apresentável. ~ation /prezn'teɪʃn/ *n* apresentação *f*. ~er *n* apresentador *m*

presently /'prezntlɪ/ *adv* dentro em pouco, daqui a pouco; (*Amer: now*) neste momento

preservative /prɪ'zɜ:vətɪv/ *n* preservativo *m*

preserv|e /prɪ'zɜ:v/ *vt* preservar; (*maintain; culin*) conservar □ *n* reserva *f*; (*fig*) área *f*, terreno *m*; (*jam*) compota *f*. ~ation /prezə'veɪʃn/ *n* conservação *f*

preside /prɪ'zaɪd/ *vi* presidir (over a)

presiden|t /'prezɪdənt/ *n* presidente *mf*. ~cy *n* presidência *f*. ~tial /-'denʃl/ *a* presidencial

press /pres/ *vt/i* carregar (on em); (*squeeze*) espremer; (*urge*) pressionar; (*iron*) passar a ferro □ *n* imprensa *f*; (*mech*) prensa *f*; (*for wine*) lagar *m*. be ~ed for estar apertado com falta de. ~ on (with) continuar (com), prosseguir (com). ~ conference entrevista *f* coletiva. ~-stud *n* mola *f*, botão *m* de pressão

pressing /'presɪŋ/ *a* premente, urgente

pressure /'preʃə(r)/ *n* pressão *f* □ *vt* fazer pressão sobre. ~-cooker *n* panela *f* de pressão. ~ group grupo *m* de pressão

pressurize /'preʃəraɪz/ *vt* pressionar, fazer pressão sobre

prestige /pre'sti:ʒ/ *n* prestígio *m*

prestigious /pre'stɪdʒəs/ *a* prestigioso

presumably /prɪ'zju:məblɪ/ *adv* provavelmente

presum|e /prɪ'zju:m/ *vt* presumir. ~e to tomar a liberdade de, atrever-se a. ~ption /-'zʌmpʃn/ *n* presunção *f*

presumptuous /prɪ'zʌmptʃʊəs/ *a* presunçoso

pretence /prɪ'tens/ *n* fingimento *m*; (*claim*) pretensão *f*; (*pretext*) desculpa *f*, pretexto *m*

pretend /prɪ'tend/ *vt/i* fingir (to do fazer). ~ to (*lay claim to*) ter pretensões a, ser pretendente a; (*profess to have*) pretender ter pretentious /prɪ'tenʃəs/ a pretencioso

pretext /'pri:tekst/ n pretexto m

pretty /'prɪtɪ/ a (-ier, -iest) bonito, lindo □ adv bastante

prevail /prɪ'veɪl/ vi prevalecer. ~ on sb to convencer alguéma. ~ing a dominante

prevalen|t /'prevələnt/ a geral, dominante. ~ce n frequência f

prevent /prɪ'vent/ vt impedir (from doing de fazer). ~able a que se pode evitar, evitável. ~ion /-ʃn/ n prevenção f. ~ive a preventivo

preview /'pri:vju:/ n pré-estréia f, (P) ante-estréia f

previous /'pri:vɪəs/ a precedente, anterior. ~ to antes de. ~ly adv antes, anteriormente

pre-war /pri:'wɔ:(r)/ a do pré-guerra, (P) de antes da guerra

prey /preɪ/ n presa f □ vi ~ on dar caça a; (worry) preocupar, atormentar. bird of ~ ave f de rapina, predador m

price /praɪs/ n preço m □ vt marcar o preço de. ~less a inestimável; (colloq: amusing) impagável

prick /prɪk/ vt picar, furar □ n picada f. ~ up one's ears arrebitar a(s) orelha(s)

prickle /'prɪkl/ n pico m, espinho m; (sensation) picada f. ~y a espinhoso, que pica; (person) irritável

pride /praɪd/ n orgulho m □ vpr ~ o.s. on orgulhar-se de

priest /pri:st/ n padre m, sacerdote m. ~hood n sacerdócio m; (clergy) clero m

prim /prɪm/ a (primmer, primmest) formal, cheio de nove-horas; (prudish) pudico

primary /'praɪmərɪ/ a primário; (chief, first) primeiro. ~ school escola f primária

prime¹ /praɪm/ a primeiro, principal; (first-rate) de primeira qualidade. P~ Minister Primeiro-Ministro m. ~ number número m primo

prime² /praɪm/ vt apontar, aprestar; (with facts) preparar; (surface) preparar, aparelhar. ~r /-ə(r)/ n (paint) aparelho m

primeval /praɪ'mi:vl/ a primitivo

primitive /'prɪmɪtɪv/ a primitivo

primrose /'prɪmrəʊz/ n primavera f, prímula f

prince /prɪns/ n príncipe m

princess /prɪn'ses/ n princesa f

principal /'prɪnsəpl/ a principal □ n (schol) diretor m, (P) director m. ~ly adv principalmente

principle /'prɪnsəpl/ n princípio m. in/on ~ em/por princípio

print /prɪnt/ vt imprimir; (write) escrever em letra de imprensa □ n marca f, impressão f; (letters) letra f de imprensa; (photo) prova (fotográfica) f; (engraving) gravura f. out of ~ esgotado. ~-out n cópia f impressa. ~ed matter impressos mpl

print|er /'prɪntə(r)/ n tipógrafo m; (comput) impressora f. ~ing n impressão f, tipografia f

prior /'praɪə(r)/ a anterior, precedente. ~ to antes de

priority /praɪ'ɒrətɪ/ n prioridade f

prise /praɪz/ vt forçar (com alavanca). ~ open arrombar

prison /'prɪzn/ n prisão f. ~er n prisioneiro m

pristine /'prɪsti:n/ a primitivo; (condition) perfeito, como novo

privacy /'prɪvəsɪ/ n privacidade f, intimidade f; (solitude) isolamento m

private /'praɪvət/ a privado; (confidential) confidencial; (lesson, life, house etc) particular; (ceremony) íntimo □ n soldado m raso. in ~ em particular; (of ceremony) na intimidade. ~ly adv particularmente; (inwardly) no fundo, interiormente

privet /'prɪvɪt/ n (bot) alfena f, ligustro m

privilege /'prɪvəlɪdʒ/ n privilégio m. ~d a privilegiado. be ~d to ter o privilégio de

prize /praɪz/ n prêmio m, (P) prémio m □ a premiado; (fool etc) perfeito □ vt ter em grande apreço, apreciar muito. ~-giving n distribuição f de prêmios, (P) prémios. ~-winner n premiado m, vencedor m

pro¹ /prəʊ/ n the ~s and cons os prós e os contras

pro- /prəʊ/ pref (acting for) pro-; (favouring) pró-

probab|le /'prɒbəbl/ a provável. ~ility /-'bɪlətɪ/ n probabilidade f. ~ly adv provavelmente

probation /prə'beɪʃn/ n (testing) estágio m, tirocínio m; (jur) liberdade f condicional. ~ary a probatório

probe /prəʊb/ n (med) sonda f; (fig: investigation) inquérito m □ vt/i ~ (into) sondar, investigar

problem /'prɒbləm/ n problema m □ a difícil. ~atic /-'mætɪk/ a problemático

procedure /prə'si:dʒə(r)/ n procedimento m, processo m, norma f

proceed /prə'si:d/ vi prosseguir, ir para diante, avançar. ~ to do passar a fazer. ~ with sth continuar or avançar com alguma coisa. ~ing n procedimento m

proceedings /prə'si:dɪŋz/ npl (jur) processo m; (report) ata f, (P) acta f

proceeds /'prəʊsi:dz/ npl produto m, luco m, proventos mpl

process /'prəʊses/ n processo m □ vt tratar; (photo) revelar. **in ~** em curso. **in the ~ of doing** sendo feito

procession /prə'seʃn/ n procissão f, cortejo m

proclaim /prə'kleɪm/ vt proclamar. **~amation** /prɒklə'meɪʃn/ n proclamação f

procure /prə'kjʊə(r)/ vt obter

prod /prɒd/ vt/i (pt **prodded**) (push) empurrar; (poke) espetar; (fig: urge) incitar □ n espetadela f; (fig) incitamento m

prodigal /'prɒdɪgl/ a pródigo

prodigious /prə'dɪdʒəs/ a prodigioso

prodigy /'prɒdɪdʒɪ/ n prodígio m

produce[1] /prə'dju:s/ vt/i produzir; (bring out) tirar, extrair; (show) apresentar, mostrar; (cause) causar, provocar; (theat) pôr em cena. **~er** n produtor m. **~tion** /-'dʌkʃn/ n produção f; (theat) encenação f

produce[2] /'prɒdju:s/ n produtos (agrícolas) mpl

product /'prɒdʌkt/ n produto m

productiv|**e** /prə'dʌktɪv/ a produtivo. **~ity** /prɒdʌk'tɪvəti/ n produtividade f

profan|**e** /prə'feɪn/ a profano; (blasphemous) blasfemo. **~ity** /-'fænəti/ n profanidade f

profess /prə'fes/ vt professar. **~ to do** alegar fazer

profession /prə'feʃn/ n profissão f. **~al** a profissional; (well done) de profissional; (person) que exerce uma profissão liberal □ n profissional mf

professor /prə'fesə(r)/ n professor m (universitário)

proficien|**t** /prə'fɪʃnt/ a proficiente, competente. **~cy** n proficiência f, competência f

profile /'prəʊfaɪl/ n perfil m

profit /'prɒfɪt/ n proveito m; (money) lucro m □ vi (pt **profited**) **~ by** aproveitar-se de; **~ from** tirar proveito de. **~able** a proveitoso; (of business) lucrativo, rentável

profound /prə'faʊnd/ a profundo. **~ly** adv profundamente

profus|**e** /prə'fju:s/ a profuso. **~ely** adv profusamente, em abundância. **~ion** /-ʒn/ n profusão f

program /'prəʊgræm/ n (computer) **~** programa m □ vt (pt **programmed**) programar. **~mer** n programador m

programme /'prəʊgræm/ n programa m

progress[1] /'prəʊgres/ n progresso m. **in ~** em curso, em andamento

progress[2] /prə'gres/ vi progredir. **~ion** /-ʃn/ n progressão f

progressive /prə'gresɪv/ a progressivo; (reforming) progressista. **~ly** adv progressivamente

prohibit /prə'hɪbɪt/ vt proibir (**sb from doing** alg de fazer)

project[1] /prə'dʒekt/ vt projetar, (P) projectar □ vi ressaltar, sobressair. **~ion** /-ʃn/ n projeção f, (P) projecção f; (protruding) saliência f, ressalto m

project[2] /'prɒdʒekt/ n projeto m, (P) projecto m

projectile /prə'dʒektaɪl/ n projétil m, (P) projéctil m

projector /prə'dʒektə(r)/ n projetor m, (P) projector m

proletari|**at** /prəʊlɪ'teərɪət/ n proletariado m. **~an** a & n proletário (m)

proliferat|**e** /prə'lɪfəreɪt/ vi proliferar. **~ion** /-'reɪʃn/ n proliferação f

prolific /prə'lɪfɪk/ a prolífico

prologue /'prəʊlɒg/ n prólogo m

prolong /prə'lɒŋ/ vt prolongar

promenade /prɒmə'nɑ:d/ n passeio m □ vt/i passear

prominen|**t** /'prɒmɪnənt/ a (projecting; important) proeminente; (conspicuous) bem à vista, conspícuo. **~ce** n proeminência f. **~tly** adv bem à vista

promiscu|**ous** /prə'mɪskjʊəs/ a promíscuo, de costumes livres. **~ity** /prɒmɪ'skju:əti/ n promiscuidade f, liberdade f de costumes

promis|**e** /'prɒmɪs/ n promessa f □ vt/i prometer. **~ing** a promissor; (of business) promissor

promot|**e** /prə'məʊt/ vt promover. **~ion** /-'məʊʃn/ n promoção f

prompt /prɒmpt/ a pronto, rápido; imediato; (punctual) pontual □ adv em ponto □ vt levar; (theat) soprar, servir de ponto para. **~er** n ponto m. **~ly** adv prontamente; pontualmente. **~ness** n prontidão f

prone /prəʊn/ a deitado (de bruços). **~ to** propenso a

prong /prɒŋ/ n (of fork) dente m

pronoun /'prəʊnaʊn/ n pronome m

pronounc|**e** /prə'naʊns/ vt pronunciar; (declare) declarar. **~ounced** a pronunciado. **~ouncement** n declaração f. **~unciation** /-ʌnsɪ'eɪʃn/ n pronúncia f

proof /pru:f/ n prova f; (of liquor) teor m alcoólico, graduação f □ a **~ against** à prova de

prop /prɒp/ n suporte m; (lit & fig) apoio m, esteio m □ vt (pt **propped**) sustentar, suportar, apoiar. **~ against** apoiar contra

prop² /prɒp/ *n* (*colloq: theat*) acessório *m*, (*P*) adereço *m*

propaganda /prɒpə'gændə/ *n* propaganda *f*

propagat|e /'prɒpəgeɪt/ *vt/i* propagar(-se). **~ion** /-'geɪʃn/ *n* propagação *f*

propel /prə'pel/ *vt* (*pt* **propelled**) propulsionar, impelir

propeller /prə'pelə(r)/ *n* hélice *f*

proper /'prɒpə(r)/ *a* correto, (*P*) correcto; (*seemly*) conveniente; (*real*) propriamente dito; (*colloq: thorough*) belo. **~ noun** substantivo *m* próprio. **~ly** *adv* corretamente, (*P*) correctamente; (*rightly*) com razão, acertadamente; (*accurately*) propriamente

property /'prɒpəti/ *n* (*house*) imóvel *m*; (*land, quality*) propriedade *f*; (*possessions*) bens *mpl*

prophecy /'prɒfəsɪ/ *n* profecia *f*

prophesy /'prɒfɪsaɪ/ *vt/i* profetizar. **~ that** predizer que

prophet /'prɒfɪt/ *n* profeta *m*. **~ic** /prə'fetɪk/ *a* profético

proportion /prə'pɔːʃn/ *n* proporção *f*. **~al**, **~ate** *adjs* proporcional

proposal /prə'pəʊzl/ *n* proposta *f*; (*of marriage*) pedido *m* de casamento

propos|e /prə'pəʊz/ *vt* propor □ *vi* pedir em casamento. **~e to do** propor-se fazer. **~ition** /prɒpə'zɪʃn/ *n* proposição *f*; (*colloq: matter*) caso *m*, questão *f*

propound /prə'paʊnd/ *vt* propor

proprietor /prə'praɪətə(r)/ *n* proprietário *m*

propriety /prə'praɪətɪ/ *n* propriedade *f*, correção *f*, (*P*) correcção *f*

propulsion /prə'pʌlʃn/ *n* propulsão *f*

prosaic /prə'zeɪk/ *a* prosaico

prose /prəʊz/ *n* prosa *f*

prosecut|e /'prɒsɪkjuːt/ *vt* (*jur*) processar. **~ion** /-'kjuːʃn/ *n* (*jur*) acusação *f*

prospect¹ /'prɒspekt/ *n* perspectiva *f*

prospect² /prə'spekt/ *vt/i* pesquisar, prospectar

prospective /prə'spektɪv/ *a* futuro; (*possible*) provável

prosper /'prɒspə(r)/ *vi* prosperar

prosper|ous /'prɒspərəs/ *a* próspero. **~ity** /-'sperətɪ/ *n* prosperidade *f*

prostitut|e /'prɒstɪtjuːt/ *n* prostituta *f*. **~ion** /-'tjuːʃn/ *n* prostituição *f*

prostrate /'prɒstreɪt/ *a* prostrado

protect /prə'tekt/ *vt* proteger. **~ion** /-ʃn/ *n* proteção *f*, (*P*) protecção *f*. **~ive** *a* protetor, (*P*) protector. **~or** *n* protetor *m*, (*P*) protector *m*

protégé /'prɒtɪʒeɪ/ *n* protegido *m*. **~e** *n* protegida *f*

protein /'prəʊtiːn/ *n* proteína *f*

protest¹ /'prəʊtest/ *n* protesto *m*

protest² /prə'test/ *vt/i* protestar. **~er** *n* (*pol*) manifestante *mf*

Protestant /'prɒtɪstənt/ *a* & *n* protestante (*mf*). **~ism** /-ɪzəm/ *n* protestantismo *m*

protocol /'prəʊtəkɒl/ *n* protocolo *m*

prototype /'prəʊtətaɪp/ *n* protótipo *m*

protract /prə'trækt/ *vt* prolongar, arrastar

protrud|e /prə'truːd/ *vi* sobressair, sair do alinhamento. **~ing** *a* saliente

proud /praʊd/ *a* (**er, -est**) orgulhoso. **~ly** *adv* orgulhosamente

prove /pruːv/ *vt* provar, demonstrar □ *vi* **~ (to be) easy/*etc*** verificar-se ser fácil/*etc*. **~ o.s.** dar provas de si. **~n** /-n/ *a* provado

proverb /'prɒvɜːb/ *n* provérbio *m*. **~ial** /prə'vɜːbɪəl/ *a* proverbial

provid|e /prə'vaɪd/ *vt* prover, munir (**sb with sth** alg de alguma coisa) □ *vi* **~ for** providenciar para; (*person*) prover de, cuidar de; (*allow for*) levar em conta. **~ed**, **~ing (that)** *conj* desde que, contanto que

providence /'prɒvɪdəns/ *n* providência *f*

province /'prɒvɪns/ *n* província *f*; (*fig*) competência *f*

provincial /prə'vɪnʃl/ *a* provincial; (*rustic*) provinciano

provision /prə'vɪʒn/ *n* provisão *f*; (*stipulation*) disposição *f*. **~s** (*pl food*) provisões *fpl*

provisional /prə'vɪʒənl/ *a* provisório. **~ly** *adv* provisoriamente

proviso /prə'vaɪzəʊ/ *n* (*pl* **-os**) condição *f*

provo|ke /prə'vəʊk/ *vt* provocar. **~cation** /prɒvə'keɪʃn/ *n* provocação *f*. **~cative** /-'vɒkətɪv/ *a* provocante

prowess /'praʊɪs/ *n* proeza *f*, façanha *f*

prowl /praʊl/ *vi* rondar □ *n* **be on the ~** andar à espreita. **~er** *n* pessoa *f* que anda à espreita

proximity /prɒk'sɪmətɪ/ *n* proximidade *f*

proxy /'prɒksɪ/ *n* **by ~** por procuração

prude /pruːd/ *n* puritano *m*, pudico *m*

pruden|t /'pruːdnt/ *a* prudente. **~ce** *n* prudência *f*

prune¹ /pruːn/ *n* ameixa *f* seca

prune² /pruːn/ *vt* podar

pry /praɪ/ *vi* bisbilhotar. **~ into** meter o nariz em, intrometer-se em

psalm /saːm/ *n* salmo *m*

pseudo- /'sjuːdəʊ/ *pref* pseudo-

pseudonym /'sjuːdənɪm/ *n* pseudónimo *m*, (*P*) pseudónimo *m*

psychiatr|y /saɪ'kaɪətrɪ/ *n* psiquiatria *f*. **~ic** /-ɪ'ætrɪk/ *a* psiquiátrico. **~ist** *n* psiquiatra *mf*

psychic /'saɪkɪk/ a psíquico; (person)
com capacidade de telepatia

psychoanalys|e /saɪkəʊˈænəlaɪz/ vt
psicanalisar. ~t /-ɪst/ n psicanalista
mf

psychoanalysis /saɪkəʊəˈnæləsɪs/ n
psicanálise f

psycholog|y /saɪˈkɒlədʒɪ/ n psicolo-
gia f. ~ical /-əˈlɒdʒɪkl/ a psicológico.
~ist n psicólogo m

psychopath /'saɪkəʊpæθ/ n psicopata
mf

pub /pʌb/ n pub m

puberty /'pjuːbətɪ/ n puberdade f

public /'pʌblɪk/ a público; (holiday)
feriado. in ~ em público. ~ house
pub m. ~ relations relações fpl
públicas. ~ school escola f particular; (Amer) escola f oficial. ~-
spirited a de espírito cívico,
patriótico. ~ly adv publicamente

publication /pʌblɪˈkeɪʃn/ n publicação f

publicity /pʌˈblɪsətɪ/ n publicidade f

publicize /'pʌblɪsaɪz/ vt fazer publicidade de

publish /'pʌblɪʃ/ vt publicar. ~er n
editor m. ~ing n publicação f. ~ing
house editora f

pucker /'pʌkə(r)/ vt/i franzir

pudding /'pʊdɪŋ/ n pudim m; (dessert)
doce m

puddle /'pʌdl/ n poça f de água, charco m

puerile /'pjʊəraɪl/ a pueril

puff /pʌf/ n baforada f □ vt/i lançar
baforadas; (breathe hard) arquejar,
ofegar. ~ at (cigar etc) dar baforadas
em. ~ out (swell) inchar(-se). ~-
pastry n massa f folhada

puffy /'pʌfɪ/ a inchado

pugnacious /pʌɡˈneɪʃəs/ a belicoso,
combativo

pull /pʊl/ vt/i puxar; (muscle) distender □ n puxão m; (fig: influence)
influência f, empenho m. give a ~
dar um puxão. ~ a face fazer uma
careta. ~ one's weight (fig) fazer a
sua quota-parte. ~ sb's leg brincar
com alguém, meter-se com alguém.
~ away or out (auto) arrancar. ~
down puxar para baixo; (building)
demolir. ~ in (auto) encostar-se. ~
off tirar; (fig) sair-se bem em, conseguir alcançar. ~ out partir; (extract)
arrancar, tirar. ~ through sair-se
bem. ~ o.s. together recompor-se,
refazer-se. ~ up puxar para cima;
(uproot) arrancar; (auto) parar

pulley /'pʊlɪ/ n roldana f

pullover /'pʊləʊvə(r)/ n pulôver m

pulp /pʌlp/ n polpa f; (for paper) pasta f de papel

pulpit /'pʊlpɪt/ n púlpito m

pulsat|e /pʌlˈseɪt/ vi pulsar, bater,
palpitar. ~ion /-ˈseɪʃn/ n pulsação f

pulse /pʌls/ n pulso m. feel sb's ~
tirar o pulso de alguém

pulverize /'pʌlvəraɪz/ vt (grind, defeat) pulverizar

pummel /'pʌml/ vt (pt pummelled)
esmurrar

pump¹ /pʌmp/ n bomba f □ vt/i bombear; (person) arrancar or extrair informações de. ~ up encher com
bomba

pump² /pʌmp/ n (shoe) sapato m

pumpkin /'pʌmpkɪn/ n abóbora f

pun /pʌn/ n trocadilho m, jogo m de
palavras

punch¹ /pʌntʃ/ vt esmurrar, dar um
murro or soco; (perforate) furar, perfurar; (a hole) fazer □ n murro m, soco
m; (device) furador m. ~-line n
remate m. ~-up n (colloq) pancadaria
f

punch² /pʌntʃ/ n (drink) ponche m

punctual /'pʌŋktʃʊəl/ a pontual.
~ity /-ˈælətɪ/ n pontualidade f

punctuat|e /'pʌŋktʃʊeɪt/ vt pontuar.
~ion /-ˈeɪʃn/ n pontuação f

puncture /'pʌŋktʃə(r)/ n (in tyre) furo
m □ vt/i furar

pundit /'pʌndɪt/ n autoridade f, sumi-
dade f

pungent /'pʌndʒənt/ a acre, pungente

punish /'pʌnɪʃ/ vt punir, castigar.
~able a punível. ~ment n punição
f, castigo m

punitive /'pjuːnɪtɪv/ a (expedition,
measure etc) punitivo; (taxation etc)
penalizador

punt /pʌnt/ n (boat) chalana f

punter /'pʌntə(r)/ n (gambler) jogador m; (colloq: customer) freguês m

puny /'pjuːnɪ/ a (-ier, -iest) fraco, débil

pup(py) /'pʌp(ɪ)/ n cachorro m, ca-
chorrinho m

pupil /'pjuːpl/ n aluno m; (of eye) pupila f

puppet /'pʌpɪt/ n (lit & fig) fantoche
m, marionete f

purchase /'pɜːtʃəs/ vt comprar (from
sb de alg) □ n compra f. ~r /-ə(r)/ n
comprador m

pur|e /'pjʊə(r)/ a (-er, -est) puro. ~ely
adv puramente. ~ity n pureza f

purgatory /'pɜːɡətrɪ/ n purgatório m

purge /pɜːdʒ/ vt purgar; (pol) sanear
□ n (med) purgante m; (pol) saneamento m

purif|y /'pjʊərɪfaɪ/ vt purificar.
~ication /-ɪˈkeɪʃn/ n purificação f

puritan /'pjʊərɪtən/ n puritano m.
~ical /-ˈtænɪkl/ a puritano

purple /'pɜːpl/ a roxo, purpúreo □ n
roxo m, púrpura f

purport /pə'pɔːt/ vt dizer-se, (P) dar a entender. ~ to be pretender ser

purpose /'pɜːpəs/ n propósito m; (determination) firmeza f. on ~ de propósito. to no ~ em vão. ~-built a construído especialmente.

purposely /'pɜːpəslɪ/ adv de propósito, propositadamente

purr /pɜːr/ n ronrom m □ vi ronronar

purse /pɜːs/ n carteira f; (Amer) bolsa f □ vt franzir

pursue /pə'sjuː/ vt perseguir; (go on with) prosseguir; (engage in) entregar-se a, dedicar-se a. ~r /-ə(r)/ n perseguidor m

pursuit /pə'sjuːt/ n perseguição f; (fig) atividade f, (P) actividade f

pus /pʌs/ n pus m

push /pʊʃ/ vt/i empurrar; (button) apertar; (thrust) enfiar; (colloq: recommend) insistir □ n empurrão m; (effort) esforço m; (drive) energia f. be ~ed for (time etc) estar com pouco. be ~ing thirty/etc (colloq) estar beirando os trinta/etc. ~ on (sl) dar o fora em alguém. ~ s.o. around fazer alguém de bobo. ~ back repelir. ~-chair n carrinho m (de criança). ~er n fornecedor m (de droga). ~ off (sl) dar o fora. ~ on continuar. ~-over n canja f, coisa f fácil. ~ up (lift) levantar; (prices) forçar o aumento de. ~-up n (Amer) flexão f. ~y a (colloq) agressivo, furão

put /pʊt/ vt/i (pt put, pres p putting) colocar, pôr; (question) fazer. ~ the damage at a million estimar os danos em um milhão. I'd ~ it at a thousand eu diria mil. ~ sth tactfully dizer alg coisa com tato. ~ across comunicar. ~ away guardar. ~ back repor; (delay) retardar, atrasar. ~ by pôr de lado. ~ down pôr em lugar baixo; (write) anotar; (pay) pagar; (suppress) sufocar, reprimir. ~ forward (plan) submeter. ~ in (insert) introduzir; (fix) instalar; (submit) submeter. ~ in for fazer um pedido, candidatar-se. ~ off (postpone) adiar; (disconcert) desanimar; (displease) desagradar. ~ s.o. off sth tirar o gosto de alguém por alg coisa. ~ on (clothes) pôr; (radio) ligar; (light) acender; (speed, weight) ganhar; (accent) adotar. ~ out pôr para fora; (stretch) esticar; (extinguish) extinguir, apagar; (disconcert) desconcertar; (inconvenience) incomodar. ~ up levantar; (building) erguer, construir; (notice) colocar; (price) aumentar; (guest) hospedar; (offer) oferecer. ~-up job embuste m. ~ up with suportar

putrefy /'pjuːtrɪfaɪ/ vi putrefazer-se, apodrecer

putty /'pʌtɪ/ n massa de vidraceiro f, betume m

puzzl|e /'pʌzl/ n puzzle m, quebra-cabeça m □ vt deixar perplexo, intrigar □ vi quebrar a cabeça. ~ing a intrigante

pygmy /'pɪgmɪ/ n pigmeu m

pyjamas /pə'dʒaːməz/ npl pijama m

pylon /'paɪlɒn/ n poste m

pyramid /'pɪrəmɪd/ n pirâmide f

python /'paɪθn/ n píton m

Q

quack[1] /kwæk/ n (of duck) grasnido m □ vi grasnar

quack[2] /kwæk/ n charlatão m

quadrangle /'kwɒdræŋgl/ n quadrángulo m; (of college) pátio m quadrangular

quadruped /'kwɒdrʊped/ n quadrúpede m

quadruple /'kwɒdrʊpl/ a & n quádruplo (m) □ vt/i /kwɒ'druːpl/ quadruplicar. ~ts /-plɪts/ npl quadrigêmeos mpl, (P) quadrigémeos mpl

quagmire /'kwæɡmaɪə(r)/ n pântano m, lamaçal m

quail /kweɪl/ n codorniz f

quaint /kweɪnt/ a (-er, -est) pitoresco; (whimsical) estranho, bizarro

quake /kweɪk/ vi tremer □ n (colloq) tremor m de terra

Quaker /'kweɪkə(r)/ n quaker mf, quacre m

qualification /kwɒlɪfɪ'keɪʃn/ n qualificação f; (accomplishment) habilitação f; (diploma) diploma m, título m; (condition) requisito m, condição f; (fig) restrição f, reserva f

qualif|y /'kwɒlɪfaɪ/ vt qualificar; (fig: moderate) atenuar, moderar; (fig: limit) pôr ressalvas ou restrições a □ vi (fig: be entitled to) ter os requisitos (for para); (sport) classificar-se. he ~ied as a vet ele formou-se em veterinária. ~ied a formado; (able) qualificado, habilitado; (moderated) atenuado; (limited) limitado

quality /'kwɒlətɪ/ n qualidade f

qualm /kwaːm/ n escrúpulo m

quandary /'kwɒndərɪ/ n dilema m

quantity /'kwɒntətɪ/ n quantidade f

quarantine /'kwɒrəntiːn/ n quarentena f

quarrel /'kwɒrəl/ n zanga f, questão f, discussão f □ vi (pt quarrelled) zangar-se, questionar, discutir. ~some a conflituoso, brigão

quarry[1] /'kwɒrɪ/ n (prey) presa f, caça f

quarry[2] /'kwɒrɪ/ n (*excavation*) pedreira f

quarter /'kwɔːtə(r)/ n quarto m; (*of year*) trimestre m; (*Amer: coin*) quarto m de dólar, 25 cêtimos mpl; (*district*) bairro m, quarteirão m. ~s (*lodgings*) alojamento m, residência f; (*mil*) quartel m □ vt dividir em quarto; (*mil*) aquartelar. **from all ~s** de todos os lados. ~ **of an hour** quarto m de hora. **(a) ~ past six** seis e quinze. **(a) ~ to seven** quinze para as sete. ~**-final** n (*sport*) quarta f de final. ~**ly** a trimestral □ adv trimestralmente

quartet /kwɔː'tet/ n quarteto m

quartz /kwɔːts/ n quartzo m □ a (*watch etc*) de quartzo

quash /kwɒʃ/ vt reprimir; (*jur*) revogar

quaver /'kweɪvə(r)/ vi tremer, tremular □ n (*mus*) colcheia f

quay /kiː/ n cais m

queasy /'kwiːzɪ/ a delicado. **feel ~** estar enjoado

queen /kwiːn/ n rainha f; (*cards*) dama f

queer /kwɪə(r)/ a (-er, -est) estranho; (*slightly ill*) indisposto; (*sl: homosexual*) bicha, maricas (sl); (*dubious*) suspeito □ n (sl) bicha m, maricas m (sl)

quell /kwel/ vt reprimir, abafar, sufocar

quench /kwentʃ/ vt (*fire, flame*) apagar; (*thirst*) matar, saciar

query /'kwɪərɪ/ n questão f □ vt pôr em dúvida

quest /kwest/ n busca f, procura f. **in ~ of** em demanda de

question /'kwestʃən/ n pergunta f, interrogação f; (*problem, affair*) questão f □ vt perguntar, interrogar; (*doubt*) pôr em dúvida or em causa. **in ~** em questão or em causa. **out of the ~** fora de toda a questão. **there's no ~ of** nem pensar em. **without ~** sem dúvida. ~ **mark** ponto m de interrogação. ~**able** a discutível

questionnaire /kwestʃə'neə(r)/ n questionário m

queue /kjuː/ n fila f, (P) bicha f □ vi (*pres p queuing*) fazer fila, (P) fazer bicha

quibble /'kwɪbl/ vi tergiversar, usar de evasivas; (*raise petty objections*) discutir por coisas insignificantes

quick /kwɪk/ a (-er, -est) rápido □ adv depressa. **be ~** despachar-se. **have a ~ temper** exaltar-se facilmente. ~**ly** adv rapidamente, depressa. ~**ness** n rapidez f

quicken /'kwɪkən/ vt/i apressar(-se)

quicksand /'kwɪksænd/ n areia f movediça

quid /kwɪd/ n invar (sl) libra f

quiet /'kwaɪət/ a (-er, -est) quieto, sossegado, tranquilo □ n quietude f, sossego m, tranquilidade f. **keep ~** calar-se. **on the ~** às escondidas, na calada. ~**ly** adv sossegadamente, silenciosamente. ~**ness** n sossego m, tranquilidade f, calma f

quieten /'kwaɪətn/ vt/i sossegar, acalmar(-se)

quilt /kwɪlt/ n coberta f acolchoada. **(continental)** ~ edredão m de penas □ vt acolchoar

quince /kwɪns/ n marmelo m

quintet /kwɪn'tet/ n quinteto m

quintuplets /'kwɪn'tjuːplɪts/ npl quíntuplos mpl

quip /kwɪp/ n piada f □ vt contar piadas

quirk /kwɜːk/ n mania f, singularidade f

quit /kwɪt/ vt (pt quitted) deixar □ vi ir-se embora; (*resign*) demitir-se. ~ **doing** (*Amer*) parar de fazer

quite /kwaɪt/ adv completamente, absolutamente; (*rather*) bastante. ~ **(so)!** isso mesmo!, exatamente! ~ **a few** bastante, alguns/algumas. ~ **a lot** bastante

quiver /'kwɪvə(r)/ vi tremer, estremecer □ n tremor m, estremecimento m

quiz /kwɪz/ n (pl quizzes) teste m; (*game*) concurso m □ vt (pt quizzed) interrogar

quizzical /'kwɪzɪkl/ a zombeteiro

quorum /'kwɔːrəm/ n quorum m

quota /'kwəʊtə/ n cota f, quota f

quotation /kwəʊ'teɪʃn/ n citação f; (*estimate*) orçamento m. ~ **marks** aspas fpl

quote /kwəʊt/ vt citar; (*estimate*) fazer um orçamento □ n (*colloq: passage*) citação f; (*colloq: estimate*) orçamento m

R

rabbi /'ræbaɪ/ n rabino m

rabbit /'ræbɪt/ n coelho m

rabble /'ræbl/ n turba f. **the ~** a ralé, a gentalha, o povinho

rabid /'ræbɪd/ a (*fig*) fanático, ferrenho; (*dog*) raivoso

rabies /'reɪbiːz/ n raiva f

race[1] /reɪs/ n corrida f □ vt (*horse*) fazer correr □ vi correr, dar uma corrida; (*rush*) ir em grande or a toda (a) velocidade. ~**-track** n pista f

race[2] /reɪs/ n (*group*) raça f □ a racial

racecourse /'reɪskɔːs/ n hipódromo m

racehorse /'reɪshɔːs/ n cavalo m de corrida

racial /'reɪʃl/ a racial

racing /'reɪsɪŋ/ n corridas fpl. ~ **car** carro m de corridas

racis|t /'reɪsɪst/ a & n racista (mf). ~**m** /-zəm/ n racismo m

rack[1] /ræk/ n (for luggage) portabagagem m, bagageiro m; (for plates) escorredor m de prato □ vt ~ **one's brains** dar tratos à imaginação

rack[2] /ræk/ n **go to** ~ **and ruin** arruinar-se; (of buildings etc) cair em ruínas

racket[1] /'rækɪt/ n (sport) raquete f, (P) raqueta f

racket[2] /'rækɪt/ n (din) barulheira f; (swindle) roubalheira f; (sl: business) negociata f (colloq)

racy /'reɪsɪ/ a (-ier, -iest) vivo, vigoroso

radar /'reɪdɑː(r)/ n radar m □ a de radar

radian|t /'reɪdɪənt/ a radiante. ~**ce** n brilho m

radiator /'reɪdɪeɪtə(r)/ n radiador m

radical /'rædɪkl/ a & n radical (m)

radio /'reɪdɪəʊ/ n (pl -os) rádio f; (set) (aparelho de) rádio m □ vt transmitir pelo rádio. ~ **station** estação f de rádio, emissora f

radioactiv|e /reɪdɪəʊ'æktɪv/ a radioativo, (P) radioactivo. ~**ity** /-'tɪvətɪ/ n radioatividade f, (P) radioactividade f

radiograph|er /reɪdɪ'ɒɡrəfə(r)/ n radiologista mf. ~**y** n radiografia f

radish /'rædɪʃ/ n rabanete m

radius /'reɪdɪəs/ n (pl -dii /-dɪaɪ/) raio m

raffle /'ræfl/ n rifa f □ vt rifar

raft /rɑːft/ n jangada f

rafter /'rɑːftə(r)/ n trave f, viga f

rag[1] /ræg/ n farrapo m; (for wiping) trapo m; (pej: newspaper) jornaleco m. ~**s** npl farrapos mpl, andrajos mpl. **in** ~**s** maltrapilho. ~ **doll** boneca f de trapos

rag[2] /ræg/ vt (pt **ragged**) zombar de

rage /reɪdʒ/ n raiva f, fúria f □ vi estar furioso; (of storm) rugir; (of battle) estar acesa. **be all the** ~ (colloq) fazer furor, estar na moda (colloq)

ragged /'ræɡɪd/ a (clothes, person) esfarrapado, roto; (edge) esfiapado, esgarçado

raid /reɪd/ n (mil) ataque m; (by police) batida f; (by criminals) assalto m □ vt fazer um ataque or uma batida or um assalto. ~**er** n atacante m, assaltante m

rail /reɪl/ n (of stairs) corrimão m; (of ship) amurada f; (on balcony) parapeito m; (for train) trilho m; (for cur-

tain) varão m. **by** ~ por estrada, (P) caminho de ferro

railings /'reɪlɪŋz/ npl grade f

railroad /'reɪlrəʊd/ n (Amer) = **railway**

railway /'reɪlweɪ/ n estrada f, (P) caminho m de ferro. ~ **line** linha f do trem. ~ **station** estação f ferroviária, (P) estação f de caminho de ferro

rain /reɪn/ n chuva f □ vi chover. ~ **forest** floresta f tropical. ~-**storm** n tempestade f com chuva. ~-**water** n água f da chuva

rainbow /'reɪnbəʊ/ n arco-íris m

raincoat /'reɪnkəʊt/ n impermeável m

raindrop /'reɪndrɒp/ n pingo m de chuva

rainfall /'reɪnfɔːl/ n precipitação f, pluviosidade f

rainy /'reɪnɪ/ a (-ier, -iest) chuvoso

raise /reɪz/ vt levantar, erguer; (breed) criar; (voice) levantar; (question) fazer; (price etc) aumentar, subir; (funds) angariar; (loan) obter □ n (Amer) aumento m

raisin /'reɪzn/ n passa f

rake /reɪk/ n ancinho m □ vt juntar, alisar com ancinho; (search) revolver, remexer. ~ **in** (money) ganhar a rodos. ~-**off** n (colloq) percentagem f (colloq). ~ **up** desenterrar, ressuscitar

rally /'rælɪ/ vt/i reunir(-se); (reassemble) reagrupar(-se), reorganizar(-se); (health) restabelecer(-se); (strength) recuperar as forças □ n (recovery) recuperação f; (meeting) comício m, assembléia f; (auto) rally m, rali m

ram /ræm/ n (sheep) carneiro m □ vt (pt **rammed**) (beat down) calcar; (push) meter à força; (crash into) bater contra

rambl|e /'ræmbl/ n caminhada f, perambulação f □ vi perambular, vaguear. ~**e on** divagar. ~**er** n caminhante mf; (plant) trepadeira f. ~**ing** a (speech) desconexo

ramp /ræmp/ n rampa f

rampage /ræm'peɪdʒ/ vi causar distúrbios violentos

rampant /'ræmpənt/ a **be** ~ viceiar, florescer; (diseases etc) grassar

rampart /'ræmpɑːt/ n baluarte m; (fig) defesa f

ramshackle /'ræmʃækl/ a (car) desconjuntado; (house) caindo aos pedaços

ran /ræn/ see **run**

ranch /rɑːntʃ/ n rancho m, estância f. ~**er** n rancheiro m

rancid /'rænsɪd/ a rançoso

rancour /'ræŋkə(r)/ n rancor m

random /'rændəm/ a feito, tirado etc ao acaso □ n at ~ ao acaso, a esmo, aleatoriamente

randy /'rændɪ/ a (-ier, -iest) lascivo, sensual

rang /ræŋ/ see ring

range /reɪndʒ/ n (distance) alcance m; (scope) âmbito m; (variety) gama f, variedade f; (stove) fogão m; (of voice) registro m, (P) registo m; (of temperature) variação f □ vt dispor, ordenar □ vi estender-se; (vary) variar. ~ of mountains cordilheira f, serra f. ~r n guarda m florestal

rank¹ /ræŋk/ n fila f, fileira f; (mil) posto m; (social position) classe f, categoria f □ vt/i ~ among contar(-se) entre. the ~ and file a massa

rank² /ræŋk/ a (-er, -est) (plants) luxuriante; (smell) fétido; (out-and-out) total

ransack /'rænsæk/ vt (search) espionar, revistar, remexer; (pillage) pilhar, saquear

ransom /'rænsəm/ n resgate m □ vt resgatar. hold to ~ prender como refém

rant /rænt/ vi usar linguagem bombástica

rap /ræp/ n pancadinha f seca □ vt/i (pt rapped) bater, dar uma pancada seca em

rape /reɪp/ vt violar, estuprar □ n violação f, estupro m

rapid /'ræpɪd/ a rápido. ~ity /rə-'pɪdətɪ/ n rapidez f

rapids /'ræpɪdz/ npl rápidos mpl

rapist /'reɪpɪst/ n violador m, estuprador m

rapport /ræ'pɔː(r)/ n bom relacionamento m

rapt /ræpt/ a absorto. ~ in mergulhado em

rapture /'ræptʃə(r)/ n êxtase m. ~ous a extático; (welcome etc) entusiástico

rare¹ /reə(r)/ a (-er, -est) raro. ~ely adv raramente, raras vezes. ~ity n raridade f

rare² /reə(r)/ a (-er, -est) (culin) mal passado

rarefied /'reərɪfaɪd/ a rarefeito; (refined) requintado

raring /'reərɪŋ/ a ~ to (colloq) impaciente por, louco por (colloq)

rascal /'rɑːskl/ n (dishonest) patife m; (mischievous) maroto m

rash¹ /ræʃ/ n erupção f cutânea, irritação f na pele (colloq)

rash² /ræʃ/ a (-er, -est) imprudente, precipitado. ~ly adv imprudentemente, precipitadamente

rasher /'ræʃə(r)/ n fatia f (de presunto or de bacon)

rasp /rɑːsp/ n lixa f grossa, (P) lima f grossa

raspberry /'rɑːzbrɪ/ n framboesa f

rasping /'rɑːspɪŋ/ a áspero

rat /ræt/ n rato m, (P) ratazana f. ~ race (fig) luta renhida para vencer na vida, arrivismo m

rate /reɪt/ n (ratio) razão f; (speed) velocidade f; (price) tarifa f; (of exchange) taxa m de câmbio m; (of interest) taxa f. ~s (taxes) impostos mpl municipais, taxas fpl □ vt avaliar; (fig: consider) considerar. at any ~ de qualquer modo, pelo menos. at the ~ of à razão de. at this ~ desse jeito, desse modo

ratepayer /'reɪtpeɪə(r)/ n contribuinte mf

rather /'rɑːðə(r)/ adv (by preference) antes; (fairly) muito, bastante; (a little) um pouco. I would ~ go preferia ir

ratify /'rætɪfaɪ/ vt ratificar. ~ication /-ɪ'keɪʃn/ n ratificação f

rating /'reɪtɪŋ/ n (comm) rating m, (P) valor m; (sailor) praça f, marinheiro m; (radio, TV) índice m de audiência

ratio /'reɪʃɪəʊ/ n (pl -os) proporção f

ration /'ræʃn/ n ração f □ vt racionar

rational /'ræʃnəl/ a racional; (person) sensato, razoável. ~ize vt racionalizar

rattle /'rætl/ vt/i matraquear; (of door, window) bater; (of bottles) chocalhar; (colloq) agitar, mexer com os nervos de □ n (baby's toy) guizo m, chocalho m; (of football fan) matraca f; (sound) matraquear m, chocalhar m. ~ off despejar (colloq)

rattlesnake /'rætlsneɪk/ n cobra f cascavel

raucous /'rɔːkəs/ a áspero, rouco

ravage /'rævɪdʒ/ vt devastar, causar estragos a. ~s npl devastação f, estragos mpl

rave /reɪv/ vi delirar; (in anger) urrar. ~ about delirar (de entusiasmo) com

raven /'reɪvn/ n corvo m

ravenous /'rævənəs/ a esfomeado; (greedy) voraz

ravine /rə'viːn/ n ravina f, barranco m

raving /'reɪvɪŋ/ a ~ lunatic doido m varrido □ adv ~ mad loucamente

ravish /'rævɪʃ/ vt (rape) violar; (enrapture) arrebatar, encantar. ~ing a arrebatador, encantador

raw /rɔː/ a (-er, -est) cru; (not processed) bruto; (wound) em carne viva; (weather) frio e úmido, (P) húmido; (immature) inexperiente, verde. ~ deal tratamento m injusto. ~ material matéria-prima f

ray /reɪ/ n raio m

raze /reɪz/ vt arrasar

razor /'reɪzə(r)/ n navalha f de barba. ~-blade n lâmina f de barbear

re /riː/ prep a respeito de, em referência a, relativo a

re- /riː/ pref re-

reach /riːtʃ/ vt chegar a atingir; (contact) contatar; (pass) passar □ vi estender-se, chegar □ n alcance m. out of ~ fora de alcance. ~ for estender a mão para agarrar. within ~ of ao alcance de; (close to) próximo de

react /rɪ'ækt/ vi reagir

reaction /rɪ'ækʃn/ n reação f, (P) reacção f. ~ary a & n reacionário (m), (P) reaccionário (m)

reactor /rɪ'æktə(r)/ n reator m, (P) reactor m

read /riːd/ vt/i (pt read /red/) ler; (fig: interpret) interpretar; (study) estudar; (of instrument) marcar, indicar □ n (colloq) leitura f. ~ about ler um artigo sobre. ~ out ler em voz alta. ~able a agradável or fácil de ler; (legible) legível. ~er n leitor m; (book) livro m de leitura. ~ing n leitura f, (of instrument) registro m, (P) registo m

readily /'redɪlɪ/ adv de boa vontade, prontamente; (easily) facilmente

readiness /'redmɪs/ n prontidão f. in ~ pronto (for para)

readjust /riːə'dʒʌst/ vt reajustar □ vi readaptar-se

ready /'redɪ/ a (-ier, -iest) pronto □ n at the ~ pronto para disparar. ~-made a pronto. ~ money dinheiro m vivo, (P) dinheiro m de contado, pagamento m à vista. ~-to-wear a prêt-à-porter

real /rɪəl/ a real, verdadeiro; (genuine) autêntico □ adv (Amer: colloq) realmente. ~ estate bens mpl imobiliários

realis|t /'rɪəlɪst/ n realista mf. ~m /-zəm/ n realismo m. ~tic /'lɪstɪk/ a realista. ~tically /'lɪstɪkəlɪ/ adv realisticamente

reality /rɪ'æləti/ n realidade f

realiz|e /'rɪəlaɪz/ vt dar-se conta de, aperceber-se de, perceber; (fulfil; turn into cash) realizar. ~ation /-'zeɪʃn/ n consciência f, noção f; (fulfilment) realização f

really /'rɪəlɪ/ adv realmente, na verdade

realm /relm/ n reino m; (fig) domínio m, esfera f

reap /riːp/ vt (cut) ceifar; (gather; fig) colher

reappear /riːə'pɪə(r)/ vi reaparecer. ~ance n reaparição f

rear¹ /rɪə(r)/ n traseira f, retaguarda f □ a traseiro, de trás, posterior. bring up the ~ ir na retaguarda, fechar a marcha. ~-view mirror espelho m retrovisor

rear² /rɪə(r)/ vt levantar, erguer; (children, cattle) criar □ vi (of horse etc) empinar-se. ~ one's head levantar a cabeça

rearrange /riːə'reɪndʒ/ vt arranjar doutro modo, reorganizar

reason /'riːzn/ n razão f □ vt/i raciocinar, argumentar. ~ with sb procurar convencer alguém. within ~ razoável. ~ing n raciocínio m

reasonable /'riːznəbl/ a razoável

reassur|e /riːə'ʃʊə(r)/ vt tranqüilizar, sossegar. ~ance n garantia f. ~ing a animador, reconfortante

rebate /'riːbeɪt/ n (refund) reembolso m; (discount) desconto m, abatimento m

rebel¹ /'rebl/ n rebelde mf

rebel² /rɪ'bel/ vi (pt rebelled) rebelar-se, revoltar-se, sublevar-se. ~lion n rebelião f, revolta f. ~lious a rebelde

rebound¹ /rɪ'baʊnd/ vi repercutir, ressoar; (fig: backfire) recair (on sobre)

rebound² /'riːbaʊnd/ n ricochete m

rebuff /rɪ'bʌf/ vt receber mal, repelir (colloq) □ n rejeição f

rebuild /riː'bɪld/ vt (pt rebuilt) reconstruir

rebuke /rɪ'bjuːk/ vt repreender □ n reprimenda f

recall /rɪ'kɔːl/ vt chamar, mandar regressar; (remember) lembrar-se de □ n (summons) ordem f de regresso

recant /rɪ'kænt/ vi retratar-se, (P) retractar-se

recap /'riːkæp/ vt/i (pt recapped) (colloq) recapitular □ n recapitulação f

recapitulat|e /riːkə'pɪtʃʊleɪt/ vt/i recapitular. ~ion /-'leɪʃn/ n recapitulação f

recede /rɪ'siːd/ vi recuar, retroceder. his hair is ~ing ele fica ficando com entradas. ~ing a (forehead, chin) recuado, voltado para dentro

receipt /rɪ'siːt/ n recibo m; (receiving) recepção f. ~s (comm) receitas fpl

receive /rɪ'siːv/ vt receber. ~r /-ə(r)/ n (of stolen goods) receptador m; (phone) fone m, (P) auscultador m; (radio/TV) receptor m. (official) ~r síndico m de massa falida

recent /'riːsnt/ a recente. ~ly adv recentemente

receptacle /rɪ'septəkl/ n recipiente m, receptáculo m

reception /rɪ'sepʃn/ n recepção f; (welcome) acolhimento m. ~ist n recepcionista mf

receptive /rɪ'septɪv/ a receptivo

recess /rɪ'ses/ n recesso m; (of legislature) recesso m; (*Amer: schol*) recreio m

recession /rɪ'seʃn/ n recessão f, depressão f

recharge /ri:'tʃɑ:dʒ/ vt tornar a carregar, recarregar

recipe /'resəpɪ/ n (*culin*) receita f

recipient /rɪ'sɪpɪənt/ n recipiente *mf*; (*of letter*) destinatário m

reciprocal /rɪ'sɪprəkl/ a recíproco

reciprocate /rɪ'sɪprəkeɪt/ vt/i reciprocar(-se), retribuir, fazer o mesmo

recital /rɪ'saɪtl/ n (*music etc*) recital m

recite /rɪ'saɪt/ vt recitar; (*list*) enumerar

reckless /'reklɪs/ a inconsciente, imprudente, estouvado

reckon /'rekən/ vt/i calcular; (*judge*) considerar; (*think*) supor, pensar. ~ **on** contar com, depender de. ~ **with** contar com, levar em conta. ~**ing** n conta(s) f (*pl*)

reclaim /rɪ'kleɪm/ vt (*demand*) reclamar; (*land*) recuperar

recline /rɪ'klaɪn/ vt/i reclinar(-se). ~**ing** a (*person*) reclinado; (*chair*) reclinável

recluse /rɪ'klu:s/ n solitário m, recluso m

recognition /rekəg'nɪʃn/ n reconhecimento m. **beyond** ~ irreconhecível. **gain** ~ ganhar nome, ser reconhecido

recognize /'rekəgnaɪz/ vt reconhecer. ~**able** /'rekəgnaɪzəbl/ a reconhecível

recoil /rɪ'kɔɪl/ vi recuar; (*gun*) dar coice □ n recuo m; (*gun*) coice m. ~ **from doing** recusar-se a fazer

recollect /rekə'lekt/ vt recordar-se de. ~**ion** /-ʃn/ n recordação f

recommend /rekə'mend/ vt recomendar. ~**ation** /-'deɪʃn/ n recomendação f

recompense /'rekəmpens/ vt recompensar □ n recompensa f

reconcile /'rekənsaɪl/ vt (*people*) reconciliar; (*facts*) conciliar. ~**e o.s. to** resignar-se a, conformar-se com. ~**iation** /-sɪlɪ'eɪʃn/ n reconciliação f

reconnaissance /rɪ'kɒnɪsns/ n reconhecimento m

reconnoitre /rekə'nɔɪtə(r)/ vt/i (*pres p* -tring) (*mil*) reconhecer, fazer um reconhecimento (de)

reconsider /ri:kən'sɪdə(r)/ vt reconsiderar

reconstruct /ri:kən'strʌkt/ vt reconstruir. ~**ion** /-ʃn/ n reconstrução f

record /rɪ'kɔ:d/ vt registar; (*disc, tape etc*) gravar. ~ **that** referir/relatar que. ~**ing** n (*disc, tape etc*) gravação f

record /'rekɔ:d/ n (*register*) registro m, (P) registo m; (*mention*) menção f, nota f; (*file*) arquivo m; (*mus*) disco

m; (*sport*) record(e) m □ a record(e) *invar*. **have a (criminal)** ~ ter cadastro. **off the** ~ (*unofficial*) oficioso; (*secret*) confidencial. ~**-player** n toca-discos m *invar*, (P) gira-discos m *invar*

recorder /rɪ'kɔ:də(r)/ n (*mus*) flauta f de ponta; (*techn*) instrumento m registrador

recount /rɪ'kaʊnt/ vt narrar em pormenor, relatar

re-count /'ri:kaʊnt/ n (*pol*) nova contagem f

recoup /rɪ'ku:p/ vt compensar; (*recover*) recuperar

recourse /rɪ'kɔ:s/ n recurso m. **have** ~ **to** recorrer a

recover /rɪ'kʌvə(r)/ vt recuperar □ vi restabelecer-se. ~**y** n recuperação f, (*health*) recuperação f, restabelecimento m

recreation /rekrɪ'eɪʃn/ n recreação f, recreio m; (*pastime*) passatempo m. ~**al** a recreativo

recrimination /rɪkrɪmɪ'neɪʃn/ n recriminação f

recruit /rɪ'kru:t/ n recruta m □ vt recrutar. ~**ment** n recrutamento m

rectangle /'rektæŋgl/ n retângulo m, (P) rectângulo m. ~**ular** /-'tæŋgjʊlə(r)/ a retangular, (P) rectangular

rectify /'rektɪfaɪ/ vt retificar, (P) rectificar

recuperate /rɪ'kju:pəreɪt/ vt/i recuperar(-se)

recur /rɪ'kɜ:(r)/ vi (*pt* recurred) repetir-se; (*come back*) voltar (**to** a)

recurrent /rɪ'kʌrənt/ a freqüente, (P) frequente, repetido, periódico. ~**ce** n repetição f

recycle /ri:'saɪkl/ vt reciclar

red /red/ a (redder reddest) encarnado, vermelho; (*hair*) ruivo □ n encarnado m, vermelho m. **in the** ~ em déficit. ~ **carpet** (*fig*) recepção f solene, tratamento m especial. **R**~ **Cross** Cruz f Vermelha. ~**-handed** a em flagrante (delito), com a boca na botija (*colloq*). ~ **herring** (*fig*) pista f falsa. ~**-hot** a escaldante, incandescente. ~ **light** luz f vermelha. ~ **tape** (*fig*) papelada f, burocracia f. ~ **wine** vinho m tinto

redden /'redn/ vt/i avermelhar(-se); (*blush*) corar, ruborizar-se

redecorate /ri:'dekəreɪt/ vt decorar/pintar de novo

redeem /rɪ'di:m/ vt (*sins etc*) redimir; (*sth pawned*) tirar do prego (*colloq*); (*voucher etc*) resgatar. ~**emption** /rɪ'dempʃn/ n resgate m; (*of honour*) salvação f

redirect /ri:daɪ'rekt/ vt (*letter*) reendereçar

redness /'rednɪs/ *n* vermelhidão *f*, cor *f* vermelha

redo /ri:'du:/ *vt* (*pt* **-did**, *pp* **-done**) refazer

redress /rɪ'dres/ *vt* reparar; (*set right*) remediar, emendar. ~ **the balance** restabelecer o equilíbrio □ *n* reparação *f*

reduc|e /rɪ'dju:s/ *vt* reduzir; (*temperature etc*) baixar. ~**tion** /rɪ'dʌkʃn/ *n* redução *f*

redundan|t /rɪ'dʌndənt/ *a* redundante, supérfluo; (*worker*) desempregado. **be made** ~**t** ficar desempregado. ~**cy** *n* demissão *f* por excesso de pessoal

reed /ri:d/ *n* cara *f*, junco *m*; (*mus*) palheta *f*

reef /ri:f/ *n* recife *m*

reek /ri:k/ *n* mau cheiro *m* □ *vi* cheirar mal, tresandar. **he** ~**s of wine** ele está com cheiro de vinho

reel /ri:l/ *n* carretel *m*; (*spool*) bobina *f* □ *vi* cambalear, vacilar □ *vt* ~ **off** recitar (*colloq*)

refectory /rɪ'fektərɪ/ *n* refeitório *m*

refer /rɪ'fɜ:(r)/ *vt/i* (*pt* **referred**) ~ **to** referir-se a; (*concern*) aplicar-se a, dizer respeito a; (*consult*) consultar; (*direct*) remeter a

referee /refə'ri:/ *n* árbitro *m*; (*for job*) pessoa *f* que dá referências □ *vt* (*pt* **refereed**) arbitrar

reference /'refrəns/ *n* referência *f*; (*testimonial*) referências *fpl*. **in** ~ **or with** ~ **to** com referência a. ~ **book** livro *m* de consulta

referendum /refə'rendəm/ *n* (*pl* **-dums** *or* **-da**) referendo *m*, plebiscito *m*

refill[1] /ri:'fɪl/ *vt* encher de novo; (*pen etc*) carga *f* nova, (*P*) recarga *f*

refill[2] /'ri:fɪl/ *n* (*pen etc*) carga *f* nova, (*P*) recarga *f*

refine /rɪ'faɪn/ *vt* refinar. ~**d** *a* refinado; (*taste, manners etc*) requintado. ~**ment** *n* (*taste, manners etc*) refinamento *m*, requinte *m*; (*tech*) refinação *f*. ~**ry** /-ərɪ/ *n* refinaria *f*

reflect /rɪ'flekt/ *vt/i* refletir, (*P*) reflectir (**on/upon** em). ~**ion** /-ʃn/ *n* reflexão *f*; (*image*) reflexo *m*. ~**or** *n* refletor *m*, (*P*) reflector *m*

reflective /rɪ'flektɪv/ *a* refletor, (*P*) reflector; (*thoughtful*) refletido, (*P*) reflectido, ponderado

reflex /'ri:fleks/ *a* & *n* reflexo (*m*)

reflexive /rɪ'fleksɪv/ *a* (*gram*) reflexivo, (*P*) reflexo

reform /rɪ'fɔ:m/ *vt/i* reformar(-se) □ *n* reforma *f*. ~**er** *n* reformador *m*

refract /rɪ'frækt/ *vt* refratar, (*P*) refractar

refrain[1] /rɪ'freɪn/ *n* refrão *m*, estribilho *m*

refrain[2] /rɪ'freɪn/ *vi* abster-se (**from** de)

refresh /rɪ'freʃ/ *vt* refrescar; (*of rest etc*) restaurar. ~ **one's memory** avivar *or* refrescar a memória. ~**ing** *a* refrescante; (*of rest etc*) reparador. ~**ments** *npl* refeição *f* leve; (*drinks*) refrescos *mpl*

refresher /rɪ'freʃə(r)/ *n* ~ **course** curso *m* de reciclagem

refrigerat|e /rɪ'frɪdʒəreɪt/ *vt* refrigerar. ~**or** *n* frigorífico *m*, refrigerador *m*, geladeira *f*

refuel /ri:'fju:əl/ *vt/i* (*pt* **refuelled**) reabastecer(-se) (de combustível)

refuge /'refju:dʒ/ *n* refúgio *m*, asilo *m*. **take** ~ refugiar-se

refugee /refju'dʒi:/ *n* refugiado *m*

refund[1] /rɪ'fʌnd/ *vt* reembolsar

refund[2] /'ri:fʌnd/ *n* reembolso *m*

refus|e[1] /rɪ'fju:z/ *vt/i* recusar(-se). ~**al** *n* recusa *f*. **first** ~**al** preferência *f*, primeira opção *f*

refuse[2] /'refju:s/ *n* refugo *m*, lixo *m*. ~**-collector** *n* lixeiro *m*, (*P*) homem *m* do lixo

refute /rɪ'fju:t/ *vt* refutar

regain /rɪ'geɪn/ *vt* recobrar, recuperar

regal /'ri:gl/ *a* real, régio

regalia /rɪ'geɪlɪə/ *npl* insígnias *fpl*

regard /rɪ'gɑ:d/ *vt* considerar; (*gaze*) olhar □ *n* consideração *f*, estima *f*; (*gaze*) olhar *m*. ~**s** cumprimentos *mpl*; (*less formally*) lembranças *fpl*, saudades *fpl*. **as** ~**s**, ~**ing** *prep* no que diz respeito a, quanto a. ~**less** *adv* apesar de tudo. ~**less of** apesar de

regatta /rɪ'gætə/ *n* regata *f*

regenerate /rɪ'dʒenəreɪt/ *vt* regenerar

regen|t /'ri:dʒənt/ *n* regente *mf*. ~**cy** *n* regência *f*

regime /reɪ'ʒi:m/ *n* regime *m*

regiment /'redʒɪmənt/ *n* regimento *m*. ~**al** /-'mentl/ *a* de regimento, regimental. ~**ation** /-en'teɪʃn/ *n* arregimentação *f*, disciplina *f* excessiva

region /'ri:dʒən/ *n* região *f*. **in the** ~ **of** por volta de. ~**al** *a* regional

regist|er /'redʒɪstə(r)/ *n* registro *m*, (*P*) registo *m* □ *vt* (*record*) anotar; (*notice*) fixar, registar, prestar atenção a; (*birth, letter*) registar, (*P*) registar; (*vehicle*) matricular; (*emotions etc*) exprimir □ *vi* inscrever-se. ~**er office** registro *m*, (*P*) registo *m*. ~**ration** /-'streɪʃn/ *n* registro *m*, (*P*) registo *m*; (*for course*) inscrição *f*, matrícula *f*. ~**ration (number)** número *m* de placa

registrar /redʒɪ'strɑ:(r)/ *n* oficial *m* do registro, (*P*) registo civil; (*univ*) secretário *m*

regret /rɪ'gret/ n pena f, pesar m; (repentance) remorso m. I have no ~s não estou arrependido □ vt (pt regretted) lamentar, sentir (to do fazer); (feel repentance) arrepender-se de, lamentar. ~fully adv com pena, pesarosamente. ~table a lamentável. ~tably adv infelizmente

regular /'regjʊlə(r)/ a regular; (usual) normal; (colloq: thorough) perfeito, verdadeiro, autêntico □ n (colloq: client) cliente mf habitual. ~ity /-'lærətɪ/ n regularidade f. ~ly adv regularmente

regulat|e /'regjʊleɪt/ vt regular. ~ion /-'leɪʃn/ n regulação f; (rule) regulamento m, regra f

rehabilitat|e /ri:ə'bɪlɪteɪt/ vt reabilitar. ~ion /-'teɪʃn/ n reabilitação f

rehash /ri:'hæʃ/ vt apresentar sob nova forma, (P) cozinhar (colloq)

rehash² /'ri:hæʃ/ n (fig) apanhado m, (P) cozinhado m (colloq)

rehears|e /rɪ'hɜ:s/ vt ensaiar. ~al n ensaio m. dress ~al ensaio m geral

reign /reɪn/ n reinado m □ vi reinar (over em)

reimburse /ri:ɪm'bɜ:s/ vt reembolsar. ~ment n reembolso m

rein /reɪn/ n rédea f

reincarnation /ri:ɪnka:'neɪʃn/ n reencarnação f

reindeer /'reɪndɪə(r)/ n invar rena f

reinforce /ri:ɪn'fɔ:s/ vt reforçar. ~ment n reforço m. ~ments reforços mpl. ~d concrete concreto m armado, (P) cimento m or betão m armado

reinstate /ri:ɪn'steɪt/ vt reintegrar

reiterate /ri:'ɪtəreɪt/ vt reiterar

reject¹ /rɪ'dʒekt/ vt rejeitar. ~ion /-ʃn/ n rejeição f

reject² /'ri:dʒekt/ n (artigo de) refugo m

rejoic|e /rɪ'dʒɔɪs/ vi regozijar-se (at/ over com). ~ing n regozijo m

rejuvenate /rɪ'dʒu:vəneɪt/ vt rejuvenescer

relapse /rɪ'læps/ n recaída f □ vi recair

relate /rɪ'leɪt/ vt relatar; (associate) relacionar □ vi ~ to ter relação com, dizer respeito a; (get on with) entender-se com. ~d a aparentado; (ideas etc) afim, relacionado

relation /rɪ'leɪʃn/ n relação f; (person) parente mf. ~ship n parentesco m; (link) relação f; (affair) ligação f

relative /'relətɪv/ n parente mf □ a relativo. ~ly adv relativamente

relax /rɪ'læks/ vt/i relaxar(-se); (fig) descontrair(-se). ~ation /ri:læk-'seɪʃn/ n relaxamento m; (fig) descontração f, (P) descontracção f;

(recreation) distração f, (P) distracção f ~ing a relaxante

relay¹ /'ri:leɪ/ n turma f, (P) turno m. ~ race corrida f de revezamento, (P) estafetas

relay² /rɪ'leɪ/ vt (message) retransmitir

release /rɪ'li:s/ vt libertar, soltar; (mech) desengatar, soltar; (bomb, film, record) lançar; (news) dar, publicar; (gas, smoke) soltar □ n libertação f; (mech) desengate m; (bomb, film, record) lançamento m; (news) publicação f; (gas, smoke) emissão f. new ~ estréia f

relegate /'relɪgeɪt/ vt relegar

relent /rɪ'lent/ vi ceder. ~less a implacável, inexorável, inflexível

relevan|t /'reləvənt/ a relevante, pertinente, a propósito. be ~ to ter a ver com. ~ce n pertinência f, relevância f

reliab|le /rɪ'laɪəbl/ a de confiança, com que se pode contar; (source etc) fidedigno; (machine etc) seguro, confiável. ~ility /-'bɪlətɪ/ n confiabilidade f

reliance /rɪ'laɪəns/ n (dependence) segurança f; (trust) confiança f, fé f (on em)

relic /'relɪk/ n relíquia f. ~s vestígios mpl, ruínas fpl

relief /rɪ'li:f/ n alívio m; (assistance) auxílio m, assistência f; (outline, design) relevo m. ~ road estrada f alternativa

relieve /rɪ'li:v/ vt aliviar; (help) socorrer; (take over from) revezar, substituir; (mil) render

religion /rɪ'lɪdʒən/ n religião f

religious /rɪ'lɪdʒəs/ a religioso

relinquish /rɪ'lɪŋkwɪʃ/ vt abandonar, renunciar a

relish /'relɪʃ/ n prazer m, gosto m; (culin) molho m condimentado □ vt saborear, apreciar, gostar de

relocate /ri:ləʊ'keɪt/ vt/i transferir (-se), mudar(-se)

reluctan|t /rɪ'lʌktənt/ a relutante (to em), pouco inclinado (to a). ~ce n relutância f. ~tly adv a contragosto, relutantemente

rely /rɪ'laɪ/ vi ~ on contar com; (depend) depender de

remain /rɪ'meɪn/ vi ficar, permanecer. ~s npl restos mpl; (ruins) ruínas fpl. ~ing a restante

remainder /rɪ'meɪndə(r)/ n restante m, remanescente m

remand /rɪ'ma:nd/ vt reconduzir à prisão para detenção provisória □ n on ~ sob prisão preventiva

remark /rɪ'ma:k/ n observação f, comentário m □ vt observar, comen-

tar □ *vi* ~ on fazer observações *or*
comentários sobre. ~able *a* notável
remarr|y /riːˈmærɪ/ *vt/i* tornar a ca-
sar(-se) (com). ~iage *n* novo casamento *m*
remed|y /ˈremədɪ/ *n* remédio *m* □ *vt*
remediar. ~ial /rɪˈmiːdɪəl/ *a* (*med*)
corretivo, (*P*) correctivo
rememb|er /rɪˈmembə(r)/ *vt* lembrar-
se de, recordar-se de. ~rance *n*
lembrança *f*, recordação *f*
remind /rɪˈmaɪnd/ *vt* (fazer) lembrar
(sb of sth alg coisa a alguém). ~ sb
to do lembrar a alguém que faça. ~er
n o que serve para fazer lembrar;
(*note*) lembrete *m*
reminisce /remɪˈnɪs/ *vi* (re)lembrar
(coisas passadas). ~nces *npl* remi-
niscências *fpl*
reminiscent /remɪˈnɪsnt/ *a* ~ of que
faz lembrar, evocativo de
remiss /rɪˈmɪs/ *a* negligente, descuidado
remission /rɪˈmɪʃn/ *n* remissão *f*;
(*jur*) comutação *f* (de pena)
remit /rɪˈmɪt/ *vt* (*pt* remitted)
(*money*) remeter. ~tance *n* remessa
f (de dinheiro)
remnant /ˈremnənt/ *n* resto *m*; (*trace*)
vestígio *m*; (*of cloth*) retalho *m*
remorse /rɪˈmɔːs/ *n* remorso *m*. ~ful
a arrependido, com remorsos. ~less
a implacável
remote /rɪˈməʊt/ *a* remoto, distante;
(*person*) distante; (*slight*) vago, leve.
~ control comando *m* à distância,
telecomando *m*. ~ly *adv* de longe;
vagamente
remov|e /rɪˈmuːv/ *vt* tirar, remover;
(*lead away*) levar; (*dismiss*) demitir;
(*get rid of*) eliminar. ~al *n* remoção
f; (*dismissal*) demissão *f*; (*from
house*) mudança *f*
remunerat|e /rɪˈmjuːnəreɪt/ *vt* remu-
nerar. ~ion /-ˈreɪʃn/ *n* remunera-
ção *f*
rename /riːˈneɪm/ *vt* rebatizar, (*P*) re-
baptizar
render /ˈrendə(r)/ *vt* retribuir; (*ser-
vices*) prestar; (*mus*) interpretar;
(*translate*) traduzir. ~ing *n* (*mus*)
interpretação *f*; (*plaster*) reboco *m*
renegade /ˈrenɪgeɪd/ *n* renegado *m*
renew /rɪˈnjuː/ *vt* renovar; (*resume*)
retomar. ~able *a* renovável. ~al *n*
renovação *f*; (*resumption*) reatamento
m
renounce /rɪˈnaʊns/ *vt* renunciar a;
(*disown*) renegar, repudiar
renovat|e /ˈrenəveɪt/ *vt* renovar.
~ion /-ˈveɪʃn/ *n* renovação *f*
renown /rɪˈnaʊn/ *n* renome *m*. ~ed *a*
conceituado, célebre, de renome
rent /rent/ *n* aluguel *m*, (*P*) aluguer

m, renda *f* □ *vt* alugar, arrendar. ~al
n (*charge*) aluguel *m*, (*P*) aluguer *m*,
renda *f*; (*act of renting*) aluguel *m*, (*P*)
aluguer *m*
renunciation /rɪnʌnsɪˈeɪʃn/ *n* renúncia *f*
reopen /riːˈəʊpən/ *vt/i* reabrir(-se).
~ing *n* reabertura *f*
reorganize /riːˈɔːgənaɪz/ *vt/i* reorga-
nizar(-se)
rep /rep/ *n* (*colloq*) vendedor *m*, cai-
xeiro-viajante *m*
repair /rɪˈpeə(r)/ *vt* reparar, consertar □ *n* reparo *m*, conserto *m*. in good
~ em bom estado (de conservação)
repartee /repaːˈtiː/ *n* resposta *f* pron-
ta e espirituosa
repatriat|e /riːˈpætrɪeɪt/ *vt* repatriar.
~ion /ˈeɪʃn/ *n* repatriamento *m*
repay /riːˈpeɪ/ *vt* (*pt* repaid) pagar,
devolver, reembolsar; (*reward*)
recompensar. ~ment *n* pagamento
m, reembolso *m*
repeal /rɪˈpiːl/ *vt* revogar □ *n*
revogação *f*
repeat /rɪˈpiːt/ *vt/i* repetir(-se) □ *n*
repetição *f*; (*broadcast*) retrans-
missão *f*. ~edly *adv* repetidas vezes,
repetidamente
repel /rɪˈpel/ *vt* (*pt* repelled) repelir.
~lent *a & n* repelente (*m*)
repent /rɪˈpent/ *vi* arrepender-se (of
de). ~ance *n* arrependimento *m*.
~ant *a* arrependido
repercussion /riːpəˈkʌʃn/ *n* re-
percussão *f*
repertoire /ˈrepətwaː(r)/ *n* repertório
m
repertory /ˈrepətrɪ/ *n* repertório *m*
repetit|ion /repɪˈtɪʃn/ *n* repetição *f*.
~ious /-ˈtɪʃəs/, ~ive /rɪˈpetətɪv/ *a* re-
petitivo
replace /rɪˈpleɪs/ *vt* colocar no mesmo
lugar, repor; (*take the place of*)
substituir. ~ment *n* reposição *f*; (*sub-
stitution*) substituição *f*; (*person*)
substituto *m*
replenish /rɪˈplenɪʃ/ *vt* voltar a encher, reabastecer; (*renew*) renovar
replica /ˈreplɪkə/ *n* réplica *f*, cópia *f*,
reprodução *f*
reply /rɪˈplaɪ/ *vt/i* responder, replicar
□ *n* resposta *f*, réplica *f*
report /rɪˈpɔːt/ *vt* relatar; (*notify*) informar; (*denounce*) denunciar, apresentar queixa de □ *vi* fazer um
relatório. ~ (on) (*news item*) fazer
uma reportagem (sobre). ~ to (*go*)
apresentar-se a □ *n* (*in newspapers*)
reportagem *f*; (*of company, doctor*)
relatório *m*; (*schol*) boletim *m* escolar; (*sound*) detonação *f*; (*rumour*) ru-
mores *mpl*. ~edly *adv* segundo
consta. ~er *n* repórter *m*

repose /rɪˈpəʊz/ n repouso m

repossess /riːpəˈzes/ vt reapossar-se de, retomar de

represent /reprɪˈzent/ vt representar. ~ation /-ˈteɪʃn/ n representação f

representative /reprɪˈzentətɪv/ a representativo □ n representante mf

repress /rɪˈpres/ vt reprimir. ~ion /-ʃn/ n repressão f. ~ive a repressor, repressivo

reprieve /rɪˈpriːv/ n suspensão f temporária; (temporary relief) tréguas fpl □ vt suspender temporariamente; (fig) dar tréguas a

reprimand /ˈreprɪmɑːnd/ vt repreender □ n repreensão f, reprimenda f

reprint /ˈriːprɪnt/ n reimpressão f, reedição f □ vt /riːˈprɪnt/

reprisals /rɪˈpraɪzlz/ npl represálias fpl

reproach /rɪˈprəʊtʃ/ vt censurar, repreender (sb for sth alguém por alg coisa, alg coisa a alguém) □ n censura f. above ~ irrepreensível. ~ful a repreensivo, reprovador. ~fully adv reprovadoramente

reproduc|e /riːprəˈdjuːs/ vt/i reproduzir(-se). ~tion /-ˈdʌkʃn/ n reprodução f. ~tive /-ˈdʌktɪv/ a reprodutivo, reprodutor

reptile /ˈreptaɪl/ n réptil m

republic /rɪˈpʌblɪk/ n república f. ~an a & n republicano (m)

repudiate /rɪˈpjuːdɪeɪt/ vt repudiar, rejeitar

repugnan|t /rɪˈpʌgnənt/ a repugnante. ~ce n repugnância f

repuls|e /rɪˈpʌls/ vt repelir, repulsar. ~ion /-ʃn/ n repulsa f. ~ive a repulsivo, repelente, repugnante

reputable /ˈrepjʊtəbl/ a respeitado, honrado; (firm, make etc) de renome, conceituado

reputation /repjʊˈteɪʃn/ n reputação f

repute /rɪˈpjuːt/ n reputação f. ~d /-ɪd/ a suposto, putativo. ~d to be tido como, tido na conta de. ~dly /-ɪdlɪ/ adv segundo consta, com fama de

request /rɪˈkwest/ n pedido m □ vt pedir, solicitar (of, from a)

requiem /ˈrekwɪəm/ n réquiem m; (mass) missa f de réquiem

require /rɪˈkwaɪə(r)/ vt requerer. ~d a requerido; (needed) necessário, preciso. ~ment n (fig) requisito m; (need) necessidade f, (demand) exigência f

requisite /ˈrekwɪzɪt/ a necessário □ n coisa necessária f, requisito m. ~s (for travel etc) artigos mpl

requisition /rekwɪˈzɪʃn/ n requisição f □ vt requisitar

resale /ˈriːseɪl/ n revenda f

rescue /ˈreskjuː/ vt salvar, socorrer (from de) □ n salvamento m; (help) socorro m, ajuda f. ~r /-ə(r)/ n salvador m

research /rɪˈsɜːtʃ/ n pesquisa f, investigação f □ vt/i pesquisar, fazer investigação (into sobre). ~er n investigador m

resembl|e /rɪˈzembl/ vt assemelhar-se a, parecer-se com. ~ance n semelhança f, similaridade f (to com)

resent /rɪˈzent/ vt ressentir(-se de), ficar ressentido com. ~ful a ressentido. ~ment n ressentimento m

reservation /rezəˈveɪʃn/ n (booking) reserva f; (Amer) reserva f (de índios)

reserve /rɪˈzɜːv/ vt reservar □ n reserva f; (sport) suplente mf. in ~ de reserva. ~d a reservado

reservoir /ˈrezəvwɑː(r)/ n (lake, supply etc) reservatório m; (container) depósito m

reshape /riːˈʃeɪp/ vt remodelar

reshuffle /riːˈʃʌfl/ vt (pol) remodelar □ n (pol) reforma f (do Ministério)

reside /rɪˈzaɪd/ vi residir

residen|t /ˈrezɪdənt/ a residente □ n morador m, habitante mf; (foreigner) residente mf; (in hotel) hóspede mf. ~ce n residência f; (official) residência f, lar m. ~ce permit visto m de residência

residential /rezɪˈdenʃl/ a residencial

residue /ˈrezɪdjuː/ n resíduo m

resign /rɪˈzaɪn/ vt (post) demitir-se. ~ o.s. to resignar-se a □ vi demitir-se de. ~ation /rezɪgˈneɪʃn/ n resignação f; (from job) demissão f. ~ed a resignado

resilien|t /rɪˈzɪlɪənt/ a (springy) elástico; (person) resistente. ~ce n elasticidade f; (of person) resistência f

resin /ˈrezɪn/ n resina f

resist /rɪˈzɪst/ vt/i resistir (a). ~ance n resistência f. ~ant a resistente

resolut|e /ˈrezəluːt/ a resoluto. ~ion /-ˈluːʃn/ n resolução f

resolve /rɪˈzɒlv/ vt resolver. ~ to do resolver fazer □ n resolução f. ~d a (resolute) resoluto; (decided) resolvido (to a)

resonan|t /ˈrezənənt/ a ressonante. ~ce n ressonância f

resort /rɪˈzɔːt/ vi ~ to recorrer a, valer-se de □ n recurso m; (place) estância f, local m turístico. as a last ~ em último recurso. seaside ~ praia f, balneário m, (P) estância f balnear

resound /rɪˈzaʊnd/ vi reboar, ressoar (with com). ~ing a ressoante; (fig) retumbante

resource /rɪˈsɔːs/ n recurso m. ~s recursos mpl, riquezas fpl. ~ful a

expedito, engenhoso, desembaraçado.
~fulness *n* expediente *m*, engenho *m*

respect /rɪ'spekt/ *n* respeito *m* □ *vt*
respeitar. with ~ to a respeito de,
com respeito a, relativamente a.
~ful *a* respeitoso

respectab|le /rɪ'spektəbl/ *a* respeitá-
vel; (*passable*) passável, aceitável.
~ility /-'bɪlətɪ/ *n* res-peitabilidade *f*

respective /rɪ'spektɪv/ *a* respectivo.
~ly *adv* respectivamente

respiration /respə'reɪʃn/ *n* respiração *f*

respite /'respaɪt/ *n* pausa *f*, trégua *f*,
folga *f*

respond /rɪ'spɒnd/ *vi* responder (to
a); (*react*) reagir (to a)

response /rɪ'spɒns/ *n* resposta *f*; (*reaction*) reação *f*, (P) reacção *f*

responsib|le /rɪ'spɒnsəbl/ *a* respon-
sável; (*job*) de responsabilidade.
~ility /-'bɪlətɪ/ *n* responsabilidade
f

responsive /rɪ'spɒnsɪv/ *a* receptivo,
que reage bem. ~ to sensível a

rest¹ /rest/ *vt/i* descansar, repousar;
(*lean*) apoiar(-se) □ *n* descanso *m*, repouso *m*; (*support*) suporte *m*. ~-
room *n* (*Amer*) banheiro *m*, (P) toa-
letes *mpl*

rest² /rest/ *vi* (*remain*) ficar □ *n* (*remainder*) resto *m* (of de). the ~ (of
the) (*others*) os outros. it ~s with
him cabe a ele

restaurant /'restrɒnt/ *n* restaurante
m

restful /'restfl/ *a* sossegado, repou-
sante, tranquilo, (P) tranquilo

restitution /restɪ'tjuːʃn/ *n* restituição
f; (*for injury*) indenização *f*, (P)
indemnização *f*

restless /'restlɪs/ *a* agitado, desasso-
segado

restor|e /rɪ'stɔː(r)/ *vt* restaurar; (*give
back*) restituir, devolver. ~ation
/restə'reɪʃn/ *n* restauração *f*

restrain /rɪ'streɪn/ *vt* conter, reprimir. ~ o.s. controlar-se. ~ sb
from impedir alguém de. ~ed *a* comedido, reservado. ~t *n* controle *m*;
(*moderation*) moderação *f*, comedi-
mento *m*

restrict /rɪ'strɪkt/ *vt* restringir,
limitar. ~ion /-ʃn/ *n* restrição *f*.
~ive *a* restritivo

result /rɪ'zʌlt/ *n* resultado *m* □ *vi* resultar (from de). ~ in resultar em

resume /rɪ'zjuːm/ *vt/i* reatar, retomar; (*work, travel*) recomeçar.
~ption /rɪ'zʌmpʃn/ *n* reatamento *m*,
retomada *f*; (*of work*) recomeço *m*

résumé /'rezjuːmeɪ/ *n* resumo *m*

resurgence /rɪ'sɜːdʒəns/ *n* reapareci-
mento *m*, ressurgimento *m*

resurrect /rezə'rekt/ *vt* ressuscitar.
~ion /-ʃn/ *n* ressureição *f*

resuscitat|e /rɪ'sʌsɪteɪt/ *vt* ressusci-
tar, reanimar. ~ion /-'teɪʃn/ *n*
reanimação *f*

retail /'riːteɪl/ *n* retalho *m* □ *a* & *adv* a
retalho □ *vt/i* vender(-se) a retalho.
~er *n* retalhista *mf*

retain /rɪ'teɪn/ *vt* reter; (*keep*) conservar, guardar

retaliat|e /rɪ'tælieɪt/ *vi* retaliar, exer-
cer represálias, desforrar-se. ~ion
/-'eɪʃn/ *n* retaliação *f*, represália *f*,
desforra *f*

retarded /rɪ'tɑːdɪd/ *a* retardado, atrasado

retch /retʃ/ *vi* fazer esforço para vomitar, estar com ânsias de vômito

retention /rɪ'tenʃn/ *n* retenção *f*

retentive /rɪ'tentɪv/ *a* retentivo. ~
memory boa memória *f*

reticen|t /'retɪsnt/ *a* reticente. ~ce *n*
reticência *f*

retina /'retɪnə/ *n* retina *f*

retinue /'retɪnjuː/ *n* séquito *m*, comitiva *f*

retire /rɪ'taɪə(r)/ *vi* reformar-se,
aposentar-se; (*withdraw*) retirar-se;
(*go to bed*) ir deitar-se □ *vt*
reformar, aposentar. ~d *a* reformado,
aposentado. ~ment *n* reforma *f*,
aposentadoria *f*, (P) aposentação *f*

retiring /rɪ'taɪərɪŋ/ *a* reservado, retraído

retort /rɪ'tɔːt/ *vt/i* retrucar, retorquir
□ *n* réplica *f*

retrace /riː'treɪs/ *vt* ~ one's steps
refazer o mesmo caminho; (*fig*) recordar, recapitular

retract /rɪ'trækt/ *vt/i* retratar(-se);
(*wheels*) recolher; (*claws*) encolher, recolher

retreat /rɪ'triːt/ *vi* retirar-se; (*mil*) retirar, bater em retirada □ *n* retirada *f*;
(*seclusion*) retiro *m*

retrial /riː'traɪəl/ *n* novo julgamento
m

retribution /retrɪ'bjuːʃn/ *n* castigo
(merecido) *m*; (*vengeance*) vingança *f*

retrieve /rɪ'triːv/ *vt* ir buscar; (*rescue*) salvar; (*recover*) recuperar; (*put
right*) reparar. ~ *n* recuperação *f*.
information ~al (*comput*) acesso *m*
à informação. ~er *n* (*dog*) perdi-
gueiro *m*, (P) cobrador *m*

retrograde /'retrəgreɪd/ *a* retrógrado
□ *vt* retroceder, recuar

retrospect /'retrəspekt/ *n* in ~ em
retrospecto, (P) retrospectivamente.
~ive /-'spektɪv/ *a* retrospectivo; (*of
law, payment*) retroativo, (P) retroac-
tivo

return /rɪ'tɜːn/ *vi* voltar, regressar,
retornar (to, a) □ *vt* devolver; (*compli-*

ment, visit) retribuir; (*put back*) pôr de volta □ *n* volta *f*, regresso *m*, retorno *m*; (*profit*) lucro *m*, rendimento *m*; (*restitution*) devolução *f*. in ~ for em troca de. ~ *journey* viagem *f* de volta. ~ match (*sport*) desafio *m* de desforra. ~ ticket bilhete *m* de ida e volta. many happy ~s (of the day) muitos parabéns

reunion /riːˈjuːnɪən/ *n* reunião *f*

reunite /riːjuːˈnaɪt/ *vt* reunir

rev /rev/ *n* (*colloq: auto*) rotação *f* □ *vt/i* (*pt* revved) ~ (up) (*colloq: auto*) acelerar (o motor)

reveal /rɪˈviːl/ *vt* revelar; (*display*) expor. ~ing *a* revelador

revel /ˈrevl/ *vi* (*pt* revelled) divertir-se. ~ in deleitar-se com. ~ry *n* festas *fpl*, festejos *mpl*

revelation /revəˈleɪʃn/ *n* revelação *f*

revenge /rɪˈvendʒ/ *n* vingança *f*; (*sport*) desforra *f* □ *vt* vingar

revenue /ˈrevənjuː/ *n* receita *f*, rendimento *m*. Inland R~ Fisco *m*

reverberate /rɪˈvɜːbəreɪt/ *vi* ecoar, repercutir

revere /rɪˈvɪə(r)/ *vt* reverenciar, venerar

reverend /ˈrevərənd/ *a* reverendo. R~ Reverendo

reverent /ˈrevərənt/ *a* reverente. ~ce *n* reverência *f*, veneração *f*

reverse /rɪˈvɜːs/ *a* contrário, inverso □ *n* contrário *m*; (*back*) reverso *m*; (*gear*) marcha *f* à ré, (*P*) atrás □ *vt* virar ao contrário; (*order*) inverter; (*turn inside out*) virar do avesso; (*decision*) anular □ *vi* (*auto*) fazer marcha à ré, (*P*) atrás. ~al *n* inversão *f*, mudança *f* em sentido contrário; (*of view etc*) mudança *f*

revert /rɪˈvɜːt/ *vi* ~ to reverter a

review /rɪˈvjuː/ *n* (*inspection; magazine*) revista *f*; (*of a situation*) revisão *f*; (*critique*) crítica *f* □ *vt* revistar, passar revista em; (*situation*) rever; (*book, film etc*) fazer a crítica de. ~er *n* crítico *m*

revise /rɪˈvaɪz/ *vt* rever; (*amend*) corrigir. ~ion /-ɪʒn/ *n* revisão *f*; (*amendment*) correção *f*

revive /rɪˈvaɪv/ *vt/i* ressuscitar, reavivar; (*play*) reapresentar; (*person*) reanimar(-se). ~al *n* reflorescimento *m*, renascimento *m*

revoke /rɪˈvəʊk/ *vt* revogar, anular, invalidar

revolt /rɪˈvəʊlt/ *vt/i* revoltar(-se) □ *n* revolta *f*

revolting /rɪˈvəʊltɪŋ/ *a* (*disgusting*) repugnante

revolution /revəˈluːʃn/ *n* revolução *f*. ~ary *a* & *n* revolucionário (*m*). ~ize *vt* revolucionar

revolve /rɪˈvɒlv/ *vi* girar. ~ing door porta *f* giratória

revolver /rɪˈvɒlvə(r)/ *n* revólver *m*

revulsion /rɪˈvʌlʃn/ *n* repugnância *f*, repulsa *f*

reward /rɪˈwɔːd/ *n* prémio *m*, (*P*) prémio *m*; (*for criminal, for lost/ stolen property*) recompensa *f* □ *vt* recompensar. ~ing *a* compensador; (*task etc*) gratificante

rewind /riːˈwaɪnd/ *vt* (*pt* rewound) rebobinar

rewrite /riːˈraɪt/ *vt* (*pt* rewrote, *pp* rewritten) reescrever

rhetoric /ˈretərɪk/ *n* retórica *f*. ~al /rɪˈtɒrɪkl/ *a* retórico; (*question*) pro forma

rheumatic /ruːˈmætɪk/ *a* reumático. ~sm /ˈruːmətɪzm/ *n* reumatismo *m*

rhinoceros /raɪˈnɒsərəs/ *n* (*pl* -oses) rinoceronte *m*

rhubarb /ˈruːbɑːb/ *n* ruibarbo *m*

rhyme /raɪm/ *n* rima *f*; (*poem*) versos *mpl* □ *vt/i* (fazer) rimar

rhythm /ˈrɪðəm/ *n* ritmo *m*. ~ic(al) /ˈrɪðmɪk(l)/ *a* rítmico, compassado

rib /rɪb/ *n* costela *f*

ribbon /ˈrɪbən/ *n* fita *f*. in ~s em tiras

rice /raɪs/ *n* arroz *m*

rich /rɪtʃ/ *a* (-er, -est) rico; (*food*) rico em açúcar e gordura. ~es *npl* riquezas *fpl*. ~ly *adv* ricamente. ~ness *n* riqueza *f*

rickety /ˈrɪkətɪ/ *a* (*shaky*) desconjuntado

ricochet /ˈrɪkəʃeɪ/ *n* ricochete *m* □ *vi* (*pt* ricocheted /-ʃeɪd/) fazer ricochete, ricochetear

rid /rɪd/ *vt* (*pt* rid, *pres p* ridding) desembaraçar (of de). get ~ of desembaraçar-se de, livrar-se de

riddance /ˈrɪdns/ *n* good ~! que alívio!, vai com Deus!

ridden /ˈrɪdn/ *see* ride

riddle¹ /ˈrɪdl/ *n* enigma *m*; (*puzzle*) charada *f*

riddle² /ˈrɪdl/ *vt* ~ with crivar de

ride /raɪd/ *vi* (*pt* rode, *pp* ridden) andar de bicicleta, a cavalo, de carro) □ *vt* (*horse*) montar; (*bicycle*) andar de; (*distance*) percorrer □ *n* passeio *m* or volta *f* (de carro, a cavalo etc); (*distance*) percurso *m*. ~r /-ə(r)/ *n* cavaleiro *m*, amazona *f*; (*cyclist*) ciclista *mf*; (*in document*) aditamento *m*

ridge /rɪdʒ/ *n* aresta *f*; (*of hill*) cume *m*

ridicule /ˈrɪdɪkjuːl/ *n* ridículo *m* □ *vt* ridicularizar

ridiculous /rɪˈdɪkjʊləs/ *a* ridículo

riding /ˈraɪdɪŋ/ *n* equitação *f*

rife /raɪf/ *a* be ~ estar espalhado; (*of illness*) grassar. ~ with cheio de riff-raff /'rɪfræf/ n gentinha f, povinho m, ralé f

rifle /'raɪfl/ n espingarda f □ vt revistar e roubar, saquear

rift /rɪft/ n fenda f, brecha f; (fig: dissension) desacordo m, desavença f, desentendimento m

rig¹ /rɪg/ vt (pt rigged) equipar □ n (for oil) plataforma f de poço de petróleo. ~out enfarpelar (colloq). ~-out n (colloq) roupa f, farpela f (colloq). ~ up arranjar

rig² /rɪg/ vt (pt rigged) (pej) manipular. ~ged a (election) fraudulento

right /raɪt/ a (correct, moral) certo, correto, (P) correcto; (fair) justo; (not left) direito; (suitable) certo, próprio □ n (entitlement) direito m; (not left) direita f; (not evil) o bem □ vt (a wrong) reparar; (sth fallen) endireitar □ adv (not left) à direita; (directly) direito; (exactly) mesmo, bem; (completely) completamente. be ~ (person) ter razão (to em). be in the ~ ter razão. on the ~ à direita. put ~ acertar, corrigir. ~ of way (auto) prioridade f. ~ angle n ângulo reto m, (P) recto. ~ away logo, imediatamente. ~-hand a à ou de direita. ~-handed a (person) destro. ~-wing a (pol) de direita

righteous /'raɪtʃəs/ a justo, virtuoso

rightful /'raɪtfl/ a legítimo. ~ly adv legitimamente, legalmente

rightly /'raɪtlɪ/ adv devidamente, corretamente, (P) correctamente; (with reason) justificadamente

rigid /'rɪdʒɪd/ a rígido. ~ity /rɪ-'dʒɪdətɪ/ n rigidez f

rigmarole /'rɪgmərəʊl/ n (speech: procedure) embrulhada f

rig|our /'rɪgə(r)/ n rigor m. ~orous a rigoroso

rile /raɪl/ vt (colloq) irritar, exasperar

rim /rɪm/ n borda f; (of wheel) aro m

rind /raɪnd/ n (on cheese, fruit) casca f; (on bacon) pele f

ring¹ /rɪŋ/ n (on finger) anel m; (for napkin, key etc) argola f; (circle) roda f, círculo m; (boxing) ringue m; (arena) arena f; (of people) quadrilha f □ vt rodear, cercar. ~ road n estrada f periférica or perimetral

ring² /rɪŋ/ vt/i (pt rang, pp rung) tocar; (of words etc) soar □ n toque m; (colloq: phone call) telefonadela f (colloq). ~ the bell tocar a campainha. ~ back telefonar de volta. ~ off desligar. ~ up telefonar (a)

ringleader /'rɪŋliːdə(r)/ n cabeça m, cérebro m

rink /rɪŋk/ n rinque m de patinação

rinse /rɪns/ vt passar uma água, enxaguar □ n enxaguadura f, (P) enxuagadela f; (hair tint) rinsagem f

riot /'raɪət/ n distúrbio m, motim m; (of colours) festival m □ vi fazer distúrbios or motins. run ~ desenfrear-se, descontrolar-se; (of plants) crescer em matagal. ~er n desordeiro m

riotous /'raɪətəs/ a desenfreado, turbulento, desordeiro

rip /rɪp/ vt/i (pt ripped) rasgar(-se) □ n rasgão m. ~ off (sl: defraud) defraudar, enrolar (sl). ~-off n (sl) roubalheira f (colloq)

ripe /raɪp/ a (-er, -est) maduro. ~ness n madureza f, (P) amadurecimento m

ripen /'raɪpn/ vt/i amadurecer

ripple /'rɪpl/ n ondulação f leve; (sound) murmúrio m □ vt/i encrespar(-se), agitar(-se), ondular

rise /raɪz/ vi (pt rose, pp risen) subir, elevar-se; (stand up) erguer-se, levantar-se; (rebel) sublevar-se; (sun) nascer; (curtain, prices) subir □ n (increase) aumento m; (slope) subida f, ladeira f; (origin) origem f. give ~ to originar, causar, dar origem a. ~r /-ə(r)/ n early ~r madrugador m

rising /'raɪzɪŋ/ n (revolt) insurreição f □ a (sun) nascente

risk /rɪsk/ n risco m □ vt arriscar. at ~ em risco, em perigo. at one's own ~ por sua conta e risco. ~ doing (venture) arriscar-se a fazer. ~y a arriscado

risqué /'rɪskeɪ/ a picante

rite /raɪt/ n rito m. last ~s últimos sacramentos mpl

ritual /'rɪtʃʊəl/ a & n ritual (m)

rival /'raɪvl/ n & a rival (mf); (fig) concorrente (mf), competidor (m) □ vt (pt rivalled) rivalizar com. ~ry n rivalidade f

river /'rɪvə(r)/ n rio m □ a fluvial

rivet /'rɪvɪt/ n rebite m □ vt (pt riveted) rebitar; (fig) prender, cravar. ~ing a fascinante

road /rəʊd/ n estrada f; (in town) rua f; (small; fig) caminho m. ~-block n barricada f. ~-map n mapa m das estradas. ~ sign n sinal m, placa f de sinalização. ~ tax imposto m de circulação. ~-works npl obras fpl

roadside /'rəʊdsaɪd/ n beira f da estrada

roadway /'rəʊdweɪ/ n pista f de rolamento, (P) rodagem

roadworthy /'rəʊdwɜːðɪ/ a em condições de ser utilizado na rua/estrada

roam /rəʊm/ vi errar, andar sem destino □ vt percorrer

roar /rɔː(r)/ n berro m, rugido m; (of thunder) ribombo m, troar m; (of sea, *wind*) bramido *m* □ *vt/i* berrar, rugir; (*of lion*) rugir; (*of thunder*) ribombar, troar; (*of sea, wind*) bramir. ~ **with laughter** rir às gargalhadas

roaring /'rɔːrɪŋ/ *a* (*trade*) florescente; (*success*) enorme; (*fire*) com grandes chamas

roast /rəʊst/ *vt/i* assar □ *a* & *n* assado (*m*)

rob /rɒb/ *vt* (*pt* **robbed**) roubar (**sb of sth** alg coisa de alguém); (*bank*) assaltar; (*deprive*) privar (**of** de). ~**ber** *n* ladrão *m*. ~**bery** *n* roubo *m*; (*of bank*) assalto *m*

robe /rəʊb/ *n* veste *f* comprida e solta; (*dressing-gown*) robe *m*. ~**s** *npl* (*of judge etc*) toga *f*

robin /'rɒbɪn/ *n* papo-roxo *m*, (*P*) pintarroxo *m*

robot /'rəʊbɒt/ *n* robô *m*, (*P*) robot *m*, autómato *m*, (*P*) autómato *m*

robust /rəʊ'bʌst/ *a* robusto

rock[1] /rɒk/ *n* rocha *f*, (*boulder*) penhasco *m*, rochedo *m*; (*sweet*) pirulito *m*, (*P*) chupa-chupa *m* comprido. **on the** ~**s** (*colloq: of marriage*) em crise; (*colloq: of drinks*) com gelo. ~**-bottom** *n* ponto *m* mais baixo □ *a* (*of prices*) baixíssimo (*colloq*)

rock[2] /rɒk/ *vt/i* balouçar(-se); (*shake*) abanar, sacudir; (*child*) embalar □ *n* (*mus*) rock *m*. ~**ing-chair** *n* cadeira *f* de balanço, (*P*) cadeira *f* de baloiço. ~**ing-horse** *n* cavalo *m* de balanço, (*P*) cavalo *m* de baloiço

rocket /'rɒkɪt/ *n* foguete *m*

rocky /'rɒkɪ/ *a* (-**ier**, -**iest**) (*ground*) pedregoso; (*hill*) rochoso; (*colloq: unsteady*) instável; (*colloq: shaky*) tremido (*colloq*)

rod /rɒd/ *n* vara *f*, vareta *f*; (*mech*) haste *f*; (*for curtains*) bastão *m*, (*P*) varão *m*; (*for fishing*) vara (de pescar) *f*

rode /rəʊd/ *see* ride

rodent /'rəʊdnt/ *n* roedor *m*

rodeo /rəʊ'deɪəʊ/ *n* (*pl* -**os**) rode(i)o *m*

roe /rəʊ/ *n* ova(s) *f* (*pl*) de peixe

rogue /rəʊg/ *n* (*dishonest*) patife *m*, velhaco *m*; (*mischievous*) brincalhão *m*

role /rəʊl/ *n* papel *m*

roll /rəʊl/ *vt/i* (fazer) rolar; (*into ball or cylinder*) enrolar(-se) □ *n* rolo *m*; (*list*) rol *m*, lista *f*; (*bread*) pãozinho *m*; (*of ship*) balanço *m*; (*of drum*) rufar *m*; (*of thunder*) ribombo *m*. **be** ~**ing in money** (*colloq*) nadar em dinheiro (*colloq*). ~ **over** (*turn over*) virar-se ao contrário. ~ **up** *vi* (*colloq*) aparecer □ *vt* (*sleeves*) arregaçar; (*umbrella*) fechar. ~**-call** *n* chamada *f*. ~**ing-pin** *n* rolo *m* de pastel

roller /'rəʊlə(r)/ *n* cilindro *m*; (*wave*)

vagalhão *m*; (*for hair*) rolo *m*. ~**-blind** *n* estore *m*. ~**-coaster** *n* montanha *f* russa. ~**-skate** *n* patim *m* de rodas

rolling /'rəʊlɪŋ/ *a* ondulante

Roman /'rəʊmən/ *a* & *n* romano (*m*). **R**~ **Catholic** *a* & *n* católico (*m*). ~ **numerals** algarismos *mpl* romanos

romance /rəʊ'mæns/ *n* (*love affair*) romance *m*; (*fig*) poesia *f*

Romania /rʊ'meɪnɪə/ *n* Roménia *f*, (*P*) Roménia *f*. ~**n** *a* & *n* romeno (*m*)

romantic /rəʊ'mæntɪk/ *a* romântico. ~**ally** *adv* românticamente. ~**ism** *n* romantismo *m*. ~**ize** *vi* fazer romance □ *vt* romantizar

romp /rɒmp/ *vi* brincar animadamente □ *n* brincadeira *f* animada. ~**ers** *npl* macacão *m* de bebê, (*P*) fato *m* de bebé

roof /ruːf/ *n* (*pl* **roofs**) telhado *m*; (*of car*) teto *m*, (*P*) capota *f*; (*of mouth*) palato *m*, céu *m* da boca □ *vt* cobrir com telhado. **hit the** ~ (*colloq*) ficar furioso. ~**ing** *n* material *m* para telhados. ~**-rack** *n* porta-bagagem *m*. ~**-top** *n* cimo *m* do telhado

rook[1] /rʊk/ *n* (*bird*) gralha *f*

rook[2] /rʊk/ *n* (*chess*) torre *f*

room /ruːm/ *n* quarto *m*, divisão *f*; (*bedroom*) quarto *m* de dormir; (*large hall*) sala *f*; (*space*) espaço *m*, lugar *m*. ~**s** (*lodgings*) apartamento *m*, cômodos *mpl*. ~**-mate** *n* companheiro *m* de quarto. ~**y** *a* espaçoso; (*clothes*) amplo, largo

roost /ruːst/ *n* poleiro *m* □ *vi* empoleirar-se. ~**er** *n* (*Amer*) galo *m*

root[1] /ruːt/ *n* raiz *f*; (*fig*) origem *f* □ *vt/i* enraizar(-se), radicar(-se). ~ **out** extirpar, erradicar. **take** ~ criar raízes. ~**less** *a* sem raízes, desenraizado

root[2] /ruːt/ *vi* ~ **about** revolver, remexer. ~ **for** (*Amer sl*) torcer por

rope /rəʊp/ *n* corda *f* □ *vt* atar. **know the** ~**s** estar por dentro (do assunto). ~ **in** convencer a participar de

rosary /'rəʊzərɪ/ *n* rosário *m*

rose[1] /rəʊz/ *n* rosa *f*; (*nozzle*) ralo *m* (de regador). ~**-bush** *n* roseira *f*

rose[2] /rəʊz/ *see* rise

rosé /'rəʊzeɪ/ *n* rosé *m*

rosette /rəʊ'zet/ *n* roseta *f*

rosewood /'rəʊzwʊd/ *n* pau-rosa *m*

roster /'rɒstə(r)/ *n* lista (de serviço) *f*, escala *f* de serviço

rostrum /'rɒstrəm/ *n* tribuna *f*; (*for conductor*) estrado *m*; (*sport*) pódium *m*

rosy /'rəʊzɪ/ *a* (-**ier**, -**iest**) rosado; (*fig*) risonho

rot /rɒt/ *vt/i* (*pt* **rotted**) apodrecer □ *n*

putrefação f, podridão f; (sl: nonsense) disparate m, asneiras fpl

rota /'rəʊtə/ n escala f de serviço

rotary /'rəʊtərɪ/ a rotativo, giratório

rotat|e /rəʊ'teɪt/ vt/i (fazer) girar, (fazer) revolver; (change round) alternar. ~**ing** a rotativo. ~**ion** /-ʃn/ n rotação f

rote /rəʊt/ n by ~ de cor, maquinalmente

rotten /'rɒtn/ a podre; (corrupt) corrupto; (colloq: bad) mau, ruim. ~ **eggs** ovos mpl podres. **feel** ~ (ill) não se sentir nada bem

rotund /rəʊ'tʌnd/ a rotundo, redondo

rough /rʌf/ a (-er, -est) rude; (to touch) áspero, rugoso; (of ground) acidentado, irregular; (violent) violento; (of sea) agitado, encapelado; (of weather) tempestuoso; (not perfect) tosco, rudimentar; (of estimate etc) aproximado □ n (ruffian) rufia m, desordeiro m □ adv (live) ao relento; (play) bruto □ vt ~ **it** viver de modo primitivo, não ter onde morar (colloq). ~ **out** fazer um esboço preliminar de. ~**-and-ready** a grosseiro mas eficiente. ~ **paper** rascunho m, borrão m. ~**ly** adv asperamente, rudemente; (approximately) aproximadamente. ~**ness** n rudeza f, aspereza f; (violence) brutalidade f

roughage /'rʌfɪdʒ/ n alimentos mpl fibrosos

roulette /ru:'let/ n roleta f

round /raʊnd/ a (-er, -est) redondo □ n (circle) círculo m; (slice) fatia f; (postman's) entrega f; (patrol) ronda f; (of drinks) rodada f; (competition) partida f, rodada f; (boxing) round m; (of talks) ciclo m, série f □ prep & adv em volta de (de), em torno (de) □ vt arredondar; (cape, corner) dobrar, virar. **come** ~ (into consciousness) voltar a si. **go** ou **come** ~ **to** (a friend etc) dar um pulo na casa de. ~ **about** (nearby) por aí; (fig) mais ou menos. ~ **of applause** salva f de palmas. ~ **off** terminar. ~**-shouldered** a curvado. ~ **the clock** noite e dia sem parar. ~ **trip** viagem f de ida e volta. ~ **up** (gather) juntar; (a figure) arredondar. ~**-up** n (of cattle) rodeio m; (of suspects) captura f

roundabout /'raʊndəbaʊt/ n carrossel m; (for traffic) rotatória f, (P) rotunda f □ a indireto, (P) folho m

rous|e /raʊz/ vt acordar, despertar. **be ~ed** (angry) exaltar-se, inflamar-se, ser provocado. ~**ing** a (speech) inflamado, exaltado; (music) vibrante; (cheers) frenético

rout /raʊt/ n derrota f; (retreat) deban-

dada f □ vt derrotar; (cause to retreat) pôr em debandada

route /ru:t/ n percurso m, itinerário m; (naut, aviat) rota f

routine /ru:'ti:n/ n rotina f; (theat) número m □ a de rotina, rotineiro. **daily** ~ rotina f diária

rov|e /rəʊv/ vt/i errar (por), vaguear (em/por). ~**ing** a (life) errante

row[1] /rəʊ/ n fila f, fileira f; (in knitting) carreira f. **in a** ~ (consecutive) em fila

row[2] /rəʊ/ vt/i remar. ~**ing** n remo m. ~**ing-boat** n barco m a remo

row[3] /raʊ/ n (colloq: noise) barulho m, bagunça f, banzé m (colloq); (colloq: quarrel) discussão f, briga f. ~ (with) vi (colloq) brigar (com), discutir (com)

rowdy /'raʊdɪ/ a (-ier, -iest) desordeiro

royal /'rɔɪəl/ a real

royalty /'rɔɪəltɪ/ n família real f; (payment) direitos mpl (de autor, de patente, etc)

rub /rʌb/ vt/i (pt rubbed) esfregar; (with ointment etc) esfregar, friccionar □ n esfrega f; (with ointment etc) fricção f. ~ **it in** repisar/insistir em. ~ **off on** comunicar-se a, transmitir-se a. ~ **out** (with rubber) apagar

rubber /'rʌbə(r)/ n borracha f. ~ **band** elástico m. ~ **stamp** carimbo m. ~**-stamp** vt aprovar sem questionar. ~**y** a semelhante à borracha

rubbish /'rʌbɪʃ/ n (refuse) lixo m; (nonsense) disparates mpl. ~ **dump** n lixeira f. ~**y** a sem valor

rubble /'rʌbl/ n entulho m

ruby /'ru:bɪ/ n rubi m

rucksack /'rʌksæk/ n mochila f

rudder /'rʌdə(r)/ n leme m

ruddy /'rʌdɪ/ a (-ier, -iest) avermelhado; (of cheeks) corado, vermelho; (sl: damned) maldito (colloq)

rude /ru:d/ a (-er, -est) mal-educado, malcriado, grosseiro. ~**ly** adv grosseiramente, malcriadamente. ~**ness** n má-educação f, má-criação f, grosseria f

rudiment /'ru:dɪmənt/ n rudimento m. ~**ary** /-'mentrɪ/ a rudimentar

rueful /'ru:fl/ a contrito, pesaroso

ruffian /'rʌfɪən/ n desordeiro m

ruffle /'rʌfl/ vt (feathers) eriçar; (hair) despentear; (clothes) amarrotar; (fig) perturbar □ n (frill) franzido m, (P) folho m

rug /rʌg/ n tapete m; (covering) manta f

rugged /'rʌgɪd/ a rude, irregular; (coast, landscape) acidentado; (character) forte; (features) marcado ruin /'ru:ɪn/ n ruína f □ vt arruinar; (fig) estragar. ~ous a desastroso

rule /ru:l/ n regra f; (regulation) regulamento m; (pol) governo m □ vt governar; (master) dominar; (jur) decretar; (decide) decidir □ vi governar. as a ~ regra geral, por via de regra. ~ out excluir. ~d paper papel m pautado. ~r /-ə(r)/ n (sovereign) soberano m; (leader) governante m; (measure) régua f

ruling /'ru:lɪŋ/ a (class) dirigente; (pol) no poder □ n decisão f

rum /rʌm/ n rum m

rumble /'rʌmbl/ vi ribombar, ressoar; (of stomach) roncar □ n ribombo m, estrondo m

rummage /'rʌmɪdʒ/ vt revistar, remexer

rumour /'ru:mə(r)/ n boato m, rumor m □ vt it is ~ed that corre o boato de que, consta que

rump /rʌmp/ n (of horse etc) garupa f; (of fowl) mitra f. ~ steak n bife m de alcatra

run /rʌn/ vi (pt ran, pp run, pres p running) correr; (flow) correr; (pass) passar; (function) andar, funcionar; (melt) derreter, pingar; (bus etc) circular; (play) estar em cartaz; (colour) desbotar; (in election) candidatar-se (for a) □ vt (manage) dirigir, gerir; (a risk) correr; (a race) participar em; (water) deixar correr; (a car) ter, manter □ n corrida f; (excursion) passeio m, ida f; (rush) corrida f, correria f; (in cricket) ponto m. be on the ~ estar foragido. have the ~ of ter à sua disposição. in the long ~ a longo prazo. ~ across encontrar por acaso, dar com. ~ away fugir. ~ down descer correndo; (of vehicle) atropelar; (belittle) dizer mal de, denegrir. be ~ down estar exausto. ~ in (engine) ligar. ~ into (meet) encontrar por acaso; (hit) bater em, ir de encontro a. ~ off vt (copies) tirar; (water) deixar correr □ vi fugir. ~-of-the-mill a vulgar. ~ out esgotar-se; (lease) expirar. I ran out of sugar o açúcar acabou. ~ over (of vehicle) atropelar. ~ up deixar acumular. the ~-up to o período que precede

runaway /'rʌnəweɪ/ n fugitivo m □ a fugitivo; (horse) desembestado; (vehicle) desgovernado; (success) grande

rung¹ /rʌŋ/ n (of ladder) degrace m

rung² /rʌŋ/ see ring²

runner /'rʌnə(r)/ n (person) corredor m; (carpet) passadeira f. ~ bean feijão m verde. ~-up n segundo classificado m

running /'rʌnɪŋ/ n corrida f; (functioning) funcionamento m □ a con-

secutivo, seguido; (water) corrente. be in the ~ (competitor) ter probabilidades de êxito. four days ~ quatro dias seguidos or a fio. ~ commentary reportagem f, comentário m

runny /'rʌnɪ/ a derretido

runway /'rʌnweɪ/ n pista f de decolagem, (P) descolagem

rupture /'rʌptʃə(r)/ n ruptura f; (med) hérnia f □ vt/i romper(-se), rebentar

rural /'rʊərəl/ a rural

ruse /ru:z/ n ardil m, estratagema m, manha f

rush¹ /rʌʃ/ n (plant) junco m

rush² /rʌʃ/ vi (move) precipitar-se, (be in a hurry) apressar-se □ vt fazer, mandar etc a toda a pressa; (person) pressionar; (mil) tomar de assalto □ n tropel m; (haste) pressa f. in a ~ às pressas. ~ hour rush m, (P) hora f de ponta

rusk /rʌsk/ n bolacha f, biscoito m

russet /'rʌsɪt/ a castanho avermelhado □ n maçã f reineta

Russia /'rʌʃə/ n Rússia f. ~n a & n russo (m)

rust /rʌst/ n (on iron, plants) ferrugem f □ vt/i enferrujar(-se). ~-proof a inoxidável. ~y a ferrugento, enferrujado; (fig) enferrujado

rustic /'rʌstɪk/ a rústico

rustle /'rʌsl/ vt/i restolhar, (fazer) farfalhar; (Amer: steal) roubar. ~ up (colloq: food etc) arranjar

rut /rʌt/ n sulco m; (fig) rotina f. in a ~ numa vida rotineira

ruthless /'ru:θlɪs/ a implacável

rye /raɪ/ n centeio m

S

sabbath /'sæbəθ/ n (Jewish) sábado m; (Christian) domingo m

sabbatical /sə'bætɪkl/ n (univ) período m de licença

sabot|age /'sæbətɑ:ʒ/ n sabotagem f □ vt sabotar. ~eur /-'tɜ:(r)/ n sabotador m

sachet /'sæʃeɪ/ n saché m

sack /sæk/ n saco m, saca f □ vt (colloq) despedir. get the ~ (colloq) ser despedido

sacrament /'sækrəmənt/ n sacramento m

sacred /'seɪkrɪd/ a sagrado

sacrifice /'sækrɪfaɪs/ n sacrifício m; (fig) sacrifício m □ vt sacrificar

sacrileg|e /'sækrɪlɪdʒ/ n sacrilégio m. ~ious /-'lɪdʒəs/ a sacrílego

sad /sæd/ a (sadder, saddest) (person) triste; (story, news) triste. ~ly

adv tristemente; (*unfortunately*) infelizmente. ~ness *n* tristeza *f*
sadden /'sædn/ *vt* entristecer
saddle /'sædl/ *n* sela *f* □ *vt* (*horse*) selar. ~ sb with sobrecarregar alguém com
sadis|m /'seɪdɪzəm/ *n* sadismo *m*. ~t /-ɪst/ *n* sádico *m*. ~tic /sə'dɪstɪk/ *a* sádico
safe /seɪf/ *a* (-er, -est) (*not dangerous*) seguro; (*out of danger*) fora de perigo; (*reliable*) confiável. ~ from salvo de risco de □ *n* cofre *m*, caixa-forte *f*. ~ and sound são e salvo. ~ conduct salvo-conduto *m*. ~ keeping custódia *f*, proteção *f*. to be on the ~ side por via das dúvidas. ~ly *adv* (*arrive etc*) em segurança; (*keep*) seguro
safeguard /'seɪfgɑːd/ *n* salvaguarda *f* □ *vt* salvaguardar
safety /'seɪftɪ/ *n* segurança *f*. ~-belt *n* cinto *m* de segurança. ~-pin *n* alfinete *m* de fralda. ~-valve *n* válvula *f* de segurança
sag /sæg/ *vi* (*pt* sagged) afrouxar
saga /'sɑːɡə/ *n* saga *f*
sage[1] /seɪdʒ/ *n* (*herb*) salva *f*
sage[2] /seɪdʒ/ *a* sensato, prudente □ *n* sábio *m*
Sagittarius /sædʒɪ'teərɪəs/ *n* (*astrol*) Sagitário *n*
said /sed/ *see* say
sail /seɪl/ *n* vela *f*; (*trip*) viagem *f* em barco a vela □ *vi* navegar; (*leave*) partir; (*sport*) velejar □ *vt* navegar. ~ing *n* navegação *f* à vela. ~ing-boat *n* barco *m* à vela
sailor /'seɪlə(r)/ *n* marinheiro *m*
saint /seɪnt/ *n* santo *m*. ~ly *a* santo, santificado
sake /seɪk/ *n* for the ~ of em consideração a. for my/your/its own ~ por mim/por isso
salad /'sæləd/ *n* salada *f*. ~ dressing *n* molho *m* para salada
salary /'sælərɪ/ *n* salário *m*
sale /seɪl/ *n* venda *f*; (*at reduced prices*) liquidação *f*. for ~ "vende-se". on ~ à venda. ~s assistant, (*Amer*) ~s clerk vendedor *m*. ~s department departamento *m* de vendas
sales|man /'seɪlzmən/ *n* (*pl* -men) (*in shop*) vendedor *m*; (*traveller*) caixeiro-viajante *m*. ~woman *n* (*pl* -women) (*in shop*) vendedora *f*; (*traveller*) caixeira-viajante *f*
saline /'seɪlaɪn/ *a* salino □ *n* salina *f*
saliva /sə'laɪvə/ *n* saliva *f*
sallow /'sæləʊ/ *a* (-er, -est) amarelado
salmon /'sæmən/ *n* (*pl invar*) salmão *m*
saloon /sə'luːn/ *n* (*on ship*) salão *m*; (*bar*) botequim *m*. ~ (car) sedã *m*

salt /sɔːlt/ *n* sal *m* □ *a* salgado □ *vt* (*season*) salgar; (*cure*) pôr em salmoura. ~-cellar *n* saleiro *m*. ~-water *n* água *f* salgada, água *f* do mar. ~y *a* salgado
salutary /'sæljʊtrɪ/ *a* salutar
salute /sə'luːt/ *n* saudação *f* □ *vt/i* saudar
salvage /'sælvɪdʒ/ *n* (*naut*) salvamento *m*; (*of waste*) reciclagem *f* □ *vt* salvar
salvation /sæl'veɪʃn/ *n* salvação *f*
same /seɪm/ *a* mesmo (as que) □ *pron* the ~ o mesmo □ *adv* the ~ o mesmo. all the ~ (*nevertheless*) mesmo assim, apesar de tudo. at the ~ time (*at once*) ao mesmo tempo
sample /'sɑːmpl/ *n* amostra *f* □ *vt* experimentar, provar
sanatorium /sænə'tɔːrɪəm/ *n* (*pl* -iums) sanatório *m*
sanctify /'sæŋktɪfaɪ/ *vt* santificar
sanctimonious /sæŋktɪ'məʊnɪəs/ *a* santarrão, carola
sanction /'sæŋkʃn/ *n* (*approval*) aprovação *f*; (*penalty*) pena *f*, sanção *f* □ *vt* sancionar
sanctity /'sæŋktɪtɪ/ *n* santidade *f*
sanctuary /'sæŋktʃʊərɪ/ *n* (*relig*) santuário *m*; (*refuge*) refúgio *m*; (*for animals*) reserva *f*
sand /sænd/ *n* areia *f*; (*beach*) praia *f* □ *vt* (*with sandpaper*) lixar
sandal /'sændl/ *n* sandália *f*
sandbag /'sændbæg/ *n* saco *m* de areia
sandbank /'sændbæŋk/ *n* banco *m* de areia
sandcastle /'sændkɑːsl/ *n* castelo *m* de areia
sandpaper /'sændpeɪpə(r)/ *n* lixa *f* □ *vt* lixar
sandpit /'sændpɪt/ *n* caixa *f* de areia
sandwich /'sænwɪdʒ/ *n* sanduíche *m*, (*P*) sandes *f invar* □ *vt* ~ed between encaixado entre. ~ course curso *m* profissionalizante envolvendo estudo teórico e estágio em local de trabalho
sandy /'sændɪ/ *a* (-ier, iest) arenoso; (*beach*) arenoso; (*hair*) ruivo
sane /seɪn/ *a* (-er, -est) (*not mad*) são *m*; (*sensible*) sensato, ajuizado
sang /sæŋ/ *see* sing
sanitary /'sænɪtrɪ/ *a* sanitário; (*system*) sanitário. ~ towel, (*Amer*) ~ napkin toalha *f* absorvente
sanitation /sænɪ'teɪʃn/ *n* condições *fpl* sanitárias, saneamento *m*
sanity /'sænɪtɪ/ *n* sanidade *f*
sank /sæŋk/ *see* sink
Santa Claus /'sæntəklɔːz/ *n* Papai Noel *m*
sap /sæp/ *n* seiva *f* □ *vt* (*pt* sapped) esgotar, minar

sapphire /'sæfaɪə(r)/ n safira f

sarcas|m /'sɑ:rkæzəm/ n sarcasmo m. ~**tic** /sɑ:r'kæstɪk/ a sarcástico

sardine /sɑ:'di:n/ n sardinha f

sardonic /sɑ:'dɒnɪk/ a sardônico

sash /sæʃ/ n (around waist) cinto m; (over shoulder) faixa f. ~**window** n janela f de guilhotina

sat /sæt/ see **sit**

satanic /sə'tænɪk/ a satânico

satchel /'sætʃl/ n sacola f

satellite /'sætəlaɪt/ n satélite m. ~ **dish** antena f de satélite. ~ **television** televisão f via satélite

satin /'sætɪn/ n cetim m

satir|e /'sætaɪə(r)/ n sátira f. ~**ical** /sə'tɪrɪkl/ a satirical. ~**ist** /'sætərɪst/ n satirista mf. ~**ize** /'sætəraɪz/ vt satirizar

satisfact|ion /sætɪs'fækʃn/ n satisfação f. ~**ory** /'fæktərɪ/ a satisfatório

satisfy /'sætɪsfaɪ/ vt satisfazer; (convince) convencer; (fulfil) atender. ~**ing** a satisfatório

saturat|e /'sætʃəreɪt/ vt saturar; (fig) ~**ed** a (wet) encharcado; (fat) saturado. ~**ion** /'reɪʃn/ n saturação f

Saturday /'sætədɪ/ n sábado m

sauce /sɔ:s/ n molho m; (colloq: cheek) atrevimento m

saucepan /'sɔ:spən/ n panela f, (P) caçarola f

saucer /'sɔ:sə(r)/ n pires m invar

saucy /'sɔ:sɪ/ a (-ier, -iest) picante

Saudi Arabia /saʊdɪə'reɪbɪə/ n Arábia f Saudita

sauna /'sɔ:nə/ n sauna f

saunter /'sɔ:ntə(r)/ vi perambular

sausage /'sɒsɪdʒ/ n salsicha f, linguiça f; (precooked) salsicha f

savage /'sævɪdʒ/ a (wild) selvagem; (fierce) cruel; (brutal) brutal □ n selvagem mf □ vt atacar ferozmente. ~**ry** n selvageria f, ferocidade f

sav|e /seɪv/ vt (rescue) salvar; (keep) guardar; (collect) colecionar; (money) economizar; (time) ganhar; (prevent) evitar, impedir (from de) □ n (sport) salvamento m □ prep salvo, exceto. ~**er** n poupador m. ~**ing** n economia f, poupança f. ~**ings** npl economias fpl

saviour /'seɪvɪə(r)/ n salvador m

savour /'seɪvə(r)/ n sabor m □ vt saborear. ~**y** a (tasty) saboroso; (not sweet) salgado

saw[1] /sɔ:/ see **see**[1]

saw[2] /sɔ:/ n serra f □ vt (pt sawed, pp sawn or sawed) serrar

sawdust /'sɔ:dʌst/ n serragem f

saxophone /'sæksəfəʊn/ n saxofone m

say /seɪ/ vt/i (pt said /sed/) □ n have a ~ (in) opinar sobre alg coisa. have one's ~ exprimir sua opinião. **I** ~! olhe! or escute!, provérbio m

scab /skæb/ n casca f, crosta f; (colloq: blackleg) fura-greve mf invar

scaffold /'skæfəʊld/ n cadafalso m, andaime m. ~**ing** /-əldɪŋ/ n andaime m

scald /skɔ:ld/ vt escaldar, queimar □ n escaldadura f

scale[1] /skeɪl/ n (of fish etc) escama f

scale[2] /skeɪl/ n (ratio, size) escala f; (mus) escala f; (of salaries, charges) tabela f. **on a small/large/etc ~** numa pequena/grande/etc escala □ vt (climb) escalar. ~ **down** reduzir

scales /skeɪlz/ npl (for weighing) balança f

scallop /'skɒləp/ n (culin) concha f de vieira; (shape) concha f de vieira

scalp /skælp/ n couro m cabeludo □ vt escalpar

scalpel /'skælpl/ n bisturi m

scamper /'skæmpə(r)/ vi sair correndo

scampi /'skæmpɪ/ npl camarões mpl fritos

scan /skæn/ vt (pt scanned) (intently) perscrutar, esquadrinhar; (quickly) passar os olhos em; (med) examinar; (radar) explorar □ n (med) exame m

scandal /'skændl/ n (disgrace) escândalo m; (gossip) fofoca f. ~**ous** a escandaloso

Scandinavia /skændɪ'neɪvɪə/ n Escandinávia f. ~**n** a & n escandinavo (m)

scanty /'skæntɪ/ a (-ier, -iest) escasso; (clothing) sumário

scapegoat /'skeɪpɡəʊt/ n bode m expiatório

scar /skɑ:(r)/ n cicatriz f □ vt (pt scarred) marcar; (fig) deixar marcas

scarc|e /skeəs/ a (-er, -est) escasso, raro. **make o.s. ~e** (colloq) sumir, dar o fora (colloq). ~**ity** n escassez f. ~**ely** adv mal, apenas

scare /skeə(r)/ vt assustar, apavorar. **be ~d** estar com medo (of de) □ n pavor m, pânico m. **bomb ~** pânico m causado por suspeita de bomba num local

scarecrow /'skeəkrəʊ/ n espantalho m

scarf /skɑ:f/ n (pl scarves) (oblong) cachecol m; (square) lenço m de cabelo

scarlet /'skɑ:lət/ a escarlate m

scary /'skeərɪ/ a (-ier, -iest) (colloq) assustador, apavorante

scathing /'skeɪðɪŋ/ a mordaz

scatter /'skætə(r)/ vt (strew) espalhar; (disperse) dispersar □ vi espalhar-se

scavenge /'skævɪndʒ/ vi procurar

comida *etc* no lixo. ~**r** /-ə(r)/ *n* (*person*) que procura comida *etc* no lixo; (*animal*) que se alimenta de carniça
scenario /sɪ'nɑːrɪəʊ/ *n* (*pl* -**os**) sinopse *f*, resumo *m* detalhado
scene /siːn/ *n* cena *f*, (*of event*) cenário *m*; (*sight*) vista *f*, panorama *m*. **behind the** ~**s** nos bastidores. **make a** ~ fazer um escândalo
scenery /'siːnərɪ/ *n* cenário *m*, paisagem *f*; (*theat*) cenário *m*
scenic /'siːnɪk/ *a* pitoresco, cênico
scent /sent/ *n* (*perfume*) perfume *m*, fragância *f*; (*trail*) rastro *m*, pista *f* □ *vt* (*discern*) sentir. ~**ed** *a* perfumado
sceptic /'skeptɪk/ *n* cético *m*. ~**al** *a* cético. ~**ism** /-sɪzəm/ *n* ceticismo *m*
schedule /'ʃedjuːl/ *n* programa *m*; (*timetable*) horário *m* □ *vt* marcar, programar. **according to** ~ conforme planejado. **behind** ~ atrasado. **on** ~ (*train*) na hora; (*work*) em dia. ~**d flight** *n* vôo *m* regular
scheme /skiːm/ *n* esquema *m*; (*plan of work*) plano *m*; (*plot*) conspiração *f*, maquinação *f* □ *vi* planejar, (*P*) planear; (*pej*) intrigar, maquinar, tramar
schism /'sɪzəm/ *n* cisma *f*
schizophreni|**a** /skɪtsəʊ'friːnɪə/ *n* esquizofrenia *f*. ~**c** /-'frenɪk/ *a* esquizofrênico, (*P*) esquizofrénico
scholar /'skɒlə(r)/ *n* erudito *m*, estudioso *m*, escolar *m*. ~**ly** *a* erudito. ~**ship** *n* erudição *f*, saber *m*; (*grant*) bolsa *f* de estudo
school /skuːl/ *n* escola *f*; (*of university*) escola *f*, faculdade *f* □ *a* (*age, year, holidays*) escolar □ *vt* ensinar; (*train*) treinar, adestrar. ~**ing** *n* instrução *f*; (*attendance*) escolaridade *f*
school|**boy** /'skuːlbɔɪ/ *n* aluno *m*. ~**girl** *n* aluna *f*
school|**master** /'skuːlmɑːstə(r)/, ~**mistress**, ~**teacher** *ns* professor *m*, professora *f*
schooner /'skuːnə(r)/ *n* escuna *f*; (*glass*) copo *m* alto
sciatica /saɪ'ætɪkə/ *n* ciática *f*
scien|**ce** /'saɪəns/ *n* ciência *f*. ~**ce fiction** ficção *f* científica. ~**tific** /-'tɪfɪk/ *a* científico
scientist /'saɪəntɪst/ *n* cientista *mf*
scintillate /'sɪntɪleɪt/ *vi* cintilar; (*fig: person*) brilhar
scissors /'sɪzəz/ *npl* (**pair of**) ~ tesoura *f*
scoff[1] /skɒf/ *vi* ~ **at** zombar de, (*P*) troçar de
scoff[2] /skɒf/ *vt* (*sl: eat*) devorar, tragar
scold /skəʊld/ *vt* ralhar com. ~**ing** *n* repressão *f*, (*P*) descompostura *f*
scone /skɒn/ *n* (*culin*) scone *m*, bolinho *m* para o chá

scoop /skuːp/ *n* (*for grain, sugar etc*) pá *f*; (*ladle*) concha *f*; (*news*) furo *m* □ *vt* ~ **out** (*hollow out*) escavar, tirar com concha *or* pá. ~ **up** (*lift*) apanhar
scoot /skuːt/ *vi* (*colloq*) fugir, mandar-se (*colloq*), (*P*) pôr-se a milhas (*colloq*)
scooter /'skuːtə(r)/ *n* (*child's*) patinete *f*, (*P*) trotinete *m*; (*motor cycle*) motoreta *f*, lambreta *f*
scope /skəʊp/ *n* âmbito *m*; (*fig: opportunity*) oportunidade *f*
scorch /skɔːtʃ/ *vt/i* chamuscar(-se), queimar de leve. ~**ing** *a* (*colloq*) escaldante, abrasador
score /skɔː(r)/ *n* (*sport*) contagem *f*, escore *m*; (*mus*) partitura *f* □ *vt* marcar com corte(s), riscar; (*a goal*) marcar; (*mus*) orquestrar □ *vi* marcar pontos; (*keep score*) fazer a contagem; (*football*) marcar um gol, (*P*) golo. **a** ~ (**of**) (*twenty*) uma vintena (de), vinte. ~**s** muitos, dezenas. **on that** ~ nesse respeito, quanto a isso. ~**board** *n* marcador *m*. ~**r** /-ə(r)/ *n* (*score-keeper*) marcador *m*; (*of goals*) autor *m*
scorn /skɔːn/ *n* desprezo *m* □ *vt* desprezar. ~**ful** *a* desdenhoso, escarninho. ~**fully** *adv* com desdém, desdenhosamente
Scorpio /'skɔːpɪəʊ/ *n* (*astr*) Escorpião *m*
scorpion /'skɔːpɪən/ *n* escorpião *m*
Scot /skɒt/ *n*, ~**tish** *a* escocês (*m*)
Scotch /skɒtʃ/ *a* escocês □ *n* uísque *m*
scotch /skɒtʃ/ *vt* pôr fim a, frustrar
scot-free /skɒt'friː/ *a* impune □ *adv* impunemente
Scotland /'skɒtlənd/ *n* Escócia *f*
Scots /skɒts/ *a* escocês. ~**man** *n* escocês *m*. ~**woman** *n* escocesa *f*
scoundrel /'skaʊndrəl/ *n* patife *m*, canalha *m*
scour[1] /'skaʊə(r)/ *vt* (*clean*) esfregar, arear. ~**er** *n* esfregão *m* de palha de aço *or* de nylon
scour[2] /'skaʊə(r)/ *vt* (*search*) percorrer, esquadrinhar
scourge /skɜːdʒ/ *n* açoite *m*; (*fig*) flagelo *m*
scout /skaʊt/ *n* (*mil*) explorador *m* □ *vi* ~ **about (for)** andar à procura de
Scout /skaʊt/ *n* escoteiro *m*, (*P*) escuteiro *m*. ~**ing** *n* escotismo *m*, (*P*) escutismo *m*
scowl /skaʊl/ *n* carranca *f*, ar *m* carrancudo □ *vi* fazer um ar carrancudo
scraggy /'skrægɪ/ *a* (-**ier**, -**iest**) descarnado, ossudo
scramble /'skræmbl/ *vi* trepar; (*crawl*) avançar de rastros, rastejar, arrastar-se □ *vt* (*eggs*) mexer □ *n* luta *f*, confusão *f*
scrap[1] /skræp/ *n* bocadinho *m*. ~**s**

npl restos *mpl* □ *vt* (*pt* scrapped) jogar fora, (P) deitar fora; (*plan etc*) abandonar, pôr de lado. ~-book *n* álbum *m* de recortes. ~ heap monte *m* de ferro-velho. ~-iron *n* ferro *m* velho, sucata *f*. ~ merchant sucateiro *m*. ~-paper *n* papel *m* de rascunho. ~py *a* fragmentário

scrap² /skræp/ *n* (*colloq: fight*) briga *f*, pancada *f* (*colloq*), rixa *f*

scrape /skreɪp/ *vt* raspar; (*graze*) esfolar, arranhar □ *vi* (*graze, rub*) roçar □ *n* (*act of scraping*) raspagem *f*; (*mark*) raspão *m*, esfoladura *f*; (*fig*) encrenca *f*, maus lençóis *mpl*. ~ through escapar pela tangente, (P) à tangente; (*exam*) passar pela tangente, (P) à tangente. ~ together conseguir juntar. ~r /-ə(r)/ *n* raspadeira *f*

scratch /skrætʃ/ *vt/i* arranhar(-se); (*a line*) riscar; (*to relieve itching*) coçar(-se) □ *n* arranhão *m*; (*line*) risco *m*; (*wound with claw, nail*) unhada *f*. start from ~ começar do princípio. up to ~ à altura, ao nível requerido

scrawl /skrɔ:l/ *n* rabisco *m*, garrancho *m*, garatuja *f* □ *vt/i* rabiscar, fazer garranchos, garatujar

scrawny /'skrɔ:nɪ/ *a* (-ier, -iest) descarnado, ossudo, magricela

scream /skri:m/ *vt/i* gritar □ *n* grito *m* (agudo)

screech /skri:tʃ/ *vi* guinchar, gritar; (*of brakes*) chiar, guinchar □ *n* guincho *m*, grito *m* agudo

screen /skri:n/ *n* écran *m*, tela *f*; (*folding*) biombo *m*; (*fig: protection*) manto *m* (*fig*), capa *f* (*fig*) □ *vt* resguardar, tapar; (*film*) passar; (*candidates etc*) fazer a triagem de. ~ing *n* (*med*) exame *m* médico

screw /skru:/ *n* parafuso *m* □ *vt* aparafusar, atarraxar. ~ up (*eyes, face*) franzir; (*sl: ruin*) estragar. ~ up one's courage cobrar coragem

screwdriver /'skru:draɪvə(r)/ *n* chave *f* de parafusos *or* de fenda

scribble /'skrɪbl/ *vt/i* rabiscar, garatujar □ *n* rabisco *m*, garatuja *f*

script /skrɪpt/ *n* escrita *f*; (*of film*) roteiro *m*, (P) guião *m*. ~-writer *n* (*film*) roteirista *m*, (P) autor *m* do guião

Scriptures /'skrɪptʃəz/ *npl* the ~ a Sagrada Escritura

scroll /skrəʊl/ *n* rolo *m* (de papel ou pergaminho); (*archit*) voluta *f* □ *vt/i* (*comput*) passar na tela

scrounge /skraʊndʒ/ *vt* (*colloq: cadge*) filar (*sl*), (P) cravar (*sl*) □ *vi* (*beg*) parasitar, viver às custas de alguém. ~r /-ə(r)/ *n* parasita *mf*, filão *m* (*sl*), (P) crava *mf* (*sl*)

scrub¹ /skrʌb/ *n* (*land*) mato *m*

scrub² /skrʌb/ *vt/i* (*pt* scrubbed) esfregar, lavar com escova e sabão; (*colloq: cancel*) cancelar □ *n* esfrega *f*

scruff /skrʌf/ *n* by the ~ of the neck pelo cangote, (P) pelo cachaço

scruffy /'skrʌfɪ/ *a* (-ier, -iest) desmazelado, desleixado, mal ajambrado (*colloq*)

scrum /skrʌm/ *n* rixa *f*; (*Rugby*) placagem *f*

scruple /'skru:pl/ *n* escrúpulo *m*

scrupulous /'skru:pjʊləs/ *a* escrupuloso. ~ly *adv* escrupulosamente. ~ly clean impecavelmente limpo

scrutin|y /'skru:tɪnɪ/ *n* averiguação *f*, escrutínio *m*. ~ize *vt* examinar em detalhes

scuff /skʌf/ *vt* (*scrape*) esfolar, safar □ *n* esfoladura *f*

scuffle /'skʌfl/ *n* tumulto *m*, briga *f*

sculpt /skʌlpt/ *vt/i* esculpir. ~or *n* escultor *m*. ~ure /-tʃə(r)/ *n* escultura *f* □ *vt/i* esculpir

scum /skʌm/ *n* (*on liquid*) espuma *f*; (*pej: people*) gentinha *f*, escumalha *f*, ralé *f*

scurf /skɜ:f/ *n* películas *fpl*; (*dandruff*) caspa *f*

scurrilous /'skʌrɪləs/ *a* injurioso, insultuoso

scurry /'skʌrɪ/ *vi* dar corridinhas; (*hurry*) apressar-se. ~ off escapulir-se

scurvy /'skɜ:vɪ/ *n* escorbuto *m*

scuttle¹ /'skʌtl/ *n* (*bucket, box*) balde *m* para carvão

scuttle² /'skʌtl/ *vt* (*ship*) afundar abrindo rombos *or* as torneiras de fundo

scuttle³ /'skʌtl/ *vi* ~ away *or* off fugir, escapulir-se

scythe /saɪð/ *n* gadanha *f*, foice *f* grande

sea /si:/ *n* mar *m* □ *a* do mar, marinho, marítimo. at ~ no alto mar, ao largo. all at ~ desnorteado. by ~ por mar. ~bird ave *f* marinha. ~-green *a* verde-mar. ~ horse cavalo-marinho *m*, hipocampo *m*. ~ level nível *m* do mar. ~ lion leão-marinho *m*. ~ shell concha *f*. ~-shore *n* litoral *m*; (*beach*) praia *f*. ~ water água *f* do mar

seaboard /'si:bɔ:d/ *n* litoral *m*, costa *f*

seafarer /'si:feərə(r)/ *n* marinheiro *m*, navegante *m*

seafood /'si:fu:d/ *n* marisco(s) *m* (*pl*)

seagull /'si:gʌl/ *n* gaivota *f*

seal¹ /si:l/ *n* (*animal*) foca *f*

seal² /si:l/ *n* selo *m*, sinete *m* □ *vt* selar; (*with wax*) lacrar. ~ing-wax *n* lacre *m*. ~ off (*area*) vedar

seam /si:m/ *n* (*in cloth etc*) costura *f*; (*of mineral*) veio *m*, filão *m*. ~less *a* sem costura

seaman /'si:mən/ n (pl -men) marinheiro m, maritimo m

seamy /'si:mɪ/ a ~ side lado m (do) avesso; (fig) lado m sórdido

seance /'seɪɑːns/ n sessão f espírita

seaplane /'si:pleɪn/ n hidroavião m

seaport /'si:pɔ:t/ n porto m de mar

search /sɜ:tʃ/ vt/i revistar, dar busca (a); (one's heart, conscience etc) examinar □ n revista f, busca f; (quest) procura f, busca f; (official) inquérito m. in ~ of à procura de. ~ for procurar. ~-party n equipe f de busca. ~-warrant n mandado m de busca. ~ing a (of look) penetrante; (of test etc) minucioso

searchlight /'sɜ:tʃlaɪt/ n holofote m

seasick /'si:sɪk/ a enjoado. ~ness n enjôo m, P enjoo m

seaside /'si:saɪd/ n costa f, praia f, beira-mar f. ~ resort n balneário m, praia f

season /'si:zn/ n (of year) estação f; (proper time) época f; (cricket, football etc) temporada f □ vt temperar; (wood) secar. in ~ na época. ~able a apropriado à estação. ~al a sazonal. ~ed a (of people) experimentado. ~ing n tempero m. ~-ticket n (train etc) passe m; (theatre etc) assinatura f

seat /si:t/ n assento m; (place) lugar m; (of bicycle) selim m; (of chair) assento m; (of trousers) fundilho m □ vt sentar; (have seats for) ter lugares sentados para. be ~ed, take a ~ sentar-se. ~ of learning centro m de cultura. ~-belt n cinto m de segurança

seaweed /'si:wi:d/ n alga f marinha

seaworthy /'si:wɜ:ðɪ/ a navegável, em condições de navegabilidade

secateurs /'sekəts:z/ npl tesoura f de poda

seclu|de /sɪ'klu:d/ vt isolar. ~ded a isolado, retirado. ~sion /sɪ'klu:ʒn/ n isolamento m

second¹ /'sekənd/ a segundo □ n segundo m; (in duel) testemunha f. ~ (gear) (auto) segunda f (velocidade). the ~ of April dois de Abril. ~s (goods) artigos mpl de segunda or de refugo □ adv (in race etc) em segundo lugar □ vt secundar. ~-best a escolhido em segundo lugar. ~-class a de segunda classe. ~-hand a de segunda mão □ n (on clock) ponteiro m dos segundos. ~-rate a medíocre, de segunda ordem. ~ thoughts dúvidas fpl. on ~ thoughts pensando melhor. ~ly adv segundo, em segundo lugar

second² /sɪ'kɒnd/ vt (transfer) destacar (to para)

secondary /'sekəndrɪ/ a secundário. ~ school escola f secundária

secrecy /'si:krəsɪ/ n segredo m

secret /'si:krɪt/ a secreto □ n segredo m. in ~ em segredo. ~ agent n agente mf secreto. ~ly adv em segredo, secretamente

secretar|y /'sekrətrɪ/ n secretário m, secretária f. S~y of State ministro m de Estado, (P) Secretário m de Estado; (Amer) ministro m dos Negócios Estrangeiros. ~ial /-'teərɪəl/ a (work, course etc) de secretária

secret|e /sɪ'kri:t/ vt segregar; (hide) esconder. ~ion /-ʃn/ n secreção f

secretive /'si:krətɪv/ a misterioso, reservado

sect /sekt/ n seita f. ~arian /teərɪən/ a sectário

section /'sekʃn/ n seção f, (P) secção f; (of country, community etc) setor m, (P) sector m; (district of town) zona f

sector /'sektə(r)/ n setor m, (P) sector m

secular /'sekjʊlə(r)/ a secular, leigo, P laico; (art, music etc) profano

secure /sɪ'kjʊə(r)/ a seguro, em segurança; (firm) seguro, sólido; (in mind) tranquilo, P tranquilo □ vt prender bem or com segurança; (obtain) conseguir, arranjar; (ensure) assegurar; (windows, doors) fechar bem. ~ly adv solidamente; (safely) em segurança

securit|y /sɪ'kjʊərətɪ/ n segurança f; (for loan) fiança f, caução f. ~ies npl (finance) títulos mpl

sedate /sɪ'deɪt/ a sereno, comedido □ vt (med) tratar com sedativos

sedation /sɪ'deɪʃn/ n (med) sedação f. under ~ sob o efeito de sedativos

sedative /'sedətɪv/ n (med) sedativo m

sedentary /'sedntrɪ/ a sedentário

sediment /'sedɪmənt/ n sedimento m, depósito m

seduce /sɪ'dju:s/ vt seduzir

seduct|ion /sɪ'dʌkʃn/ n sedução f. ~ive /-tɪv/ a sedutor, aliciante

see¹ /si:/ vt/i (pt saw, pp seen) ver; (escort) acompanhar. ~ about or to tratar de, encarregar-se de. ~ off vt (wave goodbye) ir despedir-se de; (chase) through (task) levar a cabo; (not be deceived by) não se deixar enganar por. ~ (to it) that assegurar que, tratar de fazer com que. ~ing that visto que, uma vez que. ~ you later! (colloq) até logo! (colloq)

see² /si:/ n sé f, bispado m

seed /si:d/ n semente f; (fig: origin) germe(n) m; (tennis) cabeça f de série; (pip) caroço m. go to ~ produzir sementes; (fig) desmazelar-se (colloq).

seedy 364 senior

~ling *n* planta *f* brotada a partir da semente

seedy /'si:dɪ/ *a* (-ier -iest) (com um ar) gasto, surrado; (*colloq: unwell*) abatido, deprimido, em baixo astral (*colloq*)

seek /si:k/ *vt* (*pt* sought) procurar; (*help etc*) pedir

seem /si:m/ *vi* parecer. ~ingly *adv* aparentemente, ao que parece

seemly /'si:mlɪ/ *adv* decente, conveniente, próprio

seen /si:n/ *see* see[1]

seep /si:p/ *vi* (*ooze*) filtrar-se; (*trickle*) pingar, escorrer, passar. ~age *n* infiltração *f*

see-saw /'si:sɔ:/ *n* gangorra *f*, (P) balanço *m*

seethe /si:ð/ *vi* ~ with (*anger*) ferver de; (*people*) fervilhar de

segment /'segmənt/ *n* segmento *m*; (*of orange*) gomo *m*

segregat|e /'segrigeit/ *vt* segregar, separar. ~ion /-'geiʃn/ *n* segregação *f*

seize /si:z/ *vt* agarrar, (P) deitar a mão a, apanhar; (*take possession by force*) apoderar-se de; (*by law*) apreender, confiscar, (P) apresar □ *vi* ~ on (*opportunity*) aproveitar. ~ up (*engine etc*) grimpar, emperrar. be ~d with (*fear, illness*) ter um ataque de

seizure /'si:ʒə(r)/ *n* (*med*) ataque *m*, crise *f*; (*law*) apreensão *f*, captura *f*

seldom /'seldəm/ *adv* raras vezes, raramente, raro

select /sɪ'lekt/ *vt* escolher, selecionar, (P) seleccionar □ *a* seleto, (P) selecto. ~ion /-ʃn/ *n* seleção *f*, (P) selecção *f*; (*comm*) sortido *m*

selective /sɪ'lektɪv/ *a* seletivo, (P) selectivo

self /self/ *n* (*pl* selves) the ~ o eu, o ego

self- /self/ *pref* ~-assurance *n* segurança *f*. ~-assured *a* seguro de si. ~-catering *a* em que os hóspedes tem facilidades de cozinhar. ~-centred *a* egocêntrico. ~-confidence *n* autoconfiança *f*, confiança *f* em si mesmo. ~-confident *a* que tem confiança em si mesmo. ~-conscious *a* inibido, constrangido. ~-contained *a* independente. ~-control *n* autodomínio *m*. ~-controlled *a* senhor de si. ~-defence *n* legítima defesa *f*. ~-denial *n* abnegação *f*. ~-employed *a* autônomo. ~-esteem *n* amor *m* próprio. ~-evident *a* evidente. ~-indulgent *a* que não resiste a tentações; (*for ease*) comodista. ~-interest *n* interesse *m* pessoal. ~-portrait *n* auto-retrato *m*. ~-possessed *a* senhor de si. ~-reliant *a* independente, seguro de si.

~-respect *n* amor *m* próprio. ~-righteous *a* que se tem em boa conta. ~-sacrifice *n* abnegação *f*, sacrifício *m*. ~-satisfied *a* cheio de si, convencido (*colloq*). ~-seeking *a* egoísta. ~-service *a* auto-serviço, self-service. ~-styled *a* pretenso. ~-sufficient *a* auto-suficiente. ~-willed *a* voluntarioso

selfish /'selfɪʃ/ *a* egoísta; (*motive*) interesseiro. ~ness *n* egoísmo *m*

selfless /'selflɪs/ *a* desinteressado

sell /sel/ *vt/i* (*pt* sold) vender(-se). ~ by date ~ off liquidar. be sold out estar esgotado. ~-out *n* (*show*) sucesso *m*; (*colloq: betrayal*) traição *f*. ~er *n* vendedor *m*

Sellotape /'seləʊteɪp/ *n* fita *f* adesiva, (P) fitacola *f*

semantic /sɪ'mæntɪk/ *a* semântico. ~s *n* semântica *f*

semblance /'sembləns/ *n* aparência *f*

semen /'si:mən/ *n* sêmen *m*, (P) sémen *m*, esperma *m*

semester /sɪ'mestə(r)/ *n* (*Amer: univ*) semestre *m*

semi- /'semɪ/ *pref* semi-, meio

semibreve /'semɪbri:v/ *n* (*mus*) semibreve *f*

semicirc|le /'semɪsɜ:kl/ *n* semicírculo *m*. ~ular /-sɜ:kjʊlə(r)/ *a* semicircular

semicolon /semɪ'kəʊlən/ *n* ponto-e-vírgula *m*

semi-detached /semɪdɪ'tætʃt/ *a* ~ house casa *f* geminada

semifinal /semɪ'faɪnl/ *n* semifinal *f*, (P) meiafinal *f*

seminar /'semɪnɑ:(r)/ *n* seminário *m*

seminary /'semɪnərɪ/ *n* seminário *m*

semiquaver /'semɪkweɪvə(r)/ *n* (*mus*) semicolcheia *f*

Semit|e /'si:maɪt/ *a & n* semita (*mf*). ~ic /sɪ'mɪtɪk/ *a & n* (*lang*) semítico (*m*)

semitone /'semɪtəʊn/ *n* (*mus*) semitom *m*

semolina /semə'li:nə/ *n* sêmola *f*, (P) sêmola *f*, semolina *f*

senat|e /'senɪt/ *n* senado *m*. ~or /-ətə(r)/ *n* senador *m*

send /send/ *vt/i* (*pt* sent) enviar, mandar. ~ back devolver. ~ for (*person*) chamar, mandar vir; (*help*) pedir. ~ (away *or* off) for encomendar, mandar vir (por carta). ~-off *n* despedida *f*, bota-fora *m*. ~ up (*colloq*) parodiar. ~er *n* expedidor *m*, remetente *m*

senil|e /'si:naɪl/ *a* senil. ~ity /sɪ'nɪlətɪ/ *n* senilidade *f*

senior /'si:nɪə(r)/ *a* mais velho, mais idoso (to que); (*in rank*) superior; (*in service*) mais antigo; (*after surname*) sênior, (P) sénior □ *n* pessoa *f* mais velha; (*schol*) finalista *mf*. ~ citizen

pessoa f de idade or da terceira idade.
~ity /-'ɒrəti/ n (in age) idade f; (in service) antiguidade f

sensation /sen'seiʃn/ n sensação f. ~al a sensacional. ~alism n sensacionalismo m

sense /sens/ n sentido m; (wisdom) bom senso m; (sensation) sensação f; (mental impression) sentimento m. ~s (sanity) razão f □ vt pressentir. make ~ fazer sentido. make ~ of compreender. ~less a disparatado, sem sentido; (med) sem sentidos, inconsciente

sensible /'sensəbl/ a sensato, razoável; (clothes) prático

sensitive /'sensətiv/ a sensível (to a); (touchy) susceptível. ~ity /-'tivəti/ n sensibilidade f

sensory /'sensəri/ a sensorial

sensual /'senʃuəl/ a sensual. ~ity /-'æləti/ n sensualidade f

sensuous /'senʃuəs/ a sensual

sent /sent/ see send

sentence /'sentəns/ n frase f; (jur: decision) sentença f; (punishment) pena f □ vt ~ to condenar a

sentiment /'sentimənt/ n sentimento m; (opinion) modo m de ver

sentimental /sentr'mentl/ a sentimental. ~ity /-men'tæləti/ n sentimentalidade f, sentimentalismo m. ~ value valor m estimativo

sentry /'sentri/ n sentinela f

separable /'sepərəbl/ a separável

separate¹ /'seprət/ a separado, diferente. ~s npl (clothes) conjuntos mpl. ~ly adv separadamente, em separado

separat|e² /'sepəreit/ vt/i separar (-se). ~ion /-'reiʃn/ n separação f

September /sep'tembə(r)/ n setembro m

septic /'septik/ a séptico, infectado

sequel /'si:kwəl/ n resultado m, sequela f, (P) sequela f; (of novel, film) continuação f

sequence /'si:kwəns/ n sequência f, (P) sequência f

sequin /'si:kwin/ n lantejoula f

serenade /serə'neid/ n serenata f □ vt fazer uma serenata para

seren|e /si'ri:n/ a sereno. ~ity /-'enəti/ n serenidade f

sergeant /'sɑ:dʒənt/ n sargento m

serial /'siəriəl/ n folhetim m □ a (number) de série. ~ize /-laiz/ vt publicar em folhetim

series /'siəri:z/ n invar série f

serious /'siəriəs/ a sério; (very bad, critical) grave, sério. ~ly adv seriamente, gravemente, a sério. take ~ly levar a sério. ~ness n seriedade f, gravidade f

sermon /'sɜ:mən/ n sermão m

serpent /'sɜ:pənt/ n serpente f

serrated /si'reitid/ a (edge) serr(e)ado, com serrilha

serum /'siərəm/ n (pl -a) soro m

servant /'sɜ:vənt/ n criado m, criada f, empregado m, empregada f

serv|e /sɜ:v/ vt/i servir; (a sentence) cumprir; (jur: a writ) entregar; (mil) servir, prestar serviço; (apprenticeship) fazer □ n (tennis) saque m, (P) serviço m. ~e as/to servir de/para. ~e its purpose servir para o que é (colloq), servir os seus fins. it ~es you/him etc right é bem feito. ~ing n (portion) dose f, porção f

service /'sɜ:vis/ n serviço m; (relig) culto m; (tennis) saque m (P) serviço m; (maintenance) revisão f. ~s (mil) forças fpl armadas □ vt (car etc) fazer a revisão de. of ~ to útil a, de utilidade a. ~ area área f de serviço. ~ charge serviço m. ~ station posto m de gasolina

serviceable /'sɜ:visəbl/ a (of use, usable) útil, prático; (durable) resistente; (of person) prestável

serviceman /'sɜ:vismən/ n (pl -men) militar m

serviette /sɜ:vi'et/ n guardanapo m

servile /'sɜ:vail/ a servil

session /'seʃn/ n sessão f; (univ) ano m académico, (P) académico; (Amer: univ) semestre m. in ~ (sitting) em sessão, reunidos

set /set/ vt (pt set, pres p setting) pôr, colocar; (put down) pousar; (limit etc) fixar; (watch, clock) regular; (example) dar; (exam, task) marcar; (in plaster) engessar □ vi (of sun) pôr-se; (of jelly) endurecer, solidificar(-se) □ n (of people) círculo m, roda f; (of books) coleção f, (P) colecção f; (of tools, chairs etc) jogo m; (TV, radio) aparelho m; (hair) mise f; (theat) cenário m; (tennis) partida f, set.m □ a fixo; (habit) inveterado; (jelly) duro, sólido; (book) do programa, (P) adoptado; (meal) a preço fixo. be ~ on doing estar decidido a fazer. ~ about or to começar a, pôr-se a. ~ back (plans etc) atrasar; (sl: cost) custar. ~-back n revés m, contratempo m, atraso m de vida (colloq). ~ fire to atear fogo a, (P) deitar fogo a. ~ free pôr em liberdade. ~ in (rain etc) pegar. ~ off or out partir, começar a viajar. ~ off (mechanism) pôr para funcionar, (P) pôr a funcionar; (bomb) explodir; (by contrast) realçar. ~ out (state) expor; (arrange) dispôr. ~ sail, içar as velas. ~ square esquadro m. ~ the table pôr a mesa. ~ theory teoria f de conjuntos. ~-to n briga f.

~ up (*establish*) fundar, estabelecer.
~-up *n* (*system*) sistema *m*, organização *f*; (*situation*) situação *f*
settee /se'ti:/ *n* sofá *m*
setting /'setɪŋ/ *n* (*framework*) quadro *m*; (*of jewel*) engaste *m*; (*typ*) composição *f*; (*mus*) arranjo *m* musical
settle /'setl/ *vt* (*arrange*) resolver; (*date*) marcar; (*nerves*) acalmar; (*doubts*) esclarecer; (*new country*) colonizar, povoar; (*bill*) pagar □ *vi* assentar; (*in country*) estabelecer-se; (*in house, chair etc*) instalar-se; (*weather*) estabilizar-se. ~ down acalmar-se; (*become orderly*) assentar; (*sit, rest*) instalar-se. ~ for aceitar. ~ up (with) fazer contas (com); (*fig*) ajustar contas (com). ~r /-ə(r)/ *n* colono *m*, colonizador *m*
settlement /'setlmənt/ *n* (*agreement*) acordo *m*; (*payment*) pagamento *m*; (*colony*) colónia *f*, (*P*) colónia *f*; (*colonization*) colonização *f*
seven /'sevn/ *a* & *n* sete (*m*). ~th *a* & *n* sétimo (*m*)
seventeen /sevn'ti:n/ *a* & *n* dezessete (*m*), (*P*) dezassete (*m*). ~th *a* & *n* décimo sétimo (*m*)
seventy /'sevntɪ/ *a* & *n* setenta (*m*). ~ieth *a* & *n* septuagésimo (*m*)
sever /'sevə(r)/ *vt* cortar. ~ance *n* corte *m*
several /'sevrəl/ *a* & *pron* vários, diversos
severe /sɪ'vɪə(r)/ *a* (-er, -est) severo; (*pain*) forte, violento; (*illness*) grave; (*winter*) rigoroso. ~ely *adv* severamente; (*seriously*) gravemente. ~ity /sɪ'verɪtɪ/ *n* severidade *f*; (*seriousness*) gravidade *f*
sew /səʊ/ *vt/i* (*pt* sewed, *pp* sewn *or* sewed) coser, costurar. ~ing *n* costura *f*. ~ing-machine *n* máquina *f* de costura
sewage /'sju:ɪdʒ/ *n* efluentes *mpl* dos esgotos, detritos *mpl*
sewer /'sju:ə(r)/ *n* cano *m* de esgoto
sewn /səʊn/ *see* sew
sex /seks/ *n* sexo *m* □ *a* sexual. have ~ ter relações. ~ maniac tarado *m* sexual. ~y *a* sexy *invar*, que tem sexappeal
sexist /'seksɪst/ *a* & *n* sexista *mf*
sexual /'sekʃʊəl/ *a* sexual. ~ harassment assédio *m* sexual. ~ intercourse relações *fpl* sexuais. ~ity /'ælətɪ/ *n* sexualidade *f*
shabby /'ʃæbɪ/ *a* (-ier, -iest) (*clothes, object*) gasto, surrado; (*person*) maltrapilho, mal vestido; (*mean*) miserável. ~ily *adv* miseravelmente
shack /ʃæk/ *n* cabana *f*, barraca *f*
shackles /'ʃæklz/ *npl* grilhões *mpl*, algemas *fpl*

shade /ʃeɪd/ *n* sombra *f*; (*of colour*) tom *m*, matiz *m*; (*of opinion*) matiz *m*; (*for lamp*) abat-jour *m*, quebra-luz *m*; (*Amer: blind*) estore *m* □ *vt* resguardar da luz; (*darken*) sombrear. a ~ bigger/*etc* ligeiramente maior/*etc*. in the ~ à sombra
shadow /'ʃædəʊ/ *n* sombra *f* □ *vt* cobrir de sombra; (*follow*) seguir, vigiar. S~ Cabinet gabinete *m* formado pelo partido da oposição. ~y *a* ensombrado, sombreado; (*fig*) vago, indistinto
shady /'ʃeɪdɪ/ *a* (-ier, -iest) sombreiro, (*P*) que dá sombra; (*in shade*) à sombra; (*fig: dubious*) suspeito, duvidoso
shaft /ʃɑːft/ *n* (*of arrow, spear*) haste *f*; (*axle*) eixo *m*, veio *m*; (*of mine, lift*) poço *m*; (*of light*) raio *m*
shaggy /'ʃægɪ/ *a* (-ier, -iest) (*beard*) hirsuto; (*hair*) desgrenhado; (*animal*) peludo, felpudo
shake /ʃeɪk/ *vt* (*pt* shook, *pp* shaken) abanar, sacudir; (*bottle*) agitar; (*belief, house etc*) abalar □ *vi* estremecer, tremer □ *n* (*violent*) abanão *m*, safanão *m*; (*light*) sacudidela *f*. ~ hands with apertar a mão de. ~ off (*get rid of*) sacudir, livrar-se de. ~ one's head (*to say no*) fazer que não com a cabeça. ~ up agitar. ~-up *n* (*upheaval*) reviravolta *f*
shaky /'ʃeɪkɪ/ *a* (-ier, -iest) (*hand, voice*) trémulo, (*P*) trémulo; (*unsteady, unsafe*) pouco firme, inseguro; (*weak*) fraco
shall /ʃæl/; *unstressed* /ʃəl/ *v aux* I/we ~ do (*future*) farei/faremos. I/you/he ~ do (*command*) eu hei de/você há de/tu hás de/ele há de fazer
shallot /ʃə'lɒt/ *n* cebolinha *f*, (*P*) chalota *f*
shallow /'ʃæləʊ/ *a* (-er, -est) pouco fundo, raso; (*fig*) superficial
sham /ʃæm/ *n* fingimento *m*; (*jewel etc*) imitação *f*; (*person*) impostor *m*, fingido *m* □ *a* fingido; (*false*) falso □ *vt* (*pt* shammed) fingir
shambles /'ʃæmblz/ *npl* (*colloq: mess*) balbúrdia *f*, trapalhada *f*
shame /ʃeɪm/ *n* vergonha *f* □ *vt* (*fazer*) envergonhar. it's a ~ é uma pena. what a ~! que pena! ~ful *a* vergonhoso. ~less a sem vergonha, descarado; (*immodest*) despudorado, desavergonhado
shamefaced /'ʃeɪmfeɪst/ *a* envergonhado
shampoo /ʃæm'pu:/ *n* xampu *m*, (*P*) champô *m*, shampoo *m* □ *vt* lavar com xampu, (*P*) champô *or* shampoo
shan't /ʃɑːnt/ = shall not
shanty /'ʃæntɪ/ *n* barraca *f*. ~ town favela *f*, (*P*) bairro(s) *m*(*pl*) da lata

shape /ʃeɪp/ n forma f □ vt moldar □
vi ~ (up) andar bem, fazer progressos. take ~ concretizar-se,
avançar. ~less a informe, sem forma;
(of body) deselegante, disforme
shapely /ʃeɪplɪ/ a (-ier, -iest) (leg, person) bem feito, elegante
share /ʃeə(r)/ n parte f, porção f;
(comm) acção f, (P) acção f □ vt/i par-
tilhar (with com, in de)
shareholder /ʃeəhəʊldə(r)/ n accionista mf, (P) accionista mf
shark /ʃɑːk/ n tubarão m
sharp /ʃɑːp/ a (-er, -est) (knife, pencil
etc) afiado; (pin, point etc) pontiagudo,
aguçado; (words, reply) áspero; (of
bend) fechado; (acute) agudo; (sudden) brusco; (dishonest) pouco honesto; (well-defined) nítido; (brisk)
rápido, vigoroso; (clever) vivo □ adv
(stop) de repente □ n (mus) sustenido
m. six o'clock ~ seis horas em
ponto. ~ly adv (harshly) rispida-
mente; (suddenly) de repente
sharpen /ʃɑːpən/ vt aguçar; (pencil)
fazer a ponta de, (P) afiar; (knife etc)
afiar, amolar. ~er n afiadeira f, (de
pencil) apontador m, (P) apára-lápis
m, (P) afia-lápis m
shatter /ʃætə(r)/ vt/i despedaçar
(-se), esmigalhar(-se); (hopes) des-
truir(-se); (nerves) abalar(-se). ~ed a
(upset) passado; (exhausted) estoura-
do (colloq)
shave /ʃeɪv/ vt/i barbear(-se), fazer a
barba (de) □ n have a ~e barbear-se.
have a close ~e (fig) escapar por
um triz. ~en a raspado, barbeado.
~er n aparelho m de barbear, (P)
máquina f de barbear, (P)
pincel m para a barba. ~ing-brush n
pincel m para a barba. ~ing-cream n
creme m de barbear
shaving /ʃeɪvɪŋ/ n apara f
shawl /ʃɔːl/ n xale m, (P) xaile m
she /ʃiː/ pron ela □ n fêmea f
sheaf /ʃiːf/ n (pl sheaves) feixe m; (of
papers) maço m, molho m
shear /ʃɪə(r)/ vt (pp shorn or
sheared) (sheep etc) tosquiar
shears /ʃɪəz/ npl tesoura f para jardim
sheath /ʃiːθ/ n (pl ~s /ʃiːðz/) bainha
f; (condom) preservativo m, camisa-
de-Vénus f
sheathe /ʃiːð/ vt embainhar
shed¹ /ʃed/ n (hut) casinhola f; (for
cows) estábulo m
shed² /ʃed/ vt (pt shed, pres p shedding)
perder, deixar cair; (spread) espalhar;
(blood, tears) deitar, derramar. ~
light on lançar luz sobre
sheen /ʃiːn/ n brilho m, lustre m
sheep /ʃiːp/ n (pl invar) carneiro m,
ovelha f. ~-dog n cão m de pastor

sheepish /ʃiːpɪʃ/ a encabulado. ~ly
adv com um ar encabulado
sheepskin /ʃiːpskɪn/ n pele f de carneiro; (leather) carneira f
sheer /ʃɪə(r)/ a mero, simples; (steep)
ingreme, a pique; (fabric) diáfano,
transparente □ adv a pique, verticalmente
sheet /ʃiːt/ n lençol m; (of glass, metal) chapa f, placa f; (of paper) folha f
sheikh /ʃeɪk/ n xeque m, sheik m
shelf /ʃelf/ n (pl shelves) prateleira f
shell /ʃel/ n (of egg, nut etc) casca f; (of
mollusc) concha f; (of ship, tortoise)
casco m; (of building) estrutura f,
armação f; (of explosive) cartucho m
□ vt descascar; (mil) bombardear
shellfish /ʃelfɪʃ/ n (pl invar) crus-
táceo m; (as food) marisco m
shelter /ʃeltə(r)/ n abrigo m, refúgio
m □ vt abrigar; (protect) proteger;
(harbour) dar asilo a □ vi abrigar-se,
refugiar-se. ~ed a (life etc) protegido;
(spot) abrigado
shelve /ʃelv/ vt pôr em prateleiras;
(fit with shelves) pôr prateleiras em;
(fig) engavetar, pôr de lado
shelving /ʃelvɪŋ/ n (shelves) prateleiras fpl
shepherd /ʃepəd/ n pastor m □ vt
guiar. ~'s pie empadão m de batata
e carne moída
sheriff /ʃerɪf/ n xerife m
sherry /ʃerɪ/ n Xerez m
shield /ʃiːld/ n (armour, heraldry) escudo m; (screen) antepara m □ vt proteger (from contra, de)
shift /ʃɪft/ vt/i mudar de posição,
deslocar(-se); (exchange, alter) mudar
de □ n mudança f; (workers; work)
turno m. make ~ arranjar-se
shiftless /ʃɪftlɪs/ a (lazy) molengão,
preguiçoso
shifty /ʃɪftɪ/ a (-ier, -iest) velhaco,
duvidoso
shimmer /ʃɪmə(r)/ vi luzir suavemente □ n luzir m
shin /ʃɪn/ n perna f. ~-bone n tíbia f,
canela f. ~-pad n (football) cane-
leira f
shine /ʃaɪn/ vt/i (pt shone) (fazer)
brilhar, (fazer) reluzir; (shoes) engraxar □ n lustro m. ~e a torch (on)
iluminar com uma lanterna de mão.
the sun is ~ing faz sol
shingle /ʃɪŋgl/ n (pebbles) seixos mpl
shingles /ʃɪŋglz/ npl med zona f,
herpes-zóster f
shiny /ʃaɪnɪ/ a (-ier, -iest) brilhante;
(of coat, trousers) lustroso
ship /ʃɪp/ n barco m, navio m □ vt (pt
shipped) transportar; (send) mandar
por via marítima; (load) embarcar.
~ment n (goods) carregamento m;

(*shipping*) embarque *m*. ~per *n* expedidor *m*. ~ping *n* navegação *f*; (*ships*) navios *mpl*
shipbuilding /'ʃɪpbɪldɪŋ/ *n* construção *f* naval
shipshape /'ʃɪpʃeɪp/ *adv* & a em (perfeita) ordem, impecável
shipwreck /'ʃɪprek/ *n* naufrágio *m*. ~ed *a* naufragado. be ~ed naufragar
shipyard /'ʃɪpjɑːd/ *n* estaleiro *m*
shirk /ʃɜːk/ *vt* fugir a, furtar-se a, (*P*) baldar-se a (*sl*). ~er *n* parasita *mf*
shirt /ʃɜːt/ *n* camisa *f*; (*of woman*) blusa *f*. in ~-sleeves em mangas de camisa
shiver /'ʃɪvə(r)/ *vi* arrepiar-se, tiritar □ *n* arrepio *m*
shoal /ʃəʊl/ *n* (*of fish*) cardume *m*
shock /ʃɒk/ *n* choque *m*, embate *m*; (*electr*) choque *m* elétrico, (*P*) eléctrico; (*med*) choque *m* □ *a* de choque □ *vt* chocar. ~ absorber (*mech*) amortecedor *m*. ~ing *a* chocante; (*colloq: very bad*) horrível
shod /ʃɒd/ *see* shoe
shodd|y /'ʃɒdɪ/ *a* (-ier, -iest) mal feito, ordinário, de má qualidade. ~ily *adv* mal
shoe /ʃuː/ *n* sapato *m*; (*footwear*) calçado *m*; (*horse*) ferradura *f*; (*brake*) sapata *f*, (*P*) calço *m* (de travão) □ *vt* (*pt* shod, *pres p* shoeing) (*horse*) ferrar. ~ polish *n* pomada *f*, (*P*) graxa *f* para sapatos. ~-shop *n* sapataria *f*. on a ~-string (*colloq*) com/por muito pouco dinheiro, na pindaíba (*colloq*)
shoehorn /'ʃuːhɔːn/ *n* calçadeira *f*
shoelace /'ʃuːleɪs/ *n* cordão *m* de sapato, (*P*) atacador *m*
shoemaker /'ʃuːmeɪkə(r)/ *n* sapateiro *m*
shone /ʃɒn/ *see* shine
shoo /ʃuː/ *vt* enxotar □ *int* xô
shook /ʃʊk/ *see* shake
shoot /ʃuːt/ *vt* (*pt* shot) (*gun*) disparar; (*glance, missile*) lançar; (*kill*) matar a tiro; (*wound*) ferir a tiro; (*execute*) executar, fuzilar; (*hunt*) caçar; (*film*) filmar, rodar □ *vi* disparar, atirar (at contra, sobre); (*bot*) rebentar; (*football*) rematar □ *n* (*bot*) rebento *m*. ~ down abater (a tiro). ~ in/out(*rush*) entrar/sair correndo or disparado. ~ up(*spurt*) jorrar; (*grow quickly*) crescer a olhos vistos, dar um pulo; (*prices*) subir em disparada. ~ing *n* (*shots*) tiroteio *m*. ~ing-range *n* carreira *f* de tiro. ~ing star estrela *f* cadente
shop /ʃɒp/ *n* loja *f*; (*workshop*) oficina *f* □ *vi* (*pt* shopped) fazer compras. ~ around procurar, ver o que há. ~

assistant empregado *m*, caixeiro *m*; vendedor *m*. ~-floor *n* (*workers*) trabalhadores *mpl*. ~per *n* comprador *m*. ~-soiled, (*Amer*) ~-worn *adjs* enxovalhado. ~ steward delegado *m* sindical. ~ window vitrina *f*, (*P*) montra *f*. talk ~ falar de coisas profissionais
shopkeeper /'ʃɒpkiːpə(r)/ *n* lojista *mf*, comerciante *mf*
shoplift|er /'ʃɒplɪftə(r)/ *n* gatuno *m* de lojas. ~ing *n* furto *m* em lojas
shopping /'ʃɒpɪŋ/ *n* (*goods*) compras *fpl*. go ~ ir às compras. ~ bag sacola *f* de compras. ~ centre centro *m* comercial
shore /ʃɔː(r)/ *n* (*of sea*) praia *f*, costa *f*; (*of lake*) margem *f*
shorn /ʃɔːn/ *see* shear □ a tosquiado. ~ of despojado de
short /ʃɔːt/ *a* (-er, -est) curto; (*person*) baixo; (*brief*) breve, curto; (*curt*) seco, brusco. be ~ of (*lack*) ter falta de □ *adv* (*abruptly*) bruscamente, de repente. cut ~ abreviar; (*interrupt*) interromper □ *n* (*electr*) curto-circuito *m*; (*film*) curta-metragem *f*, short *m*. ~s (*trousers*) calção *m*, (*P*) calções *mpl*, short *m*, (*P*) shorts *mpl*. a ~ time atrás pouco tempo. he is called Tom for ~ o diminutivo dele é Tom. in ~ em suma. ~-change *vt* (*cheat*) enganar. ~ circuit (*electr*) curto-circuito *m* ~-circuit*vt*/*i* (*electr*) fazer or dar um curto-circuito (em). ~ cut atalho *m*. ~-handed a com falta de pessoal. ~ list pré-seleção *f*, (*P*) pré-selecção *f*. ~-lived a de pouca duração. ~-sighted a míope, (*P*) curto de vista. ~-tempered a irritadiço. ~ story conto *m*. ~ wave (*radio*) onda(s) *f*(*pl*) curta(s)
shortage /'ʃɔːtɪdʒ/ *n* falta *f*, escassez *f*
shortbread /'ʃɔːtbred/ *n* shortbread *m*, biscoito *m* de massa amanteigada
shortcoming /'ʃɔːtkʌmɪŋ/ *n* falha *f*, imperfeição *f*
shorten /'ʃɔːtn/ *vt*/*i* encurtar(-se), abreviar(-se), diminuir
shorthand /'ʃɔːthænd/ *n* estenografia *f*. ~ typist estenodactilógrafa *f*
shortly /'ʃɔːtlɪ/ *adv* (*soon*) em breve, dentro em pouco
shot /ʃɒt/ *see* shoot □ *n* (*firing, bullet*) tiro *m*; (*person*) atirador *m*; (*pellets*) chumbo *m*; (*photograph*) fotografia *f*; (*injection*) injeção *f*, (*P*) injecção *f*; in golf, billiards) tacada *f*. go like a ~ir disparado. have a ~ (at sth)experimentar (fazer alg coisa). ~-gun *n* espingarda *f*, caçadeira *f*
should /ʃʊd/; *unstressed* /ʃəd/ *v aux* you ~ help me você devia me ajudar. I ~ have stayed devia ter

ficado. I ~ like to gostaria de or gostava de. if he ~ come se ele vier

shoulder /'ʃəʊldə(r)/ n ombro m □ vt (responsibility) tomar, assumir; (burden) carregar, arcar com. ~-blade n (anat) omoplata f. ~-pad n enchimento m de ombro, ombreira f

shout /ʃaʊt/ n grito m, brado m; (very loud) berro m □ vt/i gritar (at com); (very loudly) berrar (at com). ~ down fazer calar com gritos. ~ing n gritaria f, berraria f

shove /ʃʌv/ n empurrão m □ vt/i empurrar; (colloq: put) meter, enfiar. ~ off (colloq: depart) começar a andar (colloq), dar o fora (colloq), (P) cavar (colloq)

shovel /'ʃʌvl/ n pá f; (machine) escavadora f □ vt (pt shovelled) remover com pá

show /ʃəʊ/ vt (pt showed, pp shown) mostrar; (of dial, needle) marcar; (put on display) expor; (film) dar, passar □ vi ver-se, aparecer, estar à vista □ n mostra f, demonstração f, manifestação f; (ostentation) alarde m, espalhafato m; (exhibition) mostra f, exposição f; (theatre, cinema) espetáculo m, (P) espectáculo m, show m. for ~ para fazer vista. ~ exposto, em exposição. ~-down n confrontação f. ~-jumping n concurso m hípico. ~ in mandar entrar. ~ off vt exibir, ostentar □ vi exibir-se, querer fazer figura. ~-off n exibicionista mf. ~ out acompanhar à porta. ~-piece n peça f digna de se expor. ~ up ser claramente visível, ver-se bem; (colloq: arrive) aparecer. ~ing n (performance) atuação f, performance f; (cinema) exibição f

shower /'ʃaʊə(r)/ n (of rain) aguaceiro m, chuvarada f, (of blows etc) saraivada f; (in bathroom) chuveiro m, ducha f, (P) duche m □ vt ~ with cumular de, encher de □ vi tomar um banho de chuveiro or uma ducha, (P) um duche. ~-y a chuvoso

showerproof /'ʃaʊəpruːf/ a impermeável

shown /ʃəʊn/ see show

showroom /'ʃəʊrʊm/ n espaço m de exposição, show-room m; (for cars) stand m

showy /'ʃəʊɪ/ a (-ier, -iest) vistoso; (too bright) berrante; (pej) espalhafatoso

shrank /ʃræŋk/ see shrink

shred /ʃred/ n tira f, retalho m, farrapo m; (fig) mínimo m, sombra f □ vt (pt shredded) reduzir a tiras, estrançalhar; (culin) desfiar. ~der n trituradora f; (for paper) fragmentadora f

shrewd /ʃruːd/ a (-er, -est) astucioso,

fino, perspicaz. ~ness n astúcia f, perspicácia f

shriek /ʃriːk/ n grito m agudo, guincho m □ vt/i gritar, guinchar

shrift /ʃrɪft/ n give sb short ~ tratar alguém com brusquidão, despachar alguém sem mais cerimônias, (P) cerimónias

shrill /ʃrɪl/ a estridente, agudo

shrimp /ʃrɪmp/ n camarão m

shrine /ʃraɪn/ n (place) santuário m; (tomb) túmulo m; (casket) relicário m

shrink /ʃrɪŋk/ vt/i (pt shrank, pp shrunk) encolher; (recoil) recolher-se. ~ from esquivar-se a, fugir a (+ inf)/de (+ noun), retrair-se de. ~-age n encolhimento m; (comm) contração f

shrivel /'ʃrɪvl/ vt/i (pt shrivelled) encarquilhar(-se)

shroud /ʃraʊd/ n mortalha f □ vt (veil) encobrir, envolver

Shrove /ʃrəʊv/ n ~ Tuesday Terçafeira f gorda or de Carnaval

shrub /ʃrʌb/ n arbusto m. ~bery n arbustos mpl

shrug /ʃrʌg/ vt (pt shrugged) ~ one's shoulders encolher os ombros □ n encolher m de ombros. ~ off não dar importância a

shrunk /ʃrʌŋk/ see shrink. ~en a encolhido; (person) mirrado, chupado

shudder /'ʃʌdə(r)/ vi arrepiar-se, estremecer, tremer □ n arrepio m, tremor m, estremecimento m. I ~ to think tremo só de pensar

shuffle /'ʃʌfl/ vt (feet) arrastar; (cards) embaralhar □ vi arrastar os pés □ n marcha f arrastada

shun /ʃʌn/ vt (pt shunned) evitar, fugir de

shunt /ʃʌnt/ vt/i (train) mudar de linha, manobrar

shut /ʃʌt/ vt (pt shut, pres p shutting) fechar □ vi fechar-se; (shop, bank etc) encerrar, fechar. ~ down or up fechar. ~-down n encerramento m. ~ in or up trancar. ~ up vi (colloq: stop talking) calar-se □ vt (colloq: silence) mandar calar. ~ up! (colloq) cale-se!, cale a boca!

shutter /'ʃʌtə(r)/ n taipais mpl, (P) portada f de madeira; (of laths) persiana f; (in shop) taipais mpl; (photo) obturador m

shuttle /'ʃʌtl/ n (of spaceship) ônibus m espacial. ~ service (plane) ponte f aérea; (bus) navete f

shuttlecock /'ʃʌtlkɒk/ n volante m

shy /ʃaɪ/ a (-er, -est) tímido, acanhado, envergonhado □ vi (horse) espantar-se (at com); (fig) assustar-se (at away from com). ~ness n timidez f, acanhamento m, vergonha f

Siamese /saɪə'miːz/ a & n siamês (m). ~ **cat** gato m siamês

Sicily /'sɪsɪlɪ/ n Sicília f

sick /sɪk/ a doente; (humour) negro. be ~ (vomit) vomitar. be ~ of estar farto de. feel ~ estar enjoado. ~**bay** n enfermaria f. ~**leave** n licença f por doença ~**room** n quarto m de doente

sicken /'sɪkn/ vt (distress) desesperar; (disgust) repugnar □ vi be ~ing for flu começar a pegar uma gripe (colloq)

sickle /'sɪkl/ n foice f

sickly /'sɪklɪ/ a (-ier, -iest) (person) doentio, achacado; (smell) enjoativo; (pale) pálido

sickness /'sɪknɪs/ n doença f; (vomiting) náusea f, vômito m, (P) vómito m

side /saɪd/ n lado m; (of road, river) beira f; (of hill) encosta f; (sport) equipe f, (P) equipa f □ a lateral □ vi ~ **with** tomar o partido de. on the ~ (extra) nas horas vagas; (secretly) pela calada. ~ **by** ~ lado a lado. ~**car** n sidecar m. ~**effect** n efeito m secundário. ~**show** n espetáculo m, (P) espectáculo m suplementar. ~**step** vt (pt -stepped) evitar. ~**track** vt (fazer) desviar dum propósito

sideboard /'saɪdbɔːd/ n aparador m

sideburns /'saɪdbɜːnz/ npl suíças fpl, costeletas fpl, (P) patilhas fpl

sidelight /'saɪdlaɪt/ n (auto) luz f lateral, (P) farolim m

sideline /'saɪdlaɪn/ n atividade f, (P) actividade f secundária; (sport) linha f lateral

sidelong /'saɪdlɒŋ/ adv & a de lado

sidewalk /'saɪdwɔːk/ n (Amer) passeio m

sideways /'saɪdweɪz/ adv & a de lado

siding /'saɪdɪŋ/ n desvio m, ramal m

sidle /'saɪdl/ vi ~ **up (to)** avançar furtivamente (para), chegar-se furtivamente (a)

siege /siːdʒ/ n cerco m

siesta /sɪ'estə/ n sesta f

sieve /sɪv/ n peneira f; (for liquids) coador m □ vt peneirar; (liquids) passar, coar

sift /sɪft/ vt peneirar; (sprinkle) polvilhar. ~ **through** examinar minuciosamente, esquadrinhar

sigh /saɪ/ n suspiro m □ vt/i suspirar

sight /saɪt/ n vista f; (scene) cena f; (on gun) mira f □ vt avistar, ver, divisar. at or on ~ à vista. catch ~ of avistar. in ~ à vista, visível. lose ~ of perder de vista. out of ~ longe dos olhos

sightsee|ing /'saɪtsiːɪŋ/ n visita f, turismo m. go ~ing visitar lugares turísticos. ~**r** /'saɪtsiːə(r)/ n turista mf

sign /saɪn/ n sinal m; (symbol) signo m □ vt (in writing) assinar □ vi (make a sign) fazer sinal. ~ **on** or **up** (worker) assinar contrato. ~**language** n mímica f

signal /'sɪgnəl/ n sinal m □ vi (pt signalled) fazer signal □ vt comunicar (por sinais); (person) fazer sinal para. ~**box** n cabine f de sinalização

signature /'sɪgnətʃə(r)/ n assinatura f. ~ **tune** indicativo m musical

signet-ring /'sɪgnɪtrɪŋ/ n anel m de sinete

significan|t /sɪg'nɪfɪkənt/ a importante; (meaningful) significativo. ~**ce** n importância f; (meaning) significado m. ~**tly** adv (much) sensivelmente

signify /'sɪgnɪfaɪ/ vt significar

signpost /'saɪnpəʊst/ n poste m de sinalização □ vt sinalizar

silence /'saɪləns/ n silêncio m □ vt silenciar, calar. ~**r** /-ə(r)/ n (on gun) silenciador m; (on car) silencioso m

silent /'saɪlənt/ a silencioso; (not speaking) calado; (film) mudo. ~**ly** adv silenciosamente

silhouette /sɪlu'et/ n silhueta f □ vt be ~**d against** estar em silhueta contra

silicon /'sɪlɪkən/ n silicone m. ~ **chip** circuito m integrado

silk /sɪlk/ n seda f. ~**en**, ~**y** adjs sedoso

sill /sɪl/ n (of window) parapeito m; (of door) soleira f, limiar m

sill|y /'sɪlɪ/ a (-ier, -iest) tolo, idiota. ~**iness** n tolice f, idiotice f

silo /'saɪləʊ/ n (pl -os) silo m

silt /sɪlt/ n aluvião m, sedimento m

silver /'sɪlvə(r)/ n prata f; (silverware) prataria f, pratas fpl □ a de prata. ~ **paper** papel m prateado. ~ **wedding** bodas fpl de prata. ~**y** a prateado; (sound) argentino

silversmith /'sɪlvəsmɪθ/ n ourives m

silverware /'sɪlvəweə(r)/ n prataria f, pratas fpl

similar /'sɪmɪlə(r)/ a ~ **to** semelhante (a), parecido (com). ~**ity** /-ə'lærətɪ/ n semelhança f. ~**ly** adv de igual modo, analogamente

simile /'sɪmɪlɪ/ n símile m, comparação f

simmer /'sɪmə(r)/ vt/i cozinhar em fogo brando; (fig: smoulder) ferver, fremir; ~ **down** acalmar(-se)

simple /'sɪmpl/ a (-er, -est) simples. ~**e-minded** a simples; (feebleminded) pobre de espírito, tolo. ~**icity** /-'plɪsətɪ/ n simplicidade f.

~y *adv* simplesmente; (*absolutely*) absolutamente, simplesmente

simpleton /'smpltən/ *n* simplório *m*

simplif|y /'smplfa(r)/ *vt* simplificar. ~**ication** /-'keʃn/ *n* simplificação *f*

simulat|e /'smjulert/ *vt* simular, imitar. ~**ion** /-'leʃn/ *n* simulação *f*, imitação *f*

simultaneous /sml'temɪəs/ *a* simultâneo, concomitante. ~**ly** *adv* simultaneamente

sin /sɪn/ *n* pecado *m* □ *vi* (*pt* **sinned**) pecar

since /sɪns/ *prep* desde □ *adv* desde então □ *conj* desde que; (*because*) uma vez que, visto que. ~ **then** desde então

sincer|e /sm'sɪə(r)/ *a* sincero. ~**ely** *adv* sinceramente. ~**ity** /-'serətɪ/ *n* sinceridade *f*

sinew /'smju:/ *n* (*anat*) tendão *m*. ~**s** músculos *mpl*. ~**y** *a* forte, musculoso

sinful /'smfl/ *a* (*wicked*) pecaminoso; (*shocking*) escandaloso

sing /sɪŋ/ *vt/i* (*pt* **sang**, *pp* **sung**) cantar. ~**er** *n* cantor *m*

singe /smdʒ/ *vt* (*pres p* **singeing**) chamuscar

single /'sɪŋgl/ *a* único, só; (*unmarried*) solteiro; (*bed*) de solteiro; (*room*) individual; (*ticket*) de ida, simples □ *n* (*ticket*) bilhete *m* de ida or simples; (*record*) disco *m* de 45 r.p.m. ~**s** (*tennis*) singulares *mpl* □ *vt* ~ **out** escolher. **in** ~-**file** em fila indiana. ~-**handed** *a* sem ajuda, sozinho. ~-**minded** *a* decidido, aferrado à sua ideia, tenaz. ~ **parent** pai *m* solteiro, mãe *f* solteira. **singly** *adv* um a um, um por um

singsong /'smsɒŋ/ *n* **have a** ~ cantar em coro □ *a* (*voice*) monótono, monocórdico

singular /'sɪŋgjulə(r)/ *n* singular *m* □ *a* (*uncommon; gram*) singular; (*noun*) no singular. ~**ly** *adv* singularmente

sinister /'smɪstə(r)/ *a* sinistro

sink /sɪŋk/ *vt* (*pt* **sank**, *pp* **sunk**) (*ship*) afundar, ir a pique; (*well*) abrir; (*invest money*) empatar; (*lose money*) enterrar □ *vi* afundar-se; (*of ground*) ceder; (*of voice*) baixar □ *n* pia *f*, (*P*) lava-louça *m*. ~ **in** (*fig*) ficar gravado, entrar (*colloq*). ~ **or swim** ou vai ou racha

sinner /'smə(r)/ *n* pecador *m*

sinuous /'smjuəs/ *a* sinuoso

sinus /'saməs/ *n* (*pl* -**es**) (*anat*) seio (nasal) *m*. ~**itis** /samə'saɪtɪs/ *n* sinusite *f*

sip /sɪp/ *n* gole *m* □ *vt* (*pt* **sipped**) bebericar, beber aos golinhos

siphon /'saɪfn/ *n* sifão *m* □ *vt* ~ **off** extrair por meio de sifão

sir /sɜ:(r)/ *n* senhor *m*. **S**~ (*title*) Sir *m*. **Dear S**~ Exmo Senhor. **excuse me,** ~ desculpe, senhor. **no,** ~ não, senhor

siren /'saɪərən/ *n* sereia *f*, sirene *f*

sirloin /'sɜ:lɔɪn/ *n* lombo *m* de vaca

sissy /'sɪsɪ/ *n* maricas *m*

sister /'sɪstə(r)/ *n* irmã *f*; (*nun*) irmã *f*, freira *f*; (*nurse*) enfermeira-chefe *f*. ~-**in-law** (*pl* ~**s-in-law**) cunhada *f*. ~**ly** *a* fraterno, fraternal

sit /sɪt/ *vt/i* (*pt* **sat**, *pres p* **sitting**) sentar(-se); (*of committee etc*) reunir-se. ~ **for an exam** fazer um exame, prestar uma prova. **be** ~**ting** estar sentado. ~ **around** não fazer nada. ~ **down** sentar-se. ~-**in** *n* ocupação *f*. ~**ting** *n* reunião *f*, sessão *f*; (*in restaurant*) serviço *m*. ~**ting-room** *n* sala *f* de estar. ~ **up** endireitar-se na cadeira; (*not go to bed*) passar a noite acordado

site /saɪt/ *n* local *m*. (*building*) ~ terreno *m* para construção, lote *m* □ *vt* localizar, situar

situat|e /'sɪtʃuert/ *vt* situar. **be** ~**ed** estar situado. ~**ion** /-'erʃn/ *n* (*position, condition*) situação *f*; (*job*) emprego *m*, colocação *f*

six /sɪks/ *a* & *n* seis (*m*). ~**th** *a* & *n* sexto (*m*)

sixteen /sɪk'sti:n/ *a* & *n* dezesseis *m*, (*P*) dezasseis (*m*). ~**th** *a* & *n* décimo sexto (*m*)

sixt|y /'sɪkstɪ/ *a* & *n* sessenta (*m*). ~**ieth** *a* & *n* sexagésimo (*m*)

size /saɪz/ *n* tamanho *m*; (*of person, garment etc*) tamanho *m*, medida *f*; (*of shoes*) número *m*; (*extent*) grandeza *f* □ *vt* ~ **up** calcular o tamanho de; (*colloq: judge*) formar um juízo sobre, avaliar. ~**able** *a* bastante grande, considerável

sizzle /'sɪzl/ *vi* chiar, rechinar

skate[1] /skeɪt/ *n* (*pl invar*) (*fish*) (ar)raia *f*

skat|e[2] /skeɪt/ *n* patim *m* □ *vi* patinar. ~**er** *n* patinador *m*. ~**ing** *n* patinação *f*. ~**ing-rink** *n* rinque *m* de patinação

skateboard /'skeɪtbɔ:d/ *n* skate *m*

skelet|on /'skelɪtən/ *n* esqueleto *m*; (*framework*) armação *f*. ~**on crew** *or* ~**on staff** pessoal *m* reduzido. ~**on key** chave *f* mestra. ~**al** *a* esquelético

sketch /sketʃ/ *n* esboço *m*, croqui(s) *m*; (*theat*) sketch *m*, peça *f* curta e humorística; (*outline*) idéia *f* geral, esboço *m* □ *vt* esboçar, delinear □ *vi* fazer esboços. ~-**book** *n* caderno *m* de desenho

sketchy /'sketʃɪ/ *a* (-**ier** -**iest**) incompleto, esboçado

skewer /'skjuə(r)/ *n* espeto *m*

ski /ski:/ n (pl -s) esqui m □ vi (pt ski'd or skied, pres p skiing) esquiar; (go skiing) fazer esqui. ~er n esquiador m. ~ing n esqui m

skid /skɪd/ vi (pt skidded) derrapar, patinar □ n derrapagem f

skilful /'skɪlfl/ a hábil, habilidoso. ~ly adv habilmente, com perícia

skill /skɪl/ n habilidade f, jeito m; (craft) arte f. ~s aptidões fpl. ~ed a hábil, habilidoso; (worker) especializado

skim /skɪm/ vt (pt skimmed) tirar a espuma de; (milk) desnatar, tirar a nata de; (pass or glide over) deslizar sobre, roçar □ vi ~ through ler por alto, passar os olhos por. ~med milk leite m desnatado

skimp /skɪmp/ vt (use too little) poupar em □ vi ser poupado

skimpy /'skɪmpɪ/ a (-ier, -iest) (clothes) sumário; (meal) escasso, racionado (fig)

skin /skɪn/ n (of person, animal) pele f; (of fruit) casca f □ vt (pt skinned) (animal) esfolar, tirar a pele de; (fruit) descascar. ~-diving n mergulho m, caça f submarina

skinny /'skɪnɪ/ a (-ier, -iest) magricela, escanzelado

skint /skɪnt/ a (sl) sem dinheiro, na última lona (sl), (P) nas lonas

skip¹ /skɪp/ vi (pt skipped) saltar, pular; (jump about) saltitar; (with rope) pular corda □ vt (page) saltar; (class) faltar a □ n salto m. ~ping rope n corda f de pular

skip² /skɪp/ n (container) container m grande para entulho

skipper /'skɪpə(r)/ n capitão m

skirmish /'skɜːmɪʃ/ n escaramuça f

skirt /skɜːt/ n saia f □ vt contornar, ladear. ~ing-board n rodapé m

skit /skɪt/ n (theat) paródia f, sketch m satírico

skittle /'skɪtl/ n pino m. ~s npl boliche m, (P) jogo m de laranjinha

skive /skaɪv/ vi (sl) eximir-se de um dever, evitar trabalhar (sl)

skulk /skʌlk/ vi (move) rondar furtivamente; (hide) esconder-se

skull /skʌl/ n caveira f, crânio m

skunk /skʌŋk/ n (animal) gambá m

sky /skaɪ/ n céu m. ~-blue a & n azul-celeste (m)

skylight /'skaɪlaɪt/ n clarabóia f

skyscraper /'skaɪskreɪpə(r)/ n arranha-céus m invar

slab /slæb/ n (of marble) placa f; (of paving-stone) laje f; (of metal) chapa f; (of cake) fatia f grossa

slack /slæk/ a (-er, -est) (rope) bambo, frouxo; (person) descuidado, negligente; (business) parado, fraco; (period, season) morto □ n the ~ (in rope) a parte bamba □ vt/i (be lazy) estar com preguiça, fazer cera (fig)

slacken /'slækən/ vt/i (speed, activity etc) afrouxar, abrandar

slacks /slæks/ npl calças fpl

slag /slæg/ n escória f

slain /sleɪn/ see slay

slam /slæm/ vt (pt slammed) bater violentamente com; (throw) atirar; (sl: criticize) criticar, malhar □ vi (door etc) bater violentamente □ n (noise) bater m, pancada f

slander /'slɑːndə(r)/ n calúnia f, difamação f □ vt caluniar, difamar. ~ous a calunioso, difamatório

slang /slæŋ/ n calão m, gíria f. ~y a de calão

slant /slɑːnt/ vt/i inclinar(-se); (news) apresentar de forma tendenciosa □ n inclinação f; (bias) tendência f; (point of view) ângulo m. be ~ing ser/estar inclinado or em declive

slap /slæp/ vt (pt slapped) (strike) bater, dar uma palmada em; (on face) esbofetear, dar uma bofetada em; (put forcefully) atirar com □ n palmada f, bofetada f □ adv em cheio. ~-up a (sl: excellent) excelente

slapdash /'slæpdæʃ/ a descuidado; (impetuous) precipitado

slapstick /'slæpstɪk/ n farsa f com palhaçadas

slash /slæʃ/ vt (cut) retalhar, dar golpes em; (sever) cortar; (a garment) golpear; (fig: reduce) reduzir drasticamente, fazer um corte radical em □ n corte m, golpe m

slat /slæt/ n (in blind) ripa f, (P) lâmina f

slate /sleɪt/ n ardósia f □ vt (colloq: criticize) criticar severamente

slaughter /'slɔːtə(r)/ vt chacinar, massacrar; (animals) abater □ n chacina f, massacre m, mortandade f; (animals) abate m

slaughterhouse /'slɔːtəhaʊs/ n matadouro m

slave /sleɪv/ n escravo m □ vi mourejar, trabalhar como um escravo. ~-driver n (fig) o que obriga os outros a trabalharem como escravos, condutor m de escravos. ~ry /-ərɪ/ n escravatura f

slavish /'sleɪvɪʃ/ a servil

slay /sleɪ/ vt (pt slew, pp slain) matar

sleazy /'sliːzɪ/ a (-ier, -iest) (colloq) esquálido, sórdido

sledge /sledʒ/ n trenó m. ~-hammer n martelo m de forja, marreta f

sleek /sliːk/ a (-er, -est) liso, macio e lustroso

sleep /sliːp/ n sono m □ vi (pt slept) dormir □ vt ter lugar para, alojar. go to ~ ir dormir, adormecer. put to ~ (*kill*) mandar matar. ~ around ser promíscuo. ~er *n* aquele que dorme; (*rail: beam*) dormente *m*; (*berth*) couchette *f*. ~ing-bag *n* saco *m* de dormir. ~ing-car *n* carro-dormitório *m*, carruagemcama *f*, (*P*) vagon-lit *m*. ~less *a* insone; (*night*) em claro, insone. ~-walker *n* sonâmbulo *m*

sleep|y /'sli:pɪ/ *a* (-ier, -iest) sonolento. be ~y ter *or* estar com sono. ~ily *adv* meio dormindo

sleet /sli:t/ *n* geada *f* miúda □ *vi* cair geada miúda

sleeve /sli:v/ *n* manga *f*; (*of record*) capa *f*. up one's ~ de reserva, escondido. ~less *a* sem mangas

sleigh /sleɪ/ *n* trenó *m*

sleight /slaɪt/ *n* ~ of hand prestidigitação *f*, passe *m* de mágica

slender /'slendə(r)/ *a* esguio, esbelto; (*fig: scanty*) escasso. ~ness *n* aspecto *m* esguio, esbelteza *f*, elegância *f*; (*scantiness*) escassez *f*

slept /slept/ *see* sleep

sleuth /slu:θ/ *n* (*colloq*) detective *m*

slew¹ /slu:/ *vi* (*turn*) virar-se

slew² /slu:/ *see* slay

slice /slaɪs/ *n* fatia *f* □ *vt* cortar em fatias; (*golf, tennis*) cortar

slick /slɪk/ *a* (*slippery*) escorregadio; (*cunning*) astuto, habilidoso; (*unctuous*) melífluo □ *n* (oil) ~ mancha *f* de óleo

slid|e /slaɪd/ *vt/i* (*pt* slid) escorregar, deslizar □ *n* escorregadela *f*, escorregão *m*; (*in playground*) escorrega *m*; (*for hair*) prendedor *m*, (*P*) travessa *f*, (*photo*) diapositivo *m*, slide *m*. ~e-rule *n* régua *f* de cálculo. ~ing *scale* escala *f* móvel

slight /slaɪt/ *a* (-er, -est) (*slender, frail*) delgado, franzino; (*inconsiderable*) leve, ligeiro □ *vt* desconsiderar, desfeitear □ *n* desconsideração *f*, desfeita *f*. the ~est *a* o/a menor. not in the ~est em absoluto. ~ly *adv* ligeiramente, um pouco

slim /slɪm/ *a* (slimmer, slimmest) magro, esbelto; (*chance*) pequeno, remoto □ *vi* (*pt* slimmed) emagrecer. ~ness *n* magreza *f*, esbelteza *f*

slim|e /slaɪm/ *n* lodo *m*. ~y *a* lodoso; (*slippery*) escorregadio; (*fig: servile*) servil, bajulador

sling /slɪŋ/ *n* (*weapon*) funda *f*; (*for arm*) tipóia *f* □ *vt* (*pt* slung) atirar, lançar

slip /slɪp/ *vt/i* (*pt* slipped) escorregar; (*move quietly*) mover-se de mansinho □ *n* escorregadela *f*, escorregão *m*; (*mistake*) engano *m*, lapso *m*; (*petti-coat*) combinação *f*; (*of paper*) tira *f* de papel. give the ~ to livrar-se de, escapar(-se) de. ~ away esgueirar-se. ~ by passar sem se dar conta, passar despercebido. ~-cover *n* (*Amer*) capa *f* para móveis. ~ into (*go*) entrar de mansinho, enfiar-se em; (*clothes*) enfiar. ~ of the tongue lapso *m*. ~ped disc disco *m* deslocado. ~-road *n* acesso *m* a autoestrada. ~ sb's mind passar pela cabeça de alguém. ~ up (*colloq*) cometer uma gafe. ~-up *n* (*colloq*) gafe *f*

slipper /'slɪpə(r)/ *n* chinelo *m*

slippery /'slɪpərɪ/ *a* escorregadio; (*fig: person*) que não é de confiança, sem escrúpulos

slipshod /'slɪpʃɒd/ *a* (*person*) desleixado, desmazelado; (*work*) feito sem cuidado, desleixado

slit /slɪt/ *n* fenda *f*; (*cut*) corte *m*; (*tear*) rasgão *m* □ *vt* (*pt* slit, *pres p* slitting) fender; (*cut*) fazer um corte em, cortar

slither /'slɪðə(r)/ *vi* escorregar, resvalar

sliver /'slɪvə(r)/ *n* (*of cheese etc*) fatia *f*; (*splinter*) lasca *f*

slobber /'slɒbə(r)/ *vi* babar-se

slog /slɒg/ *vt* (*pt* slogged) (*hit*) bater com força □ *vi* (*walk*) caminhar com passos pesados e firmes; (*work*) trabalhar duro □ *n* (*work*) trabalheira *f*, (*walk, effort*) estafa *f*

slogan /'sləʊgən/ *n* slogan *m*, lema *m*, palavra *f* de ordem

slop /slɒp/ *vt/i* (*pt* slopped) transbordar, entornar. ~s *npl* (*dirty water*) água(s) *f(pl)* suja(s); (*liquid refuse*) despejos *mpl*

slope /sləʊp/ *vt/i* inclinar(-se), formar declive □ *n* (*of mountain*) encosta *f*, (*of street*) rampa *f*, ladeira *f*. ~ing *a* inclinado, em declive

sloppy /'slɒpɪ/ *a* (-ier, -iest) (*ground*) molhado, com poças de água; (*food*) aguado; (*clothes*) desleixado; (*work*) descuidado, feito de qualquer jeito *or* maneira (*colloq*); (*person*) desmazelado; (*maudlin*) piegas

slosh /slɒʃ/ *vt* entornar; (*colloq: splash*) esparrinhar; (*sl: hit*) bater em, dar (uma) sova em □ *vi* chapinhar

slot /slɒt/ *n* ranhura *f*; (*in timetable*) horário *m*, (*TV*) espaço *m*; (*aviat*) slot *m* □ *vt/i* (*pt* slotted) enfiar(-se), meter(-se), encaixar (-se). ~-machine *n* (*for stamps, tickets etc*) distribuidor *m* automático; (*for gambling*) caça-níqueis *m*, (*P*) slot machine *f*

sloth /sləʊθ/ *n* preguiça *f*, indolência *f*; (*zool*) preguiça *f*

slouch /slaʊtʃ/ *vi* (*stand, move*) andar com as costas curvadas; (*sit*) sentar em má postura slovenly /'slʌvnlı/ a desmazelado, desleixado

slow /sləʊ/ a (-er, -est) lento, vagaroso □ adv devagar, lentamente □ vt/i ~ (up or down) diminuir a velocidade, afrouxar; (auto) desacelerar. be ~ (clock etc) atrasar-se, estar atrasado. in ~ motion em câmara lenta. ~ly adv devagar, lentamente, vagarosamente

slow|coach /'sləʊkəʊtʃ/, (Amer) ~poke ns lesma m/f, pastelão m (fig)

sludge /slʌdʒ/ n lama f, lodo m

slug /slʌɡ/ n lesma f

sluggish /'slʌɡıʃ/ a (slow) lento, moroso; (lazy) indolente, preguiçoso

sluice /slu:s/ n (gate) comporta f; (channel) canal m □ vt lavar com jorros de água

slum /slʌm/ n favela f, (P) bairro m da lata; (building) cortiço m

slumber /'slʌmbə(r)/ n sono m □ vi dormir

slump /slʌmp/ n (in prices) baixa f, descida f; (in demand) quebra f na procura; (econ) depressão f □ vi (fall limply) cair, afundar-se; (of price) baixar bruscamente

slung /slʌŋ/ see sling

slur /slɜ:(r)/ vt/i (pt slurred) (speech) pronunciar indistintamente, mastigar □ n (in speech) som m indistinto; (discredit) nódoa f, estigma m

slush /slʌʃ/ n (snow) neve f meio derretida. ~ fund (comm) fundo m para subornos. ~y a (road) coberto de neve derretida, lamacento

slut /slʌt/ n (dirty woman) porca f, desmazelada f; (immoral woman) desavergonhada f

sly /slaı/ a (slyer, slyest) (crafty) manhoso; (secretive) sonso □ n on the ~ na calada. ~ly adv (craftily) astutamente; (secretively) sonsamente

smack¹ /smæk/ n palmada f, (on face) bofetada f □ vt dar uma palmada em ou tapa em; (on the face) esbofetear, dar uma bofetada em □ adv (colloq) em cheio, direto

smack² /smæk/ vi ~ of sth cheirar a alg coisa

small /smɔ:l/ a (-er, -est) pequeno □ n ~ of the back zona f dos rins □ adv (cut etc) em pedaços pequenos, aos bocadinhos. ~ change trocado m, dinheiro m miúdo. ~ talk conversa f fiada, bate-papo m. ~ness n pequenez f

smallholding /'smɔ:lhəʊldıŋ/ n pequena propriedade f

smallpox /'smɔ:lpɒks/ n varíola f

smarmy /'sma:mı/ a (-ier, -iest) (colloq) bajulador, puxa-saco (colloq)

smart /sma:t/ a (-er, -est) elegante;

(clever) esperto, vivo; (brisk) rápido □ vi (sting) arder, picar. ~ly adv elegantemente, com elegância; (cleverly) com esperteza, vivamente; (briskly) rapidamente. ~ness n elegância f

smarten /'sma:tn/ vt/i ~ (up) arranjar, dar um ar mais cuidado a. ~ (o.s.) up embelezar-se, arrumar-se, (P) pôr-se elegante/bonito; (tidy) arranjar-se

smash /smæʃ/ vt/i (to pieces) despedaçar(-se), espatifar(-se) (colloq); (a record) quebrar; (opponent) esmagar; (ruin) (fazer) falir; (of vehicle) espatifar(-se) □ n (noise) estrondo m; (blow) pancada f forte, golpe m; (collision) colisão f; (tennis) smash m

smashing /'smæʃıŋ/ a (colloq) formidável, estupendo (colloq)

smattering /'smætərıŋ/ n leves noções fpl

smear /smıə(r)/ vt (stain; discredit) manchar; (coat) untar, besuntar □ n mancha f, nódoa f; (med) esfregaço m

smell /smel/ n cheiro m, odor m; (sense) cheiro m, olfato m, (P) olfacto m □ vt/i (pt smelt or smelled) ~ (of) cheirar (a). ~y a malcheiroso

smelt¹ /smelt/ see smell

smelt² /smelt/ vt (ore) fundir

smile /smaıl/ n sorriso m □ vi sorrir. ~ing a sorridente, risonho

smirk /smɜ:k/ n sorriso m falso or afetado, (P) afectado

smithereens /smıðə'ri:nz/ npl to or in ~ em pedaços mpl

smock /smɒk/ n guarda-pó m

smog /smɒɡ/ n mistura f de nevoeiro e fumaça, smog m

smoke /sməʊk/ n fumo m, fumaça f □ vt fumar; (bacon etc) fumar, defumar □ vi fumar, fumegar. ~-screen n (lit & fig) cortina f de fumaça. ~less a (fuel) sem fumo. ~r /-ə(r)/ n (person) fumante mf, (P) fumador m. smoky a (air) enfumaçado, fumacento

smooth /smu:ð/ a (-er, -est) liso; (soft) macio; (movement) regular, suave; (manners) lisonjeiro, conciliador, suave □ vt alisar. ~ out (fig) aplanar, remover. ~ly adv suavemente, facilmente

smother /'smʌðə(r)/ vt (stifle) abafar, sufocar; (cover, overwhelm) cobrir (with de); (suppress) abafar, reprimir

smoulder /'sməʊldə(r)/ vi (lit & fig) arder, abrasar-se

smudge /smʌdʒ/ n mancha f, borrão m □ vt/i sujar(-se), manchar(-se), borrar(-se)

smug /smʌɡ/ a (smugger, smuggest) presunçoso, convencido (colloq). ~ly adv presunçosamente. ~ness n presunção f

smuggl|e /'smʌgl/ vt contrabandear, fazer contrabando de. ~er n contrabandista mf. ~ing n contrabando m

smut /smʌt/ n fuligem f. ~ty a cheio de fuligem; (colloq: obscene) indecente, sujo (colloq)

snack /snæk/ n refeição f ligeira. ~bar n lanchonete f, (P) snack(-bar) m

snag /snæg/ n (obstacle) obstáculo m; (drawback) problema m, contra m; (in cloth) rasgão m; (in stocking) fio m puxado

snail /sneɪl/ n caracol m. at a ~'s pace em passo de tartaruga

snake /sneɪk/ n serpente f, cobra f

snap /snæp/ vt/i (pt snapped) (whip, fingers) (fazer) estalar; (break) estalar(-se), partir(-se) com um estalo, rebentar; (say) dizer irritadamente □ n estalo m; (photo) instantâneo m; (Amer: fastener) mola f □ a súbito, repentino. ~ at (bite) abocanhar, tentar morder; (speak angrily) retrucar asperamente. ~ up (buy) comprar rapidamente

snappish /'snæpɪʃ/ a irritadiço

snappy /'snæpɪ/ a (-ier, -iest) (colloq) vivo, animado. make it ~ (colloq) vai rápido!, apresse-se! (colloq)

snapshot /'snæpʃɒt/ n instantâneo m

snare /sneə(r)/ n laço m, cilada f, armadilha f

snarl /snɑːl/ vi rosnar □ n rosnadela f

snatch /snætʃ/ vt (grab) agarrar, apanhar; (steal) roubar. ~ from sb arrancar de alguém □ n (theft) roubo m; (bit) bocado m, pedaço m

sneak /sniːk/ vi (slink) esgueirar-se furtivamente; (sl: tell tales) fazer queixa, delatar □ vt (sl: steal) rapinar (colloq) □ n (sl) dedo-duro m, queixinhas mf (sl). ~ing a secreto. ~y a sonso

sneer /snɪə(r)/ n sorriso m de desdém □ vi sorrir desdenhosamente

sneeze /sniːz/ n espirro m □ vi espirrar

snide /snaɪd/ a (colloq) sarcástico

sniff /snɪf/ vi fungar □ vt/i ~ (at) (smell) cheirar; (dog) farejar. ~ at (fig: in contempt) desprezar □ n fungadela f

snigger /'snɪgə(r)/ n riso m abafado □ vi rir dissimuladamente

snip /snɪp/ vt (pt snipped) cortar com tesoura □ n pedaço m, retalho m; (sl: bargain) pechincha f

snipe /snaɪp/ vi dar tiros de emboscada. ~r /-ə(r)/ n franco-atirador m

snivel /'snɪvl/ vi (pt snivelled) choramingar, lamuriar-se

snob /snɒb/ n esnobe mf, (P) snob mf. ~bery n esnobismo m, (P) snobismo m. ~bish a esnobe, (P) snob

snooker /'snuːkə(r)/ n snooker m, sinuca f

snoop /snuːp/ vi (colloq) bisbilhotar, meter o nariz em toda a parte. ~ on espiar, espionar. ~er n bisbilhoteiro m

snooty /'snuːtɪ/ a (-ier, -iest) (colloq) convencido, arrogante (colloq)

snooze /snuːz/ n (colloq) soneca f (colloq) □ vi (colloq) tirar uma soneca

snore /snɔː(r)/ n ronco m □ vi roncar

snorkel /'snɔːkl/ n tubo m de respiração, snorkel m

snort /snɔːt/ n resfôlego m, bufido m □ vi resfolegar, bufar

snout /snaʊt/ n focinho m

snow /snəʊ/ n neve f □ vi nevar. be ~ed under (fig: be overwhelmed) estar sobrecarregado (fig). ~-bound a bloqueado pela neve. ~-drift n banco m de neve. ~-plough n limpa-neve m. ~y a nevado, coberto de neve

snowball /'snəʊbɔːl/ n bola f de neve □ vi atirar bolas de neve (em); (fig) acumular-se, ir num crescendo, aumentar rapidamente

snowdrop /'snəʊdrɒp/ n (bot) furaneve m

snowfall /'snəʊfɔːl/ n nevada f, (P) nevão m

snowflake /'snəʊfleɪk/ n floco m de neve

snowman /'snəʊmæn/ n (pl -men) boneco m de neve

snub /snʌb/ vt (pt snubbed) desdenhar, tratar com desdém □ n desdém m

snuff[1] /snʌf/ n rapé m

snuff[2] /snʌf/ vt ~ out (candles, hopes etc) apagar, extinguir

snuffle /'snʌfl/ vi fungar

snug /snʌg/ a (snugger, snuggest) (cosy) aconchegado; (close-fitting) justo

snuggle /'snʌgl/ vt/i (nestle) aninhar-se, aconchegar-se; (cuddle) aconchegar

so /səʊ/ adv tão, de tal modo; (thus) assim, deste modo □ conj por isso, portanto, por consequente. ~ am I eu também. ~ does he ele também. that is ~ é isso. I think ~ acho que sim. five or ~ uns cinco. ~ as to de modo a. ~ far até agora, até aqui. ~ long! (colloq) até já! (colloq). ~ many tantos. ~ much tanto. ~ that para que, de modo que. ~-and-~ n fulano m. ~-called a pretenso, soidisant. ~-so a & adv assim assim, mais ou menos

soak /səʊk/ vt/i molhar(-se), ensopar(-se), enchacar(-se). leave to ~ pôr de molho. ~ in or up vt absorver, embeber. ~ through repassar. ~ing a ensopado, encharcado soap /səʊp/ n sabão m. (toilet) ~ sabonete m □ vt ensaboar. ~ opera (radio) novela f radiofónica, (P) radiofónica; (TV) telenovela f. ~ flakes flocos mpl de sabão. ~ powder sabão m em pó. ~y a ensaboado

soar /sɔː(r)/ vi voar alto; (go high) elevar-se; (hover) pairar

sob /sɒb/ n soluço m □ vi (pt sobbed) soluçar

sober /ˈsəʊbə(r)/ a (not drunk, calm, of colour) sóbrio; (serious) sério, grave □ vt/i ~ up (fazer) ficar sóbrio, (fazer) curar a bebedeira (colloq)

soccer /ˈsɒkə(r)/ n (colloq) futebol m

sociable /ˈsəʊʃəbl/ a sociável

social /ˈsəʊʃl/ a social; (sociable) sociável; (gathering, life) de sociedade □ n reunião f social. ~ly adv socialmente; (meet) em sociedade. ~ security previdência f social; (for old age) pensão f. ~ worker assistente m social

socialis|t /ˈsəʊʃəlɪst/ n socialista mf. ~m /-zəm/ n socialismo m

socialize /ˈsəʊʃəlaɪz/ vi socializar-se, reunir-se em sociedade. ~ with frequentar, (P) frequentar, conviver com

society /səˈsaɪətɪ/ n sociedade f

sociolog|y /səʊsɪˈɒlədʒɪ/ n sociologia f. ~ical /-əˈlɒdʒɪkl/ a sociológico. ~ist n sociólogo m

sock¹ /sɒk/ n meia f curta; (men's) meia f (curta), (P) peúga f; (women's) soquete f

sock² /sɒk/ vt (sl: hit) esmurrar, dar um murro em (colloq)

socket /ˈsɒkɪt/ n cavidade f, (for lamp) suporte m; (electr) tomada f, (of tooth) alvéolo m

soda /ˈsəʊdə/ n soda f. (baking) ~ (culin) bicarbonato m de soda. ~ (-water) água f gasosa, soda f limonada, (P) água f gaseificada

sodden /ˈsɒdn/ a ensopado, empapado

sodium /ˈsəʊdɪəm/ n sódio m

sofa /ˈsəʊfə/ n sofá m

soft /sɒft/ a (-er, -est) (not hard, feeble) mole; (not rough, not firm) macio; (gentle, not loud, not bright) suave; (tender-hearted) sensível; (fruit) sem caroço; (wood) de coníferas; (drink) não alcoólico. ~-boiled a (egg) quente. ~ spot (fig) fraco m. ~ly adv docemente. ~ness n moleza f; (to touch) maciez f; (gentleness) suavidade f, brandura f

soften /ˈsɒfn/ vt/i amaciar, amolecer; (tone down, lessen) abrandar

software /ˈsɒftweə(r)/ n software m

soggy /ˈsɒgɪ/ a (-ier, -iest) ensopado, empapado

soil¹ /sɔɪl/ n solo m, terra f

soil² /sɔɪl/ vt/i sujar(-se). ~ed a sujo

solace /ˈsɒlɪs/ n consolo m; (relief) alívio m

solar /ˈsəʊlə(r)/ a solar

sold /səʊld/ see sell □ a ~ out esgotado

solder /ˈsəʊldə(r)/ n solda f □ vt soldar

soldier /ˈsəʊldʒə(r)/ n soldado m □ vi ~ on (colloq) perseverar com afinco, batalhar (colloq)

sole¹ /səʊl/ n (of foot) planta f, sola f do pé; (of shoe) sola f

sole² /səʊl/ n (fish) solha f

sole³ /səʊl/ a único. ~ly adv unicamente

solemn /ˈsɒləm/ a solene. ~ity /səˈlemnətɪ/ n solenidade f. ~ly adv solenemente

solicit /səˈlɪsɪt/ vt (seek) solicitar □ vi (of prostitute) aproximar-se de homens na rua

solicitor /səˈlɪsɪtə(r)/ n advogado m

solicitous /səˈlɪsɪtəs/ a solícito

solid /ˈsɒlɪd/ a sólido; (not hollow) maciço, cheio, compacto; (gold etc) maciço; (meal) substancial □ n sólido m ~s (food) alimentos mpl sólidos. ~ity /səˈlɪdətɪ/ n solidez f. ~ly adv solidamente

solidarity /sɒlɪˈdærətɪ/ n solidariedade f

solidify /səˈlɪdɪfaɪ/ vt/i solidificar(-se)

soliloquy /səˈlɪləkwɪ/ n monólogo m, solilóquio m

solitary /ˈsɒlɪtrɪ/ a solitário, só; (only one) um único. ~ confinement prisão f celular, solitária f

solitude /ˈsɒlɪtjuːd/ n solidão f

solo /ˈsəʊləʊ/ n (pl -os) solo m □ a solo. ~ flight vôo m solo. ~ist n solista mf

soluble /ˈsɒljʊbl/ a solúvel

solution /səˈluːʃn/ n solução f

solve /sɒlv/ vt resolver, solucionar. ~able a resolúvel, solúvel

solvent /ˈsɒlvənt/ a (dis)solvente; (comm) solvente □ n (dis)solvente m

sombre /ˈsɒmbə(r)/ a sombrio

some /sʌm/ a (quantity) algum(a); (number) alguns, algumas, uns, umas; (unspecified, some or other) um(a)... qualquer, uns... quaisquer, umas... quaisquer; (a little) um pouco de, algum; (a certain) um certo; (contrasted with others) uns, umas, alguns, algumas, certos, certas □ pron uns, umas, algum(a), alguns, algumas; (a little) um pouco, algum □ adv (approximately) uns, umas. will you have ~ coffee/etc? você quer café/etc? ~ day algum dia. ~ of my friends alguns dos meus amigos. ~ people say... algumas pessoas dizem... ~ time ago algum tempo atrás somebody /'sʌmbədɪ/ *pron* alguém □ *n* be a ~ ser alguém

somehow /'sʌmhaʊ/ *adv* (*in some way*) de algum modo, de alguma maneira; (*for some reason*) por alguma razão

someone /'sʌmwʌn/ *pron* & *n* = somebody

somersault /'sʌməsɔːlt/ *n* cambalhota *f*; (*in the air*) salto *m* mortal □ *vi* dar uma cambalhota/um salto mortal

something /'sʌmθɪŋ/ *pron* & *n* uma/alguma/qualquer coisa *f*, algo. ~ good/*etc* uma coisa boa/*etc*, qualquer coisa de bom/*etc*. ~ like um pouco como

sometime /'sʌmtaɪm/ *adv* a certa altura, um dia □ *a* (*former*) antigo. ~ last summer a certa altura no verão passado. I'll go ~ hei de ir um dia

sometimes /'sʌmtaɪmz/ *adv* às vezes, de vez em quando

somewhat /'sʌmwɒt/ *adv* um pouco, um tanto (ou quanto)

somewhere /'sʌmweə(r)/ *adv* (*position*) em algum lugar; (*direction*) para algum lugar

son /sʌn/ *n* filho *m*. ~-in-law *n* (*pl* ~s-in-law) genro *m*

sonar /'səʊnɑː(r)/ *n* sonar *m*

sonata /sə'nɑːtə/ *n* (*mus*) sonata *f*

song /sɒŋ/ *n* canção *f*. ~-bird *n* ave *f* canora

sonic /'sɒnɪk/ *a* ~ boom estrondo *m* sónico, (*P*) sónico

sonnet /'sɒnɪt/ *n* soneto *m*

soon /suːn/ *adv* (-er, -est) em breve, dentro em pouco, daqui a pouco; (*early*) cedo. as ~ as possible o mais rápido possível. I would ~er stay preferia ficar. ~ after pouco depois. ~er or later mais cedo ou mais tarde

soot /sʊt/ *n* fuligem *f*. ~y *a* coberto de fuligem

sooth|e /suːð/ *vt* acalmar, suavizar; (*pain*) aliviar. ~ing *a* (*remedy*) calmante, suavizante; (*words*) confortante

sophisticated /sə'fɪstɪkeɪtɪd/ *a* sofisticado, refinado, requintado; (*machine etc*) sofisticado

soporific /sɒpə'rɪfɪk/ *a* soporífico

sopping /'sɒpɪŋ/ *a* encharcado, ensopado

soppy /'sɒpɪ/ *a* (-ier, -iest) (*colloq: sentimental*) piegas; (*colloq: silly*) bobo

soprano /sə'prɑːnəʊ/ *n* (*pl* ~s) & *adj* soprano (*m f*)

sorbet /'sɔːbeɪ/ *n* (*water-ice*) sorvete *m* feito sem leite

sorcerer /'sɔːsərə(r)/ *n* feiticeiro *m*

sordid /'sɔːdɪd/ *a* sórdido

sore /sɔː(r)/ *a* (-er, -est) dolorido; (*vexed*) aborrecido (at, with com) □ *n* ferida *f*. have a ~ throat ter a garganta inflamada, ter dores de garganta

sorely /'sɔːlɪ/ *adv* fortemente, seriamente

sorrow /'sɒrəʊ/ *n* dor *f*, mágoa *f*, pesar *m*. ~ful *a* pesaroso, triste

sorry /'sɒrɪ/ *a* (-ier, -iest) (*state, sight etc*) triste. be ~ to/that (*regretful*) sentir muito/que, lamentar que; be ~ about/for (*repentant*) ter pena de, estar arrependido de. feel ~ for ter pena de. ~! desculpe!, perdão!

sort /sɔːt/ *n* género *m*, (*P*) género *m*, espécie *f*, qualidade *f*. of a (*colloq*) uma espécie de (*colloq, pej*). out of ~s indisposto □ *vt* separar por grupos; (*tidy*) arrumar. ~ out (*problem*) resolver; (*arrange, separate*) separar, distribuir

soufflé /'suːfleɪ/ *n* (*culin*) suflê *m*, (*P*) soufflé *m*

sought /sɔːt/ *see* seek

soul /səʊl/ *n* alma *f*. the life and ~ of (*fig*) a alma *f* de (*fig*)

soulful /'səʊlfl/ *a* emotivo, expressivo, cheio de sentimento

sound¹ /saʊnd/ *n* som *m*, barulho *m*, ruído *m* □ *vt/i* soar; (*seem*) dar a impressão de, parecer, (as if que). ~ a horn tocar uma buzina, buzinar. ~ barrier barreira *f* de som. ~ like parecer ser, soar como. ~-proof *a* à prova de som □ *vt* fazer o isolamento sonoro de, isolar. ~-track *n* (*of film*) trilha *f* sonora, (*P*) banda *f* sonora

sound² /saʊnd/ *a* (-er, -est) (*healthy*) saudável, sadio; (*sensible*) sensato, acertado; (*secure*) firme, sólido. ~ asleep profundamente adormecido. ~ly *adv* solidamente

sound³ /saʊnd/ *vt* (*test*) sondar; (*med; views*) auscultar

soup /suːp/ *n* sopa *f*

sour /'saʊə(r)/ *a* (-er, -est) azedo □ *vt/i* azedar, envinagrar

source /sɔːs/ *n* fonte *f*; (*of river*) nascente *f*

souse /saʊs/ *vt* (*throw water on*) atirar água em cima de; (*pickle*) pôr em vinagre; (*salt*) pôr em salmoura

south /saʊθ/ *n* sul *m* □ *a* a sul, do sul; (*of country, people etc*) meridional □ *adv* a, ao/para o sul. S~ Africa/America África *f*/América *f* do Sul. S~ African/American *a* & *n* sul-africano (*m*)/sul-americano (*m*). ~-east *n* sudeste *m*. ~erly /'sʌðəlɪ/ *a* do sul, meridional. ~ward *a* ao sul. ~ward(s) *adv* para o sul. ~-west *n* sudoeste *m*

southern /'sʌðən/ *a* do sul, meridional, austral

souvenir /suːvəˈnɪə(r)/ n recordação f, lembrança f

sovereign /ˈsɒvrɪn/ n & a soberano (m). ~ty n soberania f

Soviet /ˈsəʊvɪət/ a soviético. the S~ Union a União Soviética

sow¹ /səʊ/ vt (pt sowed, pp sowed or sown) semear

sow² /saʊ/ n (zool) porca f

soy /sɔɪ/ n ~ sauce molho m de soja

soya /ˈsɔɪə/ n soja f. ~-bean semente f de soja

spa /spaː/ n termas fpl

space /speɪs/ n espaço m; (room) lugar m; (period) espaço m, período m □ a (research etc) espacial □ vt ~ out espaçar

space|craft /ˈspeɪskraːft/ n (pl invar), ~ship n nave espacial f

spacious /ˈspeɪʃəs/ a espaçoso

spade /speɪd/ n (gardener's) pá f de ferro; (child's) pá f. ~s (cards) espadas fpl

spadework /ˈspeɪdwɜːk/ n (fig) trabalho m preliminar

spaghetti /spəˈgetɪ/ n espaguete m, (P) esparguete m

Spain /speɪn/ n Espanha f

span¹ /spæn/ n (of arch) vão m; (of wings) envergadura f; (of time) espaço m, duração f; (measure) palmo m □ vt (pt spanned) (extend across) transpor; (measure) medir em palmos; (in time) abarcar, abranger, estender-se por

span² /spæn/ see spick

Spaniard /ˈspænɪəd/ n espanhol m

Spanish /ˈspænɪʃ/ a espanhol □ n (lang) espanhol m

spaniel /ˈspænɪəl/ n spaniel m, epagneul m

spank /spæŋk/ vt dar palmadas or chineladas no. ~ing n (with hand) palmada f; (with slipper) chinelada f

spanner /ˈspænə(r)/ n (tool) chave f de porcas; (adjustable) chave f inglesa

spar /spaː(r)/ vi (pt sparred) jogar boxe, esp para treino; (fig: argue) discutir

spare /speə(r)/ vt (not hurt; use with restraint) poupar; (afford to give) dispensar, ceder □ a (in reserve) de reserva, de sobra; (tyre) sobressalente; (bed) extra; (room) de hóspedes □ n (part) sobressalente m. ~ time horas fpl vagas. have an hour to ~ dispôr de uma hora. have no time to ~ não ter tempo a perder

sparing /ˈspeərɪŋ/ a poupado. be ~ of poupar em, ser poupado com. ~ly adv frugalmente

spark /spaːk/ n centelha f, faísca f □ vt lançar faíscas. ~ off (initiate) desencadear, provocar. ~(ing)-plug n vela f de ignição

sparkle /ˈspaːkl/ vi cintilar, brilhar □ n brilho m, cintilação f

sparkling /ˈspaːklɪŋ/ a (wine) espumante

sparrow /ˈspærəʊ/ n pardal m

sparse /spaːs/ a esparso; (hair) ralo. ~ly adv (furnished etc) escassamente

spasm /ˈspæzəm/ n (of muscle) espasmo m; (of coughing, anger etc) ataque m, acesso m

spasmodic /spæzˈmɒdɪk/ a espasmódico; (at irregular intervals) intermitente

spastic /ˈspæstɪk/ n deficiente mf motor

spat /spæt/ see spit¹

spate /speɪt/ n (in river) enxurrada f, cheia f. a ~ of (letters etc) uma avalanche de

spatter /ˈspætə(r)/ vt salpicar (with de, com)

spawn /spɔːn/ n ovas fpl □ vi desovar □ vt gerar em quantidade

speak /spiːk/ vt/i (pt spoke, pp spoken) falar (to/with sb about sth com alguém de/sobre alg coisa); (say) dizer. ~ out/up falar abertamente; (louder) falar mais alto. ~ one's mind dizer o que se pensa. so to ~ por assim dizer. English/Portuguese spoken fala-se português/inglês

speaker /ˈspiːkə(r)/ n (in public) orador m; (loudspeaker) alto-falante m; (of a language) pessoa f de língua nativa

spear /spɪə(r)/ n lança f

spearhead /ˈspɪəhed/ n ponta f de lança □ vt (lead) estar à frente de, encabeçar

special /ˈspeʃl/ a especial. ~ity /-ɪˈælətɪ/ n especialidade f. ~ly adv especialmente. ~ty n especialidade f

specialist /ˈspeʃəlɪst/ n especialista mf

specialize /ˈspeʃəlaɪz/ vi especializar-se (in em). ~d a especializado

species /ˈspiːʃiːz/ n (pl invar) espécie f

specific /spəˈsɪfɪk/ a específico. ~ally adv especificamente, explicitamente

specif|y /ˈspesɪfaɪ/ vt especificar. ~ication /-ɪˈkeɪʃn/ n especificação f. ~ications npl (of work etc) caderno m de encargos

specimen /ˈspesɪmɪn/ n espécime(n) m, amostra f

speck /spek/ n (stain) mancha f pequena; (dot) pontinho m, pinta f; (particle) grão m

speckled /ˈspekld/ a salpicado, manchado

specs /speks/ *npl* (*colloq*) óculos *mpl*

spectacle /'spektəkl/ *n* espetáculo *m*, (*P*) espectáculo *m*. **(pair of) ~s** (par *m* de) óculos *mpl*

spectacular /spek'tækjʊlə(r)/ *a* espetacular, (*P*) espectacular

spectator /spek'teɪtə(r)/ *n* espectador *m*

spectre /'spektə(r)/ *n* espectro *m*, fantasma *m*

spectrum /'spektrəm/ *n* (*pl* **-tra**) espectro *m*; (*of ideas etc*) faixa *f*, gama *f*, leque *m*

speculat|e /'spekjʊleɪt/ *vi* especular, fazer especulações *or* conjeturas, (*P*) conjecturas (about sobre); (*comm*) especular, fazer especulação (in em). **~ion** /-'leɪʃn/ *n* especulação *f*, conjetura *f*, (*P*) conjectura *f*; (*comm*) especulação *f*. **~or** *n* especulador *m*

speech /spiːtʃ/ *n* (*faculty*) fala *f*; (*diction*) elocução *f*; (*dialect*) falar *m*; (*address*) discurso *m*. **~less** *a* mudo, sem fala (with com, de)

speed /spiːd/ *n* velocidade *f*, rapidez *f* □ *vt/i* (*pt* **sped** /sped/) (*move*) ir depressa *or* a grande velocidade; (*send*) despedir, mandar; (*pt* **speeded**) (*drive too fast*) ultrapassar o limite de velocidade. **~ limit** limite *m* de velocidade. **~ up** acelerar(-se). **~ing** *n* excesso *m* de velocidade

speedometer /spiː'dɒmɪtə(r)/ *n* velocímetro *m*, (*P*) conta-quilómetros *m inv*

speed|y /'spiːdɪ/ *a* (**-ier**, **-iest**) rápido; (*prompt*) pronto. **~ily** *adv* rapidamente; (*promptly*) prontamente

spell[1] /spel/ *n* (*magic*) sortilégio *m*

spell[2] /spel/ *vt/i* (*pt* **spelled** *or* **spelt**) escrever; (*fig: mean*) significar, ter como resultado. **~ out** soletrar; (*fig: explain*) explicar claramente. **~ing** *n* ortografia *f*

spell[3] /spel/ *n* (*short period*) período *m* curto, breve espaço *m* de tempo; (*turn*) turno *m*

spend /spend/ *vt* (*pt* **spent**) (*money, energy*) gastar (on em); (*time, holiday*) passar. **~er** *n* gastador *m*

spendthrift /'spendθrɪft/ *n* perdulário *m*, esbanjador *m*

spent /spent/ *see* **spend** □ *a* (*used*) gasto

sperm /spɜːm/ *n* (*pl* **sperms** *or* **sperm**) (*semen*) esperma *m*, sémen *m*, (*P*) sémen *m*; (*cell*) espermatozóide *m*

spew /spjuː/ *vt/i* vomitar, lançar

sphere /sfɪə(r)/ *n* esfera *f*

spherical /'sferɪkl/ *a* esférico

spic|e /spaɪs/ *n* especiaria *f*, condimento *m*; (*fig*) picante *m* □ *vt* condimentar. **~y** *a* condimentado; (*fig*) picante

spick /spɪk/ *a* **~ and span** novo em folha, impecável

spider /'spaɪdə(r)/ *n* aranha *f*

spik|e /spaɪk/ *n* (*of metal etc*) bico *m*, espigão *m*, ponta *f*. **~y** *a* guarnecido de bicos *or* pontas

spill /spɪl/ *vt/i* (*pt* **spilled** *or* **spilt**) derramar(-se), entornar(-se), espalhar(-se). **~ over** transbordar, extravasar

spin /spɪn/ *vt/i* (*pt* **spun**, *pres p* **spinning**) (*wool, cotton*) fiar; (*web*) tecer; (*turn*) (fazer) girar, (fazer) rodopiar. **~ out** (*money, story*) fazer durar; (*time*) (fazer) parar □ *n* volta *f*; (*aviat*) parafuso *m*. **go for a ~** dar uma volta *or* um giro. **~-drier** *n* centrifugadora *f* para a roupa, secadora *f*. **~ning-wheel** *n* roda *f* de fiar. **~-off** *n* bónus *m*, (*P*) bónus *m* inesperado; (*by-product*) derivado *m*

spinach /'spɪnɪdʒ/ *n* (*plant*) espinafre *m*; (*as food*) espinafres *mpl*

spinal /'spaɪnl/ *a* vertebral. **~ cord** espina *f* dorsal

spindl|e /'spɪndl/ *n* roca *f*, fuso *m*; (*mech*) eixo *m*. **~y** *a* alto e magro; (*of plant*) espigado

spine /spaɪn/ *n* espinha *f*, coluna *f* vertebral; (*prickle*) espinho *m*, pico *m*; (*of book*) lombada *f*

spineless /'spaɪnlɪs/ *a* (*fig: cowardly*) covarde, sem fibra (*fig*)

spinster /'spɪnstə(r)/ *n* solteira *f*; (*pej*) solteirona *f*

spiral /'spaɪərəl/ *a* (em) espiral; (*staircase*) em caracol □ *n* espiral *f* □ *vi* (*pt* **spiralled**) subir em espiral

spire /spaɪə(r)/ *n* agulha *f*, flecha *f*

spirit /'spɪrɪt/ *n* espírito *m*; (*boldness*) coragem *f*, brio *m*. **~s** (*morale*) moral *m*; (*drink*) bebidas *fpl* alcoólicas, (*P*) bebidas *fpl* espirituosas. **in high ~s** alegre □ *vt* **~ away** dar sumiço em, arrebatar. **~-level** *n* nível *m* de bolha de ar

spirited /'spɪrɪtɪd/ *a* fogoso; (*attack, defence*) vigoroso, enérgico

spiritual /'spɪrɪtʃʊəl/ *a* espiritual

spiritualism /'spɪrɪtʃʊəlɪzəm/ *n* espiritismo *m*

spit[1] /spɪt/ *vt/i* (*pt* **spat** *or* **spit**, *pres p* **spitting**) cuspir; (*of rain*) chuviscar; (*of cat*) bufar □ *n* cuspe *m*, (*P*) cuspo *m*. **the ~ting image of** o retrato vivo de, a cara chapada de (*colloq*)

spit[2] /spɪt/ *n* (*for meat*) espeto *m*; (*of land*) restinga *f*, (*P*) língua *f* de terra

spite /spaɪt/ *n* má vontade *f*, despeito *m*, rancor *m* □ *vt* aborrecer, mortificar. **in ~ of** a despeito de, apesar de. **~ful** *a* rancoroso, maldoso. **~fully** *adv* rancorosamente, maldosamente

spittle /'spɪtl/ n cuspe m, (P) cuspo m, saliva f

splash /splæʃ/ vt salpicar, respingar □ vi esparrinhar, esparramar-se. ~ (about) chapinhar □ n (act, mark) salpico m; (sound) chape m; (of colour) mancha f. make a ~ (striking display) fazer um vistão, causar furor

spleen /spli:n/ n (anat) baço m. vent one's ~ on sb descarregar a neura em alguém (colloq)

splendid /'splendɪd/ a esplêndido, magnífico; (excellent) estupendo (colloq), ótimo, (P) óptimo

splendour /'splendə(r)/ n esplendor m

splint /splɪnt/ n (med) tala f

splinter /'splɪntə(r)/ n lasca f, estilhaço m; (under the skin) farpa f, lasca f □ vi estilhaçar-se, lascar-se. ~ group grupo m dissidente

split /splɪt/ vt/i (pt split, pres p splitting) rachar, fender(-se); (divide, share) dividir; (tear) romper(-se) □ n racha f, fenda f; (share) quinhão m, parte f; (pol) cisão f. ~ on (sl: inform on) denunciar. ~ one's sides rebentar de risa. ~ up (of couple) separar-se. a ~ second uma fração de segundo. ~ting headache dor f de cabeça forte

splurge /splɜ:dʒ/ n (colloq) espalhafato m, estardalhaço m □ vi (colloq: spend) gastar os tubos, (P) gastar à doida (colloq)

spool /spu:l/ n (of sewing machine) bobina f; (for cotton thread) carretel m, carrinho m; (naut; fishing) carretel m

splutter /'splʌtə(r)/ vi falar cuspindo; (engine) cuspir; (fat) crepitar

spoil /spɔɪl/ vt (pt spoilt or spoiled) estragar; (pamper) mimar □ n ~(s) (plunder) despojo(s) m(pl), espólios mpl. ~sport n desmancha-prazeres mf invar. ~t a (pampered) mimado, estragado com mimos

spoke[1] /spəʊk/ n raio m

spoke[2], **spoken** /spəʊk, 'spəʊkən/ see speak

spokes|man /'spəʊksmən/ n (pl -men) ~woman n (pl -women) porta-voz mf

sponge /spʌndʒ/ n esponja f □ vt (clean) lavar com esponja; (wipe) limpar com esponja □ vi ~ on (colloq: cadge) viver à custa de. ~ bag bolsa f de toalete. ~ cake pão-de-ló m. ~r /-ə(r)/ n parasita mf (colloq) (sl). spongy a esponjoso

sponsor /'spɒnsə(r)/ n patrocinador m; (for membership) (sócio) proponente m □ vt patrocinar; (for membership) propor. ~ship n patrocínio m

spontaneous /spɒn'teɪnɪəs/ a espontâneo

spoof /spu:f/ n (colloq) paródia f

spooky /'spu:kɪ/ a (-ier, -iest) (colloq) fantasmagórico, que dá arrepios

spool /spu:l/ n (of sewing machine) bobina f; (for thread, line) carretel m, (P) carrinho m

spoon /spu:n/ n colher f. ~-feed vt (pt -fed) alimentar de colher; (fig: help) dar na bandeja para (fig). ~ful n (pl ~fuls) colherada f

sporadic /spə'rædɪk/ a esporádico, acidental

sport /spɔ:t/ n esporte m, (P) desporto m. (good) ~ (sl: person) gente f fina, (P) bom tipo m (colloq), (P) bestial □ vt (display) exibir, ostentar. ~s car/coat carro m/casaco m esporte, (P) de desporto. ~y a (colloq) esportivo, (P) desportivo

sporting /'spɔ:tɪŋ/ a esportivo, (P) desportivo. a ~ chance uma certa possibilidade de sucesso, uma boa chance

sports|man /'spɔ:tsmən/ n (pl -men), ~woman (pl -women) desportista mf. ~manship n (spirit) espírito m esportivo, (P) desportivo; (activity) esportismo m, (P) desportismo m

spot /spɒt/ n (mark, stain) mancha f; (in pattern) pinta f, bola f; (drop) gota f; (place) lugar m, ponto m; (pimple) borbulha f, espinha f; (TV) spot m televisivo □ vt (pt spotted) manchar; (colloq: detect) descobrir, detectar (colloq). a ~ of (colloq) um pouco de. be in a ~ (colloq) estar numa encrenca (colloq), (P) estar metido numa alhada (colloq). on the ~ no local; (there and then) ali mesmo, logo ali. ~-on a (colloq) certo. ~ check inspeção f, (P) inspecção f de surpresa; (of cars) fiscalização f de surpresa. ~ted a manchado; (with dots) de pintas, de bolas; (animal) malhado. ~ty a (with pimples) com borbulhas

spotless /'spɒtlɪs/ a impecável, imaculado

spotlight /'spɒtlaɪt/ n foco m; (cine, theat) refletor m, holofote m

spouse /spaʊz/ n cônjuge mf, esposo m

spout /spaʊt/ n (of vessel) bico m; (of liquid) esguicho m, jorro m; (pipe) cano m □ vi jorrar, esguichar. up the ~ (sl: ruined) liquidado (sl)

sprain /spreɪn/ n entorse f, mau jeito m □ vt torcer, dar um mau jeito a

sprang /spræŋ/ see spring

sprawl /sprɔ:l/ vi (sit) estirar-se, esparramar-se; (fall) estatelar-se; (town) estender-se, espraiar-se

spray[1] /spreɪ/ n (of flowers) raminho m, ramalhete m

spray² /spreɪ/ n (water) borrifo m, salpico m; (from sea) borrifo m de espuma; (device) bomba f, aerossol m; (for perfume) vaporizador m, atomizador m □ vt aspergir, borrifar, pulverizar; (with insecticide) pulverizar. ~-gun n (for paint) pistola f

spread /spred/ vt/i (pt spread) (extend, stretch) estender(-se); (news, fear, illness etc) alastrar(-se), espalhar(-se), propagar(-se); (butter etc) passar; (wings) abrir □ n (expanse) expansão f, extensão f; (spreading) propagação f; (paste) pasta f para passar pão; (colloq: meal) banquete m. ~-eagled a de braços e pernas abertos. ~-sheet n (comput) folha f de cálculo

spree /spri:/ n go on a ~ (colloq) cair na farra

sprig /sprɪg/ n raminho m

sprightly /'spraɪtlɪ/ a (-ier, -iest) vivo, animado

spring /sprɪŋ/ vi (pt sprang, pp sprung) (arise) nascer; (jump) saltar, pular □ vt (produce suddenly) sair-se com; (a surprise) fazer (on sb a alguém) □ n salto m, pulo m; (device) mola f; (season) primavera f; (of water) fonte f, nascente f. ~ from vir de, originar, provir de. ~-clean vt fazer limpeza geral. ~ onion cebolinha f. ~ up surgir

springboard /'sprɪŋbɔːd/ n trampolim m

springtime /'sprɪŋtaɪm/ n primavera f

springy /'sprɪŋɪ/ a (-ier, -iest) elástico

sprinkle /'sprɪŋkl/ vt (with liquid) borrifar, salpicar; (with salt, flour) polvilhar (with de). ~ sand/etc espalhar areia/etc. ~r /-ə(r)/ n (in garden) regador m; (for fires) sprinkler m

sprinkling /'sprɪŋklɪŋ/ n (amount) pequena quantidade f; (number) pequeno número m

sprint /sprɪnt/ n (sport) corrida f de pequena distância, sprint m □ vi correr em sprint or a toda a velocidade; (sport) correr

sprout /spraʊt/ vt/i brotar, germinar; (put forth) deitar □ n (on plant etc) broto m. (Brussels) ~s couves f pl de Bruxelas

spruce /spruːs/ a bem arrumado □ vt ~ o.s. up arrumar(-se)

sprung /sprʌŋ/ see spring □ a (mattress etc) de molas

spry /spraɪ/ a (spryer, spryest) vivo, ativo, (P) activo; (nimble) ágil

spud /spʌd/ n (sl) batata f

spun /spʌn/ see spin

spur /spɜː(r)/ n (of rider) espora f; (fig: stimulus) aguilhão m; (fig)

espora f (fig) □ vt (pt spurred) esporear, picar com esporas; (fig: incite) aguilhoar, esporear. on the ~ of the moment impulsivamente

spurious /'spjʊərɪəs/ a falso, espúrio

spurn /spɜːn/ vt desdenhar, desprezar, rejeitar

spurt /spɜːt/ vi jorrar, esguichar; (fig: accelerate) acelerar subitamente, dar um arranco súbito □ n jorro m, esguicho m; (of energy, speed) arranco m, surto m

spy /spaɪ/ n espião m □ vt (make out) avistar, descortinar □ vi ~ (on) espiar, espionar. ~ out descobrir. ~ing n espionagem f

squabble /'skwɒbl/ vi discutir, brigar □ n briga f, disputa f

squad /skwɒd/ n (mil) pelotão m; (team) equipe f, (P) equipa f. firing ~ pelotão m de fuzilamento. flying ~ brigada f móvel

squadron /'skwɒdrən/ n (mil) esquadrão m; (aviat) esquadrilha f; (naut) esquadra f

squalid /'skwɒlɪd/ a esquálido, sórdido. ~or n sordidez f

squall /skwɔːl/ n borrasca f

squander /'skwɒndə(r)/ vt desperdiçar

square /skweə(r)/ n quadrado m; (in town) largo m, praça f, (T-square) régua-tê f; (set-square) esquadro m □ a (of shape) quadrado; (metre, mile etc) quadrado; (honest) direito, honesto; (of meal) abundante, substancial. (all) ~ (quits) quite(s) □ vt (math) elevar ao quadrado; (settle) acertar □ vi (agree) concordar. go back to ~ one recomeçar tudo do princípio, voltar à estaca zero. ~ brackets parênteses mpl retos, (P) rectos. ~ up to enfrentar. ~ly adv diretamente, (P) directamente; (fairly) honestamente

squash /skwɒʃ/ vt (crush) esmagar; (squeeze) espremer; (crowd) comprimir, apertar □ n (game) squash m; (Amer: marrow) abóbora f. lemon ~ limonada f. orange ~ laranjada f. ~y a mole

squat /skwɒt/ vi (pt squatted) acocorar-se, agachar-se; (be a squatter) ser ocupante ilegal □ a (dumpy) atarracado. ~ter n ocupante mf ilegal de casa vazia, posseiro m

squawk /skwɔːk/ n grasnido m, crocito m □ vi grasnar, crocitar

squeak /skwiːk/ n guincho m, chio m; (of door, shoes etc) rangido m □ vi guinchar, chiar; (of door, shoes etc) ranger. ~y a (shoe etc) que range; (voice) esganiçado

squeal /skwiːl/ vi dar gritos agudos,

guinchar □ *n* grito *m* agudo, guincho *m*. ~(**on**) (*sl: inform on*) delatar, (*P*) denunciar

squeamish /'skwi:mıʃ/ *a* (*nauseated*) que enjoa à toa

squeeze /skwi:z/ *vt* (*lemon, sponge etc*) espremer; (*hand, arm*) apertar; (*extract*) arrancar, extorquir (**from** de) □ *vi* (*force one's way*) passar à força, meter-se por □ *n* aperto *m*, apertão *m*; (*hug*) abraço *m*; (*comm*) restrições *fpl* de crédito

squelch /skweltʃ/ *vi* chapinhar *or* fazer chape-chape na lama

squid /skwıd/ *n* lula *f*

squiggle /'skwıgl/ *n* rabisco *m*, floreado *m*

squint /skwınt/ *vi* ser estrábico *or* vesgo; (*with half-shut eyes*) franzir os olhos □ *n* (*med*) estrabismo *m*

squirm /skwɜ:m/ *vi* (re)torcer-se, contorcer-se

squirrel /'skwırəl/ *n* esquilo *m*

squirt /skwɜ:t/ *vt/i* esguichar □ *n* esguicho *m*

stab /stæb/ *vt* (*pt* **stabbed**) apunhalar; (*knife*) esfaquear □ *n* punhalada *f*; (*with knife*) facada *f*; (*of pain*) pontada *f*; (*colloq: attempt*) tentativa *f*

stabilize /'steıbəlaız/ *vt* estabilizar

stable[1] /'steıbl/ *a* (**-er, -est**) estável. ~**ility** /stə'bılətı/ *n* estabilidade *f*

stable[2] /'steıbl/ *n* cavalariça *f*, estrebaria *f*. ~**-boy** *n* moço *m* de estrebaria

stack /stæk/ *n* pilha *f*, montão *m*; (*of hay etc*) meda *f* □ *vt* ~ (**up**) empilhar, amontoar

stadium /'steıdıəm/ *n* estádio *m*

staff /stɑ:f/ *n* pessoal *m*; (*in school*) professores *mpl*; (*mil*) estado-maior *m*; (*stick*) bordão *m*, cajado *m*; (*mus*) (*pl* **staves**) pauta *f* □ *vt* prover de pessoal

stag /stæg/ *n* veado (macho) *m*, cervo *m*. ~**-party** (*colloq*) reunião *f* masculina; (*before wedding*) despedida *f* de solteiro

stage /steıdʒ/ *n* (*theatre*) palco *m*; (*phase*) fase *f*, ponto *m*; (*platform in hall*) estrado *m* □ *vt* encenar, pôr em cena; (*fig: organize*) organizar. **go on the** ~ seguir a carreira teatral, ir para o teatro (*colloq*). ~**-door** entrada *f* dos artistas. ~**-fright** *n* nervosismo *m*

stagger /'stægə(r)/ *vi* vacilar, cambalear □ *vt* (*shock*) atordoar, chocar; (*holidays etc*) escalonar. ~**ing** *a* atordoador, chocante

stagnant /'stægnənt/ *a* estagnado, parado

stagnat|e /stæg'neıt/ *vi* estagnar. ~**ion** /-ʃn/ *n* estagnação *f*

staid /steıd/ *a* sério, sensato, estável

stain /steın/ *vt* manchar, pôr nódoa em; (*colour*) tingir, dar cor a □ *n* mancha *f*, nódoa *f*; (*colouring*) corante *m*. ~**ed glass window** vitral *m*. ~**less steel** aço *m* inoxidável

stair /steə(r)/ *n* degrau *m*. ~**s** escada(s) *f(pl)*

stair|case /'steəkeıs/, ~**way** /-weı/ *ns* escada(s) *f(pl)*, escadaria *f*

stake /steık/ *n* (*post*) estaca *f*, poste *m*; (*wager*) parada *f*, aposta *f* □ *vt* (*area*) demarcar, delimitar; (*wager*) jogar, apostar. **at** ~ em jogo. **have a** ~ **in** ter interesse em. ~ **a claim to** reivindicar

stale /steıl/ *a* (**-er, -est**) estragado, velho; (*bread*) duro, mofado; (*smell*) rançoso; (*air*) viciado; (*news*) velho

stalemate /'steılmeıt/ *n* (*chess*) empate *m*; (*fig: deadlock*) impasse *m*, beco-sem-saída *m*

stalk[1] /stɔ:k/ *n* (*of plant*) caule *m*

stalk[2] /stɔ:k/ *vi* andar com ar empertigado □ *vt* (*prey*) perseguir furtivamente, tocaiar

stall /stɔ:l/ *n* (*in stable*) baia *f*; (*in market*) tenda *f*, barraca *f*. ~**s** (*theat*) poltronas *fpl* de orquestra; (*cinema*) platéia *f*, (*P*) plateia *f* □ *vt/i* (*auto*) enguiçar, (*P*) ir abaixo. ~ (**for time**) ganhar tempo

stalwart /'stɔ:lwət/ *a* forte, rijo; (*supporter*) fiel

stamina /'stæmınə/ *n* resistência *f*

stammer /'stæmə(r)/ *vt/i* gaguejar □ *n* gagueira *f*, (*P*) gaguez *f*

stamp /stæmp/ *vt/i* ~ (**one's foot**) bater com o pé (no chão), pisar com força □ *vt* estampar; (*letter*) estampilhar, selar; (*with rubber stamp*) carimbar. ~ **out** (*fire, rebellion etc*) esmagar; (*disease*) erradicar □ *n* estampa *f*; (*for postage*) selo *m*; (*fig: mark*) cunho *m*. (**rubber**) ~ carimbo *m*. ~**-collecting** *n* filatelia *f*

stampede /stæm'pi:d/ *n* (*scattering*) debandada *f*; (*of horses, cattle etc*) tresma/hada *f*, debandada *f*; (*fig: rush*) corrida *f* □ *vt/i* (*fazer*) debandar; (*horses, cattle etc*) tresmalhar

stance /stæns/ *n* posição *f*, postura *f*

stand /stænd/ *vi* (*pt* **stood**) estar em pé; (*keep upright position*) ficar em pé; (*rise*) levantar-se; (*be situated*) encontrar-se, ficar, situar-se; (*pol*) candidatar-se (**for** por) □ *vt* pôr (de pé), colocar; (*tolerate*) suportar, agüentar, (*P*) aguentar □ *n* posição *f*; (*support*) apoio *m*; (*mil*) resistência *f*; (*at fair*) stand *m*, pavilhão *m*; (*in street*) quiosque *m*; (*for spectators*) arquibancada *f*, (*P*) bancada *f*; (*Amer: witness-box*) banco *m* das testemunhas. ~ **a**

chance ter uma possibilidade. ~ back recuar. ~ by or around estar parado sem fazer nada. ~ by (be ready) estar a postos; (promise, person) manter-se fiel a. ~ down desistir, retirar-se. ~ for representar, simbolizar; (colloq: tolerate) aturar. ~ in for substituir. ~ out (be conspicuous) sobressair. ~ still estar/ficar imóvel. ~ still! não se mexa!, quieto! ~ to reason ser lógico. ~ up levantar-se, pôr-se em or de pé. ~ up for defender, apoiar. ~ up to enfrentar. ~-by a (for emergency) de reserva; (ticket) de stand-by □ n (at airport) stand-by m. on ~-by (mil) de prontidão; (med) de plantão. ~-in n substituto m, suplente mf. ~-offish a (colloq: aloof) reservado, distante

standard /'stændəd/ n norma f, padrão m; (level) nível m; (flag) estandarte m, bandeira f. ~s (morals) princípios mpl □ a regulamentar; (average) standard, normal. ~ lamp abajur m de pé. ~ of living padrão m de vida, (P) nível m de vida

standardize /'stændədaɪz/ vt padronizar

standing /'stændɪŋ/ a em pé, de pé invar; (army, committee etc) permanente □ n posição f; (reputation) prestígio m; (duration) duração f. ~ order (at bank) ordem f permanente. ~-room n lugares mpl em pé

standpoint /'stændpɔɪnt/ n ponto m de vista

standstill /'stændstɪl/ n paralisação f. at a ~ parado, paralisado. bring/come to a ~ (fazer) parar, paralisar(-se), imobilizar (-se)

stank /stæŋk/ see stink

staple[1] /'steɪpl/ n (for paper) grampo m, (P) agrafo m □ vt (paper) grampear, (P) agrafar. ~r /-ə(r)/ n grampeador m, (P) agrafador m

staple[2] /'steɪpl/ a principal, básico □ n (comm) artigo m básico

star /sta:(r)/ n estrela f; (cinema) estrela f, vedeta f; (celebrity) celebridade f □ vi (pt starred) (of film) ter no papel principal, (P) ter como actor principal □ vi ~ in ser a vedeta or ter o papel principal em. ~dom n celebridade f, estrelato m

starch /sta:tʃ/ n amido m, fécula f; (for clothes) goma f □ vt pôr em goma, engomar. ~y a (of food) farináceo, feculento; (fig: of person) rígido, formal

stare /steə(r)/ vi ~ at olhar fixamente □ n olhar m fixo

starfish /'sta:fɪʃ/ n (pl invar) estrela-do-mar f

stark /sta:k/ a (-er, -est) (desolate) ári-

do, desolado; (severe) austero, severo; (utter) completo, rematado; (fact etc) brutal □ adv completamente. ~ naked nu em pêlo, (P) em pelota (colloq)

starling /'sta:lɪŋ/ n estorninho m

starlit /'sta:lɪt/ a estrelado

starry /'sta:rɪ/ a estrelado. ~-eyed a (colloq) sonhador, idealista

start /sta:t/ vt/i começar; (machine) ligar, pôr em andamento; (fashion etc) lançar; (leave) partir; (cause) causar, provocar; (jump) sobressaltar-se, estremecer; (of car) arrancar, partir □ n começo m, início m; (of race) largada f, partida f; (lead) avanço m; (jump) sobressalto m, estremecimento m. by fits and ~s aosarrancos, intermitentemente. for a ~ para começar. give sb a ~ sobressaltar alguém, pregar um susto a alguém. ~ to do começar a or pôr-se a fazer. ~er n (auto) arranque m; (competitor) corredor m; (culin) entrada f. ~ing-point n ponto m de partida

startl|**e** /'sta:tl/ vt (make jump) sobressaltar, pregar um susto a; (shock) alarmar, chocar. ~ing a alarmante; (surprising) surpreendente

starv|**e** /sta:v/ vi (suffer) passar fome; (die) morrer de fome. be ~ing (colloq: very hungry) ter muita fome, morrer de fome (colloq) □ vt fazer passar fome a; (deprive) privar. ~ation /-'veɪʃn/ n fome f

stash /stæʃ/ vt (sl) guardar, esconder, enfurnar (colloq)

state /steɪt/ n estado m, condição f; (pomp) pompa f, gala f; (pol) Estado m □ a de Estado, do Estado; (school) público; (visit etc) oficial □ vt afirmar (that que); (views) exprimir; (fix) marcar, fixar. in a ~ muito abalado

stateless /'steɪtlɪs/ a apátrida

stately /'steɪtlɪ/ a (-ier, -iest) majestoso. ~ home solar m, palácio m

statement /'steɪtmənt/ n declaração f; (of account) extrato m, (P) extracto m de conta

statesman /'steɪtsmən/ n (pl -men) homem m de estado, estadista m

static /'stætɪk/ a estático □ n (radio, TV) estática f, interferência f

station /'steɪʃn/ n (position) posto m; (rail, bus, radio) estação f; (rank) condição f, posição f social □ vt colocar. ~-wagon n perua f, (P) carrinha f. ~ed at or in (mil) estacionado em

stationary /'steɪʃnrɪ/ a estacionário, parado, imóvel; (vehicle) estacionado, parado

stationer /'steɪʃənə(r)/ n dono m de

papelaria. ~'s shop papelaria f. ~y n artigos mpl de papelaria; (*writing-paper*) papel m de carta

statistic /stə'tɪstɪk/ n dado m estatístico. ~s n (*as a science*) estatística f. ~al a estatístico

statue /'stætʃu:/ n estátua f

stature /'stætʃə(r)/ n estatura f

status /'steɪtəs/ n (*pl* -uses) situação f, posição f, categoria f; (*prestige*) prestígio m, importância f, status m. ~ quo status quo m. ~ symbol símbolo m de status

statut|e /'stætʃu:t/ n estatuto m, lei f. ~ory /-ʊtrɪ/ a estatutário, regulamentar; (*holiday*) legal

staunch /stɔ:ntʃ/ a (-er, -est) (*friend*) fiel, leal

stave /steɪv/ n (*mus*) pauta f □ vt ~ off (*keep off*) conjurar, evitar; (*delay*) adiar

stay /steɪ/ vi estar, ficar, permanecer; (*dwell temporarily*) ficar, alojar-se, hospedar-se; (*spend time*) demorar-se □ vt (*hunger*) enganar □ n estada f, visita f, permanência f. ~ behind ficar para trás. ~ in ficar em casa. ~ put (*colloq*) não se mexer (*colloq*). ~ up (*late*) deitar-se tarde. ~ing-power n resistência f

stead /sted/ n in my/your/*etc* no meu/teu/*etc* lugar. stand in good ~ ser muito útil

steadfast /'stedfa:st/ a firme, constante

stead|y /'stedɪ/ a (-ier, -iest) (*stable*) estável, firme, seguro; (*regular*) regular, constante; (*hand, voice*) firme □ vt firmar, fixar, estabilizar; (*calm*) acalmar. go ~y with (*colloq*) namorar. ~ily adv firmemente; (*regularly*) regularmente, de modo constante

steak /steɪk/ n bife m

steal /sti:l/ vt/i (*pt* stole, *pp* stolen) roubar (from sb de alguém). ~ away/in/*etc* sair/entrar/*etc* furtivamente, esgueirar-se. ~ the show pôr os outros na sombra

stealth /stelθ/ n by ~ furtivamente, na calada, às escondidas. ~y a furtivo

steam /sti:m/ n vapor m de água; (*on window*) condensação f □ vt (*cook*) cozinhar a vapor. ~ up (*window*) embaciar. □ vi soltar vapor, fumegar; (*move*) avançar. ~-engine n máquina f a vapor; (*locomotive*) locomotiva f a vapor. ~ iron ferro m a vapor. ~y a (*heat*) úmido, (P) húmido

steamer /'sti:mə(r)/ n (*ship*) (barco a) vapor m; (*culin*) utensílio m para cozinhar a vapor

steamroller /'sti:mrəʊlə(r)/ n cilindro m a vapor, rolo m compressor

steel /sti:l/ n aço m □ a de aço □ vpr ~ o.s. endurecer-se, fortalecer-se. ~ industry siderurgia f

steep¹ /sti:p/ vt (*soak*) mergulhar, pôr de molho; (*permeate*) passar, impregnar. ~ed in (*fig: vice, misery etc*) mergulhado em; (*fig: knowledge, wisdom etc*) impregnado de, repassado de

steep² /sti:p/ a (-er, -est) íngreme, escarpado; (*colloq*) exagerado, exorbitante. rise ~ly (*slope*) subir a pique; (*price*) disparar

steeple /'sti:pl/ n campanário m, torre f

steeplechase /'sti:pltʃeɪs/ n (*race*) corrida f de obstáculos

steer /stɪə(r)/ vt/i guiar, conduzir, dirigir; (*ship*) governar; (*fig*) guiar, orientar. ~ clear of evitar passar perto de. ~ing n (*auto*) direção f, (P) direcção f. ~ing-wheel n (*auto*) volante m

stem¹ /stem/ n caule m, haste f; (*of glass*) pé m; (*of pipe*) boquilha f; (*of word*) radical m □ vi (*pt* stemmed) ~ from provir de, vir de

stem² /stem/ vt (*pt* stemmed) (*check*) conter; (*stop*) estancar

stench /stentʃ/ n mau cheiro m, fedor m

stencil /'stensl/ n estêncil m, (P) stencil m □ vt (*pt* stencilled) (*document*) policopiar

step /step/ vi (*pt* stepped) ir andar □ vt ~ up aumentar □ n passo m, passada f; (*of stair, train*) degrau m; (*action*) medida f, passo m. ~s (*ladder*) escada f. in ~ no mesmo passo, a passo certo; (*fig*) em conformidade (with com). ~ down (*resign*) demitir-se. ~ in (*intervene*) intervir. ~-ladder n escada f portátil. ~ping-stone n (*fig: means to an end*) ponte f, trampolim m

stepbrother /'stepbrʌðə(r)/ n meio-irmão m. ~daughter n nora f, (P) enteada f. ~father n padrasto m. ~mother n madrasta f. ~sister n meio-irmã f. ~son n genro m, (P) enteado m

stereo /'sterɪəʊ/ n (*pl* -os) estéreo m; (*record-player etc*) equipamento m or sistema m estéreo □ a estéreo invar. ~phonic /-ə'fɒnɪk/ a estereofônico, (P) estereofónico

stereotype /'sterɪətaɪp/ n estereótipo m. ~d a estereotipado

steril|e /'steraɪl/ a estéril. ~ity /stə'rɪlətɪ/ n esterilidade f

sterilize /'sterɪlaɪz/ vt esterilizar. ~ation /-'zeɪʃn/ n esterilização f

sterling /'stɜ:lɪŋ/ n libra f esterlina □ a esterlino; (*silver*) de lei; (*fig*) excelente, de (primeira) qualidade stern¹ /stɜ:n/ a (-er, -est) severo

stern² /stɜ:n/ n (of ship) popa f, ré f

stethoscope /'steθəskəʊp/ n estetoscópio m

stew /stju:/ vt/i estufar, guisar; (fruit) cozer □ n ensopado m. ~ed fruit compota f

steward /'stjʊəd/ n (of club etc) ecônomo m, (P) econômo m, administrador m; (on ship etc) camareiro m (de bordo), (P) criado m (de bordo). ~ess /-'des/ n aeromoça f, (P) hospedeira f

stick¹ /stɪk/ n pau m; (for walking) bengala f; (of celery) talo m

stick² /stɪk/ vt (pt stuck) (glue) colar; (thrust) cravar, espetar; (colloq: put) enfiar, meter; (sl: endure) agüentar, (P) aguentar, aturar, suportar □ vi (adhere) colar, aderir; (remain) ficar enfiado or metido; (be jammed) emperrar, ficar engatado. ~ in one's mind ficar na memória. be stuck with sb/sth (colloq) não conseguir descartar-se de alguém/alg coisa (colloq). ~ out vt (head) esticar; (tongue etc) mostrar □ vi (protrude) sobressair. ~ to (promise) ser fiel a. ~-up n (sl) assalto m à mão armada. ~ up for (colloq) tomar o partido de, defender. ~ing-plaster n esparadrapo m, (P) adesivo m

sticker /'stɪkə(r)/ n adesivo m, etiqueta f (adesiva)

stickler /'stɪklə(r)/ n be a ~ for fazer grande questão de, insistir em

sticky /'stɪkɪ/ a (-ier, -iest) pegajoso; (label, tape) adesivo; (weather) abafado, mormacento

stiff /stɪf/ a (-er, -est) teso, hirto, rigido; (limb, joint; hard) duro; (unbending)' inflexível; (price) elevado, puxado (colloq), (penalty) severo; (drink) forte; (manner) reservado, formal. be bored/scared ~ (colloq) estar muito aborrecido/com muito medo (colloq). ~ neck torcicolo m. ~ness n rigidez f

stiffen /'stɪfn/ vt/i (harden) endurecer; (limb, joint) emperrar

stifl|e /'staɪfl/ vt/i abafar, sufocar. ~ing a sufocante

stigma /'stɪgmə/ n estigma m. ~tize vt estigmatizar

stile /staɪl/ n degrau m para passar por cima de cerca

stiletto /strʹletəʊ/ n (pl -os) estilete m. ~ heel n salto m alto fino

still¹ /stɪl/ a imóvel, quieto; (quiet) sossegado □ n silêncio m, sossego m □ adv ainda; (nevertheless) apesar disso, apesar de tudo. keep ~! fique quieto!, não se mexa! ~ life natureza f morta. ~ness n calma f

still² /stɪl/ n (apparatus) alambique m

stillborn /'stɪlbɔ:n/ a natimorto, (P) nado-morto

stilted /'stɪltɪd/ a afetado, (P) afectado

stilts /stɪlts/ npl pernas de pau fpl, (P) andas fpl

stimul|ate /'stɪmjʊleɪt/ vt estimular. ~ant n estimulante m. ~ating a estimulante. ~ation /-'leɪʃn/ n estimulação f

stimulus /'stɪmjʊləs/ n (pl -li /-laɪ/) (spur) estímulo m

sting /stɪŋ/ n picada f; (organ) ferrão m □ vt (pt stung) picar □ vi picar, arder. ~ing nettle urtiga f

stingy /'stɪndʒɪ/ a (-ier, -iest) pão-duro m, sovina (with com)

stink /stɪŋk/ n fedor m, catinga f, mau cheiro m □ vi (pt stank or stunk, pp stunk) ~ (of) cheirar (a), tresandar (a) □ vt ~ out (room etc) empestar. ~ing a malcheiroso. ~ing rich (sl) podre de rico (colloq)

stinker /'stɪŋkə(r)/ n (sl: person) cara m horroroso (colloq); (sl: sth difficult) osso m duro de moer

stint /stɪnt/ vi ~ on poupar em, apertar em □ n (work) tarefa f, parte f, quinhão m

stipulat|e /'stɪpjʊleɪt/ vt estipular. ~ion /-'leɪʃn/ n condição f, estipulação f

stir /stɜ:r/ vt/i (pt stirred) (move) mexer(-se), mover(-se); (excite) excitar; (a liquid) mexer □ n agitação f, rebuliço m. ~ up (trouble etc) provocar, fomentar. ~ring a excitante

stirrup /'strəp/ n estribo m

stitch /stɪtʃ/ n (in sewing; med) ponto m; (in knitting) malha f, ponto m; (pain) pontada f □ vt coser. in ~es (colloq) às gargalhadas (colloq)

stoat /stəʊt/ n arminho m

stock /stɒk/ n (comm) estoque m, (P) stock m, provisão f; (finance) valores mpl, fundos mpl; (family) família f, estirpe f; (culin) caldo m; (flower) goivo m □ a (goods) corrente, comum; (hackneyed) estereotipado □ vt (shop etc) abastecer, fornecer; (sell) vender □ vi ~ up with abastecer-se de. in ~ em estoque. out of ~ esgotado. take ~ (fig) fazer um balanço. ~-car n stock-car m. ~-cube n cubo m de caldo. ~ market Bolsa f (de Valores). ~-still a, adv imóvel. ~-taking n (comm) inventário m

stockbroker /'stɒkbrəʊkə(r)/ n corretor m da Bolsa

stocking /'stɒkɪŋ/ n meia f

stockist /'stɒkɪst/ n armazenista m

stockpile /'stɒkpaɪl/ n reservas fpl □ vt acumular reservas de, estocar

stocky /'stɒkɪ/ a (-ier, -iest) atarracado

stodg|e /stɒdʒ/ *n* (*colloq*) comida *f* pesada (*colloq*). ~**y** *a* (*of food, book*) pesado, maçudo

stoic /'stəʊɪk/ *n* estóico *m*. ~**al** *a* estoico.~**ism** /-sɪzəm/ *n* estoicismo *m*

stoke /stəʊk/ *vt* (*boiler, fire*) alimentar, carregar

stole[1] /stəʊl/ *n* (*garment*) estola *m*

stole[2], **stolen** /stəʊl, 'stəʊlən/ *see* steal

stomach /'stʌmək/ *n* estômago *m*; (*abdomen*) barriga *f*, ventre *m* □ *vt* (*put up with*) aturar. ~-**ache** *n* dor *f* de estômago; (*abdomen*) dores *fpl* de barriga

ston|e /stəʊn/ *n* pedra *f*; (*pebble*) seixo *m*; (*in fruit*) caroço *m*; (*weight*) 6,348 kg; (*med*) cálculo *m*, pedra *f* □ *vt* apedrejar; (*fruit*) tirar o caroço de. with-in a ~e's throw of (*de*). ~e-**cold** gelado. ~e-**deaf** totalmente surdo. ~**ed** *a* (*colloq: drunk*) bêbado *m* (*colloq*); (*colloq: drugged*) drogado. ~**y** *a* pedregoso. ~**y-broke** *a* (*sl*) duro, liso (*sl*)

stonemason /'stəʊnmeɪsn/ *n* pedreiro *m*

stood /stʊd/ *see* stand

stooge /stuːdʒ/ *n* (*colloq: actor*) ajudante *mf*; (*colloq: puppet*) antoche *m*, (*P*) comparsa *mf*, parceiro *m*

stool /stuːl/ *n* banco *m*, tamborete *m*

stoop /stuːp/ *vi* (*bend*) curvar-se, baixar-se; (*condescend*) condescender, dignar-se. ~ to sth rebaixar-se para (fazer) alg coisa □ *n* walk with a ~ andar curvado

stop /stɒp/ *vt/i* (*pt* stopped) parar; (*prevent*) impedir (from de); (*hole, leak etc*) tapar, vedar; (*pain, noise etc*) parar; (*colloq: stay*) ficar □ *vi* (*bus*) parada *f*, (*P*) paragem *f*; (*full stop*) ponto *m* final. put a ~ to pôr fim a. ~ it! acabe logo com isso! ~-**over** *n* (*break in journey*) parada *f*, (*P*) paragem *f*; (*port of call*) escala *f*. ~**press** *n* notícia *f* de última hora. ~-**watch** *n* cronômetro *m*, (*P*) cronómetro *m*

stopgap /'stɒpgæp/ *n* substituto *m* provisório, tapa-buracos *mpl* (*colloq*) □ *a* temporário

stoppage /'stɒpɪdʒ/ *n* parada *f*, (*P*) paragem *f*; (*of work*) paralisação *f* de trabalho; (*of pay*) suspensão *f*

stopper /'stɒpə(r)/ *n* rolha *f*, tampa *f*

storage /'stɔːrɪdʒ/ *n* (*of goods, food etc*) armazenagem *f*, armazenamento *m*. in cold ~ em frigorífico

store /stɔː(r)/ *n* reserva *f*, provisão *f*; (*warehouse*) armazém *m*, entreposto *m*; (*shop*) grande armazém *m*; (*Amer*) loja *f*; (*in computer*) memória *f* □ *vt* (*for future*) pôr de reserva, juntar, fazer provisão de; (*in warehouse*)

armazenar. be in ~ estar guardado. have in ~ for reservar para. set ~ by dar valor a. ~-**room** *n* depósito *m*, almotarifado *m*, (*P*) armazém *m*

storey /'stɔːrɪ/ *n* (*pl* -eys) andar *m*

stork /stɔːk/ *n* cegonha *f*

storm /stɔːm/ *n* tempestade *f* □ *vt* tomar de assalto □ *vi* enfurecer-se. a ~ in a teacup uma tempestade num copo de água. ~**y** *a* tempestuoso

story /'stɔːrɪ/ *n* estória *f*, (*P*) história *f*; (*in press*) artigo *m*, matéria *f*; (*Amer: storey*) andar *m*; (*colloq: lie*) cascata *f*, (*P*) peta *f*. ~-**teller** *n* contador *m* de estórias, (*P*) histórias

stout /staʊt/ *a* (-er, -est) (*fat*) gordo, corpulento; (*strong, thick*) resistente, sólido, grosso; (*brave*) resoluto □ *n* cerveja *f* preta forte

stove /stəʊv/ *n* (*for cooking*) fogão *m* (de cozinha)

stow /stəʊ/ *vt* ~ (*away*) (*put away*) guardar, arrumar; (*hide*) esconder □ *vi* ~ away viajar clandestinamente

stowaway /'stəʊəweɪ/ *n* passageiro *m* clandestino

straddle /'strædl/ *vt* (*sit*) escarranchar-se em, montar; (*stand*) pôr-se de pernas abertas sobre

straggle /'strægl/ *vi* (*lag behind*) desgarrar-se, ficar para trás; (*spread*) estender-se desordenadamente. ~**r** /-ə(r)/ *n* retardatário *m*

straight /streɪt/ *a* (-er, -est) direito; (*tidy*) em ordem; (*frank*) franco, direto, (*P*) directo; (*of hair*) liso; (*of drink*) puro □ *adv* (*in straight line*) reto; (*directly*) direito, direto, (*P*) directo, diretamente, (*P*) directamente □ *n* linha *f* reta, (*P*) recta. ~ ahead *or* on (*sempre*) em frente. ~ away logo, imediatamente. go ~ viver honestamente. keep a ~ face não se desmanchar, manter um ar sério

straighten /'streɪtn/ *vt* endireitar; (*tidy*) arrumar, pôr em ordem

straightforward /streɪt'fɔːwəd/ *a* franco, sincero; (*easy*) simples

strain[1] /streɪn/ *n* (*breed*) raça *f*; (*streak*) tendência *f*, veia *f*

strain[2] /streɪn/ *vt* (*rope*) esticar, puxar; (*tire*) cansar; (*filter*) filtrar, passar; (*vegetables, tea etc*) coar; (*med*) distender, torcer; (*fig*) forçar, pôr à prova □ *vi* esforçar-se □ *n* tensão *f*; (*fig: effort*) esforço *m*; (*med*) distensão *f*. ~**s** (*music*) melodias *fpl*. ~ one's ears apurar o ouvido. ~**ed** *a* forçado; (*relations*) tenso. ~**er** *n* coador *m*, (*P*) passador *m*

strait /streɪt/ *n* estreito *m*. ~**s** estreito *m*; (*fig*) apuros *mpl*, dificuldades *fpl*. ~-**jacket** *n* camisa-de-força *f*. ~-**laced** *a* severo, puritano

strand /strænd/ *n* (*thread*) fio *m*; (*lock of hair*) mecha *f*, madeixa *f*

stranded /'strændɪd/ *a* (*person*) em dificuldades, deixado para trás, abandonado

strange /streɪndʒ/ *a* (-er, -est) estranho. ~ly *adv* estranhamente. ~ness *n* estranheza *f*

stranger /'streɪndʒə(r)/ *n* estranho *m*, desconhecido *m*

strangle /'stræŋgl/ *vt* estrangular, sufocar

stranglehold /'stræŋglhəʊld/ *n* have a ~ on ter domínio sobre

strangulation /stræŋgjʊ'leɪʃn/ *n* estrangulamento *m*

strap /stræp/ *n* (*of leather etc*) correia *f*; (*of dress*) alça *f*; (*of watch*) pulseira *f* com correia □ *vt* (*pt* **strapped**) prender com correia

strapping /'stræpɪŋ/ *a* robusto, grande

strata /'streɪtə/ *see* **stratum**

stratagem /'strætədʒəm/ *n* estratagema *m*

strategic /strə'tiːdʒɪk/ *a* estratégico; (*of weapons*) de longo alcance

strategy /'strætədʒɪ/ *n* estratégia *f*

stratum /'strɑːtəm/ *n* (*pl* **strata**) estrato *m*, camada *f*

straw /strɔː/ *n* palha *f*; (*for drinking*) canudo *m*, (*P*) palhinha *f*. the last ~ a última gota *f*

strawberry /'strɔːbrɪ/ *n* (*fruit*) morango *m*; (*plant*) morangueiro *m*

stray /streɪ/ *vi* (*deviate from path etc*) extraviar-se, desencaminhar-se, afastar-se (from de); (*lose one's way*) perder-se; (*wander*) vagar, errar □ *a* perdido, extraviado; (*isolated*) isolado, raro, esporádico □ *n* animal *m* perdido *or* vadio

streak /striːk/ *n* risca *f*, lista *f*; (*strain*) veia *f*; (*period*) período *m*. ~ of lightning relâmpago *m* □ *vt* listrar, riscar □ *vi* ir como um raio. ~er *n* (*colloq*) pessoa *f* que corre nua em lugares públicos. ~y *a* listrado, riscado. ~y bacon toucinho *m* entremeado com gordura

stream /striːm/ *n* riacho *m*, córrego *m*, regato *m*; (*current*) corrente *f*; (*fig: flow*) jorro *m*, torrente *f*; (*school*) nível *m*, grupo *m* □ *vi* correr; (*of banner, hair*) flutuar; (*sweat*) escorrer, pingar

streamer /'striːmə(r)/ *n* (*of paper*) serpentina *f*; (*flag*) flâmula *f*, bandeirola *f*

streamline /'striːmlaɪn/ *vt* dar forma aerodinâmica a; (*fig*) racionalizar. ~d *a* (*shape*) aerodinâmico

street /striːt/ *n* rua *f*. the man in the ~ (*fig*) o homem da rua. ~ lamp poste *m* de iluminação

streetcar /'striːtkɑː(r)/ *n* (*Amer*) bonde *m*, (*P*) carro *m* eléctrico

strength /streŋθ/ *n* força *f*; (*of wall*) solidez *f*; (*of fabric etc*) resistência *f*. on the ~ of à base de, em virtude de

strengthen /'streŋθn/ *vt* fortificar, fortalecer, reforçar

strenuous /'strenjʊəs/ *a* enérgico; (*arduous*) árduo, estrênuo, (*P*) estrénuo; (*tiring*) fatigante, esgotante. ~ly *adv* esforçadamente, energicamente

stress /stres/ *n* acento *m*; (*pressure*) pressão *f*, tensão *f*; (*med*) stress *m* □ *vt* acentuar, sublinhar; (*sound*) acentuar. ~ful *a* estressante

stretch /stretʃ/ *vt* (*pull taut*) esticar; (*arm, leg, neck*) estender, esticar; (*clothes*) alargar; (*truth*) torcer □ *vi* estender-se; (*after sleep etc*) espreguiçar-se; (*of clothes*) alargar-se □ *n* extensão *f*, trecho *m*; (*period*) período *m*; (*of road*) troço *m* □ *a* (*of fabric*) com elasticidade. at a ~ sem parar. ~ one's legs esticar as pernas

stretcher /'stretʃə(r)/ *n* maca *f*, padiola *f*. ~-bearer *n* padioleiro *m*, (*P*) maqueiro *m*

strew /struː/ *vt* (*pt* **strewed**, *pp* **strewed** *or* **strewn**) (*scatter*) espalhar; (*cover*) juncar, cobrir

stricken /'strɪkən/ *a* ~ with atacado *or* acometido de

strict /strɪkt/ *a* (-er, -est) estrito, rigoroso. ~ly *adv* estritamente. ~ly speaking a rigor. ~ness *n* severidade *f*, rigor *m*

stride /straɪd/ *vi* (*pt* **strode** *pp* **stridden**) caminhar a passos largos □ *n* passada *f*. make great ~s (*fig*) fazer grandes progressos. take sth in one's ~ fazer alg coisa sem problemas

strident /'straɪdnt/ *a* estridente

strife /straɪf/ *n* conflito *m*, dissensão *f*, luta *f*

strike /straɪk/ *vt* (*pt* **struck**) bater (em); (*blow*) dar; (*match*) riscar, acender; (*gold etc*) descobrir; (*of clock*) soar, dar, bater (horas); (*of lightning*) atingir □ *vi* fazer greve; (*attack*) atacar □ *n* greve *f*; (*mil*) ataque *m*; (*find*) descoberta *f*. on ~ em greve. ~ a bargain fechar negócio. ~ off *or* out riscar. ~ up (*mus*) começar a tocar; (*friendship*) travar

striker /'straɪkə(r)/ *n* grevista *mf*

striking /'straɪkɪŋ/ *a* notável, impressionante; (*attractive*) atraente

string /strɪŋ/ *n* corda *f*, fio *m*; (*of violin, racket etc*) corda *f*; (*of pearls*) fio *m*; (*of onions, garlic*) réstia *f*; (*of lies etc*) série *f*; (*row*) fila *f* □ *vt* (*pt* **strung**) (*thread*) enfiar. pull ~s usar pistolão, (*P*) puxar os cordelinhos. ~ out espaçar-se. ~ed a (instrument) de cordas. ~y a filamentoso, fibroso; (meat) com nervos

stringent /'strindʒənt/ a rigoroso, estrito

strip[1] /strip/ vt/i (pt stripped) (undress) despir(-se); (machine) desmontar; (deprive) despojar, privar. ~per /ə(r)/ n artista mf de striptease; (solvent) removedor m

strip[2] /strip/ n tira f; (of land) faixa f. comic ~ história f em quadrinhos, (P) banda f desenhada. ~ light tubo m de luz fluorescente

stripe /straip/ n risca f, lista f, barra f. ~d a listrado, com listras

strive /straiv/ vi (pt strove, pp striven) esforçar-se (to por)

strode /strəʊd/ see stride

stroke[1] /strəʊk/ n golpe m; (of pen) penada f, (P) traço m; (in swimming) braçada f; (in rowing) remada f; (med) ataque m, congestão f. ~ of genius rasgo m de genialidade. ~ of luck golpe m de sorte

stroke[2] /strəʊk/ vt (with hand) acariciar, fazer festas em

stroll /strəʊl/ vi passear, dar uma volta □ n volta f, (P) giro m. ~ in/etc entrar/etc tranquilamente

strong /strɒŋ/ a (-er, -est) forte; (shoes, fabric etc) resistente. be a hundred/etc ~ ser em número de cem/etc. ~-box n cofre-forte m. ~-language linguagem f grosseira, palavrões mpl. ~-minded a resoluto, firme. ~-room n casa-forte f. ~ly adv (greatly) fortemente, grandemente; (with energy) com força; (deeply) profundamente

stronghold /'strɒŋhəʊld/ n fortaleza f, (fig) baluarte m, bastião m

strove /strəʊv/ see strive

struck /strʌk/ see strike □ a ~ on (sl) apaixonado por

structur|e /'strʌktʃə(r)/ n estrutura f, (of building etc) edifício m, construção f. ~al a estrutural, de estrutura, de construção

struggle /'strʌgl/ vi (to get free) debater-se; (contend) lutar; (strive) esforçar-se (to, for por) □ n luta f, (effort) esforço m. have a ~ to ter dificuldade em. ~ to one's feet levantar-se a custo

strum /strʌm/ vt (pt strummed) (banjo etc) dedilhar

strung /strʌŋ/ see string

strut /strʌt/ n (support) suporte m, escora f □ vi (pt strutted) (walk) pavonear-se

stub /stʌb/ n (of pencil, cigarette) ponta f; (of tree) cepo m, toco m; (counterfoil) talão m, canhoto m □ vt (pt stubbed) ~ one's toe dar uma topada. ~ out esmagar

stubble /'stʌbl/ n (on chin) barba f por fazer; (of crop) restolho m

stubborn /'stʌbən/ a teimoso, obstinado. ~ly adv obstinadamente, teimosamente. ~ness n teimosia f, obstinação f

stubby /'stʌbi/ a (-ier, -iest) (finger) curto e grosso; (person) atarracado

stuck /stʌk/ see stick[2] □ a emperrado. ~-up a (colloq: snobbish) convencido, esnobe

stud[1] /stʌd/ n tacha f; (for collar) botão m de colarinho □ vt (pt studded) enfeitar com tachas. ~ded with salpicado de

stud[2] /stʌd/ n (horses) haras m. ~ (-farm) n coudelaria f. ~(-horse) n garanhão m

student /'stju:dnt/ n (univ) estudante mf, aluno m; (schol) aluno m □ a (life, residence) universitário

studied /'stʌdid/ a estudado

studio /'stju:diəʊ/ n (pl -os) estúdio m. ~ flat estúdio m

studious /'stju:diəs/ a (person) estudioso; (deliberate) estudado. ~ly adv (carefully) cuidadosamente

study /'stʌdi/ n estudo m; (office) escritório m □ vt/i estudar

stuff /stʌf/ n substância f, matéria f; (sl: things) coisa(s) f (pl) □ vt encher; (animal) empalhar; (cram) apinhar, encher ao máximo; (culin) rechear; (block up) entupir; (put) enfiar, meter. ~ing n enchimento m; (culin) recheio m

stuffy /'stʌfi/ a (-ier, -iest) abafado, mal arejado; (dull) enfadonho

stumbl|e /'stʌmbl/ vi tropeçar. ~e across or on dar com, encontrar por acaso, topar com. ~ing-block n obstáculo m

stump /stʌmp/ n (of tree) cepo m, toco m; (of limb) coto m; (of pencil, cigar) ponta f

stumped /stʌmpt/ a (colloq: baffled) atrapalhado, perplexo

stun /stʌn/ vt (pt stunned) aturdir, estontear

stung /stʌŋ/ see sting

stunk /stʌŋk/ see stink

stunning /'stʌnɪŋ/ a aturdoador; (colloq: delightful) fantástico, sensacional

stunt[1] /stʌnt/ vt (growth) atrofiar. ~ed a atrofiado

stunt[2] /stʌnt/ n (feat) façanha f, proeza f; (trick) truque m; (aviat) acrobacia f aérea. ~ man n dublê m, (P) duplo m

stupefy /'stju:pɪfaɪ/ vt estupefazer, (P) estupeficar

stupendous /stjuː'pendəs/ a estupendo, assombroso, prodigioso

stupid /'stjuːpɪd/ a estúpido, obtuso. ~ity /-'pɪdətɪ/ n estupidez f. ~ly adv estupidamente

stupor /'stjuːpə(r)/ n estupor m, torpor m

sturdy /'stɜːdɪ/ a (-ier, -iest) robusto, vigoroso, forte

stutter /'stʌtə(r)/ vi gaguejar □ n gagueira f, (P) gaguez f

sty /staɪ/ n (pigsty) pocilga f, chiqueiro m

stye /staɪ/ n (on eye) terçol m, terçolho m

styl|e /staɪl/ n estilo m; (fashion) moda f; (kind) gênero m, (P) género m, tipo m; (pattern) feitio m, modelo m □ vt (design) desenhar, criar. in ~e (live) em grande estilo; (do things) com classe. ~e sb's hair fazer um penteado em alguém. ~ist n (of hair) cabeleireiro m

stylish /'staɪlɪʃ/ a elegante, na moda

stylized /'staɪlaɪzd/ a estilizado

stylus /'staɪləs/ n (pl -uses) (of record-player) agulha f, safira f

suave /swɑːv/ a polido, de fala mansa, (P) melífluo

sub- /sʌb/ pref sub-

subconscious /sʌb'kɒnʃəs/ a & n subconsciente (m)

subcontract /sʌbkən'trækt/ vt dar de subempreitada

subdivide /sʌbdɪ'vaɪd/ vt subdividir

subdue /səb'djuː/ vt (enemy, feeling) dominar, subjugar; (sound, voice) abrandar. ~d a (weak) submisso; (quiet) recolhido; (light) velado

subject[1] /'sʌbdʒɪkt/ a (state etc) dominado □ n sujeito m; (schol, univ) disciplina f, matéria f; (citizen) súdito m. ~-matter n conteúdo m, tema m, assunto m. ~ to sujeito a

subject[2] /səb'dʒekt/ vt submeter. ~ion /-kʃn/ n submissão f

subjective /sʌb'dʒektɪv/ a subjetivo, (P) subjectivo

subjunctive /səb'dʒʌŋktɪv/ a & n subjuntivo (m), (P) conjuntivo (m)

sublime /sə'blaɪm/ a sublime

submarine /sʌbmə'riːn/ n submarino m

submerge /səb'mɜːdʒ/ vt submergir □ vi submergir, mergulhar

submissive /səb'mɪsɪv/ a submisso

submi|t /səb'mɪt/ vt/i (pt submitted) submeter(-se) (to a); (jur: argue) alegar. ~ssion /-ʃn/ n submissão f

subnormal /sʌb'nɔːml/ a subnormal; (temperature) abaixo do normal

subordinate[1] /sə'bɔːdɪnət/ a subordinado, subalterno; (gram) subordinado □ n subordinado m, subalterno m

subordinate[2] /sə'bɔːdɪneɪt/ vt subordinar (to a)

subpoena /səb'piːnə/ n (pl -as) (jur) citação f, intimação f

subscribe /səb'skraɪb/ vt/i subscrever, contribuir (to para). ~ to (theory, opinion) subscrever, aceitar; (newspaper) assinar. ~r /-ə(r)/ n subscritor m, assinante m

subscription /səb'skrɪpʃn/ n subscrição f; (to newspaper) assinatura f

subsequent /'sʌbsɪkwənt/ a subsequente, (P) subsequente, posterior. ~ly adv subsequentemente, a seguir, posteriormente

subservient /səb'sɜːvɪənt/ a servil, subserviente

subside /səb'saɪd/ vi (flood, noise etc) baixar; (land) ceder, afundar; (wind, storm, excitement) abrandar. ~nce /-əns/ n (of land) afundamento m

subsidiary /səb'sɪdɪərɪ/ a subsidiário □ n (comm) filial f, sucursal f

subsid|y /'sʌbsədɪ/ n subsídio m, subvenção f. ~ize /-ɪdaɪz/ vt subsidiar, subvencionar

subsist /səb'sɪst/ vi subsistir. ~ on viver de. ~ence n subsistência f. ~ence allowance ajudas fpl de custo

substance /'sʌbstəns/ n substância f

substandard /sʌb'stændəd/ a de qualidade inferior

substantial /səb'stænʃl/ a substancial. ~ly adv substancialmente

substantiate /səb'stænʃɪeɪt/ vt comprovar, fundamentar

substitut|e /'sʌbstɪtjuːt/ n (person) substituto m, suplente mf (for de); (thing) substituto m (for de) □ vt substituir (for por). ~ion /-'tjuːʃn/ n substituição f

subterfuge /'sʌbtəfjuːdʒ/ n subterfúgio m

subtitle /'sʌbtaɪtl/ n subtítulo m

subtle /'sʌtl/ a (-er, -est) sutil, (P) subtil. ~ty n sutileza f, (P) subtileza f

subtotal /'sʌbtəʊtl/ n soma f parcial

subtract /səb'trækt/ vt subtrair, diminuir. ~ion /-kʃn/ n subtração f, diminuição f

suburb /'sʌbɜːb/ n subúrbio m, arredores mpl. ~an /sə'bɜːbən/ a dos subúrbios, suburbano. ~ia /sə'bɜːbɪə/ n (pej) os arredores

subver|t /səb'vɜːt/ vt subverter. ~sion /-ʃn/ n subverção f. ~sive /-sɪv/ a subversivo

subway /'sʌbweɪ/ n passagem f subterrânea; (Amer: underground) metropolitano m

succeed /sək'siːd/ vi ser bem sucedido, ter êxito. ~ in doing sth conseguir fazer alg coisa □ vt (follow) suceder a. ~ing a seguinte, sucessivo success /sək'ses/ n sucesso m, êxito m

succession /sək'seʃn/ n sucessão f; (series) série f. in ~ seguidos, consecutivos

successive /sək'sesɪv/ a sucessivo, consecutivo

successor /sək'sesə(r)/ n sucessor m

succinct /sək'sɪŋkt/ a sucinto

succulent /'sʌkjʊlənt/ a suculento

succumb /sə'kʌm/ vi sucumbir

such /sʌtʃ/ a & pron tal, semelhante, assim; (so much) tanto □ adv tanto. ~ a book/etc un tal livro/etc or um livro/etc assim. ~ books/etc tais livros/etc or livros/etc assim. ~ courage/ etc tanta coragem/etc. ~ a big house uma casa tão grande. as ~ como tal. ~ as como, tal como. there's no ~ thing uma coisa dessa não existe. ~-and-such a & pron tal e tal

suck /sʌk/ vt chupar; (breast) mamar. ~ in or up (absorb) absorver, aspirar; (engulf) tragar. ~ up to puxar o saco a (colloq). ~ one's thumb chupar o dedo. ~er n (sl: greenhorn) trouxa mf (colloq); (bot) broto m

suckle /'sʌkl/ vt amamentar, dar de mamar a

suction /'sʌkʃn/ n sucção f

sudden /'sʌdn/ a súbito, repentino. all of a ~ de repente, de súbito. ~ly adv subitamente, repentinamente. ~ness n subitaneidade f, brusquidão f

suds /sʌdz/ npl espuma f de sabão; (soapy water) água f de sabão

sue /suː/ vt (pres p suing) processar

suede /sweɪd/ n camurça f

suet /'suːɪt/ n sebo m

suffer /'sʌfə(r)/ vt/i sofrer; (tolerate) tolerar, suportar. ~er n sofredor m, o que sofre; (patient) doente mf, vítima f. ~ing n sofrimento m

suffice /sə'faɪs/ vi bastar, chegar, ser suficiente

sufficien|t /sə'fɪʃnt/ a suficiente, bastante. ~cy n suficiência f, quantidade f suficiente. ~tly adv suficientemente

suffix /'sʌfɪks/ n sufixo m

suffocat|e /'sʌfəkeɪt/ vt/i sufocar. ~ion n sufocação f, asfixia f. ~ing a sufocante, asfixiante

sugar /'ʃʊɡə(r)/ n açúcar m □ vt adoçar, pôr açúcar em. ~-bowl n açucareiro m. ~-lump n torrão m de açúcar, (P) quadradinho m de açúcar. brown ~ açúcar m preto, (P) açúcar m amarelo. ~y a açucarado; (fig: too sweet) delico-doce

suggest /sə'dʒest/ vt sugerir. ~ion /-tʃn/ n sugestão f. ~ive a sugestivo; (improper) brejeiro, picante. be ~ive of sugerir, fazer lembrar

suicid|e /'suːɪsaɪd/ n suicídio m. commit ~e suicidar-se. ~al /-'saɪdl/ a suicida

suit /suːt/ n terno m, (P) fato m; (woman's) costume m, (P) saia-casaco m; (cards) naipe m □ vt convir a; (of garment, style) ficar bem em; (adapt) adaptar. follow ~ (fig) seguir o exemplo. ~ability n (of action) conveniência f, oportunidade f; (of candidate) aptidão f. ~able a conveniente, apropriado (for para). ~ably adv convenientemente. ~ed a be ~ed to ser feito para, servir para. be well ~ed (matched) combinar-se bem; (of people) ser o ideal

suitcase /'suːtkeɪs/ n mala f (de viagem)

suite /swiːt/ n (of rooms; mus) suite f, (P) suite f; (of furniture) mobília f

suitor /'suːtə(r)/ n pretendente m

sulk /sʌlk/ vi amuar, ficar emburrado. ~y a amuado, emburrado (colloq)

sullen /'sʌlən/ a carrancudo

sulphur /'sʌlfə(r)/ n enxofre m. ~ic /-'fjʊərɪk/ a ~ic acid ácido m sulfúrico

sultan /'sʌltən/ n sultão m

sultana /sʌl'tɑːnə/ n (fruit) passa f branca, (P) sultana f

sultry /'sʌltrɪ/ a (-ier, -iest) abafado, opressivo; (fig) sensual

sum /sʌm/ n soma f; (amount of money) soma f, quantia f, importância f; (in arithmetic) conta f □ vt (pt summed) somar. ~ up recapitular, resumir; (assess) avaliar, medir

summar|y /'sʌmərɪ/ n sumário m, resumo m □ a sumário. ~ize vt resumir

summer /'sʌmə(r)/ n verão m, estio m □ a de verão. ~-time n verão m, época f de verão. ~y a estival, próprio de verão

summit /'sʌmɪt/ n cume m, cimo m. ~ conference (pol) conferência f de cúpula, (P) reunião f de cimeira

summon /'sʌmən/ vt mandar chamar; (to meeting) convocar. ~ up (strength, courage etc) chamar a si, fazer apelo a

summons /'sʌmənz/ n (jur) citação f, intimação f □ vt citar, intimar

sump /sʌmp/ n (auto) cárter m

sumptuous /'sʌmptʃʊəs/ a suntuoso, (P) sumptuoso, luxuoso

sun /sʌn/ n sol m □ vt (pt sunned) ~ o.s. aquecer-se ao sol. ~glasses npl óculos mpl de sol. ~-roof n teto m solar. ~-tan n bronzeado m. ~-tanned a bronzeado. ~-tan oil n óleo m de bronzear

sunbathe /'sʌnbeɪð/ vi tomar um banho de sol

sunburn /'sʌnbɜ:n/ n queimadura f de sol. ~t a queimado pelo sol

Sunday /'sʌndɪ/ n domingo m. ~ **school** catecismo m

sundial /'sʌndaɪəl/ n relógio m de sol

sundown /'sʌndaʊn/ n = sunset

sundr|y /'sʌndrɪ/ a vários, diversos. ~ies npl artigos mpl diversos. all and ~y todo o mundo

sunflower /'sʌnflaʊə(r)/ n girassol m

sung /sʌŋ/ see sing

sunk /sʌŋk/ see sink

sunken /'sʌŋkən/ a (ship etc) afundado; (eyes) fundo

sunlight /'sʌnlaɪt/ n luz f do sol, sol m

sunny /'sʌnɪ/ a (-ier -iest) (room, day etc) ensolarado

sunrise /'sʌnraɪz/ n nascer m do sol

sunset /'sʌnset/ n pôr m do sol

sunshade /'sʌnʃeɪd/ n (awning) toldo m; (parasol) pára-sol m, (P) guarda-sol m

sunshine /'sʌnʃaɪn/ n sol m, luz f do sol

sunstroke /'sʌnstrəʊk/ n (med) insolação f

super /'su:pə(r)/ a (colloq: excellent) formidável

superb /su:'pɜ:b/ a soberbo, esplêndido

supercilious /su:pə'sɪlɪəs/ a (haughty) altivo; (disdainful) desdenhoso

superficial /su:pə'fɪʃl/ a superficial. ~ity /-ɪ'ælətɪ/ n superficialidade f. ~ly adv superficialmente

superfluous /su:'pɜ:flʊəs/ a supérfluo

superhuman /su:pə'hju:mən/ a sobre-humano

superimpose /su:pərɪm'pəʊz/ vt sobrepor (on a)

superintendent /su:pərɪn'tendənt/ n superintendente m; (of police) comissário m, chefe m de polícia

superior /su:'pɪərɪə(r)/ a & n superior (m). ~ity /-'ɒrətɪ/ n superioridade f

superlative /su:'pɜ:lətɪv/ a supremo, superlativo □ n (gram) superlativo m

supermarket /'su:pəma:kɪt/ n supermercado m

supernatural /su:pə'nætʃrəl/ a sobrenatural

superpower /'su:pəpaʊə(r)/ n superpotência f

supersede /su:pə'si:d/ vt suplantar, substituir

supersonic /su:pə'sɒnɪk/ a supersónico, (P) supersônico

superstiti|on /su:pə'stɪʃn/ n superstição f. ~ous a /-'stɪʃəs/ supersticioso

superstore /'su:pəstɔ:(r)/ n hipermercado m

supertanker /'su:pətæŋkə(r)/ n superpetroleiro m

supervis|e /'su:pəvaɪz/ vt supervisar, fiscalizar. ~ion /-'vɪʒn/ n supervisão f. ~or n supervisor m; (shop) chefe mf de seção; (firm) chefe mf de serviço. ~ory /'su:pəvaɪzərɪ/ a de supervisão

supper /'sʌpə(r)/ n jantar m; (late at night) ceia f

supple /'sʌpl/ a flexível, maleável

supplement[1] /'sʌplɪmənt/ n suplemento m. ~ary /-'mentrɪ/ a suplementar

supplement[2] /'sʌplɪment/ vt suplementar

supplier /sə'plaɪə(r)/ n fornecedor m

suppl|y /sə'plaɪ/ vt suprir, prover; (comm) fornecer, abastecer □ n provisão f; (of goods, gas etc) fornecimento m, abastecimento m □ a (teacher) substituto. ~ies (food) víveres mpl; (mil) suprimentos mpl. ~y and demand oferta e procura

support /sə'pɔ:t/ vt (hold up, endure) suportar; (provide for) sustentar, suster; (back) apoiar, patrocinar; (sport) torcer por □ n apoio m; (techn) suporte m. ~er n partidário m; (sport) torcedor m

suppos|e /sə'pəʊz/ vt/i supor. ~e that supondo que, na hipótese de que. ~ed a suposto. he's ~ed to do ele deve faz. (believed to) consta que ele faz. ~edly /-ɪdlɪ/ adv segundo dizem; (probably) supostamente, em princípio. ~ing conj se. ~ition /sʌpə'zɪʃn/ n suposição f

suppress /sə'pres/ vt (put an end to) suprimir; (restrain) conter, reprimir; (stifle) abafar, sufocar; (psych) recalcar. ~ion /-ʃn/ n supressão f; (restraint) repressão f; (psych) recalque m, (P) recalcamento m

suprem|e /su:'pri:m/ a supremo. ~acy /-eməsɪ/ n supremacia f

surcharge /'sɜ:tʃa:dʒ/ n sobretaxa f, (on stamp) sobrecarga f

sure /ʃʊə(r)/ a (-er -est) seguro, certo □ adv (colloq: certainly) deveras, não há dúvida que, de certeza. be ~ about or of ter a certeza de. be ~ to (not fail) não deixar de. he is ~ to find out ele vai descobrir com certeza. make ~ assegurar. ~ly adv com certeza, certamente

surety /'ʃʊərətɪ/ n (person) fiador m; (thing) garantia f

surf /sɜ:f/ n (waves) ressaca f, rebentação f. ~er n surfista mf. ~ing n surfe m, (P) surf m, jacaré-na-praia m

surface /'sɜ:fɪs/ n superficie f □ a superficial □ vt/i revestir; (rise, become known) emergir. ~ mail via f marítima surfboard /'sɜːfbɔːd/ n prancha f de surfe, (P) surf

surfeit /'sɜːfɪt/ n excesso m (of de)

surge /sɜːdʒ/ vi (waves) ondular, encapelar-se; (move forward) avançar □ n (wave) onda f, vaga f; (motion) arremetida f

surgeon /'sɜːdʒən/ n cirurgião m

surg|ery /'sɜːdʒərɪ/ n cirurgia f; (office) consultório m; (session) consulta f; (consulting hours) horas fpl de consulta. ~ical a cirúrgico

surly /'sɜːlɪ/ a (-ier, -iest) carrancudo, trombudo

surmise /sə'maɪz/ vt imaginar, supor, calcular □ n conjetura f, (P) conjectura f; hipótese f

surmount /sə'maʊnt/ vt sobrepujar, vencer, (P) superar

surname /'sɜːneɪm/ n sobrenome m, (P) apelido m

surpass /sə'pɑːs/ vt superar, ultrapassar, exceder

surplus /'sɜːpləs/ n excedente m, excesso m; (finance) saldo m positivo □ a excedente, em excesso

surpris|e /sə'praɪz/ n surpresa f □ vt surpreender. ~ed a surpreendido, admirado (at com). ~ing a surpreendente. ~ingly adv surpreendentemente

surrender /sə'rendə(r)/ vi render-se □ vt (hand over; mil) entregar □ n (mil) rendição f; (of rights) renúncia f

surreptitious /ˌsʌrep'tɪʃəs/ a subreptício, furtivo

surrogate /'sʌrəgeɪt/ n delegado m. ~ mother mãe f de aluguel, (P) aluguer

surround /sə'raʊnd/ vt rodear, cercar; (mil etc) cercar. ~ing a circundante, vizinho. ~ings npl arredores mpl; (setting) meio m, ambiente m

surveillance /sɜː'veɪləns/ n vigilância f

survey¹ /sə'veɪ/ vt (landscape etc) observar; (review) passar em revista; (inquire about) pesquisar; (land) fazer o levantamento de; (building) vistoriar, inspecionar, (P) inspeccionar. ~or n (of buildings) fiscal m; (of land) agrimensor m

survey² /'sɜːveɪ/ n (inspection) vistoria f, inspecção f, (P) inspecção f; (general view) panorâmica f; (inquiry) pesquisa f

survival /sə'vaɪvl/ n sobrevivência f; (relic) relíquia f, vestígio m

surviv|e /sə'vaɪv/ vt/i sobreviver (a). ~or n sobrevivente mf

susceptib|le /sə'septəbl/ a (prone) susceptível (to a); (sensitive, impressionable) susceptível, sensível. ~ility /-'bɪlətɪ/ n susceptibilidade f

suspect¹ /sə'spekt/ vt suspeitar; (doubt, distrust) desconfiar de, suspeitar de

suspect² /'sʌspekt/ a & n suspeito (m)

suspen|d /sə'spend/ vt (hang, stop) suspender; (from duty etc) suspender. ~ded sentence suspensão f de pena. ~sion n suspensão f. ~sion bridge ponte f suspensa or pênsil

suspender /sə'spendə(r)/ n (presilha de) liga f. ~ belt n cintaliga f, (P) cinta f de ligas. ~s (Amer: braces) suspensórios mpl

suspense /sə'spens/ n ansiedade f, incerteza f; (in book etc) suspense m, tensão f

suspicion /sə'spɪʃn/ n suspeita f; (distrust) desconfiança f; (trace) vestígio m, (P) traço m

suspicious /səs'pɪʃəs/ a desconfiado; (causing suspicion) suspeito. be ~ of desconfiar de. ~ly adv de modo suspeito

sustain /sə'steɪn/ vt (support) suster, sustentar; (suffer) sofrer; (keep up) sustentar; (jur: uphold) sancionar; (interest, effort) manter. ~ed effort esforço m contínuo

sustenance /'sʌstɪmans/ n (food) alimento m, sustento m

swagger /'swægə(r)/ vi pavonear-se, andar com arrogância

swallow¹ /'swɒləʊ/ vt/i engolir. ~ up (absorb, engulf) devorar, tragar

swallow² /'swɒləʊ/ n (bird) andorinha f

swam /swæm/ see swim

swamp /swɒmp/ n pântano m, brejo m □ vt (flood, overwhelm) inundar, submergir. ~y a pantanoso

swan /swɒn/ n cisne m

swank /swæŋk/ vi (colloq: show off) gabar-se, mostrar-se (colloq)

swap /swɒp/ vt/i (pt swapped) (colloq) trocar (for por) □ n (colloq) troca f

swarm /swɔːm/ n (of insects, people) enxame m □ vi formigar. ~ into or round invadir

swarthy /'swɔːðɪ/ a (-ier, -iest) moreno, trigueiro

swat /swɒt/ vt (pt swatted) (fly etc) esmagar, esborrachar

sway /sweɪ/ vt/i oscilar, balançar(-se); (influence) mover, influenciar □ n oscilação f, balanceio m; (rule) domínio m, poder m

swear /sweə(r)/ vt/i (pt swore, pp sworn) jurar; (curse) praguejar, rogar pragas (at contra). ~ by jurar por; (colloq: recommend) ter grande fé em. ~-word n palavrão m

sweat /swet/ n suor m □ vi suar. ~y a suado

sweater /'swetə(r)/ n suéter m, (P) camisola f

sweatshirt /'swetʃɜːt/ n suéter m de malha or algodão

swede /swiːd/ n couve-nabo f

Swede /swiːd/ n sueco m. ~n en n Suécia f. ~ish a & n sueco (m)

sweep /swiːp/ vt/i (pt swept) varrer; (go majestically) avançar majestosamente; (carry away) arrastar; (chimney) limpar □ n (with broom) varredela f; (curve) curva f; (movement) gesto m largo. (chimney)~ limpa-chaminés m. ~ing a (gesture) largo; (action) de grande alcance. ~ing statement generalização f fácil

sweet /swiːt/ a (-er -est) doce; (colloq: charming) doce, gracinha; (colloq: pleasant) agradável □ n doce m. ~ corn milho m. ~ pea ervilha-de-cheiro f. ~ shop confeitaria f. have a ~ tooth gostar de doce. ~ly adv docemente. ~ness n doçura f

sweeten /'swiːtn/ vt adoçar; (fig: mitigate) suavizar. ~er n (for tea, coffee) adoçante m (artificial); (colloq: bribe) agrado m

sweetheart /'swiːthɑːt/ n namorado m, namorada f; (term of endearment) querido m, querida f, amor m

swell /swel/ vt/i (pt swelled, pp swollen or swelled) (expand) inchar; (increase) aumentar □ n (of sea) ondulação f □ a (colloq: excellent) excelente; (colloq: smart) chique. ~ing n (med) inchação f, inchaço m

swelter /'sweltə(r)/ vi fazer um calor abrasador; (person) abafar (com calor)

swept /swept/ see sweep

swerve /swɜːv/ vi desviar-se, dar uma guinada

swift /swift/ a (-er, -est) rápido, veloz. ~ly adv rapidamente. ~ness n rapidez f

swig /swig/ vt (pt swigged) (colloq: drink) emborcar, beber em longos tragos □ n (colloq) trago m, gole m

swill /swil/ vt passar por água □ n (pig-food) lavagem f, (P) lavadura f

swim /swim/ vi (pt swam, pp swum, pres p swimming) nadar; (room, head) rodar □ vt atravessar a nado; (distance) nadar □ n banho m. ~mer n nadador m. ~ming n natação f. ~ming-bath, ~ming-pool ns piscina f. ~ming-cap n touca f de banho. ~ming-costume, ~suit ns maiô m, (P) fato m de banho. ~ming-trunks npl calção m de banho

swindle /'swindl/ vt trapacear, fraudar, (P) vigarizar □ n vigarice f. ~r /-ə(r)/ n vigarista mf

swine /swain/ npl (pigs) porcos mpl □

n (pl invar) (colloq: person) animal m, canalha m (colloq)

swing /swiŋ/ vt/i (pt swung) balançar(-se); (turn round) girar □ n (seat) balanço m; (of opinion) reviravolta f; (mus) swing m; (rhythm) ritmo m. in full ~ no máximo, em plena atividade, (P) actividade. ~ round (of person) virar-se. ~-bridge/door ns ponte f/porta f giratória

swipe /swaip/ vt (colloq: hit) bater em, dar uma pancada em (colloq); (colloq: steal) afanar, roubar (colloq) □ n (colloq: hit) pancada f (colloq)

swirl /swɜːl/ vi rodopiar, redemoinhar □ n turbilhão m, redemoinho m

swish /swiʃ/ vt/i sibilar, zunir, (fazer) cortar o ar; (with brushing sound) roçar □ a (colloq) chique

Swiss /swis/ a & n suíço (m)

switch /switʃ/ n interruptor m; (change) mudança f □ vt (transfer) transferir; (exchange) trocar □ vi desviar-se. ~ off desligar

switchboard /'switʃbɔːd/ n (telephone) PBX m, mesa f telefónica

Switzerland /'switsələnd/ n Suíça f

swivel /'swivl/ vt/i (pt swivelled) (fazer) girar. ~ chair cadeira f giratória

swollen /'swəʊlən/ see swell □ a inchado

swoop /swuːp/ vi (bird) lançar-se, cair (down on sobre); (police) dar uma batida policial, (P) rusga

sword /sɔːd/ n espada f

swore /swɔː(r)/ see swear

sworn /swɔːn/ see swear □ a (enemy) jurado, declarado; (ally) fiel

swot /swɒt/ vt/i (pt swotted) (colloq: study) estudar muito, (P) marrar (sl) □ n (colloq) estudante n muito aplicado, (P) marrão m (sl)

swum /swʌm/ see swim

swung /swʌŋ/ see swing

sycamore /'sikəmɔː(r)/ n (maple) sicómoro m, (P) sicómoro m; (Amer: plane) plátano m

syllable /'siləbl/ n sílaba f

syllabus /'siləbəs/ n (pl -uses) programa m

symbol /'simbl/ n símbolo m. ~ic(al) /-'bɒlik(l)/ a simbólico. ~ism n simbolismo m

symbolize /'simbəlaiz/ vt simbolizar

symmetr|y /'simətri/ n simetria f. ~ical /si'metrikl/ a simétrico

sympath|ize /'simpəθaiz/ vi ~ with ter pena de, condoer-se de; (fig) compartilhar os sentimentos de. ~r n simpatizante mf

sympath|y /'simpəθi/ n (pity) pena f, compaixão f; (solidarity) solidariedade f; (condolences) pêsames mpl, condolências fpl. be in ~y with estar de acordo com. ~etic /-'θetɪk/ a compreensivo, simpático; (*likeable*) simpático; (*showing pity*) compassivo. ~etically /-'θetɪklɪ/ adv compassivamente; (*fig*) compreensivamente

symphony /'sɪmfənɪ/ n sinfonia f □ a sinfônico, (P) sinfônico. ~ic /-'fɒnɪk/ a sinfônico, (P) sinfónico

symptom /'sɪmptəm/ n sintoma m. ~atic /-'mætɪk/ a sintomático (of de)

synagogue /'sɪnəgɒg/ n sinagoga f

synchronize /'sɪŋkrənaɪz/ vt sincronizar

syndicate /'sɪndɪkət/ n sindicato m

syndrome /'sɪndrəʊm/ n (*med*) síndrome m, (P) síndroma m

synonym /'sɪnənɪm/ n sinônimo m, (P) sinónimo m. ~ous /sɪ'nɒnɪməs/ a sinônimo, (P) sinónimo (with de)

synopsis /sɪ'nɒpsɪs/ n (pl -opses /-si:z/) sinopse f, resumo m

syntax /'sɪntæks/ n sintaxe f

synthesis /'sɪnθəsɪs/ n (pl -theses /-si:z/) síntese f

synthetic /sɪn'θetɪk/ a sintético

syphilis /'sɪfɪlɪs/ n sífilis f

Syria /'sɪrɪə/ n Síria f. ~n a & n sírio (m)

syringe /sɪ'rɪndʒ/ n seringa f □ vt seringar

syrup /'sɪrəp/ n (*liquid*) xarope m; (*treacle*) calda f de açúcar. ~y a (*fig*) melado, enjoativo

system /'sɪstəm/ n sistema m; (*body*) organismo m; (*order*) método m. ~atic /sɪstə'mætɪk/ a sistemático

T

tab /tæb/ n (*flap*) lingueta f; (*for fastening, hanging*) aba f; (*label*) etiqueta f; (*loop*) argola f; (*Amer colloq: bill*) conta f. keep ~s on (*colloq*) vigiar

table /'teɪbl/ n mesa f; (*list*) tabela f, lista f □ vt (*submit*) apresentar; (*postpone*) adiar. at ~ à mesa. lay or set the ~ pôr a mesa. ~ of contents índice m (das matérias). turn the ~s inverter as posições. ~-cloth n toalha de mesa f. ~-mat n descanso m. ~ tennis pingue-pongue m

tablespoon /'teɪblspu:n/ n colher f grande de sopa. ~ful n (pl ~fuls) colher f de sopa cheia

tablet /'tæblɪt/ n (*of stone*) lápide f, placa f; (*drug*) comprimido m

tabloid /'tæblɔɪd/ n tablóide m. ~ journalism (*pej*) jornalismo m sensacionalista, imprensa f marron

taboo /tə'bu:/ n & a tabu (m)

tacit /'tæsɪt/ a tácito

taciturn /'tæsɪtɜ:n/ a taciturno

tack /tæk/ n (*nail*) tacha f; (*stitch*)

ponto m de alinhavo; (*naut*) amura f; (*fig: course of action*) rumo m □ vt (*nail*) pregar com tachas; (*stitch*) alinhavar □ vi (*naut*) bordejar. ~ on (*add*) acrescentar, juntar

tackle /'tækl/ n equipamento m, apetrechos mpl; (*sport*) placagem f □ vt (*problem etc*) atacar; (*sport*) placar; (*a thief etc*) agarrar-se a

tacky /'tækɪ/ a (-ier, -iest) peganhento, pegajoso

tact /tækt/ n tato m, (P) tacto m. ~ful a cheio de tato, (P) tacto, diplomático. ~fully adv com tato, (P) tacto. ~less a sem tato, (P) tacto. ~lessly adv sem tato, (P) tacto

tactic /'tæktɪk/ n (*expedient*) tática f, (P) táctica f. ~s n(pl) (*procedure*) tática f, (P) táctica f. ~al a tático, (P) táctico

tadpole /'tædpəʊl/ n girino m

tag /tæg/ n (*label*) etiqueta f; (*on shoelace*) agulheta f; (*phrase*) chavão m, clichê m □ vi (*pt* tagged) etiquetar; (*add*) juntar □ vi ~ along (*colloq*) andar atrás, seguir

Tagus /'teɪgəs/ n Tejo m

tail /teɪl/ n cauda f, rabo m; (*of shirt*) fralda f. ~s! (*tossing coin*) coroa! □ vt (*follow*) seguir, vigiar □ vi ~ away or off diminuir, baixar. ~-back n (*traffic*) fila f, (P) bicha f. ~-end n parte f traseira, cauda f. ~-light n (*auto*) farolete m traseiro, (P) farolim m da rectaguarda

tailor /'teɪlə(r)/ n alfaiate m □ vt (*garment*) fazer; (*fig: adapt*) adaptar. ~-made a feito sob medida, (P) por medida. ~-made for (*fig*) feito para, talhado para

tainted /'teɪntɪd/ a (*infected*) contaminado; (*decayed*) estragado; (*fig*) manchado

take /teɪk/ vt/i (*pt* took, *pp* taken) (*get hold of*) agarrar em, pegar em; (*capture*) tomar; (*a seat, a drink; train, bus etc*) tomar; (*carry*) levar (to a, para); (*contain, escort*) levar; (*tolerate*) suportar, agüentar, (P) aguentar; (*choice, exam*) fazer; (*photo*) tirar; (*require*) exigir. be ~n by or with ficar encantado com. be ~n ill adoecer. it ~s time to leva tempo para. ~ after parecer-se a. ~-away n (*meal*) comida f para levar, takeaway m; (*shop*) loja f que só vende comida para ser consumida em outro lugar. ~ away levar. ~ away from sb/sth tirar de alguém de alg coisa. ~ back aceitar de volta; (*return*) devolver; (*accompany*) acompanhar; (*statement*) retirar, retratar. ~ down (*object*) tirar para baixo; (*notes*) tirar, tomar. ~ in (*garment*) meter para dentro; (*include*) incluir; (*cheat*) enganar, levar (*colloq*) (*grasp*) compreender; (*receive*) receber. ~ it that supor que. ~ off *vt* (*remove*) tirar; (*mimic*) imitar, macaquear □ *vi* (*aviat*) descolar, levantar vôo. ~-off *n* imitação *f*; (*aviat*) decolagem *f*, (P) descolagem *f*. ~ on (*task*) encarregar-se de; (*staff*) admitir, contratar. ~ out tirar; (*on an outing*) levar para sair. ~ over *vt* tomar conta de, assumir a direção, (P) direcção de □ *vi* tomar o poder. ~ over from (*relieve*) render, substituir; (*succeed*) suceder a. ~-over *n* (*pol*) tomada *f* de poder; (*comm*) take-over *m*. ~ part participar or tomar parte (in em). ~ place ocorrer, suceder. ~ sides tomar partido. ~ sides with tomar o partido de. ~ to gostar de, simpatizar com; (*activity*) tomar gosto por, entregar-se a. ~ up (*object*) apanhar, pegar em; (*hobby*) dedicar-se a; (*occupy*) ocupar, tomar

takings /ˈteɪkɪŋz/ *npl* receita *f*

talcum /ˈtælkəm/ *n* talco *m*. ~ powder pó *m* talco

tale /teɪl/ *n* conto *m*, história *f*

talent /ˈtælənt/ *n* talento *m*. ~ed *a* talentoso, bem dotado

talk /tɔːk/ *vt/i* falar; (*chat*) conversar □ *n* conversa *f*; (*mode of speech*) fala *f*; (*lecture*) palestra *f*. small ~ conversa *f* banal. ~ into doing convencer a fazer. ~ nonsense dizer disparates. ~ over discutir. ~ shop falar de assuntos profissionais. ~ to o.s. falar sozinho, falar com os seus botões. there's ~ of fala-se de. ~er *n* conversador *m*. ~ing-to *n* (*colloq*) descompostura *f*

talkative /ˈtɔːkətɪv/ *a* falador, conversador, tagarela

tall /tɔːl/ *a* (-er, -est) alto. ~ story (*colloq*) história *f* do arco-da-velha

tallboy /ˈtɔːlbɔɪ/ *n* cômoda *f*, (P) cómoda *f* alta

tally /ˈtælɪ/ *vi* corresponder (with a), conferir (with com)

tambourine /tæmbəˈriːn/ *n* tamborim *m*, pandeiro *m*

tame /teɪm/ *a* (-er, -est) manso; (*domesticated*) domesticado; (*dull*) insipido □ *vt* amansar, domesticar

tamper /ˈtæmpə(r)/ *vi* ~ with mexer indevidamente em; (*text*) alterar

tampon /ˈtæmpən/ *n* (*med*) tampão *m*; (*sanitary towel*) toalha *f* higiênica

tan /tæn/ *vt/i* (*pt* tanned) queimar, bronzear; (*hide*) curtir □ *n* bronzeado *m* □ *a* castanho amarelado

tandem /ˈtændəm/ *n* (*bicycle*) tandem *m*. in ~ em tandem, um atrás do outro

tang /tæŋ/ *n* (*taste*) sabor *m* or gosto

m característico; (*smell*) cheiro *m* característico

tangent /ˈtændʒənt/ *n* tangente *f*

tangerine /tændʒəˈriːn/ *n* tangerina *f*

tangible /ˈtændʒəbl/ *a* tangível

tangle /ˈtæŋgl/ *vt* emaranhar, enredar □ *n* emaranhado *m*. become ~d emaranhar-se, enredar-se

tank /tæŋk/ *n* tanque *m*, reservatório *m*; (*for petrol*) tanque *m*, (P) depósito *m*; (*for fish*) aquário *m*; (*mil*) tanque *m*

tankard /ˈtæŋkəd/ *n* caneca *f* grande

tanker /ˈtæŋkə(r)/ *n* carro-tanque *m*, camião-cisterna *m*; (*ship*) petroleiro *m*

tantaliz|e /ˈtæntəlaɪz/ *vt* atormentar, tantalizar. ~ing *a* tentador

tantamount /ˈtæntəmaʊnt/ *a* be ~ to equivalar a

tantrum /ˈtæntrəm/ *n* chilique *m*, ataque *m* de mau gênio, (P) génio, birra *f*

tap¹ /tæp/ *n* (*for water etc*) torneira *f* □ *vt* (*pt* tapped) (*resources*) explorar; (*telephone*) gram-pear. on ~ (*colloq*: *available*) disponível

tap² /tæp/ *vt/i* (*pt* tapped) bater levemente. ~-dance *n* sapateado *m*

tape /teɪp/ *n* (*for dressmaking*) fita *f*; (*sticky*) fita *f* adesiva. (*magnetic*) ~ fita *f* (magnética) □ *vt* (*tie*) atar, prender; (*stick*) colar; (*record*) gravar. ~-measure *n* fita *f* métrica. ~-recorder gravador *m*

taper /ˈteɪpə(r)/ *n* vela *f* comprida e fina □ *vt/i* ~ (off) estreitar(-se), afilar(-se). ~ed, ~ing *adjs* (*fingers etc*) afilado; (*trousers*) afunilado

tapestry /ˈtæpɪstrɪ/ *n* tapeçaria *f*

tapioca /tæpɪˈəʊkə/ *n* tapioca *f*

tar /tɑː(r)/ *n* alcatrão *m* □ *vt* (*pt* tarred) alcatroar

target /ˈtɑːgɪt/ *n* alvo *m* □ *vt* ter como alvo

tariff /ˈtærɪf/ *n* tarifa *f*; (*on import*) direitos *mpl* aduaneiros

Tarmac /ˈtɑːmæk/ *n* macadame (alcatroado) *m*; (*runway*) pista *f*

tarnish /ˈtɑːnɪʃ/ *vt/i* (fazer) perder o brilho; (*stain*) manchar

tarpaulin /tɑːˈpɔːlɪn/ *n* lona *f* impermeável (alcatroada *or* encerada)

tart¹ /tɑːt/ *a* (-er, -est) ácido; (*fig*: *cutting*) mordaz, azedo

tart² /tɑːt/ *n* (*culin*) torta *f* de fruta, (P) tarte *f*; (*sl*: *prostitute*) prostituta *f*, mulher *f* da vida (*sl*) □ *vt* ~ up (*colloq*) embonecar(-se)

tartan /ˈtɑːtn/ *n* tecido *m* escocês □ *a* escocês

tartar /ˈtɑːtə(r)/ *n* (*on teeth*) tártaro *m*, (P) pedra *f*. ~ sauce molho *m* tártaro

task /tɑːsk/ *n* tarefa *f*, trabalho *m*.

take to ~ repreender, censurar. ~
force (*mil*) força-tarefa *f*
tassel /'tæsl/ *n* borla *f*
taste /teɪst/ *n* gosto *m*; (*fig: sample*)
amostra *f* □ *vt* (*eat, enjoy*) saborear;
(*try*) provar; (*perceive taste of*) sentir
o gosto de □ *vi* ~ of *or* like ter o sabor
de. have a ~ of (*experience*) provar.
~ful *a* de bom gosto. ~fully *adv* com
bom gosto. ~less *a* insípido, insosso;
(*fig: not in good taste*) sem gosto; (*fig:
in bad taste*) de mau gosto
tasty /'teɪstɪ/ *a* (-ier, -iest) saboroso,
gostoso
tat /tæt/ *see* tit²
tatter|s /'tætəz/ *npl* farrapos *mpl*.
~ed /-əd/ *a* esfarrapado
tattoo /tə'tuː/ *vt* tatuar □ *n* tatuagem *f*
tatty /'tætɪ/ *a* (-ier, -iest) (*colloq*) enxovalhado, em mau estado
taught /tɔːt/ *see* teach
taunt /tɔːnt/ *vt* escarnecer de, zombar
de □ *n* escárnio *m*. ~ing *a* escarninho
Taurus /'tɔːrəs/ *n* (*astr*) Touro *m*, (*P*)
Taurus *m*
taut /tɔːt/ *a* esticado, retesado; (*fig: of
nerves*) tenso
tawdry /'tɔːdrɪ/ *a* (-ier, -iest) espalhafatoso e ordinário
tawny /'tɔːnɪ/ *a* fulvo
tax /tæks/ *n* taxa *f*, imposto *m*;
(*on income*) imposto *m* de renda, (*P*)
sobre o rendimento □ *vt* taxar, lançar
impostos sobre, tributar; (*fig: put to
test*) pôr à prova. ~-collector *n* cobrador *m* de impostos. ~-free *a* isento de imposto. ~ relief isenção *f* de
imposto. ~ return declaração *f* do
imposto de renda, (*P*) sobre o
rendimento. ~ year ano *m* fiscal.
~able *a* tributável, passível de
imposto. ~ation /-'seɪʃn/ *n* impostos
mpl, tributação *f*. ~ing *a* penoso, difícil
taxi /'tæksɪ/ *n* (*pl* -is) táxi *m* □ *vi* (*pt*
taxied, *pres p* taxiing) (*aviat*) rolar
na pista, taxiar. ~-cab *n* táxi *m*. ~-
driver *n* motorista *mf* de táxi. ~-
rank, (*Amer*) ~ stand ponto *m* de
táxis, (*P*) praça *f* de táxis
taxpayer /'tækspeɪə(r)/ *n* contribuinte *mf*
tea /tiː/ *n* chá *m*. high ~ refeição *f*
leve à noite. ~-bag *n* saquinho *m* de
chá. ~-break *n* intervalo *m* para o
chá. ~-cosy *n* abafador *m*. ~-leaf *n*
folha *f* de chá. ~-set *n* serviço *m* de
chá. ~-shop *n* salão *m* *or* casa *f* de
chá. ~-time *n* hora *f* do chá. ~-
towel *n* pano *m* de prato
teach /tiːtʃ/ *vt* (*pt* taught) ensinar,
lecionar, (*P*) leccionar (sb sth alg
coisa a alguém) □ *vi* ensinar, ser

professor. ~er *n* professor *m*. ~ing
n ensino *m*; (*doctrines*) ensinamen-
to(s) *m* (*pl*) □ *a* pedagógico, de ensino; (*staff*) docente
teacup /'tiːkʌp/ *n* xícara *f* de chá, (*P*)
chávena *f*
teak /tiːk/ *n* teca *f*
team /tiːm/ *n* equipe *f*, (*P*) equipa *f*; (*of
oxen*) junta *f*; (*of horses*) parelha *f* □ *vi*
~ up juntar-se, associar-se (with a).
~-work *n* trabalho *m* de equipe, (*P*)
equipa
teapot /'tiːpɒt/ *n* bule *m*
tear¹ /teə(r)/ *vt* (*pt* tore, *pp* torn)
rasgar(-se); (*snatch*) arrancar, puxar;
(*rush*) lançar-se, ir numa correria;
(*fig*) dividir □ *n* rasgão *m*. ~ o.s.
away arrancar-se (from de)
tear² /tɪə(r)/ *n* lágrima *f*. ~-gas *n*
gases *mpl* lacrimogênios, (*P*) lacrimo-
génios
tearful /'tɪəfl/ *a* lacrimoso, choroso.
~ly *adv* choroso, com (as) lágrimas
nos olhos
tease /tiːz/ *vt* implicar; (*make fun of*)
caçoar de
teaspoon /'tiːspuːn/ *n* colher *f* de chá.
~ful *n* (*pl* -fuls) colher *f* de chá
cheia
teat /tiːt/ *n* (*of bottle*) bico *m*; (*of animal*) teta *f*
technical /'teknɪkl/ *a* técnico. ~ity
/-'kælətɪ/ *n* questão *f* de ordem
técnica. ~ly *adv* tecnicamente
technician /tek'nɪʃn/ *n* técnico *m*
technique /tek'niːk/ *n* técnica *f*
technolog|y /tek'nɒlədʒɪ/ *n* tecnolo-
gia *f*. ~ical /-ə'lɒdʒɪkl/ *a* tecnológico
teddy /'tedɪ/ *a* ~ (-bear) ursinho *m* de
pelúcia, (*P*) peluche
tedious /'tiːdɪəs/ *a* maçante
tedium /'tiːdɪəm/ *n* tédio *m*
tee /tiː/ *n* (*golf*) tee *m*
teem¹ /tiːm/ *vi* ~ (with) (*swarm*) pulular (de), fervilhar (de), abundar
(em)
teem² /tiːm/ *vi* ~ (with rain) chover
torrencialmente
teenage /'tiːneɪdʒ/ *a* juvenil, de/para
adolescente. ~r /-ə(r)/ *n* jovem *mf*,
adolescente *mf*
teens /tiːnz/ *npl* in one's ~ na ado-
lescência, entre os 13 e os 19 anos
teeter /'tiːtə(r)/ *vi* cambalear, vacilar
teeth /tiːθ/ *see* tooth
teethe /tiːð/ *vi* começar a ter dentes.
~ing troubles (*fig*) problemas *mpl*
iniciais
teetotaller /tiː'təʊtlə(r)/ *n* abstêmio
m, (*P*) abstémio *m*
telecommunications /telɪkəmjuːnɪ-
'keɪʃnz/ *npl* telecomunicações *fpl*
telegram /'telɪgræm/ *n* telegrama *m*
telegraph /'telɪgrɑːf/ *n* telégrafo *m* □

a telegráfico. ~**ic** /-'græfɪk/ *a* telegráfico

telepath|y /tɪ'lepəθɪ/ *n* telepatia *f*. ~**ic** /telɪ'pæθɪk/ *a* telepático

telephone /'telɪfəʊn/ *n* telefone *m □ vt* (*person*) telefonar a; (*message*) telefonar □ *vi* telefonar. ~ **book** lista *f* telefônica, (P) telefónica, guia *m* telefônico, (P) telefónico. ~ **box**, ~ **booth** cabine *f* telefônica, (P) telefónica. ~ **call** chamada *f*. ~ **directory** lista *f* telefônica, (P) telefónica, guia *m* telefônico, (P) telefónico. ~ **number** número *m* de telefone

telephonist /tɪ'lefənɪst/ *n* (*in exchange*) telefonista *mf*

telephoto /telɪ'fəʊtəʊ/ *n* ~ **lens** teleobjetiva *f*, (P) teleobjectiva *f*

telescop|e /'telɪskəʊp/ *n* telescópio *m □ vt/i* encaixar(-se). ~**ic** /-'skʊpɪk/ *a* telescópico

teletext /'telɪtekst/ *n* teletexto *m*

televise /'telɪvaɪz/ *vt* televisionar

television /telɪvɪʒn/ *n* televisão *f*. ~ **set** aparelho *m* de televisão, televisor *m*

telex /'teleks/ *n* telex *m □ vt* transmitir por telex, telexar

tell /tel/ *vt* (*pt* told) dizer (**sb** sth alg coisa a alguém); (*story*) contar; (*distinguish*) distinguir, diferençar □ *vi* (*know*) ver-se, saber. **I told you so** bem lhe disse. ~ **of** falar de. ~ **off** (*colloq: scold*) ralhar, dar uma bronca em. ~ **on** (*have effect on*) afetar, (P) afectar; (*colloq: inform on*) fazer queixa de (*colloq*). ~-**tale** *n* mexeriqueiro *m*, fofoqueiro *m □ a* (*revealing*) revelador. **tales** mexericar, fofocar

telly /'telɪ/ *n* (*colloq*) TV *f* (*colloq*)

temp /temp/ *n* (*colloq*) empregado *m* temporário

temper /'tempə(r)/ *n* humor *m*, disposição *f*; (*anger*) mau humor *m □ vt* temperar. **keep/lose one's** ~ manter a calma/perder a calma *or* a cabeça, zangar-se

temperament /'temprəmənt/ *n* temperamento *m*. ~**al** /'mentl/ *a* caprichoso

temperance /'tempərəns/ *n* (*in drinking*) moderação *f*, sobriedade *f*

temperate /'tempərət/ *a* moderado, comedido; (*climate*) temperado

temperature /'temprətʃə(r)/ *n* temperatura *f*. **have a** ~ estar com *or* ter febre

tempest /'tempɪst/ *n* tempestade *f*, temporal *m*

tempestuous /tem'pestʃʊəs/ *a* tempestuoso

template /'templ(e)ɪt/ *n* molde *m*

temple[1] /'templ/ *n* templo *m*

temple[2] /'templ/ *n* (*anat*) têmpora *f*, fonte *f*

tempo /'tempəʊ/ *n* (*pl* -**os**) (*mus*) tempo *m*; (*pace*) ritmo *m*

temporar|y /'temprərɪ/ *a* temporário, provisório. ~**ily** *adv* temporariamente, provisoriamente

tempt /tempt/ *vt* tentar. ~ **sb to do** dar a alguém vontade de fazer, tentar alguém a fazer. ~**ation** /-'teɪʃn/ *n* tentação *f*. ~**ing** *a* tentador

ten /ten/ *a & n* dez (*m*)

tenaci|ous /tɪ'neɪʃəs/ *a* tenaz. ~**ity** /-'æsətɪ/ *n* tenacidade *f*

tenant /'tenənt/ *n* inquilino *m*, locatário *m*

tend[1] /tend/ *vt* tomar conta de, cuidar de

tend[2] /tend/ *vi* ~ **to** (*be apt to*) tender a, ter tendência para

tendency /'tendənsɪ/ *n* tendência *f*

tender[1] /'tendə(r)/ *a* (*soft, delicate*) terno; (*sore, painful*) sensível, dolorido; (*loving*) terno, meigo. ~-**hearted** *a* compassivo. ~**ly** *adv* (*lovingly*) ternamente, meigamente; (*delicately*) delicadamente. ~**ness** *n* (*love*) ternura *f*, meiguice *f*

tender[2] /'tendə(r)/ *vt* (*money*) oferecer; (*apologies, resignation*) apresentar □ *vi* ~ (**for**) apresentar orçamento (para) □ *n* (*comm*) orçamento *m*. **legal** ~ (*money*) moeda *f* corrente

tendon /'tendən/ *n* tendão *m*

tenement /'tenəmənt/ *n* prédio *m* de apartamentos de renda moderada; (*Amer: slum*) prédio *m* pobre

tenet /'tenɪt/ *n* princípio *m*, dogma *m*

tennis /'tenɪs/ *n* tênis *m*, (P) ténis *m*. ~ **court** quadra *f* de tênis, (P) court *m* de ténis

tenor /'tenə(r)/ *n* (*meaning*) teor *m*; (*mus*) tenor *m*

tense[1] /tens/ *n* (*gram*) tempo *m*

tense[2] /tens/ *a* (-**er**, -**est**) tenso □ *vt* (*muscles*) retesar

tension /'tenʃn/ *n* tensão *f*

tent /tent/ *n* tenda *f*, barraca *f*. ~-**peg** *n* estaca *f*

tentacle /'tentəkl/ *n* tentáculo *m*

tentative /'tentətɪv/ *a* provisório; (*hesitant*) hesitante. ~**ly** *adv* tentativamente, a título experimental; (*hesitantly*) hesitantemente

tenterhooks /'tentəhʊks/ *npl* **on** ~ em suspense

tenth /tenθ/ *a & n* décimo (*m*)

tenuous /'tenjʊəs/ *a* tênue, (P) ténue

tepid /'tepɪd/ *a* tépido, morno

term /tɜːm/ *n* (*word*) termo *m*; (*limit*) prazo *m*, termo *m*; (*schol etc*) período *m*, trimestre *m*; (*Amer*) semestre *m*; (*of imprisonment*) (duração de) pena *f*. ~**s** (*conditions*) condições *fpl □ vt* designar, denominar, chamar. **on good/**

bad ~s de boas/más relações. not on
speaking ~s de relações cortadas.
come to ~s with chegar a um acordo
com; (become resigned to) resignar-se
a. ~ of office (pol) mandato m

terminal /'tɜ:mɪnl/ a terminal, final;
(illness) fatal, mortal □ n (oil, computer) terminal m; (rail) estação f
terminal; (electr) borne m. (air) ~
terminal m (de avião)

terminat|e /'tɜ:mɪneɪt/ vt terminar,
pôr termo a □ vi terminar. ~ion
/-'neɪʃn/ n término m, (P) terminação f, termo m

terminology /tɜ:mɪ'nɒlədʒɪ/ n termi-
nologia f

terminus /'tɜ:mɪnəs/ n (pl -ni /-naɪ/)
(rail, coach) estação f terminal

terrace /'terəs/ n terraço m; (in culti-
vation) socalco m, (houses) casas fpl
em fileira contínua, lance m de
casas. the ~s (sport) arquibancada
f. ~d house casa f ladeada por outras
casas

terrain /te'reɪn/ n terreno m

terrib|le /'terəbl/ a terrível. ~y adv
terrivelmente; (colloq: very) extremamente, espantosamente

terrific /tə'rɪfɪk/ a terrífico, tremendo; (colloq: excellent; great) tremendo.
~ally adv (colloq: very) tremenda-
mente (colloq); (colloq: very well) lindamente, maravilhosamente

terrif|y /'terɪfaɪ/ vt aterrar, ater-
rorizar. be ~ied ter pavor de

territorial /terɪ'tɔ:rɪəl/ a territorial

territory /'terɪtərɪ/ n território m

terror /'terə(r)/ n terror m, pavor m

terroris|t /'terərɪst/ n terrorista mf.
~m /-zəm/ n terrorismo m

terrorize /'terəraɪz/ vt aterrorizar,
aterrar

terse /tɜ:s/ a conciso, lapidar; (curt)
lacônico, (P) lacónico

test /test/ n teste m, exame m, prova f;
(schol) prova f, teste m; (of goods) controle m (of machine etc) ensaio m; (of
strength) prova f □ vt examinar;
(check) controlar; (try) ensaiar;
(pupil) interrogar. put to the ~ pôr
à prova. ~ match jogo m internacional. ~-tube proveta f. ~-tube
baby bebê m de proveta

testament /'testəmənt/ n testamento
m. Old/New T~ Antigo/Novo Testamento m

testicle /'testɪkl/ n testículo m

testify /'testɪfaɪ/ vt/i testificar, testemunhar, depor

testimonial /testɪ'məʊnɪəl/ n carta f
de recomendação

testimony /'testɪmənɪ/ n testemunho
m

tetanus /'tetənəs/ n tétano m

tether /'teðə(r)/ vt prender com corda
□ n be at the end of one's ~ não
poder mais, estar nas últimas

text /tekst/ n texto m

textbook /'tekstbʊk/ n compêndio m,
manual m, livro m de texto

textile /'tekstaɪl/ n & a têxtil (m)

texture /'tekstʃə(r)/ n (of fabric) tex-
tura f; (of paper) grão m

Thai /taɪ/ a & n tailandês (m). ~land
n Tailândia f

Thames /temz/ n Tâmisa m

than /ðæn; unstressed /ðən/ conj que,
do que; (with numbers) de. more/less
~ ten mais/menos de dez

thank /θæŋk/ vt agradecer. ~ you!
obrigado! ~s! (colloq) (P) obrigadinho! (colloq). ~s npl agradecimentos
mpl. ~s to graças a. T~sgiving
(Day) (Amer) Dia m de Ação, (P) Acção de Graças

thankful /'θæŋkfl/ a grato, agradecido, reconhecido (for por). ~ly adv
com gratidão; (happily) felizmente

thankless /'θæŋklɪs/ a ingrato, mal
agradecido

that /ðæt/; unstressed /ðət/ a & pron
(pl those) esse/essa, esses/essas;
(more distant) aquele/aquela, aqueles
/aquelas; (neuter) isso invar; (more
distant) aquilo invar □ adv tão, tanto,
de tal modo □ rel pron que □ conj que.
~ boy esse/aquele rapaz. what is ~?
o que é isso? who is ~? quem é? is ~
you? é você? give me ~ (one) dá-me
esse. ~ is (to say) isto é, quer dizer.
after ~ depois disso. the day ~ o dia
em que. ~ much tanto assim, tanto
como isto

thatch /θætʃ/ n colmo m. ~ed a de
colmo. ~ed cottage casa f com telhado de colmo

thaw /θɔ:/ vt/i derreter(-se), degelar;
(food) descongelar □ n degelo m, der-
retimento m

the /before vowel ðɪ/, before consonant
ðə/, stressed ði:/ a o, a (pl os, as). of
~, from ~ do, da (pl dos, das). at ~,
to ~ ao, à (pl aos, às), para o/a/os/
as. in ~ no, na (pl nos, nas). by ~
hour a cada hora □ adv all ~ better
tanto melhor. ~ more... ~ more...
quanto mais... tanto mais...

theatre /'θɪətə(r)/ n teatro m

theatrical /θɪ'ætrɪkl/ a teatral

theft /θeft/ n roubo m

their /ðeə(r)/ a deles, delas, seu

theirs /ðeəz/ poss pron o(s) seu(s), a(s)
sua(s), o(s) deles, a(s) delas. it is ~ é
(o) deles/delas or o seu

them /ðem/; unstressed /ðəm/ pron os,
as; (after prep) eles, elas. (to) ~ lhes

theme /θi:m/ n tema m

themselves /ðəm'selvz/ pron eles

mesmos/próprios, elas mesmas/ próprias; (*reflexive*) se; (*after prep*) si (mesmos, próprios). by ~ sozinhos. with ~ consigo

then /ðen/ *adv* (*at that time*) então, nessa altura; (*next*) depois, em seguida; (*in that case*) então, nesse caso; (*therefore*) então, portanto, por conseguinte □ *a* (de) então. from ~ on desde então

theolog|y /θɪˈɒlədʒɪ/ *n* teologia *f*. ~ian /θɪəˈlɒdʒən/ *n* teólogo *m*

theorem /ˈθɪərəm/ *n* teorema *m*

theor|y /ˈθɪərɪ/ *n* teoria *f*. ~etical /ˈretɪk/ *a* teórico

therapeutic /θerəˈpjuːtɪk/ *a* terapêutico

therap|y /ˈθerəpɪ/ *n* terapia *f*. ~ist *n* terapeuta *mf*

there /ðeə(r)/ *adv* aí, ali, lá; (*over there*) lá, acolá □ *int* (*triumphant*) pronto, aí está; (*consoling*) então, vamos lá. he goes ~ ele vai aí *or* lá. he goes *or* vai ele. ~ is, ~ are há. ~ you are (*giving*) toma. ~ and then logo ali. ~abouts *adv* por aí. ~after *adv* daí em diante, depois disso. ~by *adv* desse modo

therefore /ˈðeəfɔː(r)/ *adv* por isso, portanto, por conseguinte

thermal /ˈθɜːml/ *a* térmico

thermometer /θəˈmɒmɪtə(r)/ *n* termómetro *m*, (P) termómetro *m*

Thermos /ˈθɜːməs/ *n* garrafa *f* térmica, (P) termo *m*

thermostat /ˈθɜːməstæt/ *n* termostato *m*

thesaurus /θɪˈsɔːrəs/ *n* (*pl* -ri /-raɪ/) dicionário *m* de sinónimos, (P) sinónimos

these /ðiːz/ *see* this

thesis /ˈθiːsɪs/ *n* (*pl* theses /-siːz/) tese *f*

they /ðeɪ/ *pron* eles, elas. ~ say (that)... diz-se *or* dizem que...

thick /θɪk/ *a* (-er, -est) espesso, grosso; (*colloq: stupid*) estúpido □ *adv* = thickly □ *n* the ~ of no meio do de. ~-skinned *a* insensível. ~ly *adv* espessamente; (*spread*) em camada espessa. ~ness *n* espessura *f*, grossura *f*

thicken /ˈθɪkən/ *vt/i* engrossar, espessar(-se). the plot ~s o enredo complica-se

thickset /θɪkˈset/ *a* (*person*) atarracado

thief /θiːf/ *n* (*pl* thieves /θiːvz/) ladrão *m*, gatuno *m*

thigh /θaɪ/ *n* coxa *f*

thimble /ˈθɪmbl/ *n* dedal *m*

thin /θɪn/ *a* (thinner, thinnest) (*slender*) estreito, fino, delgado; (*lean, not plump*) magro; (*sparse*) ralo, escasso;

(*flimsy*) leve, fino; (*soup*) aguado; (*hair*) ralo □ *adv* = thinly □ *vt/i* (*pt thinned*) (*of liquid*) diluir(-se); (*of fog etc*) dissipar(-se); (*of hair*) rarear. ~ out (*in quantity*) diminuir, reduzir; (*seedlings etc*) desbastar. ~ly *adv* (*sparsely*) esparsamente. ~ness *n* (*of board, wire etc*) finura *f*, (*of persons*) magreza *f*

thing /θɪŋ/ *n* coisa *f*. ~s (*belongings*) pertences *mpl*. the best ~ is to o melhor é. for one ~ em primeiro lugar. just the ~ exatamente o que era preciso. poor ~ coitado

think /θɪŋk/ *vt/i* (*pt thought*) pensar (*about, of em*); (*carefully*) refletir, (P) reflectir (*about, of em*). I ~ so eu acho que sim. ~ better of it (*change one's mind*) pensar melhor. ~ nothing of achar natural. ~ of (*hold opinion of*) pensar de, achar de. ~ over pensar bem em. ~-tank *n* comissão *f* de peritos. ~ up inventar. ~er *n* pensador *m*

third /θɜːd/ *a* terceiro □ *n* terceiro *m*; (*fraction*) terço *m*. ~-party insurance seguro *m* contra terceiros. ~-rate *a* inferior, mediocre. T~ World Terceiro Mundo *m*. ~ly *adv* em terceiro lugar

thirst /θɜːst/ *n* sede *f*. ~y *a* sequioso, sedento. be ~y estar com *or* ter sede. ~ily *adv* sofregamente

thirteen /θɜːˈtiːn/ *a & n* treze (*m*). ~th *a & n* décimo terceiro (*m*)

thirt|y /ˈθɜːtɪ/ *a & n* trinta (*m*). ~ieth *a & n* trigésimo (*m*)

this /ðɪs/ *a & pron* (*pl* these) este, esta □ *pron* isto *pron* isto invar. ~ one este, esta. these ones estes, estas. ~ boy este rapaz. ~ is isto é. after ~ depois disto. like ~ assim. ~ is the man este é o homem. ~ far até aqui. ~ morning esta manhã. ~ Wednesday esta quarta-feira

thistle /ˈθɪsl/ *n* cardo *m*

thorn /θɔːn/ *n* espinho *m*, pico *m*. ~y *a* espinhoso; (*fig*) bicudo, espinhoso

thorough /ˈθʌrə/ *a* conscencioso; (*deep*) completo, profundo; (*cleaning, washing*) a fundo. ~ly *adv* (*clean, study etc*) completo, a fundo; (*very*) perfeitamente, muito bem

thoroughbred /ˈθʌrəbred/ *n* (*horse etc*) puro-sangue *m invar*

thoroughfare /ˈθʌrəfeə(r)/ *n* artéria *f*. no ~ passagem *f* proibida

those /ðəʊz/ *see* that

though /ðəʊ/ *conj* se bem que, embora, conquanto □ *adv* (*colloq*) contudo, no entanto

thought /θɔːt/ *see* think □ *n* pensamento *m*; idéia *f*. on second ~s pensando bem thoughtful /ˈθɔːtfl/ a pensativo; (*considerate*) atencioso, solícito. ~ly adv pensativamente; (*considerately*) com consideração, atenciosamente

thoughtless /ˈθɔːtlɪs/ a irrefletido, (P) irreflectido; (*inconsiderate*) pouco atencioso. ~ly adv sem pensar; (*inconsiderately*) sem consideração

thousand /ˈθaʊznd/ a & n mil(*m*).~s of milhares de. ~th a & n milésimo (*m*)

thrash /θræʃ/ vt surrar, espancar; (*defeat*) dar uma surra or sova em. ~ about debater-se. ~ out debater a fundo, discutir bem

thread /θred/ n fio m; (*for sewing*) linha f de coser; (*of screw*) rosca f □ vt enfiar. ~ one's way abrir caminho, furar

threadbare /ˈθredbeə(r)/ a puído, surrado

threat /θret/ n ameaça f

threaten /ˈθretn/ vt/i ameaçar. ~ingly adv com ar ameaçador, ameaçadoramente

three /θriː/ a & n três (*m*)

thresh /θreʃ/ vt (*corn etc*) malhar, debulhar

threshold /ˈθreʃəʊld/ n limiar m, soleira f; (*fig*) limiar m

threw /θruː/ see throw

thrift /θrɪft/ n economia f, poupança f. ~y a económico, (P) económico, poupado

thrill /θrɪl/ n arrepio m de emoção, frêmito m, (P) frémito m □ vt excitar(-se), emocionar(-se), (*fazer*) vibrar. be ~ed estar/ficar encantado. ~ing a excitante, emocionante

thriller /ˈθrɪlə(r)/ n livro m or filme m de suspense

thrive /θraɪv/ vi (*pt* thrived *or* throve, *pp* thrived *or* thriven) prosperar, florescer; (*grow strong*) crescer, dar-se bem (on com). ~ing a próspero

throat /θrəʊt/ n garganta f. have a sore ~ ter dores de garganta

throb /θrɒb/ vi (*pt* throbbed) (*wound, head*) latejar; (*heart*) palpitar, bater; (*engine; fig*) vibrar, trepidar □ n (*of pain*) latejo m, espasmo m; (*of heart*) palpitação f, batida f; (*of engine*) vibração f, trepidação f. ~bing a (*pain*) latejante

throes /θrəʊz/ npl in the ~ of (*fig*) às voltas com, no meio de

thrombosis /θrɒmˈbəʊsɪs/ n trombose f

throne /θrəʊn/ n trono m

throng /θrɒŋ/ n multidão f □ vt/i apinhar(-se); (*arrive*) afluir

throttle /ˈθrɒtl/ n (*auto*) válvula-borboleta f, estrangulador m, acelerador m de mão □ vt estrangular

through /θruː/ prep através de, por; (*during*) durante; (*by means or way of, out of*) por; (*by reason of*) por, por causa de □ adv através; (*entirely*) completamente, até o fim □ a (*train, traffic etc*) direto, (P) directo. be ~ ter acabado (with com); (*telephone*) estar ligado. come or go ~ (*cross, pierce*) atravessar. get ~ (*exam*) passar. be wet ~ estar ensopado or encharcado

throughout /θruːˈaʊt/ prep durante, por todo. ~ the country por todo o país afora. ~ the day durante todo o dia, pelo dia afora □ adv completamente; (*place*) por toda a parte; (*time*) durante todo o tempo

throw /θrəʊ/ vt (*pt* threw, *pp* thrown) atirar, jogar, lançar; (*colloq: baffle*) desconcertar □ n arremesso m; (*of dice*) lance m. ~ a party (*colloq*) dar uma festa. ~ away deitar fora, (P) deitar fora. ~ off (*get rid of*) livrar-se de. ~ out (*person*) expulsar; (*reject*) rejeitar. ~ over (*desert*) abandonar, deixar. ~ up (*one's arms*) levantar; (*resign from*) abandonar; (*colloq: vomit*) vomitar

thrush /θrʌʃ/ n (*bird*) tordo m

thrust /θrʌst/ vt (*pt* thrust) arremeter, empurrar, impelir □ n empurrão m, arremetida f. ~ into (*put*) enfiar em, mergulhar em. ~ upon (*force on*) impôr a

thud /θʌd/ n som m surdo, baque m

thug /θʌɡ/ n bandido m, facínora m, malfeitor m

thumb /θʌm/ n polegar m □ vt (*book*) manusear. ~ a lift pedir carona, (P) boleia. under sb's ~ completamente dominado por alguém. ~-index n índice m de dedo

thumbtack /ˈθʌmtæk/ n (*Amer*) percevejo m

thump /θʌmp/ vt/i bater (em), dar pancadas (em); (*with fists*) dar murros (em); (*piano*) martelar (em); (*of heart*) bater com força □ n pancada f; (*thud*) baque m. ~ing a (*colloq*) enorme

thunder /ˈθʌndə(r)/ n trovão m, trovoada f; (*loud noise*) estrondo m □ vi (*weather, person*) trovejar. ~ past passar como um raio. ~y a (*weather*) tempestuoso

thunderbolt /ˈθʌndəbəʊlt/ n raio m e ribombo m de trovão; (*fig*) raio m fulminante (*fig*)

thunderstorm /ˈθʌndəstɔːm/ n tempestade f com trovoadas, temporal m

Thursday /ˈθɜːzdɪ/ n quinta-feira f

thus /ðʌs/ adv assim, desta maneira. ~ far até aqui

thwart /θwɔːt/ vt frustrar, contrariar

thyme /taɪm/ n tomilho m

tiara /trˈɑːrə/ n tiara f, diadema m

tic /tɪk/ n tique m

tick¹ /tɪk/ n (sound) tique-taque m; (mark) sinal (V) m; (collog: moment) instantinho m □ vi fazer tique-taque □ vt ~ (off) marcar com sinal (V). ~ off (collog: scold) dar uma bronca em (collog). ~ over (engine, factory) funcionar em marcha lenta, (P) no "ralenti"

tick² /tɪk/ n (insect) carrapato m

ticket /'tɪkɪt/ n bilhete m; (label) etiqueta f; (for traffic offence) aviso m de multa. ~-collector n (railway) guarda m. ~-office n bilheteira f

tickle /'tɪkl/ vt fazer cócegas; (fig: amuse) divertir □ n cócegas fpl, comichão m

ticklish /'tɪklɪʃ/ a coceguento, sensível a cócegas; (fig) delicado, melindroso

tidal /'taɪdl/ a de marés, que tem marés. ~ wave onda f gigantesca; (fig) onda f de sentimento popular

tiddly-winks /'tɪdlɪwɪŋks/ n (game) jogo m da pulga

tide /taɪd/ n maré f; (of events) marcha f, curso m. high ~ maré f cheia, preia-mar f. low ~ maré f baixa, baixa-mar f □ vt ~ over (help temporarily) agüentar, (P) aguentar

tidy /'taɪdɪ/ a (-ier, -iest) (room) arrumado; (appearance, work) asseado, cuidado; (methodical) bem ordenado; (collog: amount) belo (collog) □ vt arrumar, arranjar. ~ily adv com cuidado. ~iness n arrumação f, ordem f

tie /taɪ/ vt (pres p tying) atar, amarrar, prender; (link) ligar, vincular; (a knot) dar, fazer □ vi (sport) empatar □ n fio m, cordel m; (necktie) gravata f; (link) laço m, vínculo m; (sport) empate m. ~ in with estar ligado com, relacionar-se com. ~ up amarrar, atar; (animal) prender; (money) imobilizar; (occupy) ocupar

tier /tɪə(r)/ n cada fila f, camada f, prateleira f etc colocada em cima de outra; (in stadium) bancada f; (of cake) andar m; (of society) camada f

tiff /tɪf/ n arrufo m

tiger /'taɪgə(r)/ n tigre m

tight /taɪt/ a (-er, -est) (clothes) apertado, justo; (rope) esticado, tenso; (control) rigoroso; (knot, schedule, lid) apertado; (collog: drunk) embriagado (collog) □ adv = tightly be in a ~ corner (fig) estar em apuros or num aperto, (P) estar entalado (collog). ~-fisted a sovina, pão-duro, (P) agarrado (collog). ~ly adv bem; (squeeze) com força

tighten /'taɪtn/ vt/i (rope) esticar; (bolt, control) apertar. ~ up on apertar o cinto

tightrope /'taɪtrəʊp/ n corda f (de acrobacias). ~ walker funâmbulo m

tights /taɪts/ npl collants mpl, meias-colant fpl

tile /taɪl/ n (on wall, floor) ladrilho m, azulejo m; (on roof) telha f □ vt ladrilhar, pôr azulejos em; (roof) telhar, cobrir com telhas

till¹ /tɪl/ vt (land) cultivar

till² /tɪl/ prep & conj = until

till³ /tɪl/ n caixa (registadora) f

tilt /tɪlt/ vt/i inclinar(-se), pender □ n (slope) inclinação f. (at) full ~ a toda a velocidade

timber /'tɪmbə(r)/ n madeira f (de construção); (trees) árvores fpl

time /taɪm/ n tempo m; (moment) momento m; (epoch) época f, tempo m; (by clock) horas fpl; (occasion) vez f; (rhythm) compasso m. ~s (multiplying) vezes □ vt escolher a hora para; (measure) marcar o tempo; (sport) cronometrar; (regulate) acertar. at ~s às vezes. for the ~ being por agora, por enquanto. from ~ to ~ de vez em quando. have a good ~ divertir-se. have no ~ for não ter paciência para. in no ~ num instante. in ~ a tempo; (eventually) com o tempo. in two days ~ daqui a dois dias. on ~ na hora, (P) a horas. take your ~ não se apresse. what's the ~? que horas são? ~ bomb bomba-relógio f. ~-limit m prazo m. ~ off tempo m livre. ~-sharing n time-sharing m. ~ zone fuso m horário

timeless /'taɪmlɪs/ a intemporal; (unending) eterno

timely /'taɪmlɪ/ a oportuno

timer /'taɪmə(r)/ n (techn) relógio m; (with sand) ampulheta f

timetable /'taɪmteɪbl/ n horário m

timid /'tɪmɪd/ a tímido; (fearful) assustadiço, medroso. ~ly adv timidamente

timing /'taɪmɪŋ/ n (measuring) cronometragem f; (of artist) ritmo m; (moment) cálculo m do tempo, timing m. good/bad ~ (moment) momento m bem/mal escolhido

tin /tɪn/ n estanho m; (container) lata f □ vt (pt tinned) estanhar; (food) enlatar. ~ foil papel m de alumínio. ~-opener n abridor m de latas, (P) abre-latas m. ~ plate lata f, folha-(de-Flandes) f. ~ned foods conservas fpl. ~ny a (sound) metálico

tinge /tɪndʒ/ vt ~ (with) tingir (de); (fig) dar um toque (de) □ n tom m, matiz m; (fig) toque m

tingle /'tɪŋgl/ vi (sting) arder; (prickle) picar □ n ardor m; (prickle) picadela f

tinker /'tɪŋkə(r)/ n latoeiro m ambulante □ vi ~ (with) mexer (em), tentar consertar

tinkle /'tɪŋkl/ n tinido m, tilintar m □ vt/i tilintar

tinsel /'tɪnsl/ n fio m prateado/dourado, enfeites mpl metálicos de Natal; (fig) falso brilho m, ouropel m

tint /tɪnt/ n tom m, matiz m; (for hair) tintura f, tinta f □ vt tingir, colorir

tiny /'taɪnɪ/ a (-ier, -iest) minúsculo, pequenino

tip[1] /tɪp/ n ponta f. (have sth) on the ~ of one's tongue ter alg coisa na ponta da língua

tip[2] /tɪp/ vt/i (pt tipped) (tilt) inclinar(-se); (overturn) virar(-se); (pour) colocar, (P) deitar; (empty) despejar(-se) □ n (money) gorjeta f; (advice) sugestão f, dica f (colloq); (for rubbish) lixeira f. ~ off avisar, prevenir. ~-off n (warning) aviso m; (information) informação f

tipsy /'tɪpsɪ/ a ligeiramente embriagado, alegre, tocado

tiptoe /'tɪptəʊ/ n on ~ na ponta dos pés

tir|e[1] /'taɪə(r)/ vt/i cansar(-se) (of de). ~eless a incansável, infatigável. ~ing a fatigante, cansativo

tire[2] /'taɪə(r)/ n (Amer) pneu m

tired /'taɪəd/ a cansado, fatigado. ~ of (sick of) farto de. ~ out morto de cansaço

tiresome /'taɪəsəm/ a maçador, aborrecido, chato (sl)

tissue /'tɪʃuː/ n tecido m; (handkerchief) lenço m de papel. ~-paper n papel m de seda

tit[1] /tɪt/ n (bird) chapim m, canário-da-terra m

tit[2] /tɪt/ n give ~ for tat pagar na mesma moeda

titbit /'tɪtbɪt/ n petisco m

titillate /'tɪtɪleɪt/ vt excitar, titilar, (P) dar gozo a

title /'taɪtl/ n título m. ~-deed n título m de propriedade. ~-page n página f de rosto, (P) frontispício m. ~-role n papel m principal

titter /'tɪtə(r)/ vi rir com riso abafado

to /tuː/, unstressed /tə/ prep a, para; (as far as) até; (towards) para; (of attitude) para (com) □ adv push or pull ~ (close) fechar. ~ Portugal a/ for a short time) a Portugal; (to stay) para Portugal. ~ the baker's para o padeiro, (P) ao padeiro. ~ do/sit/etc (infinitive) fazer/sentar-se/etc; (expressing purpose) para fazer/para se sentar/etc. it's ten ~ six six são dez para as seis, faltam dez para as seis. go ~ and fro andar de um lado para outro. husband/etc-~-be n futuro marido

m/etc. ~-do n (fuss) agitação f, alvoroço m

toad /təʊd/ n sapo m

toadstool /'təʊdstuːl/ n cogumelo m venenoso

toady /'təʊdɪ/ n lambe-botas mf, puxa-saco m □ vi puxar saco

toast /təʊst/ n fatia f de pão torrado, torrada f; (drink) brinde m, saúde f □ vt (bread) torrar; (drink to) brindar, beber à saúde de. ~er n torradeira f

tobacco /tə'bækəʊ/ n tabaco m

tobacconist /tə'bækənɪst/ n vendedor m de tabaco, homem m da tabacaria (colloq). ~'s shop tabacaria f

toboggan /tə'bɒgən/ n tobogã m, (P) toboggan m

today /tə'deɪ/ n & adv hoje (m)

toddler /'tɒdlə(r)/ n criança f que está aprendendo a andar

toe /təʊ/ n dedo m do pé; (of shoe, stocking) biqueira f □ vt ~ the line andar na linha. on one's ~s alerta, vigilante. ~-hold n apoio (precário) m. ~-nail n unha f do dedo do pé

toffee /'tɒfɪ/ n puxa-puxa m, (P) caramelo m. ~-apple n maçã f caramelizada

together /tə'geðə(r)/ adv junto, juntamente, juntos; (at the same time) ao mesmo tempo. ~ with juntamente com. ~ness n camaradagem f, companheirismo m

toil /tɔɪl/ vi labutar □ n labuta f, labor m

toilet /'tɔɪlɪt/ n banheiro m, (P) casa f de banho; (grooming) toalete f. ~-paper n papel m higiênico, (P) higiênico. ~-roll n rolo m de papel higiênico, (P) higiênico. ~ water água-de-colônia f

toiletries /'tɔɪltrɪz/ npl artigos mpl de toalete

token /'təʊkən/ n sinal m, prova f; (voucher) cheque m; (coin) ficha f □ a simbólico

told /təʊld/ see tell □ a all ~ (all in all) ao todo

tolerabl|e /'tɒlərəbl/ a tolerável; (not bad) sofrível, (work, play) razoavelmente. ~y adv (work, play) razoavelmente

toleran|t /'tɒlərənt/ a tolerante (of para com). ~ce n tolerância f. ~tly adv com tolerância

tolerate /'tɒləreɪt/ vt tolerar

toll[1] /təʊl/ n pedágio m, (P) portagem f. death ~ número m de mortos. take its ~ (of age) fazer sentir o seu peso

toll[2] /təʊl/ vt/i (of bell) dobrar

tomato /tə'mɑːtəʊ/ n (pl -oes) tomate m

tomb /tuːm/ n túmulo m, sepultura f

tomboy /'tɒmbɔɪ/ n menina f levada (E masculinizada), (P) maria-rapaz f

tombstone /'tu:mstəʊn/ n lápide f, pedra f tumular

tome /təʊm/ n tomo m, volume m

tomfoolery /tɒm'fu:lərɪ/ n disparates mpl, imbecilidades fpl

tomorrow /tə'mɒrəʊ/ n & adv amanhã (m). ~ morning/night amanhã de manhã/à noite

ton /tʌn/ n tonelada f (= 1016 kg). (metric) ~ tonelada f (= 1000 kg). ~s of (colloq) montes de (colloq), (P) carradas de (colloq)

tone /təʊn/ n tom m; (of radio, telephone etc) sinal m; (colour) tom m, tonalidade f; (med) tonicidade f □ vt ~ down atenuar □ vi ~ in combinarse, harmonizar-se (with com). ~ up (muscles) tonificar. ~-deaf a sem ouvido musical

tongs /tɒŋz/ n tenaz f; (for sugar) pinça f; (for hair) pinça f

tongue /tʌŋ/ n língua f. ~-in-cheek a & adv ser a sério, com ironia. ~-tied a calado. ~-twister n trava-língua m

tonic /'tɒnɪk/ n (med) tónico m, (P) tónico m; (mus) tónica f, (P) tónica f □ a tónico, (P) tónico

tonight /tə'naɪt/ adv & n hoje à noite, logo à noite, esta noite (f)

tonne /tʌn/ n (metric) tonelada f

tonsil /'tɒnsl/ n amígdala f

tonsillitis /tɒnsɪ'laɪtɪs/ n amigdalite f

too /tu:/ adv demasiado, demais; (also) também, igualmente; (colloq: very) muito. ~ many a demais, demasiados. ~ much a & adv demais, demasiado

took /tʊk/ see take

tool /tu:l/ n (carpenter's, plumber's etc) ferramenta f; (gardener's) utensílio m; (fig: person) joguete m. ~-bag n saco m de ferramenta

toot /tu:t/ n toque m de buzina □ vt/i ~ (the horn) buzinar, tocar a buzina

tooth /tu:θ/ n (pl teeth) dente m. ~less a desdentado

toothache /'tu:θeɪk/ n dor f de dentes

toothbrush /'tu:θbrʌʃ/ n escova f de dentes

toothpaste /'tu:θpeɪst/ n pasta f de dentes, dentifrício m

toothpick /'tu:θpɪk/ n palito m

top¹ /tɒp/ n (highest point; upper part) alto m, cimo m, topo m; (of hill; fig) cume m; (upper surface) cimo m, topo m; (surface of table) tampo m; (lid) tampa f; (of bottle) rolha f; (of list) cabeça f □ a (shelf etc) de cima, superior; (in rank) primeiro; (best) melhor; (distinguished) eminente; (maximum) máximo □ vt (pt topped) (exceed) ultrapassar, ir acima de. from ~ to bottom de alto a baixo. on ~ of em

cima de; (fig) além de. on ~ of that ainda por cima. ~ gear (auto) a velocidade mais alta. ~ hat chapéu m alto. ~-heavy a mais pesado na parte de cima. ~ secret ultra-secreto. ~ up encher. ~ped with coberto de

top² /tɒp/ n (toy) pião m. sleep like a ~ dormir como uma pedra

topic /'tɒpɪk/ n tópico m, assunto m

topical /'tɒpɪkl/ a da atualidade, (P) actualidade, corrente

topless /'tɒplɪs/ a com o peito nu, topless

topple /'tɒpl/ vt/i (fazer) desabar, (fazer) tombar, (fazer) cair

torch /tɔːtʃ/ n (electric) lanterna f elétrica, (P) eléctrica; (flaming) archote m, facho m

tore /tɔː(r)/ see tear¹

torment¹ /'tɔːment/ n tormento m

torment² /tɔː'ment/ vt atormentar, torturar; (annoy) aborrecer, chatear

torn /tɔːn/ see tear¹

tornado /tɔː'neɪdəʊ/ n (pl -oes) tornado m

torpedo /tɔː'piːdəʊ/ n (pl -oes) torpedo m □ vt torpedear

torrent /'tɒrənt/ n torrente f. ~ial /tə'renʃl/ a torrencial

torrid /'tɒrɪd/ a (climate etc) tórrido; (fig) intenso, ardente

torso /'tɔːsəʊ/ n (pl -os) torso m

tortoise /'tɔːtəs/ n tartaruga f

tortoiseshell /'tɔːtəsʃel/ n (for ornaments etc) tartaruga f

tortuous /'tɔːtʃʊəs/ a (of path etc) que dá muitas voltas, sinuoso; (fig) tortuoso, retorcido

torture /'tɔːtʃə(r)/ n tortura f, suplício m □ vt torturar. ~r /-ə(r)/ n carrasco m, algoz m, torturador m

Tory /'tɔːrɪ/ a & n (colloq) conservador (m), (P) tóri (m)

toss /tɒs/ vt atirar, jogar, (P) deitar; (shake) agitar, sacudir □ vi agitar-se, debater-se. ~ a coin, ~ up tirar cara ou coroa

tot¹ /tɒt/ n criancinha f; (colloq: glass) copinho m

tot² /tɒt/ vt/i (pt totted) ~ up (colloq) somar

total /'təʊtl/ a & n total (m) □ vt (pt totalled) (find total of) totalizar; (amount to) elevar-se a, montar a. ~ity /-'tælətɪ/ n totalidade f. ~ly adv totalmente

totalitarian /təʊtælɪ'teərɪən/ a totalitário

totter /'tɒtə(r)/ vi cambalear, andar aos tombos; (of tower etc) oscilar

touch /tʌtʃ/ vt/i tocar; (of ends, gardens etc) tocar-se; (tamper with) mexer em; (affect) comover □ n (sense) ta-to m, (P) tacto m; (contact) toque m; (of colour) toque *m*, retoque *m*. a ~ of (*small amount*) um pouco de. get in ~ with entrar em contato, (*P*) contacto com. lose ~ perder contato, (*P*) contacto. ~ **down** (*aviat*) aterrissar, (*P*) aterrar. ~ **off** disparar; (*cause*) dar início a, desencadear. ~ **on** (*mention*) tocar em. ~ **up** retocar. ~**and-go** *a* (*risky*) arriscado; (*uncertain*) duvidoso, incerto. ~**line** *n* linha *f* lateral

touching /'tʌtʃɪŋ/ *a* comovente, comovedor

touchy /'tʌtʃɪ/ *a* melindroso, suscetível, (*P*) susceptível, que se ofende facilmente

tough /tʌf/ *a* (-er, -est) (*hard, difficult*) duro; (*strong*) forte, resistente □ *n* ~ (*guy*) valentão *m*, durão *m* (*collog*). ~ **luck!** (*collog*) pouca sorte! (*P*) dureza *f*, (*strength*) força *f*, resistência *f*

toughen /'tʌfn/ *vt/i* (*person*) endurecer; (*strengthen*) reforçar

tour /tʊə(r)/ *n* viagem *f*; (*visit*) visita *f*; (*by team etc*) tournée *f* □ *vt* visitar. on ~ em tournée

tourism /'tʊərɪzəm/ *n* turismo *m*

tourist /'tʊərɪst/ *n* turista *mf* □ *a* turístico. ~ **office** agência *f* de turismo

tournament /'tʊərnəmənt/ *n* torneio *m*

tousle /'taʊzl/ *vt* despentear, esguedelhar

tout /taʊt/ *vi* angariar clientes (for para) □ *vt* (*try to sell*) tentar revender □ *n* (*hotel etc*) angariador *m*; (*ticket*) cambista *m*, (*P*) revendedor *m*

tow /təʊ/ *vt* rebocar □ *n* reboque *m*. on ~ a reboque. ~ **away** (*vehicle*) rebocar. ~**path** *n* caminho *m* de sirga. ~**rope** *n* cabo *m* de reboque

toward(s) /təˈwɔːd(z)/ *prep* para, em direção, (*P*) direcção a, na direção, (*P*) direcção de; (*of attitude*) para com; (*time*) por volta de

towel /'taʊəl/ *n* toalha *f*; (*tea towel*) pano *m* de prato □ *vt* (*pt* towelled) esfregar com a toalha. ~**rail** *n* toalheiro *m*. ~**ling** *n* atoalhado *m*, (*P*) pano *m* turco

tower /'taʊə(r)/ *n* torre *f* □ *vi* ~ **above** dominar. ~ **block** prédio *m* alto. ~**ing** *a* muito alto; (*fig: of rage etc*) violento

town /taʊn/ *n* cidade *f*. go to ~ (*collog*) perder a cabeça (*collog*). ~ **council** município *m*. ~ **hall** câmara *f* municipal. ~ **planning** urbanização *f*

toxic /'tɒksɪk/ *a* tóxico

toy /tɔɪ/ *n* brinquedo *m* □ *vi* ~ **with** (*object*) brincar com; (*idea*) considerar, cogitar

trace /treɪs/ *n* traço *m*, rastro *m*, sinal *m*; (*small quantity*) traço *m*, vestígio *m* □ *vt* seguir *or* encontrar a pista de; (*draw*) traçar; (*with tracing-paper*) decalcar

tracing /'treɪsɪŋ/ *n* decalque *m*, desenho *m*. ~**paper** *n* papel *m* vegetal

track /træk/ *n* (*of person etc*) rastro *m*, pista *f*; (*race-track, of tape*) pista *f*; (*record*) faixa *f*; (*path*) trilho *m*, carreiro *m*; (*rail*) via *f* □ *vt* seguir a pista *or* a trajetória, (*P*) trajectória de. keep ~ of manter-se em contato com; (*keep oneself informed*) informar-se. ~ **down** (*find*) encontrar, descobrir; (*hunt*) seguir a pista de. ~ **suit** conjunto *m* de jogging, (*P*) fato *m* de treino

tract /trækt/ *n* (*land*) extensão *f*; (*anat*) aparelho *m*

tractor /'træktə(r)/ *n* trator *m*, (*P*) tractor *m*

trade /treɪd/ *n* comércio *m*; (*job*) ofício *m*, profissão *f*; (*swap*) troca *f* □ *vt/i* comerciar (em), negociar (em) □ *vt* (*swap*) trocar. ~ **in** (*used article*) trocar. ~**in** *n* troca *f*. ~ **mark** marca *f* de fábrica. ~ **on** (*exploit*) tirar partido de, abusar de. ~ **union** sindicato *m*. ~**r** /-ə(r)/ *n* negociante *mf*, comerciante *mf*

tradesman /'treɪdzmən/ *n* (*pl* -men) comerciante *m*

trading /'treɪdɪŋ/ *n* comércio *m*. ~ **estate** zona *f* industrial

tradition /trəˈdɪʃn/ *n* tradição *f*. ~**al** *a* tradicional

traffic /'træfɪk/ *n* (*trade*) tráfego *m*, tráfico *m*; (*on road*) trânsito *m*, tráfego *m*; (*aviat*) tráfego *m* □ *vi* (*pt* trafficked) traficar (in em). ~ **circle** (*Amer*) giratória *f*, (*P*) rotunda *f*. ~ **island** ilha *f* de pedestres, (*P*) refúgio *m* para peões. ~ **jam** engarrafamento *m*. ~**lights** *npl* sinal *m* luminoso, (*P*) semáforo *m*. ~ **warden** guarda *mf* de trânsito. ~**ker** *n* traficante *mf*

tragedy /'trædʒədɪ/ *n* tragédia *f*

tragic /'trædʒɪk/ *a* trágico

trail /treɪl/ *vt/i* arrastar(-se), rastejar; (*of plant, on ground*) rastejar; (*of plant, over wall*) trepar; (*track*) seguir □ *n* (*of powder, smoke etc*) esteira *f*, rastro *m*, (*P*) rasto *m*; (*track*) pista *f*; (*beaten path*) trilho *m*

trailer /'treɪlə(r)/ *n* reboque *m*; (*Amer: caravan*) reboque *m*, caravana *f*, trailer *m*; (*film*) trailer *m*, apresentação *f* de filme

train /treɪn/ *n* (*rail*) trem *m*, (*P*) comboio *m*; (*procession*) fila *f*; (*of dress*) cauda *f*; (*retinue*) comitiva *f* □ *vt* (*instruct, develop*) educar, formar, treinar; (*plant*) guiar; (*sportsman, animal*) treinar; (*aim*) assestar, apon-

tar □ *vi* estudar, treinar-se. ~ed *a*
(*skilled*) qualificado; (*doctor etc*)
diplomado. ~er *n* (*sport*) treinador
m; (*shoe*) tênis *m*. ~ing *n* treino *m*

trainee /treɪ'niː/ *n* estagiário *m*

trait /treɪt/ *n* traço *m*, característica *f*

traitor /'treɪtə(r)/ *n* traidor *m*

tram /træm/ *n* bonde *m*, (P) (carro)
eléctrico *m*

tramp /træmp/ *vi* marchar (com passo pesado) □ *vt* percorrer, palmilhar □
n som *m* de passos pesados; (*vagrant*)
vagabundo *m*, andarilho *m*; (*hike*)
longa caminhada *f*

trample /'træmpl/ *vt/i* ~ (on) pisar
com força; (*fig*) menosprezar

trampoline /'træmpəliːn/ *n* (lona *f*
usada como) trampolim *m*

trance /trɑːns/ *n* (*hypnotic*) transe *m*;
(*ecstasy*) êxtase *m*, arrebatamento *m*;
(*med*) estupor *m*

tranquil /'træŋkwɪl/ *a* tranqüilo, (P)
tranquilo, sossegado. ~lity /-'kwɪləti/
n tranqüilidade *f*, (P) tranquilidade *f*,
sossego *m*

tranquillizer /'træŋkwɪlaɪzə(r)/ *n*
(*drug*) tranqüilizante *m*, (P) tranqui-
lizante *m*, calmante *m*

transact /træn'zækt/ *vt* (*business*) fazer, efetuar, (P) efectuar. ~ion /-kʃn/
n transação *f*, (P) transacção *f*

transcend /træn'send/ *vt* trans-
cender. ~ent *a* transcendente

transcribe /træn'skraɪb/ *vt* trans-
crever. ~pt, ~ption /-ɪpʃn/ *ns*
transcrição *f*

transfer¹ /træns'fɜː(r)/ *vt* (*pt* trans-
ferred) transferir; (*power, property*)
transmitir □ *vi* mudar, ser transferi-
do; (*change planes etc*) fazer transfe-
rência. ~ the charges (*telephone*)
ligar a cobrar

transfer² /'trænsfɜː(r)/ *n* trans-
ferência *f*; (*of power, property*)
transmissão *f*; (*image*) decalcomania *f*

transfigure /træns'fɪgə(r)/ *vt* trans-
figurar

transform /træns'fɔːm/ *vt* transfor-
mar. ~ation /-ə'meɪʃn/ *n* trans-
formação *f*. ~er *n* (*electr*) transfor-
mador *m*

transfusion /træns'fjuːʒn/ *n* (*of
blood*) transfusão *f*

transient /'trænzɪənt/ *a* transitório,
transiente, efêmero, (P) efémero, passageiro

transistor /træn'zɪstə(r)/ *n* (*device,
radio*) transistor *m*

transit /'trænsɪt/ *n* trânsito *m*. in ~
em trânsito

transition /træn'zɪʃn/ *n* transição *f*.
~al *a* transitório

transitive /'trænsətɪv/ *a* transitivo

transitory /'trænsɪtəri/ *a* transitório

translate /trænz'leɪt/ *vt* traduzir.
~ion /-ʃn/ *n* tradução *f*. ~or *n* tradu-
tor *m*

translucent /trænz'luːsnt/ *a* translúcido

transmit /trænz'mɪt/ *vt* (*pt* transmitted) transmitir. ~ssion *n*
transmissão *f*. ~tter *n* transmissor *m*

transparent /træns'pærənt/ *a* transparente. ~cy *n* transparência *f*;
(*photo*) diapositivo *m*

transpire /træn'spaɪə(r)/ *vi* (*secret
etc*) transpirar; (*happen*) suceder,
acontecer

transplant¹ /træns'plɑːnt/ *vt* trans-
plantar

transplant² /'trænsplɑːnt/ *n* (*med*)
transplantação *f*, transplante *m*

transport¹ /træn'spɔːt/ *vt* (*carry, delight*) transportar. ~ation /'teɪʃn/ *n*
transporte *m*

transport² /'trænspɔːt/ *n* (*of goods,
delight etc*) transporte *m*

transpose /træn'spəʊz/ *vt* transpor

transverse /'trænzvɜːs/ *a* transversal

transvestite /trænz'vestaɪt/ *n* travesti *mf*

trap /træp/ *n* armadilha *f*, ratoeira *f*,
cilada *f* □ *vt* (*pt* trapped) apanhar na
armadilha; (*cut off*) prender,
bloquear. ~per *n* caçador *m* de armadilha (esp de peles)

trapdoor /træp'dɔː(r)/ *n* alçapão *m*

trapeze /trə'piːz/ *n* trapézio *m*

trash /træʃ/ *n* (*worthless stuff*) porcaria *f*; (*refuse*) lixo *m*; (*nonsense*) disparates *mpl*. ~ can *n* (*Amer*) lata *f* do
lixo, (P) caixote *m* do lixo. ~y *a* que
não vale nada, porcaria

trauma /'trɔːmə/ *n* trauma *m*, trau-
matismo *m*. ~tic /-'mætɪk/ *a* traumá-
tico

travel /'trævl/ *vi* (*pt* travelled) viajar; (*of vehicle, bullet, sound*) ir □ *vt*
percorrer □ *n* viagem *f*. ~ agent
agente *mf* de viagem. ~ler *n* viajante
mf. ~ler's cheque cheque *m* de
viagem. ~ling *n* viagem *f*, viagens
fpl, viajar *m*

travesty /'trævəsti/ *n* paródia *f*, caricatura *f*

trawler /'trɔːlə(r)/ *n* traineira *f*, (P)
arrastão *m*

tray /treɪ/ *n* tabuleiro *m*, bandeja *f*

treacherous /'tretʃərəs/ *a* traiçoeiro

treachery /'tretʃəri/ *n* traição *f*,
perfídia *f*, deslealdade *f*

treacle /'triːkl/ *n* melaço *m*

tread /tred/ *vt/i* (*pt* trod, *pp* trodden)
(*step*) pisar; (*walk*) andar, caminhar;
(*walk along*) seguir □ *n* passo *m*, maneira *f* de andar; (*of tyre*) trilho *m*. ~
sth into (*carpet*) esmigalhar alg coisa sobre/em

treason /'tri:zn/ n traição f

treasure /'treʒə(r)/ n tesouro m ▢ vt ter o maior apreço por; (store) guardar bem guardado. ~r n tesoureiro m

treasury /'treʒərɪ/ n (building) tesouraria f; (department) Ministério m das Finanças or da Fazenda; (fig) tesouro m

treat /tri:t/ vt/i tratar ▢ n (pleasure) prazer m, regalo m; (present) mimo m, gentileza f. ~ sb to sth convidar alguém para alg coisa

treatise /'tri:tɪz/ n tratado m

treatment /'tri:tmənt/ n tratamento m

treaty /'tri:tɪ/ n (pact) tratado m

treble /'trebl/ a triplo ▢ vt/i triplicar ▢ n (mus: voice) soprano m. ~y adv triplamente

tree /tri:/ n árvore f

trek /trek/ n viagem f penosa; (walk) caminhada f ▢ vi (pt trekked) viajar penosamente; (walk) caminhar

trellis /'trelɪs/ n grade f para trepadeiras, treliça f

tremble /'trembl/ vi tremer

tremendous /trɪ'mendəs/ a (fearful, huge) tremendo; (colloq: excellent) fantástico, formidável

tremor /'tremə(r)/ n tremor m, estremecimento m. (earth) ~ abalo (sísmico) m, tremor m de terra

trench /trentʃ/ n fossa f, vala f; (mil) trincheira f

trend /trend/ n tendência f; (fashion) moda f. ~y a (colloq) na última moda, (P) na berra (colloq)

trepidation /trepɪ'deɪʃn/ n (fear) receio m, apreensão f

trespass /'trespəs/ vi entrar ilegalmente (on em). no ~ing entrada f proibida. ~er n intruso m

trestle /'tresl/ n cavalete m, armação f de mesa. ~-table n mesa f de cavaletes

trial /'traɪəl/ n (jur) julgamento m, processo m; (test) ensaio m, experiência f, prova f; (ordeal) provação f. on ~ em julgamento. ~ and error tentativas fpl

triangle /'traɪæŋgl/ n triângulo m. ~ular /-'æŋgjʊlə(r)/ a triangular

tribe /traɪb/ n tribo f. ~al a tribal

tribulation /trɪbjʊ'leɪʃn/ n tribulação f

tribunal /traɪ'bju:nl/ n tribunal m

tributary /'trɪbjʊtərɪ/ n afluente m, tributário m

tribute /'trɪbju:t/ n tributo m. pay ~ to prestar homenagem a, render tributo a

trick /trɪk/ n truque m; (prank) partida f; (habit) jeito m ▢ vt enganar. do the ~ (colloq: work) dar resultado

trickery /'trɪkərɪ/ n trapaça f

trickle /'trɪkl/ vi pingar, gotejar, escorrer ▢ n fio m de água etc; (fig: small number) punhado m

tricky /'trɪkɪ/ a (crafty) manhoso; (problem) delicado, complicado

tricycle /'traɪsɪkl/ n triciclo m

trifle /'traɪfl/ n ninharia f, bagatela f; (sweet) sobremesa f feita de pão-de-ló e frutas e creme ▢ vi ~ with brincar com. a ~ um pouquinho, (P) um cochinho

trifling /'traɪflɪŋ/ a insignificante

trigger /'trɪgə(r)/ n (of gun) gatilho m ▢ vt ~ (off) (initiate) desencadear, despoletar

trill /trɪl/ n trinado m, gorjeio m

trilogy /'trɪlədʒɪ/ n trilogia f

trim /trɪm/ a (trimmer, trimmest) bem arranjado, bem cuidado; (figure) elegante, esbelto ▢ vt (pt trimmed) (cut) aparar; (sails) orientar, marear; (ornament) enfeitar, guarnecer (with com) ▢ n (cut) aparadela f, corte m leve; (decoration) enfeite m; (on car) acabamento(s) m(pl), estofado m. in ~ em ordem; (fit) em boa forma. ~ming(s) n(pl) (dress) enfeite m; (culin) guarnição f, acompanhamento m

Trinity /'trɪnətɪ/ n the (Holy) ~ a Santíssima Trindade

trinket /'trɪŋkɪt/ n bugiganga f, (jewel) bijuteria f, berloque m

trio /'tri:əʊ/ n (pl -os) trio m

trip /trɪp/ vi (pt tripped) (stumble) tropeçar, dar um passo em falso; (go or dance lightly) andar/dançar com passos leves ▢ vt ~ (up) fazer tropeçar, passar uma rasteira a ▢ n (journey) viagem f; (outing) passeio m, excursão f; (stumble) tropeção m, passo m em falso

tripe /traɪp/ n (food) dobrada f, tripas fpl; (colloq: nonsense) disparates mpl

triple /'trɪpl/ a triplo, tríplice ▢ vt/i triplicar. ~ts /-plɪts/ npl trigémeos mpl, (P) trigémeos mpl

triplicate /'trɪplɪkət/ n in ~ em triplicata

tripod /'traɪpɒd/ n tripé m

trite /traɪt/ a banal, corriqueiro

triumph /'traɪəmf/ n triunfo m ▢ vi triunfar (over sobre); (exult) exultar, rejubilar-se. ~al /-'ʌmfl/ a triunfal. ~ant /-'ʌmfənt/ a triunfante. ~antly /-'ʌmfəntlɪ/ adv em triunfo, triunfantemente

trivial /'trɪvɪəl/ a insignificante

trod, trodden /trɒd, 'trɒdn/ see tread

trolley /'trɒlɪ/ n carrinho m. (tea-)~ carrinho m de chá

trombone /trɒm'bəʊn/ n (mus) trombone m

troop /tru:p/ n bando m, grupo m. ~s

(mil) tropas *fpl* □ *vi* ~ in/out entrar/
sair em bando *or* grupo. ~ing the
colour a saudação da bandeira. ~er
n soldado *m* de cavalaria

trophy /'trəʊfɪ/ *n* troféu *m*

tropic /'trɒpɪk/ *n* trópico *m*. ~s
trópicos *mpl*. ~al *a* tropical

trot /trɒt/ *n* trote *m* □ *vi (pt trotted)*
trotar; *(of person)* correr em passos
curtos, ir num *or* a trote *(colloq).* on
the ~ *(colloq)* a seguir, a fio. ~ out
(colloq: produce) exibir; *(colloq: state)*
desfiar

trouble /'trʌbl/ *n (difficulty)* dificul-
dade(s) *f(pl)*, problema(s) *m(pl)*;
(distress) desgosto(s) *m(pl)*, aborreci-
mento(s) *m(pl)*; *(pains, effort)* cuidado *m*, trabalho *m*, maçada *f*;
(inconvenience) transtorno *m*, incómodo *m*, *(P)* incómodo *m*; *(med)*
doença *f*. ~(s) *(unrest)* agitação *f*,
conflito(s) *m(pl)* □ *vt/i (bother)* inco-
modar(-se), *(P)* maçar(-se); *(worry)*
preocupar(-se); *(agitate)* perturbar.
be in ~ estar em apuros, estar em
dificuldades. get into ~ meter-se em
encrenca/apuros. it is not worth the
~ não vale a pena. ~-maker *n* desordeiro *m*, provocador *m*. ~-shooter
n mediador *m*, negociador *m*. ~d *a*
agitado, perturbado; *(of sleep)* agitado; *(of water)* turvo

troublesome /'trʌblsəm/ *a* problemático, importuno, *(P)* maçador

trough /trɒf/ *n (drinking)* bebedouro
m; *(feeding)* comedouro *m*. ~ *(of low
pressure)* depressão *f*, linha *f* de
baixa pressão

trounce /traʊns/ *vt (defeat)* esmagar;
(thrash) espancar

troupe /truːp/ *n (theat)* companhia *f*,
troupe *f*

trousers /'traʊzəz/ *npl* calça *f*, *(P)*
calças *fpl*. short ~ calções *mpl*

trousseau /'truːsəʊ/ *n (pl -s /-əʊz/) (of
bride)* enxoval *m* de noiva

trout /traʊt/ *n, (pl invar)* truta *f*

trowel /'traʊəl/ *n (garden)* colher *f* de
jardineiro; *(for mortar)* trolha *f*

truan|t /'truːənt/ *n* absenteísta *mf*,
(P) absentista *mf*; *(schol)* gazeteiro *m*.
play ~t fazer gazeta. ~cy *n* absenteísmo *m*, *(P)* absentismo *m*

truce /truːs/ *n* trégua(s) *f(pl)*,
armistício *m*

truck /trʌk/ *n (lorry)* camião *m*; *(barrow)* carro *m* de bagageiro; *(wagon)*
vagão *m* aberto. ~-driver *n* motorista *mf* de camião, *(P)* camionista *mf*

truculent /'trʌkjʊlənt/ *a* agressivo,
brigão

trudge /trʌdʒ/ *vi* caminhar com dificuldade, caminhar a custo, arrastar-
se

true /truː/ *a* (-er, -est) verdadeiro; *(accurate)* exato, *(P)* exacto; *(faithful)*
fiel. come ~ *(happen)* realizar-se,
concretizar-se. it is ~ é verdade

truffle /'trʌfl/ *n* trufa *f*

truism /'truːɪzəm/ *n* truísmo *m*, verdade *f* evidente, *(P)* verdade *f* do Amigo Banana *(colloq)*

truly /'truːlɪ/ *adv* verdadeiramente;
(faithfully) fielmente; *(truthfully)* sinceramente

trump /trʌmp/ *n* trunfo *m* □ *vt* jogar
trunfo, trunfar. ~ up forjar, inventar.
~ card carta *f* de trunfo; *(colloq:
valuable resource)* trunfo *m*

trumpet /'trʌmpɪt/ *n* trombeta *f*

truncheon /'trʌntʃən/ *n* cassetete *m*,
(P) cassetête *m*

trundle /'trʌndl/ *vt/i* (fazer) rolar rui-
dosamente/pesadamente

trunk /trʌŋk/ *n (of tree, body)* tronco
m; *(of elephant)* tromba *f*; *(box)* mala *f*
grande; *(Amer, auto)* mala *f*. ~s *(for
swimming)* calção *m* de banho. ~ call
n chamada *f* interurbana. ~ road *n*
estrada *f* nacional

truss /trʌs/ *n (med)* funda *f* □ *vt* atar,
amarrar

trust /trʌst/ *n* confiança *f*; *(association)* truste *m*, *(P)* trust *m*, consórcio
m; *(foundation)* fundação *f*; *(responsibility)* responsabilidade *f*; *(jur)* fideicomisso *m* □ *vt (rely on)* ter confiança
em, confiar em; *(hope)* esperar □ *vi* ~
in *or* to confiar em. in ~ em
fideicomisso. on ~ *(without proof)*
sem verificação prévia; *(on credit)* a
crédito. ~ sb with confiar em
alguém. ~ed *a (friend etc)* de confiança, seguro. ~ful, ~ing *adjs*
confiante. ~y *a* fiel

trustee /trʌs'tiː/ *n* administrador *m*;
(jur) fideicomissário *m*

trustworthy /'trʌstwɜːðɪ/ *a* (digno)
de confiança

truth /truːθ/ *n (pl -s /truːðz/)* verdade
f. ~ful *a (account etc)* verídico; *(person)* verdadeiro, que fala verdade.
~fully *adv* sinceramente

try /traɪ/ *vt/i (pt tried)* tentar, experimentar; *(be a strain on)* cansar, pôr à
prova; *(jur)* julgar □ *n (attempt)* tentativa *f*, experiência *f*; *(Rugby)* ensaio
m. ~ for *(post, scholarship)* candidatar-se a; *(record)* tentar alcançar. ~
on *(clothes)* provar. ~ out
experimentar. ~ to do tentar fazer.
~ing *a* difícil

tsar /zɑː(r)/ *n* czar *m*

T-shirt /'tiːʃɜːt/ *n* T-shirt *f*, camiseta *f*
de algodão de mangas curtas

tub /tʌb/ *n* selha *f*; *(colloq: bath)* tina *f*,
banheira *f*

tuba /'tjuːbə/ *n (mus)* tuba *f*

tubby /'tʌbɪ/ a (-ier, -iest) baixote e gorducho

tub|e /tjuːb/ n tubo m; (colloq: railway) metrô m. **inner** ~**e** câmara f de ar. ~**ing** n tubos mpl, tubagem f

tuber /'tjuːbə(r)/ n tubérculo m

tuberculosis /tjuːbɜːkjʊ'ləʊsɪs/ n tuberculose f

tubular /'tjuːbjʊlə(r)/ a tubular

tuck /tʌk/ n (fold) prega f cosida; (for shortening or ornament) refego m □ vt/i fazer pregas; (put) guardar, meter, enfiar; (hide) esconder. ~ **in** or **into** (colloq: eat) atacar. ~ **in** (shirt) meter as fraldas para dentro; (blanket) prender em; (person) cobrir bem, aconchegar. ~**-shop** n (schol) loja f de balas, (P) pastelaria f (junto à escola)

Tuesday /'tjuːzdɪ/ n terça-feira f

tuft /tʌft/ n tufo m

tug /tʌg/ vt/i (pt tugged) puxar com força; (vessel) rebocar □ n (boat) rebocador m; (pull) puxão m. ~ **of war** cabo-de-guerra m, (P) jogo m da guerra

tuition /tju:'ɪʃn/ n ensino m

tulip /'tjuːlɪp/ n tulipa f

tumble /'tʌmbl/ vi tombar, baquear, dar um trambolhão □ n tombo m, trambolhão m. ~**-drier** n máquina f de secar (roupa)

tumbledown /'tʌmbldaʊn/ a em ruínas

tumbler /'tʌmblə(r)/ n copo m

tummy /'tʌmɪ/ n (colloq: stomach) estômago m; (colloq: abdomen) barriga f. ~**-ache** n (colloq) dor f de barriga/de estômago

tumour /'tjuːmə(r)/ n tumor m

tumult /'tjuːmʌlt/ n tumulto m. ~**uous** /-'mʌltʃʊəs/ a tumultuado, barulhento, agitado

tuna /'tjuːnə/ n (pl invar) atum m

tune /tjuːn/ n melodia f □ vt (engine) regular; (piano etc) afinar □ vi ~ **in** (to) (radio, TV) ligar (em), (P) sintonizar. ~ **up** afinar. **be in/out of** ~ (instrument) estar afinado/desafinado; (singer) cantar afinado/desafinado. ~**ful** a melodioso, harmonioso. ~**r** n afinador m; (radio) sintonizador m

tunic /'tjuːnɪk/ n túnica f

Tunisia /tjuː'nɪzɪə/ n Tunísia f. ~**n** a & n tunisiano (m), (P) tunisino (m)

tunnel /'tʌnl/ n túnel m □ vi (pt tunnelled) abrir um túnel (into em)

turban /'tɜːbən/ n turbante m

turbine /'tɜːbaɪn/ n turbina f

turbo- /'tɜːbəʊ/ pref turbo-

turbot /'tɜːbət/ n rodovalho m

turbulen|t /'tɜːbjʊlənt/ a turbulento. ~**ce** n turbulência f

tureen /tə'riːn/ n terrina f

turf /tɜːf/ n (pl turfs or turves) gramado m, (P) relva f, relvado m □ vt ~ **out** (colloq) jogar fora, (P) deitar fora. **the** ~ (racing) turfe m, hipismo m. ~ **accountant** corretor m de apostas

turgid /'tɜːdʒɪd/ a (speech, style) pomposo, empolado

Turk /tɜːk/ n turco m. ~**ey** n Turquia f. ~**ish** /-ʃ/ a □ n (lang) turco m

turkey /'tɜːkɪ/ n peru m

turmoil /'tɜːmɔɪl/ n agitação f, confusão f, desordem f. **in** ~ em ebulição

turn /tɜːn/ vt/i virar(-se), voltar(-se), girar; (change) transformar(-se) (into em); (become) ficar, tornar-se; (corner) virar, dobrar; (page) virar, voltar □ n volta f; (in road) curva f; (of mind, events) mudança f; (occasion, opportunity) vez f; (colloq) ataque m, crise f; (colloq: shock) susto m. **do a good** ~ prestar (um) serviço. **in** ~ por sua vez, sucessivamente. **speak out of** ~ dizer o que não se deve, cometer uma indiscrição. **take** ~**s** revezar-se. ~ **of the century** virada f do século. ~ **against** virar-se or voltar-se contra. ~ **away** vi virar-se or voltar-se para o outro lado □ vt (avert) desviar; (reject) recusar; (send back) mandar embora. ~ **back** vi (return) devolver; (vehicle) dar meia volta, voltar para trás □ vt (fold) dobrar para trás. ~ **down** recusar; (fold) dobrar para baixo; (reduce) baixar. ~ **in** (hand in) entregar; (colloq: go to bed) deitar-se. ~ **off** (light etc) apagar; (tap) fechar; (road) virar (para rua transversal). ~ **on** (light etc) acender, ligar; (tap) abrir. ~ **out** vt (light) apagar; (empty) esvaziar, despejar; (pocket) virar do avesso; (produce) produzir □ vi (transpire) vir a saber-se, descobrir-se; (colloq: come) aparecer. ~ **round** virar-se, voltar-se. ~ **up** vi aparecer, chegar; (be found) aparecer □ vt (find) desenterrar; (increase) aumentar; (collar) levantar. ~**-out** n assistência f. ~**-up** n (of trousers) dobra f

turning /'tɜːnɪŋ/ n rua f transversal; (corner) esquina f. ~**-point** n momento m decisivo

turnip /'tɜːnɪp/ n nabo m

turnover /'tɜːnəʊvə(r)/ n (pie, tart) pastel m, empada f; (money) faturamento m, (P) facturação f; (of staff) rotatividade f

turnpike /'tɜːnpaɪk/ n (Amer) auto-estrada f com pedágio, (P) portagem f

turnstile /'tɜːnstaɪl/ n (gate) torniquete m, borboleta f turntable /'tɜːnteɪbl/ n (for record) prato m do toca-disco, (P) giradiscos; (record-player) toca-disco m, (P) giradiscos m

turpentine /'tɜːpəntam/ n terebintina f, aguarrás m

turquoise /'tɜːkwɔɪz/ a turquesa invar

turret /'tʌrɪt/ n torreão m, torrinha f

turtle /'tɜːtl/ n tartaruga-do-mar f. ~-neck a de gola alta

tusk /tʌsk/ n (tooth) presa f; (elephant's) defesa f, dente m

tussle /'tʌsl/ n luta f, briga f

tutor /'tjuːtə(r)/ n professor m particular; (univ) professor m universitário

tutorial /tjuː'tɔːrɪəl/ n (univ) seminário m

TV /tiː'viː/ n tevê f

twaddle /'twɒdl/ n disparates mpl

twang /twæŋ/ n (mus) som m duma corda esticada; (in voice) nasalação f □ vt/i (mus) (fazer) vibrar, dedilhar

tweet /twiːt/ n pio m, pipilo m □ vi pipilar

tweezers /'twiːzəz/ npl pinça f

twelve /twelv/ a & n doze (m). ~ (o'clock) doze horas. ~fth a & n décimo segundo (m). T~fth Night véspera f de Reis

twenty /'twentɪ/ a & n vinte (m). ~ieth a & n vigésimo (m)

twice /twaɪs/ adv duas vezes

twiddle /'twɪdl/ vt/i ~ (with) (fiddle with) torcer, brincar (com). ~ one's thumbs girar os polegares

twig /twɪɡ/ n galho m, graveto m

twilight /'twaɪlaɪt/ n crepúsculo m □ a crepuscular

twin /twɪn/ n & a gêmeo (m), (P) gémeo (m) □ vt (pt twinned) (pair) emparelhar, emparceirar. ~ beds par m de camas de solteiro. ~ning n emparelhamento m

twine /twaɪn/ n guita f, cordel m □ vt/i (weave together) entrançar; (wind) enroscar(-se)

twinge /twɪndʒ/ n dor f aguda e súbita, pontada f; (fig) pontada f, (P) ferroada f

twinkle /'twɪŋkl/ vi cintilar, brilhar □ n cintilação f, brilho m

twirl /twɜːl/ vt/i (fazer) girar; (moustache) torcer

twist /twɪst/ vt torcer; (weave together) entrançar; (roll) enrolar; (distort) torcer, deturpar □ vi (rope etc) torcer-se, enrolar-se; (road) dar voltas or curvas, serpentear □ n (act of twisting) torcedura f, (P) torcedela f, (of rope) nó m; (of events) reviravolta f. ~ sb's arm (fig) forçar alguém

twit /twɪt/ n (colloq) idiota mf

twitch /twɪtʃ/ vt/i contrair(-se) □ n (tic) tique m; (jerk) puxão m

two /tuː/ a & n dois (m). in or of ~ minds indeciso. put ~ and ~ together tirar conclusões. ~-faced a de duas caras, hipócrita. ~-piece n (garment) duas-peças m invar. ~-seater n (car) carro m de dois lugares. ~-way a (of road) mão dupla

twosome /'tuːsəm/ n par m

tycoon /taɪ'kuːn/ n magnata m

tying /'taɪɪŋ/ see tie

type /taɪp/ n (example, print) tipo m; (kind) tipo m, gênero m, (P) género m; (colloq: person) cara m, (P) tipo m (colloq) □ vt/i (write) bater à máquina, datilografar, (P) dactilografar

typescript /'taɪpskrɪpt/ n texto m datilografado, (P) dactilografado

typewriter /'taɪpraɪtə(r)/ n máquina f de escrever. ~ten /-ɪtn/ a batido à máquina, datilografado, (P) dactilografado

typhoid /'taɪfɔɪd/ n ~ (fever) febre f tifóide

typhoon /taɪ'fuːn/ n tufão m

typical /'tɪpɪkl/ a típico. ~ly adv tipicamente

typify /'tɪpɪfaɪ/ vt ser o (protó)tipo de, tipificar

typing /'taɪpɪŋ/ n datilografia f, (P) dactilografia f

typist /'taɪpɪst/ n datilógrafa f, (P) dactilógrafa f

tyranny /'tɪrənɪ/ n tirania f. ~ical /tɪ'rænɪkl/ a tirânico

tyrant /'taɪərənt/ n tirano m

tyre /'taɪə(r)/ n pneu m

U

ubiquitous /juː'bɪkwɪtəs/ a ubíquo, onmipresente

udder /'ʌdə(r)/ n úbere m

UFO /'juːfəʊ/ n OVNI m

ugly /'ʌɡlɪ/ a (-ier, -iest) feio. ~iness n feiúra f, (P) fealdade f

UK abbr see United Kingdom

ulcer /'ʌlsə(r)/ n úlcera f

ulterior /ʌl'tɪərɪə(r)/ a ulterior. ~ motive razão f inconfessada, segundas intenções fpl

ultimate /'ʌltɪmət/ a último, derradeiro; (definitive) definitivo; (maximum) supremo; (basic) fundamental. ~ly adv finalmente

ultimatum /ʌltɪ'meɪtəm/ n (pl -ums) ultimato m

ultra- /'ʌltrə/ pref ultra-, super-

ultraviolet /ʌltrə'vaɪələt/ a ultravioleta

umbilical /ʌm'bɪlɪkl/ a ~ cord cordão m umbilical

umbrage /'ʌmbrɪdʒ/ n take ~ (at sth) ofender-se or melindrar-se (com alg coisa)

umbrella /ʌm'brelə/ n guardachuva m

umpire /'ʌmpaɪə(r)/ n (sport) árbitro m □ vt arbitrar

umpteen /'ʌmptiːn/ a (sl) sem conta, montes de (colloq). for the ~th time (sl) pela centésima or enésima vez

UN abbr (United Nations) ONU f

un- /ʌn/ pref não, pouco

unable /ʌn'eɪbl/ a be ~ to do ser incapaz de/não poder fazer

unabridged /ʌnə'brɪdʒd/ a (text) integral

unacceptable /ʌnək'septəbl/ a inaceitável, inadmissível

unaccompanied /ʌnə'kʌmpənɪd/ a só, desacompanhado

unaccountable /ʌnə'kaʊntəbl/ a (strange) inexplicável; (not responsible) que não tem que dar contas

unaccustomed /ʌnə'kʌstəmd/ a desacostumado. ~ to não acostumado or não habituado a

unadulterated /ʌnə'dʌltəreɪtɪd/ a (pure, sheer) puro

unaided /ʌn'eɪdɪd/ a sem ajuda, sozinho, por si só

unanimous /juː'nænɪməs/ a unânime. ~ity /-ə'nɪmətɪ/ n unanimidade f. ~ously adv unânimemente, por unanimidade

unarmed /ʌn'ɑːmd/ a desarmado, indefeso

unashamed /ʌnə'ʃeɪmd/ a desavergonhado, sem vergonha. ~ly /-ɪdlɪ/ adv sem vergonha

unassuming /ʌnə'sjuːmɪŋ/ a modesto, despretencioso

unattached /ʌnə'tætʃt/ a (person) livre

unattainable /ʌnə'teɪnəbl/ a inacessível

unattended /ʌnə'tendɪd/ a (person) desacompanhado; (car, luggage) abandonado

unattractive /ʌnə'træktɪv/ a sem atrativos, (P) atractivos; (offer) de pouco interesse

unauthorized /ʌn'ɔːθəraɪzd/ a não-autorizado, sem autorização

unavoidable /ʌnə'vɔɪdəbl/ a inevitável. ~y adv inevitavelmente

unaware /ʌnə'weə(r)/ a be ~ of desconhecer, ignorar, não ter consciência de. ~s /-eəz/ adv (unexpectedly) inesperadamente. catch sb ~s apanhar alguém desprevenido

unbalanced /ʌn'bælənst/ a (mind, person) desequilibrado

unbearable /ʌn'beərəbl/ a insuportável

unbeatable /ʌn'biːtəbl/ a imbatível. ~en a não vencido, invicto; (unsurpassed) insuperado

unbeknown(st) /ʌnbɪ'nəʊn(st)/ a ~ to (colloq) sem o conhecimento de

unbelievable /ʌnbɪ'liːvəbl/ a inacreditável, incrível

unbend /ʌn'bend/ vi (pt unbent) (relax) descontrair. ~ing a inflexível

unbiased /ʌn'baɪəst/ a imparcial

unblock /ʌn'blɒk/ vt desbloquear, desobstruir; (pipe) desentupir

unborn /ʌn'bɔːn/ a por nascer; (future) vindouro, futuro

unbounded /ʌn'baʊndɪd/ a ilimitado

unbreakable /ʌn'breɪkəbl/ a inquebrável

unbridled /ʌn'braɪdld/ a desequilibrado, (P) desenfreado

unbroken /ʌn'brəʊkən/ a (intact) intato, (P) intacto, inteiro; (continuous) ininterrupto

unburden /ʌn'bɜːdn/ vpr ~ o.s. (open one's heart) desabafar (to com)

unbutton /ʌn'bʌtn/ vt desabotoar

uncalled-for /ʌn'kɔːldfɔː(r)/ a injustificável, gratuito

uncanny /ʌn'kænɪ/ a (-ier, -iest) estranho, misterioso

unceasing /ʌn'siːsɪŋ/ a incessante

unceremonious /ʌnserɪ'məʊnɪəs/ a sem cerimônia, (P) cerimónia, brusco

uncertain /ʌn'sɜːtn/ a incerto. be ~ whether não saber ao certo se, estar indeciso quanto a. ~ty n incerteza f

unchanged /ʌn'tʃeɪndʒd/ a inalterado, sem modificação. ~ing a inalterável, imutável

uncivilized /ʌn'sɪvɪlaɪzd/ a não civilizado, bárbaro

uncle /'ʌŋkl/ n tio m

uncomfortable /ʌn'kʌmfətəbl/ a (thing) desconfortável, incômodo, (P) incómodo; (unpleasant) desagradável. feel or be ~ (uneasy) sentir-se or estar pouco à vontade

uncommon /ʌn'kɒmən/ a pouco vulgar, invulgar, fora do comum. ~ly adv invulgarmente, excepcionalmente

uncompromising /ʌn'kɒmprəmaɪzɪŋ/ a intransigente

unconcerned /ʌnkən'sɜːnd/ a (indifferent) indiferente (by a)

unconditional /ʌnkən'dɪʃənl/ a incondicional

unconscious /ʌn'kɒnʃəs/ a inconsciente (of de). ~ly adv inconscientemente. ~ness n inconsciência f

unconventional /ʌnkən'venʃənl/ a não convencional, fora do comum

uncooperative /ʌnkəʊ'ɒpərətɪv/ a

(*person*) pouco cooperativo, do contra (*colloq*)

uncork /ʌn'kɔ:k/ *vt* desarrolhar, tirar a rolha de

uncouth /ʌn'ku:θ/ *a* rude, grosseiro

uncover /ʌn'kʌvə(r)/ *vt* descobrir, revelar

unctuous /'ʌŋktʃʊəs/ *a* untuoso, gorduroso; (*fig*) melífluo

undecided /ʌndɪ'saɪdɪd/ *a* (*irresolute*) indeciso; (*not settled*) por decidir, pendente

undeniable /ʌndɪ'naɪəbl/ *a* inegável, incontestável

under /'ʌndə(r)/ *prep* debaixo de, sob; (*less than*) com menos de; (*according to*) conforme, segundo □ *adv* por baixo, debaixo. ~ **age** menor de idade. ~ **way** em preparo

under- /'ʌndə(r)/ *pref* sub-

undercarriage /'ʌndəkærɪdʒ/ *n* (*aviat*) trem *m* de aterrissagem, (*P*) trem *m* de aterragem

underclothes /'ʌndəkləʊðz/ *npl* see underwear

undercoat /'ʌndəkəʊt/ *n* (*of paint*) primeira mão *f*, (*P*) primeira demão *f*

undercover /ʌndə'kʌvə(r)/ *a* (*agent, operation*) secreto

undercurrent /'ʌndəkʌrənt/ *n* corrente *f* subterrânea; (*fig*) filão *m* (*fig*), tendência *f* oculta

undercut /ʌndə'kʌt/ *vt* (*pt* undercut, *pres p* undercutting) (*comm*) vender a preços mais baixos que

underdeveloped /ʌndədɪ'veləpt/ *a* atrofiado; (*country*) subdesenvolvido

underdog /ʌndə'dɒg/ *n* desprotegido *m*, o mais fraco (*colloq*)

underdone /'ʌndədʌn/ *a* (*of meat*) mal passado

underestimate /ʌndə'restɪmeɪt/ *vt* subestimar, não dar o devido valor a

underfed /ʌndə'fed/ *a* subalimentado, subnutrido

underfoot /ʌndə'fʊt/ *adv* debaixo dos pés; (*on the ground*) no chão

undergo /ʌndə'gəʊ/ *vt* (*pt* -went, *pp* -gone) (*be subjected to*) sofrer; (*treatment*) ser submetido a

undergraduate /ʌndə'grædʒʊət/ *n* estudante *mf* universitário

underground[1] /ʌndə'graʊnd/ *adv* debaixo da terra; (*fig: secretly*) clandestinamente

underground[2] /'ʌndəgraʊnd/ *a* subterrâneo; (*fig: secret*) clandestino □ *n* (*rail*) metro(politano) *m*

undergrowth /'ʌndəgrəʊθ/ *n* mato *m*

underhand /'ʌndəhænd/ *a* (*deceitful*) sonso, dissimulado

underlie /ʌndə'laɪ/ *vt* (*pt* -lay, *pp* -lain, *pres p* -lying) estar por baixo de. ~**lying** *a* subjacente

underline /ʌndə'laɪn/ *vt* sublinhar

undermine /ʌndə'maɪn/ *vt* minar, solapar

underneath /ʌndə'ni:θ/ *prep* sob, debaixo de, por baixo de □ *adv* abaixo, em baixo, por baixo

underpaid /ʌndə'peɪd/ *a* mal pago

underpants /'ʌndəpænts/ *npl* (*man's*) cuecas *fpl*

underpass /'ʌndəpa:s/ *n* (*for cars, people*) passagem *f* inferior

underprivileged /ʌndə'prɪvɪlɪdʒd/ *a* desfavorecido

underrate /ʌndə'reɪt/ *vt* subestimar, depreciar

underside /'ʌndəsaɪd/ *n* lado *m* inferior, base *f*

underskirt /'ʌndəskɜ:t/ *n* anágua *f*

understand /ʌndə'stænd/ *vt/i* (*pt* -stood) compreender, entender. ~**able** *a* compreensível. ~**ing** *a* compreensivo □ *n* compreensão *f*; (*agreement*) acordo *m*, entendimento *m*

understatement /'ʌndəsteɪtmənt/ *n* versão *f* atenuada da verdade, litotes *f*

understudy /'ʌndəstʌdɪ/ *n* substituto *m*

undertak|e /ʌndə'teɪk/ *vt* (*pt* -took, *pp* -taken) empreender; (*responsibility*) assumir. ~**e** to encarregar-se de. ~**ing** *n* (*task*) empreendimento *m*; (*promise*) compromisso *m*

undertaker /'ʌndəteɪkə(r)/ *n* agente *m* funerário, papa-defuntos *m* (*colloq*)

undertone /'ʌndətəʊn/ *n* in an ~ a meia voz

undervalue /ʌndə'vælju:/ *vt* avaliar por baixo, subestimar

underwater /ʌndə'wɔ:tə(r)/ *a* submarino □ *adv* debaixo de água

underwear /'ʌndəweə(r)/ *n* roupa *f* interior or de baixo

underweight /'ʌndəweɪt/ *a* be ~ estar com o peso abaixo do normal, ter peso a menos

underwent /ʌndə'went/ *see* undergo

underworld /'ʌndəwɜ:ld/ *n* (*of crime*) submundo *m*, bas-fonds *mpl*

underwriter /'ʌndəraɪtə(r)/ *n* segurador *m*; (*marine*) underwriter *m*

undeserved /ʌndɪ'zɜ:vd/ *a* imerecido, injusto

undesirable /ʌndɪ'zaɪərəbl/ *a* indesejável, inconveniente

undies /'ʌndɪz/ *npl* (*colloq*) roupa *f* de baixo *or* interior

undignified /ʌn'dɪgnɪfaɪd/ *a* pouco digno, sem dignidade

undisputed /ʌndɪ'spju:tɪd/ *a* incontestado

undo /ʌn'du:/ *vt* (*pt* -did, *pp* -done /dʌn/) desfazer; (*knot*) desfazer, desatar; (*coat, button*) abrir. leave ~ nenão fazer, deixar por fazer. ~ing *n* desgraça *f*, ruína *f*

undoubted /ʌn'dautɪd/ *a* indubitável. ~ly *adv* indubitavelmente

undress /ʌn'dres/ *vt/i* despir(-se). get ~ed despir-se

undue /ʌn'dju:/ *a* excessivo, indevido. ~ly *adv* excessivamente, indevidamente

undulate /'ʌndjʊleɪt/ *vi* ondular

undying /ʌn'daɪɪŋ/ *a* eterno, perene

unearth /ʌn'ɜ:θ/ *vt* desenterrar; (*fig*) descobrir

unearthly /ʌn'ɜ:θlɪ/ *a* sobrenatural, misterioso. ~ **hour** (*colloq*) hora *f* absurda *or* inconveniente

uneasy /ʌn'i:zɪ/ *a* (*ill at ease*) pouco à vontade; (*worried*) preocupado

uneconomic /ʌni:kə'nɒmɪk/ *a* antieconômico. ~al *a* antieconômico

uneducated /ʌn'edʒʊkeɪtɪd/ *a* (*person*) inculto, sem instrução

unemploy|ed /ʌnɪm'plɔɪd/ *a* desempregado. ~ment *n* desemprego *m*. ~ment benefit auxílio-desemprego *m*

unending /ʌn'endɪŋ/ *a* interminável, sem fim

unequal /ʌn'i:kwəl/ *a* desigual. ~led *a* sem igual, inigualável

unequivocal /ʌnɪ'kwɪvəkl/ *a* inequívoco, claro

uneven /ʌn'i:vn/ *a* desigual, irregular

unexpected /ʌnɪk'spektɪd/ *a* inesperado. ~ly *a* inesperadamente

unfair /ʌn'feə(r)/ *a* injusto (to com). ~ness *n* injustiça *f*

unfaithful /ʌn'feɪθfl/ *a* infiel

unfamiliar /ʌnfə'mɪlɪə(r)/ *a* estranho, desconhecido. be ~ with desconhecer, não conhecer, não estar familiarizado com

unfashionable /ʌn'fæʃənəbl/ *a* fora de moda

unfasten /ʌn'fɑ:sn/ *vt* (*knot*) desatar, soltar; (*button*) abrir

unfavourable /ʌn'feɪvərəbl/ *a* desfavorável

unfeeling /ʌn'fi:lɪŋ/ *a* insensível

unfinished /ʌn'fɪnɪʃt/ *a* incompleto, inacabado

unfit /ʌn'fɪt/ *a* sem preparo físico, fora de forma; (*unsuitable*) impróprio (for para)

unfold /ʌn'fəʊld/ *vt* desdobrar; (*expose*) expor, revelar □ *vi* desenrolar-se

unforeseen /ʌnfɔ:'si:n/ *a* imprevisto, inesperado

unforgettable /ʌnfə'getəbl/ *a* inesquecível

unforgivable /ʌnfə'gɪvəbl/ *a* imperdoável, indesculpável

unfortunate /ʌn'fɔ:tʃənət/ *a* (*unlucky*) infeliz; (*regrettable*) lamen-

tável. it was very ~ that foi uma pena que ~ly *adv* infelizmente

unfounded /ʌn'faʊndɪd/ *a* (*rumour etc*) infundado, sem fundamento

unfriendly /ʌn'frendlɪ/ *a* pouco amável, antipático, frio

unfurnished /ʌn'fɜ:nɪʃt/ *a* sem mobília

ungainly /ʌn'geɪnlɪ/ *a* desajeitado, desgracioso

ungodly /ʌn'gɒdlɪ/ *a* ímpio. ~ **hour** (*colloq*) hora *f* absurda, às altas horas (*colloq*)

ungrateful /ʌn'greɪtfl/ *a* ingrato

unhapp|y /ʌn'hæpɪ/ *a* (-ier, -iest) infeliz, triste; (*not pleased*) descontente, pouco contente (with com). ~ily *adv* infelizmente. ~iness *n* infelicidade *f*, tristeza *f*

unharmed /ʌn'hɑ:md/ *a* incólume, são e salvo, ileso

unhealthy /ʌn'helθɪ/ *a* (-ier, -iest) (*climate etc*) doentio, insalubre; (*person*) adoentado, com pouca saúde

unheard-of /ʌn'hɜ:dɒv/ *a* inaudito, sem precedentes

unhinge /ʌn'hɪndʒ/ *vt* (*person, mind*) desequilibrar

unholy /ʌn'həʊlɪ/ *a* (-ier, -iest) (*person, act etc*) ímpio; (*colloq: great*) incrível, espantoso

unhook /ʌn'hʊk/ *vt* desenganchar; (*dress*) despertar

unhoped /ʌn'həʊpt/ *a* ~ for inesperado

unhurt /ʌn'hɜ:t/ *a* ileso, incólume

unicorn /'ju:nɪkɔ:n/ *n* unicórnio *m*

uniform /'ju:nɪfɔ:m/ *n* uniforme *m* □ *a* uniforme, sempre igual. ~ity /'fɔ:mətɪ/ *n* uniformidade *f*. ~ly *adv* uniformemente

unif|y /'ju:nɪfaɪ/ *vt* unificar. ~ication /-ɪ'keɪʃn/ *n* unificação *f*

unilateral /ju:nɪ'lætrəl/ *a* unilateral

unimaginable /ʌnɪ'mædʒɪnəbl/ *a* inimaginável

unimportant /ʌnɪm'pɔ:tnt/ *a* sem importância, insignificante

uninhabited /ʌnɪn'hæbɪtɪd/ *a* desabitado

unintentional /ʌnɪn'tenʃənl/ *a* involuntário, não proposital

uninterest|ed /ʌn'ɪntrəstɪd/ *a* desinteressado (in em), indiferente (in a). ~ing *a* desinteressante, sem interesse

union /'ju:nɪən/ *n* união *f*; (*trade union*) sindicato *m*. ~ist *n* sindicalista *mf*; (*pol*) unionista *mf*. U~ **Jack** bandeira *f* britânica

unique /ju:'ni:k/ *a* único, sem igual

unisex /'ju:nɪseks/ *a* unisexo

unison /'ju:nɪsn/ *n* in ~ em uníssono

unit /'ju:nɪt/ n unidade f; (of furniture) peça f, unidade f, (P) módulo m

unite /ju:'naɪt/ vt/i unir(-se). U~d Kingdom n Reino m Unido. U~d Nations (Organization) n Organização f das Nações Unidas. U~ States (of America) Estados mpl Unidos (da América)

unity /'ju:nətɪ/ n unidade f; (fig: harmony) união f

universal /ju:nɪ'vɜ:sl/ a universal

universe /'ju:nɪvɜ:s/ n universo m

university /ju:nɪ'vɜ:sətɪ/ n universidade f □ a universitário; (student, teacher) universitário, da universidade

unjust /ʌn'dʒʌst/ a injusto

unkempt /ʌn'kempt/ a desmazelado, desleixado; (of hair) despenteado, desgrenhado

unkind /ʌn'kaɪnd/ a desagradável, duro. ~ly adv mal

unknowingly /ʌn'nəʊɪŋlɪ/ adv sem saber, inconscientemente

unknown /ʌn'nəʊn/ a desconhecido □ n the ~ o desconhecido

unleaded /ʌn'ledɪd/ a sem chumbo

unless /ʌn'les/ conj a não ser que, a menos que, salvo se, se não

unlike /ʌn'laɪk/ a diferente □ prep ao contrário de

unlikely /ʌn'laɪklɪ/ a improvável

unlimited /ʌn'lɪmɪtɪd/ a ilimitado

unload /ʌn'ləʊd/ vt descarregar

unlock /ʌn'lɒk/ vt abrir (com chave)

unluck|y /ʌn'lʌkɪ/ a (-ier, -iest) infeliz, sem sorte; (number) que dá azar. be ~y ter pouca sorte. ~ily adv infelizmente

unmarried /ʌn'mærɪd/ a solteiro, celibatário

unmask /ʌn'ma:sk/ vt desmascarar

unmistakable /ʌnmɪs'teɪkəbl/ a (voice, person) inconfundível; (clear) claro, inequívoco

unmitigated /ʌn'mɪtɪgeɪtɪd/ a (absolute) completo, absoluto

unmoved /ʌn'mu:vd/ a impassível; (indifferent) indiferente (by a), insensível (by a)

unnatural /ʌn'nætʃrəl/ a que não é natural; (wicked) desnaturado

unnecessary /ʌn'nesəsərɪ/ a desnecessário; (superfluous) supérfluo, dispensável

unnerve /ʌn'nɜ:v/ vt desencorajar, desmoralizar, intimidar

unnoticed /ʌn'nəʊtɪst/ a despercebido

unobtrusive /ʌnəb'tru:sɪv/ a discreto

unofficial /ʌnə'fɪʃl/ a oficioso, que não é oficial; (strike) ilegal, inautorizado

unorthodox /ʌn'ɔ:θədɒks/ a pouco ortodoxo, não ortodoxo

unpack /ʌn'pæk/ vt (suitcase etc) desfazer; (contents) desembalar, desempacotar □ vi desfazer a mala

unpaid /ʌn'peɪd/ a não remunerado; (bill) a pagar

unpalatable /ʌn'pælətəbl/ a (food, fact etc) desagradável, intragável

unparalleled /ʌn'pærəleld/ a sem paralelo, incomparável

unpleasant /ʌn'pleznt/ a desagradável (to com); (person) antipático

unplug /ʌn'plʌg/ vt (pt -plugged) (electr) desligar a tomada, (P) tirar a ficha da tomada

unpopular /ʌn'pɒpjʊlə(r)/ a impopular

unprecedented /ʌn'presɪdentɪd/ a sem precedentes, inaudito, nunca visto

unpredictable /ʌnprə'dɪktəbl/ a imprevisível

unprepared /ʌnprɪ'peəd/ a sem preparação, improvisado; (person) desprevenido

unpretentious /ʌnprɪ'tenʃəs/ a despretencioso, sem pretensões

unprincipled /ʌn'prɪnsəpld/ a sem princípios, sem escrúpulos

unprofessional /ʌnprə'feʃənl/ a (work) de amador; (conduct) sem consciência profissional

unprofitable /ʌn'prɒfɪtəbl/ a não lucrativo

unqualified /ʌn'kwɒlɪfaɪd/ a sem habilitações; (success etc) total, absoluto. be ~ to não estar habilitado para

unquestionable /ʌn'kwestʃənəbl/ a incontestável, indiscutível

unravel /ʌn'rævl/ vt (pt unravelled) desenredar, desemaranhar; (knitting) desmanchar

unreal /ʌn'rɪəl/ a irreal

unreasonable /ʌn'ri:znəbl/ a pouco razoável, disparatado; (excessive) excessivo

unrecognizable /ʌn'rekəgnaɪzəbl/ a irreconhecível

unrelated /ʌnrɪ'leɪtɪd/ a (facts) desconexo, sem relação (to com); (people) não aparentado (to com)

unreliable /ʌnrɪ'laɪəbl/ a que não é de confiança

unremitting /ʌnrɪ'mɪtɪŋ/ a incessante, infatigável

unreservedly /ʌnrɪ'zɜ:vɪdlɪ/ adv sem reservas

unrest /ʌn'rest/ n agitação f, distúrbios mpl

unrivalled /ʌn'raɪvld/ a sem igual, incomparável

unroll /ʌn'rəʊl/ vt desenrolar

unruffled /ʌn'rʌfld/ a calmo, tranqüilo, imperturbável

unruly /ʌn'ru:lɪ/ a indisciplinado, turbulento

unsafe /ʌnˈseɪf/ a (*dangerous*) que não é seguro, perigoso; (*person*) em perigo

unsaid /ʌnˈsed/ a leave ~ não mencionar, não dizer, deixar algo por dizer

unsatisfactory /ʌnsætɪsˈfæktərɪ/ a insatisfatório, pouco satisfatório

unsavoury /ʌnˈseɪvərɪ/ a desagradável, repugnante

unscathed /ʌnˈskeɪðd/ a ileso, incólume

unscrew /ʌnˈskruː/ vt desenroscar, desparafusar

unscrupulous /ʌnˈskruːpjʊləs/ a sem escrúpulos, pouco escrupuloso, sem consciência

unseemly /ʌnˈsiːmlɪ/ a inconveniente, indecoroso, impróprio

unsettle /ʌnˈsetl/ vt perturbar, agitar. ~d a perturbado; (*weather*) instável, variável; (*bill*) não saldado

unshakeable /ʌnˈʃeɪkəbl/ a (*person, belief etc*) inabalável

unshaven /ʌnˈʃeɪvn/ a com a barba por fazer, por barbear

unsightly /ʌnˈsaɪtlɪ/ a feio

unskilled /ʌnˈskɪld/ a inexperiente; (*work, worker*) não especializado; (*labour*) mão-de-obra *f* não especializada

unsociable /ʌnˈsəʊʃəbl/ a insociável, misantropo

unsophisticated /ʌnsəˈfɪstɪkeɪtɪd/ a insofisticado, simples

unsound /ʌnˈsaʊnd/ a pouco sólido. of ~ mind (*jur*) não estar em plena posse das suas faculdades mentais (*jur*)

unspeakable /ʌnˈspiːkəbl/ a indescritível; (*bad*) inqualificável

unspecified /ʌnˈspesɪfaɪd/ a não especificado, indeterminado

unstable /ʌnˈsteɪbl/ a instável

unsteady /ʌnˈstedɪ/ a (*step*) vacilante, incerto; (*ladder*) instável; (*hand*) pouco firme

unstuck /ʌnˈstʌk/ a (*not stuck*) descolado. come ~ (*colloq: fail*) falhar

unsuccessful /ʌnsəkˈsesfl/ a (*candidate*) mal sucedido; (*attempt*) malogrado, fracassado. be ~ não ter êxito. ~ly adv em vão

unsuit|able /ʌnˈs(j)uːtəbl/ a impróprio, pouco apropriado, inadequado (for para). ~ed a inadequado (to para)

unsure /ʌnˈʃʊə(r)/ a incerto

unsuspecting /ʌnsəˈspektɪŋ/ a sem desconfiar de nada, insuspeitado

untangle /ʌnˈtæŋgl/ vt desemaranhar, desenredar

unthinkable /ʌnˈθɪŋkəbl/ a impensável, inconcebível

untid|y /ʌnˈtaɪdɪ/ a (-ier, -iest) (*room, desk etc*) desarrumado; (*appearance*) desleixado, desmazelado; (*hair*) despenteado. ~ily adv sem cuidado. ~iness n desordem *f*; (*of appearance*) desmazelo *m*

untie /ʌnˈtaɪ/ vt (*knot, parcel*) desatar, desfazer; (*person*) desamarrar

until /ənˈtɪl/ prep até. not ~ não antes de □ conj até que

untimely /ʌnˈtaɪmlɪ/ a inoportuno, intempestivo; (*death*) prematuro

untold /ʌnˈtəʊld/ a incalculável

untoward /ʌntəˈwɔːd/ a inconveniente, desagradável

untrue /ʌnˈtruː/ a falso

unused¹ /ʌnˈjuːzd/ a (*new*) novo, por usar; (*not in use*) não utilizado

unused² /ʌnˈjuːst/ a ~ to não habituado a, não acostumado a

unusual /ʌnˈjuːʒʊəl/ a insólito, fora do comum. ~ly adv excepcionalmente

unveil /ʌnˈveɪl/ vt descobrir; (*statue, portrait etc*) desvelar

unwanted /ʌnˈwɒntɪd/ a (*useless*) que já não serve; (*child*) indesejado

unwarranted /ʌnˈwɒrəntɪd/ a injustificado

unwelcome /ʌnˈwelkəm/ a desagradável; (*guest*) indesejável

unwell /ʌnˈwel/ a indisposto

unwieldy /ʌnˈwiːldɪ/ a difícil de manejar, pouco jeitoso

unwilling /ʌnˈwɪlɪŋ/ a relutante (to em), pouco disposto (to a)

unwind /ʌnˈwaɪnd/ vt/i (pt unwound /ʌnˈwaʊnd/) desenrolar(-se); (*colloq: relax*) descontrair(-se)

unwise /ʌnˈwaɪz/ a imprudente, insensato

unwittingly /ʌnˈwɪtɪŋlɪ/ adv sem querer

unworthy /ʌnˈwɜːðɪ/ a indigno

unwrap /ʌnˈræp/ vt (pt unwrapped) desembrulhar, abrir, desfazer

unwritten /ʌnˈrɪtn/ a (*agreement*) verbal, tácito

up /ʌp/ adv (*to higher place*) cima, para cima, para o alto; (*in higher place*) em cima, no alto; (*out of bed*) acordado, de pé; (*up and dressed*) pronto; (*finished*) acabado; (*sun*) alto □ prep no cimo de, em cima de, no alto de. ~ the street/river/etc pela rua/pelo rio/etc acima □ vt (pt upped) (*increase*) aumentar. be ~ against defrontar, enfrentar. be ~ in (*colloq*) saber. be ~ to (do) estar fazendo; (*plot*) estar tramando; (*task*) estar à altura de. feel ~ to doing (*able*) sentir-se capaz de fazer. it is ~ to you depende de você. come or go ~ subir. have ~s and downs (*fig*) ter (os seus) altos e baixos. walk ~ and down andar dum lado para o outro or para a frente e para trás. ~-and-coming *a* prometedor. ~-market *a* requintado, fino

upbringing /'ʌpbrɪŋɪŋ/ *n* educação *f*

update /ʌp'deɪt/ *vt* atualizar, (P) actualizar

upheaval /ʌp'hiːvl/ *n* pandemônio *m*, (P) pandemónio *m*, revolução *f* (*fig*); (*social, political*) convulsão *f*

uphill /'ʌphɪl/ *a* ladeira acima, ascendente; (*fig: difficult*) árduo □ *adv* /ʌp'hɪl/ go ~ subir

uphold /ʌp'həʊld/ *vt* (*pt* upheld) sustentar, manter, apoiar

upholster /ʌp'həʊlstə(r)/ *vt* estofar. ~y *n* estofados *mpl*, (P) estofo(s) *m* (*pl*)

upkeep /'ʌpkiːp/ *n* manutenção *f*

upon /ə'pɒn/ *prep* sobre

upper /'ʌpə(r)/ *a* superior □ *n* (*of shoe*) gáspea *f*. have the ~ hand estar por cima, estar em posição de superioridade. ~ class aristocracia *f*. ~most *a* (*highest*) o mais alto, superior

upright /'ʌpraɪt/ *a* vertical; (*honourable*) honesto, honrado, (P) recto

uprising /'ʌpraɪzɪŋ/ *n* insurreição *f*, sublevação *f*, levantamento *m*

uproar /'ʌprɔː(r)/ *n* tumulto *m*, alvoroço *m*

uproot /ʌp'ruːt/ *vt* desenraizar; (*fig*) erradicar, desarraigar

upset[1] /ʌp'set/ *vt* (*pt* upset, *pres p* upsetting) (*overturn*) entornar, virar; (*plan*) contrariar, transtornar; (*stomach*) desarranjar; (*person*) contrariar, transtornar, incomodar □ *a* aborrecido

upset[2] /'ʌpset/ *n* transtorno *m*; (*of stomach*) indisposição *f*; (*distress*) choque *m*

upshot /'ʌpʃɒt/ *n* resultado *m*

upside-down /ʌpsaɪd'daʊn/ *adv* (*lit & fig*) ao contrário, de pernas para o ar

upstairs /ʌp'steəz/ *adv* (*at/to*) em/para cima, no/para o andar de cima □ *a* /'ʌpsteəz/ (*flat etc*) de cima, do andar de cima

upstart /'ʌpstɑːt/ *n* arrivista *mf*

upstream /ʌp'striːm/ *adv* rio acima, contra a corrente

upsurge /'ʌpsɜːdʒ/ *n* recrudescência *f*, recrudescimento *m*; (*of anger*) acesso *m*, ataque *m*

uptake /'ʌpteɪk/ *n* be quick on the ~ pegar rapidamente as coisas; (*fig*) ser de compreensão rápida, ser vivo

up-to-date /ʌptə'deɪt/ *a* moderno, atualizado, (P) actualizado

upturn /'ʌptɜːn/ *n* melhoria *f*

upward /'ʌpwəd/ *a* ascendente, voltado para cima. ~s *adv* para cima

uranium /jʊ'remɪəm/ *n* urânio *m*

urban /'ɜːbən/ *a* urbano

urbane /ɜː'beɪn/ *a* delicado, cortês, urbano

urge /ɜːdʒ/ *vt* aconselhar vivamente (to a) □ *n* (*strong desire*) grande vontade *f*. ~ on (*impel*) incitar

urgen|**t** /'ɜːdʒənt/ *a* urgente. be ~t urgir. ~cy *n* urgência *f*

urinal /jʊə'raɪnl/ *n* urinol *m*

urin|**e** /'jʊərɪn/ *n* urina *f*. ~ate *vi* urinar

urn /ɜːn/ *n* urna *f*; (*for tea, coffee*) espécie *f* de samovar

us /ʌs; *unstressed* /əs/ *pron* nos; (*after preps*) nós. with ~ conosco. he knows ~ ele nos conhece

US *abbr* United States

USA *abbr* United States of America

usable /'juːzəbl/ *a* utilizável

usage /'juːzɪdʒ/ *n* uso *m*

use[1] /juːz/ *vt* usar, utilizar, servir-se de; (*exploit*) servir-se de; (*consume*) gastar, usar, consumir. ~ up esgotar, consumir. ~r /-ə(r)/ *n* usuário *m*, (P) utente *mf*. ~r-friendly *a* fácil de usar

use[2] /juːs/ *n* uso *m*, emprego *m*. in ~ em uso. it is no ~ shouting/*etc* não serve de nada *or* não adianta gritar/*etc*. make ~ of servir-se de. of ~ útil

used[1] /juːzd/ *a* (*second-hand*) usado

used[2] /juːst/ *pt* he ~ to ele costumava, ele tinha por costume *or* hábito □ *a* ~ to acostumado a, habituado a

use|**ful** /'juːsfl/ *a* útil. ~less *a* inútil; (*person*) incompetente

usher /'ʌʃə(r)/ *n* vagalume *m*, (P) arrumador *m* □ *vt* ~ in mandar entrar. ~ette *n* vagalume *m*, (P) arrumadora *f*

usual /'juːʒəl/ *a* usual, habitual, normal. as ~ como de costume, como habitualmente. at the ~ time na hora de costume, (P) à(s) hora(s) de costume. ~ly *adv* habitualmente, normalmente

USSR *abbr* URSS

usurp /juː'zɜːp/ *vt* usurpar

utensil /juː'tensl/ *n* utensílio *m*

uterus /'juːtərəs/ *n* útero *m*

utilitarian /juːtɪlɪ'teərɪən/ *a* utilitário

utility /juː'tɪlətɪ/ *n* utilidade *f*. (public) ~ serviço *m* público. ~ room área *f* de serviço (para as máquinas de lavar a roupa e a louça)

utilize /'juːtɪlaɪz/ *vt* utilizar

utmost /'ʌtməʊst/ *a* (*furthest, most intense*) extremo. the ~ care/*etc* (*greatest*) o maior cuidado/*etc* □ *n* do one's ~ fazer todo o possível

utter[1] /'ʌtə(r)/ *a* completo, absoluto. ~**ly** *adv* completamente

utter[2] /'ʌtə(r)/ *vt* proferir; (*sigh, shout*) dar. ~**ance** *n* expressão *f*

U-turn /'ju:tɜ:n/ *n* retorno *m*

V

vacan|t /'veɪkənt/ *a* (*post, room, look*) vago; (*mind*) vazio; (*seat, space, time*) desocupado, livre. ~**cy** *n* (*post*) vaga *f*; (*room in hotel*) vago *m*

vacate /və'keɪt/ *vt* vagar, deixar vago

vacation /və'keɪʃn/ *n* férias *fpl*

vaccinat|e /'væksmeɪt/ *vt* vacinar. ~**ion** /-'neɪʃn/ *n* vacinação *f*

vaccine /'væksi:n/ *n* vacina *f*

vacuum /'vækjʊəm/ *n* (*pl* -**cuums** *or* -**cua**) vácuo *m*, vazio *m*. ~ **flask** garrafa *f* térmica, (*P*) termo(s) *m*. ~ **cleaner** aspirador *m* de pó

vagina /və'dʒaɪnə/ *n* vagina *f*

vagrant /'veɪɡrənt/ *n* vadio *m*, vagabundo *m*

vague /veɪɡ/ *a* (-**er**, -**est**) vago; (*outline*) impreciso. **be** ~ **about** ser vago acerca de, não precisar. ~**ly** *adv* vagamente

vain /veɪn/ *a* (-**er**, -**est**) (*conceited*) vaidoso; (*useless*) vão, inútil; (*fruitless*) infrutífero. **in** ~ em vão. ~**ly** *adv* em vão

valentine /'væləntaɪn/ *n* (*card*) cartão *m* do dia de São Valentim

valet /'vælɪt, 'væleɪ/ *n* (*manservant*) criado *m* de quarto; (*of hotel*) camareiro *m* □ *vt* (*car*) lavar e limpar o interior

valiant /'væliənt/ *a* corajoso, valente

valid /'vælɪd/ *a* válido. ~**ity** /və'lɪdəti/ *n* validade *f*

validate /'vælɪdeɪt/ *vt* validar, confirmar, ratificar

valley /'væli/ *n* vale *m*

valuable /'væljʊəbl/ *a* (*object*) valioso, de valor; (*help, time etc*) precioso. ~**s** *npl* objetos *mpl*, (*P*) objectos *mpl* de valor

valuation /væljʊ'eɪʃn/ *n* avaliação *f*

value /'vælju:/ *n* valor *m* □ *vt* avaliar; (*cherish*) dar valor a. ~ **added tax** imposto *m* de valor adicional, (*P*) acrescentado. ~**r** /-ə(r)/ *n* avaliador *m*

valve /vælv/ *n* (*anat, techn, of car tyre*) válvula *f*; (*of bicycle tyre*) pipo *m*; (*of radio*) lâmpada *f*, válvula *f*

vampire /'væmpaɪə(r)/ *n* vampiro *m*

van /væn/ *n* (*large*) camião *m*; (*small*) camionete *f*, comercial *m*; (*milkman's, baker's etc*) camionete *f*; (*rail*) bagageiro *m*, (*P*) furgão *m*

vandal /'vændl/ *n* vândalo *m*. ~**ism** /-əlɪzəm/ *n* vandalismo *m*

vandalize /'vændəlaɪz/ *vt* destruir, estragar

vanguard /'vænɡɑ:d/ *n* vanguarda *f*

vanilla /və'nɪlə/ *n* baunilha *f*

vanish /'vænɪʃ/ *vi* desaparecer, sumir-se, desvanecer-se

vanity /'vænəti/ *n* vaidade *f*. ~ **case** bolsa *f* de maquilagem

vantage-point /'vɑ:ntɪdʒpɔɪnt/ *n* (bom) ponto *m* de observação

vapour /'veɪpə(r)/ *n* vapor *m*; (*mist*) bruma *f*

vari|able /'veərɪəbl/ *a* variável. ~**ation** /-'eɪʃn/ *n* variação *f*. ~**ed** /-ɪd/ *a* variado

variance /'veərɪəns/ *n* **at** ~ em desacordo (with com)

variant /'veərɪənt/ *a* diverso, diferente □ *n* variante *f*

varicose /'værɪkəʊs/ *a* ~ **veins** varizes *fpl*

variety /və'raɪəti/ *n* variedade *f*; (*entertainment*) variedades *fpl*

various /'veərɪəs/ *a* vários, diversos, variados

varnish /'vɑ:nɪʃ/ *n* verniz *m* □ *vt* envernizar; (*nails*) pintar

vary /'veərɪ/ *vt/i* variar. ~**ing** *a* variado

vase /vɑ:z/ *n* vaso *m*, jarra *f*

vast /vɑ:st/ *a* vasto, imenso. ~**ly** *adv* imensamente, infinitamente. ~**ness** *n* vastidão *f*, imensidão *f*, imensidade *f*

vat /væt/ *n* tonel *m*, dorna *f*, cuba *f*

VAT /vi:eɪ'ti:, væt/ *abbr* ICM *m*, (*P*) IVA *m*

vault[1] /vɔ:lt/ *n* (*roof*) abóbada *f*; (*in bank*) casa-forte *f*; (*tomb*) cripta *f*; (*cellar*) adega *f*

vault[2] /vɔ:lt/ *vt/i* saltar □ *n* salto *m*

vaunt /vɔ:nt/ *vt/i* gabar(-se), ufanar(-se) (de), vangloriar(-se)

VD *abbr see* **venereal disease**

VDU *abbr see* **visual display unit**

veal /vi:l/ *n* (*meat*) vitela *f*

veer /vɪə(r)/ *vi* virar, mudar de direção, (*P*) direcção

vegan /'vi:ɡən/ *a* & *n* vegetariano (*m*) estrito

vegetable /'vedʒɪtəbl/ *n* hortaliça *f*, legume *m* □ *a* vegetal

vegetarian /vedʒɪ'teərɪən/ *a* & *n* vegetariano (*m*)

vegetate /'vedʒɪteɪt/ *vi* vegetar

vegetation /vedʒɪ'teɪʃn/ *n* vegetação *f*

vehement /'vi:əmənt/ *a* veemente. ~**ly** *adv* veementemente

vehicle /'vi:ɪkl/ *n* veículo *m*

veil /veɪl/ *n* véu *m* □ *vt* velar, cobrir com véu; (*fig*) esconder, disfarçar

vein /veɪn/ *n* (*in body; mood*) veia *f*; (*in rock*) veio *m*, filão *m*; (*of leaf*) nervura *f*

velocity /vɪˈlɒsətɪ/ n velocidade f
velvet /ˈvelvɪt/ n veludo m. ~y a ave-
ludado
vendetta /venˈdetə/ n vendeta f
vending-machine /ˈvendɪŋməʃiːn/ n
vendedora f automática, (P) máquina
f de distribuição
vendor /ˈvendə(r)/ n vendedor m.
street ~ vendedor m ambulante
veneer /vəˈnɪə(r)/ n folheado m; (fig)
fachada f, máscara f
venerable /ˈvenərəbl/ a venerável
venereal /vəˈnɪərɪəl/ a venéreo. ~
disease doença f venérea
venetian /vəˈniːʃn/ a ~ blinds persiana f
Venezuela /venɪzˈweɪlə/ n Venezuela
f. ~n a & n venezuelano (m)
vengeance /ˈvendʒəns/ n vingança.
with a ~ furiosamente, em excesso,
com mais força do que se pretende
venison /ˈvenɪzn/ n carne f de veado
venom /ˈvenəm/ n veneno m. ~ous
/ˈvenəməs/ a venenoso
vent¹ /vent/ n (in coat) abertura f
vent² /vent/ n (hole) orifício m, abertura f; (for air) respiradouro m □ vt
(anger) descarregar (on para cima
de). give ~ to (fig) desabafar, dar
vazão a
ventilat|e /ˈventɪleɪt/ vt ventilar.
~ion /-ˈleɪʃn/ n ventilação f. ~or n
ventilador m
ventriloquist /venˈtrɪləkwɪst/ n ven-
tríloquo m
venture /ˈventʃə(r)/ n empreendimento m arriscado, aventura f □ vt/i
arriscar(-se)
venue /ˈvenjuː/ n porto m de encontro
veranda /vəˈrændə/ n varanda f
verb /vɜːb/ n verbo m
verbal /ˈvɜːbl/ a verbal; (literal) literal
verbatim /vɜːˈbeɪtɪm/ adv literalmente, palavra por palavra
verbose /vɜːˈbəʊs/ a palavroso, prolixo
verdict /ˈvɜːdɪkt/ n veredicto m;
(opinion) opinião f
verge /vɜːdʒ/ n beira f, borda f □ vi ~
on estar à beira de. on the ~ of
doing prestes a fazer
verify /ˈverɪfaɪ/ vt verificar
veritable /ˈverɪtəbl/ a autêntico, verdadeiro
vermicelli /vɜːmɪˈselɪ/ n aletria f
vermin /ˈvɜːmɪn/ n animais mpl noci-
vos; (lice, fleas etc) parasitas mpl
vermouth /ˈvɜːməθ/ n vermute m
vernacular /vəˈnækjʊlə(r)/ n vernáculo m; (dialect) dialeto m, (P) dialecto m
versatil|e /ˈvɜːsətaɪl/ a versátil; (tool)
que serve para vários fins. ~ity
/-ˈtɪlətɪ/ n versatilidade f

verse /vɜːs/ n (poetry) verso m, poesia
f; (stanza) estrofe f; (of Bible)
versículo m
versed /vɜːst/ a ~ in versado em, conhecedor de
version /ˈvɜːʃn/ n versão f
versus /ˈvɜːsəs/ prep contra
vertebra /ˈvɜːtɪbrə/ n (pl -brae /-briː/)
vértebra f
vertical /ˈvɜːtɪkl/ a vertical. ~ly adv
verticalmente
vertigo /ˈvɜːtɪɡəʊ/ n vertigem f
verve /vɜːv/ n verve f, vivacidade f
very /ˈverɪ/ adv muito □ a (actual)
mesmo, próprio; (exact) preciso, exato, (P) exacto. the ~ day/etc o
próprio or o mesmo dia/etc. at the
~ end mesmo or precisamente no
fim. the ~ first/best/etc (emph) o
primeiro/melhor/etc de todos. ~
much muito. ~ well muito bem
vessel /ˈvesl/ n vaso m
vest¹ /vest/ n corpete m, (P) camisola f
interior; (Amer: waistcoat) colete m
vest² /vest/ vt conferir (in a). ~ed
interests interesses mpl
vestige /ˈvestɪdʒ/ n vestígio m
vestry /ˈvestrɪ/ n sacristia f
vet /vet/ n (colloq) veterinário m □ vt
(pt vetted) (candidate etc) examinar
atentamente, estudar
veteran /ˈvetərən/ n veterano m.
(war) ~ veterano m de guerra
veterinary /ˈvetərɪnərɪ/ a veterinário. ~ surgeon veterinário m
veto /ˈviːtəʊ/ n (pl -oes) veto m; (right)
direito m de veto □ vt vetar, opor o
veto a
vex /veks/ vt aborrecer, irritar,
contrariar. ~ed question questão
f muito debatida, assunto m controverso
via /ˈvaɪə/ prep por, via
viab|le /ˈvaɪəbl/ a viável. ~ility
/-ˈbɪlətɪ/ n viabilidade f
viaduct /ˈvaɪədʌkt/ n viaduto m
vibrant /ˈvaɪbrənt/ a vibrante
vibrat|e /vaɪˈbreɪt/ vt/i (fazer) vibrar.
~ion /-ʃn/ n vibração f
vicar /ˈvɪkə(r)/ n (Anglican) pastor m;
(Catholic) vigário m, pároco m. ~age
n presbitério m
vicarious /vɪˈkeərɪəs/ a vivido indiretamente, (P) indirectamente
vice¹ /vaɪs/ n (depravity) vício m
vice² /vaɪs/ n (techn) torno m
vice- /vaɪs/ pref vice-. ~-chairman
vice-presidente m. ~-chancellor n
vice-chanceler m; (univ) reitor m. ~-
consul n vice-cônsul m. ~-president
n vice-presidente m
vice versa /ˈvaɪsˈvɜːsə/ adv vice-
versa
vicinity /vɪˈsɪnətɪ/ n vizinhança f,

cercania(s) *fpl*, arredores *mpl*. in the ~ of nos arredores de

vicious /'vɪʃəs/ *a* (*spiteful*) mau, maldoso; (*violent*) brutal, feroz. ~ circle círculo *m* vicioso. ~ly *adv* maldosamente; (*violently*) brutalmente, ferozmente

victim /'vɪktɪm/ *n* vítima *f*

victimize /'vɪktɪmaɪz/ *vt* perseguir. ~ation /-'zeɪʃn/ *n* perseguição *f*

victor /'vɪktə(r)/ *n* vencedor *m*

victory /'vɪktərɪ/ *n* vitória *f*. ~ious /-'tɔːrɪəs/ *a* vitorioso

video /'vɪdɪəʊ/ *a* video □ *n* (*pl* -os) (*colloq*) video □ *vt* (*record*) gravar em video. ~ cassette video-cassete *f*. ~ recorder videocassete *m*

vie /vaɪ/ *vi* (*pres p* vying) rivalizar, competir (with com)

view /vjuː/ *n* vista *f* □ *vt* ver; (*examine*) examinar; (*consider*) considerar, ver; (*a house*) visitar, ver. in my ~ a meu ver, na minha opinião. in ~ of em vista de. on ~ em exposição, à mostra; (*open to the public*) aberto ao público. with a ~ to com a intenção de, com o fim de. ~er *n* (*TV*) telespectador *m*; (*for slides*) visor *m*

viewfinder /'vjuːfaɪndə(r)/ *n* visor *f*

viewpoint /'vjuːpɔɪnt/ *n* ponto *m* de vista

vigil /'vɪdʒɪl/ *n* vigília *f*; (*over corpse*) velório *m*; (*relig*) vigília *f*

vigilant /'vɪdʒɪlənt/ *a* vigilante. ~ce *n* vigilância *f*. ~te /ˌvɪdʒɪ'læntɪ/ *n* vigilante *m*

vigour /'vɪgə(r)/ *n* vigor *m*. ~orous /'vɪgərəs/ *a* vigoroso

vile /vaɪl/ *a* (*base*) infame, vil; (*colloq: bad*) horroroso, péssimo

vilify /'vɪlɪfaɪ/ *vt* difamar

villa /'vɪlə/ *n* vivenda *f*, vila *f*; (*country residence*) casa *f* de campo

village /'vɪlɪdʒ/ *n* aldeia *f*, povoado *m*. ~r *n* aldeão *m*, aldeã *f*

villain /'vɪlən/ *n* patife *m*, mau-caráter *m*. ~y *n* infâmia *f*, vilania *f*

vindicate /'vɪndɪkeɪt/ *vt* vindicar, justificar. ~ion /-'keɪʃn/ *n* justificação *f*

vindictive /vɪn'dɪktɪv/ *a* vingativo

vine /vaɪn/ *n* (*plant*) vinha *f*

vinegar /'vɪnɪgə(r)/ *n* vinagre *m*

vineyard /'vɪnjəd/ *n* vinha *f*, vinhedo *m*

vintage /'vɪntɪdʒ/ *n* (*year*) ano *m* de colheita de qualidade excepcional □ *a* (*wine*) de colheita excepcional e de um determinado ano; (*car*) de museu (*colloq*), fabricado entre 1917 e 1930

vinyl /'vaɪnɪl/ *n* vinil *m*

viola /vɪ'əʊlə/ *n* (*mus*) viola *f*, violeta *f*

violate /'vaɪəleɪt/ *vt* violar. ~ion /-'leɪʃn/ *n* violação *f*

violent /'vaɪələnt/ *a* violento. ~ce *n* violência *f*. ~tly *adv* violentamente, com violência

violet /'vaɪələt/ *n* (*bot*) violeta *f*; (*colour*) violeta *m* □ *a* violeta

violin /vaɪə'lɪn/ *n* violino *m*. ~ist *n* violinista *mf*

VIP /viːaɪ'piː/ *abbr* (*very important person*) VIP *m*, personalidade *f* importante

viper /'vaɪpə(r)/ *n* víbora *f*

virgin /'vɜːdʒɪn/ *a* & *n* virgem (*f*); ~ity /və'dʒɪnətɪ/ *n* virgindade *f*

Virgo /'vɜːgəʊ/ *n* (*astr*) Virgem *f*, (P) virgo *m*

virile /'vɪraɪl/ *a* viril, varonil. ~ity /vɪ'rɪlətɪ/ *n* virilidade *f*

virtual /'vɜːtʃʊəl/ *a* que é na prática embora não em teoria, verdadeiro. a ~ failure/*etc* praticamente um fracasso/*etc*. ~ly *adv* praticamente

virtue /'vɜːtʃuː/ *n* (*goodness, chastity*) virtude *f*; (*merit*) mérito *m*. by or in ~ of por or em virtude de

virtuoso /ˌvɜːtʃʊ'əʊsəʊ/ *n* (*pl* -si /-siː/) virtuoso *m*, virtuose *mf*. ~ity /-'ɒsətɪ/ *n* virtuosidade *f*, virtuosismo *m*

virtuous /'vɜːtʃʊəs/ *a* virtuoso

virulent /'vɪrʊlənt/ *a* virulento. ~ce /-ləns/ *n* virulência *f*

virus /'vaɪərəs/ *n* (*pl* -es) vírus *m*; (*colloq: disease*) virose *f*

visa /'viːzə/ *n* visto *m*

viscount /'vaɪkaʊnt/ *n* visconde *m*. ~ess /-ɪs/ *n* viscondessa *f*

viscous /'vɪskəs/ *a* viscoso

vise /vaɪs/ *n* (*Amer: vice*) torno *m*

visible /'vɪzəbl/ *a* visível. ~ility /-'bɪlətɪ/ *n* visibilidade *f*. ~ly *adv* visivelmente

vision /'vɪʒn/ *n* (*dream, insight*) visão *f*; (*seeing, sight*) vista *f*, visão *f*

visionary /'vɪʒənərɪ/ *a* visionário; (*plan, scheme etc*) fantasista, quimérico □ *n* visionário *m*

visit /'vɪzɪt/ *vt* (*pt* visited) (*person*) visitar, fazer uma visita a; (*place*) visitar □ or estar de visita □ *n* (*tour, call*) visita *f*; (*stay*) estada *f*, visita *f*. ~or *n* visitante *mf*; (*guest*) visita *f*

visor /'vaɪzə(r)/ *n* viseira *f*; (*in vehicle*) visor *m*

vista /'vɪstə/ *n* vista *f*, panorama *m*

visual /'vɪʒʊəl/ *a* visual. ~ display unit terminal *m* de vídeo. ~ly *adv* visualmente

visualize /'vɪʒʊəlaɪz/ *vt* visualizar; (*foresee*) imaginar, prever

vital /'vaɪtl/ *a* vital. ~ statistics estatísticas *fpl* demográficas; (*colloq: woman*) medidas *fpl*

vitality /vaɪ'tælətɪ/ *n* vitalidade *f*

vitamin /'vɪtəmɪn/ *n* vitamina *f*

vivacious /vɪ'veɪʃəs/ *a* cheio de vida,

vivo, animado. ~ity /-'væsətɪ/ n vivacidade f, animação f

vivid /'vɪvɪd/ a vívido; (imagination) vivo. ~ly adv vividamente

vivisection /vɪvɪ'sekʃn/ n vivissecção f

vixen /'vɪksn/ n raposa f fêmea

vocabulary /və'kæbjʊlərɪ/ n vocabulário m

vocal /'vəʊkl/ a vocal; (fig: person) eloqüente, (P) eloquente. ~ cords cordas fpl vocais. ~ist n vocalista mf

vocation /və'keɪʃn/ n vocação f; (trade) profissão f. ~al a vocacional, profissional

vociferous /və'sɪfərəs/ a vociferante

vodka /'vɒdkə/ n vodka m

vogue /vəʊg/ n voga f, moda f, popularidade f. in ~ em voga, na moda

voice /vɔɪs/ n voz f □ vt (express) exprimir

void /vɔɪd/ a vazio; (jur) nulo, sem validade □ n vácuo m, vazio m. make ~ anular, invalidar. ~ of sem, destituído de

volatile /'vɒlətaɪl/ a (substance) volátil; (fig: changeable) instável

volcano /vɒl'keɪnəʊ/ n (pl -oes) vulcão m. ~ic /-ænɪk/ a vulcânico

volition /və'lɪʃn/ n of one's own ~ de sua própria vontade

volley /'vɒlɪ/ n (of blows etc) saraivada f, (of gunfire) salva f; (tennis) voleio m. ~ball n voleibol m, vôlei m

volt /vəʊlt/ n volt m. ~age n voltagem f

voluble /'vɒljʊbl/ a falante, loquaz

volume /'vɒljuːm/ n (book, sound) volume m; (capacity) capacidade f

voluntar|y /'vɒləntərɪ/ a voluntário; (unpaid) não-remunerado. ~ily /-trəlɪ/ adv voluntariamente

volunteer /vɒlən'tɪə(r)/ n voluntário m □ vi oferecer-se (to do para fazer); (mil) alistar-se como voluntário □ vt oferecer espontaneamente

voluptuous /və'lʌptʃʊəs/ a voluptuoso, sensual

vomit /'vɒmɪt/ vt/i (pt vomited) vomitar □ n vómito m, (P) vômito m

voodoo /'vuːduː/ n vodu m

voracious /və'reɪʃəs/ a voraz. ~ously adv vorazmente. ~ty /və-'ræsətɪ/ n voracidade f

vot|e /vəʊt/ n voto m; (right) direito m de voto □ vt/i votar. ~er n eleitor m. ~ing n votação f; (poll) escrutínio m

vouch /vaʊtʃ/ vi ~ for responder por, garantir

voucher /'vaʊtʃə(r)/ n (for meal, transport) vale m; (receipt) comprovante m

vow /vaʊ/ n voto m □ vt (loyalty etc) jurar (to a). ~ to do jurar fazer

vowel /'vaʊəl/ n vogal f

voyage /'vɔɪɪdʒ/ n viagem (por mar) f. ~r /-ə(r)/ n viajante m

vulgar /'vʌlgə(r)/ a ordinário, grosseiro; (in common use) vulgar. ~ity /-'gærətɪ/ n (behaviour) grosseria f, vulgaridade f

vulnerab|le /'vʌlnərəbl/ a vulnerável. ~ility /-'bɪlətɪ/ n vulnerabilidade f

vulture /'vʌltʃə(r)/ n abutre m, urubu m

vying /'vaɪɪŋ/ see vie

W

wad /wɒd/ n bucha f, tampão m; (bundle) maço m, rolo m

wadding /'wɒdɪŋ/ n enchimento m

waddle /'wɒdl/ vi bambolear-se, rebolar-se, gingar

wade /weɪd/ vi ~ through (fig) avançar a custo por; (mud, water) patinhar em

wafer /'weɪfə(r)/ n (biscuit) bolacha f de baunilha; (relig) hóstia f

waffle[1] /'wɒfl/ n (collog: talk) lengalenga f, papo m, conversa f; (collog: writing) □ vi (collog) escrever muito sem dizer nada de importante

waffle[2] /'wɒfl/ n (culin) waffle m

waft /wɒft/ vi flutuar □ vt espalhar, levar suavemente

wag /wæg/ vt/i (pt wagged) abanar, agitar, sacudir

wage[1] /weɪdʒ/ vt (campaign, war) fazer

wage[2] /weɪdʒ/ n ~(s) (weekly, daily) salário m, ordenado m. ~claim n pedido m de aumento de salário. ~earner n trabalhador m assalariado. ~freeze n congelamento m de salários

wager /'weɪdʒə(r)/ n (bet) aposta f □ vt apostar (that que)

waggle /'wægl/ vt/i abanar, agitar, sacudir

wagon /'wægən/ n (horse-drawn) carroça f; (rail) vagão m de mercadorias

waif /weɪf/ n criança f abandonada

wail /weɪl/ vi lamentar-se, gemer lamentosamente □ n lamentação f, gemido m lamentoso

waist /weɪst/ n cintura f. ~line n cintura f

waistcoat /'weɪskəʊt/ n colete m

wait /weɪt/ vt/i esperar □ n espera f. ~ for esperar. ~ on servir. lie in ~ (for) estar escondido à espera de, armar uma emboscada (para). keep sb ~ing fazer alguém esperar. ~ing-list n lista *f* de espera. ~ing-room *n* sala *f* de espera

wait|er /ˈweɪtə(r)/ *n* garçon *m*, (P) criado *m* (de mesa). ~ress *n* garçonete *f*, (P) criada *f* (de mesa)

waive /weɪv/ *vt* renunciar a, desistir de

wake¹ /weɪk/ *vt/i* (*pt* woke, *pp* woken) ~ (up) acordar, despertar □ *n* (*before burial*) velório *m*

wake² /weɪk/ *n* (*ship*) esteira (de espuma) *f*. in the ~ of (*following*) atrás de, em seguida a

waken /ˈweɪkən/ *vt/i* acordar, despertar

Wales /weɪlz/ *n* País *m* de Gales

walk /wɔːk/ *vi* andar, caminhar; (*not ride*) ir a pé; (*stroll*) passear □ *vt* (*streets*) andar por, percorrer; (*distance*) andar, fazer a pé, percorrer; (*dog*) (levar para) passear □ *n* (*stroll*) passeio *m*, volta *f*; (*excursion*) caminhada *f*; (*gait*) passo *m*, maneira *f* de andar; (*pace*) passo *m*; (*path*) caminho *m*. it's a 5-minute ~ são 5 minutos a pé. ~ of life meio *m*, condição *f* social. ~ out (*go away*) sair; (*go on strike*) fazer greve. ~ out on abandonar. ~-over *n* vitória *f* fácil

walker /ˈwɔːkə(r)/ *n* caminhante *mf*

walkie-talkie /wɔːkɪˈtɔːkɪ/ *n* walkie-talkie *m*

walking /ˈwɔːkɪŋ/ *n* andar (a pé) *m*, marcha *f* □ *a* (*colloq: dictionary*) vivo. ~-stick *n* bengala *f*

Walkman /ˈwɔːkmæn/ *n* walkman *m*

wall /wɔːl/ *n* parede *f*; (*around land*) muro *m*; (*of castle, town; fig*) muralha *f*; (*of stomach etc*) parede(s) *f* (*pl*) □ *vt* (*city*) fortificar; (*property*) murar. go to the ~ sucumbir, falir; (*firm*) ir à falência. up the ~ (*colloq*) fora de si

wallet /ˈwɒlɪt/ *n* carteira *f*

wallflower /ˈwɔːlflaʊə(r)/ *n* (*bot*) goivo *m*. be a ~ (*fig*) tomar chá de cadeira, (P) levar banho de cadeira

wallop /ˈwɒləp/ *vt* (*pt* walloped) (*sl*) espancar (*colloq*) □ *n* (*sl*) pancada *f* forte

wallow /ˈwɒləʊ/ *vi* (*in mud*) chafurdar, atolar-se; (*fig*) regozijar-se

wallpaper /ˈwɔːlpeɪpə(r)/ *n* papel *m* de parede □ *vt* forrar com papel de parede

walnut /ˈwɔːlnʌt/ *n* (*nut*) noz *f*; (*tree*) nogueira *f*

walrus /ˈwɔːlrəs/ *n* morsa *f*

waltz /wɔːls/ *n* valsa *f* □ *vi* valsar

wan /wɒn/ *a* pálido

wand /wɒnd/ *n* (*magic*) varinha *f* mágica *or* de condão

wander /ˈwɒndə(r)/ *vi* andar ao acaso, vagar, errar; (*river*) serpentear; (*mind, speech*) divagar; (*stray*) extraviar-se. ~er *n* vagabundo *m*, andarilho *m*. ~ing *a* errante

wane /weɪn/ *vi* diminuir, minguar; (*decline*) declinar □ *n* on the ~ em declínio; (*moon*) no quarto minguante

wangle /ˈwæŋgl/ *vt* (*colloq*) conseguir algo através de pistolão

want /wɒnt/ *vt* querer (to do fazer); (*need*) precisar (de); (*ask for*) exigir, requerer □ *vi* ~ for ter falta de □ *n* (*need*) necessidade *f*, precisão *f*; (*desire*) desejo *m*; (*lack*) falta *f*, carência *f*. for ~ of por falta de. I ~ you to go eu quero que você vá. ~ed (*criminal*) procurado pela polícia; (*in ad*) precisa(m)-se

wanting /ˈwɒntɪŋ/ *a* falho, falto (in de). be found ~ não estar à altura

wanton /ˈwɒntən/ *a* (*playful*) travesso, brincalhão; (*cruelty, destruction etc*) gratuito; (*woman*) despudorado

war /wɔː(r)/ *n* guerra *f*. at ~ em guerra. on the ~-path em pé de guerra

warble /ˈwɔːbl/ *vt/i* gorjear

ward /wɔːd/ *n* (*in hospital*) enfermaria *f*; (*jur: minor*) pupilo *m*; (*pol*) círculo *m* eleitoral □ *vt* ~ off (*a blow*) aparar; (*anger*) desviar; (*danger*) prevenir, evitar

warden /ˈwɔːdn/ *n* (*of institution*) diretor *m*, (P) director *m*; (*of park*) guarda *m*

warder /ˈwɔːdə(r)/ *n* guarda (de prisão) *m*, carcereiro *m*

wardrobe /ˈwɔːdrəʊb/ *n* (*place*) armário *m*, guarda-roupa *m*, (P) guarda-fato *m*, (P) roupeiro *m*; (*clothes*) guarda-roupa *m*

warehouse /ˈweəhaʊs/ *n* (*pl* -s /-haʊzɪz/) armazém *m*, depósito *m* de mercadorias

wares /weəz/ *npl* (*goods*) mercadorias *fpl*, artigos *mpl*

warfare /ˈwɔːfeə(r)/ *n* guerra *f*

warhead /ˈwɔːhed/ *n* ogiva (de combate) *f*

warlike /ˈwɔːlaɪk/ *a* marcial, guerreiro; (*bellicose*) belicoso

warm /wɔːm/ *a* (-er, -est) quente; (*hearty*) caloroso, cordial. be *or* feel ~ estar com *or* ter *or* sentir calor □ *vt/i* ~ (up) aquecer(-se). ~-hearted *a* afetuoso, (P) afectuoso, com calor humano. ~ly *adv* (*heartily*) calorosamente. wrap up ~ly agasalhar-se bem. ~th *n* calor *m*

warn /wɔːn/ *vt* avisar, prevenir. ~ sb off sth (*advise against*) pôr alguém de prevenção *or* de pé atrás com alg coisa; (*forbid*) proibir alg coisa a alguém. ~ing *n* aviso *m*. ~ing light lâmpada *f* de advertência. without ~ing sem aviso, sem prevenir

warp /wɔːp/ vt/i (wood etc) empenar; (fig: pervert) torcer, deformar, desvirtuar. ~ed a (fig) deturpado, pervertido

warrant /ˈwɒrənt/ n autorização f; (for arrest) mandato (de captura) m; (comm) título m de crédito, warrant m □ vt justificar; (guarantee) garantir

warranty /ˈwɒrəntɪ/ n garantia f

warring /ˈwɔːrɪŋ/ a em guerra; (rival) contrário, antagónico, (P) antagónico

warrior /ˈwɒrɪə(r)/ n guerreiro m

warship /ˈwɔːʃɪp/ n navio m de guerra

wart /wɔːt/ n verruga f

wartime /ˈwɔːtaɪm/ n in ~ em tempo de guerra

wary /ˈweərɪ/ a (-ier, -iest) cauteloso, prudente

was /wɒz/; unstressed /wəz/ see be

wash /wɒʃ/ vt/i lavar(-se); (flow over) molhar, inundar □ n lavagem f; (dirty clothes) roupa f para lavar; (of ship) esteira f; (of paint) fina camada f de tinta. have a ~ lavar-se. ~-basin n pia f, (P) lavatório m. ~-cloth n (Amer: face-cloth) toalha f de rosto. ~ one's hands of lavar as mãos de. ~ out (cup etc) lavar; (stain) tirar lavando. ~-out n (sl) fiasco m. ~-room n (Amer) banheiro m, (P) casa f de banho. ~ up lavar a louça; (Amer: wash oneself) lavar-se. ~able a lavável. ~ing n (dirty) roupa f suja; (clean) roupa f lavada. ~ing-machine n máquina f de lavar roupa. ~ing-powder n detergente m em pó. ~ing-up n lavagem f da louça

washed-out /wɒʃtˈaʊt/ a (faded) desbotado; (exhausted) exausto

washer /ˈwɒʃə(r)/ n (machine) máquina f de lavar roupa, louça f, (P) loiça f; (ring) anilha f

wasp /wɒsp/ n vespa f

wastage /ˈweɪstɪdʒ/ n desperdício m, perda f. natural ~ desgaste m natural

waste /weɪst/ vt desperdiçar, esbanjar; (time) perder □ vi ~ away consumir-se □ a (useless) inútil; (material) de refugo □ n desperdício m, perda f; (of time) perda f; (rubbish) lixo m. lay ~ assolar, devastar. ~ (land) (desolate) região f desolada, ermo m; (unused) (terreno) baldio m. ~-disposal unit triturador m de lixo. ~ paper papéis mpl velhos. ~-paper basket cesto m de papéis

wasteful /ˈweɪstfl/ a dispendioso; (person) esbanjador, gastador, perdulário

watch /wɒtʃ/ vt/i ver bem, olhar com atenção, observar; (game, TV) ver; (guard, spy on) vigiar; (be careful about) tomar cuidado com □ n vigia f, vigilância f; (naut) quarto m; (for telling time) relógio m. ~-dog n cão m de guarda. ~ out (look out) estar à espreita (for de); (take care) acautelar-se. ~-strap n correia f, pulseira f do relógio. ~-tower n torre f de observação. ~ful a atento, vigilante

watchmaker /ˈwɒtʃmeɪkə(r)/ n relojoeiro m

watchman /ˈwɒtʃmən/ n (pl -men) (of building) guarda m. (night-)~ guarda-noturno m

watchword /ˈwɒtʃwɜːd/ n lema m, divisa f

water /ˈwɔːtə(r)/ n água f □ vt regar □ vi (of eyes) lacrimejar, chorar. ~ down juntar água a, diluir; (milk, wine) aguar, batizar, (P) baptizar (colloq); (fig: tone down) suavizar. ~-closet n WC m, banheiro m, (P) lavabos mpl. ~-colour n aquarela f. ~-ice n sorvete m. ~-lily n nenúfar m. ~-main n cano m principal da rede. ~-melon n melancia f. ~-pistol n pistola f de água. ~-polo pólo m aquático. ~-skiing n esqui m aquático. ~-wheel n roda f hidráulica

watercress /ˈwɔːtəkres/ n agrião m

waterfall /ˈwɔːtəfɔːl/ n queda f de água, cascata f

watering-can /ˈwɔːtərɪŋkæn/ n regador m

waterlogged /ˈwɔːtəlɒgd/ a saturado de água; (land) empapado, alagado; (vessel) inundado, alagado

watermark /ˈwɔːtəmɑːk/ n (in paper) marca-d'água f, filigrana f

waterproof /ˈwɔːtəpruːf/ a impermeável; (watch) à prova d'água

watershed /ˈwɔːtəʃed/ n (fig) momento m decisivo; (in affairs) ponto m crítico

watertight /ˈwɔːtətaɪt/ a à prova d'água, hermético; (fig: argument etc) inequívoco, irrefutável

waterway /ˈwɔːtəweɪ/ n via f navegável

waterworks /ˈwɔːtəwɜːks/ n (place) estação f hidráulica

watery /ˈwɔːtərɪ/ a (colour) pálido; (eyes) lacrimoso; (soup) aguado; (tea) fraco

watt /wɒt/ n watt m

wav|e /weɪv/ n onda f; (in hair; radio) onda f; (sign) aceno m □ vt acenar com; (sword) brandir; (hair) ondular □ vi acenar (com a mão); (hair etc) ondular; (flag) tremular. ~eband n faixa f de onda. ~e goodbye dizer adeus. ~elength n comprimento m de onda. ~y a ondulado

waver /'weɪvə(r)/ *vi* vacilar; (*hesitate*) hesitar

wax[1] /wæks/ *n* cera *f* □ *vt* encerar; (*car*) polir. ~en, ~y *adjs* de cera

wax[2] /wæks/ *vi* (*of moon*) aumentar, crescer

waxwork /'wækswɜ:k/ *n* (*dummy*) figura *f* de cera. ~s *npl* (*exhibition*) museu *m* de figuras de cera

way /weɪ/ *n* (*road, path*) caminho *m*, estrada *f*, rua *f* (to para); (*distance*) percurso *m*; (*direction*) (P) direção *f*; (*manner*) modo *m*, maneira *f*; (*means*) meios *mpl*; (*respect*) respeito *m*. ~s (*habits*) costumes *mpl* □ *adv* (*colloq*) consideravelmente, de longe. be in the ~ atrapalhar. be on one's *or* the ~ estar a caminho. by the ~ a propósito. by ~ of por, via, através. get one's own ~ conseguir o que quer. give ~ (*yield*) ceder; (*collapse*) desabar; (*auto*) dar a preferência. in a ~ de certo modo. make one's ~ ir. that ~ dessa maneira. this ~ desta maneira. ~ in entrada *f*. ~ out saída *f*. ~out *a* (*colloq*) excêntrico

waylay /wer'leɪ/ *vt* (*pt* -laid) (*assail*) armar uma cilada para; (*stop*) interceptar

wayward /'weɪwəd/ *a* (*wilful*) teimoso; (*perverse*) caprichoso, difícil

WC /dʌb(ə)lju:'si:/ *n* WC *m*, banheiro *m*, (P) casa *f* de banho

we /wi:/ *pron* nós

weak /wi:k/ *a* (-er, -est) fraco; (*delicate*) frágil. ~en *vt*/*i* enfraquecer; (*give way*) fraquejar. ~ly *adv* fracamente. ~ness *n* fraqueza *f*; (*fault*) ponto *m* fraco. a ~ness for (*liking*) um fraco por

weakling /'wi:klɪŋ/ *n* fraco *m*

wealth /welθ/ *n* riqueza *f*; (*riches, resources*) riquezas *fpl*; (*quantity*) abundância *f*

wealthy /'welθɪ/ *a* (-ier, -iest) rico

wean /wi:n/ *vt* (*baby*) desmamar; (*from habit etc*) desabituar

weapon /'wepən/ *n* arma *f*

wear /weə(r)/ *vt* (*pt* wore *pp* worn) (*have on*) usar, trazer; (*put on*) pôr; (*expression*) ter; (*damage*) gastar. ~ black/red/*etc* vestir-se de preto/vermelho/*etc* □ *vi* (*last*) durar; (*become old, damaged etc*) gastar-se □ *n* (*use*) uso *m*; (*deterioration*) gasto *m*, uso *m*; (*endurance*) resistência *f*; (*clothing*) roupa *f*. ~ and tear desgaste *m*. ~ down gastar; (*person*) extenuar. ~ off passar. ~ on (*time*) passar lentamente. ~ out gastar; (*tire*) cansar, esgotar

wear|y /'wɪərɪ/ *a* (-ier, -iest) fatigado, cansado; (*tiring*) fatigante, cansativo □ *vi* ~y of cansar-se de. ~ily *adv* com

lassidão, cansadamente. ~iness *n* fadiga *f*, cansaço *m*

weasel /'wi:zl/ *n* doninha *f*

weather /'weðə(r)/ *n* tempo *m* □ *a* meteorológico □ *vt* (*survive*) aguentar, (P) aguentar, resistir a. under the ~ (*colloq: ill*) indisposto, achacado. ~-beaten *a* curtido pelo tempo. ~-forecast *n* boletim *m* meteorológico. ~-vane *n* cata-vento *m*

weathercock /'weðəkɒk/ *n* (*lit & fig*) cata-vento *m*

weav|e[1] /wi:v/ *vt* (*pt* wove, *pp* woven) (*cloth etc*) tecer; (*plot*) urdir, criar □ *n* (*style*) tipo *m* de tecido. ~er /-ə(r)/ *n* tecelão *m*, tecelã *f*. ~ing *n* tecelagem *f*

weave[2] /wi:v/ *vi* (*move*) serpear; (*through traffic, obstacles*) zigueza-guear

web /web/ *n* (*of spider*) teia *f*; (*fabric*) tecido *m*; (*on foot*) membrana *f* interdigital. ~bed *a* (*foot*) palmado. ~bing *n* (*in chair*) tira *f* de tecido forte. ~-footed *a* palmípede

wed /wed/ *vt*/*i* (*pt* wedded) casar(-se)

wedding /'wedɪŋ/ *n* casamento *m*. ~-cake *n* bolo *m* de noiva. ~-ring *n* aliança *f* (de casamento)

wedge /wedʒ/ *n* calço *m*, cunha *f*; (*cake*) fatia *f*; (*of lemon*) quarto *m*; (*under wheel etc*) calço *m*, cunha *f* □ *vt* calçar; (*push*) meter *or* enfiar à força; (*pack in*) entalar

Wednesday /'wenzdɪ/ *n* quartafeira *f*

weed /wi:d/ *n* erva *f* daninha □ *vt*/*i* arrancar as ervas, capinar. ~-killer *n* herbicida *m*. ~ out suprimir, arrancar. ~y *a* (*fig: person*) fraco

week /wi:k/ *n* semana *f*. a ~ today/tomorrow de hoje/de amanhã a oito dias. ~ly *a* semanal □ *a* & *n* (*periodical*) (jornal) semanário (*m*) □ *adv* semanalmente, todas as semanas

weekday /'wi:kdeɪ/ *n* dia *m* de semana

weekend /'wi:kend/ *n* fim-de-semana *m*

weep /wi:p/ *vt*/*i* (*pt* wept) chorar (for sb por alguém). ~ing willow (salgueiro-)chorão *m*

weigh /weɪ/ *vt*/*i* pesar. ~ anchor levantar âncora *or* ferro, zarpar. ~ down (*weight*) sobrecarregar; (*bend*) envergar; (*fig*) acabrunhar. ~ up (*colloq: examine*) pesar

weight /weɪt/ *n* peso *m*. lose ~ emagrecer. put on ~ engordar. ~less *a* imponderável. ~-lifter *n* halterofilista *m*. ~-lifting *n* halterofilia *f*. ~y *a* pesado; (*subject etc*) de peso; (*influential*) influente

weighting /'weɪtɪŋ/ *n* suplemento *m* salarial

weir /wɪə(r)/ n represa f, açude m

weird /wɪəd/ a (-er, -est) misterioso; (strange) estranho, bizarro

welcome /'welkəm/ a agradável; (timely) oportuno □ int (seja) benvindo! □ n acolhimento m □ vt acolher, receber; (as greeting) dar as boas vindas a. be ~e ser bem-vindo. you're ~e! (after thank you) não tem de quê!, de nada! ~e to do livre para fazer. ~ing a acolhedor

weld /weld/ vt soldar □ n solda f. ~er n soldador m. ~ing n soldagem f, soldadura f

welfare /'welfeə(r)/ n bem-estar m; (aid) assistência f, previdência f social. W~ State Estado-Providência m

well¹ /wel/ n (for water, oil) poço m; (of stairs) vão m; (of lift) poço m

well² /wel/ adv (better, best) bem □ a bem! as ~ (invar) □ int bem! as ~. we may as ~ go é melhor irmos andando. as ~ as tão bem como; (in addition) assim como. be ~ (healthy) ir or passar bem. do ~ (succeed) sairse bem, ser bem sucedido. very ~ muito bem. ~ done! bravo!, muito bem! ~-behaved a bem comportado, educado. ~-being n bem-estar m. ~-bred a (bem) educado. ~-done a (of meat) bem passado. ~-dressed a bem vestido. ~-heeled a (colloq: wealthy) rico. ~-informed a versado, bem informado. ~-known a (bem-) conhecido. ~-meaning a bem intencionado. ~-off a rico, próspero. ~-read a instruído. ~-spoken a bem-falante. ~-timed a oportuno. ~-to-do a rico. ~-wisher n admirador m, simpatizante mf

wellington /'welɪŋtən/ n (boot) bota f alta de borracha

Welsh /welʃ/ a galês □ n (lang) galês m. ~man n galês m. ~woman n galesa f

wend /wend/ vt ~ one's way dirigirse, seguir o seu caminho

went /went/ see go

wept /wept/ see weep

were /wɜ:(r)/; unstressed /wə(r)/ see be

west /west/ n oeste m. the W~ (pol) o Oeste, o Ocidente □ a ocidental, do oeste □ adv ao oeste, para o oeste. W~ Indian a & n antilhano (m). the W~ Indies as Antilhas. ~erly a ocidental, oeste. ~ward a para o oeste. ~ward(s) adv para o oeste

western /'westən/ a ocidental, do oeste; (pol) ocidental □ n (film) filme m de cowboys, bangue-bangue m

westernize /'westənaɪz/ vt ocidentalizar

wet /wet/ a (wetter, wettest) molhado; (of weather) chuvoso, de chuva; (colloq: person) fraco. get ~ molharse □ vt (pt wetted) molhar. ~ blanket (colloq) desmancha-prazeres mf invar (colloq). ~ paint pintado de fresco. ~ suit roupa f de mergulho

whack /wæk/ vt (colloq) bater em □ n (colloq) pancada f. ~ed a (colloq) morto de cansaço, rebentado (colloq). ~ing a (sl) enorme, de todo o tamanho

whale /weɪl/ n baleia f

wharf /wɔ:f/ n (pl wharfs) cais m

what /wɒt/ a (interr, excl) que. ~ time is it? que horas são? ~ an idea! que idéia! □ pron (interr) (o) quê, como, o que, qual, quais; (object) o que; (after prep) que; (that which) o que, aquilo que. ~? (o) quê?, como? ~ is it? o que é? ~ is your address? qual é o seu endereço? ~ is your name? como se chama? ~ can you see? o que é que você pode ver? this is ~ I write with é com isto que escrevo. that's ~ I need é disso que eu preciso. do ~ you want faça o que or aquilo que quiser. ~ about me/ him/etc? e eu/ele/etc? ~ about doing sth? e se fizéssemos alg coisa? ~ for? para quê?

whatever /wɒt'evə(r)/ a ~ book/etc qualquer livro/etc que seja □ pron (no matter what) qualquer que seja; (anything that) o que quer que, tudo o que. nothing ~ absolutamente nada. ~ happens aconteça o que acontecer. do ~ you like faça o que quiser

whatsoever /wɒtsəʊ'evə(r)/ a & pron = whatever

wheat /wi:t/ n trigo m

wheedle /'wi:dl/ vt convencer, persuadir, levar a

wheel /wi:l/ n roda f □ vt empurrar □ vi rodar, rolar. at the ~ (of vehicle) ao volante; (helm) ao leme

wheelbarrow /'wi:lbærəʊ/ n carrinho m de mão

wheelchair /'wi:ltʃeə(r)/ n cadeira f de rodas

wheeze /wi:z/ vi respirar ruidosamente □ n respiração f difícil

when /wen/ adv, conj & pron quando. the day/moment ~ o dia/momento em que

whenever /wen'evə(r)/ conj & adv (at whatever time) quando quer que, quando; (every time that) (de) cada vez que, sempre que

where /weə(r)/ adv, conj & pron onde, aonde; (in which place) em que, onde; (whereas) enquanto que, ao passo que. ~ is he going? aonde é que ele vai? ~abouts adv onde □ n paradeiro m.

~by *adv* pelo que. ~upon *adv* após o que, depois do que
whereas /wear'æz/ *conj* enquanto que, ao passo que
wherever /wear'eva(r)/ *conj* & *adv* onde quer que. ~ **can** it be? onde pode estar?
whet /wet/ *vt* (*pt* **whetted**) (*appetite, desire*) aguçar, despertar
whether /'weða(r)/ *conj* se. **not know** ~ não saber se. ~ I **go** or **not** caso eu vá ou não
which /wɪtʃ/ *interr* a & *pron* qual, que. ~ **bag** is yours? qual das malas é a sua? ~ is your coat? qual é o seu casaco? **do you know** ~ **he's taken**? sabe qual/quais é que ele levou? □ *rel pron* que, o qual; (*referring to whole sentence*) o que; (*after prep*) que, o qual, cujo. at ~ em qual/que. **from** ~ do qual/que. **of** ~ do qual/de que. **to** ~ para o qual/o que
whichever /wɪtʃ'eva(r)/ *a* ~ **book/** *etc* qualquer livro/*etc* que seja, seja que livro/*etc* for. **take** ~ **book you wish** leve o livro que quiser □ *pron* qualquer, quaisquer
whiff /wɪf/ *n* (*of fresh air*) sopro *m*, lufada *f*; (*smell*) baforada *f*
while /waɪl/ *n* (espaço de) tempo *m*, momento *m*. **once in a** ~ de vez em quando □ *conj* (*when*) enquanto; (*although*) embora; (*whereas*) enquanto que □ *vt* ~ **away** (*time*) passar
whim /wɪm/ *n* capricho *m*
whimper /'wɪmpa(r)/ *vi* gemer; (*baby*) choramingar □ *n* gemido *m*; (*baby*) choro *m*
whimsical /'wɪmzɪkl/ *a* (*person*) caprichoso; (*odd*) bizarro
whine /waɪn/ *vi* lamuriar-se, queixar-se; (*dog*) ganir □ *n* lamúria *f*, queixume *m*; (*dog*) ganido *m*
whip /wɪp/ *n* chicote *m* □ *vt* (*pt* **whipped**) chicotear; (*culin*) bater □ *vi* (*move*) ir a toda a pressa. ~-**round** *n* (*colloq*) coleta *f*, vaquinha *f*. ~ **up** excitar; (*cause*) provocar; (*colloq: meal*) preparar rapidamente. ~**ped cream** creme *m* chantilly
whirl /wɜːl/ *vt/i* (fazer) rodopiar, girar □ *n* rodopio *m*
whirlpool /'wɜːlpuːl/ *n* redemoinho *m*
whirlwind /'wɜːlwɪnd/ *n* redemoinho *m* de vento, turbilhão *m*
whirr /wɜː(r)/ *vi* zunir, zumbir
whisk /wɪsk/ *vt/i* (*snatch*) levar/tirar bruscamente; (*culin*) bater; (*flies*) sacudir □ *n* (*culin*) batedeira *f*. ~ **away** (*brush away*) sacudir
whisker /'wɪska(r)/ *n* fio *m* de barba. ~**s** *npl* (*of animal*) bigode *m*; (*beard*) barba *f*; (*sideboards*) suiças *fpl*

whisky /'wɪskɪ/ *n* uisque *m*
whisper /'wɪspa(r)/ *vt/i* sussurrar, murmurar; (*of stream, leaves*) sussurrar □ *n* sussurro *m*, murmúrio *m*. in a ~ baixinho, em voz baixa
whist /wɪst/ *n* uiste *m*, (*P*) whist *m*
whistle /'wɪsl/ *n* assobio *m*; (*instrument*) apito *m* □ *vt/i* assobiar; (*with instrument*) apitar
Whit /wɪt/ *a* ~ **Sunday** domingo *m* de Pentecostes
white /waɪt/ *a* (-er, -est) branco, alvo; (*pale*) pálido □ *n* (*colour; of eyes; person*) branco *m*; (*of egg*) clara (de ovo) *f*. **go** ~ (*turn pale*) empalidecer; (*of hair*) branquear, embranquecer. ~ **coffee** café *m* com leite. ~-**collar worker** empregado *m* de escritório. ~ **elephant** (*fig*) trambolho *m*, elefante *m* branco. ~ **lie** mentirinha *f*. ~**ness** *n* brancura *f*, alvura *f*
whiten /'waɪtn/ *vt/i* branquear
whitewash /'waɪtwɒʃ/ *n* cal *f*; (*fig*) encobrimento *m* □ *vt* caiar; (*fig*) encobrir
Whitsun /'wɪtsn/ *n* Pentecostes *m*
whittle /'wɪtl/ *vt* ~ **down** aparar, cortar aparas; (*fig*) reduzir gradualmente
whiz /wɪz/ *vi* (*pt* **whizzed**) (*through air*) zunir, sibilar; (*rush*) passar a toda a velocidade. ~-**kid** *n* (*colloq*) prodígio *m*
who /huː/ *interr pron* quem □ *rel pron* que, o(a) qual, os(as) quais
whoever /huː'eva(r)/ *pron* (*no matter who*) quem quer que, seja quem for; (*the one who*) aquele que
whole /haʊl/ *a* inteiro, todo; (*not broken*) intacto. **the** ~ **house/***etc* toda a casa/*etc* □ *n* totalidade *f*; (*unit*) todo *m*. **as a** ~ no conjunto, como um todo. **on the** ~ de um modo geral. ~-**hearted** *a* de todo o coração; (*person*) dedicado. ~-**heartedly** *adv* sem reservas, sinceramente
wholefood /'haʊlfuːd/ *n* comida *f* integral
wholemeal /'haʊlmiːl/ *a* ~ **bread** pão *m* integral
wholesale /'haʊlseɪl/ *n* venda *f* por grosso *or* por atacado □ *a* (*firm*) por grosso, por atacado; (*fig*) sistemático, em massa □ *adv* (*in large quantities*) por atacado; (*fig*) em massa, em grande escala. ~**r** /-a(r)/ *n* grossista *mf*, atacadista *mf*
wholesome /'haʊlsam/ *a* sadio, saudável
wholewheat /'haʊlwiːt/ *a* = **wholemeal**
wholly /'haʊlɪ/ *adv* inteiramente, completamente
whom /huːm/ *interr pron* quem □ *rel*

pron (*that*) que; (*after prep*) quem, que, o qual

whooping cough /'hu:pɪŋkɒf/ *n* coqueluche *f*

whore /hɔ:(r)/ *n* prostituta *f*

whose /hu:z/ *rel pron* & *a* cujo, de quem □ *interr pron* de quem. ~ hat is this?, ~ is this hat? de quem é este chapéu? ~ son are you? de quem é que o senhor é filho?

why /waɪ/ *adv* porque, por que motivo, por que razão, porquê. she doesn't know ~ he's here ela não sabe porque or por que motivo ele estáaqui. she doesn't know ~ ela não sabe porquê. do you know ~? você sabe porquê? □ *int* (*protest*) ora, ora essa; (*discovery*) oh. ~ yes/ *etc*

wick /wɪk/ *n* torcida *f*, mecha *f*, pavio *m*

wicked /'wɪkɪd/ *a* mau, malvado; (*mischievous, spiteful*) maldoso. ~ly *adv* maldosamente. ~ness *n* maldade *f*, malvadeza *f*

wicker /'wɪkə(r)/ *n* verga *f*, vime *m*. ~-work *n* trabalho *m* de verga *or* de vime

wicket /'wɪkɪt/ *n* (*cricket*) arco *m*

wide /waɪd/ *a* (-er, -est) largo; (*extensive*) vasto, grande, extenso. two metres ~ com dois metros de largura □ *adv* longe; (*fully*) completamente. open ~ (*door, window*) abrir-se de par em par, escancarar(-se); (*mouth*) abrir bem. ~ awake desperto, acordado. far and ~ por toda a parte. ~ly *adv* largamente; (*travel, spread*) muito; (*generally*) geralmente; (*extremely*) extremamente

widen /'waɪdn/ *vt/i* alargar(-se)

widespread /'waɪdspred/ *a* muito espalhado, difundido

widow /'wɪdəʊ/ *n* viúva *f*. ~ed *a* (*man*) viúvo; (*woman*) viúva. be ~ed enviuvar, ficar viúvo *or* viúva. ~er *n* viúvo *m*. ~hood *n* viuvez *f*

width /wɪdθ/ *n* largura *f*

wield /wi:ld/ *vt* (*axe etc*) manejar; (*fig: power*) exercer

wife /waɪf/ *n* (*pl* wives) mulher *f*, esposa *f*

wig /wɪg/ *n* cabeleira (postiça) *f*, (*judge's etc*) peruca *f*

wiggle /'wɪgl/ *vt/i* remexer(-se), retorcer(-se), mexer(-se) dum lado para outro

wild /waɪld/ *a* (-er, -est) selvagem; (*of plant*) silvestre; (*mad*) louco; (*enraged*) furioso, violento □ *adv* a esmo; (*without control*) à solta. ~s *npl* regiões *fpl* selvagens. ~-goose chase falsa pista *f*, tentativa *f* inútil. ~ly

adv violentamente; (*madly*) loucamente

wildcat /'waɪldkæt/ *a* ~ strike greve *f* ilegal

wilderness /'wɪldənɪs/ *n* deserto *m*

wildlife /'waɪldlaɪf/ *n* animais *mpl* selvagens

wile /waɪl/ *n* artimanha *f*; (*cunning*) astúcia *f*, manha *f*

wilful /'wɪlfl/ *a* (*person*) voluntarioso; (*act*) intencional, propositado

will[1] /wɪl/ *v aux* you ~ sing/he ~ do/*etc* tu cantarás/ele fará/*etc*. (*1st person: future expressing will or intention*) I ~ sing/we ~ do/*etc* eu cantarei/nós faremos/*etc*. ~ you have a cup of coffee? quer tomar um cafézinho? ~ you shut the door? quer fazer o favor de fechar a porta?

will[2] /wɪl/ *n* vontade *f*; (*document*) testamento *m*. at ~ à vontade, quando or como se quiser □ *vt* (*wish*) querer; (*bequeath*) deixar em testamento. ~-power *n* força *f* de vontade

willing /'wɪlɪŋ/ *a* pronto, de boa vontade. ~ to disposto a. ~ly *adv* (*with pleasure*) de boa vontade, de bom grado; (*not forced*) voluntariamente. ~ness *n* boa vontade *f*, disposição *f* (to do em fazer)

willow /'wɪləʊ/ *n* salgueiro *m*

willy-nilly /wɪlɪ'nɪlɪ/ *adv* de bom ou de mau grado, quer queira ou não

wilt /wɪlt/ *vi* murchar, definhar

wily /'waɪlɪ/ *a* (-ier, -iest) manhoso, matreiro

win /wɪn/ *vt/i* (*pt* won, *pres p* winning) ganhar □ *n* vitória *f*. ~ over *vt* convencer, conquistar

winc|e /wɪns/ *vi* estremecer, contrair-se. without ~ing sem pestanejar

winch /wɪntʃ/ *n* guincho *m* □ *vt* içar com guincho

wind[1] /wɪnd/ *n* vento *m*; (*breath*) fôlego *m*; (*flatulence*) gases *mpl*. get ~ of (*fig*) ouvir rumor de. put the ~ up (*sl*) assustar. in the ~ no ar. ~ instrument (*mus*) instrumento *m* de sopro. ~-swept *a* varrido pelo vento

wind[2] /waɪnd/ *vt/i* (*pt* wound) enrolar(-se); (*wrap*) envolver, pôr em volta; (*of path, river*) serpentear. ~ (up) (*clock etc*) dar corda em. ~ up (*end*) terminar, acabar; (*fig: speech etc*) concluir; (*firm*) liquidar. he'll ~ up in jail (*collog*) ele vai acabar na cadeia. ~ing *a* (*path*) sinuoso; (*staircase*) em caracol

windfall /'wɪndfɔ:l/ *n* fruta *f* caída; (*fig: money*) sorte *f* grande

windmill /'wɪndmɪl/ *n* moinho *m* de vento

window /'wɪndəʊ/ *n* janela *f*; (*of shop*) vitrine *f*, (*P*) montra *f*; (*counter*) guichê *m*, (P) guichet *m*. ~-box *n* jardineira *f*, (P) floreira *f*. ~-cleaner *n* limpador *m* de janelas. ~-dressing *n* decoração *f* de vitrines; (*fig*) apresentação *f* cuidadosa. ~-ledge *n* peitoril *m*. ~-pane *n* vidro *m*, vidraça *f*. go ~-shopping ir ver vitrines. ~-sill *n* peitoril *m*

windpipe /ˈwɪndpaɪp/ *n* traquéia *f*, (P) traqueia *f*

windscreen /ˈwɪndskriːn/ *n* pára-brisa *m*, (P) pára-brisas *m invar.* ~-wiper /-waɪpə(r)/ *n* limpador *m* de pára-brisa

windshield /ˈwɪndʃiːld/ *n* (*Amer*) = windscreen

windsurf|er /ˈwɪndsɜːfə(r)/ *n* surfista *mf*. ~ing *n* surfe *m*

windy /ˈwɪndɪ/ *a* (-ier, -iest) ventoso. it is very ~ está ventando muito

wine /waɪn/ *n* vinho *m*. ~ bar bar *m* para degustação de vinhos. ~-cellar *n* adega *f*, cave *f*. ~-grower *n* vinicultor *m*. ~-growing *n* vinicultura *f*. ~-list *n* lista *f* de vinhos. ~-tasting *n* prova *f* or degustação *f* de vinhos. ~ waiter garçon *m*

wineglass /ˈwaɪnɡlɑːs/ *n* copo *m* de vinho; (*with stem*) cálice *m*

wing /wɪŋ/ *n* asa *f*; (*mil*) flanco *m*; (*archit*) ala *f*; (*auto*) pára-lamas *m invar*, (P) guarda-lamas *m invar*. ~s (*theat*) bastidores *mpl*. under sb's ~ debaixo das asas de alguém. ~ed *a* alado

wink /wɪŋk/ *vi* piscar o olho; (*light, star*) cintilar, piscar □ *n* piscadela *f*. not sleep a ~ não pregar olho

winner /ˈwɪnə(r)/ *n* vencedor *m*

winning /ˈwɪnɪŋ/ *see* win □ *a* vencedor, vitorioso; (*number*) premiado; (*smile*) encantador, atraente. ~-post *n* meta *f*, poste *m* de chegada *f*. ~s *npl* ganhos *mpl*

wint|er /ˈwɪntə(r)/ *n* inverno *m* □ *vi* hibernar. ~ry *a* de inverno, invernoso; (*smile*) glacial

wipe /waɪp/ *vt* limpar; (*dry*) enxugar, limpar □ *n* limpadela *f*. ~ off limpar. ~ out (*destroy*) aniquilar, limpar (*colloq*); (*cancel*) cancelar. ~ up enxugar

wir|e /ˈwaɪə(r)/ *n* arame *m*; (*colloq: telegram*) telegrama *m*. (electric) ~e fio elétrico *m*, (P) eléctrico □ *vt* (*a house*) montar a instalação elétrica em; (*colloq: telegraph*) telegrafar. ~e netting rede *f* de arame. ~ing *n* (*electr*) instalação *f* elétrica, (P) eléctrica

wireless /ˈwaɪəlɪs/ *n* rádio *f*; (*set*) rádio *m*

wiry /ˈwaɪərɪ/ *a* (-ier, -iest) magro e rijo

wisdom /ˈwɪzdəm/ *n* sagacidade *f*, sabedoria *f*; (*common sense*) bom senso

m, sensatez *f*. ~ tooth dente *m* (do) sizo

wise /waɪz/ *a* (-er, -est) (*person*) sábio, avisado, sensato; (*look*) entendedor. ~ guy (*colloq*) sabichão *m* (*colloq*), sabetudo *m* (*colloq*). none the ~r sem entender nada. ~ly *adv* sensatamente

wisecrack /ˈwaɪzkræk/ *n* (*colloq*) (boa) piada *f*

wish /wɪʃ/ *n* (*desire, aspiration*) desejo *m*, vontade *f*; (*request*) pedido *m*; (*greeting*) desejo *m*, voto *m*. I have no ~ to go não tenho nenhum desejo or nenhuma vontade de ir □ *vt* (*desire, bid*) desejar; (*want*) apetecer, ter vontade de, desejar (to do fazer) □ *vi* ~ for desejar. ~ sb well desejar felicidades a alguém. I don't ~ to go não me apetece ir, não tenho vontade de ir, não desejo ir. I ~ he'd leave eu gostaria que ele partisse. with best ~es (*formal: in letter*) com os melhores cumprimentos, com saudações cordiais; (*on greeting card*) com desejos or votos (for de)

wishful /ˈwɪʃfl/ *a* ~ thinking sonhar acordado

wishy-washy /ˈwɪʃɪwɒʃɪ/ *a* sem expressão, fraco, inexpressivo

wisp /wɪsp/ *n* (*of hair*) pequena mecha *f*; (*of smoke*) fio *m*

wistful /ˈwɪstfl/ *a* melancólico, saudoso

wit /wɪt/ *n* inteligência *f*; (*humour*) presença *f* de espírito, humor *m*; (*person*) senso *m* de humor. be at one's ~'s or ~s' end não saber o que fazer. keep one's ~s about one estar alerta. live by one's ~s ganhar a vida de maneira suspeita. scared out of one's ~s apavorado

witch /wɪtʃ/ *n* feiticeira *f*, bruxa *f*. ~craft *n* feitiçaria *f*, bruxaria *f*, magia *f*

with /wɪð/ *prep* com; (*having*) de; (*because of*) de; (*at the house of*) em casa de. the man ~ the beard o homem de barbas. fill/*etc* ~ encher/*etc* de. laughing/shaking/*etc* ~ a rir/a tremer/*etc* de. I'm not ~ you (*colloq*) não estou compreendendo-o

withdraw /wɪðˈdrɔː/ *vt/i* (*pt* withdrew, *pp* withdrawn) retirar (-se); (*money*) tirar. ~al *n* retirada *f*; (*med*) estado *m* de privação. ~n *a* (*person*) retraído, fechado

wither /ˈwɪðə(r)/ *vt/i* murchar, secar. ~ed *a* (*person*) mirrado. ~ing *a* (*fig: scornful*) desdenhoso

withhold /wɪðˈhəʊld/ *vt* (*pt* withheld) negar, recusar; (*retain*) reter; (*conceal, not tell*) esconder (from de)

within /wɪˈðɪn/ *prep* & *adv* dentro (de), por dentro (de); (*in distances*) a menos de. ~ a month (before) dentro de um mês. ~ sight à vista

without /wɪˈðaʊt/ prep sem. ~ fail sem falta. go ~ saying não ser preciso dizer

withstand /wɪðˈstænd/ vt (pt withstood) resistir a, opor-se a

witness /ˈwɪtnɪs/ n testemunha f; (evidence) testemunho m □ vt testemunhar, presenciar; (document) assinar como testemunha. bear ~ to testemunhar, dar testemunho de. ~-box n banco m das testemunhas

witticism /ˈwɪtɪsɪzəm/ n dito m espirituoso

witty /ˈwɪtɪ/ a (-ier, -iest) espirituoso

wives /ˈwaɪvz/ see wife

wizard /ˈwɪzəd/ n feiticeiro m; (fig: genius) gênio m, (P) génio m

wizened /ˈwɪznd/ a encarquilhado

wobbl|e /ˈwɒbl/ vi (of jelly, voice, hand) tremer; (stagger) cambalear, vacilar; (of table, chair) balançar. ~y a (trembling) trêmulo; (staggering) cambaleante, vacilante; (table, chair) pouco firme

woe /wəʊ/ n dor f, infortúnio m

woke, woken /wəʊk, ˈwəʊkən/ see wake

wolf /wʊlf/ n (pl wolves /wʊlvz/) lobo m □ vt (food) devorar. cry ~ dar alarme falso. ~-whistle n assobio m de admiração

woman /ˈwʊmən/ n (pl women) mulher f. ~hood n as mulheres, o sexo feminino; (maturity) maturidade f. ~ly a feminino

womb /wuːm/ n seio m, ventre m; (med) útero m; (fig) seio m

women /ˈwɪmɪn/ see woman. ~'s movement movimento m feminista

won /wʌn/ see win

wonder /ˈwʌndə(r)/ n admiração f; (thing) maravilha f □ vt perguntar-se a si mesmo (if se) □ vi admirar-se (at de, com), ficar admirado, espantar-se (at com); (reflect) pensar (about em). it is no ~ não admira (that que)

wonderful /ˈwʌndəfl/ a maravilhoso. ~ly adv maravilhosamente. it works ~ly funciona às mil maravilhas

won't /wəʊnt/ = will not

wood /wʊd/ n madeira f, pau m; (for burning) lenha f. ~(s) n (pl) (area) bosque m, mata f, floresta f. ~ed a arborizado. ~en a de or em madeira, de pau; (fig: stiff) rígido; (fig: inexpressive) inexpressivo de pau

woodcut /ˈwʊdkʌt/ n gravura f em madeira

woodland /ˈwʊdlənd/ n região f arborizada, bosque m, mata f

woodlouse /ˈwʊdlaʊs/ n (pl -lice /laɪs/) baratinha f, tatuzinho m

woodpecker /ˈwʊdpekə(r)/ n (bird) pica-pau m

woodwind /ˈwʊdwɪnd/ n (mus) instrumentos mpl de sopro de madeira

woodwork /ˈwʊdwɜːk/ n (of building) madeiramento m; (carpentry) carpintaria f

woodworm /ˈwʊdwɜːm/ n caruncho m

woody /ˈwʊdɪ/ a (wooded) arborizado; (like wood) lenhoso

wool /wʊl/ n lã f. ~len a de lã. ~lens npl roupas fpl de lã. ~ly a de lã; (vague) confuso □ n (colloq: garment) roupa f de lã

word /wɜːd/ n palavra f; (news) notícia(s) f(pl); (promise) palavra f □ vt exprimir, formular. by ~ of mouth de viva voz. have a ~ with dizer duas palavras a. in other ~s em outras palavras. ~-perfect a que sabe de cor seu papel, a lição etc. ~ processor processador m de textos. ~ing n termos mpl, redação f, (P) redacção f. ~y a prolixo

wore /wɔː(r)/ see wear

work /wɜːk/ n trabalho m; (product, book etc) obra f; (building etc) obras fpl. at ~ no trabalho. out of ~ desempregado. ~s npl (techn) mecanismo m; (factory) fábrica f □ vt/i (of person) trabalhar; (techn) (fazer) funcionar, (fazer) andar; (of drug etc) agir, fazer efeito; (farm, mine) explorar; (land) lavrar. ~ sb (make work) fazer alguém trabalhar. ~ in introduzir, inserir. ~ loose soltar-se. ~ off (get rid of) descarregar. ~ out vt (solve) resolver; (calculate) calcular; (devise) planejar □ vi (succeed) resultar; (sport) treinar-se. ~-station n estação f de trabalho. ~-to-rule n greve f de zelo. ~ up vt criar □ vi (to climax) ir num crescendo. ~ed up (person) enervado, transtornado, agitado

workable /ˈwɜːkəbl/ a viável, praticável

workaholic /wɜːkəˈhɒlɪk/ n be a ~ (colloq) trabalhar como um possesso (colloq)

worker /ˈwɜːkə(r)/ n trabalhador m, trabalhadora f; (factory) operário m

working /ˈwɜːkɪŋ/ a (day, clothes, hypothesis, lunch etc) de trabalho. the ~ class(es) a classe operária, a(s) class(es) trabalhadora(s), o proletariado. ~-class a operário, trabalhador. ~ mother mãe f que trabalha. ~ party comissão f consultiva, de estudo etc. ~s npl mecanismo m. in ~ order em condições de funcionamento

workman /ˈwɜːkmən/ n (pl -men)

trabalhador m; (factory) operário m.
~ship n trabalho m, execução f, mão-
de-obra f; (skill) arte f, habilidade f.
workshop /ˈwɜːkʃɒp/ n oficina f
world /wɜːld/ n mundo m □ a
mundial. a ~ of muito(s), grande
quantidade de, um mundo de. ~-
wide a mundial, universal
worldly /ˈwɜːldlɪ/ a terreno; (devoted
to the affairs of life) mundano. ~
goods bens mpl materiais. ~-wise a
com experiência do mundo
worm /wɜːm/ n verme m; (earth-
worm) minhoca f □ vt ~ one's way
into insinuar-se, introduzir-se, enfiar-se. ~-eaten a (wood) caruncho-
so; (fruit) bichado, bichoso
worn /wɔːn/ see wear □ a usado. ~-
out (thing) completamente gasto;
(person) esgotado
worr|y /ˈwʌrɪ/ vt/i preocupar(-se) □ n
preocupação f. don't ~y fique des-
cansado, não se preocupe. ~ied a
preocupado. ~ying a preocupante,
inquietante
worse /wɜːs/ a & adv pior □ n pior m.
get ~ piorar. from bad to ~ de mal a
pior. ~ luck pouca sorte, pena
worsen /ˈwɜːsn/ vt/i piorar
worship /ˈwɜːʃɪp/ n (reverence)
reverência f, veneração f; (religious)
culto m □ vt (pt worshipped) adorar,
venerar □ vi fazer as suas devoções,
praticar o culto. ~per n (in church)
fiel m. Your/His W~ Vossa/Sua
Excelência f
worst /wɜːst/ a & n (the) ~ (o/a) pior
(mf) □ adv pior. if the ~ comes to
the ~ se o pior acontecer, na pior
das hipóteses. do one's ~ fazer todo
o mal que se quiser. get the ~ of it
ficar a perder. the ~ (thing) that o
pior que
worth /wɜːθ/ a be ~ valer; (deser-
ving) merecer □ n valor m, mérito m.
ten pounds ~ of dez libras de. it's ~
it, it's ~ while vale a pena. it's not
~ my while não vale a pena. it's ~
waiting/etc vale a pena esperar/etc.
for all one's ~ (colloq) dando tudo
por tudo. ~less a sem valor
worthwhile /ˈwɜːθwaɪl/ a que vale a
pena; (cause) louvável, meritório
worthy /ˈwɜːðɪ/ a (-ier, -iest) (deser-
ving) digno, merecedor (of de); (laudable) meritório, louvável □ n (person)
pessoa f ilustre
would /wʊd/; unstressed /wəd/ v aux
he ~ do/you ~ sing/etc (conditional
tense) ele faria/você cantaria/etc. he
~ have done ele teria feito. she ~
come every day (used to) ela vinha or
costumava vir aqui todos os dias. ~
you please come here? chegue aqui

por favor. ~ you like some tea? você
quer um chazinho? he ~n't go (re-
fused to) ele não queria ir. ~-be
author/doctor/etc aspirante a
autor/médico/etc
wound[1] /wuːnd/ n ferida f □ vt ferir.
the ~ed os feridos mpl
wound[2] /waʊnd/ see wind[2]
wove, woven /wəʊv, ˈwəʊvn/ see
weave
wrangle /ˈræŋgl/ vi disputar, discutir,
brigar □ n disputa f, discussão f, briga
f
wrap /ræp/ vt (pt wrapped) ~ (up)
embrulhar (in em); (in cotton wool,
mystery etc) envolver (in em) □ vi ~
up (dress warmly) abrigar-se bem,
agasalhar-se bem □ n xale m. ~ped
up in (engrossed) absorto em, mergulhado em. ~per n (of sweet) papel
m; (of book) capa f de papel. ~ing n
embalagem f
wrath /rɒθ/ n ira f. ~ful a irado
wreak /riːk/ vt ~ havoc (of storm etc)
fazer estragos
wreath /riːθ/ n (pl -s /-ðz/) (of flowers,
leaves) coroa f, grinalda f
wreck /rek/ n (sinking) naufrágio m;
(ship) navio m naufragado; restos mpl
de navio; (remains) destroços mpl;
(vehicle) veículo m destroçado □ vt
destruir; (ship) fazer naufragar, afundar; (fig: hope) acabar. be a nervous
~ estar com os nervos arrasados.
~age n (pieces) destroços mpl
wren /ren/ n (bird) carriça f
wrench /rentʃ/ vt (pull) puxar;
(twist) torcer; (snatch) arrancar
(from a) □ n (pull) puxão m; (of
ankle, wrist) torcedura f; (tool) chave
f inglesa; (fig) dor f de separação
wrest /rest/ vt arrancar (from a)
wrestl|e /ˈresl/ vi lutar, debater-se
(with com or contra). ~er n lutador
m. ~ing n luta f
wretch /retʃ/ n desgraçado m,
miserável mf; (rascal) miserável mf
wretched /ˈretʃɪd/ a (pitiful, poor)
miserável; (bad) horrível, desgraçado
wriggle /ˈrɪgl/ vt/i remexer(-se), contorcer-se
wring /rɪŋ/ vt (pt wrung) (twist,
clothes) torcer. ~ out of (obtain from)
arrancar a. ~ing wet encharcado de;
(person) encharcado até os ossos
wrinkle /ˈrɪŋkl/ n (on skin) ruga f;
(crease) prega f □ vt/i enrugar(-se)
wrist /rɪst/ n pulso m. ~-watch n
relógio m de pulso
writ /rɪt/ n (jur) mandado m judicial
write /raɪt/ vt/i (pt wrote, pp written) escrever. ~ back responder. ~
down escrever, tomar nota de. ~ off
(debt) dar por liquidado; (vehicle) des-

tinar à sucata. ~-off n perda f total.
~ out (in full) escrever por extenso.
~ up (from notes) redigir. ~-up n
relato m; (review) crítica f
writer /'raɪtə(r)/ n escritor m, autor
m
writhe /raɪð/ vi contorcer(-se)
writing /'raɪtɪŋ/ n escrita f. ~s
(works) escritos mpl, obras fpl. in ~
por escrito. ~-paper n papel m de
carta
written /'rɪtn/ see **write**
wrong /rɒŋ/ a (incorrect, mistaken)
mal, errado; (unfair) injusto; (wicked)
mau; (amiss) que não está bem; (mus:
note) falso; (clock) que não está certo
□ adv mal □ n mal m; (injustice)
injustiça f □ vt (be unfair to) ser injusto com; (do a wrong to) fazer mal a.
what's ~? qual é o problema? **what's**
~ **with it?** (amiss) o que é que não
vai bem?; (morally) que mal há nisso?, que mal tem? **he's in the** ~ (his
fault) ele não tem razão. **go** ~ (err)
desencaminhar-se; (fail) ir mal;
(vehicle) quebrar. ~**ly** adv mal;
(blame etc) sem razão, injustamente
wrongful /'rɒŋfl/ a injusto, ilegal
wrote /rəʊt/ see **write**
wrought /rɔ:t/ a ~ **iron** ferro m
forjado. ~**-up** a excitado
wrung /rʌŋ/ see **wring**
wry /raɪ/ a (**wryer, wryest**) torto;
(smile) forçado. ~ **face** careta f

X

Xerox /'zɪərɒks/ n fotocópia f, xerox
m □ vt fotocopiar, xerocar, tirar um
xerox de
Xmas /'krɪsməs/ n Christmas
X-ray /'eksreɪ/ n raio X m; (photograph) radiografia f □ vt radiografar.
have an ~ tirar uma radiografia
xylophone /'zaɪləfəʊn/ n xilofone m

Y

yacht /jɒt/ n iate m. ~**ing** n iatismo
m, andar m de iate; (racing) regata f
de iate
yank /jæŋk/ vt (colloq) puxar bruscamente □ n (colloq) puxão m
Yank /jæŋk/ n (colloq) ianque mf
yap /jæp/ vi (pt **yapped**) latir
yard[1] /ja:d/ n (measure) jarda f (=
0,9144 m). ~**age** n medida f em jardas
yard[2] /ja:d/ n (of house) pátio m;
(Amer: garden) jardim m; (for storage) depósito m
yardstick /'ja:dstɪk/ n jarda f; (fig)
bitola f, craveira f

yarn /ja:n/ n (thread) fio m; (colloq:
tale) longa história f
yawn /jɔ:n/ vi bocejar; (be wide open)
abrir-se, escancarar-se □ n bocejo m.
~**ing** a escancarado
year /jɪə(r)/ n ano m. school/tax ~
ano m escolar/fiscal. **be ten**/etc ~**s**
old ter dez/etc anos de idade. ~-book
n anuário m. ~**ly** a anual □ adv
anualmente
yearn /jɜ:n/ vi ~ **for, to** desejar, ansiar por, suspirar por. ~**ing** n desejo
m, anseio m (**for** de)
yeast /ji:st/ n levedura f
yell /jel/ vt/i gritar, berrar □ n grito
m, berro m
yellow /'jeləʊ/ a amarelo; (colloq: cowardly) covarde, poltrão □ n amarelo m
yelp /jelp/ n (of dog etc) ganido m □ vi
ganir
yen /jen/ n (colloq: yearning) grande
vontade f (**for** de)
yes /jes/ n & adv sim (m). ~-**man** n
(colloq) lambe-botas m invar, puxa-
saco m
yesterday /'jestədɪ/ n & adv ontem
(m). ~ **morning/afternoon/even-
ing** ontem de manhã/à tarde/à
noite. **the day before** ~ anteontem.
~ **week** há oito dias, há uma semana
yet /jet/ adv ainda; (already) já □ conj
contudo, no entanto, porém. **as** ~ até agora,
por enquanto. **his best book** ~ o seu
melhor livro até agora
yew /ju:/ n teixo m
Yiddish /'jɪdɪʃ/ n idiche m
yield /ji:ld/ vt (produce) produzir, dar;
(profit) render; (surrender) entregar □
vi (give way) ceder □ n produção f;
(comm) rendimento m
yoga /'jəʊgə/ n ioga f
yoghurt /'jɒgət/ n iogurte m
yoke /jəʊk/ n jugo m, canga f; (of garment) pala f □ vt jungir; (unite) unir,
ligar
yokel /'jəʊkl/ n caipira m, labrego m
yolk /jəʊk/ n gema f (de ovo) f
yonder /'jɒndə(r)/ adv acolá, além
you /ju:/ pron (familiar) tu, você (pl
vocês); (polite) vós, o(s) senhor(es),
a(s) senhora(s); (object: familiar) te,
lhe (pl vocês); (polite) o(s), a(s), lhes,
vós, o(s) senhor(es), a(s) senhora(s);
(after prep) ti, si, você (pl vocês); (polite) vós, o senhor, a senhora (pl os
senhores, as senhoras); (indefinite)
se; (after prep) si, você. **with** ~ (familiar) contigo, consigo, com você (pl
com vocês); (polite) com o senhor/a
senhora (pl convosco, com os senho-
res/as senhoras). **I know** ~ (familiar) eu te conheço, eu o/a
conheço (pl eu os/as conheço); (polite) eu vos conheço, conheço o

senhor/a senhora (*pl* conheço os se-
nhores/as senhoras). ~ can see the
sea você pode ver o mar
young /jʌŋ/ *a* (-er, -est) jovem, novo,
moço □ *n* (*people*) jovens *mpl*, a juventude *f*, a mocidade *f*; (*of animals*) crias
fpl, filhotes *mpl*
youngster /'jʌŋstə(r)/ *n* jovem *mf*,
moço *m*, rapaz *m*
your /jɔ:(r)/ *a* (*familiar*) teu, tua, seu,
sua (*pl* teus, tuas, seus, suas); (*polite*)
vosso, vossa, do senhor, da senhora
(*pl* vossos, vossas, dos senhores, das
senhoras)
yours /jɔ:z/ *poss pron* (*familiar*) o
teu, a tua, o seu, a sua (*pl* os teus, as
tuas, os seus, as suas); (*polite*) o vosso, a vossa, o/a do senhor, o/a da
senhora (*pl* os vossos, as vossas;
os/as do(s) senhor(es), os/as da(s)
senhora(s)). a book of ~ um livro
seu. ~ sincerely/faithfully atenciosamente, com os cumprimentos de
yourself /jɔ:'self/ (*pl* -selves /-'selvz/)
pron (*familiar*) tu mesmo/a, você
mesmo/a (*polite*) vós mesmo/a, o
senhor mesmo, a senhora mesma
(*pl* vós mesmos/as, os senhores mes-
mos/as, as senhoras mesmas); (*reflexive: familiar*) te, a ti mesmo/a, se, a si mes-
mo/a (*polite*) a você mesmo/a,
ao senhor mesmo, à senhora
mesma (*pl* aos senhores mesmos,
às senhoras mesmas); (*after prep:
familiar*) ti mesmo/a, si mesmo/a,
você mesmo/a (*pl* vocês mesmos/as);
(*after prep: polite*) vós mesmo/a, o
senhor mesmo, a senhora mesma
(*pl* vós mesmos/as, os senhores
mesmos, as senhoras mesmas). with
~ (*familiar*) contigo mesmo/a, consigo mesmo/a, com você (*pl* com
vocês); (*polite*) convosco, com o senhor, com a senhora (*pl* com os senhores, com as senhoras). by ~
sozinho
youth /ju:θ/ *n* (*pl* -s /-ðz/) mocidade *f*,
juventude *f*; (*young man*) jovem *m*,
moço *m*. ~ club centro *m* de jovens.

~ hostel albergue *m* da juventude.
~ful *a* juvenil, jovem
yo-yo /'jəʊjəʊ/ *n* (*pl* -os) ioiô *m*
Yugoslav /'ju:ɡəsla:v/ *a* & *n* iogoslavo
(*m*), (*P*) jugoslavo (*m*). ~ia /-'sla:vɪə/
n Iogoslávia *f*, (*P*) Jugoslávia *f*

Z

zany /'zeɪnɪ/ *a* (-ier, -iest) tolo, bobo
zeal /zi:l/ *n* zelo *m*
zealous /'zeləs/ *a* zeloso. ~ly *adv* ze-
losamente
zebra /'zebrə, 'zi:brə/ *n* zebra *f*. ~
crossing faixa *f* para pedestres, (*P*)
passagem *f* para peões
zenith /'zenɪθ/ *n* zênite *m*, (*P*) zénite
m, auge *m*
zero /'zɪərəʊ/ *n* (*pl* -os) zero *m*. ~
hour a hora H. below ~ abaixo de
zero
zest /zest/ *n* (*gusto*) entusiasmo *m*;
(*fig: spice*) sabor *m* especial; (*lemon
or orange peel*) casca *f* de limão/la-
ranja ralada
zigzag /'zɪɡzæɡ/ *n* ziguezague *m* □ *a* &
adv em ziguezague □ *vi* (*pt* zig-
zagged) ziguezaguear
zinc /zɪŋk/ *n* zinco *m*
zip /zɪp/ *n* (*vigour*) energia *f*, alma *f*.
~(-fastener) fecho *m* ecler □ *vt* (*pt*
zipped) fechar o fecho eclerde □ *vi* ir
a toda a velocidade. Z~ code (*Amer*)
CEP de endereçamento postal *m*, (*P*)
código *m* postal
zipper /'zɪpə(r)/ *n* = zip(-fastener)
zodiac /'zəʊdɪæk/ *n* zodíaco *m*
zombie /'zɒmbɪ/ *n* zumbi *m*; (*colloq*)
zumbi *m*, (*P*) autómato *m*
zone /zəʊn/ *n* zona *f*
zoo /zu:/ *n* jardim *m* zoológico
zoolog|y /zəʊ'ɒlədʒɪ/ *n* zoologia *f*.
~ical /-ə'lɒdʒɪkl/ *a* zoológico. ~ist *n*
zoólogo *m*
zoom /zu:m/ *vi* (*rush*) sair roando ~
lens zum *m*, zoom *m*. ~ off *or* past
passar zunindo
zucchini /zu:'ki:nɪ/ *n* (*pl* *invar*)
(*Amer*) courgette *f*

Portuguese Verbs · Verbos portugueses

Introduction
Portuguese verbs can be divided into three categories: regular verbs, those with spelling peculiarities determined by their sound and irregular verbs.

Regular verbs
in -ar (*e.g.* comprar)
Present: compr|o, ~as, ~a, ~amos, ~ais, ~am
Future: comprar|ei, ~ás, ~á, ~emos, ~eis, ~ão
Imperfect: compr|ava, ~avas, ~ava, ~ávamos, ~áveis, ~avam
Preterite: compr|ei, ~aste, ~ou, ~amos (*P*: ~ámos), ~astes, ~aram
Pluperfect: compr|ara, ~aras, ~ara, ~áramos, ~áreis, ~aram
Present subjunctive: compr|e, ~es, ~e, ~emos, ~eis, ~em
Imperfect subjunctive: compr|asse, ~asses, ~asse, ~ássemos, ~ásseis, ~assem
Future subjunctive: compr|ar, ~ares, ~ar, ~armos, ~ardes, ~arem
Conditional: comprar|ia, ~ias, ~ia, ~íamos, ~íeis, ~iam
Personal infinitive: comprar, ~es, ~, ~mos, ~des, ~em
Present participle: comprando
Past participle: comprado
Imperative: compra, comprai

in ~er (*e.g.* bater)
Present: bat|o, ~es, ~e, ~emos, ~eis, ~em
Future: bater|ei, ~ás, ~á, ~emos, ~eis, ~ão
Imperfect: bat|ia, ~ias, ~ia, ~íamos, ~íeis, ~iam
Preterite: bat|i, ~este, ~eu, ~emos, ~estes, ~eram
Pluperfect: bat|era, ~eras, ~era, ~êramos, ~êreis, ~eram
Present subjunctive: bat|a, ~as, ~a, ~amos, ~ais, ~am
Imperfect subjunctive: bat|esse, ~esses, ~esse, ~êssemos, ~êsseis, ~essem
Future subjunctive: bat|er, ~eres, ~er, ~ermos, ~erdes, ~erem
Conditional: bater|ia, ~ias, ~ia, ~íamos, ~íeis, ~iam
Personal infinitive: bater, ~es, ~, ~mos, ~des, ~em
Present participle: batendo
Past participle: batido
Imperative: bate, batei

in ~ir (*e.g.* admitir)
Present: admit|o, ~es, ~e, ~imos, ~is, ~em
Future: admitir|ei, ~ás, ~á, ~emos, ~eis, ~ão
Imperfect: admit|ia, ~ias, ~ia, ~íamos, ~íeis, ~iam
Preterite: admit|i, ~iste, ~iu, ~imos, ~istes, ~iram
Pluperfect: admit|ira, ~iras, ~ira, ~íramos, ~íreis, ~iram
Present subjunctive: admit|a, ~as, ~a, ~amos, ~ais, ~am
Imperfect subjunctive: admit|isse, ~isses, ~isse, ~íssemos, ~ísseis, ~issem
Future subjunctive: admit|ir, ~ires, ~ir, ~irmos, ~irdes, ~irem
Conditional: admitir|ia, ~ias, ~ia, ~íamos, ~íeis, ~iam
Personal infinitive: admitir, ~es, ~, ~mos, ~des, ~em
Present participle: admitindo
Past participle: admitido
Imperative: admite, admiti

Regular verbs with spelling changes:

-ar verbs:
in -car (*e.g.* ficar)
Preterite: fiquei, ficaste, ficou, ficamos (*P*: ficámos), ficais, ficam
Present subjunctive: fique, fiques, fique, fiquemos, fiqueis, fiquem

in -çar (*e.g.* abraçar)
Preterite: abracei, abraçaste, abraçou, abraçamos (*P*: abraçámos), abraçastes, abraçaram
Present subjunctive: abrace, abraces, abrace, abracemos, abraceis, abracem

in -ear (*e.g.* passear)
Present: passeio, passeias, passeia, passeamos, passeais, passeiam
Present subjunctive: passeie, passeies, passeie, passeemos, passeeis, passeiem
Imperative: passeia, passeai

in -gar (*e.g.* apagar)
Preterite: apaguei, apagaste, apagou, apagamos (*P*: apagámos), apagastes, apagaram
Present subjunctive: apague, apagues, apague, apaguemos, apagueis, apaguem

in -oar (*e.g.* voar)
Present: vôo (*P*: voo), voas, voa, voamos, voais, voam

averiguar
Preterite: averigüei (*P*: averiguei), averiguaste, averiguou, averiguamos (*P*: averiguámos), averiguastes, averiguaram
Present subjunctive: averigúe, averigúes, averigúe, averigüemos (*P*: averiguemos), averigüeis (*P*: averigueis), averigúem

enxaguar
Present: enxáguo, enxáguas, enxágua, enxaguamos, enxaguais, enxáguam
Preterite: enxagüei (*P*: enxaguei), enxaguaste, enxaguou, enxaguamos (*P*: enxaguámos), enxaguastes, enxaguaram
Present subjunctive: enxágüe, enxágües, enxágüe, enxagüemos, enxagüeis, enxágüem (*P*: enxágue, enxágues, enxágue, enxaguemos, enxagueis, enxáguem)
Similarly: aguar, desaguar

saudar
Present: saúdo, saúdas, saúda, saudamos, saudais, saúdam
Present subjunctive: saúde, saúdes, saúde, saudemos, saudeis, saúdem
Imperative: saúda, saudai

-er verbs:
in -cer (*e.g.* tecer)
Present: teço, teces, tece, tecemos, teceis, tecem
Present subjunctive: teça, teças, teça, teçamos, teçais, teçam

in -ger (*e.g.* proteger)
Present: protejo, proteges, protege, protegemos, protegeis, protegem
Present subjunctive: proteja, protejas, proteja, protejamos, protejais, protejam

in -guer (*e.g.* erguer)
Present: ergo, ergues, ergue, erguemos, ergueis, erguem
Present subjunctive: erga, ergas, erga, ergamos, ergais, ergam

in -oer (*e.g.* roer)
Present: rôo (*P*: roo), róis, rói, roemos, roeis, roem
Imperfect: roía, roías, roía, roíamos, roíeis, roíam
Preterite: roí, roeste, roeu, roemos, roestes, roeram
Past participle: roído
Imperative: rói, roei

-ir verbs:
in -ir with -e- in stem (*e.g.* vestir)
Present: visto, vestes, veste, vestimos, vestis, vestem

Present subjunctive: vista, vistas, vista, vistamos, vistais, vistam
Similarly: mentir, preferir, refletir, repetir, seguir, sentir, servir

in -ir with -o- in stem (*e.g.* dormir)
Present: durmo, dormes, dorme, dormimos, dormis, dormem
Present subjunctive: durma, durmas, durma, durmamos, durmais, durmam
Similarly: cobrir, descobrir, tossir

in -ir with -u- in the stem (*e.g.* subir)
Present: subo, sobes, sobe, subimos, subis, sobem
Similarly: consumir, cuspir, fugir, sacudir, sumir

in -air (*e.g.* sair)
Present: saio, sais, sai, saímos, saís, saem
Imperfect: saía, saías, saía, saíamos, saíeis, saíam
Preterite: saí, saíste, saiu, saímos, saístes, saíram
Pluperfect: saíra, saíras, saíra, saíramos, saíreis, saíram
Present subjunctive: saia, saias, saia, saiamos, saiais, saiam
Imperfect subjunctive: saísse, saísses, saísse, saíssemos, saísseis, saíssem
Future subjunctive: sair, saíres, sair, sairmos, sairdes, saírem
Personal infinitive: sair, saíres, sair, sairmos, sairdes, saírem
Present participle: saindo
Past participle: saído
Imperative: sai, sai

in -gir (*e.g.* dirigir)
Present: dirijo, diriges, dirige, dirigimos, dirigis, dirigem
Present subjunctive: dirija, dirijas, dirija, dirijamos, dirijais, dirijam

in -guir (*e.g.* distinguir)
Present: distingo, distingues, distingue, distinguimos, distinguis, distinguem
Present subjunctive: distinga, distingas, distinga, distingamos, distingais, distingam

in -uir (*e.g.* atribuir)
Present: atribuo, atribuis, atribui, atribuímos, atribuís, atribuem
Imperfect: atribuía, atribuías, atribuía, atribuíamos, atribuíeis, atribuíam
Preterite: atribuí, atribuíste, atribuiu, atribuímos, atribuístes, atribuíram
Pluperfect: atribuíra, atribuíras, atribuíra, atribuíramos, atribuíreis, atribuíram

Present subjunctive: atribua, atribuas, atribua, atribuamos, atribuais, atribuam

Imperfect subjunctive: atribuísse, atribuísses, atribuísse, atribuíssemos, atribuísseis, atribuíssem

Future subjunctive: atribuir, atribuíres, atribuir, atribuirmos, atribuirdes, atribuírem

Personal infinitive: atribuir, atribuíres, atribuir, atribuirmos, atribuirdes, atribuírem

Present participle: atribuindo

Past participle: atribuído

Imperative: atribui, atribuí

proibir
Present: proíbo, proíbes, proíbe, proibimos, proibis, proíbem

Present subjunctive: proíba, proíbas, proíba, proibamos, proibais, proíbam

Imperative: proíbe, proibi

Similarly: coibir

reunir
Present: reúno, reúnes, reúne, reunimos, reunis, reúnem

Present subjunctive: reúna, reúnas, reúna, reunamos, reunais, reúnam

Imperative: reúne, reuni

in -struir *(e.g. construir)* - like atribuir except:
Present: construo, constróis/construis, constrói/construi, construímos, construís, constroem/construem

Imperative: constrói/construi, construí

in -duzir *(e.g. produzir)*
Present: produzo, produzes, produz, produzimos, produzis, produzem

Imperative: produz(e), produzi

Similarly: luzir, reluzir

Irregular verbs

caber
Present: caibo, cabes, cabe, cabemos, cabeis, cabem

Preterite: coube, coubeste, coube, coubemos, coubestes, couberam

Pluperfect: coubera, couberas, coubera, coubéramos, coubéreis, couberam

Present subjunctive: caiba, caibas, caiba, caibamos, caibais, caibam

Imperfect subjunctive: coubesse, coubesses, coubesse, coubéssemos, coubésseis, coubessem

Future subjunctive: couber, couberes, couber, coubermos, couberdes, couberem

dar
Present: dou, dás, dá, damos, dais, dão

Preterite: dei, deste, deu, demos, destes, deram

Pluperfect: dera, deras, dera, déramos, déreis, deram

Present subjunctive: dê, dês, dê, demos, deis, dêem

Imperfect subjunctive: desse, desses, desse, déssemos, désseis, dessem

Future subjunctive: der, deres, der, dermos, derdes, derem

Imperative: dá, dai

dizer
Present: digo, dizes, diz, dizemos, dizeis, dizem

Future: direi, dirás, dirá, diremos, direis, dirão

Preterite: disse, disseste, disse, dissemos, dissestes, disseram

Pluperfect: dissera, disseras, dissera, disséramos, disséreis, disseram

Present subjunctive: diga, digas, diga, digamos, digais, digam

Imperfect subjunctive: dissesse, dissesses, dissesse, disséssemos, dissésseis, dissessem

Future subjunctive: disser, disseres, disser, dissermos, disserdes, disserem

Conditional: diria, dirias, diria, diríamos, diríeis, diriam

Present participle: dizendo

Past participle: dito

Imperative: diz, dizei

estar
Present: estou, estás, está, estamos, estais, estão

Preterite: estive, estiveste, esteve, estivemos, estivestes, estiveram

Pluperfect: estivera, estiveras, estivera, estivéramos, estivéreis, estiveram

Present subjunctive: esteja, estejas, esteja, estejamos, estejais, estejam

Imperfect subjunctive: estivesse, estivesses, estivesse, estivéssemos, estivésseis, estivessem

Future subjunctive: estiver, estiveres, estiver, estivermos, estiverdes, estiverem

Imperative: está, estai

fazer
Present: faço, fazes, faz, fazemos, fazeis, fazem

Future: farei, farás, fará, faremos, fareis, farão

Preterite: fiz, fizeste, fez, fizemos, fizestes, fizeram

Pluperfect: fizera, fizeras, fizera, fizéramos, fizéreis, fizeram

Present subjunctive: faça, faças, faça, façamos, façais, façam
Imperfect subjunctive: fizesse, fizesses, fizesse, fizéssemos, fizésseis, fizessem
Future subjunctive: fizer, fizeres, fizer, fizermos, fizerdes, fizerem
Conditional: faria, farias, faria, faríamos, farieis, fariam
Present participle: fazendo
Past participle: feito
Imperative: faz(e), fazei

frigir
Present: frijo, freges, frege, frigimos, frigis, fregem
Present subjunctive: frija, frijas, frija, frijamos, frijais, frijam
Imperative: frege, frigi

ir
Present: vou, vais, vai, vamos, ides, vão
Imperfect: ia, ias, ia, íamos, íeis, iam
Preterite: fui, foste, foi, fomos, fostes, foram
Pluperfect: fora, foras, fora, fôramos, fôreis, foram
Present subjunctive: vá, vás, vá, vamos, vades, vão
Imperfect subjunctive: fosse, fosses, fosse, fôssemos, fôsseis, fossem
Future subjunctive: for, fores, for, formos, fordes, forem
Present participle: indo
Past participle: ido
Imperative: vai, ide

haver
Present: hei, hás, há, hemos/havemos, haveis/heis, hão
Preterite: houve, houveste, houve, houvemos, houvestes, houveram
Pluperfect: houvera, houveras, houvera, houvéramos, houvéreis, houveram
Present subjunctive: haja, hajas, haja, hajamos, hajais, hajam
Imperfect subjunctive: houvesse, houvesses, houvesse, houvéssemos, houvésseis, houvessem
Future subjunctive: houver, houveres, houver, houvermos, houverdes, houverem
Imperative: há, havei

ler
Present: leio, lês, lê, lemos, ledes, lêem
Imperfect: lia, lias, lia, líamos, líeis, liam
Preterite: li, leste, leu, lemos, lestes, leram
Pluperfect: lera, leras, lera, lêramos, lêreis, leram

Present subjunctive: leia, leias, leia, leiamos, leiais, leiam
Imperfect subjunctive: lesse, lesses, lesse, lêssemos, lêsseis, lessem
Future subjunctive: ler, leres, ler, lermos, lerdes, lerem
Present participle: lendo
Past participle: lido
Imperative: lê, lede
Similarly: crer

odiar
Present: odeio, odeias, odeia, odiamos, odiais, odeiam
Present subjunctive: odeie, odeies, odeie, odiemos, odieis, odeiem
Imperative: odeia, odiai
Similarly: incendiar

ouvir
Present: ouço (*P also*: oiça), ouves, ouve, ouvimos, ouvis, ouvem
Present subjunctive: ouça, ouças, ouça, ouçamos, ouçais, ouçam (*P also*: oiça, oiças, oiça, oiçamos, oiçais, oiçam)

pedir
Present: peço, pedes, pede, pedimos, pedis, pedem
Present subjunctive: peça, peças, peça, peçamos, peçais, peçam
Similarly: despedir, impedir, medir

perder
Present: perco, perdes, perde, perdemos, perdeis, perdem
Present subjunctive: perca, percas, perca, percamos, percais, percam

poder
Present: posso, podes, pode, podemos, podeis, podem
Preterite: pude, pudeste, pôde, pudemos, pudestes, puderam
Pluperfect: pudera, puderas, pudera, pudéramos, pudéreis, puderam
Present subjunctive: possa, possas, possa, possamos, possais, possam
Imperfect subjunctive: pudesse, pudesses, pudesse, pudéssemos, pudésseis, pudessem
Future subjunctive: puder, puderes, puder, pudermos, puderdes, puderem

polir
Present: pulo, pules, pule, polimos, polis, pulem
Present subjunctive: pula, pulas, pula, pulamos, pulais, pulam
Imperative: pule, poli

pôr
Present: ponho, pões, põe, pomos, pondes, põem

Future: porei, porás, porá, poremos, poreis, porão
Imperfect: punha, punhas, punha, púnhamos, púnheis, punham
Preterite: pus, puseste, pôs, pusemos, pusestes, puseram
Pluperfect: pusera, puseras, pusera, puséramos, puséreis, puseram
Present subjunctive: ponha, ponhas, ponha, ponhamos, ponhais, ponham
Imperfect subjunctive: pusesse, pusesses, pusesse, puséssemos, pusésseis, pusessem
Future subjunctive: puser, puseres, puser, pusermos, puserdes, puserem
Conditional: poria, porias, poria, poríamos, poríeis, poriam
Present participle: pondo
Past participle: posto
Imperative: põe, ponde
Similarly: compor, depor, dispor, opor, supor etc

prover
Present: provejo, provês, provê, provemos, provedes, provêem
Present subjunctive: proveja, provejas, proveja, provejamos, provejais, provejam
Imperative: provê, provede

querer
Present: quero, queres, quer, queremos, quereis, querem
Preterite: quis, quiseste, quis, quisemos, quisestes, quiseram
Pluperfect: quisera, quiseras, quisera, quiséramos, quiséreis, quiseram
Present subjunctive: queira, queiras, queira, queiramos, queirais, queiram
Imperfect subjunctive: quisesse, quisesses, quisesse, quiséssemos, quisésseis, quisessem
Future subjunctive: quiser, quiseres, quiser, quisermos, quiserdes, quiserem
Imperative: quer, querei

requerer
Present: requeiro, requeres, requer, requeremos, requereis, requerem
Present subjunctive: requeira, requeiras, requeira, requeiramos, requeirais, requeiram
Imperative: requer, requerei

rir
Present: rio, ris, ri, rimos, rides, riem
Present subjunctive: ria, rias, ria, riamos, riais, riam
Imperative: ri, ride
Similarly: sorrir

saber
Present: sei, sabes, sabe, sabemos, sabeis, sabem
Preterite: soube, soubeste, soube, soubemos, soubestes, souberam
Pluperfect: soubera, souberas, soubera, soubéramos, soubéreis, souberam
Present subjunctive: saiba, saibas, saiba, saibamos, saibais, saibam
Imperfect subjunctive: soubesse, soubesses, soubesse, soubéssemos, soubésseis, soubessem
Future subjunctive: souber, souberes, souber, soubermos, souberdes, souberem
Imperative: sabe, sabei

ser
Present: sou, és, é, somos, sois, são
Imperfect: era, eras, era, éramos, éreis, eram
Preterite: fui, foste, foi, fomos, fostes, foram
Pluperfect: fora, foras, fora, fôramos, fôreis, foram
Present subjunctive: seja, sejas, seja, sejamos, sejais, sejam
Imperfect subjunctive: fosse, fosses, fosse, fôssemos, fôsseis, fossem
Future subjunctive: for, fores, for, formos, fordes, forem
Present participle: sendo
Past participle: sido
Imperative: sê, sede

ter
Present: tenho, tens, tem, temos, tendes, têm
Imperfect: tinha, tinhas, tinha, tínhamos, tínheis, tinham
Preterite: tive, tiveste, teve, tivemos, tivestes, tiveram
Pluperfect: tivera, tiveras, tivera, tivéramos, tivéreis, tiveram
Present subjunctive: tenha, tenhas, tenha, tenhamos, tenhais, tenham
Imperfect subjunctive: tivesse, tivesses, tivesse, tivéssemos, tivésseis, tivessem
Future subjunctive: tiver, tiveres, tiver, tivermos, tiverdes, tiverem
Present participle: tendo
Past participle: tido
Imperative: tem, tende

trazer
Present: trago, trazes, traz, trazemos, trazeis, trazem
Future: trarei, trarás, trará, traremos, trareis, trarão
Preterite: trouxe, trouxeste, trouxe, trouxemos, trouxestes, trouxeram

Pluperfect: trouxera, trouxeras, trouxera, trouxéramos, trouxéreis, trouxeram
Present subjunctive: traga, tragas, traga, tragamos, tragais, tragam
Imperfect subjunctive: trouxesse, trouxesses, trouxesse, trouxéssemos, trouxésseis, trouxessem
Future subjunctive: trouxer, trouxeres, trouxer, trouxermos, trouxerdes, trouxerem
Conditional: traria, trarias, traria, traríamos, traríeis, trariam
Imperative: traze, trazei

valer
Present: valho, vales, vale, valemos, valeis, valem
Present subjunctive: valha, valhas, valha, valhamos, valhais, valham

ver
Present: vejo, vês, vê, vemos, vedes, vêem
Imperfect: via, vias, via, víamos, vieis, viam
Preterite: vi, viste, viu, vimos, vistes, viram
Pluperfect: vira, viras, vira, víramos, víreis, viram

Present subjunctive: veja, vejas, veja, vejamos, vejais, vejam
Imperfect subjunctive: visse, visses, visse, vissemos, vísseis, vissem
Future subjunctive: vir, vires, vir, virmos, virdes, virem
Present participle: vendo
Past participle: visto
Imperative: vê, vede

vir
Present: venho, vens, vem, vimos, vindes, vêm
Imperfect: vinha, vinhas, vinha, vínhamos, vínheis, vinham
Preterite: vim, vieste, veio, viemos, viestes, vieram
Pluperfect: viera, vieras, viera, viéramos, viéreis, vieram
Present subjunctive: venha, venhas, venha, venhamos, venhais, venham
Imperfect subjunctive: viesse, viesses, viesse, viéssemos, viésseis, viessem
Future subjunctive: vier, vieres, vier, viermos, vierdes, vierem
Present participle: vindo
Past participle: vindo
Imperative: vem, vinde